HUXFORD'S
OLD BOOK
VALUE GUIDE

Fourth Edition

COLLECTOR BOOKS
A Division of Schroeder Publishing Co., Inc.

The current values in this book should be used only as a guide. They are not intended to set prices, which vary from one section of the country to another. Auction prices as well as dealer prices vary greatly and are affected by condition as well as demand. Neither the Author nor the Publisher assumes responsibility for any losses that might be incurred as a result of consulting this guide.

On the Cover:

Wells, H.G. *The Outline of History*. The Review, New York, 1922. $12.50

Osborn, Fairfield. *Our Plundered Planet*. Little, Brown & Co., Boston, 1948. $4.00

Nicolay, Helen. *MacArthur of Bataan*. D Appleton-Century Co., 1942. $6.00

Michener, James A. *Return to Paradise*. Random House, New York, 1951. $3.50

Wolfe, Tom. *The Right Stuff*. FSG, 1979. $40.00

Defoe, Daniel. *Robinson Crusoe*. Grosset & Dunlap, New York, 1946. $25.00

Swift, Jonathan. *Gulliver's Travels*. Oxford University Press, 1977. $15.00

Sagan, Carl. *Comet*. Random House New York, 1985. $6.00

Churchill, Winston. *Painting As A Pastime*. Cornerstone Library, New York, 1965. $20.00

Ovid. *Metamorphosis*. Philadelphia, 1899. $8.00

Wiggin, Kate Douglas. *The Arabian Nights*. Scribner's, 1936. $95.00

Little Bo Peep. M. A. Donahue & Co. $10.00

Wharton, Edith. *The Age of Innocence*. D. Appleton & Co., and Pictorial Review Company, New York, 1920. $4.00

Day, Clarence. *Life with Father*. Sun Dial Press, 1943. $10.00

Carlin, John. *Memoir of Elder Garrett*. Philadelphia, 1870. $12.00

Thalheimer, M.E. *The New Eclectic History of the U.S.* American Book Co., 1904. $8.00

Harvey, Thomas. *English Grammar*. Wilson, Hinkle & Co., 1868. $20.00

Additional copies of this book may be ordered from:

COLLECTOR BOOKS
P.O. Box 3009
Paducah, Kentucky 42002-3009

@$19.95. Add $2.00 for postage and handling.

Copyright: Schroeder Publishing Co., Inc. 1992

This book or any part thereof may not be reproduced without the written consent of the Author and Publisher.

1 2 3 4 5 6 7 8 9 0

Introduction

This book was compiled to help the owner of old books evaluate his holdings and find a buyer for them. Most of us have a box, trunk, stack, or bookcase of old books. Chances are they are not rare books, but they may have value. Two questions that we are asked most frequently are 'Can you tell me the value of my old books?' and 'Where can I sell them?' *Huxford's Old Book Value Guide* will help answer both of these questions. Not only does this book place retail values on over 25,000 old books, it also lists scores of buyers along with the type of material each is interested in purchasing. Note that we list retail values (values that an interested party would be willing to pay to obtain possession of the book). These prices are taken from recent dealers' selling lists. Most of the listings are coded (A1, S7, etc.) before the price. This coding refers to a specific dealer's listing for that book. When two or more dealers have listed the same book, their codes will be listed alphabetically in the description line. Please refer to the section titled 'Book Sellers' for codes.

If you were to sell your books to a dealer, you should expect to receive no more than 50% of the values listed in this book, unless the dealer has a specific buyer in mind for some of your material. In many cases, a dealer will pay less than 50% of retail for a book to stock.

Do not ask a dealer to evaluate your old books unless you intend to sell them to him. Most antiquarian book dealers in the larger cities will appraise your books and ephemera for a fee that ranges from a low of $10.00 per hour to $50.00 per hour. If you have an extensive library of rare books, the $50.00-an-hour figure would be money well spent (assuming, of course, the appraiser to be qualified and honest).

Huxford's Old Book Value Guide places values on the more common holdings that many seem to accumulate. You will notice that the majority of the books listed are in the $10.00 to $25.00 range. Many such guides list only the rare, almost non-existent books that the average person will never see. The format is very simple: listings are alphabetized first by the name of the author, translator, editor, or illustrator; if more than one book is listed for a particular author, each title is listed alphabetically under his or her name. When pseudonyms are known, names have been cross-referenced. Dust jackets or wrappers are noted when present, and sizes (when given) are approximate. Condition may be noted in the listing as well.

Mint condition refers to books that are perfect, in as-issued condition with no defects. Books in near-mint condition are perfect, but not as crisp as those graded mint. Excellent condition books show only a little wear from reading (such as very small marks on binding); they are not as crisp as those graded higher, but they still have no major defects. Books rated very good may show wear but must have no tears on pages, binding, or dust jacket (if issued). A rating of good applies to an average used book that has all of its pages and yet may have small tears and other defects. The term reading copy (some dealers also use 'poor') describes a book having major defects; however, its text must be complete. Ex-library books are always indicated as such; they may be found in any condition. This rule also applies to any Book Club edition. Some of our booksellers indicate intermediate grades with a + or ++, or VG-EX. We have endeavored to use the grade that best corresponded to the description of condition as given in each dealer's listing. If you want to check further on the condition of a specific book, please consult the bookseller indicated. Please note that the condition stated in the description is for the book only, not for the dust jacket.

In the back of the book we have listed buyers of books and book-related material. When you correspond with these dealers, be sure to enclose a self-addressed, stamped envelope if you want a reply. Please do not send lists of books for an appraisal. If you wish to sell your books, quote the price that you want or negotiate price only on the items the buyer is interested in purchasing. When you list your books, do so by author, full title, publisher and place, date, and edition. Indicate condition, noting any defects on cover or contents.

When shipping your books, first wrap each book in paper such as brown kraft or a similar type of material. Never use newspaper for the inner wrap, since newsprint tends to rub off. (It may, however, be used as a cushioning material within the outer carton.) Place your books in a sturdy corrugated box, and use a good shipping tape to seal it. Tape impregnated with nylon string is preferable, as it will not tear.

Books shipped by parcel post may be sent at a special fourth class book rate, which is much lower than regular parcel post zone rates.

Listing of Standard Abbreviations

Am ....American
AEG..all edge gilt
/ ....and, also, with,
    or indicates dual title book
AP ....proof, advance proof,
    advance uncorrected proof, or galley
ARC................advance reading or review copy
bdg..binding, bound
decor................................decoration, decorated
bl...blue
blk...black
BOMC..............................Book of Month Club
brd...boards
c..circa
cbdg...comb binding
dj...dust jacket
dtd...dated
E...east, eastern
ed...edition
Eng..............................England, English
ep...end pages
ES...errata slip
ERB Inc...................Edgar Rice Burroughs Inc.
EX...excellent
fld...folding, folder
G...good
GPO..................Government Printing Office
gr..green
HrdCvr...hard cover
Ils...illustrated
imp..impression
intl...initialed
inscr...inscribed
Inst...Institute
Internat..international
Intro..introduction
lg..large
Lib...library
Ltd..limited
M...mint
MIT.......................MA Institute of Technology
MOMA......................Museum of Modern Art
MPA..........................Museum of Primitive Art
Mus...museum
NM..near mint
N...north, northern

Nat...National
nd...no date
ne...no edition given
np..no place given
orig...original
p..page, pages
PB...paperback
pl...plate
Pr..press
Pub............................publisher, publishing
repro...reproduction
RS...review slip
S..south, southern
s/wrp..shrink wrap
sbdg...spiral binding
SF...Science Fiction
SftCvr...soft cover
sgn...signature, signed
sm...small
TB...textbook
TEG...top edge gilt
Trans..translated
U...University
UP...................................uncorrected proof
VG...very good
W..west, western
w/..............................indicates laid in material
wht...white
wrp...wrappers
xl...ex-library
yel..yellow
#d...numbered
12mo...about 7" tall
16mo...6" to 7" tall
24mo...5" to 6" tall
32mo...4" to 5" tall
48mo...less than 4" tall
64mo...about 3" tall
sm 8vo...7½" to 8" tall
8vo...8" to 9" tall
sm 4to.............................about 10" tall, quarto
4to.............................between 11" to 13" tall
folio...13" or larger
elephant folio.............................23" or larger
atlas folio...25"
double elephant folio................larger than 25"

AARONSON, Sam. *Sam Aaronson Lecture No 1.* nd. np. sgn. 18 p. VG. J3. $3.00

ABBEY, Edward. *Abbey's Road.* 1979. Dutton. 1st HrdCvr ed. dj. EX. K2. $175.00

ABBEY, Edward. *Appalachian Wilderness.* 1970. NY. 1st ed. folio. as issued. K2. $75.00

ABBEY, Edward. *Appalachian Wilderness.* 1973. Dutton. 2nd ed. sm quarto. dj. VG. K2. $65.00

ABBEY, Edward. *Beyond the Wall.* 1984. Holt Rinehart Winston. UP. wrp. EX. K2. $250.00

ABBEY, Edward. *Beyond the Wall.* 1984. Holt Rinehart Winston. 1st ed. dj. EX. K2. $125.00

ABBEY, Edward. *Beyond the Wall.* 1984. Holt Rinehart Winston. 1st ed. sgn. wrp. VG. K2. $85.00

ABBEY, Edward. *Blk Sun.* 1971. Simon Schuster. 1st ed. dj. EX. H3. $125.00

ABBEY, Edward. *Blk Sun.* 1971. Simon Schuster. 1st ed. inscr/dtd 1971. dj. EX. K2. $400.00

ABBEY, Edward. *Cactus Country.* 1973. NY. Time Life. 1st ed. EX. B13. $65.00

ABBEY, Edward. *Cactus Country.* 1973. Time Life. Am Wilderness Series. sgn. EX. K2. $125.00

ABBEY, Edward. *Desert Images.* 1979.Chanticleer/Harcourt Brace. sgn. slipcase. K2. $400.00

ABBEY, Edward. *Desert Images.* 1979. Harcourt Brace. 1st ed. sgn. slipcase. B13. $375.00

ABBEY, Edward. *Desert Solitaire.* 1968. NY. Ils Peter Parnell. 1st ed. dj. EX. C4. $175.00

ABBEY, Edward. *Fire on the Mt.* 1962. Dial. 1st ed. inscr. clipped dj. EX. B13. $1500.00

ABBEY, Edward. *Fool's Progress.* 1988. Holt. 1st ed. sgn. dj. K2. $125.00

ABBEY, Edward. *Good News.* 1980. Dutton. ARC. inscr. RS. EX. K2. $250.00

ABBEY, Edward. *Good News.* 1980. Dutton. UP. inscr. wrp. EX. K2. $475.00

ABBEY, Edward. *Good News.* 1980. Dutton. 1st ed. dj. EX. K2. $45.00

ABBEY, Edward. *Good News.* 1980. Dutton. 1st SftCvr ed. sgn. wrp. EX. K2. $100.00

ABBEY, Edward. *Hayduke Lives!* 1989. Little Brn. UP. EX. K2. $85.00

ABBEY, Edward. *Hayduke Lives!* 1990. Boston. 1st ed. sgn Peacock. as issued. EX. K2. $55.00

ABBEY, Edward. *Hidden Canyon.* 1977. Penguin. Ils/sgn John Blaustein. SftCvr ed. EX. K2. $45.00

ABBEY, Edward. *Jonathan Troy.* 1954. Dodd Mead. 1st ed. dj. EX. B13. $1500.00

ABBEY, Edward. *Journey Home. Some Words in Defense of the Am W.* 1977. Dutton. 1st ed. dj. EX. K2. $65.00

ABBEY, Edward. *Monkey Wrench Gang.* 1975. Lippincott. ARC. yel printed wrp. EX. K2. $150.00

ABBEY, Edward. *Monkey Wrench Gang.* 1975. Lippincott. 1st ed. sgn. dj. EX. K2. $300.00

ABBEY, Edward. *Monkey Wrench Gang.* 1978. Canongate. 1st Eng ed. dj. EX. K2. $125.00

ABBEY, Edward. *Monkey Wrench Gang.* 1985. Dream Garden. 10th Anniversary ed. inscr/sgn. dj. B13. $250.00

ABBEY, Edward. *Monkey Wrench Gang.* 1985. Dream Garden. 10th Anniversary ed. sgn. dj. K2. $125.00

ABBEY, Edward. *Slickrock.* 1971. Sierra Club. 1st ed. dj. EX. K2. $250.00

ABBEY, Edward. *Slumgullion Stew.* 1984. Dutton. 1st ed. sgn. dj. EX. K2. $125.00

ABBEY, Edward. *Sunset Canyon.* 1971. London. Talmy Franklin. 1st ed. inscr. dj. EX. K2. $200.00

ABBEY, Edward. *Vox Clamantis Indeserto.* 1989. Rydal Pr. Ltd ed. 1/225. sgn. H3. $125.00

ABBEY, Edward. *1 Life at a Time, Please.* 1988. Holt. UP. wrp. EX. K2. $200.00

ABBEY, Edward. *1 Life at a Time, Please.* 1988. Holt. 1st HrdCvr ed. inscr. dj. EX. K2. $125.00

ABBEY & NICHOLS. *In Praise of Mt Lions.* 1984. Sierra Club. 1/600. pamphlet. sgns. K2. $175.00

ABBEY & NICHOLS. *Resist Much, Obey Little.* 1985. Dream Garden. 1st ed. sgn. wrp. EX. K2. $100.00

ABBOT, Anthony. *Murder of the Circus Queen.* 1934. Collins Crime Club. dj. VG. P1. $20.00

ABBOT, W.J. *Panama & the Canal in Pictures & Prose.* 1913. Syndicate Pub. 1st ed. 4to. 412 p. F2. $20.00

ABBOTT, Jacob. *Hist of Queen Elizabeth.* 1849. Harper. Ils. red bdg. VG. C1. $22.00

ABBOTT, John. *Hist of Hernando Cortez.* 1855. Harper. 1st ed. 348 p. VG. F2. $50.00

ABBOTT, John. *Life of Gen Ulysses S Grant.* 1868. Boston. 12mo. 312 p. G. G4. $29.00

ABDULLAH, Achmed. *Honorable Gentleman & Others.* 1919. Putnam. 1st ed. EX. R3. $17.50

ABDULLAH, Achmed. *Night Drums.* 1921. McCann. 1st ed. VG. $17.50

ABDULLAH & ABBOTT. *Shadow of the Master.* nd. London. dj. VG. R3. $15.00

ABDULLAH & BALDWIN. *Broadway Interlude.* 1929. Payson Clarke. VG. R3. $10.00

ABDULLAH & BALDWIN. *Broadway Interlude.* 1929. Payson Clarke. 7th print. VG. P1. $15.00

ABE, Kobo. *Beyond the Curve.* 1991. Tokyo/NY. Kodansha. ARC. wrp. EX. K2. $30.00

ABE, Kobo. *Inter Ice Age 4.* nd. Book Club. dj. VG. P1. $4.50

ABE, Kobo. *Inter Ice Age 4.* 1970. Knopf. UP. EX. very scarce. K2. $25.00

ABELL, A. *Talks With Great Composers.* 1955. NY. 1st ed. dj. VG. B3. $40.00

ABERCONWAY, Christabel. *Dictionary of Cat Lovers.* 1949. London. 1st ed. EX. $45.00

ABERT, J.W. *Through Country of Comanches in Fall of Year 1845.* 1970. San Francisco. 1st ed. lg 4to. EX. $50.00

ABISH, Walter. *How German Is It?* 1980. New Directions. 1st ed. dj. EX. B13. $45.00

ABRAHAMS, Peter. *Jamaica.* 1957. London. 1st ed. dj. EX. B13. $75.00

ABRAMS, R.V. *Para.* 1986. 7 Suns. 1st ed. M. R3. $17.95

ACHESON, Dean. *Present at the Creation.* nd. Norton. 1st ed. dj. EX. $15.00

ACKER, Kathy. *Literal Madness.* 1987. Grove Pr. 1st ed. sgn. dj. EX. K2. $45.00

ACKERMAN, Alan. *Esoterist.* 1971. Paul Diamond. 1st ed. 45 p. NM. J3. $20.00

ACKERMAN, Alan. *Here's My Card.* 1978. Las Vegas. GBC Pr. 109 p. NM. J3. $3.00

ACKERMAN, Alan. *Magic Mafia Effects.* 1970. Ackerman. 1st ed. 39 p. NM. J3. $28.00

ACKERMAN, Carl. *George Eastman.* 1930. Boston. 1st ed. 522 p. dj. VG. B3. $47.50

ACKERMAN, F.J. *Famous Monsters of Film Land.* 1986. Image Inc. 1st ed. M. R3. $10.95

ACKERMAN, F.J. *Frankenscience Monster.* 1969. Ace. P1. $8.00

ACKERMAN, F.J. *Gernsback Awards 1926. Vol 1.* 1982. Triton Books. 1st ed. dj. EX. F5. $20.00

ACKERMAN, F.J. *Lon of a 1000 Faces.* 1983. Morrison Raven-Hill. 1st ed. 1/200. sgns. EX. R3. $100.00

ACKERMAN, Isabel. *Harmony in Flower Design.* 1939. Dodd. apparent 1st ed. 115 p. dj. VG. B10. $8.50

ACKERMAN, Robert. *Ywain, Knight of the Lion.* 1987. Cretien. PB. M. C1. $5.50

ACKROYD, Peter. *Chatterton.* 1987. Grove Pr. UP of 1st Am ed. wrp. EX. C4. $40.00

ACKROYD, Peter. *1st Light.* 1989. Grove Pr. UP of 1st Am ed. wrp. EX. C4. $30.00

ACKWORTH, R.C. *Dr Kildare Assigned to Trouble.* 1963. Whitman. VG. P1. $10.00

ACOSTA, J.R. *Palacio del Quetzalpapalotl.* 1964. Mexico. 1st ed. 4to. F2. $75.00

ACOSTA, O.Z. *Revolt of the Cockroach People.* 1973. Straight Arrow Books. 1st ed. dj. EX. K2. $35.00

ADAIR, Ian. *Balloon-O-Dove.* nd. Devon, Eng. Supreme Magic. 11 p. SftCvr. J3. $3.00

ADAIR, Ian. *Caberet Dove Act.* nd. Devon, Eng. Supreme Magic. 21 p. SftCvr. NM. J3. $4.00

ADAIR, Ian. *Dove Magic Finale.* 1960. Devon, Eng. Supreme Magic. 18 p. SftCvr. NM. J3. $7.00

ADAIR, Ian. *Doves From Silks.* nd. Devon, Eng. Supreme Magic. 10 p. SftCvr. NM. J3. $4.00

ADAIR, Ian. *Magic on the Wing.* nd. Devon, Eng. Supreme Magic. 24 p. SftCvr. NM. J3. $4.00

ADAIR, Ian. *Rainbow Dove Routines.* nd. Devon, Eng. Supreme Magic. 17 p. SftCvr. NM. J3. $4.00

ADAIR, Ian. *Watch the Birdie.* nd. Devon, Eng. Supreme Magic. SftCvr. NM. J3. $4.00

ADAM, S.F. *Nearer, My God, to Thee.* 1887. Stokes. apparent 1st ed. VG. B10. $6.00

ADAMIC, Louis. *From Many Lands.* 1940. Harper. 1st ed. 350 p. VG. B10. $10.00

ADAMIC, Louis. *Grandsons. Story of Am Lives.* 1935. Harper. sgn. dj. H3. $40.00

ADAMIC, Louis. *House in Antigua: A Restoration.* 1937. Harper. 1st ed. sgn. dj. EX. $75.00

ADAMIC, Louis. *House in Antigua: A Restoration.* 1937. Harper. 1st ed. 300 p. F2. $20.00

ADAMIC, Louis. *Lucas, King of the Balucas.* 1935. Los Angeles. Arthur Whipple. Ltd ed. presentation. H3. $30.00

ADAMS, A.B. *John James Audubon.* nd. Putnam. not Book Club ed. 510 p. dj. EX. B10. $7.00

ADAMS, Alice. *Caroline's Daughters.* 1991. Knopf. UP. wrp. EX. B13. $50.00

ADAMS, Alice. *Return Trips.* 1985. Knopf. sgn. dj. EX. H3. $45.00

ADAMS, Alice. *To See You Again.* 1982. Knopf. sgn. dj. EX. H3. $60.00

ADAMS, Andy. *Egyptian Scarab Mystery.* nd. Grosset Dunlap. VG. P1. $3.50

ADAMS, Ansel. *My Camera in the Nat Parks.* 1950. Houghton Mifflin. 1st ed. folio. sgn. sbdg. dj. VG. B13. $425.00

ADAMS, Ansel. *Photographs of SW.* 1976. Boston. 1st ed. dj. EX. B3. $65.00

ADAMS, Ansel. *Taos Pueblo.* 1977. NY Graphic Soc. facsimile of 1930 ed. 1/950. sgn. slipcase. M. $450.00

ADAMS, Ansel. *Yosemite & Range of Light.* 1980. Time Life. Special ed. sgn. dj. EX. $100.00

ADAMS, Arthur. *Quimby.* 1988. St Martin. 1st ed. dj. EX. F5. $12.00

ADAMS, C.F. *Contraband.* nd. Knopf. VG. P1. $12.50

ADAMS, C.F. *Decoy.* 1945. Books Inc. 2nd ed. VG. P1. $12.50

ADAMS, C.F. *Mine Moder-in-Law.* c 1880s. Lowell, MA. issued by Hood Sarsaparilla. 12mo. wrp. $30.00

ADAMS, C.F. *Sabotage.* 1940. Dutton. 1st ed. dj. VG. P1. $40.00

ADAMS, C.F. *Up Jumped the Devil.* 1943. Reynal Hitchcock. 1st ed. dj. VG. P1. $25.00

ADAMS, Clifton. *Hassle & the Medicine Man.* nd. Book Club. dj. VG. P1. $4.00

ADAMS, Daniel. *Geography; or, Description of World in 3 Parts.* 1814. Boston. w/atlas. VG. $75.00

ADAMS, Daniel. *Scholar's Arithmetic; or, Federal Accountant.* 1808. Keene, NH. 5th ed. 216 p. TB. T5. $25.00

ADAMS, Douglas. *Dirk Gently's Holistic Detective Agency.* 1987. NY. 1st ed. dj. M. C1. $10.00

ADAMS, Douglas. *Life, the Universe, & Everything.* 1982. Harmony. 1st ed. dj. EX. P1. $20.00

ADAMS, Douglas. *Long Dark Tea Time of the Soul.* 1989. Simon Schuster. 1st ed. dj. RS. EX. P1. $20.00

ADAMS, Douglas. *Restaurant at the End of the Universe.* nd. Book Club. dj. EX. P1. $4.50

ADAMS, Douglas. *Restaurant at the End of the Universe.* nd. Harmony. 4th ed. dj. EX. P1. $15.00

ADAMS, Douglas. *Restaurant at the End of the Universe.* 1980. Harmony. dj. VG. R3. $10.00

ADAMS, Douglas. *So Long & Thanks for All the Fish.* 1984. Pan. 1st ed. dj. EX. P1. $20.00

ADAMS, Douglas. *So Long & Thanks for All the Fish.* 1985. Harmony. 1st ed. M. R3. $15.00

ADAMS, E.L. *Death Charter.* nd. Coward McCann. 2nd ed. VG. P1. $12.50

ADAMS, E.L. *On the Wings of Flame.* nd. Grosset Dunlap. VG. P1. $10.00

ADAMS, E.L. *Pirates of the Air.* 1929. Grosset Dunlap. VG. P1. $15.00

ADAMS, E.L. *Racing Around the World.* nd. Grosset Dunlap. VG. P1. $10.00

ADAMS, E.L. *Wings of the Navy.* nd. Grosset Dunlap. dj. VG. P1. $20.00

ADAMS, E.L. *15 Days in the Air.* nd. Grosset Dunlap. VG. P1. $7.00

ADAMS, Frederick. *Conquest of the Tropics.* 1914. Doubleday. 1st ed. 368 p. gilt gr bdg. F2. $20.00

ADAMS, Henry. *Democracy.* 1880. Holt. 1st ed. state D bdg. K2. $225.00

ADAMS, Henry. *Mont-Saint-Michel & Chartres.* 1913. Houghton Mifflin. 2nd ed. 4to. G. R5. $50.00

ADAMS, Henry. *Mont-Saint-Michel & Chartres.* 1957. Ltd Ed Club. Ils/sgn Samuel Chamberlain. 4to. slipcase. VG. $70.00

ADAMS, J.T. *Adams Family.* 1930. Literary Guild. 1st ed. 364 p. EX. B10. $6.50

ADAMS, J.T. *Am's Tragedy.* 1934. NY. 1st ed. dj. VG. $18.00

ADAMS, N.M. *5th Horseman.* nd. Book Club. dj. VG. P1. $2.75

ADAMS, Nehemiah. *S-Side View of Slavery; or, 3 Months in the S in 1854.* 1855. Boston. 12mo. 222 p. bl bdg. xl. G. G4. $48.00

ADAMS, R.F. *Old-Time Cowhand.* 1961. Macmillan. Revised ed. 2nd print. VG. $20.00

ADAMS, R.F. *Rampaging Herd.* 1959. OK U. 1st ed. 463 p. dj. T5. $75.00

ADAMS, R.F. *6-Guns & Saddle Leather.* 1954. OK U. 1st ed. dj. VG. $78.00

ADAMS, R.F. *6-Guns & Saddle Leather.* 1982. Cleveland. dj. M. K1. $35.00

ADAMS, Richard. *Maia.* 1985. Knopf. 1st ed. dj. VG. P1. $15.00

ADAMS, Richard. *Shardik.* 1974. Simon Schuster. 1st ed. dj. EX. $15.00

ADAMS, Richard. *Ship's Cat.* 1977. London. Cape. 1st ed. dj. EX. B13. $65.00

ADAMS, Richard. *Ship's Cat.* 1977. NY. Knopf. 1st ed. dj. EX. B13. $65.00

ADAMS, Richard. *Watership Down.* 1972. Macmillan. inscr. dj. EX. H3. $150.00

ADAMS, Richard. *Watership Down.* 1972. Sydney. 1st Australian ed. dj. EX. $150.00

ADAMS, S.H. *Clarion.* 1914. Houghton Mifflin. 1st ed. 417 p. VG. B10. $5.00

ADAMS & KIMBALL. *Heroines of the Sky.* 1942. Garden City. Ils 1st ed. 295 p. dj. T5. $47.50

ADAMS & NEWHALL. *Flat Lux.* 1967. NY. 1st ed. folio. dj. EX. P4. $75.00

ADAMSON, David. *Ruins of Time.* 1975. Praeger. 1st ed. 8vo. 272 p. dj. G. F2. $20.00

ADAMSON, Joy. *Living Free.* 1961. Book Club. 159 p. dj. VG. B10. $4.50

ADDAMS, Charles. *Addams & Evil.* 1947. NY. 2nd print. G. $7.00

ADDAMS, Charles. *Charles Addams' Mother Goose.* 1967. NY. 1st ed. dj. VG. B3. $30.00

ADDAMS, Charles. *Drawn & Quartered.* 1942. NY. not 1st ed. dj. VG. B3. $25.00

ADDAMS, Charles. *Favorite Haunts.* 1976. Simon Schuster. VG. P1. $15.00

ADDAMS, Charles. *Groaning Brd.* 1964. NY. 1st ed. dj. VG. B3. $45.00

ADDAMS, Jane. *2nd 20 Years at Hull House.* 1930. NY. 1st ed. sgn. VG. B3. $77.50

ADDINGTON, Sarah. *Great Adventure of Mrs Santa Cluas.* 1923. Little Brn. 1 pl missing. VG. B7. $25.00

ADDISON, Joseph. *Sir Roger de Coverly Papers.* 1945. Heritage. 12 clr pls. slipcase. EX. T1. $20.00

ADDISON & STEELE. *Spectator.* 1977. London. Donaldson. sm octavo. 8 vols. G. H3. $200.00

ADE, George. *Fables in Slang & More Fables in Slang.* 1960. stiff wrp. VG. C1. $4.50

ADE, George. *More Fables.* 1902. Stone. Ils. 16mo. 218 p. $20.00

ADE, George. *Old-Time Saloon. Not Wet, Not Dry, Just Hist.* 1931. Long Smith. Ltd ed. sgn. gilt bdg. H3. $85.00

ADE, George. *People You Know.* 1903. NY/London. 1st ed. inscr. VG. $45.00

ADLER, Bill. *Dear Beatles.* 1966. Wonder Books. VG. P1. $5.00

ADLER, Elmer. *In the World of Books.* 1964. NY. Grolier. 1/800. 8vo. $15.00

ADLER, Elmer. *On Books.* 1953. KS U. sm 8vo. EX. $10.00

ADLER, Warren. *Blood Ties.* 1979. Putnam. 1st ed. dj. VG. P1. $15.00

ADLER, Warren. *Casanova Embrace.* 1978. Putnam. 1st ed. dj. VG. P1. $12.50

ADLER, Warren. *War of the Roses.* 1981. NY. 1st ed. dj. EX. C4. $30.00

ADLER & DAVIS. *You Gotta Have Heart.* 1990. NY. Donald Fine. 1st ed. inscr. 354 p. dj. EX. H3. $50.00

ADNEY & CHAPELLE. *Bark Canoes & Skin Boats of N Am.* 1964. WA. 4to. A6. $50.00

ADRION, Alexander. *Adrion's Zauber-Kabinett.* 1980. Koln, Germany. 1st ed. German text. slipcase. J3. $24.00

AESOP. *Fables.* 1933. Ltd Ed Club. Trans Samuel Croxall. 1/1500. slipcase. EX. C4. $150.00

AGASSIZ, Laura. *Tessie: Story of My Life.* 1928. private print. 12mo. inscr. 121 p. EX. $40.00

AGASSIZ & AGASSIZ. *Journey in Brazil.* 1887. Houghton Mifflin. Ils. 540 p. F2. $50.00

AGEE, James. *Letters of James Agee to Father Flye.* 1962. NY. 1st ed. dj. EX. $25.00

AGNEW, Georgette. *Let's Pretend.* 1927. London. Saville. sgns. 4to. TEG. slipcase. H3. $375.00

AGRINIER, Pierre. *Sacrifical Mass Burial at Mirmar, Chiapas, Mexico.* 1978. Provo. 4to. 52 p. wrp. F2. $15.00

AGUILAR, Grace. *Home Influence: A Tale.* 1851. Harper. New ed. VG. R5. $20.00

AHEARN, Allen. *Book Collecting.* 1989. Putnam. 1st ed. dj. M. $15.00

AHELEZNOVA, Irina. *Vasilisa the Beautiful. Russian Fairy Tales.* 1966. np. Ils. 8vo. 213 p. dj. VG. $30.00

AHERN, Allen. *Book Collecting: Book of 1st Books.* 1986. 4th ed. 1/350. dj. EX. C1. $19.00

AHERN, G.P. *Important Philippine Woods.* 1901. Manila. Ils. 8vo. VG. $145.00

AICKMAN, Robert. *Cold Hand in Mine.* nd. Book Club. dj. VG. P1. $6.00

AICKMAN, Robert. *Painted Devils.* 1979. Scribner. 1st ed. dj. EX. R3. $25.00

AIKEN, Conrad. *Charnel Rose.* 1918. 4 Seasons. 1st ed. dj. VG. B13. $85.00

AIKEN, Conrad. *Preludes for Memnon.* 1931. Scribner. sgn. H3. $85.00

AIKEN, Joan. *Castle Barebane.* 1976. Viking. ARC. VG. R3. $15.00

AIKEN, Joan. *Castle Barebane.* 1976. Viking. 1st ed. dj. VG. P1. $15.00

AIKEN, Joan. *Foul Matter.* 1983. Doubleday. 1st ed. dj. VG. P1. $12.50

AIKEN, Joan. *Gr Flash.* nd. Holt. 1st ed. dj. VG. R3. $15.00

AIKEN, Joan. *Stolen Lake.* 1981. 1st Am ed. dj. EX. C1. $14.50

AIKEN, Joan. *Stolen Lake.* 1981. 1st ed. dj. VG. C1. $9.50

AIKEN, Joan. *Touch of Chill.* 1980. Delacorte. 1st ed. dj. EX. R3. $15.00

AIKEN, Joan. *World Well Lost.* 1971. Doubleday. 1st ed. dj. EX. R3. $20.00

AIKEN, John. *Wolves of Willoughby Chase.* nd. Doubleday. dj. VG. P1. $10.00

AIKIN, John. *Essays on Song Writing.* 1774. London. Johnson. 2nd ed. octavo. 286 p. contemporary calf. H3. $225.00

AIKIN, S.C. *Theatrical Exhibitions: A Sermon.* 1836. Cleveland. 19 p. wrp. T5. $75.00

AINSWORTH, W.H. *Novels.* 1903. NY. Taylor. Cabinet ed. 1/1000. 20 vols. H3. $850.00

AIRD, Catherine. *His Burial Too.* 1973. Crime Club. dj. VG. P1. $12.50

AIRD, Catherine. *Parting Breath.* 1977. Collins Crime Club. 1st ed. dj. VG. P1. $12.50

ALAIN-FOURNIER. *Big Meaulnes.* 1932. Crosby Continental. 1st ed. wht wrp. VG. H3. $100.00

ALAN, Don. *Pretty Sneaky.* 1956. Chicago. Ireland Pub. 1st ed. 48 p. SftCvr. EX. J3. $3.00

ALAN, Don. *Rubber Circus.* 1980. Magic Inc. 7th print. SftCvr. NM. J3. $2.00

ALASTAIR. *50 Drawings by Alastair.* 1925. Knopf. Ltd ed. 1/1025. TEG. VG. $60.00

ALBAUGH, W.A. *Confederate Arms.* 1957. Bonanza. dj. VG. B3. $27.50

ALBAUGH, W.A. *Confederate Handguns.* 1943. Bonanza. dj. VG. B3. $50.00

ALBAUGH, W.A. *Photographic Supplement of Confederate Swords.* 1979. Orange, VA. 2nd ed. dj. EX. $35.00

ALBEE, Edward. *Counting the Ways & Listening.* 1977. Atheneum. 1st ed. dj. EX. H3. $50.00

ALBEE, Edward. *Delicate Balance.* 1966. Atheneum. 1st ed. dj. EX. H3. $60.00

ALBEE, Edward. *Lady From Dubuque: A Play.* 1980. Atheneum. sgn. dj. M. H3. $85.00

ALBEE, Edward. *Malcolm.* 1966. Atheneum. 1st ed. dj. EX. H3. $50.00

ALBEE, Edward. *Seascape.* 1975. Atheneum. 1st ed. inscr/sgn. dj. EX. H3. $100.00

ALBEE, Edward. *Seascape: A Play.* 1975. Atheneum. Play/1st ed. dj. EX. H3. $50.00

ALBEE, Edward. *Tiny Alice.* 1965. Atheneum. 1st ed. dj. EX. H3. $75.00

ALBEE, Edward. *Tiny Alice.* 1966. Jonathan Cape. 1st UK ed. dj. VG. H3. $50.00

ALBEE, Edward. *Tiny Alice: A Play.* 1965. Atheneum. Play/1st ed. sgn. dj. EX. H3. $150.00

ALBEE, Edward. *Who's Afraid of VA Woolf?* 1964. Jonathan Cape. 1st UK ed. dj. EX. H3. $75.00

ALBEE, Edward. *Zoo Story.* 1960. NY. 1st ed. sgn. as issued. K2. $85.00

ALBENICE. *Reel Magic.* 1941. Nat Louis. 1st ed. 55 p. NM. J3. $12.50

ALBERS, Josef. *Poems & Drawings. Gedichte und Zeichnungen.* 1961. NY. oblong 8vo. dj. VG. $30.00

ALBERT, M.H. *Chiselers.* nd. (1957?) London. Muller. 1st ed. wrp. EX. rare. T9. $30.00

ALBERT, M.H. *Don Is Dead.* 1972. Gold Medal T2527. PB Orig. wrp. EX. T9. $20.00

ALBERTO ACUNA, Luis. *El Arte de Los Indios Colombianos.* 1935. Bogota. 1st ed. 8vo. 78 p. xl. F2. $25.00

ALBO, R.J. *Magic of Okito.* nd. np. blk/orange/gr bdg. J3. $20.00

ALBRAND, Martha. *After Midnight.* nd. Random House. 2nd ed. VG. P1. $7.50

ALBRAND, Martha. *Linden Affair.* 1956. Random House. 1st ed. dj. VG. P1. $30.00

ALBRAND, Martha. *Mask of Alexander.* 1955. Random House. 1st ed. dj. VG. P1. $20.00

ALBRAND, Martha. *Remembered Anger.* 1946. Little Brn. 2nd ed. dj. VG. P1. $10.00

ALBRAND, Martha. *Without Orders.* 1944. Sun Dial. dj. VG. P1. $5.50

ALBRECHTSBERGER, J.G. *Methods of Harmony, Figured Base, & Composition...* c1830. London. Cocks. 2nd ed. 2 vols. H3. $200.00

ALBRIGHT, H.P. *Albright's Advanced Card Magic.* nd. Colon, MI. Abbott. 19 p. SftCvr. EX. J3. $3.00

ALBURGER, James. *Get Your Act Together.* 1981. San Diego. Alburger. 2nd print. 149 p. NM. J3. $9.00

ALCOHOLICS ANON. *Alcoholics Anon.* 1950. NY. dj. EX. P4. $250.00

ALCOHOLICS ANON. *Alcoholics Anon.* 1955. NY. 2nd ed. 14th print. dj. VG. B3. $20.00

ALCOTT, Bronson. *Journals of Bronson Alcott.* 1938. Little Brn. 1st ed. VG. $35.00

ALCOTT, L.M. *Aunt Jo's Scrapbook.* 1879. Roberts Bros. red cloth. VG. $25.00

ALCOTT, L.M. *Little Women.* nd. (1929) Saalfield. Ils Brundage. 630 p. VG. B10. $5.00

ALCOTT, L.M. *Little Women.* nd. Winston. Ils CM Burd. 8vo. 496 p. VG. $20.00

ALCOTT, L.M. *Old-Fashioned Girl.* 1911. Grosset. 328 p. dj. VG. B10. $3.50

ALDEN, Raymond. *Why the Chimes Rang & Other Stories.* 1924. Indianapolis. Ils Katharine Sturges. VG. $25.00

ALDEN. *Flush Decks & 4 Pipes.* 1965. Annapolis. 1st ed. 107 p. lg wrp. G. B3. $65.00

ALDINGTON, Richard. *All Men Are Enemies.* 1933. London. Chatto Windus. 1st ed. dj. VG. H3. $75.00

ALDINGTON, Richard. *Dream in the Luxembourg.* 1930. Chatto Windus. 1st ed. dj. EX. H3. $25.00

ALDINGTON, Richard. *Love & the Luxembourg.* 1930. Covici Friede. Ltd ed. 1/475. sgn. slipcase. H3. $100.00

ALDINGTON, Richard. *2 Stories.* 1930. np. Mathews Marrot. Ltd ed. 1/530. sgn. dj. EX. H3. $100.00

ALDINI (Alex Weiner). *Magic Sermonettes.* 1962. Colon, MI. Abbott. 31 p. SftCvr. NM. J3. $3.00

ALDINI (Alex Weiner). *Novel Concepts With Cards.* 1970. Calgary. Micky Hades Enterprises. SftCvr. EX. J3. $4.00

ALDISS, B.W. *Barefoot in the Head.* 1969. Doubleday. 1st Am ed. dj. VG. R3. $12.50

ALDISS, B.W. *Billion-Year Spree.* 1973. Doubleday. dj. VG. P1. $17.50

ALDISS, B.W. *Billion-Year Spree.* 1975. Corgi. P1. $3.50

ALDISS, B.W. *Brothers of the Head.* 1977. London. 1st ed. dj. EX. R3. $25.00

ALDISS, B.W. *Canopy of Time.* 1961. British SF Book Club. dj. VG. P1. $7.50

ALDISS, B.W. *Decade of the 1940s.* 1975. Macmillan. 1st ed. dj. VG. P1. $20.00

ALDISS, B.W. *Decade of the 1940s.* 1975. St Martin. 1st ed. dj. EX. R3. $17.50

ALDISS, B.W. *Earthworks.* 1965. Doubleday. 1st ed. dj. VG. P1. $35.00

ALDISS, B.W. *Enemies of the System.* 1978. Harper Row. 1st ed. dj. xl. P1. $10.00

ALDISS, B.W. *Enemies of the System.* 1978. Harper. 1st Am ed. dj. EX. R3. $20.00

ALDISS, B.W. *Frankenstein Unbound.* 1973. Random House. 1st Am ed. dj. RS. EX. R3. $30.00

ALDISS, B.W. *Frankenstein Unbound.* 1975. private print. 1st ed. 1/150. sgn. M. R3. $30.00

ALDISS, B.W. *Frankenstein Unbound.* 1976. Alternate Worlds Record. 1st ed. M. R3. $15.00

ALDISS, B.W. *Galactic Empires 2.* nd. Book Club. VG. P1. $4.50

ALDISS, B.W. *Hell's Cartographers.* 1976. Harper. 1st ed. dj. EX. R3. $20.00

ALDISS, B.W. *Hell's Cartographers.* 1976. Orbit. P1. $4.00

ALDISS, B.W. *Helliconia Spring.* 1982. Atheneum. 1st ed. dj. EX. P1. $15.95

ALDISS, B.W. *Helliconia Spring.* 1982. Jonathan Cape. 2nd ed. dj. EX. P1. $15.00

ALDISS, B.W. *Helliconia Winter.* 1985. Atheneum. 1st Am ed. dj. EX. R3. $30.00

ALDISS, B.W. *Island Called Moreau.* 1981. Simon Schuster. 1st ed. dj. EX. R3. $20.00

ALDISS, B.W. *Malacia Tapestry.* 1977. Harper Row. 1st ed. dj. EX. P1. $15.00

ALDISS, B.W. *Neanderthal Planet.* nd. Book Club. 1st ed. dj. VG. P1. $4.50

ALDISS, B.W. *Pile.* 1979. Holt Rinehart Winston. no dj issued. P1. $15.00

ALDISS, B.W. *Report on Probability.* 1969. Doubleday. 1st Am ed. dj. VG. R3. $30.00

ALDISS, B.W. *Rude Awakening.* 1978. Weidenfeld Nicolson. 1st ed. dj. VG. P1. $25.00

ALDISS, B.W. *Soldier Erect.* 1972. Coward McCann. 1st Am ed. dj. EX. R3. $20.00

ALDISS, B.W. *Space Odysseys.* 1976. Doubleday. 1st Am ed. dj. RS. EX. R3. $20.00

ALDISS, B.W. *Space Odysseys.* 1976. Doubleday. 1st ed. dj. EX. P1. $15.00

ALDISS, B.W. *Space Opera.* nd. Book Club. dj. VG. P1. $4.50

ALDISS, B.W. *Space Opera.* 1975. Doubleday. 1st Am ed. dj. EX. R3. $17.50

ALDISS, B.W. *8-Minute Hour.* 1974. Doubleday. 1st ed. dj. EX. R3. $22.50

ALDISS & WILKS. *Pile-Petals From St Klaed's Computer.* 1979. Holt. 1st Am ed. dj. EX. R3. $25.00

ALDOUS, Alan. *Lady's Eyes Were Gr.* 1951. Skeffington. xl. P1. $6.00

ALDRICH, B.S. *Cutters.* nd. Grosset. 275 p. dj. VG. B10. $3.00

ALDRICH, B.S. *Wht Bird Flying.* 1931. NY. 1st ed. dj. VG. B3. $15.00

ALDRICH, T.B. *Works.* 1897. Riverside Pr. Ltd ed. 1/250. 10 vols. H3. $2000.00

ALDRICH, T.B. *Writings.* 1911. Houghton Mifflin. Ponkapong ed. 10 vols. gilt red morocco. VG. $200.00

ALDRIDGE, Alan. *Beatles Ils Lyrics.* 1969. Delacorte. folio. 156 p. repaired dj. H3. $75.00

ALEXANDER, David. *Most Men Don't Kill.* 1951. Random House. 1st ed. dj. VG. P1. $15.00

ALEXANDER, David. *Pennies From Hell.* 1960. Lippincott. 1st ed. dj. VG. P1. $25.00

ALEXANDER, E.P. *Civil War Railroads & Models.* 1977. NY. Ils 1st ed. 255 p. dj. T5. $22.50

ALEXANDER, Grand Duke. *Once a Grand Duke.* 1932. NY. sgn. dj. VG. B3. $50.00

ALEXANDER, H.C. *Richard Cadbury of Birmingham.* 1906. Hodder Stoughton. 8vo. 448 p. V1. $18.50

ALEXANDER, Hartley. *Mythology of All Races: Latin Am Vol 11.* 1965. NY. reprint of 1920 ed. xl. F2. $10.00

ALEXANDER, Lloyd. *El Dorado Adventure.* 1987. Dutton. 1st ed. dj. EX. P1. $12.95

ALEXANDER, Lloyd. *Kestrel.* 1982. Dutton. 1st ed. dj. EX. P1. $15.00

ALEXANDER, M. *Hogarth's Times.* 1956. Rodale Mini Books. 1st ed. glassine wrp. EX. $10.00

ALEXANDER, Mary. *William Patterson Alexander in KY, the Marquesas, HI.* 1934. Honolulu. private print. VG. $40.00

ALEXANDER, Patrick. *Death of a Thin-Skinned Animal.* 1977. Dutton. 1st ed. dj. VG. P1. $15.00

ALEXANDER, Ruth. *Ghost Train.* 1928. Readers Lib. dj. VG. P1. $17.50

ALEXANDER, The Magician. *Magic Show Book.* 1950. Macmillan. 4th print. 145 p. dj. EX. J3. $11.00

ALEXANDER. *Mosby's Men.* 1907. NY/WA. 1st ed. VG. C2. $225.00

ALEXANDROV. *Math Content, Method, & Meaning.* 1963. Cambridge. 3 vols. slipcases. VG. C2. $55.00

ALEY, H.C. *1st 100 Years: Centennial Hist of Mahoning Co...* 1946. Youngstown. 113 p. decor wrp. T5. $17.50

ALGER, Edwin. *Phil Hardy's Triumph.* nd. Grosset Dunlap. dj. VG. P1. $7.50

ALGER, Horatio. *Adrift in NY.* nd. World. dj. VG. P1. $15.00

ALGER, Horatio. *Facing the World.* nd. World. dj. VG. P1. $15.00

ALGER, Horatio. *Helen Ford.* 1866. Porter Coates. 297 p. G. T5. $32.50

ALGER, Horatio. *Paul the Peddler.* nd. Donohue. decor brd. VG. P1. $12.50

ALGER, Horatio. *Phil the Fiddler.* nd. Donohue. decor brd. VG. P1. $15.00

ALGER, Horatio. *Risen From the Ranks.* nd. Hurst. VG. P1. $15.00

ALGER, Horatio. *Strong & Steady.* nd. Donohue. VG. P1. $15.00

ALGREN, Nelson. *Chicago: City on the Make.* 1951. Doubleday. 1st ed. sgn McMurtry. dj. EX. H3. $125.00

ALGREN, Nelson. *Man With the Golden Arm.* nd. Crest. EX. B4. $5.00

ALGREN, Nelson. *Man With the Golden Arm.* 1949. Doubleday. 1st ed. sgn McMurtry. dj. EX. H3. $125.00

ALGREN, Nelson. *Man With the Golden Arm.* 1949. Doubleday. 1st ed. 343 p. VG. B10. $15.00

ALGREN, Nelson. *Man With the Golden Arm.* 1961. Eng Ace H414. 1st ed. B4. $6.00

ALGREN, Nelson. *Nelson Algren's Own Book of Lonesome Monsters.* 1963. Geis/Random House. 1st ed. sgn McMurtry. dj. EX. H3. $125.00

ALGREN, Nelson. *Neon Wilderness.* 1947. Doubleday. 1st ed. dj. EX. H3. $100.00

ALGREN, Nelson. *Walk on the Wild Side.* nd. Farrar Straus Cudahy. 1st ed. sgn McMurtry. dj. EX. R3. $150.00

ALGREN, Nelson. *Walk on the Wild Side.* 1956. NY. 1st print. dj. EX. $50.00

ALGREN, Nelson. *Walk on the Wild Side.* 1960. Eng Ace H258. 1st Ace PB ed. VG. B4. $15.00

ALGREN, Nelson. *Who Lost an Am?* 1963. Macmillan. 1st ed. dj. EX. H3. $40.00

ALGREN, Nelson. *Who Lost an Am?* 1963. Macmillan. 1st ed. inscr/sgn. dj. H3. $100.00

ALIKI. *Weed Is a Flower: Life of George WA Carver.* 1965. Prentice Hall. 1st ed. dj. EX. B13. $45.00

ALINSKY, Saul. *John L Lewis: Unauthorized Biography.* 1949. Putnam. 1st Am ed. 387 p. dj. VG. B10. $8.50

ALIREZA, Marianne. *At the Drop of a Veil.* 11th print. inscr/sgn. dj. EX. C1. $7.50

ALLBEURY, Ted. *Children of Tender Years.* 1985. Beaufort. 1st ed. dj. VG. P1. $15.00

ALLEE, M.H. *Little Am Girl.* 1938. Houghton Mifflin. 8vo. 237 p. xl. very worn. V1. $4.00

ALLEN, A. *Golden Plover & Other Birds.* 1939. Ithica. 1st ed. dj. VG. B3. $32.50

ALLEN, Betsy. *Clue in Bl.* nd. Grosset Dunlap. dj. VG. P1. $6.00

ALLEN, D. *Wolves of Minong.* 1979. Boston. 1st ed. 499 p. dj. VG. B3. $45.00

ALLEN, Dave. *Little Night Reading.* 1974. Roger Schlesinger. 1st ed. dj. EX. P1. $20.00

ALLEN, Dick. *SF: The Future.* nd. Harcourt Brace Jovanovich. VG. P1. $10.00

ALLEN, E.R. *Samuel L Allen: Intimate Recollections & Letters.* 1920. Phil. 8vo. 311 p. xl. V1. $10.00

ALLEN, E.T. *Practical Forestry in the Pacific NW.* 1911. Portland, OR. EX. $45.00

ALLEN, G.H. *Yankee in the Far E.* 1915. NY. Clinton. 1st ed. 285 p. dj. EX. B10. $4.50

ALLEN, G.W. *Our Naval War With France.* 1909. Boston. 1st ed. VG. $15.00

ALLEN, Gracie. *How To Become President.* 1940. Duell Sloan Pearce. 1st ed. sm octavo. 94 p. dj. VG. H3. $85.00

ALLEN, Hervey. *Action at Aquila.* 1938. Farrar Rinehart. 369 p. G. S1. $4.00

ALLEN, Hervey. *Anthony Adverse.* 1933. Farrar. 1st ed. VG. V5. $12.00

ALLEN, Hervey. *Anthony Adverse.* 1937. Ltd Ed Club. 3 vols. boxed. EX. $30.00

ALLEN, Hugh. *House of Goodyear.* 1949. np. Ils Revised ed. 691 p. dj. T5. $35.00

ALLEN, Hugh. *Story of the Airship.* 1931. Akron. Ils. 84 p. w/orig envelope. T5. $37.50

ALLEN, J. *Capt J Allen's Expedition.* 1846. WA. 8vo. 18 p. disbound. $25.00

ALLEN, Ken. *Do-It-Yourself Lecture No 1.* 1957. Allen. 1st ed. 29 p. cbdg. EX. J3. $3.00

ALLEN, Ken. *Pilfered Patter No 1.* 1958. Union City, NJ. 1st ed. 23 p. cbdg. J3. $3.00

ALLEN, Ken. *TIPS (Tricks, Ideas, Patter, & Suggestions).* 1959. Ken Allen Products. 1st ed. 23 p. SftCvr. EX. J3. $3.00

ALLEN, L.F. *Rural Architecture.* 1860. NY. orig bdg. VG. C2. $95.00

ALLEN, Lewis. *Indian Fairy Tales.* 1912. Boston. Luce. 1st ed. VG. K2. $35.00

ALLEN, Maury. *Where Have You Gone, Joe Dimaggio?* 1975. 1st ed. dj. EX. C1. $9.50

ALLEN, Minerva. *Like Spirits of the Past Trying To Break Out & Walk to W.* 1974. Albuquerque. Wowapi. wrp. EX. K2. $35.00

ALLEN, R. *Covered Bridges of the NE.* 1957. Brattleboro. 1st ed. 121 p. dj. VG. B3. $27.50

ALLEN, R.L. *Am Farm Book.* 1850. NY. Ils Saxton. VG. $50.00

ALLEN, R.S. *Revolution in the Sky.* 1964. Brattleboro, VT. 1st ed. sgn. 232 p. T5. $47.50

ALLEN, Robert. *Lucky Forward.* 1947. NY. 1st ed. dj. VG. B3. $30.00

ALLEN, Thomas. *Commerce & Navigation of Valley of the MS.* 1847. St Louis. Chambers Knapp. 8vo. 32 p. wrp/string ties. $450.00

ALLEN, W.B. *Lion City of Africa.* 1890. Lathrop. 1st ed. sgn. EX. R3. $100.00

ALLEN, W.C. *Quaker Diary in the Orient.* 1915. San Jose, CA. Wright-Eley. 8vo. 101 p. V1. $14.00

ALLEN, WARE, & GARRISON. *Slave Songs of the US.* 1867. NY. Simpson. 1st ed. octavo. 115 pages. orig brn bdg. VG. H3. $400.00

ALLEN, Warner. *Uncounted Hour.* 1936. Constable. 1st ed. VG. P1. $30.00

ALLEN, Woody. *Getting Even.* 1971. NY. 1st ed. 1st issue dj. EX. T9. $90.00

ALLEN & AVERY. *1st Nugget.* 1893. San Francisco. 1st ed. VG. $60.00

ALLEN & BRICKMAN. *Annie Hall.* 1977. United Artists. quarto. 167 p. wrp. VG. H3. $125.00

ALLEN & DAY. *Steam Wells & Other Thermal Activity at Geysers.* 1927. Carnegie. 106 p. wrp. VG. $65.00

ALLEN & KELLEY. *Fun by the Ton.* 1941. Hastings House. 1st ed. octavo. dj. H3. $50.00

ALLEN PRESS. *Allen Pr Biography...* 1981. Greenbrae, CA. Orig ed. 1/140. folio. slipcase. EX. H3. $1750.00

ALLEN PRESS. *Book of Genesis...* 1970. Kentfield, CA. Ils Blair Hughes-Stanton. 1/140. EX. H3. $600.00

ALLINGHAM, Margery. *China Governess.* 1963. Chatto Windus. 1st ed. dj. VG. P1. $25.00

ALLINGHAM, Margery. *Crime & Mr Campion.* nd. Book Club. dj. VG. P1. $7.50

ALLINGHAM, Margery. *Mind Readers.* 1965. Morrow. 3rd ed. P1. $15.00

ALLINGHAM, Margery. *More Work for the Undertaker.* 1949. Doubleday Book Club. G. P1. $7.50

ALLINGHAM, Margery. *Mr Campion's Clowns.* 1967. Chatto Windus. 1st ed. dj. VG. P1. $25.00

ALLINGHAM, Margery. *Pearls Before Swine.* 1945. Crime Club. 1st ed. VG. P1. $15.00

ALLINSON, W.J. *Memorials of Rebecca Jones.* 1849. Phil. Longstreth. 2nd ed. 372 p. V1. $8.50

ALLISON, Sam. *Wells Fargo & Danger Station.* 1958. Whitman. HrdCvr ed. VG. P1. $15.00

ALLWRIGHT, Michael. *Neighbors.* 1968. Walker. 1st ed. dj. EX. F5. $15.00

ALMENDROS, Nestor. *Man With a Camera.* 1984. Farrar Straus. UP. wrp. EX. K2. $40.00

ALOTTA, R.I. *Stop the Evil: Story of WH Howe of 116th PA Volunteers.* nd. San Rafael. dj. EX. $15.00

ALOTTA, Robert. *Civil War Justice: Union Army Executions Under Lincoln.* 1989. Wht Mane. 234 p. dj. M. S1. $24.95

ALPERN, Andrew. *Apartments for the Affluent.* 1975. NY. 1st ed. VG. G1. $20.00

ALTMAN, Thomas. *Kiss Daddy Goodbye.* 1980. Doubleday. 1st HrdCvr ed. dj. EX. F5. $10.00

ALTSHELER, J.A. *Soldier of Manhattan.* 1897. NY. 1st ed. G. $35.00

ALVERSON, Charles. *Not Sleeping, Just Dead.* 1977. Houghton Mifflin. dj. EX. P1. $12.50

ALVERSON, Margaret. *60 Years of CA Song.* 1913. Oakland. 1st ed. inscr. VG. $35.00

ALVORD, C.W. *MS Valley in British Politics.* 1917. Arthur Clark. 2 vols. VG. $125.00

AMADO, Jorge. *Miracle of the Birds.* 1983. Targ Ed. Ltd ed. 1/250. sgn. dj. EX. K2. $85.00

AMADO, Jorge. *Violent Land.* 1945. Knopf. 1st ed. dj. EX. K2. $85.00

AMALFI (W.F. Tunnah). *Santa's Workshop & Other Christmas Magic.* 1957. Brimingham, Eng. 1st ed. SftCvr. EX. J3. $12.00

AMARAL. *Will James: Gilt-Edged Cowboy.* 1967. Los Angeles. 1st ed. 206 p. dj. EX. B3. $45.00

AMBASZ, Emilio. *Italy: New Domestic Landscape.* 1972. NY. MOMA. 1st ed. dj. VG. R5. $45.00

AMBERG, George. *Art in Modern Ballet.* 1946. Pantheon. 1st ed. folio. slipcase. H3. $75.00

AMBLER, C.H. *Hist of Trans in OH Valley.* 1932. Arthur Clark. EX. $85.00

AMBLER, Eric. *Background to Danger.* 1943. Triangle. Photoplay/2nd ed. dj. G. P1. $15.00

AMBLER, Eric. *Care of Time.* 1981. Farrar Straus Giroux. Deluxe 1st ed. 1/300. sgn. slipcase. H3. $75.00

AMBLER, Eric. *Intrigue.* 1960. Knopf. VG. P1. $9.25

AMBLER, Eric. *Levanter.* 1972. Weidenfeld Nicolson. 1st ed. dj. VG. P1. $15.00

AMERICAN HERITAGE. *Eisenhower: Am Hero, Hist Record of His Life.* 1969. Am Heritage. 1st ed. 144 p. dj. EX. B10. $6.25

AMES, Delano. *Murder, Maestro, Please.* 1952. Hodder Stoughton. VG. P1. $15.00

AMES, Delano. *She Shall Have Murder.* 1949. Rinehart. 1st ed. VG. P1. $15.00

AMES, Winslow. *Italian Drawings...15th-19th Centuries.* 1963. Shorewood. slipcase. EX. B4. $20.00

AMIS, Kingsley. *Anti-Death League.* 1966. Harcourt Brace World. 1st ed. dj. VG. P1. $20.00

AMIS, Kingsley. *Girl, 20.* 1972. Harcourt. 1st ed. dj. EX. F5. $12.00

AMIS, Kingsley. *Golden Age of SF.* 1981. Hutchinson. 1st ed. dj. EX. P1. $20.00

AMIS, Kingsley. *Gr Man.* 1969. London. Cape. 1st ed. 8vo. dj. R4. $40.00

AMIS, Kingsley. *Gr Man.* 1970. NY. 1st Am ed. dj. EX. $30.00

AMIS, Kingsley. *I Like It Here.* 1958. London. Gollancz. 1st ed. sm 8vo. dj. EX. R4. $25.00

AMIS, Kingsley. *I Want It Now.* 1969. Harcourt Brace World. 1st ed. P1. $12.00

AMIS, Kingsley. *Jake's Thing.* 1978. Hutchinson. 1st ed. dj. EX. P1. $17.50

AMIS, Kingsley. *James Bond Dossier.* 1965. New Am Lib. 1st ed. dj. VG. P1. $35.00

AMIS, Kingsley. *My Enemy's Enemy.* 1962. Gollancz. 1st ed. sm 8vo. 224 p. EX. R4. $40.00

AMIS, Kingsley. *New Maps of Hell.* 1960. Gollancz. 1st ed. dj. xl. P1. $20.00

AMIS, Kingsley. *Riverside Villas Murder.* 1973. Harcourt Brace. 2nd ed. VG. P1. $7.50

AMIS, Kingsley. *Russian Hide & Seek.* 1980. Hutchinson. 1st ed. dj. VG. P1. $20.00

AMIS, Kingsley. *Stanley & the Women.* 1984. Summit. ARC of 1st Am ed. wrp. EX. C4. $10.00

AMIS, Kingsley. *Stanley & the Women.* 1984. Summit. ARC. inscr. printed wrp. K2. $45.00

AMIS, Martin. *Money.* 1985. Viking. 1st Am ed. inscr. dj. EX. K2. $50.00

AMIS & CONQUEST. *Egyptologists.* 1966. Random House. 1st ed. dj. VG. P1. $22.50

AMMAR, Michael. *Encore III.* 1983. Bluefield, WV. 1st ed. 91 p. dj. NM. J3. $22.50

AMMAR, Michael. *Michael Ammar's 3rd Nat Tour Notes.* nd. Austin. Ammar. SftCvr. EX. J3. $8.00

AMMAR, Michael. *Success & Magic Progress Guide.* 1984. Bluefield, WV. 1st ed. SftCvr. VG. J3. $8.00

AMMAR, Michael. *Topit Book.* 1989. Austin, TX. 2nd print. 119 p. dj. NM. J3. $22.50

AMMEN, Daniel. *Atlantic Coast.* nd. NY. Brussel. 248 p. PB. G. S1. $6.00

AMMEN, Daniel. *Atlantic Coast.* 1883. NY. 273 p. VG. T5. $39.50

AMOS, Alan. *Borderline Murder.* 1947. Crime Club. 1st ed. VG. P1. $12.00

AMOS, Alan. *Fatal Harvest.* 1957. Crime Club. 1st ed. dj. VG. P1. $17.50

AMRAM, David. *Vibrations: Adventures & Musical Times of David Amram.* 1968. Macmillan. 1st ed. 469 p. dj. EX. B10. $4.50

AMUNATEGUI SOLAR, Domingo. *Hist of Chile.* 1925. Letras Chilenas. Lib of Congress duplicate. 259 p. rebound. F2. $15.00

ANATOLE, Roy; see Weiss, Joe.

ANAWALT, Patricia. *Indian Clothing Before Cortes.* 1981. OK U. 1st ed. 4to. 232 p. dj. G. F2. $50.00

ANAYA, Rudolfo. *Lord of the Dawn.* 1987. NM U. 1st ed. 159 p. F2. $16.50

ANDERSEN, H.C. *Andersen's Fairy Tales.* 1942. Heritage. Ils Kredel. slipcase. T1. $20.00

ANDERSEN, H.C. *Danish Storybook.* 1848. NY. Ils. 187 p. $75.00

ANDERSEN, H.C. *Fairy Tales.* nd. (1915) NY. Hurst. sm 4to. 160 p. VG. $45.00

ANDERSEN, H.C. *Fairy Tales.* nd. (1924) London. Hodder Stoughton. Ils/sgn Nielsen. 1/500. H3. $4500.00

ANDERSEN, H.C. *Fairy Tales.* 1924. London. Ils Nielsen. Ltd ed. 1/500. 12 clr pls. orig bdg. dj. VG. H3. $3750.00

ANDERSEN, H.C. *Fairy Tales.* 1960. Odense, Denmark. Ils Pederson/Frolich. 1st ed. 4 vols. TEG. M. $65.00

ANDERSEN, H.C. *Fairy Tales. Retold by Vera Gissing.* 1981. Cathay Books. Ils Dagmar Berkova. 4to. 264 p. dj. VG. $22.00

ANDERSEN, H.C. *Hans C Anderson's Life & Stories.* 1942. Ltd Ed Club. Ils/sgn Fritz Kridel. 2 vols. slipcase. boxed. VG. $50.00

ANDERSON, Anne. *Old Mother Goose Nursery Rhyme Book.* nd. (c 1945) Nelson. Ils Anderson. 4to. 128 p. EX. $40.00

ANDERSON, C.B. *Bookselling in Am & the World.* 1975. Ils 1st ed. dj. VG. K3. $15.00

ANDERSON, C.W. *Big Red.* 1943. NY. 1st ed. dj. VG. T5. $15.00

ANDERSON, C.W. *Blk, Bay, & Chestnut: Profiles of 20 Favorite Horses.* 1939. Macmillan. 1st ed. oblong 4to. VG. $35.00

ANDERSON, C.W. *Touch of Greatness.* 1945. NY. Ils 1st ed. 96 p. dj. VG. T5. $12.50

ANDERSON, Chester. *Fox & Hare.* 1980. Entwhistle. 1st ed. 1/200. sgn. dj. EX. R3. $35.00

ANDERSON, Chester. *Pink Palace.* 1963. Gold Medal 1374. 1st ed. B4. $20.00

ANDERSON, Dave. *Yankees.* 1980. Random House. Stated 1st ed. 212 p. VG. B10. $8.00

ANDERSON, Edward. *Campfire Stories: Sketches of the Union Army in the SW.* 1896. Chicago. 1st ed. VG. $45.00

ANDERSON, Gene. *Part-Time Pro.* 1976. Anderson. 1st ed. sgn. 30 p. NM. J3. $5.00

ANDERSON, Gerry. *Capt Scarlet & the Mysterons.* 1967. Armada. 1st UK ed. sgn. wrp. EX. scarce. F5. $15.00

ANDERSON, Isabel. *Circling S Am.* 1928. Boston. Marshall Jones. 1st ed. dj. F2. $15.00

ANDERSON, Jean. *Processor Cooking.* 1979. Morrow. 2nd ed. 8vo. 446 p. dj. EX. B10. $4.75

ANDERSON, Jervis. *This Was Harlem.* 1982. NY. 1st ed. 390 p. dj. VG. B3. $17.50

ANDERSON, Jervis. *This Was Harlem: A Cultural Portrait 1900-1950.* 1982. Farrar Straus. UP. tall wrp. EX. B13. $50.00

ANDERSON, Kenneth. *Blk Panther of Sivanipalli.* 1970. Chicago/NY/San Francisco. 2nd print. dj. EX. $20.00

ANDERSON, Madge. *Heroes of the Puppet Stage.* 1923. Harcourt. Ils. VG. B7. $23.00

ANDERSON, Margaret. *Druid's Gift.* 1989. NY. 1st ed. dj. EX. C1. $9.50

ANDERSON, Marian. *My Lord, What a Morning.* 1956. Viking. 1st ed. clipped dj. VG. B13. $45.00

ANDERSON, Maxwell. *Candle in the Wind.* 1941. Anderson House. 1st ed. dj. EX. H3. $60.00

ANDERSON, Maxwell. *Feast of Ortolans.* 1938. Dramatists Play Service. 1st ed. 38 p. yel wrp. H3. $45.00

ANDERSON, Maxwell. *High Tor.* 1937. Anderson House. 1st ed. dj. H3. $85.00

ANDERSON, Maxwell. *Key Largo.* 1939. Anderson House. 1st ed. dj. EX. H3. $100.00

ANDERSON, Maxwell. *Mary of Scotland.* 1933. Anderson House. Special Ltd ed. 1/550. H3. $200.00

ANDERSON, Maxwell. *Masque of Kings.* 1936. Anderson House. 1st ed. dj. VG. H3. $100.00

ANDERSON, Maxwell. *Star Wagon.* 1937. Anderson House. 1st ed. dj. EX. H3. $85.00

ANDERSON, Maxwell. *Storm Operation.* 1944. Anderson House. 1st ed. dj. EX. H3. $25.00

ANDERSON, Maxwell. *Valley Forge: A Play in 3 Acts.* 1934. Anderson House. Ltd ed. 1/200. sgn. full leather. H3. $125.00

ANDERSON, Maxwell. *Wingless Victory.* 1936. Anderson House. 1st ed. dj. EX. H3. $85.00

ANDERSON, Michael. *Unholy.* 1987. St Martin. 1st ed. M. R3. $15.95

ANDERSON, Otto. *Bowed-Harp.* 1930. London. Reeves. octavo. fld map. 319 p. dj. EX. H3. $75.00

ANDERSON, Poul. *Agent of the Terran Empire.* 1965. Chilton. 1st ed. dj. EX. R3. $60.00

ANDERSON, Poul. *Avatar.* 1978. Berkley Putnam. 1st ed. dj. EX. R3. $15.00

ANDERSON, Poul. *Avatar.* 1978. Berkley Putnam. 1st ed. sgn. dj. EX. F5. $25.00

ANDERSON, Poul. *Boat of a Million Years.* 1989. Tor Books. 1st ed. dj. EX. F5. $17.50

ANDERSON, Poul. *Broken Sword.* 1954. Abelard. 1st ed. dj. VG. R3. $45.00

ANDERSON, Poul. *Corridors of Time.* nd. Book Club. dj. VG. P1. $4.50

ANDERSON, Poul. *Dancer From Atlantis.* nd. Book Club. dj. EX. P1. $5.00

ANDERSON, Poul. *Dark Between the Stars.* 1981. Berkley. 1st HrdCvr ed. inscr to Simak. dj. EX. F5. $20.00

ANDERSON, Poul. *Day of Their Return.* nd. Book Club. dj. VG. P1. $4.50

ANDERSON, Poul. *Earth Book of Stormgate.* 1978. Berkley. 1st ed. dj. EX. R3. $15.00

ANDERSON, Poul. *Enemy Stars.* 1959. Lippincott. 1st ed. dj. VG. P1. $60.00

ANDERSON, Poul. *Flandry of Terra.* 1965. Chilton. 1st ed. sgn. dj. EX. F5. $40.00

ANDERSON, Poul. *Homeward & Beyond.* 1975. Doubleday. 1st ed. dj. EX. R3. $17.50

ANDERSON, Poul. *Infinite Voyage.* 1969. Crowell Collier. 1st ed. dj. xl. P1. $7.50

ANDERSON, Poul. *King of YS Vol 1.* nd. Book Club. dj. VG. P1. $6.00

ANDERSON, Poul. *Merman's Children.* 1979. Berkley Putnam. 1st ed. dj. EX. R3. $17.50

ANDERSON, Poul. *Merman's Children.* 1979. Berkley Putnam. 1st ed. dj. xl. P1. $5.00

ANDERSON, Poul. *Merman's Children.* 1979. Berkley Putnam. 1st ed. sgn. dj. EX. F5. $20.00

ANDERSON, Poul. *Midsummer Tempest.* 1974. Doubleday. 1st ed. dj. EX. R3. $45.00

ANDERSON, Poul. *Mirkheim.* nd. Book Club. dj. EX. P1. $4.50

ANDERSON, Poul. *Operation Chaos.* 1971. Doubleday. 1st ed. dj. xl. VG. P1. $7.50

ANDERSON, Poul. *Orbit Unlimited.* 1978. Gregg Pr. 1st ed. dj. EX. P1. $45.00

ANDERSON, Poul. *Orion Shall Rise.* 1983. Phantasia. 1st ed. 1/600. sgn. boxed. P1/R3. $45.00

ANDERSON, Poul. *Orion Shall Rise.* 1983. Timescape. ARC. dj. RS. EX. R3. $35.00

ANDERSON, Poul. *Orion Shall Rise.* 1983. Timescape. 1st ed. dj. EX. P1. $16.95

ANDERSON, Poul. *Perish by the Sword.* 1959. Macmillan. 1st ed. dj. EX. F5. $65.00

ANDERSON, Poul. *Perish by the Sword.* 1959. Macmillan. 2nd ed. xl. P1. $15.00

ANDERSON, Poul. *There Will Be Time.* nd. Book Club. 1st ed. dj. VG. P1. $4.50

ANDERSON, Poul. *Vault of the Ages.* 1952. Winston. 1st ed. VG. P1. $30.00

ANDERSON, Poul. *Vault of the Ages.* 1979. Gregg Pr. 1st ed. dj. EX. P1. $15.00

ANDERSON, Poul. *Winter of the World.* nd. Book Club. dj. EX. P1. $4.50

ANDERSON, Poul. *2 Worlds.* 1978. Gregg Pr. 1st ed. dj. EX. R3. $20.00

ANDERSON, R.B. *Flatey Books & Recently Discovered Vatican Manuscripts...* 1908. London. Narroena Soc. 4to. 176 p. gilt gr bdg. F2. $65.00

ANDERSON, R.G. *Villon.* 1937. Lippincott. 1st ed. dj. EX. H3. $40.00

ANDERSON, R.M. *Birds of IA.* 1907. Davenport, IA. rebound. VG. T3. $30.00

ANDERSON, Robert. *Spanish-Am Modernism: Selected Bibliography.* 1970. Tucson. 1st ed. sgn. VG. G1. $18.00

ANDERSON, Robert. *Tea & Sympathy.* 1953. Random House. early ed. sgn. H3. $75.00

ANDERSON, Rufus. *Hist of Sandwich Islands Mission.* 1870. Boston. Congregational Pub. 408 p. A5. $60.00

ANDERSON, Sherwood. *Alice & the Lost Novel.* 1929. London. Mathews Marrot. 1st ed. 1/500. sgn. EX. B13. $85.00

ANDERSON, Sherwood. *Alice & the Lost Novel.* 1929. London. Mathews Marrot. Ltd ed. 1/530. sgn. dj. H3. $125.00

ANDERSON, Sherwood. *Harlan Miners Speak.* 1932. NY. 1st ed. 348 p. G. B3. $45.00

ANDERSON, Sherwood. *Marching Men.* 1917. John Lane. 1st ed. sgn. gilt red bdg. w/RSVP card. H3. $250.00

ANDERSON, Sherwood. *Marching Men.* 1917. NY. 1st ed. VG. $80.00

ANDERSON, Sherwood. *Mid-Am Chants.* 1918. Bodley Head. sgn. yel buckram. dj. H3. $600.00

ANDERSON, Sherwood. *Plays: Winesburg & Others.* 1937. Scribner. 1st ed. dj. EX. H3. $125.00

ANDERSON, Sherwood. *Poor Wht.* 1920. NY. Heubsch. sgn. bl/yel bdg. H3. $85.00

ANDERSON, Sherwood. *Selective, Annotated Bibliography of Douglas G Rogers.* 1976. NJ. 1st ed. bl bdg. $17.50

ANDERSON, Sherwood. *Sherwood Anderson Reader.* 1947. Houghton Mifflin. 1st ed. dj. EX. C4. $40.00

ANDERSON, Sherwood. *Storyteller's Story.* 1924. NY. Heubsch. sgn. yel/brn bdg. dj. H3. $100.00

ANDERSON, Sherwood. *Tar: Midwest Childhood.* 1926. Boni Liveright. Deluxe 1st ed. 1/350. sgn. H3. $100.00

ANDERSON, Thomas. *Your Own Beloved Sons.* 1956. Random House. 1st ed. sgn. dj. EX. K2. $90.00

ANDERSON & DICKSON. *Earthman's Burden.* 1957. Gnome. 1st ed. dj. EX. R3. $85.00

ANDERSON & DICKSON. *Earthman's Burden.* 1957. Gnome. 1st ed. dj. VG. P1. $75.00

ANDERSON & MARSHALL. *Newspaper Magic.* 1968. Magic Inc. 2nd print. 144 p. SftCvr. NM. J3. $6.00

ANDREAE, Percy. *Prohibition Movement.* 1915. Chicago. 421 p. G. $15.00

ANDREAS, A.T. *Hist of Chicago.* 1884-1886. Chicago. 1st ed. 3 vols. EX. $550.00

ANDRESS, Lesley. *Caper.* 1980. Putnam. 1st ed. dj. VG. P1. $17.50

ANDREWS, A.H. *City That a Cow Kicked Over.* c 1881. Chicago. 8vo. wrp. A4. $35.00

ANDREWS, E.D. *Gift To Be Simple Songs, Dances, Rituals: Am Shakers.* 1940. NY. 1st ed. 170 p. dj. VG. B3. $40.00

ANDREWS, E.D. *People Called Shakers.* 1953. NY. 1st ed. dj. w/2 orig photos laid in. B3. $45.00

ANDREWS, H.J. *Indian Idol Mystery.* 1938. Modern Pub. 1st ed. dj. VG. P1. $30.00

ANDREWS, J.W. *Prelude to Icaros.* 1936. NY. 1st ed. 1/1500. sgn. dj. EX. $25.00

ANDREWS, John. *Viking's Daughter.* 1989. Doubleday. 1st ed. dj. M. R3. $18.95

ANDREWS, L.V. *Jaguar Woman.* 1985. Harper Row. 4th ed. dj. H3. $50.00

ANDREWS, M.P. *Dixie Book of Days.* 1912. Phil. EX. $15.00

ANDREWS, M.R.S. *Perfect Tribute.* 1911. Scribner. 47 p. S1. $5.50

ANDREWS, R.C. *Meet Your Ancestors.* 1945. Viking. 1st ed. 259 p. VG. B10. $4.25

ANDREWS, V.C. *My Sweet Audrina.* 1982. Poseidon. 1st ed. dj. VG. P1. $14.95

ANDREWS, Val. *Coin & Card Magic of Bobby Bernard.* 1982. NY. Magico Magazine. 1st ed. 123 p. NM. J3. $12.00

ANDREWS, Val. *From Here to Obscurity: Comedy Magic of Val Andrews.* 1960. Colon, MI. Abbott. SftCvr. NM. J3. $3.00

ANDREZEL, Pierre. *Angelic Avengers.* nd. Book Club. P1. $2.00

ANDRIST, R.K. *Am Heritage Hist of the Confident Years.* 1969. Heritage. G. S1. $10.00

ANDRONIK, C.M. *Quest for a King.* 1989. NY. 1st Am ed. dj. M. C1. $14.00

ANDRUS, Jerry. *Kurious Kards.* 1973. Albany, OR. 1st ed. sgn. NM. J3. $11.00

ANDRUS, Jerry. *More Sleightly Slanted.* 1977. Albany, OR. 2nd print. sgn. NM. J3. $6.00

ANDRUS, Jerry. *5-Dollar Trix.* 1973. Albany, OR. 1st ed. sgn. 52 p. NM. J3. $11.00

ANGEL & MACINTOSH. *Tiger's Milk: Women of Nicaragua.* 1987. Seaver Books. 1st Am ed. 142 p. dj. F2. $15.00

ANGELL, G.T. *Humane Horse Book.* c 1888. Boston. Ils. 56 p. wrp. G. T5. $7.50

ANGELOU, Maya. *Heart of a Woman.* 1981. Random House. UP. wrp. EX. B13. $85.00

ANGELOU, Maya. *Singin' & Swingin' & Gettin' Merry Like Christmas.* 1976. Random House. 1st ed. B13. $45.00

ANGLE, P.M. *Bloody Williamson: Chapter in Am Lawlessness.* 1952. NY. 1st ed. EX. T1. $25.00

ANGLE, P.M. *Here I Have Lived.* 1935. Springfield. 1st ed. dj. EX. B3. $32.50

ANGLE, P.M. *Lincoln Reader.* 1947. Rutgers. 564 p. dj. VG. S1. $7.00

ANGLE, P.M. *Living Lincoln: Man, Mind, Times, War, Reconstructed...* 1955. Rutgers. 1st ed. 673 p. dj. B10. $10.00

ANGLE, P.M. *Pioneers, Narratives of Noah Harris Letts...* 1972. Chicago. Ils. TEG. VG. T5. $22.50

ANNEMANN, Theo. *Annemann's Complete 1-Man Mental & Psychic Routine.* 1934. Max Holden. 1st ed. SftCvr. NM. J3. $3.00

ANNEMANN & CRIMMINS. *Annemann's Card Magic.* 1977. Dover. 188 p. NM. J3. $2.00

ANNEMANN & CRIMMINS. *Annemann's Practical Mental Effects.* 1963. Louis Tannen. 310 p. gilt bdg. EX. J3. $12.00

ANON. *Adventure Stories for Boys.* nd. Odhams. dj. VG. P1. $15.00

ANON. *Adventures of an Atom.* 1880. Hurst. 1st ed. G. R3. $50.00

ANON. *Anna Pawlowa.* 1913. Berlin. Ils. C1. $14.00

ANON. *Arms & Armor of Medieval Knight: Ils Hist.* 1988. 1st ed. dj. EX. C1. $27.00

ANON. *Art of Confectionary.* 1866. Boston. 12mo. VG. A4. $50.00

ANON. *Avon Ghost Reader.* 1946. Avon. 1st ed. wrp. EX. R3. $20.00

ANON. *Battle of Dorking.* 1871. Putnam. 1st Am ed. G. R3. $50.00

ANON. *Bawdy Ballads & Lusty Lyrics.* 1935. Indianapolis. Maxwell Drake. VG. C1. $12.50

ANON. *Beyond the Stars.* 1986. Cathay Books. EX. P1. $10.00

ANON. *Big Book of Animal Stories.* nd. (1946) John Martins House. 1st ed. dj. B10. $9.00

ANON. *BJ & the Bear Annual.* 1981. Grandreams. VG. P1. $20.00

ANON. *Blake's 7 Annual 1979.* 1978. World. VG. P1. $20.00

ANON. *Bonanza Annual.* 1965. World. G. P1. $30.00

ANON. *Buck Rogers Annual 1982.* 1981. Stafford Pemberton. HrdCvr ed. VG. P1. $15.00

ANON. *Century of Thrillers.* 1934. Daily Express. VG. P1. $35.00

ANON. *Century of Thrillers.* 1937. President Pr. 1st ed. 3 vols. VG. R3. $40.00

ANON. *Chips Annual 1980.* 1979. World. VG. P1. $20.00

ANON. *Come Not Lucifer.* 1945. London. 1st ed. dj. EX. R3. $17.50

ANON. *Creeps.* 1932. Philip Allan. 1st ed. VG. P1. $40.00

ANON. *Dallas Annual.* 1981. Grandreams. EX. P1. $20.00

ANON. *Date With Danger.* 1986. Cathay Books. EX. P1. $10.00

ANON. *Day the Sun Stood Still.* nd. Book Club. dj. VG. P1. $4.50

ANON. *Delek Annual 1978.* 1977. World. VG. P1. $40.00

ANON. *Detective Omnibus.* 1936. Dial. VG. P1. $20.00

ANON. *Dr Who Annual 1975.* 1975. World. VG. P1. $20.00

ANON. *Dr Who Annual 1980.* 1980. World. VG. P1. $20.00

ANON. *Dr Who Annual.* 1968. World. VG. P1. $30.00

ANON. *Equality; or, Hist of Lithconia.* 1947. Prime Pr. 1st ed. 1/500. dj. EX. R3. $45.00

ANON. *Fatal Fascination.* 1964. Little Brn. 1st ed. dj. VG. P1. $15.00

ANON. *Favorite Spy Stories.* 1981. Octopus. VG. P1. $10.00

ANON. *Gabriel Over the Wht House.* 1933. Farrar Rinehart. VG. P1. $30.00

ANON. *Girl From UNCLE Annual.* 1967. World. VG. P1. $25.00

ANON. *Girl From UNCLE Annual.* 1968. World. VG. P1. $30.00

ANON. *Girl From UNCLE Annual.* 1969. World. VG. P1. $30.00

ANON. *Hart to Hart Annual 1983.* 1982. Stafford Pemberton. VG. P1. $20.00

ANON. *Home Cookbook of Chicago.* 1874. Chicago. VG. A4. $35.00

ANON. *Incredible Hulk Annual 1979.* 1978. World. HrdCvr ed. VG. P1. $15.00

ANON. *Joe 90 Annual.* 1968. Century 21. VG. P1. $20.00

ANON. *Johnny Weissmuller: Tarzan of the Screen.* 1934. Big Little Book. VG. P1. $85.00

ANON. *King Arthur & the 2-Fold Quest.* 1921. Tintagel. 1st ed. 133 p. VG. C1. $49.50

ANON. *Land of the Giants Annual.* 1970. World. VG. P1. $25.00

ANON. *Logan's Run Annual.* 1978. Brn Watson. VG. P1. $20.00

ANON. *Man From UNCLE Annual.* 1966. World. VG. P1. $30.00

ANON. *Mission Impossible Annual.* 1969. Atlas. VG. P1. $25.00

ANON. *My Best Detective Story.* 1936. Faber Faber. 5th print. G. P1. $15.00

ANON. *Napoleon Bonaparte, His Own Historian.* 1818. London. 8vo. rebound. VG. A4. $150.00

ANON. *New Avengers Annual.* 1977. Brn Watson. EX. P1. $25.00

ANON. *Operation Vittles Cookbook.* 1949. Berlin. VG. $15.00

ANON. *Paine Wiehl & Co Keystone Cookbook.* c 1888. Phil. Paine Wiehl. 16mo. wrp. A4. $25.00

ANON. *Pic-Nic Party; or, Alfred Morton.* 1880. Chicago. Rosy Dawn Series. 12mo. VG. C1. $19.50

ANON. *Poles in Am.* 1933. Chicago Century Progress. souvenir phamplet. 4to. VG. G1. $30.00

ANON. *Professionals Annual 1982.* 1981. Stafford Pemberton. VG. P1. $20.00

ANON. *Return of the Saint Annual.* 1978. Stafford. EX. P1. $25.00

ANON. *Sapphire & Steel Annual.* 1980. World. VG. P1. $25.00

ANON. *Shudders.* 1932. Philip Allan. 1st ed. VG. P1. $40.00

ANON. *Slavery Rhymes. Addressed to the Friends of Liberty.* 1837. NY. 84 p. orig wrp. $125.00

ANON. *Space 1999 Annual.* 1975. World. VG. P1. $25.00

ANON. *Star Trek Annual 1971.* 1970. World. VG. P1. $30.00

ANON. *Starsky & Hutch Annual 1979.* 1978. Stafford. VG. P1. $20.00

ANON. *Tales From Beyond the Grave.* 1982. London. 1st ed. dj. EX. R3. $15.00

ANON. *Tarzan Annual.* 1967. World. VG. P1. $30.00

ANON. *Tarzan Annual.* 1973. Brn Watson. VG. P1. $25.00

ANON. *Tarzan Television Picture Storybook.* 1967. PBS. G. P1. $20.00

ANON. *Thrillers.* 1929. Clode. 1st ed. VG. R3. $25.00

ANON. *Thrills.* nd. Assn Newspapers. VG. P1. $25.00

ANON. *Thrills.* 1935. London. 1st ed. VG. R3. $20.00

ANON. *Tomorrow's Voices.* 1984. Dial. dj. RS. EX. P1. $17.50

ANON. *TV Comic Album 1967.* 1966. TV Pub. G. P1. $25.00

ANON. *TV Comic Album 1971.* 1970. Polystyle. VG. P1. $25.00

ANON. *Wee Folks' Life of Christ.* nd. (1920) Altemus. Wee Books for Wee People. 91 p. B10. $5.00

ANON. *Winter's Tales 5.* 1959. Macmillan. 1st ed. dj. xl. P1. $7.50

ANON. *150 Years Service to Am Health.* 1944. Schieffelin. 1st ed? 73 p. VG. B10. $6.75

ANON. *2000 AD Annual 1978.* 1977. IPC Magazines. VG. P1. $10.00

ANON. *4 Thrilling Adventure Novels.* nd. Odhams. G. P1. $20.00

ANON. *5 Fates.* nd. Book Club. P1. $4.50

ANON. *50 Masterpieces of Mystery.* nd. Odhams. P1. $35.00

ANON. *6 Million-Dollar Man Annual 1977.* 1976. Stafford. VG. P1. $22.50

ANOUILH, Jean. *Fables.* 1962. 1st ed. French text. presentation. C1. $12.50

ANSON, Jay. *666.* 1981. Simon Schuster. 1st ed. dj. VG. P1. $15.00

ANSTEY, F. *Humor & Fantasy.* 1931. London. 1st ed. VG. R3. $25.00

ANTHOLOGY. *Adventures of Nanabush: Ojibway Indian Stories.* 1979. Toronto. Doubleday. 1st Canadian ed. dj. EX. B13. $60.00

ANTHOLOGY. *Afterwards. Novelists on Their Novels.* 1969. Harper Row. dj. EX. K2. $35.00

ANTHOLOGY. *Am Indian Prose & Poetry.* 1974. Putnam/Capricorn. ARC. dj. EX. K2. $45.00

ANTHOLOGY. *Am Indian Reader: Anthropology.* 1972. San Francisco. Indian Hist. wrp. EX. K2. $35.00

ANTHOLOGY. *Am Indian Speaks.* 1969. SD U. wrp. VG. K2. $40.00

ANTHOLOGY. *Antologia de la Literatura Fantastica.* 1940. Sudamericana. wrp. EX. K2. $175.00

ANTHOLOGY. *Best Am Short Stories.* 1986. Houghton Mifflin. UP. wrp. EX. K2. $45.00

ANTHOLOGY. *Best of the Diner's Club Magazine.* 1962. Regents Am. 1st ed. dj. EX. B13. $45.00

ANTHOLOGY. *Borzoi Anthology of Latin Am Literature.* 1977. Knopf. 1st ed. 2 vols. wrp. EX. K2. $75.00

ANTHOLOGY. *Canadian Journal of Native Studies.* 1989. Brandon, Manitoba. Special Issue. VG. K2. $25.00

ANTHOLOGY. *Carriers of the Dream Wheel.* 1975. Harper Row. dj. EX. K2. $50.00

ANTHOLOGY. *Dancing Teepees: Poems of Am Indian Youth.* 1989. NY. Holiday. 1st ed. dj. EX. B13. $45.00

ANTHOLOGY. *Firebird 1.* 1982. Penguin/Allen Lane. 1st ed. 1st issue. wrp. EX. K2. $35.00

ANTHOLOGY. *Heart Throbs: Old Scrapbook.* 1905. Grosset Dunlap. 469 p. gr bdg. new dj. VG. B10. $4.25

ANTHOLOGY. *Hist of Police Dept of Columbus, OH.* 1908. Columbus. 1st ed. 248 p. VG. B3. $77.50

ANTHOLOGY. *I Tell You Now: Autobiographical Essays Native Am Writers.* 1987. NE U. AP. VG. K2. $65.00

ANTHOLOGY. *IA Writer's Workshop Cookbook.* 1986. Frederick Fell. 1st ed. wrp. EX. K2. $65.00

ANTHOLOGY. *Little Review Anthology.* 1953. NY. Review/1st ed. dj. VG. $40.00

ANTHOLOGY. *Man To Send Rain Clouds.* 1974. Seaver/Viking. dj. EX. very scarce. K2. $125.00

ANTHOLOGY. *Merlin & Woman: Book of 2nd Merlin Conference.* 1988. London. 1st ed. dj. M. C1. $21.50

ANTHOLOGY. *Mom, the Flag, & Apple Pie.* 1976. Doubleday. 1st ed. dj. EX. K2. $45.00

ANTHOLOGY. *New Fiction.* 1975. IL U. UP. wrp. EX. K2. $125.00

ANTHOLOGY. *Our Word: Guerrilla Poems From Latin Am.* 1968. Grossman. 1st ed. wrp. VG. K2. $20.00

ANTHOLOGY. *River Reflections.* 1984. E Woods. 1st ed. dj. EX. K2. $35.00

ANTHOLOGY. *Survival This Way.* 1987. AZ U. ARC. dj. EX. K2. $50.00

ANTHOLOGY. *This Remembered Earth.* 1981. Albuquerque. 1st ed. dj. EX. K2. $45.00

ANTHOLOGY. *Voices of the Rainbow.* 1975. Seaver/Viking. dj. EX. K2. $100.00

ANTHOLOGY. *7 Short Stories.* 1967. Prague. Orbis. 2nd ed. dj. VG. K2. $45.00

ANTHONY, A.W. *Expedition to Guadalupe Island, Mexico, in 1922.* 1922. Academy of Sciences. wrp. F2. $10.00

ANTHONY, Evelyn. *Albatross.* 1983. Putnam. 1st ed. dj. VG. P1. $14.95

ANTHONY, Evelyn. *Ave of the Dead.* 1982. Coward McCann. 1st ed. dj. VG. P1. $12.50

ANTHONY, Evelyn. *Co of Saints.* 1984. Putnam. 1st ed. dj. VG. P1. $15.00

ANTHONY, Evelyn. *Janus Imperative.* 1980. Coward McCann. 1st ed. dj. VG. P1. $12.50

ANTHONY, Evelyn. *Return.* 1978. Coward McCann. 1st ed. dj. EX. P1. $12.00

ANTHONY, Evelyn. *Silver Falcon.* 1977. Coward McCann. 1st ed. dj. VG. P1. $12.00

ANTHONY, Gordon. *Ballet: Camera Studies.* 1937. London. Bles. 1st ed. 1/100. sgn. folio. 241 p. TEG. H3. $400.00

ANTHONY, Gordon. *Sleeping Princess.* 1940. London. Routledge. 1st ed. folio. orig bdg. EX. H3. $100.00

ANTHONY, Irvin. *Voyages Unafraid.* 1930. Phil. Macrae Smith. 1st ed. VG. C1. $17.50

ANTHONY, Joseph. *Life in New Bedford 100 Years Ago.* 1922. Old Dartmouth Hist Soc. 1st ed. G. $30.00

ANTHONY, Piers. *Bearing an Hour Glass.* 1984. Del Rey. 1st ed. dj. EX. R3. $20.00

ANTHONY, Piers. *Being a Gr Mother.* 1987. Del Rey. 1st ed. dj. VG. P1. $16.95

ANTHONY, Piers. *Bl Adept.* 1981. Del Rey. 1st ed. dj. EX. F5. $17.00

ANTHONY, Piers. *Double Exposure.* nd. Book Club. dj. VG. P1. $6.00

ANTHONY, Piers. *Double Exposure.* 1982. Doubleday. 1st Compilation ed. dj. EX. F5. $10.00

ANTHONY, Piers. *Juxtaposition.* 1982. Del Rey. 1st ed. dj. EX. F5/P1. $16.00

ANTHONY, Piers. *Night Mare.* 1982. Del Rey. 1st HrdCvr ed. dj. EX. F5. $10.00

ANTHONY, Piers. *On a Pale Horse.* 1983. Del Rey. 1st ed. dj. EX. F5. $15.00

ANTHONY, Piers. *Orn.* nd. Book Club. dj. VG. P1. $4.50

ANTHONY, Piers. *Out of Phaze.* 1987. Ace Putnam. 1st ed. dj. EX. F5. $15.00

ANTHONY, Piers. *Out of Phaze.* 1987. Ace Putnam. 1st ed. sgn. dj. EX. P1. $17.95

ANTHONY, Piers. *Pornucopia.* 1989. Tafford. 1st ed. dj. F5/R3. $20.00

ANTHONY, Piers. *Pornucopia.* 1989. Tafford. 1st ed. sgn. dj. EX. P1. $25.00

ANTHONY, Piers. *Robot Adept.* 1988. Ace Putnam. 1st ed. dj. EX. P1. $16.95

ANTHONY, Piers. *Shade of the Tree.* 1986. Tor Books. 1st ed. dj. EX. P1. $15.95

ANTHONY, Piers. *Split Infinity.* 1980. Del Rey. 1st ed. dj. EX. F5. $17.00

ANTHONY, Piers. *Unicorn Point.* 1989. Ace Putnam. 1st ed. dj. EX. F5. $15.00

ANTHONY, Piers. *Wielding a Red Sword.* 1986. Del Rey. 1st ed. dj. EX. P1. $16.95

ANTHONY, Piers. *With a Tangled Skein.* 1985. Del Rey. 1st ed. dj. EX. P1. $14.95

ANTON, Ferdinand. *Ancient Mexican Art.* 1969. NY. Putnam. 1st Am ed. lg 4to. dj. F2. $75.00

ANTON, Ferdinand. *Ancient Peruvian Textiles.* 1987. NY. Thames Hudson. 1st ed. 4to. dj. F2. $45.00

ANTON & DOCKSTADER. *Pre-Columbian Art & Later Indian Tribal Arts.* nd. (1968) Abrams. 264 p. dj. F2. $30.00

ANTONY, Paul. *Ian Fleming's Incredible Creation.* 1965. 3 Star. P1. $7.50

APPEL, Benjamin. *Hell's Kitchen.* 1977. Pantheon. 1st ed. dj. VG. P1. $15.00

APPEL, David. *Comanche.* 1951. Cleveland. Ils Daugherty. 1st ed. dj. VG. B3. $27.50

APPLE, A.E. *Mr Chang of Scotland Yard.* 1926. Chelsea House. 1st ed. VG. P1. $30.00

APPLEBY, John. *Bad Summer.* 1958. Washburn. 1st ed. VG. P1. $10.00

APPLEBY, John. *Stars in the Water.* 1952. Werner Laurie. dj. xl. P1. $5.00

APPLEBY, John. *Stuffed Swan.* 1956. Hodder Stoughton. 1st ed. dj. xl. P1. $7.50

APPLEMAN, Philip. *Shame the Devil.* 1981. Crown. 1st ed. dj. EX. F5. $15.00

APPLETON, Victor. *Don Sturdy & Big Snake Hunters.* 1925. Grosset. Ils Rogers. dj. VG. B10. $6.50

APPLETON, Victor. *Don Sturdy in Land of Giants.* 1930. Grosset. 244 p. VG. B10. $2.75

APPLETON, Victor. *Tom Swift & His Diving Seacopter.* nd. Grosset Dunlap. dj. VG. P1. $7.50

APPLETON, Victor. *Tom Swift & His Flying Lab.* nd. Grosset Dunlap. dj. VG. P1. $5.00

APPLETON, Victor. *Tom Swift & His Megascope Space Prob.* nd. Grosset Dunlap. decor brd. VG. P1. $5.00

APPLETON, Victor. *Tom Swift & His Outpost in Space.* nd. Grosset Dunlap. dj. VG. P1. $7.50

APPLETON, Victor. *Tom Swift & His Polar-Ray Dynasphere.* nd. Grosset Dunlap. decor brd. VG. P1. $5.00

APPLETON, Victor. *Tom Swift & His Submarine Boat.* nd. Grosset Dunlap. VG. P1. $15.00

APPLETON, Victor. *Tom Swift & His Wireless Message.* nd. Grosset Dunlap. dj. VG. P1. $17.50

APPLETON, Victor. *Tom Swift & His Wizard Camera*. nd. Grosset Dunlap. VG. P1. $12.50

APPLETON, Victor. *Tom Swift in the Race to the Moon*. nd. Collins. decor brds. VG. P1. $5.00

APTHEKER, H. *Hist of Negro People of US*. 1951. NY. 1st ed. 942 p. dj. VG. B3. $27.50

ARBUTHNOT, Joan. *More Profit Than Gold*. 1936. Scribner. 1st ed. 287 p. F2. $15.00

ARBUTHNOT, M.H. *Children & Books*. 1957. Scott Foresman. Revised ed. VG. $25.00

ARBUTHNOT, M.H. *Early Children's Books & Their Ils*. nd. Godine. dj. EX. $75.00

ARBUTHNOT, M.H. *Yankee Doodle Literary Sampler*. 1974. Crowell. 1st ed. folio. $35.00

ARCH, E.L. *Man With 3 Eyes*. 1967. Avalon. 1st ed. dj. EX. R3. $12.50

ARCH, E.L. *Man With 3 Eyes*. 1967. Avalon. 1st ed. dj. xl. P1. $7.50

ARCHER, Frank. *Out of the Bl*. 1964. Doubleday Crime Club. 1st ed. dj. xl. P1. $5.00

ARCHER, J.C. *Tale of 5 Little Pixies*. nd. Donohue. Pixie Book Series. 12mo. 16 p. $16.00

ARCHER, Jeffrey. *Quiver Full of Arrows*. nd. Linden Pr/Simon Schuster. VG. P1. $10.00

ARCHER, Jeffrey. *1st Among Equals*. 1984. Linden Pr. 1st ed. dj. EX. P1. $15.45

ARCHER, Laird. *Balkan Journal: Unofficial Observer in Greece*. nd. np. Ils. 254 p. dj. VG. T5. $17.50

ARCHER, William. *Eng Dramatists of Today*. 1882. London. Sampson Low/Marston Searle Rivington. 1st ed. H3. $100.00

ARCHER, William. *Masks or Faces?* 1888. Longman Gr. 1st ed. octavo. 232 p. VG. scarce. H3. $100.00

ARCHIEGAS, German. *Caribbean: Sea of the New World*. 1946. Knopf. 1st Am ed. 464 p. F2. $10.00

ARD, William. *Like Ice She Was*. 1960. Monarch Books 147. PB Orig. T9. $45.00

ARDEN, William. *Goliath Scheme*. 1971. Dodd Mead. 1st ed. dj. VG. P1. $15.00

ARDEN, William. *Mystery of the Dancing Devil*. 1976. Random House. 1st ed. xl. G. P1. $5.00

ARDIES, Tom. *Pandemic*. 1973. Doubleday. dj. xl. P1. $5.00

ARENAL, Humberto. *Sun Beats Down*. 1959. Hill Wang. 1st ed. wrp. VG. K2. $30.00

ARIA, Mrs. E. *Costume: Fanciful, Hist, & Theatrical*. 1906. London. Ils. 8vo. 259 p. TEG. VG. T1. $45.00

ARIOSTO, Ludovico. *Orlando Furioso*. 1823. London. Murray. 9 vols. VG. H3. $200.00

ARIS, Ernest. *Wee Peter Pug*. c 1900. Saalfield. 12mo. VG. $22.00

ARISTOPHANES. *Birds*. 1959. Ltd Ed Club. Ils/sgn Marian Perry. 4to. slipcase. EX. $55.00

ARISTOPHANES. *Frogs*. 1937. Ltd Ed Club. Ils/sgn John Austen. 4to. VG. $45.00

ARISTOPHANES. *Lysistrata*. 1962. Heritage. Ils Picasso. EX. C1. $12.50

ARKSEY, Laura. *Am Diaries Vol 1: Diaries Written 1492-1844*. 1983. Gale. 1st ed. VG. $65.00

ARLEN, Michael. *Ghost Stories*. nd. Collins. VG. P1. $35.00

ARLEN, Michael. *Gr Hat*. 1924. Collins. 7th ed. VG. P1. $15.00

ARLEN, Michael. *Hell!, Said the Duchess*. 1934. Doubleday. 1st ed. VG. R3. $15.00

ARLEY, Catherine. *Woman of Straw*. 1958. Random House. 1st ed. clipped dj. EX. F5. $20.00

ARMISTEAD, Wilson. *Anthony Benezet From Orig Memoir, Revised, With Addition*. 1859. London. Bennett. 16mo. 144 p. VG. V1. $22.00

ARMITAGE, John. *Hist of Brazil*. 1836. London. 1st ed. 8vo. 2 vols. VG. T1. $250.00

ARMITAGE, Merle. *Dance Memoranda*. 1946. Duell Sloan Pearce. 2nd ed. quarto. dj. H3. $100.00

ARMITAGE, Merle. *George Gershwin*. 1938. Longman Gr. 1st ed. presentation. 252 p. VG. H3. $275.00

ARMITAGE, Merle. *Igor Strawinsky*. 1936. NY. Schirmer. octabo. 16 pls. 158 p. dj. slipcase. M. H3. $200.00

ARMITAGE, Merle. *Schoenberg*. 1937. NY. Schirmer. 1st ed. octavo. 319 p. VG. H3. $125.00

ARMITAGE. *30 Years With Fighting Dogs*. 1935. WA. 1st ed. 193 p. VG. B3. $125.00

ARMOUR, J.O. *Packers: Private Car Lines & the People*. 1906. Phil. 1st ed. VG. $50.00

ARMOUR, Richard. *It All Started With Hippocrates*. 1966. McGraw Hill. 1st ed. w/sgn letter. H3. $40.00

ARMOUR, Richard. *Light Armor*. nd. (1954) McGraw. 1st ed? 118 p. VG. B10. $4.00

ARMOUR, Richard. *Light Armour*. 1954. 1st ed. dj. EX. C1. $12.00

ARMSTRONG, Charlotte. *Balloon Man*. nd. Book Club. dj. VG. P1. $4.50

ARMSTRONG, Charlotte. *Better To Eat You*. 1954. Doubleday Book Club. VG. P1. $7.50

ARMSTRONG, Charlotte. *Blk-Eyed Stranger*. 1952. Peter Davies. 1st ed. VG. P1. $10.00

ARMSTRONG, Charlotte. *Dram of Poison*. nd. Book Club. dj. VG. P1. $4.50

ARMSTRONG, Gregory. *Dragon Has Come*. 1974. Harper Row. 1st ed. dj. EX. $15.00

ARMSTRONG, Louis. *Louis Armstrong: A Self-Portrait*. 1971. NY. Eakins Pr. oblong octavo. 50 p. red wrp. EX. H3. $40.00

ARMSTRONG, Margaret. *Man With No Face*. 1943. Tower. dj. VG. P1. $10.00

ARNDT & OLSON. *German-Am Newspapers & Periodicals 1732-1955*. 1961. Heidelberg. xl. VG. G1. $25.00

ARNO, Luisa. *Medieval Health Handbook*. 1976. Braziller. 1st ed. slipcase. M. C1. $22.00

ARNOLD, E.L. *Phra, the Phoenician*. nd. Lupton. G. R3. $15.00

ARNOLD, Edwin. *Japonica*. 1891. NY. Ils Robert Blum. 1st ed. 4to. TEG. VG. $15.00

ARNOLD, Edwin. *Light of Asia*. 1976. Ltd Ed Club. Ils/sgn Ayers Houghtelling. slipcase. VG. $45.00

ARNOLD, George. *Magician's Own Book; or, Whole Art of Conjuring*. 1857. Dick/Fitzgerald. 1st ed. 362 p. gilt bdg. VG. J3. $38.00

ARNOLD, Matthew. *Culture & Anarchy/ Friendship's Garland/Literature & Dogma*. 1883. NY. 3 vols. 8vo. VG. $80.00

ARNOLD, Matthew. *Works*. 1903-1904. London. Macmillan. Deluxe ed. 15 vols. H3. $1250.00

ARNOLD & THREULSEN. *Mediterranean Sweep: Air Stories From El Alamein to Rome.* 1944. NY. 1st ed. dj. EX. $20.00

ARNOW, H.S. *Seedtime on the Cumberland.* 1960. Macmillan. 1st ed. sgn. dj. EX. B13. $125.00

ARONOWITZ & HAMILL. *Hemingway Life & Death of Man.* 1961. Lancer. P1. $3.75

ARQUETTE, Cliff. *Charley Weaver's Letters From Mama.* 1959. Winston. 6th print. sgn. 64 p. dj. VG. H3. $25.00

ARR, E.H. *New Eng Bygones.* 1880. Phil. Lippincott. 1st ed. 214 p. VG. $50.00

ARRIGHI, Mel. *Turkish Wht.* 1977. Harcourt. 1st ed. dj. EX. F5. $12.00

ARROWSMITH, G.E. *Magical Mentalia.* 1942. London. Max Andrews. 66 p. VG. J3. $3.00

ARROWSMITH, G.E. *Magical Originalia.* nd. London. Max Andrews. EX. J3. $3.00

ARROWSMITH, Nancy. *Field Guide to Little People.* 1977. 1st ed. dj. EX. C1. $12.50

ARTHUR, S.C. *Old New Orleans: Hist of Vieux Carre.* 1944. Harmanson. 6th ed. 146 p. wrp. VG. B10. $4.25

ARTHUR, T.S. *Bar Rooms at Brantley.* nd. (1877) Phil. Porter Coates. 1st ed. 437 p. VG. B10. $17.50

ARTHUR & CARPENTER. *Hist of VA From Its Earliest Settlement to Present Time.* 1852. Lippincott Ganbo. 1st ed. 332 p. VG. $75.00

ARTZYBASHEFF, Boris. *Colum, Padraic. Creatures.* 1927. NY. 1st ed. VG. $20.00

ASBURY, Herbert. *French Quarter.* 1936. NY. 1st ed. 8vo. 462 p. VG. G4. $12.00

ASBURY, Herbert. *Methodist St (Bishop Asbury).* 1927. NY. 1st ed. 354 p. dj. VG. B3. $30.00

ASBURY, Herbert. *Not at Night!* 1928. Macy Macius. 1st ed. VG. R3. $25.00

ASCH, Sholem. *Nazarene.* 1939. Putnam. 1/500. presentation. H3. $40.00

ASH, Brian. *Visual Encyclopedia of SF.* 1977. Harmony Books. 1st ed. dj. EX. R3. $25.00

ASHBEE, H.S. *Iconography of Don Quixote 1605-1895.* 1895. London. 1st ed. quarto. rebound. VG. $200.00

ASHBEE, J.E. *Essex House Song Book.* 1904. London. Essex House. Ltd ed. 1/200. 2 vols. VG. H3. $400.00

ASHBERY, John. *Self-Portrait in a Convex Mirror.* 1975. Viking. sgn. dj. EX. H3. $45.00

ASHBERY, John. *Wave.* 1984. Viking. 2nd print. sgn. dj. H3. $45.00

ASHBERY & SCHUYLER. *Nest of Ninnies.* 1969. NY. 1st ed. inscr. dj. EX. C4. $300.00

ASHBRIDGE, Elizabeth. *Some Account of the Life of Elizabeth Ashbridge.* nd. Phil. Friends Bookstore. 24 mo. 59 p. V1. $14.00

ASHBROOK, H. *Murder of Steven Kester.* 1931. Coward McCann. VG. P1. $20.00

ASHDOWN, Clifford. *From a Surgeon's Diary.* 1977. Oswald Train. 1st ed. dj. EX. P1. $10.00

ASHDOWN, Clifford. *Queen's Treasure.* 1975. Oswald Train. 1st ed. dj. EX. P1. $10.00

ASHE, Geoffrey. *Discovery of King Arthur.* 1985. dj. EX. C1. $12.50

ASHE, Geoffrey. *King Arthur's Avalon: Story of Glastonbury.* 1957. London. 1st ed. dj. VG. scarce. C1. $29.50

ASHE, Geoffrey. *King Arthur's Avalon: Story of Glastonbury.* 1958. NY. 1st Am ed. dj. VG. C1. $19.50

ASHE, Geoffrey. *Search for King Arthur.* 1st Am ed. dj. M. C1. $14.00

ASHE, Gordon. *Crime-Haters.* nd. Book Club. dj. VG. P1. $4.50

ASHE, Gordon. *Pack of Lies.* nd. Book Club. dj. VG. P1. $4.50

ASHE, Gordon. *Sleepy Death.* 1953. John Long. 1st ed. dj. VG. P1. $20.00

ASHENHURST, John. *World's Fair Murders.* 1933. Houghton Mifflin. 1st ed. VG. R3. $20.00

ASHER & ADAMS. *New Topographical Map of the State of NY.* 1869. NY. 1st ed. folio. 16 maps. orig wrps. C1. $135.00

ASHFORD, Jeffrey. *Recipe for Murder.* 1980. Walker. dj. EX. P1. $12.50

ASHLEY, Clifford. *Yankee Whaler.* 1938. Boston. Popular ed. 4to. VG. $75.00

ASHLEY, Clifford. *Yankee Whaler.* 1942. Garden City. 1st ed. 156 p. VG. B3. $50.00

ASHLEY, Doris. *King Arthur & the Knights of the Round Table.* c 1900. Tuck McKay. Ils Dixon/Pentiak. VG. C1. $29.50

ASHLEY, Elizabeth. *Actress.* 1978. Evans Book Club. 252 p. dj. EX. B10. $3.75

ASHLEY, Michael. *Hist of the SF Magazine 1926-1955.* 1976-1977. Regnery. 1st Am ed. 3 vols. djs. EX. R3. $50.00

ASHMORE, Wendy. *Lowland Maya Settlement Patterns.* 1981. Albuquerque, NM. 1st ed. 465 p. dj. F2. $30.00

ASHTON, Francis. *Alas, the Great City.* 1947. London. 1st ed. dj. EX. R3. $35.00

ASHTON, John. *Romances of Chivalry: Told & Ils in Facsmilie.* 1890. London. VG. C1. $44.00

ASHTON. *Richard Lindner.* nd. (1969) NY. sm folio. pls. dj. EX. C2. $105.00

ASIMOV, Isaac. *Adventures of Lucky Starr.* nd. Book Club. dj. VG. P1. $7.50

ASIMOV, Isaac. *Asimov Chronicles.* 1989. Dark Harvest. Ltd ed. 1/500. sgn. slipcase. M. R3. $75.00

ASIMOV, Isaac. *Asimov on Astronomy.* nd. Bonanza. dj. EX. P1. $10.00

ASIMOV, Isaac. *Asimov on SF.* nd. Book Club. dj. VG. P1. $7.50

ASIMOV, Isaac. *Asimov on SF.* 1981. Doubleday. 1st ed. dj. EX. R3. $20.00

ASIMOV, Isaac. *Asimov's Annotated Paradise.* 1974. Doubleday. 1st ed. dj. EX. R3. $27.50

ASIMOV, Isaac. *Asimov's Guide to Halley's Comet.* nd. Book Club. dj. VG. P1. $4.50

ASIMOV, Isaac. *Asimov's Guide to Science.* 1972. Basic Books. dj. EX. R3. $15.00

ASIMOV, Isaac. *Asimov's Mysteries.* 1968. Doubleday. 1st ed. dj. VG. R3. $25.00

ASIMOV, Isaac. *Before the Golden Age.* 1974. Doubleday. 1st ed. dj. VG. P1. $15.00

ASIMOV, Isaac. *Beginning & the End.* 1977. Doubleday. 1st ed. dj. EX. R3. $17.50

ASIMOV, Isaac. *Best Mysteries of Isaac Asimov.* 1986. Doubleday. 1st ed. dj. RS. EX. P1. $20.00

ASIMOV, Isaac. *Buy Jupiter.* nd. Book Club. dj. VG. P1. $4.50

ASIMOV, Isaac. *Complete Robot.* nd. Book Club. dj. VG. P1. $7.50

ASIMOV, Isaac. *Complete Stories Vol 1.* 1990. Doubleday. 1st ed. dj. EX. P1. $22.95

ASIMOV, Isaac. *Double Planet.* 1967. Abelard Schuman. Revised ed. dj. VG. P1. $20.00

ASIMOV, Isaac. *Early Asimov.* nd. Book Club. dj. VG. P1. $6.00

ASIMOV, Isaac. *Earth Is Room Enough.* nd. Book Club. dj. VG. P1. $6.00

ASIMOV, Isaac. *End of Eternity.* 1955. Doubleday. 1st ed. dj. EX. R3. $250.00

ASIMOV, Isaac. *Exploring the Earth & Cosmos.* 1982. Crown. 1st ed. dj. VG. R3. $20.00

ASIMOV, Isaac. *Extra-Terrestrial Civilizations.* 1979. Crown. 1st ed. dj. EX. R3. $15.00

ASIMOV, Isaac. *Fact & Fancy.* 1962. Doubleday. 1st ed. dj. EX. P1. $35.00

ASIMOV, Isaac. *Fantastic Voyage 2.* 1987. Doubleday. 1st ed. dj. VG. P1. $18.95

ASIMOV, Isaac. *Fantastic Voyage.* nd. Book Club. dj. VG. P1. $4.50

ASIMOV, Isaac. *Far As Human Eye Could See.* 1987. Doubleday. 1st ed. dj. RS. P1. $20.00

ASIMOV, Isaac. *Far Ends of Time & Earth.* 1979. Doubleday. 1st ed. dj. EX. P1. $20.00

ASIMOV, Isaac. *Foundation & Earth.* 1986. Doubleday. 1st ed. dj. EX. P1. $16.95

ASIMOV, Isaac. *Foundation & Empire.* 1952. Gnome. 1st ed. dj. VG. R3. $200.00

ASIMOV, Isaac. *Foundation & Empire.* 1952. Gnome. 1st ed. inscr. dj. EX. K2. $350.00

ASIMOV, Isaac. *Foundation Trilogy.* nd. Book Club. dj. VG. P1. $6.00

ASIMOV, Isaac. *Foundation Trilogy.* nd. Doubleday. 3 vols. djs. EX. R3. $75.00

ASIMOV, Isaac. *Foundation.* nd. Doubleday. dj. xl. P1. $10.00

ASIMOV, Isaac. *Foundation's Edge.* nd. Book Club. dj. VG. P1. $5.00

ASIMOV, Isaac. *Foundation's Edge.* 1982. Doubleday. 1st ed. dj. EX. P1/R3. $20.00

ASIMOV, Isaac. *Foundation's Edge.* 1982. Whispers. 1st ed. 1/1000. sgn. no dj issued. EX. P1. $85.00

ASIMOV, Isaac. *Gods Themselves.* nd. Book Club. dj. VG. P1. $4.50

ASIMOV, Isaac. *Gods Themselves.* 1972. Doubleday. 1st ed. dj. EX. R3. $80.00

ASIMOV, Isaac. *Hugo Winners Vol 3.* 1977. Doubleday. 1st ed. dj. EX. R3. $35.00

ASIMOV, Isaac. *I, Robot.* nd. Book Club. dj. VG. P1. $5.00

ASIMOV, Isaac. *I, Robot.* nd. SF Book Club. dj. EX. R3. $10.00

ASIMOV, Isaac. *I, Robot.* 1950. Grosset Dunlap. dj. VG. P1. $65.00

ASIMOV, Isaac. *In Memory Yet Gr.* 1979. Doubleday. dj. EX. R3. $20.00

ASIMOV, Isaac. *Lucky Starr & the Moons of Jupiter.* nd. Doubleday. dj. xl. P1. $7.50

ASIMOV, Isaac. *Lucky Starr & the Rings of Saturn.* 1978. Gregg Pr. dj. VG. P1. $17.50

ASIMOV, Isaac. *Murder at the Aba.* nd. Book Club. dj. VG. P1. $6.00

ASIMOV, Isaac. *Murder at the Aba.* 1976. Doubleday. 1st ed. dj. VG. P1. $20.00

ASIMOV, Isaac. *Naked Sun.* nd. SF Book Club. dj. EX. R3. $10.00

ASIMOV, Isaac. *Naked Sun.* 1959. British SF Book Club. dj. VG. P1. $7.50

ASIMOV, Isaac. *Nebula Award Stories 8.* 1973. Harper. 1st ed. dj. EX. R3. $40.00

ASIMOV, Isaac. *Nemesis.* 1989. Doubleday. 1st ed. dj. EX. P1. $18.95

ASIMOV, Isaac. *Of Matters Great & Sm.* 1975. Doubleday. 1st ed. dj. EX. R3. $17.50

ASIMOV, Isaac. *Of Matters Great & Sm.* 1975. Doubleday. 1st ed. inscr. dj. EX. K2. $45.00

ASIMOV, Isaac. *Opus 100.* 1969. Houghton Mifflin. 1st ed. dj. VG. P1. $50.00

ASIMOV, Isaac. *Opus 200.* 1979. Houghton Mifflin. 1st ed. dj. VG. P1. $20.00

ASIMOV, Isaac. *Opus 300.* 1984. Houghton Mifflin. UP. EX. R3. $50.00

ASIMOV, Isaac. *Pebble in the Sky.* 1950. Doubleday. 1st ed. inscr. dj. EX. R3. $200.00

ASIMOV, Isaac. *Planet That Wasn't.* 1976. Doubleday. 1st ed. dj. EX. B13. $45.00

ASIMOV, Isaac. *Prelude to Foundation.* nd. Book Club. dj. VG. P1. $5.00

ASIMOV, Isaac. *Robot Novels.* nd. Book Club. dj. VG. P1. $6.00

ASIMOV, Isaac. *Robots & Empire.* nd. Book Club. dj. VG. P1. $4.50

ASIMOV, Isaac. *Robots & Empire.* 1985. Doubleday. 1st ed. dj. EX. P1. $16.95

ASIMOV, Isaac. *Robots & Empire.* 1985. Doubleday. 1st ed. dj. RS. EX. P1. $20.00

ASIMOV, Isaac. *Robots of Dawn.* nd. Book Club. dj. VG. P1. $5.00

ASIMOV, Isaac. *Robots of Dawn.* 1983. Doubleday. 1st ed. dj. EX. R3. $25.00

ASIMOV, Isaac. *SF A to Z.* 1982. Houghton Mifflin. 1st ed. dj. RS. EX. R3. $22.50

ASIMOV, Isaac. *SF Weight-Loss Book.* 1983. Crown. 1st ed. dj. EX. F5. $18.00

ASIMOV, Isaac. *SF Weight-Loss Book.* 1983. Crown. 1st ed. dj. VG. P1. $15.00

ASIMOV, Isaac. *Stars, Like Dust.* nd. Book Club. VG. P1. $3.50

ASIMOV, Isaac. *Sun Shines Bright.* 1984. Granada. dj. EX. P1. $15.00

ASIMOV, Isaac. *Treasury of Humor.* 1971. Houghton Mifflin. 1st ed. dj. EX. F5. $18.00

ASIMOV, Isaac. *View From a Height.* 1963. Doubleday. 1st ed. dj. EX. R3. $30.00

ASIMOV, Isaac. *X Stands for Unknown.* 1984. Doubleday. 1st ed. dj. VG. P1. $15.00

ASIMOV, Isaac. *13 Short Fantasy Novels.* 1984. Greenwich House. 1st ed. dj. VG. P1. $15.00

ASIMOV, Isaac. *2nd Foundation.* 1971. Avon N306. 12th print. Lib PB bdg. VG. P1. $3.00

ASIMOV, Isaac. *3 by Asimov.* 1981. Targ Ed. Ltd Ed Pr Book. 1/250. sgn. H3. $125.00

ASIMOV, Isaac. *9 Tomorrows.* nd. Book Club. dj. VG. P1. $6.00

ASIMOV & CIARDI. *Limericks: Too Gross.* 1978. Norton. 1st ed. dj. EX. R3. $20.00

ASIMOV & SILVERBERG. *Nightfall.* nd. Quality Book Club. dj. EX. P1. $5.00

ASPIRIN, Robert. *Sanctuary.* 1981. Doubleday. 1st HrdCvr ed. sgn. dj. EX. F5. $15.00

ASPRIN, Robert. *Bug Wars.* 1979. St Martin. 1st ed. dj. VG. P1. $15.00

ASPRIN, Robert. *Mything Persons.* 1984. Donning. 1st ed. 1/1200. sgn. boxed. EX. R3. $45.00

ASQUITH, Cynthia. *This Mortal Coil.* 1947. Arkham House. 1st ed. dj. EX. R3. $65.00

ASQUITH, Cynthia. *This Mortal Coil.* 1947. Arkham House. 1st ed. dj. VG. P1. $50.00

ASTAIRE, Fred. *Steps in Time.* 1959. NY. 1st ed. dj. VG. B3. $22.50

ASTLEY, Thea. *Hunting the Wild Pineapple.* 1991. Putnam. 1st Am ed. M. K2. $19.95

ASTOR, J.J. *Journey in Other Worlds.* 1894. Appleton. 1st ed. VG. R3. $50.00

ASTURIAS, M.A. *Gr Pope.* 1971. Delacorte/Lawrence. 1st Am ed. dj. EX. K2. $50.00

ASTURIAS, M.A. *Gr Pope.* 1971. Delacorte/Lawrence. 2nd print. dj. EX. K2. $25.00

ASTURIAS DE BARRIOS, Linda. *Comalapa: Native Dress & Its Significance.* 1985. Ixchel Mus. 1st ed. Eng text. wrp. F2. $35.00

ATGET, Eugene. *Vision of Paris.* 1963. NY. dj. EX. $65.00

ATHAS, Daphne. *Entering Ephesus.* 1971. Viking. 1st ed. sgn. dj. EX. C4. $30.00

ATHEARN, R.G. *Westward the Briton.* 1953. Scribner. 1st ed. sgn. dj. A5. $40.00

ATHEARN, R.G. *William Tecumseh Sherman & Settlement of the W.* 1956. Norman, OK. 1st ed. 371 p. dj. A5. $35.00

ATHELING, William. *More Issues at Hand.* 1970. Advent. 1st ed. dj. VG. P1. $35.00

ATHERTON, Gertrude. *Blk Oxen.* nd. AL Burt. Photoplay ed. VG. P1. $20.00

ATHERTON, Gertrude. *Horn of Life.* 1942. Appleton. 1st ed. bl bdg. VG. B10. $6.75

ATHERTON, Gertrude. *Rulers of Kings.* 1904. Harper. 1st ed. 412 p. G. B10. $4.50

ATHERTON, Gertrude. *Wht Morning.* 1918. Stokes. VG. R3. $15.00

ATKESON, M.M. *Shining Hours.* nd. (1927) Century. Ils Eloise Burns. 277 p. VG. B10. $3.75

ATKINS, Mary. *Diary of Mary Atkins: Sabbatical in 1860s.* 1937. Mills College. Ltd 1st ed. 1/500. VG. $45.00

ATKINSON, T.W. *Oriental & W Siberia: Narrative of 7 Years' Exploration.* 1859. Phil. VG. $95.00

ATTANASIO, A.A. *Arc of the Dream.* 1986. Bantam. AP. wrp. EX. $30.00

ATTANASIO, A.A. *Beast Marks.* 1984. Zeising. Ltd ed. 1/250. sgn. M. R3. $40.00

ATTANASIO, A.A. *Beast Marks.* 1984. Zeising. 1st ed. M. R3. $25.00

ATTANASIO, A.A. *In Other Worlds.* 1985. Morrow. 1st ed. RS. M. R3. $15.00

ATTAWAY, William. *Calypso Song Book.* 1957. McGraw Hill. Ils Charmatz. 1st ed. 65 p. dj. EX. H3. $50.00

ATTAWAY, William. *Calypso Song Book.* 1957. NY. 1st ed. dj. VG. B3. $25.00

ATTENBOROUGH, David. *Tribal Eye.* 1976. Norton. 1st ed. dj. F2. $20.00

ATTERIDGE, Helen. *At the Sgn of the Silver Cup.* nd. (1926) Kennedy. 1st ed? 260 p. VG. B10. $4.50

ATTOE, David. *Lion at the Door.* 1989. Little Brn. 1st ed. M. K2. $17.95

ATWAN & FORER. *Why We Write.* 1986. Harper Row. 1st ed. wrp. EX. K2. $30.00

ATWATER, G.P. *Annals of a Parish.* 1928. np. Ils. 67 p. VG. T5. $15.00

ATWOOD, Margaret. *Bluebird's Egg & Other Stories.* 1986. Houghton Mifflin. sgn. dj. EX. C4. $50.00

ATWOOD, Margaret. *Bodily Harm.* 1982. Simon Schuster. UP of 1st Am ed. wrp. EX. $45.00

ATWOOD, Margaret. *Canadian Monsters.* 1977. Cambridge. 1st ed. dj. EX. K2. $35.00

ATWOOD, Margaret. *Dancing Girls & Other Stories.* 1982. Simon Schuster. UP of 1st Am ed. wrp. EX. K2. $40.00

ATWOOD, Margaret. *Life Before Man.* 1979. Simon Schuster. sgn. H3. $50.00

ATWOOD, Margaret. *Murder in the Dark.* 1983. Coach House. 1st ed. wrp. EX. B13. $45.00

ATWOOD, Margaret. *Selected Poems.* 1976. Simon Schuster. sgn. H3. $75.00

ATWOOD, Margaret. *Surfacing.* 1972. Toronto. 1st ed. as issued. K2. $65.00

ATWOOD, Margaret. *To See Our World.* 1980. Morrow. 1st ed. quarto. dj. EX. K2. $65.00

AUBREY, Edmund. *Sherlock Holmes in Dallas.* 1980. Dodd Mead. 1st ed. dj. VG. P1. $25.00

AUCHINCLOSS, Louis. *Edith Wharton: A Woman in Her Time.* 1971. NY. 1st ed. sgn. dj. EX. T9. $45.00

AUCHINCLOSS, Louis. *Reading Henry James.* 1975. MN U. 1st ed. dj. EX. C4. $20.00

AUCHINCLOSS, Louis. *Reflections of a Jacobite.* 1961. London. 1st ed. VG. B2. $40.00

AUDEMARS, Pierre. *And 1 for the Dead.* 1981. Walker. dj. VG. P1. $12.50

AUDEN, W.H. *Academic Graffiti.* 1972. Random House. 1st Am ed. dj. EX. $17.00

AUDEN, W.H. *City Without Walls & Other Poems.* c 1969. Random House. 1st ed. dj. EX. $15.00

AUDEN, W.H. *City Without Walls.* 1969. London. Faber. 1st ed. clipped dj. EX. B13. $50.00

AUDEN, W.H. *Collected Longer Poems.* 1968. London. Faber. long unbound galleys. VG. B13. $175.00

AUDEN, W.H. *Dance of Death.* 1933. London. Faber. 1st ed. dj. VG. H3. $150.00

AUDEN, W.H. *Shield of Achilles.* 1955. Random House. 1st ed. dj. EX. B13. $45.00

AUDEN & ISHERWOOD. *Ascents of F6.* 1937. Random House. 1st Am ed. H3. $100.00

AUDEN & ISHERWOOD. *Dog Beneath the Skin; or, Where Is Francis?* 1935. London. Faber. 1st ed. dj. EX. H3. $200.00

AUDEN & ISHERWOOD. *On the Frontier.* 1938. London. Faber. 1st ed. dj. scarce. H3. $100.00

AUDEN & KALLMAN. *Elizabethan Song Book.* 1957. London. Faber. 1st ed. quarto. 240 p. dj. VG. H3. $125.00

AUDEN & KALLMAN. *Magic Flute.* 1956. Random House. 1st ed. dj. EX. H3. $65.00

AUDEN & KALLMAN. *Magic Flute.* 1957. London. Faber. 1st Eng ed. dj. EX. H3. $75.00

AUDUBON, J.J. *Birds of Am.* 1856. NY. 2nd Octavo ed. 500 pls. brn morocco. B10. $15000.00

AUDUBON, J.J. *Birds of Am.* 1856. NY. 500 pls. 7 vols. brn morocco. H3. $17500.00

AUDUBON, J.J. *Birds of Am.* 1946. Macmillan. 435 clr pls. EX. $50.00

AUEL, J.M. *Clan of the Cave Bear.* nd. Crown. 19th print. dj. EX. P1. $15.00

AUEL, J.M. *Clan of the Cave Bear.* 1980. NY. presentation. B3. $37.50

AUEL, J.M. *Mammoth Hunters.* nd. Book Club. dj. EX. P1. $4.50

AUEL, J.M. *Mammoth Hunters.* 1985. Crown. 1st ed. sgn. dj. EX. P1. $25.00

AUEL, J.M. *Plains of Passage.* nd. Crown. 2nd ed. sgn. dj. EX. P1. $25.00

AUEL, J.M. *Plains of Passage.* 1990. Crown. UP. wrp. EX. B13. $25.00

AUEL, J.M. *Valley of Horses.* 1982. Crown. 1st ed. dj. EX. P1. $20.00

AUGHEY, J.H. *Fighting Preacher.* 1899. Rhodes McClure. 1st ed. 361 p. VG. $95.00

AUGUR, Helen. *Zapotec.* 1954. Doubleday. 1st ed. dj. F2. $20.00

AUGUST, John. *Advance Agent.* 1944. Tower. 2nd ed. dj. VG. P1. $7.50

AUGUSTA & BURIAN. *Prehistoric Animals.* nd. London. Revised ed. quarto. dj. VG. $35.00

AUNGST, D.M. *2 Canals of Lebanon Co.* 1968. Lebanon. 48 p. wrp. G. T5. $15.00

AURAND, A.M. *Little-Known Facts About Bundling.* 1938. Harrisburg. Ils. 32 p. wrp. VG. $20.00

AUSLANDER, Joseph. *Sunrise Trumpets.* 1924. NY. 1st ed. VG. C1. $11.00

AUSLANDER & HILL. *Winged Horse Anthology.* 1929. Doubleday. 1st ed. dj. VG. B10. $10.00

AUSTEN, Jane. *Complete Novels of Jane Austen.* nd. Modern Lib Giant G58. 1364 p. dj. EX. B10. $6.75

AUSTEN, Jane. *Emma.* 1816. London. Murray. 1st ed. 3 vols. rebacked. VG. H3. $7500.00

AUSTEN, Jane. *Mansfield Park.* 1814. London. 1st ed. 3 vols. rebacked. VG. H3. $10000.00

AUSTEN, Jane. *Northanger Abbey/ Persuasion.* 1818. London. 1st ed. 4 vols. EX. H3. $4000.00

AUSTEN, Jane. *Novels of Jane Austen.* 1911. Edinburgh. Grant. Winchester ed. 12 vols. EX. H3. $2500.00

AUSTEN, Jane. *Persuasion.* 1977. Westport, CT. Ils/sgn Buonpastore. 1/1600. slipcase. EX. T5. $50.00

AUSTEN, Jane. *Pride & Prejudice.* 1813. London. 2nd ed. 3 vols. rebound. H3. $2750.00

AUSTEN, Jane. *Sense & Sensibility.* 1957. Ltd Ed Club. Ils Helen Sewell. slipcase. VG. $35.00

AUSTEN, Jane. *Sense & Sensibility.* 1957. Ltd Ed Club. Ils Helen Sewell. 1/1500. slipcase. EX. C4. $50.00

AUSTER, Paul. *City of Glass.* 1985. Sun/Moon Pr. sgn. H3. $40.00

AUSTER, Paul. *Ghosts.* 1986. Sun/Moon Pr. 1st ed. dj. M. C4. $50.00

AUSTER, Paul. *In the Country of Last Things.* 1987. Viking. 1st ed. sgn. dj. EX. K2. $45.00

AUSTER, Paul. *Music of Chance.* 1990. NY. UP. EX. K2. $30.00

AUSTER, Paul. *Wall Writing.* 1976. Berkeley. 1st ed. 1/500. sgn. wrp. EX. T9. $40.00

AUSTIN, Alicia. *Age of Dreams.* 1978. Grant. 1st ed. dj. EX. R3. $40.00

AUSTIN, F.B. *Red Flag.* nd. 1st ed. dj. EX. R3. $20.00

AUSTIN, F.B. *Road to Glory.* 1935. Grosset Dunlap. dj. VG. R3. $10.00

AUSTIN, F.B. *Saga of the Sea.* 1929. Macmillan. 1st ed. dj. EX. R3. $25.00

AUSTIN, F.B. *War God Walks Again.* 1926. Doubleday. dj. VG. R3. $17.50

AUSTIN, G.K. *Practical Magic With Patter.* nd. London. Ltd 2nd ed. 92 p. decor brd. EX. J3. $9.00

AUSTIN, Hugh. *Murder in Triplicate.* 1935. Sun Dial. VG. P1. $9.25

AUSTIN, Mary. *Land of Journey's End.* nd. (1924) Century. not 1st ed. 459 p. VG. B10. $8.75

AUSTIN, R.B. *Early Am Medical Imprints: Guide to Works Printed 1668-1820.* 1961. WA. 1st ed. wrp. EX. A5. $20.00

AUTOMOTIVE QUARTERLY. *Automobile Quarterly World of Cars.* 1972. 1st ed. 2nd print. 223 p. dj. EX. S1. $20.00

AVALLONE, Michael. *Man From Avon.* nd. Avon G1307. PB Orig. inscr. NM. T9. $25.00

AVALLONE, Michael. *Tall Dolores.* 1953. Perma Star 244. PB Orig. VG. T9. $25.00

AVEDON, Richard. *Avedon Photographs 1947-1977.* 1978. NY. 1st ed. sgn. EX. G1. $100.00

AVEDON & BALDWIN. *Nothing Personal.* 1964. NY. 1st ed. boxed. VG. B3. $95.00

AVELEYRA ARROYO DE ANDA, Luis. *Prehistoria de Mexico.* 1950. Mexico. Ils 1st ed. 167 p. dj. F2. $15.00

AVENI & COLLIER. *Selected Bibliography of Native Am Astronomy.* 1978. Colgate U. 148 p. wrp. w/supplement. F2. $20.00

AVENI & HARTUNG. *Maya City Planning & the Calendar.* 1986. Phil. Am Philosophical Soc. 87 p. F2. $20.00

AVERY, Richard; see Cooper, Edmund.

AVEY, Elijah. *Capture & Execution of John Brn.* 1906. Chicago. Ils. EX. $40.00

AVITABILE, Gunhild. *Chao Shao-an: Meister der Sudchinesischen Lingnan-Schule.* 1988. Frankfurt. Ils. wrp. D4. $30.00

AVITAL, Samuel. *Centre du Silence Mime Workbook.* 1977. Wisdom Garden Books. 2nd print. 158 p. EX. J3. $8.00

AXSOM, R.H. *Prints of Ellsworth Kelly: Catalog Raisonne 1949-1985.* 1987. Hudson Hills. dj. D4. $50.00

AYDEN, Erje. *Crazy Gr of 2nd Ave.* 1965. Canyon Books. 1st HrdCvr ed. dj. VG. K2. $50.00

AYER, I.W. *Life in the Wilds of Am.* 1880. Grand Rapids. A4. $75.00

AYER & TAVES. *3 Lives of Harriet Hubbard Ayer.* 1957. Lippincott. 1st ed. dj. B10. $5.75

AYERS, A.B. *Mexican Architecture.* 1926. NY. 1st ed. G. T5. $95.00

AYLING, Keith. *Combat Aviation.* 1943. Harrisburg. Ils 1st ed. 253 p. G. T5. $22.50

AZELROD, George. *Will Success Spoil Rock Hunter?* 1956. Random House. 1st ed. dj. EX. H3. $50.00

BABCOCK, Havilah. *Best of Babcock.* 1974. NY. 1st ed. dj. VG. B3. $30.00

BABCOCK, Havilah. *Jaybirds Go to Hell on Friday.* 1965. Holt Rinehart Winston. 1st ed. dj. VG. B13. $50.00

BABCOCK, Havilah. *Tales of Quails & Such.* 1951. NY. 1st ed. dj. VG. B3. $60.00

BABCOCK, W.M. *Selections From Letters & Diaries.* 1922. Albany. 110 p. wrp. EX. $55.00

BABSON, J. *Hist of Town of Gloucester, Cape Ann, Including...Rockport.* 1860. Gloucester. 1st ed. fld map. G. $40.00

BABSON, J. *Notes & Additions to Hist of Gloucester: Part 1.* 1876. Gloucester. 1st ed. VG. $17.50

BABSON, Marian. *Death Beside the Sea.* 1982. Walker. 1st ed. dj. VG. P1. $12.95

BABSON, Marian. *Death in Fashion.* 1986. Doubleday Book Club. VG. P1. $7.50

BACHELLER, Irving. *Eben Holden's Last Day A-Fishing.* 1907. NY. Ils Potter. 60 p. T5. $19.50

BACHMAN, Richard; see King, Stephen.

BACHMANN, Lawrence. *Lorelei.* 1957. Crime Club. dj. VG. P1. $7.50

BACHMANN & WALLACE. *Land Between.* 1957. Los Angeles. 1/500. dj. EX. $35.00

BACHRACH, William. *Outline of Swimming: Encyclopedia of Sport.* 1924. Chicago. Bradwell. 1st ed. presentation. 224 p. R4. $40.00

BACON, Edgar. *Narrangansett Bay.* 1904. NY. 1st ed. 8vo. VG. $35.00

BACON, Edward. *Archaeology Discoveries in the 1960s.* 1971. Praeger. 1st ed. 4to. 293 p. dj. F2. $12.50

BACON, Edward. *Digging for Hist.* 1960. London. A4. $25.00

BACON, Edward. *Digging for Hist.* 1960. NY. John Day. 1st ed. 4to. 318 p. dj. F2. $15.00

BACON, Edward. *Great Archaeologists.* 1976. Bobbs Merrill. 1st Am ed. 4to. 428 p. dj. F2. $25.00

BACON, Francis. *Essays; or, Counsels Civill & Morall.* 1944. Ltd Ed Club. 1/1100. sgn Bruce Rogers. slipcase. EX. C4. $125.00

BACON, Francis. *Works.* 1825-1934. London. Pickering. 16 vols. VG. H3. $1500.00

BACON, Francis. *Works.* 1765. London. Millar. 5 vols. G. H3. $500.00

BACON, Frank. *Lightnin'.* nd. Grosset Dunlap. Photoplay ed. G. P1. $12.50

BACON, Leonard. *Legend of Quincibald.* 1928. Harper. 1st ed. 76 p. B10. $12.00

BACON, M.H. *Valiant Friend: Life of Lucretia Mott.* 1980. NY. Walker. 2nd ed. 8vo. 265 p. dj. VG. V1. $12.00

BACON, Martha. *3rd Road.* 1971. Little Brn. 1st ed. dj. B10. $4.25

BACON, Peggy. *Leftover Elf.* 1952. Harper. Ils. 8vo. 58 p. dj. VG. $15.00

BACON. *Hist of 55th Field Artillery Brigade in WWII.* 1920. Memphis. 1st ed. folio. 340 p. G. B3. $65.00

BADEN-POWELL, B.H. *Short Account of Land Revenue...in British India.* 1894. Oxford. 1st ed. VG. T1. $40.00

BADEN-POWELL & BADEN-POWELL. *How Girls Can Help Their Country.* 1917. 1st ed. 154 p. G. B3. $100.00

BADGER, J.D. *Arthuriad.* 1972. Toronto. 1st ed. VG. C1. $29.00

BADGER, Joseph. *Memoir of Rev Joseph Badger...* 1851. Hudson, OH. 185 p. T5. $250.00

BAEDEKER, Karl. *Argentine Republic.* 1914. Barcelona. 4 maps. VG. $25.00

BAEDEKER, Karl. *Egypt & the Sudan.* 1914. 22 maps. 85 plans. 55 vignettes. dj. EX. $110.00

BAEDEKER, Karl. *Greece.* 1894. 8 maps. 15 plans. 1 panorama. VG. $60.00

BAEDEKER, Karl. *London & Its Environs.* 1892. 3 maps. 15 plans. VG. $12.00

BAEDEKER, Karl. *London & Its Environs.* 1900. 4 maps. 21 plans. VG. $8.00

BAEDEKER, Karl. *Mediterranean, Seaports, & Sea Routes.* 1911. Leipzig. 38 maps. 49 plans. 608 p. VG. $95.00

BAEDEKER, Karl. *N Germany.* 1897. 33 maps. 56 plans. VG. $40.00

BAEDEKER, Karl. *S Italy & Sicily.* 1896. 25 maps. 17 plans. VG. $10.00

BAEDEKER, Karl. *Switzerland.* 1893. 39 maps. 12 plans. 12 panoramas. G. $8.00

BAER, Gerhard. *Peru: Indiner Gestern und Heute.* 1972. Basel. German text. sq 4to. wrp. F2. $15.00

BAGBY, George. *Better Dead.* 1978. Crime Club. 1st ed. dj. xl. P1. $5.00

BAGBY, George. *Blood Will Tell.* nd. Book Club. dj. VG. P1. $4.00

BAGBY, George. *Corpse Candle.* 1967. Crime Club. 1st ed. dj. xl. P1. $5.00

BAGBY, George. *Golden Creep.* 1982. Crime Club. 1st ed. P1. $5.00

BAGBY, George. *I Could Have Died.* 1979. Crime Club. 1st ed. dj. xl. P1. $5.00

BAGBY, George. *Sitting Duck.* 1981. Crime Club. 1st ed. dj. xl. P1. $5.00

BAGBY, George. *Starting Gun.* 1948. Crime Club. 1st ed. G. P1. $12.50

BAGBY, George. *Tough Get Going.* 1977. Crime Club. 1st ed. dj. VG. P1. $12.50

BAGLEY, Desmond. *Enemy.* 1977. Collins. dj. EX. P1. $15.00

BAGLEY, Desmond. *Spoilers.* 1969. Collins. 1st ed. dj. EX. P1. $22.50

BAGLEY, Desmond. *Tightrope Men.* 1973. Doubleday. 1st ed. dj. xl. P1. $5.00

BAGLEY, Desmond. *Windfall.* 1982. Collins. 1st ed. dj. EX. P1. $17.50

BAIGELL, Matthew. *Am Scene: Am Painting of the 1930s.* 1974. Praeger. dj. D4. $50.00

BAILEY, H.C. *Cat's Whisker.* 1945. Doubleday Doran. G. P1. $7.50

BAILEY, H.C. *Meet Mr Fortune.* 1942. Book League. VG. P1. $15.00

BAILEY, H.C. *Shadow on the Wall.* 1934. Crime Club. 1st ed. VG. P1. $15.00

BAILEY, Herbert. *Art & Science of Book Pub.* 1970. Harper. 1st ed. 216 p. EX. B10. $4.00

BAILEY, J.O. *Pilgrims Through Time & Space.* 1947. Argus Books. 1st ed. dj. VG. R3. $30.00

BAILEY, J.T. *Francesco Bartolozzi.* 1907. London. Ils. 4to. wrp. VG. $50.00

BAILEY, Janet. *Chicago Houses.* 1981. NY. 1st ed. G1. $25.00

BAILEY, K.P. *OH Co of VA & the W Movement 1748-1792.* 1939. Arthur Clark. EX. $100.00

BAILEY, L.H. *Standard Cyclopedia of Horticulture.* 1935. NY. Ils. 3 vols. T5. $85.00

BAILEY, Olga. *Mollie Bailey.* 1943. Dallas. Harben-Spotts. 1st ed. octavo. 160 p. dj. EX. H3. $65.00

BAILEY, Pearl. *Duey's Tale.* 1975. Harcourt Brace. 1st ed. dj. EX. B13. $45.00

BAILEY, Pearl. *Raw Pearl.* 1968.1st ed. sgn. dj. EX. C1. $9.50

BAILEY, Pearl. *Talking to Myself.* 1971. 3rd imp? sgn. dj. EX. C1. $7.50

BAILEY, R.G. *Hells Canyon.* 1943. Lewiston, ID. Ltd 1st ed. sgn. dj. VG. T1. $125.00

BAILEY, R.H. *Forward to Richmond.* 1983. Time Life. 176 p. decor bdg. S1. $9.50

BAILEY & DUNN. *Memoir.* 1933. Ithica. Ils. 180 p. wrp. A5. $40.00

BAIN, John. *Cigarettes in Fact & Fancy.* 1906. Boston. 190 p. reading copy. T5. $25.00

BAINBRIDGE, John. *Biography of Idea/Story of Mutual Fire & Casualty Insurance.* 1952. Doubleday. 1st ed. 381 p. dj. VG. B10. $4.25

BAINES, Keith. *Morte d'Arthur: Rendition in Modern Idiom.* c 1986. Bramhill House. dj. EX. C1. $5.00

BAINES, Thomas. *N Goldfields Diary of Thomas Baines 1869-1872.* 1946. Chatto Windus. 1st ed. 3 vols. djs. VG. $200.00

BAIRD, BREWER, & RIDGWAY. *Hist of N Am Birds.* 1874. Little Brn. 3 vols. clr pls. VG. T3. $500.00

BAIRD, BREWER, & RIDGWAY. *Water Birds of N Am.* 1884. Boston. Little Brn. 2 vols. VG. T3. $250.00

BAIRD, James. *Classical Manual of Epitome of Ancient Geography.* 1871. NY. VG. C1. $15.00

BAIRD, S.F. *On the Serpents of NY.* 1854. Albany. 1st ed. 1st issue. 8vo. G. rare. T1. $200.00

BAIRD, Thomas. *Where Time Ends.* 1988. Harper. 1st ed. dj. EX. F5. $15.00

BAKER, Al. *Magical Ways & Means.* 1941. Carl Waring Jones. 1st ed. 3rd imp. EX. J3. $22.50

BAKER, Al. *Mental Magic.* 1949. Carl Waring Jones. 1st imp. 116 p. dj. NM. J3. $21.00

BAKER, Al. *Pet Secrets.* 1951. Carl Waring Jones. 2nd ed. 111 p. NM. J3. $22.50

BAKER, Charles. *Bibliography of British Book Ils 1860-1900.* 1978. Birmingham, Eng. Ils. 1/1000. dj. EX. A4. $50.00

BAKER, Dorothy. *Young Man With a Horn.* 1938. Houghton Mifflin. 1st ed. octavo. 243 p. dj. EX. H3. $75.00

BAKER, Fred. *Events: Complete Scenario of the Film.* Blk Cat B287. 1st ed. B4. $6.00

BAKER, G.M. *Manual...Bayonet Excercise & Instructions for Officers...* 1866. Buffalo, NY. 16mo. 98 p. EX. A6. $35.00

BAKER, H.L. *Cylinder Printing Machines...Study of Principal Types.* 1918. United Typothetae of Am. Ils Cottrell. EX. $95.00

BAKER, James. *Pictures From Bohemia Drawn With Pen & Pencil.* c 1880. London. 1st ed. EX. $20.00

BAKER, Jim. *Big Ditch: Story of OH Canals.* 1965. Pioneer Pr. Ils. G. T5. $15.00

BAKER, Michael. *Doyle Diary.* 1978. Paddington. dj. VG. P1. $20.00

BAKER, Nicholson. *Mezzanine.* 1988. Weidenfeld Nicolson. 1st ed. sgn. dj. EX. K2. $45.00

BAKER, Nina. *Inca Gold.* 1938. Wilde. 1st ed. dj. EX. R3. $15.00

BAKER, P.G. *12 Centuries of Rome.* 1934. Dodd Mead. 753 p. purple bdg. $7.00

BAKER, Richard. *Arthurian Legends: Ils Anthology.* c 1985. Dorset. Ils. dj. C1. $12.00

BAKER, Richard. *Arthurian Literature 4.* 1985. 1st Eng ed. EX. C1. $39.50

BAKER, Russell. *Rescue of Miss Yaskell & Other Pipe Dreams.* 1983. Congdon Weed. 1st ed. inscr. dj. EX. K2. $45.00

BAKER, S.J. *Time Is an Enemy.* 1958. Mystery House. VG. P1. $10.00

BAKER, Scott. *Night Child.* 1979. Berkley Putnam. 1st ed. dj. EX. P1. $15.00

BAKER, Will. *Dawn Stone.* 1975. Capra. Chapbook Series. 1/60. sgn. EX. K2. $20.00

BAKER & BAKER. *Doctor Who: Ultimate Foe.* 1988. WH Allen. dj. EX. P1. $14.00

BAKER & LARSEN. *Wit Kit.* 1953. Yogi Magic Mart. 1st ed. SftCvr. VG. J3. $2.00

BALCH, Glenn. *Indian Paint.* 1942. Grosset. Famous Horse Stories Series. 244 p. dj. VG. B10. $3.75

BALCHIN, Nigel. *Seen Dimly Before Dawn.* 1964. Reprint Soc. dj. VG. P1. $7.50

BALCOMB, Mary. *Nicolai Fechin.* 1985. Flagstaff. 2nd print. dj. EX. G1. $28.00

BALDICK, Robert. *Life of JK Huysmans.* 1955. Clarendon. 1st ed. 425 p. dj. R4. $50.00

BALDT, L.I. *Clothing for Women: Selection, Design, & Construction.* 1916. Lippincott. Ils. 8vo. 454 p. VG. $25.00

BALDWIN, Charles. *Universal Biographical Dictionary.* 1825. NY. 444 p. G. T5. $35.00

BALDWIN, Faith. *Skyscraper.* 1931. Grosset. Photoplay ed. B10. $3.75

BALDWIN, James. *Blues for Mr Charlie.* 1964. Dial. 1st ed. sgn. dj. EX. K2. $350.00

BALDWIN, James. *Blues for Mr Charlie.* 1965. London. Joseph. 1st ed. sgn. dj. EX. K2. $225.00

BALDWIN, James. *Devil Finds Work.* 1976. Dial. UP. wrp. EX. B13. $150.00

BALDWIN, James. *Fire Next Time.* 1963. Dial. 1st ed. sgn. dj. EX. B13. $200.00

BALDWIN, James. *Go Tell It on the Mt.* 1954. London. 1st Eng ed. dj. EX. B13. $350.00

BALDWIN, James. *Go Tell It on the Mt.* 1963. Knopf. 1st ed. sgn. very scarce. B13. $375.00

BALDWIN, James. *Going To Meet the Man.* 1965. NY. 1st ed. dj. EX. $35.00

BALDWIN, James. *If Beale St Could Talk.* 1974. Dial. UP. wrp. EX. K2. $135.00

BALDWIN, James. *If Beale St Could Talk.* 1974. Dial. 1st ed. sgn. dj. EX. B13. $150.00

BALDWIN, James. *Just Above My Head.* 1979. Dial. Ltd ed. 1/500. sgn. pub slipcase. EX. K2. $150.00

BALDWIN, James. *No Name in the Street.* 1972. Dial. UP. wrp. RS. w/photo & promotional sheet. K2. $150.00

BALDWIN, James. *Nobody Knows My Name.* 1961. Dial. ARC. dj. RS. EX. K2. $250.00

BALDWIN, James. *Nobody Knows My Name.* 1961. Dial. 1st ed. dj. EX. K2. $50.00

BALDWIN, James. *Notes of a Native Son.* 1955. Beacon. 1st ed. sgn Jimmy Baldwin. dj. EX. K2. $750.00

BALDWIN, James. *Price of the Ticket: Collected Nonfiction 1948-1985.* 1985. St Martin. inscr. dj. H3. $100.00

BALDWIN, James. *1 Day When I Was Lost (Le Jour Ou J'Etais Perdu).* 1973. Paris. Stock. 1st French ed. sgn. wrp. EX. B13. $200.00

BALDWIN, James. *1 Day When I Was Lost.* 1972. London. Joseph. 1st ed. sgn. dj. EX. K2. $275.00

BALDWIN, James. *1 Day When I Was Lost.* 1973. Dial. ARC of 1st Am ed. sgn. dj. RS. w/photo. EX. K2. $275.00

BALDWIN, James. *Price of the Ticket: Collected Nonfiction 1948-1985.* 1985. NY. Ltd ed. 1/150. sgn. slipcase. EX. $200.00

BALDWIN, John. *Ancient Am in Notes on Am Archaeology.* 1872. Harper. Ils. 299 p. gilt bdg. F2. $35.00

BALDWIN, Thomas. *Vital Records of Hardwick, MA to the Year 1850.* 1917. Boston. 1st ed. VG. $40.00

BALDWIN & AVEDON. *Nothing Personal.* 1965. Dell. 1st PB ed. sgn. wrp. EX. B13. $125.00

BALDWIN & CAZAC. *Little Man Little Man.* 1976. Dial. ARC. dj. EX. w/pub material. EX. B13. $85.00

BALDWIN & GIOVANNI. *Dialogue.* 1973. Lippincott. ARC. sgns. dj. EX. B13. $400.00

BALDWIN & MEAD. *Rap on Race.* 1971. Lippincott. UP. sgn Baldwin. wrp. EX. B13. $275.00

BALL, John. *Cop Cade.* 1978. Crime Club. 1st ed. dj. VG. P1. $12.50

BALL, John. *Dragon Hotel.* 1969. Walker/Weatherhill. 1st ed. inscr. dj. EX. B13. $85.00

BALL, John. *Killing in the Market.* 1978. Doubleday Book Club. VG. P1. $7.50

BALL, John. *Notes of a Naturalist in S Am.* 1887. London. clr map. VG. T1. $20.00

BALL, John. *Phase-3 Alert.* 1977. Little Brn. 1st ed. dj. EX. P1. $17.50

BALLANTYNE, R.M. *Gorilla Hunters.* nd. AL Burt. VG. R3. $30.00

BALLARD, J.G. *Bar Sinister.* 1960. Crime Club. 1st ed. dj. xl. P1. $6.00

BALLARD, J.G. *Concrete Island.* 1974. Farrar. 1st Am ed. dj. EX. R3. $60.00

BALLARD, J.G. *Concrete Island.* 1974. Jonathan Cape. 1st ed. dj. xl. P1. $12.50

BALLARD, J.G. *Crash.* 1973. Farrar. 1st Am ed. dj. EX. R3. $65.00

BALLARD, J.G. *Crash.* 1973. Farrar. 1st ed. dj. VG. P1. $25.00

BALLARD, J.G. *Crystal World.* nd. Book Club. dj. VG. P1. $7.50

BALLARD, G. *Day of Creation.* 1987. Lester/Orpen Denys. 1st ed. dj. EX. P1. $20.00

BALLARD, J.G. *Day of Creation.* 1988. Farrar. 1st Am ed. dj. EX. F5. $15.00

BALLARD, J.G. *Day of Creation.* 1988. NY. UP. sgn. K2. $75.00

BALLARD, J.G. *Drowned World & Wind From Nowhere.* nd. Book Club. dj. VG. P1. $7.50

BALLARD, J.G. *Drowned World & Wind From Nowhere.* 1965. Doubleday. 1st ed. dj. EX. R3. $135.00

BALLARD, J.G. *Drowned World.* 1962. Berkley. 1st ed. wrp. EX. F5. $10.00

BALLARD, J.G. *Drowned World.* 1962. London. 1st ed. dj. scarce. K2. $200.00

BALLARD, J.G. *Drowned World.* 1981. Dragon Dream Pr. dj. EX. R3. $30.00

BALLARD, J.G. *Empire of the Sun.* 1984. London. 1st ed. 1st issue. dj. EX. $50.00

BALLARD, J.G. *Empire of the Sun.* 1984. NY. 1st Am ed. dj. VG. B3. $75.00

BALLARD, J.G. *High-Rise.* 1975. Holt. 1st Am ed. dj. EX. R3. $50.00

BALLARD, J.G. *High-Rise.* 1975. Jonathan Cape. 1st ed. dj. xl. P1. $12.50

BALLARD, J.G. *Kindness of Women.* 1991. Farrar Straus. UP of 1st Am ed. wrp. EX. C4. $35.00

BALLARD, J.G. *Memories of the Space Age.* 1988. Arkham House. 1st ed. dj. M. R3. $16.95

BALLARD, J.G. *Terminal Beach.* 1964. Gollancz. HrdCvr ed. dj. EX. K2. $150.00

BALLARD, J.G. *Unlimited Dream Co.* 1979. Holt Rinehart Winston. 1st ed. dj. VG. P1. $15.00

BALLARD, W.T. *Dealing Out Death.* 1948. McKay. 1st ed. dj. VG. F5. $17.00

BALLEM, John. *Judas Conspiracy.* 1976. Musson. dj. VG. P1. $12.50

BALLINGER, B.S. *Beacon in the Night.* 1960. Boardman. dj. VG. P1. $15.00

BALLINGER, B.S. *Corsican.* 1974. Dodd Mead. 1st ed. dj. VG. P1. $15.00

BALLINGER, B.S. *Darkening Door.* 1952. Harper. 1st ed. dj. VG. P1. $20.00

BALLINGER, W.A. *Rebellion.* 1967. Howard Baker. 1st ed. dj. EX. P1. $15.00

BALLINGER & HORNBAKER. *Stouse Collection: Arts of Costa Rica.* 1974. KS U Mus of Art. oblong 4to. wrp. F2. $10.00

BALLOU, M.M. *Due S; or, Cuba Past & Present.* 1885. Boston/NY. 1st ed. EX. C1. $49.00

BALLOU, M.M. *Equatorial Am.* 1892. Houghton Mifflin. 1st ed. 371 p. F2. $25.00

BALMER, Edwin. *Keeban.* nd. Grosset Dunlap. VG. P1. $10.00

BALMER & WYLIE. *After Worlds Collide.* 1934. AL Burt. dj. EX. R3. $25.00

BALMER & WYLIE. *After Worlds Collide.* 1934. Lippincott. 1st ed. dj. xl. R3. $75.00

BALSHOFER, MILLER, & BERGSTEN. *1 Reel a Week.* 1967. CA U. 1st ed. octavo. 218 p. dj. EX. H3. $40.00

BALZAC, Honore; see De Balzac, Honore.

BAMBARA, T.C. *Sea Birds Are Still Alive.* 1977. Random House. 1st ed. dj. EX. B13. $45.00

BAMBERG, Theodore. *Quality Magic.* 1921. Will Goldston. Ltd 1st ed. 98 p. VG. J3. $12.00

BAMBERT & PARRISH. *Okito on Magic.* 1952. Chicago. Drane. 1st ed. dj. NM. J3. $27.50

BANCROFT, Aaron. *Essay: Life of George WA.* 1807. Worcester. G1. $35.00

BANCROFT, Alberta. *Lost Village.* 1927. Doran. 1st ed. 130 p. gr bdg. EX. B10. $15.00

BANCROFT, George. *Hist of Formation of Constitution of US.* 1883. Appleton. 3rd ed. 2 vols. EX. $85.00

BANCROFT, H.H. *Hist of AK 1730-1885.* 1886. San Francisco. 1st ed. VG. $75.00

BANCROFT, H.H. *Hist of Central Am.* 1886-1887. San Francisco. 3 vols. rebound. F2. $100.00

BANCROFT, H.H. *Hist of Mexico.* 1883-1888. San Francisco. Bancroft. 6 vols. rebound. F2. $150.00

BANCROFT, H.H. *Native Races of the Pacific States of N Am.* 1883-1886. San Francisco. 5 vols. rebound. F2. $125.00

BANCROFT, H.H. *Works.* 1886-1890. Hist Co Pub. 39 vols. VG. H3. $2500.00

BANCROFT & BARCLAY. *Persuasive to Unity.* 1974. Phil. Stuckey. 12mo. 336 p. G. V1. $10.00

BANCROFT LIBRARY. *Mexico: Ancient & Modern.* 1962. CA U. 1st ed. 95 p. wrp. F2. $35.00

BANDY, Father. *Isn't That Good!?! Magic of Johnny Brn.* 1974. Mesquite, TX. 101 p. NM. J3. $12.50

BANGS, J.K. *Coffee & Repartee.* c 1893. Harper. 1st Am ed. G. $12.00

BANGS, J.K. *From Pillar to Post.* 1916. NY. 1st ed. 339 p. VG. T5. $12.50

BANGS, J.K. *Houseboat on the Styx.* 1896. Harper. VG. P1. $30.00

BANGS, J.K. *Pursuit of the Houseboat.* 1897. Harper. 1st ed. sm 8vo. VG. $20.00

BANKES, George. *Peru Before Pizarro.* 1977. Oxford. 1st ed. dj. xl. F2. $10.00

BANKS, Iain. *State of the Art.* 1989. Zeising. 1st ed. M. R3. $16.00

BANKS, Iain. *Wasp Factory.* 1984. Houghton Mifflin. 1st ed. dj. VG. P1. $15.00

BANKS, L.R. *Return of the Indian.* 1986. Doubleday. 1st ed. dj. EX. P1. $12.95

BANKS, Russell. *Affliction.* 1989. NY. ARC. inscr. printed wrp. K2. $50.00

BANKS, Russell. *Book of Jamaica.* 1980. Houghton Mifflin. 1st ed. dj. EX. $50.00

BANKS, Russell. *Family Life.* 1975. NY. 1st/PB Orig ed. sgn. wrp. EX. B3. $125.00

BANKS, Russell. *Success Stories.* 1986. Harper. 1st ed. dj. M. $10.00

BANKS, Russell. *Success Stories.* 1986. NY. ARC. dj. RS. w/photo. EX. K2. $35.00

BANKS, Russell. *Trailer Park.* 1981. Houghton Mifflin. UP. dj. EX. K2. $65.00

BANKS, Russell. *Waiting To Freeze.* 1969. Lillabulero Pr. 1st ed. wrp. EX. K2. $85.00

BANNERMAN, Helen. *Hist du Petit Negre Sambo.* 1921. Stokes. French text. 24mo. dj. NM. T1. $125.00

BANNING & BANNING. *6 Horses.* 1930. Appleton Century. 410 p. A5. $60.00

BANNISTER, Manly. *Conquest of Earth.* 1957. Avalon. 1st ed. dj. EX. R3. $15.00

BAQUEDANO, Elizabeth. *Aztec Sculpture.* 1984. British Mus. 1st ed. 96 p. wrp. F2. $15.00

BAR-ZOHAR, Michael. *Spy Who Died Twice.* 1975. Houghton. 1st ed. 212 p. dj. VG. B10. $4.00

BARAKA, Amiri. *Selected Poetry of Amiri Baraka.* 1979. Morrow. UP. wrp. EX. B13. $85.00

BARAKA & BARAKA. *Confirmation: An Anthology of African-Am Women.* 1983. Morrow. UP. scarce. B13. $125.00

BARBEAU, Clayton. *Dante & Gentucca.* 1974. Capra. Chapbook Series. 1/100. sgn. EX. K2. $20.00

BARBEAU, Marius. *Cote the Wood Carver.* 1943. Ryerson Pr. 1st ed. VG. $50.00

BARBELLION, W.N.P. *Journal of a Disappointed Man.* 1919. Chatto Windus. 1st Eng ed. scarce. $65.00

BARBER, J.W. *CT Hist Collections.* 1836. New Haven. 2nd ed. map. VG. A4. $125.00

BARBER, Lynn. *Heyday of Nat Hist.* 1980. Doubleday. 1st Am ed. dj. EX. $15.00

BARBER, Richard. *Arthurian Legends: Ils Anthology.* 1985. Dorset. dj. EX. C1. $12.50

BARBER, Richard. *Paston's Family in the War of Roses.* 1981. London. Folio Soc. Ils. EX. C1. $15.00

BARBER, Richard. *Tournaments.* 1978. Ils Dalton. 1st Eng ed. NM. C1. $10.00

BARBOUR, R.H. *All Hands Stand By!* 1942. Appleton. 1st ed. 261 p. dj. VG. B10. $6.25

BARBOUR, W.A. *Chilton's Auto Repair Manual 1978.* 1977.1128 p. VG. S1. $15.00

BARCLAY, Bill; see Moorcock, Michael.

BARCLAY, John. *Memoirs of Rise, Progress, & Persecutions...N of Scotland.* 1835. Phil. Nathan Kite. 16mo. 354 p. V1. $16.00

BARCLAY, John. *Selection From Letters & Papers of the Late John Barclay.* 1847. Phil. Longstreth. 1st Am ed. 8vo. 328 p. G. V1. $25.00

BARCLAY, Robert. *Apologie de la Vraie Theologie Chretienne.* 1797. London. Phillips. 8vo. 652 p. V1. $50.00

BARCLAY, Robert. *Apology for the True Christian Divinity.* 1850. Phil. Friends Bookstore. 8vo. 548 p. G. V1. $10.00

BARCLAY, Robert. *Apology for the True Christian Divinity.* 1908. Phil. Friends Bookstore. bdg copy. V1. $14.00

BARCLAY, Robert. *Catechism & Confession of Faith.* 1878. Phil. Friends Book Assn. 12mo. G. V1. $12.00

BARCLAY, Robert. *Theologiae Vere Christianae Apologia.* 1729. London. J Sowle. 2nd ed. 12mo. 492 p. V1. $60.00

BARCLAY, Robert. *Treatise on Church Government.* 1822. Phil. Conrad. 16mo. 124 p. G. V1. $25.00

BARCLAY, Robert. *Truth Triumphant Through Spiritual Warfare...* 1831. Phil. BC Stanton. 8vo. 2 vols only. G. V1. $40.00

BARCLAY, Robert. *Views of Christian Doctrine Taken From Barclay's Apology.* 1882. Phil. Friends Bookstore. 294 p. VG. V1. $12.00

BARCYNSKA, Countess. *Yesterday Is Tomorrow.* 1950. Rich Cowan. dj. VG. P1. $10.00

BARD, N.P. *Bullhorn Reukus.* 1964. NY. 1st ed. inscr/sgn. dj. VG. T5. $15.00

BARD, N.P. *Bullhorn Ruckus.* 1964. Vantage Pr. 1st ed. 249 p. dj. VG. B10. $3.75

BARDECHE & BRASILLACH. *Hist of Motion Pictures.* 1938. MOMA. 1st ed. octavo. 412 p. dj. EX. very scarce. H3. $85.00

BARDON, Minna. *Murder Does Light Housekeeping.* nd. Phoenix Pr. 1st ed? 250 p. VG. B10. $4.00

BARING-GOULD, W.S. *Book of Werewolves.* 1973. reprint of 1865 ed. dj. VG. C1. $12.00

BARING-GOULD, W.S. *Nero Wolfe of W 35th St.* 1970. Bantam. P1. $5.00

BARING-GOULD, W.S. *Sherlock Holmes of Baker St.* 1962. NY. 1st ed. 336 p. dj. VG. T5. $15.00

BARJAVEL, Rene. *Ice People.* nd. Book Club. dj. EX. P1. $4.50

BARK, C.V. *See the Living Crocodiles.* 1968. Walker. 1st ed. dj. EX. P1. $12.50

BARKER, Clive. *Cabal.* 1988. Poseidon Pr. 1st ed. dj. EX. P1. $18.95

BARKER, Clive. *Damnation Game.* nd. Book Club. dj. EX. P1. $6.00

BARKER, Clive. *Damnation Game.* 1987. Ace Putnam. 1st Am ed. dj. EX. R3. $25.00

BARKER, Clive. *Damnation Game.* 1987. Ace Putnam. 1st ed. dj. EX. P1. $25.00

BARKER, Clive. *In the Flesh.* nd. Book Club. dj. EX. P1. $6.00

BARKER, Clive. *In the Flesh.* 1987. Poseidon. ARC. dj. EX. K2. $45.00

BARKER, Clive. *Inhuman Condition.* nd. Book Club. dj. EX. P1. $6.00

BARKER, Clive. *Inhuman Condition.* 1986. Poseidon. 1st ed. dj. EX. P1. $20.00

BARKER, Clive. *Weaveworld.* 1987. Collins. 1st ed. dj. EX. P1. $25.00

BARKER, E.S. *When Dogs Barked Treed.* 1946. Albuquerque. 1st ed. dj. VG. B3. $45.00

BARKER, Felix. *Oliviers.* 1953. Phil. 1st ed. dj. VG. B3. $25.00

BARKER, Joseph. *Recollections of 1st Settlement of OH.* 1958. Marietta. Ils. 96 p. VG. T5. $17.50

BARKER & DANFORTH. *Hunting & Trapping on Upper Magalloway River...* 1882. Boston. Ils. sgn. 232 p. VG. T5. $45.00

BARNAO, Jack. *Hammerlocke.* 1986. Scribner. 1st ed. dj. VG. P1. $13.95

BARNARD, Robert. *At Death's Door.* nd. BOMC. dj. EX. P1. $7.50

BARNARD, Robert. *Bodies.* nd. Book Club. dj. VG. P1. $5.00

BARNARD, Robert. *Bodies.* 1986. Scribner. 1st ed. dj. VG. P1. $13.95

BARNARD, Robert. *Cherry Blossom Corpse.* 1987. Scribner. 1st ed. dj. VG. P1. $14.95

BARNARD, Robert. *Corpse in a Gilded Cage.* nd. Book Club. dj. VG. P1. $4.50

BARNARD, Robert. *Corpse in a Gilded Cage.* 1984. Scribner. 1st ed. dj. EX. P1. $15.00

BARNARD, Robert. *Death in a Cold Climate.* 1981. Doubleday Book Club. VG. P1. $7.50

BARNARD, Robert. *Death of an Old Goat.* 1974. Collins Crime Club. 1st ed. dj. xl. P1. $5.00

BARNARD, Robert. *Fete Fatale.* 1985. Scribner. 1st ed. dj. EX. P1. $13.95

BARNARD, Robert. *Out of the Blackout.* nd. Book Club. dj. VG. P1. $4.00

BARNARD, Robert. *Political Suicide.* 1986. Scribner. 1st ed. dj. VG. P1. $13.95

BARNARD, Robert. *School for Murder.* nd. Book Club. dj. VG. P1. $4.50

BARNARD, Robert. *Skeleton in the Grass.* nd. Book Club. dj. VG. P1. $4.50

BARNES, A.K. *Interplanetary Hunter.* 1956. Gnome. dj. VG. P1. $15.00

BARNES, A.K. *Interplanetary Hunter.* 1956. Gnome. 1st ed. dj. EX. R3. $20.00

BARNES, Catherine. *Cinderella; or, Glass Slipper.* nd. Harrison Co. apparent 1st ed. dj. VG. B10. $5.00

BARNES, Djuna. *Book of Repulsive Women.* 1915. Bruno Chapbook. 1st ed. pamphlet. EX. K2. $450.00

BARNES, Djuna. *Creatures in an Alphabet.* nd. Dial. UP. yel wrp. EX. K2. $150.00

BARNES, Djuna. *Nightwood.* 1937. Harcourt Brace. 1st Am ed. inscr/dtd 1941. dj. VG. K2. $875.00

BARNES, Djuna. *Nightwood.* 1937. NY. 1st Am ed. 211 p. dj. VG. T5. $65.00

BARNES, John. *Sin of Origin.* 1988. Cogdon. 1st ed. dj. EX. F5. $15.00

BARNES, John. *Who Will Get Your Money?* 1972. Morrow Book Club. 250 p. dj. VG. B10. $3.50

BARNES, Julian; see Kavanagh, Dan.

BARNES, Linda. *Snake Tattoo.* nd. Book Club. dj. VG. P1. $4.50

BARNES, Linda. *Trouble of Fools.* 1987. St Martin. 1st ed. dj. EX. P1. $15.95

BARNES, M.A. *Edna, His Wife: Am Idyll.* 1935. Houghton Mifflin. presentation. dj. H3. $75.00

BARNES, Margaret. *Brief Gaudy Hour.* 1949. Book Club. dj. VG. C1. $5.00

BARNES. *JFK, Scrimshaw Collector.* 1969. Boston. 1st ed. 4to. clr pls. dj. EX. C2. $45.00

BARNES. *W Grazing Grounds & Forest Ranges.* 1913. Chicago. 1st ed. VG. C2. $97.00

BARNETT, Correlli. *1st Churchill: Marlborough, Soldier & Statesman.* 1974. NY. 1st Am ed. dj. EX. $18.00

BARNEY, N.C. *Nouvelles Pensees de L'Amazone.* 1939. Mercure de France. 1/200. yel wrp. EX. H3. $150.00

BARNEY, W.L. *Flawed Victory: New Perspective on the Civil War.* 1975. Praeger. 215 p. VG. S1. $5.00

BARNHOLTH, W.I. *Cuyahoga-Tuscarawas Portage: A Documentary Hist.* 1954. Summit Co Hist Soc. wrp. G. T5. $17.50

BARNSTONE, H. *Gaveston That Was.* 1967. NY. 2nd print. dj. VG. B3. $60.00

BARNUM, P.T. *Struggles & Triumphs; or, 40 Years' Recollections.* 1876. NY. Courier. Author ed. VG. H3. $85.00

BARR, A.H. *Masters of Modern Art.* 1958. MOMA. Revised 3rd ed. VG. G1. $20.00

BARR, James. *Scottish Covenanters.* 1947. Glasgow. Smith. 2nd ed. dj. B10. $7.00

BARR, Robert. *From Whose Bourne.* 1893. London. 1st ed. VG. R3. $50.00

BARR, Robert. *Over the Border.* 1903. Stokes. 1st ed. pictorial bdg. EX. F5. $25.00

BARRETT, John. *Panama Canal: What It Is, What It Means.* 1913. Pan Am Union. Ils. 120 p. F2. $15.00

BARRETT, Jospeh H. *Abraham Lincoln & His Presidency.* 1904. Cincinnati. Clarke. Ils 1st ed. 2 vols. T5. $95.00

BARRETT, Thomas. *Great Hanging at Gainesville.* 1961. TX State Hist Assn. reprint of 1885 ed. S1. $15.00

BARRETT. *Denver Murders.* 1946. NY. 1st ed. dj. VG. B3. $15.00

BARRIE, J.M. *Admirable Crichton.* nd. London/NY/Toronto. Ils Hugh Thompson. 4to. VG. $95.00

BARRIE, J.M. *Dear Brutus.* 1939. Hodder Stoughton. 17th print. EX. P1. $7.25

BARRIE, J.M. *Farewell Miss Julie Logan.* 1932. Hodder Stoughton. EX. P1. $7.25

BARRIE, J.M. *Greenwood Hat.* nd. Scribner. 1st Am/A ed. VG. $8.00

BARRIE, J.M. *Little Minister.* 1896. Scribner. 1st Uniform ed. 2 vols. VG. B10. $10.00

BARRIE, J.M. *Little Minister: Maude Adams Ed.* 1898. Russell. Ils AC Gilbert. 1st ed. B7. $85.00

BARRIE, J.M. *Little Wht Bird.* 1902. Caxton. 1st ed. TEG. VG. $10.00

BARRIE, J.M. *Margaret Ogilvy.* 1896. Scribner. 1st Am ed. TEG. VG. scarce. B10. $25.00

BARRIE, J.M. *My Lady Nicotine.* 1890. London. Hodder Stoughton. TEG. H3. $300.00

BARRIE, J.M. *Peter & Wendy.* nd. Grosset Dunlap. Photoplay ed. VG. B10. $9.25

BARRIE, J.M. *Peter Pan in Kensington Gardens.* 1907. NY. Ils Rackham. 1st Trade ed. EX. $200.00

BARRIE, J.M. *Peter Pan in Kensington Gardens.* 1930. Scribner. Little People Lib. 1st ed. $25.00

BARRIE, J.M. *Sentimental Tommy.* 1896. London. 1st ed. 2nd issue. VG. $15.00

BARRINGER, Leslie. *Joris of the Rock.* 1928. London. 1st ed. dj. VG. C1. $19.50

BARRINGER, Leslie. *Joris of the Rock.* 1929. Doubleday. 1st Am ed. G. R3. $35.00

BARRINGER, Leslie. *Kay, the Left-Handed.* 1935. Doubleday. 1st ed. VG. R3. $25.00

BARRINGTON, P.V. *Night of Violence.* 1959. Hammond Hammond. VG. P1. $10.00

BARRON, Neil. *Anatomy of Wonder.* 1976. Bowker. 1st ed. VG. R3. $20.00

BARRON, Neil. *Anatomy of Wonder.* 1987. Bowker. 3rd ed. M. R3. $39.95

BARRON, O.E.D. *Ashland, Dear Old Ashland!* 1915. Columbus. 1st ed. 40 p. wrp. G. T5. $12.50

BARRY, Charles. *Mouls House Mystery.* nd. McKinlay Stone MacKenzie. VG. P1. $10.00

BARRY, Iris. *DW Griffith: Am Film Master.* 1940. MOMA Lib Series. EX. $20.00

BARRY, Jerome. *Extreme License.* 1958. Crime Club. 1st ed. dj. G. P1. $8.00

BARRY, Joe. *Fall Guy.* 1958. Mystery House. 1st ed. VG. P1. $10.00

BARRY, Joe. *Triple Cross.* 1946. Mystery House. dj. VG. P1. $20.00

BARRY, P. *Barry's Fruit Garden.* 1884. Orange Judd. New ed. VG. $35.00

BARRY, Philip. *Here Come the Clowns.* 1939. Coward McCann. 1st ed. dj. EX. H3. $125.00

BARRYMORE, Ethel. *Memories.* 1955. Harper. 1st ed. 310 p. EX. B10. $5.00

BARSTOW, George. *Hist of NH From Its Discovery in 1614 to 1819.* 1842. Concord. 1st ed. 456 p. ES. VG. T1. $50.00

BARTECCHI, C.E. *Soc Trang: Vietnam Odyssey.* 1980. Boulder. Ils. 181 p. dj. M. T5. $11.95

BARTH, John. *Chimera.* 1972. NY. 1st ed. dj. EX. $35.00

BARTH, John. *Chimera.* 1972. Random House. Ltd ed. 1/300. sgn. EX. H3. $85.00

BARTH, John. *Don't Count On It: A Note on the No of 1001 Nights.* 1984. Northridge, CA. Lord John. Ltd ed. 1/150. sgn. gilt bdg. H3. $100.00

BARTH, John. *End of the Road.* 1962. London. 1st ed. dj. EX. B13. $100.00

BARTH, John. *Floating Opera.* 1968. Secker Warburg. dj. VG. P1. $15.00

BARTH, John. *Giles Goat Boy; or, The Revised New Syllabus.* 1966. Doubleday. inscr. dj. H3. $75.00

BARTH, John. *Letters: A Novel.* 1979. Putnam. sgn. dj. H3. $75.00

BARTH, John. *Todd Andrews to the Author: A Letter From Letters.* 1979. Northridge, CA. Ltd ed. 1/300. sgn. H3. $125.00

BARTHELEME, Peter. *Tart, With a Silken Finish.* 1988. St Martin. 1st ed. dj. EX. F5. $14.00

BARTHELEMY, Charles. *Histoire Bretagne: Old & Modern Tours.* 1858. El Cie. full leather. VG. R5. $25.00

BARTHELME, Donald. *Dead Father.* 1975. Farrar Straus. 1st ed. sgn. dj. EX. K2. $40.00

BARTHELME, Donald. *Guilty Pleasures.* 1974. NY. ARC. dj. RS. EX. $30.00

BARTHELME, Donald. *Guilty Pleasures.* 1974. NY. 1st Am ed. dj. EX. $20.00

BARTHELME, Donald. *Here in the Village.* 1978. Northridge, CA. Ltd ed. 1/275. sgn. H3. $100.00

BARTHELME, Donald. *King.* 1900. NY. 1st ed. dj. M. C1. $17.00

BARTHELME, Donald. *Overnight to Many Distant Cities.* 1983. Putnam. UP. wrp. EX. K2. $65.00

BARTHELME, Donald. *Presents.* nd. Dallas. Ltd ed. 1/376. sgn. w/4 collages. EX. T9. $45.00

BARTHELME, Donald. *Sam's Bar.* 1987. Doubleday. 1st ed. dj. M. $10.00

BARTHELME, Donald. *Snow Wht.* 1967. Atheneum. 1st ed. dj. EX. K2. $75.00

BARTHELME, Donald. *Snow Wht.* 1967. Atheneum. 1st ed. dj. M. H3. $100.00

BARTHELME, Donald. *60 Stories.* 1981. Putnam. Ltd ed. 1/500. sgn. slipcase. H3. $100.00

BARTHES, Roland. *Critical Essays.* 1972. Evanston. ARC. sgn. RS. EX. B13. $250.00

BARTHES, Roland. *Pleasure of the Text.* 1975. Hill Wang. 1st ed. sgn. dj. EX. B13. $200.00

BARTHOLOW, Roberts. *Manual of Hypodermic Medication.* 1869. Phil. 1st ed. 150 p. VG. T5. $75.00

BARTLETT, J.H. *John H Dillingham (1839-1910): Teacher, Minister, Editor.* 1911. Knickerbocker. 8vo. 190 p. VG. V1. $10.00

BARTLETT, J.R. *Glossary of Words...Usually Regarded As Peculiar to US.* 1859. Little Brn. 524 p. VG. A5. $45.00

BARTLETT, R.M. *Sky Pioneer.* 1947. NY. Ils 1st ed. 153 p. G. T5. $17.50

BARTLETT, Richard. *New Country: Am Frontier 1776-1890.* 1974. Oxford. 487 p. EX. T4. $10.00

BARTLETT, Ruth. *Ancient Treasures of Am: Pre-Columbian Exhibition.* 1987. Friends of Angel Mounds. 4to. F2. $10.00

BARTLETT, W.H. *Canadian Scenery Ils.* 1842. London. 1st ed. 117 pls. 2 vols. EX. H3. $2250.00

BARTON, W.E. *Life of Abraham Lincoln.* 1925. Indianapolis. Ils. 2 vols. T5. $35.00

BARTOSZEWSKI, W. *Righteous Among Nations.* 1969. London. Earlscourt. 8vo. 834 p. B10. $15.00

BARTRAM, EVANS, & WEISER. *Journey From PA to Onondaga in 1743.* Imprint Soc. 1st ed. EX. $20.00

BARTTER, M.A. *Way to Ground 0.* 1988. Greenwood. HrdCvr ed. P1. $39.95

BARZMAN, Ben. *Twinkle, Twinkle, Little Star.* nd. Book Club. dj. VG. P1. $4.00

BARZMAN, Ben. *Twinkle, Twinkle, Little Star.* 1960. Putnam. 1st ed. P1. $20.00

BARZUN & TAYLOR. *Catalog of Crime: Revised & Enlarged Ed.* 1989. Harper Row. 1st ed. dj. EX. T9. $35.00

BASAURI, Carlos. *Tojolabales, Tzeltales y Mayas.* 1931. Mexico. Spanish text. sm 4to. 163 p. wrp. F2. $30.00

BASKIN, Leonard. *Ars Anatomica.* 1972. NY. 1/2500. sgn. loose as issued. slipcase. EX. $125.00

BASS, Rick. *Watch.* 1989. NY. Norton. ARC. wrp. EX. K2. $25.00

BASSETT, Ronald. *Tinfish Run.* 1977. Harper. 1st ed. dj. EX. F5. $14.00

BASSETT, S.W. *Shining Headlands.* 1937. Book League. 264 p. dj. EX. B10. $4.00

BASSETT, Sarah Jarmy. *Memoir of Sarah Jarmy Bassett.* 1848. Phil. Harmstead. 24mo. 48 p. V1. $9.00

BATCHELDER, J.B. *Gettysburg: What To See & How To See It.* c 1878. Boston. Ils. 12mo. 148 p. gr bdg. G4. $28.00

BATE, W.J. *John Keats by Walter Jackson Bate.* 1963. Cambridge. 1st ed. dj. EX. C4. $35.00

BATEMAN, James. *2nd Century of Orchidaceous Plants.* 1867. London. 1st ed. 100 pls. orig cloth. EX. H3. $4000.00

BATES, Alfred. *Drama: Its Hist, Literature, & Influence on Civilization.* 1903. Athenian Soc. 1/75. 20 vols. TEG. H3. $4000.00

BATES, Elisha. *Doctrines of Friends; or, Principles of Christian Religion.* 1825. Mt Pleasant. Bates. 1st ed. 12mo. 320 p. G. V1. $25.00

BATES, H.E. *Down the River.* 1937. NY. Holt. Ils Agnes Parker. 1st ed. EX. $50.00

BATES, H.E. *Naturalist on the River Amazon.* 1915. London. Popular ed. sm 8vo. 394 p. VG. $15.00

BATES, Marston. *Land & Wildlife of S America.* 1964. NY. Time. 1st ed. 4to. 200 p. F2. $10.00

BATES, Marston. *Where Winter Never Comes.* 1952. Scribner. 1st/A ed. 310 p. dj. F2. $15.00

BATES, N.B. *E of the Andes & W of Nowhere.* 1947. Scribner. Ils. 237 p. F2. $25.00

BATES, W.G. *Address Delivered in New Courthouse...1874.* 1974. Springfield. 1st ed. 96 p. dj. VG. T5. $22.50

BATES & GOULD. *Eng Country Houses.* 1897. Boston. 100 pls. folio. EX. $40.00

BATESON, F.W. *Cambridge Bibliography of Eng Literature.* 1941. Macmillan. 1st ed. 4 vols. lg octavo. H3. $250.00

BATTELLI, Giulio. *Lezioni di Paleographia.* 1949. Vatican. 3rd ed. xl. VG. G1. $25.00

BATTEN, Jack. *Straight No Chaser.* 1989. Macmillan. 1st Canadian ed. dj. EX. P1. $19.95

BATTLE, Helen. *Every Wall Shall Fall.* nd. (1969) Hewitt House. not Book Club ed. 317 p. dj. VG. B10. $4.50

BAUDELAIRE, Charles. *Intimate Journals.* 1947. Marcel Rodd. Trans Isherwood. dj. EX. H3. $50.00

BAUDER, Donald. *Capt Money & the Golden Girl: J David Affair.* 1985. San Diego. 1st ed. dj. EX. C1. $9.50

BAUDEZ, Claude. *Central Am.* 1970. Geneva. Nagel. 1st ed. dj. F2. $30.00

BAUER, Joel. *Hustle, Hustle: The Magic Business.* 1983. Joel Bauer. 144 p. NM. J3. $15.00

BAUER, Maria. *Foundations Unearthed.* 1948. 3rd print. 64 p. SftCvr. VG. C1. $12.50

BAUER, Steven. *Saturday.* 1980. Berkley Putnam. 1st ed. dj. VG. P1. $15.00

BAUGHMAN, R.W. *KS in Maps.* 1961. Topeka. Ils. 104 p. M. A5. $20.00

BAUM, F.J. *To Please a Child.* 1961. Chicago. 1st ed. dj. EX. B3. $85.00

BAUM, L.F. *Dorothy & the Wizard in Oz.* 1920. Reilly Lee. decor brd. VG. P1. $75.00

BAUM, L.F. *Enchanted Island of Yew.* nd. Donohue. Ils Fanny Cory. 3rd ed. 8vo. 242 p. EX. $150.00

BAUM, L.F. *Enchanted Island of Yew.* 1903. Donohue. VG. P1. $125.00

BAUM, L.F. *Land of Oz.* c 1920s. Reilly Lee. decor brd. VG. P1. $90.00

BAUM, L.F. *Land of Oz.* c 1960s. reprint of 1904 ed. EX. $12.50

BAUM, L.F. *Land of Oz.* nd. Reilly Lee. Popular ed. VG. R3. $40.00

BAUM, L.F. *Lost Princess of Oz.* 1941. Reilly Lee. dj. VG. P1. $100.00

BAUM, L.F. *Magic of Oz.* 1931. Reilly Lee. dj. VG. P1. $125.00

BAUM, L.F. *Magical Monarch of Mo.* c 1920s. Bobbs Merrill. VG. P1. $100.00

BAUM, L.F. *Magical Monarch of Mo.* nd. Donohue. decor brd. VG. P1. $75.00

BAUM, L.F. *Marvelous Land of Oz.* 1904. Reilly Britton. 1st ed. 2nd issue. VG. $85.00

BAUM, L.F. *Master Key.* 1901. Indianapolis. 1st ed. G. B3. $65.00

BAUM, L.F. *Master Key.* 1974. Hyperion. EX. R3. $15.00

BAUM, L.F. *Mother Goose in Prose.* 1897. Chicago. Way Williams. Ils Maxfield Parrish. 1st ed. VG. H3. $4000.00

BAUM, L.F. *Mother Goose in Prose.* 1901. Chicago. Hills. Ils Parrish. 2nd ed. VG. $600.00

BAUM, L.F. *Patchwork Girl of Oz.* 1919. Reilly Britton. 1st ed. 1st state. EX. $150.00

BAUM, L.F. *Phoebe Daring.* 1912. Reilly Britton. decor brd. VG. P1. $75.00

BAUM, L.F. *Rinkitink in Oz.* c 1920s. Reilly Lee. dj. VG. P1. $125.00

BAUM, L.F. *Road to Oz.* 1941. Reilly Lee. dj. VG. P1. $100.00

BAUM, L.F. *Surprising Adventures of Magical Monarch of Mo & His People.* 1947. Indianapolis. Ils Evelyn Copelman. 197 p. VG. T5. $22.50

BAUM, L.F. *Tik-Tok of Oz.* nd. Reilly Lee. decor brd. VG. P1. $60.00

BAUM, L.F. *Tin Woodman of Oz.* 1937. Reilly Lee. dj. VG. P1. $120.00

BAUM, L.F. *Twinkle & Chubbins.* 1911. Chicago. Ils Bancroft. 1st ed. VG. B3. $200.00

BAUM, L.F. *Wizard of Oz.* 1920. Bobbs Merrill. 5th ed. VG. P1. $75.00

BAUM, L.F. *Wizard of Oz.* 1939. Grosset Dunlap. Ils Oskar Lebeck. Abridged ed. dj. EX. P1. $35.00

BAUM, L.F. *Wonderful Wizard of Oz.* 1900. Chicago/NY. Hill. 1st ed. 1st state. variant C bdg. VG. H3. $4000.00

BAUMANN, Elwood. *Rip-Roaring Races & Rallies.* 1981. 118 p. dj. M. S1. $5.00

BAUMANN, Hans. *Gold & Gods of Peru.* 1963. Oxford U. 1st Eng ed. 180 p. dj. F2. $15.00

BAUR, J.I.H. *Nature in Abstraction.* 1958. NY. Ils 1st ed. dj. T5. $22.50

BAXLEY. *What I Saw on the W Coast of N & S Am & HI Islands.* 1865. Appleton. 1st ed. 632 p. A5. $140.00

BAXT, George. *I!, Said the Demon.* 1969. Random House. 2nd ed. dj. xl. P1. $6.00

BAXTER, Ian. *10 on Deck.* 1970. Melbourne. 1st Australian ed. 39 p. NM. J3. $4.00

BAXTER, MANVELL, & WOLLENBERG. *Penguin Film Review.* 1946-1949. London. Penguin. 9 parts in 1 vol. sm octavo. VG. H3. $125.00

BAXTER, N.N. *Gallant 14th: Story of an IN Civil War Regiment.* 1986. Guild Pr. 205 p. pb. M. S1. $12.00

BAXTER, Richard. *Guilty Women.* 1943. Quality Pr. 7th ed. dj. EX. P1. $8.50

BAY, J.C. *Heroine of the Frontier: Miriam Colt in KS in 1856.* 1941. Torch Pr. Ltd ed. w/pub card. EX. K1. $22.50

BAYARD, A.P. *Hill Country Tunes: Instrumental Folk Music of SW PA.* 1944. Phil. presentation. dj. VG. $25.00

BAYER, O.W. *An Eye for An Eye.* 1946. Tower. VG. P1. $7.50

BAYER, William. *Pattern Crimes.* nd. BOMC. dj. VG. P1. $7.50

BAYER, William. *Peregrine.* 1981. Congdon Lattes. 1st ed. dj. EX. P1. $15.00

BAYLER & CARNES. *Last Man Off Wake Island.* 1943. Indianapolis. 1st ed. 367 p. dj. VG. B3. $25.00

BAYLEY, B.J. *Garments of Caesar.* 1976. Doubleday. 1st ed. dj. EX. R3. $12.50

BAYLEY, B.J. *Garments of Caesar.* 1976. Doubleday. 1st ed. dj. xl. P1. $5.00

BAYLEY, B.J. *Rod of Light.* 1987. Arbor House. 1st ed. dj. EX. P1. $15.95

BAYLY, William. *Collection of the Several Writings.* 1830. Phil. Gould. reprint of 1676 ed. 8vo. 400 p. V1. $25.00

BEACH, Joseph. *20th-Century Novel: Studies in Technique.* 1932. Appleton. not 1st ed. 569 p. G. B10. $3.25

BEACH, Lewis. *Goose Hangs High.* 1924. Little Brn. inscr. H3. $60.00

BEACH, Rex. *Winds of Chance.* nd. Hodder Stoughton. dj. VG. P1. $12.50

BEACH, Sylvia. *Shakespeare & Co.* 1959. Harcourt Brace. 1st ed. dj. EX. R3. $25.00

BEADLE, Erastus. *In NE in '57.* 1923. NY Public Lib. 1st Separate ed. 89 p. wrp. VG. $22.50

BEADLE, J.H. *Mysteries & Crimes of Mormonism.* 1870. Nat Pub Co. 540 p. EX. $70.00

BEADLE, J.H. *Undeveloped W; or, 5 Years in the Territories.* 1873. Phil. VG. $80.00

BEAGLE, P.S. *Fantasy Worlds of Peter Beagle.* 1978. Viking. 1st ed. dj. VG. P1. $20.00

BEAGLE, P.S. *Fantasy Worlds of Peter Beagle.* 1978. Viking. 2nd ed. dj. VG. P1. $12.50

BEAGLE, P.S. *Folk of the Air.* 1986. Del Rey. dj. EX. P1. $16.95

BEAGLE, P.S. *Lila the Werewolf.* 1974. Capra. 1/75. sgn. no dj issued. EX. K2. $85.00

BEAGLE, Peter. *Last Unicorn.* 1968. Viking. 1st ed. dj. EX. R3. $75.00

BEAHM, George. *Stephen King Companion.* 1989. Andrews McMeel. P1. $10.95

BEALE, Marie. *Flight Into Am's Past.* 1932. Putnam. 1st ed. 296 p. F2. $20.00

BEALS, Carleton. *Banana Gold.* 1932. Lippincott. Ils Merida. 1st ed. 367 P. F2. $20.00

BEALS, Carleton. *Dawn Over the Amazon.* 1943. Duell Sloan Pearce. EX. P1. $12.50

BEALS, Carleton. *Lands of the Dawning Morrow.* 1948. Bobbs Merrill. 1st ed. 336 p. F2. $10.00

BEALS, Carleton. *Nomads & Empire Builders.* 1960. Chilton. 1st ed. 322 p. F2. $15.00

BEALS, Carleton. *Passaconway in the Wht Mts.* 1916. Boston. 1st ed. photos. VG. C2. $27.00

BEAN, W.G. *Stonewall's Man Sandie Pendleton.* 1987. Broadfoot Pub. 252 p. dj. M. S1. $25.00

BEAR, Greg. *Blood Music.* nd. Book Club. dj. VG. P1. $5.00

BEAR, Greg. *Blood Music.* 1985. Arbor House. 1st ed. M. R3. $40.00

BEAR, Greg. *Eon.* 1985. Bluejay. 1st ed. dj. EX. F5. $50.00

BEAR, Greg. *Eternity.* 1988. Warner. 1st ed. dj. EX. F5. $20.00

BEAR, Greg. *Forge of God.* 1987. Tor Books. 1st ed. dj. VG. P1. $17.95

BEAR, Greg. *Forge of God.* 1987. Tor Books. 3rd ed. dj. VG. P1. $12.50

BEAR, Greg. *Wind From the Burning Woman.* 1983. Arkham House. 1st ed. 2nd print. M. R3. $13.95

BEARD, C.A. *Am in Midpassage.* 1939. Macmillan. 400 p. G. S1. $7.00

BEARD, Charles. *Whither Mankind: Panorama of Modern Civilization.* 1928. Longman. 1st ed. dj. VG. B10. $6.25

BEARD, Dan. *Hardly a Man Is Now Alive.* 1939. NY. 1st ed. 361 p. dj. VG. B3. $35.00

BEARD & BEARD. *Rise of Am Civilization.* 1930. London. Cape. 1 vol ed. 828 p. AEG. boxed. $85.00

BEARD & GRAHAM. *Eyelids of Morning.* 1973. Greenwich. 1st ed. dj. EX. B3. $125.00

BEARDSLEY, Aubrey. *Morte d'Arthur.* 1909. Dutton. 2nd ed. 1/500 for US. thick 4to. gilt bdg. C2. $350.00

BEARE, George. *Bee Sting Deal.* 1972. Houghton Mifflin. 1st ed. dj. xl. P1. $5.00

BEARLEY, H.C. *Time Telling Through the Ages.* 1919. NY. VG. $15.00

BEATLES. *Beatle Up to Date.* 1964. Lancer. VG. B4. $4.00

BEATLES. *Yel Submarine.* 1968. Signet. 128 p. EX. B4. $5.00

BEATON, Cecil. *Fair Lady.* 1964. NY/Chicago/San Francisco. 1st ed. dj. EX. $35.00

BEATON, W. *City That Made Itself (Seattle).* 1914. Seattle. Ltd 1st ed. 1/300. folio. 275 p. B3. $75.00

BEATTIE, Ann. *Distortions.* 1976. NY. 1st ed. sgn. dj. EX. T9. $85.00

BEATTIE, Ann. *Love Always.* 1985. Random House. UP. inscr. VG. K2. $65.00

BEATTIE, Ann. *Secrets & Surprises.* 1978. Random House. ARC. sgn. dj. EX. K2. $65.00

BEATTIE, Ann. *Spectacles.* 1985. NY. Workman. sgn. dj. EX. K2. $65.00

BEATTIE, Ann. *Where You'll Find Me.* 1986. Simon Schuster. 1st ed. sgn. dj. EX. B13. $50.00

BEATTIE, James. *Essays on Poetry & Music As They Affect the Mind...* 1778. Edinburgh. sm quarto. 555 p. full calf. VG. H3. $350.00

BEATTIE, William. *Scotland Ils.* 1830. London. 2 vols. VG. $200.00

BEATTIE, William. *Scotland Ils.* 1843. London. 2 vols. Menderson/Bisset bdg. EX. $250.00

BEATTY, A. *Essays on Practical Agriculture.* 1844. Maysville, KY. 1st ed. G. $120.00

BEATTY, Mabel. *Resurrection of Merion Lloyd.* 1929. Thornton Butterworth. EX. P1. $10.00

BEAULIEU & GEORGANO. *Early Days on the Road.* 1976. 219 p. dj. EX. S1. $16.50

BEAUMONT, Charles. *Intruder.* 1959. Putnam. 1st ed. dj. EX. R3. $60.00

BEAUMONT, Charles. *Selected Stories.* 1988. Dark Harvest. 1st ed. M. R3. $35.00

BEAUMONT, Charles. *Shadow Play.* 1964. Panther 1767. 1st Eng ed. wrp. VG. T9. $30.00

BEAUMONT & FLETCHER. *Works.* 1904. London. Bell Bullen. Varorium ed. 4 vols. 8vo. VG. A4. $100.00

BEAUMONT & FLETCHER. *Works.* 1912. Edinburgh. Ballantyne. 14 vols. VG. H3. $450.00

BEAZLEY, J.D. *Attic-Blk Figure.* 1928. London. 8vo. 50 p. VG. $100.00

BECHDOLT, Jack. *Torch.* 1948. Prime Pr. 1st ed. sgn. dj. EX. R3. $25.00

BECK, Christopher. *People of the Chasm.* nd. London. 1st ed. dj. VG. R3. $75.00

BECK, H.C. *Jersey Genesis.* 1945. New Brunswick. 1st ed. dj. VG. B3. $22.50

BECK, H.H. *Cuba's Fight for Freedon & the War With Spain.* nd. (1898) Globe Pub. 1st ed. EX. B10. $10.00

BECK, James. *Vanishing Rights of the States.* 1926. Doran. 1st ed. 126 p. VG. B10. $6.50

BECK, L.A. *Dreams & Delights.* 1926. Dodd Mead. 1st ed. VG. P1. $30.00

BECK, L.A. *Garden of Vision.* 1929. Copp Clark. 1st ed. dj. VG. P1. $40.00

BECK, L.A. *Perfume of the Rainbow.* 1937. Benn. 2nd ed. VG. P1. $25.00

BECK, L.A. *Splendor of Asia: Story & Teachings of the Buddha.* 1926. Dodd Mead. 1st ed. 269 p. VG. B10. $4.75

BECK, L.A. *Treasure of Ho.* 1926. Collins. 2nd ed. VG. P1. $20.00

BECK, L.A. *9th Vibration.* 1922. Dodd Mead. 1st ed. VG. R3. $15.00

BECK, M.E. *Daniel Wheeler.* 1895. London. Hicks. 12mo. 120 p. V1. $12.50

BECK, Robert. *Mama Blk Widow.* 1969. Holloway House 176. PB Orig. VG. T9. $15.00

BECKER, Bob. *Devil Bird.* 1933. Reilly Lee. 1st ed. VG. R3. $35.00

BECKER, Larry. *Mentalism for Magicians.* 1981. Busby Corin Inc. 1st ed. 66 p. NM. J3. $7.00

BECKER G.F. *Atlas to Accompany a Monograph on Geology...Pacific Slope.* 1887. US Geol Survey. folio. wrp. A5. $150.00

BECKETT, Samuel. *All Strange Away.* c1976. NY. Gotham Book Mart. 1/200. sgns. slipcase. EX. H3. $500.00

BECKETT, Samuel. *Imagination Dead Imagine.* 1965. London. 1st ed. 1/100. sgn. as issued. M. K2. $350.00

BECKETT, Samuel. *Imagination Dead Imagine.* 1965. London. Calder Boyars. Ltd ed. 1/100. sgn. slipcase. H3. $225.00

BECKETT, Samuel. *Lessness.* 1970. Calder Boyars. 1st Eng ed. inscr. stiff wrp. H3. $150.00

BECKETT, Samuel. *Lost Ones.* 1972. Calder Boyers. Ltd ed. 1/100. sgn. AEG. H3. $200.00

BECKETT, Samuel. *Malone Dies.* 1956. Grove Pr. 1/500. acetate dj. EX. K2. $125.00

BECKETT, Samuel. *Not I.* 1973. Faber. 1st UK ed. sgn. stiff wrp. H3. $150.00

BECKETT, Samuel. *Play.* 1964. London. Faber. 1st ed. dj. EX. H3. $75.00

BECKETT, Samuel. *Zone.* 1972. Dolmen/Calder Boyars. Ltd ed. 1/250. sgn. slipcase. H3. $250.00

BECKMAN, Eveyln. *She Asked for It.* 1970. Hamish Hamilton. dj. xl. P1. $5.00

BECKWITH, Henry. *Lovecraft's Providence.* 1986. Grant. Enlarged 2nd ed. M. R3. $15.00

BEDDALL, Barbara. *Wallace & Bates in the Tropics.* 1969. Macmillan. 1st ed. 241 p. dj. F2. $15.00

BEDEL, Frederick. *Airplane: Practical Discussion of Principles...Flight.* 1924. Van Nostrand. Revised 4th ed. VG. $50.00

BEDEN, Wilanne. *Mind Call.* 1981. Atheneum. 1st ed. dj. RS. EX. R3. $12.50

BEDFORD-JONES, H. *Breeze in the Moonlight.* 1926. Putnam. 1st ed. P1. $35.00

BEDFORD-JONES, H. *D'Artagnan's Letter.* 1931. Covici Friede. 1st ed. dj. EX. R3. $40.00

BEDFORD-JONES, H. *King's Passport.* 1928. Putnam. 1st ed. VG. R3. $15.00

BEDFORD-JONES, H. *Salute to Cyrano.* 1931. Longman. 1st ed. dj. EX. R3. $40.00

BEDFORD-JONES, H. *Shadow.* 1930. Fiction League. 1st ed. dj. VG. R3. $25.00

BEDFORD-JONES, H. *When D'Artagnan Was Young.* 1932. Doubleday. 1st ed. EX. R3. $45.00

BEDFORD-JONES, H. *2nd Mate.* nd. Garden City. wrp. VG. R3. $25.00

BEDIER, Joseph. *Roman de Tristan et Iseut.* 1926. Paris. reprint of 1902 ed. TEG. C1. $49.50

BEDIER & BELLOC. *Tristan & Iseult.* 1960. Ltd Ed Club. Ils/sgn Ivanoff. 1/1500. slipcase. C1. $59.00

BEEBE, Lucius. *Legends of the Comstock Lode.* 1950. Oakland, CA. 1st ed. sgn. 79 p. dj. VG. T5. $22.50

BEEBE, William. *Arcturus Adventure.* nd. Putnam. Author ed. 1/50. EX. $400.00

BEEBE, William. *Arcturus Adventure.* 1926. NY. 1st ed. lg 8vo. TEG. EX. $65.00

BEEBE, William. *High Jungle.* 1949. Duell Sloan Pearce. 1st/I ed. 380 p. dj. F2. $25.00

BEEBE, William. *High Jungle.* 1949. Duell Sloan Pearce. 2nd print. dj. F2. $20.00

BEEBE, William. *Pheasants: Their Lives & Homes.* 1936. Doubleday. 2 vols in 1. dj. VG. B10. $21.00

BEEBE & GLEGG. *When Beauty Rode the Rails.* 1962. NY. 1st ed. 223 p. dj. VG. B3. $37.50

BEECHER, G.A. *Bishop of the Great Plains.* 1950. Phil. 1st ed. dj. VG. B3. $12.50

BEECHER, H.W. *Star Papers.* 1855. NY. 12mo. 359 p. G. G4. $15.00

BEECHER & STOWE. *Am Woman's Home.* 1869. NY. JB Ford. 1st ed. rebound. VG. R5. $120.00

BEECHER & STOWE. *Am Woman's Home.* 1869. NY. 1st ed. AEG. VG. C2. $115.00

BEECROFT, John. *Plain & Fancy Cats: A Collection.* 1958. Rinehart. Book Club ed. 426 p. dj. VG. B10. $4.00

BEEDING, Francis. *Secret Weapon.* 1944. Books Inc. 2nd ed. VG. P1. $7.50

BEEDING, Francis. *Spellbound.* 1945. Tower. Photoplay ed. dj. VG. P1. $20.00

BEEDING, Francis. *12 Disguises.* 1946. Books Inc. dj. VG. P1. $15.00

BEEDING, Francis. *5 Flamboys.* 1929. Little Brn. 1st ed. VG. P1. $20.00

BEELER, Joe. *Cowboys & Indians.* 1967. Norman. 1st ed. dj. EX. G1. $40.00

BEERBOHM, Max. *Around Theatres.* 1930. Knopf. 1st Am ed. 2 vols. VG. H3. $65.00

BEERBOHM, Max. *Christmas Garland.* 1912. London. 1st ed. VG. C1. $79.00

BEERBOHM, Max. *Observations.* 1925. London. 1st ed. 4to. VG. $40.00

BEERBOHM, Max. *Survey.* 1921. London. Heinemann. 1st Trade ed. 4to. VG. $90.00

BEERBOHM, Max. *Things New & Old.* 1923. Heinemann. Deluxe 1st ed. 1/380. sgn. AEG. H3. $225.00

BEERS, Andrew. *Webster's Albany Almanack.* 1815. Webster. sm pamphlet. G. R5. $15.00

BEERS, H.P. *Guide to Archives of Government of CSA.* 1968. WA. EX. $30.00

BEESON, Lewis. *Congregationalism, Slavery, & the Civil War.* 1966. Lansing, MI. pamphlet. VG. S1. $5.00

BEESON, Lewis. *Impact of the Civil War on Presbyterian Church in MI.* 1965. Lansing, MI. pamphlet. S1. $5.00

BEESON, Lewis. *Methodist Episcopal Church in MI During the Civil War.* 1965. Lansing, MI. pamphlet. VG. S1. $5.00

BEESON, Lewis. *MI Catholicism in the Era of the Civil War.* 1965. Lansing, MI. pamphlet. VG. S1. $5.00

BEEZLEY, William. *Judas at Jockey Club & Other Episodes of Porfirian, Mexico.* 1987. NE U. 1st ed. 181 p. dj. F2. $15.00

BEGBIE, Harold. *Cage.* nd. Hodder Stoughton. VG. P1. $7.50

BEGBIE, Harold. *Day That Changed the World.* nd. Hodder Stoughton. VG. P1. $7.50

BEHAN, Brendan. *Borstal Boy.* 1958. London. 1st ed. dj. EX. $40.00

BEHAN, Brendan. *Confessions of an Irish Rebel.* 1965. Lancer. 1st PB ed. EX. B4. $6.00

BEHM, Marc. *Eye of the Beholder.* 1980. Dial. 1st ed. dj. EX. C4. $50.00

BEHN, Noel. *Kremlin Letter.* nd. Book Club. dj. VG. P1. $2.75

BEHNKE, Leo. *Impromptu Magic From the Magic Castle.* 1980. Tarcher. 1st ed. 235 p. dj. NM. J3. $12.00

BEHNKE, Leo. *Party Magic From the Magic Castle.* 1980. Tarcher. 1st ed. 239 p. dj. NM. J3. $12.00

BEHRMAN, S.N. *Amphitryon 38.* 1939. Random House. 1st ed. dj. H3. $60.00

BEHRMAN, S.N. *Dunnigan's Daughter.* 1946. Random House. 1st ed. dj. EX. B13. $65.00

BEHRMAN, S.N. *End of Summer.* 1936. Random House. 1st ed. dj. VG. H3. $100.00

BEHRMAN, S.N. *No Time for Comedy.* 1939. Random House. 1st ed. dj. VG. H3. $100.00

BEHRMAN, S.N. *Rain From Heaven.* nd. (1935) Random House. not 1st ed. 250 p. G. B10. $3.25

BEHRMAN, S.N. *Rain From Heaven.* 1935. Random House. 1st ed. dj. VG. H3. $75.00

BEHRMAN, S.N. *Talley Method.* 1941. Random House. 1st ed. dj. EX. H3. $65.00

BEINHART, Larry. *You Get What You Pay For.* 1988. Morrow. 1st ed. dj. EX. F5. $15.00

BEIRNE, F.F. *Amiable Baltimoreans.* 1951. NY. 1st ed. dj. VG. B3. $15.00

BEIRNE, F.F. *War of 1812.* 1949. NY. 1st ed. dj. VG. $10.00

BELANEY, Robert. *Massacre at the Carmes in 1792.* 1855. London. 8vo. VG. $80.00

BELASCO, David. *Plays Produced Under the Stage Direction of David Belasco.* 1925. NY. 1st ed. presentation. VG. H3. $85.00

BELASCO, David. *Return of Peter Grimm.* 1912. Dodd Mead. 1st ed. VG. R3. $22.50

BELASCO & BYRNE. *Fairy Tales Told by 7 Travelers at Red Lion Inn.* 1906. NY. Ils Bleekman. VG. A4. $25.00

BELDEN, G.P. *Belden, the Wht Chief.* 1872. Cincinnati/NY. early issue. EX. $75.00

BELDEN & BELDEN. *So Fell the Angels.* 1956. Boston. 1st ed. dj. VG. $10.00

BELFRAGE, Cedric. *Away From It All.* nd. Literary Guild. 411 p. dj. EX. B10. $3.50

BELGION, Montgomery. *Reading for Profit.* 1945. Pelican. VG. P1. $10.00

BELKNAP & BELKNAP. *Gunnar Widforss, Painter of the Grand Canyon.* 1969. Flagstaff. Ils 1st ed. sgn. T5. $32.50

BELL, A.G. *Mechanism of Speech.* 1908. NY. 3rd ed. gilt bdg. EX. $65.00

BELL, Clare. *Ratha's Creature.* 1983. Atheneum. 1st ed. dj. EX. P1. $10.95

BELL, D.W. *Ravenswood & Other Poems.* 1963. Hanover. Stygian Pub. Ltd ed. 1/250. sgn. H3. $45.00

BELL, Edward. *Pre-Hellenic Architecture in the Aegean.* 1926. London. sm 8vo. 213 p. dj. EX. $15.00

BELL, G.B. *Golden Troubadour.* 1980. McGraw Hill. 1st ed. dj. EX. P1. $12.50

BELL, Gertrude. *Persian Pictures.* c 1923. Boni Liveright. lg 8vo. VG. $20.00

BELL, Josephine. *Fall Over Cliff.* 1956. Macmillan. 1st ed. dj. VG. P1. $25.00

BELL, Josephine. *Fennister Affair.* 1970. Hodder Stoughton. 2nd ed. dj. VG. P1. $10.00

BELL, Josephine. *No Escape.* 1966. Macmillan. 1st ed. dj. VG. P1. $12.50

BELL, Josephine. *Question of Inheritance.* 1980. Hodder Stoughton. dj. VG. P1. $8.50

BELL, Josephine. *Wolf! Wolf!* 1980. Walker. 1st ed. dj. VG. P1. $15.00

BELL, M.S. *WA Square Ensemble.* 1983. NY. 1st ed. sgn. dj. EX. T9. $60.00

BELL, Neil. *So Perish the Roses.* 1940. Macmillan. 1st ed. 512 p. dj. EX. B10. $3.50

BELL, W.D. *Karamojo Safari.* 1949. NY. 1st ed. VG. B3. $50.00

BELL, W.D. *Moon Colony.* nd. Goldsmith. P1. $7.00

BELL, W.D. *Moon Colony.* 1937. Goldsmith. 1st ed. dj. EX. R3. $50.00

BELLAH, J.W. *Bones of Napoleon.* 1940. Appleton. 1st ed. 266 p. VG. B10. $5.50

BELLAIRS, George. *Surfeit of Suspects.* 1964. Thriller Book Club. dj. xl. P1. $5.00

BELLAIRS, John. *Dark Secret of Weatherend.* 1984. Dial. 1st ed. dj. VG. P1. $15.00

BELLAIRS, John. *Spell of the Sorcerer's Skull.* nd. Dial. 2nd ed. dj. VG. P1. $12.50

BELLAIRS, John. *Spell of the Sorcerer's Skull.* 1984. Dial. 1st ed. dj. xl. P1. $6.00

BELLAMANN, Henry. *Victoria Grandolet.* 1943. Simon Schuster. 281 p. dj. VG. B10. $3.25

BELLAMY, Edward. *Equality.* 1899. Appleton. wrp. VG. R3. $20.00

BELLAMY, Edward. *Looking Backward 2000-1887.* nd. Routledge. VG. P1. $20.00

BELLAMY, Edward. *Looking Backward 2000-1887.* 1890. Boston/NY. VG. C1. $12.50

BELLAMY, Edward. *Looking Backward 2000-1887.* 1942. Modern Lib. dj. VG. P1. $10.00

BELLAMY, Edward. *Looking Backward 2000-1887.* 1945. World. VG. P1. $15.00

BELLAMY, Edward. *Looking Backward 2000-1887.* 1946. Tower. 2nd ed. dj. VG. P1. $12.50

BELLAMY, Frank. *Time View.* 1985. Who Dares. 1st UK ed. wrp. EX. F5. $10.00

BELLEM, R.L. *Bl Murder.* 1987. Dennis McMillan. 1st ed. wrp. M. R3. $10.00

BELLOC, Hilaire. *Gr Overcoat.* 1912. NY. Ils Chesterton. 1st ed. VG. $50.00

BELLOC, Hilaire. *Heroic Poem in Praise of Wine.* 1932. London. Peter Davies. Ltd ed. 1/100. sgn. H3. $150.00

BELLOW, Saul. *Dangling Man.* 1946. London. Lehmann. 1st Eng ed. dj. EX. K2. $250.00

BELLOW, Saul. *Dangling Man.* 1946. London. Lehmann. 1st Eng ed. dj. VG. H3. $150.00

BELLOW, Saul. *Dean's December.* 1982. Harper Row. ARC. dj. RS. EX. H3. $40.00

BELLOW, Saul. *Dean's December.* 1982. Harper Row. sgn. gilt red bdg. slipcase. H3. $125.00

BELLOW, Saul. *Dean's December.* 1982. Harper Row. UP. wrp. EX. K2. $200.00

BELLOW, Saul. *Dean's December.* 1982. NY. 1st ed. dj. EX. $25.00

BELLOW, Saul. *Henderson the Rain King.* 1959. Viking. 1st ed. presentation. dj. EX. H3. $300.00

BELLOW, Saul. *Herzog.* 1964. Viking. 1st ed. sgn. dj. EX. B13. $100.00

BELLOW, Saul. *Him With His Foot in His Mouth & Other Stories.* 1984. Harper. UP. wrp. EX. B13. $85.00

BELLOW, Saul. *Last Analysis.* 1965. Viking. 1st Pub ed. presentation. dj. H3. $150.00

BELLOW, Saul. *Last Analysis.* 1966. Weidenfeld Nicholson. 1st British ed. dj. VG. H3. $30.00

BELLOW, Saul. *Mr Sammler's Planet.* 1970. NY. 1st ed. sgn. dj. EX. $65.00

BELLOW, Saul. *Mr Sammler's Planet.* 1970. Viking. 1st ed. dj. VG. P1. $15.00

BELLOW, Saul. *Mr Sammler's Planet.* 1970. Viking. dj. w/sgn on mounted card. H3. $60.00

BELLOW, Saul. *Nobel Lecture.* 1979. Targ Ed. Ltd ed. 1/350. sgn. H3. $100.00

BELLOW, Saul. *Seize the Day.* 1956. NY. 1st ed. dj. VG. B3. $65.00

BELLOW, Saul. *Seize the Day.* 1956. Viking. 1st ed. dj. EX. H3. $85.00

BELLOW, Saul. *To Jerusalem & Back.* 1976. Viking. 1st ed. presentation. dj. EX. H3. $125.00

BELLOW, Saul. *Victim.* 1947. NY. 1st ed. sgn. 249 p. VG. T5. $75.00

BELLOWS, A.J. *Philosophy of Eating.* 1922. St Louis. 1st ed. G. C2. $40.00

BELLOWS, John. *Letters & Memoir, Edited by His Wife.* 1904. Holt. 8vo. 392 p. xl. G. V1. $20.00

BELT, Thomas. *Naturalist in Nicaragua.* 1874. London. Murray. 1st ed. EX. $195.00

BELTRAN, Miriam. *Cuzco: Window on Peru.* 1970. Knopf. Ils. 226 p. F2. $15.00

BEMA, J. *Tommy Wonder Entertains.* 1983. Busby Magic. 1st ed. 41 p. EX. J3. $9.00

BEME, S. *Complete Card Linking.* 1979. Sweden. El Duco. SftCvr. EX. J3. $6.00

BEMELMANS, Ludwig. *Donkey Inside.* 1941. NY. Ltd ed. 1/175. boxed. VG. B3. $75.00

BEMELMANS, Ludwig. *Donkey Inside.* 1941. Viking. Ltd ed. 1/175. sgn. slipcase. H3. $225.00

BEMELMANS, Ludwig. *Donkey Inside.* 1941. Viking. 1st ed. 8vo. 224 p. dj. VG. $20.00

BEMELMANS, Ludwig. *Father, Dear Father.* 1953. Viking. Ltd ed. 1/151. sgn laid in. boxed. H3. $250.00

BEMELMANS, Ludwig. *Father, Dear Father.* 1953. Viking. 1st ed. dj. VG. H3. $30.00

BEMELMANS, Ludwig. *How To Travel Incognito.* 1952. Boston. 1st ed. dj. EX. $20.00

BEMELMANS, Ludwig. *Madeline & the Gypsies.* 1959. Viking. VG. B7. $35.00

BEMELMANS, Ludwig. *Parsley.* 1953. Harper. oblong 4to. VG. $25.00

BEMELMANS, Ludwig. *World of Bemelmans.* 1955. NY. 1st ed. dj. EX. $20.00

BEMMANN, Hans. *Stone & the Flute.* 1986. Viking. 1st ed. dj. VG. P1. $20.00

BEN-ALLAH. *Rudolph Valentino: His Romantic Life & Death.* 1926. Hollywood. Ben-Allah. octavo. 132 p. gr/blk wrp. VG. H3. $75.00

BENCHLEY, Robert. *Chips Off the Old Benchley.* nd. BOMC. P1. $7.50

BENCHLEY, Robert. *Chips Off the Old Benchley.* 1949. Harper Book Club. 360 p. dj. B10. $4.25

BENCHLEY, Robert. *Of All Things.* 1921. Garden City. 1st ed. dj. G. $50.00

BENDIRE, Charles. *Life Hist of N Am Birds.* 1892 & 1985. GPO. 2 vols. VG. T3. $125.00

BENEDICT, H.A. *Fagots.* 1895. Buffalo. Moulton. inscr. 12mo. gilt tan bdg. H3. $50.00

BENET, S.V. *Ballads & Poems 1915-1930.* 1931. Doubleday Doran. Ltd ed. 1/201. slipcase. H3. $250.00

BENET, S.V. *Barefoot Saint.* 1929. Doubleday Doran. Ltd ed. 1/367. sgn. slipcase. H3. $85.00

BENET, S.V. *Beginning of Wisdom.* 1921. Holt. sgn. dj. H3. $150.00

BENET, S.V. *Burning City.* 1936. Farrar Rinehart. ARC. inscr. dj. H3. $250.00

BENET, S.V. *Burning City.* 1936. Farrar Rinehart. Ltd ed. 1/275. sgn. slipcase. H3. $125.00

BENET, S.V. *Devil & Daniel Webster.* 1939. Farrar Rinehart. 1st ed. dj. H3. $125.00

BENET, S.V. *James Shore's Daughter.* 1934. Doubleday Doran. Ltd ed. 1/307. sgn. slipcase. H3. $125.00

BENET, S.V. *John Brn's Body.* 1928. Doubleday Doran. 376 p. VG. S1. $15.00

BENET, S.V. *John Brn's Body.* 1954. Rinehart. Ils Kredel. 368 p. G. S1. $4.00

BENET, S.V. *Johnny Pye & the Fool Killer.* 1938. Weston, VT. Countryman Pr. Ltd ed. sgn. slipcase. H3. $100.00

BENET, W.R. *Dust Which Is God.* 1941. Dodd Mead. Ltd ed. 1/246. sgn. H3. $85.00

BENET, W.R. *Rip Tide.* 1932. Duffield Gr. 1st ed. 1/1200. presentation. dj. H3. $75.00

BENET & BENET. *Book of Am.* 1933. Farrar Rinehart. Ltd ed. 1/125. sgns. slipcase. H3. $150.00

BENEZIT, E. *Dictionnaire Critique et Documentaire des Pientres.* 1960. Paris. Librairie Grund. 8 vols. gr bdg. EX. H3. $350.00

BENFORD, Gregory. *Across the Sea of Suns.* 1984. Timescape. 1st ed. dj. EX. R3. $20.00

BENFORD, Gregory. *Against Infinity.* 1983. Timescape. 1st ed. dj. EX. R3. $20.00

BENFORD, Gregory. *Great Sky River.* 1987. Bantam. UP. wrp. EX. R3. $40.00

BENFORD, Gregory. *Great Sky River.* 1987. Bantam. 1st ed. dj. EX. P1. $17.95

BENFORD, Gregory. *Heart of the Comet.* 1986. Bantam. 1st ed. dj. VG. P1. $17.95

BENFORD, Gregory. *In Alien Flesh.* 1986. Tor Books. 1st ed. dj. EX. F5. $20.00

BENFORD, Gregory. *In the Ocean of the Night.* nd. Book Club. dj. EX. P1. $4.50

BENFORD, Gregory. *Stars in Shroud.* 1978. Berkley. 1st ed. dj. EX. R3. $17.50

BENFORD, Gregory. *Timescape.* nd. Simon Schuster. 2nd ed. dj. VG. P1. $12.50

BENFORD, Gregory. *Timescape.* 1980. Simon Schuster. AP. wrp. EX. F5. $90.00

BENFORD, Gregory. *Timescape.* 1980. Simon Schuster. 1st ed. dj. EX. R3. $60.00

BENFORD & BRIN. *Heart of the Comet.* nd. Book Club. dj. EX. P1. $5.00

BENGTSSON, F.G. *Long Ships.* 1954. Knopf. 1st Am ed. dj. EX. R3. $25.00

BENGTSSON, F.G. *Red Orm.* 1943. Scribner. 1st ed. dj. VG. F5. $17.50

BENNENT, J.A.W. *Essays on Malory.* 1963. Oxford. 1st ed. dj. VG. C1. $85.00

BENNETT, Arnold. *Ghost.* nd. Jarrolds. VG. P1. $20.00

BENNETT, Arnold. *Loot of Cities.* 1972. Oswald Train. 1st ed. dj. EX. P1. $20.00

BENNETT, Arnold. *Matador of the 5 Towns.* 1912. London. Methuen. 1st ed. VG. C1. $14.00

BENNETT, Arnold. *Riceyman Steps.* 1923. G. K3. $20.00

BENNETT, Doug. *New Stars of Magic Vol 2.* 1984. Tannen Magic. J3. $10.00

BENNETT, E.A. *Dream of Destiny.* 1932. London. 1st ed. dj. EX. $45.00

BENNETT, E.A. *Man From the N.* 1898. London. 1st ed. 1st issue. VG. $200.00

BENNETT, F.M. *Steam Navy of the US.* 1896. Pittsburgh. 8vo. 953 p. VG. $175.00

BENNETT, Horace. *Bennett's Best.* 1975. Jerry Mentzer. 1st ed. 113 p. EX. J3. $12.00

BENNETT, James. *Much-Loved Books.* 1927. NY. 1st ed. VG. G1. $15.00

BENNETT, John. *Doctor to the Dead.* 1946. Rinehart. 1st ed. dj. VG. R3. $20.00

BENNETT, K. *Passport for a Renegade.* 1955. Doubleday Book Club. VG. P1. $7.50

BENNETT, R.A. *Bowl of Baal.* 1975. Donald Grant. dj. VG. P1. $15.00

BENNETT, R.A. *Branded.* nd. AL Burt. VG. P1. $10.00

BENNETT, R.A. *Into the Primitive.* 1980. McClurg. 1st ed. VG. R3. $45.00

BENNETT, R.A. *Thyra: Romance of the Polar Pit.* 1901. Holt. 1st ed. VG. R3. $37.50

BENNETT, Sanford. *Old Age: Cause & Prevention.* nd. (1912) NY. probably 1st ed. 394 p. G. B10. $4.00

BENNETT, Wendall. *Ancient Arts of the Andes.* 1954. MOMA. 1st ed. 187 p. dj. F2. $25.00

BENNETT, Wendell. *Excavations at La Mata, Maracay, Venezuela.* 1937. Am Mus Nat Hist. 1st ed. wrp. F2. $25.00

BENNETT & KIBBEE. *Bennett Playbill.* 1970. Holt. 1st ed. 332 p. dj. VG. B10. $4.25

BENOIT, Pierre. *Atlantida.* 1920. Duffield. 1st ed. VG. R3. $25.00

BENSON, A.C. *Thread of Gold.* 1907. Dutton. 1st ed. VG. P1. $20.00

BENSON, Adolph. *Sweden & the Am Revolution.* 1926. New Haven. 1st ed. VG. G1. $30.00

BENSON, Ben. *Broken Shield.* nd. Book Club. dj. VG. P1. $4.50

BENSON, Ben. *Silver Cobweb.* nd. Book Club. dj. VG. P1. $4.50

BENSON, E.F. *Alan.* 1925. Doran. 1st ed. VG. P1. $15.00

BENSON, E.F. *House of Defense.* 1906. NY. VG. R3. $15.00

BENSON, E.F. *Image in the Sand.* 1905. Lippincott. 1st ed. VG. R3. $27.50

BENSON, E.F. *Visible & Invisible.* 1924. Doubleday. 1st ed. VG. R3. $35.00

BENSON, Elizabeth. *City-States of the Maya: Art & Architecture.* 1986. Denver. 1st ed. 171 p. wrp. F2. $20.00

BENSON, Elizabeth. *Maya World.* 1967. Crowell. 1st ed. sm 4to. 172 p. dj. F2. $30.00

BENSON, Elizabeth. *Maya World.* 1977. Crowell. Revised ed. dj. F2. $20.00

BENSON, Elizabeth. *Mochica: Culture of Peru.* 1972. Praeger. 1st ed. 4to. dj. F2. $35.00

BENSON, Elizabeth. *Olmec & Their Neighbors.* 1981. Dumbarton Oaks. Ils. 346 p. F2. $30.00

BENSON, Elizabeth. *Pre-Columbian Metallurgy of S Am.* 1979. Dumbarton Oaks. 1st ed. 207 p. F2. $20.00

BENSON, Jane. *Quaker Pioneers in Russia.* 1902. London. Headley. 12mo. 120 p. V1. $12.00

BENSON, Nettie. *Mexico & Spanish Cortes.* 1976. TX U. 4th print. dj. F2. $15.00

BENSON, R.H. *Dawn of All.* 1945. Burns Oates Washburne. VG. P1. $12.50

BENSON, R.H. *King's Achievement.* nd. Hutchinson. VG. P1. $5.00

BENSON, Stella. *Man Who Missed the Bus.* 1928. London. Mathews Marrot. Ltd ed. 1/530. dj. H3. $40.00

BENSON, Theodora. *Man From the Tunnel.* 1950. Appleton. 1st Am ed. dj. VG. R3. $17.50

BENSON. *Life Among the Choctaw Indians.* 1860. Cincinnati. 1st ed. gilt blk bdg. VG. C1. $225.00

BENT, Newell. *Am Polo.* 1929. NY. 1st ed. 8vo. 407 p. dj. VG. $50.00

BENTLEY, E.C. *Elephant's Work.* 1950. Knopf. 1st ed. dj. VG. P1. $25.00

BENTLEY, E.C. *Trent's Last Case.* nd. Thomas Nelson. dj. VG. P1. $25.00

BENTLEY, E.C. *Trent's Last Case.* 1946. Tower. dj. VG. P1. $12.50

BENTLEY, Eric. *Playwright As Thinker.* 1946. Reynal Hitchcock. 1st ed. octavo. 382 p. VG. H3. $25.00

BENTLEY, James. *Secrets of Mt Sinai.* 1986. 1st Am ed. dj. VG. K3. $15.00

BENTLEY, Nicolas. *Events of That Week.* 1972. St Martin. 1st ed. dj. xl. P1. $5.00

BENTLEY, Nicolas. *Tongue-Tied Canary.* nd. Thriller Book Club. dj. VG. P1. $6.00

BENTLEY & HUMPHREYS. *Snow Crystals.* 1931. NY. 1st ed. EX. $225.00

BENTLEY & HUMPHREYS. *Snow Crystals.* 1931. NY. 1st ed. folio. VG. $195.00

BENTON, J.A. *CA Pilgrim: A Series of Lectures.* 1853. Sacramento. Ils Charles Nahl. rebound. VG. $120.00

BENTON, J.L. *Talent for Murder.* 1942. Gateway. VG. P1. $12.50

BENTON, Kenneth. *Craig & the Midas Touch.* 1975. Walker. 1st ed. dj. EX. F5. $12.00

BENTON, Kenneth. *24th Level.* 1970. Dodd Mead. dj. EX. P1. $7.00

BENTON, T.H. *Artist in Am.* 1937. McBride. 3rd print. sgn. VG. $50.00

BENTON, William. *Eye la View.* 1975. Capra. Chapbook Series. 1/50. sgn. EX. K2. $20.00

BENY, Roloff. *In Italy.* 1974. NY. 1st ed. dj. VG. B3. $45.00

BENY, Roloff. *Persia Bridge of Turquoise.* 1975. Toronto. 1st ed. dj. VG. B3. $80.00

BENY, Roloff. *To Everything There Is a Season.* 1969. London. Ils. dj. A4. $50.00

BERCKMAN, Evelyn. *Heir of Starvelings.* 1967. Doubleday. 1st ed. P1. $5.00

BERCKMAN, Evelyn. *She Asked for It.* 1970. Hamish Hamilton. dj. xl. P1. $5.00

BERESFORD, J.D. *Hampdenshire Wonder.* 1975. Garland. M. R3. $30.00

BERG, AVADON, & LEWIS. *Berg Book.* 1983. Wichita. 1st ed. 315 p. dj. NM. J3. $29.00

BERGE, Victor. *Pearl Diver: Adventuring Over & Under S Seas.* nd. (1930) Garden City. 368 p. VG. B10. $4.75

BERGER, Josef. *Swordfisherman Jim.* 1939. Little Brn. Ils Ashley. 1st ed. 296 p. dj. VG. B10. $4.00

BERGER, Klaus. *Odilon Redon: Fantasy & Clr.* 1965. NY. probably 1st Am ed. VG. G1. $60.00

BERGER, Meyer. *8 Million.* 1942. Book Club. 334 p. dj. G. B10. $3.25

BERGER, Thomas. *Arthur Rex.* 1978. Delacorte. 1st ed. dj. EX. scarce. C1. $15.00

BERGER, Thomas. *Crazy in Berlin.* 1958. Scribner. inscr. dj. H3. $125.00

BERGER, Thomas. *Granted Wishes: 3 Stories.* 1984. Northridge, CA. Lord John. 1/250. sgn. H3. $85.00

BERGER, Thomas. *Little Big Man.* 1964. Dial. sgn label on title pg. H3. $100.00

BERGER, Thomas. *Little Big Man.* 1964. Dial. 1st ed. sgn. dj. EX. K2. $250.00

BERGER, Thomas. *Neighbors.* 1980. Delacorte. 3rd ed. dj. EX. P1. $12.50

BERGQUIST, Lillian. *Your Shot, Darling!* 1948. Morrow. 2nd ed. P1. $7.00

BERGSTROM, E. *Old Glass Paperweights.* 1963. NY. 4th print. dj. EX. $20.00

BERKELEY, Anthony. *Roger Sheringham & the Vane Mystery.* 1927. Collins. 1st ed. VG. P1. $35.00

BERKELEY, Anthony. *Silk Stocking Murders.* 1928. Doubleday Doran. xl. G. P1. $10.00

BERKELEY, Anthony. *Trail & Error.* 1965. Hodder Stoughton. dj. VG. P1. $20.00

BERLAND, Samuel. *Amazing Tricks With Paper Cups.* 1968. Caddy. SftCvr. EX. J3. $3.00

BERLAND, Samuel. *Book of Routines Vol 1.* 1950. Chicago. 1st ed. SftCvr. VG. J3. $3.00

BERLAND, Samuel. *Close-Up Magic of Sam Berland.* 1986. Chicago. 1st ed. sgn. M. J3. $20.00

BERLAND, Samuel. *Match-Effex*. nd. Chicago. 1st ed. SftCvr. EX. J3. $3.00

BERLAND, Samuel. *New & Orig Tricks With Watches*. 1942. Chicago. 1st ed. 64 p. EX. J3. $4.00

BERLAND, Samuel. *20 Tricks With Wiztax*. nd. Chicago. 3rd ed. SftCvr. EX. J3. $2.00

BERLIN, W.M. *How To Be a Better Ventriloquist*. 1975. Seattle. stapled manuscript. NM. J3. $3.00

BERLO, Janet. *Art of Pre-Hispanic Mesoamerica: Annotated Bibliography*. 1985. Boston. Hall. 1st ed. 272 p. F2. $40.00

BERLYN, Michael. *Eternal Enemy*. 1990. Morrow. bound galley proof of 1st ed. wrp. EX. F5. $20.00

BERMAN, Mitch. *Time Capsule*. 1987. Putnam. 1st ed. dj. EX. F5. $15.00

BERMAN, Wallace. *Wallace Berman Retrospective*. 1978. Los Angeles. Ils. M. B4. $15.00

BERNAL, Ignacio. *Hist of Mexican Archaeology*. 1980. Thames. 1st ed. 208 p. F2. $15.00

BERNAL, Ignacio. *Olmec World*. 1969. CA U. 1st ed. 4to. 273 p. F2. $40.00

BERNAL, Ignacio. *Olmec World*. 1973. CA U. 2nd print. 4to. dj. F2. $25.00

BERNAL, Ignacio. *100 Great Masterpieces of Mexican Mus of Anthropology*. 1969. Abrams. 1st ed. 162 p. dj. F2. $50.00

BERNANOS, G. *Diary of a Country Priest*. 1986. Ltd Ed Club. Ils/sgn Fritz Eichenberg. slipcase. VG. $85.00

BERNARD, Seymour. *Child's Garden of Relatives*. 1950. Doubleday. Ils Edna Eicke. 1st ed. VG. B7. $25.00

BERNDT, R.C. *World of the 1st Australians*. 1964. Angus Robertson. 1st ed. 8vo. VG. $65.00

BERNHARDT, Sarah. *Dans les Nuages*. 1878. Paris. Charpentier. 1st ed. quarto. 94 p. gray wrp. portfolio. H3. $300.00

BERNSTEIN & WOODWARD. *All the President's Men*. 1974. Simon Schuster. Book Club ed. 349 p. dj. B10. $4.25

BERRA, Tim. *William Beebe: An Annotated Bibliography*. 1977. Archon Books. 1st ed. 157 p. dj. F2. $25.00

BERRALL, Julia. *Flowers & Table Settings*. 1951. Crowell. Ils. folio. dj. EX. $25.00

BERRIN, Kathleen. *Feathered Serpents & Flowering Trees*. 1988. Fine Arts Mus. 1st ed. sq 4to. dj. F2. $45.00

BERRY, C.D. *Loss of the Sultana*. 1892. Lansing, MI. Ils 1st ed. 426 p. fair. T5. $150.00

BERRY, Chuck. *Chuck Berry: The Autobiography*. 1987. Harmony Books. 1st ed. octavo. 346 p. dj. EX. H3. $40.00

BERRY, David. *Pocket Pool*. c 1975. Peppermint Pr. Ltd ed. 1/100. slipcase. H3. $45.00

BERRY, J.S. *Magic for the New World*. 1986. Paris. SftCvr. VG. J3. $18.00

BERRY, Jim. *Moon Stallion*. 1982. Evans. 1st ed. dj. VG. P1. $12.50

BERRY, John. *Krishna Fluting*. 1959. Macmillan. VG. P1. $7.50

BERRY, Wendell. *Gift of Good Land*. 1981. N Point Pr. 1st ed. sgn. dj. EX. B13. $50.00

BERRY, Wendell. *November 26, 1963*. 1964. NY. Ils Ben Shahn. slipcase. VG. T5. $25.00

BERRY, Wendell. *Remembering*. 1988. N Point Pr. 1st ed. sgn. dj. EX. B13. $45.00

BERRY, Wendell. *Reverdure*. nd. np. CO College Pr. 1st ed. 1/100. sgn. wrp. EX. K2. $175.00

BERRY, Wendell. *Salad*. 1980. N Point Pr. 1st ed. dj. gr wrp. EX. scarce. B13. $45.00

BERRY, Wendell. *Sayings & Doings*. 1975. Lexington. Gnomon. 1st ed. sgn. EX. B13. $65.00

BERRY, Wendell. *Wheel*. 1982. N Point Pr. 1st ed. sgn. dj. EX. B13. $50.00

BERRY, Wendell. *Wild Birds*. 1986. N Point Pr. 1st ed. sgn. dj. EX. B13. $45.00

BERRY, William. *Buffalo Land: Untamed Wilderness*. 1961. Macmillan. 1st ed. VG. B10. $4.50

BERRYMAN, John. *Dream Songs*. 1969. NY. 1st ed. dj. EX. $40.00

BERRYMAN, John. *Homage to Mistress Bradstreet*. 1956. NY. Ils Ben Shahn. 1st ed. dj. VG. T5. $95.00

BERTIN, Jack. *Brood of Helios*. 1966. Arcadia. 1st ed. dj. VG. P1. $12.50

BERTIN, Jack. *Interplanetary Adventures*. 1970. Lenox Hill VG. P1. $9.25

BERTON, Pierre. *Impossible Railway: Building of Canadian Pacific*. 1972. Knopf. 1st ed. 574 p. dj. EX. T4. $15.00

BERTON, Ralph. *Remembering Bix*. 1974. NY. 1st ed. dj. VG. B3. $27.50

BERTRAM, Charles. *Magician in Many Lands*. 1911. London. Routledge. 315 p. EX. J3. $120.00

BERTRAM, Ross. *Bertram on Sleight of Hand*. 1983. Magic Ltd. 1st ed. 255 p. dj. NM. J3. $65.00

BERTRAM, Ross. *Magic & Methods of Ross Bertram*. 1978. Magic Ltd. 1st ed. 163 p. dj. NM. J3. $33.00

BERTRAND, Louis. *Private Life of Louis XVI*. 1929. Carrier. 1st Am ed. 189 p. EX. B10. $5.00

BESHOAR. *Out of the Depths*. 1957. Denver. dj. VG. B3. $20.00

BEST, Herbert. *25th Hour*. 1940. Random House. 1st ed. dj. EX. R3. $60.00

BESTER, Alfred. *Computer Connection*. nd. Book Club. dj. VG. P1. $5.00

BESTER, Alfred. *Computer Connection*. 1975. Berkley Putnam. 1st ed. dj. EX. R3. $20.00

BESTER, Alfred. *Demolished Man*. 1953. Shasta. 2nd print. dj. EX. R3. $65.00

BESTER, Alfred. *Extro*. 1975. Eyre Methuen. dj. EX. P1. $20.00

BESTER, Alfred. *Golem 100*. 1980. Simon Schuster. 1st ed. dj. EX. F5. $16.00

BESTER, Alfred. *Star Light, Star Bright Vol 2*. 1976. Berkley Putnam. 1st ed. dj. VG. P1. $20.00

BESTIC. *Praise the Lord & Pass the Contribution*. 1971. NY. 1st ed. dj. VG. B3. $17.50

BESTON, H. *Outermost House*. 1928. NY. 1st ed. dj. VG. B3. $85.00

BETETA, Ramon. *Jarano*. 1970. TX U. 1st ed. 163 p. dj. F2. $20.00

BETHANCOURT, T.E. *Instruments of Darkness*. 1979. Holiday. 1st ed. dj. EX. F5. $16.50

BETJEMAN, John. *Ghastly Good Taste*. 1970. London. Anthony Blond. Ltd ed. 1/200. sgn. slipcase. H3. $65.00

BETTELHEIM, Bruno. *Uses of Enchantment*. 1977. Knopf. 6th print. EX. P1. $7.50

BETTLE, Jane. *Extracts From Memorandums of Jane Bettle*. 1843. Phil. 1st ed. 12mo. 116 p. VG. V1. $16.00

BETTS, Doris. *Heading W*. 1981. Knopf. 1st ed. dj. EX. $10.00

BEVAN, J.G. *Memoirs of Life of Isaac Penington...* 1831. Thomas Kite. 12mo. V1. $16.00

BEVANS, John. *Brief View of Doctrines of Christian Religion...of Friends*. nd. Phil. Friends Bookstore. 16mo. 124 p. EX. V1. $10.00

BEVANS, Joseph Gurney. *Piety Promoted in Brief Memorials & Dying Expressions...* 1813. NY. Samuel Wood. 16mo. 300 p. V1. $15.00

BEVERIDGE, A.J. *Life of John Marshall.* 1916. Boston. 1st ed. 4 vols. EX. $50.00

BEVIS, H.U. *Alien Abductors.* 1971. Lenox Hill. dj. VG. P1. $10.00

BEVIS, H.U. *To Luna With Love.* 1971. Lenox Hill. dj. xl. P1. $5.00

BEYER, G.E. *LA Herpetology: Checklist of Batrachians & Reptiles.* 1900. New Orleans. 8vo. 22 p. wrp. G. scarce. T1. $50.00

BEYER, Hermann. *Mexican Bone Rattles.* 1934. Tulane U. 1st ed. 4to. wrp. F2. $15.00

BEYER, W.G. *Minions of the Moon.* 1950. Gnome. 1st ed. P1. $15.00

BEYNON, John. *Stowaway to Mars.* 1953. London. 1st ed. VG. R3. $10.00

BIART, Lucien. *Aztecs.* 1900. McClurg. 343 p. VG. F2. $30.00

BIBESCO, Marthe. *Crusade for the Anemone: Letters From the Holy Land.* 1932. NY. 1st ed. 180 p. dj. G. T5. $32.50

BIBESCO, Marthe. *Egyptian Day.* 1930. NY. 1st ed. 184 p. G. T5. $22.50

BIBESCO, Marthe. *Katia.* nd. London. 1st ed. 5 pls. 264 p. G. T5. $35.00

BIBESCO, Marthe. *Worlds Apart.* 1935. NY. 1st ed. 274 p. G. T5. $22.50

BIBESCO, Marthe. *8 Paradises.* 1923. NY. 1st ed. 261 p. G. T5. $22.50

BIBLE. *Biblia. Das 1st: Die Gantze Helige Schrifft.* 1926-1938. Munich. Bremer Pr. 1/365. 5 vols. folio. H3. $1500.00

BIBLE. *Book of Common Prayer & Psalter.* 1844. Phil. George. mini book. VG. $30.00

BIBLE. *Book of Ruth.* 1944. Heritage Pr. Ils Arthur Szyk. slipcase. M. T1. $20.00

BIBLE. *Eng Bible.* 1903-1905. Doves Pr. Ltd ed. 1/500. 5 vols. lg quarto. VG. H3. $5000.00

BIBLE. *New Testament.* 1840. Keene. Polyglott School Series. 422 p. G. B10. $5.00

BICKHAM, Jack. *Day 7.* 1988. Tor Books. 1st ed. RS. M. R3. $17.95

BIDDLE, George. *Yes & No of Contemporary Art.* 1957. Cambridge. Harvard. 1st ed. inscr. dj. EX. B13. $45.00

BIDERMAN, Bob. *Strange Inheritance.* 1985. Pluto Pr. 1st UK ed. dj. EX. F5. $14.00

BIEBER, R.P. *S Trails to CA in 1849.* 1937. Glendale. Clark. Hist Series. 1st ed. dj. VG. $100.00

BIEK, Leo. *Archaeology & the Microscope.* 1965. London. Lutterworth Pr. 2nd print. 287 p. dj. F2. $10.00

BIERCE, Ambrose. *Collected Works.* 1909. NY. Neale. 12 vols. octavo. TEG. EX. H3. $750.00

BIERCE, Ambrose. *Collected Writings.* 1946. Citadel. 1st ed. dj. EX. R3. $15.00

BIERCE, Ambrose. *Fiend's Delight.* 1873. NY. Luyster. 1st Am ed. orig bdg. EX. B10. $750.00

BIERCE, Ambrose. *In the Midst of Life.* 1924. Boni. VG. R3. $12.50

BIERCE, Ambrose. *Tales of Soldiers & Civilians.* 1943. Ltd Ed Club. Ils/sgn Paul Landacre. slipcase. VG. $55.00

BIERCE, Ambrose. *Vision of Doom.* 1980. Donald Grant. 1st ed. dj. EX. P1. $12.00

BIERCE, Ambrose. *Write It Right.* 1909. NY. 1st ed. author's copy w/inscr. H3. $4500.00

BIERCE, Ambrose. *21 Letters of Ambrose Bierce.* 1922. Cleveland. George Kirk. 1/50 on Japan Vellum. sgn. EX. H3. $350.00

BIERCE, L.V. *Hist Reminiscences of Summit Co.* 1961. Akron. reprint of 1854 ed. T5. $65.00

BIERHORST, John. *Monkey's Haircut & Other Stories Told by the Mayas.* 1986. Morrow. Ils Parker. 1st ed. dj. F2. $15.00

BIERHORST, John. *Mythology of Mexico & Central Am.* 1990. Morrow. 1st ed. 239 p. dj. F2. $15.00

BIERHORST, John. *Mythology of S Am.* 1988. Morrow. 1st ed. 4to. dj. F2. $16.00

BIERSTADT, Edward. *Lord Dunsany, the Dramatist.* 1919. Little Brn. Revised 1st ed. VG. R3. $25.00

BIGELOW, Jacob. *Brief Expositions of Rational Medicine.* 1858. Phillips Sampson. VG. $30.00

BIGGERS, E.D. *Behind That Curtain.* nd. Grosset Dunlap. VG. P1. $15.00

BIGGERS, E.D. *House Without a Key.* 1941. Triangle. 4th ed. VG. P1. $9.25

BIGGERS, E.D. *Love Insurance.* 1914. Bobbs Merrill. 1st ed. VG. P1. $35.00

BIGGERS, E.D. *7 Keys to Baldpate.* nd. Collier. xl. VG. P1. $7.50

BIGGERS & RITCHIE. *Inside the Lines.* 1915. Bobbs Merrill. 1st ed. VG. P1. $35.00

BIGGLE, Lloyd. *Light That Never Was.* 1974. Elmfield Pr. dj. P1. $16.50

BIGGLE, Lloyd. *Monument.* nd. Book Club. dj. VG. P1. $4.50

BIGGLE, Lloyd. *Monument.* 1946. Doubleday. 1st ed. dj. EX. R3. $20.00

BIGGLE, Lloyd. *Monument.* 1975. New Eng Lib. dj. EX. P1. $16.50

BIGGLE, Lloyd. *Silence Is Deadly.* nd. Book Club. dj. EX. P1. $4.50

BIGGLE, Lloyd. *Watchers of the Dark.* 1966. Rapp Whiting. 1st ed. dj. VG. P1. $20.00

BIGGLE, Lloyd. *World Menders.* 1973. Elmfield Pr. 1st Eng ed. dj. EX. P1. $16.50

BIGGLESTONE & SCHULTZ. *Elizabethan Costuming for Years 1550-1580.* 1979. 1st ed. stiff wrp. EX. C1. $7.00

BILENKIN, Dmitri. *Uncertainty Principle.* 1978. Macmillan. dj. EX. P1. $12.50

BILENKIN, Dmitri. *Uncertainty Principle.* 1978. Macmillan. 1st ed. M. R3. $15.00

BILL, A.H. *Beleaguered City: Richmond 1861-1865.* 1946. Knopf. 1st ed. G. S1. $20.00

BILL, A.H. *Highroads of Peril.* 1926. Little Brn. 1st ed. EX. R3. $15.00

BILLIAN, Otto. *Brazil.* 1982. Brazil. 1st ed. sm 4to. 84 p. F2. $15.00

BILLINGS, J.D. *Hardtack & Coffee.* 1960. Lakeside Classic. 483 p. TEG. T5. $25.00

BILLINGS, J.D. *His Sayings.* 1866. NY. G. $25.00

BILYEU, Richard. *Tanelorn Archives.* 1981. Pandora. Trade PB. 1/900. P1. $7.95

BILYEU, Richard. *Tanelorn Archives.* 1981. Pandora. 1/250. sgn. P1. $20.00

BILYEU, Richard. *Tanelorn Archives.* 1981. Pandora. HrdCvr ed. 1/350. EX. P1. $15.95

BINDER, Eando. *Enslaved Brains.* nd. Avalon. dj. xl. P1. $6.00

BINDER, Eando. *Enslaved Brains.* 1965. Avalon. 1st ed. clipped dj. EX. F5. $22.00

BINDING, Paul. *Separate Country: Literary Journey Through Am S.* 1979. Paddington. 1st ed. dj. EX. B13. $45.00

BINFORD, Lewis. *For Theory Building in Archaeology.* 1981. Academic Pr. 2nd print. 419 p. F2. $10.00

BING, Rudolf. *Knight at the Opera.* nd. Putnam. not Book Club ed. dj. VG. B10. $4.00

BING, Rudolf. *5000 Nights at the Opera.* 1972. Doubleday Book Club. 345 p. dj. VG. B10. $3.50

BINGHAM, A.M. *Portrait of an Explorer: Hiram Bingham.* 1989. Ames. IA U Pr. 1st ed. dj. F2. $35.00

BINGHAM, Hiram. *Across S America.* 1911. Houghton Mifflin. Ils. 405 p. F2. $45.00

BINGHAM, Hiram. *Bartimeus of Sandwich Islands.* c 1870. Boston. 12mo. 58 p. VG. $35.00

BINGHAM, Hiram. *Inca Land.* 1922. Houghton Mifflin. 1st ed. 365 p. scarce. F2. $75.00

BINGHAM, Hiram. *Lost City of the Incas: Story of Machu Picchu & Builders.* 1948. Duell Sloan. 1st ed. 263 p. F2. $21.00

BINGHAM, John. *Good Old Charlie.* 1968. Simon Schuster. 1st ed. dj. xl. P1. $6.00

BINNS, Archie. *Laurels Are Cut Down.* 1937. Reynal Hitchcock. inscr. dj. H3. $75.00

BINNS, W.M. *1st Century of Eng Porcelain.* 1906. London. 1st ed. 251 p. VG. T5. $195.00

BINYON, Laurence. *Madness of Merlin.* 1947. Macmillan. 1st ed. dj. EX. C1. $59.50

BIOCCA, Ettore. *Yanoama.* 1969. London. George Allen. 1st ed. 333 p. dj. F2. $20.00

BIRBECK, Morris. *Letters From IL.* 1818. London. 8vo. 114 p. scarce. G4. $74.00

BIRBECK, Morris. *Notes on a Journey in Am...VA to Territory of IL.* 1818. Dublin. 2 vols. rebound. EX. T1. $180.00

BIRCHMORE, F. *Around the World on a Bicycle.* 1939. Athens, GA. 1st ed. 1/2500. VG. B3. $32.50

BIRD, Brandon. *Hawk Watch.* 1954. Doubleday Book Club. dj. VG. P1. $10.00

BIRD, R.M. *City Looking Glass: Phil Comedy in 5 Acts.* 1933. NY. 1st ed. 1/450. VG. C1. $15.00

BIRD. *Navies in the Mts.* 1962. NY. 1st ed. dj. VG. B3. $45.00

BIRKBY, Carel. *Pagel Story.* 1948. Hodder Stoughton. 1st ed. octavo. 242 p. dj. EX. H3. $50.00

BIRKHEAD, Edith. *Tale of Terror.* c 1920. 1st Am ed. VG. scarce. K3. $20.00

BIRMINGHAM, Stephen. *CA Rich.* 1980. Simons. 4to. $20.00

BIRMINGHAM, Stephen. *Our Crowd.* 1967. Harper Row. 1st ed. 4to. dj. EX. $12.00

BIRMINGHAM, Stephen. *Real Lace.* 1973. Harper Row. 1st ed. 4to. dj. EX. $12.00

BIRMINGHAM, Stephen. *Right People.* nd. Book Club. 307 p. dj. VG. B10. $3.50

BIRMINGHAM, Stephen. *Right People.* 1968. Little Brn. 1st ed. $12.00

BIRNEY, Hoffman. *Zealots of Zion.* 1931. Phil. 1st ed. 317 p. dj. VG. B3. $37.50

BISCHOFF, David. *Star Spring.* nd. Berkley. 1st ed. PB. VG. C1. $7.50

BISCHOFF & BAILEY. *Tin Woodman.* 1979. Doubleday. 1st ed. dj. EX. R3. $12.50

BISHOP, Elizabeth. *Complete Poems 1927-1979.* 1982. Farrar Straus. UP. wrp. EX. B13. $85.00

BISHOP, G.A. *Chicago's Accomplishments & Leaders.* 1932. Chicago. 1st ed. dj. EX. $13.00

BISHOP, I.B. *Isabel Bishop.* 1974. Tucson. Ltd ed. 1/2500. dj. EX. P1. $25.00

BISHOP, I.B. *6 Months in Sandwich Islands.* 1894. NY. 1st Am ed. fld map. 422 p. VG. B3. $75.00

BISHOP, Jim. *Day Lincoln Was Shot.* 1955. Book Club. 230 p. dj. VG. B10. $4.25

BISHOP, Joseph. *Goethals: Genius of the Panama Canal.* 1930. Harper. 1st ed. 493 p. gilt bdg. F2. $25.00

BISHOP, Joseph. *Uncle Sam's Panama Canal & World Hist.* 1913. World Syndicate. Ils. 234 p. poor. F2. $7.50

BISHOP, Michael. *Ancient of Days.* 1985. Arbor House. 1st ed. dj. EX. F5. $22.00

BISHOP, Michael. *Blooded on Arachne.* 1982. Arkham House. 1st ed. M. R3. $13.95

BISHOP, Michael. *Catacomb Years.* 1979. Berkley Putnam. 1st ed. dj. EX. R3. $15.00

BISHOP, Michael. *No Enemy But Time.* nd. Book Club. dj. VG. P1. $5.00

BISHOP, Michael. *Stolen Faces.* 1977. Harper Row. 1st ed. dj. EX. P1. $15.00

BISHOP, Michael. *Transfigurations.* nd. Book Club. dj. VG. P1. $5.00

BISHOP, Michael. *Transfigurations.* 1979. Berkley Putnam. 1st ed. dj. EX. R3. $20.00

BISHOP, Michael. *Transfigurations.* 1980. Gollancz. 1st ed. dj. VG. P1. $20.00

BISHOP, Michael. *Who Made Stevie Crye?* 1984. Arkham House. 1st ed. M. R3. $15.95

BISHOP, Michael. *1 Winter in Eden.* 1983. Arkham House. 1st ed. M. R3. $13.95

BISHOP, N.H. *4 Months in a Sneak-Box.* 1889. Edinburgh. 1st Eng ed. 322 p. fair. T5. $75.00

BISHOP, Paul. *Citadel Run.* 1987. Tor Books. 1st ed. dj. EX. F5. $13.00

BISHOP, Ron. *Laughter All the Way.* 1968. Goodliffe Pub. 130 p. VG. J3. $6.00

BISHOP, W.A. *Winged Peace.* 1944. NY. 1st Am ed. 175 p. G. T5. $15.00

BISHOP, W.A. *Winged Peace.* 1944. Toronto. 1st Canadian ed. 175 p. dj. VG. B3. $30.00

BISHOP & BRODEUR. *Altar of the Legion.* 1926. Little Brn. 1st/only ed. VG. C1. $45.00

BISPHAM, David. *Quaker Singer's Recollections.* 1920. Macmillan. 1st ed. 8vo. 401 p. V1. $18.00

BISSETT, James. *Tramps & Ladies.* 1959. NY. 1st ed. dj. VG. B3. $27.50

BISSON, Laurence. *Short Hist French Literature.* 1945. Pelican. 2nd ed. P1. $3.00

BJERKOE, E.H. *Cabinetmakers of Am.* 1957. Doubleday. 1st ed. dj. D4. $50.00

BJORK, K.O. *W of the Great Divide: Norwegian Migration to Pacific Coast.* 1958. Northfield. 1st ed. dj. VG. $25.00

BJORKLUND, H.C. *Chalk Talkies.* 1929. Minneapolis. 1st ed. SftCvr. EX. J3. $4.00

BJORKLUND, L. *Faces of the Frontier.* 1967. NY. 1st ed. dj. EX. $35.00

BJORN, Thyra. *Papa's Daughter.* nd. Rinehart. 238 p. VG. B10. $3.50

BLACH, Ernest. *Amateur Circus Life.* 1916. Macmillan. 1st ed. octavo. 190 p. VG. H3. $75.00

BLACK, Archibald. *Transport Aviation.* 1926. Chicago. Ils. 245 p. T5. $95.00

BLACK, Campbell. *Letters From the Dead.* 1985. Villard. 1st ed. dj. EX. F5. $15.00

BLACK, F.R. *Ill-Starred Prohibition Cases.* 1931. Boston. 1st ed. presentation. VG. B3. $25.00

BLACK, Gavin. *Bitter Tea.* 1971. Harper Row. 1st ed. dj. xl. P1. $6.00

BLACK, Gavin. *Cold Jungle.* 1969. Harper Row. 1st ed. dj. xl. P1. $6.00

BLACK, Gavin. *Dragon for Christmas.* 1963. Harper Row. 1st ed. dj. xl. P1. $7.50

BLACK, Gavin. *Eyes Around Me.* 1964. Collins. dj. xl. P1. $6.00

BLACK, Gavin. *Wind of Death.* 1967. Collins. 1st ed. dj. xl. P1. $6.00

BLACK, Gavin. *You Want To Die, Johnny?* 1966. Harper Row. 1st ed. dj. VG. P1. $20.00

BLACK, Glenn. *Angel Site: An Archaeological, Hist, & Ethnological Study.* 1967. Indianapolis. 1st ed. 2 vols. slipcase. EX. F2. $40.00

BLACK, Lionel. *Breakaway.* 1970. Collins Crime Club. dj. VG. P1. $15.00

BLACK, Lionel. *Flood.* 1971. Stein Day. dj. VG. P1. $12.50

BLACK, Lionel. *Life & Death of Peter Wade.* 1974. Stein Day. 1st ed. dj. VG. P1. $12.50

BLACK, Lionel. *Provincial Crime.* 1960. Cassell. 1st ed. dj. VG. P1. $20.00

BLACK, William. *Magic Ink & Other Stories.* 1892. NY. 1st Am ed. VG. R3. $20.00

BLACK & BLACK. *Florence & Some Tuscan Cities.* 1905. London. 75 pls. TEG. VG. T1. $50.00

BLACK SUN PRESS. *Books of the Blk Sun Pr.* 1930. Blk Sun. Ils. wrp. H3. $250.00

BLACKBURN, H. *Randolph Caldecott: His Early Art Career.* 1886. London. 1st ed. gilt gr bdg. EX. $200.00

BLACKBURN, John. *Bound To Kill.* 1963. Mill Morrow. 1st ed. dj. xl. P1. $7.50

BLACKBURN, John. *Colonel Bogus.* 1964. Jonathan Cape. 1st ed. dj. xl. P1. $7.50

BLACKBURN, John. *Cyclops Goblet.* 1977. Jonathan Cape. dj. EX. P1. $22.50

BLACKBURN, John. *Dead Man's Handle.* 1978. Jonathan Cape. 1st ed. dj. EX. P1. $22.50

BLACKBURN, John. *Gaunt Woman.* 1962. Morrow. 1st ed. dj. VG. P1. $30.00

BLACKBURN, John. *Ring of Roses.* 1965. Jonathan Cape. dj. xl. P1. $7.50

BLACKBURN, John. *Scent of New-Mown Hay.* nd. Book Club. dj. VG. P1. $4.50

BLACKBURN, John. *Wreath of Roses.* 1965. Mill Morrow. dj. xl. P1. $7.50

BLACKBURN, Paul. *In, On, or About the Premises.* 1968. Grossman/Cape Goliard. EX. B4. $20.00

BLACKBURN & ECONOMOU. *Anthology of Troubadour Poetry.* 1978. CA U. dj. NM. C1. $15.00

BLACKER, Irwin. *Cortes & the Aztec Conquest.* 1965. Am Heritage. 1st ed. 153 p. F2. $12.50

BLACKER. *ABC Collecting Old Continental Pottery.* 1913. London. 1st ed. C2. $45.00

BLACKFORD, C.M. *Trials & Trial of Jefferson Davis.* 1900. Richmond. 1st ed. wrp. EX. $45.00

BLACKMORE, R.D. *Lorna Doone.* 1943. Heritage. Ils John Austen. slipcase. EX. T1. $20.00

BLACKMORE, R.D. *Slain by the Doones.* 1895. Dodd Mead. 1st ed. VG. $45.00

BLACKMUR, R.P. *Expense of Greatness.* 1940. Arrow Eds. 1st ed. sgn. dj. EX. B13. $150.00

BLACKSTOCK, Lee. *All Men Are Murderers.* 1958. Crime Club. 1st ed. dj. VG. P1. $15.00

BLACKSTONE, Harry. *Blackstone's Modern Card Tricks & Secrets of Magic.* 1941. Garden City. 301 p. dj. VG. J3. $12.00

BLACKSTONE, Harry. *Blackstone's Modern Card Tricks.* 1932. AL Burt. 204 p. VG. J3. $6.00

BLACKSTONE, Harry. *Blackstone's Modern Card Tricks.* 1958. Garden City. New/Revised ed. 164 p. dj. NM. J3. $6.00

BLACKSTONE, Harry. *Blackstone's Secrets of Magic.* 1932. George Sully. 3rd print. 265 p. EX. J3. $11.00

BLACKSTONE, Harry. *Blackstone's Tricks Anyone Can Do.* 1948. Permabooks. 1st ed. 232 p. EX. J3. $3.00

BLACKSTONE, Sidney. *Progress of Love & Miscellanies.* nd. (1928) Dorrance. probably 1st ed. 101 p. VG. B10. $5.00

BLACKSTONE, William. *Commentaries on the Laws of Eng.* 1766-1770. Dublin. 1st ed. 4 vols. octavo. H3. $1750.00

BLACKWELL, A.S. *Little Grandmother of Russian Revolution.* 1919. Boston. not 1st ed. inscr. 348 p. VG. B10. $17.00

BLACKWOOD, Algernon. *Bright Messenger.* 1922. Dutton. 1st ed. VG. R3. $30.00

BLACKWOOD, Algernon. *Day & Night Stories.* 1917. Dutton. 1st ed. VG. R3. $30.00

BLACKWOOD, Algernon. *Doll & 1 Other.* 1946. Arkham House. 1st ed. dj. EX. R3. $45.00

BLACKWOOD, Algernon. *Dudley Nand Gilderoy.* 1929. Dutton. 1st ed. dj. VG. R3. $50.00

BLACKWOOD, Algernon. *Episodes Before 30.* 1924. Dutton. 1st ed. VG. R3. $27.50

BLACKWOOD, Algernon. *Fruit Stoners.* 1935. Dutton. 1st ed. sgn. dj. EX. $75.00

BLACKWOOD, Algernon. *Human Chord.* 1972. Tom Stacey. dj. VG. P1. $15.00

BLACKWOOD, Algernon. *Julius Le Vallon.* 1916. Dutton. 1st Am ed. VG. R3. $30.00

BLACKWOOD, Algernon. *Prisoner in Fairyland.* 1913. Macmillan. 1st ed. VG. R3. $30.00

BLACKWOOD, Algernon. *Promise of Air.* 1938. Dutton. New ed. dj. VG. R3. $25.00

BLACKWOOD, Algernon. *Tales of Uncanny & Supernatural.* 1967. London. Springs Books. 6th ed. 426 p. VG. B10. $5.75

BLADES, William. *Petateuch of Printing.* 1891. 1st Am ed. K3. $40.00

BLAFFER, Sarah. *Blk Man of Zinacantan.* 1972. TX U. 1st ed. 194 p. dj. F2. $20.00

BLAGOWIDOW, George. *Last Train From Berlin.* 1977. Doubleday. 1st ed. dj. VG. P1. $12.50

BLAINE, John. *Lost City.* nd. Grosset Dunlap. dj. VG. P1. $7.50

BLAINE, John. *Magic Talisman.* 1989. Manuscript Pr. decor brd. P1. $25.00

BLAINE, John. *Rocket's Shadow.* nd. Grosset Dunlap. dj. VG. P1. $7.50

BLAIR, C. *Silent Victory.* 1975. Phil. 1st ed. 1072 p. dj. VG. B3. $32.50

BLAIR, W.A. *Raft Pilot's Log.* 1930. Arthur Clark. EX. $135.00

BLAISDELL, A.F. *Stories of the Civil War.* 1894. Boston. Ils. VG. $45.00

BLAISDELL, F.E. *Orig Magic.* 1976. Magic Ltd. 251 p. NM. J3. $14.00

BLAKE, George. *Major Magic.* 1968. Leeds, Eng. 1st ed. 55 p. EX. J3. $5.00

BLAKE, George. *Master Magic.* 1961. Leeds, Eng. 1st ed. 32 p. NM. J3. $4.00

BLAKE, Nicholas. *End of Chapter.* 1957. Collins Crime Club. 1st ed. dj. VG. P1. $20.00

BLAKE, Nicholas. *Whisper in the Gloom.* 1954. Collins Crime Club. 1st ed. dj. VG. P1. $30.00

BLAKE, Peter. *Marcel Breuer: Sun & Shadow.* 1955. NY. 1st ed. VG. G1. $100.00

BLAKE, William. *Ils of Book of Job.* 1903. Appleton. facsimile of 1826 ed. G. $20.00

BLAKE, William. *Marriage of Heaven & Hell.* 1927. London. Dent. lg 8vo. VG. V1. $100.00

BLAKE, William. *Pilgrim's Progress.* 1942. Heritage. slipcase. A6. $18.00

BLANC, Suzanne. *Rose Window.* 1968. Cassell. dj. VG. P1. $15.00

BLANCHAN, Neltje. *Am Flower Garden.* 1909. NY. Ltd ed. 1/1050. gilt bdg. VG. $75.00

BLANCHAN, Neltje. *Bird Neighbors & Birds That Hunt & Are Hunted.* 1932. Doubleday. 1st ed. 498 p. VG. B10. $20.00

BLANCHAN, Neltje. *Bird Neighbors.* nd. Garden City. 233 p. VG. B10. $3.50

BLANCHARD, A.E. *Friend Dorothy.* 1898. Phil. GW Jacobs. 12mo. 320 p. poor. V1. $3.50

BLANCHARD & RICK. *Debate on Slavery.* 1846. Cincinnati. Moore. 482 p. S1. $45.00

BLANCKE, W.W. *Juarez of Mexico.* 1971. Praeger. 1st ed. 152 p. dj. F2. $15.00

BLANDING, Don. *Vagabonds House.* 1940. NY. 25th print. sgn. special leather. VG. B3. $20.00

BLANK, Clair. *Beverly Gray's Career.* 1935. Grosset. 254 p. dj. VG. B10. $3.00

BLANK & SEYMOUR. *CA Artists' Cookbook.* 1982. NY. 1st ed. pls. dj. EX. $45.00

BLANKFORT, Michael. *I Met a Man.* 1937. Bobbs Merrill. 1st ed. dj. VG. H3. $30.00

BLASER, Werner. *Architecture & Nature.* 1984. Basel. oblong 4to. VG. G1. $40.00

BLATCHLEY, W.S. *Notes on Flora & Fauna of Subtropical FL.* 1932. Indianapolis. EX. $50.00

BLATCHLEY, W.S. *S Am As I Saw It.* 1934. Indianapolis. 1st ed. fld map. 391 p. F2. $20.00

BLATTY, W.P. *Legion.* nd. Book Club. dj. VG. P1. $4.00

BLATTY, W.P. *9th Configuration.* 1978. Harper. 1st ed. dj. EX. F5. $25.00

BLAU, E.E. *Queen's Falcon.* nd. Collier. VG. P1. $10.00

BLAVATSKY, H.P. *Practical Occultism & Occultism Versus the Occult Arts.* 1919. Hollywood, CA. 32mo. red bdg. scarce. G. T1. $45.00

BLECHMAN, R.C. *Juggler of Our Lady: Medieval Legend Adapted by Blechman.* 1953. Holt. 1st ed. VG. B7. $58.00

BLEECK, Oliver; see Thomas, Ross.

BLEEDING, Francis. *Secret Weapon.* 1944. Books Inc. 2nd ed. VG. P1. $7.50

BLEEDING, Francis. *Spellbound.* 1945. Tower. Photoplay ed. dj. VG. P1. $20.00

BLEEKER, Sylvester. *General Tom Thumb's 3 Years' Tour Around the World...* 1872. NY. Booth. 1st ed. octavo. 144 p. gray wrp. H3. $75.00

BLEILER, E.E. *Checklist of SF & Supernatural Fiction.* 1978. Firebell. 1st ed. dj. EX. P1. $35.00

BLEILER, E.F. *Checklist of Fantastic Literature.* 1948. Shasta. 2nd print. dj. EX. R3. $90.00

BLEILER, E.F. *Checklist of Fantastic Literature.* 1958. Shasta. presentation. sm 8vo. rust bdg. $55.00

BLEILER & DIKTY. *Best SF Stories 1949.* 1949. Frederick Fell. 1st ed. dj. VG. R3. $22.50

BLEILER & DIKTY. *Year's Best SF Novels 1952.* 1952. Frederick Fell. 1st ed. dj. EX. R3. $35.00

BLIGH, W. *Voyage to the S Seas.* 1975. Ltd Ed Club. Ils/sgn Singleton & Dunstan. 4to. slipcase. VG. $55.00

BLINDLOSS, Harold. *Broken Trail.* 1926. Stokes. 1st Am ed. 314 p. VG. B10. $3.75

BLINDLOSS, Harold. *Dust of Conflict.* 1907. Stokes. 1st ed. pictorial bdg. F5. $15.00

BLISH, James. *And All the Stars a Stage.* 1972. Faber. 1st ed. dj. VG. P1. $25.00

BLISH, James. *Anywhen.* 1971. London. 1st Eng ed. dj. EX. R3. $35.00

BLISH, James. *Blk Easter.* 1968. Faber. 1st ed. dj. xl. P1. $17.50

BLISH, James. *Blk Easter/Day After Judgment.* 1980. Gregg Pr. 1st ed. EX. R3. $35.00

BLISH, James. *Day After Judgment.* 1971. Doubleday. 1st ed. dj. EX. R3. $75.00

BLISH, James. *Dr Mirabilis.* 1964. London. 1st ed. dj. EX. R3. $35.00

BLISH, James. *Earthman Come Home.* 1955. Putnam. 1st ed. dj. EX. R3. $90.00

BLISH, James. *Earthman Come Home.* 1965. Faber. 2nd ed. dj. EX. P1. $20.00

BLISH, James. *Frozen Year.* 1957. Ballantine. 1st ed. dj. VG. P1. $75.00

BLISH, James. *Jack of Eagles.* 1952. Greenberg. 1st ed. dj. EX. R3. $60.00

BLISH, James. *Midsummer Century.* 1973. Faber. 1st ed. dj. VG. P1. $15.00

BLISH, James. *Seedling Stars.* 1957. Gnome. dj. EX. P1. $18.25

BLISH, James. *Star Dwellers.* 1961. Putnam. 1st ed. dj. EX. F5. $85.00

BLISH, James. *Star Dwellers.* 1961. Putnam. 1st ed. dj. xl. P1. $7.50

BLISH, James. *Star Trek Reader II.* nd. Book Club. dj. VG. P1. $7.50

BLISH, James. *Star Trek Reader.* nd. Book Club. dj. VG. P1. $7.50

BLISH, James. *Torrent of Faces.* nd. Book Club. dj. VG. P1. $4.50

BLITZ, Signor. *50 Years in the Magic Circle.* 1871. Hartford. 1st ed. 432 p. J3. $15.00

BLOCH, Richard. *These Are a Few of My Favorite Things.* 1985. Collectors Workshop. 29 p. SftCvr. NM. J3. $5.00

BLOCH, Robert. *Am Gothic.* 1974. Simon Schuster. 1st ed. dj. xl. VG. R3. $15.00

BLOCH, Robert. *Atoms & Evil.* 1962. Gold Medal. 1st ed. wrp. EX. R3. $35.00

BLOCH, Robert. *Bloch & Bradbury.* 1972. Peacock. 1st ed. wrp. EX. R3. $17.50

BLOCH, Robert. *Blood Runs Cold.* 1961. Simon Schuster. 1st ed. dj. EX. B13. $125.00

BLOCH, Robert. *Blood Runs Cold.* 1961. Simon Schuster. 1st ed. dj. xl. P1. $20.00

BLOCH, Robert. *Cold Chills.* 1977. Doubleday. 1st ed. dj. VG. P1. $30.00

BLOCH, Robert. *Complete Robert Bloch.* 1986. Fandom Unltd. Ils. P1. $10.00

BLOCH, Robert. *Dead Beat.* 1960. Simon Schuster. 1st ed. dj. VG. P1. $25.00

BLOCH, Robert. *Dragons & Nightmares.* 1968. Mirage. 1st ed. dj. EX. R3. $50.00

BLOCH, Robert. *Fear Today, Gone Tomorrow.* 1971. Award. 1st ed. wrp. EX. R3. $35.00

BLOCH, Robert. *Night World.* Simon Schuster. 2nd ed. dj. xl. P1. $10.00

BLOCH, Robert. *Opener of the Way.* 1945. Arkham House. 1st ed. dj. EX. R3. $250.00

BLOCH, Robert. *Pyscho House.* 1990. Tor Books. 1st ed. dj. EX. P1. $16.95

BLOCH, Robert. *Scarf.* 1947. Dial. 1st ed. dj. VG. R3. $27.50

BLOCH, Robert. *Unholy Trinity.* 1986. Scream. 1st ed. wrp. M. R3. $80.00

BLOCH & MUNG. *Angel.* 1977. Ward Ritchie. dj. EX. P1. $7.50

BLOCHMAN, L.G. *Diagnosis: Homicide.* 1950. Lippincott. 1st ed. dj. VG. P1. $30.00

BLOCHMAN, L.G. *See You at the Morgue.* 1944. Books Inc. 2nd ed. VG. P1. $7.50

BLOCK, Lawrence. *Ariel.* 1980. Arbor House. 1st ed. dj. EX. F5. $32.50

BLOCK, Lawrence. *Babe in the Woods.* Nov 1960. Monarch Books 172. 1st ed. VG. T9. $55.00

BLOCK, Lawrence. *Burglar in the Closet.* nd. Book Club. dj. VG. P1. $5.00

BLOCK, Lawrence. *Burglar Who Painted Like Mondrian.* 1983. Arbor House. 1st ed. dj. EX. F5. $20.00

BLOCK, Lawrence. *Burglar Who Studied Spinoza.* nd. Book Club. dj. VG. P1. $4.50

BLOCK, Lawrence. *Code of Arms.* 1981. Marek. 1st ed. dj. EX. P1. $20.00

BLOCK, Lawrence. *Girl With the Long Gr Heart.* 1965. Fawcett Gold Medal K1555. 1st ed. wrp. EX. T9. $25.00

BLOCK, Lawrence. *Random Walk.* 1988. Tor Books. 1st ed. dj. EX. P1. $4.50

BLOCK, Lawrence. *When the Sacred Gin Mill Closes.* nd. Book Club. dj. VG. P1. $4.50

BLOCK, Lawrence. *2 for Tanner.* 1968. Fawcett Gold Medal D1896. 1st ed. wrp. EX. T9. $35.00

BLOM, Frans. *Maya Skull From the Uloa Valley, Republic of Honduras.* 1933. Tulane. Ils. 24 p. wrp. F2. $15.00

BLOMBERG, Rolf. *Buried Gold & Anacondas.* 1959. NY. Nelson. 1st ed. 144 p. dj. F2. $25.00

BLOODWORTH, Dennis. *Trapdoor.* 1980. Weidenfeld Nicolson. 1st UK ed. dj. EX. F5. $16.00

BLOOR, E.R. *We Are Many.* 1949. NY. 1st ed. dj. VG. B3. $15.00

BLOSS, R.S. *Pony Express: Great Gamble.* 1959. Howell. Ils. 159 p. dj. A5. $35.00

BLOUNT, Margaret. *Animal Land: Creatures of Children's Fiction.* 1977. Avon. EX. P1. $7.50

BLOUT, B.B. *Eyes-Light.* 1941. NY. Nat Process Co. 1st ed. presentation. dj. VG. H3. $125.00

BLOUT, William. *Blount Journal 1790-1796.* 1955. TN Hist Comm. 1st ed. VG. $30.00

BLOWER, A.H. *Akron at the Turn of the Century 1890-1913.* 1955. Akron. 1st ed. 373 p. VG. T5. $17.50

BLOWER, J.G. *Brief Hist of Trimble Township, Athens Co, OH.* nd. (1967) np. Ils. 120 p. T5. $19.50

BLOXAM, Andrew. *Diary of Andrew Bloxam...1824-1825.* 1925. Bernice Bishop Mus. 1st ed. VG. $45.00

BLUE, A.G. *Fortunes of War.* 1967. Fallbrook, CA. Ils. 96 p. wrp. VG. T5. $37.50

BLUE, Tyson. *Unseen King.* 1989. Starmont. 1st ed. wrp. M. R3. $9.95

BLUM, Daniel. *Pictorial Hist of Am Theatre 1860-1970.* 1972. Crown. 3rd ed. folio. 416 p. dj. EX. H3. $40.00

BLUM & ASSOCIATES. *Utopiates.* 1965. NY. dj. VG. C2. $55.00

BLUM. *Old World Lace.* 1920. NY. 1st ed. 81 p. VG. C2. $45.00

BLUMENTHAL, Joseph. *Typographic Years.* 1928. NY. Grolier. 1/300. 8vo. slipcase. EX. $30.00

BLUMER, Kenneth. *Roller Coaster World.* 1978. Severn House. dj. EX. P1. $18.25

BLUMER, Kenneth. *Shark N.* 1979. Severn House. dj. VG. P1. $15.00

BLUMIN, S.M. *Short Season of Sharon Springs.* 1980. Ithica. 128 p. dj. EX. S1. $4.50

BLUMLEIN, Michael. *Movements of Mts.* 1987. St Martin. 1st ed. dj. EX. F5. $16.00

BLUNDEN, Edward. *Bonadventure: Random Journey of Atlantic Holiday.* 1932. London. 1st ed. dj. VG. $115.00

BLUNT, W.S. *Art of Botanical Ils.* 1951. NY. 2nd print. dj. EX. C2. $155.00

BLUNT, W.S. *Love Lyrics & Songs of Proteus.* 1892. Hammersmith. 1/300. orig vellum. EX. H3. $600.00

BLUNT, W.S. *My Diaries.* 1921. Knopf. 1st Am ed. 2 vols. TEG. VG. $25.00

BLUNT, W.S. *Poems.* 1923. Knopf. 1st ed. C1. $10.00

BLUTSTEIN, Howard. *Area Handbook for Cuba.* 1971. GPO. 1st ed. 503 p. F2. $10.00

BLY, Robert. *Iron John: Book About Men.* 1990. Reading, MA. 1st ed. 1/100. sgn. as issued. M. $175.00

BLY, Robert. *Towards a New Am Poetics.* 1978. Blk Sparrow. sgns. as issued. M. $175.00

BLYTH, R.H. *Haiku.* 1969. Hokuseido. 4 vols. djs. VG. B3. $70.00

BLYTHE & MILLER. *Life & Works of David G Blythe.* 1950. Pittsburgh. 1st ed. 142 p. dj. VG. B3. $35.00

BOARD, John. *Polo.* 1955. Woodstock. 1st Am ed. 8vo. 228 p. dj. EX. $35.00

BOARDE, C.L. *Mainly Mental Vol 2: Book Tests.* 1950. Boarde. 1st ed. 133 p. sbdg. EX. J3. $85.00

BOARDMAN, G.D. *Church.* 1901. Scribner. 1st ed. 221 p. VG. B10. $5.00

BOARDMAN & WYATT. *Forgotten Arthurian Poetry.* 1989. Gr Chapel Pr. Ils/sgn Boardman. 1/250. C1. $17.50

BOAZ, Franz. *Anthropology & Modern Life.* 1928. Norton. dj. VG. K2. $50.00

BOAZ, Franz. *Ethnology of the Kwakiutl.* 1921. WA. 2 vols. VG. A6. $95.00

BOAZ, Franz. *Social Organization of Kwatkiuti Indians.* 1895. US Nat Mus. 400 p. VG. A5. $120.00

BOBO, J.B. *Modern Coin Magic.* 1952. Minneapolis. 2nd ed. 358 p. EX. J3. $12.00

BOBO, J.B. *Watch This One!* 1947. Oakland, CA. 124 p. EX. J3. $10.00

BOCCACCIO, Giovanni. *Decameron de Jean Boccace.* 1757-1761. Paris. 5 vols. octavo. AEG. H3. $2500.00

BODARD, Lucien. *Gr Hell.* 1971. Dutton. 1st ed. 8vo. 291 p. dj. F2. $15.00

BODDINGTON, Craig. *Am: Men & Their Guns That Made Her Great.* nd. (1981) Petersen. 186 p. dj. M. B10. $10.00

BODE, Barbara. *No Bells To Toll.* 1989. Scribner. 1st ed. 559 p. dj. F2. $20.00

BODE, Wilhelm. *Antique Rugs From the Near E.* 1922. NY. 3rd ed. 4to. VG. A4. $75.00

BODELSEN, Anders. *Freezing Down.* nd. Book Club. dj. VG. P1. $4.50

BODELSEN, Anders. *Straus.* 1974. Harper Row. dj. EX. P1. $12.50

BODENHEIM, M. *Minna & Myself.* 1918. NY. Pagan. 1st ed. latter issue. VG. $35.00

BODGER, J. *How the Heather Looks.* 1965. NY. dj. VG. B3. $35.00

BODIN, Ed. *Scare Me.* 1940. Tremaine. 1st ed. sgn. VG. R3. $30.00

BODKIN, B.A. *Treasury of Am Folklore.* nd. (1944) Crown. 932 p. VG. B10. $4.00

BOELDEKE, Alfred. *With Graciela to the Headhunters.* 1958. McKay. 1st ed. 166 p. dj. F2. $15.00

BOGAN, Louise. *Body of This Death.* 1923. McBride. 1st ed. EX. $300.00

BOGAN, Louise. *Collected Poems 1923-1953.* 1954. NY. Noonday. 1st ed. dj. EX. B13. $65.00

BOGAN & SMITH. *Golden Journey.* 1965. Reilly Lee. 1st ed. inscr. dj. EX. K2. $85.00

BOGARDUS, A.H. *Field, Cover, & Trap Shooting.* 1891. NY. Revised 3rd ed. VG. P1. $45.00

BOGART, W.G. *Crazy Indian.* 1987. Tattered Pages. 1st ed. 1/200. wrp. EX. F5. $15.00

BOGGS, Stanley. *Salvadoran Varieties of Wheeled Figurines.* 1973. Miami. 1st ed. 4to. 32 p. wrp. F2. $15.00

BOGLE, Donald. *Brn Sugar: 80 Years of Am's Blk Female Superstars.* 1980. Harmony Books. 1st ed. quarto. 208 p. dj. VG. H3. $75.00

BOHR. *Atomic Physics & Human Knowledge.* 1958. NY. 1st ed. dj. VG. C2. $25.00

BOILEAU & NARCEJAC. *Choice Cuts.* 1966. Dutton. 1st ed. dj. VG. P1. $8.50

BOJARSKI, Richard. *Films of Bela Lugosi.* 1980. Citadel. 1st ed. dj. EX. R3. $25.00

BOK, Hannes. *Memorial Portfolio.* 1970. Bokanalia. VG. R3. $50.00

BOLAN, Marc. *Warlock of Love.* 1969. Great Britain. Lupus Music. complimentary copy. VG. K2. $75.00

BOLES, P.D. *Deadline.* 1957. Macmillan. 1st ed. dj. EX. F5. $25.00

BOLGAR & KOVACS. *Indian Art From Mexico to Peru.* 1983. Budapest. sm 4to. dj. F2. $45.00

BOLINDER, Gustaf. *Indians on Horseback.* 1957. London. 1st ed. 189 p. dj. F2. $20.00

BOLINGBROKE, H.S.J. *Works.* 1809. London. Johnson. 8 vols. octavo. H3. $500.00

BOLITHO, Hector. *Batsford Century.* 1943.1st ed. dj. VG. K3. $18.00

BOLLANDIANI, Socii. *Bibliitheca Hagiographica Latina Antiquae et Mediae Aetatis.* 1898-1899. Bruxellis. 2 vols. xl. G1. $75.00

BOLLENS & SCHMANDT. *Metropolis: Its People, Politics, & Economic Life.* 1965. NY. 1st ed. dj. EX. T1. $22.00

BOLLER, H.A. *Among the Indians.* 1959. Lakeside Classic. Ils. fld map. 461 p. VG. T5. $25.00

BOLLINGER, E.T. *Rails That Climb.* 1950. Santa Fe. WC Jones ed. 1/550. sgn. VG. K1. $75.00

BOLTON, H.E. *Rim of Christendom.* 1936. Macmillan. 1st ed. dj. VG. $45.00

BOLTON, H.W. *Hist of 2nd Regiment of IL Volunteer Infantry.* 1899. Chicago. VG. A4. $100.00

BOLTON, Herbert. *Pageant in Wilderness: Story of Escalante Expedition...1776.* 1950. UT Hist Soc. 1st ed. dj. VG. $40.00

BOLTON, S.K. *Famous Givers & Their Gifts.* nd. (1896) Crowell. Ils. 382 p. VG. B10. $6.25

BOLTON, W.F. *Alcuin & Beowulf: 18th-Century View.* 1978. Rutgers. dj. EX. C1. $19.00

BONAFOUX, Pascal. *Impressionsts: Portraits & Confidences.* 1986. NY. 1st Am ed. slipcase. M. G1. $60.00

BONANNI, Filippo. *Gabinetto Armonico Pieno d'Istrumenti Sonori Indicati.* 1772. Rome. 1st ed. 151 pls. EX. B10/H3. $6000.00

BONAPARTE, Marie. *Life & Works of Edgar A Poe: Psycho-Analytic Interpretation.* 1949. Imago Pub. 1st Eng ed. VG. $50.00

BONAVIA, Duccio. *Mural Painting in Ancient Peru.* 1985. Bloomington, IN. 1st ed. 4to. dj. F2. $45.00

BOND, E.P. *Words by the Way 2nd Series.* 1901. Swarthmore. 16mo. 167 p. VG. V1. $6.00

BOND, E.P. *Words by the Way.* 1901. Swarthmore. 16mo. 167 p. VG. V1. $8.50

BOND, G.B. *Buffy Finds a Star.* 1970. Whitman. VG. P1. $7.50

BOND, J.W. *MN & Its Resources.* 1856. Chicago/Phil. 1st ed. VG. $45.00

BOND, Nelson. *Lancelot Biggs: Spaceman.* 1950. Doubleday. 1st ed. dj. VG. R3. $25.00

BOND, Nelson. *Mr Mergenthwirker's Lobblies.* 1946. Coward McCann. 1st ed. dj. EX. R3. $50.00

BOND, Nelson. *Mr Mergenthwirker's Lobblies.* 1946. Coward McCann. 1st ed. dj. VG. R3. $25.00

BOND, Nelson. *31st of February.* 1949. Gnome. 1st ed. dj. VG. P1. $35.00

BONE & ADSHEAD. *Little Boy & His House.* 1937. Jr Literary Guild/Winston. 1st ed. B10. $10.00

BONETT & BONETT. *Murder on the Costa Brava.* 1968. Walker. VG. P1. $7.50

BONFIGLIOLI, Kyril. *After You With the Pistol.* 1980. Crime Club. 1st ed. dj. xl. P1. $5.00

BONHAM, B.L. *Heroes of the Wild W.* 1970. Whitman. VG. P1. $6.00

BONHAM-CARTER, Victor. *Strategy of Victory 1914-1918.* 1963. NY. 1st ed. 417 p. dj. VG. T5. $12.50

BONIFACE, Marjorie. *Murder As an Ornament.* 1940. Crime Club. 1st ed. VG. P1. $20.00

BONNYCASTLE, R.H. *Canada As It Was, Is, & May Be.* 1852. London. 1st ed. VG. $135.00

BOONE & CROCKETT. *Records of N Am Big Game.* 1952. NY. 1st ed. dj. VG. B3. $135.00

BOOTH, Abraham. *Reign of Grace: From Its Rise to Its Consummation.* 1831. Hamilton Robb. New Enlarged ed. 395 p. fair. $35.00

BOOTH, C.G. *Cat & the Clock.* nd. Grosset Dunlap. VG. P1. $10.00

BOOTH, John. *Dramatic Magic.* 1988. Ridgeway. 1st ed. 240 p. dj. NM. J3. $30.00

BOOTH, John. *Forging Ahead in Magic.* 1939. Kanter's Magic Shop. 1st ed. 154 p. EX. J3. $15.00

BOOTH, John. *Forging Ahead in Magic.* 1944. Kanter's Magic Shop. 2nd print. 154 p. VG. J3. $10.00

BOOTH, John. *Marvels of Mystery.* 1953. Kanter's Magic Shop. 4th print. 155 p. NM. J3. $10.00

BOOTH, John. *Wonders of Magic.* 1986. Ridgeway. 1/1000. 285 p. NM. J3. $20.00

BOOTH, M.B. *Lights of Child Land.* 1902. Putnam. Ils A Farnsworth-Drew. 8vo. 193 p. VG. $25.00

BOOTH, Martin. *Bad Track.* 1980. Collins Crime Club. 1st ed. dj. xl. P1. $5.00

BOOTHBY, Guy. *Bid for Fortune.* 1929. Ward Lock. G. P1. $15.00

BOOTHBY, Guy. *Dr Nikola.* 1896. Appleton. G. P1. $20.00

BOOTHBY, Guy. *Farwell Kikola.* 1901. Lippincott. VG. P1. $25.00

BOOTHBY, Guy. *In Strange Company.* 1894. London. 1st ed. VG. R3. $30.00

BOOTHBY, Guy. *Lady of the Island.* 1904. London. 1st ed. VG. R3. $35.00

BOOTHE, Clare. *Kiss the Boys Goodbye.* 1939. Random House. 1st ed. dj. EX. H3. $45.00

BOOTON, Kage. *Who Knows Julie Gordon?* 1980. Crime Club. 1st ed. dj. VG. P1. $12.50

BORDEAUX, Henry. *Georges Guynemer.* 1918. New Haven. Ils. 256 p. fair. T5. $12.50

BORGENICHT, Miriam. *Bad Medicine.* 1984. Macmillan. 1st ed. dj. EX. P1. $15.00

BORGENICHT, Miriam. *Corpse in Diplomacy.* 1949. Mill Morrow. xl. VG. P1. $5.00

BORGENICHT, Miriam. *Margin for Doubt.* nd. Book Club. dj. VG. P1. $4.50

BORGENICHT, Miriam. *Roadblock.* 1973. Bobbs Merrill. dj. VG. P1. $6.50

BORGENICHT, Miriam. *Tomorrow Trap.* 1969. Crime Club. dj. xl. P1. $4.50

BORGES, J.L. *Aspectos de la Literatura Gauchesca.* 1950. Montevideo. Numero. 1/1000. wrp. VG. K2. $185.00

BORGES, J.L. *Atlas.* 1985. Dutton. ARC. dj. RS. EX. K2. $50.00

BORGES, J.L. *Book of Fantasy.* 1988. Viking. 1st ed. dj. EX. P1. $19.95

BORGES, J.L. *Book of Sand.* 1977. Dutton. 1st ed. dj. EX. K2. $45.00

BORGES, J.L. *Cardinal Points of Borges.* 1971. OK U. 1st ed. dj. EX. K2. $65.00

BORGES, J.L. *Chronicles of Bustos Domecq.* 1976. Dutton. UP. wrp. EX. K2. $100.00

BORGES, J.L. *Congress.* 1974. London. Enitharmon. 1st ed. 1/300. sgn. dj. EX. K2. $450.00

BORGES, J.L. *Dr Brodie's Report.* 1974. London. Lane. 1st Eng ed. dj. EX. K2. $45.00

BORGES, J.L. *Ficciones.* 1962. Grove Pr. 1st ed. dj. EX. K2. $275.00

BORGES, J.L. *Gold of the Tigers.* 1977. Dutton. ARC. dj. RS. w/promotional sheet. EX. K2. $85.00

BORGES, J.L. *Hist de la Eternidad.* 1936. Buenos Aires. 1st ed. orig wrp. scarce. K2. $450.00

BORGES, J.L. *In Praise of Darkness.* 1974. Dutton. ARC. sgn. dj. RS. w/photo & promotional sheet. K2. $30.00

BORGES, J.L. *In Praise of Darkness.* 1975. London. Lane. 1st Eng ed. K2. $45.00

BORGES, J.L. *Intro to Am Literature.* 1971. KY U. 1st ed. dj. EX. K2. $85.00

BORGES, J.L. *Intro to Eng Literature.* 1974. Lexington. ARC. sgn. dj. RS. EX. K2. $250.00

BORGES, J.L. *Irish Strategies.* nd. Dolmen Ed. Ltd ed. 1/350. sgns. slipcase. H3. $125.00

BORGES, J.L. *Labyrinths.* 1962. New Directions. 1st ed. sgn. dj. EX. very scarce. K2. $750.00

BORGES, J.L. *Other Inquisitions.* 1964. Austin. 1st ed. as issued. EX. K2. $225.00

BORGES, J.L. *Other Inquisitions.* 1964. Austin. TX U. 1st ed. sgn. dj. EX. B13. $400.00

BORGES, J.L. *Personal Anthology.* 1967. Grove Pr. 1st ed. dj. EX. K2. $100.00

BORGES & BIOY-CASARES. *6 Problems for Don Isidro Parodi.* 1981. Dutton. 1st ed. dj. EX. K2. $40.00

BORGES & CASARES. *Extraordinary Tales.* 1971. Herder. ARC. sgn Borges. dj. RS. EX. B13. $350.00

BORHEGYI, Stephan. *Archaelogical Reconnaissance of Chikultic, Chiapas, Mexico.* 1968. Tulane. F2. $10.00

BORKENAU, Franz. *Spanish Cockpit.* 1937. London. 303 p. wrp. G. T5. $8.50

BORLAND, Hal. *Country Editor's Boy.* 1970. Lippincott. Family Bookshelf/2nd ed. 313 p. dj. EX. B10. $4.00

BORLAND, Hal. *This Hill This Valley.* 1957. 1st ed. dj. VG. B3. $22.50

BORN, Franz. *Jules Vernes: Man Who Invented Future.* 1967. Scholastic. VG. P1. $3.50

BOROS, Eva. *Mermaids.* 1956. Farrar Straus. 1st ed. dj. VG. B13. $45.00

BORROW, George. *Works.* 1923. London. Constable. Norwich ed. 1/775. 16 vols. octavo. H3. $1500.00

BORSI, Franco. *Leon Battista Alberti.* 1977. NY. 1st Am ed. VG. G1. $95.00

BOSCH & BRUEGEL. *Masters of Art.* 1967. Harcourt Brace. 123 p. dj. slipcase. D4. $20.00

BOSTOCK, F.C. *Training of Wild Animals.* 1903. Century. 1st ed. octavo. 256 p. red bdg. G. H3. $50.00

BOSTWICK, A.E. *Librarian's Open Shelf.* 1920. 1st ed. VG. K3. $20.00

BOSWELL, James. *Life of Samuel Johnson, LLD.* 1791. London. 1st ed. give issue. contemporary tree calf. VG. H3. $3500.00

BOSWELL, James. *Life of Samuel Johnson.* nd. Internat Collectors Lib. 1st ed. EX. B10. $5.00

BOSWELL, James. *Life of Samuel Johnson.* 1823. London. Richardson. Ils Malone. 4 vols. octavo. rebound. H3. $450.00

BOSWELL, James. *Life of Samuel Johnson.* 1826.Talboys Wheeler/Pickering. 1/50. 4 vols. H3. $400.00

BOSWELL, James. *Life of Samuel Johnson.* 1859. London. Routledge. 4 vols. gilt bdg. G. R5. $90.00

BOSWELL, James. *Life of Samuel Johnson.* 1922. Doubleday Page. Temple Bar ed. 1/785. 10 vols. octavo. H3. $750.00

BOSWELL, James. *Life of Samuel Johnson.* 1925. Bath. George Bayntun. 1st ed. 2 vols. red bdg. EX. C4. $80.00

BOSWELL, James. *Life of Samuel Johnson.* 1939. Ltd Ed Club. 8vo. 3 vols. VG. $65.00

BOSWORTH, C. *Breeding Your Own.* 1939. Derrydale. 1/1250. VG. B3. $70.00

BOTKIN, B.A. *Sidewalks in Am.* 1954. Bobbs Merrill. 1st ed. EX. B10. $4.75

BOTT & CLEPHANE. *Our Mothers.* 1932. London. Gollancz. 2nd ed. G. R5. $20.00

BOTTOMLEY, Gordon. *Gruach & Britain's Daughter.* nd. (1921) Boston. 1st ed? 121 p. VG. B10. $8.75

BOUCHER, Anthony. *Case of the Baker Street Irregulars.* 1940. 2nd print. very scarce. C1. $12.00

BOUCHER, Anthony. *Case of the Solid Key.* 1941. Simon Schuster. 1st ed. xl. G. P1. $10.00

BOUCHER, Anthony. *Case of the 7 of Cavalry.* 1954. Macmillan. dj. VG. P1. $30.00

BOUCHER, Anthony. *Great Am Detective Stories.* 1945. NY. 1st ed. dj. VG. T9. $30.00

BOUCHER, Anthony. *Great Am Detective Stories.* 1945. Tower. 2nd ed. VG. P1. $12.50

BOUCHER, Anthony. *Treasury of Great SF Vol 2.* nd. Book Club. dj. VG. P1. $5.00

BOUCHER & MCCOMAS. *Best From Fantasy & SF.* 1952. Little Brn. 1st ed. dj. EX. R3. $45.00

BOUDIN, Kathy. *Bust Book: What To Do Until the Lawyer Comes.* 1970. Blk Cat B232. 1st PB ed. VG. B4. $4.00

BOULDING, Elise. *Joy That Is Set Before Us.* 1956. Phil. Young Friends. 12mo. SftCvr. V1. $6.00

BOULLE, Pierre. *Bridge on the River Kwai.* 1954. Vanguard. UP. EX. B13. $75.00

BOULLE, Pierre. *Photographer.* 1968. Vanguard. 1st ed. dj. EX. F5. $15.00

BOULTON, Rudyerd. *Traveling With the Birds.* 1933. NY. Ils Walter Alois Weber. 64 p. dj. VG. T5. $17.50

BOUNDS, S.J. *Dimension of Horror.* 1953. Hamilton Panther. dj. VG. P1. $35.00

BOURGEAU, Art. *Wolfman.* 1989. Fine. 1st ed. dj. EX. F5. $16.00

BOURKE-WHITE, Margaret. *Dear Fatherland Rest Quietly.* 1946. NY. 1st ed. dj. VG. B3. $37.50

BOURKE-WHITE, Margaret. *Portrait of Myself.* 1963. NY. 1st ed. dj. VG. G1. $39.00

BOURKE-WHITE, Margaret. *Shooting the Russian War.* 1942. NY. 2nd print. inscr/sgn. 298 p. dj. G. T5. $150.00

BOUSSEL, Patrice. *Leonardo da Vinci.* nd. Chartwell. dj. EX. P1. $75.00

BOUTELL, Anita. *Death Has a Past.* 1944. Books Inc. dj. VG. P1. $12.00

BOUTELLE, S.H. *Julia Morgan, Architect.* 1988. NY. 1st ed. VG. G1. $25.00

BOVA, Ben. *Aliens.* 1977. St Martin. 1st ed. dj. EX. $10.00

BOVA, Ben. *Analog Science Fact Reader.* 1974. St Martin. dj. VG. P1. $12.50

BOVA, Ben. *Cyberbooks.* 1989. Tor Books. 1st ed. dj. EX. F5. $14.00

BOVA, Ben. *End of Exile.* 1975. Dutton. dj. RS. EX. P1. $35.00

BOVA, Ben. *Exiles.* 1977. St Martin. 1st ed. dj. EX. R3. $17.50

BOVA, Ben. *High Road.* 1981. Houghton Mifflin. 1st ed. dj. EX. P1. $17.50

BOVA, Ben. *Kinsman.* nd. Book Club. dj. EX. P1. $4.00

BOVA, Ben. *Man Changes the Weather.* nd. Addison Wesley. 2nd ed. dj. xl. P1. $6.00

BOVA, Ben. *Many Worlds of SF.* nd. Book Club. dj. VG. P1. $4.50

BOVA, Ben. *Millennium.* 1976. Random House. 1st ed. sgn. dj. EX. F5. $22.00

BOVA, Ben. *Privateers.* 1985. Tor Books. 1st ed. dj. VG. P1. $15.95

BOVA, Ben. *Seeds of Tomorrow.* 1977. McKay. 1st ed. dj. EX. R3. $20.00

BOVA, Ben. *Star-Crossed.* 1975. Chilton. 1st ed. dj. EX. R3. $30.00

BOVA, Ben. *Through Eyes of Wonder.* 1975. Addisonian. 1st ed. dj. EX. F5. $15.00

BOVA, Ben. *Voyages II: The Alien Within.* 1986. Tor Books. 1st ed. dj. EX. P1. $15.95

BOVA, Ben. *Weather Makers.* 1967. Holt. 1st ed. dj. EX. R3. $25.00

BOVA, Ben. *When the Sky Burned.* 1973. Walker. 1st ed. clipped dj. EX. F5. $22.00

BOVA, Ben. *Winds of Altair.* 1973. Dutton. 1st ed. VG. P1. $12.50

BOWDEN, E.T. *James Thurber: A Biography.* 1969. Columbus. 1st/only ed. 353 p. dj. EX. $15.00

BOWEN, Elizabeth. *Heat of the Day.* 1949. Knopf. 2nd ed. dj. VG. P1. $10.00

BOWEN, Elizabeth. *House in Paris.* 1936. Knopf. 1st ed. dj. VG. P1. $20.00

BOWEN, Marjorie. *Kecksies & Other Twilight Tales.* 1976. Arkham House. 1st ed. M. R3. $8.95

BOWEN, Mrs. C.E. *Battle & Victory: Story of a Painter's Life.* nd. Dutton. VG. B10. $5.00

BOWEN, R.S. *Dave Dawson With the Air Corps.* nd. Saalfield. G. P1. $5.00

BOWEN, R.S. *Dave Dawson With the RAF.* nd. Saalfield. G. P1. $5.00

BOWEN, R.S. *Red Randall at Midway.* nd. Grosset Dunlap. VG. P1. $7.50

BOWEN, R.S. *Red Randall on Active Duty.* nd. Grosset Dunlap. dj. VG. P1. $15.00

BOWEN, R.S. *Top Secret.* 1969. Whitman. VG. P1. $7.50

BOWEN, Sandra. *Mysteries of the Crystal Skulls Revealed.* 1988. Pacifica, CA. 2nd print. 298 p. wrp. F2. $20.00

BOWER, B.M. *Flying U Strikes.* 1942. Triangle. 6th ed. VG. P1. $10.00

BOWER, B.M. *Rim O' the World.* 1919. McClelland Stewart. decor brd. VG. P1. $15.00

BOWERS, C.G. *Rhododendrons & Azaleas.* 1936. NY. 1st ed. sgn. VG. $50.00

BOWERS, C.G. *Tragic Era: The Revolution After Lincoln.* 1929. Houghton Mifflin. 567 p. G. S1. $6.00

BOWERS, T.L. *Gold Trail.* 1983. Avalon. 1st ed. dj. EX. F5. $10.00

BOWERSMITH, Isaac. *Veterinary Surgery.* 1872. Westerville, OH. 1st ed. 12mo. 219 p. $20.00

BOWIE, W.R. *Sunrise in the S: Life of Mary Cooke Branch Munford.* 1942. Richmond. 1st ed. dj. EX. $25.00

BOWKA, C.M. *Greek Experience.* nd. (1957) World. 210 p. VG. B10. $5.25

BOWKER, Richard. *Dover Beach.* 1987. Bantam. UP. wrp. EX. R3. $25.00

BOWKER, Richard. *Marlborough Street.* 1987. Doubleday. 1st ed. dj. RS. EX. P1. $17.50

BOWLES, Jane. *Collected Work of Jane Bowles.* 1956. Farrar Straus. 1st ed. dj. EX. B13. $75.00

BOWLES, Jane. *In the Summer House.* 1954. Random House. 1st ed. dj. K2. $100.00

BOWLES, Jane. *Out in the World. Selected Letters of Jane Bowles 1935-1970.* 1985. Blk Sparrow. 1/500. dj. EX. K2. $25.00

BOWLES, Paul. *Call at Corazon.* 1988. Peter Owen. 1st Eng ed. dj. EX. K2. $45.00

BOWLES, Paul. *In the Red Room.* 1981. Sylvester Orphanos. 1/330. sgn. sq octavo. EX. K2. $125.00

BOWLES, Paul. *Let It Come Down.* 1952. Random House. 1st ed. dj. EX. $50.00

BOWLES, Paul. *Let It Come Down.* 1980. Blk Sparrow. Ltd ed. sgn. H3. $60.00

BOWLES, Paul. *Midnight Mass.* 1981. Blk Sparrow. Ltd ed. sgn. H3. $85.00

BOWLES, Paul. *Scenes.* 1968. Blk Sparrow. Ltd Sgn ed. 1/250. inscr. EX. K2. $200.00

BOWLES, Paul. *She Woke Me Up So I Killed Her.* 1985. San Francisco. Cadmus. 1st ed. 1/126. sgn. acetate dj. EX. K2. $125.00

BOWLES, Paul. *Sheltering Sky.* 1949. London. Lehmann. 1st ed. 1st issue dj. VG. K2. $650.00

BOWLES, Paul. *Sheltering Sky.* 1949. New Directions. VG. K2. $85.00

BOWLES, Paul. *Sheltering Sky.* 1949. New Directions. 1st ed. dj. VG. K2. $300.00

BOWLES, Paul. *Spider's House.* 1982. Blk Sparrow. Ltd ed. sgn. H3. $60.00

BOWLES, Paul. *Their Heads Are Gr & Their Hands Are Bl.* 1963. Random House. 1st ed. dj. EX. K2. $75.00

BOWLES, Paul. *Thicket of Spring 1926-1969.* 1972. Blk Sparrow. Ltd ed. 1/200. sgn. dj. EX. H3. $125.00

BOWLES, Paul. *Thicket of Spring.* 1972. Blk Sparrow. Ltd ed. 1/26. sgn. acetate dj. EX. K2. $350.00

BOWLES, Paul. *Things Gone & Things Still Here.* 1977. Blk Sparrow. Ltd ed. 1/250. sgn. H3. $100.00

BOWLES, Paul. *Up Above the World.* 1966. Simon Schuster. 1st ed. dj. EX. B13. $55.00

BOWLES, Paul. *Without Stopping.* 1972. Putnam. UP. tall wrp/proof dj. EX. K2. $275.00

BOWLES, Paul. *Yallah.* 1957. McDowell Obolensky. 1st ed. dj. EX. scarce. B13. $275.00

BOWLES, Paul. *2 Years Beside the Strait. Tangier Journal 1987-1989.* 1990. London. Owen. 1st ed. 1/75. sgn. dj. EX. K2. $185.00

BOWLES, Samuel. *Across the Continent.* 1865. Springfield, MA. 12mo. A4. $90.00

BOWLES, Samuel. *Our New W: Records of Travel Between MS River & Pacific...* 1859. Hartford. Dennison. 524 p. A5. $60.00

BOWMAN, Anne. *Bear Hunters of the Rocky Mts.* 1863. Crosby Nichols. 1st ed. VG. $30.00

BOWMAN, Isaiah. *Desert Trails of Atacama.* 1924. Am Geog Soc. 1st ed. 362 p. F2. $25.00

BOWMAN, Martin. *Encyclopedia of US Military Aircraft.* nd. London. Bison Books. 1st ed. 224 p. VG. B10. $6.50

BOWMAN, S.M. *Sherman & His Campaigns: A Military Biography.* 1865. NY. 1st ed. 8vo. 512 p. VG. B3. $40.00

BOWMAN & BORER. *Modern Watch Repairing & Adjusting.* 1941. NY. 3rd ed. EX. $30.00

BOWMAN & DICKINSON. *Westward From Rio.* 1936. Chicago. Willett. Ils 352 p. dj. F2. $15.00

BOWRING, John. *Servian Popular Poetry.* 1827. London. later bdg. $30.00

BOWRING, John. *Specimens of Polish Poets.* 1827. London. later bdg. $30.00

BOX, Edgar; see Vidal, Gore.

BOY SCOUTS OF AMERICA. *Official Handbook for Boys.* 1913. Doubleday. Ils. 416 p. G. $125.00

BOYCE, A.O. *Records of a Quaker Family: Richardsons of Cleveland.* 1889. London. Newman. 4to. 294 p. V1. $40.00

BOYCE, Chris. *Catchworld.* 1977. Doubleday. dj. EX. P1. $15.00

BOYCE, W.D. *Australia & New Zealand Ils.* 1922. Chicago. Ils 1st ed. dj. EX. T1. $30.00

BOYD, Blanche McCrary. *Mourning the Death of Magic.* 1977. Macmillan. 1st ed. dj. M. $10.00

BOYD, Blanche McCrary. *Redneck Way of Knowledge.* 1982. Knopf. UP. wrp. EX. B13. $50.00

BOYD, Jason P. *Recent Indian Wars Under Lead of Sitting Bull.* 1891. Pub Union. VG. $30.00

BOYD, John. *Barnard's Planet.* 1975. Berkley. 1st ed. dj. EX. R3. $15.00

BOYD, John. *Girl With the Jade Gr Eyes.* 1978. Viking. 1st ed. dj. EX. P1. $15.00

BOYD, John. *Gorgon Festival.* 1972. Weybright Talley. 1st ed. dj. VG. P1. $17.50

BOYD, John. *IQ Merchant.* 1972. Weybright Talley. 1st ed. dj. EX. R3. $15.00

BOYD, John. *Rakehells of Heaven.* 1969. Weybright Talley. 1st ed. dj. VG. P1. $17.50

BOYD, John. *Sex & the High Command.* 1970. Weybright Talley. 1st ed. dj. VG. R3. $15.00

BOYD, Madeleine. *Thomas Wolfe: The Discovery of a Genius.* 1981. Thomas Wolfe Soc. 1/350. 4to. 12 p. wrp. M. C4. $40.00

BOYD, Martin. *Nuns in Jeopardy.* nd. Harcourt. reprint of Sun ed. dj. B10. $5.50

BOYD, T. *Simon Girty: Wht Savage.* 1928. NY. 1st ed. 252 p. dj. VG. B3. $27.50

BOYD, William. *Brazzaville Beach.* 1990. London Ltd Ed. 1st ed. 1/150. sgn. tissue dj. EX. B13. $175.00

BOYD, William. *Good Man in Africa.* 1982. Morrow. UP of 1st Am ed. sgn. wrp. EX. K2. $150.00

BOYD, William. *Ice Cream War.* 1982. London. 1st ed. dj. EX. B13. $100.00

BOYD, William. *School Ties.* 1985. Morrow. ARC. K2. $45.00

BOYD & HARRIS. *Great Am Baseball Card Book.* 1975. Warner. P1. $2.00

BOYINGTON, Pappy. *Baa Baa Blk Sheep.* 1958. NY. sgn. dj. VG. B3. $35.00

BOYKIN, Edward. *Congress & the Civil War.* 1955. McBride. 352 p. dj. VG. S1. $9.50

BOYLAN, J.P. *Tales of the Nineties.* 1952. private print. 1st ed. 137 p. EX. B10. $8.00

BOYLE, E.V. *Garden of Pleasure.* 1895. London. Ils. 16mo. 220 p. full gr calf. T5. $22.50

BOYLE, Kay. *Short Stories.* 1929. Ed Narcisse. 1/20 on Arches. wrp. EX. H3. $400.00

BOYLE, Kay. *Short Stories.* 1929. Ed Narcisse. 1st ed. 1/15 on Japan. sgn. case. EX. H3. $1500.00

BOYLE, Kay. *Underground Woman.* 1975. Doubleday. dj. H3. $75.00

BOYLE, Kay. *Words That Must Somehow Be Said.* 1985. N Point Pr. sgn. dj. H3. $60.00

BOYLE, T.C. *Descent of Man.* 1st UK ed. dj. EX. T9. $70.00

BOYLE, T.C. *Descent of Man.* 1979. Boston. Little Brn. 1st ed. sgn. as issued. K2. $200.00

BOYLE, T.C. *Descent of Man.* 1979. Little Brn. 1st ed. dj. EX. K2. $150.00

BOYLE, T.C. *Descent of Man.* 1979. Little Brn. 1st ed. sgn. dj. B13. $225.00

BOYLE, T.C. *Descent of Man.* 1980. London. Gollancz. 1st Eng ed. dj. EX. B13. $65.00

BOYLE, T.C. *E Is E.* 1990. NY. ARC. K2. $40.00

BOYLE, T.C. *Greasy Lake & Other Stories.* 1985. Viking. dj. H3. $40.00

BOYLE, T.C. *Only the Dead Know Brooklyn.* 1985. Stoddard. 1st ed. dj. EX. P1. $15.00

BOYLE, T.C. *Water Music.* 1981. Little Brn. 1st ed. sgn. dj. EX. K2. $100.00

BRACE, Charles. *Hungary in 1851.* 1853. NY. 8vo. 419 p. $35.00

BRACK, Gene. *Mexico Views Manifest Destiny 1821-1846.* 1975. NM U. 1st ed. 194 p. dj. F2. $15.00

BRACKE, W. *Wheat Country.* 1950. NY. 1st ed. dj. VG. B3. $17.50

BRACKETT, Leigh. *Best of Leigh Brackett.* nd. Book Club. dj. EX. P1. $6.00

BRACKETT, Leigh. *Best of SF Book Club.* 1977. SF Book Club. 1st ed. dj. EX. R3. $8.50

BRACKETT, Leigh. *Long Tomorrow.* nd. Book Club. dj. xl. P1. $3.50

BRACKETT, Leigh. *Long Tomorrow.* 1955. Doubleday. 1st ed. dj. VG. R3. $85.00

BRACKETT, Leigh. *No Good From a Corpse.* 1944. Coward McCann. 1st ed. inscr. dj. EX. R3. $125.00

BRACKETT, Leigh. *Starmen.* 1952. Gnome. 1st ed. dj. EX. R3. $125.00

BRACKETT, Leigh. *Sword of Rhianon.* 1979. Gregg Pr. 1st Am ed. EX. R3. $45.00

BRADBURY, Edward P.; see Moorcock, Michael.

BRADBURY, Ray. *Anthem Sprinters & Other Antics.* 1963. NY. 1st ed. presentation. wrp. EX. T9. $40.00

BRADBURY, Ray. *Anthem Sprinters.* 1963. Dial. 1st ed. inscr. dj. R3. $300.00

BRADBURY, Ray. *Collected Works of Buck Rogers in the 25th Century.* 1969. Chelsea House. 1st ed. dj. EX. R3. $30.00

BRADBURY, Ray. *Dandelion Wine.* 1957. Doubleday. 1st ed. inscr. dj. EX. R3. $175.00

BRADBURY, Ray. *Dark Carnival.* 1947. Arkham House. 1st ed. dj. VG. R3. $400.00

BRADBURY, Ray. *Death Is a Lonely Business.* 1985. Knopf. 1st ed. inscr. dj. EX. R3. $50.00

BRADBURY, Ray. *Death Is a Lonely Business.* 1986. London. 1st ed. dj. VG. $25.00

BRADBURY, Ray. *Fahrenheit 451.* nd. Macmillan. 3rd/Photoplay ed. P1. $15.00

BRADBURY, Ray. *Fahrenheit 451.* 1953. Ballantine. 1st ed. sgn. VG. R3. $75.00

BRADBURY, Ray. *Fahrenheit 451.* 1954. London. 1st Eng ed. dj. VG. R3. $125.00

BRADBURY, Ray. *Fahrenheit 451.* 1982. Ltd Ed Club. Ils/sgn Mugnaini. aluminum bdg. slipcase. $140.00

BRADBURY, Ray. *Forever & the Earth.* 1984. Athens, OH. 1st ed. 1/300. sgn. 43 p. EX. T5. $75.00

BRADBURY, Ray. *Golden Apples of the Sun.* 1953. Doubleday. 1st ed. dj. EX. K2. $95.00

BRADBURY, Ray. *Golden Apples of the Sun.* 1953. Doubleday. 1st ed. inscr. dj. EX. R3. $250.00

BRADBURY, Ray. *Golden Apples of the Sun.* 1953. Garden City. dj. VG. C2. $75.00

BRADBURY, Ray. *Golden Apples of the Sun.* 1953. London. 1st ed. dj. VG. R3. $75.00

BRADBURY, Ray. *Haunted Computer.* 1981. Knopf. 1st ed. dj. EX. R3. $15.00

BRADBURY, Ray. *Ils Man.* 1951. Doubleday. 1st ed. dj. EX. B13. $175.00

BRADBURY, Ray. *Machineries of Joy.* 1964. Doubleday. 1st ed. inscr. dj. EX. R3. $250.00

BRADBURY, Ray. *Martian Chronicles.* nd. Book Club. dj. VG. P1. $5.00

BRADBURY, Ray. *Martian Chronicles.* 1950. Doubleday. 1st ed. inscr/sgn. dj. $150.00

BRADBURY, Ray. *Martian Chronicles.* 1974. Ltd Ed Club. Ils/sgn Joseph Mugnaini. sgn Bradbury. slipcase. $150.00

BRADBURY, Ray. *Medicine for Melancholy.* 1959. Doubleday. 1st ed. inscr. dj. EX. R3. $225.00

BRADBURY, Ray. *Mummies of Guanajuato.* 1978. Abrams. Ils Archie Lieberman. 1st ed. 4to. wrp. F2. $15.00

BRADBURY, Ray. *Old Ahab's Friend & Friend to Noah, Speaks His Piece.* 1971. Glendale. Roy Squires. pamphlet. 1/485. presentation. wrp. H3. $75.00

BRADBURY, Ray. *Pillar of Fire.* nd. printed for author. 74 p. orange covers. EX. R3. $200.00

BRADBURY, Ray. *R Is for Rocket.* nd. Doubleday. 2nd ed. dj. xl. P1. $7.50

BRADBURY, Ray. *Something Wicked This Way Comes.* 1962. Simon Schuster. 1st ed. inscr. dj. EX. R3. $250.00

BRADBURY, Ray. *Something Wicked This Way Comes.* 1963. London. 1st Eng ed. dj. EX. R3. $150.00

BRADBURY, Ray. *Switch on the Night.* 1955. Pantheon. 1st ed. dj. EX. R3. $400.00

BRADBURY, Ray. *Switch on the Night.* 1955. Pantheon. 1st ed. dj. VG. P1. $250.00

BRADBURY, Ray. *This Attic Where the Meadow Greens.* 1979. Lord John. Ltd ed. 1/300. sgn. H3. $60.00

BRADBURY, Ray. *Timeless Stories for Today & Tomorrow.* 1952. Bantam. 1st ed. inscr. wrp. EX. R3. $50.00

BRADBURY, Ray. *Toynbee Convector.* nd. Book Club. dj. VG. P1. $7.50

BRADBURY, Ray. *Toynbee Convector.* 1988. Knopf. 1st ed. dj. EX. F5. $17.50

BRADBURY, Ray. *Twice 22.* 1966. Doubleday. dj. xl. P1. $7.50

BRADBURY, Ray. *Twin Heiroglyphs That Swim the River.* 1978. Lord John. Ltd ed. 1/300. sgn. H3. $75.00

BRADBURY, Ray. *When Elephants Last in the Dooryard Bloomed.* 1973. Knopf. 1st ed. sgn. dj. EX. R3. $32.50

BRADBURY, Ray. *When Elephants Last in the Dooryard Bloomed.* 1975. Hart-Davis MacGibbon. 1st ed. dj. EX. P1. $35.00

BRADBURY, Ray. *Where Robot Mice & Robot Men.* 1977. Knopf. 1st ed. dj. EX. R3. $17.50

BRADBURY, Ray. *Wonderful Ice Cream Suit.* 1972. London. 1st Eng ed. dj. EX. R3. $40.00

BRADBURY, Ray. *Zen & the Art of Writing.* 1973. Capra. 1st ed. inscr. wrp. R3. $50.00

BRADBURY, Ray. *Zen & the Art of Writing.* 1973. Capra. 1st ed. 1/250. sgn. dj. K2. $85.00

BRADBURY, Ray. *Zen & the Art of Writing/The Joy of Writing.* 1973. Capra Chapbook Series. 1/250. sgn. H3. $50.00

BRADDON, George. *Microbe's Kiss.* 1940. Faber. 1st ed. dj. VG. P1. $30.00

BRADFIELD, Scott. *Dream of the Wolf.* 1990. Knopf. UP. wrp. EX. B13. $45.00

BRADFIELD, Scott. *Secret Life of Houses.* 1988. Unwin Hyman. 1st Eng ed. dj. RS. scarce. B13. $85.00

BRADFORD, Gamaliel. *Confederate Portraits.* 1914. Boston. 1st ed. 291 p. VG. B3. $45.00

BRADFORD, Gamaliel. *Daughters of Eve.* 1930. Boston. 1st ed. sgn. VG. $30.00

BRADFORD, R. *Old Man Adam & His Chillun.* 1928. NY. 1st ed. VG. B3. $22.50

BRADFORD, Roark. *John Henry.* 1939. Harper. 1st ed. dj. EX. H3. $100.00

BRADFORD, Ruth. *Journal & Letters of Ruth Bradford.* 1838. Hartford. Prospect Pr. Ltd 1st ed. 1/350. VG. $45.00

BRADLEY, Douglas. *Africa & Am: Curator's Choice.* 1986. Notre Dame. Snite Mus. wrp. F2. $15.00

BRADLEY, M.Z. *Catch Trap.* 1979. Ballantine. 1st ed. dj. VG. P1. $22.50

BRADLEY, M.Z. *City of Sorcery.* nd. Book Club. dj. VG. P1. $4.50

BRADLEY, M.Z. *Dark Satanic.* 1972. Berkley. 1st ed. wrp. EX. F5. $12.50

BRADLEY, M.Z. *Darkover Landfall.* nd. Book Club. dj. VG. P1. $4.50

BRADLEY, M.Z. *Firebrand.* 1987. Simon Schuster. 1st ed. dj. EX. P1. $19.95

BRADLEY, M.Z. *House Between the Worlds.* 1980. Doubleday. 1st ed. dj. EX. R3. $15.00

BRADLEY, M.Z. *Mists of Avalon.* nd. Book Club. dj. EX. C1. $9.00

BRADLEY, M.Z. *Mists of Avalon.* 1982. Knopf. 1st ed. dj. EX. R3. $50.00

BRADLEY, M.Z. *Mists of Avalon.* 1982. NY. not 1st ed. sgn. dj. VG. B3. $45.00

BRADLEY, M.Z. *Ruins of Isis.* 1978. Norfolk. Starblaze ed. VG. C1. $7.50

BRADLEY, M.Z. *Star of Danger.* 1979. Gregg Pr. 1st ed. no dj issued. EX. P1. $30.00

BRADLEY, M.Z. *Storm Queen!* 1979. Gregg Pr. 1st ed. no dj issued. EX. P1. $30.00

BRADLEY, M.Z. *Survey Ship.* 1980. Ace. 1st Trade ed. PB. M. C1. $12.00

BRADLEY, M.Z. *Sword of Aldones.* 1977. Gregg Pr. 1st ed. sgn. no dj issued. EX. P1. $60.00

BRADLEY, M.Z. *Winds of Darkover.* 1979. Gregg Pr. 1st ed. no dj issued. EX. P1. $30.00

BRADLEY, M.Z. *World Wreckers.* 1979. Gregg Pr. 1st ed. no dj issued. P1. $30.00

BRADLEY, Scully. *Walt Whitman's Backward Glances.* 1947. Phil. Ils 1st ed. sgn. EX. T1. $45.00

BRADLEY, V.A. *Book Collector's Handbook of Values.* 1976-1977. NY. Revised Enlarged ed. dj. VG. $75.00

BRADLEY, W.A.W. *Story of Flamenca.* 1923. 1st ed. 1/750. VG. C1. $12.00

BRADLEY, William. *Bradley's Atlas of the World.* 1888. Phil. Bradley. folio. 75 maps. half leather. C1. $425.00

BRADSHAW, Gillian. *Hawk of May.* 1980. Simon Schuster. 1st ed. dj. EX. F5. $20.00

BRADSHAW, Gillian. *In Winter's Shadow.* nd. Book Club. dj. M. C1. $7.50

BRADY, C.T. *Islands of Surprise.* 1915. McClurg. 1st ed. VG. R3. $25.00

BRADY, Leo. *Edge of Doom.* 1949. Dutton. 1st ed. dj. VG. P1. $12.50

BRADY, Ryder. *Instar.* 1976. Doubleday. ARC. dj. EX. F5. $23.00

BRADY, Ryder. *Instar.* 1976. Doubleday. dj. EX. P1. $12.50

BRAGDON, O.D. *Facts & Figures; or, Useful Information for People of LA.* 1872. New Orleans. orig wrp. VG. $80.00

BRAHM, Helen. *Rubens: Paintings...in Princess Gate Collection.* 1989. London. D4. $18.50

BRAHMS, Caryl. *Footnotes to the Ballet.* 1936. Holt. 1st ed. octavo. 268 p. VG. H3. $40.00

BRAINERD, Eleanor. *For Love of Mary Ellen.* 1912. Harper. Ils O'Neil. 1st ed. VG. $18.00

BRAINERD, George. *Maya Civilization.* 1954. SW Mus. 1st ed. 2 fld maps. 93 p. F2. $12.50

BRAINERD, George. *Maya Civilization.* 1963. SW Mus. Ils. 93 p. F2. $10.00

BRAITHWAITE, J.B. *Memoirs of Anna Braithwaite.* 1905. London. Headley. 12mo. 201 p. VG. V1. $12.00

BRAITHWAITE, J.B. *Memoirs of Joseph John Gurney: Study for Young Men...* 1902. London. Headley. 3rd ed. 12mo. 486 p. VG. V1. $27.00

BRAITHWAITE, Martha. *Memorials of Christine Majolier Alsop.* 1882. Phil. Longstreth. 12mo. 248 p. VG. V1. $12.00

BRAITHWAITE, W.C. *Spiritual Guidance in Quaker Experience.* 1909. London. Headley. 1st ed. 12mo. 85 p. VG. V1. $7.00

BRAITHWAITE, W.C. *2nd Period of Quakerism.* 1919. London. Macmillan. 8vo. 668 p. VG. V1. $30.00

BRAITHWAITE & HODGKIN. *Message & Mission of Quakerism.* 1912. Phil. Winston. 1st ed. 12mo. 115 p. VG. V1. $10.00

BRAMAH, Ernest. *Kai Lung Unrolls His Mat.* 1928. Doubleday. 1st ed. VG. R3. $20.00

BRAMAH, Ernest. *Kai Lung's Golden Hours.* 1923. Doran. decor brd. VG. P1. $45.00

BRAMAH, Ernest. *Mirror of Kong Ho.* 1930. NY. 1st ed. dj. VG. B3. $65.00

BRAMAH, Ernest. *Wallet of Kai Lung.* nd. Doran. decor brd. VG. P1. $45.00

BRAMHALL, Marion. *Murder Is Contagious.* 1949. Crime Club. 1st ed. dj. VG. P1. $15.00

BRAMHALL, Marion. *Tragedy in Bl.* 1945. Crime Club. 1st ed. VG. P1. $17.50

BRANCH, E.D. *Hunting of the Buffalo.* 1929. Appleton. VG. A5. $40.00

BRANCH, E.M. *Men Call Me Lucky.* 1985. Friends of Lib Soc Miami U. 1/500. wrp. C4. $25.00

BRANCH, H.P. *Poems.* 1895. Temperance Power. 1st ed? 8vo. VG. B10. $10.00

BRAND, Christianna. *3-Cornered Halo.* 1957. Michael Joseph. dj. VG. P1. $25.00

BRAND, Max. *Best W Stories Vol 2.* 1985. Dodd Mead. 1st ed. dj. VG. P1. $13.95

BRAND, Max. *Calling Dr Kildare.* 1944. Triangle. dj. VG. P1. $10.00

BRAND, Max. *Longhorn Feud.* 1941. Triangle. 4th print. dj. VG. P1. $14.95

BRAND, Max. *Lost Wolf.* 1986. Dodd Mead. 1st ed. dj. VG. P1. $14.95

BRAND, Max. *Smoking Land.* 1980. Capra. 1st ed. wrp. EX. F5. $10.00

BRAND, Max. *20 Notches.* 1932. Dodd Mead. 1st ed. dj. EX. B13. $125.00

BRANDAU, R.S. *Hist of Homes & Gardens of TN.* 1936. Nashville. 1st ed. 1/1500. EX. $175.00

BRANDEL, Marc. *Lizard's Tail.* 1979. Simon Schuster. 1st ed. dj. EX. F5. $25.00

BRANDEN & BRANDEN. *Who Is Ayn Rand: An Analysis of Novels.* 1962. Random House. 1st ed. dj. EX. C4. $40.00

BRANDON, Henry. *As We Are: Interviews in London Sunday Times.* 1961. 1st ed. dj. EX. $15.00

BRANDON, J.G. *Murder at the Yard.* 1936. Wright Brn. xl. P1. $8.50

BRANDON, Michael. *Nonce.* 1944. Coward McCann. 1st ed. dj. VG. R3. $75.00

BRANDON, William. *Dangerous Dead.* 1943. Dodd Mead. 1st ed. VG. P1. $20.00

BRANDT, E.N. *Saturday Evening Post Reader of W Stories.* 1960. Doubleday. Book Club ed. 358 p. dj. EX. B10. $3.75

BRANDT, Tom; see Dewey, Thomas B.

BRANIGAN, Keith. *Roman Villa in SW Eng.* 1977. 1st ed. EX. C1. $17.50

BRANLEY, Franklyn. *Lodestar Rocket Ship to Mars.* 1951. Crowell. 1st ed. dj. VG. P1. $17.50

BRANNON, W.T. *Yel Kid Weil.* 1948. Chicago. 1st ed. dj. VG. B3. $20.00

BRANSON, Ann. *Journal of Ann Branson.* 1892. Phil. WH Pile's Sons. 8vo. 408 p. G. V1. $12.00

BRANSON, L.H. *Magic of India.* 1973. Pinchpenny. reprint. 103 p. EX. J3. $7.00

BRASCH, R. *Mexico: Country of Contrasts.* 1967. Australia. Longman Gr. 1st ed. 4to. 210 p. dj. F2. $10.00

BRASHEAR, J.A. *John A Brashear: Autobiography of Man Who Loved Stars.* 1924. NY. Ils. 262 p. G. T5. $22.50

BRASSEY, Anne. *Last Voyage in the Sunbeam.* 1889. London. 1st ed. EX. $50.00

BRASSEY, Anne. *Voyage in the Sunbeam, Our Home on the Ocean for 11 Months.* 1885. Chicago. Belford Clarke. possible 1st ed. 488 p. F2. $20.00

BRAUDE, J.M. *Treasury of Wit & Humor.* 1965. Prentice Hall. 2nd ed. dj. VG. P1. $7.50

BRAUTIGAN, Richard. *Abortion: Hist Romance.* 1971. Taiwan piracy ed. sgn. dj. EX. K2. $200.00

BRAUTIGAN, Richard. *All Watched Over by Machines of Loving Grace.* 1967. Communication Co. 1st ed. variant yel wrp. K2. $350.00

BRAUTIGAN, Richard. *Confederate General From Big Sur.* 1964. Grove Pr. ARC. RS. EX. K2. $375.00

BRAUTIGAN, Richard. *Confederate General From Big Sur.* 1970. London. 1st Eng ed. as issued. K2. $75.00

BRAUTIGAN, Richard. *Confederate General From Big Sur.* 1970. London. Cape. UP of 1st Eng ed. laminated wrp. EX. K2. $150.00

BRAUTIGAN, Richard. *Dreaming of Babylon.* 1942. Delacorte. UP. wrp. EX. B13. $185.00

BRAUTIGAN, Richard. *Dreaming of Babylon.* 1942. Delacorte/Lawrence. ARC. RS. K2. $65.00

BRAUTIGAN, Richard. *Dreaming of Babylon: A Private Eye Novel 1942.* nd. np. Seymour Lawrence. unbound photocopied sheets. K2. $125.00

BRAUTIGAN, Richard. *Hawkline Monster.* 1974. NY. 1st Am ed. dj. EX. $16.50

BRAUTIGAN, Richard. *In Watermelon Sugar.* 1968. 4 Seasons. Writing 21. 1st ed. wrp. EX. K2. $45.00

BRAUTIGAN, Richard. *Pill Versus the Springhill Mine Disaster.* 1968. 4 Seasons. Writing 20. 1st ed. pictorial wrp. EX. K2. $55.00

BRAUTIGAN, Richard. *Rommel Drives on Deep Into Egypt.* 1970. Delacorte/Lawrence. 1st ed. dj. EX. K2. $65.00

BRAUTIGAN, Richard. *So the Wind Won't Blow It All Away.* 1982. Delacorte/Lawrence. UP. wrp. EX. K2. $50.00

BRAUTIGAN, Richard. *So the Wind Won't Blow It All Away.* 1982. NY. AP. as issued. K2. $45.00

BRAUTIGAN, Richard. *Sombero Fallout.* 1977. London. Cape. ARC. dj. EX. K2. $65.00

BRAUTIGAN, Richard. *Tokyo-MT Express.* 1979. Targ Ed. Ltd ed. 1/350. sgn. EX. B13. $125.00

BRAUTIGAN, Richard. *Tokyo-MT Express.* 1979. Targ Ed. Ltd ed. 1/350. sgn. glassine dj. EX. K2. $150.00

BRAUTIGAN, Richard. *Tokyo-MT Express.* 1980. Delacorte. 3rd ed. dj. VG. P1. $10.00

BRAUTIGAN, Richard. *Tokyo-MT Express.* 1980. Delacorte/Lawrence. 1st ed. sgn. vignettes. dj. EX. K2. $150.00

BRAUTIGAN, Richard. *Willard & His Bowling Trophies.* 1975. Simon Schuster. 1st ed. dj. EX. K2. $30.00

BRAUTIGAN, Richard. *Willard & His Bowling Trophies.* 1975. Simon Schuster. 1st ed. dj. VG. P1. $20.00

BRAUTIGAN, Richard. *4 New Poets.* 1957. Inferno. 1st ed. printed wht wrp. EX. scarce. K2. $350.00

BRAWLEY, Benjamin. *Negro Builders & Heros.* 1937. Chapel Hill. Ils 1st ed. 315 p. VG. B3. $45.00

BRAY, Mary. *Sea Trip in Clipper Ship Days.* 1920. Richard Badger. 1st ed. VG. $25.00

BRAYBROOKE, Neville. *TS Eliot: Symposium for His 70th Birthday.* 1958. Farrar Straus Cudahy. 1st ed. dj. EX. H3. $100.00

BRAYER, H.O. *Pikes Peak; or, Busted.* 1954. Evanston, IL. 1/750. A5. $40.00

BRAYSHAW, A.N. *Quakers: Their Story & Message.* 1927. Macmillan. 12mo. 301 p. G. V1. $12.00

BREADY, J.W. *This Freedom – Whence?* 1942. Am Tract Soc. Revised ed. sgn. EX. B10. $12.00

BRECHT, Bertolt. *Private Life of the Master Race.* 1944. New Directions. 1st ed. dj. EX. H3. $75.00

BRECHT, Bertolt. *Threepenny Opera.* 1982. NY. Ils/sgn Levine. 1st ed. 1/2000. 4to. 155 p. slipcase. T5. $75.00

BRECK, Joseph. *Flower Garden; or, Breck's Book of Flowers.* 1851. Boston. Jewett. Ils. $20.00

BREEN, Jon. *Murder CA Style.* 1987. St Martin. 1st ed. dj. EX. F5. $10.00

BREEN, Walter. *Darkover Concordance.* 1979. Pennyfarthing. EX. P1. $17.50

BREESKIN, Adelyn. *Graphic Art of Mary Cassatt.* 1967. Smithsonian. 1st ed. square 8vo. dj. EX. $50.00

BREIG, J.A. *Devil You Say (Letters From Hell)!* 1952. Bruce. dj. VG. P1. $6.75

BRENGLE, R.L. *Arthur King of Britain.* later print. stiff wrp. VG. C1. $25.00

BRENNAN, J.P. *Borders Just Beyond.* 1986. Donald Grant. 1st ed. 1/750. sgn. M. R3. $40.00

BRENNAN, J.P. *Chronicles of Lucius Leffing.* 1977. Donald Grant. 1st ed. dj. EX. P1. $15.00

BRENNAN, J.P. *Stories of Darkness & Dread.* 1973. Arkham House. 1st ed. M. R3. $6.00

BRENNAN, J.P. *60 Selected Poems.* 1985. New Establishment. 1st ed. wrp. M. R3. $15.00

BRENNAN, J.P. *60 Selected Poems.* 1985. New Establishment. 1st HrdCvr ed. 1/532. M. R3. $35.00

BRENNER, Anita. *Idols Behind Altars.* 1929. NY. 2nd ed. 359 p. dj. VG. B3. $40.00

BRENNER, Anita. *Wind That Swept Mexico.* 1943. NY. 1st ed. dj. VG. B3. $57.50

BRENNER, Anita. *Your Mexican Holiday.* 1935. Putnam. Ils Merida/Garduno. 7 fld maps. VG. F2. $10.00

BRENNER, Leah. *Artist Grows Up in Mexico.* 1953. Beechhurst Pr. 1st ed. 144 p. dj. F2. $20.00

BRENNER, Leah. *Boyhood of Diego Rivera.* 1964. Barnes. Ils Rivera. 1st ed. dj. F2. $15.00

BRERETON, F.S. *Great Aeroplane.* c 1911. London. 1st ed. EX. R3. $75.00

BRESLER, Fenton. *Mystery of Georges Simenon.* 1983. Beaufort. 1st ed. dj. EX. P1. $18.95

BRESLOW & BRESLOW. *Residential Works 1966-1977.* 1977. NY. 1st Am ed. VG. G1. $40.00

BRETNOR, Reginald. *Modern SF.* 1953. Coward McCann. 1st ed. dj. EX. $50.00

BRETT, John. *Who'd Hire Brett?* 1981. St Martin. 1st ed. dj. EX. F5. $14.00

BRETT, Leo. *Alien Ones.* 1969. Arcadia. dj. VG. P1. $10.00

BRETT, Simon. *Dead Giveaway.* nd. BOMC. dj. VG. P1. $7.50

BRETT, Simon. *Murder in the Title.* 1983. Gollancz. 1st ed. dj. EX. P1. $20.00

BRETT, Simon. *Shock to the System.* 1985. Scribner. 1st ed. dj. VG. P1. $13.95

BREVICK, Harold. *Books Were Opened.* 1947. Thule Pub. probably 1st ed. VG. B10. $4.00

BREWER, Gil. *Killer Is Loose.* March 1954. Gold Medal. 1st ed. wrp. EX. T9. $25.00

BREWER, Reginald. *Delightful Diverson.* 1935. reprint ed. dj. VG. K3. $20.00

BREWER, William. *Up & Down CA in 1860-1864.* 1949. CA U. 1st ed. dj. VG. $45.00

BREWER. *Art of Aviation.* 1910. London. 1st ed. 11 fld pls. 253 p. VG. C2. $195.00

BREWINGTON. *Chesapeake Bay Log Canoes.* 1937. Newport News. 1st ed. 113 p. VG. B3. $35.00

BREWSTER, David. *Letters on Natural Magic, Addressed to Sir Walter Scott.* 1834. London. John Murray. 352 p. G. J3. $48.00

BREWSTER, David. *Letters on Natural Magic, Addressed to Sir Walter Scott.* 1868. London. William Tegg. New ed. 424 p. VG. J3. $110.00

BREYER, Sigfried. *Battleships & Battle Cruisers 1905-1970.* 1973. Garden City. Ils. 480 p. dj. G. T5. $22.50

BREYTENBACH, Breyten. *True Confessions of an Albino Terrorist.* 1984. London. Faber. 1st Eng ed. dj. EX. K2. $30.00

BRICKER & TOOLEY. *Landmarks of Mapmaking: Ils Hist of Maps & Mapmakers.* 1976. Dorset. folio. M. A5. $40.00

BRIDGE, Ann. *And Then You Came.* 1949. NY. 1st Am ed. VG. C1. $16.50

BRIDGMAN, L.J. *Kewts: Their Trip in US.* 1902. Caldwell. VG. B7. $55.00

BRIFFAULT, Robert. *Europa: Days of Ignorance.* 1935. Scribner. 410 p. xl. VG. B10. $10.00

BRIFFAULT, Robert. *Mothers.* 1931. NY. 1st 1 Vol Abridged ed. dj. G. B3. $22.50

BRIGGS, K.M. *Personnel of Fairyland.* 1954. NY. Ils. dj. VG. C1. $19.50

BRIGGS, Philip. *Escape From Gravity.* 1955. Lutterworth. 1st ed. dj. VG. P1. $15.00

BRIGGS, Philip. *Silent Planet.* 1957. Lutterworth. dj. VG. P1. $15.00

BRIGHAM, C.S. *Paul Revere's Engravings.* 1954. Worcester, MA. 4to. dj. EX. $85.00

BRIGHAM, C.S. *Paul Revere's Engravings.* 1969. NY. Ils. 4to. dj. VG. T6. $95.00

BRIGHT, R. *Life & Death of Little Joe.* 1944. NY. 1st ed. dj. VG. B3. $20.00

BRIMM. *Seaplanes: Maneuvering, Maintaining, Operating.* 1937. NY. Ils. 140 p. EX. C2. $55.00

BRIN, David. *Postman.* 1985. Bantam. 1st ed. dj. EX. P1. $20.00

BRIN, David. *Uplift War.* 1987. Phantasia. 1st ed. M. R3. $75.00

BRINE, M.D. *Boys & Girls of Marble Dale.* 1888. NY. Ils. 304 p. G. T5. $25.00

BRINE, M.D. *Zigzag Journeys in the Orient: Adriatic to the Baltic.* 1882.Boston. pls. 320 p. G. T5. $22.50

BRINE, Mary. *Grandma's Memories.* 1888. Dutton. Ils Paget/others. VG. B7. $45.00

BRINGHAM, William. *Guatemala: Land of the Quetzal, a Sketch.* 1887. Scribner. 1st ed. 2 fld map. 453 p. F2. $65.00

BRINGS, Lawrence. *Master Stunt Book.* 1964. Minneapolis. 11th print. 431 p. dj. NM. J3. $5.00

BRINKLEY, Roberta. *Eng Poetry of 17th Century.* 1936. Norton. 1st ed. 584 p. VG. B10. $5.00

BRINTON, Anna. *Then & Now. Quaker Essays: Hist & Contemporary.* 1960. Phil. PA U. 12mo. 352 p. dj. VG. V1. $12.00

BRINTON, Crane. *Hist of W Morals.* 1959. 1st ed. dj. VG. C1. $6.50

BRINTON, Howard. *Byways in Quaker Hist.* 1944. Wallingford. Pendle Hill. 8vo. 246 p. dj. VG. V1. $10.00

BRINTON, Howard. *Children of Light: In Honor of Rufus M Jones.* 1938. Macmillan. 1st ed. 8vo. 416 p. VG. V1. $16.00

BRINTON, Howard. *Critique by Eternity.* 1943. Wallingford. Pendle Hill. 12mo. 56 p. VG. V1. $6.00

BRINTON, Howard. *Vocal Ministry & Quaker Worship.* 1928. Phil. 16mo. 32 p. dj. V1. $8.50

BRION, Marcel. *Bartolome de las Casas.* 1929. Dutton. 1st ed. 315 p. VG. F2. $30.00

BRISTOL, J.E. *Missing Ingredient: Unilateral Disarmament.* nd. Phil. Friends Peace Service. 12mo. 8 p. wrp. VG. V1. $5.00

BRISTOL, L.H. *Profits in Advance.* 1932. Harper. 1st ed. inscr. 180 p. VG. B10. $5.00

BRITLAND, David. *Angel Card Rise, Plus.* 1985. London. Martin Breese. 28 p. SftCvr. NM. J3. $6.00

BRITLAND, David. *Card Kenetics.* 1988. London. Martin Breese. 2nd ed. 42 p. SftCvr. M. J3. $8.00

BRITTEN, William. *Art Magic; or, Mundane...Super-Mundane Spiritism.* 1876. NY. Britten. Ils. 467 p. VG. $65.00

BROCK, Edwin. *I Never Saw It Lit.* 1974. Capra. Chapbook Series. 1/75. sgn. EX. K2. $20.00

BROCK, Lynn. *Murder at the Inn.* nd. Grosset Dunlap. VG. P1. $10.00

BROCK, Rose; see Hansen, Joseph.

BROCK. *Hist of Fireworks.* 1949. London. Ils 1st ed. dj. VG. C2. $50.00

BROCKBANK, Elizabeth. *Edward Burrough: A Wrestler for Truth, 1634-1662.* 1949. London. Bannisdale Pr. 1st ed. 12mo. 174 p. dj. V1. $15.00

BROCKETT, L.P. *Men of Our Day.* 1868. Zeigler McCurdy. 653 p. rebound. VG. S1. $30.00

BROCKWAY, Fenner. *Bermondsey Story: Life of Alfred Salter.* 1951. Allen Unwin. 1st print. 12mo. 246 p. dj. VG. V1. $8.00

BROD, Max. *Franz Kafka: A Biography of Max Brod.* 1960. Schocken. 2nd/Enlarged ed. dj. EX. C4. $20.00

BRODIE, F.M. *No Man Knows My Hist.* 1946. NY. 2nd ed. dj. VG. B3. $27.50

BROER, L.R. *Sanity Plea: Novels of Vonnegut.* 1989. UMI Research Pr. dj. EX. P1. $35.00

BROMFIELD, Louis. *Animals & Other People.* 1955. NY. 1st ed. dj. EX. $20.00

BROMFIELD, Louis. *Awake & Rehearse.* 1929. Stokes. Ltd ed. 1/500. sgn. dj. boxed. H3. $40.00

BROMFIELD, Louis. *From My Experience: Pleasures & Miseries of Life on Farm.* 1955. NY. Ils 1st ed. 355 p. dj. VG. T5. $12.50

BROMFIELD, Louis. *Modern Hero.* 1932. NY. 1st ed. 450 p. G. T5. $12.50

BROMFIELD, Louis. *Strange Case of Miss Annie Spragg.* 1928. NY. 1st ed. 314 p. G. T5. $15.00

BROMFIELD, Louis. *Until the Daybreak.* 1942. Harper. 1st ed. 325 p. dj. G. B10. $4.00

BROMWELL, W.J. *Hist of Immigration to the US 1819-1855.* 1856. NY. VG. $70.00

BRONOWSKI, Jacob. *Face of Violence.* 1955. Braziller. 1st ed. inscr. dj. EX. B13. $100.00

BRONTE, BRONTE, & BRONTE. *Life & Works of the Sisters Bronte.* c 1899. Harper. Thornfield/Ltd Deluxe ed. 1/150. 7 vols. H3. $850.00

BRONTE, BRONTE, & BRONTE. *Life & Works of the Sisters Bronte.* c 1899. Harper. Thornfield/Regular ed. 7 vols. octavo. VG. H3. $300.00

BRONTE, BRONTE, & BRONTE. *Novels of the Sisters Bronte.* 1907. Edinburgh. Grant. Thornton ed. 12 vols. octavo. VG. H3. $1500.00

BRONTE, BRONTE, & BRONTE. *Novels of the 3 Bronte Sisters.* 1922. London. Ils Dulac. 6 vols. 12mo. EX. A4. $275.00

BRONTE, BRONTE, & BRONTE. *Shakespeare Head Bronte.* 1931. Basil Blackwell. 1/1000. 11 vols. octavo. djs. H3. $2000.00

BRONTE, Charlotte. *Emma.* 1981. NY. Everest House. UP. later print. wrp. EX. B13. $45.00

BRONTE, Charlotte. *Jane Eyre.* 1848. Harper. 1st Am ed. orig wrp. VG. H3. $5000.00

BRONTE, Charlotte. *Jane Eyre. An Autobiography.* 1847. Smith Elder. 1st ed. 3 vols. orig cloth. slipcases. H3. $25000.00

BRONTE, Charlotte. *Villette.* 1853. Harper. 1st Am ed. orig wrp. EX. rare. H3. $2000.00

BRONTE, Charlotte. *Villette.* 1853. London. 1st ed. 3 vols. w/1st state pub catalog. H3. $1250.00

BROOKE, Avery. *Celtic Prayers.* 1981. 3rd print. stiff wrp. EX. C1. $6.50

BROOKE, Geoffrey. *Horse Sense & Horsemanship of Today.* 1926. NY. Ils. 179 p. VG. T5. $22.50

BROOKE, Ken. *Ken Brooke's Magic, the Unique Years.* 1980. Devon, Eng. Supreme Magic. 222 p. dj. NM. J3. $21.00

BROOKE, L.L. *Golden Goose Book.* nd. Warne. VG. B7. $52.00

BROOKE, Rupert. *Letters From Am.* 1916. Scribner. 1st Am ed. H3. $50.00

BROOKES, G.S. *Friend Anthony Benezet.* 1937. Phil. PA U. 1st ed. 8vo. 516 p. V1. $18.50

BROOKES, John. *Sm Garden.* 1978. NY. 1st ed. dj. EX. $35.00

BROOKNER, Anita. *Hotel du Lac.* 1984. London. 1st ed. dj. EX. $65.00

BROOKNER, Anita. *Providence.* 1982. London. Cape. 1st ed. dj. EX. B13. $75.00

BROOKS, Alfred. *Blazing AK Trails.* 1953. AK U. Ils dj. EX. A6. $45.00

BROOKS, Charles. *Frightful Plays!* 1922. Ils Flory. 1st Am ed. VG. C1. $5.00

BROOKS, Charles. *Hints to Pilgrims.* 1921. Yale. 1st Am ed. VG. C1. $7.00

BROOKS, Charles. *Prologue.* 1931. Ils Flory. 1st Am ed. VG. C1. $7.00

BROOKS, Charles. *Roads to the N.* 1928. NY. 1st Am ed. VG. C1. $6.50

BROOKS, Charles. *Roundabout to Canterbury.* 1926. Harcourt Brace. 1st Am ed. VG. C1. $7.50

BROOKS, Charles. *There's Pippins & Cheese To Come.* 1917. 1st ed. VG. C1. $7.50

BROOKS, Gwendolyn. *Bronzeville Boys & Girls.* 1956. Harper Row. 1st ed. dj. EX. B13. $250.00

BROOKS, Gwendolyn. *In the Mecca.* 1968. NY. 1st ed. sgn. dj. EX. T9. $55.00

BROOKS, Gwendolyn. *To Disembark.* 1981. Chicago. 3rd World Pr. later print. inscr. wrp. EX. B13. $35.00

BROOKS, J.G. *Social Unrest: Studies in Labor & Socialist Movements.* 1903. Macmillan. 1st ed. 8vo. 394 p. EX. R4. $30.00

BROOKS, Joe. *Lg Trout for the W Fly Fisherman.* 1970. S Brunswick. 1st ed. dj. EX. C2. $55.00

BROOKS, Juanita. *Mt Meadows Massacre.* 1966. Norman. Ils. 316 p. dj. A5. $30.00

BROOKS, Noah. *1st Across the Continent.* 1904. Scribner. $75.00

BROOKS, Phillips. *Easter Angels.* c 1920s? Nister/Dutton. stiff wrp. B10. $6.50

BROOKS, R.M. *38th NCB Saga.* nd. np. Ils. 155 p. G. T5. $65.00

BROOKS, S.W. *Garden With a House Attached.* 1904. Boston. Badger. 1st ed. 8vo. 118 p. gr bdg. G. B10. $8.50

BROOKS, Terry. *Magic Kingdom for Sale: Sold.* nd. np. 1st Am ed. VG. C1. $7.50

BROOKS, Terry. *Sword of Shannara.* 1977. Random House. ARC. wrp. VG. R3. $35.00

BROOKS, V.W. *Flowering of New Eng.* 1941. Ltd Ed Club. Ils/sgn RJ Holden. 1/1500. sgn. slipcase. C4. $50.00

BROOKS, V.W. *Sir Hans Sloane: Great Collector & His Circle.* 1954. London. 1st ed. dj. VG. C2. $25.00

BROOKS, V.W. *World of WA Irving.* 1944. Dutton Book Club. 387 p. VG. B10. $3.75

BROOKS & WARREN. *Understanding Fiction.* 1943. Appleton. 9th print. sgn Brooks. dj. EX. B13. $50.00

BROSMAN, John. *Future Tense.* 1978. St Martin. 1st ed. dj. EX. R3. $25.00

BROSSARD, Chandler. *Inside World of Adolph Hitler.* 1966. Gold Medal 1744. Ils. RS. EX. B4. $25.00

BROSSARD, Chandler. *1st Time.* 1957. Pyramid 260. 1st PB ed. B4. $4.00

BROTHERS GRIMM. *Complete Fairy Tales.* 1981. Avenel. facsimile of c 1800s 1st ed. EX. C1. $5.00

BROTHERS GRIMM. *Deutsche Sagen.* 1816. Berlin. VG. $400.00

BROTHERS GRIMM. *Fairy Tales of the Brothers Grimm.* 1909. London. 1st Trade ed. 40 pls. VG. H3. $750.00

BROTHERS GRIMM. *German Popular Stories.* 1823-1826. London. 1st Eng ed. 1st issue. 2 vols. Zaehnsdorf bdg. H3. $8500.00

BROTHERSTON, Gordon. *Image of the New World.* 1979. Thames Hudson. 1st ed. 324 p. dj. F2 $20.00

BROTHERWELL, Don. *Science in Archaeology.* 1963. Basic Books. 1st ed. 95 pls. 595 p. F2. $12.50

BROUGH, R.B. *Life of Sir John Falstaff.* 1858. London. Ils Cruikshank. rebound. A4. $225.00

BROUGHTON, Jack. *Thud Ridge.* 1969. Phil. 1st ed. dj. G. T5. $12.50

BROUSSAIS, F.J.V. *Treatise on Physiology Applied to Pathology...* 1826. Phil. full leather. G. $100.00

BROUSSEAU, Kate. *Mongolism.* 1928. Williams Wilkins. 1st ed. lg 8vo. 210 p. EX. $25.00

BROWN, A.B. *Democratic Leadership.* 1938. Allen Unwin. 1st ed. wrp. G. V1. $8.00

BROWN, A.C. *Dismal Swamp Canal.* 1946. Am Neptune Inc. 1st ed. 65 p. wrp. G. B3. $25.00

BROWN, A.C. *Study in Origins of Arthurian Romance.* 1968. Haskel House. reprint of 1903 ed. M. C1. $24.00

BROWN, A.C. *Wild Bill Donovan, the Last Hero.* 1982. Times. 1st ed. dj. EX. P1. $24.95

BROWN, A.J. *Hist of Newton Co, MS From 1834-1894.* 1984. Jackson, MS. 1st ed. 472 p. $160.00

BROWN, Adna. *From VT to Damascus, Returning by Way of...Constantinople.* 1895. Boston. Ellis. Ils. 8vo. 212 p. scarce. $75.00

BROWN, Alexander. *Galvanized Yankees.* 1963. IL U. 243 p. dj. A5. $40.00

BROWN, Alice. *Paradise.* 1905. Houghton Mifflin. 1st ed. 388 p. VG. B10. $6.00

BROWN, Bob. *Complete Book of Cheese.* 1955. Gramercy. 1st ed. 314 p. VG. B10. $3.50

BROWN, Bob. *1450-1950.* 1929. Blk Sun. 1st ed. 1/150. wrp. boxed. EX. H3. $850.00

BROWN, Carnaby. *Sm Change.* 1958. Roy. VG. P1. $7.50

BROWN, Charles. *Journal & Letters of Capt Charles W Brn.* 1935. np. 1st ed. 110 p. stiff wrp. VG. $20.00

BROWN, D.S. *Lynchburg's Pioneer Quakers & Their Meeting House.* 1936. Lynchburg. Bell. 12mo. 180 p. dj. VG. V1. $12.50

BROWN, E.V. *Quaker Aspects of Truth.* nd. London. Swarthmore. 12mo. 156 p. VG. V1. $8.00

BROWN, Edward. *Wadsworth Memorial.* 1875. Wadsworth. 232 p. VG. T5. $75.00

BROWN, F.C. *Letters & Lettering.* 1921. Boston. Ils. 214 p. G. T5. $22.50

BROWN, F.D. *Tales of Old Eddyville.* 1966. Eddyville, IA. 1st ed. sgn. VG. $17.50

BROWN, F.M. *Am's Yesterday.* 1937. Lippincott. 1st ed. 319 p. F2. $20.00

BROWN, Forman. *Sm Wonder.* 1980. Scarcrow. presentation. gilt teal bdg. dj. EX. H3. $45.00

BROWN, Fredric. *And the Gods Laughed.* 1987. Phantasia. Ltd ed. 1/475. sgn. M. R3. $125.00

BROWN, Fredric. *And the Gods Laughed.* 1987. Phantasia. 1st ed. dj. EX. P1. $35.00

BROWN, Fredric. *Angels & Spaceships.* 1954. Dutton. 1st ed. P1. $40.00

BROWN, Fredric. *Before She Kills.* 1984. Dennis McMillan. 1st ed. 1/350. sgn Nolan. M. R3. $65.00

BROWN, Fredric. *Best of Fredric Brn.* nd. Book Club. dj. VG. P1. $7.50

BROWN, Fredric. *Brother Monster.* 1987. Dennis McMillan. 1st ed. 1/400. sgn Altschuler. M. R3. $50.00

BROWN, Fredric. *Case of the Dancing Sandwiches.* 1985. Dennis McMillan. 1st ed. 1/400. sgn Block. M. R3. $55.00

BROWN, Fredric. *Far Cry.* 1951. Dutton. 1st ed. dj. VG. P1. $90.00

BROWN, Fredric. *Freak Show Murders.* 1985. Dennis McMillan. 1st ed. 1/350. sgn Lupoff. M. R3. $50.00

BROWN, Fredric. *Gibbering Night.* 1991. Macmillan. dj. EX. P1. $35.00

BROWN, Fredric. *Happy Ending.* 1990. Macmillan. 1st ed. 1/450. dj. EX. P1. $35.00

BROWN, Fredric. *Homicide Sanitarium.* 1985. Dennis McMillan. 1st ed. wrp. M. R3. $10.00

BROWN, Fredric. *Lights in the Sky Are Stars.* nd. SF Book Club. dj. EX. R3. $12.50

BROWN, Fredric. *Madman's Holiday.* 1985. Dennis McMillan. 1st ed. 1/350. sgn Baird. M. R3. $65.00

BROWN, Fredric. *Martians Go Home.* nd. SF Book Club. dj. EX. R3. $12.50

BROWN, Fredric. *Mrs Murphy's Underpants.* 1963. Dutton. 1st ed. xl. P1. $50.00

BROWN, Fredric. *Murderers.* 1961. Dutton. 1st ed. dj. EX. C4. $75.00

BROWN, Fredric. *Night of the Jabberwock.* 1950. Dutton. 1st ed. dj. EX. R3. $150.00

BROWN, Fredric. *Nightmare in Darkness.* 1987. Dennis McMillan. 1st ed. 1/425. sgn Linn Brn. M. R3. $50.00

BROWN, Fredric. *Office.* 1958. Dutton. 1st ed. dj. VG. P1. $250.00

BROWN, Fredric. *Office.* 1958. Dutton. 1st ed. dj. xl. P1. $100.00

BROWN, Fredric. *Office.* 1987. Dennis McMillan. 1st ed. 1/425. sgn Philip Jose Farmer. M. R3. $55.00

BROWN, Fredric. *Office.* 1987. Macmillan. 1st ed. dj. EX. P1. $45.00

BROWN, Fredric. *Paradox Lost.* 1973. Random House. 1st ed. dj. EX. R3. $40.00

BROWN, Fredric. *Paradox Lost.* 1973. Random House. 1st ed. dj. xl. P1. $20.00

BROWN, Fredric. *Pardon My Ghoulish Laughter.* 1986. Dennis McMillan. 1st ed. 1/400. sgn Donald Westlake. M. R3. $55.00

BROWN, Fredric. *Pardon My Ghoulish Laughter.* 1986. Macmillan. dj. EX. P1. $30.00

BROWN, Fredric. *Red Is the Hue of Hell.* 1986. Dennis McMillan. 1st ed. 1/400. sgn Walt Sheldon. M. R3. $50.00

BROWN, Fredric. *Screaming Mimi.* nd. Book Club. dj. VG. P1. $5.00

BROWN, Fredric. *Screaming Mimi.* 1949. NY. Correct 1st ed. dj. EX. T9. $85.00

BROWN, Fredric. *Selling Death Short.* 1988. Dennis McMillan. 1st ed. 1/450. sgn Francis Nevins. M. R3. $50.00

BROWN, Fredric. *Sex Life on Planet Mars.* 1986. Dennis McMillan. 1st ed. 1/400. sgn Willeford. M. R3. $55.00

BROWN, Fredric. *Space on My Hands.* 1951. Shasta. 1st ed. sgn. dj. EX. R3. $225.00

BROWN, Fredric. *Water Walker.* 1990. Macmillan. 1st ed. dj. P1. $35.00

BROWN, Fredric. *What Mad Universe.* nd. Book Club. dj. VG. P1. $7.50

BROWN, Fredric. *What Mad Universe.* 1949. Dutton. 1st ed. dj. EX. R3. $175.00

BROWN, Fredric. *What Man Universe.* 1978. Pennyfarthing. dj. EX. R3. $30.00

BROWN, Fredric. *Whispering Death.* 1989. Dennis McMillan. 1st ed. 1/450. M. R3. $50.00

BROWN, Fredric. *Who Was That Blond.* 1988. Dennis McMillan. 1st ed. 1/450. sgn Alan Nourse. M. R3. $50.00

BROWN, Fredric. *3-Corpse Parlay.* 1988. Dennis McMillan. 1st ed. 1/450. sgn Max Collins. M. R3. $50.00

BROWN, Fredric. *30 Corpses Every Thursday.* 1986. Macmillan. 1/375. sgn Gualt. dj. EX. P1. $30.00

BROWN, Fredric. *30 Corpses Every Thursday.* 1986. Macmillan. 1st ed. 1/375. sgn Gault. M. R3. $50.00

BROWN, Fredric. *5-Day Nightmare.* 1962. Dutton. 1st ed. dj. EX. F5. $25.00

BROWN, G.M. *Ponce De Leon Land & FL War Record.* 1902. St Augustine. sgn. 180 p. orig wrp. VG. $45.00

BROWN, G.W. *Reminiscences of Gov RJ Walker With True Story Rescue of KS.* 1902. Rockford, IL. Ils. 204 p. VG. B3. $50.00

BROWN, Harry. *End of a Decade.* 1940. New Directions. dj. VG. B4. $20.00

BROWN, James. *Autobiography.* 1915. Cuyahoga Falls. 52 p. journal bdg. G. T5. $15.00

BROWN, L.K. *Account of Meetings...Within the Baltimore Yearly Meeting.* 1875. Phil. T Ellwood Zell. 16mo. 64 p. lacks map. V1. $12.00

BROWN, Larry. *Big Bad Love.* 1990. Algonquin Books. UP. wrp. EX. C4. $60.00

BROWN, M.M. *Study of John D Rockefeller: Wealthiest Man in the World.* 1905. Cleveland. 1st ed. EX. $25.00

BROWN, Mary. *Unlikely Ones.* nd. Book Club. dj. VG. P1. $4.50

BROWN, Mary. *Unlikely Ones.* 1986. McGraw Hill. 1st ed. dj. EX. P1. $15.95

BROWN, Paul. *Insignia of the Services.* 1941. NY. Ils. G. T5. $8.50

BROWN, Percy. *Am Martyrs to Science Through the Roentgen Rays.* 1936. Springfield. Ils 1st ed. 276 p. VG. T5. $22.50

BROWN, R.G. *Waters of Centaurus.* 1970. Doubleday. 1st ed. dj. EX. R3. $30.00

BROWN, Rosellen. *Some Deaths in the Delta & Other Poems.* 1970. MA U. 1st ed. sgn. dj. EX. scarce. T9. $55.00

BROWN, Slater. *Spaceward Bound.* 1955. Prentice Hall. VG. P1. $15.00

BROWN, T.A. *Hist of the Am Stage.* 1870. NY. Dick/Fitzgerald. 1st ed. octavo. 421 p. VG. H3. $200.00

BROWN, Thurlow. *Minnie Herman...* 1854. Auburn, NY. Miller. 472 p. G. B10. $12.00

BROWN, Wenzell. *Dark Drums.* 1950. Appleton Century Crofts. dj. EX. P1. $15.00

BROWN, Wenzell. *Murder Seeks an Agent.* 1947. Arcadia House. 1st ed. dj. VG. F5. $20.00

BROWN, William R. *Horse of the Desert.* 1947. NY. Ils. 218 p. dj. VG. B3. $85.00

BROWN & BROWN. *Cookout Book.* 1961. Ward Richie. apparent 1st ed. 144 p. VG. B10. $4.50

BROWN & LEACH. *Help Wanted! Experiences...Quaker Conscientious Objectors.* 1940. Phil. 3rd ed. 12mo. SftCvr. VG. V1. $8.00

BROWN & REYNOLDS. *SF Carnival.* 1953. Shasta. 1st ed. dj. EX. R3. $50.00

BROWN & TUCKER. *James Brn: The Godfather of Soul.* 1986. Macmillan. 1st ed. octavo. 336 p. dj. VG. H3. $25.00

BROWN. *Chicago Wht Sox.* 1952. NY. 1st ed. sgn. photos. 248 p. VG. $30.00

BROWNE, C.W. *Santa Claus Visit.* nd. (1905) Chicago. Donohue. Santa Claus Series. 76 p. VG. $50.00

BROWNE, G.A. *Hazard.* 1973. Arbor House. dj. VG. P1. $12.50

BROWNE, Howard. *Paper Gun.* 1985. Macmillan. dj. EX. P1. $35.00

BROWNE, Howard. *Paper Gun.* 1985. Macmillan. 1st ed. 1/350. sgn. M. R3. $50.00

BROWNE, Thomas. *Religio Medici.* 1939. Ltd Ed Club. printed/sgn JH Nash. slipcase. EX. C4. $65.00

BROWNE, Thomas. *Works.* 1928. London. Faber Gwyer. 1/210. sgn. 6 vols. TEG. H3. $400.00

BROWNE & AUSTIN. *Who's Who on the Stage.* 1906. NY. Brn/Austin. 1st ed. lg octavo. 232 p. VG. H3. $200.00

BROWNE & DE ROY KOCH. *Who's Who on the Stage 1908.* 1908. NY. Dodge. octavo. 467 p. VG. H3. $125.00

BROWNE & DOLE. *New Am & the Far E.* 1910. Boston. 9 vols. AEG. EX. A6. $95.00

BROWNING, E.B. *Lady Geraldine's Courtship.* 1876. Miller Pub. Ils Hennessy. VG. B10. $12.00

BROWNING, E.B. *Sonnets From the Portuguese.* 1936. NY. Ils Pogany. 1st ed. TEG. EX. $40.00

BROWNING, E.B. *Sonnets From the Portuguese.* 1948. Ltd Ed Club. Ils/sgn Valenti Angelo. 1/1500. slipcase. C4. $50.00

BROWNING, E.B. *Sonnets From the Portuguese.* 1962. London. 1st ed. boxed. EX. $45.00

BROWNING, Robert. *Complete Works.* 1910. NY. Fred De Fau. 1/100. 12 vols. octavo. VG. H3. $1500.00

BROWNING, Robert. *Parleyings With Certain People.* 1887. London. 1st ed. VG. $20.00

BROWNING, Robert. *Pied Piper of Hamelin.* nd. (c 1903) London/NY. Ils Payne. VG. $60.00

BROWNING, Robert. *Pied Piper of Hamelin.* 1910. Rand McNally. Ils Hope Dunlap. VG. B7. $55.00

BROWNING, Robert. *Poetical Works.* 1888-1894. London. 17 vols. EX. $100.00

BROWNING, Robert. *Ring & the Book.* 1949. Ltd Ed Club. Ils/sgn Carl Schultheiss. 4to. 2 vols. slipcase. $60.00

BROWNING, Robert. *Works.* 1912. London. Elder. Centenary ed. 1/500. 10 vols. octavo. H3. $1000.00

BROWNLOW, Kevin. *Parades Gone By.* 1968. NY. 1st Am ed. dj. ES. EX. $70.00

BROWNLOW, W.G. *Sketches of Rise, Progress, & Decline of Secession.* 1862. Phil. 1st ed. 12mo. 458 p. G. G4. $37.00

BROXON, M.D. *Too Long a Sacrifice.* nd. Book Club. dj. VG. P1. $4.50

BROXON, M.D. *Too Long a Sacrifice.* 1984. Bluejay. PB. VG. C1. $4.50

BRUACHAC, Joseph. *Return of the Sun: Native Am Tales From the NE Woodlands.* 1989. Freedom, CA. Crossing Pr. 1st ed. dj. EX. B13. $45.00

BRUCCOLI, M.J. *Reconquest of Mexico.* 1974. Vanguard. 1st ed. 253 p. dj. F2. $15.00

BRUCCOLI, M.J. *Ross Macdonald.* 1984. San Diego. 1st ed. dj. EX. T9. $25.00

BRUCCOLI, M.J. *Scott Fitzgerald: Descriptive Bibliography.* 1972. Pittsburgh. 1st ed. EX. G1. $40.00

BRUCE, Edward. *Art in Federal Buildings.* 1936. WA. Ils. 309 p. T5. $145.00

BRUCE, Robert. *Lacandon Dream Symbolism.* 1979. Mexico. Ltd ed. 1/1000. 2 vols in 1. 363 p. F2. $40.00

BRUCE. *Hist of Milwaukee.* 1922. Chicago. Ils. 3 vols. VG A6. $75.00

BRUCHAC, Joseph. *For the Child To Be Born.* 1974. Cold Mt. 1/150. sgn. EX. K2. $45.00

BRUCHAC, Joseph. *Road to Blk Mt.* 1976. Thorp Springs. 1st ed. wrp. EX. K2. $50.00

BRUEHLER & BRUEHLER. *Orig Prints.* 1931. Cleveland. Ils. G. T5. $45.00

BRUETTE, William. *Am Duck, Goose, & Brant Shooting.* 1929. NY. 1st ed. VG. G1. $22.00

BRUETTE, William. *Training the Hound.* 1908. Chicago. 1st ed. 219 p. VG. B3. $20.00

BRUHN-TILKE. *Pictorial Hist of Costume.* 1965. NY. Praeger. sm folio. dj. slipcase. EX. $45.00

BRUKOWSKI, Charles. *At Terror St & Agony Way.* 1968. Blk Sparrow. 1st ed. 1/800. wrp. EX. K2. $85.00

BRUNDAGE, B.C. *Lord of Cuzco.* 1967. Norman. 1st ed. 458 p. dj. F2. $25.00

BRUNDAGE, Frances. *Adventures of Jack.* 1921. Rochester. Ils. sm folio. 14 p. wrp. VG. T1. $40.00

BRUNER, GOODNOW, & AUSTIN. *Study of Thinking.* 1956. Wiley. 1st ed. dj. EX. $15.00

BRUNHOUSE, Robert. *Pursuit of the Ancient Maya.* 1975. Albuquerque. 1st ed. 252 p. dj. F2. $25.00

BRUNNER, Bernard. *Face of Night.* 1967. Frederick Fell. 1st ed. dj. xl. $5.00

BRUNNER, John. *Devil's Work.* 1970. Norton. 1st ed. dj. EX. R3. $45.00

BRUNNER, John. *Devil's Work.* 1970. Norton. 1st ed. dj. xl. P1. $20.00

BRUNNER, John. *From This Day Forward.* 1972. Doubleday. 1st ed. dj. xl. P1. $5.00

BRUNNER, John. *Plague on Both Your Causes.* 1969. Hodder Stoughton. 1st ed. dj. xl. P1. $7.50

BRUNNER, John. *Players at the Game of People.* nd. Book Club. dj. EX. P1. $4.50

BRUNNER, John. *Quicksand.* nd. Book Club. dj. VG. P1. $4.50

BRUNNER, John. *Sheep Look Up.* 1972. Harper Row. 1st ed. dj. EX. R3. $35.00

BRUNNER, John. *Sheep Look Up.* 1972. Harper Row. 1st ed. dj. xl. P1. $6.00

BRUNNER, John. *Shockwave Rider.* nd. Book Club. dj. VG. P1. $4.50

BRUNNER, John. *Stand on Zanzibar.* 1968. Doubleday. 1st ed. VG. R3. $35.00

BRUNNER, John. *Stone That Never Came Down.* nd. Book Club. dj. VG. P1. $4.50

BRUNNER, John. *Stone That Never Came Down.* 1976. New Eng Lib. VG. P1. $7.50

BRUNNER, John. *Times Without Number.* 1983. 1st Am ed. sgn. PB. EX. C1. $6.50

BRUNNER, John. *Total Eclipse.* nd. Book Club. dj. EX. P1. $4.50

BRUNNER, John. *Total Eclipse.* 1974. Doubleday. 1st ed. dj. EX. R3. $15.00

BRUNNER, John. *Wrong End of Time.* 1971. Doubleday. 1st ed. dj. EX. R3. $27.50

BRUNO, Harry. *Wings Over Am.* 1944. Halcyon. 1st ed. 4to. $10.00

BRUNSWIK, Egon. *Experimentelle Psychologie in Demonstrationen.* 1935. Verlag. 1st ed. tall 8vo. 166 p. VG. B10. $6.50

BRUSH, Katherine. *Young Man of Manhattan.* 1930. Farrar. not 1st ed. 325 p. VG. B10. $3.50

BRUSSEL, I.R. *Anglo-Am 1st Eds 1826-1900 E to W.* 1935. London. xl. G. T6. $90.00

BRUSSOF, Valery. *Republic of the S Cross.* 1918. London. 1st ed. VG. R3. $35.00

BRYAN, Anthony. *Politics of the Porfiriato: Research Review.* 1973. Bloomington, IN. 35 p. wrp. F2. $7.50

BRYAN, Christopher. *Night of the Wolf.* 1983. Harper Row. 1st ed. dj. EX. F5. $17.00

BRYAN, Christopher. *Night of the Wolf.* 1983. Harper Row. 1st ed. dj. VG. P1. $15.00

BRYAN, J.A. *OH Register.* 1835. Columbus. 128 p. T5. $125.00

BRYAN, M.E. *Her Husband's Ghost.* c 1900. Westbrook. wrp. G. R3. $20.00

BRYAN, Michael. *Biographical & Critical Dictionary of Painters & Engravers.* 1816. London. 2 vols. rebound. $125.00

BRYANT, Billy. *Children of Old Man River.* 1936. NY. 1st ed. sgn. dj. VG. B3. $37.50

BRYANT, Edward. *Among the Dead.* 1973. Macmillan. 1st ed. dj. VG. P1. $22.50

BRYANT, Edward. *Cinnabar.* 1976. Macmillan. 1st ed. dj. EX. R3. $15.00

BRYANT, G.E. *Chelsea Porcelain Toys.* 1925. London. 1/600. sgn. EX. $300.00

BRYANT, Marguerite. *Heights.* 1924. Duffield. EX. P1. $7.50

BRYANT, Paul. *Bear.* 1974. Boston. 1st ed. dj. EX. B3. $17.50

BRYANT, W.C. *Letters of a Traveler.* 1850. NY. 12mo. 442 p. xl. G4. $24.00

BRYANT, W.C. *Poems.* 1947. Ltd Ed Club. Ils/sgn Thomas Nason. full leather. slipcase. VG. $75.00

BRYANT. *Logging.* 1914. NY. 1st ed. VG. C2. $35.00

BRZEZINSKI, Zbigniew. *Power & Principle: Memoirs...1977-1981.* 1983. Farrar. 1st ed. 587 p. dj. NM. B10. $6.00

BUCHAN, John. *Castle Gay.* 1934. Hodder Stoughton. 7th print. VG. P1. $15.00

BUCHAN, John. *Far Islands & Other Tales of Fantasy.* 1984. Donald Grant. dj. EX. P1. $17.00

BUCHAN, John. *Free Fishers.* 1936. Hodder Stoughton. 8th ed. dj. VG. P1. $20.00

BUCHAN, John. *Island of Sheep.* 1938. Hodder Stoughton. 7th ed. dj. VG. P1. $20.00

BUCHAN, John. *John Buchan by His Wife & Friends.* 1947. Hodder Stoughton. VG. P1. $20.00

BUCHAN, John. *Memory Hold the Door.* nd. BOMC. P1. $10.00

BUCHAN, John. *Nelson's Hist of the War Vol 21.* 1918. Thomas Nelson. dj. VG. P1. $16.50

BUCHAN, John. *Path of the King.* nd. Nelson. dj. VG. P1. $17.50

BUCHAN, John. *Prester John.* 1910. Doran. 1st A ed. 272 p. VG. B10. $15.00

BUCHAN, John. *Prester John.* 1936. London. dj. EX. R3. $17.50

BUCHAN, John. *Witchwood.* 1927. Houghton Mifflin. 1st ed. VG. R3. $20.00

BUCHAN, John. *3 Hostages.* nd. Grosset Dunlap. VG. P1. $10.00

BUCHAN, Perdita. *Called Away.* 1980. Atlantic. 1st ed. dj. EX. F5. $13.00

BUCHANAN, A.R. *Navy's Air War.* 1946. NY. Ils. 432 p. scarce. T5. $65.00

BUCHNER, Alexander. *Folk Music Instruments.* 1972. Crown. folio. 292 p. dj. VG. H3. $60.00

BUCK, C.N. *Memoirs of Charles N Buck...1791-1841.* 1941. Walnut House. 1st ed. VG. B10. $16.25

BUCK, C.W. *Under the Sun.* 1902. Sheltman. 1st ed. EX. R3. $17.50

BUCK, Frank. *Wild Cargo.* 1932. NY. Ils 1st ed. 8vo. gilt bdg. VG. T1. $25.00

BUCK, K.M. *Wayland-Dietrich Saga.* 1924-1929. Ils Goodman. 8 vols. VG. T6. $250.00

BUCK, Pearl. *All Men Are Brothers.* 1948. Ltd Ed Cub. Ils/sgn Miguel Covarrubias. 4to. 2 vols. VG. $135.00

BUCKINGHAM, Geoffrey. *It's Easier Than You Think.* 1952. London. Clarke. 1st ed. sgn. 191 p. dj. EX. J3. $36.00

BUCKINGHAM, Nash. *Flood Lines: Tales of Shooting & Fishing.* 1938. Derrydale. 1/1250. sgn. as issued. EX. $375.00

BUCKINGHAM, Nash. *Hallowed Years.* 1953. Harrisburg. 1st ed. dj. EX. $50.00

BUCKINGHAM, Nash. *Mark Right! Tales of Shooting & Fishing.* 1936. Derrydale. 1st ed. 1/1250. EX. $250.00

BUCKINGHAM, Nash. *Ole Miss'.* 1937. Derrydale. 1/1250. EX. $275.00

BUCKLE, Richard. *Modern Ballet Design.* 1955. London. Blk. 1st ed. octavo. 128 p. dj. VG. H3. $60.00

BUCKLEY, A.H. *Card Control.* 1946. Buckley. 1st ed. 219 p. NM. J3. $37.00

BUCKLEY, A.H. *Card Control.* 1946. Buckley. 1st ed. 219 p. VG. J3. $26.00

BUCKLEY, A.H. *Principles & Deceptions.* 1948. Buckley. 1st ed. 224 p. NM. J3. $30.00

BUCKLEY, J. *Travels in 3 Continents: Europe, Africa, & Asia.* 1895. Hunt Eaton. 8vo. 614 p. VG. $25.00

BUCKLEY, W.F. *Saving the Queen.* 1976. Doubleday. dj. VG. P1. $12.50

BUCKLEY, W.F. *Stained Glass.* nd. Book Club. dj. VG. P1. $4.50

BUCKLEY, William. *United Nations Journal: Delegate's Odyssey.* 1974. Putnam. dj. VG. $10.00

BUCKLEY & COOK. *Gems of Mental Magic.* 1947. Chicago. 1st ed. 132 p. EX. J3. $15.00

BUDAY, G. *Hist of the Christmas Card.* 1964. London. dj. EX. $20.00

BUDGE. *Nile: Notes for Travelers in Egypt.* 1905. London/Cairo. 9th ed. 808 p. VG. $80.00

BUDRYS, Algis. *Man of Earth.* 1958. Ballantine. 1st ed. wrp. EX. R3. $25.00

BUDRYS, Algis. *Michaelmas.* 1977. Berkley. 1st ed. dj. EX. R3. $15.00

BUEGELEISEN, Sally. *Into the Wind: Story of Max Conrad.* 1973. NY. 1st ed. inscr by Conrad. dj. VG. T5. $12.50

BUEL, J.W. *Heroes of the Dark Continent.* 1890. Phil. Ils. 576 p. T5. $25.00

BUGLIOSI, Vincent. *Till Death Us Do Part.* 1978. Norton. 1st ed. dj. EX. $18.00

BUIJTENHUIJS, Robert. *Mau Mau: 20 Years After, Myth & Survivors.* 1973. The Hague. 170 p. wrp. VG. T5. $19.50

BUKOWSKI, Charles. *Hollywood.* 1989. Blk Sparrow. 1st ed. 1/500. sgn. acetate dj. EX. K2. $50.00

BUKOWSKI, Charles. *Mockingbird Wish Me Luck.* 1972. Los Angeles. 1st Trade ed. presentation. wrp. EX. T9. $60.00

BULAU, Alwin. *Footprints of Assurance.* 1953. Macmillan. 1st ed. 4to. dj. EX. $40.00

BULLA, Clyde. *Sword in the Tree.* 2nd print. xl. C1.$12.00

BULLEN, F.T. *Cruise of the Cachalot*. 1899. Appleton. Ils. VG. T1. $35.00

BULLINS, Ed. *5 Plays*. 1969. Bobbs Merrill. 1st ed. dj. EX. H3/K2. $45.00

BULLIVANT, C.H. *Home Fun: Conjuring, Ventriloquism, Theatrical...* ca 1910. Nelson. 8vo. 459 p. VG. $28.00

BULLIVANT, C.H. *Home Fun: Conjuring, Ventriloquism, Theatrical...* 1910. Dodge. xl. G. J3. $2.00

BULLOCH, J.D. *Secret Service of the Confederate States in Europe*. 1959. Yoseloff. 460 p. VG. S1. $7.00

BULLOCK, Barbara. *Wynn Bullock*. 1971. Scrimshaw. 4to. dj. EX. $30.00

BULLOCK, Charles. *Home Words for the Heart & Hearth*. 1879. London. Hand/Heart Pub. Ils Weir/Barnes. B10. $6.00

BULLOCK, Helen. *Hist of Harrison Co*. 1961. Cadiz Public Lib. inscr. 48 p. wrp. T5. $12.50

BULLRICH, Francisco. *New Directions in Latin Am Architecture*. 1969. Braziller. 1st ed. 4to. 128 p. dj. F2. $20.00

BULMER, Kenneth. *Insane City*. 1978. Severn House. 1st ed. dj. VG. P1. $17.50

BULMER, Kenneth. *New Writings in SF 28*. 1976. Sidwick Jackson. 1st ed. dj. xl. P1. $5.00

BULMER, Kenneth. *Roller Coaster World*. 1978. Severn House. dj. EX. P1. $20.00

BULMER, Kenneth. *Shark N*. 1979. Severn House. dj. VG. P1. $15.00

BULWER-LYTTON, Edward. *Last Days of Pompeii*. nd. Hurst. decor brd. VG. P1. $10.00

BULWER-LYTTON, Edward. *Last Days of Pompeii*. 1956. Ltd Ed Club. Ils/sgn Kurt Craemer. 4to. slipcase. VG. $50.00

BULWER-LYTTON, Edward. *Last of the Barons*. nd. Collins. VG. P1. $10.00

BULWER-LYTTON, Edward. *Novels & Romances*. 1897. Little Brn. 18 vols. octavo. TEG. EX. H3. $750.00

BULWER-LYTTON, Edward. *Rienzi, Last of the Roman Tribunes*. 1904. Scribner. VG. P1. $10.00

BULWER-LYTTON, Edward. *Works*. c1890. Boston. Estes. Ed des Amateurs. 1/74. 32 vols. octavo. H3. $2500.00

BULWER-LYTTON, Edward. *Works*. 1877-1883. London. Routledge. 39 vols. sm octavo. H3. $2500.00

BULWER-LYTTON, Edward. *Works*. 1891. Boston. Estes. Warwick ed. 1/100. 31 vols. Postethwaite bdg. H3. $2000.00

BULYCHEV, Kirell. *Half a Life*. 1977. Macmillan. 1st ed. dj. RS. EX. R3. $17.50

BUNCE, Frank. *So Young a Body*. nd. Inner Sanctum Mystery. 216 p. dj. VG. B10. $3.00

BUNNELL, L.H. *Winona & Its Environs on the MS in Ancient & Modern Days*. 1897. Winona, MN. 1st ed. EX. $65.00

BUNYAN, John. *Pilgrim's Progress*. 1929. Macmillan. Ils HJ Ford. VG. B7. $50.00

BUNYAN, John. *Pilgrim's Progress*. 1941. Ltd Ed Club. Ils William Blake. 1/1500. slipcase. EX. C4. $100.00

BURBANK, Addison. *Guatemala Profile*. 1939. Coward McCann. 1st ed. 296 p. F2. $10.00

BURBANK, Addison. *Mexican Frieze*. 1940. Coward McCann. 1st ed. 268 p. dj. F2. $17.50

BURBANK. *Photographic Negative*. 1988. NY. Scovill Series. VG. C2. $65.00

BURD, V.A. *Ruskin Family Letters...1801-1843*. 1973. NY. Ils. 2 vols. EX. T1. $38.00

BURGER, Eugene. *Audience Involvement...a Lecture*. nd. Excelsior. 27 p. SftCvr. NM. J3. $5.00

BURGER, Eugene. *Eugene Burger on Matt Schulien's Fablous Card Discoveries*. 1983. Arlington Heights. 1st ed. 45 p. SftCvr. NM. J3. $8.00

BURGER, Eugene. *Intimate Power*. 1983. Arlington Heights. 1st ed. SftCvr. NM. J3. $12.00

BURGER, Eugene. *Performance of Close-Up Magic*. 1987. Kaufman/Greenberg. 1st ed. sgn. dj. NM. J3. $28.00

BURGESS, Anthony. *Any Old Iron*. 1989. 1st Am ed. dj. M. C1. $18.00

BURGESS, Anthony. *Clockwork Orange*. 1963. Norton. 1st Am ed. dj. EX. H3. $100.00

BURGESS, Anthony. *Enderby's Dark Lady*. 1984. McGraw Hill. 1st ed. dj. VG. P1. $14.95

BURGESS, Anthony. *Ernest Hemingway & His World*. 1978. Thomas Hudson. 1st ed. dj. EX. H3. $50.00

BURGESS, Anthony. *Little Wilson & Big God*. 1988. Penguin. VG. P1. $12.50

BURGESS, Anthony. *Long Trip to Teatime*. 1976. Dempsey Squires. dj. EX. P1. $15.00

BURGESS, Anthony. *Napoleon Symphony*. 1974. Knopf. 1st ed. dj. xl. P1. $5.00

BURGESS, Anthony. *Piano Players*. 1986. Arbor House. 1st ed. dj. VG. P1. $16.95

BURGESS, Anthony. *Piano Players*. 1986. Hutchinson. dj. EX. P1. $17.50

BURGESS, Anthony. *Shakespeare*. 1970. Knopf. 1st Am ed. 48 clr pls. dj. EX. C4. $35.00

BURGESS, Anthony. *Tremor of Intent*. 1966. NY. 1st ed. dj. VG. $20.00

BURGESS, Anthony. *1985*. 1978. Little Brn. 1st ed. dj. VG. P1. $17.50

BURGESS, Gelett. *Romance of the Commonplace*. 1902. Elder Shepard. EX. $75.00

BURGESS, Gelett. *Vivette*. 1897. Boston. Copeland Day. 1st ed. EX. B13. $85.00

BURGESS, George. *Journal of a Surveying Trip Into W PA...in 1795*. 1965. Mt Pleasant, MI. Cumming. 1st ed. VG. $20.00

BURGESS, T.W. *Adventures of Blacky the Crow*. nd. Grosset Dunlap. dj. VG. P1. $8.00

BURGESS, T.W. *Adventures of Buster Bear*. 1943. McClelland Stewart. VG. P1. $7.50

BURGESS, T.W. *Adventures of Jimmy Skunk*. 1927. Little Brn. decor brd. VG. P1. $12.50

BURGESS, T.W. *Adventures of Longlegs the Heron*. nd. Grosset Dunlap. VG. P1. $5.00

BURGESS, T.W. *Adventures of Old Mr Toad*. 1927. Little Brn. VG. B10. $4.25

BURGESS, T.W. *Adventures of Old Mr Toad*. 1964. Little Brn. decor brd. VG. P1. $4.00

BURGESS, T.W. *Adventures of Sammy Jay*. 1964. Little Brn. decor brd. VG. P1. $7.50

BURGESS, T.W. *Adventures of Unc' Billy Possum*. 1917. Little Brn. decor brd. VG. P1. $12.50

BURGESS, T.W. *Billy Mink*. nd. Grosset Dunlap. VG. P1. $7.50

BURGESS, T.W. *Bird Book for Children*. 1930. Boston. B3. $27.50

BURGESS, T.W. *Book of Nature Lore*. nd. Bonanza. 3rd ed. dj. VG. P1. $12.50

BURGESS, T.W. *Book of Nature Lore*. 1965. Bonanza. reprint. dj. B10. $5.00

BURGESS, T.W. *Burgess Animal Book for Children*. 1929. Boston. Ils Fuertes. later print. VG. $20.00

BURGESS, T.W. *Flower Book for Children*. 1923. Boston. 1st ed. VG. B3. $20.00

BURGESS, T.W. *Jerry Muskrat at Home.* nd. Grosset Dunlap. VG. P1. $10.00

BURGESS, T.W. *Mother W Wind Where Stories.* c 1941. np. Ils Cady. 16mo. 244 p. VG. $25.00

BURGESS, T.W. *Seashore Book for Children.* 1929. Boston. 1st ed. EX. B3. $65.00

BURGIN, Richard. *Conversations With Jorge Luis Borges.* 1969. Holt Rinehart Winston. ARC. sgn Borges. dj. RS. w/photo. EX. B13. $200.00

BURGUNDER, H.B. *Magic of Flight.* 1966. NY. Ils. 80 p. T5. $19.50

BURKE, A.D. *Driven to Murder.* 1986. Atlantic Monthly. 1st ed. dj. EX. P1. $15.95

BURKE, Bernard. *Genealogical & Heraldic Dictionary...British Empire.* 1858. London. sm 4to. 1190 p. G4. $44.00

BURKE, E. *On Conciliation With the Colonies.* 1975. Ltd Ed Club. Ils/sgn Lynd Ward. slipcase. VG. $40.00

BURKE, Edmund. *Reflections on the Revolution in France.* 1790. London. 1st ed. 1st issue. EX. $350.00

BURKE, Edmund. *Works.* 1826. London. Rivington. 16 vols. octavo. H3. $500.00

BURKE, Edmund. *Works.* 1854. London. 6 vols. sm octavo. H3. $200.00

BURKE, Edmund. *Writings & Speeches.* 1901. Little Brn. Beaconsfield ed. 1/1000. 12 vols. TEG. H3. $450.00

BURKE, Edmund. *3 Memorials on French Affairs...1791-1793.* 1797. London. 8vo. $95.00

BURKE, J.F. *Crazy Woman Blues.* 1978. Dutton. 1st ed. inscr. dj. NM. T9. $25.00

BURKE, J.L. *Blk Cherry Blues.* 1988. Boston. ARC. sgn. K2. $65.00

BURKE, J.L. *Blk Cherry Blues.* 1989. Little Brn. 1st ed. dj. EX. F5. $16.00

BURKE, J.L. *Blk Cherry Blues.* 1989. Little Brn. 1st ed. sgn. dj. EX. T9. $35.00

BURKE, J.L. *Heaven's Prisoners.* 1988. Holt. 1st ed. dj. EX. B13. $45.00

BURKE, J.L. *Lay Down My Sword & Shield.* 1971. Crowell. UP. sgn. VG. K2. $950.00

BURKE, J.L. *Morning for Flamingos.* 1990. Little Brn. 1st ed. sgn. dj. M. C4. $45.00

BURKE, J.L. *Neon Rain.* 1987. Holt. inscr/sgn. dj. EX. K2. $85.00

BURKE, J.L. *Neon Rain.* 1987. NY. 1st ed. sgn. dj. EX. T9. $65.00

BURKE, J.L. *To the Bright & Shining Sun.* 1970. Scribner. dj. EX. K2. $350.00

BURKE, John. *Angry Silence: A Novel.* 1961. Hodder Stoughton. 1st ed. 8vo. dj. EX. R4. $30.00

BURKE, Jonathan. *Alien Landscapes.* 1955. Mus Pr. xl. P1. $10.00

BURKE, Richard. *Chinese Red.* 1942. Putnam. 1st ed. xl. P1. $7.50

BURKE, Richard. *Dead Take No Bows.* 1941. Houghton Mifflin. 1st ed. VG. P1. $30.00

BURKE, Richard. *Murder on High Heels.* 1940. Gateway. xl. G. P1. $10.00

BURKE, Thomas. *Limehouse Nights.* nd. Daily Express. dj. VG. P1. $9.25

BURKE, Thomas. *Wind & the Rain.* 1924. Doran. 1st ed. pictorial bdg. EX. F5. $20.00

BURKETT, Charles. *Farmers' Veterinarian.* 1909. Judd. Farm Life Series. 1st ed. 275 p. dj. EX. B10. $4.50

BURKS, A.J. *Blk Medicine.* 1966. Arkham House. 1st ed. dj. EX. R3. $35.00

BURLAND, C.A. *Ancient Maya.* 1967. London. Weidenfild. 1st ed. 112 p. dj. F2. $15.00

BURLAND, Cottie. *Montezuma.* 1973. Putnam. 1st ed. 269 p. dj. F2. $25.00

BURLAND, Harris. *Princess Thora.* 1978. Arno. EX. R3. $45.00

BURLEY, W.J. *Charles & Elizabeth.* 1981. Walker. 1st ed. dj. EX. P1. $12.50

BURLEY, W.J. *Wycliffe & the Schoolgirls.* 1976. Gollancz. dj. EX. P1. $15.00

BURLINGHAME, H.J. *Magician's Handbook, Tricks, & Secrets.* 1942. Wilcox Follett. 298 p. decor brd. J3. $15.00

BURLINGHAME, H.J. *Tricks & Secrets of Hermann the Great.* 1942. Chicago. 1st ed. wrp. VG. C2. $27.00

BURN, Gordon. *Somebody's Husband, Somebody's Son.* nd. Book Club. dj. VG. P1. $4.50

BURN, Richard. *Justice of the Peace & Parish Officer.* 1825. London. Cadell. 24th ed. 5 vols. VG. H3. $500.00

BURNAP, W.A. *What Happened During 1 Man's Lifetime 1840-1920.* 1923. Fergus Falls, MN. 1st ed. 461 p. VG. $80.00

BURNET, Dana. *Pool.* 1945. Knopf. 1st ed. 53 p. dj. EX. B10. $5.00

BURNETT, F.H. *Editha's Burglar.* Boston. Ils Sandham. 1st ed. 12mo. VG. A4. $50.00

BURNETT, F.H. *Little Lord Fauntleroy.* 1914. Scribner. Ils Reginald Birch. cream bdg. VG. C1. $8.50

BURNETT, F.H. *Little Pilgrim's Progress.* 1895. NY. 1st ed. VG. $30.00

BURNETT, F.H. *Lost Prince.* 1915. William Briggs. decor brd. VG. P1. $25.00

BURNETT, F.H. *Making of a Marchioness.* 1901. NY. 1st ed. VG. $17.50

BURNETT, F.H. *Sara Crewe; or, What Happened at Miss Munchins.* 1895. Scribner. VG. B7. $52.50

BURNETT, F.H. *Secret Garden.* 1962. Phil. Ils Tasha Tudor. gilt red bdg. VG. T1. $35.00

BURNETT, F.H. *1 I Knew the Best of All: Memory of Mind of a Child.* 1893. Scribner. sgn mounted on endpaper. H3. $250.00

BURNETT, Virgil. *Towers at the Edge of the World.* 1980. St Martin. 1st ed. dj. EX. P1. $15.00

BURNETT, W.R. *Asphalt Jungle.* 1949. Knopf. 1st ed. dj. VG. T9. $75.00

BURNETT, W.R. *Asphalt Jungle.* 1950. London. Macdonald. 1st UK ed. dj. w/photo. NM. T9. $70.00

BURNETT, W.R. *Conant.* 1961. Popular Giant G538. 1st/PB Orig ed. wrp. NM. T9. $35.00

BURNETT, W.R. *Dark Hazard.* 1933. Harper. 1st ed. VG. P1. $25.00

BURNETT, W.R. *Dark Hazard.* 1933. Harper. 1st ed. xl. P1. $10.00

BURNETT, W.R. *Goodbye, Chicago.* 1981. St Martin. 1st ed. dj. EX. T9. $15.00

BURNETT, W.R. *High Sierra.* 1940. Knopf. 1st ed. dj. NM. T9. $165.00

BURNETT, W.R. *Iron Man.* 1930. Lincoln Macveagh Dial. 1st ed. VG. P1. $30.00

BURNETT, W.R. *It's Always 4 O'Clock.* 1956. Random House. 1st ed. dj. EX. T9. $40.00

BURNETT, W.R. *Little Caesar.* 1944. Armed Services ed. EX. T9. $45.00

BURNETT, W.R. *Little Men, Big World.* 1951. NY. 1st ed. dj. VG. T9. $75.00

BURNETT, W.R. *Mi Amigo.* 1959. Knopf. 1st ed. xl. P1. $5.00

BURNETT, W.R. *Underdog.* 1957. Knopf. 1st ed. orange dj. EX. T9. $40.00

BURNETTE, Robert. *Tortured Am.* 1971. Prentice Hall. 1st ed. dj. VG. K2. $45.00

BURNHAM, Clara. *Flutterbye.* 1910. Boston. Ils 1st ed. gilt bdg. EX. $20.00

BURNHOUSE, Robert. *Frans Blom, Maya Explorer.* 1976. NM U. 1st ed. 291 p. F2. $20.00

BURNS, E.B. *Eadweard Muybridge in Guatemala.* 1986. Berkeley, CA. 1st ed. oblong 4to. 136 p. dj. F2. $45.00

BURNS, Fox. *Roving Outdoorsman.* nd. Terre Haute. 1st ed. inscr. dj. EX. $35.00

BURNS, Rex. *Angle of Attack.* 1979. Harper Row. 1st ed. dj. VG. P1. $15.00

BURNS, Robert. *Complete Poetical Works.* 1847. NY. 2nd Am ed. 12mo. T1. $35.00

BURNS, Robert. *Poems, Chiefly in Scottish Dialect.* 1797. Edinburgh. 1st ed. 1st issue. VG. H3. $750.00

BURNS, Robert. *Poems, Chiefly in Scottish Dialect.* 1878. London. 3rd ed. 1st ed w/Burns frontispiece. $300.00

BURNS, Robert. *Poetical Works.* nd. London. Collins. 8vo. AEG. VG. $25.00

BURNS, Robert. *Poetical Works.* 1958. London. Oxford. 8vo. AEG. EX. $35.00

BURNS, Robert. *Works.* 1800. Liverpool. Davies Creech. 1st Collected ed. 4 vols. H3. $750.00

BURNS, Tex; see L'Amour, Louis.

BURR, H.M. *Cave Boys.* 1923. Assn Pr. 1st ed. VG. R3. $15.00

BURR & HINTON. *Life of Gen Philip H Sheridan.* 1888. Providence. Ils 445 p. G. G4. $30.00

BURROUGH, Edward. *Memoir of the Life & Religious Labors.* 1890. Phil. Friends Bookstore. 16mo. 239 p. VG. V1. $12.50

BURROUGHS, E.R. *Apache Devil.* 1933. NY. Ils Studley Burroughs. dj. VG. B3. $70.00

BURROUGHS, E.R. *At the Earth's Core.* nd. Book Club. Photoplay ed. dj. VG. P1. $6.00

BURROUGHS, E.R. *At the Earth's Core.* 1922. Grosset Dunlap. clr Canon dj. VG. R3. $25.00

BURROUGHS, E.R. *At the Earth's Core.* 1922. McClurg. 1st ed. EX. B13. $350.00

BURROUGHS, E.R. *At the Earth's Core.* 1962. Canaveral. 1st ed. dj. VG. P1. $50.00

BURROUGHS, E.R. *Beasts of Tarzan.* Grosset Dunlap. WWII ed. clr Canon dj. VG. R3. $10.00

BURROUGHS, E.R. *Beasts of Tarzan.* nd. AL Burt. VG. P1. $10.00

BURROUGHS, E.R. *Beasts of Tarzan.* 1916. McClurg. clr Canon dj. VG. R3. $60.00

BURROUGHS, E.R. *Beasts of Tarzan.* 1917. AL Burt. clr Canon dj. VG. R3. $15.00

BURROUGHS, E.R. *Beasts of Tarzan.* 1937. Big Little Book. VG. P1. $75.00

BURROUGHS, E.R. *Beyond 30 & the Man-Eater.* 1957. SF/Fantasy. 1st ed. dj. EX. R3. $60.00

BURROUGHS, E.R. *Carson of Venus.* 1939. ERB Inc. 1st ed. dj. EX. R3. $350.00

BURROUGHS, E.R. *Carson of Venus.* 1963. Canaveral. 1st ed. dj. VG. P1. $60.00

BURROUGHS, E.R. *Cave Girl.* c 1920s. Grosset Dunlap. clr Canon dj. G. R3. $20.00

BURROUGHS, E.R. *Cave Girl.* c 1940s. Dell. wrp. VG. R3. $20.00

BURROUGHS, E.R. *Cave Girl.* 1925. McClurg. 1st ed. fair. P1. $25.00

BURROUGHS, E.R. *Cave Girl.* 1962. Canaveral. 1st ed. dj. VG. P1. $60.00

BURROUGHS, E.R. *Chessmen of Mars.* 1922. McClurg. 1st ed. VG. P1. $75.00

BURROUGHS, E.R. *Escape on Venus.* 1946. ERB Inc. 1st ed. dj. EX. R3. $150.00

BURROUGHS, E.R. *Escape on Venus.* 1946. ERB Inc. 1st ed. dj. VG. P1. $75.00

BURROUGHS, E.R. *Escape on Venus.* 1963. Canaveral. dj. VG. P1. $60.00

BURROUGHS, E.R. *Eternal Lover.* 1927. Grosset Dunlap. clr Canon dj. G. R3. $15.00

BURROUGHS, E.R. *Fighting Man of Mars.* 1948. ERB Inc. VG. P1. $15.00

BURROUGHS, E.R. *Fighting Man of Mars.* 1962. Canaveral. dj. xl. P1. $20.00

BURROUGHS, E.R. *Fighting Man of Mars.* 1962. Canaveral. 1st ed. 249 p. dj. EX. R4. $35.00

BURROUGHS, E.R. *Girl From Hollywood.* 1923. Macaulay. 1st ed. EX. P1. $200.00

BURROUGHS, E.R. *Girl From Hollywood.* 1923. Macauley. 3rd ed. VG. P1. $75.00

BURROUGHS, E.R. *Girl From Hollywood.* 1925. Macaulay. clr Canon dj. EX. R3. $75.00

BURROUGHS, E.R. *Gods of Mars.* 1919. Chicago. Ils Schoonover. 1st ed. 348 p. VG. T5. $125.00

BURROUGHS, E.R. *Gods of Mars.* 1920. Grosset Dunlap. gr bdg. clr Canon dj. VG. R3. $17.50

BURROUGHS, E.R. *Gods of Mars/Warlord of Mars.* nd. Book Club. dj. VG. P1. $5.00

BURROUGHS, E.R. *I Am a Barbarian.* 1967. ERB Inc. 1st ed. dj. EX. B3. $47.50

BURROUGHS, E.R. *John Carter of Mars.* 1964. Canaveral. 1st ed. dj. EX. F5. $80.00

BURROUGHS, E.R. *Jungle Girl.* 1933. London. 1st Eng ed. dj. EX. R3. $125.00

BURROUGHS, E.R. *Jungle Girl.* 1973. Tom Stacey. 1st ed. dj. EX. P1. $20.00

BURROUGHS, E.R. *Jungle Tales of Tarzan.* 1919. Chicago. Ils St John. 1st ed. 1st bdg. T5. $75.00

BURROUGHS, E.R. *Jungle Tales of Tarzan.* 1919. McClurg. clr Canon dj. VG. R3. $42.50

BURROUGHS, E.R. *Jungle Tales of Tarzan.* 1923. Grosset Dunlap. VG. P1. $25.00

BURROUGHS, E.R. *Jungle Tales of Tarzan.* 1949. Methuen. 14th ed. VG. P1. $12.50

BURROUGHS, E.R. *Lad & the Lion.* 1964. Canaveral. dj. VG. P1. $60.00

BURROUGHS, E.R. *Land of Terror.* 1944. ERB Inc. 1st ed. VG. R3. $100.00

BURROUGHS, E.R. *Land of Terror.* 1944. ERB Inc. 1st ed. dj. VG. $180.00

BURROUGHS, E.R. *Land of Terror.* 1963. Canaveral. 1st ed. dj. VG. P1. $50.00

BURROUGHS, E.R. *Land That Time Forgot.* 1925. Grosset Dunlap. clr Canon dj. EX. R3. $30.00

BURROUGHS, E.R. *Land That Time Forgot.* 1962. Canaveral. dj. VG. P1. $60.00

BURROUGHS, E.R. *LLana of Gathol.* 1948. ERB Inc. 1st ed. dj. EX. R3. $125.00

BURROUGHS, E.R. *Llana of Gathol.* 1948. ERB Inc. 1st ed. dj. VG. P1. $75.00

BURROUGHS, E.R. *Lost on Venus.* 1935. ERB Inc. 1st ed. dj. VG. R3. $375.00

BURROUGHS, E.R. *Lost on Venus.* 1940. ERB Inc. red bdg. clr Canon dj. EX. R3. $35.00

BURROUGHS, E.R. *Lost on Venus.* 1963. Canaveral. dj. VG. P1. $60.00

BURROUGHS, E.R. *Mad King.* 1927. Grosset Dunlap. clr Canon dj. EX. R3. $35.00

BURROUGHS, E.R. *Man-Eater.* 1974. Fantasy. 1st Separate ed. wrp. EX. R3. $15.00

BURROUGHS, E.R. *Mastermind of Mars.* 1928. Grosset. Ils St John. 312 p. red bdg. dj. VG. B10. $15.00

BURROUGHS, E.R. *Monster Men.* 1929. McClurg. 1st ed. VG. $60.00

BURROUGHS, E.R. *Monster Men.* 1962. Canaveral. dj. VG. P1. $50.00

BURROUGHS, E.R. *Moon Maid.* 1927. Grosset Dunlap. clr Canon dj. VG. R3. $25.00

BURROUGHS, E.R. *Moon Men.* 1962. Canaveral. dj. VG. P1. $50.00

BURROUGHS, E.R. *Mucker.* 1921. Grosset Dunlap. clr Canon dj. VG. R3. $25.00

BURROUGHS, E.R. *Mucker.* 1963. Canaveral. 1st ed. dj. VG. P1. $75.00

BURROUGHS, E.R. *Pellucidar.* nd. Grosset Dunlap. VG. P1. $11.00

BURROUGHS, E.R. *Pellucidar.* 1924. Grosset Dunlap. clr Canon dj. G. R3. $15.00

BURROUGHS, E.R. *Pellucidar.* 1935. Methuen. 3rd ed. VG. P1. $18.25

BURROUGHS, E.R. *Pellucidar.* 1962. Canaveral. 1st ed. dj. VG. P1. $50.00

BURROUGHS, E.R. *Pirates of Venus.* 1940. ERB Inc. red bdg. dj. EX. R3. $125.00

BURROUGHS, E.R. *Pirates of Venus.* 1962. Canaveral. dj. VG. P1. $60.00

BURROUGHS, E.R. *Princess of Mars & Fighting Man of Mars.* 1964. Dover. wrp. EX. R3. $7.50

BURROUGHS, E.R. *Princess of Mars.* 1970. Doubleday Book Club. 179 p. dj. VG. B10. $3.50

BURROUGHS, E.R. *Return of Tarzan.* 1916. AL Burt. dk gr bdg. clr Canon dj. VG. R3. $25.00

BURROUGHS, E.R. *Return of Tarzan.* 1927. Grosset Dunlap. clr Canon dj. EX. R3. $35.00

BURROUGHS, E.R. *Return of Tarzan.* 1927. Grosset Dunlap. VG. P1. $17.50

BURROUGHS, E.R. *Return of Tarzan.* 1940. Grosset Dunlap. VG. P1. $15.00

BURROUGHS, E.R. *Return of Tarzan.* 1967. Whitman. VG. P1. $10.00

BURROUGHS, E.R. *Savage Pellucidar.* 1963. Canaveral. 1st ed. dj. VG. P1. $75.00

BURROUGHS, E.R. *Son of Tarzan.* 1917. McClurg. 1st ed. clr Canon dj. VG. R3. $75.00

BURROUGHS, E.R. *Son of Tarzan.* 1918. AL Burt. clr Canon dj. VG. R3. $20.00

BURROUGHS, E.R. *Son of Tarzan.* 1940. Grosset Dunlap. VG. P1. $15.00

BURROUGHS, E.R. *Swords of Mars/ Synthetic Men.* 1974. Doubleday Book Club. 345 p. dj. VG. B10. $3.50

BURROUGHS, E.R. *Synthetic Men of Mars.* 1948. ERB Inc. clr Canon dj. VG. R3. $15.00

BURROUGHS, E.R. *Tales of 3 Planets.* 1964. Canaveral. 1st ed. dj. EX. P1. $75.00

BURROUGHS, E.R. *Tanar of Pellucidar.* 1931. Grosset Dunlap. dj. EX. R3. $75.00

BURROUGHS, E.R. *Tanar of Pellucidar.* 1962. Canaveral. dj. EX. P1. $50.00

BURROUGHS, E.R. *Tarzan, Lord of the Jungle.* 1929. Grosset Dunlap. clr Canon dj. G. R3. $10.00

BURROUGHS, E.R. *Tarzan, Lord of the Jungle.* 1929. Grosset Dunlap. VG. P1. $25.00

BURROUGHS, E.R. *Tarzan, Lord of the Jungle.* 1948. Grosset Dunlap. VG. P1. $7.00

BURROUGHS, E.R. *Tarzan & Journey of Terror.* 1950. Whitman. Ils. 16mo. VG. $15.00

BURROUGHS, E.R. *Tarzan & the Ant Men.* nd. Grosset Dunlap. VG. P1. $15.00

BURROUGHS, E.R. *Tarzan & the City of Gold.* 1935. Grosset Dunlap. J Allen St John dj. VG. F5. $40.00

BURROUGHS, E.R. *Tarzan & the City of Gold.* 1940. Grosset Dunlap. dj. EX. R3. $175.00

BURROUGHS, E.R. *Tarzan & the City of Gold.* 1940. Whitman. G. R3. $5.00

BURROUGHS, E.R. *Tarzan & the City of Gold.* 1966. Whitman. decor brd. EX. P1. $7.00

BURROUGHS, E.R. *Tarzan & the Forbidden City.* 1938. ERB Inc. 1st ed. dj. $175.00

BURROUGHS, E.R. *Tarzan & the Foreign Legion.* 1948. ERB Inc. 1st ed. dj. VG. R3. $50.00

BURROUGHS, E.R. *Tarzan & the Golden Lion.* nd. Grosset Dunlap. VG. P1. $15.00

BURROUGHS, E.R. *Tarzan & the Jewels of Opar.* nd. AL Burt. VG. P1. $11.50

BURROUGHS, E.R. *Tarzan & the Jewels of Opar.* nd. Grosset Dunlap. dj. EX. P1. $45.00

BURROUGHS, E.R. *Tarzan & the Jewels of Opar.* 1918. McClurg. 1st ed. clr Canon dj. VG. R3. $60.00

BURROUGHS, E.R. *Tarzan & the Jewels of Opar.* 1919. AL Burt. clr Canon dj. VG. R3. $17.50

BURROUGHS, E.R. *Tarzan & the Jewels of Opar.* 1919. McClurg. 2nd ed. dj. VG. P1. $90.00

BURROUGHS, E.R. *Tarzan & the Leopard Men.* 1935. ERB Inc. 1st ed. clr Canon dj. xl. G. R3. $20.00

BURROUGHS, E.R. *Tarzan & the Lion Man.* 1934. Grosset Dunlap. clr Canon dj. G. R3. $15.00

BURROUGHS, E.R. *Tarzan & the Lion Man.* 1940. ERB Inc. red bdg. clr Canon dj. EX. R3. $35.00

BURROUGHS, E.R. *Tarzan & the Lost Empire.* c 1940s. Dell. wrp. VG. R3. $22.50

BURROUGHS, E.R. *Tarzan & the Lost Empire.* 1929. Metropolitan Books. 1st ed. orange bdg. VG. $65.00

BURROUGHS, E.R. *Tarzan & the Lost Empire.* 1931. Grosset Dunlap. dj. VG. P1. $30.00

BURROUGHS, E.R. *Tarzan & the Lost Safari.* nd. Whitman. decor brd. VG. P1. $17.50

BURROUGHS, E.R. *Tarzan & the Lost Safari.* 1966. Whitman. 1st ed. EX. R3. $10.00

BURROUGHS, E.R. *Tarzan & the Madman.* 1964. Canaveral. 1st ed. dj. EX. R3. $100.00

BURROUGHS, E.R. *Tarzan & the Madman.* 1964. Canaveral. 1st ed. dj. VG. P1. $65.00

BURROUGHS, E.R. *Tarzan at the Earth's Core.* 1930. Metropolitan Books. 1st ed. clr Canon dj. G. R3. $50.00

BURROUGHS, E.R. *Tarzan at the Earth's Core.* 1930. Metropolitan Books. 1st ed. VG. B3. $115.00

BURROUGHS, E.R. *Tarzan of the Apes.* 1914. Chicago. McClure. 1st ed. G. B3. $400.00

BURROUGHS, E.R. *Tarzan of the Apes.* 1914. NY. 1st ed. gilt red bdg. B3. $300.00

BURROUGHS, E.R. *Tarzan of the Apes.* 1915. AL Burt. dj. EX. R3. $150.00

BURROUGHS, E.R. *Tarzan of the Apes.* 1964. Whitman. decor brd. VG. P1. $15.00

BURROUGHS, E.R. *Tarzan the Invincible.* 1948. ERB Inc. clr Canon dj. VG. R3. $10.00

BURROUGHS, E.R. *Tarzan the Terrible.* nd. Grosset Dunlap. VG. P1. $10.00

BURROUGHS, E.R. *Tarzan the Terrible.* 1921. McClurg. 1st ed. clr Canon dj. VG. R3. $75.00

BURROUGHS, E.R. *Tarzan the Terrible.* 1940. Grosset Dunlap. dj. EX. R3. $175.00

BURROUGHS, E.R. *Tarzan the Untamed.* 1920. McClurg. 1st ed. clr Canon dj. VG. R3. $60.00

BURROUGHS, E.R. *Tarzan the Untamed.* 1922. Grosset Dunlap. dj. VG. P1. $60.00

BURROUGHS, E.R. *Tarzan Triumphant.* 1940. ERB Inc. red bdg. clr Canon dj. VG. R3. $27.50

BURROUGHS, E.R. *Thuvia, Maid of Mars.* 1921. Grosset Dunlap. clr Canon dj. VG. R3. $25.00

BURROUGHS, E.R. *Thuvia, Maid of Mars.* 1921. Grosset Dunlap. VG. P1. $25.00

BURROUGHS, E.R. *War Chief.* 1927. McClurg. 1st ed. EX. B13. $325.00

BURROUGHS, E.R. *Warlord of Mars.* 1919. McClurg. 1st ed. 1st state. P1. $100.00

BURROUGHS, E.R. *Warlord of Mars.* 1919. McClurg. 1st ed. 8vo. 296 p. R4. $100.00

BURROUGHS, E.R. *Warlord of Mars.* 1920. Grosset Dunlap. G. R3. $10.00

BURROUGHS, E.R. *Warlord of Mars.* 1920. Grosset Dunlap. VG. P1. $25.00

BURROUGHS, John. *Accepting the Universe.* 1920. Houghton Mifflin. sgn. dj. EX. K2. $350.00

BURROUGHS, John. *In the Catskills.* 1910. Boston. 1st ed. VG. $25.00

BURROUGHS, John. *Squirrels & Other Fur-Bearers.* 1900. Houghton Mifflin. clr pls. VG. T3. $15.00

BURROUGHS, Stephen. *Memoirs.* 1811. Albany. 2 vols in 1. VG. scarce. G4. $59.00

BURROUGHS, W.S. *Alf's Smile.* 1973. Gottingen. Expanded Media Eds. 1/99. sgn. wrp. EX. K2. $125.00

BURROUGHS, W.S. *APO-33.* 1967. San Francisco. Beach Books. 1st ed. wrp. EX. scarce. B13. $100.00

BURROUGHS, W.S. *APO-33.* 1968. San Francisco. Beach Books. 2nd ed. 2nd print. EX. K2. $25.00

BURROUGHS, W.S. *Cities of the Red Night.* 1981. Holt Rinehart Winston. 1st ed. inscr. dj. EX. K2. $50.00

BURROUGHS, W.S. *Exterminator!* 1973. Viking. UP. wrp. EX. K2. $85.00

BURROUGHS, W.S. *Exterminator!* 1973. Viking. 1st ed. dj. xl. P1. $10.00

BURROUGHS, W.S. *Naked Lunch.* 1959. Grove Pr. 1st Am ed. dj. EX. C4. $75.00

BURROUGHS, W.S. *Naked Lunch.* 1964. London. Calder/Olympia. ARC of 1st ed. rare. K2. $350.00

BURROUGHS, W.S. *Nova Express.* 1964. Grove Pr. 1st Am ed. sgn. dj. EX. K2. $85.00

BURROUGHS, W.S. *Nova Express.* 1966. London. AP. sgn. K2. $185.00

BURROUGHS, W.S. *Place of Dead Roads.* 1984. NY. Ltd ed. 1/300. sgn. slipcase. EX. $145.00

BURROUGHS, W.S. *Place of Dead Roads.* 1984. NY. 1st ed. inscr. dj. EX. K2. $50.00

BURROUGHS, W.S. *Queer.* 1985. Viking. ARC of 1st ed. dj. EX. K2. $45.00

BURROUGHS, W.S. *Roosevelt After Inauguration.* 1964. NY. pamphlet. 1/500. sgn. K2. $150.00

BURROUGHS, W.S. *Soft Machine.* 1966. Grove Pr. ARC. dj. w/photo. EX. K2. $125.00

BURROUGHS, W.S. *Ticket That Exploded.* 1967. NY. 1st ed. dj. EX. $35.00

BURROUGHS, W.S. *W Lands.* 1987. Viking. 1st ed. inscr. dj. EX. K2. $50.00

BURROUGHS & GINSBERG. *Yage Letters.* 1966. City Lights. VG. B4. $5.00

BURROUGHS & GYSIN. *Exterminator.* 1960. San Francisco. 1st ed. 1/1000. wrp. EX. K2. $75.00

BURROWS, George. *On Disorders of the Cerebral Circulation...* 1848. Phil. Ils. 216 p. G. T5. $95.00

BURTIS, Thompson. *Flying Blk Birds.* nd. Grosset Dunlap. dj. VG. P1. $9.25

BURTIS, Thompson. *Wing for Wing.* nd. Grosset Dunlap. VG. P1. $7.50

BURTON, H.P. *Favorite Stories by Famous Writers.* 1932. NY. VG. $10.00

BURTON, Miles. *Hardway Diamonds Mystery.* 1930. Mystery League. 1st ed. VG. P1. $18.25

BURTON, Miles. *Return from the Dead.* 1959. Collins Crime Club. 1st ed. dj. xl. P1. $7.50

BURTON, Miles. *Secret of High Eldersham.* 1931. Mystery League. 1st ed. VG. P1. $18.25

BURTON, R.F. *Arabian Nights.* nd. Internat Collector Lib. 472 p. TEG. B10. $6.25

BURTON, R.F. *Book of 1000 Nights & a Night.* nd. private print. Burton Club. 16 vols. octavo. EX. H3. $200.00

BURTON, R.F. *Book of 1000 Nights & a Night.* 1934. Heritage. Ils Valenti Angelo. 6 vols in 3. slipcase. VG. T1. $45.00

BURTON, R.F. *City of the Saints & Across the Rocky Mts to CA.* 1862. Harper. 573 p. A5. $400.00

BURTON, R.F. *Kasidah of Haji Abdu el-Yezdi.* 1937. Ltd Ed Club. 1/2250. glassine dj. slipcase. EX. $65.00

BURTON, R.F. *Kasidah of Haji Abdu el-Yezdi.* 1937. Ltd Ed Club. Ils/sgn Valenti Angelo. 1/1500. slipcase. EX. C4. $100.00

BURTON, R.F. *Tales From Arabian Nights.* 1978. Avenel. 1st ed. 871 p. EX. B10. $5.00

BURTON, Richard. *Brodie the Devil Drives.* 1967. NY. 1st ed. dj. VG. B3. $22.50

BURTON, Richard. *Midsummer Memory.* 1910. Minneapolis. Brooks. Ltd ed. 1/500. sgn. H3. $75.00

BURTON, Warren. *District School As It Was.* 1838. NY. Revised ed. 156 p. rebacked. T5. $20.00

BUSBY, A.B. *2 Summers Among the Musquakies.* 1886. Vinton, IA. 1st ed. VG. K1. $450.00

BUSBY, F.M. *Cage of Man.* nd. Book Club. dj. VG. P1. $3.75

BUSBY, F.M. *Long View.* 1976. Berkley Putnam. dj. EX. P1. $17.50

BUSBY, Jeff. *Into the 4th Dimension...& Beyond.* 1980. Magic Inc. 2nd print. 17 p. NM. J3. $4.00

BUSBY, Jeff. *Larry Jennings Exclusive Release No 2.* 1977. Oakland, CA. 2nd ed. SftCvr. NM. J3. $4.00

BUSBY & HOLTHAM. *Main Line Kill.* 1968. Walker. 1st ed. dj. EX. F5. $14.00

BUSCH, F.X. *Prisoners at the Bar.* 1952. Indianapolis. 1st ed. dj. VG. B3. $15.00

BUSCH, Frederick. *Breathing Trouble & Other Stories.* 1973. Calder Boyars. 1st ed. dj. EX. K2. $65.00

BUSCH, Frederick. *Hawkes: A Guide to His Fictions.* 1973. Syracuse. 1st ed. dj. EX. K2. $85.00

BUSCH, Frederick. *I Wanted a Year Without Fall.* 1971. Calder Boyars. 1st ed. inscr/sgn. dj. EX. K2. $125.00

BUSCH, Frederick. *I Wanted a Year Without Fall.* 1971. London. 1st ed. dj. EX. scarce. T9. $90.00

BUSCH, Frederick. *Mutual Friend*. 1978. Harvester. 1st Eng ed. inscr. dj. EX. K2. $45.00

BUSCH, Wilhelm. *Max & Maurice: Story of 2 Rascals in 7 Pranks*. 1963. Munich. Ils. EX. $15.00

BUSER, H.J. *How To Pitch Real Curves*. 1924. Wichita. 1st ed. wrp. VG. K1. $30.00

BUSH, Charles. *Friends School in Wilmington (DE)*. 1948. Wilmington. 8vo. 129 p. dj. G. V1. $9.00

BUSH, Christopher. *Case of the Curious Client*. 1948. Macmillan. 1st ed. VG. P1. $15.00

BUSH, Christopher. *Case of the Running Man*. 1959. Macmillan. 1st ed. VG. P1. $12.50

BUSH, Christopher. *Case of the Russian Cross*. 1958. Macmillan. 1st ed. xl. P1. $5.00

BUSH, Christopher. *Case of the Silken Petticoat*. 1954. Macmillan. 2nd ed. dj. xl. P1. $20.00

BUSH, Christopher. *Case of the Tudor Queen*. 1938. Holt. 1st ed. dj. EX. F5. $25.00

BUSH, Christopher. *Dead Man Twice*. 1930. Crime Club. 1st ed. VG. P1. $20.00

BUSH, Christopher. *Perfect Murder Case*. 1933. Heinemann. 5th ed. VG. P1. $12.50

BUSH, George. *Theological Dictionary*. 1831. Phil. VG. A4. $30.00

BUSH, Vannevar. *Modern Arms & Free Men*. 1949. Book Club. dj. VG. B10. $3.50

BUSH-BROWN, James & Louise. *Am's Garden Book*. 1958. Scribner. Revised Enlarged ed. 752 p. dj. VG. B10. $9.25

BUSHNELL, Adelyn. *Strange Gift*. 1951. Coward McCann. 1st ed. dj. VG. F5. $15.00

BUSHNELL, G.H.S. *Peru*. nd. Praeger. 1st ed. 207 p. dj. F2. $25.00

BUSHNELL, G.H.S. *1st Am*. 1968. McGraw Hill. 1st ed. 144 p. dj. F2. $15.00

BUSHNELL & DIGBY. *Ancient Am Pottery*. 1955. London. Faber. 1st ed. 4to. dj. F2. $40.00

BUSLETT, O.A. *Det Femtende Regiment WI Frivillige*. 1894. Decorah, IA. 1st ed. VG. $125.00

BUTLER, Don. *Hist of the Hudson*. 1982. 336 p. S1. $17.50

BUTLER, Gerald. *Kiss the Blood Off My Hands*. 1946. Farrar Rinehart. 1st ed. dj. xl. P1. $7.50

BUTLER, Ivan. *Horror in the Cinema*. 1970. Zwemmer & Barnes. 2nd ed. P1. $7.50

BUTLER, John. *Sketches of Mexico*. 1894. Hunt Eaton. 1st ed. 12mo. 316 p. F2. $30.00

BUTLER, Joyce. *Pages From a Journal*. 1976. Book Club. 171 p. NM. B10. $4.50

BUTLER, M.M. *Romance in Lakewood St*. 1962. Cleveland. Ils. sgn. 47 p. dj. VG. T5. $12.50

BUTLER, O.E. *Clay's Ark*. nd. Book Club. dj. EX. P1. $4.50

BUTLER, O.E. *Clay's Ark*. 1984. St Martin. 1st ed. VG. R3. $15.00

BUTLER, O.E. *Dawn*. 1987. Warner. 1st ed. dj. EX. P1. $15.95

BUTLER, O.E. *Mind of My Mind*. 1977. Doubleday. 2nd ed. dj. VG. P1. $17.50

BUTLER, O.E. *Wild Seed*. 1980. Doubleday. 1st ed. dj. EX. P1/R3. $30.00

BUTLER, Paul. *Jim Ravel's Theatrical Pickpocketing*. 1988. Magical Pub. 1st ed. 137 p. dj. NM. J3. $22.50

BUTLER, Pierce. *Checklist of 15th-Century Books in Newberry Lib*. 1933. Chicago. Ltd 1st ed. 1/850. VG. G1. $50.00

BUTLER, R.O. *Countrymen of Bones*. 1983. Horizon. 1st ed. sgn. dj. EX. K2. $50.00

BUTLER, R.O. *Sun Dogs*. 1982. Horizon. 1st ed. sgn. dj. EX. K2. $50.00

BUTLER, Ragan. *Capt Nash & the Wrath Inheritance*. 1975. Heywood. 1st UK ed. dj. EX. F5. $20.00

BUTLER, Samuel. *Erewhon: Over the Range*. 1931. NY. 4 clr pls. G. R5. $20.00

BUTLER, William. *Wild N Land*. 1904. NY. 1st ed. VG. $65.00

BUTLER-BOWDEN, W. *Book of Margery Kempe: Modern Version*. 1944. Devin. 1st ed? 243 p. EX. B10. $7.50

BUTTERFIELD, C.W. *Hist Account of Expedition Against Sandusky...1782*. 1873. Cincinnati. 403 p. TEG. T5. $125.00

BUTTERFIELD, M.D. *1st Lady*. 1964. Morrow. 1st Am ed. tall 8vo. dj. VG. B10. $5.00

BUTTERTON, M.L. *Metric 16*. 1972. Durham, NC. 1st ed. inscr. dj. EX. T5. $32.50

BUTTERWORTH, Hezekiah. *Over the Andes; or, Our Boys in New S America*. 1897. Boston. Wilde. Ils Sandham. 1st ed. 370 p. F2. $25.00

BUTTERWORTH, Michael. *Virgin on the Rocks*. 1985. Crime Club. dj. EX. P1. $12.95

BUTTERWORTH, W.E. *Flying Army*. 1971. NY. Ils. 196 p. dj. G. T5. $22.50

BUZZATI, Dino. *Tartar Steppe*. 1952. Farrar Straus. 1st Am ed. dj. EX. C4. $35.00

BYERLY, A.E. *Ferugs; or, Fergusson-Webster Settlement With Hist...* 1932-1934. Elora, Ontario, Canada. 1st ed. inscr. T5. $45.00

BYERS, Chester. *Cowboy Roping & Rope Tricks*. 1966. Dover. 99 p. NM. J3. $2.00

BYNNER, Witter. *Journey With Genius: Recollections...Concerning DL Lawrence*. 1951. NY. John Day. 1st ed. dj. EX. C4. $25.00

BYNNER, Witter. *New Poems*. 1960. Knopf. Ltd ed. 1/1750. inscr. dj. H3. $85.00

BYRD, R.E. *Alone*. 1938. NY. 1st ed. VG. $15.00

BYRD, R.E. *Little Am*. 1930. NY. 1st ed. sgn. dj. VG. B3. $27.50

BYRD, R.E. *Little Am*. 1930. Putnam. 1st ed. 422 p. VG. B10. $8.75

BYRD, R.O. *Quaker Ways in Foreign Policy*. nd. Toronto U. 8vo. 230. dj. VG. V1. $8.00

BYRNE, Donn. *Hangman's House*. nd. Grosset Dunlap. Photoplay ed. VG. P1. $13.75

BYRNE, M.S.C. *Elizabethan Home: Discovered in 2 Dialogues*. 1930. Cobden Sanderson. 2nd ed. 8vo. R4. $25.00

BYRNES, L.G. *Hist of 94th Infantry Division in WWII*. 1948. WA. 1st ed. 527 p. T5. $65.00

BYRON, Lord G.G. *Don Juan*. 1926. London/NY. Ils John Austen. 1st ed. dj. VG. $95.00

BYRON, Lord G.G. *Ravenna Journal*. 1928. London. 1st Ed Club. 1/500. VG. $95.00

BYRON, Lord G.G. *Seige of Corinth: A Poem*. 1816. London. Murray. 2nd ed. rebound. EX. C4. $50.00

BYRON, Lord G.G. *Works*. 1832. London. Murray. 17 vols. 12mo. VG. H3. $650.00

BYRON, Lord G.G. *Works*. 1898. London. Murray. Special ed. 1/250. lg octavo. TEG. H3. $3500.00

CABELL, J.B. *Cords of Vanity*. 1920. Revised ed. VG. C1. $5.00

CABELL, J.B. *Cream of the Jest*. nd. Modern Lib. VG. P1. $7.50

CABELL, J.B. *Eagles' Shadow*. 1904. Doubleday Page. Ils Grefe. 1st ed. inscr. H3. $450.00

CABELL, J.B. *Figures of Earth*. nd. Grosset Dunlap. dj. VG. P1. $25.00

CABELL, J.B. *Figures of Earth*. 1926. 7th print. VG. C1. $4.50

CABELL, J.B. *Gentleman From Chicago*. 1973. Harper Row. AP. wrp. EX. F5. $35.00

CABELL, J.B. *Jurgen*. nd. Grosset Dunlap. VG. P1. $12.50

CABELL, J.B. *Jurgen*. 1949. Bodley Head. 13th ed. dj. VG. P1. $15.00

CABELL, J.B. *Jurgen*. 1976. Ltd Ed Club. Ils/sgn Virgil Burnett. slipcase. VG. $45.00

CABELL, J.B. *King Was in His Counting House*. 1938. Farrar. 1st ed. dj. EX. R3. $35.00

CABELL, J.B. *Ladies & Gentlemen*. 1934. McBride. Ltd ed. 1/153. sgn. slipcase. H3. $175.00

CABELL, J.B. *Line of Love*. 1905. London/NY. Harper. Ils Pyle. presentation. H3. $125.00

CABELL, J.B. *Line of Love*. 1921. NY. 8vo. VG. $25.00

CABELL, J.B. *Music From Behind the Moon*. 1926. John Day. 1/3000. EX. P1. $90.00

CABELL, J.B. *Silver Stallion*. 1926. Lg Paper/1st ed. 1/850. sgn. C1. $10.00

CABELL, J.B. *Smire*. 1937. 1st ed. VG. C1. $6.00

CABELL, J.B. *Something About Eve*. 1927. McBride. 1st ed. dj. VG. F5. $45.00

CABELL, J.B. *Something About Eve*. 1927. McBride. 1st ed. 1/850. sgn. H3. $60.00

CABELL, J.B. *Something About Eve*. 1927. NY. McBride. Lg Paper/1st ed. 1/850. sgn. VG. C1. $75.00

CABELL, J.B. *Sonnets From Antan With an Editorial Note*. 1929. Fountain Pr. Ltd ed. 1/718. sgn. H3. $75.00

CABELL, J.B. *Straws & Prayer Books*. 1924. 1st Trade ed. VG. C1. $7.00

CABELL, J.B. *Straws & Prayer Books*. 1930. Storisende ed. 1/1590. VG. C1. $10.00

CABELL, J.B. *Way of Ecben*. 1929. McBride. Ltd ed. 1/850. sgn. slipcase. H3. $125.00

CABELL, J.B. *Works*. 1927. NY. McBride. Storisende ed. 1/1590. 15 vols. VG. H3. $300.00

CABEZAS, Omar. *Fire From the Mt: Making of a Sandinista*. 1985. NY. 1st ed. dj. M. T1. $22.00

CABLE, G.W. *Amateur Garden*. 1914. NY. 1st ed. EX. $35.00

CABLE, G.W. *Old Creole Days*. 1883. NY. 2 vols. $35.00

CABLE, G.W. *Old Creole Days/Scenes of Cable's Romances...* 1943. Heritage Pr. Ils John Cosgrove. slipcase. M. T1. $20.00

CABLE, Mary. *Lost New Orleans*. 1980. NY. 1st ed. 235 p. $12.50

CADBURY, H.J. *Jesus & Judiasm & the Emphasis of Jesus*. 1962. Indianapolis. John Woolman. 12mo. 22 p. V1. $5.00

CADBURY, H.J. *Quaker Relief During the Siege of Boston*. nd. Wallingford. Pendle Hill. 8vo. 23 p. pamphlet. V1. $5.00

CADBURY, Henry. *Rufus Jones Centennial 1863-1963*. 1963. 5 Years Meeting. 4to. 20 p. VG. V1. $12.00

CADWELL, Dorothy. *Murder on the House*. 1976. Musson. 1st ed. dj. xl. P1. $5.00

CADY, A.C. *Am Continent & Its Inhabitants Before Discovery of Columbus*. 1892. Phil. Antiquarian ed. 4to. AEG. VG. T1. $45.00

CAESAR, Irving. *Sing a Song of Safety*. 1937. NY. Ils Rose O'Neill. 1st ed. sgn. 71 p. G. B3. $60.00

CAESAR, Julius. *Gallic Wars*. 1954. Ltd Ed Club. Ils/sgn Bruno Bramanti. 4to. slipcase. VG. $50.00

CAFFIN & CAFFIN. *Dancing & Dancers of Today*. 1912. Dodd Mead. 1st ed. quarto. 301 p. VG. H3. $175.00

CAGE, John. *Year From Monday: New Lectures & Writings*. 1967. Wesleyan U. 1st ed. dj. EX. $30.00

CAGLE & MASON. *Sea War in Korea*. 1957. Annapolis. tall 8vo. dj. VG. $30.00

CAHILL, James. *Distant Mts: Chinese Painting of Late Ming Dynasty...* 1982. NY. 1st ed. 302 p. dj. EX. T5. $45.00

CAHILL, James. *Hills Beyond a River*. 1976. NY. Ils 1st ed. 198 p. dj. EX. T5. $75.00

CAHILL, James. *Parting at the Shore*. 1978. NY. 1st ed. 281 p. dj. EX. T5. $45.00

CAHLANDER & BAIZERMAN. *Double-Woven Treasures From Old Peru*. 1985. St Paul. 1st ed. 4to. wrp. F2. $35.00

CAHN, Sammy. *I Should Care*. 1974. Arbor House. 1st ed. inscr. 318 p. dj. EX. H3. $85.00

CAHPIN, H.M. *Artistic Motives in the US Flag*. 1930. Roger Williams Pr. Ils. 4to. EX. $60.00

CAHRTERS, Ann. *Kerouac*. 1974. Warner. 1st PB ed. VG. B4. $8.00

CAHUN, Leon. *Adventures of Capt Mago*. 1889. Scribner. 1st ed? EX. R3. $85.00

CAIGER, G. *Dolls on Display: Japan in Miniature*. nd. (c 1933) Tokyo. Hokuseido. 1st ed. silk/tassel bdg. boxed. EX. R4. $150.00

CAIGER, Stephen. *British Honduras*. 1951. London. Allen. 1st ed. 240 p. F2. $20.00

CAIN, J.M. *Baby in the Icebox & Other Short Fiction*. 1981. Holt. 1st ed. dj. EX. T9. $25.00

CAIN, J.M. *Butterfly*. 1947. Knopf. 1st ed. dj. EX. F5. $40.00

CAIN, J.M. *Butterfly*. 1947. Knopf. 1st ed. dj. xl. P1. $10.00

CAIN, J.M. *Cain X-3*. 1969. Knopf. 1st Collected ed. inscr. dj. H3. $250.00

CAIN, J.M. *Cloud 9*. 1984. Mysterious Pr. UP. EX. K2. $40.00

CAIN, J.M. *Cloud 9*. 1984. Mysterious Pr. 1st ed. dj. EX. P1. $17.50

CAIN, J.M. *Institute*. 1976. Mason Charter. 1st ed. dj. VG. P1. $17.50

CAIN, J.M. *Love's Lovely Counterfeit*. 1942. NY. 1st ed. dj. VG. T9. $95.00

CAIN, J.M. *Love's Lovely Counterfeit*. 1945. Tower. VG. P1. $10.00

CAIN, J.M. *Mildred Pierce*. 1941. Knopf. 1st ed. dj. VG. T9. $65.00

CAIN, J.M. *Mildred Pierce*. 1945. Cleveland. Tower. 1st Photoplay ed. dj. EX. T9. $35.00

CAIN, J.M. *Mildred Pierce*. 1945. World. Photoplay ed. VG. P1. $11.50

CAIN, J.M. *Our Government*. 1930. Knopf. 1st ed. sans dj. VG. T9. $45.00

CAIN, J.M. *Past All Dishonor*. 1946. Knopf. 1st ed. dj. EX. T9. $45.00

CAIN, J.M. *Postman Always Rings Twice*. nd. Grosset Dunlap. dj. VG. P1. $20.00

CAIN, J.M. *Postman Always Rings Twice.* 1934. London. Jonathan Cape. 1st ed. dj. VG. T9. $35.00

CAIN, J.M. *Rainbow's End.* 1975. Mason Charter. inscr/sgn. dj. H3. $125.00

CAIN, J.M. *Rainbow's End.* 1975. NY. Mason Charter. 1st ed. dj. T9. $30.00

CAIN, J.M. *Serenade.* 1937. Knopf. 1st ed. dj. xl. P1. $25.00

CAIN, J.M. *Serenade.* 1943. Tower. VG. P1. $15.00

CAIN, J.M. *3 of Hearts.* 1949. Robert Hale. VG. P1. $25.00

CAIN, Paul. *Fast 1.* 1949. Paris. 1st French ed. sans dj. VG. T9. $45.00

CAIN, Paul. *Fast 1.* 1978. S IL U. 1st print. sgn. dj. EX. T9. $35.00

CAIN & HOOPES. *Cain: Biography of James M Cain.* 1982. Holt. 1st ed. dj. EX. R3. $30.00

CAINE, Hall. *Bondman.* nd. Lupton. 357 p. TEG. VG. B10. $3.50

CAINE, Hall. *Eternal City.* 1902. Grosset Dunlap. Ils. 449 p. VG. B10. $3.50

CAINES, Jeanette. *Just Us Women.* 1982. Harper. Ils Pat Cummings. 1st ed. clipped dj. EX. B13. $45.00

CAIRD, Janet. *Murder Reflected.* 1965. Geoffrey Bles. 1st ed. dj. xl. P1. $7.50

CAIRNES, J.E. *Slave Power.* 1969. Harper Row. 410 p. G. S1. $4.00

CALDECOTT, Moyra. *Bran Son of Llyr.* 1985. Frome. 1st ed. M. C1. $6.00

CALDECOTT, Moyra. *Crystal Legends.* 1990. 1st ed. PB. M. C1. $12.50

CALDECOTT, Moyra. *Crystal Legends.* 1990. 1st ed. sgn. stiff card covers. C1. $10.00

CALDECOTT, Moyra. *Gr Lady & the King of Shadows: Glastonbury Legend.* 1989. Gothic Image Pr. 1st ed. PB. M. C1. $11.50

CALDECOTT, Moyra. *Taliesin & Avagddu.* 1985. (1st 1983) Ils Gusman. 2nd imp. M. C1. $6.00

CALDECOTT, Moyra. *Tall Stones.* 1977. Hill Wang. 1st ed. dj. EX. F5. $15.00

CALDECOTT, Moyra. *Temple of the Sun.* 1977. Hill Wang. 1st ed. dj. EX. F5. $15.00

CALDECOTT, Moyra. *Women in Celtic Myth.* 1988. London. 1st ed. M. C1. $8.50

CALDWELL, Ben. *Blk Quartet.* 1970. Signet. B4. $5.00

CALDWELL, Erskine. *All Night Long.* 1942. Book League. 283 p. dj. VG. B10. $3.50

CALDWELL, Erskine. *All Night Long.* 1942. Duell. 1st ed. 283 p. dj. VG. B10. $7.00

CALDWELL, Erskine. *All Night Long: Novel of Guerrilla Warfare in Russia.* 1942. Duell Sloan Pearce. Ltd ed. sgn. dj. H3. $150.00

CALDWELL, Erskine. *God's Little Acre.* 1948. Falcon. dj. VG. P1. $12.50

CALDWELL, Erskine. *House in the Uplands.* 1946. Duell. 1st ed. 238 p. VG. B10. $12.00

CALDWELL, Erskine. *Kneel to the Rising Sun & Other Stories.* 1935. Viking. Ltd ed. 1/300. sgn. slipcase. H3. $175.00

CALDWELL, Erskine. *Message for Genevieve.* 1933. Mt Vernon, ME. pamphlet. Ils/sgn Morang. 1/100. H3. $600.00

CALDWELL, Erskine. *Sacrilege of Alan Kent.* 1936. Falmouth Book House. Ltd ed. 1/300. sgn. slipcase. H3. $175.00

CALDWELL, Erskine. *Say Is This the USA?* 1941. NY. 1st ed. VG. B3. $67.50

CALDWELL, Erskine. *Summertime Island.* 1968. World. sgn. H3. $75.00

CALDWELL, Erskine. *Tenant Farmer.* 1935. Phalanx Pr. 1st ed. wrp. scarce. B13. $125.00

CALDWELL, Erskine. *Tenant Farmer.* 1935. Phalanx Pr. sgn. gr/orange wrp. H3. $150.00

CALDWELL, Erskine. *This Very Earth.* 1948. NY. 1st ed. 254 p. dj. T5. $25.00

CALDWELL, Erskine. *Tobacco Road/GA Boy/Sure Hand of God: 3 Great Novels of S.* 1947. Little Brn. inscr. dj. H3. $150.00

CALDWELL, Erskine. *We Are the Living.* 1933. Viking. Ltd ed. 1/250. sgn. H3. $250.00

CALDWELL, Steven. *Aliens in Space.* 1979. Crescent. dj. EX. P1. $7.50

CALDWELL, Steven. *Aliens in Space.* 1980. Crescent. decor brd. EX. P1. $5.00

CALDWELL, Steven. *Settlers in Space.* 1980. Crescent. decor brd. EX. P1. $5.00

CALDWELL, Taylor. *Dialogues With the Devil.* 1967. Doubleday. 1st ed. P1. $7.00

CALDWELL, Taylor. *Late Clara Beame.* 1963. Crime Club. 1st ed. dj. VG. P1. $12.50

CALDWELL & BOURKE-WHITE. *You Have Seen Their Faces.* 1937. NY. 1st Lg SftCvr ed. photos. VG. B3. $45.00

CALDWELL & BOURKE-WHITE. *You Have Seen Their Faces.* 1937. Viking. 1st ed. inscr. dj. EX. very scarce. B13. $375.00

CALKINS, F. *Jackson Hole.* 1973. NY. 1st ed. 299 p. dj. VG. B3. $20.00

CALL, F.O. *Spell of French Canada.* 1926. Boston. Page. 1st ed. 372 p. VG. B10. $5.00

CALLAGHAN, Morley. *That Summer in Paris.* 1963. NY. 1st ed. dj. EX. B3. $27.50

CALLAWAY, Henry. *Memoir of James Parnell With Extracts From His Writings.* 1846. London. Gilpin. 16mo. 124 p. xl. V1. $14.50

CALLCOTT, Margaret. *Negro in MD Politics 1870-1912.* nd. (1969) John Hopkins. 1st ed? 199 p. B10. $10.00

CALLEN, Larry. *Cabbage Patch & Just-Right Family.* 1984. Parker. 1st ed. sm 4to. dj. EX. B10. $4.50

CALLENDER, James. *Yesterdays on Brooklyn Hgts.* 1927. NY. Ltd ed. sgn. EX. G1. $30.00

CALLOW, Edward. *Old London Taverns.* 1901. NY. 12mo. A4. $25.00

CALLOWAY, Cab. *Of Minnie the Moocher & Me.* 1976. NY. 1st ed. dj. VG. B3. $20.00

CALLOWAY & ROLLINS. *Of Minnie the Moocher & Me.* 1976. Crowell. 1st ed. octavo. 282 p. dj. EX. H3. $50.00

CALTHROP, D.C. *Eng Costume.* 1907. London. Blk. Ils Hollar/Dightons. A4. $125.00

CALVINO, Italo. *Baron in the Trees.* 1959. Random House. 1st ed. inscr. dj. EX. B13. $650.00

CALVINO, Italo. *Castle of Crossed Destinies.* 1977. Harcourt Brace. 8 clr prints. dj. EX. K2. $65.00

CALVINO, Italo. *Cosmicomics.* 1968. Harcourt Brace. ARC. inscr. EX. K2. $350.00

CALVINO, Italo. *Mr Palomar.* 1985. Harcourt Brace. UP. wrp. EX. K2. $50.00

CALVINO, Italo. *Path to the Nest of Spiders.* 1957. Beacon Pr. 1st ed. inscr. dj. EX. scarce. K2. $650.00

CALVINO, Italo. *T Zero.* 1969. Harcourt Brace. ARC. inscr. EX. scarce. K2. $350.00

CALVINO, Italo. *Time & the Hunter.* 1970. London. Cape. 1st ed. dj. EX. B13. $100.00

CALVINO, Italo. *Watcher & Other Stories.* 1971. Harcourt Brace. 1st Am. ed. dj. EX. C4. $75.00

CALVINO, Italo. *Watcher.* 1971. Harcourt Brace. ARC. inscr. dj. EX. K2. $350.00

CAMDEN, John. *Hundredth Acre.* 1905. Turner. 1st ed. VG. P1. $20.00

CAMERON, C.W. *Handbook of Horror.* nd. Devon, England. 43 p. SftCvr. EX. J3. $6.00

CAMERON, Don. *Dig Another Grave.* 1946. Mystery House. VG. P1. $9.25

CAMERON, Don. *Wht for a Shroud.* nd. Boardman. dj. VG. P1. $15.00

CAMERON, J.R. *Motion Pictures With Sound.* 1929. Cameron Pub. 1st ed. 393 p. dj. VG. H3. $60.00

CAMERON, John. *Astrologer.* 1972. Random House. 1st ed. dj. EX. F5. $14.00

CAMPAN, Madame. *Memoirs of Private Life of Marie Antionette.* 1823. Phil.$75.00

CAMPBELL, Albert. *Report Upon the Pacific Wagon Roads.* 1859.6 fld maps. A5. $225.00

CAMPBELL, Alice. *Murder in Paris.* nd. Farrar Rinehart. VG. P1. $12.50

CAMPBELL, Alice. *Murder in Paris.* nd. Grosset Dunlap. G. P1. $3.50

CAMPBELL, Alice. *Veiled Murder.* 1949. Random House. 1st ed. P1. $10.00

CAMPBELL, Bruce. *Secret of Skeleton Island.* 1949. Grosset Dunlap. VG. P1. $6.00

CAMPBELL, E.C. *Geneva, OH: Building of Am City 1866-1966.* 1966. Geneva, OH. Ils. dj. G. T5. $19.50

CAMPBELL, G.H. *Campbells Are Coming.* 1947. NY. 1st ed. xl. G. B3. $32.50

CAMPBELL, George. *Wht & Blk: Outcome of a Visit to the US.* 1879. NY. G. $75.00

CAMPBELL, H.J. *Beyond the Visible.* 1952. Hamilton. 1st ed. dj. VG. P1. $25.00

CAMPBELL, J.F. *Hist & Bibliography of New Practical Navigator.* 1964. Peabody Mus. 1st ed. 1/1000. G. $55.00

CAMPBELL, J.L. *Jest for Fun, Trick-Tion-Ary.* 1988. Waukesha, WI. 1st ed. M. J3. $6.50

CAMPBELL, J.W. *Analog 2.* 1964. Doubleday. 1st ed. dj. RS. EX. R3. $25.00

CAMPBELL, J.W. *Astounding July.* 1984. S IL U. facsimile of 1939 ed. M. R3. $15.00

CAMPBELL, J.W. *Astounding SF Anthology.* 1951. Simon Schuster. 1st ed. dj. VG. P1. $75.00

CAMPBELL, J.W. *Atomic Story.* 1947. Holt. 1st ed. dj. EX. R3. $50.00

CAMPBELL, J.W. *Biographical Sketches...* 1838. Columbus. 279 p. fair. T5. $42.50

CAMPBELL, J.W. *Blk Star Passes.* 1953. Fantasy. 1st ed. P1. $35.00

CAMPBELL, J.W. *Cloak of Aesir.* 1952. Shasta. 1st ed. dj. EX. R3. $40.00

CAMPBELL, J.W. *Cloak of Aesir.* 1976. Hyperion. EX. R3. $20.00

CAMPBELL, J.W. *Collected Editorials From Analog.* 1984. Doubleday. 1st ed. dj. EX. R3. $27.50

CAMPBELL, J.W. *From Unknown Worlds.* 1952. London. VG. R3. $25.00

CAMPBELL, J.W. *Incredible Planet.* 1949. Fantasy. Ltd 1st ed. 1/250. sgn. dj. EX. R3. $200.00

CAMPBELL, J.W. *Invaders From the Infinite.* 1961. Gnome. 1st ed. dj. EX. R3. $30.00

CAMPBELL, J.W. *Moon Is Hell!* 1951. Fantasy. 1st ed. dj. EX. R3. $65.00

CAMPBELL, J.W. *Moon Is Hell!* 1951. Fantasy. 1st ed. dj. G. P1. $35.00

CAMPBELL, J.W. *Who Goes There?* 1948. Shasta. 1st ed. dj. EX. R3. $95.00

CAMPBELL, J.W. *Who Goes There?* 1976. Hyperion. EX. R3. $20.00

CAMPBELL, John. *Council of Dogs.* 1809. Phil. 12mo. wrp. EX. $150.00

CAMPBELL, John. *World's Displayed: For Benefit of Young People.* 1819. Phil. Bailey. 12mo. wrp. EX. $90.00

CAMPBELL, Joseph. *Masks of God: Primitive Mythology.* 1959. np. 1st ed. dj. VG. B3. $27.50

CAMPBELL, Julie. *Rin Tin Tin's Rinty.* 1954. Whitman. EX. P1. $25.00

CAMPBELL, Julie. *Trixie Belden & Mystery Off Glen Road.* 1956. Whitman. decor brd. VG. P1. $10.00

CAMPBELL, Keith. *Darling Don't!* 1950. MacDonald. dj. VG. P1. $7.00

CAMPBELL, Kimberlee. *Protean Text.* 1988. Garland. 1st ed. M. C1. $24.50

CAMPBELL, Marion. *Dark Twin.* 1973. London. Turnstone. 1st ed. dj. EX. very scarce. C1. $32.50

CAMPBELL, Ramsey. *Ancient Images.* 1989. Scribner. 1st ed. dj. RS. EX. P1. $20.00

CAMPBELL, Ramsey. *Cold Print.* 1985. Scream. 1st ed. 1/250. sgn. M. R3. $100.00

CAMPBELL, Ramsey. *Dark Feasts.* 1987. Robinson. 1st ed. sgn. dj. EX. P1. $30.00

CAMPBELL, Ramsey. *Demons by Daylight.* 1973. Arkham House. 1st ed. M. R3. $30.00

CAMPBELL, Ramsey. *Face That Must Die.* 1983. Scream. 1st ed. 1/100. sgn. M. R3. $450.00

CAMPBELL, Ramsey. *Height of the Scream.* 1976. Arkham House. 1st ed. M. R3. $8.95

CAMPBELL, Ramsey. *Hungry Moon.* 1986. Macmillan. dj. EX. P1. $18.95

CAMPBELL, Ramsey. *Influence.* 1988. Macmillan. 1st ed. dj. VG. P1. $14.95

CAMPBELL, Ramsey. *New Tales of the Cthulhu Mythos.* 1980. Arkham House. 3rd print. M. R3. $14.95

CAMPBELL, Ramsey. *Obsession.* 1985. Macmillan. 1st ed. dj. EX. R3. $15.00

CAMPBELL, Ramsey. *Parasite.* 1980. Macmillan. 1st ed. dj. VG. P1. $20.00

CAMPBELL, Ramsey. *Scared Stiff.* 1987. Scream. Ltd ed. 1/250. sgn. M. R3. $80.00

CAMPBELL, Ramsey. *Scared Stiff.* 1987. Scream. 1st ed. M. R3. $25.00

CAMPBELL, Robert. *Alice in La-La Land.* 1987. Poseidon. 1st ed. dj. VG. P1. $16.95

CAMPBELL, Robert. *In La-La Land We Trust.* 1986. Mysterious Pr. 1st ed. dj. VG. P1. $15.95

CAMPBELL, Roy. *Mithraic Emblems.* 1936. London. 1st Trade ed. dj. T5. $25.00

CAMPBELL, Thomas. *Poetical Works.* nd. NY. Crowell. 8vo. G. $25.00

CAMPBELL & DAYTON. *Crystal Cups.* 1983. Calgary. Micky Hades Internat. NM. J3. $4.00

CAMPBELL & DUNN. *Child's 1st Book.* 1864. Richmond. orig wrp. VG. $250.00

CAMPBELL & ROBINSON. *Skeleton Key to Finnegan's Wake.* 1944. Harcourt Brace. 1st ed. dj. EX. C4. $45.00

CAMPBELL & WOOLERY. *Bethany Years.* 1941. Huntington. 1st ed. 290 p. VG. B3. $22.50

CAMPBELL. *S Highlander & His Homeland.* 1921. NY. 2nd print. 1/1500. VG. C2. $65.00

CAMPEN, R.N. *Architecture of the W Reserve 1800-1900.* 1971. Cleveland. Ils. 260 p. dj. VG. T5. $65.00

CAMPEN, R.N. *OH: An Architectural Portrait.* 1973. Chagrin Falls. 1st ed. 320 p. dj. VG. T5. $25.00

CAMPOS, Jilieta. *Bajo el Signo de Ix Bolon.* 1988. Ltd 1st ed. 1/1500. 4to. dj. F2. $40.00

CAMUS, Albert. *Caligula & 3 Other Plays.* 1958. Knopf. 1st Am ed. dj. EX. H3. $75.00

CAMUS, Albert. *Exile & the Kingdom.* 1958. NY. 1st Am ed. dj. VG. $20.00

CAMUS, Albert. *Possessed.* 1960. Knopf. Trans O'Brien. 1st Am ed. dj. EX. H3. $75.00

CAMUS, Albert. *Resistance, Rebellion, & Death.* 1961. London. Review 1st ed. dj. VG. $35.00

CANBY, H.S. *Brandywine.* 1941. NY/Toronto. Ils Wyeth. VG. $30.00

CANBY, Vincent. *Unnatural Scenery.* 1979. Knopf. 1st ed. 274 p. dj. NM. B10. $4.50

CANETTI, Elias. *Crowds & Power.* 1962. London. Gollancz. 1st ed. dj. EX. B13. $75.00

CANFIELD, Dorothy. *Basque People.* 1931. Harcourt. 1st ed. dj. VG. $7.00

CANFIELD, Dorothy. *Home Fires in France.* 1918. Holt. 1st ed. 306 p. VG. B10. $9.00

CANFIELD, Dorothy. *Raw Material.* 1924. London. 1st ed. inscr. EX. $40.00

CANIFF, Milton. *April Kane & the Dragon Lady.* nd. Whitman. VG. P1. $9.25

CANIN, Ethan. *Emperor of the Air: Stories.* 1988. Houghton Mifflin. 1st ed. dj. EX. C4. $30.00

CANNELL, J.C. *Secrets of Houdini.* 1973. Dover. 279 p. NM. J3. $4.00

CANNING, Victor. *Burning Eye.* 1960. Hodder Stoughton. 1st UK ed. dj. EX. F5. $20.00

CANNING, Victor. *Circle of the Gods.* 1979. London. dj. EX. C1. $8.00

CANNING, Victor. *Crimson Chalice.* 1st Am ed. dj. M. C1. $14.00

CANNING, Victor. *Fight of the Gray Goose.* 1973. Morrow. 1st ed. dj. EX. F5. $13.00

CANNING, Victor. *Man From the Turkish Slave.* 1954. Hodder Stoughton. dj. VG. P1. $16.50

CANNING, Victor. *Mr Finchley Goes to Paris.* 1938. Carrick Evans. 1st ed. dj. VG. P1. $27.25

CANNING, Victor. *Python Project.* 1968. Morrow. 1st ed. dj. EX. $15.00

CANNON, Richard. *Hist Records of 10th or N Lincolnshire Regiment.* 1847. London. 3 clr pls. A4. $110.00

CANTON, William. *Invisible Playmate.* 1907. NY. Ils Brock. 12mo. VG. A4. $25.00

CANTOR, Eddie. *As I Remember Them.* 1963. Duell Sloan Pearce. 1st ed. sgn. 144 p. dj. EX. H3. $75.00

CAPE, Tony. *Cambridge Theorem.* 1990. Doubleday. ARC. EX. K2. $15.00

CAPEK, Karel. *Absolute at Lg.* 1927. Macmillan. 1st ed. dj. EX. R3. $75.00

CAPEK, Karel. *Absolute at Lg.* 1974. Hyperion. wrp. EX. R3. $10.00

CAPEK, Karel. *Power & Glory.* 1938. Allen Unwin. 1st ed. dj. EX. H3. $75.00

CAPELLANUS, Andreas. *Art of Courtly Love.* 1978. pb. VG. C1. $3.50

CAPERTON, H.L. *Legends of VA.* 1931. Richmond. 1st ed. 74 p. T5. $17.50

CAPON, Paul. *World at Bay.* 1954. Winston. 1st ed. xl. VG. P1. $7.50

CAPOTE, Truman. *Breakfast at Tiffany's.* 1958. Random House. ARC. sgn Goyen. dj. RS. EX. K2. $275.00

CAPOTE, Truman. *Breakfast at Tiffany's.* 1958. Random House. 1st ed. dj. EX. B13. $250.00

CAPOTE, Truman. *Christmas Memory.* 1956. NY. 1st ed. slipcase. as issued. EX. K2. $40.00

CAPOTE, Truman. *Grass Harp.* 1952. Random House. 1st ed. dj. EX. scarce. K2. $300.00

CAPOTE, Truman. *In Cold Blood.* 1965. Random House. ARC. wrp. EX. C4. $150.00

CAPOTE, Truman. *In Cold Blood.* 1965. Random House. 1st ed. dj. EX. B13. $75.00

CAPOTE, Truman. *Muses Are Heard.* 1956. NY. 1st ed. as issued. K2. $85.00

CAPOTE, Truman. *Music for Cameleons.* 1982. NY. 1/350. sgn. as issued. K2. $200.00

CAPOTE, Truman. *Other Voices Other Rooms.* 1947. Random House. 1st ed. dj. EX. K2. $250.00

CAPOTE, Truman. *Selected Writings of Truman Capote.* 1963. Random House 1st ed. dj. VG. K2. $50.00

CAPOTE, Truman. *Thanksgiving Visitor.* 1967. London. 1st ed. dj. VG. $35.00

CAPOTE, Truman. *Thanksgiving Visitor.* 1967. Random House. 1st ed. slipcase. EX. B13. $75.00

CAPOTE, Truman. *Thanksviging Visitor.* 1967. Random House. Ltd ed. sgn. slipcase. H3. $200.00

CAPOTE, Truman. *1 Christmas.* 1983. Random House. ARC. slipcase. RS. B13. $85.00

CAPOTE, Truman. *1 Christmas.* 1983. Random House. Ltd ed. 1/500. sgn. slipcase. H3. $150.00

CAPOTE & AVEDON. *Observations.* 1959. Simon Schuster. 1st ed. glassine dj. boxed. EX. K1. $200.00

CAPP, Al. *Life & Times of the Schmoo.* 1948. NY. 1st ed. lg wrp. VG. B3. $40.00

CAPPER, Mary. *Memoir of Mary Capper, Late of Birmingham, England...* 1888. Phil. Friends Bookstore. 12mo. 454 p. VG. V1. $8.50

CAPSTICK, P.H. *Death in the Long Grass.* 1977. St. Martin. dj. VG. P1. $10.00

CAPUTO, Philip. *Del Corso's Gallery.* 1983. Holt Rinehart Winston. 1st ed. dj. B4. $15.95

CAPUTO, Philip. *Rumor of War.* 1977. Holt. 1st ed. dj. EX. K1. $50.00

CARD, O.S. *Abyss.* 1989. Legend. 1st ed. dj. EX. P1. $30.00

CARD, O.S. *Folk of the Fringe.* 1989. Phantasia. Ltd ed. 1/475. sgn. M. R3. $125.00

CARD, O.S. *Folk of the Fringe.* 1989. Phantasia. 1st ed. M. R3. $22.00

CAREY, A.A. *Memoirs of a Murder Man.* 1930. Doubleday Doran. 1st ed. VG. P1. $18.25

CAREY, Chris. *Do the Stuff That's You!* 1980. Tamarac, FL. Show-Pro. 1st ed. sgn. EX. J3. $8.00

CAREY, Chris. *Find the Stuff That's You.* 1989. Atlanta. 1st ed. dj. NM. J3. $20.00

CAREY, M.V. *Mystery of the Singing Serpent.* nd. Random House. EX. P1. $7.50

CAREY, Peter. *Oscar & Lucinda.* 1988. Queensland. 1st ed. dj. EX. B13. $125.00

CAREY, Vin. *Sleeving: How To Do It, What To Do With It.* nd. Am Magic Co. stapled manuscript. NM. J3. $5.00

CARLETON, George. *Our Artist in Peru.* 1886. Carleton Pub. 1st ed. 8vo. F2. $40.00

CARLETON, J.H. *Special Report of Mt Meadows Massacre.* 1902. GPO. 17 p. wrp. VG. A5. $50.00

CARLINSKY, Dan. *World's Greatest Monster Quiz.* nd. Berkley. 2nd ed. P1. $2.75

CARLON, Patricia. *See Nothing...Say Nothing.* 1968. Walker. dj. VG. P1. $7.00

CARLTON, A.B. *Wonderlands of the W With Sketches of the Mormons.* 1891. np. Vg. $50.00

CARLTON, H.W. *Spaniels: Their Breaking for Sport & Field Trials.* 1926. London. Revised 4th ed. 16mo. EX. A4. $27.50

CARLTON, Paul. *Magician's Handy Book of Cigarette Tricks.* 1933. RJ Reynolds Tobacco Co. 1st ed. 36 p. VG. J3. $4.00

CARLYLE, Thomas. *French Revolution: A Hist.* 1857. London. 12mo. 2 vols. full leather. VG. T5. $175.00

CARLYLE, Thomas. *French Revolution: A Hist.* 1956. Ltd Ed Club. Ils/sgn Bernard Lamotte. 4to. slipcase. VG. $90.00

CARLYLE, Thomas. *Hist of Friedrich II of Prussia, Called Frederick the Great.* c 1900. Scribner. 8 vols. octavo. VG. H3. $125.00

CARLYON, Richard. *Dark Lord of Pengersick.* 1980. Farrar Straus Giroux. 1st ed. dj. EX. P1. $15.00

CARMACK, Robert. *Quiche Mayas of Utatlan.* 1981. OK U. 1st ed. 4to. 435 p. dj. F2. $30.00

CARMACK, Robert. *Toltec Influence on the Post-Classic Culture Hist Guatemala.* nd. Tulane. F2. $15.00

CARMAN, J.N. *From Camelot to Joyous Guard.* 1974. KS U. M. C1. $14.50

CARMER, Carl. *Dark Trees to the Wind.* 1949. Sloan. 1st ed. sgn. 370 p. dj. VG. $27.00

CARMER, Carl. *Dark Trees to the Wind.* 1949. Sloan. 2nd ed. sgn. VG. $7.50

CARMER, Carl. *Genesee Fever.* 1941. Rinehart. 1st ed. 360 p. dj. B10. $15.00

CARMER, Carl. *Listen for a Lonesome Drum.* 1950. Sloan. sgn. VG. $7.50

CARMER, Carl. *Songs of the Rivers of Am.* 1942. NY. 1st ed. dj. VG. B3. $85.00

CARMICHAEL, Harry. *False Evidence.* 1976. Collins Crime Club. 1st ed. dj. xl. P1. $5.00

CARMICHAEL, Harry. *Most Deadly Hate.* 1974. Dutton. 1st ed. dj. EX. P1. $17.50

CARMICHAEL, Harry. *Of Unsound Mind.* 1962. Crime Club. 1st ed. dj. xl. P1. $7.50

CARMICHAEL, Harry. *Quiet Woman.* 1972. Saturday Review. 1st ed. dj. xl. P1. $7.50

CARMICHAEL, Harry. *Remote Control.* 1971. McCall. 1st ed. dj. VG. P1. $15.00

CARMICHAEL, J. *Who's Who in the Major Leagues Baseball.* 1939. Chicago. 7th ed. EX. $120.00

CARNELL, John. *Gateway to Tomorrow.* 1954. London. 1st ed. sgn. dj. EX. R3. $25.00

CARNELL, John. *Jinns & Jitters.* 1946. London. 1st ed. dj. EX. R3. $25.00

CARNEY, John. *Conjuror's Journal.* 1973. Carney. 1st ed. stapled manuscript. NM. J3. $4.00

CARO, Dennis. *Devine War.* 1986. Arbor House. 1st ed. dj. RS. EX. P1. $17.50

CARO, Dennis. *Devine War.* 1986. Arbor House. 1st ed. RS. EX. R3. $16.00

CARO, Dennis. *Man in the Dark Suit.* 1980. Pocket Books. UP. 1st ed. VG. R3. $15.00

CARPENTER, Don. *Hard Rain Falling.* 1966. NY. 1st ed. sgn. dj. VG. T9. $55.00

CARPENTER, F.B. *6 Months at the Wht House With Abraham Lincoln.* 1866. NY. 12mo. 359 p. G. G4. $37.00

CARPENTER, Frances. *Wonder Tales of Dogs & Cats.* 1955. Doubleday. Ils Ezra Keats. 8vo. 255 p. VG. $16.00

CARPENTER, Leonard. *Conan the Raider.* 1986. Tor Books. 1st ed. wrp. EX. F5. $8.00

CARPENTER, W.M. *Kipling's College.* 1929. Evanston, IL. 1st ed. 1/100. 8vo. 58 p. EX. R4. $75.00

CARPENTIER, Alejo. *Kingdom of This World.* 1957. Knopf. 1st Am ed. 12mo. dj. EX. C4. $40.00

CARR, Albert. *World & William Walker.* 1963. Harper Row. 1st ed. 289 p. dj. F2. $25.00

CARR, CASE, & DELLAR. *Hip.* 1986. London. Faber. Ils. lg wrp. B4. $15.00

CARR, Charles. *Colonists of Space.* 1954. Ward Lock. dj. VG. P1. $18.25

CARR, Charles. *Salamander War.* 1955. Ward Lock. dj. EX. P1. $18.25

CARR, Clark E. *Stephen A Douglas: His Life & Public Services...* 1909. Chicago. 1st ed. sgn. EX. $50.00

CARR, Harry. *Old Mother Mexico.* 1931. Houghton Mifflin. 1st ed. 270 p. F2. $12.50

CARR, J.D. *Arabian Nights Murder.* 1949. Hamish Hamilton. VG. P1. $25.00

CARR, J.D. *Below Suspicion.* 1949. Harper. 1st ed. dj. VG. P1. $27.50

CARR, J.D. *Bride of Newgate.* 1950. Harper. 1st ed. VG. P1. $20.00

CARR, J.D. *Captain Cut-Throat.* 1955. Hamish Hamilton. 1st ed. VG. P1. $40.00

CARR, J.D. *Captain Cut-Throat.* 1955. Harper. 1st ed. dj. EX. P1. $80.00

CARR, J.D. *Dead Sleep Lightly.* 1983. Crime Club. 1st ed. M. R3. $12.00

CARR, J.D. *Devil in Velvet.* 1951. Harper. dj. VG. P1. $20.00

CARR, J.D. *Emperor's Snuffbox.* 1946. Books Inc. dj. VG. P1. $15.00

CARR, J.D. *Hag's Nook.* 1933. Hamish Hamilton. 1st ed. VG. P1. $75.00

CARR, J.D. *He Who Whispers.* 1946. Harper. 1st ed. dj. EX. B13. $125.00

CARR, J.D. *He Who Whispers.* 1971. Hamish Hamilton. dj. xl. P1. $7.50

CARR, J.D. *House at Satan's Elbow.* 1965. Harper Row. 1st ed. dj. VG. P1. $20.00

CARR, J.D. *Hungry Goblin.* 1972. Harper Row. 1st ed. dj. VG. P1. $20.00

CARR, J.D. *It Walks by Night.* 1930. Harper. 4th ed. VG. P1. $50.00

CARR, J.D. *Life of Sir Arthur Conan Doyle.* 1949. NY. 1st ed. C1. $17.50

CARR, J.D. *Life of Sir Arthur Conan Doyle.* 1975. Vintage. VG. P1. $7.50

CARR, J.D. *Man Who Could Not Shudder.* nd. Collier. VG. P1. $9.25

CARR, J.D. *Most Secret.* 1964. Hamish Hamilton. 1st ed. dj. EX. P1. $45.00

CARR, J.D. *Papa – La Bas.* 1968. Harper. 1st ed. dj. EX. F5. $25.00

CARR, J.D. *Patrick Butler for the Defense.* 1956. Harper. 1st ed. xl. Lib bdg. VG. P1. $7.50

CARR, J.D. *Poison in Jest.* nd. Harper. VG. P1. $18.25

CARR, J.D. *Poison in Jest.* 1977. Hamish Hamilton. dj. EX. P1. $15.00

CARR, J.D. *Problem of the Gr Capsule.* nd. (1939) Grosset. 286 p. VG. B10. $3.50

CARR, J.D. *Problem of the Gr Capsule.* 1939. Harper. 1st ed. xl. VG. P1. $18.25

CARR, J.D. *Problem of the Gr Capsule.* 1945. Books Inc. 2nd ed. VG. P1. $10.00

CARR, J.D. *Sleeping Sphinx.* 1947. Harper. 1st ed. P1. $15.00

CARR, J.D. *Till Death Do Us Part.* nd. Collier. VG. P1. $15.00

CARR, J.D. *Till Death Do Us Part.* 1944. Harper. 1st ed. dj. EX. F5. $50.00

CARR, J.D. *To Wake the Dead.* 1937. Hamish Hamilton. 1st ed. VG. P1. $50.00

CARR, J.D. *To Wake the Dead.* 1944. Books Inc. dj. VG. P1. $20.00

CARR, J.D. *3rd Bullet.* 1954. Harper. 1st ed. dj. EX. B13. $75.00

CARR, Jayge. *Leviathan's Deep.* nd. Book Club. dj. VG. P1. $4.50

CARR, Jayge. *Leviathan's Deep.* 1979. Doubleday. dj. EX. P1. $13.75

CARR, Jayge. *Rabelaisian Reprise.* 1988. Doubleday. ARC. dj. RS. EX. F5. $17.50

CARR, Jayge. *Rabelaisian Reprise.* 1988. Doubleday. 1st ed. M. R3. $13.00

CARR, Jayge. *Treasure in the Heart of the Maze.* 1985. Doubleday. 1st ed. dj. RS. EX. P1. $17.50

CARR, Nick. *Am's Secret Service Ace: Operator 5.* 1985. Starmont. 1st ed. wrp. M. R3. $9.95

CARR, Nick. *Flying Spy: G-8.* 1989. Starmont. 1st ed. wrp. M. R3. $9.95

CARR, R.S. *Beyond Infinity.* 1951. Fantasy. Ltd ed. 1/350. sgn. dj. EX. R3. $65.00

CARR, R.S. *Beyond Infinity.* 1951. Fantasy. 1st ed. dj. EX. R3. $20.00

CARR, R.S. *Room Beyond.* 1948. Appleton. 1st ed. dj. EX. F5. $32.00

CARR, Robyn. *Bl Falcon.* 1981. 1st ed. dj. VG. C1. $5.00

CARR, Terry. *Best SF of the Year No 6.* 1977. Holt. 1st ed. dj. EX. R3. $15.00

CARR, Terry. *Cirque.* 1977. Bobbs Merrill. 1st ed. EX. R3. $20.00

CARR, Terry. *Cirque.* 1977. Bobbs Merrill. 2nd ed. dj. VG. P1. $12.50

CARR, Terry. *Cirque.* 1987. Doubleday. dj. EX. P1. $12.95

CARR, Terry. *Classic SF.* 1978. Harper Row. ARC. RS. EX. R3. $15.00

CARR, Terry. *Classic SF.* 1978. Harper Row. 1st ed. dj. EX. R3. $10.00

CARR, Terry. *Creatures From Beyond.* nd. Book Club. dj. VG. P1. $4.00

CARR, Terry. *Fellowship of the Stars.* nd. Book Club. dj. VG. P1. $4.00

CARR, Terry. *Fellowship of the Stars.* 1974. Simon Schuster. 1st ed. dj. RS. EX. R3. $15.00

CARR, Terry. *Infinite Arena.* 1977. Nelson. 1st ed. dj. EX. R3. $15.00

CARR, Terry. *Into the Unknown.* 1973. Nelson. 1st ed. dj. EX. R3. $12.50

CARR, Terry. *Step Outside Your Mind.* 1969. London. 1st Eng ed. dj. EX. R3. $12.50

CARR, Terry. *Universe 3.* 1973. Random House. 1st ed. dj. EX. R3. $12.50

CARR, Terry. *Universe 5.* 1974. Random House. 1st ed. dj. RS. EX. R3. $12.50

CARR, Terry. *Universe 7.* 1977. Doubleday. 2nd ed. dj. EX. P1. $7.00

CARR, Terry. *Year's Finest Fantasy.* 1978. Berkley Putnam. 1st ed. dj. VG. $9.00

CARREL, Alexis. *Man the Unknown.* 1938. Halcyon. 4to. 346 p. VG. $20.00

CARRELL, P. *Hitler Moves E.* 1963. Boston. 1st Am ed. dj. VG. B3. $95.00

CARRINGTON, Grant. *Time's Fool.* 1981. Doubleday. 1st ed. dj. EX. P1. $9.25

CARRINGTON, Hereward. *Magic for Everyone.* 1943. World. 3rd print. 138 p. VG. J3. $4.00

CARRINGTON, Hereward. *Side Show & Animal Tricks.* 1913. Wilson. 1st ed. 66 p. SftCvr. EX. J3. $6.00

CARROLL, Alice. *Complete Guide to Modern Knitting & Crocheting.* 1949. NY. VG. $20.00

CARROLL, Alice. *Good Housekeeping Needlework Encyclopedia.* 1947. NY. 1st ed. dj. EX. $22.00

CARROLL, James. *Madonna Red.* 1976. Little Brn. 1st ed. dj. EX. F5. $12.00

CARROLL, Jim. *Book of Nods.* 1986. NY. 1st ed. sgn. HrdCvr. scarce. as issued. K2. $65.00

CARROLL, Jim. *Living at the Movies.* 1981. Penguin. 1st ed. EX. B4. $5.00

CARROLL, Jonathan. *Land of Laughs.* 1980. Viking. 1st ed. dj. EX. K2. $125.00

CARROLL, Jonathan. *Sleeping in Flame.* 1989. Doubleday. 1st ed. dj. VG. P1. $15.00

CARROLL, Jonathan. *Voice of Our Shadow.* 1983. Viking. 1st ed. dj. VG. P1. $45.00

CARROLL, Jose. *52 Lovers Vol 1.* 1988. Madrid. Frakson. 1st ed. 165 p. dj. J3. $45.00

CARROLL, Lewis. *Alice in Wonderland.* 1930. Blk Sun. Ils Laurencin. 1/350 on Rives. H3. $3500.00

CARROLL, Lewis. *Alice's Adventures in Wonderland.* 1871. London. presentation. full red morocco. VG. H3. $4000.00

CARROLL, Lewis. *Alice's Adventures in Wonderland.* 1897. Altemus. VG. P1. $12.50

CARROLL, Lewis. *Alice's Adventures in Wonderland.* 1902. NY. Ils Newell. 192 p. TEG. G. T5. $55.00

CARROLL, Lewis. *Alice's Adventures in Wonderland.* 1932. Ltd Ed Club. 2 vols. sgn Alice Hargraves. rebound. VG. $200.00

CARROLL, Lewis. *Alice's Adventures in Wonderland.* 1983. CA U. Ils Moser. 1st ed. slipcase. w/sgn woodcut print. M. $125.00

CARROLL, Lewis. *Alice's Adventures in Wonderland/Through the Looking Glass.* 1872. London. 1st Eng ed. rebound Zaehnsdorf bdg. EX. H3. $8000.00

CARROLL, Lewis. *Alice's Adventures in Wonderland/Through the Looking Glass.* 1923. Winston. Ils Tenniel/Prittie. dj. VG. $22.00

CARROLL, Lewis. *Further Nonsense: Verse & Prose.* 1926. Appleton. Ils Bateman. 1st ed. VG. B7. $70.00

CARROLL, Lewis. *Nursery Alice.* 1890. London. Ils Tenniel. 2nd ed. orig bdg. VG. H3. $750.00

CARROLL, Lewis. *Rhyme? Reason?* 1884. Macmillan. 1st Am ed. VG. C1. $49.50

CARROLL, P.V. *Shadow & Substance.* 1937. Random House. 1st ed. dj. EX. H3. $35.00

CARROLL, P.V. *Wht Steed & Coggerers.* 1939. Random House. 1st ed. dj. EX. H3. $40.00

CARROLL, Robert. *Disappearance.* 1975. Dial. dj. xl. P1. $4.75

CARRUTH, Hayden. *Adventures of Jones.* 1895. Harper. 1st ed. VG. R3. $40.00

CARRUTH, Hayden. *N Winter.* 1964. IA City. Prairie. ARC. EX. K2. $85.00

CARRUTH, Hayden. *Sleeping Beauty.* 1982. Harper Row. UP. 144 p. EX. K2. $30.00

CARRUTH, Hayden. *Tracks End: Dakota Pioneers.* 1911. Harper. 1st ed? G. B3. $25.00

CARRUTH, Hayden. *Tracks End: Dakota Pioneers.* 1911. NY. 1st ed. 230 p. dj. VG. B3. $45.00

CARRYL, G.W. *Mother Goose for Grown-Ups.* 1900. 1st ed. VG. C1. $7.50

CARSE, Adam. *Musical Wind Instruments.* 1939. Macmillan. 1st ed. 381 p. VG. H3. $60.00

CARSE, Robert. *Beckoning Waters.* 1953. Scribner. 1st ed. dj. VG. F5. $20.00

CARSON, Rachel. *Sea Around Us.* 1951. Oxford. apparent 1st ed. 230 p. VG. B10. $3.50

CARSON, Rachel. *Sea Around Us.* 1980. Ltd Ed Club. Ils/sgn Alfred Eisenstaedt. slipcase. VG. $125.00

CARSON, Rachel. *Silent Spring.* 1962. Houghton Mifflin. 1st ed. clipped dj. EX. B13. $150.00

CARSON, W.E. *Mexico: Wonderland of the S.* 1914. Macmillan. Revised ed. 449 p. F2. $20.00

CARSON, W.G.B. *Theatre on the Frontier.* 1932. Chicago U. 1st ed. octavo. 361 p. dj. VG. H3. $85.00

CARSON. *Old Country Store.* 1954. Oxford. 1st Am ed. dj. VG. C2. $35.00

CARTER, Angela. *Fireworks.* 1981. Harper Row. 1st ed. dj. EX. P1. $17.50

CARTER, Angela. *Infernal Desire Machine of Dr Hoffman.* 1972. London. 1st ed. dj. VG. $50.00

CARTER, Angela. *Nights at the Circus.* 1984. Hogarth. dj. VG. P1. $20.00

CARTER, C.E. *Territory NW of River OH 1787-1803.* 1934. WA. 2 vols. EX. A4. $100.00

CARTER, Carrie Giles. *Life of Chauncy Giles.* 1920. Boston. 478 p. T5. $25.00

CARTER, Forrest. *Watch for Me on the Mt.* 1978. Delacorte/Friede. ARC. dj. EX. K2. $125.00

CARTER, Forrest. *Watch for Me on the Mt.* 1978. Delacorte. 1st ed. dj. EX. C4. $75.00

CARTER, Hodding. *Doomed Road of Empire.* 1963. Am Trail Series. 1st ed. dj. VG. B3. $27.50

CARTER, Huntly. *New Spirit in the Cinema.* 1930. London. Shaylor. 1st ed. octavo. 403 p. dj. EX. H3. $85.00

CARTER, J.H. *Log of the Commodore Rollingpin: His Adventures...* 1874. Carleton. 1st ed. 258 p. VG. B10. $17.00

CARTER, John. *Taste & Technique in Book Collecting.* 1949. 2nd imp. dj. VG. C1. $12.50

CARTER, Lin. *Dreams From R'Lyeh.* 1975. Arkham House. 1st ed. M. R3. $5.00

CARTER, Lin. *Flashing Swords! No 1.* nd. Book Club. dj. VG. P1. $4.00

CARTER, Lin. *Horror Wears Bl.* 1987. Doubleday. 1st ed. dj. RS. EX. P1. $17.50

CARTER, Lin. *Horror Wears Bl.* 1987. Doubleday. 1st ed. M. R3. $15.00

CARTER, Lin. *Imaginary Worlds.* 1973. Ballantine. EX. P1. $10.00

CARTER, Lin. *Invisible Death.* 1975. Doubleday. 1st ed. dj. EX. P1. $22.50

CARTER, Lin. *Kingdoms of Sorcery.* 1976. Doubleday. 1st ed. dj. EX. R3. $12.50

CARTER, Lin. *Lovecraft: Look Behind Cthulhu Mythology.* 1972. Ballantine. VG. P1. $7.50

CARTER, Lin. *Sandlewood & Jade.* 1951. Sgn of Centaur. 1st ed. wrp. EX. extremely scarce. R3. $75.00

CARTER, Lin. *Tolkien: Look Behind Lord of Rings.* 1974. Ballantine. VG. P1. $3.25

CARTER, Lin. *Volcano Ogre.* 1976. Doubleday. 1st ed. dj. EX. P1. $9.25

CARTER, Lin. *Volcano Ogre.* 1976. Putnam. 1st ed. dj. EX. R3. $8.50

CARTER, Lin. *Zarkon, Lord of the Unknown.* 1975. Doubleday. 1st ed. dj. RS. EX. R3. $15.00

CARTER, Michelle. *On Other Days While Going Home.* 1987. Morrow. 1st ed. dj. M. $10.00

CARTER, Nick. *Nick Carter Detective.* 1963. Macmillan. 1st ed. dj. VG. P1. $20.00

CARTER, Rosalynn. *1st Lady From Plains.* 1984. Boston. 1st ed. 1/750. sgn. dj. EX. B3. $40.00

CARTER, Russell. *Patriot Lad of Old CT.* nd. (1935) Phil. Penn. Ils Hargens. dj. VG. B10. $4.75

CARTER, Samuel. *Siege of Atlanta.* 1973. Bonanza. 1st ed. 425 p. dj. G. S1. $18.00

CARTER, Sidney. *Dear Bet: The Carter Letters 1861-1863.* 1978. Greenville, SC. 1st ed. wrp. EX. $25.00

CARTER, Youngman. *Mr Campion's Farthing.* 1969. Heinemann. 1st ed. dj. xl. P1. $7.00

CARTER & FIELD. *Nature Stories for Little Folk: Crooked Oak Tree...* c 1895. London. Ils. 12mo. wrp. A4. $40.00

CARTER. *1st Century of Scottish Rite Masonry in TX 1867-1967.* 1967. Waco. Ils. 508 p. A5. $30.00

CARTER. *101st Field Artillery in WWI.* 1940. Boston. 1st ed. 305 p. dj. VG. B3. $55.00

CARTIER-BRESSON, Henri. *Man & Machine.* 1971. NY. oblong 4to. dj. EX. $30.00

CARTIER-BRESSON, Henri. *World of NY.* 1968. oblong 4to. dj. EX. $35.00

CARTON, Bernard. *Conjuring for Connoisseurs.* 1921. London. Johnson. 1st ed. 32 p. SftCvr. VG. J3. $3.00

CARVER, J.A. *Rapture Effect.* 1987. Tor Books. 1st ed. dj. EX. F5. $18.00

CARVER, Raymond. *At Night the Salmon Move.* 1976. Santa Barbara. Capra. 1st ed. 1/100. sgn. no dj issued. EX. K2. $575.00

CARVER, Raymond. *At Night the Salmon Move.* 1976. Santa Barbara. Capra. 1st Trade ed. 1/1000. sgn. wrp. EX. K2. $275.00

CARVER, Raymond. *Cathedral.* 1983. Knopf. 1st ed. sgn Carver/Gallagher. dj. EX. K2. $175.00

CARVER, Raymond. *Cathedral.* 1983. Knopf. 1st ed. sgn. dj. EX. B13. $175.00

CARVER, Raymond. *Cathedral.* 1983. NY. UP. K2. $100.00

CARVER, Raymond. *Cathedral.* 1984. London. Collins. 1st ed. dj. EX. K2. $45.00

CARVER, Raymond. *Cathedral.* 1984. NY. Vintage. PB Orig. sgn. wrp. EX. K2. $85.00

CARVER, Raymond. *Early for the Dance.* 1986. Concord. Ewert. 1st HrdCvr ed. 1/36. sgn. EX. K2. $250.00

CARVER, Raymond. *Elephant.* 1988. Fairfax. Jungle Garden. 1/200. sgn. gray wrp. EX. K2. $150.00

CARVER, Raymond. *Elephant.* 1988. London. Collins Harvill. 1st ed. dj. EX. K2. $75.00

CARVER, Raymond. *Fires.* nd. 1st Eng ed. dj. EX. K2. $85.00

CARVER, Raymond. *Fires.* 1983. Capra. Ltd ed. 1/250. sgn. no dj issued. EX. K2. $125.00

CARVER, Raymond. *Fires.* 1984. Vintage. 1st Expanded Am ed. inscr. wrp. EX. K2. $175.00

CARVER, Raymond. *Furious Seasons & Other Stories.* 1977. Capra. 1st ed. 1/1200. sgn. wrp. EX. K2. $250.00

CARVER, Raymond. *Glimpses.* 1985. Northampton. Basement Pr. 1st ed/printer proof. 1/17. very rare. B13. $1500.00

CARVER, Raymond. *If It Please You.* 1984. Lord John. Ltd ed. 1/200. sgn. H3. $75.00

CARVER, Raymond. *If It Please You.* 1984. Northridge. Lord John. 1/26. sgn. no dj issued. EX. K2. $350.00

CARVER, Raymond. *In a Marine Light.* 1987. Collins Havill. 1st Eng ed. dj. EX. K2. $85.00

CARVER, Raymond. *My Father's Life.* 1986. Babcock Koontz. 1/200. sgn. wrp. C4. $90.00

CARVER, Raymond. *My Father's Life.* 1986. Derry/Ridgewood. 1st Separate ed. 1/200. sgn. wrp. EX. K2. $125.00

CARVER, Raymond. *New Path to the Waterfall.* nd. Quality PB Book Club. 1st ed. EX. K2. $20.00

CARVER, Raymond. *Painter & the Fish.* 1988. Concord. Ewart. Ils/sgn Mary Azarian. 1/26. EX. B13. $225.00

CARVER, Raymond. *Painter & the Fish.* 1988. Concord. Ewart. Ils/sgn Mary Azarian. 1/74. sgn. wrp. EX. B13. $125.00

CARVER, Raymond. *Pheasant.* 1982. Worcester. Metacom. Ltd ed. 1/26. sgn. acetate dj. EX. K2. $675.00

CARVER, Raymond. *Put Yourself in My Shoes.* 1974. Capra. 1st HrdCvr ed. 1/75. sgn. EX. scarce. K2. $500.00

CARVER, Raymond. *Put Yourself in My Shoes.* 1974. Santa Barbara. 1st ed. wrp. EX. T9. $115.00

CARVER, Raymond. *This Water.* 1985. Concord. Ewart. 1st ed. 1/100. sgn. dj. EX. B13. $100.00

CARVER, Raymond. *This Water.* 1985. Ewert. Ltd ed. 1/100. sgn. H3. $75.00

CARVER, Raymond. *This Water: Poems.* 1985. Concord. Ewert. 1/36. sgn. EX. C4. $200.00

CARVER, Raymond. *Those Days.* 1987. Elmwood. Raven. 1st ed. 1/100. sgn. wrp. EX. K2. $275.00

CARVER, Raymond. *Toes.* 1988. Concord. 1/36. as issued. K2. $175.00

CARVER, Raymond. *Ultramarine.* 1986. Random House. UP. wrp. EX. K2. $125.00

CARVER, Raymond. *Ultramarine.* 1987. Vintage. PB Orig. wrp. EX. K2. $20.00

CARVER, Raymond. *What We Talk About When We Talk About Love.* 1981. London. Collins. 1st Eng ed. dj. EX. K2. $75.00

CARVER, Raymond. *What We Talk About When We Talk About Love.* 1982. NY. Vintage. PB Orig. sgn. wrp. EX. K2. $125.00

CARVER, Raymond. *What We Talk About When We Talk About Love.* 1989. Vintage. Contemporaries ed. wrp. EX. K2. $25.00

CARVER, Raymond. *Where I'm Calling From.* 1989. Vingage. 1st Trade PB ed. wrp. EX. K2. $20.00

CARVER, Raymond. *Where Water Comes Together With Other Water.* 1985. Random House. UP. wrp. EX. K2. $200.00

CARVER, Raymond. *Where Water Comes Together With Other Water.* 1986. Vintage. PB Orig. wrp. EX. K2. $20.00

CARVER, Raymond. *Will You Please Be Quiet, Please?* 1976. McGraw Hill. 1st ed. dj. EX. B13. $500.00

CARVER, Raymond. *Will You Please Be Quiet, Please?* 1976. McGraw Hill. 1st ed. sgn. dj. M. extremely scarce. K2. $650.00

CARVER, Raymond. *Window.* 1985. Concord. Ewert. 1/136. sgn. orig envelope. very scarce. K2. $275.00

CARVER, Raymond. *Winter Insomnia.* 1970. Santa Cruz. Kayak. 1st ed. sgn. wrp. EX. K2. $250.00

CARVER, Raymond. *Winter Insomnia.* 1970. Santa Cruz. Kayak. 1st ed. wrp. EX. K2. $125.00

CARVER, Raymond. *2 Poems.* 1982. Salisbury. Scarab. 1st ed. 1/100. sgn. EX. K2. $250.00

CARVIC, Heron. *Miss Seeton Draws the Line.* 1970. Harper Row. 1st ed. dj. xl. P1. $6.00

CARY, Elizabeth. *Honore Daumier.* 1907. NY. 8vo. EX. $60.00

CASALS, Pablo. *Joys & Sorrows.* 1970. NY. 1st ed. dj. VG. B3. $20.00

CASANOVA DE SEINGALT, Jacques. *Memoirs.* 1925. Aventuros. Ils Kent. 1/1000. 12 vols. TEG. H3. $1500.00

CASANOVA DE SEINGALT, Jacques. *Memoirs.* 1925. Ils Kent. 1/1000. sm 4to. 12 vols. VG. C2. $225.00

CASAUBON, G.E. *Deceptions With a Short Card.* nd. Colon, MI. Abbott. 56 p. SftCvr. EX. J3. $5.00

CASE, David. *3rd Grave.* 1981. Arkham House. 1st ed. M. R3. $10.95

CASEWIT, C.W. *Peacemakers.* 1960. Avalon. 1st ed. dj. EX. R3. $10.00

CASEY, John. *Am Romance.* 1977. Atheneum. UP. wrp. EX. scarce. K2. $150.00

CASEY, John. *Am Romance.* 1977. NY. 1st ed. sgn. dj. EX. T9. $95.00

CASEY, John. *Am Romance.* 1977. NY. Atheneum. 1st ed. dj. EX. K2. $75.00

CASEY, John. *Testimony & Demeanor.* 1979. Knopf. ARC. dj. EX. K2. $40.00

CASEY, Michael. *Obscenities.* 1972. NH. 3rd print. K2. $20.00

CASEY. *Give the Man Room.* 1952. Indianapolis. 1st ed. 326 p. dj. VG. B3. $20.00

CASH, W.J. *Mind of the S.* 1941. Knopf. 1st ed. inscr/sgn. dj. EX. B13. $1250.00

CASH, W.J. *Mind of the S.* 1941. Knopf. 1st ed. sgn. xl. scarce. C4. $400.00

CASO, Alfonso. *Aztecs: People of the Sun.* 1970. OK U. Ils Covarrubias. 4th print. dj. F2. $20.00

CASO & BERNAL. *Urnas de Oaxaca.* 1952. Mexico. 1st ed. 1/1500. folio. 398 p. F2. $125.00

CASPARY, Vera. *Music in the Street.* nd. Grosset Dunlap. VG. P1. $4.75

CASSADY, Carolyn. *Heart Beat.* 1978. Pocket Books. 1st PB ed. B4. $6.00

CASSELLARI, Rene. *Dramas of French Crime.* 1930. London. VG. $20.00

CASSILL, R.V. *Father & Other Stories.* 1965. Simon Schuster. 1st ed. dj. EX. F5. $20.00

CASSIN, John. *Ils of the Birds of CA, TX, OR, British & Russian Am.* 1865. Phil. later issue. 50 pls. orig cloth. rebacked. VG. H3. $2500.00

CASSOU, Jean. *Antoni Clave.* 1960. Greenwich. French/Eng/Spanish/German text. D4. $125.00

CASSOU, Jean. *Picasso.* 1940. NY. Ils. 167 p. dj. VG. T5. $75.00

CASSOU & LANGUI. *Sources du Vingtiene Siecle.* 1961. Paris. 1st ed. folio. VG. G1. $50.00

CASSUTT, Michael. *Star Country.* 1986. Doubleday. 1st ed. dj. EX. P1. $12.95

CASTANEDA, Carlos. *Mexican Side of the TX Revolution.* 1971. Documentary Pr. Ltd ed. 1/500. 391 p. F2. $30.00

CASTANEDA, Carlos. *2nd Ring of Power.* 1977. Simon Schuster. 1st ed. dj. EX. R3. $10.00

CASTEDO, Leopoldo. *Baroque Prevalence in Brazilian Art.* 1964. NY. Frank. 1st ed. sm 4to. dj. F2. $20.00

CASTEDO, Leopoldo. *Hist of Latin Am Art & Architecture.* 1969. Praeger. 1st ed. 320 p. wrp. F2. $12.50

CASTILLO, Carlos. *Antologia de la Literatura Mexicana.* 1949. CA U. 2nd ed. F2. $10.00

CASTLE, J.L. *Satellite E 1.* 1954. Eyre Spottiswoode. dj. VG. P1. $7.00

CASTLE, Lewis. *Cactaceous Plants: Their Hist & Culture.* 1884. London. Ils. 93 p. VG. T5. $25.00

CASTLE, William. *HI: Past & Present.* 1917. NY. Ils. VG. T1. $25.00

CASTNER, James. *Rain Forests.* 1990. Gainsville. 1st ed. sgn. wrp. F2. $22.95

CATCHPOOL, Corder. *Letters of a Prisoner for Conscience Sake.* 1941. London. Allen Unwin. 12mo. 163 p. dj. VG. V1. $7.00

CATE, Curtis. *War of the 2 Emperors: Duel Between Napoleon & Alexander...* 1985. NY. Ils 1st ed. 487 p. dj. VG. T5. $12.50

CATHCART, William. *Baptist Encyclopedia.* 1883. Phil. Everts. 2 vols. AEG. VG. $150.00

CATHER, Willa. *April Twilights & Other Poems.* 1923. Knopf. 2nd ed. 1/450. sgn. VG. K2. $175.00

CATHER, Willa. *April Twilights.* 1903. Boston. 1st ed. orig brd. VG. scarce. H3. $900.00

CATHER, Willa. *Death Comes for the Archbishop.* 1972. Knopf. 1st ed. gift inscr. dj. EX. B13. $875.00

CATHER, Willa. *Lost Lady.* 1983. Ltd Ed Club. Ils/sgn Bailey. boxed. M. $125.00

CATHER, Willa. *Lost Lady.* 1983. Ltd Ed Club. Ils/sgn William Bailey. slipcase. VG. $95.00

CATHER, Willa. *Old Beauty.* 1948. NY. 1st ed. as issued. K2. $25.00

CATHER, Willa. *Professor's House.* 1925. Knopf. Ltd ed. 1/225. sgn. slipcase. H3. $350.00

CATHER, Willa. *Sapphira & the Slave Girl.* 1940. Knopf. Book Club ed. dj. EX. B10. $4.25

CATHER, Willa. *Sapphira & the Slave Girl.* 1940. Knopf. 1st ed. gr bdg. dj. VG. $25.00

CATHER, Willa. *Shadows on the Rock.* 1931. Knopf. Book Club ed? 280 p. dj. VG. B10. $5.00

CATHER, Willa. *Shadows on the Rock.* 1931. Knopf. Ltd ed. 1/619. sgn. dj. slipcase. H3. $400.00

CATHER, Willa. *Song of the Lark.* 1938. London. 1st Eng ed. as issued. K2. $85.00

CATHER, Willa. *1 of Ours.* 1922. Knopf. 1st ed. 1/310. sgn. EX. K2. $375.00

CATON, J.D. *Antelope & Deer of Am.* 1877. Forest & Stream. VG. T3. $125.00

CATON, J.D. *Land of the IL & Sketch of Pottowatomies.* 1876. Chicago. Fergus Hist Series. wrp. VG. A4. $50.00

CATTELL, Ann. *Mind Juggler & Other Ghost Stories.* 1966. Exposition. dj. EX. P1. $10.00

CATTON, Bruce. *Army of the Potomac: Glory Road.* 1952. Doubleday. 389 p. dj. VG. S1. $7.00

CATTON, Bruce. *Army of the Potomac: Mr Lincoln's Army.* 1962. Doubleday. 363 p. dj. VG. S1. $5.00

CATTON, Bruce. *Coming Fury: Centennial Hist of the Civil War.* 1961. Doubleday. 565 p. dj. xl. S1. $4.00

CATTON, Bruce. *Mr Lincoln's Army.* 1951. Doubleday. 372 p. VG. S1. $5.00

CATTON, Bruce. *Never Call Retreat.* 1965. Doubleday. 555 p. dj. VG. S1. $10.00

CATTON, Bruce. *Stillness at Appomattox.* 1957. Doubleday. 438 p. dj. VG. S1. $5.00

CATTON, Bruce. *Terrible Swift Sword.* 1963. Doubleday. 559 p. dj. VG. S1. $10.00

CATTON, Bruce. *This Hallowed Ground.* 1956. Doubleday. 437 p. dj. VG. S1. $10.00

CATTON, Bruce. *Waiting for the Morning Train.* 1972. Doubleday. dj. G. $17.00

CATULLUS. *Poems of Catullus: A Bilingual Ed.* 1969. CA U. Intro Peter Whigham. 1st Am ed. dj. EX. C4. $25.00

CATWIN, Bruce. *On the Blk Hill.* 1982. London. Cape. 1st ed. dj. EX. B13. $125.00

CATWIN, Bruce. *Viceroy of Ouidah.* 1980. London. Cape. 1st ed. dj. EX. B13. $150.00

CATWIN, Bruce. *Viceroy of Ouidah.* 1980. Summit. UP of 1st Am ed. wrp. EX. B13. $125.00

CAUFFMAN, Stanley. *Witch Finders.* 1934. Penn. 1st ed. VG. R3. $17.50

CAVE, Emma. *Blood Bond.* 1979. Harper Row. 1st ed. dj. EX. F5. $14.00

CAVE, H.B. *Corpse Maker.* 1988. Starmont. 1st ed. wrp. M. R3. $9.95

CAVE, H.B. *Cross on the Drum.* 1959. Doubleday. dj. EX. R3. $15.00

CAVEK, Roderick. *Private Pr.* 1971. NY. lg 8vo. dj. EX. $35.00

CAVELIER, Jean. *Journal of Jean Cavelier: Account of a Survivor...* 1938. Chicago. Inst Jesuit Hist. VG. $30.00

CAVENDISH, G. *Life & Death of Cardinal Wolsey.* 1905. Houghton Mifflin. Ils. 1/1030. EX. $40.00

CAVINO, Italo. *Watcher.* 1971. Watcher. 1st Am ed. dj. EX. R3. $20.00

CAWEIN, M.J. *Accolon of Gaul.* 1889. Louisville. Morton. 1st/only ed. M. C1. $69.00

CAYCE, H.L. *Venture Inward.* nd. Book Club. VG. $2.00

CAZOTTE, Jacques. *Devil in Love.* 1925. Boston. Ils JE Laboureur. 1/365. 87 p. VG. T5. $35.00

CECIL, Henry. *Brothers in Law.* 1955. Michael Joseph. 3rd ed. dj. VG. P1. $17.50

CELINE, L.F. *Castle to Castle.* 1968. Delacorte. 1st Am ed. dj. EX. C4. $25.00

CELINE, L.F. *Death on the Installment Plan.* 1966. New Directions. 1st Am ed. dj. EX. C4. $50.00

CERAM, C.W. *Gods, Graves, & Scholars.* 1954. Knopf. 32 pls. 428 p. dj. F2. $10.00

CERF, Bennett. *Plays of Our Time.* 1967. Book Club. 782 p. VG. B10. $3.75

CERVANTES, Carlo; see De Cervantes Saavedra, Miguel.

CERVON, Bruce. *Card Secrets of Bruce Cervon.* 1976. Los Angeles. Cervon. 1st ed. 64 p. SftCvr. EX. J3. $8.00

CERVON, Bruce. *Cervon File.* 1988. Magical Pub. 1st ed. 254 p. NM. J3. $22.00

CHABER, M.E. *Bonded Dead.* 1971. Holt Rinehart Winston. 1st ed. dj. EX. P1. $13.75

CHABER, M.E. *Day It Rained Diamonds.* 1966. Holt Rinehart Winston. 1st ed. dj. VG. P1. $13.75

CHABER, M.E. *Gr Grow the Graves.* 1970. Holt Rinehart Winston. 1st ed. dj. EX. P1. $13.75

CHABON, Michael. *Model World & Other Stories.* 1991. Morrow. ARC. EX. K2. $25.00

CHACE & LOVELL. *2 Quaker Sisters.* 1937. NY. Liveright. 1st print. 8vo. 83 p. dj. VG. V1. $15.00

CHAFFERS, W. *Hallmarks on Gold & Silverplate.* 1872. London. 4th ed. VG. C2. $40.00

CHAFFERS, W. *Hallmarks on Gold & Silverplate.* 1905. London. 9th ed. VG. $22.00

CHAGALL, Marc. *Jerusalem Windows.* 1962. Braziller. 2 orig lithos. dj. EX. H3. $1500.00

CHAGALL, Marc. *Lithographs.* 1960. Monte Carlo. Sauret. 14 orig lithos. dj. EX. H3. $3000.00

CHAGALL, Marc. *Musee Nat Message Biblique.* 1973. Paris. Ils. stiff wrp. VG. T5. $35.00

CHALFANT, E. *Goodly Heritage: Earliest Wills on an Am Frontier.* 1955. Pittsburgh. dj. EX. $22.00

CHALKER, J.L. *Messiah Choice.* 1985. Bluejay. 1st ed. dj. EX. P1. $16.95

CHALKER, J.L. *4 Lords of the Diamond.* 1983. Doubleday. 1st HrdCvr ed. dj. EX. F5. $12.00

CHALKLEY, Thomas. *Journal of Thomas Chalkley.* nd. Phil. Friends Bookstore. Stereotype ed. 12mo. 634 p. V1. $15.00

CHALMERS, A.B. *Declaring the Everlasting Truth.* 1952. Phil. Young Friends. 16mo. SftCvr. VG. V1. $6.00

CHALMERS, Harvey. *W to the Setting Sun.* 1943. Toronto. 1st ed. 362 p. VG. B10. $9.00

CHAMBERLAIN, Elinor. *Manila Hemp.* 1947. Dodd Mead. 1st ed. dj. VG. P1. $15.00

CHAMBERLAIN, Samuel. *Fair Is Our Land.* 1944. Hastings House. 4th ed. 252 p. VG. B10. $5.50

CHAMBERLAIN. *Annals of Grand Monadnock.* 1936. Concord. 1st ed. photos. fld maps. VG. C2. $35.00

CHAMBERLIN, E.R. *Fall of the House of Borgia.* 1974. NY. 1st ed. dj. EX. $15.00

CHAMBERLIN, H.D. *Riding & Schooling Horses.* 1934. Derrydale. 1/950. 199 p. G. T5. $55.00

CHAMBERS, E.K. *Sir Thomas & Some Collected Studies.* 1933. London. Sidgwick Jackson. VG. C1. $7.50

CHAMBERS, H.A. *Diary of Captain Henry A Chambers.* 1983. Broadfoot Pub. 290 p. dj. M. S1. $25.00

CHAMBERS, Jack. *NV Whalen Avenger.* nd. Saalfield. Big Little Book. G. P1. $10.50

CHAMBERS, Lenoir. *Stonewall Jackson.* 1988. Broadfoot Pub. 2 vols. boxed. M. S1. $60.00

CHAMBERS, Peter. *Bad Die Young.* 1967. Robert Hale. 1st ed. dj. xl. P1. $5.00

CHAMBERS, Peter. *Downbeat Kill.* 1964. Abelard Schuman. EX. P1. $9.25

CHAMBERS, Peter. *Lady, You're Killing Me.* 1979. Robert Hale. 1st ed. dj. xl. P1. $5.00

CHAMBERS, Peter. *Wreath for a Redhead.* 1962. Abelard Schuman. 1st ed. dj. VG. P1. $10.00

CHAMBERS, R.W. *Anne's Bridge.* 1914. Appleton. presentation. gr bdg. H3. $50.00

CHAMBERS, R.W. *Common Law.* 1911. McLeod Allen. VG. P1. $4.75

CHAMBERS, R.W. *Fighting Chance.* 1906. Appleton. presentation. H3. $40.00

CHAMBERS, R.W. *Flaming Jewel.* 1942. Triangle. dj. VG. P1. $10.00

CHAMBERS, R.W. *Gay Rebellion.* 1913. Appleton. 1st ed. VG. R3. $45.00

CHAMBERS, R.W. *Hidden Children.* nd. AL Burt. dj. EX. R3. $25.00

CHAMBERS, R.W. *In the Quarter.* c 1890s. Neely. VG. R3. $22.50

CHAMBERS, R.W. *Maid-At-Arms.* 1902. Harper. Ils Christy. presentation. H3. $60.00

CHAMBERS, R.W. *Maker of Moons.* 1954. Shroud Krueger. 1st ed. wrp. dj. EX. R3. $35.00

CHAMBERS, R.W. *Quick Action.* 1914. Appleton. 1st ed. VG. R3. $20.00

CHAMBERS, R.W. *Secret Service Operator 13.* 1934. Appleton. 1st ed. EX. F5. $10.00

CHAMBERS, R.W. *Secret Service Operator 13.* 1942. Triangle. 2nd ed. VG. P1. $7.50

CHAMBERS, R.W. *Special Messenger.* nd. Clifford's Inn. presentation. H3. $75.00

CHAMBERS, R.W. *Talkers.* 1923. Doran. 1st ed. VG. R3. $25.00

CHAMBERS, R.W. *Younger Set.* nd. AL Burt. VG. P1. $4.50

CHAMBERS, R.W. *Younger Set.* 1907. Appleton. presentation. H3. $60.00

CHAMBERS, Robert. *King in Yellow.* 1902. NY. Ils. VG. B3. $27.50

CHAMBERS, W.R. *Bluebird Weather.* 1912. Appleton. Ils Gibson. VG. $7.00

CHAMBERS, Whitman. *Coast of Intrigue.* nd. World. VG. P1. $6.50

CHAMBERS. *Chambers Encyclopedia.* 1881. London. 3rd ed. 10 vols. 8vo. EX. A4. $200.00

CHAMPION, Joseph. *New & Elegant Set of Copies in German Text With Alphabet.* 1808. Phil. oblong 8vo. wrp. $150.00

CHAMPNEY, E.W. *Romance of Russia.* 1921. Putnam. 1st ed. 352 p. VG. B10. $7.00

CHAMPNEY, E.W. *3 Vassar Girls in France...* 1888. Boston. 240 p. G. T5. $35.00

CHAMPNEY, E.W. *3 Vassar Girls in Russia & Turkey.* 1889. Boston. pls. 240 p. T5. $35.00

CHANCE, Harold. *Tradition & Challenge.* 1952. Phil. Larchwood Pr. 16mo. 70 p. dj. VG. V1. $6.00

CHANCE, John. *Race & Class in Colonial Am.* 1978. Stanford. 1st ed. 250 p. dj. F2. $20.00

CHANCE, Stephen. *Septimus & the Stone of Offering.* 1976. 1st ed. dj. VG. C1. $6.50

CHANCELLOR, P. *Bach Flower Remedies.* 1971. Keats. 1st ed? PB. VG. B10. $3.50

CHANDLER, A.B. *Hamelin Plague.* 1963. Monarch. 1st ed. wrp. EX. F5. $10.00

CHANDLER, A.B. *When the Dream Dies.* 1981. Allison Busby. dj. P1. $15.00

CHANDLER, A.B. *When the Dream Dies.* 1981. London. dj. R3. $25.00

CHANDLER, A.C. *Pan the Piper & Other Marvelous Tales.* 1922. Harper. 1st ed. VG. B7. $50.00

CHANDLER, Alice. *Dream of Order.* 1970. NE U. 1st ed. dj. EX. C1. $11.00

CHANDLER, D.G. *Campaigns of Napoleon.* 1966. NY. 1172 p. G. T5. $47.50

CHANDLER, David. *Aphrodite.* 1977. Morrow. 1st ed. dj. xl. P1. $4.75

CHANDLER, Harold. *Chandu's Magical Varieties.* 1970. Micky Hades Enterprises. Revised ed. NM. J3. $4.00

CHANDLER, Mark. *9 Lives.* 1937. Lippincott. 1st ed. dj. VG. R3. $25.00

CHANDLER, Ranmond. *Spanish Blood.* 1945. World. 1st ed. dj. VG. R3. $22.50

CHANDLER, Raymond. *Big Sleep.* 1946. Forum. Photoplay ed. dj. VG. P1. $30.00

CHANDLER, Raymond. *Big Sleep.* 1946. Tower. Photoplay ed. 1st print. dj. VG. T9. $40.00

CHANDLER, Raymond. *Farewell, My Lovely.* nd. Modern Lib. EX. P1. $18.25

CHANDLER, Raymond. *Farewell, My Lovely.* 1946. Tower. 3rd ed. dj. VG. P1. $25.00

CHANDLER, Raymond. *Farewell, My Lovely.* 1946. World. 3rd/Photoplay ed. dj. VG. P1. $25.00

CHANDLER, Raymond. *High Window.* 1945. Tower. dj. VG. P1. $17.50

CHANDLER, Raymond. *High Window.* 1946. Tower. 2nd ed. dj. VG. P1. $25.00

CHANDLER, Raymond. *Lady in the Lake.* 1944. Hamish Hamilton. VG. P1. $27.25

CHANDLER, Raymond. *Lady of the Lake.* 1946. Grosset Dunlap. 1sr Photoplay ed. dj. VG. T9. $45.00

CHANDLER, Raymond. *Little Sister.* 1949. Houghton Mifflin. 1st Am ed. VG. T9. $40.00

CHANDLER, Raymond. *Little Sister.* 1949. London. Hamish Hamilton. VG. P1. $45.00

CHANDLER, Raymond. *Long Goodbye.* 1953. Hamish Hamilton. 1st ed. VG. P1. $30.00

CHANDLER, Raymond. *Long Goodbye.* 1953. Hamish Hamilton. 2nd ed. VG. P1. $22.75

CHANDLER, Raymond. *Long Goodbye.* 1953. London. Penguin. 1st ed. dj. VG. P1. $50.00

CHANDLER, Raymond. *Mystery Omnibus.* 1944. Forum. 1st ed. VG. P1. $11.50

CHANDLER, Raymond. *Notebooks of Raymond Chandler/Eng Summer.* 1976. Ecco. 1st ed. dj. EX. K2. $40.00

CHANDLER, Raymond. *Playback.* nd. Book Club. dj. VG. P1. $3.50

CHANDLER, Raymond. *Playback.* 1958. Boston. 1st Am ed. as issued. M. K2. $85.00

CHANDLER, Raymond. *Playback.* 1958. Houghton Mifflin. 1st Am ed. dj. EX. T9. $50.00

CHANDLER, Raymond. *Raymond Chandler's Philip Marlowe: Centennial Celebration...* 1988. Knopf. UP. wrp. EX. C4. $35.00

CHANDLER, Raymond. *Raymond Chandler's Unknown Thriller: Screenplay of Playback.* 1985. Mysterious Pr. UP. wrp. EX. C4. $50.00

CHANDLER, Raymond. *Red Wind.* 1946. World. 1st ed. dj. VG. T9. $40.00

CHANDLER, Raymond. *Simple Art of Murder.* 1950. Hamish Hamilton. 2nd ed. dj. VG. P1. $25.00

CHANDLER, Raymond. *Spanish Blood.* 1946. Tower. dj. VG. P1. $25.00

CHANDLER, Raymond. *Spanish Blood.* 1946. World. 1st ed. dj. VG. T9. $45.00

CHANDLER & THAMES. *Colonial VA.* 1907. Richmond. 1st ed. 388 p. VG. B3. $37.50

CHANGE, J.N. *Blk Widow.* 1981. Robert Hale. 1st ed. dj. xl. P1. $5.00

CHANGE, J.N. *Night of the Full Moon.* 1950. MacDonald. 1st ed. dj. xl. P1. $6.00

CHANIN, Jack. *Grand Finale! Silk at Your Fingertips.* 1952. Phil. Chanin. Revised/Enlarged ed. 96 p. NM. J3. $12.00

CHANIN, Jack. *Jack Chanin Grand Finale, Silks at Your Fingertips.* 1940. Chanin. 1st ed. 13 p. SftCvr. VG. J3. $6.00

CHANIN, Jack. *JC Cigar Magic, Cigar Manipulations.* 1937. Phil. Chanin. 1st ed. 80 p. SftCvr. EX. J3. $12.00

CHANIN, Jack. *New Twist to Your Magic.* 1952. Magician's Guild of Am. 1st ed. stapled manuscript. NM. J3. $10.00

CHANNING, W.E. *Thoreau: Poet-Naturalist With Memorial Verses.* 1873. Boston. 1st ed. G. T5. $25.00

CHANNING S.A. *Crisis of Fear: Succession in SC.* 1970. Simon Schuster. 315 p. dj. S1. $15.00

CHANSLOR, Roy. *Ballad of Cat Ballou.* 1956. Little Brn. 1st ed. dj. EX. C4. $35.00

CHANT, A.G. *Legend of Glastonbury.* 1948. London. 1st ed. dj. NM. C1. $16.50

CHANT, Joy. *Gray Mane of Morning.* 1977. Allen Unwin. 1st ed. dj. EX. P1. $25.00

CHANT, Joy. *Gray Mane of Morning.* 1978. Allen Unwin. 2nd ed. P1. $11.50

CHANT, Joy. *Red Moon & Blk Mt.* nd. Book Club. dj. VG. P1. $4.75

CHANUTE, Octave. *Progress in Flying Machines.* 1976. Long Beach. facsimile of 1894 ed. dj. VG. T5. $15.00

CHAPIN, C.M. *3 Died Beside the Marble Pool.* 1936. Crime Club. 1st ed. VG. P1. $18.25

CHAPLIN, Jeremiah. *Life of Charles Sumner.* 1874. Lathrop. 504 p. G. S1. $12.00

CHAPMAN, A.E. *Ready Blade.* 1934. NY. 1st ed. VG. C1. $7.00

CHAPMAN, Charles. *Colonial Hispanic Am: A Hist.* 1933. Macmillan. 1st ed. 405 p. F2. $12.50

CHAPMAN, Elwood. *Scrambling: Zigzagging Your Way to the Top.* 1981. 1st ed. inscr. dj. EX. C1. $7.50

CHAPMAN, F.M. *Clr Key to N Am Birds.* 1912. Appleton. Ils. VG. T3. $35.00

CHAPMAN, F.M. *Warblers of N Am.* 1907. Appleton. clr pls. VG. T3. $40.00

CHAPMAN, Frank. *20 Stunners With a Nail Writer.* 1944. Lee Grey. 3rd ed. 25 p. SftCvr. M. J3. $2.00

CHAPMAN, T.J. *French in the Allegheny Valley.* 1887. Cleveland. 1st ed. presentation from author's wife. VG. T5. $125.00

CHAPMAN, Walker. *Golden Dream.* 1967. Bobbs Merrill. 1st ed. 436 p. dj. F2. $15.00

CHAPPELL, Fred. *Gaudy Place.* 1973. NY. 1st ed. presentation. dj. EX. T9. $65.00

CHAPUIS & JAQUET. *Hist of the Self-Winding Watch.* 1956. NY. Ils. 4to. dj. EX. $65.00

CHARBONNEAU, Louis. *No Place on Earth.* nd. Book Club. dj. VG. P1. $3.50

CHARHADI, D.H. *Life Full of Holes.* 1964. NY. Trans Bowles. 1st ed. dj. EX. $45.00

CHARLES, David. *Story of the Aircraft.* 1974. London. Ils. 127 p. dj. T5. $9.50

CHARLES, Neil. *24 Hours.* 1952. London. 1st ed. wrp. VG. R3. $15.00

CHARLOT, Jean. *Artist on Art: Collected Essays.* 1972. Hawaii U. 1st ed. 2 vols. slipcase. F2. $35.00

CHARNAS, Suzy McKee. *Bronze King.* 1985. Houghton Mifflin. 1st ed. dj. VG. P1. $12.95

CHARNAS, Suzy McKee. *Dorothea Dreams.* 1986. Arbor House. 1st ed. dj. RS. EX. P1. $20.00

CHARNAS, Suzy McKee. *Motherlines.* 1978. 1st ed. dj. VG. C1. $7.50

CHARNAS, Suzy McKee. *Motherlines.* 1978. Berkley Putnam. 1st ed. dj. VG. P1. $17.50

CHARNEY, D.H. *Magic: Great Illusions Revealed & Explained.* 1975. Strawberry Hill. 247 p. dj. J3. $12.00

CHARTERIS, Leslie. *Brighter Buccaneer.* 1975. Wht Lion. dj. xl. P1. $6.00

CHARTERIS, Leslie. *Call for the Saint.* 1948. Doubleday Crime Club. 1st ed. xl. VG. P1. $7.50

CHARTERIS, Leslie. *Featuring the Saint.* nd. Hodder Stoughton. VG. P1. $7.50

CHARTERIS, Leslie. *Follow the Saint.* 1940. Hodder Stoughton. 3rd ed. xl. P1. $7.50

CHARTERIS, Leslie. *Follow the Saint.* 1943. Triangle. 2nd ed. VG. P1. $10.00

CHARTERIS, Leslie. *Juan Belmonte Killer of Bulls.* nd. Book League. VG. P1. $15.00

CHARTERIS, Leslie. *Last Hero.* 1948. Hodder Stoughton. 18th print. VG. P1. $12.00

CHARTERIS, Leslie. *Saint & Mr Teal.* 1943. Triangle. VG. P1. $10.00

CHARTERIS, Leslie. *Saint at Lg.* 1945. Triangle. 5th ed. dj. VG. P1. $12.50

CHARTERIS, Leslie. *Saint Bids Diamonds.* 1942. Triangle. dj. VG. P1. $12.50

CHARTERIS, Leslie. *Saint Goes On.* 1942. Triangle. 9th print. VG. P1. $10.00

CHARTERIS, Leslie. *Saint Goes W.* 1942. Musson. 1st Canadian ed. VG. P1. $12.50

CHARTERIS, Leslie. *Saint in Miami.* 1945. Triangle. 4th ed. dj. VG. P1. $11.50

CHARTERIS, Leslie. *Saint in NY.* 1941. Triangle. 2nd ed. G. P1. $5.00

CHARTERIS, Leslie. *Saint in Trouble.* 1978. Crime Club. 1st ed. dj. VG. P1. $17.50

CHARTERIS, Leslie. *Saint on Guard.* 1944. Crime Club. 1st ed. dj. VG. P1. $35.00

CHARTERIS, Leslie. *Saint Overboard.* 1942. Triangle. 6th ed. VG. P1. $9.25

CHARTERIS, Leslie. *Saint Plays With Fire.* 1942. Triangle. VG. P1. $10.00

CHARTERIS, Leslie. *Saint Sees It Through.* 1947. Musson. 1st Canadian ed. VG. P1. $6.50

CHARTERIS, Leslie. *Saint Steps in.* 1944. Musson. dj. xl. P1. $6.50

CHARTERIS, Leslie. *Saint to the Rescue.* 1959. Crime Club. 1st ed. dj. xl. P1. $10.00

CHARTERIS, Leslie. *Saint's Getaway.* 1945. Triangle. VG. P1. $10.00

CHARTERIS, Leslie. *Trust the Saint.* 1962. Crime Club. 1st ed. dj. VG. P1. $22.50

CHARTERIS, Leslie. *Wht Rider.* nd. Ward Lock. VG. P1. $20.00

CHARTERIS, Leslie. *X Esquire.* nd. Ward Lock. VG. P1. $40.00

CHARYN, Jerome. *Man Who Grew Younger & Other Stories.* 1967. Harper. 1st ed. inscr. dj. EX. F5. $25.00

CHARYN, Jerome. *War Cries Over Ave C.* 1985. NY. Fine. UP. inscr. proof dj. EX. K2. $45.00

CHARYN, Jerome. *7th Babe.* 1979. Arbor House. UP. proof dj. scarce. B13. $65.00

CHASE, A.W. *Dr Chase's Recipes; or, Information for Everybody.* 1866. Ann Arbor. Chase. EX. $45.00

CHASE, J.H. *I'll Bury My Dead.* 1954. Dutton. 1st ed. dj. VG. P1. $10.00

CHASE, J.H. *You Have Yourself a Deal.* 1968. Walker. 1st Am ed. dj. F5. $25.00

CHASE, J.H. *You're Lonely When You're Dead.* 1951. Popular Lib 378. PB Orig. NM. T9. $15.00

CHASE, M.E. *Dawn in Lyonesse.* 1938. NY. 1st Am ed. VG. scarce. C1. $6.50

CHASE, Stuart. *Tyranny of Words.* 1938. Harcourt Brace. 1st ed. 396 p. dj. VG. B10. $4.50

CHASE, W.H. *5 Generations of Loom Builders.* 1950. Hopewell, MA. Ils. presentation. boxed. EX. $45.00

CHASE. *Memorial Life of Gen Sherman.* 1891. Chicago. Ils. 8vo. 558 p. red bdg. G4. $19.00

CHASE-RIBOUD, Barbara. *Echo of Lions.* 1989. Morrow. 1st ed. dj. EX. B13. $25.00

CHASTAIN, Thomas. *911.* nd. Book Club. VG. P1. $3.00

CHATHAM, Russell. *Angler's Coast.* 1976. NY. 1st ed. sgn. dj. EX. T9. $65.00

CHATHAM. *Anecdotes of William Pitt, 1st Earl.* 1797. London. 6th ed. 3 vols. A4. $250.00

CHATTERJEE, S. *Short Sketch of Rajah Rajendro Mullick Bahadur & Family.* 1917. Calcutta. Ils. 100 p. G. $75.00

CHATTERTON, E.K. *Eng's Greatest Statesman.* 1930. Indianapolis. 1st ed. VG. $15.00

CHATWIN, Bruce. *In Patagonia.* 1977. Summit. 1st Am ed. dj. C4. $100.00

CHATWIN, Bruce. *In Patagonia.* 1977. Summit. 1st ed. dj. EX. B13. $200.00

CHATWIN, Bruce. *Songlines.* 1987. Viking. ARC of 1st Am ed. dj. RS. EX. K2. $75.00

CHATWIN, Bruce. *Viceroy of Ouidah.* 1980. London. Cape. UP. wrp. EX. K2. $285.00

CHATWIN, Bruce. *What Am I Doing Here?* 1989. London. UP. EX. $80.00

CHATWIN & THEROUX. *Patagonia Revisited.* 1985. London. Michael Russell. 1st ed. 1/250. sgns. tissue dj. EX. B13. $275.00

CHATWIN & THEROUX. *Patagonia Revisited.* 1986. Houghton Mifflin. 1st Am ed. 62 p. dj. F2. $15.00

CHAUCER, Geoffrey. *Canterbury Tales.* 1946. Ltd Ed Club. Ils/sgn Arthur Szyk. Deluxe ed. slipcase. M. $250.00

CHAUCER, Geoffrey. *Poetical Works.* 1845. London. Pickering. Aldine ed. 6 vols. sm octavo. EX. H3. $450.00

CHAUCER, Geoffrey. *Troilus & Cressida.* 1932. Literary Guild. Ils Eric Gill. VG. B7. $38.00

CHAUCER, Geoffrey. *Troilus & Cressida.* 1939. London. Ltd Ed Club. Printed/sgn George Jones. 1/1500. slipcase. C4. $50.00

CHAUCER, Geoffrey. *Works.* 1928-1929. Blackwell. Ltd ed. 1/375. 8 vols. lg octavo. H3. $2000.00

CHAUVELOT, Robert. *Mysterious India.* 1921. Century. 1st ed. 277 p. VG. B10. $7.50

CHAUVIERRE, Marc. *Television: Les Problemes Theoretiques et Pratiques...* 1938. Paris. Dunod. 1st ed. octavo. 267 p. wrp. VG. H3. $150.00

CHAVEZ, Augustin. *Valazquez, Contemporary Mexican Artist.* 1937. Covici Friede. 1st ed. 304 p. VG. $75.00

CHAVEZ, Marion. *Encyclopedia of Dove Magic.* 1979. Tannen Magic. 1st ed. 152 p. M. J3. $20.00

CHAVEZ & CHAVEZ. *Chavez Studio of Magic, Prestidigitation, & Showmanship.* 1960. Chavez Studio. J3. $25.00

CHEETHAM, Anthony. *Life & Times of Richard III.* 1972. London. NM. C1. $12.50

CHEEVER, John. *Brigadier & the Golf Widow.* 1964. Harper Row. 1st ed. dj. VG. H3. $40.00

CHEEVER, John. *Bullet Park.* 1969. Knopf. 1st ed. dj. EX. $35.00

CHEEVER, John. *Enormous Radio & Other Stories.* 1953. Funk Wagnalls. 1st ed. EX. H3. $175.00

CHEEVER, John. *Expelled.* 1987. Sylvester Orphanos. 1/185. sgn Cheever/ Updike/Cowley/Chappell. EX. K2. $275.00

CHEEVER, John. *Oh What a Paradise It Seems.* 1982. Knopf. UP. wrp. EX. C4. $45.00

CHEEVER, John. *Whapshot Scandal.* 1964. Harper Row. 1st print. dj. EX. $125.00

CHEEVER, John. *World of Apples.* 1973. Knopf. 1st ed. dj. EX. H3. $40.00

CHEKHOV, Anton. *Sea Gull.* 1939. Scribner. 1st ed. dj. EX. H3. $75.00

CHEKHOV, Anton. *Short Stories.* 1973. Ltd Ed Club. Ils/sgn Lajos Szalay. slipcase. VG. $45.00

CHEKHOV, Anton. *2 Plays of Anton Chekhov: The Cherry Orchard/3 Sisters.* 1966. Ltd Ed Club. Ils/sgn Lajos Szalay. 1/1500. slipcase. EX. C4. $65.00

CHEKHOV, Anton. *3 Sisters.* 1969. Macmillan. Trans Jarrell. 1st ed. dj. EX. H3. $75.00

CHENEY, J. *Caxton Club Scrapbook: Early Eng Verses 1250-1650.* 1904. Chicago. Ltd ed. 1/250. G. $25.00

CHERMERE. *Papillon.* 1970. NY. 1st ed. sgn. dj. VG. B3. $50.00

CHERNIN, Kim. *Flame Bearers.* 1986. nd. np. 1st ed. dj. EX. C1. $7.50

CHERRY, Kelly. *My Life With Dr Joyce Brothers.* 1990. Algonquin Books. UP. wrp. EX. K2. $30.00

CHERRY, P.P. *Portage Path.* 1911. Akron. Ils 1st ed. 106 p. T5. $42.50

CHERRY & GARRAGO. *Worst Journey in World.* 1965. London. 584 p. maps. B3. $37.50

CHERRYH, C.J. *Brothers of Earth.* nd. Book Club. dj. VG. P1. $4.50

CHERRYH, C.J. *Brothers of Earth.* 1976. SF Book Club. 1st ed. sgn. dj. EX. R3. $25.00

CHERRYH, C.J. *Chanur's Homecoming.* 1986. DAW Books. 1st Trade HrdCvr ed. sgn. dj. EX. F5. $14.00

CHERRYH, C.J. *Chanur's Venture.* 1984. Phantasia. Ltd ed. 1/350. sgn. M. R3. $40.00

CHERRYH, C.J. *Chanur's Venture.* 1984. Phantasia. 1st ed. M. R3. $17.00

CHERRYH, C.J. *Chernevog.* 1990. Del Rey. 1st ed. sgn. dj. EX. F5. $22.00

CHERRYH, C.J. *Cuckoo's Egg.* 1985. Phantasia. Ltd ed. 1/350. sgn. dj. slipcase. P1/R3. $40.00

CHERRYH, C.J. *Cuckoo's Egg.* 1985. Phantasia. 1st ed. M. R3. $17.00

CHERRYH, C.J. *Cyteen.* 1988. Warner. 1st ed. sgn. dj. EX. F5. $25.00

CHERRYH, C.J. *Downbelow Station.* 1981. DAW Books. 1st HrdCvr ed. sgn. dj. EX. F5. $20.00

CHERRYH, C.J. *Exile's Gate.* 1988. DAW Books. 1st HrdCvr ed. 1st print. dj. EX. F5. $11.00

CHERRYH, C.J. *Kif Strike Back.* 1984. Phantasia. 1st ed. M. R3. $17.00

CHERRYH, C.J. *Kif Strike Back.* 1985. Phantasia. Ltd ed. 1/350. sgn. dj. slipcase. P1/R3. $40.00

CHERRYH, C.J. *Merchanter's Luck.* 1982. DAW Books. 1st HrdCvr ed. dj. EX. F5. $10.00

CHERRYH, C.J. *Pride of Chanur.* 1981. DAW Books. 1st HrdCvr ed. dj. EX. F5. $10.00

CHERRYH, C.J. *40,000 in Gehenna.* 1983. Phantasia. 1st ed. M. R3. $17.00

CHERRYTH & HENNEBERG. *Gr Gods.* 1980. DAW Books. 1st ed. sgn. wrp. EX. F5. $10.00

CHESBRO, G.C. *Affair of Sorcerers.* 1980. Severn House. 1st ed. dj. EX. P1. $20.00

CHESBRO, G.C. *City of Whispering Stone.* 1978. Simon Schuster. 1st ed. dj. VG. P1. $25.00

CHESBRO, G.C. *Jungle of Steel & Stone.* 1988. Mysterious Pr. 1st ed. dj. EX. F5. $15.00

CHESBRO, G.C. *Shadow of a Broken Man.* 1977. Simon Schuster. 1st ed. dj. EX. F5. $30.00

CHESBRO, G.C. *Shadow of a Broken Man.* 1977. Simon Schuster. 1st ed. dj. VG. P1. $20.00

CHESBRO, George B.; see Cross, David.

CHESSMAN, Caryl. *Cell 2455 Death Row.* 1954. NY. 1st ed. dj. VG. B3. $27.50

CHESSMAN, Caryl. *Face of Justice.* 1957. Prentice Hall. 1st ed. dj. VG. B3. $20.00

CHESTER, Alfred. *Jamie Is My Heart's Desire.* 1957. NY. 1st ed. dj. EX. T9. $40.00

CHESTER, G.R. *Cash Intrigue.* 1909. Bobbs Merrill. 1st ed. EX. R3. $25.00

CHESTER, Giraud. *Embattled Maiden.* 1951. NY. Ils 307 p. dj. VG. T5. $15.00

CHESTERFIELD, P.D.S. *Poetical Works.* 1927. London. Mathews Marrot. 1/250. VG. C4. $350.00

CHESTERTON, G.K. *Annotated Innocence of Father Brn.* 1987. Oxford. 1st ed. M. R3. $19.00

CHESTERTON, G.K. *Autobiography.* 1936. London. Hutchinson. 12mo. RS. w/sgn letter. H3. $300.00

CHESTERTON, G.K. *Autobiography.* 1936. NY. 1st ed. VG. $20.00

CHESTERTON, G.K. *Ball & the Cross.* 1910. London. 1st ed. TEG. VG. $50.00

CHESTERTON, G.K. *Defendant.* c 1920-1930. London. Dent. 131 p. G. B10. $3.75

CHESTERTON, G.K. *Father Brn Book.* 1959. Cassell. 2nd ed. xl. P1. $7.25

CHESTERTON, G.K. *Incredulity of Father Brn.* 1926. NY. Dodd. 1st ed. dj. VG. B13. $125.00

CHESTERTON, G.K. *Incredulity of Father Brn.* 1984. Hall. Lg Print ed. 271 p. B10. $5.25

CHESTERTON, G.K. *Innocence of Father Brn.* nd. (1911) Readers League. 312 p. B10. $3.50

CHESTERTON, G.K. *Innocence of Father Brn.* nd. Macaulay. VG. P1. $15.00

CHESTERTON, G.K. *Innocence of Father Brn.* 1913. Cassell. 4th print. VG. P1. $18.25

CHESTERTON, G.K. *Man Who Was Thursday.* 1946. Arrowsmith. 3rd ed. VG. P1. $20.00

CHESTERTON, G.K. *Orthodoxy.* 1911. John Lane. 1st ed. sgn. dj. EX. B13. $100.00

CHESTERTON, G.K. *Tales of the Long Bow.* 1925. Tauchnitz. VG. P1. $60.00

CHESTERTON, G.K. *What's Wrong With the World.* 1913. Cassell. 8th print. VG. P1. $20.00

CHESTNUT, Robert; see Cooper, Clarence.

CHETWIN, Grace. *Atheling.* 1988. Tor Books. 1st ed. dj. EX. F5. $16.00

CHETWIN, Grace. *Crystal Stair.* 1988. Bradbury. 1st ed. dj. VG. P1. $13.95

CHETWIN, Grace. *Riddle & the Rune.* 1987. Bradbury. 1st ed. dj. EX. P1. $13.95

CHETWIN, Grace. *Starstone.* 1989. Bradbury. 1st ed. dj. EX. P1. $14.95

CHETWYND-HAYES, R. *Dracula's Children.* 1987. William Kimber. 1st ed. sgn. dj. EX. P1. $25.00

CHETWYND-HAYES, R. *House of Dracula.* 1987. William Kimber. 1st ed. sgn. dj. EX. P1. $25.00

CHETWYND-HAYES, R. *Quiver of Ghosts.* 1984. William Kimber. 1st ed. sgn. dj. EX. P1. $30.00

CHETWYND-HAYES, R. *Tales From the Dark Lands.* 1984. William Kimber. 1st ed. dj. EX. P1. $20.00

CHEVALIER, Sarah. *Treatise on the Hair: Learn to Cultivate.* 1873. NY. 24 p. wrp. $25.00

CHEYNE, John. *Essay on Hydrocephalus Actus or Dropsey in the Brain.* 1814. Phil. full leather. VG. $400.00

CHEYNEY, Peter. *Dark Bahama.* 1950. Collins. dj. VG. P1. $9.25

CHEYNEY, Peter. *Dark Wanton.* 1948. Collins. dj. VG. P1. $9.25

CHEYNEY, Peter. *I'll Say She Does.* 1946. Book Club. VG. P1. $5.00

CHEYNEY, Peter. *Ladies Won't Wait.* 1972. Collins. dj. VG. P1. $12.50

CHEYNEY, Peter. *Lady, Behave!* 1950. Collins. dj. VG. P1. $15.00

CHEYNEY, Peter. *Man Nobody Saw.* 1949. Dodd Mead. 1st ed. dj. xl. P1. $8.00

CHEYNEY, Peter. *Sinister Errand.* 1952. Collins. Photoplay ed. dj. VG. P1. $17.50

CHEYNEY, Peter. *Uneasy Terms.* 1947. Dodd Mead. xl. P1. $6.00

CHEYNEY, Peter. *Uneasy Terms.* 1958. Collins. dj. VG. P1. $17.50

CHEYNEY, Peter. *1 of Those Things.* 1950. Dodd Mead. VG. P1. $10.00

CHICAGO ART INSTITUTE. *Primitive Art From Chicago Collections.* 1960. Chicago. Ils. 4to. wrp. F2. $12.50

CHICHESTER, J.J. *Rogues of Fortune.* 1929. Chelsea House. xl. VG. P1. $13.75

CHIDSEY, D.B. *Stronghold.* 1948. Doubleday. 1st ed. EX. F5. $13.00

CHIEF STANDING BEAR. *My People the Sioux.* 1928. Boston. 1st ed. 288 p. VG. B3. $40.00

CHILD, Hamilton. *Oneida Co Directory 1869.* 1869. Syracuse, NY. scarce. B10. $32.00

CHILD, Julia. *From Julia Child's Kitchen.* 1982. Knopf. 687 p. dj. EX. B10. $8.00

CHILD, L.M. *Isaac T Hopper: A True Life.* 1853. Boston. JP Jewett. 1st ed. 12mo. 493 p. V1. $22.50

CHILDERS, J.S. *Novel About a Wht Man & a Blk Man in the Deep S.* 1936. Farrar Rinehart. presentation. H3. $75.00

CHILDRESS, Alice. *Like 1 of the Family.* 1956. Brooklyn. 1st ed. dj. very scarce. B13. $125.00

CHILDRESS, Alice. *Those Other People.* 1989. Putnam. 1st ed. dj. EX. B13. $35.00

CHILDS, C.D. *Samuel Chamberlain: Etcher & Lithographer.* 1927. Boston. Ils 1st ed. G. T5. $12.50

CHILDS, Marquis. *Captive Hero.* 1958. Harcourt. not 1st ed/Book Club. 310 p. dj. VG. B10. $3.50

CHILDS, Timothy. *Cold Turkey.* 1979. Harper Row. dj. EX. P1. $7.00

CHIPMAN, C.P. *Last Cruise of the Electra.* 1902. Saalfield. 1st ed. 4 pls. 268 p. T5. $25.00

CHIPMAN, Donald. *Nuno de Guzman & Province of Panuco in New Spain.* 1967. Arthur Clarke. 1st ed. 322 p. F2. $35.00

CHITTENDEN, H.M. *Hist of Am Fur Trade of the Far W.* 1954. Stanford. 8vo. 2 vols. djs. EX. T1. $80.00

CHITTENDEN & SELTMAN. *Greek Art: Commemorative Cat.* 1947. London. Burlington House. 8vo. 72 p. VG. $25.00

CHITTY, Joseph. *Treatise on Law of Bills of Exchange, Checks on Banks...* 1807. London. 1st ed. VG. $100.00

CHODOROV & FIELDS. *Jr Miss.* 1942. Random House. 1st ed. dj. EX. H3. $40.00

CHOUKRI, Mohamed. *TN Williams in Tangier.* 1979. Cadmus. Trans/sgn Bowles. 1/200. sgn. wrp. EX. K2. $85.00

CHOUKRI, Mohamed. *TN Williams in Tangier.* 1979. Cadmus. 1st Trade ed. 1/1300. wrp. glassine dj. EX. K2. $45.00

CHRETIEN DE TROYES. *Erec et Enide.* 1924. Paris. C1. $9.00

CHRIS-JANER, Albert. *Eliel Sarrinen.* 1979. Chicago. Revised 1st ed. VG. G1. $35.00

CHRIST, K.D. *Boots, the Firemen's Dog.* 1936. Am Book Co. Ils Frank Dobias. 12mo. VG. $15.00

CHRISTENSEN, D.R. *Space Ghost, the Sorceress of Cyba-3.* nd. Whitman. Big Little Book. VG. P1. $7.50

CHRISTENSEN, Erwin. *Primitive Art.* 1955. Bonanza. 4to. 384 p. F2. $30.00

CHRISTIANER, L.F. *Effective Card Tricks.* nd. Thayer. 2nd ed. SftCvr. NM. J3. $2.00

CHRISTIE, Agatha. *Adventure of the Christmas Pudding.* 1960. London. Crime Club. 1st ed. dj. VG. B13. $150.00

CHRISTIE, Agatha. *Agatha Christie: An Autobiography.* 1977. Dodd Mead. 1st Am ed. photos. dj. EX. C4. $25.00

CHRISTIE, Agatha. *By the Pricking of My Thumbs.* 1968. Collins Crime Club. 1st ed. dj. VG. P1. $20.00

CHRISTIE, Agatha. *Cards on the Table.* 1937. Dodd Mead. 1st ed. VG. P1. $40.00

CHRISTIE, Agatha. *Caribbean Mystery.* 1965. Dodd Mead. 1st ed. dj. xl. P1. $6.00

CHRISTIE, Agatha. *Clocks.* 1963. Collins Crime Club. 1st ed. dj. VG. P1. $30.00

CHRISTIE, Agatha. *Crooked House.* 1950. Collins Crime Club. 1st Australian ed. dj. VG. P1. $25.00

CHRISTIE, Agatha. *Curtain.* 1975. Dodd Mead. dj. VG. P1. $15.00

CHRISTIE, Agatha. *Dead Man's Folly.* 1956. Collins Crime Club. dj. VG. P1. $30.00

CHRISTIE, Agatha. *Death Comes As the End.* 1945. London. Crime Club. 1st ed. dj. EX. B13. $225.00

CHRISTIE, Agatha. *Destination Unknown.* 1954. Collins Crime Club. dj. VG. P1. $30.00

CHRISTIE, Agatha. *Elephants Can Remember.* 1972. London. Collins. 1st ed. dj. EX. T9. $45.00

CHRISTIE, Agatha. *Funerals Are Fatal.* 1953. Doubleday Book Club. dj. VG. P1. $30.00

CHRISTIE, Agatha. *Hound of Death & Other Stories.* 1933. Odhams. 1st ed. VG. P1. $150.00

CHRISTIE, Agatha. *Hound of Death & Other Stories.* 1939. Collins Crime Club. dj. VG. P1. $45.00

CHRISTIE, Agatha. *Miss Marple Meets Murder.* nd. Book Club. dj. EX. P1. $7.50

CHRISTIE, Agatha. *Mrs McGinty's Dead.* 1952. Collins Crime Club. 1st ed. dj. VG. P1. $30.00

CHRISTIE, Agatha. *Murder of Roger Ackroyd.* nd. Grosset Dunlap. dj. VG. P1. $15.00

CHRISTIE, Agatha. *Nemesis.* nd. Dodd Mead. 3rd ed. dj. VG. P1. $12.50

CHRISTIE, Agatha. *Nemesis.* 1971. Collins Crime Club. 1st ed. dj. VG. P1. $17.50

CHRISTIE, Agatha. *Nemesis.* 1971. London. Collins. 1st ed. dj. EX. T9. $45.00

CHRISTIE, Agatha. *Ordeal by Innocence.* 1958. Collins Crime Club. 1st ed. VG. P1. $25.00

CHRISTIE, Agatha. *Passenger to Frankfurt.* nd. Dodd Mead. dj. VG. P1. $10.00

CHRISTIE, Agatha. *Passenger to Frankfurt.* 1970. Collins Crime Club. 1st ed. dj. VG. P1. $30.00

CHRISTIE, Agatha. *Pocket Full of Rye.* 1953. Collins Crime Club. 1st ed. dj. VG. P1. $30.00

CHRISTIE, Agatha. *Poirot's Early Cases.* 1974. London. Collins. 1st ed. dj. EX. T9. $35.00

CHRISTIE, Agatha. *Postern of Fate.* nd. Dodd Mead. 3rd ed. dj. EX. P1. $9.25

CHRISTIE, Agatha. *Postmark: Murder.* 1986. Doubleday Book Club. dj. EX. B10. $4.50

CHRISTIE, Agatha. *Sleeping Murder.* 1976. Collins Crime Club. dj. VG. P1. $9.25

CHRISTIE, Agatha. *They Do It With Mirrors.* 1952. Collins Crime Club. 1st ed. dj. VG. P1. $25.00

CHRISTIE, Agatha. *Under Dog.* nd. Daily Express. VG. P1. $25.00

CHRISTIE, Agatha. *13 for Luck.* 1961. Dodd Mead. 1st ed. dj. EX. B13. $50.00

CHRISTIE. *Samplers & Stitches.* 1929. London. Revised Enlarged 2nd ed. 34 pls. G. C2. $37.00

CHRISTOPHER, John. *Little People.* nd. Book Club. dj. VG. P1. $4.00

CHRISTOPHER, John. *Little People.* 1966. Simon Schuster. 1st ed. dj. xl. P1. $4.50

CHRISTOPHER, John. *Long Winter.* nd. Book Club. dj. VG. P1. $4.50

CHRISTOPHER, John. *No Blade of Grass.* nd. Book Club. dj. VG. P1. $4.50

CHRISTOPHER, John. *Pendulum.* 1968. Simon Schuster. 1st ed. dj. EX. F5. $16.00

CHRISTOPHER, John. *Pendulum.* 1968. Simon Schuster. 1st ed. dj. VG. P1. $15.00

CHRISTOPHER, John. *Wht Voyage.* nd. Book Club. dj. VG. P1. $2.75

CHRISTOPHER, Milbourne. *Ils Hist of Magic.* 1973. Crowell. 1st ed. 452 p. EX. J3. $12.00

CHRISTOPHER, Milbourne. *Milbourne Christopher's Magic Book.* 1985. Barnes Noble. 1st ed. 210 p. NM. J3. $4.00

CHRISTOPHER, Milbourne. *Panorama of Magic.* 1962. Dover. sgn. 216 p. EX. J3. $35.00

CHRISTOPHER, Milbourne. *Panorama of Magic.* 1962. Dover. 216 p. EX. J3. $12.00

CHRISTY, H.C. *Am Girl.* 1906. NY. 1st ed. VG. $55.00

CHRISTY, H.C. *Our Girls.* 1907. NY. sm 4to. VG. C2. $125.00

CHRONISTER, E. *Reminiscences of Army Life.* 1908. Eagle Grove, IA. 1st ed. orig wrp. $220.00

CHUAN, T.H. *Rough & Smooth Possibilities.* 1948. Croydon, England. 1st ed. NM. J3. $10.00

CHURCH, Richard. *Mary Shelley.* 1928. NY. 8vo. xl. $35.00

CHURCH, W.C. *Life of John Ericsson.* 1906. Scribner. 2 vols. EX. $65.00

CHURCHILL, David. *It, Us, & the Others.* 1979. Harper Row. dj. EX. P1. $7.00

CHURCHILL, Sarah. *Empty Spaces.* nd. Dodd Mead. not Book Club. dj. VG. B10. $4.00

CHURCHILL, W.S. *Aftermath.* 1929. Scribner. 1st ed. dj. EX. B13. $95.00

CHURCHILL, W.S. *Celebrity.* Macmillan Standard Lib. 302 p. dj. G. B10. $3.50

CHURCHILL, W.S. *Collected Essays.* 1976. np. Lib Imperial Hist. 1/3000. 4 vols. AEG. M. T5. $750.00

CHURCHILL, W.S. *Crossing.* 1913. Grosset Dunlap. 598 p. VG. B10. $3.50

CHURCHILL, W.S. *End of the Beginning.* 1943. Boston. 1st Am ed. dj. VG. B3. $22.50

CHURCHILL, W.S. *Far Country.* 1915. NY. 1st ed. VG. C1. $7.50

CHURCHILL, W.S. *Hist of the Eng-Speaking Peoples.* 1956-1958. London. Cassell. 1st ed. 4 vols. rebound. H3. $850.00

CHURCHILL, W.S. *Ian Hamilton's March.* 1900. NY. 1st Am ed. orig cloth. VG. H3. $1000.00

CHURCHILL, W.S. *Inside of the Cup.* 1913. Macmillan. not 1st ed. 513 p. EX. B10. $3.50

CHURCHILL, W.S. *Inside the Cup.* 1913. Grosset Dunlap. Photoplay ed. 513 p. VG. B10. $3.50

CHURCHILL, W.S. *London to Ladysmith via Pretoria.* 1900. London. 1st ed. orig bdg. VG. H3. $1500.00

CHURCHILL, W.S. *London to Ladysmith via Pretoria.* 1900. London. 1st ed. orig pictorial cloth. VG. H3. $1500.00

CHURCHILL, W.S. *Lord Randolph Churchill.* 1906. Macmillan. 1st ed. 2 vols. plum bdg. VG. H3. $400.00

CHURCHILL, W.S. *My African Journey.* 1908. London. 1st ed. Bayntun scarlet morocco bdg. EX. H3. $750.00

CHURCHILL, W.S. *My African Journey.* 1908. London. Hodder Stoughton. 1st ed. VG. B13. $450.00

CHURCHILL, W.S. *My African Journey.* 1909. Toronto. 1st Canadian ed. map. 226 p. VG. B3. $45.00

CHURCHILL, W.S. *My Early Life. A Roving Commission.* 1941. London. reprint. inscr. orig cloth. w/sgn letter. H3. $6000.00

CHURCHILL, W.S. *My Early Life: A Roving Commission.* 1949. London. reprint. inscr. H3. $3000.00

CHURCHILL, W.S. *Painting As a Pastime.* 1950. NY. Ils 1st Am ed. dj. G. T5. $25.00

CHURCHILL, W.S. *Savrola: A Tale of the Revolution in Laurania.* 1900. London. 1st Eng ed. orig cloth. H3. $1000.00

CHURCHILL, W.S. *Secret Session Speeches.* 1946. NY. 1st True ed. dj. EX. $90.00

CHURCHILL, W.S. *Step by Step: 1936-1939.* 1939. Putnam. 1st ed. dj. EX. B13. $250.00

CHURCHILL, W.S. *Story of the Malakand Field Force.* 1898. London. 1st ed. gr crushed morocco. EX. H3. $2500.00

CHURCHILL, Winston. *Savrola: A Tale of the Revolution in Laurania.* 1956. Random House. 1st ed. dj. EX. C4. $60.00

CHURCHWARD, James. *Lost Continent of Mu.* 1926. NY. 1st ed. presentation. VG. B3. $70.00

CHUTE, Carolyn. *Beans of Egypt, ME.* 1985. Ticknor Fields. UP. wrp. EX. K2. $150.00

CIARDI, John. *How Does a Poem Mean?* 1959. Houghton Mifflin. sgn. dj. H3. $30.00

CICERO, M.T. *Opera.* 1753. Padua. Typis Seminarii. 9 vols. quarto. H3. $650.00

CISNEROS, Sandra. *Woman Hollering Creek & Other Stories.* 1991. Random House. UP. EX. K2. $35.00

CIST, Charles. *Cincinnati in 1841.* 1841. Cincinnati. 1st ed. G. C2. $65.00

CLAASEN, Hermann. *Gesang Im Feuerofen.* 1947. Duesseldorf. 4to. photos. T5. $45.00

CLAFLIN & SHERIDAN. *Street Magic.* 1977. Dolphin Books. 1st ed. 156 p. EX. J3. $18.00

CLAMPITT, Amy. *Kingfisher.* 1983. Knopf. 1st HrdCvr ed. dj. EX. K2. $50.00

CLANCY, Tom. *Cardinal of the Kremlin.* 1988. Putnam. 1st ed. dj. VG. P1. $19.95

CLANCY, Tom. *Clear & Present Danger.* 1989. Putnam. 7th print. inscr. H3. $45.00

CLANCY, Tom. *Hunt for Red October.* 1984. Annapolis, MD. 1st ed. dj. EX. K2. $650.00

CLAPHAM, Richard. *Foxes, Foxhounds, & Fox Hunting.* 1922. NY. 1st Am ed? VG. G1. $40.00

CLARE, John. *Dwellers in the Wood.* 1967. Macmillan. 1st ed. thin 8vo. dj. EX. B10. $9.25

CLARENDON, Edward. *Hist of Rebellion & Civil Wars in Eng.* 1826. Clarendon. 8 vols. octavo. G. H3. $225.00

CLARENS, Carols. *Ils Hist of the Horror Film.* 1967. Putnam. 1st ed. dj. VG. R3. $17.50

CLARESON, T.D. *Spectrum of Worlds.* 1972. Doubleday. 1st ed. dj. EX. R3. $15.00

CLARESON, Thomas. *Voices for the Future Vol 3*. 1984. Bowling Gr. dj. P1. $15.00

CLARIDGE, Richard. *Tractatus Hierographicus; or, Treatise of Holy Scriptures.* 1878. NY. Wood. 2nd Am ed. 171 p. G. V1. $10.00

CLARK, Al. *Raymond Chandler in Hollywood.* 1983. Proteus. 1st Am ed. wrp. EX. T9. $20.00

CLARK, C.H. *Quakeress: A Tale.* 1905. Phil. Winston. 1st ed. 12mo. 392 p. G. V1. $4.50

CLARK, Champ. *Gettysburg: Confederate High Tide.* 1985. Time Life. 176 p. decor bdg. VG. S1. $9.50

CLARK, Curt; see Westlake, Donald E.

CLARK, D.S. *Moravian Mission of Pilgrerrug.* 1940. Bethlehem, PA. 35 p. wrp. VG. T5. $12.50

CLARK, E.H. *Carleton Case.* 1910. McLeod Allen. 1st Canadian ed. VG. P1. $4.75

CLARK, E.M. *OH Art & Artists.* 1932. Richmond, VA. Ils 509 p. G. T5. $220.00

CLARK, Eleanor. *Oysters of Lacmariaquer.* 1964. NY. 1st ed. sgn. dj. EX. T9. $50.00

CLARK, H.M. *World's Greatest Magic.* 1976. Bonanza. 2nd print. 208 p. dj. NM. J3. $10.00

CLARK, H.M. *World's Greatest Magic.* 1976. NY. Crown. 1st ed. 208 p. dj. NM. J3. $12.00

CLARK, J.A. *Walk About Zion.* 1835. Phil/Providence. orig purple cloth. G. $75.00

CLARK, J.R. *Hist of US Especially for Schools.* nd. (1876) Cincinnati. Grammer School ed. 390 p. EX. B10. $4.00

CLARK, Jocko. *Carrier Admiral.* 1967. NY. 1st ed. sgn. dj. VG. B3. $60.00

CLARK, Keith. *Encyclopedia of Cigarette Tricks.* 1952. Louis Tannen. 2nd ed. 304 p. NM. J3. $10.00

CLARK, La Verne Harrell. *They Sang for Horses.* 1966. AZ U. Ils Begay. 1st ed. presentation/inscr. dj. EX. K2. $125.00

CLARK, Larry. *Teenage Lust.* 1983. Clark. photos. wrp. EX. K2. $175.00

CLARK, Larry. *Tulsa.* 1971. Clark. photos. dj. EX. K2. $200.00

CLARK, Leonard. *Rivers Ran E.* 1953. Funk Wagnall. 366 p. dj. F2. $15.00

CLARK, M.H. *Aspire to the Heavens.* 1968. NY. 1st ed. dj. VG. B3. $25.00

CLARK, M.H. *Cradle Will Fall.* 1980. Simon Schuster. 1st ed. dj. VG. P1. $15.00

CLARK, M.H. *Stranger Is Watching.* 1977. Simon Schuster. 1st ed. dj. VG. P1. $15.00

CLARK, M.H. *Weep No More, My Lady.* 1987. Simon Schuster. 1st ed. dj. VG. P1. $15.00

CLARK, R.D. *Life of Matthew Simpson.* 1956. NY. 1st ed. EX. $40.00

CLARK, Sydney. *All the Best in Central Am.* 1946. Dodd Mead. 1st ed. 288 p. dj. F2. $15.00

CLARK, T.D. *Pleasant Hill in the Civil War.* 1972. Pleasant Hill. Ils. 76 p. dj. VG. T5. $15.00

CLARK, Tom. *Bl.* 1974. Blk Sparrow. 1st ed. 1/200. sgn. dj. EX. $12.00

CLARK, Tom. *Border.* 1985. Coffee House Pr. 1/500. sgn. dj. B4. $15.00

CLARK, Tom. *Fan Poems.* 1976. N Atlantic Books. Ils. EX. B4. $12.00

CLARK, Tom. *When Things Get Tough on Easy Street.* 1978. Blk Sparrow. Ltd ed. 1/200. sgn. H3. $15.00

CLARK, V.A. *Field Hands to Stage Hands in Haiti: Measure of Tradition...* 1983. np. 570 p. F2. $20.00

CLARK, W.V.T. *City of Leaves.* 1945. NY. Stated 1st ed. dj. EX. J2. $25.00

CLARK, W.V.T. *Track of the Cat.* 1949. NY. 1st ed. dj. VG. $35.00

CLARK, Walter. *On Roanoke Island.* c 1902. Goldsboro. 1st ed. $25.00

CLARK, William. *W With Dragoons: Journal of William Clark.* 1937. Fulton, MO. Ovid Bell Pr. 97 p. wrp. VG. $45.00

CLARK & PARADY. *Stone Monuments of the Guatemalan Piedmont & Chiapas.* 1975. np. Eng/Spanish text. 24 p. wrp. F2. $10.00

CLARKE, A.B. *Travels in Mexico & CA.* 1852. Boston. 1st ed. orig wrp. EX. H3. $1100.00

CLARKE, A.C. *Across the Sea of Stars.* nd. Book Club. dj. VG. P1. $7.50

CLARKE, A.C. *City & the Stars.* nd. Book Club. VG. P1. $3.00

CLARKE, A.C. *City & the Stars.* 1956. Harcourt Brace. 1st ed. dj. EX. C4. $100.00

CLARKE, A.C. *Deep Range.* 1957. Harcourt. 1st ed. dj. EX. R3. $225.00

CLARKE, A.C. *Exploration of Space.* nd. BOMC. dj. VG. P1. $5.00

CLARKE, A.C. *Fountains in Paradise.* 1980. Hall. Lg Print ed. 514 p. dj. EX. B10. $10.00

CLARKE, A.C. *Imperial Earth.* nd. Book Club. dj. VG. P1. $4.00

CLARKE, A.C. *Imperial Earth.* 1975. London. 1st ed. dj. EX. R3. $50.00

CLARKE, A.C. *Islands in the Sky.* 1954. Winston. 2nd ed. VG. P1. $15.00

CLARKE, A.C. *Lion of Commarre & Against the Fall.* nd. Book Club. VG. P1. $3.00

CLARKE, A.C. *Prelude to Mars.* nd. Book Club. dj. VG. P1. $7.50

CLARKE, A.C. *Prelude to Space.* 1954. Gnome. xl. P1. $10.00

CLARKE, A.C. *Prelude to Space.* 1970. Harcourt Brace World. dj. EX. P1. $15.00

CLARKE, A.C. *Profiles of the Future.* 1984. Holt. 1st ed. RS. M. R3. $20.00

CLARKE, A.C. *Promise of Space.* nd. BOMC. dj. EX. P1. $7.50

CLARKE, A.C. *Report on Planet 3.* 1972. Harper Row. 1st ed. dj. VG. P1. $25.00

CLARKE, A.C. *Sands of Mars.* nd. Book Club. dj. VG. P1. $4.50

CLARKE, A.C. *Sands of Mars.* 1952. Gnome. 1st ed. dj. EX. R3. $150.00

CLARKE, A.C. *Sentinel.* 1983. Berkley. 1st ed. 1/465. sgn. M. R3. $75.00

CLARKE, A.C. *Songs of Distant Earth.* 1986. Random House. 1st ed. 1/500. sgn. M. R3. $100.00

CLARKE, A.C. *Tales From the Wht Hart.* 1970. Harcourt Brace World. 1st ed. dj. VG. P1. $100.00

CLARKE, A.C. *Tales of 10 Worlds.* 1962. Harcourt Brace World. 1st ed. dj. VG. P1. $50.00

CLARKE, A.C. *1061: Odyssey 3.* 1988. Del Rey. 1st ed. M. R3. $17.95

CLARKE, A.C. *1984: Spring/Choice of Futures.* 1984. Ballantine. UP. wrp. EX. C4. $20.00

CLARKE, A.C. *1984: Spring/Choice of Futures.* 1984. Del Rey. 1st ed. M. R3. $14.95

CLARKE, A.H. *Hawthorne's Country.* 1910. Baker Taylor. G. $7.00

CLARKE, Anna. *Cabin 3033.* 1986. Crime Club. 1st ed. dj. EX. P1. $12.95

CLARKE, Anna. *Soon She Must Die.* 1984. Doubleday Book Club. VG. P1. $7.50

CLARKE, Anna. *We, the Bereaved.* 1983. Doubleday Book Club. VG. P1. $7.50

CLARKE, Covington. *Aces Up.* 1929. Chicago. Ils 1st ed. VG. T5. $27.50

CLARKE, D.H. *Housekeeper's Daughter.* 1940. Triangle. 5th/Photoplay ed. dj. VG. P1. $15.00

CLARKE, D.H. *Housekeeper's Daughter.* 1941. Triangle. 8th ed. dj. VG. P1. $5.50

CLARKE, D.H. *Louis Beretti.* 1943. Triangle. 11th print. dj. EX. P1. $7.00

CLARKE, Harry. *Years at the Spring.* 1920. NY. Brentano. 1st ed. folio. VG. B3. $70.00

CLARKE, I.C. *Secret Citadel.* nd. (1914) Benziger. 416 p. VG. B10. $3.75

CLARKE, James. *Man Is the Prey.* nd. (1969) Stein Day. 318 p. dj. VG. B10. $4.00

CLARKE, P.D. *Orig & Traditional Hist of Wyandots & Other Tribes of N Am.* 1870. Toronto. 16mo. VG. A4. $200.00

CLARKE, Thurston. *13 O'Clock.* 1984. Doubleday. 1st ed. RS. M. R3. $15.00

CLARKE. *Cabinet of Arts; or, General Instructor in Arts, Science, Trade.* 1817. London. 1st ed. 8vo. 859 p. rare. $150.00

CLARKE. *Pioneer Days of OR Hist.* 1905. Portland. Gill. 2 vols. VG. A5. $100.00

CLARKSON, Thomas. *Memoirs of Public & Private Life of William Penn.* 1849. London. Gilpin. New ed. 12mo. G. V1. $20.00

CLARKSON, Thomas. *Portraiture of Quakerism.* 1806. London. Longman. 1st ed. 8vo. 3 vols. VG. $150.00

CLARKSON, Thomas. *Portraiture of Quakerism.* 1806. NY. Stansbury. 1st ed. 3 vols. V1. $85.00

CLARO, Joe. *Alex Gets the Business.* 1986. Weekly Reader. VG. P1. $5.00

CLASON, C.B. *Ark of Venus.* 1955. Knopf. 1st ed. VG. P1. $20.00

CLAUDEL, Paul. *5 Great Odes.* 1967. Rapp Carroll. Trans/sgn Luce-Smith. 1st ed. 1/10. H3. $60.00

CLAUDY, C.H. *Adventures in the Unknown Series.* 1933-1934. Grosset Dunlap. 1st ed. 4 vols. VG. R3. $125.00

CLAUDY, C.H. *Bl Grotto Terror.* 1934. Grosset Dunlap. 1st ed. G. R3. $25.00

CLAUDY, C.H. *Girl Reporter.* 1930. Little Brn. 1st ed. VG. R3. $30.00

CLAUDY, C.H. *Land of No Shadow.* 1933. Grosset Dunlap. 1st ed. VG. R3. $30.00

CLAUDY, C.H. *Mystery Men of Mars.* 1933. Grosset Dunlap. 1st ed. dj. VG. R3. $40.00

CLAVELL, James. *Nobel House.* c 1981. Delacorte. Ltd ed. 1/500. sgn. slipcase. H3. $125.00

CLAVELL, James. *Noble House.* 1981. Delacorte. 1st ed. dj. EX. B10. $7.50

CLAVELL, James. *Shogun.* 1975. Atheneum Book Club. 2 vols. VG. B10. $7.00

CLAY, B.M. *Gypsy Daughter.* nd. Favorite Lib 161. G. B10. $3.50

CLAY & STERLING. *Belle of the '50s.* 1905. NY. Ils. 386 p. T5. $37.50

CLAYRE, Alasdair. *Heart of the Dragon.* 1985. Houghton Mifflin. dj. VG. P1. $20.00

CLAYTON, John. *Flower Arranging.* 1985. Gallery Books. folio. 224 p. dj. EX. $30.00

CLEARY, Jon. *Flight of Chariots.* nd. Companion Book Club. dj. EX. P1. $5.00

CLEARY, Jon. *Peter's Pence.* 1974. Doubleday Book Club. VG. P1. $7.50

CLEATOR, P.E. *Archaeology in the Making.* 1976. London/NY. Robert Hale/St Martin. 1st ed. 238 p. dj. F2. $10.00

CLEAVES, Freeman. *Old Tippecanoe.* 1939. Scribner. 1st ed. 422 p. tall 8vo. VG. B10. $16.50

CLEEVE, Brian. *Dark Blood, Dark Terror.* 1965. Random House. 1st ed. dj. EX. F5. $15.00

CLEEVE, Brian. *Dark Blood, Dark Terror.* 1965. Random House. 1st ed. dj. xl. P1. $5.00

CLEEVE, Brian. *Tread Softly This Place.* 1973. John Day. VG. P1. $2.75

CLEIFFE, Philip. *Tour de Force.* nd. Book Club. dj. EX. P1. $2.75

CLEMENS, Clara. *My Husband: Gabrilowitsch.* 1938. Harper. 1st ed. sgn. quarto. 351 p. dj. EX. H3. $75.00

CLEMENS, Samuel L.; see Twain, Mark.

CLEMENT, Hal. *Left of Africa.* 1976. Aurian Society. 1st ed. dj. EX. P1. $15.00

CLEMENT, Hal. *Needle.* 1950. Doubleday Young Moderns. dj. VG. P1. $20.00

CLEMENT, Hal. *Still River.* 1987. Del Rey. 1st ed. dj. EX. P1. $16.95

CLEMENT, Hal. *Still River.* 1987. Del Rey. 1st ed. M. R3. $19.95

CLEMENTI, Mrs. Cecil. *Through British Guiana to the Summit of Roraima.* c 1920. Dutton. Ils. fld map. 236 p. F2. $35.00

CLEMENTS, Edith. *Flowers of Coast & Sierra.* 1947. NY. Wilson. inscr. 226 p. $40.00

CLEMENTS, Edith. *Pictures of Wild Flowers.* 1954. London. Ils Whitbourne. VG. $25.00

CLERK, J. *Essay of Naval Tactics.* 1804. Edinburgh. 2nd ed. rebound. $150.00

CLEVE, Van. *How To Win a Magic Contest.* 1978. Magic Inc. 1st ed. 33 p. SftCvr. J3. $3.00

CLEVELAND, Grover. *Fishing & Shooting Sketches.* 1906. NY. 16mo. decor bdg. VG. A4. $30.00

CLIFFORD, Francis. *Amigo, Amigo.* 1973. Coward McCann. 1st Am ed. dj. RS. EX. T9. $30.00

CLIFFORD, H.B. *Boothbay Region 1906-1960.* 1961. Freeport, ME. Ils. 354 p. dj. VG. T5. $25.00

CLIFFORD, H.B. *ME & Her People.* 1958. Freeport, ME. Ils 1st ed. 327 p. dj. G. T5. $22.50

CLIFTON, Bud. *Let Him Go Hang.* 1961. Ace D-501. 1st ed. wrp. VG. T9. $25.00

CLIFTON, Bud. *Murder Specialist.* 1959. Ace D-838. PB Orig. wrp. VG. T9. $20.00

CLIFTON & RILEY. *They'd Rather Be Right.* 1957. Gnome. 1st ed. dj. EX. R3. $100.00

CLINE, Edward. *1st Prize.* 1988. Mysterious Pr. 1st ed. dj. EX. F5. $14.00

CLING & MASEL. *Hist of the 71st Infantry Division.* 1946. np. Ils Norman Nichole. 117 p. T5. $35.00

CLIVE, Paul. *Card Tricks Without Skill.* 1947. Blackpool, England. 2nd ed. 190 p. dj. EX. J3. $20.00

CLIVE, William. *Dando & the Summer Palace.* 1972. Macmillan. dj. VG. P1. $7.00

CLOPPER, Edward. *Am Family: Its Ups & Downs Through 8 Generations.* 1950. private print. 1st ed. dj. VG. $45.00

CLOSS, Hannah. *High Are the Mts.* 1959. 1st Am ed. VG. C1. $5.00

CLOSS, Hannah. *Tristan.* 1967. 1st Am ed. dj. VG. C1. $17.50

CLOUSTON, J.S. *Man From the Clouds.* 1919. Doran. 1st ed. dj. EX. R3. $50.00

CLUNN, Harold. *Face of Paris.* c 1950s. London. 310 p. dj. VG. B10. $10.00

CLUTTERBUCK, Henry. *Lectures on Blood Letting.* 1839. Phil. Haswell. VG. $375.00

CLUTTON, BIRD, & HARDING. *Batsford Guide to Vintage Cars.* 1976. 224 p. VG. S1. $6.00

CLUTTON, Cecil. *Watches.* 1965. NY. 1st ed. 4to. dj. EX. $50.00

CLYMER, Floyd. *Treasury of Early Am Automobiles 1877-1925.* 1950. 213 p. dj. VG. S1. $14.00

COATES, I.W. *Some Evidences Indian Occupancy Along...Canandaigua Outlet.* c 1890. NY. wrp. A4. $35.00

COATSWORTH, Elizabeth. *Big Gr Umbrella: Story Parade Picture Book.* 1944. Grosset Dunlap. Ils Helen Sewell. VG. B7. $25.00

COBB, I.S. *Old Judge Priest.* 1916. Doran. sgn. gilt gr bdg. H3. $50.00

COBB, I.S. *Poindexter Clr.* 1922. NY. 1st ed. VG. B3. $15.00

COBB, I.S. *Roughing It Deluxe.* 1914. NY. Doran. Ils McCutcheon. 1st ed. EX. $15.00

COBB, J.H. *Manual of Mulberry Tree...Directions for Culture of Silk.* 1883. Boston. pls. rare. C1. $65.00

COBB, Ty. *Busting 'Em.* 1914. NY. 1st ed. 282 p. VG. B3. $95.00

COBB, Vicki. *Magic...Naturally! Science Entertainments & Amusements.* 1976. Lippincott. 159 p. EX. J3. $3.00

COBLENTZ, S.A. *After 12,000 Years.* 1950. Fantasy. 1st ed. dj. EX. R3. $20.00

COBLENTZ, S.A. *Crimson Capsule.* 1967. Avalon. 1st ed. dj. EX. R3. $15.00

COBLENTZ, S.A. *Crimson Capsule.* 1967. Avalon. 1st ed. dj. xl. P1. $5.50

COBLENTZ, S.A. *Into Plutonian Depths.* 1950. Avon. 1st ed. wrp. EX. R3. $35.00

COBLENTZ, S.A. *Lizard Lords.* 1964. Avalon. 1st ed. dj. xl. R3. $10.00

COBLENTZ, S.A. *Lord of Tranerica.* 1966. Avalon. 1st ed. dj. EX. R3. $25.00

COBLENTZ, S.A. *Planet of Youth.* 1952. Fantasy. 1st ed. 1st bdg. dj. EX. R3. $25.00

COBLENTZ, S.A. *Runaway World.* 1961. Avalon. 1st ed. dj. xl. P1. $7.50

COCHRAN, C.B. *Secrets of a Showman.* 1926. Holt. octavo. 436 p. VG. H3. $65.00

COCHRAN, E.A. *Cathedral of Commerce: Woolworth Building.* 1917. Thomsen Ellis. Ils. 30 p. VG. $30.00

COCHRAN & STOBBS. *Search for the Perfect Swing.* 1968. Phil. 1st ed. dj. VG. B3. $50.00

COCHRAN. *Pabst Brewing Co: A Hist.* 1948. NY. 1st ed. 451 p. dj. VG. B3. $45.00

COCHRANE, Micky. *Baseball Fans' Game.* 1939. NY. VG. B3. $25.00

COCKBURN, James. *Review of...Causes...to Rise of Soc of Friends.* 1829. Phil. Philip Price. 1st print. 281 p. ES. G. V1. $25.00

COCKERELL, Douglas. *Bookbinding & Care of Books.* 1912. NY. Appleton. 342 p. G. $20.00

COCKTON, Henry. *Life & Adventures of Valentine Vox the Ventriloquist.* 1840. London. 60 pls. 8vo. VG. T1. $95.00

COCTEAU, Jean. *Children of the Game.* 1955. London. Havill Pr. 1st ed. dj. VG. C4. $30.00

COCTEAU, Jean. *Cocteau's World.* 1973. Dodd Mead. 8vo. dj. VG. $15.00

COCTEAU, Jean. *Journal d'un Inconnu.* 1953. Paris. Grasset. 1/56. presentation. wrp. slipcase. H3. $400.00

CODDINGTON, E.B. *Gettysburg Campaign.* 1968. NY. 1st ed. dj. VG. B3. $55.00

CODRESCU, Andre. *License To Carry a Gun.* 1970. Chicago. 1st ed. sgn. dj. EX. T9. $55.00

CODRESCU, Andre. *Serious Morning.* 1973. Capra. Chapbook Series. printer copy. sgn. EX. K2. $35.00

CODY, Liza. *Dupe.* 1981. Scribner. 1st ed. dj. EX. F5. $15.00

CODY, Morrill. *This Must Be the Place.* 1937. NY. Lee Furman. 1st Am ed. dj. EX. H3. $100.00

CODY, Sherwin. *Selection From the Great Eng Poets.* 1910. McClurg. 4th print. 576 p. TEG. VG. B10. $3.75

CODY & WETMORE. *Last of the Great Scouts: Life of Col William F Cody.* 1899. Duluth Pr. Ltd ed. 1/500. sgn. VG. H3. $350.00

COE, George. *Frontier Fighter.* 1934. Boston. presentation. lacks front fly. VG. B3. $45.00

COE, Michael. *African, Pacific, & Pre-Columbian Art in IU Art Mus.* 1986. Bloomington, IN. 1st ed. 157 p. dj. F2. $35.00

COE, Michael. *Am's 1st Civilization.* 1968. Am Heritage Pub. 1st ed. 160 p. dj. F2. $15.00

COE, Michael. *Jaguar's Children.* 1965. NY. 1st ed. 4to. dj. F2. $45.00

COE, Michael. *Mexico.* 1962. Praeger. 1st ed. 245 p. dj. F2. $20.00

COE, Michael. *Old Gods & Young Heroes.* 1982. Am Friends Israel Mus. 1st ed. oblong 4to. dj. F2. $45.00

COE, Tucker. *Kinds of Love, Kinds of Death.* nd. Book Club. dj. VG. P1. $4.50

COE, Tucker. *Kinds of Love, Kinds of Death.* nd. Random House. 2nd ed. dj. xl. P1. $5.00

COE & FLANNERY. *Early Cultures & Human Ecology in S Coast Guatemala.* 1967. Smithsonian. 4to. 135 p. F2. $25.00

COETZEE, J.M. *Dusklands.* 1974. Johannesburg. 1st ed. dj. K2. $275.00

COETZEE, J.M. *Dusklands.* 1974. Raven Pr. 1st ed. dj. C4. $250.00

COETZEE, J.M. *From the Heart of the Country.* 1977. Harper. 1st Am ed. sgn. dj. EX. C4. $125.00

COETZEE, J.M. *Life & Times of Michael K.* 1983. Viking. 1st Am ed. sgn. dj. EX. C4. $125.00

COETZEE, J.M. *Life & Times of Michael K.* 1984. Viking. UP. EX. K2. $65.00

COETZEE, J.M. *Truth in Autobiography?* 1984. Cape Town. stapled wrp. EX. K2. $85.00

COFFEY, Brian. *Blood Risk.* 1973. Bobbs Merrill. 1st ed. dj. VG. P1. $125.00

COFFEY, Brian. *Face of Fear.* 1977. Bobbs Merrill. 2nd ed. dj. xl. P1. $30.00

COFFEY, Brian. *Voice of the Night.* 1980. Doubleday. 1st ed. dj. xl. P1. $35.00

COFFIN, C.C. *My Days & Nights on the Battlefield.* 1887. Boston. 234 p. fair. T5. $25.00

COFFIN, Lewis. *Sm French Buildings.* 1921. NY. VG. G1. $50.00

COFFIN, M.H. *Battle of Sant Creek.* 1965. Waco. Morrison. 40 p. A5. $35.00

COFFIN, T.P. *Ils Book of Christmas Folklore.* 1973. Seabury. VG. B7. $25.00

COFFMAN, Virginia. *From Satan With Love.* 1983. Paitkus. dj. EX. P1. $15.00

COGGINS, Clemency. *Cenote of Sacrifice.* 1984. TX U. 1st ed. 4to. wrp. F2. $20.00

COGHILL, Dugald. *Elusive Gael.* 1928. Stirling, Scotland. 1st ed. dj. VG. C1. $7.50

COGNIAT, Raymond. *French Painting: Time of Impressionists.* 1951. London. 1st ed. dj. EX. G1. $40.00

COHAN & GREENBERG. *Exploring Joseph Cornell's Visual Poetry.* 1982. Ils. wrp. 24 p. EX. C2. $17.00

COHEN, Leonard. *Spice Box of the Earth.* 1961. Viking. 1st ed. dj. EX. B13. $125.00

COHEN, Matt. *Clrs of War.* 1977. Methuen. 1st UK ed. dj. F5. $20.00

COHEN, Mrs. O.R. *Our Darktown Pr.* 1932. NY. 1st ed. G. B3. $25.00

COHEN, O.R. *May Day Mystery.* 1929. Appleton. 1st ed. inscr. dj. VG. R3. $35.00

COHEN, Stanley. *330 Park.* 1977. Putnam. 1st ed. dj. EX. P1. $15.00

COHEN & GAUVEAU. *Billy Mitchell: Founder of Our Air Force.* 1942. NY. 1st ed. VG. $15.00

COHN, Art. *Around the World in 80 Days Almanac.* 1956. Random House. Photoplay ed. P1. $9.25

COHN, L.H. *Bibliography of Ernest Hemingway.* 1931. Random House. 1/500. EX. B13. $185.00

COHN, Nik. *King Death.* 1975. Harcourt. 1st ed. dj. EX. F5. $17.00

COHN, R.G. *Writer's Way in France.* 1960. PA U. 1st ed. VG. C1. $6.50

COKE, H.J. *Ride Over the Rocky Mts to OR & CA.* 1852. London. 1st ed. orig bdg. H3. $500.00

COKER. *Clavarias of US & Canada.* 1923. Chapel Hill. 1st ed. VG. C2. $75.00

COLASANTI, Arduino. *Volte e Soffitti Italini.* 1923. Milan. Bestetti Tumminelli. xl. scarce. D4. $90.00

COLBY, N.S. *Remembering.* 1938. Little Brn. 1st ed. 308 p. purple bdg. B10. $7.00

COLBY, W.P. *Honorable Men: My Life in CIA.* 1978. Simons. 1st ed. 493 p. EX. $16.00

COLCORD, J.C. *Songs of Am Sailormen.* 1938. NY. Revised Enlarged ed. dj. VG. C2. $45.00

COLCORD, Lincoln. *Instrument of the Gods & Other Sea Stories.* 1922. Macmillan. 1st ed. 321 p. VG. B10. $5.25

COLDEN, Cadwallader. *Life of Robert Fulton.* 1817. NY. Kirk Mercein. 8vo. V1. $150.00

COLE, A.C. *Whig Party in the S.* 1913. WA, DC. Ils. 7 fld maps. 392 p. VG. T5. $95.00

COLE, Burt. *Bl Climate.* 1977. Harper Row. 1st ed. dj. VG. P1. $12.50

COLE, Burt. *Blood Knot.* 1980. St Martin. 1st ed. dj. EX. F5. $15.00

COLE, Burt. *Funco File.* nd. Book Club. dj. VG. P1. $3.75

COLE, D.M. *Beyond Tomorrow.* 1965. Amherst Pr. 1st ed. dj. EX. R3. $65.00

COLE, E.B. *Philosophical Corps.* 1961. Gnome. 1st ed. dj. EX. P1. $20.00

COLE, Gerold. *Am Travelers to Mexico 1821-1972.* 1978. NY. Whitston. 1st ed. 139 p. F2. $25.00

COLE, W.R. *Checklist of SF Anthologies.* 1975. Arno. no dj issued. EX. R3. $35.00

COLE & COLE. *End of an Ancient Mariner.* 1933. Crime Club. 2nd ed. VG. P1. $15.00

COLE & COLE. *End of an Ancient Mariner.* 1938. Collins Crime Club. 8th print. dj. VG. P1. $20.00

COLE & HENCKEN. *New Rumley, Harrison Co, OH.* nd. Strasburg, OH. 8vo. orig paper wrp. T5. $16.00

COLE. *IA Through the Years.* 1940. IA City. 1st ed. 547 p. VG. B3. $12.50

COLEMAN, Elizabeth. *Opulent Era: Fashions of Worth, Doucet, & Pingat.* 1990. Brooklyn Mus. Ils. 208 p. D4. $29.00

COLEMAN, Jonathan. *At Mother's Request.* 1985. Atheneum. 1st ed. dj. EX. $20.00

COLERIDGE, Samuel. *Rime of the Ancient Mariner.* 1945. Heritage. Ils Edward Wilson. slipcase. EX. T1. $20.00

COLERIDGE-TAYLOR, S. *24 Negro Melodies Transcribed for the Piano: Op 59.* 1905. Boston. Oliver Ditson. Musicans Lib Series. 1st ed. VG. H3. $150.00

COLES, John. *Archaeology by Experiment.* 1973. Scribner. 1st ed. 182 p. dj. F2. $7.50

COLES, Manning. *Basle Express.* 1956. Crime Club. 1st ed. VG. P1. $15.00

COLES, Manning. *Basle Express.* 1956. Hodder Stoughton. 1st ed. dj. xl. P1. $10.00

COLES, Manning. *Not Negotiable.* 1952. Hodder Stoughton. 2nd ed. VG. P1. $20.00

COLES, Manning. *Search for a Sultan.* 1972. Wht Lion. VG. P1. $15.00

COLES, Manning. *They Tell No Tales.* 1950. Hodder Stoughton. 4th ed. VG. P1. $20.00

COLES, Manning. *Toast to Tomorrow.* 1943. Musson. dj. VG. P1. $13.75

COLES, Manning. *Without Lawful Authority.* nd. Book Club. dj. VG. P1. $5.00

COLES, Manning. *Without Lawful Authority.* 1943. Crime Club. VG. P1. $10.00

COLES, Robert. *Walker Percy: Am Search.* 1978. 1st ed. dj. EX. C1. $6.50

COLETTE. *Break of Day.* 1983. Ltd Ed Club. Ils/sgn Francoise Gilot. slipcase. VG. $110.00

COLETTE. *Collected Stories of Colette.* nd. Farrar Straus. UP. wrp. EX. B13. $65.00

COLIN, Aubrey. *Hands of Death.* 1963. Hammond Hammond. 1st ed. dj. VG. P1. $7.50

COLLIER, Edward. *Remember Them: An Hist Discourse.* 1912. E Greenbush, NY. tall 8vo. wrp. G. B10. $5.00

COLLIER, J.P. *Hist of Eng Dramatic Poetry to Time of Shakespeare...* 1831. London. Murray. 1st ed. 3 vols. EX. H3. $300.00

COLLIER. *Fire in the Sky.* 1941. Boston. 1st ed. dj. VG. B3. $15.00

COLLINGS, Michael. *Annotated Guide to Stephen King.* 1986. Starmont. 1st ed. wrp. M. R3. $9.95

COLLINGS, Michael. *Films of Stephen King.* 1986. Starmont. Ltd 1st ed. HrdCvr. M. R3. $25.00

COLLINGS, Michael. *Many Facets of Stephen King.* 1986. Starmont. Ltd 1st ed. HrdCvr. M. R3. $25.00

COLLINGS, Michael. *Reflections on the Fantastic.* 1986. Greenwood. 1st ed. RS. M. R3. $29.95

COLLINGS, Michael. *Shorter Works of Stephen King.* 1986. Starmont. Ltd 1st ed. HrdCvr. M. R3. $25.00

COLLINGS, Michael. *Stephen King As Richard Bachman.* 1986. Starmont. Ltd 1st ed. HrdCvr. M. R3. $25.00

COLLINGS, Michael. *Stephen King Phenomenon.* 1987. Starmont. 1st ed. wrp. M. R3. $9.95

COLLINGS. *Adventures on a Dude Ranch.* 1940. Indianapolis. photos. A6. $22.00

COLLINS, Elizabeth. *Memoirs of Elizabeth Collins of Upper Evesham, NJ.* 1833. Phil. Nathan Kite. 1st ed. 18mo. 144 p. VG. V1. $18.00

COLLINS, M.A. *Million-Dollar Wound.* 1986. St Martin. 1st ed. dj. EX. F5. $16.00

COLLINS, M.A. *Neon Mirage.* 1988. St Martin. 1st ed. dj. EX. F5. $15.00

COLLINS, Max. *No Cure for Death.* 1983. Walker. 1st ed. dj. VG. P1. $15.00

COLLINS, Max. *Shroud for Aquarius.* 1985. Walker. 1st ed. dj. EX. P1. $14.95

COLLINS, Michael. *Act of Fear.* 1967. Doubleday Book Club. P1. $7.50

COLLINS, Michael. *Carrying the Fire.* 1974. NY. 1st ed. dj. VG. B3. $15.00

COLLINS, Michael. *MN Strip.* 1987. Donald Fine. 1st ed. inscr. dj. EX. T9. $35.00

COLLINS, Michael. *Naked to the Sun.* 1985. Starmont. 1st ed. wrp. M. R3. $8.95

COLLINS, Paul. *Envisioned Worlds.* 1978. Void. 1st ed. M. R3. $10.00

COLLINS, W.J.T. *Romance of the Echoing Wood.* 1937. Newport. Johns. Ltd ed. 1/220. sgns. H3. $125.00

COLLINS, W.J.T. *Tales From the New Mabinogian.* 1923. London. 1st ed. VG. extermely scarce. C1. $29.50

COLLINS, Wilkie. *Moonstone.* 1946. Literary Guild. dj. VG. P1. $5.50

COLLINS. *FBI in Peace & War.* 1943. NY. inscr by Hoover. dj. VG. $60.00

COLLINS. *Indians` Last Fight; or, The Dull Knife Raid.* nd. (1915?) Girard. 1st ed. fair. C2. $89.00

COLLIS, Maurice. *Raffles.* 1968. Day. 1st Am ed. 227 p. EX. B10. $20.00

COLLIS & HOGERZEIL. *Straight On.* 1947. London. 1st ed. dj. G. C2. $37.00

COLLODI, Carl. *Pinocchio.* nd. Donohue. VG. P1. $7.50

COLLUM, Ridgwell. *Hound From the N.* nd. AL Burt. VG. P1. $7.00

COLLUM, Ridgwell. *Men Who Wrought.* nd. AL Burt. VG. P1. $5.00

COLLUM, Ridgwell. *Triumph of John Kars.* 1917. Chapman Hall. VG. P1. $10.00

COLTER, Cyrus. *Hippodrome.* 1973. Swallow Pr. 1st ed. clipped dj. EX. F5. $15.00

COLTON, James; see Hansen, Joseph.

COLTON, Walter. *Deck & Port Cruise of the Frigate Congress to CA.* 1850. Barnes. 4 clr pls. map. 408 p. A5. $80.00

COLUM, Padraic. *Frenzied Prince: Heroic Stories of Ancient Ireland.* 1943. Phil. Ils Pogany. dj. EX. $40.00

COLUM, Padric. *Boy Apprenticed to an Enchanter.* 1920. Macmillan. 1st ed. VG. scarce. C1. $59.50

COLVIN, F.H. *Aircraft Mechanics Handbook.* 1918. McGraw Hill. 5th print. VG. P1. $9.25

COLVIN, James; see Moorcock, Michael.

COLWIN, Laurie. *Passion & Affect.* 1974. Viking. 1st ed. inscr. dj. EX. B13. $45.00

COLYTON, H.J. *Sir Pagan.* 1947. Creative Age. 1st ed. dj. VG. F5. $15.00

COMAS & GENOVES. *Anthropologia Fisica en Mixico 1943-1959.* 1960. Mexico. 1st ed. 66 p. wrp. F2. $10.00

COMFORT, Alex. *Novel & Our Time.* 1948. Phoenix House. 1st ed. sm 8vo. dj. EX. R4. $15.00

COMFORT, W.L. *Son of Power.* nd. Gundy. 1st Canadian ed. VG. P1. $12.50

COMFORT, W.W. *Just Among Friends: The Quaker Way of Life.* 1952. Phil. Revised 3rd ed. 12mo. SftCvr. VG. V1. $5.00

COMFORT, W.W. *Stephen Grellet, 1773-1855.* 1942. Macmillan. 12mo. 202 p. VG. V1. $10.00

COMFORT, W.W. *William Penn & Our Liberties.* 1947. Penn Mutual. 1st ed. 12mo. 146 p. V1. $8.00

COMLY, John. *Journal of Life & Religious Labors of John Comly...* 1853. Phil. Chapman. 8vo. 645 p. full leather. V1. $32.00

COMMAGER, H.S. *Bl & Gray.* 1950. Bobbs Merrill. 2 vols. VG. S1. $14.00

COMPTON, D.G. *Ascendancies.* 1980. Berkley Putnam. 1st ed. dj. EX. F5/R3. $18.00

COMPTON, D.G. *Windows.* 1979. Berkley Putnam. 1st ed. dj. VG. P1. $12.50

COMSTOCK, E.L. *Life & Letters of Elizabeth Comstock.* 1895. London. Headley. 12mo. 511 p. G. V1. $15.00

COMSTOCK, F.A. *Gothic Vision: FL Griggs & His Work.* 1966. Boston/Oxford. 1/600. sgn. EX. $50.00

CONDE, J.A. *Cars That Hudson Built.* 1980. 211 p. dj. EX. S1. $25.00

CONDE, Nicholas. *Religion.* 1982. New Am Lib. 1st ed. dj. EX. F5. $16.50

CONDON, Eddie. *We Called It Music.* 1947. NY. 1st ed. 341 p. dj. VG. B3. $40.00

CONDON, Richard. *Manchurian Candidate.* 1959. McGraw Hill. 1st ed. inscr. dj. EX. C4. $225.00

CONDON, Richard. *Prizzi's Family.* 1986. Putnam. 1st ed. dj. EX. F5. $15.00

CONDON & O'NEAL. *Eddie Condon's Scrapbook of Jazz.* nd. (1973) Galahad Books. 250 p. dj. NM. B10. $6.25

CONDRON, CORDEN, & SULLIVAN. *Thinking Soldiers.* 1944. Peking. sgns. 246 p. dj. VG. T5. $125.00

CONE, Mary. *2 Years in CA.* 1876. Chicago. 1st ed. fld map. VG. $35.00

CONEY, M.G. *Celestial Steam Locomotive.* 1983. Houghton Mifflin. 1st ed. dj. EX. R3. $15.00

CONEY, M.G. *Girl With a Symphony in Her Fingers.* 1975. London. 1st ed. dj. EX. R3. $25.00

CONEY, M.G. *Gods of the Greataway.* 1984. Houghton Mifflin. 1st ed. dj. VG. P1. $15.95

CONEY, M.G. *Syzygy.* 1973. Elmfield Pr. dj. P1. $18.25

CONEY, M.G. *Syzygy.* 1973. London. 1st ed. dj. R3. $20.00

CONEY, M.G. *Winter's Children.* 1975. Reader's Union Book Club. dj. VG. P1. $5.00

CONEY, Michael. *Fang the Gnome.* 1988. 1st ed. dj. VG. C1. $17.00

CONFUCIUS. *Analects.* 1970. Ltd Ed Club. Ils/sgn Tseng Yu-Ho. slipcase. VG. $70.00

CONGDON, H.W. *Early Am Homes of Today.* 1963. Rutland. 1st print. 4to. slipcase. M. T1. $35.00

CONGER, E.B. *OH Woman in the Phillipines.* 1904. Akron, OH. 166 p. VG. T5. $27.50

CONGER, E.M. *Am Tanks & Tank Destroyers.* 1944. NY. Ils. 172 p. dj. EX. $45.00

CONKIN, Henry. *Through Poverty's Vale.* 1974. Syracuse. 1st ed. dj. EX. B10. $4.75

CONKLIN, George. *Ways of the Circus.* 1921. Harper. presentation. 308 p. VG. H3. $75.00

CONKLIN, Groff. *Best of SF.* 1946. Crown. 1st ed. dj. EX. R3. $35.00

CONKLIN, Groff. *Big Book of SF.* nd. Crown. 3rd ed. dj. VG. P1. $25.00

CONKLIN, Groff. *Big Book of SF.* 1950. Crown. 1st ed. dj. EX. R3. $35.00

CONKLIN, Groff. *Giants Unleashed.* 1965. Grosset Dunlap. 1st ed. dj. EX. R3. $20.00

CONKLIN, Groff. *Omnibus of SF.* 1952. Crown. 1st ed. dj. EX. R3. $25.00

CONKLIN, Groff. *Possible Worlds of SF.* 1965. Vanguard. 1st ed. dj. VG. R3. $25.00

CONKLIN, Groff. *SF Adventures in Dimension.* 1953. Vanguard. 1st ed. dj. EX. R3. $45.00

CONKLIN, Groff. *SF Adventures in Mutation.* 1955. Vanguard. 1st ed. dj. VG. P1. $35.00

CONKLIN, Groff. *SF Thinking Machines.* 1954. Vanguard. 1st ed. dj. EX. R3. $30.00

CONKLIN, Groff. *Treasury of SF.* 1948. Crown. 1st ed. sgn. dj. EX. R3. $55.00

CONKLING, M.C. *Memoirs of Mother & Wife of WA.* 1851. Auburn. 12mo. 248 p. gilt red bdg. xl. G. G4. $16.00

CONLEY, Robert. *Witch of Goingsnake & Other Stories.* 1988. OK U. ARC. dj. RS. EX. K2. $35.00

CONN, George. *Arabian Horse in Am.* 1957. Woodstock, VT. 1st ed. dj. EX. $40.00

CONNELL, E.S. *Connoisseur.* 1974. Knopf. 1st ed. inscr. dj. EX. scarce. B13. $125.00

CONNELL, E.S. *Son of the Morning Star.* 1984. N Point Pr. UP. EX. K2. $100.00

CONNELL, E.S. *Son of the Morning Star.* 1984. San Francisco. N Point Pr. 1st ed. inscr. EX. K2. $250.00

CONNELL, Evan. *Son of the Morning Star.* 1984. San Francisco. 1st ed. as issued. EX. K2. $90.00

CONNELL, Vivian. *Chinese Room.* 1942. Citadel. 1st ed. dj. EX. F5. $30.00

CONNELL, Vivian. *Golden Sleep.* 1948. Dial. 1st ed. dj. EX. F5. $27.50

CONNER, Patrick. *Oriental Architecture in the W.* 1979. London. 1st ed. VG. G1. $20.00

CONNER, Ralph. *Runner.* 1929. Doubleday. 1st ed. 481 p. M. B10. $8.25

CONNINGTON, J.J. *Eye in the Mus.* nd. Grosset Dunlap. VG. P1. $7.50

CONNOLLY, Cyril. *Ideas & Places.* 1953. Weidenfeld Nicolson. 1st ed. 280 p. dj. EX. R4. $40.00

CONNOLLY, Cyril. *Modern Movement.* 1965. London. Hamish Hamilton. 1st ed. dj. EX. B13. $150.00

CONNOLLY, Cyril. *Modern Movement.* 1966. NY. Atheneum. 1st Am ed. dj. EX. B13. $85.00

CONNOLLY, Cyril. *Rock Pool.* 1936. Scribner. Ltd Am ed. presentation. fld case. rare. H3. $750.00

CONQUEST, Joan. *Reckoning.* 1931. Macaulay. 1st ed. dj. VG. F5. $40.00

CONRAD, Earl. *Da Vinci Machine.* 1968. Fleet Pr. dj. VG. P1. $7.25

CONRAD, H.L. *Uncle Dick Wootton.* 1957. Lakeside Classic. Ils. 465 p. VG. T5. $22.50

CONRAD, Joseph. *Children of the Sea.* 1897. NY. 1st Am ed of Nigger of Narcissus. 217 p. T5. $125.00

CONRAD, Joseph. *Complete Works.* 1928. Doubleday Doran/Wise. Canterbury ed. 26 vols. octavo. TEG. H3. $350.00

CONRAD, Joseph. *Lord Jim.* 1959. Ltd Ed Club. Ils/sgn Lynd Ward. 1/1500. slipcase. EX. C4. $100.00

CONRAD, Joseph. *Lord Jim.* 1977. Easton Pr. Ils Lynd Ward. Ltd ed. full gr leather. M. T1. $40.00

CONRAD, Joseph. *Mirror of the Sea.* 1905. NY. 1st Am ed. VG. $50.00

CONRAD, Joseph. *Nostromo.* 1904. London. 1st ed. VG. scarce. $275.00

CONRAD, Joseph. *Nostromo.* 1923. Doubleday Page. VG. P1. $25.00

CONRAD, Joseph. *Notes on My Books.* 1921. Heinemann. 1/250. sgn. VG. K2. $375.00

CONRAD, Joseph. *Secret Sharer.* 1985. Ltd Ed Club. Ils/sgn Bruce Chandler. slipcase. M. $125.00

CONRAD, Joseph. *Tales of Hearsay.* 1925. Fisher Unwin. 1st ed. VG. $30.00

CONRAD, Joseph. *Typhoon.* nd. Readers Lib. dj. VG. P1. $18.25

CONRAD, Joseph. *Victory, an Island Tale.* 1915. London. 1st Eng ed. 415 p. T5. $50.00

CONRAD, Joseph. *Works.* 1921-1927. Heinemann. Ltd ed. 1/780. 20 vols. octavo. TEG. H3. $4000.00

CONRAD, Joseph. *Works.* 1925. Edinburgh/London. Grant. 20 vols. sm octavo. EX. H3. $3000.00

CONRAD, Joseph. *Youth & 2 Other Stories.* 1903. McClure Phillips. fair. $40.00

CONRAD, Jospeh. *Laughing Anne: A Play.* 1923. London. Vine Books/Morland. 1/200. sgn. K2. $850.00

CONRAN, Anthony. *Claim Claim Claim.* 1969. Guildford. 1/250. wrp. D4. $50.00

CONRAN, Terence. *House Book.* 1976. Crown. 4to. dj. EX. $9.00

CONROY, Albert; see Albert, Marvin H.

CONROY, Carol. *Beauty Wars.* 1991. Norton. 1st ed. sgn. dj. EX. B13. $45.00

CONROY, Frank. *Midair.* 1985. Dutton/Seymour Lawrence. 1st ed. sgn. dj. EX. K2. $45.00

CONROY, Frank. *Stop Time.* 1967. NY. ARC. VG. K2. $50.00

CONROY, Pat. *Boo.* 1970. McClure. 1st ed. 1/1000. VG. K2. $350.00

CONROY, Pat. *Boo.* 1970. Verona. McClure. 1st ed. dj. VG. B13. $350.00

CONROY, Pat. *Boo.* 1988. Atlanta. Old NY Book Shop. sgn. slipcase. K2. $175.00

CONROY, Pat. *Boo.* 1988. Atlanta. NY Book Shop Pr. 1st ed. 1/250. slipcase. EX. B13/K2. $150.00

CONROY, Pat. *Great Santini.* 1976. Houghton Mifflin. 1st ed. sgn. dj. EX. B13. $125.00

CONROY, Pat. *Lords of Discipline.* 1980. Houghton Mifflin. sgn. H3. $100.00

CONROY, Pat. *Prince of Tides.* 1986. Boston. 1st ed. dj. VG. B3. $35.00

CONROY, Pat. *Prince of Tides.* 1986. Houghton Mifflin. 1st ed. sgn. dj. EX. K2. $50.00

CONROY, Pat. *Water Is Wide.* 1972. Houghton Mifflin. 1st ed. dj. EX. B13. $350.00

CONSTANTINE, K.C. *Always a Body To Trade.* 1983. Godine. 1st ed. inscr. dj. EX. K2. $250.00

CONSTANTINE, K.C. *Joey's Case.* 1988. Mysterious Pr. 1st ed. dj. EX. F5. $13.00

CONTE, Christine. *Maya Culture & Costume.* 1984. Taylor Mus. 1st ed. sm 4to. F2. $20.00

CONWAY, Hugh. *Called Back.* nd. Detective Club. dj. VG. P1. $13.75

CONWAY, J.G. *Flowers E & W.* 1948. Knopf. Ils. lg 4to. 336 p. dj. $25.00

CONWAY & CONWAY. *Enchanted Islands.* 1947. Putnam. 1st ed. 280 p. dj. F2. $15.00

CONWELL, R.H. *Hist of Great Fire in Boston.* 1873. 12mo. 312 p. G. G4. $24.00

CONYBEARE, F.C. *Selections From the Septuagint.* nd. (1905) Ginn. sq 8vo. VG. B10. $4.25

COOK, Clarence. *House Beautiful.* 1980. N River Pr. 1st ed. 336 p. dj. EX. B10. $8.25

COOK, D.J. *Hands Up!; or, 20 Years of Detective Life in Mts.* 1958. Norman. dj. EX. $20.00

COOK, E.D. *Book of the Play.* 1882. Sampson Low. 4th ed. octavo. 391 p. G. H3. $60.00

COOK, E.D. *On the Stage.* 1883. Sampson Low. 1st ed. 2 vols. VG. H3. $150.00

COOK, Edward. *Life of Florence Nightingale.* 1942. NY. 2 vols in 1. VG. $20.00

COOK, Elliott. *Land Ho!* 1935. Baltimore. Remington Putnam. 1st ed. VG. $32.50

COOK, F.A. *Return From the Pole.* 1951. NY. 1st ed. 375 p. dj. VG. B3. $27.50

COOK, Glenn. *Doomstalker.* 1985. Popular Lib. UP. wrp. EX. R3. $15.00

COOK, Hugh. *Wizards & the Warriors.* 1986. Colin Smyth/Dufour. 1st ed. dj. RS. EX. P1. $18.95

COOK, J.H. *50 Years on the Old Frontier.* 1923. New Haven. Ils. 291 p. G. T5. $65.00

COOK, James. *Capt James Cook in the Pacific.* 1957. Ltd Ed Club. Ils/sgn Ingelton & Dunstan. 4to. slipcase. VG. $110.00

COOK, James. *3 Voyages of Capt James Cook Round the World.* 1821. Longman Hurst Rees Orme. 1st ed. 7 vols. octavo. EX. H3. $2250.00

COOK, Joel. *Eng, Picturesque & Descriptive.* 1882. Phil. 1st ed. 4to. AEG. EX. $35.00

COOK, R.B. *Annals of Ft Lee.* 1935. Charleston. 1st ed. 119 p. VG. $30.00

COOK, T.A. *Old Touraine.* 1892. London. 1st ed. 1/36. 2 vols. EX. $275.00

COOK, W.W. *Adrift in the Unknown.* 1925. Street Smith. wrp. VG. R3. $17.50

COOK, W.W. *Around the World in 80 Hours.* 1925. Chelsea House. 1st ed. G. R3. $17.50

COOK, W.W. *Juggling With Liberty.* 1906. Street Smith. wrp. G. R3. $12.50

COOK. *Journals of Military Expedition of Maj Gen J Sullivan...* 1887. NY. Ils. maps. 580 p. A5. $50.00

COOKE, Alistar. *Christmas Eve.* nd. Knopf. Stated 1st ed. dj. VG. B7. $28.00

COOKE, J.E. *Life of Gen Robert E Lee.* 1871. NY. 1st ed. VG. J2. $120.00

COOKE, J.E. *Outlines From the Outpost.* 1961. Chicago. Ils. 413 p. EX. T5. $25.00

COOKE, J.E. *Stonewall Jackson.* 1893. Dillingham. VG. K1. $22.50

COOKE, Jay. *Journal of Jay Cooke; or, Gibraltar Records 1865-1905.* 1935. OH State U. 1st ed. VG. $55.00

COOKSON, Catherine. *Harrogate Secret.* 1988. Summit. 1st ed. 352 p. dj. EX. B10. $5.25

COOLEY, A.A. *Complete Practical Treatise on Perfumery...* 1874. Phil. 804 p. EX. $55.00

COOLEY. *School Acres.* 1930. New Haven. 1st ed. 166 p. dj. VG. B3. $30.00

COOMBS, Charles. *Andy Burnett on Trial.* 1958. Whitman. Big Little Book. G. P1. $7.50

COOMBS, Charles. *Maverick.* 1959. Whitman. VG. P1. $15.00

COOMBS, Charles. *Water Sport Stories.* 1952. Grosset Dunlap. Young Readers Series. dj. VG. B10. $3.00

COON, Carleton. *7 Caves.* 1957. Knopf. 1st ed. 31 pls. 338 p. F2. $10.00

COONEY, Michael. *King of the Sceptered Isle.* 1st Am ed. dj. M. C1. $16.00

COONTS, Stephen. *Flight of the Intruder.* 1986. Annapolis. K2. $35.00

COOPER, Astley. *Series of Lectures on...Practice of Modern Surgery.* 1823. Boston. 1st Am ed. 8vo. 456 p. VG. G4. $69.00

COOPER, C.R. *Lions 'n Tigers 'n Everything.* 1924. Little Brn. 1st ed. octavo. 260 p. EX. H3. $50.00

COOPER, C.R. *Under the Big Top.* 1923. Little Brn. octavo. 238 p. VG. H3. $50.00

COOPER, Clarence. *Syndicate.* 1960. Newsstand Lib 513. PB Orig. wrp. NM. T9. $50.00

COOPER, Clayton. *Brazilians & Their Country.* 1917. Stokes. 1st ed. 8vo. 403 p. dj. F2. $20.00

COOPER, Douglas. *Henri de Toulouse-Lautrec.* 1966. Abrams. 152 p. dj. D4. $40.00

COOPER, Edmund. *Sea Horse in the Sky.* 1970. Putnam. dj. xl. P1. $4.75

COOPER, Edmund. *Slaves of Heaven.* 1974. Putnam. dj. EX. P1. $9.25

COOPER, Edmund. *10th Planet.* 1973. Putnam. dj. EX. P1. $9.25

COOPER, Edmund. *5 to 12.* nd. Book Club. dj. VG. P1. $4.00

COOPER, Gordon. *Dead Cities & Forgotten Tribes.* 1952. Philosophical Lib. 1st ed. 160 p. dj. F2. $12.50

COOPER, J.F. *Deerslayer.* 1929. Scribner. Ils Classics Series. Ils Wyeth. EX. $45.00

COOPER, J.F. *Deerslayer.* 1961. Ltd Ed Club. Ils/sgn Edward Wilson. 4to. slipcase. VG. $55.00

COOPER, J.F. *Last of the Mohicans.* 1884. Belforde. 358 p. VG. B10. $4.00

COOPER, J.F. *Last of the Mohicans.* 1979. Easton Pr. Ils Wilson. 1st ed. leather bdg. M. $30.00

COOPER, J.F. *Pathfinder.* 1965. Lunenburg, VT. Ltd Ed Club. Ils/sgn RM Powers. slipcase. EX. C4. $50.00

COOPER, J.F. *Technique of Contraception: Principles & Practice...* 1929. NY. 2nd ed. 271 p. EX. scarce. $50.00

COOPER, Samuel. *1st Lines of Surgery.* 1828. Boston. 3rd ed. VG. $75.00

COOPER, Susan. *Dark Is Rising.* Atheneum. PB. VG. C1. $6.00

COOPER, Susan. *Seaward.* 1983. Atheneum. 1st ed. dj. EX. P1. $10.95

COOPER & RECORD. *Evergreen Forest of Liberia.* 1931. New Haven. Ils. 153 p. wrp. fair. T5. $15.00

COOPER-OAKLY, Isabel. *Masonry & Medieval Mysticism: Traces of Hidden Tradition.* 1977. London. 2nd ed. stiff wrp. VG. C1. $17.50

COOVER, Robert. *Pinocchio in Venice.* 1991. Simon Schuster. UP. wrp. EX. K2. $35.00

COOVER, Robert. *Universal Baseball Assn, Inc.* 1968. Random House. 1st print. dj. EX. H3. $75.00

COOVER, Robert. *Water Pourer.* 1972. Bruccoli Clark. 1/50 marked not for sale. sgn. EX. B13. $100.00

COPE, S.S. *Memoir of Samuel S Cope, Son of Morris & Ann Cope.* 1867. Phil. WH Pile. 16mo. 24 p. G. V1. $8.50

COPLEY, Gordon. *Going Into the Past.* 1955. Phoenix House. 1st ed. 160 p. dj. F2. $7.50

COPPARD, A.E. *Adam & Eve & Pinch Me.* 1922. Knopf. 2nd ed. dj. VG. P1. $30.00

COPPARD, A.E. *Fearful Pleasures.* 1946. Arkham House. 1st ed. dj. EX. R3. $100.00

COPPEE. *Grant & His Campaigns: A Military Biography.* 1866. NY. 1st ed. 8vo. 521 p. G. $50.00

COPPEL, Alfred. *Gate of Hell.* 1967. Harcourt Brace World. 1st ed. dj. VG. P1. $7.00

COPPEL, Alfred. *Hastings Conspiracy.* nd. Holt Rinehart Winston. 2nd ed. dj. EX. P1. $10.00

COPPER, Basil. *And Afterward the Dark.* 1977. Arkham House. 1st ed. EX. R3. $8.95

COPPER, Basil. *From Evil's Pillow.* 1973. Arkham House. dj. EX. P1. $15.00

COPPER, Basil. *House of the Worm.* 1983. Arkham House. 1st ed. M. R3. $30.00

COPPER, Basil. *Necropolis.* 1980. Arkham House. 2nd print. M. R3. $17.50

COPPOLINO, Carl. *Crime That Never Was.* 1980. Tampa. Justice Pr. 307 p. EX. $12.00

CORBEN, Richard. *Bloodstar.* 1976. Morning Star. dj. VG. P1. $30.00

CORBEN, Richard. *Flights Into Fantasy.* 1981. Thumbtack Books. 1st ed. dj. EX. P1. $30.00

CORBETT, Jim. *Man-Eaters of Kumaon.* 1946. Oxford. 1st Am ed. dj. VG. B10. $4.50

CORDELL, Alexander. *If You Believe the Soldiers.* 1974. Doubleday. 1st ed. dj. VG. P1. $7.25

CORDER, Susanna. *Memoir of Priscilla Gurney.* 1856. Phil. Longstreth. 8vo. 228 p. V1. $18.00

CORDNER, Lynn. *Artistic Traditions of Peru.* 1978. UCLA. Ils. 4to. wrp. F2. $10.00

CORE, Sue. *Burial of the Fish.* 1949. N River Pr. 1st ed. dj. F2. $15.00

CORELLI, Marie. *Wormwood.* nd. Donohue. VG. P1. $20.00

CORI, Jacques. *Chile.* 1954. Santiago. 4th ed. 8vo. Eng/Spanish text. dj. F2. $15.00

CORKILL, Louis. *Fish Lane.* 1951. Bobbs Merrill. 1st ed. dj. VG. P1. $10.00

CORLE, Edwin. *Burro Alley.* 1938. Duell Sloan Pearce. Ltd ed. 1/1500. H3. $85.00

CORLE, Edwin. *Coarse Gold.* 1952. Duell Sloan/Little Brn. 1/1000. sgns. dj. H3. $20.00

CORLE, Edwin. *Igor Stravinsky.* 1949. Duell Sloan Pearce. 1st ed. octavo. 245 p. dj. EX. H3. $125.00

CORLEY, Corin. *Lancelot of the Lake.* 1st Eng Trans. pb. 447 p. M. C1. $12.50

CORMACK, M.B. *Star-Crossed Woman.* 1962. Crown. dj. EX. P1. $10.00

CORMAN, Cid. *At Their Word.* 1978. Blk Sparrow. 1/200. sgn. 218 p. EX. T5. $20.00

CORNE, M.E. *Death at the Manor.* 1938. Mill. 1st ed. xl. P1. $10.00

CORNELISEN, Ann. *Where It All Began.* 1990. Dutton. UP. EX. K2. $25.00

CORNELIUS, Brother. *Keith: Old Master of CA.* 1942. Putnam. 1st ed. presentation. dj. VG. $75.00

CORNELIUS, John. *Borrowed Bill Routine.* 1984. San Antonio. NM. J3. $5.00

CORNELL, J.J. *Autobiography Containing Account of Religious Experiences.* 1906. Lord Baltimore Pr. 8vo. 498 p. VG. V1. $15.00

CORNELL, J.J. *Principles of Religious Soc of Friends & Some Testimonies.* 1897. Baltimore. Isaac Walker. 16mo. 45 p. V1. $10.00

CORNELL, W.M. *Life & Public Career of Honorable Horace Greeley.* nd. Lathrop. 317 p. G. $7.00

CORNPLANTER, Jesse. *Legends of the Longhouse.* 1938. Lippincott. 1st ed. dj. VG. K2. $85.00

CORNWALLIS-WEST, Mrs. George. *Reminiscences of Lady Randolph Churchill.* 1908. NY. Ils 1st Am ed. 470 p. TEG. G. T5. $45.00

CORREDOR-MATHOES, Jose. *Tamayo.* 1987. Rizzoli. 1st ed. 128 p. F2. $25.00

CORRELL, A.B. *Murder Is an Art.* 1950. Phoenix. dj. VG. P1. $7.50

CORRELL & GOSDEN. *All About Amos 'n Andy & Their Creators, Correll & Gosden.* 1930. Rand McNally. octavo. 127 p. dj. EX. H3. $75.00

CORRIGAN, Douglas. *That's My Story.* 1938. Dutton. 1st ed. B10. $14.50

CORRIGAN, Douglas. *That's My Story.* 1938. NY. 1st ed. presentation. G. B3. $37.50

CORRIGAN, Douglas. *That's My Story.* 1939. NY. 1st ed. sgn. 221 p. dj. VG. T5. $35.00

CORSO, Gregory. *Gasoline.* nd. City Lights. 8th print. B4. $3.00

CORSSEN, K.F. *Adventures in Tomorrow.* 1950. Greenberg. dj. VG. P1. $20.00

CORTAZAR, Julio. *End of the Game.* 1967. Pantheon. 1st ed. dj. EX. K2. $125.00

CORTAZAR, Julio. *Winners.* 1965. Pantheon. 1st ed. dj. EX. K2. $65.00

CORTI, E.C. *Rise of the House of Rothschild 1770-1830.* 1928. NY. Ils 1st ed. 427 p. VG. $35.00

CORWIN, J.H. *Harp of Home; or, The Medley.* 1858. Cincinnati. 1st ed. 382 p. T5. $35.00

CORWIN, Norman. *Selected Radio Plays.* 1944. Armed Services Ed. G. B4. $8.00

CORY, C.B. *Birds of IL & WI.* 1909. Chicago. Field Mus Nat Hist. wrp. VG. T3. $45.00

CORY, C.B. *Mammals of IL & WI.* 1912. Chicago. Field Mus Nat Hist. wrp. VG. T3. $45.00

CORY, Desmond. *Feramontov.* 1966. Muller. VG. P1.$7.50

COSTA, Richard. *Edmund Wilson: Our Neighbor From Talcottville.* 1980. Syracuse U. 1st ed. 173 p. dj. w/sgn note. EX. B10. $7.25

COSTAIN, T.B. *Hist of Plantagenets.* 1962. NY. 4 vols. boxed. EX. B3. $30.00

COSTAIN, T.B. *Silver Chalice.* nd. Book Club. dj. VG. C1. $3.50

COSTAIN, T.B. *3 Edwards.* 1962. NY. VG. $15.00

COSTELLO, A. *Our Firemen.* 1887. NY. 1st ed. 1112 p. AEG. VG. $130.00

COSTELLO, A. *Police Protectors.* 1885. NY. Ils. 526 p. decor brd. VG. $110.00

COTHRAN. *Charleston Murders.* 1947. NY. 1st ed. dj. VG. B3. $17.50

COTLER, Gordon. *Mission in Blk.* nd. Book Club. dj. EX. P1. $4.50

COTLOW, Lewis. *In Search of the Primitive.* 1966. Little Brn. 1st ed. 454 p. dj. F2. $12.50

COTLOW, Lewis. *Twilight of the Primitive.* 1971. Macmillan. 1st ed. 257 p. dj. F2. $12.50

COTT, Jonathan. *Beyond the Looking Glass.* 1973. Stonehill Bowker. 2nd ed. dj. VG. P1. $25.00

COTTON, J.B. *Wall-Eyed Caesar's Ghost.* 1925. Boston. 1st ed. sgn. VG. B3. $30.00

COTTON, J.B. *Wall-Eyed Caesar's Ghost.* 1926. Boston. Ils Frederic Cotton. 1st ed. $50.00

COTTON, Joseph. *Vanity Will Get You Somewhere.* 1987. Mercury House. 1st ed. presentation. 235 p. dj. EX. H3. $50.00

COTTRELL, John. *Man of Destiny: Story of Muhammad Ali.* 1967. London. Muller. 1st ed. 363 p. EX. B10. $5.75

COUCH, N.C. *Pre-Columbian Art From Ernest Erickson Collection...* 1988. NY. 1st ed. oblong 4to. F2. $20.00

COUDENHOVE, Hans. *My African Neighbors: Man, Bird, & Beast.* 1925. Boston. Ils. 245 p. G. $35.00

COUES, Elliott. *Soldier-Scientist in the Am SW: Narrative of Travels.* 1973. AZ Hist Soc. 1st ed. 74 p. wrp. VG. $20.00

COUGHLAN, Robert. *Private World of William Faulkner.* 1962. Avon. P1. $4.50

COULSON, Juantia. *Outward Bound.* nd. Book Club. dj. VG. P1. $4.50

COULSON, Juantia. *Tomorrow's Heritage.* nd. Book Club. dj. VG. P1. $4.50

COULSON, Thomas. *Mata Hari.* 1930. Harper. 1st ed. lg 8vo. $14.00

COULTER, E.M. *Confederate States of Am 1861-1965.* 1950. LA State U. 644 p. G. S1. $7.00

COULTER, E.M. *S During Reconstruction.* 1947. LA State U. VG. S1. $7.00

COULTER, J.W. *Drama of Fiji.* nd. Rutland. Ils. dj. EX. T1. $20.00

COULTER, Stephen. *Players in a Dark Game.* 1968. Morrow. 1st ed. dj. EX. F5. $10.00

COUNSELMAN, M.E. *Half in Shadow.* 1978. Arkham House. 1st ed. dj. EX. P1. $15.00

COUNSELOR & COUNSELOR. *Wild, Woolly, & Wonderful.* 1954. NY. 1st ed. scarce. $75.00

COUPER, William. *VA Military Inst Cadets.* 1933. Charlottesville. Ils. 8vo. 272 p. VG. $75.00

COURTIER, S.H. *Ligny's Lake.* 1971. Robert Hale. 1st ed. dj. VG. P1. $15.00

COURTIER, S.H. *Ligny's Lake.* 1971. Simon Schuster. 1st ed. dj. xl. P1. $7.00

COURTNEY, Ashley. *Let's Halt Awhile.* 1943. London. Simpkin. 197 p. dj. VG. B10. $4.00

COUSE & MAPLE. *Button Classics.* 1941. Chicago. Ils. 4to. 249 p. C2. $75.00

COUSINS, Norman. *In God We Trust.* 1958. Harper Book Club. dj. EX. B10. $4.25

COUTEUR. *Ancient Glass in Winchester.* 1929. Winchester. 1st ed. 39 pls. 183 p. VG. C2. $45.00

COVARRUBIAS, Luis. *Mexican Native Dances.* 1978. Mexico. Fishgrund. 2nd ed. F2. $10.00

COVARRUBIAS, Miguel. *Arts of the S Seas.* nd. MOMA. 200 p. F2. $25.00

COVARRUBIAS, Miguel. *Eagle, Jaguar, & Serpent: Indian Art of Am.* 1954. Knopf. 1st ed. dj. F2. $85.00

COVARRUBIAS, Miguel. *Indian Art of Mexico & Central Am.* 1957. Knopf. 1st ed. 360 p. dj. F2. $85.00

COVARRUBIAS, Miguel. *John & Juan in the Jungle.* 1953. Dodd Mead. 1st ed. 64 p. VG. F2. $25.00

COVARRUBIAS, Miguel. *Mexico S: Isthmus of Tehuantepec.* 1946. Knopf. 1st ed. 427 p. F2. $30.00

COVER, A.B. *E Wind Coming.* 1979. Berkley. 1st ed. wrp. EX. F5. $12.00

COVER, James. *Notes on Jurgen.* 1928. NY. 1st ed. 1/850. VG. C1. $24.50

COVERLY, R. *Papers: From the Spectator 1711-1712.* 1945. Ltd Ed Club. Ils/sgn Gordon Ross. slipcase. VG. $50.00

COVES, Elliot. *Key to N Am Birds.* 1903. Boston. Page. 5th ed. 2 vols. VG. T3. $85.00

COWAN, James. *Daybreak.* 1896. Richmond. 1st ed. VG. R3. $50.00

COWAN, R.E. *Spanish Pr of CA.* 1931. San Francisco. JH Nash. 1/50. sgn. VG. rare. C1. $85.00

COWAN & COWAN. *Bibliography of CA 1510-1930.* 1964. Los Angels. 4 vols. 8vo. VG. $95.00

COWAN & KINDER. *Smart Women, Foolish Choices.* 1985. 1st ed. dj. EX. C1. $8.50

COWARD, Noel. *Nowel Coward Song Book.* 1953. Michael Joseph. 1st ed. quarto. 314 p. dj. VG. H3. $125.00

COWARD, Noel. *Play Parade.* 1933. Garden City. 576 p. dj. VG. B10. $3.50

COWARD, Noel. *Point Valaine.* 1935. Doubleday Doran. 1st Am ed. dj. EX. H3. $45.00

COWARD, Noel. *Post-Mortem.* 1931. Heinemann. 1st ed. dj. EX. H3. $50.00

COWARD, Noel. *Present Indicative.* 1937. Heinemann. 1st ed. octavo. 431 p. dj. VG. H3. $75.00

COWARD, Noel. *Quadrille: Romantic Comedy in 3 Acts.* 1955. Doubleday. 1st Am ed. dj. EX. H3. $50.00

COWARD, Noel. *This Happy Breed.* 1947. Doubleday. 1st ed. dj. EX. H3. $40.00

COWART, David. *Thomas Pynchon: Art of Allusion.* nd. Carbondale, IL. S IL U. long galley sheets. K2. $85.00

COWBURN, Benajamin. *No Cloak No Dagger.* nd. Adventurers Club. VG. P1. $3.75

COWELL, Adrian. *Heart of the Forest.* 1961. Knopf. 240 p. dj. VG. F2. $12.50

COWLEY, Malcolm. *Bl Juniata Collected Poems.* 1968. NY. 1st ed. dj. VG. B3. $20.00

COWLEY, Malcolm. *Exile's Return.* 1934. Norton. 1st ed. dj. EX. H3. $200.00

COWLEY, Malcolm. *Exile's Return.* 1981. Ltd Ed Club. Ils/sgn Berenice Abbott. slipcase. EX. $75.00

COWLEY, Malcolm. *Literary Situation.* 1954. Viking. 1st ed. dj. EX. H3. $75.00

COWLEY, Stewart. *Space Wreck.* 1979. Hamlin. dj. EX. P1. $10.00

COWLEY, Stewart. *Spacecraft 2000 to 2100 AD.* 1978. Chartwell. dj. EX. P1. $7.00

COWLEY, W.M. *Portable Faulkner.* 1951. Viking. 3rd ed. 756 p. VG. B10. $4.00

COWLEY & HERRIDGE. *Great Space Battles.* 1979. Chartwell. dj. EX. P1. $7.50

COWPER, Richard. *Clone.* 1973. Doubleday. 1st ed. dj. EX. P1. $10.00

COWPER, Richard. *Kuldesak.* 1972. Doubleday. 1st ed. dj. EX. F5. $16.00

COWPER, Richard. *Road to Corlay.* nd. Book Club. dj. EX. P1. $4.50

COWPER, Richard. *Story of Pepito & Corindo.* 1982. Cheap Street. 1st ed. 1/99. sgn. wrp. M. R3. $20.00

COWPER, Richard. *Unhappy Princess.* 1982. Cheap Street. 1st ed. wrp. M. R3. $20.00

COWPER, Richard. *Web of the Magi.* 1980. London. 1st ed. dj. EX. R3. $40.00

COWPER, William. *Poems.* 1782 & 1785. London. 1st ed. 2 vols. polished calf. rebacked. VG. H3. $850.00

COWPER, William. *Poems.* 1905. London. 1st ed. 27 pls. TEG. T5. $35.00

COX, Erle. *Out of the Silence.* 1928. Henkle. 1st Am ed. G. R3. $40.00

COX, Ian. *Scallop: Studies of Shell & Its Influence on Mankind.* 1957. London. Ils. 135 p. G. T5. $15.00

COX, J.D. *Atlanta.* nd. NY. Brussel. PB. G. S1. $6.00

COX, J.D. *March to the Sea.* nd. NY. Brussel. PB. VG. S1. $6.00

COX, Jack. *Nicaragua Betrayed.* 1981. Boston. 2nd print. 431 p. dj. F2. $10.00

COX, Sidney. *Swinger of Birches: Robert Frost.* 1961. Collier. EX. P1. $10.00

COXE, G.H. *Dangerous Legacy.* 1946. Knopf. dj. VG. P1. $15.00

COXE, G.H. *Easy Way To Go.* 1969. Knopf. 1st ed. dj. xl. P1. $7.50

COXE, G.H. *Fenner.* 1971. Knopf. 1st ed. dj. EX. P1. $15.00

COXE, G.H. *Groom Lay Dead.* 1947. Triangle. dj. VG. P1. $10.00

COXE, G.H. *Impetuous Mistress.* 1958. Knopf. 1st ed. 215 p. dj. EX. B10. $6.50

COXE, G.H. *Inside Man.* nd. Blk. P1. $4.00

COXE, G.H. *Murder With Pictures.* nd. Grosset Dunlap. VG. P1. $5.50

COXE, G.H. *Silent Witness.* 1973. Doubleday Book Club. VG. P1. $7.50

COXEY, J.S. *Coxey: His Own Story of the Commonwealth.* 1914. Massillon, OH. Ils. 92 p. printed wrp. VG. T5. $22.50

COYNE, John. *Fury.* 1989. Warner. 1st HrdCvr ed. dj. EX. F5. $14.00

COYNE, John. *Hobgoblin.* 1981. Putnam. 1st ed. inscr. dj. RS. EX. R3. $40.00

COYNE, John. *Piercing.* nd. Book Club. dj. VG. P1. $4.50

COYNE, John. *Piercing.* 1979. Putnam. 1st ed. dj. EX. F5. $30.00

COYNE, John. *Searing.* nd. Book Club. dj. VG. P1. $4.50

COYNE, John. *Searing.* 1980. Putnam. 1st ed. dj. EX. R3. $25.00

COZZENS, J.G. *Last Adam.* 1933. Harcourt Brace. 1st ed. xl. P1. $10.00

COZZENS, J.G. *Michael Scarlett.* 1925. Boni. 1st ed. dj. EX. B13. $200.00

COZZENS, J.G. *Son of Perdition.* 1929. Morrow. 1st ed. dj. EX. B13. $150.00

CRABB, A.L. *Peace at Bowling Gr.* 1955. Bobbs Merrill. 316 p. dj. EX. $10.00

CRABBE, George. *Poems.* 1905. Cambridge Eng Classic. 3 vols. octavo. djs. H3. $150.00

CRADOCK, Mrs. *Josephine's Christmas Party.* nd. London. Blackie. Ils Appleton. VG. B7. $48.00

CRAFTON, Allen. *Acting: Book for Beginners.* 1928. Crofts. 1st ed. 318 p. VG. B10. $4.50

CRAIG, Alisa. *Dismal Thing To Do.* nd. Book Club. dj. EX. P1. $5.00

CRAIG, Alisa. *Murder Goes Mumming.* nd. Book Club. dj. VG. P1. $5.00

CRAIG, David. *Contact Lost.* 1970. Stein Day. dj. VG. P1. $7.00

CRAIG, William. *Enemy at the Gates: Battle for Stalingrad.* 1973. NY. dj. VG. $12.00

CRAIGHEAD, F. *Track of the Grizzly.* 1979. San Francisco. 261 p. dj. VG. B3. $20.00

CRAIGHEAD. *Hawks in the Hand.* 1939. Boston. 1st ed. 290 p. dj. VG. B3. $47.50

CRAIK. *Practical Am Millwright & Miller.* 1877. Phil. fld plts. VG. C2. $95.00

CRAKE, A.D. *Doomed City.* 1911. Mowbray. Ils George Kruger. Revised ed. EX. F5. $15.00

CRAKE, A.D. *Last Abbot of Glastonbury.* 1910. London. gilt bl bdg. C1. $22.50

CRAMER, Stuart. *Secrets of Karl Germain.* 1962. Cleveland Heights. 70 p. VG. J3. $6.00

CRAMP, Arthur. *Nostrum's Quackery Pseudo-Medicine. Vol 3.* 1936. Chicago. 1st ed. G. C2. $25.00

CRANE, Caroline. *Circus Day.* 1986. Dodd Mead. 1st ed. dj. P1. $14.95

CRANE, Caroline. *Something Evil.* 1984. Doubleday Book Club. VG. P1. $7.50

CRANE, Frances. *Blk Cypress.* 1948. Random House. 1st ed. VG. P1. $15.00

CRANE, Frances. *Cinnamon Murder.* 1946. Random House. 1st ed. xl. P1. $10.00

CRANE, Frank. *Everyday Wisdom.* 1928. Wise. 2nd ed. 4to. 365 p. VG. B10. $6.00

CRANE, H. *Bridge.* 1981. Ltd Ed Club. Ils/sgn Richard Benson. 4to. slipcase. VG. $55.00

CRANE, H. *Maggie.* 1974. Ltd Ed Club. Ils/sgn Sigmund Abeles. slipcase. VG. $45.00

CRANE, Robert. *Hero's Walk.* 1954. Ballantine. dj. EX. P1. $35.00

CRANE, Robert. *Hero's Walk.* 1954. Ballantine. 1st ed. dj. EX. R3. $20.00

CRANE, Stephen. *Lanthorn Book.* 1898. NY. 1st ed. 1/125. sgn. sm folio. H3. $4000.00

CRANE, Stephen. *Little Regiment.* 1896. NY. 1st ed. 1st state. VG. $125.00

CRANE, Stephen. *Maggie: Girl of the Streets.* 1896. NY. 1st ed. VG. $75.00

CRANE, Stephen. *O'Ruddy.* 1903. NY. Stokes. 1st ed. VG. $50.00

CRANE, Stephen. *Red Badge of Courage.* 1896. Appleton. 2nd ed. VG. $35.00

CRANE, Stephen. *Red Badge of Courage.* 1944. Ltd Ed Club. Ils/sgn John S Curry. slipcase. VG. $65.00

CRANE, Stephen. *Red Badge of Courage.* 1990. Vintage Books. Intro/sgn Robert Stone. 1st ed. wrp. EX. B13. $85.00

CRANE, Stephen. *Whilomville Stories.* 1900. Harper. Ils Peter Newell. 1st ed. 12mo. EX. C4. $125.00

CRANE, Stephen. *Wounds in the Rain: War Stories.* 1900. Stokes. 1st Am ed. 12mo. TEG. gr bdg. EX. C4. $125.00

CRANE, Stephen. *3rd Violet.* 1897. NY. 1st ed. EX. $125.00

CRANE, W.E. *Bugle Blasts: Read Before the OH Commandery...* 1884. Cincinnati. 17 p. wrp. xl. VG. T5. $35.00

CRANE, Walter. *Baby's Bouquet.* nd. (c 1938) London/NY. Warne. 12mo. 56 p. VG. $40.00

CRANKSHAW, Edward. *Cracks in the Kremlin Wall.* 1951. Viking. 1st ed. 279 p. dj. EX. B10. $7.00

CRANKSHAW, Edward. *Russia & the Russians.* 1948. Viking. 3rd ed. not Book Club ed. 223 p. dj. VG. B10. $3.50

CRANSTON. *To Heaven on Horseback.* 1952. NY. 1st ed. dj. VG. B3. $15.00

CRARY, Mary. *Daughters of the Stars.* 1939. London. Hatchard. Ils Dulac. 4to. 190 p. tan bdg. VG. $55.00

CRAVEN, J.J. *Prison Life of Jefferson Davis.* 1866. NY. VG. $35.00

CRAVEN, Roy. *Ceremonial Centers of the Maya.* 1974. FL U. 1st ed. sm 4to. dj. F2. $30.00

CRAVEN. *Army Air Forces: WWII Men & Planes Vol 6.* 1955. Chicago. 1st ed. 808 p. dj. VG. B3. $70.00

CRAVENS & CRAVENS. *Blk Death.* 1977. Dutton. 1st ed. dj. VG. P1. $12.50

CRAWFORD, Caroline. *Folk Dances & Games.* 1931. Barnes. 4to. VG. B10. $9.00

CRAWFORD, Dan. *Thinking Blk.* 1912. London. 2nd ed. 485 p. G. $25.00

CRAWFORD, F.E. *Early Ancestors of the Crawfords in Am.* 1940. Cambridge, MA. Ils 1st ed. inscr. 81 p. T5. $25.00

CRAWFORD, F.M. *Khaled: Tale of Arabia.* 1891. London. 1st ed. VG. R3. $40.00

CRAWFORD, F.M. *Little City of Hope.* 1907. Macmillan. VG. P1. $10.00

CRAWFORD, F.M. *Primadonna.* nd. Review of Reviews. VG. P1. $15.00

CRAWFORD, F.M. *To Leeward.* 1911. Ward Lock. VG. P1. $12.50

CRAWFORD, F.M. *Wht Sister.* nd. Grosset Dunlap. Photoplay ed. VG. P1. $10.00

CRAWFORD, F.M. *Witch of Prague.* 1891. Macmillan. 1st Am ed. EX. R3. $50.00

CRAWFORD, G.W. *Ramsey Campbell.* 1988. Starmont. G. P1. $8.95

CRAWFORD, Hubert. *Crawford's Encyclopedia of Comic Books.* 1978. Jonathan David. 1st ed. dj. EX. R3. $20.00

CRAWFORD, Joan. *Portrait of Joan.* 1962. NY. 1st ed. presentation. dj. VG. B3. $75.00

CRAWFORD, Michael. *Tlaxcaltecans: Prehistory, Demography, Morphology...* 1976. KS U. 4to. 208 p. wrp. F2. $20.00

CRAWFORD & GRANT. *333.* 1953. Grant. 1st ed. wrp. EX. R3. $75.00

CRAWLEY & BESTERMAN. *Mystic Rose.* 1927. NY. Revised 2nd ed. 2 vols. VG. $37.50

CRAY, Ed. *Chrome Classics: Gen Motors & Its Times.* 1980. 616 p. dj. EX. S1. $10.00

CRAYON, Geoffrey. *Tales of a Traveler.* nd. Crowell. purple bdg. VG. B10. $3.75

CREASEY, John. *Alibi.* 1971. Scribner. dj. xl. P1. $5.00

CREASEY, John. *Baron & the Stone Legacy.* 1967. Scribner. dj. EX. P1. $15.00

CREASEY, John. *Baron in France.* 1976. Walker. 1st ed. dj. VG. P1. $17.50

CREASEY, John. *Baron on Board.* 1968. Walker. 1st ed. dj. EX. P1. $15.00

CREASEY, John. *Big Call.* 1975. Doubleday Book Club. VG. P1. $7.50

CREASEY, John. *Blight.* 1968. Walker. 1st ed. dj. EX. P1. $15.00

CREASEY, John. *Bundle for the Toff.* 1968. Walker. 1st ed. dj. EX. P1. $15.00

CREASEY, John. *Call for the Baron.* 1976. Walker. 1st ed. dj. VG. P1. $15.00

CREASEY, John. *Croaker.* 1973. Holt Rinehart Winston. 1st ed. dj. VG. P1. $7.50

CREASEY, John. *Death of a Racehorse.* 1962. Doubleday Book Club. VG. P1. $7.50

CREASEY, John. *Depths.* 1967. Walker. dj. VG. P1. $15.00

CREASEY, John. *Dissemblers.* 1967. Scribner. dj. VG. P1. $15.00

CREASEY, John. *Elope to Death.* 1977. Doubleday Book Club. VG. P1. $7.50

CREASEY, John. *Famine.* 1968. Walker. 1st ed. dj. EX. P1. $15.00

CREASEY, John. *Hang the Little Man.* 1964. Scribner. 1st ed. dj. VG. P1. $15.00

CREASEY, John. *Insulators.* 1973. Walker. dj. VG. P1. $15.00

CREASEY, John. *Kill the Toff.* 1966. Walker. 1st Am ed. dj. EX. F5/P1. $15.00

CREASEY, John. *Killer Strike.* 1961. Scribner. 1st ed. dj. VG. P1. $15.00

CREASEY, John. *Life for a Death.* 1973. Holt Rinehart Winston. 1st ed. dj. VG. P1. $15.00

CREASEY, John. *Missing Monoplane.* nd. Sampson Low. VG. P1. $20.00

CREASEY, John. *Murder With Mushrooms.* 1974. Doubleday Book Club. VG. P1. $7.50

CREASEY, John. *Plague of Silence.* 1968. Walker. dj. VG. P1. $15.00

CREASEY, John. *Runaway.* 1971. World. 1st ed. dj. xl. P1. $5.00

CREASEY, John. *Scene of the Crime.* 1963. Scribner. 1st ed. dj. xl. P1. $5.00

CREASEY, John. *Shadow of Death.* 1976. Doubleday Book Club. VG. P1. $7.50

CREASEY, John. *So Young To Burn.* 1968. Scribner. 1st ed. dj. VG. P1. $15.00

CREASEY, John. *Splinter of Glass.* 1973. Doubleday Book Club. VG. P1. $15.00

CREASEY, John. *Taste of Treasure.* 1966. Long. 1st ed. dj. xl. P1. $5.00

CREASEY, John. *This Man Did I Kill?* 1974. Stein Day. dj. VG. P1. $15.00

CREASEY, John. *Thunder in Europe.* 1936. Andrew Melrose. xl. G. P1. $10.00

CREASEY, John. *Thunder Maker.* 1976. Walker. 1st ed. dj. EX. P1. $15.00

CREASEY, John. *Toff & the Sleepy Cowboy.* 1974. Hodder Stoughton. 1st ed. dj. VG. P1. $15.00

CREASEY, John. *Toff & the Trip-Trip-Triplets.* 1972. Thriller Book Club. dj. EX. P1. $7.50

CREASEY, John. *Toff at the Fair.* 1968. Walker. 1st Am ed. dj. EX. F5. $15.00

CREASEY, John. *Wait for Death.* 1972. Holt Rinehart Winston. dj. xl. P1. $5.00

CREASY, E.S. *15 Decisive Battles of the World.* 1881. Am Books/Tribune. 297 p. VG. B10. $4.50

CREELEY, Robert. *Gold Diggers.* 1954. Divers Pr. 1st ed. wrp. EX. $75.00

CREELEY, Robert. *Le Fou.* 1952. Golden Goose Pr. 1st ed. 1/500. wrp. EX. C4. $500.00

CREELEY, Robert. *Pieces.* 1969. Scribner. 1st ed. dj. EX. B13. $45.00

CREELEY, Robert. *Poems 1950-1965.* 1966. Calder Boyars. 1/100. sgn. slipcase. EX. C4. $300.00

CREMER, Jan. *Jan Cremer Writes Again.* 1969. Grove Pr. 1st ed. dj. EX. K2. $35.00

CREMER, W.H. *Magician's Own Book.* c 1871. Camden Hotten. 325 p. decor brd. J3. $60.00

CREMER, W.H. *Magician's Own Book.* 1890. Chatto Windus. New ed. 325 p. J3. $20.00

CREMER, W.H. *Secret Out, 1,000 Tricks.* 1871. Edinbourgh. Grant. 307 p. EX. J3. $60.00

CRESWICKE, Louis. *S Africa & the Transvaal War.* 1900. Edinburgh. 7 vols. gilt bl bdg. EX. $250.00

CREVEL, Rene. *Mr Knife Miss Fork.* 1931. Blk Sun. Trans Boyle. Ils Max Ernst. boxed. H3. $3000.00

CREWS, Donald. *Harbor.* 1982. NY. Greenwillow. 1st ed. clipped dj. EX. B13. $45.00

CREWS, Donald. *Parade.* 1983. NY. Greenwillow. 1st ed. dj. EX. B13. $45.00

CREWS, Harry. *Blood & Grits.* 1979. Harper. 1st ed. dj. EX. C4. $35.00

CREWS, Harry. *Body.* 1990. Poseidon/Ultramarine Pr. Ltd ed. 1/40. sgn. as issued. EX. K2. $175.00

CREWS, Harry. *Car.* 1972. Morrow. 1st ed. dj. EX. B13. $200.00

CREWS, Harry. *Car.* 1973. Secker Warburg. 1st UK ed. dj. EX. C4. $100.00

CREWS, Harry. *Childhood: The Biography of a Place.* 1978. Harper. UP. wrp. EX. C4. $125.00

CREWS, Harry. *Feast of Snakes.* 1976. Atheneum. ARC of 1st ed. dj. w/newsletter. EX. C4. $175.00

CREWS, Harry. *Feast of Snakes.* 1976. Atheneum. 1st ed. dj. EX. B13/K2. $125.00

CREWS, Harry. *FL Frenzy.* 1982. Gainesville. ARC. wrp. EX. T9. $40.00

CREWS, Harry. *Gospel Singer.* 1968. Morrow. ARC of 1st ed. inscr. dj. RS. EX. C4. $800.00

CREWS, Harry. *Hawk Is Dying.* 1973. Knopf. UP. inscr. wrp. EX. C4. $275.00

CREWS, Harry. *Hawk Is Dying.* 1973. Knopf. 1st ed. dj. EX. K2. $85.00

CREWS, Harry. *Hawk Is Dying.* 1973. Knopf. 1st ed. inscr. dj. EX. C4. $150.00

CREWS, Harry. *Karate Is a Thing of the Spirit.* 1971. Morrow. 1st ed. dj. EX. B13. $175.00

CREWS, Harry. *This Thing Don't Lead to Heaven.* 1970. Morrow. 1st ed. inscr. dj. EX. C4. $300.00

CREWS, Harry. *2 by Crews.* 1984. Northridge. Lord John. 1st ed. 1/200. sgn. B13. $100.00

CRICHTON, Michael. *Eaters of the Dead.* 1976. Knopf. 1st ed. dj. EX. P1. $15.00

CRICHTON, Michael. *Great Train Robbery.* nd. BOMC. dj. VG. P1. $5.00

CRICHTON, Michael. *Jurassic Park.* 1990. Knopf. UP. wrp. EX. B13. $25.00

CRICHTON, Michael. *Sphere.* nd. Book Club. dj. VG. P1. $5.00

CRICHTON, Michael. *Terminal Man.* nd. BOMC. dj. EX. P1. $5.00

CRIDER, Bill. *Shotgun Saturday Night.* 1987. Walker. 1st ed. dj. EX. F5. $15.00

CRIDLAND, R.B. *Practical Landscape Gardening.* 1927. De La Mere. 34th ed. VG. $20.00

CRIMMINS, J.J. *Ted Annemann's Card Magic.* 1977. Dover. 188 p. NM. J3. $2.00

CRIPPS, W.J. *Old Eng Pl: Ecclesiastical, Decorative, & Domestic...* 1891. London. 4th ed. VG. $40.00

CRISP, N.J. *Brink.* 1982. Viking. ARC. wrp. EX. F5. $20.00

CRISP, N.J. *Brink.* 1982. Viking. dj. EX. P1. $15.00

CRISP, N.J. *Gotland Deal.* 1976. Viking. dj. EX. P1. $15.00

CRISP, N.J. *Gotland Deal.* 1976. Weidenfeld Nicolson. 2nd ed. P1. $10.00

CRISP, Stephen. *Christian Experiences, Gospel Labors, & Writings.* 1822. Phil. Kite. 8vo. 412 p. V1. $25.00

CRISPIN, Edmund. *Love Lies Bleeding.* 1948. Lippincott. 1st ed. VG. P1. $12.50

CRISPIN, Edmund. *Love Lies Bleeding.* 1981. Walker. dj. VG. P1. $20.00

CRISPIN, Edmund. *Moving Toy Shop.* 1946. Phil. 1st ed. dj. VG. B3. $30.00

CRITE, A.R. *Is It Nothing to You?* 1948. Boston. Episcopal Diocese of MA. 1st ed. wrp. EX. B13. $65.00

CROCE, Arlene. *Fred Astaire & Ginger Rogers.* 1972. Dutton. 1st ed. photos. dj. EX. $12.50

CROCKET, G.L. *2 Centuries in E TX.* 1972. SW Pr. facsimile ed. dj. VG. A5. $50.00

CROCKETT, W. *Hist of Lake Champlain 1609-1936.* 1936. Burlington, VT. 1st ed. 320 p. dj. VG. B3. $25.00

CROFTS, F.W. *Cask.* 1967. Norton. dj. xl. P1. $7.50

CROFTS, F.W. *Inspector French & the Cheyne Mystery.* nd. Collins. VG. P1. $25.00

CROFTS, F.W. *Inspector French's Greatest Case.* 1927. Collins. VG. P1. $25.00

CROFTS, F.W. *Ponson Case.* 1926. Collins. 10th print. P1. $25.00

CROFTS, F.W. *Sea Mystery.* 1928. Collins. 2nd ed. VG. P1. $25.00

CROKER, T.H. *Complete Dictionary of Arts & Sciences.* 1764. London. 1st ed. 3 vols. folio. VG. H3. $1500.00

CRONIN, Michael. *Night of the Party.* 1958. Ives Washburn. 1st ed. dj. VG. P1. $12.50

CROOK D.P. *N, the S, & the Powers 1861-1865.* 1974. NY. Wiley. 1st ed. 405 p. dj. EX. S1. $15.00

CROOKE, G. *21st Regiment of IA Volunteer Infantry.* 1891. Milwaukee. 1st ed. EX. scarce. K1. $200.00

CROSBY, Caresse. *Crosses of Gold.* 1925. Paris. Albert Messein. Nouvelle ed. H3. $250.00

CROSBY, Caresse. *Graven Image.* 1926. Houghton Mifflin. bl brds. H3. $200.00

CROSBY, Caresse. *Impossible Melodies.* 1928. Ed Narcisse. 1st ed. 1/44 on Van Gelder Zonen. wrp. H3. $850.00

CROSBY, Caresse. *Painted Shores.* 1927. Ed Narcisse. 1st ed. orig/glassine wrp. H3. $600.00

CROSBY, Caresse. *Passionate Years.* 1955. Alvin Redman. 1st Eng ed. dj. EX. H3. $125.00

CROSBY, Caresse. *Passionate Years.* 1963. Dial. 1st ed. inscr. dj. EX. H3. $175.00

CROSBY, Frank. *Life of Abraham Lincoln.* 1865. Potter. 1st ed. G. S1. $30.00

CROSBY, Harry. *Anthology.* nd. np. Blk Sun. 1st ed. rebound. EX. H3. $1500.00

CROSBY, Harry. *Chariot of the Sun.* 1928. Blk Sun. 1st ed. inscr. rebound. H3. $350.00

CROSBY, Harry. *Mad Queen.* 1929. Ed Narcisse. 1st ed. 1/100. orig/glassine wrp. boxed. H3. $1250.00

CROSBY, Harry. *Sleeping Together.* 1929. Blk Sun. 1/70 on Van Gelder Zonen. wrp/glassine wrp. H3. $1000.00

CROSBY, Harry. *Sonnets for Caresse.* 1927. Ed Narcisse. 4th ed. 1/44 on Japan Imperial. wrp. EX. H3. $500.00

CROSBY, Harry. *Torchbearer.* 1931. Blk Sun. 1st ed. 1/500. wrp/glassine. EX. H3. $400.00

CROSBY, Harry. *Transit of Venus.* 1929. Blk Sun. 2nd ed. 1/200. sgn. slipcase. H3. $350.00

CROSBY, Harry. *War Letters.* 1932. Blk Sun. private ed. 1/125 on Navarre. rebound. H3. $7.50

CROSBY, John. *Company of Friends.* 1977. Stein Day. 1st ed. dj. VG. P1. $12.50

CROSFIELD, H.G. *Margaret Fox of Swarthmoor Hall.* c 1913. London. Headley. 8vo. 272 p. G. V1. $12.00

CROSS, Amanda. *James Joyce Murder.* 1967. Macmillan. 2nd ed. dj. VG. P1. $10.00

CROSS, Amanda. *Question of Max.* 1976. Knopf. 1st ed. dj. xl. P1. $6.00

CROSS, J.K. *Angry Planet.* nd. Jr Literary Guild. dj. VG. P1. $10.00

CROSS, J.K. *Best Blk Magic Stories.* 1960. Faber. 1st ed. dj. EX. P1. $35.00

CROSS, J.K. *Best Horror Stories 2.* 1965. Faber. dj. EX. P1. $35.00

CROSS, J.K. *Red Journey Back.* 1954. Coward McCann. VG. P1. $15.00

CROSS, Mark. *Perilous Hazard.* 1961. Ward Lock. dj. VG. P1. $15.00

CROSS, R.A. *Prisoners of Paradise.* 1988. Watts. 1st ed. dj. EX. F5. $14.00

CROSS, Wilbur. *Ghost Ship of the Pole.* 1960. NY. 1st ed. 304 p. dj. VG. T5. $32.50

CROSSMAN, C.L. *China Trade.* 1973. Princeton. dj. VG. B3. $27.50

CROSSMAN, C.L. *China Trade: Export Paintings...Other Objects.* 1972. Pyne Pr. Ils. 4to. 275 p. dj. M. $85.00

CROTCH, William. *Elements of Musical Composition.* 1883. Longman Gr. 2nd ed. octavo. G. H3. $125.00

D'ALBAS, Andrieu. *Death of Navy: Japanese Naval Action in WWII.* 1957. NY. 1st Am ed. 362 p. dj. VG. T5. $25.00

D'AULAIRE & D'AULAIRE. *Benjamin Franklin.* 1950. Doubleday. Jr Literary Guild. dj. VG. B7. $33.00

D'HARCOURT, Raoul. *Primitive Art of Am.* 1950. Tudor. 1st Am ed. 199 p. F2. $25.00

D'ORMESSON, Jean. *Glory of the Empire.* 1974. Knopf. 1st ed. dj. EX. F5. $20.00

DABNEY, R.L. *Life & Campaigns of Lt-Gen Thomas J Jackson.* 1866. NY. Blelock. VG. $60.00

DABNEY & DABNEY. *William Henry Drayton & the Am Revolution.* nd. np. 1st ed. dj. VG. $15.00

DABOLL, Nathan. *Daboll's Schollmaster's Assistant.* 1823. New London. 240 p. full leather. fair. T5. $25.00

DACY, G.H. *4 Centuries of FL Ranching.* 1940. St Louis. 1st ed. EX. $45.00

DAGLIESH, Alice. *Davenports & Cherry Pie.* 1949. Scribner. Jr Literary Guild. Ils Gag. VG. B7. $42.00

DAHL, Roald. *Charlie & the Great Glass Elevator.* 1972. Knopf. 1st ed. dj. VG. P1. $30.00

DAHL, Roald. *Gremlins.* 1943. NY. 1st ed. G. B3. $75.00

DAHL, Roald. *My Uncle Oswald.* 1980. Knopf. 1st ed. dj. VG. P1. $15.00

DAHL, Roald. *Over to You: 10 Stories of Flyers & Flying.* 1946. Reynal Hitchcock. 1st ed. dj. VG. B13. $200.00

DAHL, Roald. *Switch Bitch.* 1974. Knopf. UP. G. C4. $25.00

DAHL, Roald. *Switch Bitch.* 1974. Knopf. 1st ed. 210 p. orange bdg. dj. M. B10. $7.50

DAHL, Roald. *2 Fables.* 1987. Farrar Straus Giroux. 1st ed. dj. EX. P1. $12.95

DAHLBERG, Edward. *Do These Bones Live.* 1941. Harcourt Brace. 1st ed. dj. EX. K2. $100.00

DAHLBERG, Edward. *Edward Dahlberg Reader.* 1967. New Directions. 1st ed. dj. EX. C4. $20.00

DAILEY, E.J. *Practical Muskrat Raising.* 1927. Columbus. Revised 3rd ed. 12mo. VG. $15.00

DAKIN, Harvey. *Frenesi.* 1945. Centaur. 1st ed. dj. VG. F5. $15.00

DALE, Jane. *Wheat for My Bread.* 1938. Artists/Writers Guild. 1st ed. sq 8vo. stiff wrp. B10. $3.75

DALEY, Brian. *Han Solo at Stars' End.* nd. Book Club. dj. VG. P1. $4.50

DALEY, Brian. *Han Solo's Revenge.* 1979. Del Rey. 1st ed. dj. VG. P1. $12.50

DALEY, Robert. *Fast 1.* 1978. Crown. 1st ed. dj. VG. P1. $20.00

DALEY, Robert. *Kill a Cop.* 1976. Crown. 1st ed. dj. VG. P1. $20.00

DALEY, Robert. *Target Bl.* 1973. Delacorte. 1st ed. dj. VG. P1. $25.00

DALGLIESH, Alice. *Long Live the King: Storybook of Eng Kings & Queens.* 1937. Scribner. Ils Lois Maloy. 1st ed. dj. VG. B7. $55.00

DALI, Salvador. *Da Da Dali.* 1966. Bremen. 1/100. sgn. German text. w/orig drawing on title p. H3. $4000.00

DALI, Salvador. *Dali.* 1968. Abrams. 1st ed. dj. EX. B3. $60.00

DALI, Salvador. *Dali's Tarot.* 1985. Salem House. sm 8vo. VG. $20.00

DALI, Salvador. *Hidden Faces.* 1944. Dial. 1st ed. 8vo. VG. $20.00

DALI, Salvador. *Jerusalem Bible.* 1970. Doubleday. 1st ed? boxed. VG. B3. $125.00

DALI, Salvador. *Secret Life of Dali.* 1942. Dial. 4th ed. sm 4to. VG. $45.00

DALI, Salvador. *50 Secrets of Magic Craftsmanship.* 1948. Dial. 1st ed. 192 p. dj. EX. $125.00

DALTON, Emmett. *When the Daltons Rhode.* 1937. Garden City. Ils 313 p. VG. B3. $27.50

DALTON, J.E. *Forged in Strong Fires.* 1948. Caxton. 1st ed. 1/1000. sgn. EX. $150.00

DALTON. *Under the Blk Flag.* 1917. Memphis. Ils. wrp. VG. C2. $65.00

DALY, C.J. *Mr Strang.* 1936. Stokes. 1st ed. VG. P1. $50.00

DALY, Elizabeth. *House Without the Door.* 1950. Hammond Hammond. 2nd ed. VG. P1. $17.50

DALY, Elizabeth. *Night Walk.* 1947. Rinehart. 1st ed. dj. VG. P1. $30.00

DALY, Elizabeth. *Wrong Way Down.* 1946. Rinehart. 1st ed. xl. P1. $10.00

DALY, J.J. *Song in His Heart.* 1951. Winston. 1st ed. quarto. dj. VG. H3. $75.00

DAMMANN, G.H. *70 Years of Chrysler.* 1974. 392 p. EX. S1. $17.50

DANA, C.A. *Recollections of the Civil War.* 1902. NY. 296 p. T5. $32.50

DANA, J.D. *Corals & Coral Islands.* 1872. Dodd Mead. 1st ed. fld chart/maps. G. $50.00

DANA, J.D. *Geol Story.* 1876. Ivison. 263 p. VG. B10. $7.00

DANA, Marion. *Mystery of the 3rd Parrot.* 1924. McClurg. 1st ed. VG. R3. $40.00

DANA, R.H. *Oration of July 4, 1814.* 1814. Cambridge. 1st ed. 22 p. self wrp. $85.00

DANA, R.H. *To Cuba & Back: A Vacation Voyage.* 1859. Boston. 1st ed. VG. $75.00

DANA, R.H. *2 Years Before the Mast.* 1841. London. 1st Eng ed. yel wrp. rare. H3. $2000.00

DANA, R.H. *2 Years Before the Mast.* 1947. Heritage. Ils Mueller. slipcase. EX. T1. $20.00

DANE, Clemence. *Arrogant Hist of Wht Ben.* 1939. Literary Guilt. dj. VG. P1. $20.00

DANE & ADDINSELL. *Come of Age.* 1938. Heinemann. 1st London ed. dj. H3. $30.00

DANE & SIMPSON. *Enter Sir John.* 1971. Tom Stacey. dj. VG. P1. $15.00

DANIEL, Glyn. *Ils Encyclopedia of Archaeology.* 1977. Crowell. 1st ed. 4to. 224 p. dj. F2. $15.00

DANIEL, J.W. *Life & Reminiscences of Jefferson Davis.* 1890. Baltimore. $70.00

DANIELS, Arthur. *Journal of Sibley's Indian Expedition During Summer of 1863.* 1980. Minneapolis. Thueson. Ltd 1st ed. 1/300. VG. $30.00

DANIELS, Jeff. *British Leyland: Truth About Cars.* 1980. 192 p. dj. EX. S1. $12.50

DANIELS, Jonathan. *Clash of Angels.* 1930. Brewer Warren. 1st ed. VG. R3. $20.00

DANIELS, Jonathan. *End of Innocence.* 1954. Lippincott. 1st ed. purple bdg. VG. B10. $5.00

DANIELS, Les. *Blk Castle.* 1978. Scribner. 1st ed. dj. EX. P1. $25.00

DANIELS, Les. *Citizen Vampire.* 1981. Scribner. 1st ed. dj. EX. R3. $25.00

DANK, G.R. *Forest of App.* 1983. Greenwillow. 1st ed. dj. EX. F5. $13.00

DANK, Milton. *Glider Gang: Eyewitness Hist of WWII Glider Combat.* 1977. Phil. 273 p. T5. $19.50

DANKER, D.F. *Man of the Plains: Recollections...1856-1882.* 1961. NE U. 350 p. dj. A5. $30.00

DANN, Jack. *Immortal.* 1978. Harper. 1st ed. dj. RS. EX. R3. $20.00

DANN, Jack. *Star Hiker.* 1977. Harper. 1st ed. dj. EX. R3. $15.00

DANN, Jack. *Wandering Stars.* nd. Book Club. dj. VG. P1. $4.50

DANN & DOZOIS. *Future Power.* 1976. Random House. dj. P1. $15.00

DANN & DOZOIS. *Future Power.* 1976. Random House. 1st ed. dj. R3. $10.00

DANOEN, Emile. *Tides of Time.* 1952. Ballantine. dj. VG. P1. $30.00

DANTE, Alighieri. *Amoroso Convivio di Dante.* 1531. Vinegia. Italian text. 18mo. scarce. V1. $275.00

DANTE, Alighieri. *Divine Comedy: Inferno.* 1970. Princeton. Trans Charles Singleton. 1st ed. 2 vols. djs. C4. $50.00

DANTE, Alighieri. *Dore Dante.* 1904. London. Cassell. Henry Irving ed. 1/1000. 3 vols in 6. H3. $1750.00

DANTE, Alighieri. *New Life.* c 1920. Camperfield Pr. Ils. VG. C1. $59.00

DANZIGER, James. *Beaton.* 1980. NY. 1st ed. VG. G1. $20.00

DARBY, Catherine. *Dream of Fair Serpents.* Popular Lib. 1st ed. EX. C1. $12.00

DARLEY, F.O. *Selected of War Lyrics With Ils.* 1864. NY. G. $18.50

DARLINGTON, C.J. *Memoirs of Charles J Darlington.* 1966. Phil. Dunlap. 2 vols. PB. VG. V1. $8.00

DARRACH, B. *Bobby Fischer Versus the Rest of the World.* 1974. NY. Review 1st ed. dj. VG. B3. $22.50

DARROW, Clarence. *Attorney for the Damned.* nd. Weinberg ed. 4th print. dj. VG. $8.50

DARROW, Clarence. *Farmington.* 1904. McClurg. 1st ed. dj. EX. B13. $125.00

DARROW, Clarence. *Farmington.* 1925. Boni Liveright. sgn. gilt bdg. H3. $250.00

DARROW, Clarence. *Story of My Life.* 1932. NY. 1st ed. dj. VG. B3. $35.00

DARROW, Clarence. *Story of My Life.* 1932. Scribner. 1/294. sgn. orig bdg. VG. H3. $850.00

DART, E.W. *Conjurors' Book of Stage Illusions.* 1974. Calgary. 1st ed. 86 p. NM. J3. $11.00

DARTON, R.J.H. *Dickens: Positively the 1st Appearance, Centenary Review.* 1933. London. Argonaut. H3. $75.00

DARTON, William. *Little Truths Better Than Great Fables.* 1800. Phil. 2 vols. wrp. EX. $300.00

DARVILL, F.T. *How To Become a Ventriliquist.* 1937. Darvill. 2nd print. 32 p. EX. J3. $6.00

DARWIN, Charles. *Descent of Man & Selection in Relation to Sex.* 1873-1874. Paris. 2nd ed. 2 vols. VG. T1. $85.00

DARWIN, Charles. *Insectivorous Plants.* 1876. Stuttgart. 1st German ed. 8vo. VG. T1. $75.00

DARWIN, Charles. *Naturalist's Voyage Round the World.* 1905. London. Murray. New ed. gr bdg. VG. C1. $24.50

DATER, H.M. *Development of Escort Carrier.* 1948. np. reprint. VG. T5. $25.00

DATER, Judy. *Imogen Cunningham: A Portrait.* 1979. Boston. 1st ed. VG. G1. $25.00

DAUDET. *Sappho.* 1930. Golden Bough Pr. Ils/sgn Majeska. 1st ed. 1/750. sgn. EX. $95.00

DAUGHERTY, James. *Daniel Boone.* 1940. Viking. 2nd print. VG. $15.00

DAUMAL, Rene. *Mt Analogue: A Novel...* 1960. Pantheon. Trans/Intro Roger Shattuck. 1st Am ed. dj. EX. C4. $30.00

DAVENPORT, Basil. *Deals With the Devil.* 1958. Dodd Mead. 1st ed. dj. EX. R3. $20.00

DAVENPORT, Basil. *SF Novel.* 1971. Advent. 2nd ed. dj. VG. P1. $15.00

DAVENPORT, Basil. *13 Ways To Dispose of a Body.* 1966. Dodd Mead. dj. VG. P1. $12.50

DAVENPORT, Basil. *13 Ways To Kill a Man.* 1966. Faber. 1st ed. dj. VG. P1. $17.50

DAVENPORT, Bishop. *New Gazetter... Geographical Dictionary of N Am & W Indies.* 1832. Baltimore. Ils. 471 p. T5. $35.00

DAVENPORT, Guy. *Belinda's World Tour.* 1991. NY. Dim Gray Bar Pr. Ils/sgn Norden. 1st ed. 1/100. sgn. EX. C4. $100.00

DAVENPORT, Guy. *Flowers & Leaves.* 1966. Highlands. Johnathan Williams. 1st ed. wrp. EX. C4. $90.00

DAVENPORT, Guy. *Goldfinch Thistle Star.* 1968. Red Ozier Pr. Special HrdCvr ed. 1/45. sgn. EX. C4. $100.00

DAVENPORT, H. *My Quest of Arabian Horse.* 1909. NY. 1st ed. 276 p. VG. B3. $45.00

DAVENTRY, Leonard. *Man of Double Deed.* 1965. Doubleday. 1st Am ed. dj. EX. R3. $15.00

DAVID, Elizabeth. *Omelette & a Glass of Wine.* 1985. Viking. 1st ed. dj. EX. B13. $25.00

DAVID, Gwen. *Pretenders.* 1969. World. 3rd ed. VG. $7.00

DAVID, Peter. *Knight's Life.* 1987. Ace. 1st ed. EX. C1. $4.50

DAVID, R.B. *Finn Burnett: Frontiersman.* 1937. Glendale. Clark. Ils. 378 p. A5. $125.00

DAVID & DAVID. *Doctor to the Islands.* (1st 1954) Boston. dj. EX. T1. $20.00

DAVIDS, Kenneth. *Softness on the Other Side of the Hole.* 1968. Grove Pr. dj. EX. B4. $15.00

DAVIDS, V.R. *Brn Magic: Book for Brn Owls.* 1925. Pearson. 2nd ed. 126 p. dj. EX. B10. $10.00

DAVIDSON, Angus. *Edward Lear.* 1950. Penguin. P1. $10.00

DAVIDSON, Avram. *And on the 8th Day.* 1964. Random House. 1st ed. dj. EX. F5. $25.00

DAVIDSON, Avram. *Best From Fantasy & SF 14th Series.* nd. Book Club. dj. VG. P1. $4.50

DAVIDSON, Avram. *Best of Avram Davidson.* 1979. Doubleday. 1st ed. dj. EX. R3. $27.50

DAVIDSON, Avram. *Enquiries of Dr Eszterhazy.* 1975. Warner. 1st ed. wrp. EX. F5. $10.00

DAVIDSON, Avram. *Joyleg.* 1971. Walker. 1st ed. dj. VG. R3. $20.00

DAVIDSON, Avram. *Peregrine Primus.* 1971. Walker. 1st ed. dj. VG. R3. $13.50

DAVIDSON, Avram. *Peregrine Primus.* 1971. Walker. 1st ed. dj. xl. P1. $10.00

DAVIDSON, Avram. *Phoenix & the Mirror.* 1969. Doubleday. 1st ed. dj. F5. $25.00

DAVIDSON, Avram. *Phoenix & the Mirror.* 1969. Doubleday. 1st ed. dj. R3. $10.00

DAVIDSON, Avram. *Strange Seas & Shores.* 1971. Doubleday. clipped dj. EX. F5. $15.00

DAVIDSON, Bill. *Cut Off.* 1972. NY. 1st ed. 202 p. dj. T5. $22.50

DAVIDSON, Bill. *Cut Off.* 1972. Stein Day. 1st ed. dj. P1. $15.00

DAVIDSON, Donald. *Outland Piper.* 1924. Houghton Mifflin. 1st ed. EX. B13. $275.00

DAVIDSON, Judith. *Jivaro.* 1985. San Diego Mus of Man. oblong 4to. 18 p. wrp. F2. $10.00

DAVIDSON, Lionel. *Long Way to Shiloh.* 1966. Gollancz. 2nd ed. dj. VG. P1. $15.00

DAVIDSON, Lionel. *Long Way to Shiloh.* 1966. Gollancz. 2nd ed. dj. xl. P1. $5.00

DAVIDSON, Lionel. *Menorah Men.* 1966. Harper Row. dj. VG. P1. $20.00

DAVIDSON, Lionel. *Under Plum Lake.* 1980. Knopf. 1st ed. dj. EX. P1. $20.00

DAVIDSON, N.J. *Knight Errant & His Doughty Deeds: Story of Amadis of Gaul.* 1911. London. Seeley. 1st ed? VG. C1. $21.50

DAVIDSON & HILL. *Subsistence USA.* 1973. NY. 1st ed. dj. EX. G1. $22.00

DAVIDSON. *TN: Old River.* 1946. NY. 1st ed. dj. VG. B3. $22.50

DAVIE, D. *Events & Wisdoms: Poems 1957-1963.* c 1964. London. Routledge/Kegan Paul. 1st ed. dj. EX. $16.00

DAVIE, Oliver. *Methods in the Art of Taxidermy.* 1894. Columbus. 1st ed. EX. $80.00

DAVIES, A.T. *Friends Ambulance Unit.* 1947. London. Allen Unwin. 1st ed. 494 p. dj. VG. V1. $12.00

DAVIES, J. *Legend of Hobey Barker.* 1966. Boston. 1st ed. dj. VG. B3. $22.50

DAVIES, L.P. *Artificial Man.* nd. Book Club. dj. VG. P1. $4.50

DAVIES, L.P. *Lampton Dreamers.* 1967. Crime Club. 1st ed. dj. xl. P1. $6.00

DAVIES, L.P. *Psychogeist.* nd. Book Club. dj. VG. P1. $4.50

DAVIES, L.P. *Shadow Before.* 1970. Crime Club. 1st ed. dj. xl. P1. $5.00

DAVIES, L.P. *Twilight Journey.* nd. Book Club. dj. VG. P1. $4.50

DAVIES, L.P. *Twilight Journey.* 1967. Herbert Jenkins. dj. xl. P1. $5.00

DAVIES, Nigel. *Aztec Empire: Toltec Resurgence.* 1987. Norman. 1st ed. 342 p. dj. F2. $30.00

DAVIES, Nigel. *Toletec Heritage From Fall of Tula to Rise of Tenochittlan.* 1980. Norman. 1st ed. 401 p. dj. F2. $25.00

DAVIES, Nigel. *Voyages to the New World.* 1979. Morrow. 1st ed. dj. F2. $20.00

DAVIES, Randall. *Eng Soc of the 18th Century in Contemporary Art.* 1907. London. Seeley. VG. $25.00

DAVIES, Rhys. *Daisy Mathews.* 1932. Golden Cockerel. 1/325. VG. $95.00

DAVIES, Rhys. *Time To Laugh.* 1937. London/Toronto. Heinemann. presentation. dj. H3. $100.00

DAVIES, Richard. *Account of Convincement, Exercises, Services, & Travels.* 1877. Phil. Friends Bookstore. 12mo. 192 p. EX. V1. $9.00

DAVIES, Richard. *Account...Travels With Spreading of Truth in N Wales.* 1877. Phil. Friends Bookstore. 12mo. 192 p. dj. EX. V1. $14.00

DAVIES, Robertson. *Diary of Samuel Marchbanks.* 1947. Toronto. Clarke Irwin. 1st ed. dj. EX. C4. $125.00

DAVIES, Robertson. *Enthusiasms of Robertson Davies.* 1979. Toronto. 1st ed. dj. VG. T9. $45.00

DAVIES, Robertson. *Table Talk of Samuel Marchbanks.* 1949. Toronto. Clarke Irwin. 1st ed. dj. EX. C4. $100.00

DAVIES, Robertson. *Tempest-Tost.* 1952. Rinehart. 1st Am ed. dj. EX. C4. $125.00

DAVIES, Thomas. *Dramatic Miscellanies.* 1794. Dublin. Price. 1st Irish ed. 12mo. 3 vols. contemporary calf. H3. $300.00

DAVIES, Thomas. *Memoirs of Life of David Garrick...* 1781. London. 3rd ed. 2 vols. contemporary calf. slipcase. H3. $175.00

DAVIES, Valentine. *Miracle on 34th St.* 1947. Harcourt Brace. 1st ed. VG. P1. $10.00

DAVIS, A.J. *Harmonial Man.* 1868. Boston. VG. $10.00

DAVIS, A.Y. *If They Come in the Morning.* 1971. NY. 3rd Pr. ARC. sgn James Baldwin. dj. RS. w/photo. EX. K2. $200.00

DAVIS, Angela. *Angela.* 1971. Leisure Books. 1st PB ed. VG. B4. $20.00

DAVIS, Arlette. *Flowers.* 1946. Paris. Hyperion. dj. EX. $75.00

DAVIS, Bette. *Lonely Life.* 1962. NY. 1st ed. dj. VG. B3. $25.00

DAVIS, Bette. *Lonely Life.* 1962. Putnam. 1st ed. presentation. dj. VG. H3. $125.00

DAVIS, Burke. *Jeb Stuart: Last Cavalier.* 1957. NY. 1st ed. dj. VG. B3. $30.00

DAVIS, Burke. *Jeb Stuart: Last Cavalier.* 1958. Bonanza. Ils. 462 p. dj. VG. S1. $20.00

DAVIS, Burke. *To Appomattox: 9 April Days 1865.* 1959. Rinehart. 433 p. dj. VG. S1. $6.00

DAVIS, C.H. *Narrative of N Polar Expedition.* 1876. WA. Ils. 696 p. A6. $150.00

DAVIS, C.H. *Report Interoceanic Canals & Railroads...Atlantic & Pacific.* 1867. WA. 14 fld maps. T5. $135.00

DAVIS, Charles. *Paper Fabrication, Clr, Finishing Machines, Tools...* 1886. Phil. 1st ed. 671 p. VG. $90.00

DAVIS, Deering. *Am Cow Pony.* 1962. Princeton. 1st ed. dj. EX. $22.00

DAVIS, E.A. *On the Night Wind's Telling.* 1946. OK U. 1st ed. 276 p. dj. F2. $20.00

DAVIS, F.C. *Lilies in Her Garden Grew.* 1951. Crime Club. 1st ed. VG. P1. $20.00

DAVIS, F.C. *Mole Men Want Your Eyes.* 1976. Shroud Krueger. 1st ed. wrp. EX. R3. $6.00

DAVIS, F.M. *Counterattack.* 1964. Whitman. VG. P1. $7.50

DAVIS, George. *Story of Barberton, OH.* 1963. Barberton. Revised ed. 77 p. T5. $22.50

DAVIS, H.R. *Soldier of Fortune.* 1897. Scribner. 1st ed. VG. $15.00

DAVIS, Hassoldt. *Jungle & the Damned.* 1952. Duell Sloan. 1st ed. 306 p. dj. F2. $25.00

DAVIS, J.F. *China: General Description of Empire & Inhabitants.* 1857. London. 1st ed. 2 vols. EX. $200.00

DAVIS, J.G. *Taller Than Trees.* 1975. Doubleday. 1st ed. dj. EX. P1. $15.00

DAVIS, Jefferson. *Report of the Secretary of War...Purchase of Camels...* 1857. WA. scarce. A5. $275.00

DAVIS, Joe. *Tiptop Entertainment & Minstrel.* 1936. Tiptop Pub. 66 p. NM. J3. $10.00

DAVIS, John. *Guggenheims: Am Epic.* 1978. Morrow. Stated 1st ed. 608 p. dj. EX. B10. $5.75

DAVIS, Keith. *Desire Charnay: Expeditionary Photographer.* 1981. NM U. 1st ed. 4to. 212 p. F2. $30.00

DAVIS, L.J. *Whence All But He Had Fled.* 1968. Viking. 1st ed. dj. EX. K2. $35.00

DAVIS, L.R. *Threat of Dragons.* 1948. Crime Club. VG. P1. $7.50

DAVIS, M.L. *Sourdough Gold.* 1933. Boston. 1st ed. 351 p. EX. $50.00

DAVIS, M.L. *We Are Alaskans.* 1931. Boston. 1st ed. VG. $35.00

DAVIS, N.A. *Campaign From TX to MD With Battle of Fredericksburg.* 1961. Austin, TX. facsimile. boxed. M. $40.00

DAVIS, O.K. *At the Emperor's Wish: Tale of New Japan.* 1905. Appleton. 1st ed. 149 p. TEG. VG. B10. $5.00

DAVIS, Peter. *Hometown.* 1982. Simon Schuster. UP. wrp. VG. B13. $35.00

DAVIS, R.H. *Lost Road.* 1913. Scribner. 1st ed. 266 p. B10. $7.50

DAVIS, R.H. *Once Upon a Time.* 1910. Scribner. 1st ed. $18.00

DAVIS, R.H. *3 Gringoes in Venezuela & Central Am.* 1896. Harper. 1st ed. F2. $35.00

DAVIS, Reuben. *Recollections of MS.* 1890. Boston. 446 p. $65.00

DAVIS, Robertson. *World of Wonders.* 1976. Viking. 1st ed. 358 p. dj. EX. J3. $17.00

DAVIS, Robertson. *5th Business.* 1970. Viking. 1st ed. 309 p. dj. NM. J3. $20.00

DAVIS, S.M. *Life & Times of Sir Philip Sidney.* 1864. Ticknor Fields. 3 vols. Chambolle-Duru bdg. H3. $1250.00

DAVIS, Terry. *Vision Quest.* nd. (1979) Viking. UP. wrp. EX. B13. $65.00

DAVIS, W.C. *Battle at Bull Run: Hist of 1st Major Campaign.* 1977. Doubleday. 1st ed. 298 p. dj. G. S1. $8.50

DAVIS, W.C. *Battle of New Market.* 1975. NY. 1st ed. EX. $10.00

DAVIS, W.C. *Brother Against Brother: The War Begins.* 1983. Time Life. Ils. 176 p. decor bdg. G. S1. $9.50

DAVIS, W.C. *Embattled Confederacy.* 1982. Doubleday. 464 p. G. S1. $17.50

DAVIS, W.C. *End of an Era.* 1982. Doubleday. 496 p. dj. EX. S1. $20.00

DAVIS, W.C. *Fighting for Time.* 1983. Doubleday. 464 p. dj. S1. $20.00

DAVIS, W.C. *Guns of 1862.* 1982. Doubleday. 460 p. dj. EX. S1. $20.00

DAVIS, W.C. *Shadows of the Storm.* 1981. Doubleday. 464 p. dj. S1. $20.00

DAVIS, W.C. *1st Blood: Ft Sumter to Bull Run.* 1983. Time Life. 176 p. EX. S1. $9.50

DAVIS, W.H. *75 Years in CA.* 1929. Howell. Argonaut ed. 1/100. VG. H3. $350.00

DAVIS & PACK. *Mexican Jewelry.* 1963. TX U. Ils. 262 p. dj. F2. $25.00

DAVISON, R.A. *Isaac Hicks: NY Merchant & Quaker, 1767-1820.* 1964. Cambridge. 1st ed. 8vo. 217 p. dj. xl. VG. V1. $10.00

DAWE, W.C. *Yel & Wht.* 1895. Boston. 1st ed. VG. $17.00

DAWES, A.L. *How Are We Governed?* nd. (1885) Boston. apparent 1st ed. 423 p. VG. B10. $6.25

DAWES, E.A. *Great Illusionists.* 1979. Chartwell Books. 1st ed. 216 p. VG. J3. $20.00

DAWES, N.T. *Packard 1942-1962.* 1975. 219 p. dj. EX. S1. $30.00

DAWES & SETTERINGTON. *Encyclopedia of Magic.* 1986. Gallery Books. 1st ed. 190 p. dj. NM. J3. $14.00

DAWKINS, Cecil. *Quiet Enemy.* 1963. NY. 1st Am ed. presentation. dj. EX. T9. $55.00

DAWSON, Fielding. *Blk Mt Book.* 1970. Croton Pr. 1st ed. dj. EX. B13. $45.00

DAWSON, Fielding. *Man Steps Into Space.* 1965. Shortstop. 1/500. intl. pamphlet. EX. K2. $25.00

DAWSON, James. *Hell Gate.* 1971. McKay. dj. VG. P1. $10.00

DAWSON, Steve. *How To Be Funny Without Being Stupid.* 1982. Magic Touch. 29 p. SftCvr. EX. J3. $3.00

DAY, David. *Tolkien Bestiary.* 1979. Ballantine. 1st ed. dj. VG. P1. $25.00

DAY, Gene. *Future Day.* 1979. Flying Buttress. 1st ed. VG. P1. $15.00

DAY, Gina. *Tell No Tales.* 1967. Hart Davis. 1st ed. dj. EX. P1. $15.00

DAY, J. *Principles of Plane Geometry, Mensuration...Surveying.* 1831. New Haven. fld plts. rebacked. VG. G4. $28.00

DAY, Judson LeRoy. *Baptists of MI & the Civil War.* 1965. Lansing, MI. 21 p. pamphlet. G. S1. $5.00

DAY, Mildred. *Story of Meridoc King of Cambria.* nd. Garland. 1st ed. M. C1. $19.50

DAY, T.R. *Manual de Algodao.* nd. Brazil. 2nd ed. inscr/dtd 1922. 146 p. F2. $25.00

DAY & DINES. *Ils of Medieval Costume in Eng Collected From Manuscripts...* 1851. London. Bosworth. 1st ed. quarto. VG. H3. $250.00

DAY. *Big Country TX.* 1947. NY. 1st ed. dj. VG. B3. $25.00

DAY-LEWIS, C. *C Day-Lewis: Poet Laureate.* 1968. Chicago/London. St James. Ltd ed. 1/100. sgn. dj. H3. $85.00

DAYTON, F.E. *Steamboat Days.* 1925. NY. Ils Adams. 1st ed. EX. $45.00

DAYTON, R.J. *Conjuror's Collage.* 1980. Calgary. 1st ed. 78 p. NM. J3. $9.00

DAYTON & KAUFMAN. *1st Lady.* 1935. Random House. 1st ed. dj. VG. H3. $75.00

DE ALARCON, D.P. *3-Cornered Hat.* 1959. Ltd Ed Club. Ils/sgn Roger Duvisin. 4to. slipcase. VG. $45.00

DE ANGELI, Marguerite. *Door in the Wall.* nd. (1949) Doubleday. Ils. dj. VG. B10. $9.00

DE ANGELI, Marguerite. *Petite Suzanne.* c 1937. Doubleday. dj. xl. B10. $5.00

DE ANGULO, Jaime. *Acumawi Language.* 1930. Columbia U. wrp. EX. K2. $85.00

DE ANGULO, Jaime. *Creation Myth of the Pomo Indians.* 1932. Anthropos. 1st ed. wrp. scarce. EX. K2. $175.00

DE ANGULO, Jaime. *Indian Tales.* 1953. NY. Wyn. 1st ed. dj. EX. scarce. K2. $150.00

DE ANGULO, Jaime. *Karok Texts.* 1931. Columbia. 1st ed. wrp. EX. K2. $85.00

DE BALZAC, Honore. *Comedie Humaine.* c 1896. Little Brn. Trans Wormeley. 1/500. VG. H3. $1000.00

DE BALZAC, Honore. *Comedie Humaine.* 1898-1899. Boston. Hardy Pratt. Ed Grand Format. 40 vols. H3. $2500.00

DE BALZAC, Honore. *Comedie Humaine.* 1896. Boston. Roberts. Trans Wormeley. 1/250. 41 vols. H3. $2500.00

DE BALZAC, Honore. *Droll Stories.* 1939. Heritage. Ils Artzybasheff. slipcase. EX. T1. $20.00

DE BALZAC, Honore. *Eugene Grandet.* 1960. Ltd Ed Club. Ils/sgn Rene Ben Sussan. 4to. slipcase. VG. $40.00

DE BALZAC, Honore. *Girl With the Golden Eyes.* 1931. Ils Ed Co. VG. $21.00

DE BALZAC, Honore. *Old Man Goriot.* 1948. Ltd Ed Club. Ils/sgn Rene Ben Sussan. 4to. slipcase. VG. $45.00

DE BALZAC, Honore. *Old Man Goriot.* 1949. Winston. 1st ed. 232 p. glassine dj. VG. B10. $4.50

DE BEAUVOIR, Simone. *Belles Images.* 1968. Collins. 2nd ed. dj. EX. P1. $15.00

DE BEAUVOIR, Simone. *Force of Circumstance.* 1965. Putnam. 1st ed. dj. EX. B13. $45.00

DE BLASIO, Edward. *All About the Beatles.* 1964. MacFadden. PB. VG. B4. $3.50

DE CAMP, L.S. *Bones of Zora.* 1983. Phantasia. Ltd ed. 1/300. sgn. M. R3. $30.00

DE CAMP, L.S. *Castle of Iron.* 1950. Gnome. 1st ed. dj. VG. R3. $37.50

DE CAMP, L.S. *Continent Makers.* 1953. Twayne. 1st ed. sgn. dj. EX. R3. $45.00

DE CAMP, L.S. *Divide & Rule.* 1948. Fantasy. Ltd ed. 1/500. sgn. dj. EX. R3. $125.00

DE CAMP, L.S. *Divide & Rule.* 1948. Fantasy. 1st ed. dj. EX. R3. $65.00

DE CAMP, L.S. *Dragon of the Ishtar Gate.* 1982. Donning. Ltd ed. sgn. boxed. M. R3. $75.00

DE CAMP, L.S. *Golden Wind.* 1969. Doubleday. 1st ed. dj. EX. R3. $40.00

DE CAMP, L.S. *Golden Wind.* 1969. Doubleday. 1st ed. dj. xl. P1. $20.00

DE CAMP, L.S. *Great Fetish.* 1978. Doubleday. 1st ed. dj. xl. P1. $5.00

DE CAMP, L.S. *Gun for Donosaur.* 1963. Doubleday. 1st ed. dj. VG. R3. $125.00

DE CAMP, L.S. *Heroic Age of Am Invention.* 1961. Doubleday. 1st ed. sgn. dj. VG. R3. $25.00

DE CAMP, L.S. *Hostage of Zir.* nd. Book Club. dj. VG. P1. $4.50

DE CAMP, L.S. *Hostage of Zir.* 1977. Berkley. 1st ed. inscr. dj. EX. R3. $20.00

DE CAMP, L.S. *Lest Darkness Fall.* 1949. Prime Pr. 1st ed. sgn. VG. R3. $25.00

DE CAMP, L.S. *Literary Swordsmen & Sorcerers.* 1976. Arkham House. 1st ed. M. R3. $10.00

DE CAMP, L.S. *Lost Continents.* 1954. Gnome. 1st ed. dj. EX. R3. $25.00

DE CAMP, L.S. *Lovecraft: A Biography.* 1976. Ballantine. VG. P1. $5.00

DE CAMP, L.S. *Miscast Barbarian.* 1975. Gerry De La Ree. 1st ed. wrp. M. R3. $15.00

DE CAMP, L.S. *Phantoms & Fancies.* 1972. Mirage. 1st ed. M. R3. $10.00

DE CAMP, L.S. *Prisoner of Zhamanak.* 1982. Phantasia. Ltd ed. 1/500. sgn. M. R3. $30.00

DE CAMP, L.S. *Prisoner of Zhamanak.* 1982. Phantasia. 1st ed. M. R3. $12.00

DE CAMP, L.S. *Rogue Queen.* 1951. Doubleday. 1st ed. dj. VG. R3. $35.00

DE CAMP, L.S. *Tritonian Ring.* 1977. Owlswick. 1st ed. sgn. dj. EX. P1. $30.00

DE CAMP, L.S. *Unbeheaded King.* 1983. Del Rey. 1st ed. dj. EX. P1. $15.00

DE CAMP, L.S. *Unbeheaded King.* 1983. Del Rey. 1st ed. sgn. dj. EX. P1. $25.00

DE CAMP, L.S. *Warlocks & Warriors.* 1970. Putnam. 1st ed. dj. EX. R3. $17.50

DE CAMP, L.S. *Wheels of If.* 1948. Shasta. 1st ed. dj. EX. R3. $85.00

DE CAMP & DE CAMP. *Ancient Ruins & Archaeology.* 1964. Doubleday Doran. Ils. 294 p. dj. F2. $10.00

DE CAMP & DE CAMP. *Bones of Zora.* 1983. Phantasia. 1st ed. 1/300. sgn. dj. slipcase. EX. P1. $35.00

DE CAMP & DE CAMP. *Dark Valley Destiny.* 1983. Bluejay. 1st ed. dj. EX. P1. $30.00

DE CAMP & DE CAMP. *Footprints on Sand.* 1981. Advent. 1st ed. dj. EX. P1. $20.00

DE CAMP & DE CAMP. *Spirits, Stars, & Spells.* 1966. Canaveral. 1st ed. M. R3. $17.50

DE CAMP & LEY. *Lands Beyond.* 1962. Rinehart. 1st ed. sgns. dj. EX. R3. $75.00

DE CAMP & PRATT. *Carnelian Cube.* 1948. Gnome. 1st ed. inscr. dj. EX. R3. $90.00

DE CAMP & PRATT. *Tales From Gavagan's Bar.* 1953. Twayne. 1st ed. dj. EX. R3. $60.00

DE CAMP & SCITHERS. *Conan Grimoire.* 1972. Mirage. 1st ed. dj. EX. R3. $60.00

DE CAPP, L.S. *Heroes & Hobgoblins.* 1981. Ils/sgn Kirk. 1st ed. 1/1250. dj. EX. C1. $26.00

DE CERVANTES SAAVEDRA, Miguel. *Don Quixote.* 1620. London. 2 vols in 1. orig bdg. G. $600.00

DE CERVANTES SAAVEDRA, Miguel. *Vida y Hechos del Ingenioso Hidalgo Don Quixote la Mancha.* 1738. London. Tonson. 1st Spanish ed. 4 vols. quarto. H3. $3000.00

DE CHANT. *Devil Birds.* 1947. NY. 1st ed. 265 p. VG. B3. $20.00

DE CIVRIEUX, Marc. *Watunna: An Orinoco Creation Cycle.* 1980. San Francisco. 1st ed. 195 p. dj. F2. $15.00

DE COSTA, J.F. *Vorkolumbische Keramik aus den Zentralanden.* nd. Mus Volkerkunde. Ils. 72 p. wrp. F2. $20.00

DE COURCY, Ken. *Australian Gambling Game of 31.* nd. Devon, Eng. Supreme Magic. NM. J3. $5.00

DE COURCY, Ken. *Automentalism, Ken De Courcy's.* 1953. London. Armstrong. 1st ed. VG. w/cards. J3. $3.00

DE COURCY, Ken. *Leo Leslie's Triple-Clr Cups & Balls.* nd. Devon, Eng. Supreme Magic. SftCvr. EX. J3. $3.00

DE DIESBACH, Ghislain. *Toys of Princes.* 1962. Chapman Hall. 1st ed. dj. VG. P1. $7.00

DE DILLMONT, Therese. *Encyclopedia of Needlework.* c 1925. Mulhouse. 24mo. EX. A4. $50.00

DE DURFORT, Clare. *Ourika.* 1977. Taylor. Trans/sgn Fowles. Ltd ed. 1/500. H3. $125.00

DE FELITTA, Frank. *Entity.* nd. Book Club. dj. VG. P1. $4.50

DE FOREST, J.D. *Indians of CT.* 1951. Hartford. Hamersly. 509 p. A5. $100.00

DE FOREST, J.W. *Union Officer in the Reconstruction.* 1948. Yale U. 211 p. G. $8.00

DE FOREST, Lee. *Father of Radio.* 1950. Chicago. 1st ed. sgn. G. B3. $87.50

DE GARMO, W.B. *Dance of Soc.* 1892. NY. 5th ed. 234 p. VG. $35.00

DE GRUYTER. *Kanawha Spectator Vol 1.* 1953. Charleston. 553 p. VG. A5. $35.00

DE HAAS, Arline. *Jazz Singer.* 1927. Grosset Dunlap. Photoplay ed. octavo. 248 p. dj. EX. H3. $200.00

DE HARTOG, Jan. *Lamb's War.* 1980. Harper Row. 2nd ed. 8vo. 443 p. dj. V1. $7.00

DE HAVEN, Tom. *Freak's Amour.* 1979. Morrow. ARC. pictorial wrp. EX. C4. $65.00

DE HEMPSEY, Sydney. *How To Do Punch & Judy.* 1977. Chicago Magic. 106 p. NM. J3. $4.00

DE JOMINI, General Baron. *Political & Military Hist of Campaign of Waterloo.* 1862. NY. fld map. 227 p. fair. T5. $45.00

DE JONG, Dola. *Whirligig of Time.* 1964. Crime Club. 1st ed. dj. xl. P1. $5.00

DE KAY, J.E. *Nat Hist of NY: Zoology, Mollosca, & Crustacea.* 1843. Wiley Putnam. Ils. VG. T3. $250.00

DE KAY, J.E. *Nat Hist of NY: Zoology-Ornithology.* 1843. Wiley Putnam. clr pls. VG. T3. $750.00

DE KAY, J.E. *Zoology of NY: Mammulia.* 1984. Wht Visscher. clr pls. rebound. VG. T3. $175.00

DE LA FAILLE, J.B. *Worms of Vincent Van Gogh.* 1970. Reynall. 1st ed. 56 clr pls. folio. dj. VG. B3. $150.00

DE LA FONTAINE, Jean. *Fables.* 1930. Ltd Ed Club. 1/1500. 2 vols. slipcase. EX. C4. $90.00

DE LA MARE, Colin. *They Walk Again.* 1942. Dutton. VG. R3. $12.50

DE LA MARE, Walter. *Come Hither.* 1923. London. 1/305. sgn. 2 vols. A4. $50.00

DE LA MARE, Walter. *News.* 1930. Faber. 1/500. sgn. xl. H3. $60.00

DE LA MARE, Walter. *On the Edge.* 1930. Faber. Ltd ed. 1/300. sgn. TEG. slipcase. H3. $85.00

DE LA MARE, Walter. *To Lucy.* 1931. Faber. Ltd ed. 1/275. sgn. H3. $60.00

DE LA MARE, Walter. *Winged Chariot.* 1951. Viking. 1st ed. presentation. clipped dj. EX. F5. $60.00

DE LA MARE, Walter. *8 Tales.* 1971. Arkham House. 1st ed. M. R3. $30.00

DE LA REE, Gerry. *Art of the Fantastic.* 1978. De La Ree. 1st ed. dj. EX. R3. $65.00

DE LA REE, Gerry. *More Fantasy by Fabian.* 1979. De La Ree. 1st ed. 1/1300. dj. EX. P1. $20.00

DE LA REE, Gerry. *Space Flight...When?* 1946. De La Ree. 1st ed. wrp. EX. R3. $50.00

DE LA REE, Gerry. *6th Book of Virgil Finlay.* 1980. De La Ree. 1/1300. dj. EX. P1. $20.00

DE LA REE & NIGRA. *Nahhes Bok Sketchbook.* 1976. De La Ree. 1st ed. wrp. EX. R3. $20.00

DE LA ROCHE, Mazo. *Return to Jalna.* 1946. Little Brn. not 1st ed. 462 p. VG. B10. $3.25

DE LA TORRE, Jose. *Ascanio's World of Knives Vol 1.* 1975. Belleville, NJ. 1st ed. 95 p. NM. J3. $7.00

DE LABORDE, J.B. *Choix de Chansons Mises en Musique.* 1881. Rouen. Lemonnyer. facsimile of 1773 ed. 4 vols in 2. H3. $600.00

DE LAWRENCE & THOMPSON. *Modern Card Effects & How To Perform Them.* 1920. Felsman. 1st ed. VG. J3. $5.00

DE LILLO, Don. *Day Room.* 1987. Knopf. UP. wrp. EX. B13. $85.00

DE LILLO, Don. *Great Jones St.* 1973. NY. 1st ed. sgn. dj. EX. T9. $75.00

DE LILLO, Don. *Mao II.* 1991. Viking. ARC. wrp. EX. K2. $45.00

DE LILLO, Don. *Names.* 1982. Knopf. 1st ed. sgn. dj. EX. B13. $100.00

DE LINT, Charles. *Jack the Giant Killer.* 1987. Ace. 1st ed. dj. VG. P1. $16.95

DE LUDES, Ignatius. *Tourist's Guide to Transylvania.* 1981. Octopus. dj. EX. P1. $15.00

DE MADARIAGA, Salvador. *Hernan Cortes: Conqueror of Mexico.* 1941. Macmillan. 1st ed. 554 p. EX. F2. $20.00

DE MARCO, Gordon. *Frisco Blues.* 1985. London. Pluto. 1st ed. dj. EX. T9. $35.00

DE MARINIS, Rick. *Scimitar.* 1977. NY. 1st ed. sgn. dj. EX. T9. $35.00

DE MARINIS, Rick. *Voice of Am: Stories.* 1991. Norton. UP. wrp. EX. K2. $25.00

DE MARTINI, Joseph. *Expedition Diamonds.* 1983. Carlton Pr. 1st ed. 160 p. dj. F2. $15.00

DE MENDELSSOHN, Peter. *Age of Churchill.* 1961. NY. Ils 1st Am ed. 650 p. dj. VG. T5. $9.50

DE MILLE, J.A. *Strange Manuscript Found in a Copper Cylinder.* 1888. Harper. 1st ed. G. R3. $30.00

DE MILLE, Richard. *2 Qualms & a Quirk.* 1973. Capra. Chapbook Series. 1/100. sgn. EX. K2. $20.00

DE MILLERET, Jean. *Entretiens Avec Jorge Luis Borges.* 1967. Paris. Belfond. 1st ed. wrp. EX. K2. $45.00

DE MILT, A.R. *Ways & Days Out of London.* 1910. NY. Baker Taylor. 1st ed. lg 8vo. EX. $20.00

DE MOLIERE, J.B.P. *Misanthrope.* 1966. Harcourt Brace. Trans/sgn Wilbur. 1st ed. 1/1500. EX. H3. $125.00

DE MONVEL, Boutet. *Our Children & Girls & Boys.* 1931. Jr Literary Guild. 4to. G. $45.00

DE MORGAN, William. *When Ghost Meets Ghost.* 1914. Holt. 1st ed. VG. R3. $20.00

DE MUSSET, Alfred. *Complete Writings.* 1905. NY. Hill. Lg Paper ed. 1/150. Levant bdg. H3. $750.00

DE NADAILLAC, Marquis. *Prehistoric America.* 1895. Putnam. Ils. 566 p. gilt bdg. F2. $50.00

DE ONIS, Harriet. *Golden Land: Anthology of Latin Am Folklore in Literature.* 1948. Knopf. 1st ed. 395 p. F2. $15.00

DE OVIEDO Y VALDES. *Conquest of Peru.* 1975. Ltd Ed Club. Ils/sgn Jack & Irene Delano. slipcase. VG. $75.00

DE PEREYRA, Diomedes. *Land of the Golden Scarabs.* 1928. Bobbs Merrill. 1st ed. dj. EX. R3. $40.00

DE QUEIROZ, Eca. *Sweet Miracle.* 1914. Mosher. 2nd ed. 33 p. wrp/dj. EX. B10. $4.50

DE QUINCEY, Thomas. *Works.* 1862-1871. London. A&C Blk. 18 vols. sm octavo. H3. $1000.00

DE REICHBERG, Jean. *Legends Vosgiennes.* 1901. Loos Mai. 8vo. 131 p. wrp. B10. $7.25

DE REY, Lester. *And Some Were Human.* 1949. Prime Pr. 1st ed. sgn. dj. EX. R3. $45.00

DE REYNA, Jorge. *Return of the Starships.* 1968. Avalon. dj. xl. P1. $5.00

DE RIO & NOHL. *Beethoven: Reminiscences...From Diary of Lady...* c 1876. London. Reeves. 1st Eng ed. octavo. 250 p. VG. H3. $20.00

DE ROGATIS, Al. *NY Giants.* 1964. Duell. 1st ed. 152 p. B10. $5.00

DE ROUGEMONT, Denis. *Love in the W World.* 1956.Revised Augmented ed. dj. VG. C1. $17.50

DE SAINT PIERRE, Bernardin. *Paul & VA.* 1839. London. Ils. Root bdg. AEG. slipcase. EX. A4. $200.00

DE SAINT-EXUPERY, Antoine. *Little Prince (Le Petit Prince).* 1956. Paris. Ils. 93 p. Bonet bdg. dj. VG. T5. $45.00

DE SAINT-EXUPERY, Antoine. *Night Flight.* 1932. Blk Sun. Trans Gilbert. H3. $100.00

DE SEINGALT, Jacques; see Casanova De Seingalt, Jacques.

DE SEVERSKY, Alexander. *Victory Through Air Power.* 1942. NY. 1st ed. inscr. dj. VG. $45.00

DE SORMO, Maitland. *Noah John Rondeau: Adirondack Hermit.* 1975. Saranac Lake. 4th ed. 204 p. dj. EX. P1. $5.00

DE SOUZA, Marc. *Let's Fake a Deal.* 1979. Harrisburg. 1st ed. EX. J3. $4.00

DE TERRA, Helmut. *Man & Mammoth in Mexico.* 1957. London. Hutchinson. 1st ed. 191 p. dj. F2. $20.00

DE VEAUX, Alexis. *Don't Explain: A Song of Billie Holiday.* 1980. Harper. 1st ed. clipped dj. EX. B13. $45.00

DE VEAUX, Alexis. *Enchanted Hair Tale.* 1987. Harper. Ils Cheryl Hanna. 1st ed. clipped dj. EX. B13. $40.00

DE VOTO, Bernard. *Across the Wide MO.* 1947. Boston. 1st ed. dj. VG. B3. $55.00

DE VOTO, Bernard. *Beyond the Wide MO.* 1947. Boston. Ltd ed. 1/265. sgn. VG. B3. $80.00

DE VOTO, Bernard. *Hour.* 1951. Houghton Mifflin. Ils William Varss. VG. $17.00

DE VRIES, A.B. *Jan Vermeer Van Delft.* c1950. London. probably 1st ed. 4to. VG. G1. $40.00

DE VRIES, Peter. *No But I Saw the Movie.* 1952. Little Brn. 1st ed. dj. EX. B13. $175.00

DE VRIES, Peter. *Tunnel of Love.* nd. Little Brn. 9th ed. dj. VG. P1. $7.00

DE WEESE, Gene. *Beepers From Outer Space.* 1985. Weekly Reader Book. decor brd. VG. P1. $5.00

DE WEESE, T.A. *Bend in the Road & How a Man of the City Found It.* 1913. NY. Ils. 208 p. TEG. T5. $25.00

DE WEESE & COULSON. *Now You See Him/Them.* 1975. Doubleday. 1st ed. dj. EX. P1. $15.00

DE WET, C.R. *3-Years' War (Boer War).* 1902. NY. 1st ed. map. plans. VG. T1. $65.00

DE WOLF, L.E. *Constable's Guide for State of PA.* 1845. Towanda, PA. 8vo. 176 p. VG. $50.00

DE ZORITA, Alonso. *Life & Labor in Ancient Mexico.* 1963. Rutgers. 1st ed. 328 p. dj. F2. $25.00

DEAL, B.H. *Grail.* c 1963. VG. C1. $22.50

DEAN, Amber. *Bullet Proof.* 1960. Crime Club. 1st ed. dj. xl. P1. $5.00

DEAN, Amber. *Call Me Pandora.* 1946. Crime Club. VG. P1. $15.00

DEAN, Amber. *Dead Man's Float.* 1944. Crime Club. EX. P1. $15.00

DEAN, Amber. *Wrap It Up.* nd. Collier. VG. P1. $10.00

DEAN, Amber. *Wrap It Up.* 1946. Crime Club. 1st ed. dj. VG. P1. $15.00

DEAN, Ellwood. *Letters & Memoranda.* 1909. OH Yearly Meeting. 12mo. 71 p. G. V1. $12.00

DEAN, Leon. *Old Wolf: Story of Israel Putnam.* 1942. Farrar. 1st ed. VG. B10. $12.00

DEAN, R.G. *Affair at Lover's Leap.* 1953. Crime Club. 1st ed. dj. VG. P1. $17.50

DEAN-SMITH, Margaret. *Playford's English Dancing Master 1651.* 1957. London. Schott. 1st ed. quarto. 90 p. dj. EX. H3. $60.00

DEANDREA, W.L. *Lunatic Fringe.* 1980. Evans. 1st ed. dj. VG. P1. $15.00

DEANDREA, W.L. *5 O'Clock Lightning.* 1982. St Martin. 1st ed. dj. VG. P1. $15.00

DEANE, Diane. *Spock's World.* 1988. Pocket. 1st ed. dj. VG. P1. $15.00

DEANE & BALDERSTON. *Dracula: Vampire Play.* 1971. Book Club. dj. VG. C1. $3.00

DEANE & BALDERSTON. *Dracula: Vampire Play.* 1971. Doubleday. 1st Revised ed. dj. EX. F5. $13.00

DEARDEN, Warren. *Free Country.* 1971. Blk Cat B318Z. 1st PB ed. B4. $4.00

DEBENHAM, Frank. *Discovery & Exploration.* 1960. Crescent. 1st ed. 4to. 272 p. dj. F2. $15.00

DEBOUCHEL, Victor. *Hist Louisiane Depuis Premieres Descouvertes Jusquen 1840.* 1841. Lelievre. 1st ed. 12mo. 197 p. G. $150.00

DEBS, E.V. *Walls & Bars.* 1927. Chicago. probable 1st ed. 248 p. EX. R4. $35.00

DEBS, E.V. *Walls & Bars.* 1927. Chicago. 1st ed. 248 p. VG. B3. $40.00

DECASTRO, Jacob. *Memoirs of J Decastro, Comedian.* 1824. Sherwood Jones. 1st ed. octavo. 279 p. VG. H3. $300.00

DECKER, Peter. *Diaries of Peter Decker: Overland to CA in 1849...* 1966. Talisman Pr. 1st ed. dj. VG. $50.00

DEDMON, Emmett. *Great Enterprises: 100 Years of YMCA Metropolitan Chicago.* 1957. 1st ed. dj. EX. C1. $8.50

DEEGAN, J.J. *Underworld of Zello.* nd. Panther Books. 1st ed. wrp. VG. R3. $15.00

DEEPING, Warwick. *I Live Again.* 1942. Knopf. 1st ed. dj. EX. F5. $22.00

DEEPING, Warwick. *Man on the Wht Horse.* 1934. Knopf. 1st Am ed. VG. C1. $12.50

DEEPING, Warwick. *Man Who Went Back.* 1940. 1st Am ed. VG. C1. $24.50

DEEPING, Warwick. *To Live Again.* 1942. London. 1st ed. dj. VG. R3. $22.50

DEFOE, Daniel. *Fortunes & Misfortunes of Famous Moll Flanders.* 1942. Heritage. Ils Marsh. slipcase. $20.00

DEFOE, Daniel. *Fortunes & Misfortunes of Moll Flanders.* nd. (1931) Bibliophilist Soc. 1st ed. 299 p. dj. VG. B10. $12.00

DEFOE, Daniel. *Novels & Selected Works.* 1928. Blackwell. Lg Paper ed. 1/530. 14 vols. octavo. H3. $750.00

DEFOE, Daniel. *Robinson Crusoe.* c 1920s. Saalfield. Ils Brundage. dj. B10. $6.50

DEFOE, Daniel. *Robinson Crusoe.* nd. (1945) Doubleday/Literary Guild. 1st ed. VG. B10. $3.50

DEFOE, Daniel. *Robinson Crusoe.* nd. Whitman 2124. 237 p. dj. VG. B10. $3.50

DEFOE, Daniel. *Robinson Crusoe.* 1866. London. 1st ed. AEG. EX. $75.00

DEFOE, Daniel. *Robinson Crusoe.* 1930. Heritage. Ils Wilson. slipcase. T1. $20.00

DEFOE, Daniel. *Robinson Crusoe.* 1946. Literary Guild. Ils Kredel. 397 p. dj. VG. B10. $4.00

DEFOE, Daniel. *Roxana: Fortunate Mistress.* 1976. Avon, CT. Ils/sgn Kroeber. 1/2000. slipcase. EX. T5. $50.00

DEFORD, M.A. *How To Write Business Letters.* 1927. Haldeman. 1st ed. wrp. scarce. F5. $12.00

DEFORD, M.A. *Latin Self-Taught.* 1926. Haldeman. 1st ed. sm wrp. EX. F5. $12.00

DEFORD, M.A. *Typewriting Self-Taught.* 1926. Haldeman. 1st ed. wrp. F5. $12.00

DEHAN, Richard. *Gilded Vanity.* 1916. Doran. 1st ed. 336 p. VG. B10. $3.75

DEIGHTON, Len. *Berlin Game.* 1983. Hutchinson. 1st ed. dj. EX. P1. $17.50

DEIGHTON, Len. *Billion-Dollar Brain.* 1966. Jonathan Cape. 1st ed. dj. VG. P1. $20.00

DEIGHTON, Len. *Billion-Dollar Brain.* 1966. Putnam. 1st ed. sgn. dj. EX. B13. $125.00

DEIGHTON, Len. *Bomber.* 1970. London. Cape. 1st ed. dj. EX. B13. $85.00

DEIGHTON, Len. *Expensive Place To Die.* 1967. London. Cape. 1st ed. dj. w/Top Secret docket. EX. B13. $100.00

DEIGHTON, Len. *Expensive Place To Die.* 1967. Putnam. ARC. sgn. self wrp. scarce. B13. $250.00

DEIGHTON, Len. *Fighter: The Story of the Battle of Britain.* 1977. London. Cape. 1st ed. dj. M. C4. $75.00

DEIGHTON, Len. *Funeral in Berlin.* 1964. London. 1st ed. dj. EX. C4. $125.00

DEIGHTON, Len. *Funeral in Berlin.* 1965. Putnam. 1st ed. sgn. dj. EX. B13. $125.00

DEIGHTON, Len. *Horse Under Water.* 1968. Putnam. 1st ed. sgn. dj. EX. B13. $125.00

DEIGHTON, Len. *Len Deighton's Continental Dossier.* 1968. London. Joseph/Dickson. laminated brd. EX. K2. $65.00

DEIGHTON, Len. *London Match.* 1985. Knopf. UP. wrp. EX. $10.00

DEIGHTON, Len. *London Match.* 1985. Knopf. 1st ed. dj. EX. P1. $17.95

DEIGHTON, Len. *Mexico Set.* 1985. Knopf. 1st ed. dj. VG. P1. $16.95

DEIGHTON, Len. *Only When I Larf.* 1968. London. Sphere. PB Orig. sgn. wrp. EX. B13. $100.00

DEIGHTON, Len. *Only When I Larf.* 1968. London. Sphere. 1st SftCvr ed. VG. K2. $45.00

DEIGHTON, Len. *Spy Sinker.* 1990. Harper Row. ARC. wrp. EX. K2. $25.00

DEIGHTON, Len. *Spy Story.* nd. Harcourt Brace. 3rd ed. dj. VG. P1. $15.00

DEIGHTON, Len. *Spy Story.* 1974. Harcourt Brace. 1st ed. sgn. dj. EX. B13. $75.00

DEIGHTON, Len. *SS-GB.* 1976. London. Cape. 1st ed. sgn. dj. EX. B13. $125.00

DEIGHTON, Len. *XPD.* 1981. Hutchinson. 1st ed. dj. VG. P1. $15.00

DEIGHTON, Len. *XPD.* 1981. Knopf. 1st ed. sgn. dj. EX. B13. $75.00

DEIGHTON, Len. *Yesterday's Spy.* Harcourt Brace. 2nd ed. dj. VG. P1. $15.00

DEIGHTON, Len. *Yesterday's Spy.* 1975. London. Cape. 1st ed. sgn. dj. EX. B13. $125.00

DEKOBRA, Maurice. *Love Clinic.* 1929. Payson Clarke. 1st ed. 2nd print. dj. EX. F5. $22.00

DEL REY, J.L. *Stellar SF Stories 4.* nd. Book Club. dj. EX. P1. $4.50

DEL REY, Lester. *And Some Were Human.* 1949. Prime Pr. 1st ed. dj. VG. P1. $45.00

DEL REY, Lester. *Best of CL Moore.* 1977. Taplinger. 1st ed. dj. EX. F5. $20.00

DEL REY, Lester. *Best of Lester Del Rey.* nd. Book Club. dj. VG. P1. $5.00

DEL REY, Lester. *Best of Lester Del Rey.* 1978. Del Rey. 1st HrdCvr ed. dj. EX. F5. $11.00

DEL REY, Lester. *Best SF Stories of the Year No 5.* 1976. Dutton. 1st ed. dj. EX. P1. $15.00

DEL REY, Lester. *Day of the Giants.* 1959. Avalon. 1st ed. dj. EX. R3. $12.50

DEL REY, Lester. *Early Del Rey.* nd. Book Club. dj. VG. P1. $6.00

DEL REY, Lester. *Fantastic SF Art.* 1975. Ballantine. 1st ed. wrp. VG. R3. $12.50

DEL REY, Lester. *Infinite Worlds of Maybe.* 1966. Holt. 1st ed. dj. EX. R3. $35.00

DEL REY, Lester. *Marooned on Mars.* 1952. Winston. 1st ed. clipped dj. EX. F5. $60.00

DEL REY, Lester. *Moon of Mutiny.* 1961. Holt Rinehart. 1st ed. xl. P1. $5.00

DEL REY, Lester. *Mortals & Monsters.* 1965. Ballantine. 1st ed. sgn. wrp. EX. R3. $15.00

DEL REY, Lester. *Outpost of Jupiter.* 1971. Holt. 1st ed. dj. EX. R3. $25.00

DEL REY, Lester. *Pirate Flag for Monterey.* 1952. Winston. 1st ed. dj. EX. R3. $25.00

DEL REY, Lester. *Preferred Risk.* 1955. Simon Schuster. 1st ed. dj. EX. R3. $35.00

DEL REY, Lester. *Rockets Through Space.* 1957. Winston. 1st ed. dj. VG. F5. $35.00

DEL REY, Lester. *Rockets Through Space.* 1957. Winston. 1st ed. xl. VG. P1. $10.00

DEL REY, Lester. *Runaway Robot.* 1965. Westminster. dj. EX. P1. $25.00

DEL REY, Lester. *Year After Tomorrow.* 1954. Winston. 1st ed. dj. EX. R3. $25.00

DELACORTA. *Diva.* 1983. Summit Books. UP. wrp. EX. K2. $45.00

DELACORTA. *Luna.* 1984. Summit Books. UP. wrp. EX. K2. $30.00

DELACOUR. *Waterfowl of the World. Vol 4.* 1964. London. 1st ed. pls. dj. NM. C2. $45.00

DELAND, Fred. *Dumb No Longer: Romance of the Telephone.* 1908. WA. Ils. 8vo. AEG. EX. T1. $40.00

DELAND, Margaret. *Encore.* 1907. Harper. Ils Stephens. 1st ed. VG. $25.00

DELAND, Margaret. *Old Garden & Other Verses.* 1894. Boston/NY. Riverside Pr. 114 p. G. T5. $45.00

DELANY, S.R. *Am Shore.* 1978. Dragon. 1st ed. inscr. M. R3. $45.00

DELANY, S.R. *Jeweled-Hinged Jaw.* 1977. Dragon. 1st ed. 1/110. sgn. M. R3. $60.00

DELANY, S.R. *Nebula Winners 13.* 1980. Harper Row. 1st ed. dj. VG. P1. $17.50

DELANY, S.R. *Nova.* nd. Book Club. dj. VG. P1. $7.50

DELANY, S.R. *Nova.* 1968. Doubleday. 1st ed. inscr. dj. EX. R3. $100.00

DELANY, S.R. *Stars in My Pocket Like Grains of Sand.* 1984. Bantam. 1st ed. dj. VG. P1. $12.50

DELANY, S.R. *Stars in My Pocket Like Grains of Sand.* 1984. Bantam. 1st ed. inscr. dj. EX. R3. $40.00

DELANY & HACKER. *Quark 1.* 1970. NY. 1st ed. sgns. wrp. EX. T9. $40.00

DELAPLANE, Stanton. *Delaplane in Mexico.* 1960. Coward McCann. 1st ed. dj. F2. $10.00

DELARRABEITI, Michael. *Hollywood Takes.* 1988. Crime Club. 1st ed. dj. EX. F5. $15.00

DELAUNAY, Charles. *Hot Discography.* 1943. Commodore Record Co. reprint of 1938 ed. sm octavo. 416 p. VG. H3. $100.00

DELAUNAY, Sonia. *Alphabet.* 1972. Crowell. 1st ed. dj. EX. B13. $100.00

DELEVOY, R.L. *Bosch: Taste of Our Time.* 1960. Crown. 144 p. dj. D4. $25.00

DELILLO, Don. *Americana.* 1989. Penguin. Contemporary Am Fiction Series. UP. wrp. EX. K2. $40.00

DELILLO, Don. *Names.* 1982. Knopf. UP. wrp. EX. C4. $100.00

DELINT, Charles. *Drink Down the Moon.* 1990. Ace. PB Orig. M. C1. $4.50

DELINT, Charles. *Riddle of the Wren.* Ace. PB Orig. VG. C1. $5.00

DELL, Anthony. *Llama Land: E & W of the Andes in Peru.* 1927. Doran. 1st ed. lg 8vo. 248 p. F2. $45.00

DELL, Floyd. *King Arthur's Socks.* 1922. NY. 1st ed. dj. EX. scarce. C1. $19.50

DELLA SANTA, E. *Salle du Perou.* 1963. Leige. Ils. French text. wrp. F2. $15.00

DELTEIL, Joseph. *Joan of Arc.* 1926. NY. Minton Balch. 1st ed. dj. EX. B13. $50.00

DELVING, Michael. *Bored to Death.* 1975. Scribner. 1st ed. dj. xl. P1. $7.50

DELVING, Michael. *Die Like a Man.* Crime Book Club. VG. C1. $4.50

DELVING, Michael. *Die Like a Man.* Detective Book Club. VG. C1. $7.50

DEMAREST, Arthur. *Viracocha.* 1981. Peabody Mus. 1st ed. 88 p. wrp. F2. $15.00

DEMARIS, Ovid. *Brothers in Blood.* 1977. Scribner. 1st ed. dj. EX. P1. $20.00

DEMBY, William. *Love Story Blk.* 1978. NY. 1st ed. wrp. EX. T9. $55.00

DEMIJOHN, Thomas. *Blk Alice.* nd. Book Club. VG. P1. $5.00

DEMILLE, Nelson. *By the Rivers of Babylon.* nd. BOMC. dj. EX. P1. $7.50

DEMILLE, Nelson. *Word of Honor.* nd. BOMC. dj. EX. P1. $7.50

DEMING, Richard. *Assignment: The Arranger.* 1969. Whitman. VG. P1. $7.50

DEMING, Richard. *Assignment: The Hideout.* 1970. Whitman. VG. P1. $7.50

DEMING, Richard. *Dragnet.* 1970. Whitman. VG. P1. $10.00

DEMING, Richard. *Famous Investigators.* 1963. Whitman. decor brd. VG. P1. $6.00

DEMING, Richard. *Gallows in My Garden.* 1952. Rinehart. dj. xl. P1. $7.50

DEMING, Richard. *Whistle Past the Graveyard.* 1954. Rinehart. 1st ed. dj. xl. P1. $7.50

DENHARD, Harold. *How To Do Rope Tricks.* 1979. Magic Inc. 6th print. 68 p. EX. J3. $3.00

DENIS, Pierre. *Argentine Republic.* 1922. London. Fisher Unwin. 1st ed. VG. F2. $20.00

DENISON, Merrill. *Klondike Mike.* 1948. Johnson Pub. 1st ed. EX. B10. $7.25

DENKER, Henry. *Experiment.* 1976. Simon Schuster. 1st ed. dj. EX. P1. $10.00

DENMARK, Harrison; see Zelazny, Roger.

DENNIS, William. *Documentary Hist of Tacna-Arica Dispute.* 1971. Kennikat Pr. reprint of 1927 ed. 262 p. F2. $15.00

DENNIS & WILLMARTH. *Blk Hist for Beginners.* 1984. Writers & Teaders. 1st ed. dj. EX. B13. $45.00

DENNIS. *Shores Inland Sea.* 1895. np. VG. C2. $20.00

DENNISON, L.R. *Devil Mt.* 1942. Hastings House. 1st ed. 271 p. F2. $20.00

DENNISON, Tim Sr. *Am Negro & His Amazing Music.* 1963. Vantage Pr. 1st ed. sgn. 76 p. dj. VG. H3. $45.00

DENSMORE, John. *Riders on the Storm: My Life With Jim Morrison & the Doors.* 1990. Delacorte. UP. wrp. EX. $10.00

DENT, J.C. *Canadian Portrait Gallery.* 1880. Toronto. Magurn. 4 vols in 2. $125.00

DENT, Lester. *Hades & Hocus-Pocus.* 1979. Pulp Pr. 1st ed. dj. EX. R3. $25.00

DENT, SCHICHNER, & MOSES. *Free S Theater by the Free S Theater.* 1969. Bobbs Merrill. 1st ed. 233 p. VG. H3. $65.00

DERING, Edward. *Diaries & Papers of Sir Edward Dering...1644-1684.* 1976. London. Her Majesty's Stationery Office. 1st ed. dj. VG. $25.00

DERLETH, August. *Adventures of Solar Pons.* 1975. Robson. dj. EX. P1. $20.00

DERLETH, August. *Beachheads in Space.* 1952. Pelligrini Cudahy. 1st ed. dj. VG. P1. $35.00

DERLETH, August. *Beyond Time & Space.* 1950. Payson Clarke. 1st ed. dj. EX. R3. $45.00

DERLETH, August. *Captive Island.* 1952. Aladdin. 1st ed. EX. R3. $20.00

DERLETH, August. *Chronicles of Solar Pons.* 1973. Mycroft Moran. dj. EX. P1. $20.00

DERLETH, August. *Chronicles of Solar Pons.* 1975. Robson. dj. EX. P1. $20.00

DERLETH, August. *Dark Mind, Dark Heart.* 1962. Arkham House. 1st ed. dj. EX. R3. $45.00

DERLETH, August. *Dark of the Moon.* 1947. Arkham House. 1st ed. inscr. dj. EX. R3. $225.00

DERLETH, August. *Dwellers in Darkness.* 1976. Arkham House. 1st ed. M. R3. $8.95

DERLETH, August. *Evening in Spring.* 1945. Stanton Lee. 1st ed. inscr. dj. EX. R3. $50.00

DERLETH, August. *Far Boundaries.* 1951. Payson Clarke. 1st ed. inscr. dj. EX. R3. $60.00

DERLETH, August. *Far Boundaries.* 1951. Pelligrini Cudahy. 1st ed. dj. VG. P1. $35.00

DERLETH, August. *Harrigan's File.* 1975. Arkham House. 1st ed. dj. EX. P1. $20.00

DERLETH, August. *House Above Cuzco.* 1969. Candlelight. 1st ed. sgn. dj. EX. R3. $25.00

DERLETH, August. *In Re: Sherlock Holmes.* 1945. Arkham House. 1st ed. VG. B3. $50.00

DERLETH, August. *Lonesome Places.* 1962. Arkham House. 1st ed. sgn. dj. VG. P1. $95.00

DERLETH, August. *Man on All Fours.* 1934. Loring Mussby. 1st ed. xl. P1. $15.00

DERLETH, August. *Mr Fairlie's Final Journey.* 1968. Mycroft Moran. 1st ed. dj. VG. P1. $25.00

DERLETH, August. *New Poetry Out of WI.* 1969. Stanton Lee. 1st ed. dj. EX. P1. $50.00

DERLETH, August. *Night Side.* 1947. Rinehart. 1st ed. 8vo. 372 p. dj. EX. R4. $40.00

DERLETH, August. *No Future for Luana.* 1945. Scribner. 1st ed. VG. P1. $30.00

DERLETH, August. *Not Long for This World.* 1948. Arkham House. 1st ed. dj. VG. R3. $100.00

DERLETH, August. *Other Side of the Moon.* 1949. Payson Clarke. 1st ed. dj. EX. R3. $35.00

DERLETH, August. *Other Side of the Moon.* 1949. Pelligrini Cudahy. VG. P1. $17.50

DERLETH, August. *Outer Reaches.* 1951. Payson Clarke. 1st ed. dj. EX. R3. $35.00

DERLETH, August. *Over the Edge.* 1964. Arkham House. 1st ed. dj. EX. R3. $40.00

DERLETH, August. *Place of Hawks.* 1935. Loring Mussey. presentation. dj. H3. $200.00

DERLETH, August. *Portals of Tomorrow.* nd. Book Club. dj. VG. P1. $5.00

DERLETH, August. *Praed St Dossier.* 1968. Arkham House. 1st ed. dj. EX. R3. $40.00

DERLETH, August. *Restless Is the River.* 1939. Scribner. presentation. dj. H3. $125.00

DERLETH, August. *Sac Prairie People.* 1948. Sauk City. 1st ed. 322 p. dj. RS. T5. $45.00

DERLETH, August. *Sleep No More.* 1944. Farrar. 1st ed. dj. EX. R3. $45.00

DERLETH, August. *Sleep No More.* 1945. Armed Services ed. 1st PB ed. VG. T9. $35.00

DERLETH, August. *Some Notes on HP Lovecraft.* 1959. Arkham House. 1st ed. sgn. wrp. VG. R3. $95.00

DERLETH, August. *Someone in the Dark.* 1941. Arkham House. 1st ed. dj. VG. R3. $300.00

DERLETH, August. *Something Near.* 1945. Arkham House. 1st ed. dj. EX. R3. $150.00

DERLETH, August. *Strange Ports of Call.* 1948. Payson Clarke. 1st ed. inscr. dj. EX. R3. $60.00

DERLETH, August. *Time To Come.* 1954. Farrar. 1st ed. dj. EX. R3. $17.50

DERLETH, August. *Travelers by Night.* 1967. Arkham House. 1st ed. dj. EX. R3. $50.00

DERLETH, August. *When Evil Wakes.* 1963. London. dj. EX. R3. $25.00

DERLETH, August. *Who Knocks?* 1946. Rinehart. 1st ed. dj. VG. R3. $20.00

DERLETH, August. *WI Harvest.* 1966. Stanton Lee. 1st ed. dj. EX. P1. $20.00

DERLETH, August. *Wind Leans W.* 1969. Candlelight. 1st ed. dj. EX. P1. $20.00

DERLETH, August. *Wind Over WI.* 1938. Scribner. presentation. sgn. dj. H3. $150.00

DERLETH, August. *Worlds of Tomorrow.* 1953. Payson Clarke. 1st ed. dj. EX. R3. $27.50

DERLETH, August. *100 Books by August Derleth.* 1962. Arkham House. 1st ed. wrp. EX. R3. $150.00

DERLETH, August. *3 Straw Men.* 1970. Candlelight Pr. 1st ed. dj. EX. P1. $20.00

DERLETH, August. *30 Years of Arkham House.* 1970. Arkham House. 1st ed. dj. EX. R3. $65.00

DERLETH & DWIG. *Boy's Way.* 1947. Stanton Lee. 1st ed. dj. EX. P1. $20.00

DERLETH & DWIG. *It's a Boy's World.* 1948. Stanton Lee. dj. EX. P1. $20.00

DERLETH & DWIG. *Wilbur, the Trusting Whippoorwill.* 1959. Stanton Lee. dj. EX. P1. $20.00

DERN, J.H. *Rememberance of Miracles.* 1971. Wilder, VT. Phineas Pr. Ltd ed. 1/100. sgn. dj. wrp. H3. $35.00

DEROUGEMONT, Denis. *Love Declared: Essays on the Myths of Love.* 1963. NY. 1st ed. dj. VG. C1. $9.50

DEROUGEMONT, Denis. *Love in the W World.* 1956. Pantheon. dj. VG. C1. $12.50

DESCOLA, Jean. *Conquistadors.* 1957. Viking. 1st ed. dj. F2. $15.00

DESCOLA, Jean. *Daily Life in Colonial Peru 1710-1820.* 1968. Macmillan. 1st Am ed. 275 p. dj. F2. $15.00

DESMOND, A.C. *Bewitching Betsy Bonaparte.* 1958. NY. 1st ed. dj. VG. $15.00

DESMOND, Alice. *Soldier of the Sun.* 1939. NY. Dodd. 1st ed. 243 p. dj. F2. $15.00

DESMOND, M.S. *Space Age Miscellany of Magic.* 1967. Manchester, NH. NM. J3. $5.00

DESMOND & MESSENGER. *Dream of Maya.* 1989. NM U. Ils. 4to. 147 p. F2. $20.00

DESSART, Gina. *Cry for the Lost.* 1959. Harper. 1st ed. dj. VG. P1. $10.00

DESTEFANO, Tony. *Sorceress.* 1977. Manor. 1st ed. wrp. EX. F5. $10.00

DETRO, Gene. *Patchen: Last Interview.* 1976. Capra. Chapbook Series. 1/60. sgn. K2. $35.00

DETZER, Diane. *Planet of Fear.* 1968. Avalon. 1st ed. dj. EX. R3. $12.50

DEUEL, Leo. *Conquistadors Without Swords.* 1967. St Martin. 1st ed. maps. 647 p. dj. F2. $20.00

DEUEL, Leo. *Flights Into Yesterday.* 1969. St Martin. 1st ed. 332 p. dj. F2. $15.00

DEVANT, David. *My Magic Life.* nd. Supreme Magic. 297 p. dj. NM. J3. $18.00

DEVERDUN, A.L. *True Mexico.* 1939. Banta. 1st ed. 304 p. dj. F2. $45.00

DEVERE, William. *Tramp Poet of the W: Jim Marshall.* 1897. NY/Chicago/London. 1st ed. EX. $20.00

DEVINS, J.H. *Vaagso Raid.* 1968. Phil. 1st ed. 222 p. dj. VG. T5. $15.00

DEVLIN, Barry. *Other Loves.* 1955. Vixen Pr. 1st ed. dj. EX. F5. $20.00

DEVOL, George. *40 Years a Gambler on the MS.* 1926. NY. 1st ed. 288 p. G. B3. $45.00

DEWDNEY & KIDD. *Indian Rock Paintings of the Great Lakes.* 1962. Toronto. 1st ed. 4to. dj. EX. $30.00

DEWEES, Rebecca. *Memoir of Rebecca Dewees, Late of Pennsville, OH.* 1833. Phil. WH Pile. 16mo. 104 p. V1. $14.00

DEWEES & DEWEES. *Hist of Westtown Boarding School 1799-1899.* 1899. Phil. Sherman. 12mo. 204 p. G. V1. $20.00

DEWEY, T.B. *Can a Mermaid Kill?* 1965. Tower. 1st ed. wrp. EX. F5. $8.00

DEWEY, T.B. *Case of Chased & Unchaste.* nd. Book Club. dj. VG. P1. $4.00

DEWEY, T.B. *Draw the Curtain Close.* 1951. Dakers. VG. P1. $20.00

DEWEY, T.B. *Go To Sleep, Jeannie.* 1959. Popular Giant G302. 1st ed. wrp. EX. T9. $20.00

DEWEY, T.B. *How Hard To Kill.* 1962. Simon Schuster. 1st ed. dj. xl. P1. $5.00

DEWEY, T.B. *Hue & Cry.* nd. Grosset Dunlap. dj. VG. P1. $20.00

DEWEY, T.B. *Love-Death Thing.* 1969. Simon Schuster. 1st ed. dj. xl. P1. $6.00

DEWEY, T.B. *Mean Streets.* 1955. Boardman. VG. P1. $20.00

DEWEY, T.B. *Mt Girl.* 1952. Gold Medal 276. PB Orig. wrp. EX. T9. $30.00

DEWEY, T.B. *Nude in NV.* 1965. Dell 8408. 1st ed. wrp. EX. T9. $25.00

DEWEY, T.B. *Run, Brother, Run.* 1954. Popular Lib 584. PB Orig. wrp. EX. T9. $25.00

DEWEY, T.B. *Taurus Trip.* 1970. Simon Schuster. 1st ed. dj. xl. P1. $7.50

DEWEY & DEWEY. *Letters From China & Japan.* 1921. NY. Dutton. 311 p. G. B3. $15.00

DEXTER, Colin. *Dead of Jericho.* 1981. St Martin. 1st ed. dj. EX. P1. $17.50

DEXTER, Colin. *Riddle of the 3rd Mile.* nd. St Martin. 2nd ed. dj. VG. P1. $12.50

DEXTER, F.T. *42 Years' Scrapbook of Ancient Firearms.* 1954. Los Angeles. Ltd ed. sgn. dj. VG. B3. $75.00

DEXTER, Pete. *Brotherly Love.* 1991. Random House. UP. glossy wrp. EX. C4. $75.00

DEXTER, Pete. *Deadwood.* 1986. Random House. ARC. wrp. EX. C4. $50.00

DEXTER, Pete. *God's Pocket.* 1983. NY. 1st ed. sgn. dj. EX. T9. $65.00

DEXTER, Pete. *Paris Trout.* 1988. Random House. UP. wrp. EX. C4. $75.00

DEXTER, Pete. *Paris Trout.* 1988. Random House. 1st ed. dj. M. C4. $45.00

DEXTER, Will. *Everybody's Book of Magic.* 1956. London. Arco. 1st ed. dj. VG. J3. $15.00

DEXTER, Will. *Identity Parade.* 1954. London. Armstrong. 1st ed. EX. J3. $3.00

DEXTER, Will. *Magic Circle Magic.* 1963. London. Clarke. 1st ed. 265 p. dj. EX. J3. $24.00

DEXTER, Will. *Sealed Vision.* 1989. Magico Magazine. 66 p. M. J3. $10.00

DEXTER, Will. *This Is Magic.* 1958. Citadel. 1st ed. 204 p. dj. J3. $6.00

DEXTER, Will. *101 Magic Secrets.* 1958. Arco. 158 p. EX. J3. $3.00

DI PRIMA, Diane. *Loba Part 1.* 1973. Capra. Chapbook Series. 1/100. sgn. EX. K2. $45.00

DI PRIMA, Diane. *Memoirs of a Beatnik.* nd. Last Gasp. EX. B4. $12.00

DI TURNO, S.G. *Diamond River.* 1963. Harcourt. 1st Am ed. 186 p. dj. F2. $15.00

DIAMOND, Frank. *Murder Rides a Rocket.* 1946. Mystery House. 1st ed. dj. VG. R3. $25.00

DIAMOND, Graham. *Dungeons of Kuba.* 1979. Playboy Pr. 1st ed. wrp. EX. F5. $7.50

DIAMOND, Hal. *Promotion in Motion.* 1981. Kensington, MD. 2nd print. 70 p. J3. $8.00

DIAZ DEL CASTILLO, Bernal. *Discovery & Conquest of Mexico 1517-1521.* 1956. Farrar. 478 p. F2. $10.00

DIBDIN, Michael. *Last Sherlock Holmes' Story.* 1978. Pantheon. 1st ed. dj. EX. P1. $25.00

DIBDIN, T.F. *Bibliomania.* 1903. Boston. 1/483. 4 vols. 2 slipcases. NM. A4. $225.00

DIBDIN, T.F. *Reminiscences of a Literary Life.* 1836. London. 2 vols. Solander cases. EX. A4. $225.00

DICHTER, Harry. *Early Am Sheet Music 1768-1889.* 1941. NY. Ils. sm 4to. 287 p. xl. VG. T6. $65.00

DICHTER, Harry. *Handbook of Am Sheet Music.* 1947. Phil. 1st ed. 100 p. wrp. EX. K1. $25.00

DICK, P.K. *Clans of the Alphane Moon.* 1964. Ace. 1st ed. EX. R3. $30.00

DICK, P.K. *Cosmic Puppets.* 1957. Ace. 1st ed. wrp. EX. R3. $25.00

DICK, P.K. *Crack in Space.* 1989. Severn House. dj. EX. P1. $25.00

DICK, P.K. *Dark-Haired Girl.* 1988. Ziesing. 1st ed. dj. EX. P1. $19.95

DICK, P.K. *Divine Invasion.* nd. Book Club. dj. VG. P1. $7.50

DICK, P.K. *Dr Bloodmoney.* 1965. Ace. 1st ed. wrp. EX. R3. $35.00

DICK, P.K. *Dr Futurity.* 1960. Ace. 1st ed. wrp. EX. R3. $35.00

DICK, P.K. *Eye in the Sky.* 1957. Ace. 1st ed. wrp. VG. R3. $20.00

DICK, P.K. *Flow My Tears, the Policeman Said.* 1974. Doubleday. 1st ed. dj. xl. VG. R3. $50.00

DICK, P.K. *Galactic Pot-Healer.* 1969. SF Book Club. 1st print. dj. EX. F5. $12.00

DICK, P.K. *Game Players of Titan.* 1963. Ace. 1st ed. wrp. EX. R3. $25.00

DICK, P.K. *Golden Man.* nd. Book Club. dj. VG. P1. $7.50

DICK, P.K. *Man in the High Castle.* nd. Book Club. dj. VG. P1. $7.50

DICK, P.K. *Man Who Japed.* 1978. Ace. 1st ed. wrp. EX. R3. $40.00

DICK, P.K. *Man Whose Teeth Were All Exactly Alike.* 1984. Ziesing. 1st ed. M. R3. $50.00

DICK, P.K. *Martian Time Slip.* 1964. Ace. 1st ed. wrp. EX. R3. $35.00

DICK, P.K. *Mary & the Giant.* 1987. Arbor House. 2nd ed. dj. EX. P1. $16.95

DICK, P.K. *Now Wait for Last Year.* 1968. MacFadden. PB Orig. wrp. EX. R3. $25.00

DICK, P.K. *Our Friends From Frolix 8.* nd. Book Club. dj. VG. P1. $10.00

DICK, P.K. *Our Friends From Frolix 8.* 1970. Ace. 1st Ace/1st HrdCvr ed. dj. EX. F5. $20.00

DICK, P.K. *Our Friends From Frolix 8.* 1989. Kinnell. dj. EX. P1. $25.00

DICK, P.K. *Our Friends From Frolix.* 1970. Ace. PB Orig. wrp. EX. R3. $20.00

DICK, P.K. *Penultimate Truth.* 1964. Belmont. 1st ed. wrp. EX. R3. $20.00

DICK, P.K. *Preserving Machine.* 1969. Ace. 1st HrdCvr ed. dj. EX. F5. $12.00

DICK, P.K. *Radio Free Albemuth.* nd. Book Club. dj. EX. P1. $7.50

DICK, P.K. *Radio Free Albemuth.* 1985. Arbor House. 1st ed. dj. EX. R3. $20.00

DICK, P.K. *Scanner Darkly.* nd. Book Club. dj. VG. P1. $7.50

DICK, P.K. *Scanner Darkly.* 1977. Doubleday. dj. EX. R3. $25.00

DICK, P.K. *Simulacra.* 1964. Ace. 1st ed. wrp. EX. R3. $20.00

DICK, P.K. *Transmigration of Timothy Archer.* 1982. Timescape. 1st ed. dj. EX. R3. $20.00

DICK, P.K. *Unteleported Man.* 1966. Ace. 1st ed. wrp. VG. R3. $30.00

DICK, P.K. *Variable Man.* 1957. Ace. 1st ed. wrp. EX. R3. $50.00

DICK, P.K. *Vulcan's Hammer.* 1960. Ace. 1st ed. wrp. EX. $35.00

DICK, P.K. *World Jones Made.* nd. Ace. 1st Separate ed. wrp. EX. R3. $10.00

DICK & NELSON. *Ganymede Takeover.* 1988. Severn House. dj. EX. P1. $25.00

DICKASON, D.H. *Daring Young Men: Story of Am Pre-Raphaelites.* 1953. Bloomington, IN. Ils 1st ed. 304 p. dj. VG. T5. $27.50

DICKENS, Charles. *Adventures of Oliver Twist.* c 1903. Oxford. Rireside ed. sm octavo. EX. H3. $100.00

DICKENS, Charles. *Am Notes for Gen Circulation.* 1842. Lea Blanchard. early Am ed. 8vo. wht wrp. G. H3. $350.00

DICKENS, Charles. *Am Notes for General Circulation.* 1855. Chapman Hall. Cheap ed. gilt gr bdg. H3. $125.00

DICKENS, Charles. *Am Notes for General Circulation.* 1868. Appleton. Popular Works ed. 8vo. brn wrp. H3. $90.00

DICKENS, Charles. *Am Notes for General Circulation.* 1975. Avon. Ils/sgn Houlihan. 1/2000. H3. $50.00

DICKENS, Charles. *Battle of Life.* 1846. London. Bradbury Evans. 1st ed. AEG. VG. H3. $200.00

DICKENS, Charles. *Bleak House.* 1852-1853. London. Bradbury Evans. 20 parts in 19. wrp. H3. $1750.00

DICKENS, Charles. *Bleak House.* 1853. Bradbury Evans. 1st ed. 8vo. gr bdg. G. H3. $1750.00

DICKENS, Charles. *Bleak House.* 1853. Harper. 1st Am ed. 12mo. 2 vols. H3. $250.00

DICKENS, Charles. *Centenary Ed of Works of Charles Dickens.* 1910-1919. Chapman Hall. 36 vols. TEG. morocco. H3. $4500.00

DICKENS, Charles. *Child's Hist of Eng.* 1854. Bradbury Evans. later imp. 3 vols. red-brn bdg. H3. $150.00

DICKENS, Charles. *Chimes.* nd. (1913) Hodder Stoughton. Ils Thompson. 1st ed. H3. $450.00

DICKENS, Charles. *Chimes.* 1845. Chapman Hall. 1st ed. 2nd state. sm 8vo. H3. $250.00

DICKENS, Charles. *Chimes.* 1845. Chapman Hall. 9th ed. gilt red bdg. H3. $100.00

DICKENS, Charles. *Chimes.* 1931. London. Ltd Ed Club. Ils/sgn Rackham. 1/1500. quarto. EX. H3. $400.00

DICKENS, Charles. *Chips From Dickens.* nd. NY. Wht Stokes Allen. 32mo. wrp. slipcase. H3. $200.00

DICKENS, Charles. *Christmas Books.* 1886-1887. Chapman Hall. facsimile. 5 vols. VG. $175.00

DICKENS, Charles. *Christmas Carol in Prose.* c 1905? Boston. Joseph Knight. Ils Gaugengigl/Chominski. H3. $50.00

DICKENS, Charles. *Christmas Carol in Prose/Chimes/Cricket on the Hearth.* 1846. Tauchnitz. Copyright ed. sm 8vo. H3. $100.00

DICKENS, Charles. *Christmas Carol.* c 1881. London. Dicks. Ils Leech. 8vo. gr wrp. H3. $50.00

DICKENS, Charles. *Christmas Carol.* 1843. Chapman Hall. 1st ed. 2nd issue. sm octavo. 166 p. H3. $4000.00

DICKENS, Charles. *Christmas Carol.* 1843. Chapman Hall. 3rd ed. sm octavo. red-brn bdg. H3. $750.00

DICKENS, Charles. *Christmas Carol.* 1844. Phil. 1st Am ed. orig bdg. VG. scarce. H3. $2500.00

DICKENS, Charles. *Christmas Carol.* 1845. Chapman Hall. 11th ed. red bdg. H3. $450.00

DICKENS, Charles. *Christmas Carol.* 1902. Roycroft. Deluxe ed. 1/100. sgn Hubbard. VG. H3. $250.00

DICKENS, Charles. *Christmas Carol.* 1902. Roycroft. VG. C1. $12.00

DICKENS, Charles. *Christmas Carol.* 1930. Mt Vernon, NY. 12mo. 2 vols. red morocco. H3. $125.00

DICKENS, Charles. *Christmas Carol.* 1932. Cheshire House. Ltd ed. 1/1200. red morocco. H3. $150.00

DICKENS, Charles. *Christmas Carol.* 1940. Monastery Hill Pr. Ils Reed. gilt red morocco. EX. H3. $300.00

DICKENS, Charles. *Christmas Stories.* nd. Books Inc. Ils. VG. P1. $7.00

DICKENS, Charles. *Cricket on the Hearth.* c1900. Putnam. Ils Coburn. gilt gr bdg. boxed. H3. $50.00

DICKENS, Charles. *Cricket on the Hearth.* 1946. London. Bradbury Evans. 1st ed. red bdg. H3. $250.00

DICKENS, Charles. *Dicken's Dictionary of London 1879: Unconventional Handbook.* 1879. London. 1st ed. 16mo. brn bdg. VG. H3. $75.00

DICKENS, Charles. *Dicken's Works Vol 1 Through Vol 20.* nd. Phil. Morris. Gadshill ed. 1/100. gilt red-brn leather. H3. $850.00

DICKENS, Charles. *Dickens-Kolle Letters.* 1910. Bibliophile Soc. 8vo. 90 p. red wrp/slipcase. H3. $85.00

DICKENS, Charles. *Dombey & Son.* nd. Chapman Hall. Ils Browne. early reprint. 8vo. gr bdg. H3. $200.00

DICKENS, Charles. *Dombey & Son.* 1848. London. Bradbury Evans. Ils Browne. 1st ed. not 1st issue. G. H3. $650.00

DICKENS, Charles. *Dombey & Son.* 1957. Ltd Ed Club. Ils/sgn Pitz. 1/1500. 2 vols. H3. $75.00

DICKENS, Charles. *George Silverman's Explanation.* 1984. Santa Susana Pr. Ils/sgn Block. 1st Book ed. 1/26. H3. $175.00

DICKENS, Charles. *Great Expectations.* 1862. Boston. Fuller. 1st ed. 12mo. 312 p. brn bdg. G. H3. $250.00

DICKENS, Charles. *Great Expectations.* 1864. London. 1st Cheap ed. orig gr cloth. VG. $210.00

DICKENS, Charles. *Great Expectations.* 1937. Edinburgh. Ltd Ed Club. Ils/sgn Ross. 1/1500. gr bdg. slipcase. H3. $150.00

DICKENS, Charles. *Great Expectations.* 1937. Ltd Ed Club. Ils/sgn Gordon Ross. slipcase. C4. $125.00

DICKENS, Charles. *Hard Times & Additional Christmas Stories.* 1871. Appleton. 8vo. 202 p. tan wrp. G. H3. $60.00

DICKENS, Charles. *Hard Times for These Times.* 1966. Ltd Ed Club. Ils/sgn Raymond. 1/1500. slipcase. H3. $60.00

DICKENS, Charles. *Haunted Man & the Ghost's Bargain.* 1848. Bradbury Evans. 1st ed. Bayntun bdg. H3. $125.00

DICKENS, Charles. *Haunted Man & the Ghost's Bargain.* 1848. London. Bradbury Evans. 1st ed. TEG. Zaehnsdorf bdg. VG. H3. $225.00

DICKENS, Charles. *Life & Adventures of Martin Chuzzlewit.* 1843-1844. Chapman Hall. 1st ed. 20 parts in 19. wrp. H3. $1250.00

DICKENS, Charles. *Life & Adventures of Martin Chuzzlewit.* 1844. Chapman Hall. 1st ed in book form. 2nd issue. boxed. H3. $450.00

DICKENS, Charles. *Life & Adventures of Nicholas Nickleby.* 1838-1839. Chapman Hall. 1st ed. 1st issue. 20 parts in 19. gr wrp. H3. $1650.00

DICKENS, Charles. *Life & Adventures of Nicholas Nickleby.* 1839. London. Ils Phiz. 1st Book ed. rebound. EX. H3. $600.00

DICKENS, Charles. *Life of Our Lord.* 1934. Simon Schuster/Merrymount. Ltd ed. 8vo. G. V1. $50.00

DICKENS, Charles. *Life of Our Lord.* 1934. London. 1st ed. VG. B3. $55.00

DICKENS, Charles. *Life of Our Lord.* 1934. Simon Schuster. sm octavo. slipcase. H3. $75.00

DICKENS, Charles. *Little Dorrit.* 1855. Bradbury Evans. Ils Browne. 20 parts in 19. wrp. H3. $2500.00

DICKENS, Charles. *Little Dorrit.* 1856. Tauchnitz. Ils Browne. Copyright ed. 4 vols. H3. $200.00

DICKENS, Charles. *Little Dorrit.* 1857. Bradbury Evans. Ils Browne. 1st ed. Bayntun bdg. EX. H3. $550.00

DICKENS, Charles. *Master Humphrey's Clock.* 1840-1841. Chapman Hall. 1st ed. 1st issue. wht wrp. boxed. H3. $2500.00

DICKENS, Charles. *Master Humphrey's Clock.* 1840-1841. Chapman Hall. 1st ed. 2nd issue. gr wrp. clamshell box. H3. $2250.00

DICKENS, Charles. *Master Humphrey's Clock.* 1840-1841. Chapman Hall. 1st ed. 4th issue. 3 vols. lg 12mo. H3. $1250.00

DICKENS, Charles. *Memoirs of Joseph Grimaldi.* 1838. NY. Colyer. 2nd Am ed. 12mo. 232 p. H3. $275.00

DICKENS, Charles. *Mrs Lirriper's Legacy.* 1864. Chapman Hall. 1st ed. 8vo. bl wrp. EX. H3. $125.00

DICKENS, Charles. *Mudfog Papers.* 1880. Holt. Leisure Hour Series. 1st Am ed. H3. $225.00

DICKENS, Charles. *Mugby Junction.* 1866. Chapman Hall. 1st ed. 8vo. 48 p. VG. H3. $125.00

DICKENS, Charles. *Mystery of Edwin Drood.* 1870. Chapman Hall. Ils Fildes. 1st ed. 8vo. gr bdg. G. H3. $300.00

DICKENS, Charles. *Mystery of Edwin Drood.* 1870. Chapman Hall. 1st ed. 2nd bdg w/variant border. H3. $250.00

DICKENS, Charles. *Nonesuch Dickens.* 1937-1938. Nonesuch. 1/877. 23 vols. lg octavo. TEG. EX. H3. $10000.00

DICKENS, Charles. *Old Curiosity Shop.* 1941. Chapman Hall. 1st Separate ed. 2nd bdg. 12mo. H3. $500.00

DICKENS, Charles. *Old Leaves: Gathered From Household Words.* 1860. Chapman Hall. 1st ed. 8vo. morocco slipcase. H3. $350.00

DICKENS, Charles. *Oliver Twist.* 1839. Cincinnati. James. early Am ed. 2 vols. 12mo. H3. $350.00

DICKENS, Charles. *Oliver Twist.* 1898. Kjobenjavn. Danish text. 8vo. VG. V1. $35.00

DICKENS, Charles. *Our Mutual Friend.* 1865. Chapman Hall. Ils Stone. 1st Book ed. 2 vols. H3. $500.00

DICKENS, Charles. *Our Mutual Friend.* 1865. Chapman Hall. 1st ed. rare variant w/2 vols in 1. H3. $500.00

DICKENS, Charles. *Our Mutual Friend.* 1865. Harper. 1st Am ed in book form. 8vo. gr bdg. H3. $125.00

DICKENS, Charles. *Personal Hist & Experience of David Copperfield.* 1849-1850. Wiley Putnam. 1st Am ed. 36 pl. buff wrp. H3. $5000.00

DICKENS, Charles. *Personal Hist & Experience of David Copperfield.* 1850. Wiley. 1st Am ed. 8vo. 2 vols. slipcase. H3. $300.00

DICKENS, Charles. *Personal Hist of David Copperfield.* c 1911. London. Westminster. quarto. 572 p. H3. $175.00

DICKENS, Charles. *Personal Hist of David Copperfield.* nd. Chapman Hall. early ed. 8vo. olive-gr bdg. EX. H3. $200.00

DICKENS, Charles. *Personal Hist of David Copperfield.* 1849-1850. Bradbury Evans. 1st ed. Solander case. H3. $8500.00

DICKENS, Charles. *Personal Hist of David Copperfield.* 1850. Bradbury Evans. Ils Browne. 1st ed in book form. 8vo. H3. $500.00

DICKENS, Charles. *Personal Hist of David Copperfield.* 1850. London. 1st ed. 40 pls. Bayntun/Riviere bdg. H3. $1000.00

DICKENS, Charles. *Pic-Nic Papers.* 1841. London. 1st ed. 2nd issue. 3 vols. 12mo. H3. $1250.00

DICKENS, Charles. *Pickwick Papers.* nd. Modern Lib. 855 p. 8vo. bl bdg. VG. B10. $3.50

DICKENS, Charles. *Pickwick Papers.* 1837. Chapman Hall. 1st ed. early issue. TEG. VG. V1. $550.00

DICKENS, Charles. *Pictures From Italy.* 1846. Bradbury Evans. Ils Palmer. 1st ed. 8vo. Zaehnsdorf bdg. H3. $350.00

DICKENS, Charles. *Plated Article by Charles Dickens.* nd. (1930) Copeland Sons. sm octavo. VG. H3. $25.00

DICKENS, Charles. *Poor Traveler/Boots at the Holly-Tree Inn/Mrs Gamp.* 1858. Bradbury Evans. 1st ed. stiff gr wrp. VG. H3. $125.00

DICKENS, Charles. *Poor Traveler/Boots at the Holly-Tree Inn/Mrs Gamp.* 1869. Chapman Hall. later reprint. 8vo. 114 p. gr wrp. G. H3. $100.00

DICKENS, Charles. *Posthumous Papers of the Pickwick Club.* c 1910. Hodder Stoughton. 26 pl. 584 p. boxed. EX. H3. $200.00

DICKENS, Charles. *Posthumous Papers of the Pickwick Club.* 1837. Chapman Hall. Ils Seymour/Phiz. 1st ed. EX. H3. $450.00

DICKENS, Charles. *Posthumous Papers of the Pickwick Club.* 1842. Tauchnitz. Copyright ed. 2 vols. H3. $175.00

DICKENS, Charles. *Posthumous Papers of the Pickwick Club.* 1945. Dodd Mead. Great Ils Classics Series. 8vo. H3. $150.00

DICKENS, Charles. *Sikes & Nancy: A Reading.* 1921. London. reprint of private print ed. Riviere bdg. H3. $4500.00

DICKENS, Charles. *Sketches by Boz.* 1839. Chapman Hall. Collected ed. gilt bl morocco. VG. H3. $350.00

DICKENS, Charles. *Sketches by Boz.* 1850. Chapman Hall. later ed. gilt gr bdg. G. H3. $125.00

DICKENS, Charles. *Sketches by Boz.* 1885. Leeds. Goodall Backhouse. 2nd ed. gr wrp. VG. H3. $30.00

DICKENS, Charles. *Sketches of Young Couples.* 1840. Chapman Hall. Ils Phiz. 1st ed. G. H3. $250.00

DICKENS, Charles. *Story of Little Dombey.* 1858. Bradbury Evans. 1st Trade ed. gr wrp. VG. H3. $100.00

DICKENS, Charles. *Sunday Under 3 Heads.* 1884. London. Jarvis. Ils. sm octavo. gray wrp. H3. $45.00

DICKENS, Charles. *Tale of 2 Cities.* 1859. Chapman Hall. 1st ed. 1st issue in book form. Goodspeed bdg. H3. $1250.00

DICKENS, Charles. *Tale of 2 Cities.* 1859. London. 1st ed. 1st issue. VG. H3. $850.00

DICKENS, Charles. *Uncommercial Traveler.* 1861. London. 1st ed. orig bdg. VG. H3. $1250.00

DICKENS, Charles. *Works.* c 1850s-1870s. Phil. Peterson. Peoples ed. 22 vols. H3. $375.00

DICKENS, Charles. *Works.* nd. London. Chapman Hall. gilt bl leather. VG. T1. $100.00

DICKENS, Charles. *Works.* 1874-1876. Chapman Hall. Lib ed. 30 vols. VG. H3. $2000.00

DICKENS, Charles. *Works.* 1874-1876. Chapman Hall. Ils Lib ed. 30 vols. gilt morocco. EX. H3. $5000.00

DICKENS, Charles. *Works.* 1897-1903. London. Gadshill ed. 36 vols. $450.00

DICKENS, Henry F. *Memories of My Father.* 1928. London. Ltd ed. 1/250. sgn. dj. VG. B3. $115.00

DICKENS & COLLINS. *No Thoroughfare.* 1867. Chapman Hall. 1st ed. 8vo. 48 p. bl wrp. VG. H3. $125.00

DICKENS & COLLINS. *Wreck of the Golden Mary.* 1956. Kentfield, CA. Allen. Ltd ed. 1/200. 8vo. 90 p. H3. $275.00

DICKENSON, Fred. *Kill 'Em With Kindness.* 1950. Bell. dj. VG. P1. $15.00

DICKESON, G.R. *Alien Art.* 1973. Dutton. 1st ed. dj. EX. P1. $25.00

DICKESON, G.R. *Ancient My Enemy.* nd. Book Club. dj. VG. P1. $4.50

DICKESON, G.R. *Ancient My Enemy.* 1974. Doubleday. 1st ed. dj. xl. P1. $7.00

DICKESON, G.R. *Final Encyclopedia.* 1984. Tor Books. 1st ed. dj. VG. P1. $18.00

DICKESON, G.R. *Masters of Everon.* nd. Book Club. dj. EX. P1. $4.50

DICKESON, G.R. *Nebula Winners 12.* 1979. Harper Row. 2nd ed. dj. EX. P1. $15.00

DICKESON, G.R. *Pritcher Mass.* 1972. Doubleday. 2nd ed. dj. EX. P1. $12.00

DICKESON, G.R. *Star Road.* 1973. Doubleday. 1st ed. sgn. dj. EX. P1. $25.00

DICKESON, G.R. *Star Road.* 1975. Robert Hale. 1st ed. dj. VG. P1. $15.00

DICKEY, Charley. *Dove Hunting.* 1976. Galahad. 1st Am ed. 112 p. dj. VG. B10. $6.75

DICKEY, Charley. *Outdoors.* 1989. Amwell Pr. Ltd ed. 1/1000. sgn. 140 p. $12.00

DICKEY, Herbert. *Misadventures of a Tropical Medico.* 1929. Dodd Mead. Ils 1st ed. 304 p. F2. $20.00

DICKEY, James. *Deliverance.* 1970. Houghton Mifflin. sgn. dj. H3. $60.00

DICKEY, James. *Enemy From Eden.* 1978. Lord John. 1/275. sgn. H3. $75.00

DICKEY, James. *Eye-Beaters, Blood, Victory, Madness, Buckhead, & Mercy.* 1970. Doubleday. Ltd ed. 1/250. sgn. slipcase. H3. $60.00

DICKEY, James. *Sorties.* 1971. Doubleday. early issue. sgn. red bdg. dj. H3. $60.00

DICKEY, James. *Spinning the Crystal Ball: Some Guesses at Future Am Poetry.* 1967. WA. Lib of Congress. 1st ed. 8vo. 22 p. wrp. EX. C4. $20.00

DICKEY, James. *Tucky the Hunter.* c 1978. Crown. Ils Marie Angel. sgn. dj. H3. $35.00

DICKINSON, C.E. *Hist of Belpre.* 1920. Parkersburg, WV. Ils 1st ed. 243 p. G. T5. $65.00

DICKINSON, Carter. *Red Widow Murders*. 1935. Morrow. 1st ed. 12mo. dj. EX. C4. $125.00

DICKINSON, Charles. *Waltz in Marathon*. 1983. NY. ARC. sgn. dj. w/pub card. T9. $45.00

DICKINSON, Emily. *Complete Poems of Emily Dickinson*. 1960. Little Brn. 1st ed. dj. EX. C4. $35.00

DICKINSON, Peter. *Devil's Children*. 1986. Delacorte. 1st ed. dj. VG. P1. $15.00

DICKINSON, Peter. *Old Eng Peep Show*. 1969. Harper Row. dj. VG. P1. $20.00

DICKINSON, Peter. *Perfect Gallows*. nd. BOMC. dj. EX. P1. $7.50

DICKINSON, Peter. *Sleep & His Brother*. 1971. Harper Row. 1st ed. G. P1. $5.00

DICKINSON, Peter. *Weathermonger*. 1974. DAW Books. 1st ed. VG. C1. $3.00

DICKINSON, Susan. *Drugged Cornet*. nd. Book Club. dj. VG. P1. $4.50

DICKS, Terrace. *Dr Who: Arc of Infinity*. 1983. Target. 1st UK ed. wrp. EX. F5. $7.50

DICKS, Terrance. *Dr Who: Wheel in Space*. 1988. Allen. EX. P1. $14.00

DICKSON, A.J. *Covered Wagon Days*. 1929. Arthur Clark. VG. $125.00

DICKSON, Carter. *Cavalier's Cup*. nd. Book Club. dj. VG. P1. $4.50

DICKSON, Carter. *Graveyard To Let*. nd. Book Club. dj. VG. P1. $5.00

DICKSON, Carter. *My Late Wives*. 1946. Morrow. P1. $20.00

DICKSON, Carter. *Skeleton in the Clock*. nd. Book Club. VG. P1. $5.00

DICKSON, Carter. *Wht Priory Murders*. 1944. Books Inc. 1st ed. VG. $15.00

DICKSON, G.R. *Alien Art*. 1973. Dutton. 1st ed. dj. EX. R3. $10.00

DICKSON, G.R. *Final Encyclopedia*. 1980. Tor Books. 1st ed. EX. R3. $25.00

DICKSON, G.R. *In Iron Years*. 1980. Doubleday. 1st ed. dj. EX. R3. $10.00

DICKSON, G.R. *R Master*. 1973. Lippincott. 1st ed. sgn. dj. VG. R3. $20.00

DICKSON, G.R. *Storm*. 1977. St Martin. 1st ed. dj. EX. R3. $25.00

DICKSON, G.R. *Tactics of Mistake*. 1971. Doubleday. 1st ed. dj. VG. R3. $50.00

DICKSON, G.R. *3 to Dorsai!* 1975. Doubleday. 1st HrdCvr Compilation ed. inscr. dj. EX. F5. $20.00

DICKSON, Harris. *Old-Fashioned Senator: Story/Biography of John S Williams*. 1925. NY. 1st ed. dj. EX. $40.00

DIDION, Joan. *Democracy*. 1984. Simon Schuster. UP. wrp. EX. K2. $35.00

DIDION, Joan. *Play It As It Lays*. 1970. Farrar Straus Giroux. 1st ed. inscr. dj. EX. H3. $150.00

DIDION, Joan. *Run River*. 1963. Ivan Obolensky. 1st ed. dj. EX. H3. $200.00

DIDION, Joan. *Salvador*. 1983. Simon Schuster. 1st ed. inscr. EX. H3. $75.00

DIDION, Joan. *Salvador*. 1983. Simon Schuster. 1st ed. 4to. 108 p. dj. F2. $15.00

DIDION, Joan. *Telling Stories*. 1978. Berkeley, CA. Friends Bancroft Lib. Keepsake ed. wrp. EX. K2. $50.00

DIDION, Joan. *Wht Album*. 1979. Simon Schuster. 1st ed. presentation. dj. EX. H3. $75.00

DIEHL, Richard. *Tula: Toltec Capital of Ancient Mexico*. 1983. Thames Hudson. 1st Am ed. 4to. dj. F2. $30.00

DIEHL, William. *Hooligans*. 1984. Villard. 1st ed. dj. EX. P1. $20.00

DIETRICH & JARROW. *Trade Show Handbook*. 1976. Magic Inc. 2nd print. 48 p. NM. J3. $4.00

DIETSCH, Ludwig. *Knaus*. 1896. Bielefeld. Velhagen Klasing. 76 p. TEG. D4. $20.00

DIGBY, Adrian. *Maya Jades*. 1978. British Mus. Ils. dj. F2. $15.00

DIGBY, J.B. *Bowden Has a Centennial*. 1954. Bowden, GA. Ils. inscr. 55 p. VG. T5. $17.50

DIGGES, Jeremiah. *Cape Cod Pilot*. 1937. Provincetown/NY. 2nd print. dj. VG. T5. $35.00

DIKTY, T.E. *Best SF Stories & Novels 1956*. nd. Book Club. dj. VG. P1. $6.00

DIKTY, T.E. *Great SF Stories About the Moon*. 1967. Frederick Fell. 1st ed. dj. VG. P1. $17.50

DILL & GARNETT. *Ideal Book*. 1931. Ltd Ed Club. 1/500. EX. C1. $16.50

DILLARD, Anne. *Teaching a Stone To Talk*. 1982. Harper Row. UP. wrp. EX. K2. $45.00

DILLARD, Annie. *Pilgrim at Tinker Creek*. 1974. Harper. tall 8vo. dj. B10. $5.50

DILLARD, Annie. *Weasel*. 1981. Claremont. Rara Avis. 1st ed. 1/190. sgn. wrp/dj. scarce. B13. $125.00

DILLARD, J.M. *Lost Years*. 1989. Pocket. dj. VG. P1. $17.95

DILLIARD, M.E. *Old Dutch Houses of Brooklyn*. 1945. NY. Ils. dj. VG. C2. $45.00

DIMAGGIO, Joe. *Baseball for Everyone*. 1948. Grosset Dunlap. Ils. 109 p. VG. $50.00

DIMAGGIO, Joe. *Lucky To Be a Yankee*. 1956. NY. 1st ed. sgn. 210 p. VG. T5. $125.00

DIMAND, M.S. *Handbook of Mohammedan Decorative Arts*. 1930. MOMA. Ltd 1st ed. 1/2000. 8vo. printed wrp. VG. T1. $50.00

DIMENT, Adam. *Dolly Dolly Spy*. 1967. Dutton. dj. EX. P1. $15.00

DIMNET, Ernest. *My Old World*. 1935. Simon Schuster. Book Club ed? 280 p. dj. VG. B10. $4.50

DIMONA, Joseph. *To the Eagle's Nest*. 1980. Morrow. 1st ed. dj. VG. P1. $15.00

DINES, Michael. *Operation Kill or Be Killed*. 1969. Robert Hale. 1st ed. dj. xl. P1. $5.00

DINESEN, Isak. *Out of Africa*. 1938. NY. Stated 1st ed. dj. VG. J2. $30.00

DINESEN, Isak. *Out of Africa*. 1938. NY. 1st ed. dj. B3. $32.50

DINNEEN, J.P. *Anatomy of a Crime*. 1954. Scribner. 1st ed. xl. P1. $5.00

DIPRIMA, Diane. *Memoirs of a Beatnik*. 1969. Traveler's Companion Series. 1st ed. wrp. B13. $50.00

DIRKS, Raymon. *Great Wall Street Scandal*. 1974. NY. 1st ed. dj. EX. T1. $22.00

DISCH, T.B. *Bad Moon Rising*. 1973. Harper. 1st ed. dj. EX. R3. $15.00

DISCH, T.B. *New Improved Sun*. 1975. Harper. 1st ed. dj. EX. R3. $20.00

DISCH, T.B. *Wht Fang Goes Dingo & Other Funny SF Stories*. 1971. London. 1st/PB Orig ed. sgn. wrp. EX. scarce. T9. $40.00

DISCH, T.M. *On Wings of Song*. 1979. St Martin. dj. EX. P1. $20.00

DISCH, T.M. *On Wings of Song*. 1979. St Martin. 1st ed. inscr. EX. K2. $45.00

DISCH, T.M. *Ringtime*. 1983. Toothpaste. Ils Mikolowski. 1st ed. 1/975. EX. K2. $30.00

DISNEY, D.M. *Hangman's Tree*. 1949. Random House. 1st ed. dj. VG. P1. $10.00

DISNEY, D.M. *Last Straw*. 1954. Crime Club. 1st ed. dj. VG. P1. $25.00

DISNEY, D.M. *Mrs Meeker's Money*. nd. Book Club. dj. xl. P1. $4.00

DISNEY, D.M. *Shadow of a Man.* 1965. Crime Club. 1st ed. dj. VG. P1. $20.00

DISNEY, D.M. *Who Rides a Tiger.* nd. Collier. VG. P1. $10.00

DISNEY, D.M. *3's a Crowd.* 1971. Crime Club. 1st ed. dj. P1. $20.00

DISNEY STUDIOS. *Donald Duck: Prize Driver.* 1956. Simon Schuster. 1st ed. sm 8vo. VG. $12.00

DISNEY STUDIOS. *Stories From Walt Disney's Fantasia.* 1940. Random House. 1st ed. 4to. dj. EX. K1. $200.00

DISNEY STUDIOS. *Sword in the Stone.* 1987. NY. Smith. dj. NM. C1. $11.00

DISSELHOFF & LINNE. *Art of Ancient Am.* 1960. Crown. 1st ed. 274 p. F2. $25.00

DISSELHOFF & LINNE. *Art of Ancient Am.* 1966. NY. Greystone. Revised ed. 270 p. dj. F2. $20.00

DISTANT, W.L. *Naturalist in Transvaal.* 1892. London. Porter. Ils. pls. EX. $150.00

DITMARS, Raymond. *Thrills of a Naturalist's Quest.* 1935. Macmillan. 1st ed. 268 p. VG. B10. $5.00

DIVINE, David. *Atom at Spithead.* 1953. Macmillan. 1st ed. xl. P1. $7.00

DIVOIRE, Fernand. *Decouvertes sur la Danse.* 1924. Paris. Les Ed G Cres et Cie. 1st ed. 1/1130. wrp. EX. H3. $150.00

DIXON, F.W. *S of the Rio Grande.* nd. Grosset Dunlap. VG. P1. $7.50

DIXON, Franklin. *Through the Air to AK.* c 1930. Grosset Dunlap. red bdg. VG. C1. $12.50

DIXON, Peter. *Bobby Benson & the Lost Herd.* 1936. Hecker. 1st ed. VG. B10. $13.00

DIXON, Roger. *Noah II.* 1975. Harwood Smart. dj. EX. P1. $15.00

DIXON, Stephen. *Work.* 1977. NY. 1st ed. sgn. wrp. EX. T9. $25.00

DIXON, Thomas. *Clansman.* 1905? Grosset Dunlap. Photoplay ed. dj. P4. $40.00

DIXON, Thomas. *Clansman.* 1905. NY. 1st ed. clr dj. B3. $20.00

DIXON, Thomas. *Fall of a Nation.* 1916. Donohue. dj. VG. R3. $35.00

DIXON, Thomas. *Sun Virgin.* 1929. Liveright. 1st ed. VG. R3. $25.00

DIXON, William. *Portfolio of Edgar Rice Burroughs' Drawings.* 1971. Train. 1st ed. sgn. VG. R3. $20.00

DIXON, Zellabelen. *Concerning Bookplates.* 1903. Chicago. Author ed. inscr. 12mo. EX. A4. $40.00

DOANE, Gustavus. *Battle Drums & Geysers.* 1970. Swallow. 1st ed. dj. VG. $35.00

DOANE, Michael. *6 Miles to Roadside Business.* 1990. Knopf. UP. EX. K2. $20.00

DOBBINS, P.H. *Fatal Finale.* 1949. Phoenix. dj. VG. P1. $10.00

DOBBS, C.R. *Freedom's Will: Society of Separatists of Zoar...* 1947. NY. sgn. 104 p. T5. $45.00

DOBIE, J.F. *Apache Gold & Yaqui Slvr.* 1939. Little Brn. Sierra Madre ed. 1/265. sgns. w/5 Ils Lea. H3. $1250.00

DOBIE, J.F. *Ben Lilly Legend.* 1950. Boston. 1st ed. dj. VG. B3. $30.00

DOBIE, J.F. *Coronado's Children.* 1931. Literary Guild. Ils Mead. orange bdg. VG. $16.00

DOBIE, J.F. *Tales of the Mustang.* 1936. TX Book Club. Ltd ed. 1/300. inscr. VG. $500.00

DOBIE, J.F. *Texan in Eng.* 1944. Little Brn. 14th print. inscr. gray bdg. dj. H3. $125.00

DOBIE, J.F. *Texan in Eng.* 1945. Boston. Little Brn. 1st ed. dj. VG. $22.50

DOBIE, J.F. *Texan in Eng.* 1945. NY. 1st ed. dj. VG. B3. $25.00

DOBIE, J.F. *Tongues of the Monte: The Mexico I Like.* 1948. London. 1st ed. VG. B2. $50.00

DOBIE, J.F. *Vaquero of the Brush Country.* 1929. SW Pr. 1st ed. VG. scarce. B2. $350.00

DOBREE, Bonamy. *William Penn, Quaker & Pioneer.* 1932. Houghton Mifflin. 1st print. 8vo. 346 p. xl. V1. $12.50

DOBSON, Austin. *At the Sgn of the Lyre.* 1885. Author ed. VG. $12.00

DOBSON, Austin. *At the Sgn of the Lyre.* 1886. London. not 1st ed. VG. C1. $3.00

DOBSON, C.C. *Did Our Lord Visit Britain...in Cornwall & Somerset?* 1967. 48 p. SftCvr. VG. C1. $4.50

DOBYNS, Henry. *Analisis Situacion Comunidades Indigenas Ambiente Nactional.* 1962. Lima, Peru. Eng/Spanish text. 16 p. wrp. F2. $10.00

DOBYNS, Stephen. *Man of Little Evils.* 1973. Atheneum. 1st ed. sgn. dj. EX. T9. $55.00

DOBYNS, Stephen. *Saratoga Headhunter.* 1985. Viking. 1st ed. sgn. dj. EX. B13. $60.00

DOBYNS, Stephen. *Saratoga Longshot.* 1976. Atheneum. 1st ed. sgn. dj. EX. T9. $45.00

DOBYNS, Stephen. *Saratoga Snapper.* 1986. Viking. 1st ed. dj. EX. P1. $15.95

DOBYNS, Stephen. *2 Deaths of Senora Puccini.* 1988. Viking. 1st ed. sgn. dj. EX. B13. $45.00

DOBYNS, Winifred. *CA Gardens.* 1931. NY. 1st ed. 4to. VG. G1. $22.00

DOBYNS & EULER. *Ghost Dance of 1889: Among Pai Indians of NW AZ.* 1967. Prescott, AZ. 1st ed. octavo. 67 p. dj. EX. H3. $45.00

DOCKERY & WYATT. *Minor Arthurian Poetry of the 19th Century.* 1989. Gr Chapel Pr. Ils Dockery. sgns. C1. $17.50

DOCKSTADER, Frederick. *Indian Art of Am.* 1973. Mus Am Indian. 1st ed. 304 p. F2. $15.00

DOCTOROW, E.L. *Lives of the Poets.* 1984. Random House. 1st ed. sgn. dj. EX. C4. $40.00

DOCTOROW, E.L. *Loon Lake.* 1980. NY. 1st ed. dj. EX. T1. $22.00

DOCTOROW, E.L. *Welcome to Hard Times.* 1960. Simon Schuster. 1st ed. dj. EX. B13. $375.00

DODD, D.O. *Letters of David O Dodd With a Biographical Sketch.* 1917. np. 1st ed. orig wrp. $95.00

DODGE, David. *Death & Taxes.* 1941. Macmillan. 1st ed. dj. VG. P1. $11.50

DODGE, David. *Lights of Skaro.* 1954. Random House. 1st ed. dj. xl. P1. $7.50

DODGE, David. *Plunder of the Sun.* 1950. Michael Joseph. dj. G. P1. $10.00

DODGE, G.M. *Battle of Atlanta.* 1910. Council Bluffs, IA. 1st ed. VG. C2. $45.00

DODGE, G.M. *Personal Recollections of Lincoln, Grant, & Sherman.* 1914. Council Bluffs, IA. Ils. G. T5. $35.00

DODGE, G.M. *Personal Recollections of President Abraham Lincoln...* 1914. Council Bluffs, IA. 1st ed. VG. $40.00

DODGE, H.H. *Mt Vernon: Its Owner & Its Story.* 1932. Phil. 1st ed. dj. EX. $15.00

DODGE, R.I. *Our Wild Indians.* 1883. Hartford. 653 p. A5. $65.00

DODGE, R.I. *Plains of the Great W & Their Inhabitants.* 1877. Putnam. 448 p. A5. $80.00

DODGE, R.J. *Isolated Splendor.* 1975. Hicksville, NY. 1st ed. 166 p. dj. VG. B3. $22.50

DODGE, T.A. *Alexander.* 1890. Boston. 2 vols. TEG. xl. T5. $125.00

DODGSON, C.L. *Curiosa Mathematica Part 2: Pillow Problems.* 1893. London. Macmillan. 1st ed. presentation. inscr. orig bdg. H3. $8000.00

DODGSON, Campbell. *Etchings of Charles Meryon.* 1921. London. Studio Ltd. lg quarto. pls. EX. $175.00

DODINGTON, George. *Diary of the Late George Bubb Dodington.* 1784. London. Wyndham. 1st ed. Lib bdg. VG. $45.00

DODSLEY, Robert. *Select Collection of Old Plays.* 1780. London. Dodsley. 12 vols. sm octavo. H3. $425.00

DODSON, Goodlette. *Exhibition Card Fans.* 1963. Haines House of Cards. 2nd print. 50 p. SftCvr. EX. J3. $20.00

DODSON, Owen. *Boy at the Window.* 1977. Popular Lib. reissue. inscr. wrp. EX. B13. $45.00

DODSON, Owen. *Come Home Early, Child.* 1977. Popular Lib. 1st ed. inscr. wrp. w/sgn post card. B13. $75.00

DOERFLINGER, William. *Magic Catalog.* 1977. Sunrise Book. 1st ed. 242 p. dj. NM. J3. $10.00

DOERR, Harriet. *Stones for Ibarra.* 1984. Viking. 1st ed. sgn. dj. EX. scarce. B13. $125.00

DOGGETT, Carita. *Dr Andrew Turnbull & the New Smyrna Colony of FL.* 1919. np. 1st ed. EX. $45.00

DOHERTY, Brian. *Father Malachy's Miracle.* 1938. Random House. 1st ed. dj. EX. H3. $75.00

DOIG, Ivan. *Dancing at the Rascal Fair.* 1987. Atheneum. ARC. printed wrp. EX. K2. $30.00

DOIG, Ivan. *Dancing at the Rascal Fair.* 1987. Atheneum. 1st ed. sgn. dj. EX. K2. $45.00

DOIG, Ivan. *Eng Creek.* 1984. Atheneum. 1st ed. sgn. dj. EX. K2. $40.00

DOIG, Ivan. *Sea Runners.* 1982. Atheneum. UP. wrp. EX. K2. $40.00

DOIG, Ivan. *Winter Brothers.* 1980. Harcourt Brace. ARC. dj. RS. w/photo laid in. EX. K2. $40.00

DOIG, Ivan. *Winter Brothers.* 1980. Harcourt Brace. UP. wrp. EX. B13. $125.00

DOLAN, E.F. *Let's Make Magic.* 1981. Doubleday. 1st ed. 96 p. dj. NM. J3. $7.00

DOLGE, Alfred. *Pianos & Their Makers.* 1911. Covina Pub. 1st ed. octavo. 478 p. EX. H3. $200.00

DOLINGER, Jane. *Gypsies of the Pampas.* 1958. Fleet Pub. 1st ed. 179 p. dj. F2. $20.00

DOLINGER, Jane. *Inca Gold.* 1968. Chicago. Henry Regnery. 1st Am ed. 189 p. dj. F2. $15.00

DOLLAR & WHEATLEY. *Handbook of Horseshoeing.* 1898. NY. 1st ed. 438 p. G. T5. $75.00

DOLMETSCH, Mabel. *Dances of Eng & France From 1450-1600.* 1949. Routledge/Kegan Paul. 1st ed. octavo. 163 p. VG. H3. $50.00

DOLMETSCH, Mabel. *Dances of Spain & Italy From 1400-1600.* 1954. Routledge/Kegan Paul. 1st ed. octavo. 174 p. G. H3. $50.00

DOLPH, E.A. *Sound Off: Soldier Songs From Yankee Doodle to Parley Voo.* 1929. NY. Ils Lawrence Schick. 4to. A4. $50.00

DOMBROWSKI, Baroness Katrina. *Fat Camel of Bagdad: New Tale of Abdallah's Adventures.* 1929. Macmillan. 1st ed. 156 p. dj. VG. $45.00

DOMBROWSKI, John. *Area Handbook for Guatemala.* 1970. GPO. 1st ed. 361 p. xl. F2. $10.00

DOMINIAN, Helen. *Apostle of Brazil: Biography of Padre Jose de Anchieta.* 1958. NY. Exposition Pr. 1st ed. 346 p. dj. F2. $20.00

DOMINIC, R.B. *Epitaph for a Lobbyist.* nd. Book Club. dj. VG. P1. $4.50

DOMMETT, W.E. *Aeroplanes & Airships.* 1919. London. Ils. 76 p. T5. $85.00

DONALD, David. *Inside Lincoln's Cabinet: Civil War Diaries of SP Chase.* 1954. Longman Gr. 342 p. dj. G. S1. $11.00

DONALD, David. *Lincoln's Herndon.* 1948. Knopf. 373 p. G. S1. $12.50

DONALDSON, S.R. *Daughter of Regals & Other Tales.* 1984. Del Rey. dj. xl. P1. $7.50

DONALDSON, S.R. *Daughter of Regals.* 1984. Del Rey. 1st ed. dj. EX. P1/R3. $15.00

DONALDSON, S.R. *Mirror of Her.* 1986. Del Rey. UP. 1st ed. wrp. EX. R3. $30.00

DONALDSON, S.R. *Wht Gold Wielder.* 1983. Ballantine. UP. wrp. EX. B13. $65.00

DONALDSON, S.R. *Wht Gold Wielder.* 1983. Del Rey. 1st ed. dj. EX. R3. $15.00

DONALDSON, S.R. *1 Tree.* 1982. Del Rey. 1st ed. dj. VG. P1. $15.00

DONAVAN, John. *Case of the Violet Smoke.* 1940. Mystery House. VG. P1. $20.00

DONCASTER, Phebe. *John Stephenson Rowntree: His Life & Work.* 1908. London. Headley. 8vo. 446 p. G. V1. $20.00

DONLEAVY, J.P. *Ginger Man.* 1961. Random House. 1st print. dj. RS. H3. $75.00

DONLEAVY, J.P. *Ginger Man.* 1965. Greenleaf Classics. 1st pb ed. EX. B4. $20.00

DONLEAVY, J.P. *Ginger Man.* 1966. Delacorte. 2nd ed. 347 p. dj. VG. B10. $4.50

DONLEAVY, J.P. *Ginger Man: A Play.* 1961. Random House. 1st print. dj. RS. EX. H3. $75.00

DONNAN, Christopher. *Moche Art of Peru.* 1979. UCLA. Ils. wrp. F2. $25.00

DONNAN, Christopher. *Pacatnamu Papers Vol 1.* 1986. UCLA. 1st ed. 188 p. F2. $35.00

DONNE, John. *Letters to Several Persons of Honor.* 1651. London. 1st ed. 318 p. rare. $595.00

DONNE, John. *Poems of John Donne.* 1968. Ltd Ed Club. Ils/sgn Imre Reiner. slipcase. EX. C4. $100.00

DONNEL, C.P. *Murder-Go-Round.* 1945. McKay. VG. P1. $10.00

DONNELLY, Elizabeth. *Army of Heroes.* 1944. Moscow. 1st ed. 171 p. VG. T5. $45.00

DONNELLY, Ignatius. *Atlantis: The Antediluvian World.* nd. NY. Gramercy. reprint of 1882 ed. 355 p. dj. F2. $10.00

DONNELLY, Ignatius. *Caesar's Column.* nd. Caspar. VG. R3. $15.00

DONNELLY, J.P. *Jacques Marquette, 1637-1675.* 1968. Chicago. 1st ed. 395 p. dj. VG. T5. $19.50

DONNELLY, R.W. *Confederate States' Marine Corps.* 1989. Wht Mane. Ils. 337 p. dj. M. S1. $24.95

DONOHUE, H.E.F. *Conversations With Nelson Algren.* 1964. Hill Wang. 1st ed. sgn McMurtry. dj. EX. H3. $125.00

DONOSO, Jose. *Charleston.* 1977. Godine. Ltd ed. 1/200. sgn. slipcase. EX. B13/K2. $85.00

DONOSO, Jose. *Charleston.* 1977. Godine. 1st Trade ed. dj. EX. K2. $35.00

DONOSO, Jose. *Sacred Families.* 1978. London. Gollancz. 1st ed. dj. EX. B13. $85.00

DOODY, M.J. *B Company 309th Engineers.* c 1919. Indianapolis. 1st ed. oblong 4to. T5. $27.50

DOOLEY, Dixie. *Mr Dixie Dooley Presents...Las Vegas Jokes.* 1988. Las Vegas. Dooley. SftCvr. M. J3. $3.50

DOOLEY, Mrs. J.H. *Dem Good Ole Times.* 1906. Doubleday Page. Ils Gutherz. 1st ed. 4to. 150 p. VG. $25.00

DOOLEY & ENGLE. *Superman at 50.* 1987. Octavia. 1st ed. M. R3. $16.95

DORAN, John. *Their Majesties' Servants.* 1890. McKay. 2 vols. TEG. VG. H3. $85.00

DORE, Gustave. *Bible in Pictures.* 1937. Wise. 444 p. fair. B10. $5.00

DORFLES, Gillo. *Kitsch: World of Bad Taste.* 1970. NY. dj. VG. $25.00

DORIVAL, Bernard. *Cezanne.* c 1948. Boston. 1st ed? 4to. dj. VG. G1. $50.00

DORMON, C. *Flowers Native to the Deep S.* 1958. Harrisburg. 1st ed. 23 clr pls. dj. VG. $35.00

DORN, Edward. *N Atlantic Turbine.* 1967. London. Fulcrum Pr. 1st ed. dj. EX. C4. $30.00

DORNER, H.B. *Window Gardening.* 1908. Bobbs Merrill. 1st ed. VG. C1. $17.50

DORNFIELD, W.C. *Dorny on Trix.* 1954. Chicago. 40 p. EX. J3. $2.00

DORNFIELD, W.C. *Trix & Chatter.* 1921. Felsman. 286 p. VG. J3. $17.00

DORRINGTON, Albert. *Radium Terrors.* 1912. Doubleday. 1st ed. VG. R3. $25.00

DORRIS, Michael. *Broken Cord.* 1989. Harper Row. 1st ed. sgn. dj. EX. K2. $50.00

DORRIS & DORRIS. *Glimpses of Hist Madison Co, KY.* 1955. Nashville, TN. 1st ed. sgns. 334 p. dj. VG. T5. $35.00

DORRIS & ERDRICH. *Crown of Columbus.* 1991. Harper Collins. ARC. wrp. EX. K2. $50.00

DORSET, C.A. *Think Before You Speak; or, 3 Wishes.* 1810. Phil. 16mo. 32 p. wrp. EX. $135.00

DORTU, M.G. *Toulouse-Lautrec et Con Oeuvre.* 1971. NY. 1st ed. 1/450. 6 vols. EX. $625.00

DOS PASSOS, John. *Panama; or, The Adventures of My 7 Uncles.* 1931. Harper. Trans/Ils Dos Passos. 1/300. sgns. slipcase. H3. $200.00

DOS PASSOS, John. *USA, the 42nd Parallel/Big Money/1919.* 1946. Houghton Mifflin. Ils Marsh. 1/365. sgns. 3 vols. TEG. slipcase. H3. $500.00

DOS PASSOS, John. *Villages Are the Heart of Spain.* 1937. Esquire Coronet. Ltd ed. 1/1200. sgn. H3. $150.00

DOS PASSOS, John. *3 Soldiers.* 1921. NY. Doran. 1st ed. 1st state. presentation. dj. slipcase/chemise. K2. $1250.00

DOSTOEVSKY, F. *Brothers Karamazov.* 1949. Heritage. Ils Fritz Eichenberg. slipcase. NM. T1. $20.00

DOSTOEVSKY, F. *House of the Dead.* 1982. Ltd Ed Club. Ils/sgn Fritz Eichenberg. slipcase. VG. $75.00

DOSTOEVSKY, F. *Idiot.* 1956. Ltd Ed Club. Ils/sgn Fritz Eichenberg. rebound. slipcase. EX. $35.00

DOSTOEVSKY, F. *Raw Youth.* 1974. Ltd Ed Club. Ils/sgn Fritz Eichenberg. 2 vols. slipcase. VG. $80.00

DOUGHTY, C.M. *Arabia Deserta.* 1923. Boni Liveright. 2 vols. VG. $75.00

DOUGHTY, C.M. *Travels in Arabia Deserta.* 1953. Ltd Ed Club. Ils Edy LeGrand. EX. C4. $100.00

DOUGLAS, A.M. *Kathie's Soldiers.* nd. (1899) Lathrop. 1st ed. VG. B10. $4.25

DOUGLAS, Bert. *Masonic Magic.* nd. Invisible Lodge. 2nd print. SftCvr. NM. J3. $4.00

DOUGLAS, C.N. *Heir of Rengarth.* 1988. Tor Books. 1st ed. dj. EX. P1. $17.95

DOUGLAS, C.N. *Keepers of Edanvant.* 1987. Tor Books. 1st ed. dj. EX. F5. $15.00

DOUGLAS, George. *House With the Gr Shutters.* 1901. London. MacQueen. presentation. gr bdg. slipcase. H3. $150.00

DOUGLAS, H.K. *I Rode With Stonewall.* 1940. Chapel Hill. VG. A6. $30.00

DOUGLAS, H.K. *I Rode With Stonewall.* 1968. Chapel Hill. 401 p. dj. M. S1. $19.95

DOUGLAS, Norman. *DH Lawrence & Maurice Magnus.* 1925. private print. orig wrp. VG. H3. $75.00

DOUGLAS, Norman. *Paneros.* c 1931. Florence. private print/Orioli. 1/250. sgn dj. H3. $200.00

DOUGLAS, Norman. *S Wind.* 1922. London. Secker. 1/125. sgn. gilt blk bdg. H3. $125.00

DOUGLAS, Norman. *S Wind.* 1928. NY. Ils Valenti Angelo. 1/250. boxed. EX. $125.00

DOUGLAS, Norman. *S Wind.* 1929. Chicago. Argus Books. Ils John Austen. 1st ed. 2 vols. EX. $75.00

DOUGLAS, Norman. *S Wind.* 1939. Heritage. Ils Petrina. slipcase. T1. $20.00

DOUGLAS, Norman. *Some Limericks.* 1967. Grove Pr. 1st ed. EX. P1. $7.00

DOUGLAS, W.O. *Justice Douglas Appeals for Rebirth of Freedom.* 1952. Phil. 12mo. 8 p. pamphlet. V1. $4.50

DOUGLASS, Frederick. *Life & Times of Frederick Douglass.* 1962. Bonanza. 640 p. dj. EX. S1. $6.00

DOVER, Robert. *Andean Music.* 1987. Bloomington. 4to. 75 p. wrp. F2. $15.00

DOW, A.B. *Reflections.* 1970. Midland. 1st ed. 192 p. dj. VG. B3. $50.00

DOW, Charles. *Anthology & Bibliography of Niagara Falls.* 1921. Lyon. 1 vol only. 689 p. VG. B10. $6.25

DOW, G.F. *Slave Ships & Slaving.* 1927. Salem, MA. 1st ed. EX. $85.00

DOW, G.F. *Slave Ships & Slaving.* 1968. Maritime Pr. 386 p. dj. VG. $21.00

DOWD & SPENDER. *Serious Business.* 1937. Scribner. Latin Am ed. dj. EX. $30.00

DOWDEY, Clifford. *Death of a Nation: Story of Lee & His Men at Gettysburg.* 1958. Knopf. 383 p. dj. G. S1. $10.00

DOWDEY, Clifford. *Lee's Last Campaign.* 1960. Bonanza. 416 p. dj. VG. S1. $22.50

DOWDEY, Clifford. *Wartime Papers of Robert E Lee.* 1961. Bramhall House. 994 p. dj. EX. S1. $10.00

DOWNES, R.C. *Hist of Lake Shore, OH.* 1952. NY. Ils 1st ed. 3 vols. T5. $95.00

DOWNEY, Fairfax. *Burton: Arabian Nights Adventurer.* 1938. Modern Age. VG. P1. $20.00

DOWNEY, Fairfax. *7th's Staghound.* 1948. NY. Ils Paul Brn. 1st ed. 230 p. dj. VG. T5. $17.50

DOWNING, Todd. *Vultures in the Sky.* 1935. Crime Club. 1st ed. VG. P1. $25.00

DOWNS, T.N. *Art of Magic.* 1921. Felsman. 2nd ed. 354 p. EX. J3. $50.00

DOWNS, T.N. *Modern Coin Manipulation.* 1900. Routledge. 1st Am ed. 178 p. EX. J3. $75.00

DOWSON, E.C. *Poetical Works.* 1934. London. 1st ed. AEG. Sangorski/Sutcliffe bdg. EX. $200.00

DOWSON, Ernest. *Pierrot of the Minute.* 1923. Grolier. 1st ed. 1/300. slipcase. EX. H3. $175.00

DOYLE, A.C. *Adventures of Sherlock Holmes.* 1892. London. 1st ed. Zaehnsdorf bdg. EX. H3. $1000.00

DOYLE, A.C. *Boys' Sherlock Holmes.* 1936. Harper. VG. P1. $20.00

DOYLE, A.C. *British Campaign in France & Flanders 1914-1918.* 1916-1920. Doran. 1st Am ed. 6 vols. octavo. VG. H3. $275.00

DOYLE, A.C. *Casebook of Sherlock Holmes.* 1927. Doran. 1st ed. dj. VG. F5. $35.00

DOYLE, A.C. *Casebook of Sherlock Holmes.* 1952. Murray. 16th print. dj. VG. P1. $25.00

DOYLE, A.C. *Complete Napoleonic Stories.* 1956. Murray. dj. VG. P1. $25.00

DOYLE, A.C. *Crowborough Ed of the Works of Doyle.* 1930. Doubleday Doran. 1/760. sgn. 24 vols. lg octavo. H3. $3000.00

DOYLE, A.C. *Desert Drama.* 1898. Lippincott. 1st Am ed. 277 p. fair. B10. $10.00

DOYLE, A.C. *Desert Drama.* 1898. Phil. 1st Am ed. VG. $75.00

DOYLE, A.C. *Duet.* 1899. NY. 1st Am ed. 1st issue. EX. $75.00

DOYLE, A.C. *Great Keinplatz Experiment.* nd. Rand McNally. VG. P1. $25.00

DOYLE, A.C. *Heaven Has Claws.* 1953. Random House. 1st ed. dj. VG. P1. $15.00

DOYLE, A.C. *His Last Bow.* nd. AL Burt. VG. P1. $7.50

DOYLE, A.C. *His Last Bow.* 1917. Murray. 2nd ed. VG. P1. $20.00

DOYLE, A.C. *Hound of the Baskervilles.* 1902. London. 1st ed. orig bdg. VG. H3. $1000.00

DOYLE, A.C. *Hound of the Baskervilles.* 1902. McClure Phillips. 1st Am ed. VG. P1. $100.00

DOYLE, A.C. *Ils Sherlock Holmes Treasury.* nd. Avenel. EX. P1. $10.00

DOYLE, A.C. *Last Galley.* 1911. Garden City. 1st Am ed. VG. C1. $19.00

DOYLE, A.C. *Memoirs of Sherlock Holmes.* 1894. NY. 1st Am ed. 1st issue. G. J2. $75.00

DOYLE, A.C. *Micah Clarke.* nd. Donohue. decor brd. VG. P1. $10.00

DOYLE, A.C. *Micah Clarke.* nd. Mershon. VG. P1. $20.00

DOYLE, A.C. *Refugees.* 1903. Harper. decor brd. P1. $17.50

DOYLE, A.C. *Rodney Stone.* nd. Nash Grayson. VG. P1. $15.00

DOYLE, A.C. *Sherlock Holmes' Long Stories.* 1954. Murray. 9th print. VG. P1. $15.00

DOYLE, A.C. *Sign of the 4 & Other Stories.* nd. Collier. VG. P1. $15.00

DOYLE, A.C. *Sir Nigel.* 1906. McClure Phillips. 1st ed. pictorial bdg. VG. F5. $20.00

DOYLE, A.C. *Study in Scarlet & Other Stories.* nd. Collier. VG. P1. $15.00

DOYLE, A.C. *Study in Scarlet Murder Mystery.* 1985. Peerage Books. EX. P1. $20.00

DOYLE, A.C. *Study in Scarlet.* 1918. Ward Lock. decor brd. VG. P1. $25.00

DOYLE, A.C. *Tales of Love & Hate.* 1960. Murray. 1st ed. P1. $10.00

DOYLE, A.C. *Treasury of Sherlock Holmes.* nd. Hanover House. P1. $10.00

DOYLE, A.C. *Valley of Fear.* 1965. John Murray. 14th print. dj. EX. P1. $20.00

DOYLE, A.C. *Wht Co & Beyond the City.* nd. Collier. VG. P1. $10.00

DOYLE, A.C. *Wht Co.* nd. Grosset Dunlap. VG. P1. $10.00

DOYLE, A.C. *Wht Co.* 1895. London. Smith Elder. 15th ed. presentation. H3. $600.00

DOYLE, A.C. *Wht Co.* 1939. Murray. 65th print. P1. $15.00

DOYLE, A.C. *Wht Co.* 1945. Musson. VG. P1. $10.00

DOYLE, A.C. *Works.* 1930. Crowborough ed. 1/760. sgn. 23 of 24 vols. P4. $600.00

DOYLE, J.E. *Chronicle of Eng BC 44-AD 1485.* 1864. London. Ils Edmund Evans. AEG. gilt red bdg. EX. $150.00

DOYLE, Kirby. *Happiness Bastard.* 1968. Essex House. B4. $5.00

DOYLE, W.B. *Centennial Hist of Summit Co & Representative Citizens.* 1908. Chicago. 1st ed. 1115 p. T5. $85.00

DOZER & HOPLEY. *Bucyrus As It Is.* 1899. Bucyrus. Ils 50 p. G. T5. $65.00

DOZOIS, Gardner. *Devil's Church.* 1951. Rinehart. dj. VG. P1. $30.00

DOZOIS, Gardner. *Strangers.* 1978. Berkley Putnam. 1st ed. dj. xl. P1. $7.50

DOZOIS, Gardner. *Year's Best SF. 3rd Annual.* 1986. Book Club. 626 p. dj. NM. B10. $4.25

DRAKE, David. *Dragon Lord.* 1979. 1st Am ed. dj. EX. C1. $21.50

DRAKE, Earl. *Regina: The Queen City.* 1955. McClelland Stewart. 1st ed. dj. VG. $20.00

DRANNON, W.F. *Chief of Scouts As Pilot to Emigrant & Government Trains...* 1901. Chicago. Ils 407 p. A5. $30.00

DRAPER, Hal. *Berkeley: New Student Revolt.* 1965. Blk Cat. 1st PB ed. VG. B4. $4.00

DRAPER, Muriel. *Music at Midnight.* 1929. Harper. octavo. 237 p. VG. H3. $50.00

DRAYTON, M. *Battle of Agincourt.* 1893. London. Whittingham. 1/50. vellum bdg. VG. $25.00

DREISER, Theodore. *Am Tragedy.* 1925. Boni Liveright. 1st issue after Trade ed. sgn. 2 vols. H3. $225.00

DREISER, Theodore. *Chains.* 1927. Boni Liveright. Ltd ed. 1/440. sgn. H3. $150.00

DREISER, Theodore. *Dawn: Hist of Myself.* 1931. Horace Liveright. Ltd ed. 1/275. sgn. TEG. gilt blk bdg. H3. $200.00

DREISER, Theodore. *Dawn: Hist of Myself.* 1931. Horace Liveright. 1st Trade ed. inscr Helen Dreiser. dj. H3. $150.00

DREISER, Theodore. *Epitaph: A Poem.* 1929. Heron Pr. Ils Fawcett. 1/1100. sgns. slipcase. H3. $200.00

DREISER, Theodore. *Gallery of Women.* 1929. Horace Liveright. Ltd ed. 1/560. sgn. 2 vols. H3. $200.00

DREISER, Theodore. *Genius.* 1915. Bodley Head/John Lane. 1st ed. presentation. slipcase. H3. $450.00

DREISER, Theodore. *Hey Rub-A-Dub-Dub.* 1920. Boni Liveright. presentation. H3. $150.00

DREISER, Theodore. *Moods, Cadenced, & Declaimed.* 1926. Boni Liveright. Ltd ed. 1/550. sgn. H3. $150.00

DREISER, Theodore. *Plays of Natural & Supernatural.* 1916. John Lane. 1st ed. 2nd issue. VG. H3. $75.00

DREISER, Theodore. *Sister Carrie.* 1907. NY. Ils 1st ed. VG. J2. $20.00

DREISER, Theodore. *Sister Carrie.* 1939. Ltd Ed Club. Ils/sgn Reginald Marsh. 1/1500. slipcase. C4. $175.00

DREISER & ANDERSON. *Harlan Miners Speak.* 1932. NY. VG. B3. $50.00

DRENNAN, Robert. *Excavations at Quachilco.* 1978. Ann Arbor. 4to. 81 p. wrp. F2. $10.00

DRENNAN, Robert. *Prehistoric... Development in Area of Tehuacan Valley.* 1979. Ann Arbor. 4to. 259 p. wrp. F2. $15.00

DRENNAN, Robert. *Regional Archaelogy in Valle de la Plata, Colombia...* 1985. Ann Arbor. 4to. 195 p. F2. $15.00

DREW, Wayland. *Willow.* 1988. Del Rey. 1st HrdCvr ed. dj. EX. F5. $13.00

DREXLER, Arthur. *Drawings.* 1962. NY. 1st ed. dj. VG. G1. $85.00

DRICKAMER, L.C. *Ft Lyon to Harper's Ferry.* 1987. Wht Mane. 273 p. dj. M. S1. $19.95

DRIGGS, Howard. *Westward Am.* 1942. Putnam. Ils. 312 p. A5. $45.00

DRINKER, Elizabeth. *Extracts From Journal of Elizabeth Drinker From 1759-1807.* 1889. Lippincott. 8vo. 423 p. V1. $45.00

DRINKWATER, John. *Abraham Lincoln.* nd. (1923) Houghton Mifflin. 19th print. dj. B10. $5.00

DRINKWATER, John. *Poet & Communication.* 1923. London. Watts. presentation. 12mo. gilt bl bdg. H3. $100.00

DRINKWATER, John. *Seeds of Time.* 1922. Houghton. 1st ed. 68 p. B10. $12.50

DRINKWATER, John. *Selected Poems.* 1922. London. Sidgwick Jackson. 1st ed. dj. EX. B13. $45.00

DRIVER, Clive. *Art of Claud Lovatt Fraser.* 1971. Phil. Rosenbach. 8vo. wrp. $20.00

DROWN & DROWN. *Mission to the Headhunters.* 1957. Harper. 1st ed. 252 p. dj. F2. $12.50

DRUITT, Robert. *Principles & Practice of Modern Surgery.* 1844. Phil. 8vo. 568 p. VG. G4. $69.00

DRUMMOND, Henry. *Monkey That Would Not Kill.* 1898. Dodd Mead. Ils Wain. 12mo. 115 p. VG. $35.00

DRUMMOND, June. *I Saw Him Die.* 1979. Gollancz. dj. EX. P1. $17.50

DRUMMOND, June. *Saboteurs.* 1969. Holt Rinehart Winston. 1st ed. dj. P1. $17.50

DRUMMOND, W.H. *Habitant & Other French-Canadian Poems.* nd. (1897) Putnam. 137 p. VG. B10. $6.00

DRURY, Allen. *Against the Gods.* 1976. Franklin Lib. gilt brn leather. M. T1. $40.00

DRURY, Allen. *Shade of Difference.* 1962. Doubleday. dj. VG. $7.00

DRYBROUGH, T.B. *Polo.* 1898. London. 1st ed. 8vo. 357 p. VG. $45.00

DRYDEN, John. *Dramatic Works.* 1931-1932. Nonesuch. Ltd ed. 1/800. 6 vols. lg octavo. H3. $1500.00

DRYDEN, John. *Dramatic Works.* 1762. London. Tonson. Ils Gravelot. 6 vols. 12mo. VG. H3. $300.00

DRYDEN, John. *Poetical Works.* 1843. London. Pickering. Aldine ed. 5 vols. sm octavo. EX. H3. $300.00

DU BOIS, Theodora. *Armed With a New Terror.* 1936. Houghton Mifflin. 1st ed. dj. VG. P1. $25.00

DU BOIS, Theodora. *High King's Daughter.* 1965. Ariel. dj. xl. P1. $5.00

DU BOIS, Theodora. *Listener.* 1953. Crime Club. 1st ed. dj. VG. P1. $15.00

DU BOIS, W.E.B. *Blk Reconstruction.* 1935. Harcourt Brace. 1st ed. orange dj. EX. B13. $675.00

DU BOIS, W.E.B. *Dark Princess.* 1928. Harcourt Brace. 1st ed. later print. sgn. rebound. EX. B13. $200.00

DU BOIS, W.E.B. *Dark Water.* 1921. Harcourt Brace. 2nd ed. sgn. EX. B13. $375.00

DU BOIS, W.E.B. *Dusk of Dawn.* 1940. NY. 1st ed. dj. VG. B3. $70.00

DU BOIS, W.E.B. *Ordeal of Mansart.* 1957. Mainstream. 1st ed. dj. VG. B13. $35.00

DU BOIS, W.E.B. *Selected Poems.* c 1960s? Ghana. 1st ed. wrp. very scarce. B13. $175.00

DU BOIS, W.E.B. *Worlds of Clr.* 1961. Mainstream. 1st ed. dj. VG. B13. $45.00

DU CANE, Florence. *Flowers & Gardens of Japan.* 1908. London. 8vo. gilt gr bdg. VG. $45.00

DU CHAILLU, P.B. *Explorations & Adventures in Equatorial Africa.* 1871. NY. 1st ed. VG. $100.00

DU CHAILLU, P.B. *Land of the Midnight Sun.* 1882. Harper. 1st Am ed. 2 vols. VG. K1. $120.00

DU CHAILLU, P.B. *Land of the Midnight Sun.* 1889. Harper. EX. $50.00

DU MAURIER, Daphne. *Classics of the Macbre.* 1987. Doubleday. 1st ed. dj. EX. P1. $18.95

DU MAURIER, Daphne. *Don't Look Now.* 1971. Doubleday. 1st ed. dj. EX. R3. $35.00

DU MAURIER, Daphne. *Echoes From the Macabre.* 1977. Doubleday. 1st Am ed. dj. EX. R3. $20.00

DU MAURIER, Daphne. *Flight of the Falcon.* 1965. Doubleday Book Club. 311 p. dj. VG. B10. $3.25

DU MAURIER, Daphne. *Golden Lands: Sir Francis Bacon, Anthony Bacon & Friends.* 1975. 1st Am ed. dj. VG. C1. $12.50

DU MAURIER, Daphne. *Jamaica Inn.* 1936. Garden City. 1st ed. dj. VG. $35.00

DU MAURIER, Daphne. *Mary Anne.* 1954. Doubleday. 1st ed. 351 p. dj. B10. $5.50

DU MAURIER, Daphne. *Rule Britannia.* 1973. Doubleday. dj. xl. P1. $5.00

DU MAURIER, George. *Peter Ibbetson.* 1963. Ltd Ed Club. Ils. 4to. slipcase. VG. $35.00

DU MAURIER, George. *Trilby.* 1894. Harper. 1st ed. gilt gr bdg. VG. $20.00

DU MAURIER, George. *Trilby.* 1894. Harper. 1st ed. 464 p. G. B10. $12.00

DUANNE, Diane. *My Enemy, My Ally.* 1984. Pocket. 1st HrdCvr ed. dj. EX. F5. $12.00

DUANNE, Diane. *Wounded Sky.* 1983. Pocket. 1st HrdCvr ed. dj. EX. F5. $12.00

DUBBS, Chris. *Ms Faust.* 1985. Richardson Steirman. 1st ed. dj. EX. F5. $15.00

DUBOIS, Felix. *Timbuctoo the Mysterious.* 1896. Longman Gr. Ils. xl. VG. $30.00

DUBUS, Andre. *Adultery & Other Choices.* 1977. Boston. Godine. UP. EX. K2. $100.00

DUBUS, Andre. *Blessings.* 1987. Raven Eds. Letterpress ed. 1/60. sgn. EX. K2. $150.00

DUBUS, Andre. *Finding a Girl in Am.* 1980. Boston. Godine. 1st ed. dj. EX. K2. $45.00

DUBUS, Andre. *Land Where My Father Died.* 1984. Stuart Wright. Ltd ed. 1/200. sgn. as issued. EX. K2. $60.00

DUBUS, Andre. *Last Worthless Evening.* 1986. Godine. UP. sgn. wrp. EX. C4. $65.00

DUBUS, Andre. *Selected Stories.* 1988. Boston. Godine. 1st ed. sgn. dj. EX. C4. $50.00

DUBUS, Andre. *Separate Flights.* 1975. Boston. Godine. 1st ed. dj. EX. K2. $75.00

DUBUS, Andre. *Separate Flights: A Novella & 7 Short Stories.* 1975. Boston. Godine. 1st ed. sgn. dj. EX. C4. $75.00

DUCHARTRE, P.L. *Comedie Italienne.* 1925. Paris. Lib de France. Nouvelle ed. quarto. 351 p. VG. H3. $75.00

DUCHARTRE, P.L. *Commedia Dell Arte et Ses Enfants.* 1955. Paris. 1st ed. quarto. 291 p. EX. H3. $85.00

DUCHARTRE, P.L. *Italian Comedy.* nd. (1929) John Day. 1st Am ed. quarto. 330 p. dj. H3. $125.00

DUCHARTRE, Saulnier. *L'Imagerie Parisienne.* 1944. Paris. 1st ed. folio. G. B3. $75.00

DUCKETT, Margaret. *Mark Twain & Bret Harte.* 1964. OK U. 1st ed. dj. EX. C4. $40.00

DUERRENMATT, Friedrich. *Quarry.* 1962. NY Graphic Soc. 1st ed. dj. EX. F5. $30.00

DUFFIE, Peter. *Quartet: 4 Exclusive Card Effects.* 1986. London. Martin Breese. 1st ed. 16 p. cbdg. M. J3. $9.50

DUFFY, Margaret. *Murder of Crows.* 1987. St Martin. 1st ed. dj. EX. F5. $10.00

DUFFY, Maureen. *Erotic World of Faery.* nd. Avon. PB. VG. C1. $5.50

DUFOUR. *9 Men in Gray.* 1963. Garden City. 1st ed. dj. VG. C2. $45.00

DUGAN. *Ploesti.* 1962. NY. 1st ed. 407 p. dj. VG. B3. $35.00

DUGGAN, Alfred. *Conscience of the King.* 1951. London. 1st ed. VG. rare. C1. $44.50

DUGGAN, Alfred. *Cunning of the Dove.* 1960. 1st Am ed. dj. xl. VG. C1. $7.50

DUGGAN, Alfred. *Family Favorites.* 1960. 1st Am ed. dj. VG. C1. $11.00

DUGGAN, Alfred. *Leopards & Lillies.* 1969. (1st 1954) dj. VG. C1. $12.50

DUGGAN, Alfred. *Lord Geoffrey's Fancy.* 1962. 1st Am ed. dj. xl. VG. C1. $8.50

DUGGAN, Alfred. *Right Line of Cerdic: Novel of Alfred the Great.* 1961. 1st Am ed. dj. VG. C1. $12.50

DUGMORE, A.R. *Romance of the Beaver.* 1914. Heinemann. VG. T3. $25.00

DUHAMEL, Georges. *Ntaire du Havre.* 1933. Paris. Mercure De France. 1st ed. later print. inscr. wrp. VG. B13. $65.00

DULL. *Battle Hist of Imperial Japanese Navy.* 1978. Annapolis. Book Club ed. dj. VG. B3. $15.00

DUMAS, Alexander. *20 Years After.* 1958. Ltd Ed Club. Ils/sgn Edy Legrand. slipcase. VG. $50.00

DUMAS, Alexandre. *Adventures in Algeria/Adventures in Spain.* 1959. Phil. 1st Am ed. 2 vols. djs. slipcase. EX. T1. $40.00

DUMAS, Alexandre. *Blk Tulip.* nd. Dean. dj. VG. P1. $15.00

DUMAS, Alexandre. *Blk Tulip.* 1907. Hurst. decor brd. P1. $25.00

DUMAS, Alexandre. *Camille.* 1937. Ltd Ed Club. Ils/sgn Marie Laurencin. 1/1500. slipcase. EX. C4. $200.00

DUMAS, Alexandre. *Chevalier d'Harmental.* 1899. Little Brn. VG. P1. $20.00

DUMAS, Alexandre. *Chevalier de Maison Rouge.* nd. Collins. VG. P1. $15.00

DUMAS, Alexandre. *Chicot the Jester.* nd. Collins. VG. P1. $20.00

DUMAS, Alexandre. *Count of Monte Christo.* 1914. Chicago. 3 vols. EX. B10. $20.00

DUMAS, Alexandre. *Count of Monte Christo.* 1941. Heritage. Ils Lynd Ward. 4 vols in 1. slipcase. EX. T1. $20.00

DUMAS, Alexandre. *Count of Monte Christo.* 1941. Ltd Ed Club. Ils/sgn Lynd Ward. 1/1500. 4 vols. slipcase. C4. $65.00

DUMAS, Alexandre. *Count of Monte Cristo Vol 1.* nd. Atheneum. VG. P1. $15.00

DUMAS, Alexandre. *Edmund Dantes.* 1911. Leslie Judge. VG. P1. $30.00

DUMAS, Alexandre. *Man in the Iron Mask.* nd. Collins. leather bdg. VG. P1. $20.00

DUMAS, Alexandre. *Memoirs of a Physician.* nd. Henneberry. VG. P1. $20.00

DUMAS, Alexandre. *Queen's Necklace.* nd. Collins. leather bdg. EX. P1. $20.00

DUMAS, Alexandre. *Taking the Bastille.* nd. Collins. VG. P1. $15.00

DUMAS, Alexandre. *Taking the Bastille.* nd. Oxford Soc. leather bdg. VG. P1. $20.00

DUMAS, Alexandre. *10 Years Later.* 1899. Fenno. VG. P1. $20.00

DUMAS, Alexandre. *20 Years Later.* 1899. Fenno. VG. P1. $20.00

DUMONT, J.P. *Headman & I.* 1978. TX U. 1st ed. 211 p. dj. F2. $20.00

DUN, John. *11 Stories Inspired by AZ Sunshine.* 1938. Roycroft. 1st ed. EX. $45.00

DUNBAR, P.L. *Li'l Gal.* 1904. Dodd Mead. 1st ed. VG. $55.00

DUNBAR, P.L. *When Malindy Sings.* 1903. NY. VG. B3. $85.00

DUNBAR, S. *Hist of Travel in Am.* 1915. Indianapolis. 4 vols. xl. $90.00

DUNCAN, D.D. *This Is War!* 1951. Harcourt Brace. 1st ed. dj. EX. K2. $125.00

DUNCAN, D.D. *This Is War!* 1951. NY. 1st ed. 4to. G. $20.00

DUNCAN, D.D. *War Without Heroes.* 1970. NY. 1st ed. VG. B3. $85.00

DUNCAN, D.D. *Yankee Nomad.* 1967. NY. 2nd ed. dj. EX. $25.00

DUNCAN, D.D. *Yankee Nomad: Photographic Odyssey.* nd. np. Ils. 479 p. dj. ES. T5. $45.00

DUNCAN, David. *Picasso's Picassos.* c 1961. NY. 102 pls. dj. EX. G1. $59.00

DUNCAN, R.L. *Dragons at the Gate.* 1975. Morrow. 3rd ed. dj. EX. P1. $15.00

DUNCAN, Robert. *Tribunals: Passages 31-35.* 1970. Plantin Pr. Ltd ed. 1/250. sgn. yel bdg. H3. $75.00

DUNCAN, Robert. *1st Decade: Selected Poems 1940-1950.* 1968. London. Fulcrum Pr. 1/150. sgn. dj. EX. C4. $100.00

DUNCAN, Thomas. *Gus the Great.* 1947. Lippincott. 1st ed. 703 p. dj. NM. J3. $13.00

DUNHAM, Curtis. *Dancing With Helen Moller, Her Own Statement of Philosophy.* 1918. John Lane. 1st ed. 4to. 115 p. R4. $75.00

DUNHILL, Alfred. *Gentle Art of Smoking.* 1954. NY. dj. EX. $20.00

DUNHILL, Ed. *MC Routines.* c 1990. Dunhill. SftCvr. M. J3. $5.00

DUNLAP, W.C. *Quaker Education in Baltimore & VA Yearly Meeting.* 1936. Phil. private print. 1st ed. 574 p. VG. V1. $16.00

DUNLOP, Anna. *Here, There, & Everywhere in Scotland.* nd. (1952) Edinburgh. 2nd ed. 72 p. dj. VG. B10. $5.25

DUNLOP, W.S. *Lee's Sharpshooters; or, Forefront of the Battle.* 1899. Little Rock. 1st ed. EX. $385.00

DUNN, Allan. *Care-Free San Francisco.* 1913. Robertson. 83 p. VG. $20.00

DUNN, J.A. *Dead Man's Gold.* nd. Gundy. VG. P1. $200.00

DUNN, Katherine. *Greek Love.* 1989. Knopf. UP. wrp. EX. B13. $100.00

DUNN, Katherine. *Truck.* 1971. Harper. 1st ed. dj. EX. C4. $75.00

DUNN, W.R. *I Stand by Sand Creek.* 1985. Old Army Pr. 158 p. A5. $25.00

DUNNE, J.G. *Quintana & Friends.* 1978. Dutton. 1st ed. inscr. dj. EX. H3. $75.00

DUNNE, J.G. *Red, Wht, & Bl.* 1987. Simon Schuster. 1st ed. inscr. M. H3. $75.00

DUNNE, J.G. *Vegas.* 1974. Random House. 1st ed. presentation. dj. EX. H3. $75.00

DUNNE, Philip. *How Gr Was My Valley.* 1990. Santa Barbara. Santa Teresa. 1st ed. sgn. M. K2. $27.50

DUNNETT, Dorothy. *Pawn in Frankincense.* 1969. NY. 1st ed. dj. VG. $25.00

DUNNING, H.M. *Over Hill & Vale.* 1956. Johnson Pub. Ils. inscr. 556 p. A5. $40.00

DUNNING, J. *Tune in Yesterday.* 1976. Englewood Cliffs. 1st ed. dj. EX. B3. $70.00

DUNNINGER, Joseph. *Dunninger's Complete Encyclopedia of Magic.* 1987. Granmercy. 1st print. 388 p. dj. NM. J3. $10.00

DUNNINGER, Joseph. *Dunninger's Monument to Magic.* 1974. Lyle Stuart. 1st ed. 222 p. dj. EX. J3. $22.00

DUNNINGER, Joseph. *Dunninger's Popular Magic & Card Tricks No 3.* 1929. Experimenter Pub. 1st ed. 95 p. J3. $5.00

DUNNINGER, Joseph. *Dunninger's Secrets.* 1974. Lyle Stuart. 1st ed. 332 p. dj. NM. J3. $10.00

DUNNINGER, Joseph. *Here's Fun for Young & Old!* c 1951. Saalfield. VG. J3. $12.00

DUNNINGER, Joseph. *Popular Magic Prepared by Science & Invention.* c 1926. Experimenter Pub. 94 p. J3. $5.00

DUNNINGER, Joseph. *100 Houdini Tricks You Can Do.* 1954. Arco. 1st ed. 144 p. dj. VG. J3. $12.00

DUNSANY, Lord. *Chairwoman's Shadow.* 1926. Putnam. 1st ed. VG. R3. $25.00

DUNSANY, Lord. *Chronicles of Rodriguez.* 1922. Putnam. 1st ed. 1/500. sgn. dj. H3. $225.00

DUNSANY, Lord. *Dreamer's Tales & Other Stories.* c 1919. NY. Modern Lib Ed. Ils Borg. H3. $3500.00

DUNSANY, Lord. *Ghosts of the Heaviside Layer.* 1980. Owlswick. dj. EX. P1. $20.00

DUNSANY, Lord. *Gods, Men, & Ghosts.* nd. Dover. Ils Sidney Sime. PB. VG. C1. $4.00

DUNSANY, Lord. *If.* 1922. Putnam. 1st ed. dj. EX. K2. $65.00

DUNSANY, Lord. *King of Elfland's Daughter.* nd. Ballantine. PB. VG. C1. $4.00

DUNSANY, Lord. *Plays of Gods & Men.* 1977. Luce. 1st ed. VG. $15.00

DUNSANY, Lord. *Plays of Near & Far.* 1923. 1st ed. VG. C1. $17.50

DUNSANY, Lord. *Rory & Brand.* 1937. 1st ed. dj. VG. C1. $29.50

DUNSANY, Lord. *Tales of War.* 1918. Talbot Pr. 1st ed. VG. P1. $75.00

DUNSANY, Lord. *Tales of 3 Hemispheres.* 1976. Owlswick. dj. EX. P1. $20.00

DUNSANY, Lord. *4th Book of Jorkens.* 1948. Arkham House. 1st ed. dj. VG. R3. $50.00

DUPUY, R.E. *St Vith: Lion in the Way.* 1949. WA. 1st ed. 252 p. dj. VG. B3. $60.00

DURAN, F.D. *Aztecs: Hist of Indies of New Spain.* 1964. Orion Pr. 1st ed. 382 p. dj. F2. $35.00

DURANT, John. *Dodgers: Ils Story of Those Unpredictable Bums.* 1948. NY. Ils. 154 p. G. T5. $22.50

DURANT, Will. *Reformation.* 1957. 2nd print. dj. EX. C1. $7.50

DURANT, Will. *Story of Civilization: Renaissance.* 1953. 5th print. dj. VG. C1. $7.50

DURAS, Marguerite. *Practicalities.* 1990. Grove Weidenfeld. AP. wrp. EX. K2. $25.00

DURAS, Marguerite. *Sea Wall.* 1952. Pellegrini Cudahy. 1st Am ed. dj. EX. C4. $75.00

DURDEN, Kent. *Gifts of an Eagle.* 1972. Simon Schuster. 2nd ed. 158 p. dj. B10. $4.50

DURHAM, David. *Hounded Down.* nd. Detective Club. dj. VG. P1. $20.00

DURHAM, Lady. *Lady Durham's Journal.* 1925. Quebec. Literary & Hist Soc. 1st ed. 199 p. wrp. VG. $45.00

DURHAM & KNIGHT. *Hitch Your Wagon.* nd. Drexel Hill. 1st ed. inscr. VG. $35.00

DURIE, Alistair. *Weird Tales.* 1979. London. 1st ed. dj. EX. R3. $30.00

DURR, Marilyn. *Hist Collection From Columbiana & Fairfield Township...1975.* 1976. Columbiana. Ils. 120 p. clr wrp. EX. T5. $12.50

DURR, R.E. *Shelter From Compassion.* 1956. Wallingford. Pendle Hill. Ils Eichenberg. 12mo. 24 p. pamphlet. V1. $2.50

DURRELL, Lawrence. *Acte.* 1965. London. Faber. 1st ed. dj. EX. H3. $40.00

DURRELL, Lawrence. *Alexandria Quartet.* 1957-1960. Faber. 1st ed. 4 vols. EX. H3. $400.00

DURRELL, Lawrence. *Alexandria Quartet.* 1962. London. Faber. 1st ed. 1/500. sgn. boxed. H3. $500.00

DURRELL, Lawrence. *Bl Thirst.* 1975. Capra. Ltd 1st ed. 1/250. sgn. H3. $100.00

DURRELL, Lawrence. *Blk Book.* 1973. London. Faber. sgn. dj. M. H3. $125.00

DURRELL, Lawrence. *Caesar's Vast Ghost: Aspects of Provence.* 1990. Arcade. UP of 1st Am ed. wrp. EX. C4. $30.00

DURRELL, Lawrence. *Constance in Love; or, Solitary Practices.* 1982. Viking. UP. wrp. EX. K2. $40.00

DURRELL, Lawrence. *Constance; or, Solitary Practices.* 1982. Viking. 1st Am ed. sgn. dj. H3. $65.00

DURRELL, Lawrence. *Descente du Styx.* 1964. France. La Murene. 1st/only ed. 1/250. sgn. wrp. H3. $250.00

DURRELL, Lawrence. *Deus Loci.* 1950. Campania, Italy. private print. 1/200. sgn. wrp. H3. $200.00

DURRELL, Lawrence. *Irish Faustus.* 1963. London. Faber. 1st ed. M. H3. $50.00

DURRELL, Lawrence. *Monsieur.* 1975. Viking. 1st Am ed. dj. H3. $85.00

DURRELL, Lawrence. *Nothing Is Lost: Sweet Self.* 1967. London. Turrett. 1st ed. 1/100. sgns. dj. H3. $200.00

DURRELL, Lawrence. *On Seeming To Presume.* 1948. London. Faber. 1st Eng ed. 1st issue. dj. H3. $100.00

DURRELL, Lawrence. *Plant Magic Man.* 1973. Capra. Chapbook Series. Review ed. EX. K2. $75.00

DURRELL, Lawrence. *Quinz; or, The Ripper's Tale.* 1985. Viking. 1st Am ed. M. H3. $60.00

DURRELL, Lawrence. *Red Limbo Lingo: A Poetry Notebook.* 1971. Faber. 1st Eng ed. 1/100. sgn. boxed. M. H3. $250.00

DURRELL, Lawrence. *Tunc.* 1968. Dutton. Review 1st Am ed. dj. H3. $100.00

DURRELL, Lawrence. *Tunc.* 1968. Dutton. 1st ed. 359 p. dj. EX. $30.00

DURRELL, Lawrence. *Tunc.* 1968. London. Faber. 1st ed. dj. EX. H3. $60.00

DURRELL & MILLER. *Private Correspondence.* 1963. Dutton. 1st ed. dj. EX. K2. $25.00

DURST, R.C.R. *Centennial Program & Hist.* 1930. np. (Cuyahoga Falls) Ils 1st ed. 34 p. T5. $32.50

DURUY, Victor. *Hist of Rome & the Roman People.* 1884-1887. Estes Lauriat. Ed De Grand Luxe. 1/250. 16 vols. H3. $750.00

DURYEA, N.L. *House of the 7 Gabblers.* 1911. Appleton. VG. P1. $5.00

DUSS, John. *Harmonists.* 1943. Harrisburg. 1st ed. 425 p. VG. T5. $35.00

DUSTIN, Fred. *Report on Indian Earthworks in Ogemaw Co, MI.* 1932. Broomfield Hills, MI. inscr. wrp. A5. $25.00

DUTHUIT, Georges. *Fauves: Braque, Derain, Van Dogen, Dufy...Vlaminck.* 1949. Geneva. 1st Trade ed. 254 p. French wrp. EX. R4. $125.00

DUTTON, C.J. *Streaked With Crimson.* nd. Collier. VG. P1. $10.00

DUTTON. *Dupont: 140 Years.* 1949. NY. Ils. 403 p. dj. VG. B3. $12.50

DUVALIER, Francois. *Tribute to...Reverend Dr Martin Luther King Jr.* 1968. Haiti. 1st ed. 8vo. 167 p. dj. very scarce. R4. $85.00

DUVALL, Marius. *Navy Surgeon in CA 1846-1847.* 1957. Howell. Ltd 1st ed. 1/600. EX. $35.00

DUYCKINCK, E.A. *Encyclopedia of Am Literature.* 1965. Gale Research. HrdCvr ed. xl. P1. $20.00

DVORKIN, David. *Budspy.* 1987. Watts. 1st ed. dj. EX. P1. $17.95

DVORKIN, David. *Seekers.* 1988. Watts. 1st ed. dj. EX. F5. $15.00

DWORKIN, Andrea. *Ice & Fire.* 1987. Weidenfeld. UP. wrp. EX. K2. $20.00

DWORKIN, Andrea. *Ice & Fire.* 1987. Weidenfeld. 1st ed. dj. EX. F5. $13.00

DWYER, K.R.; see Koontz, Dean R.

DYBEK, Stuart. *Childhood & Other Neighborhoods.* nd. Viking. UP. wrp. EX. B13. $45.00

DYER, Frederick. *Compendium of War of the Rebellion.* 1959. NY. 1st ed. 3 vols. boxed. G. $140.00

DYER, J.P. *Gallant Hood.* 1950. Indianapolis. 1st ed. dj. EX. $50.00

DYER, R.O. *Adventures of the Inkspots.* 1923. Boston. Ils LJ Bridgman. 158 p. G. T5. $22.50

DYER, T.F.T. *Ghost World.* 1898. London. 447 p. $60.00

DYER, T.H. *Pompeii: Its Hist, Buildings, & Antiquities.* 1868. London. 2nd ed. 570 p. TEG. VG. $25.00

DYESS, W.E. *Dyess Story.* 1944. NY. 1st ed. 182 p. dj. G. T5. $17.50

DYESS, W.E. *Dyess Story.* 1944. Putnam. 1st ed. dj. EX. P1. $20.00

DYKES, J. *50 Great W Ils: Bibliographical Checklist.* 1975. Northland. 1st ed. 4to. dj. EX. $75.00

DYLAN, Bob. *Tarantula.* nd. Hibbing, MN. Wimp. Pirated ed. EX. K2. $75.00

DYLAN, Bob. *Tarantula.* 1971. Macmillan. 1st ed. 137 p. dj. EX. B10. $17.00

DYLAN, Bob. *Writings & Drawings.* 1973. NY. 1st ed. EX. B3. $25.00

DYOTT, William. *William Dyott's Diary 1781-1845.* 1907. Archibald Constable. 1st ed. 2 vols. VG. $65.00

EAMES, Hugh. *Sleuths, Inc: Studies of Problem Solvers*. 1978. Lippincott. 1st ed. dj. EX. T9. $25.00

EAMES, J.D. *MGM Story*. 1975. London. Ils 1st ed. folio. 400 p. dj. VG. B3. $30.00

EAMES, J.D. *MGM Story*. 1982. NY. 2nd Revised ed. dj. EX. $30.00

EARHART, Amelia. *20 Hours 40 Minutes*. 1928. NY. Grosset. reprint ed. sgn. dj. VG. B3. $250.00

EARLHAM COLLEGE. *Earlham Review, Spring 1966*. 1966. Richmond. 8vo. 48 p. SftCvr. VG. V1. $6.00

EARLY, Eleanor. *Island Patchwork*. 1941. Houghton Mifflin. 8vo. 290 p. G. V1. $8.50

EASBY, Elizabeth. *Ancient Art of Latin Am*. 1966. Brooklyn Mus. 4to. 139 p. F2. $15.00

EASBY & SCOTT. *Before Cortes: Sculpture of Middle Am*. 1970. NY. 1st ed. 4to. 332 p. F2. $60.00

EASLEY, Bert. *Doing Magic for Youngsters*. 1948. Louis Tannen. 1st ed. glassine dj. J3. $11.00

EAST, Andy. *Agatha Christie Quiz Book*. 1976. Pocket. VG. P1. $4.00

EASTLAKE, William. *Bronc People*. 1958. Harcourt Brace. 1st ed. dj. EX. K2. $175.00

EASTLAKE, William. *Dancers in the Scalp House*. 1975. Viking. UP. EX. scarce. K2. $50.00

EASTLAKE, William. *Go in Beauty*. 1956. Harper. 1st ed. sgn. dj. EX. B13. $350.00

EASTLAKE, William. *Jack Armstrong in Tangier & Other Escapes*. 1984. Bamberger Books. Ltd ed. 1/175. dj. M. H3. $125.00

EASTLAKE, William. *Jack Armstrong in Tangier*. 1984. Flint, MI. 1/300. sgn 5 times. wrp. EX. T9. $40.00

EASTLAKE, William. *Long Naked Descent Into Boston*. nd. (1977) Viking. UP. wrp. EX. B13. $125.00

EASTLAKE, William. *Portrait of an Artist With 26 Horses*. 1965. Michael Joseph. 1st ed. dj. EX. H3. $50.00

EASTMAN, C.C. *Choice Magic*. nd. Eastman. 2nd ed. sgn. 25 p. NM. J3. $4.00

EASTMAN, Charles. *Indian Boyhood*. 1902. NY. Phillips. 1st ed. inscr. EX. K2. $225.00

EASTMAN, Charles. *Indian Today*. 1915. Doubleday Page. dj. EX. K2. $85.00

EASTMAN, Max. *Enjoyment of Poetry*. nd. (1928) Houghton. not 1st ed. 254 p. gr bdg. VG. B10. $4.50

EASTMAN, Max. *Love & Revolution*. 1964. NY. 1st ed. sgn. dj. VG. B3. $27.50

EASTMAN. *Wht Mt Guide*. 1863. Concord. 16mo. 2 fld maps. VG. $85.00

EASTON, Carol. *Straight Ahead*. 1973. NY. 1st ed. dj. VG. B3. $27.50

EASTON, M.C. *Sprints of Cavern & Hearth*. 1988. St Martin. 1st ed. dj. EX. F5. $15.00

EASTON, Nat. *Bill for Damages*. 1958. Roy. xl. VG. P1. $5.00

EASTON, Nat. *Right for Trouble*. 1960. Boardman. 1st ed. dj. VG. P1. $10.00

EASTWOOD, James. *Diamonds Are Deadly*. 1969. McKay Washburn. 1st ed. dj. xl. P1. $5.00

EATON, D.C. *Beautiful Ferns*. 1892. Boston. Joseph Knight. Ils Faxon/Emerton. VG. T3. $75.00

EATON, Harold. *Poisoners of Women*. nd. Detective Club. dj. VG. P1. $20.00

EATON, Seymour. *Roosevelt Bears: Their Travels & Adventures*. 1906. Phil. Stern. 1st ed. 4to. EX. $225.00

EBERHART, Dikkon. *Paradise*. 1983. 1st ed. dj. NM. C1. $6.50

EBERHART, M.G. *Bayou Road*. 1979. Random House. 1st ed. dj. VG. P1. $15.00

EBERHART, M.G. *Danger Money*. 1974. Random House. 1st ed. dj. EX. F5. $12.00

EBERHART, M.G. *Hangman's Whip*. nd. Book League. VG. P1. $10.00

EBERHART, M.G. *Hangman's Whip*. 1942. Triangle. VG. P1. $10.00

EBERHART, M.G. *Man Next Door*. 1943. Random House. 1st ed. dj. xl. P1. $10.00

EBERHART, M.G. *Speak No Evil*. 1941. NY. 1st ed. dj. VG. B3. $45.00

EBERHART, M.G. *While the Patient Slept*. 1933. Heinemann. 7th print. VG. P1. $10.00

EBERHART, M.G. *With This Ring*. 1941. Random House. 1st ed. VG. P1. $12.50

EBERHART, M.G. *Witness at Lg*. 1966. Random House. 1st ed. dj. EX. P1. $20.00

EBERHART, M.G. *3 Days for Emerald*. 1988. Random House. 1st ed. dj. EX. P1. $14.95

EBERHART, Richard. *Quarry*. 1964. NY. 1st ed. sgn. dj. EX. T9. $45.00

EBERHART, Richard. *Richard Eberhart: Selected Poems 1930-1965*. 1964. New Directions. sgn. wrp. H3. $25.00

EBERS, Geroge. *Bride of the Nile*. 1887. Munro. wrp. VG. R3. $20.00

EBY & FLEMING. *Hell Hath No Fury*. 1947. Dutton. 1st ed. dj. EX. F5. $27.50

ECHARD, Margaret. *I Met Murder on the Way*. 1965. Crime Club. dj. xl. P1. $6.00

ECKERT, Allan. *Frontiersman*. 1967. Boston. 1st ed. sgn. dj. VG. B3. $40.00

ECKERT, Allan. *Owls of N America*. 1974. Doubleday. 1st ed. 278 p. dj. VG. B3. $60.00

ECKERT, Allan. *Time of Terror*. 1965. Boston. 1st ed. sgn. dj. VG. B3. $20.00

ECKFELDT & DU BOIS. *New Varieties of Gold & Silver Coins...* 1850. Phil. 1st ed. H3. $2500.00

ECKSTROM, Jack. *Time of the Hedrons*. 1968. Avalon. 1st ed. dj. EX. R3. $12.50

ECO, Umberto. *Name of the Rose*. 1983. Harcourt Brace. UP of 1st Am ed. wrp. EX. C4. $100.00

ECO, Umberto. *Name of the Rose*. 1983. Harcourt Brace. 1st Am ed. dj. EX. K2. $125.00

ECO, Umberto. *Postscript to the Name of the Rose*. 1984. Harcourt Brace. 1st ed. dj. EX. B13. $45.00

ECO, Umberto. *Theory of Semiotics*. 1976. IN U. 1st Am ed. dj. EX. C4. $60.00

EDDISON, E.R. *Childhood of an Esquestrian*. 1973. Harper Row. galley sheets. EX. scarce. K2. $45.00

EDDISON, E.R. *Worm Ouroboros*. 1922. London. Cape. 1st ed. dj. EX. K2. $750.00

EDDY, C. *Down the World's Most Dangerous River (CO)*. 1929. NY. 1st ed. 293 p. dj. VG. B3. $45.00

EDDY, D.C. *Daughters of the Cross*. 1855. Boston. Wentworth. 1st ed. xl. G. R5. $25.00

EDDY, M.B.G. *Science & Health*. 1875. Boston. 1st ed. blk leather. EX. H3. $2250.00

EDE, H.S. *Savage Messiah*. 1931. NY. 8vo. VG. $30.00

EDELSON, Edward. *Great Monsters of the Movies*. 1974. Arch. VG. P1. $3.50

EDEN, Dorothy. *Voice of the Dolls/Listen to Danger*. nd. Book Club. VG. P1. $3.00

EDGERTON, Clyde. *Floatplane Notebooks.* 1988. Algonquin Books. sgn. dj. M. C4. $40.00

EDGERTON, Clyde. *Floatplane Notebooks.* 1988. Algonquin Books. 1st ed. sgn. dj. EX. K2. $35.00

EDGERTON, Clyde. *Killer Diller.* 1991. Algonquin Books. ARC. sgn. wrp. EX. K2. $45.00

EDGERTON, Clyde. *Raney.* 1990. London. Penguin. 1st UK/PB Orig ed. wrp. EX. C4. $25.00

EDGERTON, Joseph. *Some Account of Life & Religious Service of Joseph Edgerton.* 1885. Phil. Pile. 12mo. 252 p. VG. V1. $12.50

EDGEWORTH, Maria. *Novels & Tales.* 1845. Harper. Sterotype ed. 18 vols in 9. G. H3. $125.00

EDGLEY, Leslie. *Judas Goat.* 1952. Crime Club. 1st ed. dj. VG. P1. $15.00

EDIGER, Donald. *Well of Sacrifice.* 1971. Doubleday. 1st ed. 288 p. dj. F2. $25.00

EDMINSTER, F.C. *Ruffed Grouse.* 1947. NY. 1st ed. dj. VG. B3. $50.00

EDMONDS, Harry. *Secret Voyage.* 1946. McDonald. VG. P1. $10.00

EDMONDS, W.D. *Drums Along the Mohawk.* 1936. Boston. 1st ed. 592 p. Pitz dj. VG. T5. $22.50

EDMONDS, W.D. *Rome Haul.* 1929. Little Brn. 1st ed. 347 p. VG. B10. $6.50

EDMONDS, W.D. *Young Ames.* 1942. Little Brn. 1st ed. 350 p. VG. B10. $8.50

EDMUNDSON, William. *Journal of Life, Travels, Sufferings, & Labor of Love.* 1774. London. Mary Hinde. 2nd ed. 12mo. 371 p. full leather. G. V1. $110.00

EDSCHMID, Kasimir. *S America: Lights & Shadows.* 1932. Viking. 1st ed. 408 p. F2. $15.00

EDWARD, Alexander. *McQ.* 1974. Warner. 1st ed. wrp. EX. F5. $8.00

EDWARDS, A.B. *Pharaohs, Fellahs, & Explorers.* 1891. NY. 1st ed. VG. $45.00

EDWARDS, Anne. *Judy Garland Biography.* 1975. Book Club. dj. EX. B10. $4.50

EDWARDS, Anne. *Remarkable Woman: Biography of Katherine Hepburn.* 1985. Morrow Book Club. 436 p. dj. EX. B10. $3.50

EDWARDS, Billy. *Gladiators of the Prize Ring.* 1895. Chicago. T5. $195.00

EDWARDS, Clayton. *Treasury of Heroes & Heroines.* nd. (1920) Stokes. Hampton Classic Series. dj. B10. $10.00

EDWARDS, D.M. *Toll of the Arctic Seas.* 1910. NY/London. 1st ed. VG. $45.00

EDWARDS, Eleanor. *World-Famous Great Mystery Stories.* 1960. Hart. VG. P1. $15.00

EDWARDS, Emily. *Painted Walls of Mexico.* 1966. TX U. 1st ed. 4to. dj. F2. $40.00

EDWARDS, Gawain. *Earth-Tube.* 1929. Appleton. 1st ed. dj. EX. B13. $100.00

EDWARDS, Jonathan. *Treatise Concerning Religious Affections.* 1794. Boston. 1st ed. 406 p. orig leather. VG. B3. $275.00

EDWARDS, Jonathan. *Treatise Concerning Religious Affections.* 1794. Boston. Larkin. 1st ed. 406 p. rebound. B3. $295.00

EDWARDS, Leo. *Jerry Todd in the Whispering Cave.* nd. Grosset Dunlap. VG. P1. $5.00

EDWARDS, Leo. *Poppy Ott Hits the Trail.* nd. Grosset Dunlap. VG. P1. $5.00

EDWARDS, Lionel. *My 1st Horse.* 1947. London. 1st ed. oblong 8vo. VG. $12.00

EDWARDS, R.D. *St Valentine's Day Murders.* 1984. St Martin. dj. VG. P1. $12.00

EDWARDS, Samuel. *Wht Plume.* 1961. Morrow. apparent 1st ed. 314 p. dj. VG. B10. $3.75

EDWARDS, William. *Civil War Guns.* 1962. Harrisburg. 1st ed. dj. EX. $30.00

EDWARDS & HOLDSTOCK. *Realms of Fantasy.* 1983. Doubleday. dj. VG. P1. $17.95

EFFINGER, G.A. *Death in Florence.* 1978. Doubleday. 1st ed. xl. P1. $5.00

EFFINGER, G.A. *Dirty Tricks.* 1978. Doubleday. 1st ed. dj. EX. R3. $15.00

EFFINGER, G.A. *Heroics.* 1979. Doubleday. 1st ed. dj. VG. P1. $20.00

EFFINGER, G.A. *Mixed Feelings.* 1974. Harper. 1st ed. dj. EX. R3. $15.00

EFFINGER, G.A. *Nick of Time.* 1985. Doubleday. 1st ed. dj. EX. F5. $16.00

EFFINGER, G.A. *What Entrophy Means to Me.* 1972. Doubleday. 1st ed. dj. VG. P1/R3. $15.00

EFFINGER, G.A. *When Gravity Fails.* 1987. Arbor House. 1st ed. dj. EX. P1. $16.95

EGAN, Howard. *Pioneering the W 1846-1878.* 1917. Richmond, UT. 1st ed. VG. $45.00

EGAN, Lesley. *Blind Search.* nd. Book Club. dj. VG. P1. $5.00

EGAN, Lesley. *Crime for Christmas.* nd. Book Club. dj. VG. P1. $5.00

EGAN, Lesley. *Detective's Due.* 1965. Harper Row. 1st ed. dj. xl. P1. $7.50

EGAN, Lesley. *Dream Apart.* nd. Book Club. dj. VG. P1. $5.00

EGAN, Lesley. *Dream Apart.* 1978. Crime Club. 1st ed. dj. xl. P1. $7.50

EGAN, Lesley. *Hunters & the Hunted.* 1979. Doubleday. 1st ed. dj. xl. P1. $7.50

EGAN, Lesley. *Look Back on Death.* nd. Book Club. dj. VG. P1. $5.00

EGAN, Lesley. *Look Back on Death.* 1978. Doubleday Crime Club. 1st ed. dj. xl. P1. $6.00

EGAN, Lesley. *Miser.* nd. Book Club. dj. VG. P1. $5.00

EGAN, Lesley. *Motive in Shadow.* nd. Book Club. dj. VG. P1. $5.00

EGAN, Lesley. *Nameless Ones.* 1967. Harper Row. 1st ed. dj. VG. P1. $17.50

EGAN, Lesley. *Nightmare.* nd. Book Club. dj. VG. P1. $5.00

EGAN, Lesley. *Random Death.* nd. Book Club. dj. VG. P1. $5.00

EGAN, Lesley. *Scenes of Crime.* nd. Book Club. dj. VG. P1. $5.00

EGAN, Lesley. *Wine of Violence.* 1969. Harper Row. 1st ed. dj. xl. P1. $7.50

EGG, Erich. *Tiroler Geschutzguss 1400-1600.* 1961. Innsbruck. 212 p. $25.00

EGGLESTON, Edward. *Hoosier Schoolmaster.* c 1871. Orange Judd. 1st ed. 1st imp. G. $40.00

EGGLESTON, N.H. *Villages & Village Life With Hints for Their Improvement.* 1878. 1st ed. EX. $25.00

EGLETON, Clive. *Eisenhower Deception.* 1981. Atheneum. 1st ed. dj. EX. P1. $20.00

EHLE, John. *Kingstree Island.* 1959. Morrow. 1st ed. dj. EX. K2. $85.00

EHLE, John. *Move Over, Mt.* 1957. Morrow. 1st ed. dj. EX. K2. $125.00

EHLE, John. *Shepherd of the Streets: Story of the Rev JA Gusweller...* 1960. NY. Wm Sloane. 1st ed. dj. EX. C4. $75.00

EHRICH, Max. *Big Eye.* nd. Book Club. dj. VG. P1. $4.50

EHRICH, Max. *Shaitan.* 1981. Arbor House. 1st ed. dj. EX. F5. $16.00

EHRLICH, Max. *Reincarnation of Peter Proud.* nd. Book Club. dj. VG. P1. $4.50

EICHELBERGER. *Our Jungle Road to Tokyo.* 1950. NY. 1st ed. dj. VG. B3. $40.00

EICHENBERG, Fritz. *Wood & the Graver.* 1977. Imprint Soc. 1/500. sgn. slipcase. EX. $110.00

EICHLER, Alfred. *Death of an Ad Man.* 1954. Abelard Schuman. dj. VG. P1. $15.00

EICHLER, Alfred. *Election by Murder.* 1947. Lantern Pr. xl. P1. $5.00

EICHLER, Lillian. *New Book of Etiquette.* 1924. Doubleday. 1st ed. 2 vols. VG. B10. $6.00

EIGNER, Larry. *Line That May Be Cut.* 1968. London. 1/250. D4. $40.00

EIGNER, Larry. *Looks Like Nothing the Shadow Through Air.* 1972. Guildford. 1/220. D4. $45.00

EINARSEN, Arthur. *Pronghorn Antelope & Its Managment.* 1948. WA. Ils. dj. EX. T1. $25.00

EINZIG, Richard. *Classic Modern Houses in Europe.* 1981. London. 1st ed. VG. G1. $20.00

EIPPER, Paul. *Circus: Men, Beasts, & Joys of the Road.* 1931. Viking. 1st Am ed. octavo. 213 p. dj. EX. H3. $75.00

EISELEY, Loren. *Darwin's Century.* 1959. Gollancz. 1st Eng ed. dj. EX. K2. $55.00

EISELEY, Loren. *Francis Bacon & the Modern Dilemma.* 1962. NE U. 1st ed. dj. EX. K2. $45.00

EISELEY, Loren. *Notes of an Alchemist.* 1972. Scribner. 1st ed. sgn. dj. EX. B13. $60.00

EISENBERG, Larry. *Best-Laid Schemes.* 1971. Macmillan. 1st ed. dj. EX. R3. $12.50

EISENHOWER, Dwight. *Waging Peace 1956-1961.* 1965. Garden City. 1st Trade ed. inscr. gilt bl bdg. EX. $250.00

EISENHOWER & COOKE. *Gen Eisenhower on the Military Churchill.* 1970. Norton. 1st ed. dj. EX. B10. $5.00

EISENSCHIML, Otto. *Historian Without an Armchair.* 1963. Bobbs Merrill. 224 p. dj. VG. S1. $12.50

EISENSTADT, Jill. *From Rockaway.* 1987. Knopf. AP. K2. $25.00

EISENSTADT, Jill. *Kiss Out.* 1991. Knopf. UP. wrp. EX. C4. $25.00

EISENSTEIN, Phyllis. *Born to Exile.* 1978. Arkham House. 1st ed. M. R3. $8.95

EISGRUBER, Frank. *Gangland's Doom: The Shadow.* 1985. Starmont. wrp. M. R3. $9.95

EISLER, C.T. *Flemish & Dutch Drawings From the 15th-18th Centuries.* 1963. Shorewood. slipcase. EX. D4. $20.00

EISLER, C.T. *German Drawings...16th Century to Expressionism.* 1963. Shorewood. slipcase. EX. D4. $20.00

EISLER, Steven. *Space Wars, Worlds, & Weapons.* 1979. Crescent. dj. EX. P1. $6.00

EISNER, Will. *Art of Will Eisner.* 1982. Kitchen Sink Pr. 1st ed. 1/1000. sgn. dj. EX. R3. $35.00

EISNER, Will. *Hawks of the Sea.* 1986. Kitchen Sink Pr. 1st ed. wrp. M. R3. $12.95

EISTER, A. *Drawing Room Conversion.* 1950. Durham. 1st ed. dj. VG. B3. $35.00

EKHOLM, Gordon. *Maremont Collection of Pre-Columbian Art.* c 1980s. Jerusalem. Israel Mus. 4to. wrp. F2. $20.00

EKHOLM, Gordon. *Maya Sculpture in Wood.* 1964. MPA. Ils. 4to. F2. $10.00

EKLUND, Gordon. *Beyond the Resurrection.* 1973. Doubleday. 1st ed. dj. EX. P1. $20.00

EKLUND, Gordon. *Gray Space Beast.* 1976. Doubleday. 1st ed. dj. EX. R3. $8.50

ELAM, R.M. *Young Readers SF Stories.* nd. Grosset Dunlap. VG. P1. $5.00

ELAM, R.M. *Young Visitor to Mars.* nd. Grosset Dunlap. dj. VG. P1. $15.00

ELBERTUS, Fra. *Motto Book.* 1920. Roycroft. 67 p. B10. $6.50

ELBIQUET. *Supplementary Magic.* nd. Routledge. 1st ed. 200 p. EX. J3. $15.00

ELBIQUET. *TB of Magic.* nd. Routledge. 1st ed. 203 p. VG. J3. $12.00

ELDER, Michael. *Oil Seeker.* 1977. Readers Union Book Club. dj. VG. P1. $5.00

ELDER, William. *Biography of Elisha Kent Kane.* 1858. Phil. Ils. 8vo. 416 p. G. G4. $30.00

ELDIN, Peter. *Let's Make Magic.* 1985. Treasure Pr. 45 p. J3. $5.00

ELDIN, Peter. *Magic Handbook.* 1985. Simon Schuster. 1st Am ed. 3rd print. 189 p. NM. J3. $5.00

ELDRIDGE, Roger. *Shadow of the Gloom World.* 1977. Gollancz. 1st ed. dj. EX. P1. $15.00

ELFLANDSSON, Galad. *Blk Wolf.* 1979. Grant. 1st ed. dj. EX. R3. $25.00

ELGIN, S.H. *And Then There'll Be Fireworks.* 1981. Doubleday. 1st ed. dj. P1/R3. $15.00

ELGIN, S.H. *Grand Jubilee.* 1981. Doubleday. 1st ed. dj. VG. P1. $15.00

ELGIN, S.H. *12 Fair Kingdoms.* 1981. Doubleday. 1st ed. dj. EX. P1. $15.00

ELIADES & DIAL. *Only Land I Know: Hist of the Lumbee Indians.* 1975. San Francisco. Indian Hist. wrp. EX. K2. $35.00

ELIOT, David. *Training Gun Dogs To Retrieve.* 1952. NY. 1st ed. dj. EX. $17.50

ELIOT, George. *Complete Works.* c 1900. NY. Fred De Fau. 1/1000. 12 vols. TEG. VG. H3. $225.00

ELIOT, George. *Middlemarch.* 1871. Edinburgh. 1st ed. 4 vols. VG. H3. $1500.00

ELIOT, George. *Mill on the Floss.* 1840. Blackwood. 1st ed. 3 vols. H3. $450.00

ELIOT, George. *Novels.* c 1900. London. Blackwood. 8 vols in 7. H3. $750.00

ELIOT, George. *Personal Ed of George Eliot's Works.* 1901. Doubleday Page. 12 vols. VG. H3. $750.00

ELIOT, George. *Scenes of Clerical Life.* 1858. Edinburgh. 1st ed. orig bdg. VG. scarce. H3. $4500.00

ELIOT, George. *Silas Marner.* c 1910. AL Burt. VG. B10. $3.50

ELIOT, George. *Works.* c 1906. Estes. Ils Cabinet ed. 24 vols. TEG. EX. H3. $275.00

ELIOT, George. *Writings.* c 1907-1908. Houghton Mifflin. Warwickshire ed. 25 vols. H3. $1250.00

ELIOT, George. *Writings.* 1908. Houghton Mifflin. Lg Paper ed. 1/750. 25 vols. lg octavo. H3. $1250.00

ELIOT, T.S. *Anabasis.* 1930. London. Faber. Ltd ed. 1/350. presentation. slipcase. H3. $375.00

ELIOT, T.S. *Ash Wednesday.* 1930. NY. 1st ed. VG. B3. $40.00

ELIOT, T.S. *Cocktail Party.* 1949. London. Faber. 1st ed. dj. EX. H3. $125.00

ELIOT, T.S. *Confidential Clerk: A Play.* 1953. London. Faber. 1st ed. dj. EX. H3. $100.00

ELIOT, T.S. *Cultivation of Christmas Trees.* 1956. Farrar Straus Cudahy. 1st ed. EX. H3. $40.00

ELIOT, T.S. *Cultivation of Christmas Trees.* 1956. NY. Ils Enrico Arno. 1st ed. G. T5. $17.50

ELIOT, T.S. *Elder Statesman*. 1959. London. Faber. 1st ed. dj. EX. H3. $75.00

ELIOT, T.S. *Elder Statesman: A Play*. 1959. Farrar Straus Cudahy. 1st ed. dj. EX. H3. $60.00

ELIOT, T.S. *For Lancelot Andrews*. 1929. Doubleday Doran. 1st Am ed. dj. EX. K2. $275.00

ELIOT, T.S. *Idea de Una Sociedad Cristiana*. 1942. Buenos Aires. 1st Spanish ed. wrp. G. K2. $45.00

ELIOT, T.S. *Little Gidding*. 1942. London. Faber. 1st issue. sewn wrp. EX. B13. $85.00

ELIOT, T.S. *Marina*. 1930. London. Faber. Ltd ed. 1/400. sgn. H3. $175.00

ELIOT, T.S. *Murder in the Cathedral*. 1936. Harcourt Brace. 1st ed. 2nd issue. dj. EX. H3. $35.00

ELIOT, T.S. *Old Possum's Book of Practical Cats*. 1959. Harcourt Brace. dj. VG. B3. $25.00

ELIOT, T.S. *On Poetry & Poets*. 1957. Farrar Straus Cudahy. 1st ed. dj. EX. H3. $50.00

ELIOT, T.S. *Poems Written in Early Youth*. 1967. London. Faber. 1st ed. dj. EX. H3. $60.00

ELIOT, T.S. *Poetas Metafisicos y Otros Ensayos Sobre Teatro y Religion*. 1944. Buenos Aires. 1st ed. 2 vols. orig wrp. djs. K2. $75.00

ELIOT, T.S. *Poetry & Drama*. 1951. London. Faber. 1st Eng ed. dj. VG. H3. $50.00

ELIOT, T.S. *To Criticize the Critic & Other Writings*. 1965. NY. 1st ed. 188 p. dj. T5. $17.50

ELIOT, T.S. *Triumphal March*. 1931. London. Faber. Ltd ed. 1/300. sgn. H3. $200.00

ELIOT, T.S. *Wasteland*. 1922. NY. 1st ed. 1/1000. orig cloth. dj. VG. H3. $1250.00

ELIOT, T.S. *Wasteland*. 1928. Liveright. 3rd ed. VG. B10. $15.00

ELIOT, T.S. *4 Quarters*. 1943. NY. 1st ed. 2nd issue. 1/700. dj. EX. $175.00

ELIOTT, E.C. *Kemlo & the Martian Ghosts*. 1954. Thomas Nelson. dj. VG. P1. $17.50

ELIOTT, E.C. *Kemlo & the Zombie Men*. 1958. Thomas Nelson. 1st ed. dj. VG. P1. $20.00

ELKIN, Stanley. *Bad Man*. 1967. Random House. 1st ed. dj. F5. $16.00

ELKIN, Stanley. *Big Night*. 1950. Lion 41. PB Orig. 1st print. wrp. VG. T9. $20.00

ELKIN, Stanley. *Bind*. 1970. Random House. 1st ed. dj. EX. T9. $25.00

ELKIN, Stanley. *Blessington Method & Other Strange Tales*. 1964. Random House. 1st ed. dj. EX. T9. $35.00

ELKIN, Stanley. *Boswell*. 1964. Random House. 1st ed. dj. EX. K2. $90.00

ELKIN, Stanley. *Dark Fantastic*. 1983. Andre Deutsch. 1st ed. dj. EX. P1. $20.00

ELKIN, Stanley. *Dreadful Summit*. 1948. Simon Schuster. 1st ed. red bdg. VG. T9. $20.00

ELKIN, Stanley. *House of Cards*. 1967. Macdonald. 1st ed. dj. VG. P1. $15.00

ELKIN, Stanley. *Kindly Dig Your Grave & Other Wicked Stories*. 1975. Davis Pub. 1st ed. wrp. EX. T9. $30.00

ELKIN, Stanley. *Star Light Star Bright*. 1979. Random House. 1st ed. dj. VG. P1. $20.00

ELKIN, Stanley. *Stronghold*. 1974. Random House. 1st ed. dj. VG. P1. $20.00

ELKIN, Stanley. *Valentine Estate*. 1968. Random House. 1st ed. dj. EX. T9. $25.00

ELKIN, Stanley. *Winter After This Summer*. 1960. Random House. 1st ed. dj. VG. P1. $35.00

ELKINS, A.J. *Fellowship of Fear*. 1982. Walker. 2nd ed. dj. EX. P1. $11.95

ELKINTON, J.S. *Selections From the Diary of Joseph S Elkinton*. 1913. Phil. private print. 8vo. 512 p. VG. V1. $15.00

ELLIN, Stanley. *Mystery Stories*. 1956. Simon Schuster. 1st ed. inscr. VG. B13. $175.00

ELLIOT, E. *Centreville to Woodridge: Story of Sm Community*. 1976. Expo Pr. 1st ed. dj. B10. $15.00

ELLIOT, Elisabeth. *Through Gates of Splendor*. 1957. Harper. 1st ed. 256 p. F2. $12.50

ELLIOT, F.P. *Gift of Abou Hassan*. 1912. Little Brn. 1st ed. VG. R3. $25.00

ELLIOT, Frances. *Diary of Idle Woman in Spain*. 1884. London. 2 vols. A4. $100.00

ELLIOTT, Bruce. *Best in Magic*. 1956. Galahad Books. later print. 246 p. J3. $9.00

ELLIOTT, Bruce. *Classic Secrets of Magic*. 1953. Harper. 210 p. VG. J3. $10.00

ELLIOTT, Bruce. *Classic Secrets of Magic*. 1953. Harper. 210 p. xl. VG. J3. $5.00

ELLIOTT, Bruce. *Great Secrets of the Master Magicians*. 1975. Collier. 5th print. 190 p. EX. J3. $3.00

ELLIOTT, Bruce. *Magic As a Hobby*. 1958. Gramercy. 4th print. 230 p. dj. NM. J3. $6.00

ELLIOTT, Bruce. *Professional Magic Made Easy*. 1959. Gramercy. 1st print. 225 p. dj. NM. J3. $12.00

ELLIOTT, Don; see Silverberg, Robert.

ELLIOTT, J. *Transport to Disaster*. 1962. NY. 1st ed. dj. VG. B3. $25.00

ELLIOTT & GOULD. *From Approximately Coast to Coast...Its the Bob & Ray Show*. 1983. Atheneum. 2nd print. sgns. dj. EX. B13. $75.00

ELLIS, B.E. *Less Than Zero*. 1985. Simon Schuster. 1st ed. dj. EX. B13. $45.00

ELLIS, Edith. *Incarnation: Plea From the Masters*. 1951. Anthony. Ils. dj. VG. B10. $4.50

ELLIS, Edward. *Practical Manual of the Diseases of Children*. 1878. NY. Wood. 3rd ed. VG. J2. $15.00

ELLIS, George. *Metrical Romances*. 1968. NY. reprint of 1848 ed. EX. C1. $24.50

ELLIS, George. *Specimens of Early Eng Metrical Romances*. 1848. London. Bohn. G. very scarce. C1. $14.50

ELLIS, H.H. *MI in Civil War: Guide to Material in Detroit Newspapers*. 1965. Lansing, MI. 404 p. PB. G. S1. $12.50

ELLIS, Hamilton. *Pictorial Encyclopedia of Railways*. 1976. London. Hamlyn. Revised ed. dj. EX. $22.00

ELLIS, Mel. *No Man for Murder*. 1973. Holt Rinehart. dj. EX. P1. $7.50

ELLIS, N.P. *1 Who Walked Alone*. 1986. Donald Grant. 1st ed. dj. EX. P1. $25.00

ELLIS, R.H. *General Pope & US Indian Policy*. 1970. Albuquerque. Ils 1st ed. dj. VG. T5. $17.50

ELLIS, W.E. *Bovarysm: Art-Philosophy of Jules de Gauthier*. 1928. Seattle. 16mo. wrp. A4. $25.00

ELLIS, William. *Am Mission in the Sandwich Islands*. 1866. London. Pardon. wrp. scarce. $300.00

ELLIS, William. *Narrative of a Tour Through HI*. 1917. Honolulu. 1st ed. VG. $40.00

ELLISON, Harlan. *Again, Dangerous Visions*. nd. Book Club. dj. VG. P1. $7.50

ELLISON, Harlan. *Alone Against Tomorrow*. 1971. Macmillan. 1st ed. sgn. dj. EX. R3. $30.00

ELLISON, Harlan. *Approaching Oblivion*. nd. Book Club. dj. VG. P1. $7.50

ELLISON, Harlan. *Beast That Shouted Love at the Heart of the World.* 1969. Avon. 1st HrdCvr ed. dj. EX. F5. $13.00

ELLISON, Harlan. *Dangerous Visions.* nd. Book Club. dj. VG. P1. $7.50

ELLISON, Harlan. *Deathbird Stories.* 1975. Harper Row. 1st ed. dj. EX. P1. $75.00

ELLISON, Harlan. *Deathbird Stories.* 1978. Millington. dj. VG. P1. $50.00

ELLISON, Harlan. *Edge in My Voice.* 1985. Donning. ARC. proof dj. $75.00

ELLISON, Harlan. *Edge in My Voice.* 1985. Donning. 1st ed. inscr. wrp. EX. R3. $35.00

ELLISON, Harlan. *Gentleman Junkie & Other Stories of the Hung-Up Generation.* 1961. Regency RB 102. 1st ed. wrp. NM. T9. $175.00

ELLISON, Harlan. *Ils Book of Harlan Ellison.* 1978. Baronet. Ltd ed. 1/3000. sgn. EX. R3. $35.00

ELLISON, Harlan. *Ils Book of Harlan Ellison.* 1978. Baronet. 1st ed. sgn. wrp. EX. R3. $20.00

ELLISON, Harlan. *Medea: Harlan's World.* 1985. Phantasia. 1st ed. 1/725. M. R3. $40.00

ELLISON, Harlan. *Partners in Wonder.* 1971. Walker. 1st ed. sgn. dj. M. $60.00

ELLISON, Harlan. *Shatterday.* 1980. Houghton. 1st ed. dj. EX. R3. $30.00

ELLISON, Harlan. *Stalking the Nightmare.* nd. Book Club. dj. VG. P1. $7.50

ELLISON, Harlan. *Stalking the Nightmare.* 1982. Huntington Woods. 1st ed. dj. EX. B3. $20.00

ELLISON, Harlan. *Stalking the Nightmare.* 1982. Phantasia. 1st ed. sgn. dj. VG. P1. $50.00

ELLISON, Harlan. *Strange Wine.* 1978. Harper Row. 1st ed. dj. EX. R3. $50.00

ELLISON, Harlan. *Strange Wine.* 1978. Harper Row. 1st ed. sgn. dj. EX. K2. $65.00

ELLISON, Harlan. *Time of the Eye.* 1974. Panther. 1st ed. wrp. EX. F5. $12.50

ELLISON, Mary. *Support for Secession.* 1972. Chicago. 259 p. dj. VG. S1. $12.00

ELLISON, Ralph. *Casebook on Ralph Ellison's Invisible Man.* 1972. Crowell. 1st ed. sgn. wrp. EX. K2. $85.00

ELLISON, Ralph. *El Oficio de Escritor.* 1970. Mexico. 2nd Spanish ed. inscr. K2. $55.00

ELLISON, Ralph. *Invisible Man.* 1980. Franklin Lib. Ltd ed. sgn. AEG. K2. $150.00

ELLISON, Ralph. *Ralph Ellison: A Collection of Critical Essays.* 1974. Prentice Hall. ARC. inscr. dj. w/promotional sheet. EX. K2. $125.00

ELLISON, Ralph. *Shadow & Act.* 1966. New Am Lib. 1st PB ed. sgn. EX. K2. $55.00

ELLISON, Ralph. *Shadow & Act.* 1967. Secker Warburg. 1st Eng ed. inscr. dj. EX. K2. $200.00

ELLISON, Ralph. *Shadow & Act.* 1972. Vintage. Review PB ed. sgn. RS. K2. $85.00

ELLISON, Ralph. *Writers & Issues.* 1969. New Am Lib. PB Orig. inscr. EX. K2. $100.00

ELLISON & BRYANT. *Phoenix Without Ashes.* 1978. London. 1st ed. wrp. VG. R3. $15.00

ELLISON & SLUSSER. *Unrepentant Harlequin.* 1977. Borgo Pr. 1st ed. wrp. VG. R3. $10.00

ELLORY, James. *Blood on the Moon.* 1984. Mysterious Pr. 1st ed. dj. VG. P1. $15.00

ELLROY, James. *Blk Dahlia.* 1987. Mysterious Pr. 1st ed. sgn. dj. M. C4. $35.00

ELLSON, Hal. *Golden Spike.* 1952. Ballantine. 1st HrdCvr ed. clipped dj. VG. T9. $95.00

ELLSON, Hal. *Killer's Kiss.* 1959. Hillman Books 354. 1st ed. wrp. EX. T9. $25.00

ELLSON, Hal. *Tomboy.* 1950. Scribner. 1st/A ed. dj. VG. T9. $40.00

ELLSON, Hal. *Torment of the Kids.* 1961. Regency Books 108. PB Orig. wrp. NM. T9. $25.00

ELLSWORTH, Lincoln. *Beyond Horizons.* 1938. Book Club ed. Ils. 403 p. dj. VG. T5. $22.50

ELLSWORTH, Lincoln. *Exploring Today.* 1941. NY. Ils. 194 p. G. T5. $15.00

ELON, Amos. *Timetable.* 1980. Doubleday. dj. VG. P1. $15.00

ELRICK, G.S. *Bonanza the Bubble Gum Kid.* 1967. Big Little Book. VG. P1. $10.00

ELRICK, G.S. *Calcutta Affair.* 1967. Big Little Book. VG. P1. $12.50

ELRICK, G.S. *Killer Whale Trouble.* 1967. Whitman. Big Little Book. VG. P1. $6.00

ELRICK, G.S. *Lone Ranger Outwits Crazy Cougar.* Big Little Book. VG. P1. $5.00

ELRICK, G.S. *Night of Terror.* 1968. Whitman. Big Little Book. VG. P1. $7.50

ELRICK, G.S. *Tarzan & the Mark of the Red Hyena.* 1967. Big Little book. VG. P1. $15.00

ELSWYTH, Thane. *Bird Who Made Good.* 1947. NY. 1st ed. dj. VG. $25.00

ELTON, Packer. *Roy Rogers on the Trail of the Zeros.* 1954. Whitman. 1st ed. dj. EX. F5. $25.00

ELWES, Alfred. *Jaufry the Knight & the Fair Brunissende.* 1979. Newcastle. Ils 1st ed. scarce. C1. $9.50

ELWOOD, P.H. *Am Landscape & Architecture.* 1924. NY. 1st ed. EX. $275.00

ELWOOD, Roger. *And Walk Now Gently Through Fire.* 1972. Chilton. 1st ed. dj. EX. P1. $15.00

ELWOOD, Roger. *Continuum 2.* 1974. Putnam. 1st ed. dj. EX. R3. $15.00

ELWOOD, Roger. *Continuum 4.* 1975. Putnam. dj. VG. P1. $15.00

ELWOOD, Roger. *Dystopian Visions.* 1975. Prentice Hall. 1st ed. dj. VG. P1. $15.00

ELWOOD, Roger. *Far Side of Time.* 1974. Dodd Mead. 1st ed. dj. VG. P1. $15.00

ELWOOD, Roger. *Future City.* 1973. Trident. 1st ed. dj. EX. R3. $10.00

ELWOOD, Roger. *Future Kin.* 1974. Doubleday. 1st ed. dj. EX. P1. $15.00

ELWOOD, Roger. *Gifts of Asti.* 1975. Follett. 1st ed. dj. EX. R3. $10.00

ELWOOD, Roger. *Long Night of Waiting.* 1974. Auora. 1st ed. dj. EX. P1. $17.50

ELWOOD, Roger. *Other Side of Tomorrow.* 1973. Random House. 1st ed. sgn. dj. EX. R3. $15.00

ELWOOD, Roger. *Showcase.* 1973. Harper. 1st ed. dj. EX. P1. $15.00

ELWOOD, Roger. *Tomorrow.* 1975. Evans. 1st ed. dj. EX. R3. $8.50

ELWOOD, Roger. *Way Out.* 1973. Whitman. G. P1. $3.00

ELWOOD & KIDD. *Saving Worlds.* 1973. Doubleday. 1st ed. dj. EX. R3. $10.00

ELY, Alfred. *Sermon, Preached at Northampton.* 1819. Northampton. 40 p. disbound. T5. $12.50

ELY, Evelyn. *Ojos de Dios.* 1972. NM U. Ils. 4to. wrp. F2. $7.50

ELY, Sims. *Lost Dutchman Mine.* 1954. Morrow. 2nd ed. dj. VG. B3. $25.00

EMBREE, E.R. *Brn Am: Story of a New Race.* 1931. Viking. 1st ed. dj. EX. B13. $100.00

EMECHETA, Buchi. *Nowhere To Play.* 1980. Allison Busby. Ils Peter Archer. 1st ed. EX. B13. $40.00

EMERSON, Alice. *Betty Gordon & Lost Pearls.* 1927. Cupples. dj. B10. $4.00

EMERSON, J.M. *European Glimpses & Glances.* 1889. Cassell. 1st ed. bl bdg. VG. B10. $16.50

EMERSON, N.B. *Unwritten Literature of HI & Sacred Songs of the Hula.* 1909. GPO. 288 p. VG. $65.00

EMERSON, R.W. *Am Scholar.* 1901. Laurentian Pr. 1/510. 4to. VG. $60.00

EMERSON, R.W. *Complete Works.* 1903-1904. Riverside. Autograph Centenary ed. 1/600. 20 vols. H3. $2750.00

EMERSON, R.W. *Encyclopedia of Britannica.* 1926. London. 13th ed. 32 vols. quarto. VG. H3. $500.00

EMERSON, R.W. *Essays.* 1906. Dove Pr. 1/300. orig vellum. EX. H3. $500.00

EMERSON, R.W. *Nature.* 1905. Roycroft. 1/100 on Japan. sgn. 12mo. EX. A4. $150.00

EMERSON, R.W. *Poems.* 1945. Ltd Ed Club. Ils/sgn Richard & Doris Beer. slipcase. VG. $75.00

EMERY, Clayton. *Tales of Robin Hood.* 1988. PB Orig. EX. C1. $3.00

EMMENS. *Keeping & Breeding Aquarium Fishes.* 1953. Academic Pr. 1st ed. dj. VG. C2. $25.00

EMMERICH, Andre. *Art Before Columbus.* 1963. Simon Schuster. 1st ed. 256 p. dj. F2. $25.00

EMMERICH & LAPINER. *Pre-Columbian Art: Mexico, Mesoamerica, & S Am.* nd. Detroit. Hudson Mus. 4to. wrp. F2. $10.00

EMMONS, E. *Nat Hist of NY: Agriculture & Fruits.* 1851. Appleton/Wiley Putnam. 2 vols. clr pls. VG. T3. $300.00

EMMONS, E. *Nat Hist of NY: Agriculture & Insects.* 1854. NY. clr pls. VG. T3. $250.00

EMMOTT, E.R. *Loving Service: Record of Life of Martha Braithwaite.* 1896. London. Headley. 12mo. 296 p. V1. $12.00

EMORY, W.C. *Be Still.* 1929. Detroit. Lotus Pr. Ltd ed. 1/215. sgn. ES. H3. $35.00

EMORY, W.C. *Glory.* 1929. Argus Books. 1st ed. VG. H3. $20.00

EMORY, W.C. *Glory: A Play in 1 Brief Act.* 1929. Argus Books. Ltd ed. 1/75. sgn. H3. $75.00

ENCISO, Jorge. *Design Motifs of Ancient Mexico.* 1953. NY. Dover. 1st ed. 4to. F2. $25.00

ENDE, Michael. *Neverending Story.* 1983. Doubleday. 3rd ed. dj. VG. P1. $15.95

ENDE, Michael. *Neverending Story.* 1983. NY. 1st ed. dj. VG. B3. $55.00

ENDICOTT, Wendell. *Adventures in AK Along the Trail.* 1928. Stokes. presentation. VG. $40.00

ENDORE, Guy. *King of Paris.* nd. Book Club. EX. P1. $2.25

ENDORE, Guy. *Man From Limbo.* 1930. Farrar Rinehart. 1st ed. VG. R3. $12.50

ENDORE, Guy. *Methinks the Lady.* nd. Duell Sloan. 3rd ed. dj. VG. P1. $15.00

ENEY, Richard. *Fancyclopedia II.* 1959. Eney. 1st ed. 1/450. EX. R3. $45.00

ENEY, Richard. *Fancyclopedia II.* 1979. Mirage. 1st ed. wrp. M. R3. $15.00

ENGBERG, Edward. *On Civilizing the Corporation.* 1976. Capra. Chapbook Series. 1/60. sgn. EX. K2. $20.00

ENGDAHL, Sylvia. *Anywhere, Anywhen.* 1976. Atheneum. 1st ed. dj. VG. P1. $17.50

ENGDAHL, Sylvia. *Far Side of Evil.* 1972. Atheneum. 2nd ed. dj. xl. P1. $6.00

ENGDAHL, Sylvia. *Far Side of Evil.* 1975. Gollancz. dj. EX. P1. $15.00

ENGEL, Frederic. *Ancient World Preserved.* 1976. Crown. Revised Updated/1st Eng ed. 314 p. F2. $17.50

ENGEL, Howard. *Murder Sees the Light.* 1984. Viking. dj. VG. P1. $15.00

ENGEL, Howard. *Ransom Game.* 1981. Clarke Irwin. 1st ed. sgn. dj. EX. P1. $30.00

ENGEL & PILLER. *World Aflame: Russian-Am War of 1950.* 1947. Dial. 1st ed. dj. EX. R3. $27.50

ENGELS, M.T. *Heinrich Campendonk.* 1958. Verlag. 1st ed. German text. pls. dj. VG. $25.00

ENGL & ENGL. *Twilight of Ancient Peru.* 1969. McGraw. 1st ed. sm 4to. dj. F2. $35.00

ENGLAND, G.A. *Air Trust.* 1915. Wagner. 1st ed. VG. R3. $100.00

ENGLAND, G.A. *Air Trust.* 1976. Hyperion. EX. R3. $22.50

ENGLAND, G.A. *Cursed.* 1919. Sm Maynard. 1st ed. EX. R3. $70.00

ENGLAND, G.A. *Darkness & Dawn.* 1914. Sm Maynard. VG. R3. $50.00

ENGLAND, G.A. *Flying Legion.* 1920. McClurg. 1st ed. G. R3. $45.00

ENGLAND, G.A. *Out of the Abyss.* 1967. Avalon. 1st ed. dj. EX. R3. $17.50

ENGLAND, G.A. *Vikings of the Ice.* 1924. Doubleday. 1st ed. presentation. G. R3. $50.00

ENGLE, Paul. *Am Song Book of Poems.* 1934. Doubleday. 1st ed. 102 p. VG. B10. $4.50

ENGLEHARDT. *Franciscans of CA.* 1897. Harbor Springs, MI. 517 p. orig wrp. A5. $70.00

ENGLEMAN, C.F. *W Patriot & Canton Almanac for Year of Our Lord 1837.* nd. Canton. Ils. G. T5. $75.00

ENOCK, C.R. *Spanish Am: Its Romance, Reality, & Future.* c 1920. Scribner. 2 vols. F2. $20.00

ENSTROM, Robert. *Beta Colony.* 1980. Doubleday. 1st ed. dj. EX. F5. $15.00

ENSTROM, Robert. *Encounter Program.* 1977. Doubleday. dj. EX. P1. $15.00

ENTWHISTLE, William. *Arthurian Legend in Literature of Spanish Peninsula.* 1975. NY. reprint of 1925 ed. M. C1. $22.50

ENYEART, James. *Bruguiere: His Photographs & His Life.* 1977. NY. 1st ed. VG. G1. $25.00

EPICURUS. *Extant Works.* 1947. Ltd Ed Club. Ils/sgn Bruce Rogers. slipcase. VG. $145.00

EPSTEIN, Brian. *Cellar Full of Noise.* 1965. Pyramid. 1st PB ed. G. B4. $3.50

EPSTEIN, Jacob. *Art of Jacob Epstein.* 1942. Cleveland. World. VG. $50.00

ERASMUS, Desiderius. *Moriae Encomium; or, The Praise of Folly.* 1943. Ltd Ed Club. Ils/sgn Lynd Ward. 4to. slipcase. EX. C4. $75.00

ERDMAN, L.G. *Years of the Locust.* 1947. Dodd. not 1st ed. 234 p. VG. B10. $3.50

ERDRICH, Louise. *Baptism of Desire.* 1989. Harper Row. ARC. dj. EX. w/promotional material. K2. $50.00

ERDRICH, Louise. *Beet Queen.* 1986. Holt. ARC. sgn. wrp. EX. K2. $85.00

ERDRICH, Louise. *Beet Queen.* 1986. Holt. ARC. wrp. EX. K2. $35.00

ERDRICH, Louise. *Jacklight.* 1984. NY. 1st ed. sgn. wrp. EX. T9. $140.00

ERDRICH, Louise. *Love Medicine.* 1984. Holt. 1st ed. dj. EX. C4. $125.00

ERDRICH, Louise. *Tracks.* 1988. Holt. ARC. sgn. wrp. EX. K2. $75.00

ERDRICH, Louise. *Tracks.* 1988. Holt. ARC. wrp. EX. K2. $35.00

ERDSTEIN & BEAN. *Inside the 4th Reich.* 1977. St Martin. 1st ed. dj. EX. P1. $15.00

ERICHSEN, John. *On Concussion of the Spine.* 1882. NY. Bermingham. 300 p. VG. J2. $40.00

ERNST & ELUARD. *Misfortunes of the Immortals.* 1943. Blk Sun. Trans Chisholm. 1/500. VG. H3. $300.00

ERSKINE, A.R. *Hist of Studebaker Corp.* 1924. S Bend. 1st ed. presentation. 229 p. VG. B3. $60.00

ERSKINE, A.R. *Hist of Studebaker Corp.* 1924. S Bend. 1st ed. 229 p. VG. B3. $45.00

ERSKINE, Dorothy. *Crystal Boat.* 1946. 1st ed. dj. VG. C1. $6.50

ERSKINE, John. *Adam & Eve.* 1927. Bobbs Merrill. VG. P1. $12.50

ERSKINE, John. *Adam & Eve.* 1927. McClelland Stewart. 1st Canadian ed. VG. P1. $7.00

ERSKINE, John. *Private Life of Helen of Troy.* 1925. Bobbs Merrill. VG. P1. $17.50

ERSKINE, John. *Tristan & Isolde: Restoring Palamede.* 1932. 1st Am ed. VG. C1. $18.00

ERSKINE, Margaret. *Old Mrs Ommanney Is Dead.* 1955. Crime Club. 1st ed. dj. VG. P1. $30.00

ERSKINE, Michael. *Diary of Michael Erskine Describing Cattle Drive...* 1979. Nita Stewart Memorial Lib. 1st ed. 1/975. VG. $85.00

ERTE. *Erte Fashions.* 1972. London. 1st ed. VG. G1. $20.00

ERTZ, Susan. *Woman Alive.* 1936. Appleton. 1st Am ed. dj. EX. R3. $20.00

ERVINE, St. John. *People of Our Class.* 1936. Allen Unwin. 1st ed. dj. EX. H3. $40.00

ESAREY, Logan. *Hist of IN From Its Exploration to 1850.* 1915. Indianapolis. 1st ed. 515 p. VG. T1. $60.00

ESHBACH, L.A. *Of Worlds Beyond.* 1947. Fantasy. 1st ed. dj. EX. R3. $75.00

ESHBACH, L.A. *Tyrant of Time.* 1955. Fantasy. 1st ed. dj. VG. R3. $17.50

ESHBACH, L.A. *Tyrant of Time.* 1955. Fantasy. 1st ed. Grant bdg. dj. M. P1. $20.00

ESHLEMAN, Clayton. *House of Ibuki: A Poem.* 1967. Sumac Pr. Ltd ed. 1/26. sgn. gilt blk bdg. M. H3. $45.00

ESHLEMAN, Clayton. *Mexico & N.* 1962. Tokyo. Hakyu-o-do. sgn. rose wrp. H3. $60.00

ESHLEMAN, Clayton. *T'ai.* 1969. Sans Souci Pr. Ltd ed. 1/99. sgn. glassine wrp. M. H3. $50.00

ESKELUND, Karl. *Cactus of Love.* 1957. London. 1st ed. 157 p. dj. F2. $15.00

ESKELUND, Karl. *Vagabond Fever.* 1954. Rand McNally. 1st ed. 240 p. dj. F2. $15.00

ESKEW, G.L. *Cradle of Ships.* 1958. NY. 1st ed. 279 p. dj. VG. B3. $30.00

ESON, Theo. *Grandma's Corner.* 1978. Leman Pub. 42 p. VG. B10. $3.00

ESPEJEL, Carlos. *Nelson A Rockefeller Collection of Mexican Folk Art.* 1986. San Francisco. 1st ed. 4to. 79 p. F2. $20.00

ESQUIRE. *Esquire's 1945 Jazz Book.* 1945. NY. Ils. 256 p. dj. VG. $50.00

ESSOE, Gabe. *Tarzan of the Movies.* 1973. Citadel. EX. R3. $15.00

ESTEVEN, John. *By Night at Dinsmore.* 1935. Canadian Crime Club. VG. P1. $20.00

ESTLEMAN, L.D. *Downriver.* 1988. Houghton Mifflin. 1st ed. dj. EX. P1. $15.95

ESTLEMAN, L.D. *Dr Jekyll & Mr Holmes.* 1979. Doubleday. 1st ed. dj. EX. F5. $15.00

ESTLEMAN, L.D. *General Murders.* 1988. Houghton Mifflin. 1st ed. dj. EX. P1. $16.95

ESTLEMAN, L.D. *Glass Highways.* 1983. Houghton Mifflin. dj. VG. P1. $15.00

ESTLEMAN, L.D. *Lady Yesterday.* 1987. Houghton Mifflin. 1st ed. dj. EX. F5. $15.00

ESTLEMAN, L.D. *Lady Yesterday.* 1987. Houghton Mifflin. 1st ed. sgn. dj. EX. T9. $30.00

ESTLEMAN, Loren. *Roses Are Dead.* 1985. Mysterious Pr. UP. wrp. EX. C4. $45.00

ETCHISON, Dennis. *Cutting Edge.* nd. Book Club. dj. VG. P1. $5.00

ETCHISON, Dennis. *Dark Country.* 1982. Scream. 1st ed. sgn. dj. EX. R3. $175.00

ETTINGHAUSEN, Richard. *Arab Painting.* 1962. Luasanne. Treasures of Asia Series. 4to. 208 p. T5. $65.00

ETZENHOUSER, J. *From Palmyra 1830 to Independence 1894.* 1894. Independence. 1st ed. 444 p. B3. $47.50

EVANS, A.B. *Jules Verne Rediscovered.* 1988. Greenwood. 1st ed. RS. M. R3. $37.95

EVANS, B.I. *Short Hist of Eng Literature.* 1951. Pelican. 5th print. VG. P1. $5.00

EVANS, Charles. *Am Bibliography 1639-1729.* 1943. Boston. Ils Wroth. 1/40. crimson morocco. EX. H3. $10000.00

EVANS, Charles. *Friends in the 17th Century.* 1875. Phil. Friends Bookstore. 8vo. 666 p. V1. $22.00

EVANS, E.E. *Alien Minds.* 1953. Fantasy. 1st ed. VG. R3. $37.50

EVANS, E.E. *Food for Demons.* 1971. Shroud Krueger. 1st ed. wrp. EX. R3. $15.00

EVANS, E.E. *Man of Many Minds.* 1953. Fantasy. 1st ed. VG. R3. $17.50

EVANS, H.R. *Hist of Conjuring & Magic.* 1928. Kenton, OH. 1st ed. 235 p. J3. $36.00

EVANS, Oliver. *Young Man With a Screwdriver.* 1950. NE U. Forword/sgn TN Williams. 1st ed. dj. EX. K2. $175.00

EVANS, P. *Best Book of Horse Stories.* 1958. Prentice. 1st ed. 384 p. VG. B10. $3.50

EVANS, Sebastian. *High Hist of the Holy Grail.* 1907 & 1924. Dent. 2 vols. C1. $29.50

EVANS, Sebastian. *High Hist of the Holy Grail.* 1913. Everymans Ed. VG. C1. $14.50

EVANS, Thomas. *Concise Account of Religious Soc of Friends.* nd. Phil. Friends Bookstore. 12mo. 161 p. V1. $10.00

EVANS, Thomas. *Examples of Youthful Piety...Instruction of Young Persons.* 1830. Phil. Thomas Kite. 12mo. 215 p. full leather. G. V1. $18.00

EVANS, W.B. *Jonathan Evans & His Time 1759-1839, Bicentennial Biography.* 1959. Boston. Christopher Pub. 1st ed. 8vo. 192 p. dj. VG. V1. $10.00

EVANS, William. *Journal of Life & Religious Service of William Evans.* 1870. Phil. Friends Bookstore. 8vo. 710 p. VG. V1. $25.00

EVANS & EVANS. *Friend's Lib.* 1841. Phil. Rakestraw. 4to. 14 vols. full leather. V1. $250.00

EVANS & EVANS. *Piety Promoted in Collection of Dying Sayings Vol 3.* 1854. Phil. Friends Bookstore. New Complete ed. 12mo. 450 p. G. V1. $14.00

EVANS & MEGGERS. *Archaeological Investigations on the Rio Napo, E Ecuador.* 1968. Smithsonian. 1st ed. 4to. 127 p. F2. $35.00

EVANS & STIVERS. *Hist of Adams Co, OH.* 1900. W Union, OH. Ils. 946 p. xl. T5. $150.00

EVERETT, Fred. *Fun With Game Birds.* 1954. Harrisburg. EX. $25.00

EVERETT, Fred. *Fun With Trout.* 1952. Harrisburg. EX. $45.00

EVERETT, L.T. *Patrick R Cleburne, Fighting Prophet.* 1946. De Land, FL. 1st ed. wrp. EX. $25.00

EVERETT-GREEN, E. *Mystery of Alton Grange.* c 1912. London. Ils Tod. Queen Academy presentation. NM. A4. $35.00

EVERITT, G. *Eng Caricaturists & Graphic Humorists of 19th C.* 1886. London. 1st ed. rebacked. G. $145.00

EVERMANN & GOLDSBOROUGH. *Fishes of AK.* 1907. GPO. clr pls. VG. T3. $65.00

EVERMANN & GOLDSBOROUGH. *Report on Fishes Collected in Mexico & Central Am.* 1902. GPO. 4to. wrp. F2. $17.50

EVERMANN & MARSH. *Fishes of Porto Rico.* 1900. GPO. clr pls. rebound. VG. T3. $75.00

EVERSON, William. *Residual Years.* 1948. New Directions. sgn. dj. H3. $85.00

EVERSON, William. *Triptych for the Living.* 1951. Seraphim Pr. 1/200. orig vellum/red silk ties. EX. H3. $2250.00

EWES, Basil. *Empire.* 1906. Copp Clarke. 3rd ed. VG. P1. $10.00

EXLEY, Frederick. *Fan's Notes.* 1968. NY. ARC. K2. $90.00

EYDOUX, H.P. *Hist of Archaeological Discoveries.* nd. London. Leisure Arts. 4to. 112 p. dj. F2. $15.00

EYDOUX, H.P. *In Search of Lost World.* 1971. World. 1st Am ed. 344 p. dj. F2. $15.00

FABER, Theodore. *Sketches of the Internal State of France.* 1812. Phil. 1st Am ed. $65.00

FABIAN, Robert. *Fabian of the Yard.* 1950. Naldrett. 2nd ed. dj. VG. P1. $10.00

FABIAN, Stephen. *Fabian in Clr.* 1980. Starmont. 1st ed. sgn. w/8 prints. M. R3. $17.50

FABIAN, Stephen. *Letters Lovecraftian.* 1974. De La Ree. 1st ed. wrp. EX. R3. $20.00

FABIAN, Stephen. *More Fantasy by Fabian.* 1979. De La Ree. 1st ed. dj. EX. R3. $45.00

FABRE, J.H. *Book of Insects.* 1936. Tudor. Ils Detmold. 12 pls. dj. EX. K1. $75.00

FABREGA & SILVER. *Illness & Shamanistic Curing in Zinacantan.* 1973. Stanford. 1st ed. 285 p. F2. $20.00

FADIMAN, Clifton. *Lifetime Reading Plan.* 1961. Avon. VG. P1. $4.50

FAGAN, Brian. *Intro Readings in Archaeology.* 1970. Little Brn. 5th print. 366 p. wrp. F2. $5.00

FAGAN, J.B. *Treasure Island.* 1936. Cassell. 1st ed. dj. VG. H3. $35.00

FAIR, A.A. *Gold Comes in Bricks.* 1944. Triangle. VG. P1. $10.00

FAIR, A.A. *Try Anything Once.* 1962. Morrow. 1st ed. dj. VG. P1. $17.50

FAIR, R.L. *Hog Butcher.* 1966. NY. 1st ed. sgn. dj. EX. T9. $55.00

FAIRBANKS, Arthur. *Handbook of Greek Religion.* nd. AM Book. VG. B10. $5.00

FAIRBANKS, Douglas. *Laugh & Live.* 1917. NY. 1st ed. dj. EX. K1. $27.50

FAIRCHILD, David. *World Was My Garden.* 1938. Scribner. 1st ed. sgn. 494 p. VG. $30.00

FAIRCHILD, David. *World Was My Garden.* 1939. NY/London. later print. VG. $20.00

FAIRLEY & WELFARE. *Arthur C Clarke's World of Strange Powers.* 1984. Putnam. 1st ed. M. R3. $19.95

FAIRLIE, Gerald. *No Sleep for Macall.* 1955. Hodder Stoughton. 1st ed. VG. P1. $20.00

FALCONER, Lando. *Ceclia de Noel.* 1892. London. VG. R3. $17.50

FALCONER, Sovereign. *To Make Death Love Us.* 1987. Doubleday. dj. RS. EX. P1. $17.50

FALCONER, Sovereign. *To Make Death Love Us.* 1987. Doubleday. 1st ed. dj. EX. F5. $16.00

FALK, Lee. *Phantom.* 1936. Whitman. Big Little Book. fair. B10. $4.00

FALK & DAVIS. *Mandrake the Magician & the Midnight Monster.* 1939. Whitman. Better Little Book. VG. J3. $20.00

FALL, Bernard. *St Without Joy.* 1961. Stackpole. 1st ed. dj. EX. very scarce. K2. $500.00

FALLACI, O. *Nothing & So Be It.* 1972. Garden City. K2. $30.00

FALLS, D.C. *Comic Military Alphabet.* 1891. NY. 27 pls. VG. $150.00

FALSTAFF, Jake. *Book of Rabelais.* 1928. NY. Ils Guy Arnoux. 1st ed. 246 p. VG. T5. $12.50

FALSTAFF, Jake. *Pippins & Cheese.* 1960. Hollywood, CA. 149 p. wrp. VG. T5. $3.50

FALSTEIN, Louis. *Slaughter St.* 1953. Lion. PB Orig. wrp. VG. T9. $15.00

FANNER, Janet. *London Was Yesterday 1934-1939.* 1975. Viking. 1st ed. inscr. dj. EX. B13. $175.00

FANNIN, Cole. *Leave It to Beaver.* 1962. Whitman. VG. P1. $7.50

FANNIN, Cole. *Sea Hunt.* 1960. Whitman. EX. P1. $20.00

FANT & ASHLEY. *Robert Faulkner at W Point.* 1964. Random House. 1st print. dj. VG. $17.00

FANTE, John. *Ask the Dust.* 1939. Stackpole. 1st ed. orig cloth. dj. EX. H3. $450.00

FANTEL, Hans. *William Penn: Apostle of Dissent.* 1974. Morrow. 1st ed. 8vo. 298 p. dj. VG. V1. $9.50

FANTHORPE, Lionel. *Macabre Ones.* 1973. Spencer. 1st HrdCvr ed. sgn. dj. EX. F5. $28.00

FARAGO, Ladislas. *Palestine at the Crossroads.* 1937. NY. 1st ed. EX. T1. $30.00

FARAGO, Ladislas. *Patton Ordeal & Triumph.* 1964. NY. 1st ed. dj. VG. B3. $27.50

FARBER, James. *Ft Worth in the Civil War.* 1960. Belton, TX. 1st ed. EX. $25.00

FARELLI, Victor. *Can You Tell Fortunes?* 1959. London. Mason Franco. 1st ed. NM. J3. $5.00

FARJEON, Eleanor. *10 Saints.* 1936. Oxford. Ils Helen Sewell. VG. B7. $45.00

FARJEON, J.J. *Mystery Underground.* 1932. Collins. 5th print. VG. P1. $10.00

FARJEON, J.J. *Shadow of 13.* 1949. Collins Crime Club. 1st ed. dj. VG. P1. $15.00

FARLEY, R.M. *Earth Man on Venus.* 1950. Avon. 1st ed. wrp. VG. R3. $25.00

FARLEY, R.M. *Hidden Universe.* 1950. Fantasy. 1st ed. dj. EX. R3. $15.00

FARLEY, R.M. *Omnibus of Time.* 1950. Fantasy. 1st ed. dj. EX. R3. $25.00

FARLEY, R.M. *Radio Man.* 1948. Fantasy. 1st ed. 1st bdg. dj. EX. R3. $25.00

FARLEY, Walter. *Blk Stallion & Satan.* 1949. Random House. 1st ed. dj. EX. P1. $20.00

FARLEY, Walter. *Blk Stallion.* nd. Random House. dj. VG. P1. $9.25

FARMAN, E.S. *Where the MS Flows & Other Stories.* 1906. Chicago. sgn. VG. C1. $24.50

FARMER, Bob. *Tsunami.* 1987. Ontario. Farmer. 1st ed. stapled manuscript. NM. J3. $7.00

FARMER, F.M. *Food & Cookery for the Sick & Convalescent.* 1917. Boston. Ils. 12mo. 305 p. gr bdg. VG. T1. $35.00

FARMER, Frances. *Will There Really Be a Morning?* 1972. NY. 1st ed. dj. VG. B3. $20.00

FARMER, P.J. *Adventure of the Peerless Peer.* 1974. Aspen. 1st ed. dj. EX. R3. $50.00

FARMER, P.J. *Barnstormer in Oz.* 1982. Phantasia. 1st ed. 1/600. sgn. M. R3. $50.00

FARMER, P.J. *Behind the Walls of Terra.* 1982. Phantasia. 1st ed. 1/250. sgn. M. R3. $60.00

FARMER, P.J. *Book of Philip J Farmer.* 1976. London. 1st ed. dj. EX. $20.00

FARMER, P.J. *Classic Farmer 1952-1964.* nd. Book Club. dj. VG. P1. $4.50

FARMER, P.J. *Classic Farmer 1964-1973.* 1984. Crown. 1st ed. dj. EX. P1. $8.95

FARMER, P.J. *Dark Design.* 1974. London. 1st ed. sgn. dj. EX. R3. $30.00

FARMER, P.J. *Dark Design.* 1977. Berkley Putnam. 1st ed. dj. VG. P1. $20.00

FARMER, P.J. *Dark Is the Sun.* 1979. Del Rey. 1st ed. dj. EX. R3. $20.00

FARMER, P.J. *Dayworld.* 1985. Putnam. 1st ed. dj. EX. P1. $16.95

FARMER, P.J. *Doc Savage: His Apocalyptic Life.* 1973. Doubleday. 1st ed. dj. EX. $50.00

FARMER, P.J. *Fabulous Riverboat.* 1974. London. 1st Eng ed. sgn. Lib bdg. EX. R3. $50.00

FARMER, P.J. *Fabulous Riverboat.* 1980. Gregg Pr. 1st ed. M. R3. $30.00

FARMER, P.J. *Flesh.* 1960. Beacon. 1st ed. sgn. EX. R3. $50.00

FARMER, P.J. *Gates of Creation.* 1981. Phantasia. 1st ed. M. R3. $15.00

FARMER, P.J. *Gods of Riverworld.* 1983. Phantasia. 1st ed. 1/650. sgn. dj. slipcase. EX. P1. $50.00

FARMER, P.J. *Gods of Riverworld.* 1983. Putnam. 1st ed. M. R3. $15.00

FARMER, P.J. *Love Song.* 1983. Dennis McMillan. 1st HrdCvr ed. 1/500. sgn. M. R3. $75.00

FARMER, P.J. *Magic Labyrinth.* 1980. Berkley Putnam. 1st ed. dj. EX. P1. $15.00

FARMER, P.J. *Magic Labyrinth.* 1980. Berkley Putnam. 1st ed. sgn. dj. EX. R3. $25.00

FARMER, P.J. *Maker of Universes.* 1980. Phantasia. 1st ed. M. R3. $15.00

FARMER, P.J. *Private Cosmos.* 1981. Phantasia. Ltd ed. 1/250. sgn. M. R3. $45.00

FARMER, P.J. *Private Cosmos.* 1981. Phantasia. 1st ed. M. R3. $18.00

FARMER, P.J. *River of Eternity.* 1983. Phantasia. 1st ed. 1/500. sgn. M. R3. $35.00

FARMER, P.J. *Unreasoning Mask.* 1981. NY. 1st ed. DJ. EX. $20.00

FARMER, P.J. *Unreasoning Mask.* 1981. Putnam. Ltd ed. 1/500. sgn. slipcase. EX. K2. $65.00

FARMER, P.J. *Venus on the Half Shell.* 1975. Dell. 1st ed. wrp. EX. B13. $25.00

FARMER, P.J. *Your Scattered Bodies Go.* 1980. Gregg Pr. 1st ed. M. R3. $30.00

FARNHAM, Jerusha. *Log City Days: 2 Narratives on Settlement of Galesburg, IL.* 1937. Knox College. 1st ed. VG. $35.00

FARNOL, Jeffery. *Belante the Smith.* 1929. Sampson Low. VG. P1. $10.00

FARNOL, Jeffery. *Broad Highway.* 1911. Little Brn. 7th print. VG. P1. $10.00

FARNOL, Jeffery. *My Lord of Wrybourne.* 1948. Ryerson. 1st Canadian ed. dj. VG. P1. $15.00

FARNOL, Jeffery. *Way Beyond.* 1933. Ryerson. VG. P1. $10.00

FARNOL, Jeffery. *Winds of Chance.* 1924. Ryerson. VG. P1. $12.50

FARNUM. *Life in Prairie Land.* 1846. Harper. 1st ed. 480 p. G. A5. $40.00

FARR, Robert. *Electronic Criminals.* 1975. McGraw Hill. 1st ed. dj. VG. P1. $15.00

FARRAR, Geraldine. *Autobiography.* 1916. Boston. 1st ed. 116 p. dj. VG. B3. $25.00

FARRAR, Stewart. *Death in the Wrong Bed.* 1964. Walker. 1st ed. dj. xl. P1. $7.50

FARRELL, J.T. *Judith.* 1969. Schneider. Ltd ed. 1/300. sgn. stiff wrp. H3. $60.00

FARRELL, J.T. *Misunderstanding.* 1949. House of Books. Ltd ed. 1/300. sgn. H3. $50.00

FARRELL, J.T. *Silence of Hist.* 1963. Garden City. 1st ed. dj. VG. $15.00

FARRELL, J.T. *Silence of Hist.* 1963. Garden City. 1st ed. dj. w/4 p letter. B3. $95.00

FARRINGTON, S.K. *Atlantic Game Fishing.* 1937. Kennedy Bros. Ils Bogue-Hunt. presentation. 297 p. EX. $145.00

FARRINGTON, S.K. *Atlantic Game Fishing.* 1939. NY. Deluxe ed. VG. $35.00

FARRINGTON, S.K. *Ducks Came Back: Story of Ducks Unlimited.* 1945. NY. 1st ed. sgn. dj. EX. $35.00

FARRIS, John. *Corpse Next Door.* 1956. Graphic 138. 1st ed. wrp. VG. T9. $30.00

FARRIS, John. *King Windom.* 1967. Trident Pr. 1st ed. dj. EX. F5. $60.00

FARRIS, John. *Nightfall.* 1987. Tor Books. 1st ed. wrp. EX. F5. $8.00

FARRIS, John. *Son of the Endless Night.* nd. Book Club. dj. VG. P1. $5.00

FAST, Howard. *Hunter & the Trap.* 1968. Dial. 3rd ed. dj. VG. P1. $10.00

FAST, Howard. *Touch of Infinity.* 1973. Morrow. 1st ed. dj. EX. F5. $20.00

FAST, Jonathan. *Inner Circle.* nd. Book Club. dj. VG. P1. $4.50

FAST, Jonathan. *Mortal Gods.* 1978. Harper Row. 1st ed. dj. EX. P1. $15.00

FAST & FAST. *Picture Book Hist of the Jews.* 1942. Hebrew Pub. 1st ed. dj. K2. $65.00

FATOUT, Paul. *Mark Twain Speaks for Himself.* 1978. Purdue U. dj. VG. $16.00

FAUCHARD, Pierre. *Surgeon Dentist; or, Treatise on Teeth.* 1969. NY. reprint of 1746 ed. $25.00

FAULKNER, John. *Men Working.* 1941. Harcourt Brace. 1st ed. sgn. dj. EX. B13. $150.00

FAULKNER, William. *Absalom, Absalom!* 1936. Random House. Ltd ed. 1/300. sgn. TEG. H3. $1500.00

FAULKNER, William. *Absalom, Absalom!* 1936. Random House. 1st ed. VG. H3. $75.00

FAULKNER, William. *Anthology of Younger Poets.* 1932. Phil. Centaur. 1st ed. 1/500. glassine dj. EX. B13. $300.00 ·

FAULKNER, William. *As I Lay Dying.* 1930. Jonathan Cape. 1st ed. 1st issue. dj. VG. H3. $750.00

FAULKNER, William. *Bear.* 1958. Paderborn. Schoningh. pamphlet. EX. K2. $85.00

FAULKNER, William. *Dr Martino & Other Stories.* 1934. Smith Haas. 1st ed. dj. EX. H3. $500.00

FAULKNER, William. *Elmer.* 1983. Seajay Pr. 1st ed. 1/200. EX. B13. $250.00

FAULKNER, William. *Fable.* 1954. Random House. Ltd ed. 1/1000. sgn. glassine dj. EX. H3. $550.00

FAULKNER, William. *Fable.* 1954. Random House. 1st ed. dj. VG. H3. $100.00

FAULKNER, William. *Faulkner at W Point.* 1964. Random House. 1st ed. dj. EX. B13. $65.00

FAULKNER, William. *Ghost of Rowman Oak.* 1980. Yoknapatawpha Pr. 1st ed. dj. EX. B13. $30.00

FAULKNER, William. *Go Down, Moses & Other Stories.* 1942. Random House. 1st ed. dj. EX. H3. $750.00

FAULKNER, William. *Go Down, Moses.* 1942. Random House. 1st ed. dj. VG. H3. $350.00

FAULKNER, William. *Go Down, Moses.* 1942. Random House. 2nd print. dj. EX. K2. $250.00

FAULKNER, William. *Gr Bough.* 1933. Smith Haas. 1st ed. 1/360. sgn. EX. K2. $1350.00

FAULKNER, William. *Gr Bough.* 1933. Smith Haas. 1st Trade ed. dj. EX. B13. $450.00

FAULKNER, William. *Hamlet.* 1940. Random House. 1st ed. orig bdg. dj. EX. H3. $750.00

FAULKNER, William. *Hunting Stories.* 1988. Ltd Ed Club. Ils/sgn Neil Welliver. slipcase. VG. $60.00

FAULKNER, William. *Idyll in the Desert.* 1931. NY. 1st ed. 1/400. sgn. as issued. K2. $650.00

FAULKNER, William. *Intruder in the Dust.* 1948. NY. Ltd ed. 1/750. sgn. K2. $600.00

FAULKNER, William. *Intruder in the Dust.* 1948. Random House. 1st ed. dj. EX. H3. $125.00

FAULKNER, William. *Intruder in the Dust.* 1948. Random House. 2nd print. sgn. dj. EX. w/Cerf letter. K2. $1500.00

FAULKNER, William. *Intruder in the Dust.* 1948. Random House. 6th print. dj. EX. $15.00

FAULKNER, William. *Jealousy & Episode.* 1955. Faulkner Studios. Ltd ed. 1/500. EX. H3. $250.00

FAULKNER, William. *Knight's Gambit.* 1949. Random House. 1st ed. dj. EX. H3. $200.00

FAULKNER, William. *Light in August.* 1932. Smith Haas. 1st ed. dj. EX. H3. $1000.00

FAULKNER, William. *Mansion.* 1959. Random House. Ltd 1st ed. 1/500. sgn. EX. H3. $600.00

FAULKNER, William. *Mansion.* 1959. Random House. 1st ed. dj. EX. H3. $75.00

FAULKNER, William. *Marionettes.* 1975. Yoknapatawpha Pr. Special Pub Presentation ed. boxed. EX. B13. $350.00

FAULKNER, William. *Mayday.* 1978. Notre Dame. Trade ed. dj. M. scarce. C1. $17.50

FAULKNER, William. *Mirrors of the Chartres St.* 1953. Minneapolis. Faulkner Studies. 1/1000. dj. EX. B13. $275.00

FAULKNER, William. *Miss Zilphia Gant.* 1932. TX Book Club. 1st ed. 1/300. sgn. glassine dj. EX. B13/K2/H3. $1250.00

FAULKNER, William. *Mosquitoes.* 1927. Boni Liveright. 1st ed. dj. VG. H3. $1500.00

FAULKNER, William. *Mosquitoes.* 1937. Dial. 1st ed. VG. $30.00

FAULKNER, William. *New Eng Journeys.* 1954. Ford Motors. Ford Times Special ed. PB. B13. $45.00

FAULKNER, William. *New Orleans Sketches.* 1955. Tokyo. Hokuseido. 1st ed. tan wrp. EX. scarce. $200.00

FAULKNER, William. *Notes on a Horse Thief.* 1950. Levee Pr. Ltd 1st ed. 1/975. sgn. EX. H3/K2. $550.00

FAULKNER, William. *Perspective From the Brodsky Collection.* 1979. SE MO U. 1st ed. 1/2500. 4to. wrp. EX. B13. $35.00

FAULKNER, William. *Portable Faulkner.* 1946. Viking. 1st ed. dj. EX. H3. $30.00

FAULKNER, William. *Pylon.* 1935. NY. 1st ed. later state dj. VG. K2. $150.00

FAULKNER, William. *Pylon.* 1935. Smith Haas. Ltd ed. 1/310. sgn. boxed. H3. $750.00

FAULKNER, William. *Pylon.* 1935. Smith Haas. 1st ed. dj. EX. H3. $300.00

FAULKNER, William. *Pylon.* 1935. Smith Haas. 1st ed. dj. VG. B3. $200.00

FAULKNER, William. *Reivers.* 1962. Random House. Ltd ed. 1/500. sgn. H3. $500.00

FAULKNER, William. *Requiem for a Nun.* 1951. Random House. Ltd ed. 1/750. sgn. H3. $500.00

FAULKNER, William. *Requiem for a Nun.* 1951. Random House. 1st ed. dj. VG. H3. $125.00

FAULKNER, William. *Requiem for a Nun: A Play.* 1959. NY. Adapted/inscr Ruth Ford. as issued. K2. $85.00

FAULKNER, William. *Rose for Emily & Other Stories.* nd. Armed Services ed. 1st ed. wrp. VG. T9. $75.00

FAULKNER, William. *Salmagundi.* 1932. Casanova. Ltd ed. 1/525. slipcase. EX. H3. $650.00

FAULKNER, William. *Sanctuary.* 1932. Crosby Continental Ed. 1st Blk Sun ed. wrp. H3. $125.00

FAULKNER, William. *Sanctuary.* 1932. Modern Lib. dj. VG. P1. $20.00

FAULKNER, William. *Sartoris.* 1929. Harcourt Brace. 1st ed. dj. EX. H3. $1500.00

FAULKNER, William. *Soldier's Pay.* 1930. Chatto Windus. Ils/sgn Paul Cadmus. 2nd print. VG. B13. $300.00

FAULKNER, William. *Soldier's Play.* 1926. Boni Liveright. 1st ed. H3. $150.00

FAULKNER, William. *Soldier's Play.* 1930. London. 1st Eng ed. dj. EX. H3. $2500.00

FAULKNER, William. *Sound & the Fury.* 1929. Jonathan Cape. 1st ed. dj. EX. H3. $2750.00

FAULKNER, William. *Sound & the Fury.* 1931. London. 1st ed. dj. EX. H3. $1750.00

FAULKNER, William. *These 13.* 1931. Jonathan Cape. 1st ed. dj. VG. H3. $400.00

FAULKNER, William. *These 13.* 1931. NY. Cape Smith. 2nd print. EX. B13. $45.00

FAULKNER, William. *This Earth.* 1932. NY. Equinox. 1st ed. 1/100. orig mailing envelope. EX. K2. $185.00

FAULKNER, William. *This Earth. A Poem...With Drawings by Albert Beckman.* 1932. Equinox. Ltd ed. wrp. EX. H3. $250.00

FAULKNER, William. *Town.* 1957. NY. Correct 1st issue. VG. K2. $125.00

FAULKNER, William. *Town.* 1957. Random House. Ltd 1st ed. sgn. H3. $650.00

FAULKNER, William. *Unvanquished.* c1957. Berlin. Velhagen Klasing. pamphlet. wrp. EX. K2. $85.00

FAULKNER, William. *Unvanquished.* 1938. Random House. Ils Shenton. Ltd 1st ed. 1/250. sgn. H3. $1250.00

FAULKNER, William. *Unvanquished.* 1938. Random House. 1st ed. dj. EX. H3. $450.00

FAULKNER, William. *Wild Palms.* 1939. Random House. Ltd 1st ed. 1/250. sgn. slipcase. H3. $1000.00

FAULKNER, William. *Wild Palms.* 1939. Random House. 1st ed. H3. $450.00

FAULKNER, William. *Wishing Tree.* 1964. Random House. Ltd ed. 1/500. dj. slipcase. B13. $250.00

FAULKNER, William. *Wishing Tree.* 1967. Random House. Ltd ed. 1/500. dj. slipcase. H3. $200.00

FAULKNER, William. *Wishing Tree.* 1967. Random House. 1st Trade ed. dj. EX. H3. $100.00

FAULKNER & FAULKNER. *Inside Today's Home.* 1954. NY. 552 p. $35.00

FAULKNER & KERR. *Yoknapatawpha: Faulkner's Native Soil.* 1969. NY. 1st ed. 284 p. dj. VG. B3. $32.50

FAWCETT, C.H. *We Fell in Love With the Circus.* 1949. Linquist. 1st ed. octavo. 198 p. dj. VG. H3. $60.00

FAWCETT, P.H. *Exploration Fawcett.* 1953. London. 1st ed. 312 p. dj. F2. $20.00

FAY, Charles. *Mary Celeste: Odyssey of an Abandoned Ship.* 1942. Peabody Mus. Ltd 1st ed. 1/1000. VG. $25.00

FEA, Allan. *Picturesque Old Houses.* nd. London. Ils. 224 p. TEG. fair. T5. $22.50

FEARING, Kenneth. *Generous Heart.* 1954. Harcourt Brace. 1st ed. dj. VG. P1. $35.00

FEARN, J.R. *Amazon Strikes Again.* 1954. London. 1st ed. dj. EX. R3. $40.00

FEARN, J.R. *Amazon's Diamond Quest.* 1963. London. 1st ed. dj. EX. R3. $40.00

FEARN, J.R. *Golden Amazon Returns.* 1948. London. 1st ed. dj. EX. R3. $40.00

FEARN, J.R. *Golden Amazon's Triumph.* 1953. London. 1st ed. dj. EX. R3. $40.00

FEARN, J.R. *Liners of Time.* 1947. London. 1st ed. dj. EX. R3. $30.00

FEARN, J.R. *Slaves of Ajax.* nd. London. 1st ed. wrp. VG. R3. $10.00

FEARN, J.R. *Twin of the Amazon.* 1954. London. 1st ed. dj. EX. R3. $40.00

FEATHERSTONE, Donald. *Battles With Model Soldiers.* 1972. NY. VG. C1. $12.00

FEATHERSTONE, Donald. *Bowmen of Eng.* 1968. NY. 1st ed. EX. $20.00

FEBRES-CORDERO, Focion. *Origenes de la Odontologia.* 1964. Caracas. Spanish text. 131 p. F2. $10.00

FEDERN, Robert. *Bibliography Literature Francaise des Origins a Nous Jours.* 1913. Paris. VG. G1. $40.00

FEDKO, John. *Magic Classics.* 1975. Fedko Magic. 22 p. NM. J3. $4.00

FEHRENBACH, T.R. *This Kind of War.* 1963. NY. 1st ed. dj. VG. B3. $40.00

FEIFFER, Jules. *Carnal Knowledge.* 1971. NY. 1st ed. clipped dj. EX. T9. $35.00

FEIFFER, Jules. *Carnal Knowlege.* 1971. Farrar Straus. Photoplay/1st ed. dj. EX. scarce. B13. $85.00

FEIFFER, Jules. *Whitehouse Murder Case.* 1970. Blk Cat. 1st PB ed. B4. $4.00

FEININGER, Andreas. *Face of NY.* 1945. Chicago/NY. 1st ed. VG. $45.00

FEININGER, Andreas. *World Through My Eyes: 30 Years of Photography.* nd. NY. Ils. 52 p. dj. VG. T5. $45.00

FEINMAN, Jeffrey. *Magic: 193 Easy-To-Do, Impossible-To-Detect Magic Tricks.* 1980. Wanderer Books. 1st print. 126 p. EX. J3. $4.00

FEINMAN, Jeffrey. *Mysterious World of Agatha Christie.* 1975. Award Books. PB Orig. wrp. EX. T9. $15.00

FEIST, R.E. *Faerie Tale.* 1988. Doubleday. ARC. wrp. M. R3. $20.00

FEIST, R.E. *Faerie Tale.* 1988. Doubleday. 1st ed. dj. EX. F5. $18.00

FELDMAN & GARTENBERG. *Protest: Beat Generation & the Angry Young Men.* 1960. London. Panther 1075. PB Orig. B4. $4.00

FELLER, Bob. *Strikeout Story.* 1947. NY. Ils. 258 p. G. T5. $17.50

FELTHAM, Jane. *Peruvian Textiles.* 1989. Aylesbury. 1st ed. 72 p. wrp. F2. $10.00

FELTON, Mrs. *Life in Am.* 1883. Eng. Hull. 1st ed. 12mo. VG. A4. $125.00

FELTON, Rebecca. *Romantic Story of GA's Women.* 1930. Atlanta. 1st ed. orig wrp. VG. $25.00

FENISONG, Ruth. *Lost Caesar.* 1945. Crime Club. 1st ed. xl. P1. $5.00

FENISONG, Ruth. *Widows' Plight.* nd. Book Club. dj. VG. P1. $4.50

FENN, G.M. *Young Robin Hood.* c 1900. Phil. probably 1st ed. dj. C1. $29.50

FENNER, Marian. *Betty's Beautiful Nights.* 1916. NY. Ils Clara Burd. 1st ed. EX. $25.00

FENNER, T.P. *Cabin & Plantation Songs.* 1878. Putnam. octavo. 255 p. wrp. G. H3. $75.00

FENOLLOSA, Ernest. *Chinese Written Character As Medium for Poetry.* 1936. NY. Arrow Ed. 8vo. 52 p. VG. V1. $65.00

FENTON, R.W. *Big Swingers.* 1967. Prentice Hall. 1st ed. dj. EX. R3. $25.00

FERBER, Edna. *Cimarron.* 1963. Bantam. 12th print. Lib PB bdg. VG. P1. $4.00

FERBER, Edna. *Peculiar Treasure.* 1939. Doubleday Doran. Ltd ed. 1/351. sgn. TEG. H3. $150.00

FERBER, Edna. *Saratoga Trunk.* 1941. Doubleday Doran. Ltd ed. 1/562. sgn. TEG. slipcase. H3. $125.00

FERBER, Edna. *Saratoga Trunk.* 1941. Doubleday Doran. 1st ed. 352 p. xl. B10. $7.00

FERBER, Edna. *Show Boat.* 1926. Doubleday Page. Ltd ed. 1/201. sgn. TEG. slipcase. H3. $300.00

FERBER, F. *L'Aviation.* 1909. Paris. Ils. 4th print. 250 p. T5. $295.00

FERBER & KAUFMAN. *Land Is Bright.* 1941. Doubleday Doran. 1st ed. dj. EX. H3. $60.00

FERGUSON, Brad. *Crisis on Centaurus.* 1986. Pocket. 1st HrdCvr ed. dj. EX. F5. $16.00

FERGUSON, C.D. *Experiences of a Forty-Niner.* 1888. Cleveland. Ils 1st ed. 507 p. VG. T5. $125.00

FERGUSON, Neil. *Bars of Am.* 1986. Hamish Hamilton. 1st ed. dj. EX. F5. $15.00

FERGUSON, William. *Dream Reader.* 1973. Cambridge. Ferguson. sgn. wrp. H3. $35.00

FERGUSON & ROYCE. *Maya Ruins in Central Am in Clr.* 1984. NM U. 1st ed. dj. F2. $40.00

FERGUSSON, Bruce. *Shadow of His Wings.* 1987. Arbor House. 1st ed. dj. EX. P1. $16.95

FERGUSSON, Erna. *Guatemala.* 1949. Knopf. 317 p. xl. F2. $10.00

FERGUSSON, Erna. *Mexico Revisited.* 1955. Knopf. 1st ed. 346 p. F2. $15.00

FERGUSSON, Erna. *Venezuela.* 1939. Knopf. 1st ed. 346 p. F2. $10.00

FERGUSSON, William. *Maya Ruins of Mexico in Clr.* 1977. OK U. 1st ed. 246 p. dj. F2. $35.00

FERLINGHETTI, Lawrence. *Back Roads to Far Towns After Basho.* 1970. private print. inscr/sketch. VG. B4. $20.00

FERLINGHETTI, Lawrence. *Pictures of the Gone World.* 1957. City Lights. 3rd print. sgn. VG. B4. $10.00

FERLINGHETTI, Lawrence. *Secret Meaning of Things.* 1967. New Directions. 2nd print. PB. VG. B4. $3.00

FERMAN, Edward. *Best From Fantasy & SF 16th Series.* 1967. Doubleday. 1st ed. dj. EX. R3. $15.00

FERMAN & MALZBERG. *Final Stage.* 1974. Charterhouse. 1st ed. dj. VG. R3. $11.50

FERMAN & MALZBERG. *Graven Images.* 1977. Nelson. 1st ed. dj. EX. F5. $15.00

FERMAN & MALZBERG. *Graven Images.* 1977. Nelson. 1st ed. sgns. EX. R3. $25.00

FERNANDEZ, Justino. *Mexican Art.* 1970. London. Hamlyn. 4to. F2. $10.00

FERNOW, B. *Forest Conditions of Nova Scotia.* 1912. Ottawa. Ils. 5 pocket maps. VG. $85.00

FERRAND DE ALMEIDA, Luis. *Informacao de Francisco Ribeiro Sobre Colonia Do Sacramento.* 1955. Coimbra. 105 p. wrp. F2. $10.00

FERRARO, Geraldine. *Ferraro: My Story.* 1985. Bantam. Book Club ed. dj. M. B10. $4.00

FERRARS, E.X. *Breath of Suspicion.* 1973. Collins Crime Club. 1st ed. dj. xl. P1. $7.50

FERRARS, E.X. *Death in Botanist's Bay.* 1941. Hodder Stoughton. VG. P1. $25.00

FERRARS, E.X. *Designs on Life.* 1980. Crime Club. 1st ed. dj. xl. P1. $7.50

FERRARS, E.X. *Hunt the Tortoise.* 1953. Collins Crime Club. 2nd ed. dj. VG. P1. $15.00

FERRARS, E.X. *I, Said the Fly.* 1945. Crime Club. VG. P1. $15.00

FERRARS, E.X. *Thinner Than Water.* 1982. Doubleday. 1st ed. dj. VG. P1. $15.00

FERRENTINO, John. *Comedy Clubs for All Magicians.* 1984. Jenack Circus Corp. 52 p. SftCvr. EX. J3. $6.00

FERRERE, Claude. *Useless Hands.* 1926. Dutton. Review 1st ed. VG. R3. $35.00

FERRERE, John. *Sharp Practice.* 1974. Simon Schuster. 1st ed. dj. EX. R3. $75.00

FERRERE, John. *Wildwood.* 1986. Tor Books. 1st ed. dj. EX. R3. $20.00

FERREZ & NAEF. *Pioneer Photographers of Brazil 1840-1920.* 1976. NY. 1st ed. oblong 8vo. 144 p. F2. $30.00

FERRIS, David. *Memoirs of the Life of David Ferris...Written by Himself.* 1855. Phil. Merrihew Thompson. Revised ed. 16mo. 106 p. V1. $20.00

FERRIS, J. *States & Territories of the Great W.* 1856. NY. Ils. 12mo. 352 p. lacks map. G4. $28.00

FERRIS, J.C. *X-Bar-X Boys in the Haunted Gully.* 1940. Grosset. 216 p. VG. B10. $3.75

FERRIS, Paul. *High Places.* 1977. Coward McCann Goeghegan. 1st ed. dj. VG. P1. $15.00

FERRIS, Ron. *Apparitions, Animations, & Aces.* 1973. Micky Hades. 1st ed. 31 p. NM. J3. $7.00

FERRY, A.F. *When I Was at Farmington.* 1931. Chicago. Ils. 296 p. G. T5. $25.00

FEUCHTWANGER, Franz. *Art of Ancient Mexico.* 1955. Thames Hudson. 4to. 125 p. VG. F2. $35.00

FEVAL, Paul; see Bedford-Jones, H.

FEZANDIE, Clement. *Through the Earth.* 1972. Starmont. 1st ed. wrp. EX. R3. $10.00

FICK, Hermann. *Life & Deeds of Dr Martin Luther.* 1869. Schulze. 1st Am ed? 181 p. fair. B10. $7.00

FIEBEGER, C.J. *Campaign & Battle of Gettysburg.* 1915. W Point. Ils. maps. 116 p. VG. T5. $42.50

FIEDLER, Maggi. *Corky's Pet Parade.* 1946. Pied Piper Books. 32 p. dj. G. T5. $35.00

FIEGER, Erwin. *Mexico.* 1973. W Germany. 1st ed. 206 pls. 208 p. F2. $25.00

FIELD, Andrew. *Djuna: Life & Times of Djuna Barnes.* 1982. Putnam. UP. wrp. EX. K2. $25.00

FIELD, D.D. *Brainerd Family in US (Genealogy).* 1857. NY. 1st ed. 303 p. $65.00

FIELD, Eugene. *Baedeker's Conversation Dictionary in 4 Languages.* 1889. London. sgn. 16mo. gilt bdg. H3. $50.00

FIELD, Eugene. *Clink of the Ice.* nd. (1905) Chicago. Donahue. 1st ed. VG. B10. $8.50

FIELD, Eugene. *In Wink-a-Way land.* 1930. Donohue. 4to. 128 p. VG. $35.00

FIELD, Eugene. *Little Book of Profitable Tales.* 1889. Chicago. 1/250. sgn. TEG. slipcase. H3. $200.00

FIELD, Eugene. *My Book.* 1905. Chicago. Ils Seypel. 1st/only ed. sgn. H3. $250.00

FIELD, Eugene. *Sleeping World & Other Poems.* 1887. McClurg. w/sgn poem on endpaper. H3. $150.00

FIELD, Evan. *What Nigel Knew.* 1981. Potter. 1st ed. dj. EX. P1. $12.50

FIELD, H.M. *Story of the Atlantic Telegraph.* 1892. NY. 1st ed. inscr. 415 p. K1. $150.00

FIELD, R.D. *Art of Walt Disney.* 1942. Macmillan. 1st ed. 4to. 290 p. EX. R4. $185.00

FIELD, R.D. *Art of Walt Disney.* 1942. NY. Ils. 4to. VG. $85.00

FIELD, R.D. *Art of Walt Disney.* 1947. London. 3rd print. VG. C2. $175.00

FIELD, Rachel. *Calico Bush.* 1931. NY. 1st ed. presentation. VG. $70.00

FIELD, W.B. *John Leech on My Shelves.* 1970. NY. Collectors Ed. reprint of 1930 ed. H3. $40.00

FIELDING, A. *Cautley Mystery.* nd. AL Burt. dj. VG. P1. $10.00

FIELDING, A. *Death of John Tait.* 1932. Kinsey. 1st ed. VG. P1. $15.00

FIELDING, A. *Eames Erskine Case.* nd. AL Burt. VG. P1. $5.00

FIELDING, A. *Murder at the Nook.* 1930. Knopf. 1st ed. gr bdg. xl. B10. $3.75

FIELDING, Henry. *Hist of the Life of Late Mr Jonathan Wild, the Great.* 1943. Ltd Ed Club. Ils/sgn TM Cleland. 1/1500. slipcase. EX. C4. $80.00

FIELDING, Henry. *Hist of the Life of Late Mr Jonathan Wild, the Great.* 1943. Ltd Ed Club. Ils/sgn TM Cleland. 4to. slipcase. VG. $45.00

FIELDING, Henry. *Hist of Tom Jones, Foundling.* c 1920. Modern Lib. 861 p. dj. VG. B10. $3.50

FIELDING, Henry. *Hist of Tom Jones, Foundling.* 1749. London. 1st ed. 6 vols. ES. rebound. H3. $5000.00

FIELDING, Henry. *Works.* nd. London. Navarre Soc. 12 vols. TEG. VG. $95.00

FIELDING, Henry. *Works.* 1771. London. Strahan. New ed. 8 vols. thick octavo. G. H3. $300.00

FIELDS, W.C. *WC Fields by Himself.* 1973. Prentice Hall. 1st ed. octavo. 510 p. dj. EX. H3. $35.00

FIELDS & CHODOROV. *My Sister Eileen.* 1941. Random House. sgn. gr bdg. dj. H3. $175.00

FIELDS & CHODOROV. *My Sister Eileen.* 1941. Random House. 1st ed. dj. EX. H3. $150.00

FILBY & HOWARD. *Star-Spangled Books.* 1972. MD Hist Soc. quarto. 175 p. EX. H3. $40.00

FINCH, E.W. *Frontier: Army & Professional Life of EW Finch.* 1909. New Rochelle. 1st ed. VG. $85.00

FINDLAY, James. *Modern Latin Am Art: A Bibliography.* 1983. Greenwood Pr. 1st ed. 301 p. F2. $25.00

FINEMAN, Irving. *Life & Death of St Adolphe.* 1937. Covici Friede. 1/199. sgn. 16mo. H3. $30.00

FINGER, C.J. *Tales From Silver Lands.* nd. (1924) Doubleday. Ils Honore. dj. B10. $8.25

FINKEL, George. *Watch Fires to the N.* 1st Am ed. dj. VG. C1. $44.50

FINLAY, Virgil. *Astrology Sketchbook.* 1975. Grant. 1st ed. dj. EX. R3. $15.00

FINLAY, Virgil. *Book of Virgil Finlay.* 1976. Avon. lg wrp. VG. R3. $20.00

FINLAY, Virgil. *Space Travel.* 1956. World. 1st ed. dj. EX. R3. $65.00

FINLAY, Virgil. *3rd Book of Virgil Finlay.* 1979. De La Ree. 1st ed. dj. EX. R3. $75.00

FINLAY & SHEPPARD. *S Am Overland.* 1980. Australia. Angus Robertson. 1st ed. 383 p. dj. F2. $15.00

FINLEY, G.E. *Van Gogh.* 1966. Tudor. dj. VG. P1. $15.00

FINLEY, J.B. *Sketches of W Methodism.* 1854. Cincinnati. Ils 1st ed. 551 p. T5. $65.00

FINLEY & MACKENZIE. *Chinese Art.* nd. (1968) London. Revised 2nd ed. dj. B10. $7.00

FINN, C.E. *OH Canals: Public Enterprise on the Frontier.* 1956. Ft Wayne, OH. Ils. 42 p. wrp. T5. $9.50

FINNEY, C.G. *Circus of Dr Lao.* 1935. Viking. Ils Artzybashef. 1st ed. dj. VG. B3. $35.00

FINNEY, C.G. *Circus of Dr Lao.* 1949. London. Grey Walls. Ils GN Fish. 1st ed. scarce. VG. C1. $49.00

FINNEY, C.G. *Circus of Dr Lao.* 1982. Ltd Ed Club. Ils/sgn Clair Van Vliet. slipcase. VG. $55.00

FINNEY, C.G. *Unholy City.* 1937. Vanguard. 1st ed. dj. EX. R3. $50.00

FINNEY, Jack. *Assault on a Queen.* nd. Book Club. VG. P1. $2.50

FINNEY, Jack. *Body Snatchers.* 1955. NY. 1st/PB Orig ed. presentation. wrp. VG. T9. $65.00

FINNEY, Jack. *Forgotten News.* 1983. Doubleday. dj. EX. $20.00

FINNEY, Jack. *House of Numbers.* 1958. Dell. PB Orig. sgn. wrp. EX. K2. $125.00

FINNEY, Jack. *Marion's Wall.* nd. Simon Schuster. 2nd ed. dj. VG. P1. $15.00

FINNEY, Jack. *Time & Again.* nd. BOMC. dj. VG. P1. $5.00

FINNEY, Jack. *Woodrow Wilson Dime.* 1968. Simon Schuster. 1st ed. dj. EX. F5. $40.00

FIRBANK, Ronald. *New Rhythm & Other Pieces.* 1962. London. Duckworth. 1st ed. dj. R4. $40.00

FIRBANK, Ronald. *Princess Zoubaroff: A Comedy.* 1920. London. Grant Richards. 1st ed. EX. B13. $250.00

FIREBAUGH, E.M. *Physician's Wife & Things That Pertain to Her Life.* 1894. Phil/London. 1st ed. split hinges. C1. $12.50

FIREMAN, Judy. *Ultimate TV Book.* 1977. Workman. dj. EX. P1. $20.00

FIRTH, R. *Art & Life in New Guinea.* 1936. London. 1st ed. 126 p. VG. B3. $67.50

FISCHER, Bruno. *Spider Lily.* 1946. McKay. 1st ed. dj. VG. F5. $9.00

FISCHER, Erwin. *Berlin Indictment.* 1971. World. 1st ed. dj. xl. P1. $5.00

FISCHER, Ottokar. *Ils Magic.* 1944. Macmillan. 2nd print. 206 p. EX. J3. $20.00

FISCHMAN, Bernard. *Man Who Rode 10-Speed Bicycle to Moo.* 1979. Marek. dj. EX. P1. $10.00

FISH, R.L. *Brazilian Sleigh Ride.* 1965. Simon Schuster. 1st ed. dj. xl. P1. $6.00

FISH, R.L. *Rub-a-Dub-Dub.* 1971. Simon Schuster. 1st ed. dj. xl. P1. $5.00

FISH, R.L. *Trouble in Paradise.* 1975. Doubleday. dj. VG. P1. $15.00

FISH, R.L. *Whirligig.* 1970. World. 1st ed. dj. xl. P1. $6.00

FISH, R.L. *Xavier Affair.* 1969. Putnam. 1st ed. dj. xl. P1. $5.00

FISHER, Harrison. *Am Girls in Mini.* 1912. NY. 1st ed. 32 clr pls. VG. B3. $250.00

FISHER, Harrison. *Dream of Fair Women.* 1907. Grosset. EX. B3. $150.00

FISHER, Harrison. *Fair Am.* 1911. NY. 1st ed. VG. B3. $350.00

FISHER, J. *Fabulous Hoosier.* 1947. NY. 1st ed. presentation. dj. VG. B3. $25.00

FISHER, John. *Magic of Lewis Carroll.* 1973. Bramhall House. 1st print. 288 p. dj. NM. J3. $16.00

FISHER, John. *Medieval Literature of W Europe.* 1968. 2nd print. dj. VG. C1. $12.00

FISHER, John. *Paul Daniels & the Story of Magic.* 1987. London. Cape. 1st ed. dj. NM. J3. $25.00

FISHER, L.B. *18th-Century Garland.* 1951. Colonial Williamsburg. 1st ed. dj. EX. $35.00

FISHER, Lillian. *Last Inca Revolt 1780-1883.* 1966. OK U. 1st ed. 426 p. dj. F2. $30.00

FISHER, M.F.K. *Alphabet for Gourmets.* 1949. Viking. 1st ed. dj. EX. C4. $50.00

FISHER, M.F.K. *Among Friends.* 1971. NY. 1st ed. dj. VG. $30.00

FISHER, M.F.K. *Consider the Oyster.* 1941. NY. 1st ed. dj. VG. B3. $45.00

FISHER, M.F.K. *Here Let Us Feast.* 1946. NY. 1st ed. dj. VG. B3. $32.50

FISHER, M.F.K. *Serve It Forth.* 1937. NY. 1st ed. VG. T9. $145.00

FISHER, M.F.K. *With Bold Knife & Fork.* 1969. NY. 1st ed. dj. VG. B3. $27.50

FISHER, Steve. *Homicide Johnny.* 1950. Popular Lib 229. 1st print. wrp. VG. T9. $35.00

FISHER, Steve. *Night Before Murder.* 1939. Hillman Curl. 1st ed. VG. P1. $20.00

FISHER, Steve. *Sheltering Night.* 1952. Gold Medal 219. 1st ed. wrp. EX. T9. $40.00

FISHER, Steve. *Winter Kill.* 1946. Dodd Mead. 1st ed. dj. VG. T9. $30.00

FISHER, Vardis. *Children of God.* 1939. NY. 1st ed. dj. VG. B3. $27.50

FISHER, Vardis. *Intimations of Eve.* 1946. Vanguard. EX. $17.50

FISHER, Vardis. *Love & Death.* 1959. Doubleday. 1st ed. dj. EX. F5. $18.00

FISHER, Vardis. *Mothers.* 1943. NY. 1st ed. dj. EX. $25.00

FISHER, Vardis. *Valley of Vision.* 1951. Abelard Pr. 1st ed. dj. EX. $35.00

FISHER, W.H. *Top of the World.* 1926. NY. sgn. photos. 178 p. EX. $45.00

FISHER. *Trial of the Constitution.* 1862. Phil. 1st ed. 8vo. 391 p. G. G4. $30.00

FISHMAN, Jack. *7 Men of Spandau.* 1954. NY. 1st ed. 276 p. dj. VG. T5. $15.00

FISK, Nicholas. *Rag, a Bone, & a Hank of Hair.* 1982. Crown. UP of 1st ed. wrp. F5. $20.00

FISK, Nicholas. *Space Hostages.* 1984. Kestrel Books. decor brd. EX. P1. $15.00

FISKE, John. *Excursions of an Evolutionist.* 1893. Houghton. 379 p. TEG. EX. B10. $5.75

FISKE, John. *MS Valley in the Civil War.* 1900. Boston. EX. $35.00

FISKE, John. *MS Valley in the Civil War.* 1901. Riverside Pr. 12mo. 368 p. bl bdg. G4. $28.00

FISKE, John. *Witchcraft in Salem Village.* c 1902. Houghton Mifflin. 12mo. 60 p. dj. VG. $12.00

FITCH, Asa. *1st & 2nd Report of Noxious Insects of NY.* 1856. Albany. 1st ed. inscr. K1. $50.00

FITCH, G.H. *Comfort Found in Good Old Books.* 1911. NY. Ils. VG. $25.00

FITT, Mary. *Banquet Ceases.* 1949. McDonald. 1st ed. dj. VG. P1. $25.00

FITZ, Grancel. *N Am Head Hunting.* 1957. NY. 1st ed. dj. VG. $20.00

FITZGERALD, F.S. *Afternoon of an Author.* 1957. Princeton. 1st ed. as issued. K2. $100.00

FITZGERALD, F.S. *All the Sad Young Men.* 1926. NY. Scribner. 1st ed. G. $60.00

FITZGERALD, F.S. *Basil & Josephine Stories.* 1973. Scribner. UP. bl wrp. VG. w/2 pub letters. K2. $200.00

FITZGERALD, F.S. *Beautiful & Damned.* 1922. Scribner. 1st ed. 1st issue. EX. $90.00

FITZGERALD, F.S. *Beautiful & Damned.* 1950. London. 2nd ed. dj. EX. $40.00

FITZGERALD, F.S. *Dearly Beloved.* 1969. IA City. Windhover/IA U. 1st ed. 1/300. tall quarto. EX. K2. $75.00

FITZGERALD, F.S. *Diamond As Big As the Ritz.* 1946. Armed Services Ed. wrp. VG. B13. $85.00

FITZGERALD, F.S. *F Scott Fitzgerald's St Paul Plays 1911-1914.* 1978. Princeton. 1st ed. dj. EX. H3. $75.00

FITZGERALD, F.S. *Fie! Fie! Fi-Fi!* 1914. John Church. 2nd print. orig wrp. VG. H3. $2500.00

FITZGERALD, F.S. *Great Gatsby.* 1925. Scribner. 1st ed. 1st issue. Paul Horgan xl. EX. K2. $750.00

FITZGERALD, F.S. *Great Gatsby.* 1980. Ltd Ed Club. Ils/sgn Fred Meyer. slipcase. VG. $100.00

FITZGERALD, F.S. *Rubaiyat of Omar Khyyam.* 1935. Ltd Ed Club. Ils/sgn Valenti Angelo. 1/1500. slipcase. EX. C4. $100.00

FITZGERALD, F.S. *Stories of F Scott Fitzgerald.* 1951. Scribner. Intro/tipped-in sgn Cowley. 1st ed. dj. EX. C4. $100.00

FITZGERALD, F.S. *Tales of the Jazz Age.* 1922. Scribner. 1st ed. VG. $120.00

FITZGERALD, F.S. *Taps at Reveille.* 1935. Scribner. 1st ed. gr cloth. G. $60.00

FITZGERALD, F.S. *Taps at Reveille.* 1935. Scribner. 1st ed. 1st issue. variant dj. EX. very scarce. K2. $1750.00

FITZGERALD, F.S. *Taps at Reveille.* 1960. Scribner. dj. VG. $12.00

FITZGERALD, F.S. *Tender Is the Night.* 1934. Scribner. 1st ed. gr cloth. G. $50.00

FITZGERALD, F.S. *Tender Is the Night.* 1982. Ltd Ed Club. Ils/sgn Meyer & Scribner. slipcase. VG. $150.00

FITZGERALD, F.S. *Vegetable.* 1923. Scribner. 1st ed. EX. H3. $100.00

FITZGERALD, Ken. *Space-Age Photographic Atlas.* 1970. Crown. 1st ed. dj. RS. EX. R3. $15.00

FITZGERALD, Kevin. *Quiet under the Sun.* 1954. Little Brn. 1st ed. dj. VG. P1. $10.00

FITZGERALD, Nigel. *Blk Welcome.* 1962. Macmillan. 1st ed. dj. VG. P1. $15.00

FITZGERALD, Nigel. *Day of the Adder.* 1973. Collins Crime Club. dj. VG. P1. $15.00

FITZGERALD, Nigel. *Echo Answers Murder.* 1963. Macmillan. 1st ed. dj. xl. P1. $5.00

FITZGERALD, Nigel. *Midsummer Malice.* 1959. Macmillan. VG. P1. $15.00

FITZGERALD, Zelda. *Save Me the Waltz.* 1953. London. 1st ed. dj. VG. $95.00

FITZKEE, Dariel. *Card Expert Entertains.* 1948. St Raphael House. 1st ed. 171 p. NM. J3. $10.00

FITZKEE, Dariel. *Contact Mind Reading – Expanded.* 1945. St Raphael House. 2nd ed. SftCvr. EX. J3. $4.00

FITZKEE, Dariel. *Cut & Restored Rope Manipulation.* 1929. Am Studios. 1st ed. stapled manuscript. J3. $6.00

FITZKEE, Dariel. *Magic by Misdirection.* 1945. St Raphael House. 1st ed. 227 p. EX. J3. $22.00

FITZKEE, Dariel. *Rings on Your Fingers.* 1946. St Raphael House. 1st ed. 120 p. J3. $10.00

FITZKEE, Dariel. *Showmanship for Magicians.* 1945. Oakland. Magic Ltd. 4th ed. 197 p. dj. M. J3. $18.00

FITZSIMMONS, Cortland. *Sudden Silence.* 1938. Stokes. 1st ed. Grosset dj. VG. P1. $15.00

FIXEL, Lawrence. *Through Deserts of Snow.* 1975. Capra. Chapbook Series. 1/100. sgn. EX. K2. $20.00

FLACELIERE, Robert. *Literary Hist of Greece.* 1968. Mentor. VG. P1. $3.50

FLAGG, Francis. *Night People.* 1947. Fantasy. 1st ed. wrp. VG. R3. $75.00

FLAMINI. *Scarlett, Rhett, & Cast of Thousands.* 1975. NY. 1st ed. dj. EX. B3. $27.50

FLAMMARION, Camille. *Flammarion Book of Astronomy.* 1964. Simon Schuster. 1st ed. dj. EX. R3. $35.00

FLANDRAU, Charles. *Viva Mexico!* 1950. Mexico Pr. 219 p. dj. F2. $15.00

FLAUBERT, Gustave. *Bibliomania: A Tale.* 1939. Evanston, IL 1/500. 8vo. French wrp. R4. $35.00

FLAUBERT, Gustave. *Complete Works.* 1904. NY. Dunne. 10 vols. TEG. EX. H3. $1500.00

FLAUBERT, Gustave. *Salambo.* 1947. Pushkin Pr. 1st UK ed. dj. VG. F5. $18.00

FLAUBERT, Gustave. *3 Tales.* 1978. Ltd Ed Club. Ils/sgn May Neama. 4to. slipcase. VG. $40.00

FLEETWOOD, Hugh. *Redemmer.* 1979. Hamish Hamilton. 1st ed. dj. VG. P1. $12.50

FLEG, Edmond. *Wall of Weeping.* 1929. Gollancz/Dutton. Ltd ed. 1/750. sgns. H3. $75.00

FLEMING, Ian. *Chitty Chitty Bang Bang.* nd. Book Club. dj. EX. B10. $3.50

FLEMING, Ian. *Diamond Smugglers.* 1957. Jonathan Cape. 1st ed. dj. VG. P1. $35.00

FLEMING, Ian. *Dr No.* 1958. Jonathan Cape. 1st ed. VG. P1. $60.00

FLEMING, Ian. *Fleming Introduces Jamaica.* 1965. Andre Deutsch. 2nd ed. dj. EX. F5. $12.00

FLEMING, Ian. *From Russia With Love.* 1957. Jonathan Cape. 1st ed. VG. P1. $100.00

FLEMING, Ian. *Goldfinger.* 1959. Macmillan. 1st ed. dj. VG. P1. $50.00

FLEMING, Ian. *Man With the Golden Gun.* 1965. Doubleday. 3rd ed. dj. VG. P1. $25.00

FLEMING, Ian. *Man With the Golden Gun.* 1965. Jonathan Cape. 1st ed. dj. VG. P1. $40.00

FLEMING, Ian. *Man With the Golden Gun.* 1965. New Am Lib. 1st ed. dj. VG. P1. $35.00

FLEMING, Ian. *Octopussy & the Living Daylights.* 1966. Jonathan Cape. 1st ed. dj. EX. P1. $50.00

FLEMING, Ian. *Octopussy.* 1965. New Am Lib. 1st ed. 120 p. EX. B10. $6.50

FLEMING, Ian. *On Her Majesty's Secret Service.* 1963. Jonathan Cape. Ltd Eng ed. 1/250. sgn. TEG. EX. H3. $2500.00

FLEMING, Ian. *Spy Who Loved Me.* 1962. Jonathan Cape. 1st ed. dj. VG. P1. $45.00

FLEMING, Ian. *Thunderball.* 1961. Jonathan Cape. 2nd ed. dj. VG. P1. $20.00

FLEMING, Ian. *You Only Life Twice.* 1964. Jonathan Cape. 2nd ed. VG. P1. $15.00

FLEMING, Ian. *You Only Live Twice.* nd. New Am Lib. 2nd ed. VG. P1. $10.00

FLEMING, Ian. *You Only Live Twice.* 1964. New Am Lib/World. 1st ed. dj. VG. P1. $35.00

FLEMING, J.M. *Practical Violin School for Home Students.* nd. (1886) London. Gill. lg quarto. 160 p. VG. H3. $75.00

FLEMING, Peter. *Brazilian Adventure.* 1934. Scribner. 1st ed. 412 p. F2. $15.00

FLEMING, Thomas. *Officers' Wives.* 1981. Doubleday. dj. VG. $7.00

FLEMING & MARION. *Distinguished Negroes Abroad.* 1946. WA. Assn Pub. 1st ed. dj. VG. B13. $65.00

FLETCHER, Banister. *Hist of Architecture on Comparative Method.* 1950. London. 15th ed. M. T1. $35.00

FLETCHER, D.C. *Reminiscences of CA & the Civil War.* 1894. Ayer, MA. 1st ed. VG. $80.00

FLETCHER, David. *Lovable Man.* 1975. Coward McCann. 1st ed. dj. xl. P1. $5.00

FLETCHER, Helen. *Adventures in Archaeology.* 1962. Bobbs Merrill. Ils. 216 p. dj. F2. $7.50

FLETCHER, I. *Pay, Pack, & Follow.* 1959. NY. 1st ed. dj. VG. B3. $17.50

FLETCHER, J.G. *Blk Rock.* 1928. London. 1st ed. VG. B3. $30.00

FLETCHER, J.G. *Branches of Adam.* 1926. London. Faber Gwyn. 1st ed. inscr. EX. B13. $450.00

FLETCHER, J.S. *Amaranth Club.* nd. Grosset Dunlap. dj. VG. P1. $15.00

FLETCHER, J.S. *Bartenstein Mystery.* nd. AL Burt. VG. P1. $5.00

FLETCHER, J.S. *False Scent.* 1925. Macmillan. VG. P1. $15.00

FLETCHER, J.S. *Lost Mr Linthwaite.* 1923. Knopf. 1st ed. VG. P1. $20.00

FLETCHER, J.S. *Markenmore Mystery.* nd. Grosset Dunlap. dj. VG. P1. $15.00

FLETCHER, J.S. *Rayner-Slade Amalgamation.* 1922. Knopf. G. P1. $10.00

FLETCHER, J.S. *3 Days' Terror.* 1927. Clode. 1st ed. VG. R3. $22.50

FLETCHER, Lucille. *And Presumed Dead.* 1963. Random House. 1st ed. VG. P1. $10.00

FLETCHER, Lucille. *Girl in Cabin B54.* 1968. Random House. 1st ed. clipped dj. EX. F5. $16.00

FLETCHER, Lucille. *80 Dollars to Stamford.* 1975. Random House. 1st ed. dj. EX. F5. $14.00

FLEXNER, J.T. *Am Painting: 1st Flowers of the Wilderness.* 1947. Houghton Mifflin. 1st ed. 367 p. VG. B10. $12.50

FLEXNER, J.T. *John Singleton Copley.* 1948. Boston. 1st ed. 4to. dj. EX. G1. $35.00

FLICKINGER, R.C. *Greek Theater & Its Drama.* 1929. Chicago. 3rd ed. 381 p. VG. H3. $50.00

FLINT, Russel. *Morte d'Arthur.* 1923. Boston/London. 1 vol ed. VG. C1. $44.50

FLINT, Timothy. *Recollections of Last 10 Years in Valley of the MS.* 1968. S IL U. 1st ed. VG. B10. $7.00

FLORESCU, Radu. *In Search of Frankenstein.* 1975. NY Graphic Soc. 1st ed. dj. EX. P1. $20.00

FLORNOY, Bertrand. *Inca Adventure.* 1956. London. Allen. 1st ed. 212 p. dj. F2. $20.00

FLOURNOY, Valerie. *Twins Strike Back.* 1980. Dial. Ils Diane de Groat. 1st ed. clipped dj. EX. B13. $45.00

FLOWER, F.A. *Edwin McMasters Stanton: Autocrat of Rebellion.* 1905. Akron. 1st ed. VG. $45.00

FLOWER, Newman. *George Frideric Handel.* 1923. Houghton Mifflin. 1st ed. octavo. 378 p. VG. H3. $125.00

FLOWER, Pat. *Crisscross.* 1976. Collins Crime Club. 1st ed. dj. EX. P1. $12.50

FLOWER, Pat. *Crisscross.* 1977. Stein Day. dj. VG. P1. $10.00

FLOWER, Pat. *Vanishing Point.* 1977. Stein Day. 1st ed. dj. VG. P1. $10.00

FLOYD, W.H. *Phantom Riders of the Pony Express.* 1958. Dorrance. Ils. 142 p. dj. A5. $25.00

FLYNN, Errol. *My Wicked, Wicked Ways.* 1959. NY. 1st ed. dj. VG. B3. $22.50

FLYNN, Errol. *My Wicked, Wicked Ways.* 1959. Putnam. 1st ed. octavo. 438 p. dj. EX. H3. $85.00

FODOR, Laszlo. *Brazil.* 1940. Hastings House. 1st ed. 77 p. dj. F2. $15.00

FOGAZZARO, Antonio. *Saint.* 1907. Copp Clarke. decor brd. P1. $10.00

FOGLE, James. *Drugstore Cowboy.* 1990. NY. Delta/Dell. UP. PB Orig. wrp. EX. B13. $45.00

FOLDES, Jolan. *St of the Fishing Cat.* 1937. Farrar. 1st ed. 308 p. tan bdg. xl. VG. B10. $3.50

FOLEY, Edwin. *Book of Decorative Furniture.* 1911. NY. Lg Paper ed. 2 vols. TEG. VG. T1. $95.00

FOLEY, Rae. *Trust a Woman?* 1973. Dodd Mead. 1st ed. dj. VG. P1. $15.00

FOLLETT, Ken. *Lie Down With Lions.* 1986. Morrow. dj. EX. P1. $18.95

FONSECA, Lew. *How To Pitch Baseball.* 1942. Chicago. 1st ed. sgn. 107 p. VG. B3. $30.00

FONSTAD, K.W. *Atlas of Middle Earth.* 1981. Houghton Mifflin. unbound galleys. VG. B13. $125.00

FONTENAY, Charles. *Day the Oceans Overflowed.* 1964. Monarch. 1st ed. wrp. EX. F5. $9.00

FOORA, Fletcher. *Irrepressible Peccadillo.* 1962. Macmillan. 1st ed. dj. VG. P1. $20.00

FOOTE, Horton. *3 Plays.* 1962. NY. 1st ed. sgn. wrp. EX. T9. $50.00

FOOTE, Shelby. *Civil War.* 1958, 1963, & 1974. 1st ed. 3 vols. djs. VG. B3. $85.00

FOOTNER, Hulbert. *Dark Ships.* 1937. Harper. 1st ed. VG. P1. $10.00

FOOTNER, Hulbert. *Murder Runs in the Family.* 1934. Harper. 1st ed. dj. EX. F5. $35.00

FOOTNER, Hulbert. *Obeah Murders.* 1937. Harper. 1st ed. VG. P1. $27.50

FOOTNER, Hulbert. *Unneutral Murder.* 1944. Collins Crime Club. 1st ed. VG. P1. $10.00

FORBES, Alexander. *Quest for a N Air Route.* 1953. Cambridge. Ils. 138 p. dj. VG. T5. $22.50

FORBES, Allan. *Towns of New Eng & Old Eng, Ireland, & Scotland Part 1.* 1936. NY. Tudor. Ils. 2 vols in 1. G. T5. $9.50

FORBES, Bryan. *Endless Game.* 1985. Random House. ARC. wrp. w/promotional letter. EX. F5. $20.00

FORBES, E.A. *Leslie's Photographic Review of the Great War (WWI).* 1920. NY. folio. 200 p. G. B10. $18.00

FORBES, Esther. *Mirror For Witches.* 1928. Houghton Mifflin. dj. EX. R3. $20.00

FORBES, John. *Quaker Star Under 7 Flags.* 1962. Phil. PA U. 8vo. 274 p. dj. VG. V1. $10.00

FORBES, Murray. *Hollow Triumph.* 1946. Ziff Davis. 1st ed. dj. EX. F5. $25.00

FORBES, R.J. *Metallurgy in Antiquity.* 1950. Leiden. 1st ed. VG. $45.00

FORBES, Rosita. *8 Republics in Search of a Future.* 1935. London. Cassell. 2nd ed. 340 p. VG. B10. $4.75

FORBES, Stanton. *But I Wouldn't Want To Die There.* 1972. Doubleday Book Club VG. P1. $7.50

FORBES, Stanton. *Grieve for the Past.* 1963. Crime Club. 1st ed. VG. P1. $10.00

FORBES, Stanton. *If 2 of Them Are Dead.* 1968. Crime Club. 1st ed. dj. xl. P1. $5.00

FORBES & RICHARDSON. *Fishes of IL.* 1908. IL State Legislature. 2 vols. w/separate atlas. VG. T3. $85.00

FORBUSH, Bliss. *Elias Hicks: Quaker Liberal.* 1956. Columbia U. 1st ed. 8vo. sgn. 355 p. dj. V1. $14.00

FORBUSH, Bliss. *Hist of Baltimore Yearly Meeting of Friends.* 1972. Baltimore Yearly Meeting. 8vo. 1974 p. V1. $6.00

FORBUSH, Bliss. *Moses Sheppard: Quaker Philanthropist of Baltimore.* 1968. Phil. Lippincott. 12mo. 317 p. dj. VG. V1. $12.00

FORBUSH, E.H. *Useful Birds & Their Protection.* 1907. MA State Agriculture. 2nd ed. VG. T3. $45.00

FORBUSH & MASSECK. *Boys' Round Table.* 1908. Postdam, NY. 6th ed. scarce. C1. $27.50

FORCE, M.F. *From Ft Henry to Corinth.* 1881. NY. G. T5. $37.50

FORCE, Peter. *Declaration of Independence.* 1855. London. 1st ed. wrp. $45.00

FORD, Boris. *From Dryden to Johnson.* 1957. Pelican. VG. P1. $4.50

FORD, C.H. *Poems for Painters.* 1945. NY. View. 1st ed. 1/500. inscr. K2. $450.00

FORD, Corey. *Best of Corey Ford.* 1975. NY. 1st ed. dj. EX. B3. $22.50

FORD, F.M. *Brn Owl.* 1892. NY. Cassell. 12mo. VG. B2. $250.00

FORD, F.M. *Joseph Conrad: A Personal Remembrance.* 1924. Duckworth. 1st Eng ed. dj. EX. H3. $100.00

FORD, F.M. *Man Could Stand Up.* 1926. Duckworth. 1st Eng ed. dj. VG. H3. $75.00

FORD, F.M. *Mirror to France.* 1926. Duckworth. 1st Eng ed. VG. H3. $75.00

FORD, F.M. *NY Essays.* 1927. NY. Rudge. 1/750. sgn. dj. H3. $200.00

FORD, F.M. *Provence.* 1935. Lippincott. 1st ed. dj. EX. H3. $100.00

FORD, F.M. *Queen Who Flew.* 1965. Braziller. 1st Am ed. dj. EX. B13. $35.00

FORD, G. *Portrait of the Assassin.* 1965. NY. 1st ed. dj. EX. B3. $40.00

FORD, Garrett. *Science & Sorcery.* 1953. Fantasy. 1st ed. dj. VG. R3. $25.00

FORD, Henry. *Edison As I Know Him.* 1930. NY. 1st ed. dj. VG. B3. $95.00

FORD, Henry. *Ford Ideals.* 1922. Dearborn. VG. $25.00

FORD, Henry. *My Life & Work.* 1922. Garden City. dj. EX. $40.00

FORD, J.A. *Judge of Men.* 1968. Hodder Stoughton. dj. VG. P1. $7.00

FORD, J.D. *Am Cruiser in the E.* 1898. NY. Ils 1st ed. EX. $45.00

FORD, J.M. *Scholars of Night.* 1988. Tor Books. 1st ed. sgn. dj. EX. F5. $20.00

FORD, Karen. *Las Yerbas de Gente: Study of Hispano-Am Medicinal Plants.* 1975. Ann Arbor. 473 p. wrp. F2. $15.00

FORD, Leslie. *Date With Death.* 1949. Scribner. 1st ed. dj. VG. P1. $15.00

FORD, Leslie. *Murder in the OPM.* 1942. Scribner. 1st ed. VG. P1. $17.50

FORD, Leslie. *Phil Murder Story.* 1945. Scribner. dj. VG. P1. $15.00

FORD, Leslie. *Road to Folly.* nd. Collier. VG. P1. $10.00

FORD, M.H. *Legend of Parsifal.* 1904. Caldwell. 1st ed. decor bdg. VG. C1. $19.00

FORD, P.L. *Checked Love Affair.* 1903. NY. Ils Fisher. TEG. NM. A4. $50.00

FORD, P.L. *Checked Love Affair.* 1903. NY. 1st ed. EX. $25.00

FORD, P.L. *New Eng Primer.* 1899. NY. 1st ed. VG. B3. $32.50

FORD, P.L. *Wanted a Chaperon.* 1902. Dodd Mead. Ils Armstrong/Christy. 1st ed. VG. B7. $85.00

FORD, P.L. *Wanted a Matchmaker.* nd. AL Burt. Ils Christie. $7.00

FORD, Richard. *Communist.* 1987. Derry. Ils Koontz. Ltd 1st ed. 1/200. sgn. wrp. EX. B13/K2. $75.00

FORD, Richard. *Piece of My Heart.* 1976. Harper Row. 1st ed. dj. EX. K2. $175.00

FORD, Richard. *Sportswriter.* 1986. NY. Correct 1st ed. sgn. wrp. EX. T9. $85.00

FORD, Richard. *Sportswriter.* 1986. NY. 1st ed. sgn. wrp. VG. $65.00

FORD, Richard. *Sportswriter.* 1986. Vintage. PB Orig/1st ed. sgn. pictorial wrp. EX. C4. $60.00

FORD, Richard. *Wildlife.* 1990. NY. 1st ed. 1/200. sgn. slipcase. EX. $115.00

FORD, Sewell. *Wilt Thou Tourchy.* 1917. Grosset. 311 p. dj. VG. B10. $3.50

FORD, W.C. *Boston in 1775.* 1892. Hist Print Club. 1/50. wrp. VG. A4. $50.00

FORD & FORD. *Good Morning.* 1926. Dearborn, MI. Ils. 169 p. G. T5. $19.50

FORDMAN, H.J. *Rembrandt Murder.* 1931. Smith. 1st ed. dj. xl. P1. $10.00

FOREL, Auguste. *Out of My Life & Work.* 1937. Allen Unwin. 1st ed. lg 8vo. dj. EX. $30.00

FOREMAN, Grant. *Pioneer Days in Early SW.* 1926. Arthur Clark. Ltd ed. EX. $175.00

FORESTER, C.S. *Admiral Hornblower in the W Indies.* 1958. Boston/Toronto. 1st ed. dj. VG. $20.00

FORESTER, C.S. *Commodore Hornblower.* nd. BOMC. dj. VG. P1. $7.50

FORESTER, C.S. *Flying Clrs.* 1939. Little Brn. 1st ed. 294 p. xl. VG. B10. $9.25

FORESTER, C.S. *Good Shepherd.* nd. BOMC. dj. VG. P1. $7.50

FORESTER, C.S. *Hornblower & the Hotspur.* 1962. Boston/Toronto. 1st ed. dj. EX. $20.00

FORESTER, C.S. *Hornblower Companion.* 1964. Boston. 1st ed. dj. VG. T5. $32.50

FORESTER, C.S. *Lord Hornblower.* 1946. Little Brn. 1st ed. VG. P1. $25.00

FORESTER, C.S. *Lord Nelson.* 1929. Indianapolis. Ils 1st ed. 353 p. VG. T5. $25.00

FORESTER, C.S. *Ship.* 1943. Clipper Books. dj. VG. P1. $7.50

FORESTER, C.S. *Sky & the Forest.* nd. BOMC. dj. VG. P1. $7.50

FORESTER, C.S. *Sky & the Forest.* 1948. Michael Joseph. 1st ed. dj. VG. P1. $20.00

FORESTER, C.S. *To the Indies.* 1940. Boston. 1st ed. 298 p. dj. VG. T5. $17.50

FORESTER, Frank. *Complete Manual for Young Sportsmen.* 1859. NY. Townsend. VG. $80.00

FORNEY, J.W. *Life & Military Career of Winfield Scott Hancock.* c 1880. Phil. 12mo. 504 p. gilt bl bdg. G. G4. $35.00

FORREST, Anthony. *Capt Justice.* 1981. Hill. 1st ed. dj. EX. F5. $15.00

FORREST, Richard. *Death in the Willows.* 1979. Rinehart. 1st ed. dj. VG. P1. $15.00

FORRESTER, Stephen. *Art of Street Magic.* 1989. Calgary. 1st print. 1/100. sgn. NM. J3. $21.00

FORRESTER. *This 1 Mad Act.* 1937. Boston. 1st ed. VG. B3. $37.50

FORSTER, E.M. *Collected Tales of EM Forster.* 1947. Knopf. 1st ed. dj. EX. R3. $30.00

FORSTER, E.M. *Eng's Pleasant Land.* 1940. Hogarth. 1st Eng ed. dj. EX. H3. $100.00

FORSTER, E.M. *Hill of Devi.* 1953. Harcourt Brace. 1st Am ed. dj. EX. H3. $40.00

FORSTER, E.M. *Life To Come & Other Stories.* 1972. London. Arnold. 1st ed. 8vo. dj. EX. R4. $25.00

FORSTER, E.M. *Pharos & Pharillon.* 1923. London. Hogarth. 2nd ed. presentation. stiff wrp. H3. $150.00

FORSYTH, Frederick. *Day of the Jackal.* 1971. Hutchinson. 1st ed. dj. EX. scarce. B13. $150.00

FORSYTH, Frederick. *Dogs of War.* nd. Book Club. dj. VG. P1. $5.00

FORSYTH, Frederick. *Odessa File.* 1972. 1st Am ed. dj. EX. C1. $9.50

FORSYTH, Frederick. *4th Protocol.* 1984. San Francisco. Ltd ed. 1/600. sgn. 389 p. slipcase. M. T5. $65.00

FORSYTH, Frederick. *4th Protocol.* 1984. Stoddart. 1st ed. dj. EX. P1. $20.00

FORSYTH, G.A. *Thrilling Days in Army Life.* 1900. NY. 1st ed. VG. $125.00

FORSYTH, William. *Life of Cicero.* 1865. Scribner. 2 vols. gilt brn bdg. VG. C1. $34.50

FORT, Charles. *Books of Charles Ft.* 1941. Holt. 1st Collected ed. G. R3. $17.50

FORTUNE, Dion. *Goat-Foot God.* 1976. Star. 1st PB ed. wrp. EX. F5. $6.00

FORTUNE, Dion. *Moon Magic.* 1976. Star. Eng PB ed. worn. C1. $4.50

FORTUNE, R.F. *Sorcerers of Dobu Islands of W Pacific.* 1932. London. Routledge. 1st ed. VG. $65.00

FORWARD, Robert. *Starquake.* 1985. Del Rey. 1st ed. RS. $35.00

FOSDICK, H.E. *On Being a Real Person.* 1943. Harper. 2nd ed. 295 p. dj. VG. B10. $3.50

FOSS, C.F. *Jane's Combat Support Equipment 1978-1979.* 1978. NY. Ils 1st Am ed. 547 p. VG. T5. $37.50

FOSTER, A.D. *Alien.* 1979. Warner. UP. wrp. EX. B13. $100.00

FOSTER, A.D. *Cachalot.* nd. Book Club. dj. EX. P1. $4.50

FOSTER, A.D. *Clash of the Titans.* 1981. Warner. AP. wrp. EX. F5. $25.00

FOSTER, A.D. *Day of the Dissonance.* 1984. Phantasia. 1st ed. M. R3. $17.00

FOSTER, A.D. *Day of the Dissonance.* 1984. Phantasia. 1st ed. 1/375. sgn. dj. EX. P1. $40.00

FOSTER, A.D. *Into the Out Of.* 1986. Warner. 1st ed. dj. EX. P1. $15.95

FOSTER, A.D. *Krull.* 1983. Warner. UP. wrp. EX. B13. $75.00

FOSTER, A.D. *Man Who Used the Universe.* nd. Book Club. dj. EX. P1. $4.50

FOSTER, A.D. *Midworld.* nd. Book Club. 1st ed. dj. VG. P1. $4.50

FOSTER, A.D. *Midworld.* nd. British SF Book Club. dj. VG. P1. $5.00

FOSTER, A.D. *Moment of the Magician.* 1984. Phantasia. 1st ed. 1/375. sgn. dj. slipcase. EX. P1. $40.00

FOSTER, A.D. *Season of the Spellsong.* 1985. Doubleday. 1st Compiled ed. dj. EX. F5. $12.00

FOSTER, A.D. *Splinter of the Mind's Eye.* nd. Book Club. dj. VG. P1. $4.50

FOSTER, A.D. *Splinter of the Mind's Eye.* 1978. Del Rey. 1st ed. dj. EX. R3. $32.50

FOSTER, A.D. *To the Vanishing Point.* 1988. Warner. 1st ed. dj. EX. F5. $16.00

FOSTER, A.D. *Voyage to the City of the Dead.* 1984. Del Rey. 1st ed. wrp. EX. F5. $8.00

FOSTER, Coram. *Rear Admiral Byrd & the Polar Expeditions.* 1930. AL Burt. Ils. 256 p. dj. VG. T5. $15.00

FOSTER, G.C. *Mistress.* nd. (1930) Macaulay. 1st Am ed. 319 p. G. B10. $3.50

FOSTER, George. *Studies in Middle Am Anthropology.* 1976. Tulane. 4to. 107 p. F2. $25.00

FOSTER, Hal. *Prince Valiant & the Golden Princess.* 1955. Hastings House. 1st ed. dj. EX. F5. $30.00

FOSTER, Hal. *Prince Valiant & the 3 Challenges.* 1960. Hastings House. 1st ed. dj. EX. F5. $25.00

FOSTER, Hal. *Prince Valiant in the Days of King Arthur.* 1941. Hastings House. dj. EX. F5. $15.00

FOSTER, Hal. *Prince Valiant in the New World.* 1956. Hastings House. 1st ed. dj. EX. F5. $30.00

FOSTER, Hal. *Young Knight: Tale of Medieval Times.* c 1946. Kenosha, WI. rare. C1. $19.50

FOSTER, Harry. *Tropical Tramp With the Tourists.* 1925. Dodd Mead. 1st ed. 305 p. F2. $25.00

FOSTER, Josiah. *Piety Promoted.* 1830. Phil. Thomas Kite. 12mo. 368 p. leather. fair. V1. $16.50

FOSTER, Neil. *Tops Pictorial Album of Magicians.* 1966. Colon, MI. 1st ed. VG. J3. $11.00

FOSTER, Robert. *Guide to Middle Earth.* 1974. Ballantine. EX. P1. $4.50

FOSTER, W.H. *New Eng Grouse Shooting.* 1942. NY. 1st ed. 4to. VG. C2. $125.00

FOSTER, W.Z. *Political Hist of Am.* 1951. NY. 1st ed. dj. VG. $17.50

FOSTER, W.Z. *World Trade Movement.* 1956. NY. 1st ed. dj. VG. B3. $17.50

FOSTER, William. *Memoirs.* 1865. London. AW Bennett. 1st ed. 8vo. G. V1. $25.00

FOTHERGILL, John. *Fothergill Omnibus.* 1931. Eyre Spottiswoode. 1st ed. sgns. VG. H3. $200.00

FOTHERGILL, Samuel. *Memoirs of Life & Gospel Labors...* 1857. London. Cash. 2nd ed. 12mo. 456 p. V1. $22.00

FOTHERGILL, Samuel. *10 Discourses Delivered Extempore...Great Britain 1767-1770.* 1898. Phil. B Johnson. 16mo. 220 p. full leather. V1. $15.00

FOTHERGILL, Samuel. *11 Discourses Delivered Extempore at Several Meeting Houses.* 1817. Wilmington. Coale Rumford. 16mo. 263 p. poor. V1. $15.00

FOUNTAIN, Nigel. *Days Like These.* 1985. Pluto Pr. 1st UK ed. dj. EX. F5. $14.00

FOUNTAIN, Paul. *Great NW & Great Lakes Region of N Am.* 1904. London. A4. $60.00

FOURNIER, Alain. *Wanderer.* 1928. Houghton Mifflin. 1st ed. dj. VG. B13. $45.00

FOWKE, Gerard. *Archaeological Hist of OH.* 1902. Columbus. 1st ed. 760 p. VG. $95.00

FOWLER, G. *Father Goose.* 1934. NY. 1st ed. dj. VG. B3. $27.50

FOWLER, Gene. *Salute to Yesterday.* 1937. Random House. sgn. H3. $45.00

FOWLER, R.H. *Jim Mundy.* 1977. Harper. 1st ed. inscr. dj. EX. F5. $22.00

FOWLER, Sydney. *Bell St Murders.* 1932. Harrap. 3rd ed. dj. VG. P1. $20.00

FOWLES, John. *Aristos.* 1964. NY. 1st ed. dj. EX. T9. $150.00

FOWLES, John. *Brief Hist of Lyme.* 1981. Lyme Regis. Friends of Mus. 1st ed. sgn. wrp. EX. C4. $50.00

FOWLES, John. *Cinderella.* 1974. Jonathan Cape. sgn. dj. H3. $125.00

FOWLES, John. *Ebony Tower.* 1974. London. Cape. 1st ed. dj. EX. K2. $175.00

FOWLES, John. *Ebony Tower.* 1974. London. Cape. 1st ed. 12mo. dj. EX. C4. $175.00

FOWLES, John. *Intro: Remembering Cruikshank.* nd. Princeton U. reprint. 1/25. sgn. B13. $450.00

FOWLES, John. *Maggot.* 1985. Jonathan Cape. Ltd ed. 1/500. sgn. glassine wrp. H3. $150.00

FOWLES, John. *Mantissa.* 1982. Boston. Little Brn. 1/510. sgn. s/wrp. EX. K2. $75.00

FOWLES, John. *Mantissa.* 1982. Little Brn. UP. wrp. EX. B13. $100.00

FOWLES & GODWIN. *Islands.* 1978. London. Cape. Ils Godwin. 1st ed. inscr. dj. EX. K2. $100.00

FOWLES & HORVAT. *Tree.* 1979. London. Aurum. 1st ed. oblong 4to. dj. EX. B13. $85.00

FOX, Caroline. *Memories of Old Friends: Extracts From Journals & Letters.* 1882. Lippincott. 12mo. 378 p. VG. V1. $12.00

FOX, F.M. *Little Bear's Ups & Downs.* 1936. Rand McNally. Ils Frances Been. 16mo. 64 p. VG. $12.00

FOX, G.G. *Democracy & Nazism.* 1934. Chicago. Argus. 1st ed. 79 p. EX. R4. $15.00

FOX, Genevieve. *Cynthia of Bee Tree Hollow.* 1948. Little Brn. 1st ed. 212 p. EX. B10. $5.00

FOX, George. *Diario de Jorge Fox.* 1939. Friends Bookstore. Spanish Trans of Everyman ed. 12mo. V1. $6.00

FOX, George. *Gospel Truth Demonstrated in Collection of Doctrinal Books.* 1706. London. Sowle. 1st ed. full leather. G. V1. $160.00

FOX, George. *Journal; or, Hist Account of Life, Travels...* 1765. London. Richardson Clark. 3rd Corrected ed. 4to. 679 p. V1. $75.00

FOX, George. *Passages From Life & Writings of George Fox From Journal.* 1881. Phil. Friends Bookstore. 12mo. 345 p. VG. V1. $12.00

FOX, George. *Short Journal & Itinerary Journals of George Fox.* 1925. Friends Bookstore. 8vo. 403 p. TEG. dj. VG. V1. $15.00

FOX, George. *Warlord's Hill.* 1982. Times. 1st ed. dj. VG. P1. $15.00

FOX, George. *Works of George Fox.* 1831. Phil. MT Gould. 12mo. 8 vols. full leather. G. V1. $250.00

FOX, Herbert. *Disease in Captive Wild Mammals & Birds.* 1923. Phil. Lippincott. 1st ed. 8vo. gilt bl bdg. EX. $125.00

FOX, J.M. *Iron Virgin.* 1951. Little Brn. 1st ed. VG. P1. $10.00

FOX, J.M. *Operation Dancing Dog.* 1974. Walker. 1st ed. dj. VG. P1. $5.00

FOX, J.M. *Shroud for Mrs Gundy.* 1952. Little Brn. 1st ed. VG. P1. $15.00

FOX, John. *Following the Sun Flag.* 1905. NY. 1st ed. VG. B3. $40.00

FOX, John. *Heart of the Hills.* 1913. Scribner. 1st ed. 396 p. VG. B10. $7.25

FOX, John. *Knight of Cumberland.* 1913. Scribner. 1st Uniform ed. 259 p. EX. B10. $3.25

FOX, John. *Little Shepherd of Kingdom Come.* 1903. NY. 1st ed. 1st issue. EX. J2. $25.00

FOX, John. *Little Shepherd of Kingdom Come.* 1909. Scribner. Ils Yohn. TEG. VG. B10. $3.75

FOX, John. *Quiche Conquest.* 1978. NM U. 1st ed. 322 p. dj. F2. $15.00

FOX, Karrell. *Clever...Like a Fox.* 1976. Supreme Magic. 1st ed. 200 p. dj. NM. J3. $19.00

FOX, Karrell. *Comedy a la Card.* 1960. Ireland Magic. 1st ed. 28 p. EX. J3. $4.00

FOX, Karrell. *For My Next Trick.* 1986. Supreme Magic. 1st ed. 184 p. NM. J3. $26.00

FOX, Maria. *Brief Memoir of Maria Fox.* 1858. Phil. Assn Diffusion of Knowledge. 16mo. 157 p. G. V1. $10.00

FOX, Maria. *Memoirs of Maria Fox.* 1846. London. Charles Gilpin. 1st ed. 8vo. 493 p. VG. V1. $20.00

FOX, N.A. *Roughshod.* 1951. Dodd Mead. 1st ed. rebound. xl. P1. $5.00

FOX, W.P. *Dr Golf.* 1963. Lippincott. 1st ed. dj. EX. C4. $50.00

FOX, W.P. *Dr Golf.* 1963. Phil. 1st ed. dj. VG. B3. $30.00

FOX & BRADLEY. *New Medical Dictionary, Concise Explanation of Terms.* 1803. London. VG. $36.00

FOX-DAVIES, A.C. *Complete Guide to Heraldry.* nd. London/Edinburgh. Revised ed. VG. C1. $29.50

FOXX, Jack. *Wildfire.* 1978. Bobbs Merrill. 1st ed. dj. xl. P1. $7.50

FRACKELTON & SEELY. *Sagebrush Dentist.* 1947. Pasadena. 1st Revised ed. 258 p. dj. VG. T5. $25.00

FRAENKEL, Michael. *Death Is Not Enough.* 1939. London. Daniel. presentation. dj. H3. $125.00

FRANCE, Anatole. *Crainquebille.* 1949. Ltd Ed Club. Ils/sgn Bernard Lamotte. 1/1500. slipcase. EX. C4. $45.00

FRANCE, Anatole. *Crime of Sylvestre Bonnard.* 1937. Ltd Ed Club. Ils/sgn Sylvain Sauvage. 1/1500. slipcase. EX. C4. $50.00

FRANCE, Anatole. *Penguin Island.* 1909. John Lane. 1st ed. 1/500. G. R3. $25.00

FRANCE, Anatole. *Penguin Island.* 1925. Bodley Head. 12th print. VG. P1. $5.00

FRANCE, Anatole. *Works.* 1924. NY. Wells. Autograph ed. 1/1075. sgn. 30 vols. EX. H3. $500.00

FRANCES, Evan. *Ladies' Home Journal Family Diet Book.* 1973. Macmillan Book Club. dj. B10. $3.75

FRANCH, J.A. *Pre-Columbian Art.* 1983. Abrams. 1st ed. folio. photos. maps. charts. dj. F2. $100.00

FRANCIS, Dick. *Across the Board.* 1975. Harper. 1st ed. dj. EX. B13. $65.00

FRANCIS, Dick. *Bonecrack.* nd. Book Club. dj. VG. $4.00

FRANCIS, Dick. *Bonecrack.* 1972. NY. 1st ed. dj. VG. $35.00

FRANCIS, Dick. *Hot Money.* 1987. London. 1st ed. inscr. dj. EX. $45.00

FRANCIS, Dick. *Longshot.* 1990. Putnam. 1st ed. dj. EX. $18.00

FRANCIS, Dick. *Odds Against.* 1965. Harper. 1st ed. dj. EX. B13. $200.00

FRANCIS, Dick. *Reflex.* 1980. London. Michael Joseph. sgn. dj. H3. $75.00

FRANCIS, Dick. *Slayride*. 1974. NY. 1st ed. dj. EX. $45.00

FRANCIS, Dick. *Sport of Queens*. 1969. Harper. 1st ed. dj. EX. B13. $100.00

FRANCIS, Dick. *Trial Run*. 1978. London. Michael Joseph. UP. wrp. VG. B13. $125.00

FRANCIS, Phil. *FL Fish & Fishing*. 1955. NY. 1st print. dj. EX. T1. $25.00

FRANCK, A.H. *Working N From Patagonia, Journey Through SE S America*. 1921. Century. Ils. VG. $14.00

FRANCK, Harry. *Roaming Through the W Indies*. 1923. Century. 486 p. F2. $10.00

FRANCK, Harry. *Tramping Through Mexico, Guatemala, & Honduras*. 1916. Century. 1st ed. 378 p. F2. $20.00

FRANCK, Harry. *Zone Policeman 88*. 1913. Century. 1st ed. 314 p. VG. B10. $10.00

FRANCL, Joseph. *Overland Journey of Joseph Francl*. 1968. San Francisco. Wrenden. 1/540. wht dj. EX. K2. $275.00

FRANK, Alan. *Horror Movies*. 1975. Deribooks. 1st ed. wrp. EX. R3. $12.50

FRANK, Alan. *SF Now: 10 Exciting Years*. 1978. Octopus. 1st ed. lg wrp. EX. R3. $10.00

FRANK, Bruno. *Magician*. 1946. Viking. 1st ed. dj. EX. R3. $20.00

FRANK, E. *Old French Ironwork*. 1950. Cambridge. 1st ed. dj. EX. $25.00

FRANK, G.R. *Chung Ling Soo, the Man of Mystery*. 1988. Fantastic Magic Co. Ltd 1st ed. sgn by son. M. J3. $20.00

FRANK, Pat. *Alas, Babylon*. 1959. Lippincott. 1st ed. dj. EX. C4. $100.00

FRANKAU, Gilbert. *Seeds of Enchantment*. 1921. Doubleday. 1st ed. VG. R3. $17.50

FRANKFORT, Ellen. *Voice: Unauthorized Account*. 1976. NY. 1st ed. EX. T1. $25.00

FRANKLIN, Albert. *Ecuador: Portrait of a People*. 1943. Doubleday. 1st ed. 326 p. F2. $15.00

FRANKLIN, Benjamin. *Account of the Newly Invented PA Fireplace*. 1973. Hall. reprint. wrp. M. $12.00

FRANKLIN, Benjamin. *Complete Works*. 1887-1888. Putnam. Letter Pr ed. 1/600. 10 vols. EX. H3. $1250.00

FRANKLIN, Benjamin. *Experiments & Observations on Electricity*. 1774. London. 5th ed. contemporary calf. H3. $2000.00

FRANKLIN, Benjamin. *Life of Franklin*. 1794. Phil. 2nd Am ed. $75.00

FRANKLIN, Benjamin. *Life of Franklin*. 1796. Salem. G. $50.00

FRANKLIN, Benjamin. *Way to Wealth*. 1820. NY. Wood. 16mo. 44 p. $95.00

FRANKLIN, Benjamin. *Works*. 1793. London. 2 vols. $150.00

FRANKLIN, J.H. *From Slavery to Freedom: Hist of Negro Am*. 1967. Knopf. 686 p. dj. VG. S1. $7.50

FRANKLIN, Jay. *Rat Race*. 1950. Fantasy. 1st ed. 1st bdg. dj. EX. R3. $20.00

FRANKLIN, Malcolm. *Bitterweeds*. 1977. Irving, TX. 1/300. sgn. dj. EX. K2. $100.00

FRAPPIER, Jean. *Mort le Roi Artu*. 1964. Geneva/Paris. 3rd ed. French text. stiff wrp. EX. C1. $9.50

FRARY, I.T. *Thomas Jefferson: Architect & Builder*. 1931. Richmond. 1st ed. 139 p. VG. B3. $45.00

FRASER, Antonia. *Weaker Vessel*. 1984. NY. 1st Am ed. dj. VG. C1. $10.50

FRASER, Dawn. *Below the Surface*. 1965. Morrow. 1st Am ed. 250 p. dj. VG. B10. $4.50

FRASER, G.M. *Flashman & the Mt of Light*. 1991. Knopf. UP. wrp. EX. B13. $65.00

FRASER, G.M. *Flashman at the Charge*. 1973. NY. 1st ed. dj. VG. B3. $30.00

FRASER, John. *Canadian Pen & Ink Sketches*. 1890. Montreal. 8vo. 319 p. T6. $35.00

FRASER, Ronald. *City of the Sun*. 1961. Jonathan Cape. dj. xl. P1. $5.00

FRAZEE, Steve. *Apache Way*. 1969. Whitman. VG. P1. $7.50

FRAZEE, Steve. *Killer Lion*. 1966. Whitman. VG. P1. $7.50

FRAZER, Antonia. *Oxford Blood*. nd. Book Club. dj. VG. P1. $4.50

FRAZIER, I.H. *Ft Recovery*. 1941. Columbus. Ils. 31 p. wrp. VG. T5. $8.50

FREDERICK, Harold. *Gloria Mundi*. 1898. Chicago. Stone. 1st ed. VG. B3. $25.00

FREDERICK, Harold. *March Hares*. 1896. Appleton. 1st Am ed. EX. $15.00

FREDMAN, John. *Epitaph to a Bad Cop*. 1973. McKay. dj. EX. P1. $15.00

FREDMAN, John. *False Joanna*. 1970. Bobbs Merrill. dj. EX. P1. $15.00

FREEBORN, Brian. *Good Luck Mr Cain*. 1976. St Martin. 1st ed. dj. VG. P1. $12.00

FREEDMAN, Nancy. *Joshua Son of None*. nd. Book Club. dj. VG. P1. $4.50

FREELING, Nicolas. *Gadget*. 1977. Coward McCann. 1st ed. dj. VG. P1. $22.50

FREELING, Nicolas. *Night Lords*. 1978. Pantheon. 1st ed. dj. xl. P1. $5.00

FREELING, Nicolas. *Valparaiso*. 1964. Harper. 1st ed. dj. EX. F5. $14.00

FREELING, Nicolas. *Wolfnight*. 1982. Pantheon. 1st ed. dj. EX. P1. $15.00

FREEMAN, D.S. *Lee's Dispatches to Jefferson Davis 1862-1865*. 1957. Putnam. 416 p. G. S1. $12.50

FREEMAN, D.S. *Lee's Lieutenants*. 1945. NY. 3 vols. VG. B3. $35.00

FREEMAN, D.S. *Robert E Lee: A Bibliography*. 1945. Scribner. 4 vols. VG. B3. $75.00

FREEMAN, Donald. *Boston Architecture*. 1971. Boston. 2nd ed. VG. R5. $20.00

FREEMAN, F. *Hist of Cape Cod & Barnstable Co*. 1965. Yarmouth Port. facsimile of 1858 ed. 2 vols. boxed. B3. $135.00

FREEMAN, J.C. *Forgotten Rebel*. 1966. Watkins Glen. Ltd 1st ed. sgn. VG. B3. $65.00

FREEMAN, J.E. *Gatherings From an Artist's Portfolio*. 1877. Appleton. 1st ed. VG. C1. $11.50

FREEMAN, R.A. *Eye of Osiris*. nd. Hodder Stoughton. VG. P1. $30.00

FREEMAN, R.A. *Mr Pottermack's Oversight*. 1930. Dodd Mead. 1st ed. dj. VG. P1. $45.00

FREEMAN, R.A. *Mystery of Angelina Frood*. 1936. Hodder Stoughton. 7th print. VG. P1. $25.00

FREEMAN, Ruth. *Quakers & Peace*. 1947. Ithaca. Pacifist Research Bureau. 12mo. SftCvr. G. V1. $6.00

FREEMANTLE, Brian. *Betrayals*. 1989. Tor Books. 1st ed. dj. EX. P1. $18.95

FREEMANTLE, Brian. *Choice of Eddie Franks*. 1987. Tor Books. 1st ed. dj. EX. P1. $15.95

FREEMANTLE, Brian. *Deaken's War*. 1982. Hutchinson. 1st ed. dj. xl. P1. $6.00

FREEMANTLE, Brian. *See Charlie Run*. nd. BOMC. dj. EX. P1. $7.50

FREEMANTLE, Brian. *Steal*. 1986. Michael Joseph. 1st ed. dj. EX. P1. $20.00

FREMANTLE & HASKELL. *2 Views of Gettysburg.* 1964. Lakeside Classic. Ils. 264 p. VG. T5. $25.00

FREMONT, J.C. *Narrative of Exploring Expedition to Rocky Mts in 1842...* 1846. Appleton. 182 p. G. A5. $90.00

FREMONT, J.C. *Narrative of Exploring Expedition to Rocky Mts...* 1846. London. 1st ed. fld map. full calf. H3. $600.00

FREMONT, J.C. *Year of Am Travel.* 1878. Harper. 1st ed. 32 mo. VG. $200.00

FRENCH, J.L. *Ghost Story Omnibus.* 1943. Tudor. VG. R3. $12.50

FRENCH, Paul; see Asimov, Issac.

FREUCHEN, Peter. *Arctic Adventure: Life in Frozen N.* nd. (1935) Farrar Book Club. 467 p. dj. VG. B10. $6.50

FREUCHEN, Peter. *Book of 7 Seas.* 1958. Messner Book Club. 412 p. dj. VG. B10. $8.00

FREUD, Sigmund. *Die Traumdeutung.* 1900. Leipzig. 1st ed. contemporary half cloth. H3. $13500.00

FREUD, Sigmund. *Dream Psychology.* 1921. NY. McCann. 1st Am ed. gr bdg. $50.00

FREUD, Sigmund. *Moses & Monotheism.* 1939. NY. 1st Am ed. VG. C1. $19.50

FREUND, Philip. *Devious Ways.* 1963. London House. 1st ed. dj. EX. F5. $17.00

FREWIN, Anthony. *100 Years of SF Ils.* 1975. Pyramid. EX. P1. $7.50

FREY, R.W. *Hist & Legends of Rogue's Hollow.* 1958. np. 100 p. VG. T5. $17.50

FRIDAY, Bill. *I Love You Alice B Toklas.* 1968. Bantam. Photoplay ed. B4. $3.00

FRIEDENTHAL, Richard. *Wht Gods.* 1931. Harper. 1st ed. 424 p. F2. $10.00

FRIEDLER, Arkady. *River of Singing Fish.* 1951. London. Ils. 191 p. F2. $15.00

FRIEDMAN, B.J. *Dick.* 1970. Knopf. 1st ed. dj. xl. P1. $6.00

FRIEDMAN, B.J. *Lonely Guy's Book of Life.* 1978. McGraw Hill. presentation. dj. H3. $30.00

FRIEND, O.J. *Kid From Mars.* 1949. Fell. 1st ed. dj. EX. R3. $40.00

FRIENDS GENERAL CONFERENCE. *Proceedings...Conference Held at Toronto, Canada, 1904.* c 1904. Phil. 8vo. 467 p. G. V1. $12.00

FRIENDS GENERAL CONFERENCE. *Proceedings...Held at Richmond, IN, 1898.* c 1898. Phil. 8vo. 372 p. VG. V1. $12.00

FRIENDS RELIGIOUS CONGRESS. *Program of Exercises in Gen Parliament of Religions.* nd. Chicago. 8vo. fair. V1. $6.00

FRIERMAN, Jay. *Natalie Wood Collection of Pre-Columbian Ceramics...* 1969. UCLA. Ils. 4to. 92 p. F2. $40.00

FRISKE, John. *Writings.* 1902. Cambridge. Riverside. Deluxe ed. 1/1000. 24 vols. octavo. H3. $250.00

FRITH, Henry. *King Arthur & His Knights.* 1932. NY. Ils Schoonover. 1st ed. VG. $25.00

FRIZELL & GREENFIELD. *Sight-Seeing in S Am.* 1912. np. 1st ed. 299 p. F2. $30.00

FROBISHER, J.E. *Acting & Oratory.* 1879. College of Oratory & Acting. 1st ed. 415 p. H3. $75.00

FROEST, Frank. *Grell Mystery.* nd. Detective Club. dj. VG. P1. $20.00

FROEST & DILNOT. *Crime Club.* nd. Detective Club. dj. VG. P1. $20.00

FROHMAN, C.E. *Put-In-Bay: Its Hist.* 1971. Columbus. Ils. 156 p. wrp. T5. $12.50

FROHMAN, C.E. *Rebels on Lake Erie.* 1965. Columbus. Ils 1st ed. inscr. 157 p. EX. T5. $50.00

FROHMAN, Daniel. *Memories of a Manager.* 1911. Doubleday Page. 1st ed. presentation. 235 p. VG. H3. $100.00

FROISSART, John. *Chronicles of Eng, France, Spain, & Adjoining Countries.* 1805-1806. London. 2nd ed. 12 vols. octavo. VG. H3. $600.00

FROISSART, John. *Chronicles.* 1959. Ltd Ed Club. 1/1500. sgn Henry Pits. boxed. EX. $30.00

FROME, David. *Mr Pinkerton.* 1936. Grosset Dunlap. 1st Compilation ed. dj. EX. F5. $22.00

FROST, A.B. *Portfolio 12 Orig Ils Reproduced From Drawings...Pickwick.* 1908. London. Slater. India Paper ed. 12 pls. wht wrp. VG. H3. $125.00

FROST, Helen. *Oriental & Character Dances.* 1927. NY. Barnes. quarto. 118 p. VG. H3. $40.00

FROST, Jason. *Ivasion USA.* 1985. Pinnacle. 1st ed. wrp. EX. F5. $6.00

FROST, John. *Pictorial Hist of Am Navy.* 1854. NY. Ils. 440 p. VG. $65.00

FROST, Robert. *Collected Poems of Robert Frost 1939.* 1945. Holt. inscr. dj. H3. $325.00

FROST, Robert. *Complete Poems.* 1950. Ltd Ed Club. sgn Nason/Frost/Rogers. rebound. VG. $175.00

FROST, Robert. *From Snow to Snow.* 1936. NY. 1st ed. tan wrp. EX. $100.00

FROST, Robert. *Further Range.* 1936. Holt Book Club. 102 p. dj. EX. B10. $4.00

FROST, Robert. *Further Range.* 1936. Holt. 1st ed. 1/803. sgn. glassine dj. EX. B13. $275.00

FROST, Robert. *In the Clearing.* 1962. Holt. Ltd 1st ed. 1/1500. sgn. boxed. H3. $250.00

FROST, Robert. *In the Clearing.* 1962. NY. 1st ed. dj. EX. $20.00

FROST, Robert. *In the Clearing. Introduction by Robert Graves.* 1962. London. 1st ed. dj. VG. $35.00

FROST, Robert. *Masque of Mercy.* 1947. Holt. Ltd ed. 1/751. sgn. dj. boxed. H3. $200.00

FROST, Robert. *Masque of Mercy.* 1947. Holt. Ltd ed. 1/751. sgn. EX. K2. $85.00

FROST, Robert. *Masque of Mercy.* 1947. NY. 1st Trade ed. EX. $50.00

FROST, Robert. *NH: A Poem.* 1923. NY. 1st ed. VG. B3. $30.00

FROST, Robert. *NH's Child.* 1969. Albany. Ils Lesley Frost. dj. VG. B3. $22.50

FROST, Robert. *Steeple Bush.* 1947. Holt. inscr. dj. H3. $175.00

FROST, Robert. *W-Running Brook.* 1928. Holt. sgn. dj. H3. $300.00

FROST, Robert. *Witness Tree.* 1942. Holt. Ltd ed. 1/735. inscr. slipcase. H3. $450.00

FROST, Robert. *You Come Too.* 1959. NY. 1st ed. dj. EX. $35.00

FROST, W.H. *Court of King Arthur.* 1902. VG. C1. $10.00

FROTHINGHAM, Robert. *Songs of Horses: Anthology...* 1920. Cambridge, MA. 1st ed. 231 p. full leather. VG. T5. $17.50

FROTHINGHAM, T.G. *Naval Hist of World War.* 1924. Cambridge, MA. 8 fld maps. G. T5. $22.50

FRY, A.R. *John Bellers, 1654-1725: Quaker, Economist...Reformer.* 1935. London. Cassell. 1st ed. 12mo. 174 p. V1. $16.00

FRY, A.R. *Quaker Adventure.* 1943. London. Friends Service Council. 12mo. 76 p. xl. V1. $9.50

FRY, A.R. *Simple Faith.* 1956. London. 12mo. 24 p. pamphlet. V1. $3.50

FRY, Christopher. *Thor With Angels.* 1949. Oxford. 3rd imp. VG. C1. $5.00

FRY, Elizabeth. *Brief Memoir...* 1858. Phil. Assn Diffusion of Knowledge. 24mo. VG. V1. $12.00

FRYE & FEDERER. *Myths Every Child Should Know.* nd. (1914) Doubleday. Ils Frye. VG. B10. $5.00

FRYER, Donald. *Songs & Sonnets Atlantean.* 1971. Arkham House. 1st ed. M. R3. $25.00

FRYER, Jane. *Mary Frances Cookbook.* 1912. Phil. 1st ed. VG. B3. $65.00

FUCHS, Theodore. *Stage Lighting.* 1929. Little Brn. 1st ed. 499 p. dj. VG. H3. $75.00

FUENTES, Carlos. *Aura.* 1975. Farrar Straus. Bilingual 1st ed. dj. EX. C4. $30.00

FUENTES, Carlos. *Death of Artemio Cuz.* 1964. Farrar Straus. Trans Sam Hileman. 1st Am ed. dj. EX. C4. $75.00

FUENTES, Carlos. *Hyda Head.* 1978. Farrar Straus. 1st Am ed. sgn. dj. EX. C4. $90.00

FUENTES, Carlos. *Terra Nostra.* 1976. Farrar Straus. UP. 2 vols. wrp. EX. K2. $125.00

FUERST & HUME. *20th-Century Stage Decoration.* 1928. Knopf. 1st ed. 2 vols. VG. H3. $250.00

FUHRMANN & MAYOR. *Voyage d'Exploration Scientifique en Colombie.* 1914. Neuchatel. French text. 1090 p. EX. T1. $375.00

FUKUDA, K. *Japanese Stone Gardens.* 1970. Rutland. 1st ed. VG. G1. $40.00

FULDHEIM, Dorothy. *I Laughed, I Cried, I Loved...* 1966. Cleveland. Ils 1st ed. 204 p. dj. VG. T5. $15.00

FULLAM, G.T. *Journal of George Townley Fullam Boarding Officer.* 1973. AL U. 1st ed. 1/600. EX. $85.00

FULLER, J.F.C. *Generalship of Ulysses S Grant.* 1929. Murray. 1st ed. 446 p. G. S1. $22.50

FULLER, R.B. *Critical Path.* 1981. NY. 1/250. sgn. 471 p. EX. T5. $45.00

FULLER, R.B. *Untitled Epic Poem on Hist of Industrialization.* 1962. NY. 1st ed. dj. EX. $30.00

FULLER, R.B. *9 Chains to the Moon.* 1938. Phil. 1st ed. dj. VG. B3. $40.00

FULLER, Samuel. *Dead Pigeon on Beethoven St.* 1974. Pyramid V3736. 1st ed. wrp. VG. T9. $25.00

FULLERTON, Alexander. *Bury the Past.* 1954. Peter Davies. dj. VG. P1. $15.00

FULVES, Karl. *Card Under Glass.* 1979. Teaneck, NJ. SftCvr. M. J3. $4.50

FULVES, Karl. *Cards No 5, the Multiple Shift.* 1989. Teaneck, NJ. 1st ed. 48 p. M. J3. $25.00

FULVES, Karl. *Easy-To-Do Card Tricks for Children.* 1989. NY. Dover. 1st ed. SftCvr. M. J3. $2.95

FULVES, Karl. *Kaleidoscope, a Collection of New Card Tricks.* 1989. Teaneck, NJ. 1st ed. 50 p. M. J3. $25.00

FULVES, Karl. *Quick Card Tricks.* 1989. Teaneck, NJ. 1st ed. 50 p. M. J3. $25.00

FULVES, Karl. *Shape Changers.* 1979. Teaneck, NJ. 1st ed. SftCvr. M. J3. $7.50

FULVES, Karl. *Wireless II.* 1982. Teaneck, NJ. SftCvr. M. J3. $8.00

FULVES, Karl. *4-Clr Problems.* 1979. Teaneck, NJ. 1st ed. SftCvr. M. J3. $4.50

FURNEAUX, Rupert. *Legend & Reality.* 1959. London. 1st ed. dj. VG. C1. $5.00

FURNILL, John. *Culmination.* 1933. Elkin Mathews Marrot. 2nd ed. xl. VG. P1. $6.00

FURST, Arnold. *Great Magic Shows.* 1968. Magic Ltd. Special Sgn ed. SftCvr. M. J3. $5.00

FURST, Arnold. *How To Get Publicity in Newspapers & Other Media.* 1975. Magic Ltd. 95 p. M. J3. $5.00

FURST, Clyde. *Merlin.* 1930. Merrymount. 1st ed. 1/300. VG. C1. $95.00

FUTAGAWA, Shigeo. *Introduction to Coin Magic.* 1978. Borden Pub. 1st ed. 199 p. dj. M. J3. $9.00

FUTRELLE, Jacques. *Diamond Master.* 1909. Bobbs Merrill. 1st ed. VG. R3. $45.00

FYVIE, John. *Comedy Queens of the Georgian Era.* 1906. London. Constable. 2nd imp. octavo. 445 p. VG. H3. $60.00

GABORIAU, Emile. *Blackmailer*. nd. Detective Club. dj. VG. P1. $15.00

GABORIAU, Emile. *Honor of the Name*. 1902. Scribner. EX. P1. $20.00

GABORIAU, Emile. *Monsieur Lecoq*. 1902. Scribner. VG. P1. $20.00

GABORIAU, Emile. *Other People's Money*. 1902. Scribner. EX. P1. $20.00

GABORIAU, Emile. *Widow Lerouge*. 1902. Scribner. EX. P1. $20.00

GABRIELSON, I. *Birds of AK*. 1959. Harrisburg. 1st ed. 922 p. dj. VG. B3. $175.00

GADDIS, Thomas. *Birdman of Alcatraz*. 1955. NY. 1st ed. dj. VG. B3. $25.00

GADDIS, William. *Carpenter's Gothic*. 1985. Viking. ARC. inscr. dj. EX. K2. $125.00

GADDIS, William. *Carpenter's Gothic*. 1985. Viking. UP. inscr. EX. B13/K2. $200.00

GADDIS, William. *Recognitions*. 1955. Harcourt Brace World. Book Club ed. inscr. dj. EX. K2. $150.00

GADDIS, William. *Recognitions*. 1985. Penguin. UP of revised reissue. inscr. wrp. EX. K2. $150.00

GADE, J.A. *Life & Times of Tycho Brahe*. 1947. NY. 1st ed. dj. EX. $25.00

GAIL, O.W. *Rocket to the Moon*. 1931. Sears. 1st ed. VG. R3. $35.00

GAILLARD, Stephen. *Pirates of the Sky*. 1915. Rand McNally. 1st ed. VG. R3. $75.00

GAINES, E.J. *Autobiography of Miss Jane Pitman*. 1971. Dial. ARC. dj. EX. K2. $100.00

GAINHAM, Sarah. *Appointment in Vienna*. 1958. Dutton. 1st ed. dj. VG. P1. $15.00

GAINHAM, Sarah. *Cold Dark Night*. 1961. Walker. dj. VG. P1. $15.00

GAITSKILL, Mary. *Bad Behavior*. 1988. Poseidon. ARC. wrp. EX. K2. $45.00

GAITSKILL, Mary. *2 Girls, Fat & Thin*. 1991. Poseidon. UP. wrp. EX. K2. $45.00

GALANOPOULOS & BACON. *Atlantis: Truth Behind the Legend*. 1969. Bobbs Merrill. 4to. 216 p. EX. T4. $15.00

GALBREATH, C.B. *Expedition of Celoron to the OH Country in 1749*. 1921. Columbus. Ils. 140 p. T5. $35.00

GALE, E.O. *Early Chicago*. 1902. Revell. Ils Trowbridge. VG. A4. $50.00

GALE, Zona. *Bridal Pond*. 1930. Knopf. 1st ed. 260 p. VG. B10. $10.00

GALERIE, J.B. *Scultpure en Pierre de l'Ancien Mexique*. 1963. Paris. French text. 4to. F2. $35.00

GALLAGHER, Stephen. *Down River*. 1989. New Eng Lib. 1st ed. sgn. dj. EX. P1. $30.00

GALLENKAMP, Charles. *Maya: Riddle & Rediscovery of Lost Civilization*. 1959. McKay. 1st ed. 240 p. dj. F2. $20.00

GALLENKAMP, Charles. *Maya: Treasures of an Ancient Civilization*. 1985. NY. 4to. wrp. F2. $20.00

GALLICO, Paul. *Ludmina: Legend of Liechtenstein*. 1959. NY. 1st ed. 16mo. dj. EX. $15.00

GALLICO, Paul. *Sm Miracle*. 1951. London. Michael Joseph. 1st ed. dj. EX. B10. $4.50

GALLICO, Paul. *Snow Goose*. 1942. Michael Joseph. Australian ed. dj. VG. P1. $10.00

GALLINI, G.A. *Critical Observations on the Art of Dancing*. nd. (c 1770) London. 2 vols in 1. contemporary calf. very scarce. H3. $400.00

GALLOWAY, David. *Melody Jones*. 1980. London/NY. Calder/Riverrun. 1st Am ed. dj. EX. T9. $30.00

GALLUN, R.Z. *Bioblast*. 1985. Berkley. 1st ed. inscr. wrp. EX. R3. $10.00

GALLUP, Donald. *TS Eliot: A Bibliography*. 1953. NY. 1st Am ed. dj. VG. G1. $22.00

GALSWORTHY, John. *Creation of Character in Literature*. 1931. Clarendon. Ltd 1st ed. 1/250. sgn. buff wrp. H3. $35.00

GALSWORTHY, John. *Forsytes, Pendyces, & Others*. 1935. London. 1st ed. dj. VG. $30.00

GALSWORTHY, John. *Modern Comedy*. 1929. Heinemann. Ltd ed. 1/1030. sgn. TEG. H3. $65.00

GALSWORTHY, John. *Modern Comedy*. 1929. Scribner. not 1st ed. 798 p. VG. B10. $4.25

GALSWORTHY, John. *Plays of John Galsworthy*. 1929. Duckworth. Ltd ed. 1/1275. sgn. TEG. dj. H3. $250.00

GALSWORTHY, John. *Swan Song*. 1928. Heinemann. 1st ed. 1/525. sgn. TEG. dj. H3. $75.00

GALSWORTHY, John. *Works*. 1922. Scribner. Manaton ed. 1780. sgn. 30 vols. H3. $1000.00

GALSWORTHY, John. *1 More River*. 1933. Scribner. 1st ed. 365 p. xl. VG. B10. $4.75

GANDOLFI, Simon. *France Security*. 1981. Blond Briggs. 1st ed. dj. EX. P1. $15.00

GANDY. *Tabors*. 1934. NY. 1st ed. sgn. 291 p. VG. B3. $32.50

GANN, E.K. *Aviator*. nd. Arbor House. 2nd ed. dj. VG. P1. $12.50

GANN, Thomas. *Mystery Cities*. 1925. London. Duckworth. 1st ed. 252 p. F2. $35.00

GANN, W.D. *Tunnel Through the Air*. 1927. NY. 1st ed. dj. VG. B3. $40.00

GANN & THOMPSON. *Hist of the Maya*. 1931. Scribner. Ils. 264 p. F2. $30.00

GANN & THOMPSON. *Hist of the Maya*. 1937. Scribner. Ils. 264 p. F2. $25.00

GANNETT, Henry. *Lists of Elevations Principally in Part of US W of MS River*. 1877. GPO. wrp. A5. $40.00

GANOE, W.A. *Soldiers Unmasked*. 1935. Pyne Davidson. sgn. H3. $50.00

GANS, L. *Nieuwe Kunst: Nedelandse Bijdrage tot de Art Nouveau*. 1966. Utrecht. Probable 1st ed. 4to. 296 p. dj. EX. R4. $125.00

GANTHONY, Robert. *Practical Ventriloquism*. 1938. Chicago. Drake. octavo. 116 p. EX. H3. $45.00

GANTZ, K.F. *Not in Solitude*. nd. Book Club. dj. VG. P1. $4.50

GARBER, D.W. *Wildcat Banks on the Mohican Frontier*. 1975. np. 1/250. 71 p. pictorial wrp. VG. T5. $9.50

GARCIA, F. *Marked Cards & Loaded Dice*. 1962. Englewood Cliffs. 1st ed. 274 p. dj. VG. B3. $20.00

GARCIA MARQUEZ, Gabriel. *Adventura de Miguel Littin Clandestino en Chile*. 1986. Bogota. Oveja Negra. 1st ed. dj. EX. K2. $65.00

GARCIA MARQUEZ, Gabriel. *Autumn of the Patriarch*. 1975. Harper Row. UP. wrp. EX. B13/K2. $350.00

GARCIA MARQUEZ, Gabriel. *Autumn of the Patriarch*. 1977. London. Cape. 1st Eng ed. dj. EX. K2. $60.00

GARCIA MARQUEZ, Gabriel. *Chronicle of a Death Foretold*. 1982. Knopf. UP. EX. B13. $200.00

GARCIA MARQUEZ, Gabriel. *Chronicle of a Death Foretold*. 1983. Knopf. 1st ed. 1st issue dj. EX. K2. $40.00

GARCIA MARQUEZ, Gabriel. *Clandestine in Chile.* 1989. Cambridge. Granta. 1st Eng ed. dj. EX. B13. $40.00

GARCIA MARQUEZ, Gabriel. *Collected Novellas.* 1990. Harper Collins. 1st ed. inscr. dj. EX. K2. $1000.00

GARCIA MARQUEZ, Gabriel. *Collected Stories.* 1984. Harper. 1st Am ed. dj. EX. C4. $40.00

GARCIA MARQUEZ, Gabriel. *Collected Stories.* 1984. Knopf. 1st ed. EX. B13. $275.00

GARCIA MARQUEZ, Gabriel. *Doom of Damocles.* 1986. Costa Rica. Eng text. stapled wrp. EX. B13. $250.00

GARCIA MARQUEZ, Gabriel. *Gen en Su Laberinto.* 1989. Bogota. 1st ed. as issued. K2. $100.00

GARCIA MARQUEZ, Gabriel. *Gen in His Labyrinth.* 1990. Knopf. 1st ed. dj. EX. B13. $25.00

GARCIA MARQUEZ, Gabriel. *In Evil Hour.* 1979. Harper Row. UP. octavo. EX. K2. $275.00

GARCIA MARQUEZ, Gabriel. *In Evil Hour.* 1980. London. Cape. 1st Eng ed. dj. EX. B13. $45.00

GARCIA MARQUEZ, Gabriel. *Increible y Triste Hist Candida Erendira Abuela Desalmada.* 1972. Barcelona. Barral. 1st Spanish ed. wrp. B13. $450.00

GARCIA MARQUEZ, Gabriel. *Increible y Triste Hist Candida Erendira Abuela Desalmada.* 1972. Mexico. Hermes. 1st ed. orig wrp. VG. K2. $400.00

GARCIA MARQUEZ, Gabriel. *Innocent Irendira & Other Stories.* 1978. Harper. Trans Gregory Rabassa. 1st Am ed. dj. EX. C4. $40.00

GARCIA MARQUEZ, Gabriel. *Leaf Storm & Other Stories.* 1972. London. Cape. 1st Eng ed. dj. EX. B13. $85.00

GARCIA MARQUEZ, Gabriel. *Love in the Time of Cholera.* 1988. Knopf. Ltd ed. 1/350. sgn. dj. slipcase. B13. $475.00

GARCIA MARQUEZ, Gabriel. *Love in the Time of Cholera.* 1988. Knopf. 1st ed. dj. EX. B3. $45.00

GARCIA MARQUEZ, Gabriel. *No 1 Writes the Colonel & Other Stories.* 1968. Harper. Trans JS Bernstein. 1st Am ed. dj. EX. C4. $650.00

GARCIA MARQUEZ, Gabriel. *100 Years of Solitude.* 1970. NY. 1st ed. dj. K2. $375.00

GARDEN, Nancy. *Door Between.* 1987. Farrar Straus Giroux. 1st ed. dj. EX. P1. $13.95

GARDETTE & POE. *Fire Fiend & the Raven.* 1973. Gerry De La Ree. 1st ed. wrp. EX. R3. $10.00

GARDINER, C.H. *Literary Memoranda of William Hickling Prescott.* 1961. OK U. 1st ed. 2 vols. slipcase. F2. $30.00

GARDINER, Dorothy. *Lion in Wait.* 1963. Crime Club. 1st ed. dj. VG. P1. $20.00

GARDINER, S.P. *Memoirs of Life & Religious Labors of Sunderland P Gardner.* 1895. Phil. Friends Book Assn. 12mo. 687 p. VG. V1. $8.00

GARDINER, William. *Journal of Eternal Evidences of Lord's Gracious Dealings.* 1819. Phil. 1st ed. 8vo. 496 p. V1. $16.00

GARDNER, A.H. *Outline of Eng Architecture.* 1947. London. 2nd ed. dj. VG. R5. $30.00

GARDNER, A.H. *Outline of Eng Architecture.* 1949. London. 3rd ed. VG. R5. $25.00

GARDNER, Albert. *Winslow Homer: Am Artist.* 1961. Bramhall House. Ils. 263 p. A5. $35.00

GARDNER, Bess. *Mexico: Notes in the Margin.* 1937. Houghton Mifflin. 1st ed. 164 p. F2. $10.00

GARDNER, E.G. *Arthurian Legend in Italian Literature.* 1930. London. 1st ed. 349 p. dj. VG. B3. $45.00

GARDNER, E.S. *Case of Beautiful Beggar.* nd. Book Club. dj. VG. P1. $4.50

GARDNER, E.S. *Case of Blk-Eyed Blond.* 1944. Doubleday Book Club. G. P1. $6.00

GARDNER, E.S. *Case of Blond Bonanza.* 1962. Doubleday Book Club. VG. P1. $7.50

GARDNER, E.S. *Case of Careless Cupid.* nd. Blk. dj. VG. P1. $4.00

GARDNER, E.S. *Case of Careless Cupid.* 1968. Doubleday Book Club. VG. P1. $7.50

GARDNER, E.S. *Case of Crooked Candle.* 1944. Morrow. VG. P1. $15.00

GARDNER, E.S. *Case of Drowsy Mosquito.* 1943. Morrow. 1st ed. VG. P1. $25.00

GARDNER, E.S. *Case of Empty Tin.* nd. Grosset Dunlap. dj. VG. P1. $15.00

GARDNER, E.S. *Case of Ice-Cold Hands.* 1962. Morrow. 1st ed. dj. VG. P1. $15.00

GARDNER, E.S. *Case of Sulky Girl.* 1945. Triangle. 5th print. dj. VG. P1. $7.50

GARDNER, E.S. *Case of the Grinning Gorilla.* nd. Grosset Dunlap. VG. P1. $10.00

GARDNER, E.S. *Case of the Grinning Gorilla.* 1952. Morrow. 1st ed. dj. VG. P1. $45.00

GARDNER, E.S. *Case of the Stepdaughter's Secret.* 1963. Morrow. 1st ed. dj. EX. B13. $50.00

GARDNER, E.S. *Case of Vagabond Virgin.* 1948. Morrow. VG. P1. $10.00

GARDNER, E.S. *Cops on Campus/Crime in the St.* 1970. Morrow. 1st ed. dj. EX. P1. $40.00

GARDNER, E.S. *DA Calls It Murder.* 1942. Triangle. 3rd ed. VG. P1. $10.00

GARDNER, E.S. *DA Draws a Circle.* 1943. Triangle. VG. P1. $12.50

GARDNER, E.S. *Host With the Big Hat.* 1969. Morrow. 1st ed. dj. F2. $15.00

GARDNER, E.S. *Human Zero.* 1981. Morrow. 1st ed. dj. EX. R3. $30.00

GARDNER, E.S. *Mexico's Magic Square.* 1968. Morrow. 1st ed. 205 p. dj. F2. $15.00

GARDNER, E.S. *Neighborhood Frontiers.* 1954. Morrow. 1st ed. 272 p. F2. $20.00

GARDNER, E.S. *Perry Mason Omnibus.* nd. Book Club. dj. EX. P1. $7.50

GARDNER, John. *Bartleby: Art & Social Commitment.* 1964. Philological Quarterly. 1st ed. K2. $225.00

GARDNER, John. *Complete Works of Gawain Poet.* Modern Eng Version. PB. VG. C1. $3.50

GARDNER, John. *Cornermen.* 1976. Doubleday. 1st ed. dj. EX. P1. $35.00

GARDNER, John. *For Special Services.* 1982. Coward McCann. 1st ed. dj. EX. P1. $17.50

GARDNER, John. *Grendel.* 1971. 1st Eng ed. sgn. dj. EX. $100.00

GARDNER, John. *Grendel.* 1971. Knopf. Ltd ed. dj. EX. $150.00

GARDNER, John. *Life & Times of Chaucer.* 1977. 1st ed. dj. EX. C1. $22.50

GARDNER, John. *Life & Times of Chaucer.* 1977. Knopf. 1st ed. sgn. dj. EX. K2. $90.00

GARDNER, John. *Madrigal.* 1967. Frederick Muller. dj. xl. P1. $7.50

GARDNER, John. *Madrigal.* 1968. Viking. 1st ed. dj. VG. P1. $22.50

GARDNER, John. *No Deals, Mr Bond.* 1987. Putnam. 1st ed. dj. VG. P1. $13.95

GARDNER, John. *Nobody Lives Forever.* 1986. Jonathan Cape. 1st ed. dj. VG. P1. $20.00

GARDNER, John. *Nobody Lives Forever.* 1986. Putnam. 1st ed. dj. VG. P1. $13.95

GARDNER, John. *Nostradamus Traitor.* 1979. Book Club Assn. dj. VG. P1. $7.50

GARDNER, John. *October Light.* 1977. Knopf. UP. tall wrp. EX. very scarce. K2. $350.00

GARDNER, John. *On Becoming a Novelist.* 1983. Harper Row. UP. wrp. EX. K2. $125.00

GARDNER, John. *On Becoming a Novelist.* 1983. NY. AP. K2. $125.00

GARDNER, John. *On Moral Fiction.* 1978. Basic. 1st ed. dj. EX. K2. $65.00

GARDNER, John. *Resurrection.* 1966. New Am Lib. 1st ed. dj. EX. K2. $450.00

GARDNER, John. *Scorpius.* 1988. Putnam. 1st ed. dj. VG. P1. $12.95

GARDNER, John. *Secret Generations.* 1985. Putnam. dj. RS. EX. P1. $22.50

GARDNER, John. *Secret Houses.* 1987. Putnam. 1st ed. dj. VG. P1. $18.95

GARDNER, John. *Wreckage of Agathon.* 1970. NY. 1st ed. dj. EX. $90.00

GARDNER, Martin. *Order & Surprise.* 1983. Prometeus Books. 396 p. dj. M. J3. $20.00

GARDNER, S.P. *Address to the Youth & Children of Religious Soc of Friends.* 1846. Phil. TE Chapman. 16mo. 16 p. G. V1. $10.00

GARDYNE, M.E. *Oup in Ole VT & Other French Dialect Poems.* 1920. Badger Pr. 1st ed. inscr. 64 p. dj. VG. B10. $15.00

GARFIELD, Brian. *Death Sentence.* 1975. Doubleday Book Club. VG. P1. $7.50

GARFIELD, Brian. *Hit.* 1970. Macmillan. 1st ed. dj. VG. P1. $22.50

GARIS, H.R. *Uncle Wiggily's Apple Roast.* 1927. Graham. 12mo. 32 p. VG. $22.00

GARIS, Lilian. *Ghost of Melody Lane.* 1933. Grosset. Ils Doane. dj. B10. $5.00

GARIS, Lilian. *Nancy Brandons Mystery.* 1925. Grosset. Ils. 300 p. dj. VG. B10. $5.00

GARLAND, Hamlin. *Book of the Am Indian.* 1927. NY/London. later print. EX. $75.00

GARLAND, Hamlin. *Companions on the Trail.* 1931. Macmillan. 1st ed. 539 p. VG. B10. $7.00

GARLAND, Hamlin. *Member of the 3rd House: A Dramatic Story.* 1892. Chicago. Schulte. sgn. H3. $200.00

GARLAND, Hamlin. *Spirit of Sweetwater.* 1898. Curtis/Doubleday McClure. sgn. 16mo. TEG. H3. $100.00

GARMAN, Samuel. *N Am Reptiles & Batrachians.* 1884. Salem. Ils. 8vo. 46 p. wrp. G. T1. $50.00

GARNER, Alan. *Lad of the Gad.* 1981. Philomel. 1st ed. dj. EX. P1. $15.00

GARNER, J.L. *Caesar Borgia: Study of Renaissance.* 1912. McBride. 320 p. G. B10. $20.00

GARNER, William. *Us or Them War.* nd. Companions Book Club. dj. EX. P1. $4.50

GARNER, William. *Us or Them War.* 1969. Collins. xl. P1. $5.00

GARNER & STRATTON. *Domestic Architecture of Eng During the Tudor Period.* 1929. London. 1st ed. 2 vols. EX. $225.00

GARNETT, David. *Beany-Eye.* 1935. Chatto Windus. 1st ed. dj. EX. B13. $85.00

GARNETT, David. *Letters of TE Lawrence.* 1939. NY. 1st Am ed. fld maps. 896 p. T5. $45.00

GARNETT, David. *Man in the Zoo.* 1924. Macmillan. dj. VG. P1. $10.00

GARNETT, L.M.J. *Greece of the Hellenes.* 1914. London. Ils. 246 p. VG. T5. $22.50

GARNETT, Randall. *Unwise Child.* nd. Book Club. dj. VG. P1. $6.00

GARNETT, Richard. *Twilight of the Gods.* 1924. Bodley Head. Ils Keen. 1st ed. EX. A4. $75.00

GARNETT, William. *From Dusk Till Dawn.* 1931. Bodley Head. EX. P1. $10.00

GARNIER, Louis. *Dog Sled to Airplane.* 1949. Quebec. 1st ed. 298 p. T5. $25.00

GARREAU, G. *Bat Boy of the Giants.* 1948. Phil. 1st ed. dj. VG. B3. $15.00

GARRETT, A.C. *Short Life of Stephen Grellet 1773-1855.* 1914. Phil. Friends Bookstore. 16mo. 128 p. VG. V1. $8.50

GARRETT, George. *King of the Mt.* 1957. NY. 1st ed. presentation. dj. EX. T9. $70.00

GARRETT, George. *King of the Mt.* 1957. Scribner. 1st ed. inscr/sgn. dj. EX. K2. $175.00

GARRETT, George. *King of the Mt.* 1959. Eyre Spottiswoode. 1st Eng ed. dj. VG. K2. $45.00

GARRETT, George. *Sleeping Gypsy & Other Poems.* 1958. Austin. 1st ed. dj. EX. K2. $75.00

GARRETT, George. *Succession.* 1983. Doubleday. UP. inscr. tall yel wrp. K2. $65.00

GARRETT, George. *Succession.* 1983. Doubleday. 1st ed. sgn. dj. EX. C4. $60.00

GARRETT, Randall. *Pagan Passions.* 1959. Beacon. 1st ed. wrp. EX. R3. $20.00

GARRETT, Randall. *Unwise Child.* 1962. Doubleday. 1st ed. 215 p. dj. VG. B10. $10.00

GARRETT & HEYDRON. *Return to Eddarta.* 1985. Bantam. UP. 1st ed. proof dj. EX. R3. $15.00

GARRETT & HEYDRON. *Search for Ka.* 1984. Bantam. UP. 1st ed. proof cover. EX. R3. $15.00

GARRISON, Jim. *Heritage of Stone.* 1970. NY. 5th ed. dj. VG. B3. $22.50

GARRISON, Jim. *Star-Spangled Contract.* 1976. McGraw Hill. 1st ed. dj. EX. P1. $17.50

GARRISON, W.L. *Sonnets & Other Poems.* 1843. Boston. 1st ed. $85.00

GARRISON. *Principles Anatomic Ils Before Vesalius.* 1926. NY. Ils. 12mo. 58 p. EX. C2. $65.00

GARSON, Paul. *Great Quill.* 1973. Doubleday. 1st ed. dj. VG. P1. $15.00

GARSTIN, Crosbie. *Dragon & Lotus.* 1927. Stokes. 1st ed. 343 p. B10. $7.50

GARTH, Charles. *Flower Weavers: Builders of Old Mexico.* 1954. NY. Exposition Pr. 1st ed. dj. F2. $10.00

GARTH, David. *Bermuda Calling.* 1944. Thomas Allen. 1st ed. dj. VG. P1. $15.00

GARTH, Will. *Dr Cyclops.* 1974. Bookfinger. reprint of 1940 ed. VG. R3. $15.00

GARVE, Andrew. *Ascent of D13.* 1969. Thriller Book Club. dj. VG. P1. $4.50

GARVE, Andrew. *Megstone Plot.* nd. Book Club. dj. VG. P1. $4.50

GARVE, Andrew. *Riddle of Samson.* 1957. Collins Crime Club. dj. VG. P1. $15.00

GARWOOD, D. *Artist in IA (Grant Wood).* 1944. NY. 1st ed. dj. w/8 Grant Wood post cards. B3. $35.00

GARY, Romain. *Lady L.* 1959. Simon Schuster. 1st ed. 215 p. dj. EX. B10. $5.00

GASH, Joe. *Newspaper Murders.* 1985. Holt Rinehart. 1st ed. dj. VG. P1. $15.00

GASH, Joe. *Priestly Murders.* 1984. Holt Rinehart. 1st ed. dj. EX. P1. $15.00

GASH, Jonathan. *City.* 1978. St Martin. 1st ed. dj. EX. P1. $15.00

GASH, Jonathan. *Grail Tree.* 1st Am ed. dj. EX. C1. $16.50

GASH, Jonathan. *Jade Woman.* 1989. St Martin. 1st ed. dj. EX. P1. $15.00

GASKELL, Jane. *Atlan.* 1978. St Martin. 1st Am HrdCvr ed. dj. EX. F5. $20.00

GASKELL, Jane. *Serpent.* 1977. St Martin. 1st Am HrdCvr ed. dj. EX. F5. $20.00

GASKELL, Jane. *Some Summer Lands.* 1979. St Martin. 1st Am ed. dj. EX. F5. $15.00

GASPARINI & DUARTE. *Retablos del Periodo Colonial en Venezuela.* 1971. Caracas. 1st ed. 1/4000. lg 4to. dj. F2. $45.00

GASPELL, Susan. *Norma Ashe.* 1942. Phil. 1st ed. dj. VG. B3. $25.00

GASS, William. *Omensetter's Luck.* 1966. New Am Lib. 1st ed. dj. EX. scarce. B13. $175.00

GASS, William. *On Being Bl.* nd. (1976) Godine. ARC. dj. EX. B13. $100.00

GASS, William. *On Being Bl.* 1976. Boston. Godine. Review Trade ed. 1/3000. dj. EX. K2. $100.00

GASS, William. *Willie Master's Lonesome Wife.* 1971. Knopf. ARC. dj. EX. B13. $85.00

GATENBY, Rosemary. *Deadly Relations.* nd. Book Club. dj. VG. P1. $4.50

GATENBY, Rosemary. *Fugative Affair.* nd. Book Club. dj. VG. P1. $4.50

GATENBY, Rosemary. *Fugative Affair.* 1976. Dodd Mead. 1st ed. dj. VG. P1. $15.00

GATES, Josephine. *Book of Live Dolls: Omnibus for Children.* 1931. Bobbs Merrill. Ils Mabel Rogers/others. VG. B7. $38.00

GATES, Macburney. *Blk Pirate.* 1926. Grosset Dunlap. Photoplay ed. dj. VG. P1. $20.00

GATHORNE-HARDY, Robert. *Recollections of Logan Pearsall Smith: Story of Friendship.* 1950. Macmillan. 1st ed. 8vo. 259 p. VG. V1. $12.50

GAULT, W.C. *Come Die With Me.* 1959. Random House. 1st ed. VG. P1. $20.00

GAULT, W.C. *Dead Seed.* 1985. Walker. dj. EX. P1. $15.00

GAULT, W.C. *Death in Donegal Bay.* 1984. Walker. 1st ed. dj. EX. P1. $15.00

GAULT, W.C. *End of a Call Girl.* 1958. Crest Book 248. PB Orig. wrp. EX. T9. $25.00

GAULT, W.C. *Million-Dollar Tramp.* 1961. Crest Book 361. 1st ed. wrp. NM. T9. $25.00

GAULT, W.P. *OH at Vicksburg.* 1906. Columbus. Ils 1st ed. 374 p. T5. $35.00

GAULTIER, Bon. *Book of Ballads.* 1845. London. Orr. octavo. 152 p. VG. H3. $75.00

GAUTIER, Leon. *Chivalry: Everyday Life of the Medieval Knight.* 1989. reprint of c 1890s ed. M. C1. $14.50

GAUTIER, Theophile. *Mademoiselle de Maupin.* 1943. Ltd Ed Club. Ils/sgn Andre Dugo. 1/1500. slipcase. EX. C4. $35.00

GAUTIER & MERIMER. *Tales Before Supper.* nd. (1887) Brentano. apparent 1st ed. 224 p. TEG. VG. B10. $20.00

GAVIN, James M. *On to Berlin.* 1978. NY. Ils 1st ed. 336 p. dj. G. T5. $15.00

GAVIN, James M. *War & Peace in Space Age.* 1958. NY. 1st ed. 304 p. dj. G. T5. $8.50

GAWRON, Jean M. *Apology for Rain.* 1974. Doubleday. 1st ed. dj. EX. P1. $15.00

GAY, Carlo. *Chalcacingo.* 1972. Portland. Ils Frances Pratt. 1st Am ed. folio. 119 p. F2. $75.00

GAY, Carlo. *Mezcala Stone Sculpture: The Human Figure.* 1967. MPA Studies 5. 1st ed. 4to. 39 p. VG. F2. $20.00

GAY, John. *Fables.* 1793. London. Darton Harvey. pls. 8vo. 256 p. V1. $185.00

GAY, M.A.H. *Life in Dixie During the War.* 1979. Atlanta. reprint of 1897 ed. 448 p. VG. T5. $22.50

GEARE & CORBY. *Dracula's Diary.* 1982. Beaufort. 1st ed. dj. EX. P1. $17.50

GEBHART-SAYER, Angelika. *Cosmos Encoiled: Indian Art of Peruvian Amazon.* 1984. NY. Ils. 4to. wrp. F2. $15.00

GEE. *Reflections in Pike Place Markets.* 1968. Seattle. 1st ed. folio. VG. $27.50

GEHERIN, David. *Am Private Eye.* 1985. Ungar. 1st ed. dj. EX. T9. $25.00

GEIBERGER, Al. *Tempo: Golf's Master Key.* 1980. NY. 1st ed. dj. VG. B3. $25.00

GEIS, Richard. *Bongo Bum.* 1966. Brandon House. VG. B4. $12.50

GELATT, R. *Fabulous Phonograph.* 1955. Phil. 1st ed. dj. VG. B3. $30.00

GELL & GANDY. *Pompeii: Its Destruction & Rediscovery With Engravings...* 1880. NY. Ils. 4to. 70 pls. AEG. VG. T5. $45.00

GELLER, Eli. *Window Episode.* 1958. Mystery House. 1st ed. xl. P1. $5.00

GELLER, Stephen. *Pretty Poison.* 1968. Ballantine 71002. Photoplay ed. 2nd print. EX. B4. $6.00

GEMMILL, C.L. *Physiology in Aviation.* 1943. Springfield. 1st ed. 129 p. dj. VG. T5. $25.00

GENET, Jean. *Blks: A Clown Show.* 1960. Grove Pr. Trans Bernard Frechtman. 1st Am ed. dj. EX. C4. $40.00

GENSTEIN, E.S. *Stock Market Profit Without Forecasting.* 1954. Ltd 1st ed. dj. EX. $10.00

GENTHE, Arnold. *Pictures of Old China Town.* 1908. NY. Ils. G. B3. $80.00

GENTLE, Mary. *Hawk in Silver.* 1977. Lathrop. 1st ed. dj. EX. P1. $17.50

GENTRY, T.G. *Birds of the US: Nests & Eggs.* 1882. Phil. Wagenseller. clr pls. rebound. VG. T3. $350.00

GENTZ, Fred. *State of Europe Before & After the French Revolution.* 1803. London. 2nd ed. 8vo. VG. $45.00

GEOFFREY OF MONMOUTH. *Legendary Hist of Britain.* 1950. CA U. 1st ed. dj. VG. C1. $39.50

GEORGE, J.N. *Eng Pistols & Revolvers: Hist Outline of Development...* 1938. Sm Arms Pub. 8vo. 256 p. dj. VG. $75.00

GEORGE, Peter. *Commander 1.* 1965. Delacorte. 1st ed. dj. VG. P1. $20.00

GEORGIA MUSEUM OF ART. *Art of Ancient Peru: Paul A Clifford Collection.* 1969. Athens. Ils. oblong 4to. F2. $15.00

GERARD, Francis. *Secret Sceptre.* 1939. Dutton. 1st Am ed. dj. VG. C1. $44.50

GERARD, James. *Face to Face With Kaiserism.* 1918. Doran. 1st ed. 380 p. VG. B10. $3.50

GERARD, Max. *Dali.* 1968. Abrams. 1st ed. dj. EX. B3. $62.50

GERARD, Max. *Dali.* 1968. NY. 1st Am ed. VG. G1. $45.00

GERARD, Sanford. *How Good Is Your Taste.* 1946. Doubleday. 1st ed. 141 p. dj. VG. B10. $5.00

GERARDE, John. *Herball; or, Generall Historie of Plantes...* 1636. London. 3rd ed. contemporary calf. hinges repaired. VG. H3. $3000.00

GERBER, Dan. *Voice From the River.* 1990. Livingston, MT. 1st ed. sgn. wrp. EX. T9. $35.00

GERBI, Antonello. *Nature in the New World.* 1985. Pittsburgh U. 1st ed. 462 p. dj. F2. $25.00

GERDTS & BURKE. *Am Still-Life Painting.* 1971. NY. 1st ed. dj. EX. G1. $45.00

GERHARDIE, William. *Eva's Apples: A Story of Jazz & Jasper.* 1928. Duffield. 1st Am ed. dj. EX. C4. $50.00

GERROLD, David. *Chess With a Dragon.* 1987. Walker. 1st ed. dj. RS. EX. P1. $20.00

GERROLD, David. *Day for Damnation.* 1984. Timescape. 1st ed. dj. EX. P1. $16.95

GERRY, J.P. *Golden Age.* nd. Collier. 220 p. VG. B10. $4.25

GERSHAM, Otto. *Greenbacks.* 1927. Chicago. 1st ed. presentation. 312 p. G. B3. $45.00

GERSHAM. *Monster Midway.* 1953. NY. 1st ed. dj. VG. B3. $35.00

GERSHWIN, George. *Porgy & Bess.* 1935. NY. 1st ed. 1/250. sgns. orig morocco. EX. H3. $5000.00

GERSON, N.B. *Neptune.* 1976. Dodd Mead. 1st ed. dj. VG. P1. $17.50

GERSON, N.B. *Velvet Glove: Life of Dolly Madison.* 1975. Nashville. Nelson. 8vo. 264 p. dj. VG. V1. $8.50

GERUSEZ, Victor. *Paris au Bois.* 1890. Paris. 4to. EX. $100.00

GESELL, Arnold. *Embryology of Behavior.* 1945. Harper. 2nd ed. 289 p. dj. VG. B10. $7.00

GESSLER, Clifford. *Pattern of Mexico.* 1941. Appleton. 1st ed. 442 p. F2. $15.00

GETHIN, David. *Wyatt & the Moresby Legacy.* 1984. St Martin. 1st ed. dj. EX. F5. $12.00

GETMAN, Anson. *Lure of the Valley.* 1956. Pageant Pr. 1st ed. 284 p. dj. VG. B10. $10.00

GETTINGS, Fred. *Book of Tarot.* nd. London. Triune Books. apparent 1st ed. 143 p. dj. EX. B10. $5.75

GHEERBRANT, Alain. *Incas.* 1961. Orion Pr. 2nd print. 432 p. dj. F2. $25.00

GHEERBRANT, Alain. *Journey to the Far Amazon.* 1954. Simon Schuster. 2nd print. 353 p. dj. F2. $15.00

GIANCACA, Antoinette. *Mafia Princess.* 1984. Morrow Book Club. 241 p. dj. EX. B10. $3.00

GIBBINGS, Robert. *Coming Down the Seine.* 1953. London. Dent. Ltd ed. 1/75. sgn. AEG. morocco. H3. $150.00

GIBBINGS, Robert. *True Tale of Love in Tonga.* 1954. London. Dent. 1st ed. 12mo. 53 p. VG. $22.00

GIBBON, Edward. *Decline & Fall of Roman Empire.* c 1910. Wheeler. Deluxe ed. 1/1000. 12 vols. octavo. G. H3. $150.00

GIBBON, Edward. *Hist of Decline & Fall of Roman Empire.* 1777-1789. London. 6 vols. quarto. H3. $1000.00

GIBBON, Edward. *Hist of Decline & Fall of Roman Empire.* 1791-1792. London. 12 vols. octavo. H3. $400.00

GIBBON, Edward. *Hist of Decline & Fall of Roman Empire.* 1830. Phil. 8vo. 4 vols. full calf. VG. T1. $60.00

GIBBON, F.P. *Disputed VC.* 1903. Blackie & Son. Ils Stanley Wood. 1st ed. VG. F5. $30.00

GIBBONS, Daniel. *God in Us: World Faith of Quakerism.* 1928. Macmillan. 1st ed. 16mo. 100 p. dj. V1. $8.50

GIBBONS, Hannah. *Memoir of Hannah Gibbons, Late, of W Chester, PA.* 1873. Phil. Pile. 12mo. 220 p. VG. V1. $12.00

GIBBONS, Kaye. *Cure for Dreams.* 1991. Algonquin Books. ARC. wrp. EX. C4. $40.00

GIBBONS, Kaye. *Cure for Dreams.* 1991. Algonquin Books. 1st ed. sgn. dj. M. C4. $30.00

GIBBONS, Kaye. *Ellen Foster.* 1987. Chapel Hill. 1st ed. sgn. dj. EX. B13. $75.00

GIBBONS, Kaye. *Family Life.* 1990. NC Wesleyan U. 1/500. sgn. wrp. B13. $30.00

GIBBONS, Kaye. *Family Life.* 1990. NC Wesleyan U. 1/500. sgn. wrp. C4. $25.00

GIBBONS, William. *Review & Refutation of Some of Opprobrious Charges...* 1849. Phil. Chapman. 12mo. 185 p. full leather. G. V1. $20.00

GIBBS, G.W. *Collected Works.* 1948. New Haven. reprint 1928 ed. 2 vols. VG. C2. $65.00

GIBBS, Philip. *Darkened Rooms.* 1929. Doubleday Doran. VG. P1. $6.00

GIBBS, S.M. *Life's Perfected Steps; or, King's Pathway to Peace.* 1889. Chicago. 1st ed. 8vo. 136 p. AEG. R4. $20.00

GIBSON, C.D. *London As Seen By Charles Dana Gibson.* 1897. NY. 1st ed. folio. AEG. VG. T1. $65.00

GIBSON, C.D. *Sketches & Cartoons.* 1898. NY. folio. AEG. VG. T1. $65.00

GIBSON, Hugh. *Rio.* 1938. Doubleday. Ils. sgn. 263 p. F2. $15.00

GIBSON, Rebecca. *Indians of Latin Am: Exhibition of Materials in Lilly Lib.* nd. Lilly Lib. Ltd ed. 1/1500. wrp. F2. $12.50

GIBSON, W.B. *Bunco Book.* 1986. Citadel. 114 p. M. J3. $8.00

GIBSON, W.B. *Dreams.* nd. Castle Books. 1st reprint ed. dj. VG. T9. $15.00

GIBSON, W.B. *Return of the Shadow.* 1963. Belmont 90-298. 1st ed. NM. T9. $20.00

GIBSON, W.H. *Highways & Byways; or, Saunterings in NE.* 1882. NY. 4to. VG. $45.00

GIBSON, W.H. *Strolls by Starlight & Sunshine.* 1891. NY. 4to. VG. $40.00

GIBSON, W.W. *Collected Poems.* 1917. VG. C1. $9.00

GIBSON, Walter. *Crime Over Casco/Mother Goose Murder.* 1979. Crime Club. 1st ed. dj. EX. P1. $35.00

GIBSON, Walter. *Magic Explained.* 1949. Perma P54. EX. P1. $35.00

GIBSON, Walter. *Quarter of 8 & the Freak Show Murders.* 1978. Crime Club. 1st ed. dj. xl. F5. $10.00

GIBSON, Walter. *Rod Serling's the Twilight Zone.* 1963. Grosset Dunlap. dj. VG. P1. $17.50

GIBSON, Walter. *Shadow & the Golden Master.* 1984. Mysterious Pr. 1st ed. dj. EX. P1. $25.00

GIBSON, Walter. *Twilight Zone.* 1963. Grosset Dunlap. VG. P1. $20.00

GIBSON, Walter. *Weird Adventures of the Shadow.* 1960. Grosset Dunlap. 1st ed. EX. R3. $25.00

GIBSON, William. *Burning Chrome.* 1986. Arbor House. 1st ed. sgn. dj. EX. R3. $25.00

GIBSON, William. *Count 0.* 1986. Arbor House. 1st ed. sgn. dj. EX. R3. $25.00

GIBSON, William. *Neuromancer.* 1986. Phantasia. 1st ed. M. R3. $65.00

GIDE, Andre. *Montaigne: Essay in 2 Parts.* 1929. Blackamore/Liveright. Ltd ed. 1/800. sgn. gilt gr bdg. H3. $85.00

GIDE, Andre. *Theseus.* 1949. Verona. Ltd ed. 1/240. folio. orig wrp. slipcase. EX. H3. $1500.00

GIECK, Jack. *Photo Album of OH's Canal Era 1825-1913.* 1988. Kent. 2nd print. sgn. dj. M. T5. $35.00

GIEDION, S. *Walter Gropius: Work & Teamwork.* 1954. Zurich. 1st ed. EX. G1. $100.00

GIELGUD, John. *Early Stages.* 1948. Falcon Pr. New Revised ed. sgn. 249 p. VG. H3. $40.00

GIELGUD, Val. *Death at Broadcasting House.* 1935. Rich Cowan. 5th print. dj. VG. P1. $16.00

GIESY, J.U. *Jason, Son of Jason.* 1966. Avalon. dj. VG. P1. $15.00

GIESY, J.U. *Mouthpiece of Zitu.* 1965. Avalon. 1st ed. dj. EX. R3. $17.50

GIEURE, Maurice. *Georges Braque.* 1956. Paris. probably 1st ed. VG. G1. $90.00

GIFFORD, Barry. *Devil Thumbs a Ride & Other Unforgettable Films.* 1988. Grove Pr. UP. wrp. EX. C4. $30.00

GIFFORD, Barry. *Persimmons.* 1977. Berkley. 1st ed. sgn. wrp. EX. T9. $25.00

GIFFORD & HOGGARTH. *Carnival & Coca Leaf.* 1976. London. Scottish Academic Pr. 1st ed. dj. F2. $25.00

GIFFORD & KIRKPATRICK. *Ancient Maya Pottery.* 1973 & 1975. 2 folio. sgn. F2. $40.00

GIGANIT, Paul Jr. *How Many Snails?* 1988. NY. Greenwillow. Ils Donald Crews. 1st ed. clipped dj. EX. B13. $40.00

GIILMAN, Dorothy. *Mrs Pollifax & Hong Kong Buddha.* 1985. Doubleday. 1st ed. dj. EX. P1. $15.00

GIILMAN & CLIVE. *KG 200.* nd. Simon Schuster. 2nd ed. dj. VG. P1. $12.50

GILBERT, A.T. *Hist of Little Fanny.* 1825. Phil. Ils Charles. 2nd ed. 15 p. wrp. EX. $500.00

GILBERT, A.T. *My Mother: A Poem by a Lady.* 1816. Phil. Ils William Charles. 1st Am ed. wrp. EX. $950.00

GILBERT, Anthony. *And Death Came Too.* 1956. Collins Crime Club. 1st ed. xl. VG. P1. $6.00

GILBERT, Anthony. *By Hook or By Crook.* 1947. Doubleday Book Club. VG. P1. $7.50

GILBERT, Anthony. *Death Knocks 3 Times.* 1949. Crime Club. 1st ed. dj. VG. P1. $20.00

GILBERT, Anthony. *Mr Crook Lifts the Mask.* 1970. Random House. 1st ed. dj. xl. P1. $6.00

GILBERT, Anthony. *Mystery of the Open Window.* 1930. Dodd Mead. VG. P1. $25.00

GILBERT, Anthony. *No Dust in the Attic.* 1963. Random House. 1st ed. dj. VG. P1. $20.00

GILBERT, Anthony. *Ring for a Noose.* 1964. Random House. dj. xl. P1. $7.50

GILBERT, Henry. *King Arthur's Knights.* c 1930s. Ils Walter Crane. C1. $14.00

GILBERT, Michael. *Blk Seraphim.* 1984. Harper. 1st ed. dj. EX. F5. $15.00

GILBERT, Michael. *Body of a Girl.* 1972. Harper Row. 1st ed. dj. VG. P1. $12.50

GILBERT, Michael. *Country House Burglar.* nd. Book Club. dj. xl. P1. $3.50

GILBERT, Michael. *Family Tomb.* 1969. Harper. 1st ed. dj. EX. F5. $17.00

GILBERT, Michael. *Night of the 12th.* nd. Harper Row. dj. EX. P1. $10.00

GILBERT, Michael. *Overdrive.* 1967. Harper. 1st ed. dj. EX. F5. $14.00

GILBERT, Michael. *Petrella at Q.* 1977. Harper Row. 1st ed. dj. VG. P1. $12.50

GILBERT, Michael. *Trouble.* 1987. Harper Row. 1st ed. dj. EX. P1. $15.95

GILBERT, Paul. *Bertram & His Funny Animals.* 1934. Chicago. Ils Rousseff. dj. VG. B3. $27.50

GILBERT, Stuart. *James Joyce's Ulysses: A Study of Stuart Gilbert.* 1952. Knopf. Revised 2nd ed. dj. EX. C4. $35.00

GILBERT, W.S. *Foggerty's Fairy & Other Tales.* 1890. London. 1st ed. G. R3. $40.00

GILBERT, W.S. *Pinafore Picture Book.* 1908. Macmillan. Ils Woodward. 1st ed. 4to. 131 p. VG. $75.00

GILCHRIST, Alexander. *Life of William Blake.* 1863. London. 1st ed. 2 vols in 1. EX. $225.00

GILCHRIST, Ellen. *Annunciation.* 1983. Little Brn. ARC. sgn. dj. RS. B13. $100.00

GILCHRIST, Ellen. *I Cannot Get You Close Enough.* 1990. Little Brn. UP. wrp. EX. B13. $50.00

GILCHRIST, Ellen. *In the Land of Dreamy Dreams.* 1981. Fayetteville. AK U. 1st ed. sgn. dj. EX. $100.00

GILCHRIST, Ellen. *Land Surveyor's Daughter.* 1979. Fayetteville. AK U. Lost Roads. 1st ed. sgn. wrp. very scarce. $65.00

GILCHRIST, Ellen. *Light Can Be Both Wave & Particle.* 1989. Little Brn. 1st ed. sgn. dj. EX. C4. $30.00

GILES, J.H. *Damned Engineers.* 1970. Boston. 1st ed. 409 p. dj. VG. B3. $35.00

GILES, J.H. *GI Journal of Sergeant Giles.* 1965. Boston. 1st ed. dj. VG. B3. $30.00

GILES, J.H. *Miss Willie.* nd. Peoples Book Club. dj. VG. P1. $5.00

GILES, J.H. *6-Horse Hitch.* 1969. Boston. 1st ed. dj. VG. B3. $20.00

GILES, Kenneth. *Death Among the Stars.* 1969. Walker. 1st ed. dj. EX. P1. $10.00

GILHAM, William. *Manual of Instruction for Volunteers & Militia of US.* 1861. Phil. 1st ed. 743 p. T5. $195.00

GILKYSON, Walter. *Toward What Bright Land.* 1947. Scribner. 1st ed. 8vo. 522 p. dj. V1. $6.50

GILL, Bartholomew. *McGarr & Method of Descartes.* 1984. Viking. 1st ed. dj. EX. P1. $15.00

GILL, Bartholomew. *McGarr on the Cliffs of Moher.* 1978. Doubleday Book Club. VG. P1. $7.50

GILL, Brendan. *Here at the New Yorker.* 1975. NY. 1st ed. dj. VG. T1. $25.00

GILL, Brendan. *Many Masks: Life of Frank Lloyd Wright.* 1987. Putnam. 1st ed. dj. EX. $15.00

GILL, Elizabeth. *Crime Coast.* 1931. Crime Club. 1st ed. VG. P1. $20.00

GILL, Tom. *Land Hunger in Mexico.* 1951. WA. 1st ed. 86 p. F2. $10.00

GILLESPIE, Janet. *Bedlam in the Back Seat.* 1960. NY. 1st ed. dj. EX. B3. $25.00

GILLETT, J.B. *6 Years With the TX Rangers 1875-1881.* 1943. Lakeside Classic. VG. $30.00

GILLMOR, Frances. *King Danced in the Marketplace.* 1964. Tucson. 1st ed. 271 p. dj. F2. $25.00

GILLMORE, Rufus. *Ebony Bed Murder.* 1932. Mystery League. VG. P1. $10.00

GILMAN, Coburn. *Weekend Book of Travel.* 1946. McBride. 1st ed. 352 p. VG. B10. $5.50

GILMAN, Dorothy. *Elusive Mrs Pollifax.* 1971. Doubleday. 1st ed. dj. EX. F5. $16.00

GILMAN, Dorothy. *Mrs Pollifax & the Golden Triangle.* 1988. Doubleday. 1st ed. dj. EX. F5. $15.00

GILMAN, Dorothy. *Mrs Pollifax on Safari.* 1977. Doubleday. 1st ed. 182 p. dj. VG. B10. $4.75

GILMAN, Laselle. *Red Gate.* 1953. Ballantine. 1st ed. dj. VG. P1. $30.00

GILMORE, James. *Down in TN & Back by Way of Richmond.* 1864. NY. 1st ed. 222 p. VG. T5. $25.00

GILPATRICK, Guy. *Canny Mr Glencannon.* 1948. NY. galley proof/1st ed. G. B3. $60.00

GILPIN, Laura. *Rio Grande, River of Destiny.* 1949. NY. 2nd ed. dj. VG. B3. $55.00

GILPIN, Laura. *Temples in Yucatan.* 1948. Hastings House. Ils. sgn. dj. A5. $160.00

GINGERY, L.F. *Dogs & Hounds.* 1944. KS City. 1st ed. VG. $20.00

GINGRICH, Arnold. *Cast Down the Laurel.* 1935. Knopf. inscr. dj. H3. $75.00

GINGRICH, Arnold. *Well-Tempered Angler.* 1965. NY. 1st ed. dj. VG. B3. $27.50

GINSBERG, Allen. *Ankor-Wat.* 1968. London. Fulcrum Pr. AP. wht wrp. scarce. K2. $100.00

GINSBERG, Allen. *Collected Poems 1947-1980.* 1984. Harper. sgn. blk bdg. dj. H3. $50.00

GINSBERG, Allen. *Howl & Other Poems.* nd. City Lights. 4th print. B4. $3.00

GINSBERG, Allen. *Kaddish.* 1961. City Lights. 1st ed. wrp. M. $7.00

GINSBERG, Allen. *Planet News 1961-1967.* 1968. City Lights. 1st Am ed. 2nd print. EX. B4. $8.00

GINSBERG, Allen. *Scrap Leaves.* 1968. Millbrook, NY. Poets Pr. 1/150. sgn. wrp. M. H3. $50.00

GINSBERG, Allen. *Visions of the Great Rememberer.* 1974. Mulch Pr. 1/75. sgns. wrp. H3. $75.00

GINSBERG, Allen. *Wht Shroud: Poems 1980-1985.* 1986. Harper Row. Ltd ed. 1/200. sgn. slipcase. M. H3. $125.00

GINSBERG, Allen. *Wichita Vortex Sutra.* 1967. Coyote. 1st print. B4. $6.00

GINSBERG, Allen. *1st Blues: Rags, Ballads, & Harmonium Songs 1971-1974.* 1975. Full Court Pr. 1st HrdCvr ed. sgn. dj. EX. K2. $50.00

GINSBURG, Mirra. *Last Door to Aiya.* 1968. Phillips. dj. EX. P1. $22.50

GINSBURG, Mirra. *Ultimate Threshold.* 1970. Holt. 1st ed. 244 p. dj. EX. B10. $9.50

GINTY, E.B. *MO Legend.* 1938. Random House. 1st ed. dj. EX. H3. $35.00

GIONO, Jean. *Horseman on the Roof.* 1954. Knopf. 1st ed. dj. EX. B13. $35.00

GIONO, Jean. *Straw Man.* 1959. Knopf. 1st Am ed. dj. EX. C4. $30.00

GIOVANNI, Nikki. *Those Ride the Night Winds.* 1983. Morrow. UP. wrp. EX. B13. $85.00

GIOVANNI & WALKER. *Poetic Equation: Conversations Between Giovanni & Walker.* 1974. Howard U. ARC. dj. EX. K2. $65.00

GIOVANNITTI, Len. *Prisoners of Combine D.* 1957. NY. 1st ed. 541 p. dj. VG. T5. $15.00

GIPSON, M. *Mr Bear Squash You All Flat.* 1950. NY. 1st ed. G. B3. $27.50

GIRARD, Sharon. *Funeral Music & Customs in Venezuela.* 1980. Tempe. 1st ed. 8vo. wrp. F2. $15.00

GIROUARD, Mark. *Life in the Eng Country House.* nd. Penguin. NM. C1. $9.00

GIROUARD, Mark. *Return to Camelot.* 1981. Yale. 1st ed. dj. EX. C1. $19.50

GIRSBERGER, Hans. *Im Umgang mit Le Corbusier...* nd. (1981) np. (Zurich/Munich) Artemis. 1/950. orig wrp. R4. $30.00

GISSING, George. *By the Ionian Sea.* 1901. Chapman Hall. 1st ed. sm quarto. wht bdg. VG. K2. $175.00

GISSING, George. *Charles Dickens: Critical Study.* 1898. London. Blackie. 1st ed. red bdg. H3. $100.00

GISSING, George. *New Grub St.* 1891. London. Smith Elder. 1st ed. 3 vols. orig cloth. EX. H3. $4500.00

GISWOLD, Lawrence. *Tombs, Travel, & Trouble.* 1937. Hillman Curl. 1st ed. 337 p. dj. F2. $10.00

GIVENS, C.G. *All Cats Are Gray.* 1937. Bobbs Merrill. inscr. gilt red bdg. dj. H3. $60.00

GLADDEN, William. *From the Hub to Hudson & Principle Connections to Chicago...* 1869. Boston. 12mo. A4. $50.00

GLAISHER, J. *Atmosphere.* 1873. NY. 453 p. VG. $40.00

GLASCOCK, B.C. *Here's Death Valley.* 1940. Bobbs Merrill. 1st ed. dj. VG. $21.00

GLASGOW, Ellen. *Voice of the People.* 1900. NY. 1st ed. 444 p. VG. T5. $25.00

GLASPELL, Susan. *Cherished & Shared of Old.* 1940. NY. 1st ed. 24mo. VG. $15.00

GLASPELL, Susan. *Comic Artist.* 1927. NY. 1st ed. dj. VG. B3. $35.00

GLAZIER, Willard. *Ocean to Ocean on Horseback.* 1900. Phil. Ils. 544 p. EX. P4. $85.00

GLEASON, Arthur. *Our Part in the Great War.* nd. (1917) Stokes. 338 p. VG. B10. $5.00

GLEASON, W.J. *Hist of Cuyahoga Co Soldiers' & Sailors' Monument.* 1894. Cleveland. Ils. 770 p. AEG. T5. $37.50

GLEN, Lois. *Charles WS Williams: A Checklist.* 1975. Kent State. 1st ed. M. R3. $25.00

GLINES, C.V. *Doolittle's Tokyo Raiders.* 1964. NY. 1st ed. dj. EX. B3. $55.00

GLINES, C.V. *Grand Old Lady.* 1959. Cleveland. 1st ed. 250 p. dj. VG. B3. $27.50

GLINES, C.V. *Saga of the Air Mail.* 1968. Princeton. Ils 1st ed. 180 p. dj. VG. T5. $37.50

GLOAG, John. *Artorius Rex.* 1977.1st Am ed. dj. EX. C1. $21.50

GLOUGH. *Operation, Care, & Repair of Automobiles.* 1907. NY. 1st ed. 343 p. G. $90.00

GLOVER, M.B. *Science & Health.* 1875. Boston. orig cloth/wrp/slipcase. P4. $1800.00

GLOVER, T.R. *Nature & Purpose of a Christian Soc.* 1912. London. Headley. 2nd ed. 12mo. VG. V1. $6.00

GLYN, Elinor. *Beyond the Rocks.* 1906. Harper. 1st ed. 326 p. VG. B10. $3.75

GNARRA, Irene. *Philippe de Remi's la Manekine: Text, Trans, Commentary.* 1988. Garland. HrdCvr. M. C1. $22.50

GODCHAUX, Elma. *Stubborn Roots.* 1936. Macmillan. inscr. dj. H3. $50.00

GODDARD, Anthea. *Vienna Persuit.* 1976. Walker. dj. VG. P1. $7.50

GODDARD, H.H. *Criminal Imbecile: Analysis of 3 Remarkable Murder Cases.* 1916. NY. 1st ed. 2nd print. 8vo. bl bdg. G. T1. $85.00

GODDARD, Robert. *Rocket Development: Liquid Fuel Rocket Research 1929-1941.* 1948. NY. 8vo. 291 p. EX. $65.00

GODDARD, Robert. *Rockets.* 1946. NY. Am Rocket Soc. dj. EX. C2. $75.00

GODDEN, Jon. *In Her Garden.* 1981. Doubleday Book Club. VG. P1. $7.50

GODDEN, Rumer. *China Court.* 1961. Viking. 1st ed. 304 p. dj. VG. B10. $3.50

GODDEN, Rumer. *In This House of Brede.* 1969. Viking Book Club. 376 p. B10. $4.00

GODDEN, Rumer. *Mousewife.* 1951. London. 1st Eng ed. dj. VG. C1. $9.00

GODEY, John. *Snake.* nd. Putnam. 2nd ed. dj. VG. P1. $15.00

GODEY, John. *Talisman.* 1976. Putnam. 1st ed. dj. VG. P1. $20.00

GODEY, John. *3 Worlds of Johnny Handsome.* 1972. Book Club. 222 p. EX. B10. $3.50

GODFREY, Ellen. *Murder Behind Locked Doors.* 1988. St Martin. 1st ed. dj. EX. F5. $14.00

GODMAN, J.D. *Am Nat Hist.* 1826. Carey Lea. 1 vol only. VG. T3. $45.00

GODMAN, J.D. *Am Nat Hist.* 1831. Stoddard Atherton. 2nd ed. 3 vols. pls. rebacked. VG. T3. $125.00

GODMAN, J.D. *Rambles of a Naturalist With Memoir of the Author.* 1859. Assn Friends Diffusion Knowledge. 12mo. 124 p. V1. $12.00

GODWIN, Gail. *Glass People.* 1972. Knopf. 1st ed. dj. EX. K2. $65.00

GODWIN, Gail. *Violet Clay.* 1978. Knopf. 1st ed. sgn. dj. EX. C4. $35.00

GODWIN, George. *Eternal Forest.* 1929. Appleton. 1st Canadian ed. 318 p. G. B10. $4.00

GODWIN, Parke. *Beloved Exile.* PB Orig. VG. C1. $4.00

GODWIN, Parke. *Beloved Exile.* 1987. 1st German ed. 2 vols. sgn. M. C1. $14.00

GODWIN, Parke. *Fire When It Comes.* 1984. 1st ed. dj. M. C1. $12.50

GODWIN, Parke. *Firelord.* 1980. 1st ed. sgn. dj. EX. C1. $35.00

GODWIN, Parke. *Firelord.* 1982. PB Orig. sgn. C1. $7.50

GODWIN, Parke. *Invitation to Camelot.* 1st German ed. sgn. PB. EX. C1. $9.50

GODWIN, Parke. *Last Rainbow.* 1985. Bantam. 1st Trade ed. sgn. C1. $15.00

GODWIN, Parke. *Last Rainbow.* 1986. 1st mass market PB ed. sgn. M. C1. $7.50

GODWIN, Parke. *Last Rainbow.* 1988. 1st German ed. 2 vols. sgn. wrp. M. C1. $14.00

GOEBEL & GOEBEL. *General in Wht House.* 1952. NY. 276 p. dj. VG. T5. $9.50

GOERTZ. *Give Us Our Dream.* 1947. McGraw Hill. dj. VG. $7.00

GOETHE, J.W. *Goethe's Werke.* 1900. Leipzig Wien. early ed. German text. 30 vols. VG. R5. $35.00

GOETHE. *Works.* 1885. Phil. Ils. 4to. 5 vols. AEG. VG. T1. $100.00

GOGARTY, Oliver St John. *Going Native.* 1940. NY. 1st ed. dj. EX. B13. $45.00

GOGOL, Nikolai. *Chichikov's Journeys; or, Home Life in Old Russia.* 1944. Heritage. Ils Lucille Corcos. slipcase. EX. T1. $20.00

GOGOL, Nikolai. *Overcoat & Other Stories.* 1923. Knopf. 1st Am ed. dj. EX. B13. $100.00

GOINES, Donald. *Story of a Ghetto Pimp.* 1972. Holloway House BH421. 1st ed. wrp. VG. T9. $20.00

GOLD, H.L. *Bodyguard.* nd. Book Club. dj. VG. P1. $4.00

GOLD, H.L. *Galaxy Reader of SF.* 1952. Crown. 1st ed. dj. VG. R3. $40.00

GOLD, H.L. *Mind Partner.* 1961. Doubleday. dj. VG. P1. $10.00

GOLD, H.L. *4th Galaxy Reader.* 1959. Doubleday. 1st ed. dj. VG. P1. $15.00

GOLD, H.L. *5th Galaxy Reader.* 1961. Book Club. 1st ed. dj. VG. P1. $30.00

GOLD, P.D. *In FL Dawn: Romance of Hist.* 1926. Jacksonville. inscr. EX. $40.00

GOLD & FIZDALE. *Misia: Life of Misia Sert.* 1980. Knopf. 3rd ed. 337 p. B10. $6.00

GOLDBERG, I. *Tin Pan Alley: Chronicle of Am Popular Music Racket.* 1930. NY. John Day. 1st ed. VG. $35.00

GOLDEN, F.L. *For Doctors Only: Mixture of Medical Humor.* 1948. Fell Pub. 1st ed. 273 p. dj. VG. B10. $3.75

GOLDEN, H. *World of Haldeman Julius.* 1960. NY. 1st ed. 288 p. dj. VG. B3. $20.00

GOLDEN, Harry. *So What Else Is New?* nd. (1964) Putnam. 312 p. VG. B10. $3.50

GOLDHURST, Richard. *Many Are the Hearts: Agony & Triumph of US Grant.* 1975. Crowell. 1st ed. dj. G. S1. $8.00

GOLDHURST, Richard. *Tour Around the World.* 1879. Phil. Nat Pub. 810 p. G. S1. $10.00

GOLDIN, Stephen. *Assault on the Gods.* 1977. Doubleday. sgn. dj. EX. P1. $20.00

GOLDIN, Stephen. *World Called Solitude.* 1981. Doubleday. 1st ed. dj. EX. P1. $15.00

GOLDING, Louis. *Blk Frailty.* 1934. Centaur Pr. 1st ed. 1/75. sgn. EX. H3. $60.00

GOLDING, William. *Gordimer, Nadine.* 1971. Viking. 1st ed. dj. EX. B13. $50.00

GOLDING, William. *Lord of the Flies.* 1955. Coward McCann. 1st Am ed. dj. VG. scarce. K2. $175.00

GOLDING, William. *Moving Target.* 1982. Farrar Straus. UP. EX. K2. $45.00

GOLDING, William. *Spire.* 1964. Harcourt Brace. 1st Am ed. dj. VG. $35.00

GOLDING, William. *Spire.* 1964. Harcourt Brace. 1st ed. sgn. dj. w/sgn letter. B13. $125.00

GOLDING, William. *Spire.* 1964. London. 1st ed. dj. EX. $55.00

GOLDMAN, James. *Man From Greek & Roman.* nd. Book Club. dj. VG. C1. $5.00

GOLDMAN, William. *Boys & Girls Together.* 1964. Atheneum. 1st ed. inscr. dj. EX. H3. $75.00

GOLDMAN, William. *Brothers.* 1987. Warner. 1st ed. inscr. dj. w/wrp sample chapter. M. C4. $45.00

GOLDMAN, William. *Clr of Light.* 1984. Warner. 1st ed. dj. VG. P1. $17.50

GOLDMAN, William. *Father's Day.* 1971. Michael Joseph. 1st ed. VG. P1. $10.00

GOLDMAN, William. *Heat.* 1984. Warner. 1st ed. dj. VG. P1. $15.00

GOLDMAN, William. *Magic.* nd. Book Club. dj. VG. P1. $4.50

GOLDMAN, William. *Magic.* 1976. Delacorte. 1st ed. sgn. dj. EX. H3. $200.00

GOLDMAN, William. *Marathon Man.* 1974. Delacorte. 1st ed. dj. VG. P1. $30.00

GOLDMAN, William. *No Way To Treat a Lady.* nd. Harcourt Brace. 1st HrdCvr ed in author's real name. H3. $75.00

GOLDMAN, William. *Princess Bride.* 1973. NY. 1st ed. dj. VG. B3. $60.00

GOLDMAN, William. *Soldier in the Rain.* 1960. Atheneum. 1st ed. dj. EX. H3. $20.00

GOLDMAN, William. *Temple of Gold.* 1957. Knopf. 1st ed. dj. EX. H3. $100.00

GOLDMAN, William. *Wigger.* 1974. Harcourt Brace. 1st ed. presentation. dj. EX. H3. $75.00

GOLDMAN, William. *Your Turn To Curtsy, My Turn To Bow.* 1958. Doubleday. 1st ed. presentation. dj. EX. H3. $125.00

GOLDSBOROUGH, Robert. *Murder in E Minor.* nd. Book Club. dj. EX. P1. $5.00

GOLDSMITH, E.E. *Toby: Story of a Dog.* 1913. NY. Ils. 224 p. VG. T5. $15.00

GOLDSMITH, Oliver. *Deserted Village.* ca 1880s? Phil. Coates. sm 8vo. B10. $6.75

GOLDSMITH, Oliver. *Poems, Plays, & Essays.* 1854. Phillips Sampson. 1st ed. 530 p. B10. $35.00

GOLDSMITH, Oliver. *Poetical Works.* 1845. London. sm quarto. Riviere bdg. H3. $3000.00

GOLDSMITH, Oliver. *Vicar of Wakefield*. c1929. Phil. VG. G1. $75.00

GOLDSMITH, Oliver. *Vicar of Wakefield*. 1903. London. A&C Blk. 13 pls. gilt gr bdg. EX. $40.00

GOLDSMITH, Oliver. *Vicar of Wakefield*. 1939. Heritage. Ils John Austen. slipcase. EX. T1. $20.00

GOLDSMITH, Oliver. *Works*. nd. Boston. Jefferson Pr. Lib ed. 12 vols. VG. H3. $250.00

GOLDSMITH, Oliver. *Works*. 1908. Putnam. Turk's Head ed. 1/1000. 10 vols. H3. $1500.00

GOLDSMITH, Wallace. *Misfit Christmas*. 1906. Boston. Ils. VG. $22.00

GOLDSTEIN, David. *Socialism: Nation of Fatherless Children*. nd. (1903) Boston. 1st ed. 8vo. 374 p. EX. R4. $35.00

GOLDSTEIN, Lisa. *Dream Years*. 1985. Bantam. 1st ed. dj. EX. P1. $15.00

GOLDSTEIN, Lisa. *Tourist*. 1989. Simon Schuster. UP. wrp. EX. F5. $22.00

GOLDSTEIN, Marily. *Huastec Art From Pre-Columbian Mexico*. 1982. Fine Arts Mus. sq 4to. wrp. F2. $7.50

GOLDSTONE, A.H. *AH Goldstone Collection of Mystery & Detective Fiction*. 1981. CA Book Auction Galleries. 1/400. EX. T9. $175.00

GOLDTHWAITE, E.K. *Cat & Mouse*. 1946. Duell Sloan Pearce. dj. xl. P1. $5.00

GOLDTHWAITE, E.K. *Scarecrow*. 1946. Books Inc. dj. VG. P1. $10.00

GOLL, Yvan. *Lackawanna Elegy*. 1970. Sumac Pr. 1/100. sgn. gilt blk bdg. M. H3. $60.00

GOLLANCZ, Israel. *Sir Gawain & the Gr Knight*. 1940. Early Eng Text Soc. VG. C1. $15.00

GOLON, Sergeanne. *Angelique & the Demon*. 1974. Putnam. 1st ed. dj. EX. F5. $15.00

GONCALEZ SANCHEZ, Isabel. *Haciendas y Ranchos de Tlaxcala en 1712*. 1969. Mexico. Ltd 1st ed. Spanish text. wrp. F2. $30.00

GONG & GRANT. *Tong War!* 1930. NY. Ils Pedro Llanuza. 1st ed. sgn. T5. $47.50

GONZALES, Laurence. *Jambeaux*. 1979. NY. 1st ed. sgn. dj. EX. T9. $65.00

GONZALES DAVILA, Francisco. *Ancient Cultures of Mexico*. 1968. Mexico. Ils. sm 4to. 80 p. F2. $10.00

GONZALEZ-GERTH & SCHADE. *Ruben Dario Centennial Studies*. 1972. TX U. 2nd print. dj. F2. $12.50

GOOD, Kenneth. *Into the Heart*. 1991. Simon Schuster. 1st ed. 349 p. dj. F2. $17.50

GOODALE, G.L. *Wild Flowers of Am*. 1886. Boston. 2nd ed. 51 pls. VG. $375.00

GOODCHILD, George. *CO Jim*. nd. Collins Wild W Club. VG. P1. $10.00

GOODCHILD, George. *Jack-O'-Lantern*. 1930. Mystery League. 1st ed. VG. P1. $10.00

GOODEN, Stephen. *Fables*. 1936. London. 1/525. sgn. 12 pls. orig vellum. EX. H3. $1000.00

GOODGOLD & CARLINSKY. *Compleat Beatles Quiz Book*. 1975. Warner. PB. EX. B4. $4.00

GOODIS, David. *Behold This Woman*. 1947. Appleton Century. dj. VG. T9. $100.00

GOODIS, David. *Blk Friday*. 1954. Lion 224. PB Orig. wrp. EX. T9. $125.00

GOODIS, David. *Dark Passage*. 1946. NY. Messner. 1st ed. dj. EX. T9. $190.00

GOODIS, David. *Dark Passage*. 1947. World. dj. EX. T9. $85.00

GOODIS, David. *Moon in the Gutter*. 1953. Gold Medal 348. PB Orig. EX. rare. T9. $85.00

GOODIS, David. *Of Tender Sin*. 1952. Gold Medal 226. PB Orig. EX. T9. $135.00

GOODIS, David. *Shoot the Piano Player*. nd. Blk Cat BA-35. 1st Eng-language ed. wrp. VG. T9. $35.00

GOODIS, David. *Somebody's Done For*. 1967. Banner B60-111. PB Orig. EX. rare. T9. $115.00

GOODMAN, Henry. *Selected Writings of Lafcadio Hearn*. 1949. NY. 1st ed. gr bdg. VG. T1. $35.00

GOODMAN, P. *Our Visit to Niagara*. 1960. Horizon. 1st ed. dj. EX. $12.00

GOODMAN, Richard. *French Dirt: Story of a Garden in the S of France*. 1991. Chapel Hill. 1st ed. wrp. EX. B13. $45.00

GOODRICH, C.A. *Universal Traveler*. c 1836. NY. 12mo. 504 p. gilt bdg. G. G4. $45.00

GOODRICH, C.A. *Universal Traveler*. 1836. Hartford. Ils. 12mo. 610 p. VG. G4. $47.00

GOODRICH, F.B. *Man Upon the Sea: Hist of Maritime Adventures...* 1858. Phil. Ils 1st ed. 8vo. gilt red bdg. EX. T1. $110.00

GOODRICH, Lloyd. *Winslow Homer, Catalog Raisonne of His Graphic Art*. 1968. Smithsonian. 1st ed. square 8vo. dj. EX. $35.00

GOODSPEED, Bernice. *Mexican Tales*. 1937. Mexico. 1st ed. inscr. 227 p. wrp. F2. $25.00

GOODSPEED, Bernice. *Paricutin*. 1945. Am Book Co. 1st ed. inscr. stiff wrp. F2. $25.00

GOODSTONE, Tony. *Pulps*. 1970. Chelsea House. 1st ed. dj. EX. R3. $25.00

GOODWIN-SMITH, R. *Eng Domestic Metalwork*. 1937. Essex, Eng. 1st ed. dj. EX. $150.00

GOOSE, P.H. *Aquarium: Unveiling of Wonders of Deep Sea*. 1854. London. Van Voorst. 6 pls. 12mo. G. V1. $125.00

GORDIMER, Nadine. *Conservationist*. 1975. Viking. 1st Am ed. dj. EX. C4. $40.00

GORDIMER, Nadine. *July's People*. 1981. Viking. 1st Am ed. sgn. dj. EX. K2. $65.00

GORDIMER, Nadine. *Livingstone's Companion*. 1972. London. Cape. 1st ed. dj. EX. B13. $125.00

GORDIMER, Nadine. *My Son's Story*. 1990. London. Bloomsbury. UP of 1st Eng ed. wrp. VG. K2. $40.00

GORDIMER, Nadine. *Occasion for Loving*. 1963. Viking. 1st ed. dj. VG. K2. $65.00

GORDIMER, Nadine. *Soft Voice of the Serpent*. 1952. NY. 1st ed. dj. VG. $70.00

GORDIMER, Nadine. *Something Out There*. 1984. Viking. AP. wrp. EX. K2. $45.00

GORDIMER, Nadine. *Something Out There*. 1984. Viking. 1st ed. sgn. dj. EX. K2. $65.00

GORDIMER, Nadine. *Sport of Nature*. 1987. Knopf. UP. wrp. EX. C4. $30.00

GORDIMER, Nadine. *Sport of Nature*. 1987. Viking. UP. sgn. salmon wrp. EX. K2. $85.00

GORDIMER, Nadine. *World of Strangers*. 1958. London. 1st ed. as issued. K2. $55.00

GORDON, A.L. *Poems*. 1912. London. Constable. 1st Eng ed. scarce. C1. $14.50

GORDON, Caroline. *Collected Stories of Caroline Gordon*. 1981. Farrar Straus. UP. wrp. EX. B13. $125.00

GORDON, Caroline. *Penhally*. 1931. Scribner. 1st ed. 12mo. dj. EX. C4. $125.00

GORDON, Caroline. *Women on the Porch*. 1944. NY. dj. lacks fly. VG. B3. $32.50

GORDON, Cyrus. *Before Columbus.* 1971. Crown. 1st ed. 224 p. F2. $15.00

GORDON, Elsbeth. *Pre-Columbian Pottery of Peru.* 1975. Gainesville, FL. Ils. 36 p. wrp. F2. $10.00

GORDON, J.B. *Reminiscences of the Civil War.* 1905. NY. 474 p. G. T5. $45.00

GORDON, J.B. *Reminiscences of the Civil War.* 1974. Gettysburg. reprint of 1904 Scribner ed. M. $25.00

GORDON, Richard. *Captain's Table.* 1954. Michael Joseph. 1st ed. dj. VG. P1. $20.00

GORDON, Richard. *Doctor at Lg.* nd. Quality Book Club. VG. P1. $5.00

GORDON, Richard. *Doctor at Lg.* 1958. Michael Joseph. 9th print. dj. VG. P1. $20.00

GORDON, Richard. *Doctor at Sea.* 1954. Michael Joseph. 13th print. dj. VG. P1. $15.00

GORDON, Richard. *Doctor in the House.* 1952. Michael Joseph. 2nd ed. dj. VG. P1. $15.00

GORDON, Richard. *Nuts in May.* 1964. Heinemann. 1st ed. dj. VG. P1. $17.50

GORDON-MILLER, W. *Recollections of US Army.* 1845. Boston. 2nd ed. VG. $100.00

GORDON-WISE, B.A. *Reclamation of a Queen.* 1991. Greenwood. no dj issued. EX. P1. $39.95

GORENSTEIN, Shirley. *Intro to Archaeology.* 1965. Basic Books. 165 p. dj. F2. $10.00

GORENSTEIN, Shirley. *Not Forever on Earth.* 1975. Scribner. 1st ed. 153 p. dj. F2. $15.00

GORER, Geoffrey. *Africa Dances.* 1935. London. Faber. 1st ed. octavo. 363 p. VG. H3. $75.00

GORES, Joe. *Come Morning.* 1986. Mysterious Pr. 1st ed. dj. VG. P1. $15.95

GOREY, Edward. *Broken Spoke.* 1976. Dodd Mead. 1st ed. sgn. dj. EX. B13. $65.00

GOREY, Edward. *Loathsome Couple.* 1977. Dodd Mead. 1st ed. dj. VG. B7. $25.00

GOREY, Edward. *Melange.* 1981. Gotham. 1/526. sgn. wrp. H3. $60.00

GOREY, Edward. *Unstrung Harp; or, Mr Easbrass Writes a Novel.* 1953. Duell. 1st ed. VG. scarce. B10. $15.00

GOREY, Edward. *Willowdale.* 1962. Indianapolis/NY. 1st ed. wrp. VG. $25.00

GORGAS, Marie. *William Crawford Gorgas: Life & Work.* 1935. Doubleday. 359 p. xl. VG. B10. $4.50

GORHAM, Bob. *Churchill Downs 100th KY Centennial.* 1973. Churchill Downs. Ils. EX. B10. $7.50

GORLING, Lars. *491.* 1966. Grove Pr. 1st ed. dj. EX. K2. $25.00

GORMAN, Edward. *Guild.* 1987. Evans. 1st ed. dj. EX. P1. $14.95

GORMAN, Edward. *Murder in the Wings.* 1986. St Martin. 1st ed. dj. EX. F5. $16.00

GORMAN, Edward. *Murder on the Aisle.* 1987. Walker. 1st ed. dj. EX. F5. $15.00

GOSCH & HAMMER. *Last Testament of Lucky Luciano.* 1975. Little Brn. 1st ed. dj. EX. P1. $17.50

GOSLING, Paula. *Hoodwink.* 1988. Crime Club. 1st ed. dj. EX. F5. $12.00

GOSNELL, H.A. *Before the Mast in the Clippers: Diaries of Charles A Abbey.* 1937. Derrydale. 1/950. EX. $140.00

GOTTLIEB, Hinko. *Key to the Great Gate.* 1947. Simon Schuster. 1st ed. dj. EX. R3. $15.00

GOTTSCHALK, L. *Lafayette in Am 1777–1783.* c 1975. Arveyres, France. 1st/Bicentennial ed. sgn. fld maps. EX. $45.00

GOTTSHALL, Franklin. *Craft Work in Metal, Wood, Leather, & Plastics.* nd. (1954) Bruce. 1st ed? 144 p. VG. B10. $4.75

GOUDGE, Elizabeth. *Rosemary Tree.* 1956. Coward. 2nd ed. red bdg. dj. B10. $3.75

GOUDSMIT, S.A. *Alsos.* 1947. NY. Ils. 259 p. VG. T5. $19.50

GOUGH, James. *Memoirs of Life, Religious Experience, & Labors in Gospel.* 1886. Phil. Friends Bookstore. 12mo. 149 p. EX. V1. $12.00

GOULART, Ron. *Blood Countess.* 1975. Warner. 1st ed. wrp. EX. F5. $8.50

GOULART, Ron. *Camelion Corps.* 1972. Macmillan. 1st ed. dj. EX. R3. $15.00

GOULART, Ron. *Cleopatra Jones & the Casino of Gold.* 1975. Warner. 1st ed. wrp. EX. F5. $15.00

GOULART, Ron. *Death in Silver.* 1975. Golden Pr. decor brd. EX. P1. $7.50

GOULART, Ron. *Dime Detectives.* 1988. Mysterious Pr. 1st ed. dj. EX. F5. $20.00

GOULART, Ron. *Hawkshaw.* 1972. Doubleday. 1st ed. dj. EX. R3. $12.50

GOULART, Ron. *House of Death.* 1973. Warner. 1st ed. wrp. EX. F5. $7.00

GOULART, Ron. *If Dying Was All.* 1971. Ace 36300. 1st ed. wrp. EX. T9. $30.00

GOULART, Ron. *Line Up Tough Guys.* 1966. Sherbourne Pr. 1st ed. inscr. dj. EX. T9. $35.00

GOULART, Ron. *Man of Bronze.* 1933. Street Smith. 1st ed. VG. R3. $75.00

GOULART, Ron. *Nutzenbolts.* 1975. Macmillan. 1st ed. dj. EX. F5. $18.00

GOULART, Ron. *Odd Job No 101.* 1975. Scribner. 1st ed. dj. EX. P1. $20.00

GOULART, Ron. *Quest of Qui.* 1975. Golden Pr. decor brd. EX. P1. $7.50

GOULART, Ron. *Quest of the Spider.* 1933. Street Smith. 1st ed. VG. R3. $100.00

GOULART, Ron. *Secret in the Sky.* 1975. Golden Pr. decor brd. VG. P1. $5.00

GOULD, Chester. *Dick Tracy Ace Detective.* 1943. Whitman. VG. P1. $15.00

GOULD, Heywood. *Glitterburn.* 1981. St Martin. 1st ed. dj. xl. P1. $6.00

GOULD, John. *Farmer Takes a Wife.* 1946. Morrow. 3rd ed. 153 p. dj. VG. B10. $3.50

GOULD, M.T.C. *Report of Trial of Friends at Steubenville, OH.* 1829. Phil. Harding. 8vo. 340 p. orig brd. V1. $25.00

GOULD, R.F. *Hist of Free Masonry.* nd. London. Caxton. 6 vols. gilt bdg. EX. $175.00

GOULD. *Hen's Teeth.* 1983. NY. 1st ed. dj. EX. C2. $20.00

GOULDING, Michael. *Fishes & the Forest.* 1980. CA U. 1st ed. 280 p. dj. F2. $15.00

GOVER, Robert. *$100 Misunderstanding.* 1962. Grove Pr. sgn. dj. EX. H3. $85.00

GOVER, Robert. *Getting Pretty on the Table.* 1975. Capra. Chapbook Series. 1/100. sgn. EX. K2. $20.00

GOWANLOCH. *Fishes & Fishing in LA.* 1933. New Orleans. Ils. wrp. VG. C2. $27.00

GOYEN, William. *Arcadio.* 1983. Clarkson Potter. UP. EX. K2. $35.00

GOYEN, William. *Book of Jesus.* 1973. Doubleday. ARC. inscr. dj. RS. EX. B13. $125.00

GOYEN, William. *Book of Jesus.* 1973. Doubleday. 1st ed. dj. EX. H3. $30.00

GOYEN, William. *Faces of Blood Kindred.* 1960. Random House. 1st ed. dj. EX. H3. $50.00

GOYEN, William. *Ghost & Flesh.* 1952. Random House. 1st ed. dj. VG. H3. $75.00

GOYEN, William. *House of Breath.* 1950. Random House. ARC. sgn. dj. EX. K2. $275.00

GOYEN, William. *House of Breath.* 1950. Random House. 1st ed. inscr/sgn. dj. EX. B13. $275.00

GOYEN, William. *House of Breath.* 1950. Random House. 1st ed. sgn. dj. EX. K2. $150.00

GRABHORN PUBLISHING. *Catalog of Some 500 Examples of Printing...1917-1960.* Grabhorn. 1/250. 4to. 63 p. VG. V1. $150.00

GRADY, James. *6 Days of the Condor.* 1974. Norton. 1st ed. dj. EX. F5. $28.00

GRAEME, Bruce. *Murder of Some Importance.* nd. Hutchinson. 9th print. VG. P1. $10.00

GRAEME, Bruce. *Unsolved.* 1932. Lippincott. 1st ed. VG. P1. $15.00

GRAEME, Bruce. *2-Faced.* 1977. Hutchinson. dj. xl. P1. $5.00

GRAEME, David. *Vengeance of Monsieur Blackshirt.* 1971. Tom Stacey. dj. VG. P1. $12.50

GRAETZ, Heinrich. *Hist of the Jews.* 1933. NY. Dobsevage. Ils Dobsevage. 6 vols. octavo. H3. $1000.00

GRAF, O.M. *Prisoners All.* 1928. Knopf. 1st Am ed. 442 p. G. B10. $5.50

GRAFFMAN. *I Really Should Be Practicing.* 1981. NY. 1st ed. dj. VG. B3. $25.00

GRAFTON, Carol. *Traditional Patchwork Patterns.* 1974. Dover. 1st ed. 57 p. wrp. EX. B10. $2.00

GRAFTON, Sue. *Keziah Dane.* 1967. Macmillan. 1st ed. dj. EX. B13. $250.00

GRAHAM, Caroline. *Death of a Hollow Man.* 1989. Morrow. 1st Am ed. dj. EX. T9. $25.00

GRAHAM, J.A. *Aldeburg Cezanne.* nd. Book Club. dj. EX. P1. $4.50

GRAHAM, J.A. *Arthur.* nd. Book Club. dj. EX. P1. $4.50

GRAHAM, J.A. *Involvment of Arnold Wechsler.* nd. Book Club. dj. VG. P1. $4.50

GRAHAM, J.W. *Faith of a Quaker.* 1920. Cambridge U. 8vo. 444 p. G. V1. $10.50

GRAHAM, J.W. *Quaker Ministry.* 1925. London. Swarthmore. 1st ed. 12mo. 88 p. G. V1. $7.00

GRAHAM, John. *Ancient Mesoamerica: Selected Readings.* 1969. Palo Alto. Peek Pub. 4to. 300 p. wrp. F2. $15.00

GRAHAM, Philip. *Showboats: Hist of Am Inst.* 1951. Austin, TX. Ils 1st ed. 224 p. dj. VG. T5. $75.00

GRAHAM, R.B. *S Am Sketches of RB Cunninghame Graham.* 1978. OK U. 1st ed. dj. F2. $20.00

GRAHAM, Stephen. *In Quest of El Dorado.* 1923. Appleton. 1st ed. 333 p. dj. F2. $22.50

GRAHAM, Tom; see Lewis, Sinclair.

GRAHAM, W. *Reno Court of Inquiry.* 1954. Harrisburg. 1st ed. dj. VG. B3. $47.50

GRAHAM, W.A. *Story of the Little Big Horn: Custer's Last Fight.* 1926. NY. 1st ed. VG. $55.00

GRAHAM. *NY Giants: An Informal Hist.* 1952. NY. 1st ed. VG. P1. $30.00

GRAHAME, Kenneth. *Golden Age.* 1895. Chicago. Stone Kimball. 1st Am ed. VG. C1. $19.50

GRAHAME, Kenneth. *Golden Age.* 1900. London. Ils Parrish. 1st ed. TEG. red bdg. $150.00

GRAHAME, Kenneth. *Golden Age.* 1905. NY. Ils Parrish. later print. 1952 p. VG. T5. $65.00

GRAHAME, Kenneth. *Headswoman.* 1921. Bodley Head. Ltd ed. 1/75. sgn. TEG. H3. $750.00

GRAHAME, Kenneth. *Wind in the Willows.* 1908. Scribner. 1st ed. VG. B2. $85.00

GRAHAME, Kenneth. *Wind in the Willows.* 1962. Heritage Pr. EX. C1. $15.00

GRAMMONT, Count. *Secret Hist of Court of Charles the 2nd.* 1864. NY. 12mo. 329 p. VG. G4. $20.00

GRANBERG, Wilbur. *People of the Maguey.* 1970. Praeger. 1st ed. 160 p. dj. P1. $15.00

GRANCSAY, Stephen. *Catalog of Armor: John Woodman Higgins Armory.* 1961. Worcester, MA. EX. $20.00

GRAND, Gordon. *Col Weatherford & His Friends.* 1933. Derrydale. Ltd ed. 1/1450. EX. $65.00

GRANDMA MOSES. *Grandma Moses Storybook for Boys & Girls.* 1961. NY. 1st ed. 4to. dj. EX. $45.00

GRANGER, Bill. *El Murders.* 1987. Holt. 1st ed. dj. EX. P1. $16.95

GRANGER, Bill. *Hemingway's Notebook.* 1986. Crown. 1st ed. dj. VG. P1. $15.95

GRANGER, Bill. *There Are No Spies.* 1986. Warner. 1st ed. dj. VG. P1. $16.95

GRANT, Bruce. *Life & Fighting Times of Isaac Hull...* 1947. Chicago. 418 p. EX. $35.00

GRANT, C.L. *Dodd Mead Gallery of Horror.* 1983. Dodd Mead. 1st ed. dj. VG. P1. $30.00

GRANT, C.L. *For Fear of the Night.* 1987. Tor Books. 1st ed. dj. EX. F5. $15.00

GRANT, C.L. *Greystone Bay.* 1985. Tor Books. 1st ed. wrp. EX. F5. $8.00

GRANT, C.L. *Hour of the Oxrun Dead.* 1977. Doubleday. 1st ed. dj. EX. F5. $50.00

GRANT, C.L. *Last Call of Mourning.* 1979. Doubleday. 1st ed. dj. EX. F5. $75.00

GRANT, C.L. *Nightmare Seasons.* 1982. Doubleday. 1st ed. dj. RS. EX. R3. $40.00

GRANT, C.L. *Orchard.* 1986. Tor Books. 1st ed. wrp. EX. F5. $6.00

GRANT, C.L. *Ravens of the Moon.* 1978. Doubleday. 1st ed. dj. xl. P1. $7.50

GRANT, C.L. *Ravens of the Moon.* 1978. Doubleday. 1st ed. inscr. dj. EX. R3. $30.00

GRANT, C.L. *Shadows 2.* 1979. Doubleday. 1st ed. dj. VG. P1. $17.50

GRANT, C.L. *Shadows 3.* 1980. Doubleday. 1st ed. dj. EX. R3. $17.50

GRANT, C.L. *Shadows 7.* 1984. Doubleday. 1st ed. dj. EX. P1. $15.00

GRANT, C.L. *Tales From the Nightside.* 1981. Arkham House. 1st ed. M. R3. $11.95

GRANT, Donald. *RI on Lovecraft.* 1945. Donald Grant. 2nd ed. wrp. EX. R3. $45.00

GRANT, J.C. *Ethiopian.* 1935. NY. Blk Hawk Pr. 1st ed. VG. B3. $30.00

GRANT, J.C. *Ethiopian: Narrative of Soc of Human Leopards.* 1935. NY. 287 p. dj. T5. $35.00

GRANT, Joan. *Lord of the Horizon.* 1944. Methuen. 3rd ed. VG. P1. $12.00

GRANT, Maxwell. *Crime Oracle/Teeth of the Dragon.* 1975. Dover. lg wrp. VG. R3. $10.00

GRANT, Maxwell. *Living Shadow.* 1931. Simon Schuster. 1st ed. EX. R3. $100.00

GRANT, Maxwell. *Norgil the Magician.* 1977. Mysterious Pr. 2nd ed. dj. xl. P1. $12.00

GRANT, Maxwell. *Shadow Laughs.* 1931. Simon Schuster. 1st ed. decor brd. VG. R3. $75.00

GRANT, Roderick. *Private Vendetta*. 1978. Scribner. 1st ed. dj. EX. P1. $15.00

GRANT, U.S. *Memoirs*. 1885. NY. 1st ed. 2 vols. B3. $75.00

GRANT, U.S. *Personal Memoirs*. 1885 & 1886. NY. 1st ed. 2 vols. J2. $60.00

GRANT, U.S. *Personal Memoirs*. 1885. NY. 2 vols. A6. $50.00

GRASS, Gunter. *Cat & Mouse*. 1963. Harcourt Brace World. 1st Am ed. dj. EX. K2. $30.00

GRASS, Gunter. *From the Diary of the Snail*. 1973. Harcourt Brace. 1st Am ed. sgn. dj. H3. $60.00

GRASS, Gunter. *Rat*. 1986. San Diego. ARC. wrp. EX. K2. $45.00

GRASS, Gunther. *Tin Drum*. 1962. Pantheon. UP. VG. B13. $150.00

GRATTON, C.H. *SW Pacific to 1900/SW Pacific Since 1900*. 1963. Ann Arbor. 1st ed. 2 vols. djs. EX. T1. $45.00

GRAUMONT & HENSEL. *Encyclopedia of Knots & Fancy Rope Work*. 1939. NY. 1st ed. 615 p. dj. VG. B3. $75.00

GRAVATT, Glenn. *50 Modern Card Tricks You Can Do!* 1977. Magic Ltd. 2nd print. M. J3. $3.50

GRAVES, John. *Goodbye to a River*. 1960. NY. 1st ed. dj. EX. B3. $40.00

GRAVES, Robert. *Antigua, Penny, Puce*. 1936. Seizin/Constable. inscr. dj. H3. $200.00

GRAVES, Robert. *Big Gr Book*. 1962. Crowell Collier. Stated 1st ed. VG. B7. $36.00

GRAVES, Robert. *Count Belisarius*. nd. Literary Guild. 564 p. VG. B10. $3.75

GRAVES, Robert. *Goodbye to All That: An Autobiography*. 1930. Harrison Smith. 1st Am ed. dj. EX. C4. $375.00

GRAVES, Robert. *Love Respelt Again*. 1969. Doubleday. 1/1000. sgn. gilt blk bdg. dj. H3. $75.00

GRAVES, Robert. *Man Does, Woman Is*. 1964. Cassell. Ltd ed. 1/201. sgn. EX. H3. $85.00

GRAVES, Robert. *Orig Rubaiyat of Omar Khayaam*. 1968. Doubleday. Ltd ed. 1/500. sgn. slipcase. H3. $125.00

GRAVES, Robert. *Poems 1929*. 1929. London. Seizin. Ltd ed. 1/225. sgn. H3. $375.00

GRAVES, Robert. *Transformations of Lucius Otherwise Known As the Golden Ass*. 1950. Harmondsworth. 1/2000. sgn. 12mo. slipcase. H3. $200.00

GRAVES, Robert. *Watch the N Wind Rise*. 1949. NY. Creative Age. sgn. dj. H3. $150.00

GRAVES, Robert. *Wht Goddess*. 1948. 1st ed. dj. VG. C1. $14.50

GRAVES, Robert. *10 Poems More*. 1930. Paris. Hours Pr. Ltd 1st ed. 1/200. sgn. H3. $450.00

GRAVES & HODGE. *Reader Over Your Shoulder*. 1944. Readers Union/Jonathan Cape. 2nd ed. sgn. H3. $75.00

GRAY, Asa. *How Plants Grow*. 1858. Am Book Co. G. $45.00

GRAY, Berkeley. *Conquest in the Underworld*. 1974. Collins. dj. VG. P1. $10.00

GRAY, Berkeley. *Lost World of Everest*. nd. Childrens Pr. VG. P1. $7.50

GRAY, Caroline. *3rd Life*. 1988. St Martin. 1st ed. dj. EX. F5. $15.00

GRAY, Charleston. *Vagabond Lover*. 1929. AL Burt. 1st ed. VG. B10. $8.25

GRAY, Curme. *Murder in Millennium 6*. 1951. Shasta. 1st ed. dj. VG. P1. $40.00

GRAY, Curme. *Murder in Millennium 6*. 1951. Shasta. 1st ed. dj. xl. VG. R3. $25.00

GRAY, E.J. *Continued Study Units in European Backgrounds: II*. nd. Phil. FA Davis. 8vo. 60 p. VG. V1. $5.00

GRAY, E.J. *Penn*. 1938. Viking. 1st ed. 8vo. 298 p. dj. VG. V1. $6.50

GRAY, Harold. *Little Orphan Annie & Gila Monster G*. nd. Whitman. VG. P1. $10.00

GRAY, Harold. *Little Orphan Annie in the Circus*. 1927. NY. Ils. VG. $25.00

GRAY, Henry. *Anatomy: Descriptive & Surgical*. 1870. Phil. Ils. 4to. 876 p. VG. G4. $49.00

GRAY, Thomas. *Odes*. 1757. Strawberry Hill. 1st ed. Riviere bdg. H3. $2250.00

GRAY, Thomas. *Odes*. 1757. Strawberry Hill. 1st ed. 4to. disbound. A4. $550.00

GRAY, Thomas. *Poems of Mr Gray With Memoirs of His Life & Writings*. 1775. York. 1st ed. $100.00

GRAY, Zane. *To the Last Man*. 1922. Grosset Dunlap. Photoplay ed. 310 p. reading copy. B10. $3.50

GRAY & ARBUTHNOT. *Fun With Dick & Jane*. 1946. Scott Foresman. TB. VG. K1. $25.00

GRAYSON, Richard. *Death on the Cards*. 1989. St Martin. 1st ed. dj. EX. F5. $12.00

GRAZIER, Willard. *Down the Great River*. 1892. Hubbard Bros. VG. $20.00

GRAZIER, Willard. *Ocean to Ocean on Horseback*. 1896. Hubbard Bros. VG. $12.00

GREAVES, Richard. *Brewster's Million*. 1903. Chicago. Stone. 1st ed. EX. B13. $50.00

GREELEY, A.M. *God Game*. 1986. Warner. 1st ed. dj. EX. P1. $16.95

GREELEY, Andrew. *Love Song*. ARC. stiff wrp. EX. C1. $7.50

GREELEY, Horace. *Am Conflict*. 1865. Hartford. 2 vols. leather bdg. VG. A4. $50.00

GREELY, A.W. *Handbook to AK*. 1906. NY. inscr. VG. A4. $40.00

GREELY, A.W. *Polar Regions in the 20th Century*. 1928. Boston. dj. G. A6. $35.00

GREEN, A.K. *Amethyst Box*. 1905. Merrill. 1st ed. VG. F5. $20.00

GREEN, A.K. *Golden Slipper*. 1915. NY. 1st ed. dj. VG. $20.00

GREEN, A.K. *Mayor's Wife*. nd. (1907) Bobbs Merrill. 1st ed. 389 p. G. B10. $4.00

GREEN, A.K. *Miss Hurd: An Enigma*. 1894. NY. 1st ed. $45.00

GREEN, Alan. *What a Body!* nd. Book Club. dj. VG. P1. $4.50

GREEN, F.L. *Magician*. 1951. Coward McCann. 1st Am ed. dj. EX. T9. $30.00

GREEN, Gerald. *Not in Vain*. 1984. Donald Fine. 1st ed. 299 p. dj. EX. B10. $4.50

GREEN, J.H. *Secret Band of Brothers; or, Am Outlaws*. 1848. Phil. 3rd ed. VG. $45.00

GREEN, Joseph. *Conscience Interplanetary*. 1973. Doubleday. 1st ed. dj. EX. P1. $15.00

GREEN, Judith. *Lost Panecitos Benditos: Clay Eating in Oaxaca*. 1968. San Diego. 1st ed. 4to. wrp. F2. $10.00

GREEN, KEANE, & CALLANAN. *Sky Lancer*. 1946. Sydney, Australia. 1st ed. 4to. VG. T5. $225.00

GREEN, Kenneth. *Cotswolds*. 1952. Bristol. Garland. 3rd ed. 23 p. dj. VG. B10. $3.75

GREEN, Martin. *Earth Again Redeemed*. 1977. Basic Books. 1st ed. dj. EX. P1. $15.00

GREEN, Paul. *In the Valley & Other Carolina Plays*. 1928. NY. 1/160. sgn. TEG. G. T5. $35.00

GREEN, Paul. *Johnny Johnson.* 1937. NY. French. 1st ed. dj. H3. $50.00

GREEN, Paul. *Wide Fields.* 1928. NY. McBride. 1st print. VG. $50.00

GREEN, R.L. *King Arthur.* 1957. PB. VG. $3.00

GREEN, R.T. *Genealogical & Hist Notes on Culpepper Co, VA.* 1900. Culpeper, VA. 1st ed. VG. $95.00

GREEN, S.E. *Contemporary SF Fantasy & Horror Poetry.* 1989. Greenwood. 1st ed. no dj issued. EX. P1. $35.00

GREEN & GREEN. *Pioneer Mothers of Am.* 1912. Putnam. Ils. 3 vols. VG. J2. $20.00

GREEN & GRIBBLE. *Murder Mistaken.* nd. Allen. dj. xl. P1. $7.50

GREENAWAY, Kate. *A Apple Pie.* 1907. Akron. muslin p/wrp. EX. $150.00

GREENAWAY, Kate. *Almanac.* 1888. London. Rutledge. VG. V1. $85.00

GREENAWAY, Kate. *Calendar of the Seasons.* 1881. London. Marcus Ward. EX. rare. $100.00

GREENAWAY, Kate. *Day in a Child's Life.* nd. London. Routledge. 1st ed. dj. EX. H3. $950.00

GREENAWAY, Kate. *Kate Greenaway's Birthday Book for Children.* 1880. London/NY. 1st ed. AEG. red leather. VG. $145.00

GREENAWAY, Kate. *Marigold Garden.* nd. (1888) London/NY. sm 4to. VG. T1. $55.00

GREENAWAY, Kate. *Pictures From Orig Presented to John Ruskin.* 1921. London. 4to. dj. EX. A4. $315.00

GREENBERG, Martin. *Coming Attractions.* 1957. Gnome. 1st ed. dj. EX. R3. $12.50

GREENBERG, Martin. *Journey to Infinity.* 1951. Gnome. 1st ed. dj. EX. R3. $35.00

GREENBERG, Martin. *Robot & the Man.* 1953. Gnome. 1st ed. dj. VG. R3. $12.50

GREENBERG, Martin. *Travelers of Space.* 1951. Gnome. 1st ed. dj. EX. R3. $75.00

GREENBERG, Samuel. *Poems.* 1947. Holt. 1st ed. dj. EX. C4. $30.00

GREENBURG, M. *In the Ring: Treasury of Boxing Stories.* 1986. Bonanza. 1st ed. 560 p. dj. NM. B10. $7.00

GREENE, Bob. *Billion-Dollar Baby.* 1974. NY. 1st ed. dj. VG. B3. $22.50

GREENE, F.V. *Revolutionary War & Military Policy of US.* 1911. NY. 1st ed. 350 p. G. T5. $45.00

GREENE, G. *Cosmo Girl's Guide to New Etiquette.* 1971. stiff wrp. VG. C1. $9.50

GREENE, Graham. *Another Mexico.* 1939. Viking. 1st ed. 279 p. dj. F2. $45.00

GREENE, Graham. *Best of Saki.* 1961. Viking. 1st ed. VG. T9. $35.00

GREENE, Graham. *Brighton Rock & End of the Affair.* 1987. Peerage Books. dj. EX. P1. $15.00

GREENE, Graham. *Brighton Rock.* nd. Sydney. Invincible Pr. 1st Australian ed. wrp. VG. B13. $125.00

GREENE, Graham. *British Dramatists.* 1942. London. Collins. 1st ed. H3. $50.00

GREENE, Graham. *Burnt-Out Case.* 1961. Heinemann. 1st ed. dj. xl. P1. $5.00

GREENE, Graham. *Burnt-Out Case.* 1961. Heinemann. 1st Eng ed. dj. EX. H3. $85.00

GREENE, Graham. *Burnt-Out Case.* 1974. Heinemann. not 1st ed. 236 p. xl. B10. $3.50

GREENE, Graham. *Collected Stories.* 1972. Viking. 1st ed. dj. EX. C4. $60.00

GREENE, Graham. *Dr Fischer of Geneva.* 1980. Bodley Head. 1st ed. dj. EX. P1. $15.00

GREENE, Graham. *Dr Fischer of Geneva.* 1980. Simon Schuster. 1st ed. dj. EX. P1. $15.00

GREENE, Graham. *Dr Fischer of Geneva; or, The Bomb Party.* 1980. Simon Schuster. Ltd ed. 1/500. sgn. slipcase. M. H3. $175.00

GREENE, Graham. *End of the Affair.* 1951. Viking. 1st ed. dj. EX. P1. $100.00

GREENE, Graham. *Essais Catholiques.* 1953. Paris. Eds du Seuil. 1st ed. wrp. EX. B13. $85.00

GREENE, Graham. *Getting To Know the General.* 1984. Simon Schuster. 1st ed. 249 p. dj. F2. $20.00

GREENE, Graham. *Heart of the Matter.* 1948. Heinemann. 1st Eng ed. dj. G. H3. $100.00

GREENE, Graham. *Heart of the Matter.* 1948. Viking. 1st Am ed. dj. VG. H3. $100.00

GREENE, Graham. *Honorary Consul.* nd. (1973) Book Club. 315 p. VG. B10. $6.00

GREENE, Graham. *Honorary Consul.* 1973. Simon Schuster. 1st ed. dj. EX. H3. $30.00

GREENE, Graham. *How Father Quixote Became a Monsignor.* 1980. Sylvester Orphanos. 1/330. sgn. lg octavo. H3. $200.00

GREENE, Graham. *Human Factor.* nd. Simon Schuster. 2nd ed. dj. VG. P1. $12.50

GREENE, Graham. *It's a Battlefield.* 1959. Heinemann. dj. xl. P1. $5.00

GREENE, Graham. *It's a Battlefield.* 1962. Viking. dj. VG. H3. $75.00

GREENE, Graham. *J'Accuse: The Dark Side of Nice.* 1982. Bodley Head. 1st ed. Eng/French text. 72 p. gray wrp. EX. T9. $35.00

GREENE, Graham. *Lawless Road.* 1950. London. 3rd ed. 389 p. F2. $15.00

GREENE, Graham. *Le Petit Omnibus.* 1955. Paris. 1st French ed. EX. K2. $75.00

GREENE, Graham. *Little Steamroller.* 1974. Doubleday. 1st Am ed. oblong quarto. dj. EX. $100.00

GREENE, Graham. *Lord Rochester's Monkey.* 1974. Viking. 1st ed. dj. EX. H3. $60.00

GREENE, Graham. *May We Borrow Your Husband?* 1967. NY. 1st ed. dj. EX. $35.00

GREENE, Graham. *May We Borrow Your Husband? & Other Comedies of Sexual Life.* 1967. Bodley Head. Ltd ed. 1/500. sgn. dj. H3. $175.00

GREENE, Graham. *Ministry of Fear.* 1944. Sun Dial. Photoplay ed. dj. VG. P1. $17.50

GREENE, Graham. *Monsignor Quixote.* 1982. NY. Ltd ed. 1/250. slipcase. EX. $210.00

GREENE, Graham. *Monsignor Quixote.* 1982. Simon Schuster. UP. K2. $50.00

GREENE, Graham. *Orient Express.* 1933. Doubleday. 1st ed. dj. VG. F5. $175.00

GREENE, Graham. *Our Man in Havana.* nd. London. UP. wrp. VG. rare. T1. $1200.00

GREENE, Graham. *Our Man in Havana.* 1958. Heinemann. 1st ed. dj. VG. P1. $100.00

GREENE, Graham. *Petite Pompe Incendie.* 1954. Paris. 1st French ed. laminated brd. EX. K2. $85.00

GREENE, Graham. *Pleasure Dome: Collected Film Criticism 1935-1940.* 1972. London. Secker Warburg. 1st ed. dj. EX. T9. $30.00

GREENE, Graham. *Potting Shed.* 1957. Viking. 1st ed. dj. RS. EX. H3. $125.00

GREENE, Graham. *Power & the Glory.* 1962. Time Inc. 1st print. wrp. NM. T9. $25.00

GREENE, Graham. *Quick Look Behind: Footnotes to an Autobiography.* 1983. Sylvester Orphanos. Ltd ed. 1/330. sgn. slipcase. H3. $250.00

GREENE, Graham. *Reflections on Travels With My Aunt.* 1989. 1sts Co. Ltd ed. 1/250. sgn. stiff wrp. H3. $225.00

GREENE, Graham. *Sort of Life.* 1971. Simon Schuster. 1st ed. dj. EX. H3. $40.00

GREENE, Graham. *This Gun for Hire.* 1942. Triangle. Photoplay ed. dj. VG. T9. $40.00

GREENE, Graham. *Ways of Escape.* 1980. Lester/Orphen Denys. 1st ed. dj. VG. P1. $17.50

GREENE, Graham. *Yes & No/For Whom the Bell Chimes.* 1983. Bodley Head. Ltd ed. 1/750. sgn. M. H3. $200.00

GREENE, Graham. *3rd Man.* 1950. Bantam 797. 1st Separate ed. wrp. EX. T9. $55.00

GREENE, Howard. *Reverend Richard Fish Cadle, Missionary...* 1936. Waukesha, WI. Ils 1st ed. inscr. 165 p. G. T5. $35.00

GREENE, Hugh. *Am Rivals of Sherlock Holmes.* 1976. Pantheon. 1st ed. dj. EX. R3. $15.00

GREENE, Joseph. *Journey to Jupiter.* 1961. Golden Pr. decor brd. VG. P1. $10.00

GREENE, Laurence. *Filibuster: Career of William Walker.* 1937. Bobbs Merrill. 1st ed. 350 p. F2. $35.00

GREENE, Merle. *Ancient Maya Relief Sculpture.* 1967. MPA. 1st ed. 1/4000. lg 4to. boxed. F2. $40.00

GREENE, Merle. *Maya Sculpture.* 1972. Berkley. 1st ed. 4to. dj. F2. $50.00

GREENFIELD, I.A. *Tagget.* 1979. Arbor House. 1st ed. dj. EX. P1. $15.00

GREENLEAF, Stephen. *Death Bed.* 1980. Dial. 1st ed. dj. EX. P1. $20.00

GREENLEAF, Stephen. *Fatal Obsession.* 1983. Dial. dj. VG. P1. $20.00

GREENLEE, Sam. *Ammunition: Poetry & Other Raps.* 1975. London. 1st ed. inscr. wrp. EX. T9. $45.00

GREENLEE, Sam. *Baghdad Blues.* 1976. Bantam 2901. 1st ed. wrp. VG. T9. $25.00

GREENTHAL, Kathryn. *Augustus St-Gaudens: Master Sculptor.* 1985. NY. Hall. 176 p. dj. D4. $55.00

GREENWOOD, Edwin. *Deadly Dowager.* 1935. Doubleday Doran. VG. P1. $5.00

GREENWOOD, John. *Missing Mr Mosley.* 1985. Walker. dj. EX. P1. $15.00

GREENWOOD, L.B. *Sherlock Holmes & the Case of Salsina Hall.* 1989. EX. C1. $3.50

GREENWOOD, Marianne. *Tattooed Heart of Livingston.* 1965. Stein Day. 1st ed. 187 p. dj. F2. $15.00

GREER, S.S. *Quakerism; or, Story of My Life.* 1852. Phil. JW Moore. 12mo. 348 p. V1. $28.00

GREER, S.S. *Soc of Friends: A Domestic Narrative...* 1853. NY. Dodd. 12mo. 340 p. fair. V1. $20.00

GREG, Percy. *Hist of the US.* 1892. Richmond. 2 vols in 1. VG. $35.00

GREG, Perry. *Across the Zodiac.* 1974. Hyperion. reprint of 1880 ed. EX. R3. $15.00

GREGORY, David. *Elements of Astronomy, Physical & Geometrical...* 1715. London. 1st Eng ed. 2 vols. rebacked. H3. $1250.00

GREGORY, Dick. *Dick Gregory's Political Primer.* 1972. NY. 1st ed. dj. VG. B3. $15.00

GREGORY, Dick. *From the Back of the Bus.* 1962. Avon S129. 1st PB ed. B4. $6.00

GREGORY, Dick. *Nigger.* 1964. NY. 1st ed. dj. VG. B3. $27.50

GREGORY, Dick. *Shadow That Scares Me.* 1968. Pocket Books. 1st PB ed. EX. B4. $5.00

GREGORY, Franklin. *Valley of Adventure.* 1940. Triangle. VG. P1. $10.00

GREGORY, Jackson. *Border Line.* 1942. Dodd Mead. 1st ed. xl. VG. P1. $10.00

GREGORY, Jackson. *Case for Mr Paul Savoy.* 1933. Scribner. 1st ed. VG. P1. $20.00

GREGORY, Jackson. *Everlasting Whisper.* nd. Grosset Dunlap. VG. P1. $4.50

GREGORY, Jackson. *Mad O'Hara of Wild River.* 1939. Dodd. 1st ed. 272 p. G. B10. $3.75

GREGORY, Jackson. *Ru the Conqueror.* 1933. Scribner. 1st ed. dj. VG. R3. $50.00

GREGORY, Jackson. *6 Feet 4.* 1918. Grosset. 295 p. VG. B10. $3.25

GREGORY, Mason. *If 2 of Them Are Dead.* 1953. Arcadia. 1st ed. xl. P1. $5.00

GREGORY, Odin. *Caius Gracchus.* 1920. Boni Liveright. 1st ed. H3. $75.00

GREIG, Francis. *Heads You Lose.* 1982. Crown. dj. RS. P1. $15.00

GRELLET, Stephen. *Memoirs of Life & Gospel Labors.* 1860. Phil. Longstreth. 8vo. 2 vols in 1. V1. $16.00

GRENDON, Stephen. *Mr George & Other Odd Persons.* 1963. Arkham House. 1st ed. M. R3. $40.00

GRESHAM, W.L. *Nightmare Alley.* 1948. Triangle. 1st/Photoplay ed. no dj issued. EX. F5. $22.00

GRESHAM. *Monster Midway.* 1953. NY. 1st ed. dj. VG. B3. $35.00

GREX, Leo. *Mix Me a Murder.* 1978. Robert Hale. 1st ed. dj. xl. P1. $5.00

GREY, Charles. *Enterprise 2115.* nd. Merit. VG. P1. $15.00

GREY, H. *Hoods.* 1952. NY. 1st ed. VG. B3. $27.50

GREY, M.E. *Greselda.* 1904. Boston. Turner. 1st ed. 113 p. VG. B10. $5.00

GREY, R.M. *Yahweh.* 1937. Willet Clark. 1st ed. dj. EX. R3. $35.00

GREY, Zane. *AR Ames.* nd. Grosset Dunlap. VG. P1. $7.50

GREY, Zane. *Border Legion.* nd. Blk. VG. P1. $7.50

GREY, Zane. *Call of the Canyon.* 1924. Musson. VG. P1. $10.00

GREY, Zane. *Day of the Beast.* 1922. NY. 1st ed. VG. B3. $45.00

GREY, Zane. *Forlorn River.* nd. Grosset Dunlap. dj. VG. P1. $7.50

GREY, Zane. *Forlorn River.* 1927. Harper. 1st ed. VG. P1. $20.00

GREY, Zane. *Hash Knife Outfit.* nd. Blk. VG. P1. $7.50

GREY, Zane. *Heritage of the Desert.* nd. Grosset Dunlap. Photoplay ed. VG. P1. $7.50

GREY, Zane. *Heritage of the Desert.* 1910. Grosset Dunlap. later ed. sgn. H3. $75.00

GREY, Zane. *Ken Ward in the Jungle.* nd. Grosset Dunlap. VG. P1. $7.50

GREY, Zane. *Ken Ward in the Jungle.* 1940. Grosset Dunlap. red bdg. VG. B10. $3.50

GREY, Zane. *Last of the Plainsmen.* nd. Hodder Stoughton Yellowjacket. dj. VG. P1. $12.50

GREY, Zane. *Last of the Plainsmen.* 1911. Grosset Dunlap. Ils. 314 p. dj. VG. T5. $65.00

GREY, Zane. *Last Ranger.* 1983. Ian Henry. dj. EX. P1. $10.00

GREY, Zane. *Last Trail.* nd. Grosset Dunlap. VG. P1. $5.00

GREY, Zane. *Last Trail.* nd. Triangle. dj. EX. P1. $12.50

GREY, Zane. *Last Trail*. nd. Whitman. VG. P1. $12.50

GREY, Zane. *Majesty's Rancho*. nd. Blk. VG. P1. $7.50

GREY, Zane. *Raiders of Spanish Peaks*. nd. Collier. VG. P1. $7.50

GREY, Zane. *Rainbow Trail*. 1915. Harper. VG. P1. $12.50

GREY, Zane. *Rainbow Trail*. 1981. Ian Henry. dj. EX. P1. $10.00

GREY, Zane. *Real Dogs: Favorite Dog Stories*. 1926. Sun Dial. Ils. dj. B10. $12.00

GREY, Zane. *Riders of the Purple Sage*. 1912. NY. 1st ed. VG. B3. $70.00

GREY, Zane. *Robbers' Roost*. nd. Blk. VG. P1. $7.50

GREY, Zane. *Roping Lions in the Grand Canyon*. nd. Grosset Dunlap. EX. P1. $15.00

GREY, Zane. *Shepherd of Guadaloupe*. nd. Grosset Dunlap. dj. VG. P1. $12.50

GREY, Zane. *Short-Stop*. nd. Grosset Dunlap. G. P1. $7.50

GREY, Zane. *Spirit of the Border*. nd. Whitman. VG. P1. $5.00

GREY, Zane. *Spirit of the Border*. nd. World. decor brd. VG. P1. $7.50

GREY, Zane. *Spirit of the Border*. 1943. Triangle. 18th print. dj. VG. P1. $12.50

GREY, Zane. *Stairs of Sand*. nd. Collier. VG. P1. $7.50

GREY, Zane. *Stairs of Sand*. 1945. Musson. VG. P1. $12.00

GREY, Zane. *Tenderfoot*. 1982. Ian Henry. dj. EX. P1. $10.00

GREY, Zane. *Thunder Mt*. 1935. Harper. 1st ed. dj. VG. P1. $30.00

GREY, Zane. *Thundering Herd*. nd. Blk. VG. P1. $7.50

GREY, Zane. *To the Last Man*. nd. Grosset Dunlap. G. P1. $5.00

GREY, Zane. *Twin Sombreros*. nd. Collier. VG. P1. $7.50

GREY, Zane. *Twin Sombreros*. nd. Grosset Dunlap. VG. P1. $7.50

GREY, Zane. *Valley of Wild Horses*. nd. Grosset Dunlap. dj. VG. P1. $7.50

GREY, Zane. *Valley of Wild Horses*. nd. Harper. dj. VG. P1. $15.00

GREY, Zane. *Wanderer of the Wasteland*. nd. Grosset Dunlap. dj. VG. P1. $7.50

GREY, Zane. *Wanderer of the Wasteland*. 1923. NY. Ils 1st ed. 419 p. G. T5. $25.00

GREY, Zane. *Wild Horse Mesa*. nd. Blk. VG. P1. $7.00

GREY, Zane. *Wild Horse Mesa*. 1928. Gorsset Dunlap. VG. P1. $7.50

GREY, Zane. *Wildfire*. nd. Blk. VG. P1. $7.50

GREY, Zane. *Wildfire*. nd. Grosset Dunlap. VG. P1. $7.50

GREY, Zane. *Young Lion Hunter*. nd. Grosset Dunlap. decor brd. VG. P1. $12.50

GREY, Zane. *Young Pitcher*. nd. Grosset Dunlap. dj. VG. P1. $7.50

GREY, Zane. *Zane Grey's Adventures in Fishing*. 1952. NY. 1st ed. VG. C2. $55.00

GREY OWL. *Pilgrims of the Wild*. 1971. Scribner. 1st ed. dj. EX. B13. $55.00

GREY OWL. *Sajo & Her Beaver People*. 1970. Toronto. Macmillan. reprint. dj. EX. B13. $40.00

GREY OWL. *Tales of an Empty Cabin*. 1936. Dodd Mead. 1st ed. dj. EX. B13. $95.00

GRIBBLE, Leonard. *Atomic Murder*. 1947. Ziff Davis. 1st ed. dj. EX. R3. $20.00

GRIEDER, Terence. *Art & Archaeology of Pashash*. 1978. TX U. 1st ed. sm 4to. dj. F2. $25.00

GRIERSON, Francis. *Boomerang Murder*. 1951. Hutchinson. 1st ed. dj. xl. P1. $7.50

GRIERSON, Francis. *Murder at the Wedding*. nd. Literary Pr. G. P1. $7.00

GRIEVE, Symington. *Great Auk, or Gorefowl: Its Hist, Archaeology, & Remains*. 1885. London. Thomas Jack. clr pls. VG. T3. $250.00

GRIFFEN, G. *CA Expedition: Stevenson's Regiment of 1st NY Volunteers*. 1951. Oakland. 1st ed. 1/650. 4to. EX. $35.00

GRIFFIN, Charles. *Latin Am: Guide to Hist Literature*. 1971. Austin. 1st ed. 4to. 700 p. dj. F2. $50.00

GRIFFIN, W.E.B. *Aviators*. 1988. Putnam. UP. wrp. EX. F5. $20.00

GRIFFIN, Z.F. *India & Daily Life in Bengal*. 1896. Buffalo. Ils. decor bdg. EX. T1. $45.00

GRIFFITH, George. *Angel of the Revolution*. 1974. Hyperion. reprint of 1894 ed. wrp. EX. R3. $10.00

GRIFFITH, George. *Olga Romanoff*. 1974. Hyperion. reprint of 1895 ed. EX. R3. $15.00

GRIFFITH, George. *Outlaws of the Air*. 1895. Tower. 1st ed. VG. R3. $75.00

GRIFFITH, George. *Valdar the Oft-Born*. 1972. Starmont. EX. R3. $25.00

GRIFFITH, George. *World Masters*. c 1900. London. VG. R3. $60.00

GRIFFITH, John. *Journal of Life, Travels, & Labors in Work of Ministry...* 1780. Phil. Joseph Crukshank. 12mo. 538 p. poor. V1. $35.00

GRIFFITH, Samuel. *Case of Shapley Shadow*. 1960. Lippincott. 1st ed. inscr. dj. EX. B10. $6.50

GRIFFITH, William. *Bermuda Troubadours*. 1935. NY. Kendal Sharp. 1st ed. EX. C1. $14.00

GRIFFITH, Wyn. *Wales in Clr*. 1958. London. 1st ed. dj. VG. C1. $9.00

GRIFFITHS, Bryn. *Beasthoods*. 1972. London. Turret. sgn. dj. M. H3. $50.00

GRIGOR, John. *Arboriculture*. 1868. Edinburgh. 1st ed. VG. $55.00

GRILE, Dod. *Fiend's Delight*. 1873. NY. 1st ed. orig cloth. EX. H3. $750.00

GRIMBERG, Salomon. *Frida Kahlo*. 1989. Dallas. Meadows Mus. 1st ed. wrp. F2. $20.00

GRIMES, Martha. *Deer Leap*. 1985. Little Brn. 1st ed. dj. EX. P1. $15.95

GRIMES, Martha. *Old Silent*. 1989. 1st Am ed. dj. VG. C1. $3.50

GRIMES, Martha. *5 Bells & Bladebone*. 1987. Little Brn. 1st ed. dj. VG. P1. $15.95

GRIMKE, J.F. *Duty of Executors & Administrators According to Laws of SC*. 1797. NY. 1st ed. fld chart. VG. rare. $350.00

GRIMLEY, G.P. *Baltimore & OH Railroad*. 1933. Internat Geol Guidebook 30. wrp. A4. $25.00

GRIMM, Brothers; see Brothers Grimm.

GRIMWOOD, Ken. *Replay*. 1986. Arbor House. 1st ed. dj. EX. R3. $30.00

GRIMWOOD & GOODYEAR. *Intro to Decorative Woodwork*. 1936. Peoria. 1st ed. sm 4to. VG. C2. $55.00

GRINDE, D.A. *Iroquois & the Founding of the Am Nation*. 1977. San Francisco. Indian Hist. wrp. EX. K2. $40.00

GRINNELL, David. *Destiny's Orbit*. 1961. Avalon. 1st ed. dj. EX. R3. $17.50

GRINNELL, G.B. *Am Duck Shooting.* 1901. Forest/Stream. rebound. VG. $48.00

GRINNELL, Joseph. *Gold Hunting in AK.* 1901. Elgin, IL. Ils. 96 p. wrp. A6. $75.00

GRINNELL & CARTER. *Destination: Saturn.* 1967. Avalon. dj. xl. P1. $6.00

GRINNELL & CARTER. *Destination: Saturn.* 1967. Avalon. 1st ed. dj. VG. R3. $17.50

GRINNELL-MILNE, Duncan. *Killing of William Rufus: Investigation in New Forest.* 1968.1st ed. dj. VG. C1. $12.50

GRINSTEIN, H. *Rise of the Jewish Community of NY 1654-1860.* 1945. Phil. 1st ed. VG. $35.00

GRISCOM, A.B. *Peace Crusaders.* 1928. Lippincott. 12mo. 191 p. G. V1. $8.00

GRISCOM, L. *Birds of Concord.* 1949. Cambridge. 1st ed. 340 p. dj. VG. B3. $30.00

GRISMER, K.H. *Hist of St Petersburg: Hist & Biographical.* 1924. St Petersburg. 1st ed. EX. $45.00

GRISSOM, M.A. *Negro Sings a New Heaven.* 1930. Chapel Hill. 1st ed. quarto. 101 p. dj. EX. H3. $125.00

GRISWOLD, George. *Checkmate by the Colonel.* 1953. Dutton. 1st ed. dj. VG. P1. $20.00

GRISWOLD, George. *Red Pawns.* 1954. Dutton. 1st ed. dj. VG. P1. $15.00

GRISWOLD, Lawrence. *Tombs, Travel, & Trouble.* 1937. Hillman Curl. 2nd ed. 337 p. VG. B10. $5.00

GRISWOLD, R.G. *Republican Court of Am Soc in Days of WA.* 1855. NY. 4to. AEG. VG. $60.00

GRISWOLD. *Sea Island Lady.* 1939. NY. 1st ed. dj. VG. B3. $17.50

GROACH, W.S. *Skyway to Asia.* 1936. NY. 1st ed. 205 p. dj. T5. $45.00

GROHMANN, Will. *Paul Klee.* nd. Abrams. dj. VG. C2. $75.00

GROHMANN, Will. *Paul Klee.* 1954. NY. VG. G1. $90.00

GROOM, Arthur. *Flying Doctor Annual.* 1963. Dean. VG. P1. $30.00

GROOM, G.L. *Singing Sword.* 1929. NY/London. 1st ed. dj. VG. C1. $12.00

GROSS, L.S. *Redefining the Am Gothic.* 1989. UMI Research. 1st ed. dj. EX. P1. $35.00

GROSS, Milt. *Dunt Esk!* 1927. Doran. inscr. dj. EX. H3. $175.00

GROSS, Milt. *Famous Females From Hist.* 1928. NY. 1st ed. dj. VG. B3. $22.50

GROSS, Miriam. *World of Raymond Chandler.* 1977. NY. Intro/sgn Highsmith. 1st ed. clipped dj. EX. T9. $55.00

GROSSBACH, Robert. *Never Say Die.* 1979. Harper Row. 1st ed. dj. EX. P1. $15.00

GROSSO & DEVANEY. *Murder at the Harlem Mosque.* 1977. Crown. dj. EX. P1. $15.00

GROSZ, George. *Little Yes & a Big No.* 1946. NY. 1st ed. 8vo. VG. $40.00

GROTH, John. *Studio Asia.* 1952. Cleveland. 1st ed. dj. VG. B3. $17.50

GROTTA-KURSHA, Daniel. *Tolkien: Architect of Middle Earth.* 1976. Running Pr. VG. P1. $7.50

GROUSSET, Rene. *Empire of the Steppes: Hist of Central Asia.* 1970. Rutgers. 1st ed. 720 p. dj. EX. T4. $10.00

GROUSSET, Rene. *Epic of the Crusades.* 1970. Orion. Trans Lindsay. VG. B10. $5.00

GROUT, A.J. *Mosses With a Hand Lens.* 1905. NY. 2nd ed. VG. $20.00

GROUT, D.J. *Hist of W Music.* 1973.Revised ed. dj. EX. C1. $9.00

GROVE, David. *Chalcatzingo: Excavations of the Olmec Frontier.* 1984. Thames Hudson. 1st ed. 4to. dj. F2. $32.50

GROVE, Richard. *Mexican Popular Arts Today.* 1954. Taylor Mus. 1st ed. 1/2000. sbdg. F2. $15.00

GROVER, Edwin. *Book of Good Cheer.* 1916. Algonquin. Ils. 60 p. dj. VG. B10. $3.50

GROVER, Euladie O. *Sunbonnet Babies in Holland.* 1915. Chicago. 1st ed. VG. T1. $40.00

GROVER & HAMMOND. *Commonplace Book With Something for Everybody.* 1969. Grace Hoper Pr. 1st ed. 1/200. 54 p. EX. R4. $100.00

GRUB, David. *Shadow of My Bother.* 1966. Hutchinson. 1st ed. dj. EX. P1. $25.00

GRUBAR, F.S. *William Ranney: Painter of the Early W.* 1962. NY. Clarkson Potter. 1st ed. 4to. 65 p. dj. EX. R4. $75.00

GRUBB, Davis. *Barefoot Man.* 1971. Simon Schuster. 1st ed. dj. EX. R3. $15.00

GRUBB, Davis. *Night of the Hunter.* 1953. Harper. 1st ed. dj. VG. R3. $17.50

GRUBB, Davis. *12 Stories of Suspense & the Supernatural.* 1964. Scribner. 1st ed. dj. EX. R3. $100.00

GRUBB, Isabel. *J Ernest Grubb of Carrick-on-Suir.* 1928. Dublin. Talbot Pr. 12mo. VG. V1. $8.50

GRUBB, Isabel. *Quaker Homespuns 1655-1833.* 1932. London. Allenson. 1st ed. 12mo. 144 p. G. V1. $8.00

GRUBB, Sarah. *Selection From Letters of Late Sarah Grubb.* 1848. Sudbury. J Wright. 8vo. 451 p. full leather. VG. V1. $28.00

GRUBB, Sarah. *Some Account of Life & Religious Labors.* 1792. Dublin. R Jackson. 1st ed. 12mo. 435 p. V1. $25.00

GRUBER, Frank. *Brass Knuckles.* 1966. Sherbourne Pr. 1st ed. dj. EX. T9. $35.00

GRUBER, Frank. *Brass Knuckles.* 1966. Sherbourne Pr. 1st ed. dj. xl. P1. $7.50

GRUBER, Frank. *Bridge of Sand.* 1963. Dutton. 1st ed. dj. VG. P1. $25.00

GRUBER, Frank. *Laughing Fox.* 1943. Tower. VG. P1. $12.50

GRUBER, Frank. *Little Hercules.* 1965. Dutton. 1st ed. dj. xl. P1. $6.00

GRUBER, Frank. *Pulp Jungle.* 1967. Sherbourne Pr. 1st ed. dj. EX. R3. $25.00

GRUBER, Frank. *Run, Fool, Run.* 1966. Dutton. 1st ed. dj. EX. T9. $30.00

GRUBER, Frank. *Run, Fool, Run.* 1966. Dutton. 1st ed. dj. xl. P1. $5.00

GRUBER, Frank. *Simon Lash, Detective.* 1946. London. Nicholson Watson. 1st PB ed. wrp. G. T9. $25.00

GRUBER, Frank. *Spanish Prisoner.* 1969. Dutton. 1st ed. dj. xl. P1. $6.00

GRUBER, Frank. *Swing Low, Swing Dead.* 1964. Belmont L92-586. 1st ed. wrp. NM. T9. $15.00

GRUBER, Frank. *Talking Clock.* nd. Grosset Dunlap. xl. P1. $5.00

GRUBER, Frank. *Twilight Man.* 1967. Dutton. 1st ed. dj. xl. P1. $6.00

GRUBER, Frank. *20 Plus 2.* 1961. Dutton. 1st ed. dj. VG. P1. $20.00

GRUELLE, Johnny. *My Very Own Fairy Stories.* 1949. NY. reprint. VG. $15.00

GRUELLE, Johnny. *Raggedy Ann & Andy & the Camel With the Wrinkled Knees.* 1960. Bobbs Merrill. 8vo. 95 p. VG. $16.00

GRUELLE, Johnny. *Raggedy Ann & Andy & the Nice Fat Policeman.* 1960. Bobbs Merrill. 8vo. 95 p. VG. $18.00

GRUELLE, Johnny. *Raggedy Ann's Lucky Pennies.* c 1960. Donohue. 8vo. 94 p. VG. $18.00

GRUEN, John. *Keith Haring, Radiant Child.* 1991. Prentice Hall. UP. wrp. EX. K2. $25.00

GRUMMERE, A.M. *Quaker: A Study in Costume.* 1901. Phil. Ferris Leach. 1st ed. 8vo. 232 p. V1. $25.00

GRUNDY, C.R. *James Ward: His Life & Works.* 1909. London. Ils. 4to. wrp. $50.00

GRUNWALD, Henry. *Salinger: A Critical Portrait.* 1962. Harcourt Brace. UP/galley sheets. sbdg. pub wrp. K2. $275.00

GRUSA, Jiri. *Questionnaire.* 1982. Farrar Straus. UP. wrp. EX. B13. $35.00

GUARD & GRAHAM. *Francis Parnell Murphy: Governor of NH.* 1940. Roycroft. EX. $65.00

GUARESCHI, Giovanni. *Don Camillo & His Flock.* 1952. Pelligrini Cudahy. 4th print. P1. $12.50

GUDERIAN, Heinz. *Panzer Leader.* 1952. NY. 1st ed. dj. VG. B3. $47.50

GUEDALLA, Philip. *100 Years.* 1936. Hodder Stoughton. Ltd ed. 1/250. sgn. H3. $60.00

GUEDALLA, Philip. *100 Years.* 1937. Doubleday. 400 p. EX. B10. $4.50

GUELETTE. *Chinese Tales/Wonderful Adventures of Mandarin Fum-Hoam...* 1781. London. Trans Stackhouse. 2 vols in 1. VG. $225.00

GUERBER, H.A. *Stories of the Wagner Opera.* 1896. NY. Probable 1st ed. VG. C1. $9.50

GUERNSEY, A.H. *Harper's Pictorial Hist of the Civil War.* nd. Fairfax Pr. 836 p. dj. EX. S1. $50.00

GUEST, E.A. *Passing Throng.* 1923. Reilly Lee. VG. P1. $10.00

GUEST, William. *Stephen Grellet 1773-1855.* 1901. Phil. Longstreth. 12mo. 264 p. xl. V1. $8.50

GUGGENHEIM. *Mixtures.* 1952. Oxford. 1st ed. VG. C2. $35.00

GUIBERT, Rita. *7 Voices: 7 Latin Am Writers Talk to Rita Guibert.* 1973. Knopf. 1st ed. dj. EX. C4. $40.00

GUICHARD-MEILI, Jean. *Matisse: World of Art Profile.* 1967. Praeger. 256 p. dj. D4. $35.00

GUIDONI & MAGNI. *Monuments of Civilization: The Andes.* 1977. Grosset Dunlap. 189 p. dj. D4. $40.00

GUILD, Marian. *What's Cooking in Rome.* 1981. St John Baptist. 3rd ed. stiff wrp. B10. $3.50

GUILD, Nicholas. *Chain Reaction.* 1983. St Martin. 1st ed. dj. VG. P1. $15.00

GUINAGH, Kevin. *Search for Glory.* 1946. Longman. 1st ed. 220 p. dj. B10. $4.75

GUINIER, Andrey. *Radiocristallographie.* 1945. Paris. Dunod. Ils. 294 p. VG. $65.00

GUINNESS, Bryan. *Clock.* 1973. Dublin. Dolmen. 1st ed. dj. EX. H3. $30.00

GUITERMAN, Arthur. *Death & General Putnam.* 1935. NY. 1st ed. VG. $17.00

GUIZOT. *Chroniques de Jehan Froissart.* 1881. Paris. Ils. 4to. maps. AEG. EX. $200.00

GULICK, B. *Snake River Country.* 1972. Caldwell. 1st ed. 195 p. dj. EX. B3. $25.00

GULICK, Paul. *Strings of Steel.* nd. Grosset Dunlap. Photoplay ed. VG. P1. $20.00

GUMMERE, A.M. *Quaker in the Forum.* 1910. Phil. Winston. 72mo. 327 p. VG. V1. $12.50

GUNN, Alexander. *Hermitage-Zoar Notebook & Journal of Travel.* 1902. NY. 1/500. 261 p. TEG. bl morocco. slipcase. T5. $250.00

GUNN, Drewey. *Mexico in Am & British Letters.* 1974. Metuchen. Scarecrow. 1st ed. F2. $25.00

GUNN, J.E. *Alternate Worlds: Ils Hist of SF.* 1975. Prentice Hall. 1st ed. M. R3. $20.00

GUNN, J.E. *Deadlier Than the Male.* 1945. Tower. VG. P1. $10.00

GUNN, J.E. *End of the Dream.* 1975. Scribner. 1st ed. dj. EX. R3. $10.00

GUNN, J.E. *Magicians.* 1976. Scribner. 1st ed. dj. EX. R3. $10.00

GUNN, J.E. *Some Dreams Are Nightmares.* 1974. Scribner. 1st ed. dj. EX. R3. $10.00

GUNN, Thomas. *Jack Straw's Castle & Other Poems.* 1976. Farrar Straus. 1st Am ed. dj. EX. C4. $20.00

GUNSAULUS, Frank. *Monk & Knight: Hist Study in Fiction.* 1893. McClurg. 1st ed. 2 vols. EX. $25.00

GUNTHART, Lotte. *Watercolors & Drawings.* 1970. Carnegie-Mellon U. Ils. $25.00

GUNTHER, John. *Eden for 1.* 1927. Harper. 1st ed. VG. R3. $17.50

GUPPY, Nicholas. *Wai-Wai. Through the Forests of the Amazon.* 1958. Dutton. 1st ed. 373 p. dj. F2. $20.00

GURDJIEFF, G.I. *4th Way: Record of Talks Based on Teaching.* 1957. Knopf. 1st Am ed. 446 p. VG. B10. $7.00

GURGANUS, Allan. *Blessed Assurance.* 1990. Rocky Mt, NC. Ils Revised ed. 1/2000. sgn. sans dj. EX. T9. $50.00

GURGANUS, Allan. *Good Help.* 1988. Rocky Mt, NC. 1st ed. 1/1000. sgn. wrp. EX. B13. $50.00

GURGANUS, Allan. *Oldest Living Confederate Widow Tells All.* 1989. Knopf. UP. wrp. EX. C4. $100.00

GURGANUS, Allan. *Wht People: Stories.* 1991. Knopf. UP. wrp. EX. C4. $50.00

GURNEY, David. *F Certificate.* 1968. Geis. 1st ed. EX. P1. $7.50

GURNEY, E.P. *Memoirs of Eliza Paul Gurney & Others.* 1883. Phil. Longstreth. 12mo. 91 p. reading copy. V1. $8.00

GURNEY, J.J. *Essay on Habitual Exercise of Love to God.* 1840. Phil. Henry Perkins. 12mo. 242 p. fair. V1. $20.00

GURNEY, J.J. *4 Lectures on Evidences of Christianity.* 1857. Phil. Longstreth. 12mo. 176 p. fair. V1. $8.00

GURNEY, R. *Our Trees & Woodlands.* 1947. Medici Soc. 1st ed. sm 8vo. 144 p. dj. R4. $20.00

GURTEEN, S.H. *Arthurian Epic.* 1895. London/NY. 1st ed. VG. C1. $59.00

GUSTKE, Nancy. *Stately Picturesque Dream.* 1984. Gainesville. 1st ed. sm 4to. wrp. F2. $15.00

GUTHERIE, A.B. *Way W.* 1949. Sloane. 1st ed. dj. EX. B13. $85.00

GUTHORN, P.J. *Am Maps & Map Makers of the Revolution.* 1966. Monmouth Beach, NJ. 1st ed. inscr. VG. $40.00

GUTHRIE, A.B. *Big Sky.* 1947. London. 1st ed. dj. VG. $40.00

GUTHRIE, A.B. *Big Sky.* 1947. NY. 1st ed. dj. EX. $75.00

GUTHRIE, A.B. *Fair Land, Fair Land.* 1982. Houghton Mifflin. AP. wrp. EX. K2. $45.00

GUTHRIE, Woody. *Bound for Glory.* 1943. Dutton. 1st ed. dj. EX. H3. $150.00

GUTIERREZ, Ludivina. *Monumentos Coloniales de Xalapa.* 1981. Mexico. 1st ed. 1/3000. wrp. F2. $15.00

GUTTERIDGE, Lindsay. *Cold War in Country Garden.* 1971. Putnam. dj. VG. P1. $7.50

GUTTERIDGE, Lindsay. *Killer Pine.* 1974. British SF Book Club. dj. VG. P1. $4.50

GUY, David. *Football Dreams.* 1980. Seaview. UP. wrp. EX. C4. $50.00

GUY, J. *Pocket Encyclopedia of Miscellaneous Selections...* 1894. 3rd ed. G. C1. $44.00

GUY, Rosa. *Measure of Time.* 1983. Holt Rinehart Winston. UP. wrp. EX. B13. $100.00

GUYE & MICHEL. *Time & Space: Measuring Instruments From 15th-19th Century.* 1971. NY. Ils. 4to. dj. EX. $60.00

GYLES & SAYER. *Of Gods & Men: Heritage of Ancient Mexico.* 1980. Harper. 1st ed. 323 p. dj. F2. $20.00

HAAS, Dorothy. *Sir Lancelot.* 1958. Big Little Book. VG. P1. $15.00

HAAS, R.B. *William Grant Still & Fusions of Cultures in Am Music.* 1972. Blk Sparrow. 1st ed. 1/100. sgn. EX. H3. $175.00

HABBERTON, John. *Helen's Babies.* c1920s. Barse. Ils Von Hofsten. tall 8vo. VG. B10. $4.25

HABERLAND, Wolfgang. *Zentral-Mexiko.* 1974. Hamburg. German text. wrp. F2. $15.00

HACKER, Leonard. *Cinematic Design.* 1931. Boston. Special Deluxe ed. 1/100. 193 p. dj. EX. H3. $150.00

HACKER, Marilyn. *Presentation Piece: Poems.* 1974. Viking. dj. EX. C4. $30.00

HACKETT, John. *3rd World War August 1985.* nd. Book Club. P1. $4.50

HADDAD, C.A. *Academic Factor.* 1980. Doubleday Book Club. VG. P1. $7.50

HADER & HADER. *Rainbows End.* 1945. Macmillan. VG. B7. $37.00

HADFIELD, A.M. *King Arthur & the Round Table.* 1964. Ils Cammell. dj. VG. C1. $9.00

HADLEY, Harold. *Come See Them Die.* 1934. Messner. 1st ed. VG. P1. $10.00

HADLOW, S.G. *Pageant of Twinsburg in Celebration of 100th Anniversary...* nd. (1917) Twinsburg. 30 p. T5. $12.50

HAFERKORN, Henry. *War With Mexico 1846-1848.* 1970. Franklin. reprint of 1914 ed. F2. $25.00

HAGEDORN, Jessica. *Dogeaters.* 1990. Pantheon. UP. wrp. EX. K2. $35.00

HAGEMANN, E.R. *Index to Blk Mask 1920-1951.* 1982. Bowling Gr. dj. EX. P1. $20.00

HAGGARD, H.R. *After-War Settlement & Employment of Ex-Service Men...* 1916. St Catherine Pr. 1st ed. sgn. AEG. red morocco. H3. $150.00

HAGGARD, H.R. *Allan Quatermain.* nd. McKinlay. G. R3. $7.50

HAGGARD, H.R. *Allan Quatermain.* 1927. Harrap. 3rd ed. VG. P1. $15.00

HAGGARD, H.R. *Allan's Wife.* 1927. Longman Gr. VG. R3. $15.00

HAGGARD, H.R. *Ancient Allan.* 1920. Longman Gr. 1st ed. VG. P1. $60.00

HAGGARD, H.R. *Ancient Allan.* 1920. NY. 1st Am ed. 298 p. G. T5. $22.50

HAGGARD, H.R. *Ayesha: The Return of She.* 1905. Doubleday. VG. R3. $35.00

HAGGARD, H.R. *Benita.* 1965. MacDonald. dj. EX. P1. $20.00

HAGGARD, H.R. *Brethren.* 1904. McClure Phillips. 1st ed. VG. F5. $35.00

HAGGARD, H.R. *Brethren.* 1904. NY. Ils 1st Am ed. 2nd imp. 411 p. T5. $15.00

HAGGARD, H.R. *Child of Storm.* 1913. Longman Gr. 1st ed. VG. P1. $75.00

HAGGARD, H.R. *Classic Adventures.* 1986. New Orchard. 1st ed. dj. EX. P1. $19.95

HAGGARD, H.R. *Cleopatra.* nd. McKinley. VG. R3. $8.50

HAGGARD, H.R. *Cleopatra.* nd. Review of Reviews. VG. P1. $17.50

HAGGARD, H.R. *Cleopatra.* 1926. Harrap. 2nd ed. VG. P1. $15.00

HAGGARD, H.R. *Collected Novels.* 1986. Castle. 1st ed. dj. EX. P1. $15.00

HAGGARD, H.R. *Dawn.* 1924. Harrap. VG. P1. $35.00

HAGGARD, H.R. *Eric Brighteyes.* nd. WB Conkey. VG. P1. $15.00

HAGGARD, H.R. *Eric Brighteyes.* 1925. Harrap. VG. P1. $25.00

HAGGARD, H.R. *Finished.* 1962. MacDonald. dj. VG. P1. $25.00

HAGGARD, H.R. *Ivory Child.* 1916. NY. 1st Am ed. 377 p. fair. T5. $22.50

HAGGARD, H.R. *King Solomon's Mines.* nd. Readers Lib. dj. VG. P1. $20.00

HAGGARD, H.R. *Maiwa's Revenge.* 1888. Longman Gr. 1st ed. VG. F5. $60.00

HAGGARD, H.R. *Margaret.* 1907. Longman Gr. 1st ed. decor brd. P1. $20.00

HAGGARD, H.R. *Marie.* 1959. MacDonald. dj. EX. P1. $25.00

HAGGARD, H.R. *People of the Mist.* 1919. Longman Gr. VG. R3. $10.00

HAGGARD, H.R. *Queen Sheba's Ring.* 1910. NY. 1st Am ed. 326 p. T5. $35.00

HAGGARD, H.R. *Regeneration.* 1910. Longman Gr. presentation. scarce. H3. $350.00

HAGGARD, H.R. *She & Allan.* nd. London. 1st Eng ed. VG. R3. $50.00

HAGGARD, H.R. *She.* 1925. Grosset Dunlap. Photoplay ed. G. R3. $7.50

HAGGARD, H.R. *Spirit of Bambatse.* nd. McKinlay. VG. R3. $10.00

HAGGARD, H.R. *Wanderer's Necklace.* 1914. NY. 1st Am ed. 341 p. G. T5. $25.00

HAGGARD, H.R. *Works.* 1909. McKinlay Stone MacKenzie. London. Hooper Wigstead. 8 vols. H3. $1000.00

HAGGARD, H.W. *Rise of Medicine From Superstition to Science.* 1933. 1st Am ed. presentation. VG. C1. $9.50

HAGGARD, William. *Hard Sell.* 1966. Ives Washburn. 1st ed. dj. VG. P1. $17.50

HAGGARD, William. *Median Line.* 1981. Walker. 1st ed. dj. EX. P1. $15.00

HAGGARD, William. *Mischief Makers.* 1982. Doubleday Book Club. VG. P1. $7.50

HAGGARD & LANG. *World's Desire.* 1920. Hodder Stoughton. VG. P1. $20.00

HAGGERTY, T.M. *Come Stains.* 1976. Seattle Airplane Pr. EX. B4. $4.00

HAGLOCH, H.C. *Hist of Tuscarawas County, OH.* 1956. Dover Hist Soc. 1st ed. 212 p. rebound. G. T5. $15.00

HAGUE, Arnold. *Atlas to Accompany to Monograph on Geol of Eureka District.* nd. US Geol Survey. folio. wrp. A5. $125.00

HAGUE, Harlan. *Road to CA.* 1978. Glendale. Clark. Ils. 325 p. A5. $50.00

HAHN, Emily. *Animal Gardens.* 1967. Doubleday. 1st ed. 403 p. xl. VG. B10. $4.00

HAHN, Otto. *New Atoms: Progress & Some Memories.* 1950. Elsevier. EX. $45.00

HAIG-BROWN, R.L. *Fisherman's Spring.* 1951. NY. 1st ed. dj. VG. B3. $42.50

HAIG-BROWN, R.L. *River Never Sleeps.* 1946. NY. 1st ed. dj. VG. B3. $45.00

HAIG-BROWN, R.L. *River Never Sleeps.* 1946. Toronto. Collins. ARC. dj. RS. EX. $65.00

HAIG-BROWN, R.L. *W Angler.* 1947. Morrow. VG. B3. $37.50

HAIGHT, A.L. *Portrait of Latin Am As Seen by Her Printmakers.* 1946. Hastings House. Ils 1st ed. F2. $30.00

HAILBUM, Isidore. *Mutants Are Coming.* 1984. Doubleday. 1st ed. dj. RS. EX. P1. $20.00

HAILBUM, Isidore. *Walk Are Among Us.* 1975. Doubleday. 1st ed. dj. VG. P1. $15.00

HAINES, D.H. *Pro Quarterback.* 1940. Farrar. 1st ed. 266 p. dj. VG. B10. $4.25

HAINES, Lynn. *Lindberghs.* 1931. NY. 1st ed. dj. VG. B3. $27.50

HAINING, Peter. *Dead of Night.* 1989. Dorset. 1st ed. dj. EX. P1. $16.95

HAINING, Peter. *Deadly Nightshade.* 1978. Taplinger. 1st ed. dj. EX. P1. $22.50

HAINING, Peter. *Dictionary of Ghosts.* 1982. Robert Hale. 1st ed. dj. EX. P1. $20.00

HAINING, Peter. *Dr Who: A Celebration.* 1983. Allen. 1st ed. dj. EX. P1. $20.00

HAINING, Peter. *Dr Who: Time-Traveler's Guide.* 1987. Allen. dj. EX. P1. $24.95

HAINING, Peter. *HG Wells Scrapbook.* 1978. Potter. 1st Am ed. dj. EX. R3. $15.00

HAINING, Peter. *Hollywood Nightmare.* 1970. MacDonald. 1st ed. dj. EX. P1. $15.00

HAINING, Peter. *Jules Verne Companion.* 1978. Baronet. 1st ed. wrp. EX. R3. $12.50

HAINING, Peter. *Lucifer Soc.* nd. Taplinger. 2nd ed. dj. EX. P1. $15.00

HAINING, Peter. *Midnight People.* 1968. Leslie Frewin. 1st ed. dj. EX. P1. $25.00

HAINING, Peter. *Satanists.* 1970. Taplinger. 1st ed. dj. VG. P1. $17.50

HAINING, Peter. *Terror!* 1976. A&W Visual Lib. dj. EX. P1. $25.00

HAINING, Peter. *Wild Night Co.* 1971. Taplinger. 1st ed. dj. xl. P1. $7.50

HAIRE, F.H. *Folk Costume Book.* 1934. Barnes. Revised Enlarged ed. 150 p H3. $40.00

HAKES, John. *Personal Voice.* 1964. Lippincott. 1st ed. dj. w/pamphlet. EX. K2. $85.00

HALACY, D.S. *Ripcord.* 1962. Whitman. VG. P1. $5.00

HALD, A. *Contemporary Swedish Design.* 1951. Stockholm. 1st ed. 4to. EX. $35.00

HALDEMAN, H.R. *Ends of Power.* 1978. Times. 1st ed. 4to. dj. EX. $12.00

HALDEMAN, J.C. *Vector Analysis.* 1978. Berkley. 1st ed. dj. EX. R3. $8.50

HALDEMAN, Joe. *All My Sins Remembered.* 1977. St Martin. 1st Am ed. dj. EX. R3. $20.00

HALDEMAN, Joe. *All My Sins Remembered.* 1978. London. 1st Eng ed. dj. EX. R3. $15.00

HALDEMAN, Joe. *Buying Time.* 1989. Morrow. 1st ed. dj. EX. F5. $17.00

HALDEMAN, Joe. *Cosmic Laughter.* 1974. Holt. 1st ed. dj. EX. R3. $15.00

HALDEMAN, Joe. *Dealing in Futures.* 1985. Viking. 1st ed. dj. EX. P1. $16.95

HALDEMAN, Joe. *Infinite Dreams.* nd. Book Club. dj. VG. P1. $4.50

HALDEMAN, Joe. *Infinite Dreams.* 1978. St Martin. 1st ed. dj. EX. P1. $20.00

HALDEMAN, Joe. *Mindbridge.* nd. Book Club. dj. EX. P1. $4.50

HALDEMAN, Joe. *Mindbridge.* 1976. SF Book Club. inscr. dj. EX. R3. $12.50

HALDEMAN, Joe. *Mindbridge.* 1976. St Martin. 1st Am ed. dj. EX. R3. $30.00

HALDEMAN, Joe. *Nebula Award Stories 17.* 1983. Holt Rinehart Winston. 1st ed. dj. EX. P1. $16.95

HALDEMAN, Joe. *Study War No More.* 1977. St Martin. 1st ed. dj. VG. $10.00

HALDEMAN, Joe. *Worlds.* 1981. Viking. 1st ed. dj. EX. P1. $15.00

HALE, D.E. *Great Dane.* 1938. Judy Pub. 2nd ed. 8vo. 112 p. VG. $20.00

HALE, E.E. *Giants of the Republic.* 1895. Smith Simon. Salesman ed. G. S1. $8.00

HALE, Hilary. *Winter's Crimes 16.* 1984. Macmillan. 1st ed. dj. EX. P1. $15.00

HALE, J.P. *Trans-Allegheny Pioneers: Sketches of 1st Wht Settlements...* 1886. Cincinnati. 1st ed. VG. $195.00

HALE, John. *Paradise Man.* 1969. Bobbs Merrill. dj. VG. P1. $10.00

HALE, L.C. *We Discover New Eng.* 1915. Dodd Mead. VG. $10.00

HALE, Nancy. *Sgn of Jonah.* 1950. Scribner. 1st ed. dj. VG. F5. $15.00

HALE, Sarah. *Flora's Interpreter; or, Am Book of Flowers & Sentiments.* 1833. Boston. 14th ed. 265 p. G. T5. $65.00

HALE, Susan. *Men & Manners of the 18th Century.* 1898. Meadville, PA. 1st ed. VG. C1. $12.50

HALE, W.H. *Horace Greeley: Voice of the People.* 1950. Harper. 376 p. dj. VG. S1. $6.00

HALEY, Alex. *Roots.* 1976. Doubleday. presentation. dj. EX. H3. $150.00

HALEY, J.E. *Charles Goodnight: Cowman & Plainsman.* 1936. Boston. 1st ed. VG. B3. $40.00

HALIFAX, Joan. *Shaman: Wounded Healer.* 1990. Thames Hudson. Ils. 4to. wrp. F2. $12.95

HALL, A.F. *Handbook of Yosemite Nat Park.* 1921. NY. 1st ed. sgn. 347 p. A6. $27.50

HALL, A.G. *Nansen.* 1940. Viking. Ils Artzybasheff. dj. VG. $25.00

HALL, Austin. *People of the Comet.* 1948. Fantasy. 1st ed. 1st bdg. dj. EX. R3. $40.00

HALL, B. *Best Remaining Seats.* 1961. Bramhall, NY. dj. VG. B3. $22.50

HALL, Donald. *Contemporary Am Poetry.* 1962. Penguin. 1st ed. wrp. sgns contributors. wrp. EX. C4. $175.00

HALL, Donald. *Playing Around.* 1974. Little Brn. 1st ed. 248 p. dj. VG. B10. $4.00

HALL, F.B. *Quaker Worship in N Am.* c 1978. Richmond. Friends United Pr. 12mo. 150 p. EX. V1. $4.00

HALL, H.R. *Aegean Archeology.* 1915. London. 8vo. 270 p. TEG. VG. $25.00

HALL, Hal. *Cinematographic Annual 1930.* 1930. Am Soc Cinematographers. octavo. 606 p. EX. H3. $75.00

HALL, Helen. *Mexican Art: Pre-Columbian to Modern Times.* 1958-1959. Ann Arbor. Ils. 4to. wrp. F2. $15.00

HALL, J.B. *Yates Paul: His Grand Flights, His Tootings.* 1963. World. 1st ed. dj. EX. $12.00

HALL, J.W. *Tropical Freeze.* 1989. Norton. 1st ed. sgn. dj. EX. T9. $35.00

HALL, L.W. *Elementary Outline of Mental Philosophy for Use in Schools.* 1845. Cleveland. 1st ed. 201 p. G. T5. $47.50

HALL, O.M. *Murder City.* 1950. London. Barker. 1st ed. dj. VG. T9. $70.00

HALL, Radclyffe. *Well of Loneliness.* 1929. Covici Friede. Victory ed. 1/225. sgn. boxed. H3. $300.00

HALL, Roger. *19.* nd. Norton. 2nd ed. dj. VG. P1. $8.00

HALL, W.H. *Quaker Internat Work in Europe Since 1914.* 1938. Savoie. 8vo. 310 p. SftCvr. VG. V1. $8.00

HALL, W.W. *Guide to Health, Peace, & Competence.* c 1869. Springfield. Ils. 8vo. 752 p. G4. $59.00

HALL & FLINT. *Blind Spot.* 1951. Prime Pr. 1st ed. dj. EX. R3. $50.00

HALL & KRETSINGER. *Romance of the Patchwork Quilt.* 1947. Caldwell. Ils. 8vo. EX. $40.00

HALL. *Am Weasels.* 1951. Lawrence. Ils. 466 p. VG. C2. $35.00

HALLIBURTON, Richard. *New Worlds To Conquer.* 1929. Bobbs Merrill. probably 1st ed. sgn. tall 8vo. B10. $15.00

HALLIBURTON, Richard. *Royal Road to Romance.* nd. Indianapolis. tall 8vo. sgn. 399 p. gr bdg. B10. $5.00

HALLIDAY, Brett. *Blood on Biscayne Bay.* 1946. Ziff Davis. 1st ed. VG. F5. $10.00

HALLIDAY, Brett. *Date With a Dead Man.* 1959. Torquil. 1st ed. dj. EX. F5. $30.00

HALLIDAY, Brett. *Die Like a Dog.* 1959. Dodd Mead. 1st ed. dj. EX. F5. $20.00

HALLIDAY, Brett. *Dividend on Death.* 1939. Holt. 1st ed. dj. EX. F5. $35.00

HALLIDAY, Brett. *Dividend on Death.* 1942. Sun Dial. VG. P1. $10.00

HALLIDAY, Brett. *Fit To Kill.* 1958. Dodd Mead. 1st ed. dj. xl. P1. $10.00

HALLIDAY, Brett. *Homicidal Virgin.* 1960. Torquil. 1st ed. dj. xl. P1. $7.50

HALLIDAY, Brett. *Killers From the Keys.* 1961. Torquil. 1st ed. dj. xl. P1. $7.50

HALLIDAY, Brett. *Murder & the Married Virgin.* 1948. Triangle. dj. VG. P1. $12.00

HALLIDAY, Brett. *Murder & the Wanton Bride.* 1958. Torquil. 1st ed. dj. EX. F5. $30.00

HALLIDAY, Brett. *Murder in Haste.* 1961. Torquil. 1st ed. dj. EX. F5. $30.00

HALLIDAY, Brett. *Pay-Off Blood.* 1962. Torquil. 1st ed. dj. EX. F5. $30.00

HALLIDAY, Brett. *Private Practice of Michael Shayne.* 1940. Holt. 1st ed. VG. P1. $20.00

HALLIDAY, Brett. *She Woke to Darkness.* 1954. Torquil. 1st ed. dj. EX. P1. $20.00

HALLIDAY, Brett. *Taste for Cognac.* 1951. Dell. 1st Separate ed. wrp. VG. T9. $20.00

HALLIDAY, Dorothy. *Dolly & the Dr Bird.* 1971. Cassell. 1st ed. dj. xl. P1. $5.00

HALLIDAY, Fred. *Ambler.* 1983. Simon Schuster. 1st ed. dj. VG. P1. $13.95

HALLMARK EDITIONS. *House Divided: Treasury of Civil War Ils With Photos.* 1968. Hallmark Cards Inc. 61 p. dj. EX. S1. $6.00

HALLOWELL, A.D. *James & Lucretia Mott: Life & Letters.* 1884. Houghton Mifflin. 12mo. 566 p. G. V1. $35.00

HALLOWELL, Benjamin. *Autobiography.* 1883. Phil. Friends Book Assn. 1st ed. 12mo. 394 p. VG. V1. $10.00

HALLOWELL, Benjamin. *Young Friend's Manual Containing Statement Doctrines...* 1884. Phil. Friends Book Assn. 16mo. 174 p. G. V1. $10.00

HALLOWELL, Benjamin. *Young Friend's Manual.* 1868. Phil. Ellwood Zell. 2nd ed. 16mo. 174 p. G. V1. $10.00

HALLOWELL, R.P. *Quaker Invasion of MA.* 1883. Houghton Mifflin. 12mo. 227 p. G. V1. $16.00

HALPERN, Jay. *Jade Unicorn.* 1979. Macmillan. 1st ed. dj. EX. P1. $20.00

HALPIN, W.T. *Hoofbeats.* 1938. Phil/NY. Ltd ed. 1/1500. 4to. EX. $80.00

HALSEY, D.P. *Hist & Heroic Lynchburg.* 1935. Lynchburg. dj. EX. $40.00

HALSEY, F.W. *Am Authors & Their Homes.* 1901. Pott. 1st ed. 302 p. G. B10 $4.50

HALSTEAD, Murat. *Story of Cuba.* nd. Werner. 6th ed. 649 p. VG. B10. $9.50

HAMBLY, Barbara. *Quirinal Hill Affair.* 1983. St Martin. 1st ed. dj. EX. F5. $17.00

HAMBLY, Barbara. *Those Who Hunt the Night.* 1988. Del Rey. 1st ed. dj. EX. F5. $17.00

HAMERSLY, L.R. *Records of Living Officers of Navy & Marine Corps.* 1890. Phil. Hamersly. 8vo. VG. $95.00

HAMID, George. *Circus.* 1950. Sterling Pub. 1st ed. octavo. 253 p. dj. EX. H3. $45.00

HAMILTON, Alexander. *Federalist.* 1945. Heritage. 623 p. slipcase. T1. $35.00

HAMILTON, Alexander. *Splinters.* 1969. Walker. 1st ed. dj. VG. P1. $25.00

HAMILTON, Alexander. *Works.* c 1900. Putnam. Constitutional ed. 12 vols. lg octavo. H3. $450.00

HAMILTON, Anthony. *Memoirs of Count Grammont.* 1903. London. 2 vols. 8vo. VG. $60.00

HAMILTON, Bob. *Gene Autry & the Redwood Pirates.* 1946. Whitman. dj. VG. P1. $20.00

HAMILTON, Bob. *Gene Autry & the Thief River Outlaws.* 1944. Whitman. dj. VG. P1. $20.00

HAMILTON, Bruce. *To Be Hanged.* nd. Crime Club. VG. P1. $17.50

HAMILTON, Charles. *Early Day Oil Tales of Mexico.* 1966. Houston. Gulf Pub. 1st ed. 246 p. dj. F2. $25.00

HAMILTON, Donald. *Steel Mirror.* nd. Book Club. VG. P1. $4.00

HAMILTON, Edith. *Mythology.* 1942. Little Brn. Ils Savage. dj. EX. B10. $3.75

HAMILTON, Edmond. *Battle for the Stars.* nd. Book Club. dj. VG. P1. $7.50

HAMILTON, Edmond. *City at World's End.* 1951. Fell. 1st ed. dj. EX. R3. $65.00

HAMILTON, Edmond. *Star Kings.* 1949. Fell. 1st ed. dj. EX. R3. $150.00

HAMILTON, Edmond. *Star of Life.* nd. Book Club. dj. VG. P1. $7.50

HAMILTON, Patrick. *Resources of AZ.* 1885. Bancroft. Ils. 414 p. A5. $180.00

HAMILTON, Virginia. *Arilla Sun Down.* 1976. Greenwillow. 1st ed. clipped dj. EX. B13. $50.00

HAMILTON, Virginia. *Gathering.* 1981. Greenwillow. 1st ed. dj. EX. B13. $45.00

HAMILTON, Virginia. *Mystery of Drear House.* 1987. Greenwillow. 1st ed. dj. EX. B13. $40.00

HAMILTON & REILLY. *Pickwick: Play in 3 Acts.* 1927. Putnam/Knickerbocker. photos. gilt red bdg. EX. H3. $50.00

HAMLIN, T. *Benjamin Henry Latrobe.* 1955. NY. 1st ed. dj. VG. B3. $55.00

HAMMETT, Dashiell. *Adventures of Sam Spade.* 1945. Tower. 2nd ed. dj. VG. P1. $7.50

HAMMETT, Dashiell. *Big Knockover.* nd. BOMC. VG. P1. $7.50

HAMMETT, Dashiell. *Big Knockover.* nd. Random House. 2nd ed. dj. VG. P1. $15.00

HAMMETT, Dashiell. *Blood Money.* 1943. Tower. dj. VG. P1. $25.00

HAMMETT, Dashiell. *Blood Money.* 1944. Tower. 2nd ed. VG. P1. $20.00

HAMMETT, Dashiell. *Continental Op.* 1945. Bestseller Mystery. PB Orig. EX. T9. $115.00

HAMMETT, Dashiell. *Creeps by Night.* 1931. John Day. 1st ed. VG. P1. $250.00

HAMMETT, Dashiell. *Dain Curse.* 1929. Knopf. 1st ed. EX. $150.00

HAMMETT, Dashiell. *Dashiell Hammett Omnibus.* 1950. London. Cassell. 1st ed. 954 p. G. B10. $5.50

HAMMETT, Dashiell. *Glass Key*. nd. Grosset Dunlap. VG. P1. $6.00

HAMMETT, Dashiell. *Glass Key*. 1931. Grosset Dunlap. Photoplay ed. dj. VG. T9. $55.00

HAMMETT, Dashiell. *Maltese Falcon*. 1983. San Francisco. Arion Pr. 1st print. 1/400. slipcase. orig mailer. EX. T9. $450.00

HAMMETT, Dashiell. *Maltese Falcon*. 1987. Franklin Lib. 1st ed. EX. B13. $40.00

HAMMETT, Dashiell. *Man Named Thin & Other Stories*. 1962. Mercury Mystery 233. PB Orig. wrp. EX. T9. $135.00

HAMMETT, Dashiell. *Novels of Dashiell Hammett*. nd. Book Club. dj. VG. P1. $7.50

HAMMETT, Dashiell. *Red Harvest*. 1958. Panther 754. 1st UK PB ed. wrp. VG. T9. $35.00

HAMMETT, Dashiell. *Woman in the Dark*. 1988. Knopf. 1st HrdCvr ed. dj. EX. T9. $55.00

HAMMETT & COLODNY. *Battle of the Aleutians*. 1944. AK. HQ W Defense Command. 1st/only ed. bl wrp. VG. T9. $225.00

HAMMETT & RAYMOND. *Secret Agent X-9*. 1971. NY. Nostalgia Pr. 1st 1-vol/full-sized ed. 1st print. wrp. EX. T9. $35.00

HAMMIL, Joel. *Limbo*. 1980. Arbor House. 1st ed. dj. VG. P1. $12.50

HAMMOND, J.M. *Quaint & Hist Forts of N Am*. 1915. Phil. 1st ed. 309 p. T5. $145.00

HAMMOND, Keith; see Kuttner, Henry.

HAMMOND, Norman. *Lubaatun 1926-1970: British Mus in British Honduras*. 1972. London. 1st ed. wrp. F2. $15.00

HAMMOND. *On Certain Conditions of Nervous Derangement*. 1881. NY. VG. C2. $95.00

HAMMONDS, Michael. *Among the Hunted*. nd. Book Club. dj. VG. P1. $4.00

HAMPTON, B.B. *Hist of the Movies*. 1931. Covici Friede. 1st ed. octavo. 456 p. ES. scarce. H3. $100.00

HAMRI, Mohamed. *Tales of Joujouka*. 1975. Capra. Chapbook Series. 1/50. sgn. EX. K2. $20.00

HANBURY-TENISON, Robin. *Question of Survival*. 1973. Scribner. 1st ed. 272 p. F2. $15.00

HANBURY-TENISON, Robin. *Worlds Apart*. 1984. Little Brn. 1st Am ed. sm 4to. 227 p. dj. F2. $25.00

HANCE, R.A. *Destination Earth 2*. 1977. Vantage. dj. VG. P1. $10.00

HANCER, Kevin. *PB Price Guide No 1*. 1980. Overstreet. VG. P1. $15.00

HANCER, Kevin. *Price Guide to PB*. 1990. Wallace Homestead. 3rd ed. EX. P1. $16.95

HANCOCK, H.I. *Jiu-Jitsu Combat Tricks*. 1904. Putnam. 1st ed. 8vo. 151 p. EX. R4. $20.00

HANCOCK, Weston. *Lost Treasure of Cocos Island*. 1960. NY. 1st ed. dj. VG. B3. $25.00

HANDELMAN, Howard. *Military Government & the Movement Toward Democracy in S Am*. 1981. Bloomington. 1st ed. 388 p. F2. $10.00

HANDLEMAN. *Bridge to Victory*. 1943. NY. dj. VG. B3. $22.50

HANFF, H. *Apple of My Eye*. 1978. NY. 1st ed. dj. VG. B3. $25.00

HANFF, H. *84 Charing Cross Road*. 1970. NY. 1st ed. dj. VG. B3. $35.00

HANGELDIAN, A.E. *Tapis d'Orient*. 1959. Paris. 1st ed. dj. EX. $45.00

HANKE, Lewis. *Selected Writings of Lewis Hanke on Hist of Latin Am*. 1979. Tempe. 1st ed. 497 p. F2. $15.00

HANKEY, Donald. *Student at Arms 2nd Series*. 1917. Dutton. 5th ed. 246 p. B10. $5.25

HANKINS, M.L. *Women of NY*. 1861. NY. G. $125.00

HANKINS, R.M. *Lonesome River Range*. 1951. Hodder Stoughton Yellowjacket. dj. VG. P1. $10.00

HANKS & DESKEY. *Decor Designs & Interiors*. 1987. NY. 1st ed. VG. G1. $25.00

HANLEY, James. *Andersonville*. 1912. Cincinnati/NY. VG. T5. $25.00

HANLEY, James. *At Bay*. 1935. Grayson. 1st Eng ed. 1/250. sgn. dj. H3. $40.00

HANLEY, James. *Last Voyage*. 1931. London. Joiner Steele. 1st ed. 1/550. H3. $125.00

HANLEY, James. *Resurrexit Dominus*. 1934. private print. Ltd ed. 1/99. sgn. TEG. H3. $225.00

HANLEY, James. *Stoker Haslett*. 1932. London. Joiner Steele. 1st ed. 1/350. sgn. H3. $125.00

HANNA, M.C. *Cassie & Ike*. 1973. Phil. JF Blair. 8vo. 207 p. dj. VG. V1. $6.00

HANNAH, Barry. *Airships*. 1978. NY. 1st ed. sgn. dj. EX. T9. $55.00

HANNAH, Barry. *Capt Maxiumus*. 1985. Knopf. 1st ed. sgn. dj. EX. C4. $35.00

HANNAH, Barry. *Hey Jack!* 1987. Dutton Lawrence. UP. wrp. RS. w/photo. EX. K2. $45.00

HANNAH, Barry. *Never Die*. 1991. Houghton Mifflin. UP. wrp. EX. B13. $50.00

HANNAH, Barry. *Nightwatchman*. 1973. NY. 1st ed. sgn. dj. EX. C4. $100.00

HANNAY. *Poetical Works of Edgar Allan Poe*. nd. (1859) London. Complete ed. gilt gr bdg. very scarce. $160.00

HANNON, John. *Kings & Cats: Munster Fairy Tales for Young & Old*. 1909. London. Burns Oates. Ils Wain. 4to. 78 p. VG. $45.00

HANRATTY, Peter. *Last Knight of Albion*. 1st Trade PB ed. VG. C1. $3.50

HANSARD, G.A. *Book of Archery*. 1841. London. 8vo. 456 p. VG. $80.00

HANSEN, H.J. *Late 19th-Century Art*. nd. (1972) McGraw Hill. 1st ed. 4to. 264 p. dj. EX. R4. $30.00

HANSEN, Joseph. *Backtrack*. 1982. Woodstock. Foul Play. 1st ed. dj. EX. T9. $25.00

HANSEN, Joseph. *Country of Old Men*. 1991. Viking. UP. wrp. EX. K2. $45.00

HANSEN, Joseph. *Fadeout*. 1970. Harper Row. 1st ed. dj. EX. T9. $110.00

HANSEN, Joseph. *Little Dog Laughed*. 1986. Harper Row. 1st ed. dj. EX. T9. $20.00

HANSEN, Joseph. *Longleaf*. 1974. Harper Row. UP of ARC. bl wrp. EX. T9. $90.00

HANSEN, Joseph. *Lost on Twilight Road*. 1964. Nat Lib Books. 1st ed. wrp. NM. T9. $125.00

HANSEN, Joseph. *Man Everybody Was Afraid Of*. 1978. Harper Row. 1st ed. dj. EX. T9. $40.00

HANSEN, Joseph. *Obedience*. 1988. Mysterious Pr. 1st ed. dj. EX. F5. $13.00

HANSEN, Joseph. *Skinflick*. 1979. Holt Rinehart Winston. 1st ed. dj. EX. T9. $30.00

HANSEN, Joseph. *Skinflick*. 1979. Holt Rinehart Winston. 1st ed. dj. VG. P1. $12.50

HANSEN, Joseph. *Steps Going Down*. 1985. Foul Play. 1st ed. dj. EX. F5. $13.00

HANSEN, Joseph. *Strange Marriage*. 1965. Argyle Books. 1st ed. dj. EX. T9. $55.00

HANSEN, Joseph. *Todd*. 1971. Traveler's Companion. PB Orig. wrp. EX. T9. $35.00

HANSEN, Joseph. *Troublemaker.* 1975. Harper Row. 1st ed. sgn. dj. EX. T9. $55.00

HANSEN, Joseph. *1 Foot in the Boat.* 1977. Los Angeles. Momentum Pr. 1st ed. wrp. EX. T9. $20.00

HANSEN, R.P. *Deadly Purpose.* 1958. Mill Morrow. 1st ed. dj. VG. P1. $20.00

HANSEN, R.P. *There's Always a Payoff.* 1959. Mill Morrow. VG. P1. $15.00

HANSEN, Ron. *Desperadoes.* 1979. Knopf. 1st ed. dj. EX. C4. $40.00

HANSJAFOB, Heinrich. *Der Dogt Auf Huhlftein.* 1895. Freiburg. German text. G. R5. $30.00

HANSON, C.E. *Plains Rifle.* 1960. NY. 4to. plastic dj. EX. G1. $20.00

HANSON, C.T. *Loafing Down Long Island.* 1921. Century. 1st ed. VG. $25.00

HANSON, J.M. *Bull Run Remembers.* 1953. Nat Capitol Pub. 194 p. PB. G. S1. $7.00

HAPGOOD, Hutchins. *Autobiography of a Thief.* 1914. Dutton. 347 p. G. B10. $3.75

HAPGOOD & RICHARDSON. *Monte Cassino.* 1984. NY. inscr. dj. EX. $15.00

HAPLEY, George; see Woolrich, Cornell.

HARBEN, W.N. *Land of the Changing Sun.* 1975. Gregg Pr. M. R3. $25.00

HARDIE, Martin. *Eng Clr Books.* 1973. Totowa, NJ. Ils. dj. EX. T1. $40.00

HARDING, Bertita. *Amazon Throne.* nd. George Harrap. 1st Australian ed. 292 p. VG. F2. $10.00

HARDING, Bertita. *Amazon Throne.* 1941. Bobbs Merrill. Ils. 353 p. dj. F2. $12.50

HARDING, Jack. *I Like Brazil.* 1941. Bobbs Merrill. 1st ed. 355 p. F2. $10.00

HARDING, M.H. *George Rogers Clark & His Men.* 1981. KY Hist Soc. Ils. 244 p. G. T5. $17.50

HARDING, Robert. *Boy's Own Annual Vol 63 1940-1941.* 1941. Lutterworth. VG. P1. $30.00

HARDING, Walter. *Thoreau Handbook by Walter Harding.* 1959. NY U. 1st ed. dj. EX. C4. $35.00

HARDINGE, George. *Winter's Crimes 11.* 1980. St Martin. 1st ed. dj. EX. P1. $15.00

HARDOY, Jorge. *Urban Planning in Pre-Columbian Am.* 1968. Braziller. 1st ed. 128 p. dj. F2. $20.00

HARDWICK, Alice. *Little Wooden Shoes.* nd. (c 1920s) Saalfield. Ils Brundage. 8vo. VG. $15.00

HARDWICK, Elizabeth. *Ghostly Lover.* 1945. NY. 1st ed. sgn. clipped dj. EX. T9. $135.00

HARDWICK, Elizabeth. *Simple Truth.* 1955. Harcourt Brace. 1st ed. dj. EX. B13. $125.00

HARDWICK, Elizabeth. *Sleepless Nights.* 1979. Random House. 1st ed. sgn. dj. EX. C4. $45.00

HARDWICK, Michael. *Private Life of Dr Watson.* 1983. Dutton. 1st ed. dj. EX. P1. $20.00

HARDWICK, Michael. *Revenge of the Hound.* 1987. Villard Books. 1st ed. dj. EX P1. $20.00

HARDWICK, Richard. *Mystery of Blk Schooner.* 1966. Whitman. EX. P1. $12.50

HARDWICK & HARDWICK. *Sherlock Holmes Companion.* 1962. Murray. 1st ed. dj. VG. P1. $40.00

HARDY, A.S. *No 13, Rue Du Bon Diable.* 1917. Houghton. 1st ed. EX. F5. $20.00

HARDY, Lindsay. *Nightshade Ring.* 1954. Appleton Century Crofts. dj. VG. P1. $10.00

HARDY, Thomas. *Famous Tragedy of the Queen of Cornwall.* 1923. London. 1st ed. EX. $75.00

HARDY, Thomas. *Human Shows, Far Phantasies.* 1925. London. 1st ed. VG. $95.00

HARDY, Thomas. *Life's Little Ironies.* 1894. NY. 1st Am ed. EX. $45.00

HARDY, Thomas. *Oxen.* 1915. London. Hove. private circulation only. gray wrp. scarce. B13. $225.00

HARDY, Thomas. *Return of the Native.* 1878. London. 1st ed. 3 vols. VG. H3. $4000.00

HARDY, Thomas. *Return of the Native.* 1929. Harper. Ils/sgn Clare Leighton. dj. EX. $75.00

HARDY, Thomas. *Return of the Native.* 1942. Heritage. Ils Agnes Parker. slipcase. EX. T1. $20.00

HARDY, Thomas. *Song of the Soldiers.* 1914. London. Hove. 1st Separate ed. EX. K2. $200.00

HARDY, Thomas. *Tess of the D'Urbervilles.* 1891. London. 1st ed. presentation. rebound. H3. $2000.00

HARDY, Thomas. *Tess of the D'Urbervilles.* 1926. London. Macmillan. Ltd Ils ed. 1/325. sgn. VG. K2. $1000.00

HARDY, Thomas. *Woodlanders.* 1887. London. 1st ed. 1st bdg. H3. $2000.00

HARDY, Thomas. *Works.* 1919. London. Macmillan. Mellstock ed. 1/500. sgn. 37 vols. H3. $7500.00

HARDY, Thomas. *Works...in Prose & Verse.* 1917. London. Macmillan. Wessex ed. 17 vols. octavo. VG. H3. $750.00

HARDY, Thomas. *Writings in Prose & Verse.* 1920. Harper. Anniversary Ed. 1/1250. 21 vols. quarto. H3. $750.00

HARDY, William. *Little Sin.* 1958. Dodd Mead. 1st ed. dj. xl. P1. $5.00

HARE, Amory. *Tristram & Iseult.* 1930. Gaylordsville. Ils Escherick. 1/450. sgns. very rare. C1. $175.00

HARE, Cyril. *Untimely Death.* 1957. Macmillan. 1st ed. dj. xl. P1. $6.00

HARGREAVES, H.A. *N by 2000.* 1975. Peter Martin. 1st ed. dj. VG. P1. $15.00

HARING, D. *Blood on the Rising Sun.* 1943. Phil. 1st ed. 239 p. dj. VG. B3. $17.50

HARINGTON, Donald. *Cockroaches of Stay More.* 1989. Harcourt Brace. 1st ed. dj. EX. P1. $19.95

HARJO, Joy. *What Moon Drove Me to This?* 1979. NY. I Reed Books. 1st ed. EX. K2. $50.00

HARLAND, Marion. *Common Sense in the Household.* 1884. Scribner. 546 p. B10. $12.00

HARLAND, Marion. *Some Colonial Homesteads & Their Stories.* 1897. NY. 1st ed. 511 p. G. T5. $17.50

HARLOW, R.V. *Samuel Adams.* 1923. NY. 1st ed. EX. $15.00

HARM, Ray. *Ray Harm's African Sketchbook.* 1973. Louisville. 1st ed. sgn. slipcase. EX. G1. $50.00

HARMON, Tom. *Pilots Also Pray.* 1944. Crowell. dj. VG. P1. $17.50

HARNER, Michael. *Jivaro.* 1972. Doubleday. 1st ed. 233 p. dj. F2. $15.00

HARNESS, Charles. *Paradox Men.* 1984. Crown. 1st ed. dj. EX. R3. $12.50

HARPER, Frank. *Military Ski Manual.* 1943. Harrisburg. 1st ed. 393 p. T5. $25.00

HARPER, G.W. *Gypsy Earth.* 1982. Doubleday. dj. EX. P1. $15.00

HARPER, Vincent. *Mortgage on the Brain.* 1905. Doubleday. 1st ed. G. R3. $50.00

HARPER, Wilhelmina. *Yankee Yarns: Stories From NE States.* 1944. Dutton. 1st ed. 315 p. VG. B10. $6.25

HARR, J.T. *King Arthur.* 1973. 1st Eng Trans. dj. EX. C1. $17.50

HARR, J.T. *King Arthur.* 1973. Crane Russak. dj. EX. P1. $15.00

HARRAR, E.S. *Hough's Encyclopedia of Am Woods Vol 2.* 1958. NY. 1st ed. 2 vols. slipcase. VG. T5. $37.50

HARRE, T.E. *Beware After Dark!* 1945. Emerson. dj. VG. R3. $25.00

HARRER. *Wht Spider.* 1968. London. dj. VG. B3. $35.00

HARRICK, C.B. *RR Surgery: Handbook on Management of Injuries.* 1899. NY. Wood. 1st ed. 265 p. VG. $125.00

HARRIMAN, M.C. *Vicious Circle (Algonquin).* 1951. NY. 1st ed. dj. VG. B3. $22.50

HARRINGTON, Horacio. *Ordovician Trilobites of Argentina.* 1957. Lawrence U. 1st ed. 276 p. F2. $20.00

HARRINGTON, Joseph. *Last Doorbell.* nd. Book Club. dj. VG. P1. $3.00

HARRINGTON, William. *Mr Target.* 1973. Delacorte. 1st ed. dj. EX. F5. $12.00

HARRINGTON, William. *Oberst.* 1987. Donald Fine. 1st ed. dj. EX. F5. $11.00

HARRIS, A.C. *AK & the Klondike Gold Fields.* 1897. Phil. Ils 1st ed. 8vo. VG. T1. $35.00

HARRIS, Alfred. *Baroni.* 1975. Putnam. 1st ed. dj. VG. P1. $15.00

HARRIS, B.C. *Compleat Herbal.* 1978. PB. VG. C1. $3.50

HARRIS, Ben. *Fandango.* 1986. Ben Harris Magic. 1st ed. SftCvr. M. w/cards. J3. $6.00

HARRIS, Ben. *1986 World Lecture Tour Notes.* 1986.1st ed. SftCvr. M. J3. $6.00

HARRIS, C.W. *Away From the Here & Now.* 1947. Dorrance. 1st ed. R3. $30.00

HARRIS, Cicero. *Sectional Struggle.* 1902. Phil. 1st ed. $18.00

HARRIS, F.R. *Hometown Chronicles.* 1955. Greenfield, OH. Ils. 246 p. VG. T5. $19.50

HARRIS, Frank. *Bernard Shaw.* 1931. Gollancz. 1st ed. Simon Schuster. VG. $50.00

HARRIS, Frank. *Bernard Shaw.* 1931. Gollancz. 2nd ed. VG. P1. $17.50

HARRIS, Frank. *Elder Conklin.* 1894. NY. 1st ed. VG. $40.00

HARRIS, Frank. *Joan La Romee: A Drama.* nd. London. Fortune. 1/350. sgn. TEG. H3. $125.00

HARRIS, Frank. *My Life & Loves.* 1922. Harris. VG. P1. $25.00

HARRIS, Frank. *My Life Vol 2.* 1925. Harris. VG. P1. $25.00

HARRIS, Herbert. *John Creasey's Crime Collection 1984.* c 1984. Hutchinson. dj. EX. P1. $15.00

HARRIS, Hyde; see Harris, Timothy.

HARRIS, J.C. *Aaron in the Wildwoods.* 1897. Boston. 1st ed. 1st print. 270 p. T5. $25.00

HARRIS, J.C. *Tales of the Home Folks in Peace & War.* 1898. Boston. VG. $75.00

HARRIS, J.C. *Tales of the Home Folks in Peace & War.* 1898. Houghton Mifflin. 1st ed. G. $16.00

HARRIS, J.C. *Uncle Remus & His Friends.* 1892. Houghton Mifflin. Ils Frost. 1st ed. VG. $75.00

HARRIS, J.C. *Uncle Remus.* 1957. Ltd Ed Club. Ils/sgn Seong Moy. slipcase. EX. $40.00

HARRIS, J.C. *Uncle Remus: Daddy Jake...& Other Stories.* 1889. Century. Ils Kemble. 1st ed. 4to. 145 p. EX. $165.00

HARRIS, J.C. *Uncle Remus: His Songs & Sayings.* 1905. NY. Ils Frost. New Revised ed. TEG. EX. $80.00

HARRIS, J.C. *Uncle Remus: His Songs & Sayings.* 1930. London/NY. Appleton. New Revised ed. 265 p. scarce dj. VG. $45.00

HARRIS, John Benyon; see Wyndham, John.

HARRIS, John. *Old Trade of Killing.* 1966. Hutchinson. 1st ed. dj. xl. P1. $6.00

HARRIS, Macdonald. *Private Demons.* 1961. Houghton Mifflin. 1st ed. dj. EX. C4. $50.00

HARRIS, Mark. *Bang the Drum Slowly.* 1956. Knopf. ARC. wrp. VG. B13. $150.00

HARRIS, Mark. *City of Discontent.* 1952. Bobbs Merrill. 1st ed. dj. w/sgn bookplate. EX. C4. $50.00

HARRIS, Mark. *Dr Who Technical Manual.* 1983. Random House. 1st ed. dj. EX. F5. $10.00

HARRIS, Mark. *Ticket for Seamstitch.* 1957. Knopf. 1st ed. dj. EX. H3. $40.00

HARRIS, Mark. *Trumpet to the World.* 1946. Reynal Hitchcock. 1st ed. dj. EX. F5. $25.00

HARRIS, Raymond. *Shadows of the Wht Sun.* 1988. Ace. 1st HrdCvr ed. dj. EX. F5. $10.00

HARRIS, T.W. *Treatise on Insects Injurious to Vegetation.* 1862. Boston. 3rd ed. 640 p. G. B3. $135.00

HARRIS, Thomas. *Blk Sunday.* nd. Putnam. 4th ed. dj. VG. P1. $17.50

HARRIS, Thomas. *Silence of the Lambs.* ARC. stiff wrp. M. C1. $29.50

HARRIS, Thomas. *Silence of the Lambs.* 1988. NY. AP of 1st ed. clr wrp. T1. $65.00

HARRIS, Timothy. *Am Gigolo.* 1979. Delacorte. ARC. dj. RS. EX. T9. $55.00

HARRIS, Timothy. *Good Night & Goodbye.* 1979. Delacorte. 1st ed. dj. EX. T9. $35.00

HARRIS, Timothy. *Kyd for Hire.* 1977. London. Gollancz. 1st ed. sgn. dj. EX. T9. $65.00

HARRIS, Timothy. *Kyd for Hire.* 1978. Dell 11670. 1st Am ed. wrp. EX. T9. $25.00

HARRIS, Timothy. *Steelyard Blues.* 1972. Bantam B7396. PO Orig. wrp. EX. T9. $25.00

HARRIS, Wilson. *Caroline Fox.* 1946. London. Constable. 3rd print. 358 p. dj. VG. V1. $8.00

HARRIS. *Minor Encyclopedia. Vol 4.* 1803. Boston. 12mo. 307 p. G. G4. $14.00

HARRISON, B. *Visions of Glory.* 1978. NY. 1st ed. 413 p. dj. VG. B3. $27.50

HARRISON, Benjamin. *This Country of Ours.* 1899. Scribner. 360 p. G. S1. $12.00

HARRISON, Chip; see Block, Lawrence.

HARRISON, E.S. *Nome & Seward Peninsula.* 1905. Souvenir ed. 1st ed. 392 p. K1. $175.00

HARRISON, G.B. *Introducing Shakespeare.* 1947. Pelican. P1. $10.00

HARRISON, G.L. *Remains of William Penn...Plea, Mission to Eng...* 1882. Phil. private print. 1st ed. 8vo. 94 p. VG. V1. $20.00

HARRISON, H.H. *Am Birds in Clr: Land Birds.* 1948. NY. 1st ed. sgn. VG. $20.00

HARRISON, Harry. *Astounding: John W Campbell Memorial Vol.* 1973. Random House. 1st ed. dj. EX. R3. $12.50

HARRISON, Harry. *Captive Universe.* 1969. Putnam. 1st ed. dj. EX. R3. $25.00

HARRISON, Harry. *Great Balls of Fire!* 1977. Grosset Dunlap. 1st Am ed. wrp. EX. R3. $15.00

HARRISON, Harry. *Nova 1*. 1970. Delacorte. 1st ed. VG. P1. $10.00

HARRISON, Harry. *Nova 4*. 1974. Walker. 1st ed. sgn. dj. VG. P1. $25.00

HARRISON, Harry. *Queen Victoria's Revenge*. 1974. Crime Club. 1st ed. dj. EX. R3. $22.50

HARRISON, Harry. *Queen Victoria's Revenge*. 1977. Severn House. 1st ed. dj. VG. P1. $20.00

HARRISON, Harry. *Return to Eden*. 1987. Bantam. ARC. pub sgn/letter. EX. R3. $40.00

HARRISON, Harry. *SF Author's Choice 4*. 1974. Putnam. dj. VG. P1. $10.00

HARRISON, Harry. *Skyfall*. 1976. Atheneum. 1st Am ed. dj. RS. EX. R3. $15.00

HARRISON, Harry. *Skyfall*. 1976. Atheneum. 1st ed. sgn. dj. EX. F5. $24.00

HARRISON, Harry. *Stainless Steel Rat Saves the World*. 1977. Putnam. 1st ed. dj. EX. R3. $25.00

HARRISON, Harry. *Stainless Steel Rat Wants You*. nd. Book Club. dj. VG. P1. $4.50

HARRISON, Harry. *Stainless Steel Rat's Revenge*. 1970. Walker. 1st ed. sgn. dj. EX. R3. $60.00

HARRISON, Harry. *To The Stars*. nd. Book Club. dj. VG. P1. $10.00

HARRISON, Harry. *W of Eden*. 1984. Bantam. ARC. wrp. M. R3. $15.00

HARRISON, Harry. *Winter in Eden*. 1986. Bantam. 1st ed. sgn. dj. EX. P1. $25.00

HARRISON, Harry. *Worlds of Wonder*. 1969. Doubleday. 1st ed. dj. EX. R3. $15.00

HARRISON, Harry. *Year 2000*. 1970. Doubleday. 1st ed. dj. EX. R3. $10.00

HARRISON, Harry. *Year 2000*. 1970. Doubleday. 1st ed. dj. xl. P1. $5.00

HARRISON, Harry. *1 Step From Earth*. 1970. Macmillan. 1st ed. dj. EX. R3. $12.50

HARRISON, Jim. *Farmer*. 1976. Viking. 1st ed. dj. EX. K2. $40.00

HARRISON, Jim. *Farmer*. 1976. Viking. 1st ed. sgn. dj. EX. C4. $85.00

HARRISON, Jim. *Good Day To Die*. 1973. Simon Schuster. 1st ed. dj. EX. B13. $200.00

HARRISON, Jim. *Just Before Dark: Collected Non-Fiction*. 1991. Clark City Pr. 1/250. sgn. slipcase. EX. C4. $150.00

HARRISON, Jim. *Legends of the Fall*. 1979. Delacorte. Ltd ed. 1/250. sgn. 3 vols. slipcase. EX. K2. $375.00

HARRISON, Jim. *Legends of the Fall*. 1979. Delacorte. UP. red wrp. EX. C4. $150.00

HARRISON, Jim. *Locations*. 1968. Norton. 1st HrdCvr ed. dj. EX. K2. $125.00

HARRISON, Jim. *Nat World: A Bestiary*. 1981. Barrytown. Ils/sgn/inscr Guest. 1/100. no dj issued. EX. C4. $275.00

HARRISON, Jim. *Plain Song*. 1965. NY. 1st ed. sgn. wrp. scarce. T9. $125.00

HARRISON, Jim. *Selected & New Poems*. 1982. Delacorte. 1st ed. 1/250. sgn. boxed. M. B13. $175.00

HARRISON, Jim. *Sundog*. 1984. Dutton Lawrence. Ltd ed. 1/250. sgn. slipcase. EX. K2. $135.00

HARRISON, Jim. *Warlock*. 1981. Delacorte. UP. wrp. EX. B13. $175.00

HARRISON, Jim. *Warlock*. 1981. Dutton Lawrence. Ltd ed. 1/250. sgn. slipcase. EX. K2. $135.00

HARRISON, Jim. *Warlock*. 1981. NY. Delacorte. UP. yel wrp. laid into proof dj. EX. K2. $175.00

HARRISON, M.J. *Centauri Device*. 1974. Doubleday. 1st ed. dj. EX. P1. $20.00

HARRISON, M.J. *In Viriconium*. 1982. Gollancz. 1st ed. sgn. dj. EX. P1. $30.00

HARRISON, M.J. *Storm of Wings*. 1980. Doubleday. 1st ed. dj. EX. P1. $20.00

HARRISON, M.J. *Viriconium Nights*. 1985. Gollancz. 1st ed. sgn. dj. EX. P1. $25.00

HARRISON, Margaret. *Capt of the Andes*. 1943. NY. Richard Smith. 1st ed. 216 p. dj. F2. $20.00

HARRISON, Michael. *Higher Things*. nd. MacDonald. VG. P1. $20.00

HARRISON, Mrs. Burton. *Recollections Grave & Gay*. 1911. NY. 1st ed. 386 p. T5. $42.50

HARRISON, William. *Man Under Orders*. 1979. Harper. 1st ed. 194 p. dj. EX. B10. $7.00

HARRISON, William. *Theologian*. 1965. Harper. 1st ed. dj. EX. F5. $15.00

HARRISON, William. *Theologian*. 1965. NY. 1st ed. sgn. dj. EX. T9. $55.00

HARRISON & DICKSON. *Lifeship*. 1976. Harper. 1st ed. dj. RS. R3. $20.00

HARRISON & WATERS. *Burne-Jones*. 1973. NY. Putnam. 1st Am ed from Eng sheets. 4to. 209 p. dj. EX. R4. $45.00

HARRISON. *Story of Dining Fork*. 1927. Cincinnati. 1st ed. VG. C2. $39.00

HARSHA, D.A. *Life of Charles Sumner*. 1858. NY. Dayton. Ils. 329 p. G. S1. $16.00

HARSHA, J.W. *Nature, Effects, & Pardon of Sin...* 1853. NY. Dodd. 1st ed. 241 p. VG. B10. $5.00

HART, George. *Violin & Its Music*. 1881. London. Dulau/Novello. 1st ed. octavo. 484 p. VG. H3. $150.00

HART, Moss. *Winged Victory*. 1943. Random House. 1st ed. dj. H3. $45.00

HART, Susanne. *Life With Daktari*. 1969. Atheneum. 1st Am ed. 224 p. dj. VG. B10. $5.00

HART, W.S. *Law on Horseback & Other Stories*. 1935. Times-Mirror Pr. 1st ed. inscr. 223 p. dj. VG. H3. $85.00

HART, W.S. *Lighter of Flames*. 1923. Crowell. 1st ed. 1/1000. sgn. 246 p. VG. H3. $50.00

HART & KAUFMAN. *Fabulous Invalid*. 1938. Random House. 1st ed. dj. EX. H3. $75.00

HART & KAUFMAN. *George WA Slept Here*. 1940. Random House. 1st ed. dj. EX. scarce. H3. $150.00

HARTCUP, Guy. *Achievement of the Airship: Hist of Development...* 1974. London. 1st Eng ed. dj. EX. T5. $35.00

HARTE, Bret. *Her Letter*. 1905. Houghton Mifflin. Ils. TEG. VG. $25.00

HARTE, Bret. *Luck of Roaring Camp & Other Sketches*. 1875. Osgood. 1st ed. later print. inscr. EX. B13. $375.00

HARTE, Bret. *Luck of Roaring Camp*. nd. Houghton Mifflin. VG. P1. $17.50

HARTE, Bret. *Stories in Light & Shadow*. 1898. Houghton Mifflin. 16mo. 304 p. VG. $70.00

HARTE, Bret. *Writings*. c 1906. Houghton Mifflin. Autograph ed. 19 vols. lg octavo. H3. $3500.00

HARTE, Bret. *Writings*. c 1906. Houghton Mifflin. Riverside ed. 19 vols. TEG. H3. $1500.00

HARTLAND, E.S. *Science of Fairy Tales*. 1897. London/NY. VG. C1. $24.00

HARTLEY, Cecil. *Gentleman's Book of Etiquette & Fashion*. 1872. Boston. VG. $40.00

HARTLEY, E.N. *Iron Works on the Saugus.* 1957. Norman. 1st ed. 328 p. dj. VG. B3. $20.00

HARTLEY, H.W. *Tragedy of Sand Cave.* 1925. Louisville, KY. 2nd ed. G. $20.00

HARTLEY, L.P. *Boat.* 1949. Doubleday. 1st Am ed. dj. VG. R3. $45.00

HARTLEY, L.P. *Traveling Grave.* 1948. Arkham House. 1st ed. dj. EX. R3. $125.00

HARTLEY, L.P. *Traveling Grave.* 1951. London. 1st ed. dj. EX. R3. $20.00

HARTLEY, Marsden. *25 Poems.* 1923. Paris. Contact Ed. 1st ed. sgn. wrp. glassine sleeve. K2. $1350.00

HARTLEY, Norman. *Shadowplay.* 1982. Atheneum. 1st ed. dj. EX. P1. $12.95

HARTLEY, Norman. *Viking Process.* 1976. Simon Schuster. 1st ed. dj. VG. P1. $10.00

HARTWELL, David. *Dark Descent.* 1987. Tor Books. 1st ed. w/sgn ils PB. M. R3. $35.00

HARTWIG, G. *Polar & Tropical Worlds.* 1874. Springfield. 2 vols in 1. G. G4. $28.00

HARVESTER, Simon. *Bamboo Screen.* 1968. Walker. 1st ed. dj. EX. P1. $15.00

HARVESTER, Simon. *Moscow Road.* 1971. Walker. 1st ed. dj. EX. P1. $5.00

HARVESTER, Simon. *Tiger in the N.* 1963. Walker. 1st ed. dj. xl. P1. $6.00

HARVESTER, Simon. *Zion Road.* 1968. Jarrolds. dj. xl. P1. $7.50

HARVESTER, Simon. *Zion Road.* 1968. Walker. 1st ed. dj. EX. P1. $15.00

HARVEY, M.E. *Warhaven.* 1987. Franklin Watts. 1st ed. dj. RS. EX. P1. $15.95

HARVEY, T.E. *Rise of the Quakers.* 1905. London. Headley. 2nd print. 181 p. VG. V1. $9.00

HARVEY, William. *Beast With 5 Fingers.* 1947. Dutton. 1st Am ed. dj. EX. R3. $32.50

HARWELL, R.B. *More Confederate Imprints.* 1957. Richmond. wrp. EX. $40.00

HASKELL, A.L. *Some Studies in Ballet.* 1928. S Kensington. Lamley. 1st ed. 198 p. VG. H3. $350.00

HASKELL & NOUVEL. *Diaghileff: His Artistic & Private Life.* 1935. Simon Schuster. 1st ed. 359 p. dj. VG. H3. $40.00

HASKIN, Leslie. *Wild Flowers of Pacific Coast.* 1934. OR. 182 pls. $30.00

HASKINS & BENSON. *Scott Joplin.* 1978. Doubleday. 1st ed. octavo. 248 p. dj. RS. EX. H3. $50.00

HASSAUREK, Friedrich. *4 Years Among the Ecuadorians.* 1967. S IL U. reprint of 1867/1st ed. 196 p. dj. F2. $15.00

HASSIG, Ross. *Trade, Tribute, & Transportation.* 1985. OK U. 1st ed. 364 p. dj. F2. $20.00

HASSLER, Donald. *Patterns of the Fantastic.* 1983. Starmont. 1st ed. wrp. EX. R3. $7.50

HASSON, Josephs. *With the 114th in the ETO: A Combat Hist.* 1945. Camp Chaffee, AR. Ils. maps. 192 p. VG. T5. $65.00

HASSRICK, P. *Way W.* 1982. Abrams. 1/1500. dj. boxed. VG. $85.00

HASTINGS, Brook. *Demon Within.* 1953. Crime Club. 1st ed. VG. P1. $10.00

HASTINGS, Macdonald. *Cork on Water.* nd. Book Club. dj. VG. P1. $3.00

HASTINGS, Milo. *City of Endless Night.* 1920. Dodd Mead. 1st ed. G. R3. $30.00

HASTY, J.E. *Man Without a Face.* 1958. Dodd Mead. dj. VG. P1. $10.00

HASWELL, Jock. *D-Day: Intelligence & Deception.* 1980. Time Books. 1st ed. dj. EX. P1. $15.00

HATFIELD. *Am House Carpenter.* 1857. NY. Revised Enlarged 7th ed. presentation. VG. C2. $165.00

HATHAWAY, Louise. *Enchanted Hour.* 1940. Newbegin/Ward Ritchie. 1/500. EX. C1. $9.50

HATTON & PLATE. *Magicians' Tricks.* 1910. NY. 1st ed. G. C2. $65.00

HAUPTMANN, Gerhard. *Parsival.* 1915. Macmillan. 1st ed. VG. very scarce. C1. $27.50

HAUSER, Thomas. *Hawthorne Group.* 1991. Tor Books. UP. wrp. EX. B13. $20.00

HAUSMAN, Patricia. *Right Dose (Vitamins & Minerals).* 1987. Rodale. 1st ed. dj. VG. P1. $24.95

HAVARD, Henry. *France Artistique et Monumentale.* 1890s. Paris. 6 vols. folio. H3. $1750.00

HAVEN, C.C. *New Hist Manual Concerning 3 Battles at Trenton & Princeton.* 1871. Trenton. 1st ed. G. T5. $45.00

HAVEN & BELDEN. *Hist of Colt Revolver 1836-1940.* 1940. Morrow. Ils. VG. $95.00

HAVERFORD SCHOOL ASSN. *Report of the Managers.* 1840. Phil. Brn Bicking Guilbert. 8vo. 22 p. wrp. V1. $7.50

HAVERFORD SCHOOL ASSN. *Report of the Managers.* 1857. Phil. Joseph Rakestraw. 8vo. pamphlet. VG. V1. $16.00

HAVERGAL, F.R. *Swiss Letters & Alpine Poems.* c 1880. Randolph. 1st Am ed? 298 p. B10. $18.00

HAVERSTOCK. *Am Bestiary.* 1979. Abrams. 248 p. A5. $40.00

HAVIARAS, Stratis. *When the Tree Sings.* 1979. NY. 1st ed. dj. EX. T9. $45.00

HAVILAND, Virginia. *William Penn: Founder & Friend.* 1952. Abingdon Pr. 8vo. 128 p. dj. VG. V1. $6.00

HAVILAND, William. *Ancient Lowland Maya Social Organization.* 1968. Tulane. F2. $10.00

HAWK, John. *House of Sudden Sleep.* 1930. Mystery League. 1st ed. dj. VG. P1. $25.00

HAWK, P. *Off the Racket.* 1937. NY. 1st ed. 390 p. VG. B3. $47.50

HAWKES, Clarence. *Gentleman From France: An Airdale Hero.* 1924. Boston. 1st ed. 5 pls. VG. $20.00

HAWKES, Jacquetta. *Providence Island.* 1959. Random House. 1st ed. dj. EX. R3. $17.50

HAWKES, Jacquetta. *World of the Past.* 1963. Knopf. Book Club ed. 2 vols. boxed. F2. $20.00

HAWKES, John. *Beetle Leg.* 1951. New Directions. 1st ed. dj. EX. H3. $125.00

HAWKES, John. *Cannibal.* 1949. New Directions. 1st ed. dj. EX. scarce. K2. $125.00

HAWKES, John. *Goose on the Grave/The Owl: 2 Short Novels.* 1954. New Directions. 1st ed. dj. EX. H3. $125.00

HAWKES, John. *Humors of Blood & Skin: A John Hawkes Reader.* 1984. NY. 1st ed. dj. EX. $35.00

HAWKES, John. *Innocent Party.* 1966. New Directions. 1st ed. dj. EX. H3. $65.00

HAWKES, John. *Lime Twig.* 1961. New Directions. 2nd print. dj. EX. H3. $100.00

HAWKES, John. *Lunar Landscapes. Stories & Short Novels 1949-1963.* 1969. New Directions. 1st ed. dj. EX. H3. $100.00

HAWKES, John. *Passion Artist.* 1979. New Directions. 1st ed. 1/200. sgn. EX. B13. $65.00

HAWKES, John. *2nd Skin.* 1964. NY. 1st ed. dj. EX. $75.00

HAWKEY & BINGHAM. *Wild Card.* 1974. Stein Day. 1st ed. dj. EX. P1. $15.00

HAWKINS, Gerald. *Beyond Stonehenge.* 1973. Harper. Book Club ed. 319 p. F2. $10.00

HAWKINS, Gerald. *Stonehenge Decoded.* 1966. Revised Expanded ed. dj. VG. C1. $7.50

HAWKINS, J.R. *Sword of Power.* 1987. Davos. 1st HrdCvr ed. 1/1000. sgn. dj. EX. F5. $25.00

HAWKINS, John. *Life of Samuel Johnson.* 1787. Dublin. 1st ed. VG. $395.00

HAWKINS, S. *Stoner's Boy.* 1926. Cincinnati. Hawkins. inscr. H3. $50.00

HAWKINS, William. *Treatise of Pleas of the Crown. Vol 1.* 1795. London. 8vo. 659 p. +63 p tables. G. G4. $65.00

HAWKINS, William. *Treatise of Pleas of the Crown. Vol 4.* 1795. London. 8vo. 511 p. +103 p tables. G. G4. $42.00

HAWKS, Frank. *Speed.* 1931. NY. sgn. 314 p. VG. T5. $150.00

HAWTHORNE, Julian. *Mystery & Detective Stories.* 1908. Review of Reviews. P1. $15.00

HAWTHORNE, Nathaniel. *Blithedale Romance.* 1852. Ticknor. 1st ed. EX. C4. $150.00

HAWTHORNE, Nathaniel. *Complete Works.* 1886. Houghton Mifflin. Riverside ed. 12 vols. VG. H3. $200.00

HAWTHORNE, Nathaniel. *Complete Works.* 1891. Houghton Mifflin. Wayside ed. 25 vols. sm octavo. H3. $1000.00

HAWTHORNE, Nathaniel. *Dr Grimshawe's Secret.* 1883. Longman. 1st Eng ed. VG. B13. $135.00

HAWTHORNE, Nathaniel. *Marble Faun; or, Romance of Monte Beni.* 1860. Boston. 1st ed. 2nd print. 2 vols. G. T5. $195.00

HAWTHORNE, Nathaniel. *Marble Faun; or, Romance of Monte Beni.* 1894. Boston. Ils. EX. $60.00

HAWTHORNE, Nathaniel. *Marble Faun; or, Romance of Monte Beni.* 1931. Zurich. Ltd Ed Club. Ils/sgn Carl Strauss. 2 vols. slipcase. EX. C4. $60.00

HAWTHORNE, Nathaniel. *Mosses From an Old Manse.* 1854. Ticknor. 1st ed. 12mo. 2 vols. EX. C4. $125.00

HAWTHORNE, Nathaniel. *Scarlet Letter.* 1935. Heritage. Ils WA Dwiggins. slipcase. EX. T1. $20.00

HAWTHORNE, Nathaniel. *Septimus Felton; or, The Elixer of Life.* 1872. Osgood. 1st ed. VG. R3. $100.00

HAWTHORNE, Nathaniel. *Tanglewood Tales.* 1918. London. Ils/sgn Dulac. 1/500. sgn. orig vellum. EX. H3. $850.00

HAWTHORNE, Nathaniel. *Transformation.* 1860. Leipzig. Ils gilt vellum. EX. $225.00

HAWTHORNE, Nathaniel. *Writings.* 1900. Houghton Mifflin. Old Manse ed. 22 vols. octavo. H3. $300.00

HAY, Clarence. *Maya & Their Neighbor.* 1962. UT U. reprint of 1940 ed. 606 p. dj. F2. $35.00

HAY, George. *Stopwatch.* 1974. London. 1st ed. dj. EX. R3. $20.00

HAY, John. *Pioneers of OH.* 1879. Cleveland. Leader Print Co. 12mo. wrp. VG. T5. $37.50

HAY & WERNER. *Admirable Trumpeter: Biography of Gen James Wilkinson.* 1941. NY. 1st ed. VG. $15.00

HAYCRAFT, Howard. *Murder for Pleasure.* 1941. Appleton Century. 1st ed. sans dj. VG. T9. $75.00

HAYDEN, Arthur. *Chats on Old Prints: Practical Guide for the Collector.* 1906.Ils. 307 p. A5. $25.00

HAYDEN, Arthur. *Furniture Designs of Chippendale Hepplewhite & Sheraton.* 1940. Tudor. 300 p. dj. VG. B10. $20.00

HAYDEN, Sterling. *Wanderer.* 1964. Longman. 1st ed. 434 p. dj. EX. B10. $6.00

HAYES, B.H. *Am Drawings.* 1965. Shorewood. slipcase. EX. D4. $20.00

HAYES, Helen. *On Relfection.* 1968. Evans. 1st ed. 1/1000. 253 p. slipcase. EX. H3. $75.00

HAYES, J.R. *Molly Pryce: A Quaker Idyll.* 1914. Biddle Pr. 1st print. 16mo. 30 p. VG. V1. $8.50

HAYES, J.R. *Roger Morland: A Quaker Idyll.* 1915. Phil. Biddle Pr. 16mo. 23 p. VG. V1. $9.00

HAYES, J.W. *Tales of the Sierras.* 1912. NY. Ils. 136 p. wrp. A5. $35.00

HAYES, Jack. *Intrepid TX Ranger.* c 1933. Bandera, TX. wrp. A5. $90.00

HAYES, M.H. *Points of the Horse.* 1897. London. 2nd ed. 1/156. sgn. 4to. 333 p. VG. $200.00

HAYES, M.H. *Points of the Horse...Breeds & Evolution.* c 1905. London. 4th ed. xl. $150.00

HAYES, P.C. *War Verse & Other Verse.* 1914. Joliet, IL. 1st ed. presentation. 8vo. 316 p. EX. R4. $30.00

HAYES, Ralph. *Visiting Moon.* 1971. Lenox Hill. dj. xl. P1. $5.00

HAYES, Woody. *You Win With People.* 1973. Columbus. 1st ed. presentation. dj. VG. B3. $45.00

HAYES & LOOS. *Twice Over Lightly.* nd. (1972) Harcourt. not 1st ed. 343 p. VG. B10. $4.25

HAYLEY, William. *Life & Posthumous Writings of William Cowper.* 1803-1804. Chicester. Seagrave. 1st ed. 3 vols. quarto. H3. $450.00

HAYMAN, Eric. *Worship & the Common Life.* 1944. Cambridge U. 2nd ed. 16mo. 155 p. dj. EX. V1. $9.00

HAYMON, S.T. *Death of a God.* 1987. St Martin. 1st ed. sgn. dj. EX. F5. $18.00

HAYNE, P.H. *Lives of Robert Young Hayne & Hugh Swinton Legare.* 1878. Charleston. 1st ed. orig wrp. EX. $45.00

HAYS, L.F. *Hero of Hornet's Nest: Biography of Elijah Clark.* 1946. NY. sgn. VG. $37.00

HAYWARD, C.B. *Practical Aeronautics.* 1912. Chicago. Ils 1st ed. 769 p. xl. T5. $75.00

HAYWARD, J. *New Eng Gazetteer.* 1839. Concord, NH. Ils. 8vo. VG. G4. $56.00

HAZEL, Paul. *Yearwood.* 1980. Atlantic/Little Brn. 1st ed. dj. EX. P1. $20.00

HAZELTON, R.M. *In Our Midst.* 1948. NY. Island Pr. 12mo. 182 p. dj. VG. V1. $8.50

HAZEN, Marcella. *Classic Italian Cookbook.* 1973. Harper Book Club. 483 p. VG. B10. $5.00

HAZZARD, Shirley. *People in Glass Houses.* 1967. NY. 1st ed. dj. EX. $45.00

HEAD, F.B. *Journeys Across the Pampas & Among the Andes.* 1967. S IL U. reprint of 1827 ed. dj. F2. $15.00

HEAD, Matthew. *Accomplice.* 1947. Simon Schuster. 1st ed. dj. VG. P1. $20.00

HEAD, Matthew. *Smell of Money.* 1944. Tower. dj. VG. P1. $12.50

HEADLEY, J.T. *Achievements of Stanley & Other African Explorers.* 1878. Phil. 1st ed. EX. $65.00

HEADLEY, J.T. *Life & Naval Career of Admiral Farragut.* c 1865. Boston. 12mo. 342 p. gr bdg. G. G4. $14.00

HEADLEY, J.T. *Stanley's Adventures in Africa.* nd. (1882) Edgewood Co. 483 p. EX. B10. $10.00

HEALD, Tim. *Brought To Back.* 1988. Crime Club. 1st ed. dj. EX. F5. $14.00

HEALD, Tim. *Unbecoming Habits.* 1973. Stein Day. 1st ed. dj. VG. P1. $15.00

HEALY, Christopher. *Memoir of Christopher Healy.* 1886. Phil. Friends Bookstore. 12mo. 258 p. EX. V1. $9.00

HEALY, Jeremiah. *So Like Sleep.* 1987. Harper Row. 1st ed. dj. EX. P1. $15.95

HEALY, Jeremiah. *Swan Dive.* 1988. Harper Row. 1st ed. dj. EX. P1. $16.95

HEALY, Jeremiah. *Yesterday's News.* 1989. Harper Row. 1st ed. dj. EX. P1. $16.95

HEALY, R.J. *9 Tales of Space & Time.* 1954. Holt. 1st ed. VG. P1. $20.00

HEALY & MCCOMAS. *Adventures in Time & Space.* 1946. Random House. 1st ed. dj. EX. R3. $30.00

HEANEY, Seamus. *Hailstones.* 1984. Dublin. Gallery. 1st ed. 1/750. sgn. wrp. EX. K2. $125.00

HEANEY, Seamus. *N.* 1976. Oxford. 1st Am ed. sgn. dj. EX. K2. $225.00

HEANEY, Seamus. *Personal Selection.* 1982. Belfast. Ulster Mus. sgn. wrp. EX. K2. $85.00

HEANEY, Seamus. *Preoccupations. Selected Prose 1968-1978.* 1980. Farrar Straus Giroux. 1st Am ed. sgn. dj. EX. K2. $100.00

HEANEY, Seamus. *Preoccupations: Selected Prose 1968-1978.* 1980. London. Faber. sgn. dj. H3. $100.00

HEANEY, Seamus. *Station Island.* 1984. Farrar Straus Giroux. UP. wrp. EX. K2. $45.00

HEANEY, Seamus. *Station Island.* 1984. London. Faber. 1st ed. sgn. dj. EX. K2. $125.00

HEANEY, Seamus. *Station Island.* 1985. Farrar Straus Giroux. 1st ed. sgn. dj. EX. K2. $85.00

HEANEY, Seamus. *Stations.* 1975. Belfast. Ulsterman. 1st ed. sgn. stapled wrp. EX. K2. $250.00

HEANEY, Seamus. *Sweeney Astray.* 1983. Derry. Field Day. 1st ed. sgn. dj. EX. K2. $175.00

HEANEY, Seamus. *Sweeney Astray.* 1984. Farrar Straus Giroux. 1st Am ed. sgn. dj. EX. K2. $85.00

HEARD, H.F. *Doppelgangers.* 1947. Vanguard. 1st ed. dj. EX. R3. $22.50

HEARD, H.F. *Weird Tales, Terror, & Detection.* 1946. Sun Dial. dj. VG. P1. $35.00

HEARD, N.C. *House of Slammers.* 1975. Macmillan. UP. wrp. EX. B13. $75.00

HEARD. *Hist of Sioux Wars & Massacres of 1862-1863.* nd. Harper. 354 p. A5. $80.00

HEARN, C.V. *Foreign Assignment.* 1961. Adventurers Club. dj. VG. P1. $7.50

HEARN, E. *You Are As Young As Your Spine.* 1967. NY. 1st ed. 120 p. dj. VG. B3. $22.50

HEARN, Lafcadio. *Japan: An Interpretation.* 1904. NY. 1st ed. 12mo. TEG. VG. T1. $35.00

HEARN, Lafcadio. *Japanese Miscellany.* 1901. Little Brn. 1st ed. 1st issue. 12mo. EX. C4. $125.00

HEARN, Lafcadio. *Karma & Other Stories & Essays.* 1921. London. 1st Eng ed. 204 p. TEG. G. T5. $95.00

HEARN, Lafcadio. *Leaves From the Diary of an Impressionist.* 1911. Houghton Mifflin. 1/575. sm 8vo. slipcase. VG. $95.00

HEARN, Lafcadio. *Letters From the Raven.* 1908. London. Constable. 1st Eng ed. VG. $25.00

HEARN, Lafcadio. *2 Years in the French W Indies.* 1890. Harper. 1st ed. VG. $35.00

HEARON, Shelby. *Owing Jolene.* 1989. Knopf. UP. wrp. EX. B13. $35.00

HEARTSILL, W.W. *1491 Days in the Confederate Army.* 1987. Broadfoot Pub. 336 p. dj. M. S1. $30.00

HEATH, C. *Paris & Its Environs.* 1831-1833. London. 1st ed. 2 vols. EX. $250.00

HEATH, W.L. *Good Old Boys.* 1971. NY. McCall. 1st ed. dj. EX. T9. $50.00

HEATON, Mary. *Vorse: Time & the Town.* 1942. NY. 1st ed. dj. VG. w/letter by Vorse. B3. $90.00

HEBDEN, Mark. *Pel & the Prowler.* 1986. Walker. 1st ed. dj. EX. P1. $15.95

HECHT, Ben. *Fantazius Mallare: Mysterious Oath.* 1922. Covici McGee. Ltd ed. 1/2025. sgn. H3. $50.00

HECHT, Ben. *Florentine Dagger: Novel for Amateur Detectives.* 1923. Boni Liveright. 1st ed. EX. scarce. B13. $85.00

HECHT, Ben. *Jew in Love.* 1931. Covici Friede. Ltd ed. 1/150. sgn. H3. $400.00

HECHT, Ben. *Kingdom of Evil.* 1924. Covici. 1st ed. dj. EX. $60.00

HECHT, Ben. *Miracle in the Rain.* 1943. Peter Huston. 2nd ed. VG. P1. $15.00

HECHT, Ben. *1001 Afternoons in Chicago.* 1922. Covici McGee. inscr. VG. H3. $200.00

HECK, Klaus. *Before You Cast the 2nd Stone.* 1979. Dillsboro, NC. Ils. inscr. 134 p. dj. VG. T5. $42.50

HECKELMANN, Charles. *Trumpets in the Dawn.* 1958. Doubleday. 1st ed. dj. EX. F5. $18.00

HECKLEMANN, Charles. *Big Valley.* 1966. Whitman. VG. P1. $6.00

HECKMAN, Hazel. *Island Year.* 1972. WA U. Family Bookshelf ed. 255 p. dj. M. B10. $4.00

HEDIN, Sven. *Trans-Himalaja.* 1909. Leipzig. 1st ed. 2 vols. EX. $95.00

HEDRICK, Basil. *NM Frontier.* 1971. S IL U. 1st ed. 255 p. dj. F2. $15.00

HEDRICK, U.P. *Cherries of NY.* 1915. Albany. Lyon. clr pls. VG. T3. $150.00

HEDRICK, U.P. *Grapes of NY.* 1908. Albany. Lyon. clr pls. VG. T3. $200.00

HEDRICK, U.P. *Peaches of NY.* 1917. Albany. Lyon. clr pls. VG. T3. $200.00

HEDRICK, U.P. *Pears of NY.* 1921. Albany. Lyon. clr pls. VG. T3. $200.00

HEDRICK, U.P. *Plums of NY.* 1911. Albany. Lyon. clr pls. VG. T3. $150.00

HEDRICK, U.P. *Sm Fruits of NY.* 1925. Albany. clr pls. VG. T3. $150.00

HEER, Friedrich. *Medieval World.* 1961. Trans into Eng. 1st ed. dj. VG. C1. $14.00

HEGEN, Edmund. *Highways Into the Upper Amazon Basin.* 1966. FL U. 1st ed. 168 p. wrp. F2. $15.00

HEIMER, Mel. *Empty Man.* 1971. McCall. dj. VG. P1. $15.00

HEINEMANN, Larry. *Close Quarters.* 1977. Farrar Straus. 1st ed. dj. EX. C4. $100.00

HEINLEIN, R.A. *Beyond This Horizon.* 1948. Fantasy. 1st ed. G. R3. $30.00

HEINLEIN, R.A. *Beyond This Horizon.* 1948. Grosset Dunlap. VG. P1. $25.00

HEINLEIN, R.A. *Cat Who Walks Through Walls.* 1985. Putnam. ARC. M. $30.00

HEINLEIN, R.A. *Cat Who Walks Through Walls.* 1985. Putnam. 1st ed. dj. EX. F5. $20.00

HEINLEIN, R.A. *Cat Who Walks Through Walls*. 1985. Putnam. 1st ed. dj. VG. P1. $17.95

HEINLEIN, R.A. *Citizen of the Galaxy*. 1967. Scribner. 7th ed. xl. P1. $10.00

HEINLEIN, R.A. *Door Into Summer*. nd. Book Club. VG. P1. $4.50

HEINLEIN, R.A. *Farmer in the Sky*. 1950. Scribner. 1st ed. dj. EX. R3. $250.00

HEINLEIN, R.A. *Farnham's Freehold*. nd. Book Club. dj. VG. P1. $7.50

HEINLEIN, R.A. *Farnham's Freehold*. 1964. Putnam. 1st ed. dj. EX. R3. $375.00

HEINLEIN, R.A. *Friday*. 1982. Holt Rinehart Winston. 1st ed. dj. EX. P1. $20.00

HEINLEIN, R.A. *Friday*. 1982. Holt. 1st ed. inscr/sgn twice. dj. w/sgn card. EX. F5. $250.00

HEINLEIN, R.A. *Gr Hills of Earth*. 1951. Shasta. 1st ed. sgn. dj. EX. B13. $750.00

HEINLEIN, R.A. *Grumbles From the Grave*. 1989. Del Rey. 1st ed. 281 p. dj. xl. B10. $5.00

HEINLEIN, R.A. *Have Space Suit Will Travel*. 1967. Scribner. 10th ed. xl. P1. $10.00

HEINLEIN, R.A. *I Will Fear No Evil*. 1970. Putnam. 1st ed. dj. EX. P1. $100.00

HEINLEIN, R.A. *Job: Comedy of Justice*. 1984. Del Rey. dj. EX. P1. $16.95

HEINLEIN, R.A. *Job: Comedy of Justice*. 1984. Del Rey. 1st ed. dj. RS. R3. $25.00

HEINLEIN, R.A. *Job: Comedy of Justice*. 1984. Del Rey. 1st ed. 1/750. sgn. slipcase. EX. B13. $275.00

HEINLEIN, R.A. *Man Who Sold the Moon*. nd. Shasta. 3rd ed. dj. xl. P1. $12.50

HEINLEIN, R.A. *Man Who Sold the Moon*. 1950. Shasta. 3rd print. dj. M. R3. $100.00

HEINLEIN, R.A. *No of the Beast*. 1980. London. 1st ed. M. R3. $35.00

HEINLEIN, R.A. *Orphans of the Sky*. 1963. London. 1st ed. dj. EX. R3. $600.00

HEINLEIN, R.A. *Orphans of the Sky*. 1964. Putnam. 1st Am ed. dj. EX. R3. $300.00

HEINLEIN, R.A. *Past Through Tomorrow Book 1*. nd. New Eng Lib. dj. EX. P1. $35.00

HEINLEIN, R.A. *Red Planet*. 1958. Scribner. 7th ed. xl. VG. P1. $7.50

HEINLEIN, R.A. *Rocket Ship Galileo*. 1947. Scribner. 1st ed. dj. EX. R3. $350.00

HEINLEIN, R.A. *Rolling Stones*. 1961. Scribner. 6th ed. dj. xl. P1. $10.00

HEINLEIN, R.A. *Star Ship of Troopers*. 1959. Putnam. 1st ed. dj. EX. R3. $600.00

HEINLEIN, R.A. *Starman Jones*. 1953. Scribner. 1st ed. dj. VG. R3. $225.00

HEINLEIN, R.A. *Starman Jones*. 1954. London. 1st Eng ed. dj. EX. R3. $125.00

HEINLEIN, R.A. *Starship Troopers*. 1959. Putnam. 1st ed. dj. EX. B13. $600.00

HEINLEIN, R.A. *Starship Troopers*. 1959. Putnam. 1st ed. dj. xl. P1. $50.00

HEINLEIN, R.A. *Stranger in a Strange Land*. nd. Tawain. Pirate ed. dj. EX. C4. $40.00

HEINLEIN, R.A. *Stranger in a Strange Land*. 1961. NY. 1st ed. dj. EX. A6. $50.00

HEINLEIN, R.A. *Time for the Stars*. nd. Book Club. dj. VG. P1. $7.50

HEINLEIN, R.A. *Time for the Stars*. 1956. Scribner. 1st ed. dj. EX. R3. $135.00

HEINLEIN, R.A. *Time for the Stars*. 1959. Scribner. 3rd ed. xl. VG. P1. $10.00

HEINLEIN, R.A. *To Sail Beyond the Sunset*. 1987. Ace Putnam. 1st ed. dj. EX. P1. $20.00

HEINLEIN, R.A. *Tomorrow the Stars*. 1952. Garden City. 1st ed. dj. EX. P4. $90.00

HEINLEIN, R.A. *Tunnel in the Sky*. 1967. Scribner. 8th print. xl. P1. $10.00

HEINLEIN, R.A. *Universe*. 1951. Dell. 1st ed. wrp. VG. R3. $40.00

HEINLEIN, R.A. *Unpleasant Profession of Jonathan Hoag*. 1959. Gnome. 1st ed. dj. EX. R3. $135.00

HEINLEIN, R.A. *6th Column*. 1949. Gnome. 1st ed. dj. EX. R3. $325.00

HEINLEIN, R.A. *6th Column*. 1949. Gnome. 1st ed. rebound. xl. P1. $12.00

HEINMANN, Bjorn. *Heinmann Coins & Cards Sonitine, Opus 1*. 1987. Hank Lee's Magic Factory. SftCvr. M. w/accessories. J3. $10.00

HEINRICH, B. *Ravens in Winter*. 1989. Summit. UP. wrp. EX. K2. $25.00

HEINRICH, Heine. *Works*. 1893. Heinemann. Lg Paper ed. 1/100. 8 vols. octavo. H3. $2000.00

HEINS, Hardy. *Golden Anniversary Bibliography of Edgar Rice Burroughs*. 1962. Heins. 1st ed. 1/150. wrp. M. R3. $400.00

HEINTZ, C.W. *Coppacaw Story: Hist of Cuyahoga Falls, OH*. 1962. Cuyahoga Falls. Ils. 92 p. pictorial wrp. VG. T5. $9.50

HEIZER, Robert. *Man's Discovery of His Past*. 1973. Palo Alto. Peek Pub. Ils. 4to. 291 p. wrp. F2. $10.00

HELD, John. *Travels of Baron Munchausen*. 1929. Ltd Ed Club. 1/1500. sgn. 204 p. D4. $75.00

HELD, John. *Works*. 1931. Ives Washburn. 168 p. scarce. D4. $70.00

HELFERICH. *On Fractures & Dislocations*. 1899. London. Sydenham Soc. 68 pls. 162 p. VG. $75.00

HELLER, Joseph. *Catch-22*. 1961. Simon Schuster. ARC. wrp. EX. K2. $575.00

HELLER, Joseph. *Catch-22*. 1961. Simon Schuster. 1st ed. orig bdg. dj. EX. H3. $500.00

HELLER, Joseph. *Catch-22*. 1961. Simon Schuster. 2nd print. inscr. VG. C4. $50.00

HELLER, Joseph. *Catch-22*. 1973. Delacorte. UP. wrp. EX. B13. $250.00

HELLER, Joseph. *God Knows*. 1984. Knopf. Ltd ed. 1/350. dj. slipcase. $75.00

HELLER, Joseph. *Good As Gold*. 1979. Simon Schuster. Ltd ed. 1/500. sgn. slipcase. VG. $65.00

HELLER, Joseph. *Good As Gold*. 1979. Simon Schuster. Ltd ed. 1/500. slipcase. M. H3. $125.00

HELLER, Joseph. *Good As Gold*. 1979. Simon Schuster. 1st ed. inscr. dj. EX. B13. $100.00

HELLER, Joseph. *Good As Gold*. 1982. Franklin Lib. 1st ed. sgn. K2. $50.00

HELLER, Joseph. *Something Happened*. 1974. Knopf. Ltd ed. 1/350. sgn. dj. slipcase. H3. $150.00

HELLER, Joseph. *Something Happened*. 1974. Knopf. 1st ed. presentation. dj. EX. H3. $100.00

HELLER, Joseph. *Something Happened*. 1974. Knopf. 1st ed. sgn. dj. EX. B13. $85.00

HELLER, Joseph. *We Bombed in New Haven*. 1968. Knopf. 1st ed. sgn. dj. EX. K2. $65.00

HELLER, Joseph. *We Bombed in New Haven: A Play*. 1968. Knopf. 1st ed. presentation. dj. EX. H3. $150.00

HELLER & VOGEL. *No Laughing Matter*. 1986. Jonathan Cape. 1st Eng ed. dj. M. H3. $50.00

HELLMAN, Lillian. *Autumn Garden*. 1951. Little Brn. 1st ed. dj. M. H3. $85.00

HELLMAN, Lillian. *Days To Come*. 1936. Knopf. 1st ed. dj. EX. H3. $125.00

HELLMAN, Lillian. *Little Foxes*. 1939. Hamish Hamilton. 1st Eng ed. dj. H3. $100.00

HELLMAN, Lillian. *Pentimento*. 1973. Little Brn. 1st ed. dj. EX. H3. $40.00

HELLMAN, Lillian. *Searching Wind*. 1944. NY. Viking. 1st ed. dj. EX. H3. $85.00

HELLMAN, Lillian. *Toys in the Attic*. 1960. Random House. Fireside Theatre Book Club ed. dj. EX. H3. $45.00

HELLMAN, Lillian. *Unfinished Woman: A Memoir*. 1969. Little Brn. 1st ed. dj. EX. H3. $60.00

HELLMAN, Lillian. *Watch on the Rhine*. 1942. NY. private print. Ils Ltd ed. 1/349. slipcase. H3. $250.00

HELMS, MacKinley. *Journeying Through Mexico*. 1948. Little Brn. 1st ed. 297 p. dj. F2. $15.00

HELMS, Randel. *Tolkien's World*. 1974. Houghton Mifflin. 1st ed. dj. EX. P1. $20.00

HELPER, H.R. *Impending Crisis of the S: How To Meet It*. 1857. NY. 8vo. VG. T1. $35.00

HELPRIN, Mark. *Dove of the E & Other Stories*. 1975. Knopf. 1st ed. dj. EX. C4. $90.00

HELPRIN, Mark. *Dove of the E*. 1975. Knopf. 1st ed. sgn. dj. EX. $125.00

HELPRIN, Mark. *Dove of the E*. 1976. London. 1st ed. dj. EX. B13. $85.00

HELPRIN, Mark. *Soldier of the Great War*. 1991. Harcourt Brace. 1st ed. 1/250. sgn. slipcase. EX. K2. $150.00

HEMANS, Felicia. *Poems*. c 1880s. reading copy. C1. $5.00

HEMINGWAY, Ernest. *Across the River & Into the Trees*. 1950. Jonathan Cape. 1st Eng ed. dj. VG. H3. $75.00

HEMINGWAY, Ernest. *Across the River & Into the Trees*. 1950. Scribner. 1st ed. 2nd state dj. H3. $50.00

HEMINGWAY, Ernest. *By-Line: Ernest Hemingway. Selected Articles & Dispatches...* 1967. Scribner. 1st ed. dj. EX. C4. $50.00

HEMINGWAY, Ernest. *Collected Poems*. c 1950. np. Pirated ed. 24 p. VG. H3. $30.00

HEMINGWAY, Ernest. *Death in the Afternoon*. 1932. Halcoyn House. VG. $25.00

HEMINGWAY, Ernest. *Death in the Afternoon*. 1932. Scribner. 1st ed. dj. EX. K2. $275.00

HEMINGWAY, Ernest. *Ernest Hemingway, Cub Reporter*. 1970. Pittsburgh U. 1st ed. dj. EX. H3. $50.00

HEMINGWAY, Ernest. *Farewell to Arms*. 1929. 1st ed. 2nd issue. EX. B2. $50.00

HEMINGWAY, Ernest. *Farewell to Arms*. 1929. NY. Ltd ed. 1/510. sgn. vellum brd. slipcase. NM. $2500.00

HEMINGWAY, Ernest. *Farewell to Arms*. 1929. NY. 1st ed. 1st issue. dj. EX. $400.00

HEMINGWAY, Ernest. *Farewell to Arms*. 1929. Scribner. 1st ed. blk cloth. G. $45.00

HEMINGWAY, Ernest. *Farewell to Arms*. 1931. Grosset Dunlap. reprint. dj. EX. H3. $50.00

HEMINGWAY, Ernest. *Farewell to Arms*. 1949. Bantam 467. VG. B4. $7.00

HEMINGWAY, Ernest. *Fiesta*. 1927. London. Cape. 1st ed. rebound by Bayntun Reviere. EX. C4. $450.00

HEMINGWAY, Ernest. *For Whom the Bell Tolls*. 1941. Jonathan Cape. 1st UK ed. dj. G. H3. $125.00

HEMINGWAY, Ernest. *For Whom the Bell Tolls*. 1942. Ltd Ed Club. Ils/sgn Lynd Ward. slipcase. H3. $225.00

HEMINGWAY, Ernest. *For Whom the Bell Tolls*. 1942. Ltd Ed Club. Ils/sgn Lynd Ward. 1/1500. slipcase. C4. $100.00

HEMINGWAY, Ernest. *For Whom the Bells Tolls*. 1940. Scribner. 1st ed. dj. EX. H3. $250.00

HEMINGWAY, Ernest. *Garden of Eden*. 1986. Scribner. 1st ed. dj. EX. H3. $40.00

HEMINGWAY, Ernest. *God Rest You Merry Gentlemen*. 1933. House of Books Ltd. 1/300. gilt red bdg. EX. rare. H3. $600.00

HEMINGWAY, Ernest. *Gr Hills of Africa*. nd. np. Tawain. Pirated ed. dj. EX. B13. $85.00

HEMINGWAY, Ernest. *Gr Hills of Africa*. 1935. Scribner. 1st ed. dj. H3. $450.00

HEMINGWAY, Ernest. *Gr Hills of Africa*. 1935. Scribner. 1st ed. gr bdg. dj. VG. K2. $500.00

HEMINGWAY, Ernest. *Gr Hills of Africa*. 1944. London. Cape. British Armed Forces ed. wrp. EX. K2. $45.00

HEMINGWAY, Ernest. *In Our Time*. 1924. Paris. 3 Mts Pr. 1st ed. 1/170. orig brd. rebacked. H3. $8500.00

HEMINGWAY, Ernest. *In Our Time*. 1930. Scribner. 2nd Am ed. dj. VG. H3. $300.00

HEMINGWAY, Ernest. *In Our Time*. 1930. Scribner. 2nd Am ed/1st ed Intro Wilson. dj. M. C4. $1600.00

HEMINGWAY, Ernest. *In Our Time*. 1932. Crosby Continental Ed. wrp. H3. $150.00

HEMINGWAY, Ernest. *Islands in the Stream*. 1970. Scribner. 1st ed. dj. RS. EX. H3. $35.00

HEMINGWAY, Ernest. *Islands in the Stream*. 1970. Scribner. 1st ed. gr cloth. dj. VG. $25.00

HEMINGWAY, Ernest. *Kiki's Memories*. 1930. Paris. Edward Titus. Trans Samuel Putnam. orig wrp. EX. H3. $275.00

HEMINGWAY, Ernest. *Men Without Women*. 1927. Scribner. Ltd ed. dj. VG. H3. $2000.00

HEMINGWAY, Ernest. *Moveable Feast*. 1964. Jonathan Cape. 1st UK ed. dj. EX. H3. $75.00

HEMINGWAY, Ernest. *Nick Adams Stories*. 1972. Scribner. ARC. dj. EX. H3. $150.00

HEMINGWAY, Ernest. *Nick Adams Stories*. 1972. Scribner. 1st ed. dj. EX. K2. $50.00

HEMINGWAY, Ernest. *Old Man & the Sea*. nd. Scribner. dj. VG. P1. $10.00

HEMINGWAY, Ernest. *Old Man & the Sea*. 1952. Jonathan Cape. 1st Eng ed. dj. EX. H3. $200.00

HEMINGWAY, Ernest. *Old Man & the Sea*. 1952. NY. 1st ed. 1st print. dj. VG. $100.00

HEMINGWAY, Ernest. *Old Man & the Sea*. 1952. NY. 1st ed. 8-line inscr. dj. VG. H3. $4500.00

HEMINGWAY, Ernest. *Old Man & the Sea*. 1952. Scribner. 1st ed. dj. EX. H3. $150.00

HEMINGWAY, Ernest. *Short Stories of Ernest Hemingway*. c 1965. Scribner. Book Club ed. 499 p. VG. B10. $4.50

HEMINGWAY, Ernest. *Short Stories of Ernest Hemingway*. 1942. Modern Lib. dj. EX. K2. $65.00

HEMINGWAY, Ernest. *Spanish Earth*. 1938. Cleveland. Savage. 1st ed. 1/1000. orig glassine. EX. H3. $400.00

HEMINGWAY, Ernest. *Sun Also Rises*. 1926. Scribner. 1st ed. 2nd state text. 1st issue dj. H3. $7500.00

HEMINGWAY, Ernest. *Sun Also Rises*. 1930. Grosset Dunlap. reprint of 1926 ed. dj. H3. $100.00

HEMINGWAY, Ernest. *To Have & Have Not*. 1937. Scribner. 1st ed. dj. EX. K2. $450.00

HEMINGWAY, Ernest. *Torrents of Spring*. nd. Crosby Continental ed. wrp. H3. $150.00

HEMINGWAY, Ernest. *Torrents of Spring*. nd. np. Tawain. Pirated ed. dj. EX. B13. $85.00

HEMINGWAY, Ernest. *Torrents of Spring*. 1926. Scribner. 1st ed. dj. EX. H3. $1500.00

HEMINGWAY, Ernest. *Winner Take Nothing*. 1933. Scribner. 1st ed. dj. EX. K2. $275.00

HEMINGWAY, Ernest. *5th Column & the 1st 49 Stories.* 1938. Scribner. 1st ed. dj. EX. H3. $125.00

HEMINGWAY, Leicester. *My Brother, Ernest Hemingway.* 1962. Cleveland. 1st ed. dj. VG. $17.50

HEMINGWAY & MCNEIL. *Hokum: A Play in 3 Acts.* 1978. Sans Souci Pr. 1/26. sgn pub. dj. slipcase. EX. C4. $275.00

HEMINGWAY & MCNEIL. *88 Poems.* 1979. Harcourt Brace. 1st Authorized ed. dj. w/clr broadside. M. C4. $50.00

HEMLOW, Joyce. *Hist of Fanny Burney.* 1958. Clarendon. 1st ed. 528 p. dj. R4. $40.00

HEMMING, John. *Conquest of the Incas.* 1970. Harcourt. 1st Am ed. 641 p. F2. $25.00

HEMMING, John. *Machu Picchu.* 1981. Newsweek Inc. 1st ed. 4to. 172 p. dj. F2. $25.00

HEMMING, John. *Red Gold.* 1978. Harvard U. 1st ed. 677 p. dj. F2. $25.00

HEMMING, John. *Search for El Dorado.* 1978. London. Michael Joseph. 1st ed. dj. F2. $25.00

HENDERSON, David. *Felix of the Silent Forest.* 1967. NY. 1st ed. 1/2000. sgn. wrp. EX. T9. $45.00

HENDERSON, E.B. *Plantation Echoes.* 1904. Columbus. 1st ed. VG. B3. $40.00

HENDERSON, G.F.R. *Stonewall Jackson & the Am Civil War.* 1898. Longman Gr. 2 vols. gilt red morocco. VG. $75.00

HENDERSON, G.F.R. *Stonewall Jackson & the Am Civil War.* 1937. NY. Authorized Am ed. 5 maps. T5. $45.00

HENDERSON, J.Y. *Circus Doctor.* 1951. Little Brn. octavo. 238 p. dj. VG. H3. $35.00

HENDERSON, John. *World of the Ancient Maya.* 1981. Ithaca. 1st ed. 4to. 277 p. dj. F2. $30.00

HENDERSON, L.T. *Hagar.* 1978. Christian Herald. 1st ed. dj. EX. P1. $10.00

HENDERSON, M.R. *If I Should Die.* 1985. Doubleday. 1st ed. dj. VG. P1. $15.00

HENDERSON, Peter. *Gardening for Profit.* 1867. Orange Judd. Ils. G. $20.00

HENDERSON, Thomas. *Royal 4 Town of Lochmaben.* 1953. Lockerbie. Herald Pr. VG. B10. $7.00

HENDERSON, Zenna. *Anything Box.* 1966. Gollancz. 1st ed. dj. EX. F5. $30.00

HENDERSON, Zenna. *Holding Wonder.* 1971. Doubleday. 1st ed. dj. EX. R3. $65.00

HENDRICK, B.J. *Lees of VA.* 1935. Boston. Ltd ed. sgn. VG. G1. $55.00

HENDRICK, B.J. *Statesmen of the Lost Cause: Jefferson Davis & His Cabinet.* 1939. Literary Guild. 452 p. G. S1. $10.00

HENDRICK, B.J. *Sumter: 1st Day of the Civil War.* 1990. Scarborough House. dj. 286 p. dj. M. S1. $22.95

HENDRICKS, Gordon. *Photographs of Thomas Eakins.* 1972. NY. 1st ed. VG. G1. $20.00

HENDRYX, J.B. *Blood on the Yukon Trail.* 1930. Doubleday. 1st ed. 305 p. blk bdg. B10. $5.50

HENEAGE & FORD. *Sidney Sime, Master of the Mysterious.* 1980. London. 1st ed. lg wrp. M. R3. $65.00

HENFREY, Colin. *Through Indian Eyes.* 1965. Holt. 1st Am ed. 286 p. dj. F2. $20.00

HENISSART, Paul. *Winter Spy.* 1976. Simon Schuster. 1st ed. dj. VG. P1. $15.00

HENIUS, Frank. *Stories of Am.* 1944. Scribner. Ils Leo Politi. 1st/A ed. 114 p. F2. $15.00

HENLE, Fritz. *Mexico.* 1945. Chicago. Eng/Spanish text. dj. G. T5. $17.50

HENNESSEY, Caroline. *I, BITCH.* 1970. Lancer. G. B4. $8.00

HENNESSY & LINTON. *Edwin Booth in 12 Dramatic Characters.* 1872. Boston. Osgood. 1st ed. folio. AEG. gr bdg. VG. H3. $125.00

HENOCH, Edward. *Lectures on Diseases of Children.* 1882. NY. Wood. 1st ed. EX. $95.00

HENRY, Alexander. *Alexander Henry's Travels & Adventures in Years 1760-1776.* 1921. Lakeside Classic. 340 p. T5. $42.50

HENRY, G.A. *No Surrender!* 1899. NY. 1st ed. VG. $50.00

HENRY, G.A. *Yuletide Yarns.* 1899. Longman. 1st ed. G. R3. $15.00

HENRY, J.A. *Henry's Directory of Morrisania & Vicinity for 1853-1854.* 1853. Morrisania. fld map. 32 p. printed wrp. T5. $125.00

HENRY, Marguerite. *Album of Horses.* 1965. Rand McNally. not 1st ed. 112 p. dj. EX. B10. $4.25

HENRY, Marguerite. *Justin Morgan Had a Horse.* 1954. NY. Ils/sgn Wesley Dennis. 1st ed. sgn. dj. G. T5. $15.00

HENRY, O. *Complete Writings.* 1917. Doubleday Page. Deluxe ed. 1/1075. 14 vols. octavo. H3. $4500.00

HENRY, R.S. *As They Saw Forrest.* 1956. Jackson, TN. 1st ed. sgn. dj. VG. B3. $45.00

HENRY, Will. *Death of a Legend.* 1954. Random House. 1st ed. dj. EX. F5. $16.00

HENSHALL, James. *Book of the Blk Bass.* 1970. facsimile reprint of 1881 1st ed. EX. C1. $17.50

HENSLEY, J.L. *Clr Him Guilty.* 1987. Walker. 1st HrdCvr ed. dj. EX. F5. $13.00

HENSLEY, J.L. *Killing in Gold.* 1978. Crime Club. 1st ed. dj. xl. P1. $5.00

HENSLEY, J.L. *Legislative Body.* 1972. Crime Club. 1st ed. dj. xl. P1. $5.00

HENSLEY, J.L. *Minor Murders.* 1979. Crime Club. 1st ed. dj. xl. P1. $7.50

HENSLEY, J.L. *Outcasts.* 1981. Crime Club. 1st ed. dj. VG. P1. $15.00

HENSLEY, J.L. *Outcasts.* 1981. Doubleday Crime Club. 1st ed. sgn. dj. EX. T9. $25.00

HENSLEY, J.L. *Rivertown Risk.* 1977. Crime Club. 1st ed. dj. xl. P1. $7.50

HENSON, Lance. *Selected Poems 1970-1983.* 1985. Greenfield Review. 1st ed. wrp. VG. K2. $40.00

HENTOFF, Nat. *Call the Keeper.* 1966. Viking. 1st ed. dj. EX. F5. $22.00

HEPWORTH & MCNAMEE. *Resist Much, Obey Little: Some Notes on Edward Abbey.* 1985. Salt Lake City. Dream Garden. 1st ed. dj. EX. K2. $85.00

HERBERT, Brian. *Prisoners of Arionn.* 1987. Arbor House. 1st ed. dj. RS. EX. P1. $20.00

HERBERT, Frank. *Chapterhouse Dune.* 1985. Putnam. 1st ed. dj. EX. P1. $17.95

HERBERT, Frank. *Children of Dune.* nd. Berkley Putnam. 9th print. dj. VG. P1. $10.00

HERBERT, Frank. *Dosadi Experiment.* 1977. Berkley Putnam. 1st ed. dj. VG. P1. $30.00

HERBERT, Frank. *Dragon in the Sea.* 1956. Doubleday. 1st ed. dj. VG. P1. $175.00

HERBERT, Frank. *God Emperor of Dune.* 1981. Putnam. 1st ed. 1/750. sgn. slipcase. EX. K2. $75.00

HERBERT, Frank. *God Emperor of Dune.* 1981. Putnam. 1st ed. 1/750. sgn. slipcase. M. R3. $120.00

HERBERT, Frank. *Heretics of Dune.* 1984. Putnam. Ltd ed. 1/1500. sgn. slipcase. EX. K2. $75.00

HERBERT, Frank. *Nebula Winners 15.* 1981. Harper Row. 1st ed. dj. EX. R3. $20.00

HERBERT, Frank. *Wht Plague.* 1982. Putnam. Ltd ed. 1/500. sgn. slipcase. EX. K2. $75.00

HERBERT, Frank. *Wht Plague.* 1982. Putnam. 1st ed. M. R3. $15.00

HERBERT, Frank. *Worlds of Frank Herbert.* 1980. Gregg Pr. 1st HrdCvr ed. M. R3. $50.00

HERBERT, H.A. *Abolition & Its Consequences.* 1912. NY. 1st ed. EX. $37.00

HERBERT, James. *Magic Cottage.* 1987. New Am Lib. 1st ed. dj. EX. P1. $17.95

HERBERT, James. *Sepulchre.* 1987. Hodder Stoughton. 1st ed. dj. EX. P1. $20.00

HERBERT, James. *Survivor.* 1981. New Eng Lib. 5th ed. VG. P1. $4.00

HERBERT, Kathleen. *Bride of the Spear.* 1988. NY. 1st Am ed. dj. M. C1. $12.00

HERBERT & HERBERT. *Man of 2 Worlds.* 1986. Putnam. 1st ed. dj. EX. P1. $18.95

HERBERT & RANSOM. *Jesus Incident.* 1979. Putnam. 1st ed. dj. EX. R3. $25.00

HERBERT & RANSOM. *Lazarus Effect.* 1983. Putnam. 1st ed. M. R3. $25.00

HERFORD, Oliver. *Fairy Godmother-in-Law.* 1905. Scribner. 1st ed. 12mo. 104 p. VG. $20.00

HERGESHEIMER, Joseph. *Limestone Trees.* 1931. Knopf. Ltd ed. 1/75. sgn. stiff wrp. H3. $75.00

HERGESHEIMER, Joseph. *Presbyterian Child.* 1923. Knopf. Ltd ed. 1/950. sgn. H3. $20.00

HERLEY, Richard. *Stone Arrow.* 1978. 1st Am ed. dj. EX. C1. $6.50

HERLIHY, J.L. *Midnight Cowboy.* 1965. Simon Schuster. 1st ed. dj. EX. H3. $150.00

HERLIHY, J.L. *Season of the Witch.* 1971. Simon Schuster. 1st print. dj. EX. H3. $50.00

HERMAN, Frank. *How To Do Instant Impressions.* nd. Moreno Valley, CA. Suds. SftCvr. M. J3. $5.00

HERMENT, G. *Pipe.* 1957. NY. wrp. VG. $10.00

HERNANDEZ DE ALBA, Gregorio. *El Museo Del Oro 1923-1948.* 1948. Bogota. Ils. 100 clr pls. 2 clr maps. xl. F2. $100.00

HERNDON, W.L. *Exploration of Valley of the Amazon Part 1.* 1853. WA. 417 p. F2. $55.00

HERR, Michael. *Dispatches.* 1977. Knopf. 1st ed. dj. EX. C4. $75.00

HERRICK, F.H. *Am Lobster.* 1895. GPO. VG. T3. $85.00

HERRICK, Robert. *Hesperides.* 1648. London. Hunt. 1st ed. scarce variant imp. AEG. H3. $9500.00

HERRICK, William. *Itinerant.* 1967. NY. 1st ed. inscr. dj. EX. T9. $60.00

HERRIOTT, James. *James Herriot's Yorkshire.* 1979. St Martin. 1st ed. dj. VG. P1. $15.00

HERRLINGER, R. *Hist of Medical Ils.* 1970. NY. Ils. 4to. 178 p. slipcase. EX. $70.00

HERRMANN, Paul. *Conquest by Man.* 1954. Harper. 1st ed. dj. F2. $12.50

HERRON, Don. *Echoes From Vaults of Yoh-Vombis.* 1976. Herron. 1st ed. wrp. EX. R3. $10.00

HERRON, Francis. *Letters From the Argentine.* 1943. Putnam. 1st ed. 307 p. dj. F2. $15.00

HERRON, Shaun. *Bird in Last Year's Nest.* 1974. Evans. 1st ed. dj. xl. P1. $5.00

HERRON, Shaun. *Through the Dark & Hairy Wood.* 1972. Random House. 1st ed. dj. xl. P1. $5.00

HERSCHEL, Sir John. *Outlines of Astronomy.* 1858. London. 5th ed. 8vo. VG. $135.00

HERSEY, John. *Antonietta.* 1991. Knopf. UP. wrp. EX. C4. $30.00

HERSEY, John. *Child Buyer.* 1960. Knopf. 1st ed. dj. EX. H3. $30.00

HERSEY, John. *Conspiracy.* 1972. Knopf. 1st ed. presentation. dj. EX. H3. $50.00

HERSEY, John. *Fling.* 1990. Knopf. UP. wrp. EX. K2. $25.00

HERSEY, John. *Hiroshima.* 1946. Book Club. 117 p. EX. B10. $3.50

HERSEY, John. *Men on Bataan.* 1942. Knopf. 1st ed. dj. w/sgn letter. EX. H3. $200.00

HERSEY, John. *Pulpwood Editor.* 1937. NY. 1st ed. 301 p. dj. VG. B3. $45.00

HERSEY, John. *Walnut Door.* 1977. Knopf. 1st ed. dj. EX. H3. $30.00

HERTER & HERTER. *How To Get Out of the Rat Race & Live on $10 a Month.* 1965. Waseca, MN. 1st ed. VG. $25.00

HERTZ, Louis. *Collecting Model Trains.* 1956. NY. 1st ed. dj. VG. B3. $45.00

HERTZ, Louis. *Complete Book of Model Railroading.* 1957. NY. 1st ed. 3rd print. dj. VG. B3. $32.50

HERTZ, Louis. *Riding the Tin-Plate Rails.* 1944. Ramsey. VG. C2. $67.00

HERVEY, A.B. *Sea Mosses.* 1881. Boston. 1st ed. clr pls. VG. $20.00

HERVEY, J. *Am Trotter.* 1947. NY. 1st ed. dj. VG. B3. $47.50

HERZOG, Arthur. *IQ 83.* 1978. Simon Schuster. 1st ed. dj. EX. F5/P1. $15.00

HERZOG, Arthur. *Make Us Happy.* 1978. Crowell. 1st ed. dj. EX. F5. $15.00

HESKY, Olga. *Sequin Syndicate.* 1969. Dodd Mead. 1st ed. VG. P1. $6.00

HESKY, Olga. *Time for Treason.* 1967. Dodd Mead. 1st ed. dj. xl. P1. $5.00

HESSE, Hermann. *Demian.* 1948. Holt. 1st ed. dj. EX. B13. $35.00

HESSE, Hermann. *Die Morgenlandfahrt.* 1932. Berlin. Verlag. 1st ed. dj. EX. B13. $1850.00

HESSE, Hermann. *Lekture fur Minuten.* 1952. Berlin. Stampfli Cie. inscr. stiff wrp. dj. H3. $275.00

HESSE, Hermann. *Pictor's Metamorphoses.* 1982. Farrar Straus. UP. wrp. EX. B13. $40.00

HESSE, Hermann. *Sinclairs Notizbuch.* 1923. Zurich. Rascher Cie. 1/1100. sgn. EX. B13. $500.00

HESSE, Hermann. *Unterwegs.* 1911. Verlag. 1st ed. 1/500. EX. very scarce. B13. $1000.00

HESSELTINE, W.B. *Hist of the S.* 1955. (1st 1936) NY. 2nd print. dj. EX. $17.00

HESTON, C.B. Jr. *Quaker Essays.* 1930. Phil. 12mo. 47 p. EX. V1. $8.00

HEUER, Kenneth. *End of the World.* 1953. Rinehart. 1st ed. dj. EX. R3. $30.00

HEUER, Kenneth. *Men of Other Planets.* 1951. Payson Clarke. 1st ed. dj. EX. $17.50

HEWAT, A.V. *Lady's Time.* 1985. Harper Row. 1st ed. dj. EX. K2. $25.00

HEWETT, Edgar. *Ancient Andean Life.* 1939. Bobbs Merrill. 1st ed. 336 p. F2. $30.00

HEWETT, Edgar. *Ancient Life in Mexico & Central Am.* 1936. Bobbs Merrill. 1st ed. 364 p. F2. $30.00

HEWETT, Edgar. *Ancient Life in Mexico & Central Am.* 1943. Tudor. Ils. 364 p. F2. $20.00

HEWETT & MAUZY. *Landmarks of NM.* 1947. Albuquerque. 1st ed. dj. VG. B3. $40.00

HEWITT, Jean. *NY Times Lg-Type Cookbook.* nd. (1968) Golden Pr. 446 p. VG. B10. $5.50

HEWLETT, Maurice. *Halfway House: Comedy of Degrees.* 1908. Scribner. 1st ed. 424 p. TEG. VG. B10. $8.25

HEYDEN & GENDROP. *Pre-Columbian Architecture of Mesoamerica.* 1988. Rizzoli. Ils. 4to. wrp. F2. $25.00

HEYEN, William. *Noise in the Trees: Poems & a Memoir.* nd. (1974) Vanguard. apparent 1st ed. sgn. dj. EX. B10. $5.75

HEYER, Georgette. *Charity Girl.* 1970. Bodley Head. 1st ed. dj. VG. P1. $15.00

HEYER, Georgette. *Cotillion.* nd. Putnam. VG. P1. $7.50

HEYER, Georgette. *Lady of Quality.* nd. Book Club. dj. VG. P1. $4.00

HEYERDAHL, Thor. *Am Indians in the Pacific.* 1952. Oslo. 1st ed. 921 p. dj. F2. $85.00

HEYWARD, D.B. *Brass Ankle.* 1931. Farrar Rinehart. 1st Trade ed. dj. EX. H3. $300.00

HEYWARD, D.B. *Brass Ankle: Play in 3 Acts.* 1921. Farrar Rinehart. Ltd ed. 1/100. sgn. H3. $150.00

HEYWARD, D.B. *Half-Pint Flask.* 1929. Farrar Rinehart. 1st ed. 1/175. sgns. H3. $125.00

HEYWARD, D.B. *Skylines & Horizons.* 1924. Macmillan. presentation. H3. $50.00

HEYWARD & HEYWARD. *Mamba's Daughter.* 1939. Farrar Rinehart. 1st ed. dj. EX. H3. $300.00

HEYWARD & HEYWARD. *Porgy.* 1929. London. Benn. 1st Eng ed. dj. VG. H3. $75.00

HIASEN, Carl. *Native Tongue.* 1991. Knopf. ARC. pictorial wrp. EX. C4. $35.00

HIASEN, Carl. *Native Tongue.* 1991. Knopf. UP. wrp. EX. C4. $60.00

HIASEN & MONTALBANO. *Death in China.* 1984. Atheneum. 1st ed. dj. EX. K2. $50.00

HIASSEN, Carl. *Double Whammy.* 1987. Putnam. 1st ed. dj. VG. P1. $16.95

HIATT. *Silversmiths of KY.* 1954. Louisville. 135 p. VG. C2. $45.00

HIBBEN, F. *Hunting Am Lions.* 1948. NY. 1st ed. VG. B3. $50.00

HIBBEN, F. *Hunting Am Lions.* 1948. NY. 1st ed. VG. B3. $47.50

HICHENS, Robert. *Bacchante.* 1927. Cosmopolitan. G. B10. $5.00

HICHENS, Robert. *Temptation.* nd. Grosset Dunlap. Photoplay ed. dj. VG. P1. $10.00

HICHENS, Robert. *Unearthly.* 1926. Cosmopolitan. 1st ed. G. R3. $10.00

HICKENLOOPER, Frank. *Ils Hist of Monroe Co, IA.* 1896. np. 1st ed. VG. $50.00

HICKS, Edward. *Letters Including Observations on Slavery of Africans.* 1861. Phil. Chapman. 8vo. 240 p. xl. G. V1. $30.00

HICKS, Edward. *Memoirs of Life & Religious Labors of Edward Hicks.* 1851. Phil. Merrihew Thompson. 12mo. 365 p. G. V1. $24.00

HICKS, Edward. *Series of Extemporaneous Discourses.* 1825. Phil. Parker. 8vo. 322 p. G. V1. $36.00

HICKS, Elias. *Doctrinal Epistle Written...on Long Island in Year 1820...* 1824. Phil. S Potter. 12mo. V1. $35.00

HICKS, Jack. *Cutting Edges.* 1973. Harper Row. ARC. wrp. EX. K2. $45.00

HICKS, Rachel. *Memoir of Rachel Hicks, Witten by Herself.* 1880. Putnam. 12mo. 287 p. V1. $9.00

HIELSCHER, Kurt. *Picturesque Spain.* 1925. NY. 1st ed. VG. G1. $50.00

HIERONYMUSSEN, Paul. *Orders, Medals, & Decor of Britain & Europe.* 1975. London. Blanford. not 1st ed. 256 p. dj. B10. $6.50

HIGDON, H. *Crime of the Century.* 1975. NY. 1st ed. dj. VG. B3. $25.00

HIGGINS, C.A. *To CA & Back.* 1904. Doubleday. Ils. 317 p. A5. $30.00

HIGGINS, G.V. *Choice of Enemies.* 1984. Knopf. 1st ed. dj. VG. P1. $17.50

HIGGINS, G.V. *City on a Hill.* 1975. Knopf. 1st ed. dj. VG. P1. $25.00

HIGGINS, G.V. *Digger's Game.* 1973. Knopf. 1st ed. dj. EX. P1. $15.00

HIGGINS, G.V. *Digger's Game.* 1973. Knopf. 1st ed. sgn. dj. NM. T9. $35.00

HIGGINS, G.V. *Imposters.* 1986. Holt. 1st ed. dj. VG. P1. $16.95

HIGGINS, G.V. *Judgement of Deke Hunter.* 1976. Atlantic/Little Brn. 2nd ed. dj. EX. P1. $15.00

HIGGINS, G.V. *Outlaws.* 1987. Holt. 1st ed. dj. VG. P1. $18.95

HIGGINS, Jack. *Day of Judgment.* nd. Holt Rinehart. 2nd ed. dj. EX. P1. $12.50

HIGGINS, Jack. *Day of Judgment.* 1978. Collins. 1st ed. dj. VG. P1. $20.00

HIGGINS, Jack. *Luciano's Luck.* 1981. Collins. 1st ed. dj. VG. P1. $15.00

HIGGINS, Jack. *Night of the Fox.* nd. BOMC. dj. EX. P1. $7.50

HIGGINS, Jack. *Night of the Fox.* 1986. Simon Schuster. 1st ed. dj. VG. P1. $17.95

HIGGINS, Jack. *Season in Hell.* 1989. Simon Schuster. 1st ed. dj. EX. P1. $18.95

HIGGINS, Jack. *Solo.* 1980. Collins. 1st ed. dj. VG. P1. $15.00

HIGGINS, Jack. *Storm Warning.* 1976. Holt Rinehart Winston. 1st ed. dj. VG. P1. $20.00

HIGGINSON, T.W. *Army Life in a Blk Regiment.* 1982. Time Life. reprint. EX. S1. $17.50

HIGH, P.E. *These Savage Futurians.* 1969. Dobson. dj. EX. P1. $12.50

HIGHSMITH, Patricia. *Blk House.* 1988. Mysterious Pr. 1st Am ed. dj. EX. F5. $14.00

HIGHSMITH, Patricia. *Deep Water.* 1957. Harper. 1st ed. dj. VG. P1. $27.50

HIGHSMITH, Patricia. *Dog's Ransom.* 1972. Knopf. 1st ed. dj. VG. P1. $20.00

HIGHSMITH, Patricia. *Game for the Living.* 1962. Great Pan G548. 1st PB ed. inscr. wrp. EX. T9. $35.00

HIGHSMITH, Patricia. *Glass Cell.* 1964. Crime Club. dj. xl. P1. $7.50

HIGHSMITH, Patricia. *People Who Knock on the Door.* 1985. Penzler. 1st ed. dj. VG. P1. $15.95

HIGHSMITH, Patricia. *Ripley Under Ground.* nd. Book Club. dj. xl. P1. $3.00

HIGHSMITH, Patricia. *Ripley Under Ground.* 1971. Heinemann. 1st Eng ed. dj. EX. T9. $55.00

HIGHSMITH, Patricia. *Strangers on a Train.* 1950. London. 1st UK ed. presentation. sans dj. VG. T9. $165.00

HIGHSMITH, Patricia. *Strangers on a Train.* 1951. Bantam 905. 1st PB ed. Zuckerberg cover. wrp. EX. T9. $85.00

HIGHWATER, Jamake. *Eyes of Darkness.* 1985. NY. Lathrop. 1st ed. dj. EX. B13. $45.00

HIGHWATER, Jamake. *Fodor's Indian Am.* 1975. NY. McKay. 1st ed. inscr. dj. EX. K2. $75.00

HIGHWATER, Jamake. *Mick Jagger: The Singer Not the Song.* 1973. NY. 1st/PB Orig ed. sgn. wrp. EX. scarce. T9. $55.00

HIGHWATER, Jamake. *Sweet Grass Lives On.* 1980. Lippincott. 1st ed. quarto. dj. EX. K2. $75.00

HIJUELOS, Oscar. *Our House in the Last World.* 1983. Persea. 1st ed. dj. EX. K2. $65.00

HILBURN, Robert. *Elton John.* 1975. Boutwell. 1st print. octavo. 48 p. VG. H3. $50.00

HILDICK, Wallace. *Bracknell's Law.* nd. Book Club. dj. VG. P1. $4.50

HILGARTNER, Beth. *Necklace of Fallen Stars.* 1979. Little Brn. 1st ed. dj. EX. P1. $12.50

HILL, A.L. *Practical Guide Arranging Grasses, Mosses...Wild Flowers.* 1952. Crowell. Ils. 4to. 151 p. dj. EX. $16.00

HILL, Adam. *Peking Target.* 1982. Playboy. 1st ed. VG. P1. $10.00

HILL, Adam. *Sinkiang Executive.* 1978. Doubleday. 1st ed. dj. VG. P1. $15.00

HILL, Christopher. *Scorpian.* nd. (1974) St Martin. 1st ed. 224 p. dj. VG. B10. $6.25

HILL, Douglas. *Alien Citadel.* 1984. Atheneum. 1st ed. dj. EX. F5. $15.00

HILL, Douglas. *Young Legionary.* 1983. Atheneum. 1st ed. dj. EX. P1. $15.00

HILL, F.P. *Am Plays Printed 1714-1830.* 1934. Stanford. 1st ed. H3. $25.00

HILL, G.L. *Daphne Deane.* 1937. Grosset. 317 p. dj. G. B10. $3.75

HILL, G.L. *Wht Flower.* 1927. Phil. 1st ed. sgn to sister. VG. B3. $50.00

HILL, J.L. *End of the Cattle Trail.* c 1920. Long Beach. 120 p. wrp. A5. $65.00

HILL, Porter. *Bombay Marines.* 1988. Walker. 1st ed. dj. EX. F5. $14.00

HILL, Porter. *China Flyer.* 1988. Walker. 1st ed. dj. EX. F5. $14.00

HILL, R.L. *King of Wht Lady.* 1975. Putnam. 1st ed. dj. EX. P1. $17.50

HILL, Reginald. *Ruling Passion.* 1973. Harper Row. dj. xl. P1. $6.00

HILL, Reginald. *Underworld.* 1988. Scribner. 1st ed. dj. EX. P1. $14.95

HILL, Roscoe. *Nat Archives of Latin Am.* 1945. Cambridge. xl. F2. $15.00

HILL G.C. *Daniel Boone: Pioneer of KY.* 1869. Phil. Ils. 262 p. G. T5. $27.50

HILLBORN, I.H. *Views & Testimonies of Friends.* 1903. Phil. Friends Book Assn. 16mo. 31 p. VG. V1. $8.00

HILLCOURT, William. *Baden-Powell: 2 Lives of a Hero.* 1964. Putnam. 1st ed. VG. $25.00

HILLER, B.B. *Superman IV.* 1987. Scholastic Pr. 1st ed. wrp. EX. F5. $7.00

HILLERMAN, Tony. *Blessing Way.* 1970. Harpr Row. 1st ed. sgn. dj. EX. K2. $850.00

HILLERMAN, Tony. *Blessing Way.* 1989. Armchair Detective Lib. reissue. 1/26. presentation. slipcase. EX. K2. $375.00

HILLERMAN, Tony. *Ghostway.* 1984. Harper. 1st ed. dj. EX. B13. $85.00

HILLERMAN, Tony. *Jim Chee Mysteries.* 1990. Harper. ARC. dj. RS. EX. B13. $45.00

HILLERMAN, Tony. *Listening Woman.* 1978. BOMC. dj. VG. P1. $7.50

HILLERMAN, Tony. *Skinwalkers.* 1986. Harper Row. ARC. pictorial wrp. C4. $50.00

HILLERMAN, Tony. *Skinwalkers.* 1986. Harper Row. UP. brn wrp. scarce. K2. $200.00

HILLERMAN, Tony. *Skinwalkers.* 1986. Harper. ARC. wrp. F5. $24.00

HILLERMAN, Tony. *Skinwalkers.* 1988. London. Joseph. 1st Eng ed. dj. EX. K2. $35.00

HILLERMAN, Tony. *Talking God.* 1989. Harper Row. 1st ed. dj. EX. P1. $17.95

HILLERMAN, Tony. *Thief of Time.* 1988. Harper Row. ARC. inscr. printed wrp. K2. $150.00

HILLERMAN, Tony. *Thief of Time.* 1988. Harper Row. 1st ed. dj. EX. P1. $15.95

HILLIER, Bevis. *Decorative Arts of the '40s & '50s.* 1975. NY. 4to. dj. EX. $40.00

HILLIER, J.R. *Japanese Clr Prints.* nd. London/NY. Phaidon. 50 pls. VG. C1. $7.50

HILLIER, J.R. *Japanese Drawings From the 17th-19th Centuries.* 1965. Shorewood. slipcase. EX. D4. $20.00

HILTON, James. *Goodbye Mr Chips.* 1935. Boston. reprint. sgn. dj. EX. $45.00

HILTON, James. *Random Harvest.* 1941. Little Brn. 1st ed. sgn. dj. H3. $75.00

HILTON, James. *Story of Dr Wassell.* 1943. Little Brn. 1st ed. inscr. dj. EX. B13. $85.00

HILTON, James. *To You Mr Chips!* 1938. London. 1st ed. dj. EX. B13. $125.00

HILTON, James. *Was It Murder?* 1935. Harper. VG. P1. $20.00

HILTON, John. *Sonora Sketchbook.* 1947. Macmillan. 1st ed. 333 p. dj. F2. $20.00

HIMES, Chester. *All Shot Up.* 1969. London. Panther. 1st UK/PB Orig ed. VG. T9. $40.00

HIMES, Chester. *Blind Man With a Pistol.* 1969. Morrow. 1st ed. dj. EX. T9. $45.00

HIMES, Chester. *Blk on Blk.* 1973. Doubleday. 1st Collected ed. dj. EX. H3. $60.00

HIMES, Chester. *Case of Rape.* 1980. Targ Ed. Ltd ed. 1/350. sgn. dj. EX. B13/H3/K2. $100.00

HIMES, Chester. *If He Hollars Let Him Go.* 1958. Berkley. 2nd ed. VG. B4. $8.00

HIMES, Chester. *Pinktoes.* 1965. Putnam. 1st ed. dj. EX. H3. $50.00

HIMES, Chester. *Primitive.* 1955. Signet 1264. PB Orig. wrp. NM. T9. $65.00

HIMES, Chester. *Quality of Hurt.* 1972. Doubleday. 1st ed. dj. EX. H3. $50.00

HIMES, Chester. *Run Man Run.* 1966. Putnam. 1st ed. dj. EX. H3. $70.00

HIMMEL, Richard. *23rd Web.* 1977. Random House. 1st ed. dj. EX. P1. $15.00

HINCKLEY, E.P. *Redlands 1950-1960.* 1960. Claremont. Ils. 35 p. wrp. P4. $5.00

HINDUS, Milton. *Leaves of Grass, 100 Years After, New Essays.* 1955. Stanford. 1st ed. 149 p. VG. T5. $37.50

HINE, R.V. *CA's Utopian Colonies.* 1953. San Marino. 1st ed. presentation. EX. $50.00

HINES, Gustavus. *OR: Its Hist, Condition, & Prospects.* 1851. Derby Miller. 438 p. A5. $50.00

HINKEMEYER, M.T. *4th Down Death.* 1985. St Martin. 1st ed. dj. EX. P1. $13.95

HINSDALE, B.A. *Hist of Popular Education of W Reserve.* 1896. Cleveland. 23 p. G. T5. $25.00

HINSHAW, David. *Experiment in Friendship.* 1947. Putnam. 16mo. 147 p. dj. VG. V1. $7.50

HINSHAW, David. *Heroic Finland.* nd. Putnam. Family Bookshelf ed. 306 p. dj. VG. B10. $3.50

HINSHAW, David. *Rufus Jones: Master Quaker.* 1951. Putnam. sgn. 8vo. 306 p. dj. G. V1. $12.00

HINTON, J.W. *Organ Construction.* 1902. London. Weekes. 2nd ed. sgn. 200 p. VG. H3. $150.00

HINTON, S.E. *That Was Then, This Is Now.* 1971. Viking. 1st ed. dj. EX. scarce. B13. $80.00

HINTZE, N.A. *You'll Like My Mother.* nd. Putnam. 2nd ed. dj. VG. P1. $10.00

HINXMAN, Margaret. *Night They Murdered Chelsea.* 1984. Collins Crime Club. dj. VG. P1. $12.50

HINZ, Christopher. *Liege-Killer.* 1987. St. Martin. 1st ed. dj. EX. R3. $15.00

HIRES, C.E. *Short Hist Sketch of Old Merion Meeting House.* 1917. Merion, PA. 12mo. G. V1. $16.00

HIRSCHFELD, Burt. *Key W.* 1979. Morrow. 1st ed. dj. EX. F5. $16.00

HIRSCHMAN, Jack. *Cantilations.* 1974. Capra. Chapbook Series. 1/75. sgn. EX. K2. $20.00

HIRSHFELD, Albert. *Am Theatre As Seen by Hirschfeld.* 1961. NY. 1st ed. dj. VG. $25.00

HIRTH, Kenneth. *Trade & Exchange in Early Mesoamerica.* 1984. NM U. 1st ed. 338 p. F2. $25.00

HITCHCOCK, Alfred. *Ghostly Gallery.* 1962. Random House. decor brd. VG. P1. $15.00

HITCHCOCK, Alfred. *Haunted Houseful.* 1961. Random House. 1st ed. decor brd. VG. P1. $15.00

HITCHCOCK, Alfred. *Monster Mus.* 1965. Random House. dj. VG. P1. $20.00

HITCHCOCK, Alfred. *My Favorites in Suspense.* 1959. Random House. 1st ed. dj. EX. R3. $25.00

HITCHCOCK, Alfred. *Solve-Them-Yourself Mysteries.* 1963. Random House. decor brd. EX. P1. $15.00

HITCHCOCK, Alfred. *Stories Not for the Nervous.* nd. Book Club. dj. VG. P1. $5.00

HITCHCOCK, Alfred. *Stories Not for the Nervous.* 1965. Random House. 1st ed. VG. P1. $15.00

HITCHCOCK, H.R. *In Nature of Materials: Buildings of FL Wright 1887-1941.* 1942. NY. 3rd print. 413 pls. 143 p. dj. VG. B3. $95.00

HITCHCOCK, H.R. *Modern Architecture.* 1929. NY. 1st ed. 58 pls. 525 p. VG. B3. $50.00

HITCHCOCK, Ripley. *LA Purchase & Exploration, Early Hist, & Building of W.* 1904. Boston. Ils. VG. T1. $20.00

HITCHENS, Dolores. *Bank With Bamboo Door.* 1965. Simon Schuster. 1st ed. dj. xl. P1. $5.00

HITCHENS, Dolores. *Stairway to an Empty Room.* nd. Book Club. dj. VG. P1. $5.00

HITCHINS, Robert. *Egypt & Its Monuments.* 1908. Century. Ils Jules Guerin. 1st ed. 272 p. TEG. EX. $85.00

HITCHMAN, Janet. *Such a Strange Lady.* 1976. New Eng Lib. VG. P1. $4.00

HITLER, Adolph. *Hitler's Secret Book.* 1961. Grove Pr. 1st Am ed. 230 p. G. T5. $19.50

HITT, J.E. *TN Smith.* 1979. Dutton. 1st ed. dj. EX. F5. $15.00

HITT, Orrie. *Diploma Dolls.* 1961. Kozy Book. 1st ed. wrp. EX. F5. $12.00

HITTI, P.K. *Hist of the Arabs.* 1937. London. Macmillan. 767 p. VG. J2. $30.00

HJORTH, Herman. *Reproduction of Antique Furniture.* 1924. Bruce. 2nd ed. 198 p. VG. B10. $5.50

HJORTSBERG, William. *Falling Angel.* 1978. Harcourt Brace. UP. tall bl wrp. scarce. B13. $150.00

HJORTSBERG, William. *Gray Matters.* nd. Simon Schuster. 2nd ed. dj. EX. P1. $10.00

HJORTSBERG, William. *Symbiography.* 1973. Sumac Pr. 1st ed. sgn. dj. EX. B13. $55.00

HOAG, Joseph. *Journal of Life & Gospel Labors.* 1860. Sherwoods, NY. Heston. 8vo. 370 p. ES. fair. V1. $28.00

HOBAN, Russell. *Kleinzeit.* 1983. Summit Books. UP. K2. $25.00

HOBAN, Russell. *Lion of Boaz-Jachin & Jachin-Boaz.* 1973. London. Cape. UP. wrp. EX. scarce. K2. $200.00

HOBAN, Russell. *Lion of Boaz-Jachin & Jachin-Boaz.* 1983. Summit Books. UP. wrp. EX. K2. $25.00

HOBAN, Russell. *Medusa Frequency.* 1987. Atlantic. 1st ed. dj. EX. F5. $15.00

HOBAN, Russell. *Pilgermann.* 1983. Summit Books. 1st ed. dj. VG. P1. $17.50

HOBART, A.T. *Yang & Yin.* 1936. Indianapolis. 1st ed. dj. EX. $12.00

HOBART, J.H. *Quaker by Convincement: Spiritual Autobiography.* 1951. NY. McKay. 12mo. 227 p. dj. VG. V1. $8.00

HOBBS, Robert. *Odilon Redon.* 1977. Boston. 4to. dj. EX. C2. $85.00

HOBHOUSE, Stephen. *Stephen Hobhouse: Reformer, Pacifist, Christian...* 1952. Beacon. 8vo. 216 p. dj. VG. V1. $8.50

HOBHOUSE, Stephen. *William Law & the 18th-Century Quakerism.* 1927. London. Allen Unwin. 8vo. 342 p. dj. G. V1. $12.00

HOBSON, Hank. *Big Twist.* 1959. Cassell. 1st ed. dj. VG. P1. $25.00

HOBSON, Howard. *Scientific Baseball.* nd. (1949) Prentice Hall. 250 p. dj. VG. B10. $4.50

HOBSON, L.Z. *Gentleman's Agreement.* 1947. NY. ARC. dj. RS. EX. $24.00

HOBSON, R.P. *Nothing Too Good for a Cowboy.* 1955. Phil. 1st ed. dj. VG. B3. $20.00

HOCH, E.D. *Best Detective Stories 1976.* 1976. Dutton. 1st ed. dj. xl. P1. $7.50

HOCH, E.D. *Best Detective Stories 1978.* 1978. Dutton. 1st ed. dj. EX. P1. $15.00

HOCH, E.D. *Leopold's Way.* 1985. Carbondale, IL. 1st ed. dj. NM. T9. $35.00

HOCH, E.D. *Shattered Raven.* 1969. Lancer 74525. 1st ed. sgn. wrp. VG. T9. $20.00

HOCHBAUM, H.A. *Travels & Traditions of Waterfowl.* 1955. Minneapolis. 1st ed. 301 p. VG. $20.00

HOCKING, Joseph. *Man Who Almost.* 1935. Hodder Stoughton. 9th print. dj. EX. P1. $12.00

HOCKING, Joseph. *Soul of Cominic Wildthorne.* 1908. Jennings Graham. 1st ed. VG. P1. $10.00

HOCKING, Joseph. *Tommy.* nd. Hodder Stoughton. dj. VG. P1. $10.00

HODDER-WILLIAMS, Christopher. *Egg-Shaped Thing.* nd. Book Club. dj. VG. P1. $4.50

HODEL, M.P. *Enter the Lion.* 1979. Hawthorne. 1st ed. dj. EX. P1. $20.00

HODGELL, P.C. *Dark of the Moon.* 1985. Atheneum. 1st ed. dj. EX. R3. $30.00

HODGELL, P.C. *God Stalk.* 1982. Argo. 1st ed. dj. EX. P1. $15.00

HODGKIN, L.V. *Book of Quaker Saints.* 1918. London. TN Foulis. 2nd ed. 8vo. 548 p. VG. V1. $15.00

HODGKIN, L.V. *George Lloyd Hodgkin, 1880-1918.* 1921. Edinburgh. private print. 12mo. 268 p. VG. V1. $10.00

HODGKIN, L.V. *Silent Worship: Way of Wonder.* 1929. London. Swarthmore. 2nd ed. 16mo. 95 p. VG. V1. $7.00

HODGSON, Ralph. *Last Blackbird & Other Lines.* 1907. London. Allen. sgn. dj. slipcase. H3. $75.00

HODGSON, W.H. *Boats of the Glen Carrig.* 1976. Hyperion. reprint of 1920 ed. M. R3. $25.00

HODGSON, W.H. *Carnacki the Ghost Finder.* 1947. Arkham House. 1st ed. dj. EX. R3. $95.00

HODGSON, W.H. *Ghost Pirates.* 1976. Hyperion. reprint of 1909 ed. M. J3. $25.00

HODGSON, W.H. *House on the Borderland.* 1976. Hyperion. reprint of 1908 ed. M. R3. $17.50

HODGSON, W.H. *Nightland.* 1976. Hyperion. reprint of 1912 ed. wrp. EX. R3. $17.50

HODGSON, W.H. *Out of the Storm.* 1975. Donald Grant. 1st ed. dj. EX. R3. $30.00

HODGSON, William. *Select Hist Memoirs of Religious Soc of Friends.* 1881. Lippincott. 3rd ed. 12mo. 412 p. V1. $10.00

HOEBEL, E.A. *Man in the Primitive World.* 1958. McGraw. Ils 678 p. VG. F2. $7.50

HOEFLER, Paul. *1st Trans Africa Journey by Motor Truck From Indian Ocean...* 1931. NY. Ils. sgn. VG. T1. $22.00

HOEGH & DOYLE. *Timberwolf Tracks: Hist of 104th Infantry 1942-1945.* 1956. Infantry Journal. 1st ed. 444 p. VG. $65.00

HOEHLING. *Lexington Goes Down.* 1971. NY. dj. VG. B3. $20.00

HOEPPLI, R. *Parasites & Parasitic Infections in Early Medicine.* 1959. Singapore. 1st ed. 4to. dj. EX. R4. $60.00

HOFFER, Eric. *Reflections on the Human Condition.* 1973. Harper Row. sgn. dj. H3. $75.00

HOFFMAN, Abbie. *Steal Yourself Rich Book.* 1971. Hopscotch. Pirated ed. VG. B4. $25.00

HOFFMAN, Alice. *Angel Landing.* 1980. Putnam. UP. wrp. EX. K2. $45.00

HOFFMAN, Alice. *Fortune's Daughter.* 1985. Putnam. 1st ed. dj. EX. F5. $15.00

HOFFMAN, C.F. *Winter in the W.* 1882. Chicago. Fergus Hist Series. reprint. wrps. EX. A4. $30.00

HOFFMAN, Lee. *Fox.* 1976. Doubleday. 1st ed. dj. xl. P1. $5.00

HOFFMAN, Lee. *Loco.* 1969. Doubleday. 1st ed. dj. xl. P1. $5.00

HOFFMAN, Professor. *Later Magic.* 1911. Dutton. 738 p. VG. J3. $21.00

HOFFMAN, RUBIN, & SANDERS. *Vote!* 1972. PB Lib. 1st ed. VG. B4. $8.00

HOFFMAN, W.D. *Gun Gospel.* 1926. AL Burt. dj. EX. R3. $40.00

HOFFMAN, Werner. *Sculpture of Henry Laurens.* 1970. NY. 1st ed. dj. EX. $80.00

HOFLAND, Barbara. *Iwanowna; or, Maid of Moscow.* 1816. NY. 2nd Am ed. EX. $75.00

HOFMANN, W. *Sculpture of Henri Laurens.* 1970. NY. 1st ed. dj. EX. G1. $70.00

HOGAN, J.P. *Code of the Lifemaker.* 1983. Del Rey. 1st ed. dj. EX. P1/R3. $15.00

HOGAN, J.P. *Code of the Lifemaker.* 1983. Del Rey. 1st ed. dj. VG. P1. $12.50

HOGAN, J.P. *Endgame Enigma.* 1987. Bantam. 1st ed. dj. EX. P1. $16.95

HOGAN, J.P. *Voyage From Yesterday.* 1982. Doubleday. 1st ed. dj. EX. F5. $9.00

HOGAN, J.P. *Voyage From Yesteryear.* nd. Book Club. dj. VG. P1. $4.50

HOGARTH, Burne. *Dynamic Anatomy.* 1984. Watson Guptill. 11th print. dj. EX. P1. $20.00

HOGARTH, William. *Life & Works.* 1900. Phil. Barrie. Deluxe ed. 1/1000. H3. $350.00

HOIG, Stan. *W Odyssey of John Simpson Smith...* 1974. Glendale, CA. Ils. 254 p. T5. $15.00

HOKE, Helen. *Too Many Kittens.* 1947. Jr Literary Guild/McKay. Ils. VG. $22.00

HOKE, Helen. *Witches, Witches, Witches.* 1958. NY. Watts. 11th print. 230 p. NM. J3. $7.50

HOLBROOK, J. *10 Years Among the Mail Bags.* 1855. Phil. 1st ed. 432 p. fair. T5. $45.00

HOLBROOK, J. *10 Years Among the Mail Bags.* 1888. Nat Lib Assn. Ils. 8vo. VG. $20.00

HOLBROOK, Stewart. *Dreams the Am Dream.* 1957. Doubleday. 1st ed. 4to. 369 p. dj. EX. $25.00

HOLDEN, D. *House of Saud.* c 1981. Holt Rinehart. 1st Am ed. photos. dj. EX. $15.00

HOLDEN, Genevieve. *Sound an Alarm.* 1954. Crime Club. VG. P1. $7.50

HOLDEN, Max. *Programs of Famous Magicians.* 1937. NY. Holden. 1st ed. 47 p. SftCvr. EX. J3. $6.00

HOLDEN, R.C. *Snow Fury.* nd. Book Club. dj. VG. P1. $4.50

HOLDREDGE, H. *Mammy Pleasant's Partner.* 1954. NY. 1st ed. dj. VG. B3. $15.00

HOLDSTOCK, Robert. *Encyclopedia of SF.* 1978. Octopus. 1st ed. dj. EX. R3. $30.00

HOLDSTOCK, Robert. *Eye Among the Blind.* 1977. Doubleday. 1st Am ed. dj. B10. $6.75

HOLDSTOCK, Robert. *Mythago Wood.* nd. Book Club. dj. EX. C1. $4.50

HOLE, H.G. *Westtown Through the Years.* 1942. Westtown. 1st ed. 8vo. 434 p. VG. V1. $20.00

HOLIDAY & DUFTY. *Lady Sings the Blues.* 1956. Doubleday. 1st ed. octavo. dj. EX. H3. $100.00

HOLLAND, B.W. *25 Ghost Stories.* 1941. Hartsdale. 1st ed. dj. EX. R3. $20.00

HOLLAND, Cecelia. *City of God.* 1979. NY. 1st ed. dj. M. $15.00

HOLLAND, Cecelia. *Earl.* 1971. NY. 1st ed. dj. EX. $12.00

HOLLAND, Cecelia. *Home Ground.* 1981. NY. 1st ed. dj. M. $10.00

HOLLAND, J.G. *Arthur Bonnicastle.* 1905. Scribner. 401 p. G. $5.00

HOLLAND, Maurice. *Architects of Aviation.* 1951. NY. Ils 1st ed. 214 p. dj. VG. T5. $22.50

HOLLAND, R.P. *My Dog Lemon.* 1945. NY. 1st ed. dj. VG. B3. $30.00

HOLLAND, R.P. *Nip & Tuck: Penn Pub Co.* 1939. Phil. Ils Fuller. Ltd 1st ed. 1/74. sgns. slipcase. EX. $500.00

HOLLAND, R.P. *Now Listen, Warden.* nd. (1946) Barnes. 1/7500. 130 p. EX. B10. $6.75

HOLLAND, R.P. *Scattergunning.* 1951. NY. 1st ed. dj. VG. B3. $40.00

HOLLAND, R.P. *Shotgunning in Lowlands.* 1945. NY. 1st ed. 1/3500. boxed. VG. B3. $67.50

HOLLAND, R.S. *Yankee Ships in Pirate Waters.* 1931. NY. Ils Schoonover. 1st ed. VG. $20.00

HOLLAND, Robert. *Hunter.* 1971. Stein Day. 1st ed. dj. EX. F5. $15.00

HOLLAND, W.J. *To the River & Back.* 1913. Putnam. 1st ed. 387 p. F2. $25.00

HOLLEY, Marietta. *My Wayward Pardner; or, My Trials With Josiah...* 1881. Am Pub. 1st ed. gilt gr bdg. C1. $12.50

HOLLEY, Marietta. *Samantha Among the Brethren.* 1892. Funk Wagnall. Ils. 8vo. decor red cloth. VG. B10. $5.00

HOLLEY, Marietta. *Samantha in Europe.* 1896. NY. Ils. VG. $15.00

HOLLICK, Frederick. *Matron's Manual of Midwifery & Diseases of Women.* 1840. NY. 47th ed. 460 p. G. T5. $42.50

HOLLIDAY, R.C. *Literary Lanes & Other Byways.* 1925. Doran. 1st ed. 219 p. dj. VG. B10. $25.00

HOLLIDAY, R.C. *Walking Stick Papers.* 1918. Doran. 1st ed. 309 p. VG. B10. $8.00

HOLLING, H.C. *Book of Cowboys.* 1936. Platt Munk. 1st ed. 4to. dj. VG. $20.00

HOLLIS, Jim. *Teach You a Lesson.* 1955. Harper. 1st ed. dj. VG. P1. $17.50

HOLLISTER, O.J. *CO Volunteers in NM in 1862.* 1962. Lakeside Classic. 308 p. EX. T5. $25.00

HOLLO, Anselm. *Red Cats.* 1967. City Lights. 5th print. EX. B4. $3.00

HOLLOWAY, C. *TX Gun Lore.* 1951. San Antonio. 1st ed. dj. VG. B3. $32.50

HOLLOWAY, Merlyn. *Bibliography 19th-Century British Topographicals...* 1977. London. 1st ed. dj. EX. G1. $25.00

HOLLY, H.H. *Modern Dwellings.* 1878. Harper. gilt bdg. VG. C1. $65.00

HOLLY, J.H. *Encounter.* 1959. Avalon. dj. xl. P1. $6.00

HOLLY, J.H. *Mind Traders.* 1966. Avalon. 1st ed. dj. EX. R3. $12.50

HOLME, Geoffrey. *Design in the Theatre.* 1927. Boni. 1st ed. quarto. dj. VG. H3. $125.00

HOLMES, Charles. *Old Masters & Modern Art.* 1925. London. 3 vols. EX. $15.00

HOLMES, H.H. *Rocket to the Morgue.* 1942. Phantom. 1st ed. wrp. VG. R3. $20.00

HOLMES, J.C. *Death Drag: Selected Poems 1948-1979.* 1979. Poctello, ID. 1/26. sgn. wrp. EX. T9. $65.00

HOLMES, J.C. *Go.* 1952. NY. 1st ed. VG. G1. $75.00

HOLMES, J.C. *Go.* 1952. Scribner. 1st ed. inscr/sgn. dj. VG. B13. $475.00

HOLMES, J.C. *Horn.* 1958. NY. 1st ed. dj. EX. G1. $100.00

HOLMES, J.C. *Horn.* 1958. NY. 1st ed. dj. VG. B3. $50.00

HOLMES, J.C. *Horn.* 1988. Thunder Mouth Pr. 1st print. RS. B4. $15.00

HOLMES, O.W. *Dorothy Q With Ballad of Boston Tea Party.* 1893. Houghton Mifflin. Ils Pyle. 8vo. VG. $20.00

HOLMES, O.W. *Last Leaf.* 1895. Houghton Mifflin. 1st ed. VG. C1. $17.50

HOLMES, O.W. *Mortal Antipathy.* 1885. Boston. 2nd print. EX. $17.00

HOLMES, O.W. *Our 100 Days in Europe.* 1887. Boston. 1st ed. dj. EX. $30.00

HOLMES, O.W. *Works.* 1892. Houghton Mifflin. Artist ed. 1/750. 13 vols. djs. H3. $500.00

HOLMES, William. *Ancient Art of Province of Chiriqui, Colombia.* 1888. GPO. Ils. map. rebound. F2. $75.00

HOLMES. *From Spain By Sea to CA 1519-1669.* 1968. Glendale. Ils. maps. 308 p. VG. A5. $50.00

HOLT, B.B. *Rugs, Oriental & Occidental.* 1901. Chicago. Ils. 4to. A4. $75.00

HOLT, H.G. *House on Jefferson St.* 1971. Holt. 1st ed. 276 p. dj. NM. B10. $7.00

HOLT, Henry. *Call Out the Flying Squad.* 1933. Crime Club. 2nd ed. dj. VG. P1. $20.00

HOLT, Henry. *Midnight Mail.* 1931. Crime Club. 1st ed. VG. P1. $15.00

HOLT, Henry. *On the Cosmic Relations.* 1915. Boston. reprint of 1st ed. VG. $65.00

HOLT, Samuel. *What I Tell You 3 Times Is False.* 1987. Tor Books. 1st ed. dj. EX. F5. $13.00

HOLT, Victoria. *King of the Castle.* nd. Book Club. dj. VG. P1. $4.50

HOLTON, Isaac. *New Granada: 20 Months in the Andes.* 1967. S IL U. reprint of 1857 ed. dj. F2. $15.00

HOLTON, Leonard. *Corner of Paradise.* 1977. St Martin. dj. EX. P1. $15.00

HOLTON, Leonard. *Out of the Depths.* nd. Book Club. dj. VG. P1. $4.50

HOLTON, Leonard. *Touch of Jonah.* 1968. Dodd Mead. 1st ed. dj. VG. P1. $15.00

HOLZWORTH, J. *Wild Grizzlies of AK.* 1930. NY. 1st ed. 417 p. dj. VG. B3. $60.00

HOMAN, W.J. *Children & Quakerism.* 1939. Gillick Pr. 1st print. 8vo. 162 p. V1. $25.00

HOMANS, J.E. *Self-Propelled Vehicles: Treatise on All Forms Automobiles.* 1910. NY. Ils. 8vo. TEG. EX. T1. $25.00

HOMER. *Iliad.* Pope Trans. 1979. Easton Pr. 1st ed. leather bdg. M. $30.00

HOMES, Geoffrey. *Then There Were 3.* 1944. Books Inc. VG. P1. $10.00

HONCOCK, Thomas. *Principles of Peace.* 1829. Phil. 213 p. fair. T5. $15.00

HONEY, W.B. *Eng Pottery & Porcelain.* 1933. London. 1st ed. dj. VG. C2. $40.00

HONEY, W.B. *European Ceramic Art From End of Middle Ages to About 1815.* nd. Book Collector Soc. 1/250. 4to. EX. $65.00

HONOUR, Hugh. *New Golden Land.* 1975. London. 1st ed. 299 p. dj. F2. $20.00

HONSINGER, Welthy. *Beyond the Moon Gate.* nd. (1924) Abington. apparent 1st ed. 176 p. VG. B10. $6.75

HOOBLER, Thomas. *Dr Chill's Project.* 1987. Putnam. 1st ed. dj. EX. F5. $14.00

HOOD, Thomas. *Works.* 1862. London. Moxon. 8 vols. octavo. H3. $350.00

HOOD, Tom. *Jingles & Jokes for the Little Folks.* c 1865. London. 12mo. VG. A4. $35.00

HOOK, Thomas. *Shenandoah Saga.* 1973. Baltimore. Ils. sgn. wrp. T5. $10.95

HOOK, Thomas. *Sky Ship: Akron Era.* 1976. Baltimore. Ils. sgn. 148 p. VG. T5. $8.95

HOOKER, Richard. *MASH.* 1968. NY. Morrow. 1st ed. dj. scarce. EX. K2. $500.00

HOOKER, W.F. *Bullwacker: Adventures of a Frontier Freighter.* 1924. NY. Ils. 167 p. G. T5. $12.50

HOOPER, B.P. *Inquiry Into the State of the Ancient Measures.* 1721. London. 500 p. xl. VG. $200.00

HOOPER, D.M. *Popular Springer Spaniel.* 1963. London. 1st ed. dj. EX. $35.00

HOOPES, Roy. *JM Cain.* 1982. Holt. 1st ed. 684 p. dj. EX. T9. $30.00

HOOVER, Herbert. *Am Individualism.* 1922. NY. 1st ed. inscr/sgn. bl bdg. VG. $100.00

HOOVER, Herbert. *Another Heaven, Another Earth.* 1981. Viking. 1st ed. dj. EX. P1. $15.00

HOOVER, Herbert. *Challenge to Liberty.* 1934. Scribner. 1st ed. 8vo. 212 p. G. V1. $10.00

HOOVER, Herbert. *Challenge to Liberty.* 1935. NY. 3rd ed. inscr/sgn. dj. NM. $80.00

HOOVER, Herbert. *Memoirs of Herbert Hoover: Years of Adventure 1874-1920.* 1951. Macmillan. 2nd ed. 8vo. 496 p. dj. VG. V1. $14.00

HOOVER, Herbert. *Memoirs.* 1952. NY. 1st ed. 3 vols. inscr/sgn. NM. $275.00

HOOVER, Herbert. *Ordeal of Woodrow Wilson*. 1958. NY. Ltd ed. 1/500. sgn. boxed. EX. B3. $175.00

HOPE, Anthony. *God in the Car*. 1894. NY. 1st Am ed. G. $15.00

HOPE, Anthony. *Works*. 1902. Appleton. Author ed. 1/25. 15 vols. gr morocco. H3. $2000.00

HOPE. *Sorrento & Inlaid Work*. 1880. NY. 1st ed. gilt bdg. VG. C2. $55.00

HOPE-MONCRIEFF, A.R. *Romance & Legend of Chivalry*. 1934. 1st ed. bl bdg. VG. C1. $7.50

HOPKINS, A.A. *Lore of the Lock*. 1928. NY. 8vo. $50.00

HOPKINS, A.A. *Magic: Scientific Diversions & Stage Illusions...* 1977. Arno Pr. reprint of 1897 1st ed. dj. NM. J3. $18.00

HOPKINS, A.A. *Magic: Stage Illusions & Scientific Diversions...* 1901. NY. Ils. pictorial bdg. VG. H3. $300.00

HOPKINS, A.A. *20th-Century Magic*. 1898. NY. EX. C2. $65.00

HOPKINS, C.H. *Outs, Precautions, & Challenges*. 1978. Fred Mitchell. 2nd print. SftCvr. M. J3. $5.00

HOPKINS, C.H. *Outs: Precautions & Challenges*. 1940. Phil. 1st ed. 79 p. SftCvr. NM. J3. $8.00

HOPKINS, G.E. *1st Battle of Modern Naval Hist*. 1943. Richmond. 1st ed. 1/199. sgn. dj. EX. $95.00

HOPKINS, Lee. *After They Learn To Dance*. 1974. Capra. Chapbook Series. 1/75. sgn. EX. K2. $20.00

HOPKINS & SUGARMAN. *No 1 Here Gets Out Alive*. 1981. Warner. 1st PB ed. VG. B4. $8.00

HOPPE, Joanne. *Lesson Is Murder*. 1977. Harcourt Brace. 1st ed. sgn. dj. VG. P1. $17.50

HOPPER, James. *Medals of Honor*. 1929. John Day. Ils Rockwell Kent. 1st ed. wht dj. EX. B13. $45.00

HOPPER & STOUT. *Once a Clown, Always a Clown*. 1927. Little Brn. 1st ed. octavo. 238 p. VG. H3. $50.00

HORAN, J.D. *Desperate Women*. 1952. NY. VG. C1. $5.00

HORAN, Kenneth. *Remember the Day*. 1937. NY. 1st ed. dj. EX. $15.00

HORGAN, Paul. *Conquistadors in N Am Hist*. 1963. Farrar Straus. 1st ed. 303 p. F2. $15.00

HORGAN, Paul. *Of Am E & W: Selection From Writings of Paul Horgan*. 1982. Farrar Straus. UP. wrp. EX. B13. $50.00

HORGAN, Paul. *Thin Mt Air*. 1977. Farrar Straus. 1st ed. dj. xl. G. $7.00

HORLER, Sydney. *Curse of Doone*. 1930. Mystery League. 1st ed. dj. VG. P1. $20.00

HORLER, Sydney. *Evil Chateau*. nd. Grosset Dunlap. dj. EX. P1. $25.00

HORLER, Sydney. *False Face*. 1926. Doran. 1st ed. VG. P1. $20.00

HORLER, Sydney. *False Purple*. 1932. Mystery League. 1st ed. dj. VG. P1. $10.00

HORLER, Sydney. *Harlequin of Death*. 1933. John Long. xl. P1. $10.00

HORLER, Sydney. *High Hazard*. 1950. Hodder Stoughton. 3rd ed. VG. P1. $12.00

HORLER, Sydney. *Horror's Head*. 1934. Hodder Stoughton. 4th ed. VG. P1. $20.00

HORLER, Sydney. *House of Secrets*. nd. Thomas Nelson. dj. VG. P1. $17.50

HORLER, Sydney. *Man From Scotland Yard*. 1970. John Long. dj. VG. P1. $15.00

HORLER, Sydney. *Man Who Walked With Death*. nd. Grosset Dunlap. VG. P1. $7.50

HORLER, Sydney. *Mystery of the 7 Cafes*. 1935. Hodder Stoughton. 1st ed. VG. P1. $20.00

HORLER, Sydney. *Peril*. 1930. Mystery League. 1st ed. dj. EX. F5. $35.00

HORLER, Sydney. *Peril*. 1930. Mystery League. 1st ed. G. R3. $10.00

HORLER, Sydney. *Peril*. 1930. Mystery League. 1st ed. VG. P1. $25.00

HORLER, Sydney. *Tiger Standish*. 1933. Crime Club. VG. P1. $15.00

HORN, Calvin. *NM Troubled Years*. 1963. Albuquerque. 1st ed. dj. EX. $25.00

HORN, E.N. *Faster Faster*. 1946. Coward McCann. dj. xl. P1. $6.00

HORN, Maurice. *Women in the Comics*. 1977. Chelsea House. 1st ed. dj. VG. P1. $15.00

HORN, Stanley. *Hermitage: Home of Old Hickory*. 1950. NY. 1st ed. 226 p. VG. B3. $17.50

HORN & HORN. *Trader Horn*. 1927. Grosset Dunlap. Photoplay ed. dj. VG. P1. $15.00

HORNADAY. *Am Nat Hist*. 1910. NY. Ils. lg 8vo. A6. $30.00

HORNBLOW, Arthur. *Hist of the Theatre in Am: From Beginning to Present Times*. 1919. Lippincott. 1st ed. 2 vols. VG. H3. $125.00

HORNBY, C.H. *Descriptive Bibliography of Books Printed at Ashendene Pr*. 1935. Chelsea. 1/390. sgn. slipcase. EX. H3. $3000.00

HORNER, D.L. *Murder by the Dozen*. 1935. Dingwall Rock. 1st ed. VG. P1. $25.00

HORNER, H.H. *Lincoln & Greeley*. 1953. IL U. 432 p. dj. VG. S1. $9.00

HORNIG, Doug. *Dark Side*. 1986. Mysterious Pr. 1st ed. dj. EX. F5. $12.00

HORNSBY, Rogers. *My War With Baseball*. 1962. NY. 1st ed. dj. VG. B3. $27.50

HORNSTEIN, L.H. *World Literature*. nd. Mentor. 14th print. P1. $2.50

HORNUNG, E.W. *Shadow of the Rope*. 1909. Scribner. VG. P1. $15.00

HORNUNG, E.W. *Stingaree*. 1909. Scribner. VG. P1. $15.00

HOROVITZ, MCNALLY, & MELFI. *Morning, Noon, & Night: 3 1-Act Plays*. 1969. Random House. 1st ed. inscr. dj. EX. B13. $65.00

HOROWITZ, S.L. *Mohammed Bey's Routine With Okito Coin Box & More...* 1963. Tannen. 53 p. SftCvr. EX. J3. $4.00

HORRICKS, Raymond. *Count Basie & His Orchestra*. 1957. Citadel. 1st Am ed. 320 p. dj. EX. H3. $50.00

HORSLEY, Samuel. *9 Sermons on Nature of Evidence...Our Lord's Resurrection...* 1816. NY/Phil/Boston. 274 p. VG. $200.00

HORST, Louis. *Pre-Classic Dance Forms*. 1960. NY. Kamin Dance Pub. octavo. gr wrp. EX. H3. $45.00

HORSTING, Jessie. *Stephen King at the Movies*. nd. Starlog Signet. Special ed. P1. $9.95

HORTON, Guy. *Some Legal Aspects of Life Insurance Trusts*. 1927. VT. 1st ed. 8vo. 49 p. VG. B10. $4.00

HORTON, R.G. *Youth's Hist of Great Civil War in the US*. 1867. NY. 12 mo. 384 p. G4. $19.00

HORTON, R.G. *Youth's Hist of War of 1861*. 1925. Dallas. 2nd Revised ed. EX. $25.00

HORWITZ, Basil. *Mental Magic of Basil Horwitz Vol 1*. 1984. Martin Breese. 2nd ed. 64 p. SftCvr. NM. J3. $12.00

HORWOOD, William. *Callanish*. 1984. Watts. 1st ed. dj. EX. P1. $15.00

HOSE, Charles. *Natural Man: Record From Borneo.* 1926. London. Macmillan. 1st ed. VG. $95.00

HOSKINS, Robert. *Shattered People.* 1975. Doubleday. 1st ed. dj. xl. P1. $5.00

HOTCHNER, A.E. *Papa Hemingway.* 1967. Bantam. P1. $3.00

HOTTES, A.C. *1001 Garden Questions Answered.* 1934. De La Mare. not 1st ed. 293 p. VG. B10. $3.00

HOUCK, Louis. *Hist of MO From Earliest Explorations.* 1908. Chicago. 1st ed. 3 vols. VG. $175.00

HOUDINI, Harry. *Houdini's Big Little Book of Magic.* 1927. Whitman. 1st ed. 191 p. VG. J3. $27.00

HOUDINI, Harry. *Houdini's Paper Magic.* 1922. NY. Ils 1st ed. 206 p. VG. B3. $70.00

HOUDINI, Harry. *Houdini's Paper Magic.* 1941. Dutton. 5th print. 206 p. VG. $15.00

HOUDINI, Harry. *Magician Among the Spirits.* 1924. NY. 1st ed. 294 p. VG. B3. $115.00

HOUDINI, Harry. *Magician Among the Spirits.* 1972. Arno Pr. reprint of 1924 1st ed. dj. NM. J3. $15.00

HOUDINI, Harry. *Miracle Mongers & Their Methods, a Complete Expose.* 1920. Dutton. 1st ed. 240 p. VG. J3. $40.00

HOUDINI, Harry. *Miracle Mongers & Their Methods, a Complete Expose.* 1981. Prometheus. 240 p. dj. NM. J3. $10.00

HOUGH, Emerson. *Magnificient Adventure.* 1916. Appleton. 2nd ed. 355 p. G. B10. $3.00

HOUGH, H.B. *Alcoholic to His Sons.* 1954. NY. 1st ed. dj. VG. B3. $15.00

HOUGH, H.B. *Long Anchorage.* 1947. NY. 1st ed. dj. VG. B3. $15.00

HOUGH, Richard. *Buller's Victory.* 1984. Morrow. 1st ed. dj. EX. F5. $15.00

HOUGH, Richard. *Wings of Victory.* 1980. Morrow. 1st ed. dj. EX. P1. $12.50

HOUGH, S.B. *Bronze Perseus.* 1962. Walker. dj. VG. P1. $10.00

HOUGH, S.B. *Dear Daughter Dead.* 1966. Walker. 1st ed. dj. VG. P1. $10.00

HOUGH, S.B. *Frontier Incident.* 1951. Crowell. dj. EX. P1. $20.00

HOUGH, Walter. *Archaeological Field Work in NE AZ.* 1901. US Nat Mus. xl. A5. $7.00

HOUGHTON, Claude. *Beast.* 1936. Belfast. Quota Pr. Ils Kerr. 1/250. sgns. H3. $75.00

HOUGHTON, Claude. *Christina.* 1936. Heinemann. sgn. dj. H3. $50.00

HOUGHTON, Claude. *Hudson Rejoins the Herd.* 1939. London. Collins. sgn. dj. H3. $50.00

HOUGHTON, Claude. *Julian Grant Loses His Way.* 1933. Heinemann. sgn. dj. H3. $60.00

HOUGHTON, Claude. *Passing of the 3rd Floor Back.* c 1937. Queensway Pr. sgn. dj. H3. $50.00

HOUGHTON, Claude. *Strangers.* 1938. London. Collins. sgn. dj. H3. $45.00

HOUGHTON, Claude. *Tavern of Dreams.* 1919. London. Richards. inscr. dj. H3. $60.00

HOUGHTON, Claude. *This Was Ivor Trent.* 1935. Doubleday. 1st ed. B10. $5.00

HOUGHTON, Claude. *This Was Ivor Trent.* 1935. Heinemann. 1st ed. VG. P1. $12.00

HOUGHTON, Claude. *3 Fantastic Tales.* 1934. London. Joiner. sgn. TEG. H3. $75.00

HOUGRON, Jean. *Question of Character.* 1958. NY. 1st ed. dj. EX. $10.00

HOUSE, H.D. *Wild Flowers of NY.* 1918. NY U. 2 vols. clr pls. VG. T3. $75.00

HOUSE, H.D. *Wild Flowers of NY.* 1923. NY U. 2 vols. A5. $125.00

HOUSEHOLD, Goeffrey. *Sending.* 1980. Little Brn. 1st Am ed. dj. VG. R3. $10.00

HOUSEHOLD, Goeffrey. *Spanish Cave.* 1948. Coronet. 1st ed. wrp. VG. R3. $10.00

HOUSEMAN, Laurence. *Angels & Ministers.* 1922. 1st Am ed. dj. VG. C1. $9.00

HOUSMAN, A.E. *Confines of Criticism: Cambridge Inaugural 1911.* 1969. Cambridge. 1st ed. sm 8vo. 54 p. EX. R4. $30.00

HOUSMAN, A.E. *Intro Lecture: 1892.* 1937. NY. 1st ed. dj. EX. $20.00

HOUSMAN, A.E. *Last Poems.* 1922. London. 1st ed. dj. EX. $40.00

HOUSMAN, A.E. *More Poems.* 1936. London. 1st ed. dj. EX. $28.00

HOUSMAN, Laurence. *Cynthia.* 1947. Sidgwick Jackson. 1/500. sgn. slipcase. H3. $75.00

HOUSMAN, Laurence. *Golden Sovereign.* 1937. Jonathan Cape. 1st ed. dj. H3. $75.00

HOUSMAN, Laurence. *King John of Tingald.* 1937. 1st Am ed. VG. C1. $6.50

HOUSMAN, Laurence. *Stories From the Arabian Nights.* 1907. London. Ils/sgn Dulac. 1/350. orig vellum. EX. H3. $1000.00

HOUSTON, J.D. *Occurrence at Norman's Burger Castle.* 1972. Capra. Chapbook Series. 1/100. sgn. EX. K2. $20.00

HOUSTON, J.D. *3 Songs for My Father.* 1974. Capra. Chapbook Series. 1/75. sgn. EX. K2. $20.00

HOUSTON, M.B. *Moon of Delight.* 1931. NY. 1st ed. dj. EX. $10.00

HOUSTON, Robert. *Nation Thief.* 1984. NY. 1st ed. inscr. dj. EX. T9. $40.00

HOUSTON. *Critical Study of Nullification in SC.* c 1896. Cambridge. xl. VG. G4. $16.00

HOVEY, H. *Mammoth Cave of KY.* 1912. Louisville. Revised 2nd ed. fld map. 131 p. VG. B3. $35.00

HOWARD, B. *Gemstone Reading for Profit.* 1988. New Zealand. Brookfield Pr. 1st ed. 40 p. NM. J3. $20.00

HOWARD, Constance. *Ameliar Anne & the Gr Umbrella.* 1920. Macrae Smith. dj. G. B7. $43.00

HOWARD, David. *Royal Indian Hospital of Mexico City.* 1980. Tempre. 1st ed. 99 p. wrp. F2. $10.00

HOWARD, DE CAMP, & CARTER. *Conan of Cimmeria.* 1969. Lancer. 1st ed. wrp. EX. R3. $25.00

HOWARD, Hartley. *Other Side of the Door.* 1953. Collins. 1st ed. dj. xl. P1. $10.00

HOWARD, Joan. *Story of John J Audubon.* 1954. Signature Books. Ils Castellon. EX. $8.00

HOWARD, L.O. *Fighting the Insects.* 1933. NY. 1st ed. 333 p. dj. VG. B3. $22.50

HOWARD, L.R. *Rather Remarkable Father.* 1959. NY. 1st ed. dj. EX. $15.00

HOWARD, Munroe. *Call Me Brick.* 1967. NY. 1st ed. dj. EX. $12.00

HOWARD, Munroe. *Fires of Autumn.* 1961. London. 1st ed. dj. EX. $12.00

HOWARD, Munroe. *Whole Heart.* 1944. London. 1st ed. dj. EX. $14.00

HOWARD, O.O. *My Life & Experiences Among Hostile Indians.* 1907. Hartford. 1st ed. 570 p. VG. B3. $100.00

HOWARD, R.E. *Blk Colossus.* 1979. Donald Grant. 1st ed. dj. EX. P1. $35.00

HOWARD, R.E. *Coming of Conan.* 1953. Gnome. 1st ed. dj. EX. P1. $85.00

HOWARD, R.E. *Conan the Barbarian.* 1954. NY. 1st ed. as issued. K2. $100.00

HOWARD, R.E. *Conan the Conqueror.* 1953. Ace. 1st ed. wrp. VG. R3. $30.00

HOWARD, R.E. *Dark Man & Others.* 1963. Arkham House. 1st ed. dj. VG. R3. $75.00

HOWARD, R.E. *Devil in Iron.* 1976. Donald Grant. dj. EX. P1. $35.00

HOWARD, R.E. *From the Hells Beneath the Hells.* 1975. Alternate World Recording. 1st ed. sgn. M. R3. $25.00

HOWARD, R.E. *Garden of Fear.* 1945. Crawford. 1st ed. wrp. EX. R3. $10.00

HOWARD, R.E. *Hour of the Dragon.* 1977. Berkley Putnam. dj. EX. R3. $15.00

HOWARD, R.E. *Jewels of Gwahlur.* 1979. Donald Grant. 1st ed. dj. EX. P1. $35.00

HOWARD, R.E. *Lord of the Dead.* 1981. Donald Grant. 1st ed. dj. EX. R3. $25.00

HOWARD, R.E. *People of the Blk Circle.* 1974. Donald Grant. dj. EX. P1. $40.00

HOWARD, R.E. *People of the Blk Circle.* 1978. Berkley Putnam. dj. VG. P1. $25.00

HOWARD, R.E. *Post Oaks & Sand Roughs.* 1990. Donald Grant. dj. EX. P1. $25.00

HOWARD, R.E. *Queen of the Blk Coast.* 1978. Donald Grant. dj. EX. P1. $35.00

HOWARD, R.E. *Red Nails.* 1975. Donald Grant. dj. EX. P1. $50.00

HOWARD, R.E. *Red Nails.* 1979. Berkley Putnam. dj. EX. R3. $15.00

HOWARD, R.E. *Red Shadows.* 1978. Donald Grant. Ils/sgn Jeff Jones. 1st ed. dj. EX. P1. $75.00

HOWARD, R.E. *Rogues in the House.* 1976. Donald Grant. dj. EX. P1. $35.00

HOWARD, R.E. *Shadows of Dreams.* 1989. Donald Grant. 1st ed. dj. EX. P1. $25.00

HOWARD, R.E. *Son of the Wht Wolf.* 1977. Starmont. 1st ed. dj. EX. R3. $20.00

HOWARD, R.E. *Sowers of Thunder.* 1976. Donald Grant. 2nd ed. dj. EX. P1. $25.00

HOWARD, R.E. *Swords of Shahrazar.* 1976. Starmont. 1st HrdCvr ed. dj. EX. R3. $15.00

HOWARD, R.E. *Tower of the Elephant.* 1975. Donald Grant. dj. EX. P1. $35.00

HOWARD, R.E. *Vultures.* 1973. Fistioneer Books. 1st ed. dj. EX. R3. $25.00

HOWARD, R.E. *Witch Shall Be Born.* 1975. Donald Grant. dj. EX. P1. $40.00

HOWARD, R.E. *2 Against Tyre.* 1975. Macmillan. 1st ed. 1/600. EX. F5. $30.00

HOWARD, Winifred. *Vengeance of Fu Chang.* 1932. Oxford U Pr. 1st ed. inscr. dj. EX. R3. $25.00

HOWARD & DE CAMP. *Tales of Conan.* 1955. Gnome. 1st ed. dj. EX. R3. $75.00

HOWARD & LUPOFF. *Return of Skullface.* 1977. Starmont. 1st ed. dj. EX. R3. $15.00

HOWARD. *Pen Pictures of the Plains.* 1902. Denver. Reed. Ils. photos. poems. A5. $40.00

HOWATCH, Susan. *April's Grave.* 1974. Stein Day. dj. xl. P1. $5.00

HOWATT, G.M. *Let's Make Magic.* 1945. Chicago. Ireland. 1st ed. 27 p. EX. J3. $3.00

HOWBERT, A.R. *Reminiscences of the War.* 1888. Springfield, OH. 1st ed. 388 p. VG. T5. $175.00

HOWDEN-SMITH, Arthur. *Hate.* nd. Brentano. repro dj. VG. R3. $20.00

HOWDEN-SMITH, Arthur. *Treasure of the Bucoleon.* 1923. Brentano. 1st ed. repro dj. VG. R3. $20.00

HOWE, A.H. *Scientific Piano Tuning & Servicing.* 1955. Howe. octavo. 267 p. VG. H3. $35.00

HOWE, G.F. *Battle Hist of 1st Armored Division.* 1954. WA. 1st ed. dj. EX. $35.00

HOWE, W. *Professional Gunsmithing.* 1946. Plantersville, SC. 1st ed. dj. VG. B3. $65.00

HOWE & ALLEN. *Birds of MA.* 1901. Cambridge. Ltd 1st ed. 1/450 EX T1. $45.00

HOWELL, A.H. *FL Bird Life.* 1932. NY. 1st ed. 72 clr pls. VG. B3. $95.00

HOWELL, Anthony. *Imruil.* 1970. London. Barrie Jenkins. 1/50. sgn. H3. $75.00

HOWELL, James. *Familiar Letters of James Howell.* 1907. Boston. Ltd 1st ed. 1/220. 4 vols. VG. T1. $85.00

HOWELLS, W.D. *Certain Delightful Eng Towns.* 1906. Harper. inscr. TEG. gilt red bdg. H3. $75.00

HOWELLS, W.D. *Chance Acquaintance.* 1873. Boston. 1st ed. EX. $45.00

HOWELLS, W.D. *Dr Breen's Practice.* 1881. Osgood. 1st ed. 272 p. VG. B10. $16.25

HOWELLS, W.D. *My Mark Twain.* 1910. NY. 1st ed. VG. B3. $35.00

HOWELLS, W.D. *Questionable Shapes.* 1903. Harper. 1st ed. VG. R3. $35.00

HOWELLS, W.D. *Rise of Silas Lapham.* 1885. Boston. 1st ed. 2nd state. EX. $32.00

HOWELLS, W.D. *Roman Holidays & Others.* 1908. Harper. 1st ed. 302 p. TEG. B10. $8.50

HOWELLS, W.D. *Their Silver Wedding Anniversary.* 1899. NY. 2 vols. EX. $32.00

HOWELLS, W.D. *Venetian Life.* 1883. Leipzig. 8vo. AEG. EX. $110.00

HOWES, Royce. *Case of the Copy-Hook Killing.* 1945. Dutton. 1st ed. dj. VG. P1. $10.00

HOWEY, M.E. *Creative Marketing for the Magician...* 1988. Mesa, AZ. Howey. 1st ed. 51 p. w/8 cassette tapes. J3. $95.00

HOWITT, William. *Homes & Haunts of the Most Eminent British Poets.* 1847. London. Bentley. 2 vols. VG. $125.00

HOWITT, William. *Life in Germany.* 1849. London. Routledge. Ils Sargeant/Woods. VG. $125.00

HOWITT, William. *N Heights of London.* 1869. London. VG. $100.00

HOWITT, William. *Rural & Domestic Life of Germany.* 1842. London. Ils Sargeant. VG. $75.00

HOWITT, William. *Rural Life of Eng.* 1840. London. 2nd ed. Tout bdg. VG. $75.00

HOWITT, William. *Visits to Remarkable Places.* 1840. London. 1st Series. VG. $75.00

HOYLAND, J.S. *Light of Christ.* 1928. London. Swarthmore. 1st print. 16mo. VG. V1. $7.00

HOYLE, Fred. *Blk Cloud.* nd. Book Club. VG. P1. $3.00

HOYLE, Fred. *Element 79.* nd. Book Club. dj. VG. P1. $4.50

HOYLE, Fred. *October the 1st Is Too Late.* nd. Book Club. dj. VG. P1. $4.50

HOYLE, Fred. *October the 1st Is Too Late.* 1963. Harper. 1st ed. dj. EX. R3. $25.00

HOYLE, Fred. *Ossian's Ride.* 1959. Harper. 1st Am ed. dj. VG. R3. $20.00

HOYLE & GEOFFREY. *Incandescent Ones.* 1977. Harper Row. 1st ed. dj. RS. R3. $20.00

HOYLE & GEOFFREY. *Inferno.* 1973. Harper. 1st Am ed. dj. VG. R3. $12.50

HOYNE, T.T. *Intrigue on the Upper Level.* 1934. Reilly Lee. 1st ed. G. R3. $17.50

HOYT, C.K. *Interior Spaces Designed by Architects.* 1981. McGraw Hill. giant folio. dj. EX. $65.00

HOYT, Deristhe. *World's Painters & Their Pictures.* nd. (1898) Boston. Ginn. 272 p. VG. B10. $4.25

HOYT, E. *Peabody Influence.* 1968. NY. 1st ed. 302 p. dj. VG. B3. $15.00

HOYT, E.P. *Marilyn, the Tragic Venus.* 1965. NY. 1st ed. dj. EX. K1. $22.50

HOYT, Helen. *Leaves of Wild Grape.* nd. (1920) Harcourt. VG. B10. $5.00

HOYT, Richard. *Decoys.* 1980. Evans. 1st ed. dj. EX. F5. $12.00

HOYT, Richard. *Head of State.* 1985. Tor Books. 1st ed. dj. EX. P1. $15.00

HRUSKA, Alan. *Borrowed Time.* 1985. Baen. 1st ed. wrp. EX. F5. $6.00

HUBBARD, B.C. *Essay on Art & Life As Written by Vernon Lee...* 1896. NY. 1/109. sgn. T6. $150.00

HUBBARD, Bela. *Memorials of Half Century.* 1888. NY. Ils. 581 p. VG. B3. $80.00

HUBBARD, Elbert. *Book of the Roycrofters.* 1923. Roycroft. VG. $40.00

HUBBARD, Elbert. *Complete Writings.* 1914. Roycroft. Author ed. 1/1000. sgn. 20 vols. EX. H3. $2500.00

HUBBARD, Elbert. *Elbert Hubbard Book of Wise & Witty Says From Works...* nd. Whitman. apparent 1st ed. 92 p. EX. B10. $6.25

HUBBARD, Elbert. *Little Journeys to Homes of the Great.* 1922. Roycroft. Memorial ed. 14 vols. djs. EX. T1. $250.00

HUBBARD, Elbert. *Pig Pen Pete; or, Some Chums of Mine.* 1914. Roycroft. VG. $30.00

HUBBARD, Elbert. *This Then Is a William Morris Book.* 1907. Roycroft. 1/203 on Japan. sgn. 12mo. NM. A4. $175.00

HUBBARD, Kin. *Abe Martin's Barbed Wire.* 1928. Indianapolis. Stated 1st ed. dj. EX. J2. $40.00

HUBBARD, L.R. *Alien Affair.* 1986. Bridge. 1st ed. dj. EX. P1. $25.00

HUBBARD, L.R. *Battlefield Earth.* nd. Bridge. 1st ed. dj. EX. P1. $25.00

HUBBARD, L.R. *Battlefield Earth.* 1982. Bridge. 1st ed. dj. EX. R3. $30.00

HUBBARD, L.R. *Blk Genesis: Fortress of Evil.* 1986. Bridge. 1st ed. dj. EX. P1. $25.00

HUBBARD, L.R. *Child Dianetics.* 1982. Bridge. dj. EX. P1. $15.00

HUBBARD, L.R. *Death Quest.* 1986. Bridge. 1st ed. dj. EX. P1. $25.00

HUBBARD, L.R. *Death's Deputy.* 1948. Fantasy. 1st ed. dj. EX. R3. $225.00

HUBBARD, L.R. *Dianetics.* 1950. Hermitage House. 1st ed. dj. VG. K2. $250.00

HUBBARD, L.R. *Dianetics.* 1950. NY. 1st ed. 4th print. dj. w/return card. P4. $75.00

HUBBARD, L.R. *Disaster.* 1987. Bridge. ARC. wrp. M. R3. $50.00

HUBBARD, L.R. *Disaster.* 1987. Bridge. 1st ed. dj. EX. P1. $25.00

HUBBARD, L.R. *Doomed Planet.* 1987. Bridge. 1st ed. dj. EX. P1. $25.00

HUBBARD, L.R. *Enemy Within.* 1986. Bridge. 1st ed. dj. EX. P1. $25.00

HUBBARD, L.R. *Fortune of Fear.* 1986. Bridge. ARC. wrp. EX. R3. $50.00

HUBBARD, L.R. *Fortune of Fear.* 1986. Bridge. 1st ed. dj. EX. P1. $25.00

HUBBARD, L.R. *Invaders' Plan.* nd. Book Club. dj. EX. P1. $5.00

HUBBARD, L.R. *Invaders' Plan.* 1985. Bridge. 1st ed. dj. EX. P1. $25.00

HUBBARD, L.R. *Kingslayer.* 1949. Fantasy. 1st ed. dj. EX. R3. $225.00

HUBBARD, L.R. *Lives You Wished To Lead But Never Dared.* 1978. Theta Pr. 1st ed. M. R3. $75.00

HUBBARD, L.R. *Mission Earth.* c 1980s. Bridge. 1st ed. 10 vols. M. R3. $300.00

HUBBARD, L.R. *Mission Earth.* nd. Bridge. Ltd 1st ed. 1/1000. 10 vols. djs. EX. P1. $250.00

HUBBARD, L.R. *Mission Earth/Blk Genesis.* 1985 & 1986. Blk Genesis. 1st ed. 2 vols. djs. EX. T1. $90.00

HUBBARD, L.R. *My Best SF Story.* 1949. Merlin. 1st ed. dj. EX. R3. $100.00

HUBBARD, L.R. *Ole Doc Methuselah.* 1970. Theta Pr. 1st ed. dj. P1. $150.00

HUBBARD, L.R. *Ole Doc Methuselah.* 1970. Theta Pr. 1st ed. R3. $75.00

HUBBARD, L.R. *Phoenix Lectures.* 1971. Am St Hill Organization. dj. VG. P1. $20.00

HUBBARD, L.R. *Triton.* 1949. Fantasy. 1st ed. dj. EX. R3. $200.00

HUBBARD, L.R. *Villainy Victorious.* 1987. Bridge. 1st ed. dj. EX. P1. $25.00

HUBBARD, M.A. *Murder Takes the Veil.* 1950. Bruce. 2nd ed. dj. VG. P1. $15.00

HUBBARD, P.M. *Graveyard.* 1975. Atheneum. 1st ed. dj. xl. P1. $5.00

HUBBARD, P.M. *Rooted Sorrow.* 1973. Macmillan. 1st ed. dj. xl. P1. $5.00

HUBBARD, Ralph. *Wolf Song.* 1935. Garden City. 1st ed. dj. VG. B3. $27.50

HUBBARD & HUBBARD. *Justinian & Theodora.* 1906. E Aurora. Ils. 221 p. VG. T5. $47.50

HUBBELL, R.W. *4000 Years of Television.* 1942. Putnam. 1st ed. presentation. 256 p. VG. H3. $150.00

HUBBEN, William. *Exiled Pilgrim.* 1943. Macmillan. 1st ed. sgn. 12mo. 261 p. dj. VG. V1. $12.00

HUBER, Morton. *Vanishing Japan.* 1965. NY. Am Photo. dj. G. B10. $7.00

HUBIN, A.J. *Best Detective Stories 1971.* 1971. Dutton. 2nd ed. dj. xl. P1. $7.50

HUBIN, A.J. *Bibliography of Crime Fiction 1749-1975.* nd. Pub Inc. HrdCvr ed. P1. $75.00

HUCKEL, Oliver. *Wagner's Siegfried.* 1910. NY. 1st ed. VG. C1. $14.00

HUDDLE, David. *High Spirits.* 1989. Godine. 1st ed. dj. EX. K2. $17.95

HUDDLESTON, Sisley. *What's Right With Am.* 1930. Lippincott. 1st ed. 251 p. VG. B10. $5.00

HUDLESTON, F.J. *Warriors in Undress.* 1926. Boston. Ils 1st ed. 229 p. G. T5. $22.50

HUDSON, Dean. *Lust Dream.* 1962. Corinth. 1st ed. wrp. EX. F5. $8.00

HUDSON, W.H. *Bird of la Plata.* 1920. London. Ltd 1st ed. 2 vols. EX. $125.00

HUDSON, W.H. *Collected Works.* 1922-1923. Dent. 1/850. 24 vols. EX. H3. $3200.00

HUDSON, W.H. *Far Away & Long Ago: A Hist of My Early Life.* 1943. Buenos Aires. Ltd Ed Club. 1/1500. horsehair/rawhide bdg. C4. $125.00

HUDSON, W.H. *Gr Mansions.* nd. 3 Sirens Pr. Ils. 276 p. F2. $10.00

HUDSON, W.H. *Gr Mansions.* 1944. Modern Lib. dj. VG. P1. $10.00

HUDSON, W.H. *Man Napoleon.* 1915. London. Harrup. Ils Myrbach. NM. $75.00

HUDSON, W.H. *Purple Land.* nd. Dutton. Ils Henderson. 368 p. F2. $15.00

HUDSON, Walt. *Magical Puppeteer (Another Approach for Entertaining Kids).* 1980. Magic Media Ltd. M. J3. $5.00

HUDSON, Wilson. *Healer of Los Olmos & Other Mexican Lore.* 1966. S Methodist U. facsimile of 1951 ed. 139 p. F2. $10.00

HUEFFER, F.M. *Feather.* 1892. London. Unwin. 2nd ed. TEG. red bdg. EX. $125.00

HUEMER, Richard. *Dragon on the Hill Road.* 1958. Los Angeles. sgn. dj. EX. C1. $35.00

HUFFAKER, Clair. *7 Ways From Sundown.* 1961. Crest. 1st ed. wrp. EX. F5. $8.00

HUGARD, Jean. *Card Manipulations Series 1.* 1933. NY City. Holden. 1st ed. sgn. VG. J3. $7.00

HUGARD, Jean. *Close-Up Magic.* 1964. Tannen. 3rd print. 57 p. sgn. EX. J3. $3.00

HUGARD, Jean. *Coin Magic.* 1935. NY. Holden. 1st ed. EX. J3. $4.00

HUGARD, Jean. *Encyclopedia of Card Tricks.* nd. Tannen. 3rd print. 402 p. dj. NM. J3. $12.00

HUGARD, Jean. *Encyclopedia of Card Tricks.* 1937. NY. Holden. 1st ed. sgn. 403 p. Deluxe bdg. VG. J3. $32.00

HUGARD, Jean. *Hugard's Annual of Magic 1937.* 1937. NY. Holden. 1st ed. 141 p. EX. J3. $12.00

HUGARD, Jean. *Hugard's Annual of Magic 1938-1939.* 1939. NY. Holden. 1st ed. 137 p. EX. J3. $8.00

HUGARD, Jean. *Modern Magic Manual.* 1943. Harper. 4th ed. 345 p. dj. EX. J3. $15.00

HUGARD, Jean. *Sealed Mysteries of Pocket Magic Vol 1.* nd. Brooklyn. 1st ed. 14 p. SftCvr. EX. J3. $4.00

HUGARD & BRAUE. *Invisible Pass.* 1946. Brooklyn. 1st ed. 29 p. EX. J3. $9.00

HUGARD & BRAUE. *Royal Road to Card Magic.* 1947. Harper. 1st ed. 292 p. VG. J3. $15.00

HUGGINS, Nathan. *Harlem Renaissance.* 1973. Oxford. 1st PB ed. 343 p. B10. $3.50

HUGHART, Barry. *Story of the Stone.* 1988. Doubleday. 1st ed. RS. M. R3. $17.95

HUGHART, Barry. *8 Skilled Gentlemen.* 1991. Doubleday. ARC. wrp. w/pub letter. EX. F5. $15.00

HUGHES, C.E. *Memorial Address for Warren G Harding.* 1927. Memorial ed. EX. $15.00

HUGHES, Cledwyn. *He Dared Not Look Behind.* 1947. Wyn. dj. VG. P1. $15.00

HUGHES, D.B. *Blackbirder.* 1943. Duell Sloan Pierce. 1st ed. VG. P1. $15.00

HUGHES, D.B. *Blackbirder.* 1944. Tower. dj. VG. P1. $15.00

HUGHES, D.B. *Delicate Ape.* 1945. Armed Services/1st ed. EX. T9. $25.00

HUGHES, D.B. *Delicate Ape.* 1945. Tower. 1st ed. VG. P1. $10.00

HUGHES, D.B. *Delicate Ape.* 1945. Tower. 2nd ed. VG. P1. $6.00

HUGHES, D.B. *Dorothy B Hughes' Mystery Reader.* 1944. Forum. 2nd ed. VG. P1. $5.00

HUGHES, D.B. *Dread Journey.* nd. Duell Sloan Pierce. 3rd ed. dj. VG. P1. $15.00

HUGHES, D.B. *Dread Journey.* 1946. Tower. dj. VG. P1. $15.00

HUGHES, D.B. *Fallen Sparrow.* nd. Duell Sloan Pierce. VG. P1. $10.00

HUGHES, D.B. *Fallen Sparrow.* 1942. Duell Sloan Pearce. 1st ed. inscr/sgn. dj. VG. T9. $165.00

HUGHES, D.B. *Ride the Pink Horse.* nd. Collier. VG. P1. $10.00

HUGHES, J.A. *Light of the World: William Penn Lecture.* 1933. Phil. Book Committee of Friends. 12mo. 56 p. dj. VG. V1. $6.00

HUGHES, J.S. *Little Ships.* nd. (1933) Dutton. probable 1st Am ed. 187 p. VG. B10. $16.25

HUGHES, Langston. *African Treasury.* 1960. Crown. 1st ed. inscr. dj. EX. K2. $350.00

HUGHES, Langston. *Big Sea.* 1940. Knopf. 1st ed. dj. EX. B13. $250.00

HUGHES, Langston. *Clothes to the Jew.* 1927. NY. 1st ed. dj. EX. P4. $275.00

HUGHES, Langston. *I Wonder As I Wander.* 1956. NY. 1st ed. dj. VG. B3. $60.00

HUGHES, Langston. *Laughing To Keep From Crying.* 1952. Holt. 1st ed. inscr. dj. EX. K2. $575.00

HUGHES, Langston. *Not Without Laughter.* 1933. Knopf. 1st ed. inscr. H3. $350.00

HUGHES, Langston. *Shakespeare in Harlem.* 1947. Knopf. 3rd print. inscr. dj. H3. $300.00

HUGHES, Langston. *Simple Speaks His Mind.* 1950. Simon Schuster. 1st ed. sgn. wrp. EX. K2. $150.00

HUGHES, Langston. *Tambourines to Glory.* 1959. London. Gollancz. 1st ed. dj. EX. B13. $85.00

HUGHES, Langston. *1-Way Ticket.* 1949. NY. 1st ed. VG. B3. $42.50

HUGHES, Monica. *Isis Pedlar.* 1983. Atheneum. 1st ed. M. R3. $17.50

HUGHES, Monica. *Keeper of the Isis Light.* 1981. Atheneum. 1st ed. M. R3. $17.50

HUGHES, Richard. *Gypsy-Night & Other Poems.* 1922. Chicago. Ils Bianco. 1st ed. 1/63. sgn. EX. P4. $225.00

HUGHES, Richard. *Innocent Voyage.* 1944. Ltd Ed Club. Ils/sgn Lynd Ward. 1/1500. 4to. slipcase. EX. C4. $50.00

HUGHES, Rupert. *She Goes to War.* nd. Grosset Dunlap. Photoplay ed. VG. P1. $20.00

HUGHES, Ted. *Crow.* 1971. NY. sgn. dj. EX. $25.00

HUGHES, Ted. *Earth Owl & Other Moon People.* 1963. London. Ils 1st ed. dj. EX. $30.00

HUGHES, Ted. *Gaudette.* 1977. NY. 1st ed. dj. EX. $15.00

HUGHES, Ted. *Lupercal.* 1960. NY. 1st Am ed. dj. EX. $35.00

HUGHES, Ted. *Meet My Folks.* 1961. London. Ils 1st ed. dj. EX. $30.00

HUGHES, Ted. *Moon Bells & Other Poems.* 1978. London. 1st ed. decor brd. EX. $35.00

HUGHES, Ted. *Moon Bells & Other Poems.* 1986. London. New ed. w/3 new poems. M. $15.00

HUGHES, Ted. *Wodwo.* 1967. NY. 1st Am ed. dj. EX. $30.00

HUGHES, W.R. *Week's Tramp in Dickens-Land.* 1891. Chapman Hall. 1st ed. 8vo. 466 p. gr bdg. recased. H3. $85.00

HUGHES & CARRUTHERS. *Cuba Libre.* 1948. Los Angeles. Ward Ritchie. 1st ed. 1/500. EX. B13. $400.00

HUGHES & DE CARAVA. *Sweet Flypaper of Life.* 1955. Simon Schuster. 1st ed. inscr/sgn. dj. VG. B13. $650.00

HUGHES & DE CARAVA. *Sweet Flypaper of Life.* 1967. Hill Wang. New/reissue ed. dj. EX. B13. $65.00

HUGO, Richard. *Duwamish Head.* 1976. Port Townsend, WA. 1st ed. 1/1000. sgn. wrp. EX. T9. $65.00

HUGO, Richard. *Roads End at Tahola.* 1978. Slow Loris Pr. 1/64. sgn. wrp. EX. C4. $75.00

HUGO, Richard. *Run of Jacks.* 1961. MN U. dj. EX. C4. $125.00

HUGO, Victor. *Hunchback of Notre Dame.* nd. AL Burt. Photoplay ed. VG. P1. $30.00

HUGO, Victor. *Les Miserables*. 1862. NY. 1st Am ed. French text. EX. $225.00

HUGO, Victor. *Les Miserables*. 1938. Ltd Ed Club. Ils/sgn Lynd Ward. 1/1500. 5 vols. slipcase. C4. $125.00

HUGO, Victor. *Man Who Laughs*. 1967. NY. NBI Pr. 1st ed. dj. EX. C4. $60.00

HUGO, Victor. *Novels, Complete & Unabridged*. 1894. Phil. Barrie. Bibliophile ed. 1/250. 41 vols. H3. $450.00

HUGO, Victor. *Novels, Complete & Unabridged*. 1895. London. Nichols. 1/100. 26 vols. TEG. H3. $750.00

HUGO, Victor. *Oeuvres Completes*. 1885. Paris. Hetzel Cie. 53 vols. octavo. H3. $2000.00

HUGO, Victor. *Works*. c 1900. Estes. Cabinet ed. sm octavo. H3. $850.00

HUGO, Victor. *Works*. 1890. Ils. 8vo. 10 vols. TEG. EX. T1. $65.00

HUGO, Victor. *Works*. 1907. Jenson Soc. 1/500. 20 vols. octavo. TEG. VG. H3. $600.00

HUI-MING, Wang. *Birds & the Animals*. nd. (1969) Gehenna Pr. Ltd ed. 1/200. clamshell box. EX. R4. $300.00

HUIDOBRO, Vincente. *Mirror of the Mage*. 1931. Houghton Mifflin. 1st ed. VG. R3. $20.00

HUIE, W.B. *Can Do!* 1944. NY. 1st ed. 322 p. T5. $15.00

HUIE, W.B. *In the Hours of the Night*. 1975. Delacorte. 1st ed. dj. VG. P1. $20.00

HULBERT, A.B. *Forty-Niners*. 1931. Boston. 1st ed. VG. G1. $22.00

HULBERT, A.G. *Niagara River*. 1908. Putnam. 1st ed. inscr. 4to. EX. $50.00

HULFISH, D.S. *Cyclopedia of Motion-Picture Work*. 1911. Chicago. 1st ed. 2 vols. VG. rare. H3. $300.00

HULL, Burling. *Bulletin of Latest Sleights & Tricks*. 1915. Am Magic Corp. 1st ed. 31 p. SftCvr. EX. J3. $10.00

HULL, Burling. *Expert Billiard Ball Manipulation Part 1*. 1928. Stage Magic. 5th ed. 47 p. SftCvr. VG. J3. $12.00

HULL, Burling. *Gold Medal Showmanship for Magicians & Mentalists*. 1971. Calgary. 1st ed. 95 p. NM. J3. $10.00

HULL, Helen. *Heat Lightning*. nd. (1932) Coward. 328 p. EX. B10. $3.50

HULL, Henry. *Memoir of Life & Religious Labors of Henry Hull*. 1873. Phil. Friends Bookstore. Stereotype ed. 12mo. 334 p. VG. V1. $14.00

HULL, W.I. *Benjamin Furly & Quakerism in Rotterdam*. 1941. Swarthmore. 1st ed. 8vo. 314 p. EX. V1. $22.00

HULL, W.I. *Rise of Quakerism in Amsterdam, 1655-1665*. 1938. Phil. Swarthmore. 1st ed. 8vo. 346 p. EX. V1. $12.00

HULL, W.I. *1st Biographies of William Penn*. 1936. Swathmore. 1st ed. 8vo. 136 p. EX. V1. $14.00

HULME, Keri. *Te Kaihau: The Windeater*. 1987. Braziller. 1st ed. inscr. dj. EX. B13. $125.00

HULPACH, Vlad. *Heroes of Folk Tale & Legend*. nd. London. Hamlyn. 331 p. VG. B10. $6.50

HULT. *Steamboats in the Timber*. 1952. Caldwell. 1st ed. 187 p. dj. VG. B3. $25.00

HULTMAN, H.J. *This Murderous Shaft*. 1946. Phoenix Pr. 1st ed. dj. EX. F5. $8.50

HUMBLE, Richard. *Ils Hist of the Civil War*. 1987. Gallery Books. 264 p. dj. M. $17.00

HUME, Cyril. *Golden Dancer*. 1926. Doran. 1st ed. dj. EX. R3. $30.00

HUME, Cyril. *Myself & the Young Bowman*. 1932. Doubleday Doran. 1st ed. 1/1500. sgn. dj. VG. C1. $39.50

HUME, David. *Dangerous Mr Dell*. 1936. Collins. 3rd ed. VG. P1. $15.00

HUME, David. *Hist of Eng*. 1826. Oxford. Talboys Wheeler. Lg Paper ed. 1/50. 8 vols. lg octavo. H3. $1250.00

HUME, David. *Stand Up & Fight*. 1941. Collins. 1st ed. VG. P1. $22.50

HUME, Fergus. *Expedition of Capt Flick*. 1899. New Amsterdam. 1st Am ed. VG. R3. $30.00

HUME. *Here Lies VA*. 1963. NY. 1st ed. dj. VG. B3. $25.00

HUMFREVILLE. *20 Years Among Our Hostile Indians*. 1899. Hunter. 480 p. A5. $120.00

HUMPHREY, Doris. *Art of Making Dances*. 1959. Rinehart. 1st ed. octavo. 189 p. dj. VG. H3. $50.00

HUMPHREY, H. *Letters of JRR Tolkien*. 1981. Houghton Mifflin. 1st Am ed. dj. EX. R3. $17.00

HUMPHREY, M.A. *Squatter Sovereign; or, KS in the '50s*. 1883. Chicago. Coburn Newman. 1st ed. inscr. 8vo. 354 p. VG. V1. $90.00

HUMPHREY, Ron. *Juggling for Fun & Entertainment*. 1967. Rutland. 1st ed. 72 p. EX. J3. $26.00

HUMPHREY, William. *Farther Off From Heaven*. 1977. NY. 1st ed. dj. M. $15.00

HUMPHREY, William. *Home From the Hill*. 1958. Knopf. 1st ed. dj. EX. C4. $50.00

HUMPHREYS, A.A. *VA Campaign 1865*. nd. Bl/Gray Pr. 451 p. VG. S1. $6.00

HUMPHREYS, R.A. *Latin Am Hist: Guide to Literature in Eng*. 1958. London. Oxford. 1st ed. dj. F2. $20.00

HUMPHRIES. *Oriental Carpets, Runners, & Rugs....* 1910. London. thick 4to. 24 clr pls. 428 p. VG. C2. $95.00

HUNECKER, J.G. *Intimate Letters*. 1924. NY. Ltd ed. dj. VG. $12.00

HUNGERFORD, E. *Story of Baltimore & OH Railroad*. 1928. NY. 1 vol sgn. 2 vols. 1 dj. VG. B3. $62.50

HUNGERFORD, E. *Story of Rome Watertown Ogdensburg Railroad*. 1922. NY. 1st ed. 269 p. VG. B3. $30.00

HUNT, Bampton. *Gr Room Book; or, Who's Who on Stage*. 1906. NY. Warne. 1st ed. sm octavo. 452 p. VG. H3. $150.00

HUNT, C.T. *Story of Mr Circus*. 1954. Rochester. Record Pr. 1st ed. sgn. dj. NM. J3. $22.00

HUNT, E.H. *Hargrave Deception*. 1980. NY. 1st ed. dj. EX. $10.00

HUNT, Howard. *Diabolus*. 1971. Waybright. 1st ed. dj. EX. F5. $20.00

HUNT, Kyle. *Kill My Love*. nd. Book Club. xl. P1. $2.00

HUNT, Kyle. *To Kill a Killer*. 1960. Random House. 1st ed. dj. VG. P1. $20.00

HUNT, Leigh. *Essays & Poems*. 1891. London. 2 vols. VG. $42.00

HUNT, Leigh. *Feast of the Poets*. 1814. Winkle Wiley. 1st Am ed. $75.00

HUNT, Leigh. *Men, Women, & Books*. 1847. NY. 1st Am ed. 2 vols. VG. $75.00

HUNT, M.L. *Singing Among Strangers*. 1954. Lippincott. 12mo. 214 p. xl. V1. $4.50

HUNT, P. *Peter Hunt's How-To-Do-It Book*. 1952. NY. 1st ed. dj. EX. $18.00

HUNT, P. *Peter Hunt's Workbook*. 1945. NY. 4to. VG. $15.00

HUNT, Sarah. *Journal of Life & Religious Labors*. 1892. Friends Book Assn. 1st print. 12mo. 262 p. G. V1. $8.00

HUNT, Thomas. *Ghost Trails to CA*. 1974. Palo Alto. 1st ed. 262 p. $40.00

HUNT, W.E. *Hist Collections of Coshocton Co, OH.* 1876. Cincinnati. Clarke. 1st ed. 264 p. xl. T5. $65.00

HUNT, Wray. *Satan's Daughter.* 1975. New Eng Lib. VG. P1. $4.00

HUNT & HUNT. *Art of Magic.* 1967. Atheneum. 1st ed. 216 p. dj. VG. J3. $9.00

HUNT & HUNT. *Memoirs of William & Nathan Hunt From Journals & Letters.* 1858. London. Uriah Hunt. 16mo. 160 p. V1. $26.00

HUNT & LACEY. *Friends & the Use of the 5th Amendment.* 1957. Phil Yearly Meeting. 12mo. SftCvr. V1. $6.00

HUNT. *Hist of Ft Leavenworth 1827-1927.* 1927. Ft Leavenworth. presentation. 298 p. A5. $80.00

HUNTER, Alan. *Death on the Broadlands.* 1984. Walker. 1st ed. dj. EX. P1. $15.00

HUNTER, Alan. *Gently Between Tides.* 1983. Walker. 2nd ed. dj. EX. P1. $11.95

HUNTER, Alan. *Gently to the Summit.* 1961. Cassell. 1st ed. dj. VG. P1. $25.00

HUNTER, Alan. *Landed Gently.* 1957. Cassell. 1st ed. dj. VG. P1. $20.00

HUNTER, Alan. *Unhanged Man.* 1984. Walker. 1st ed. dj. EX. P1. $15.00

HUNTER, Dard. *Papermaking by Hand in India.* 1939. NY. Pynson. 1/370. sgn. decor brd. slipcase. H3. $2250.00

HUNTER, Dard. *Papermaking Pilgrimage to Japan, Korea, & China.* 1936. NY. Pynson. 1/370. sgn. decor brd. slipcase. EX. H3. $4000.00

HUNTER, Evan. *Buddwing.* 1964. NY. 1st ed. dj. EX. $12.00

HUNTER, Evan. *Every Little Crook & Nanny.* nd. Doubleday. 2nd ed. dj. VG. P1. $10.00

HUNTER, Evan. *Find the Feathered Serpent.* 1952. Winston. 1st ed. VG. R3. $15.00

HUNTER, Evan. *Last Summer.* 1968. NY. 1st ed. presentation. dj. EX. $12.00

HUNTER, Evan. *2nd Ending.* 1956. Simon Schuster. 1st ed. dj. EX. P1. $75.00

HUNTER, J.A. *Hunter.* 1952. Harper. 263 p. VG. B10. $4.00

HUNTER, J.A. *Hunter's Tracks.* 1957. NY. 1st ed. VG. $25.00

HUNTER, Mark. *Fantastic Journeys.* 1980. Walker. 1st ed. dj. RS. R3. $15.00

HUNTER, Norman. *Successful Conjuring.* 1963. Arco. Revised ed. 1st print. 256 p. dj. EX. J3. $15.00

HUNTER, Norman. *Successful Magic for Amateurs.* nd. Arco. 383 p. dj. EX. J3. $16.00

HUNTER, W.A. *Forts on PA Frontier 1753-1758.* 1960. Harrisburg. Ils. 596 p. VG. T5. $25.00

HUNTER, William. *Scrutiny of Cinema.* 1932. London. 1st ed. quarto. 87 p. VG. H3. $75.00

HUNTING, Gardner. *Vicarion.* 1927. Unity Pr. dj. VG. P1. $7.50

HUNTINGTON, Ellsworth. *Climatic Changes: Their Nature & Cause.* 1922. Yale. 1st ed. tall 8vo. VG. B10. $6.50

HUNTINGTON, Gale. *Songs the Whalemen Sang.* 1964. Barre. 1st ed. inscr. dj. EX. $30.00

HUNTINGTON, R.W. *Tabare: Epic Poem of Early Days in Paraguay.* 1934. Buenos Aires. inscr. ES. w/sgn booklet. wrp/ties. A4. $100.00

HURD & OSMOND. *Send Him Victorious.* 1969. Macmillan. 1st ed. dj. EX. F5. $15.00

HURLEY, V. *Swish of the Kris.* 1936. NY. 1st ed. VG. B3. $27.50

HURLIMANN, Bettina. *3 Centuries of Children's Books in Europe.* 1968. Cleveland. dj. EX. $45.00

HURLL, Estelle. *Memoirs of Early Italian Painters.* 1896. Houghton. 281 p. TEG. VG. B10. $5.00

HURRELL, F.G. *John Lillibud.* 1935. Kendall Sharp. 1st ed. P1. $10.00

HURSTON, Z.N. *Mules & Men.* 1935. Lippincott. 1st ed. dj. EX. C4. $675.00

HURWOOD, B.J. *Passport to the Supernatural.* 1972. Robert Hale. 1st ed. dj. VG. P1. $20.00

HUSON, W.H. *Birds of La Plata.* 1920. Dutton. Ltd 1st Am ed. 1/1500. 2 vols. VG. F2. $175.00

HUSSEY, Christopher. *Tait McKenzie: A Sculptor of Youth.* 1930. Lippincott. 1st ed. 93 pls. 4to. 107 p. dj. EX. R4. $75.00

HUSSEY, Christopher. *Tait McKenzie: A Scupture of Youth.* 1929. London. 1st ed. 93 pls. dj. EX. T1. $75.00

HUSSEY, S.F. *Brief Examination of Asa Rand's Book...* 1821. Salem. Cushing. 16mo. 237 p. G. V1. $40.00

HUSTON, John. *Frankie & Johnny.* 1930. Boni. Ils Covarrubius. dj. EX. B13. $100.00

HUTCHINGS, J.M. *In the Heart of the Sierras.* 1886. Oakland. 1st ed. fld map. VG. K1. $350.00

HUTCHINSON, A.S.M. *1 Increasing Purpose.* nd. London. VG. R3. $15.00

HUTCHINSON, Don. *Super Feds.* 1988. Starmont. 1st ed. wrp. M. R3. $9.95

HUTCHINSON, G.R. *Flying the States.* 1937. Chicago. Ils. 288 p. VG. T5. $15.00

HUTCHINSON, H. *Big Game Shooting.* 1905. London/NY. Country Life Lib Sport. 1st ed. 2 vols. VG. B3. $150.00

HUTCHINSON, H.N. *Story of Hills.* 1892. London. full leather. VG. C1. $65.00

HUTCHINSON, Jonathan. *Memoir of Jonathan Hutchinson With Selection From Letters.* 1877. Friends Book Assn. 120 p. G. V1. $9.00

HUTCHINSON, Robert. *Vesco.* 1974. NY. 1st ed. dj. VG. T1. $22.00

HUTCHINSON, W.H. *Gene Autry & the Big Valley Grab.* 1952. Whitman. dj. VG. P1. $17.50

HUTCHINSON, W.H. *Gene Autry & the Golden Ladder Gang.* 1950. Whitman. dj. VG. P1. $17.50

HUTCHINSON. *Golf.* 1895. London. 5th ed. 480 p. G. B3. $95.00

HUTTON, Laurence. *Curiosities of the Am Stage.* 1891. Harper. 1st ed. octavo. 347 p. VG. H3. $75.00

HUXLEY, Aldous. *After Many a Summer Dies the Swan.* 1939. Harper. presentation. H3. $300.00

HUXLEY, Aldous. *After Many a Summer.* 1953. Vanguard. VG. P1. $10.00

HUXLEY, Aldous. *Ape & Essence.* 1948. NY. 1st ed. dj. EX. $30.00

HUXLEY, Aldous. *Apennine.* 1930. Slide Mt. Ltd ed. 1/91. sgn. scarce. H3. $400.00

HUXLEY, Aldous. *Beyond the Mexique Bay.* 1934. Harper. 1st ed. 295 p. F2. $25.00

HUXLEY, Aldous. *Brave New World Revisited.* 1966. Chatto Windus. 6th print. dj. VG. P1. $15.00

HUXLEY, Aldous. *Brave New World.* 1932. 1st Am Trade ed. gilt bdg. EX. $80.00

HUXLEY, Aldous. *Brave New World.* 1932. London. 1st ed. 1/324. sgn. VG. $700.00

HUXLEY, Aldous. *Brave New World.* 1932. London. 1st Trade ed. dj. EX. $325.00

HUXLEY, Aldous. *Brief Candles.* 1930. Chatto Windus. sgn. gilt blk bdg. H3. $125.00

HUXLEY, Aldous. *Devils of London.* 1952. London. 1st ed. dj. VG. R3. $25.00

HUXLEY, Aldous. *Do With Me What You Will: Essays.* 1929. London. 1st ed. VG. B2. $40.00

HUXLEY, Aldous. *End & Means.* 1937. Chatto Windus. 1st ed. dj. EX. H3. $75.00

HUXLEY, Aldous. *Ends & Means.* 1937. Harper. 3rd ed. presentation. H3. $200.00

HUXLEY, Aldous. *Essays New & Old.* 1926. Chatto Windus. Ltd ed. 1/650. sgn. TEG. H3. $250.00

HUXLEY, Aldous. *Eyeless in Gaza.* 1936. Harper. 7th ed. VG. P1. $15.00

HUXLEY, Aldous. *Heaven & Hell.* 1956. Harper. 1st ed. dj. EX. H3. $50.00

HUXLEY, Aldous. *Little Mexican & Other Stories.* 1924. Chatto Windus. 1st ed. dj. EX. H3. $125.00

HUXLEY, Aldous. *Music at Night & Other Essays.* 1931. Fountain Pr. 1st ed. 1/842. sgn. 146 p. VG. T5. $95.00

HUXLEY, Aldous. *Music at Night.* 1931. Chatto Windus. 1st ed. dj. EX. H3. $125.00

HUXLEY, Aldous. *Olive Tree.* 1936. London. Ltd ed. 1/160. sgn. EX. B2. $175.00

HUXLEY, Aldous. *Point Counter Point.* 1928. Chatto Windus. 1st ed. dj. VG. H3. $75.00

HUXLEY, Aldous. *Point Counter Point.* 1928. Modern Lib. inscr. 12mo. dj. H3. $150.00

HUXLEY, Aldous. *Proper Studies.* 1927. Chatto Windus. 1st ed. dj. EX. H3. $100.00

HUXLEY, Aldous. *Texts & Pretexts.* 1932. Chatto Windus. 1st ed. dj. EX. H3. $100.00

HUXLEY, Aldous. *Vulgarity in Literature.* 1930. Chatto Windus. Ltd ed. 1/260. sgn. TEG. H3. $275.00

HUXLEY, Aldous. *Vulgarity in Literature.* 1930. London. 1st ed. dj. RS. VG. $45.00

HUXLEY, Aldous. *World of Light.* 1931. Chatto Windus. 1st ed. dj. VG. H3. $85.00

HUXLEY, Elspeth. *Love Among the Daughters.* 1968. London. 1st ed. presentation. dj. VG. $35.00

HUXLEY, Francis. *Affable Savages.* 1957. Viking. 1st ed. 287 p. dj. F2. $20.00

HUXLEY & CAPA. *Farewell to Eden.* 1964. Harper. 1st ed. 4to. dj. F2. $25.00

HUYGEN & POORTVIET. *Gnomes.* 2nd ed. EX. C1. $18.00

HUYGEN & POORTVIET. *Pop-Up Book of Gnomes.* 1977. NM. C1. $8.50

HUYGEN & POORTVIET. *Secrets of the Gnomes.* 1982. 1st ed. NM. C1. $11.00

HUYSMANS, K.J. *Against the Grain: Novel Without Plot.* 1926. Groves Michaux. 1st ed. 8vo. 299 p. R4. $50.00

HYAMAS & ORDISH. *Last of the Incas.* 1963. Simon Schuster. 1st ed. 294 p. F2. $15.00

HYDE, William. *5 Great Philosophies of Life.* 1928. Macmillan. Special ed. 296 p. VG. B10. $4.50

HYDE. *Printed Maps of Victorian London.* 1975. Folkstone. Ils 1st ed. 271 p. dj. VG. C2. $55.00

HYER, Richard. *Riceburner.* 1986. Scribner. 1st ed. dj. EX. P1. $17.00

HYMAN, Jackie. *Eyes of a Stranger.* 1987. St Martin. 1st ed. dj. EX. F5. $15.00

HYNE, C.J.C. *Lost Continent.* 1900. Harper. G. R3. $17.50

HYNE, C.J.C. *Lost Continent.* 1974. Oswald Train. dj. EX. P1. $20.00

HYNE, C.J.C. *Paradise Coal Boat.* 1897. London. 1st ed. G. R3. $25.00

HYNEMAN, Leon. *Universal Masonic Record; or, Links in Golden Chain...* 1859. Phil. 183 p. AEG. gilt bdg. VG. T5. $125.00

IAMS, Jack. *Death Draws the Line*. 1949. Morrow. 1st ed. dj. EX. F5. $27.00

IAMS, Jack. *Shot of Murder*. 1950. Morrow. 1st ed. dj. VG. P1. $17.50

IBANEZ, Felix. *Epic of Medicine*. 1962. NY. 1st ed. 295 p. dj. VG. B3. $27.50

IBARRA GRASSO, D.E. *Escritura Indigena Andina*. 1953. Bolivia. Lib of Congress duplicate. xl. rebound. F2. $30.00

IBSEN, Henrik. *Peer Ghynt*. c 1930s. Lippincott. Ils Rackham. EX. C1. $75.00

IBSEN, Henrik. *Works*. 1911. Scribner. Viking ed. 1/265. 16 vols. octavo. H3. $1500.00

IGLESIAS, Dolores. *Bibliografia e Indice da Geologia do Brasil 1951-1955*. 1957. Rio. 80 p. wrp. F2. $10.00

IGNATOW, D. *Poems*. c 1948. Decker Pr. 1st ed. dj. EX. $60.00

IHLE, S.N. *Malory's Grail Quest*. 1983. WI U. M. C1. $15.00

ILLICK, Joseph. *PA Trees*. 1928. Pa Dep Forest/Waters. 1st ed. 237 p. VG. B10. $10.00

INFIELD, G.B. *Unarmed & Unafraid*. 1970. NY. Ils 1st ed. 308 p. T5. $15.00

INGE, William. *Summer Brave & 11 Short Plays*. 1962. Random House. 1st ed. inscr. dj. EX. B13. $400.00

INGELLS, D.J. *L-1011 Tri-Star & the Lockheed Story*. 1973. Fallbrook. 1st ed. dj. EX. $35.00

INGERSOL, Jared. *Diamond Fingers*. 1970. Robert Hale. 1st ed. dj. xl. P1. $5.00

INGERSOLL, R.G. *Works*. 1929. Ingersoll League. Dresden Memorial ed. 12 vols. djs. H3. $300.00

INGHAM, H.L. *Bury Me Deep*. 1963. Hammond Hammond. VG. P1. $7.50

INGOLDSBY, Thomas. *Ingoldsby Legends*. 1907. London. Ils/sgn Rackham. 1/560. 24 clr pls. full vellum. VG. H3. $750.00

INGRAM, J.S. *Centennial Exposition*. c 1876. np. 8vo. 770 p. brn bdg. G. G4. $22.00

INNES, Hammond. *Angry Mt*. 1950. Collins. 1st ed. dj. VG. P1. $22.50

INNES, Hammond. *Campbell's Kingdom*. 1952. Collins. dj. VG. P1. $20.00

INNES, Hammond. *Maddon's Rock*. 1951. Collins. 2nd ed. dj. VG. P1. $10.00

INNES, Hammond. *Mary Deare*. 1956. Collins. 2nd ed. dj. VG. P1. $17.50

INNES, L. *Pittsburgh Glass 1797-1891: Hist & Guide for Collectors*. 1976. Boston. dj. EX. $55.00

INNES, Michael. *Ampersand Papers*. 1978. Gollancz. 1st ed. dj. EX. P1. $20.00

INNES, Michael. *Appleby & Honeybath*. 1983. Gollancz. 1st ed. dj. EX. P1. $17.50

INNES, Michael. *Appleby File*. 1975. Gollancz. 1st ed. dj. EX. P1. $15.00

INNES, Michael. *Appleby's Answer*. 1973. Gollancz. 1st ed. dj. EX. P1. $20.00

INNES, Michael. *Awkward Lie*. 1971. Dodd Mead. dj. xl. P1. $6.00

INNES, Michael. *Carson's Conspiracy*. 1984. Gollancz. 1st ed. dj. EX. P1. $17.50

INNES, Michael. *Death at the Chase*. 1970. Gollancz. 1st ed. dj. xl. P1. $6.00

INNES, Michael. *Honeybath's Haven*. 1977. Gollancz. 1st ed. dj. EX. P1. $20.00

INNES, Michael. *Sheiks & Adders*. 1982. Dodd Mead. 1st ed. dj. EX. P1. $15.00

IPCAR, Dahlov. *Dark Horn Blowing*. 1978. Viking. 1st ed. dj. EX. P1. $15.00

IRELAND, Tom. *Great Lakes: St Lawrence, Deep Waterway to the Sea*. 1934. NY/London. 1st ed. 223 p. dj. T5. $22.50

IREMONGER, Lucille. *Young Traveler in W Indies*. 1955. Dutton. 1st ed. 215 p. dj. VG. B10. $4.00

IRESON, Barbara. *April Witch & Other Strange Tales*. 1978. Scribner. 1st ed. dj. VG. P1. $20.00

IRISH, William; see Woolrich, Cornell.

IRON, Ralph. *Dreams*. c 1900. Lowell Gatefield. VG. R3. $20.00

IRVINE, Alexander. *My Lady of the Chimney Corner*. 1922. Santa Barbara. 1st Am ed? 8vo. 221 p. dj. R4. $30.00

IRVING, Henry. *Drama Addresses*. 1893. Heinemann. octavo. 163 p. VG. H3. $60.00

IRVING, John. *Berlin Stories: Last of Mr Norris/Goodbye to Berlin*. 1945. New Directions. inscr. dj. H3. $250.00

IRVING, John. *Cider House Rules*. 1985. Morrow. Special Ltd ed. 1/795. sgn. slipcase. M. H3. $150.00

IRVING, John. *Cider House Rules*. 1985. Morrow. UP. inscr. wrp. EX. K2. $125.00

IRVING, John. *Down There on a Visit*. 1962. Simon Schuster. sgn. dj. H3. $50.00

IRVING, John. *Hotel NH*. 1981. Dutton. Special Ltd ed. sgn. TEG. slipcase. H3. $125.00

IRVING, John. *Hotel NH*. 1981. Dutton. 1st ed. sgn. dj. EX. B13. $85.00

IRVING, John. *Hotel NH*. 1981. NY. Dutton. 1st ed. dj. M. $20.00

IRVING, John. *Pension Grillparzer*. nd. Logan, IA. 1st Separate ed. wrp. EX. scarce. T9. $35.00

IRVING, John. *Setting Free the Bears*. 1968. Random House. 1st ed. dj. EX. K2. $375.00

IRVING, John. *Vedanta for the W World*. 1949. Allen Unwin. inscr. dj. H3. $75.00

IRVING, John. *Water-Method Man*. 1972. Random House. UP. wrp. EX. B13. $300.00

IRVING, John. *World According to Garp*. 1978. Dutton Robbins. 1st ed. sgn. dj. EX. scarce. K2. $175.00

IRVING, John. *World According to Garp*. 1978. Dutton. Review ed. sgn. wrp. H3. $75.00

IRVING, John. *World According to Garp*. 1978. Dutton. 1st ed. dj. EX. C4. $60.00

IRVING, John. *3 by Irving*. 1980. Random House. UP. wrp. EX. C4. $45.00

IRVING, Washington. *Hist of NY*. 1825. London. 24mo. 340 p. xl. G4. $40.00

IRVING, Washington. *Legend of Sleepy Hollow*. 1928. Phil. Ils/sgn Rackham. 1/125. 8 clr pls. orig vellum. EX. H3. $1850.00

IRVING, Washington. *Legend of Sleepy Hollow*. 1931. NY. Ils Bernhardt Wall. 1/1200. slipcase. EX. $100.00

IRVING, Washington. *Life of WA*. 1887. Alden Pr. 4 vols. TEG. VG. B10. $18.00

IRVING, Washington. *Old Christmas*. 1876. London. Macmillan. Ils Caldecott. AEG. V1. $75.00

IRVING, Washington. *Oliver Goldsmith*. 1849. London. 1st ed. EX. $48.00

IRVING, Washington. *Voyages & Discoveries of Companions of Columbus*. 1831. Phil. 1st ed. 8vo. new spine. VG. T1. $110.00

IRWIN, Wallace. *Nautical Days of a Landsman*. 1904. Dodd Mead. 1st ed. 135 p. G. B10. $7.50

IRWIN, Will. *House That Shadows Built.* 1928. Doubleday Doran. 1st ed. octavo. 293 p. VG. H3. $35.00

ISAACS, Neil. *All the Moves: Hist of College Basketball.* 1975. Lippincott. 1st ed. 319 p. dj. EX. B10. $6.75

ISE, John. *Sod & Stubble: Story of KS Homestead.* 1938. NY. sgn. VG. $15.00

ISHERWOOD, B.F. *Experimental Researches in Steam Engineering.* 1863. Phil. Ils. 2 vols. EX. $275.00

ISHERWOOD, Christopher. *Christopher & His Kind.* 1976. NY. 1st ed. dj. M. $15.00

ISHERWOOD, Christopher. *Condor & the Cows.* 1949. Random House. 1st ed. dj. VG. H3. $50.00

ISHERWOOD, Christopher. *Condor & the Cows.* 1949. Random House. 1st ed. 217 p. F2. $15.00

ISHERWOOD, Christopher. *Lions & Shadows.* 1947. Norfolk. 1st Am ed. 312 p. dj. VG. T5. $35.00

ISHERWOOD, Christopher. *My Guru & His Disciple.* 1980. Farrar Straus. 1st ed. sgn/dtd 1983. dj. EX. C4. $75.00

ISHERWOOD, Christopher. *Prater Violet.* 1945. Armed Services Ed. EX. B4. $25.00

ISHERWOOD, Christopher. *Single Man.* 1964. London. 1st ed. sgn. as issued. K2. $150.00

ISHERWOOD, Christopher. *World in the Evening.* 1960. London. 1st PB ed. VG. B4. $6.00

ISHIGURO, Kazuo. *Artist of the Floating World.* 1986. Putnam. 1st ed. dj. EX. B13. $50.00

ISHIGURO, Kazuo. *Pale View of the Hills.* 1982. Putnam. UP. very scarce. K2. $275.00

ISHIGURO, Kazuo. *Remains of the Day.* 1989. Knopf. UP of 1st Am ed. wrp. EX. C4. $50.00

ISHIGURO, Kazuo. *Remains of the Day.* 1989. London. Faber. 1st ed. sgn. dj. EX. B13. $250.00

ISSACS, E.J.R. *Negro in the Am Theatre.* 1947. Theatre Arts. 1st ed. quarto. 143 p. dj. EX. H3. $100.00

ITOTE, Wartuhiu. *Mau Mau General.* 1967. Nairobi. Ils. 297 p. wrp. G. T5. $17.50

IVES, Herbert. *Airplane Photography.* 1920. Phil. Ils. 422 p. VG. $95.00

IVIMY, John. *Sphinx & the Megaliths.* 1975. Harper. 1st Am ed. 207 p. dj. F2. $10.00

JACCOMA, Richard. *Yel Peril.* 1978. Marek. 1st ed. dj. VG. P1. $25.00

JACKMAN, Stuart. *Davidson Affair.* 1966. Eerdmans. dj. VG. P1. $12.50

JACKS, L.P. *Last Legend of Smokeover.* 1939. Hodder Stoughton. dj. VG. P1. $30.00

JACKSON, Basil. *Epicenter.* 1971. Norton. 2nd ed. dj. VG. P1. $10.00

JACKSON, C.S. *Pageant of the Pioneers: Veritable Art of WH Jackson.* 1958. Minden, NE. 1st ed. 1/1000. 4to. dj. EX. R4. $45.00

JACKSON, Charles. *Eng Goldsmiths & Their Marks...* 1964. NY. 2nd ed. 745 p. dj. xl. VG. $25.00

JACKSON, Donald. *Journals of Zebulon Montgomery Pike.* 1966. OK. 1st ed. 60 pls. 2 vols. slipcase. EX. T1. $50.00

JACKSON, Elmore. *Meeting of the Minds.* 1952. McGraw Hill. 1st ed. 12mo. 200 p. dj. VG. V1. $8.50

JACKSON, H.H. *Nelly's Silver Mine.* 1921. Boston. VG. B3. $25.00

JACKSON, H.H. *Ramona.* 1959. Los Angeles. Ltd Ed Club. Ils/sgn EG Jackson. 1/1500. slipcase. EX. C4. $50.00

JACKSON, Holbrook. *Anatomy of Bibliomania.* nd. NY. 8vo. dj. EX. $15.00

JACKSON, Holbrook. *Bookman's Holiday.* 1945. London. 1st ed. VG. G1. $15.00

JACKSON, Holbrook. *1890s.* nd. NY. VG. G1. $15.00

JACKSON, John. *Dissertation: Hist & Critical on Christian Ministry.* 1855. Phil. TE Chapman. 8vo. 120 p. V1. $12.50

JACKSON, John. *Reflections on Peace & War.* 1846. Phil. TE Chapman. Enlarged 2nd ed. 16mo. 108 p. V1. $14.00

JACKSON, John. *Sermons.* 1851. Phil. TE Chapman. 16mo. 120 p. fair. V1. $12.50

JACKSON, Joseph. *Mexican Interlude.* 1936. Macmillan. 1st ed. 232 p. F2. $15.00

JACKSON, Joseph. *Notes on a Drum: Travel Sketches in Guatemala.* 1937. Macmillan. 1st ed. 276 p. dj. F2. $20.00

JACKSON, K.H. *Celtic Miscellany.* 1982. Penguin. VG. C1. $4.00

JACKSON, L.R. *Peter Pater Book for Children.* 1918. Chicago. Ils BF Wright. 4to. VG. A4. $50.00

JACKSON, R. *Airships.* 1973. NY. 1st ed. 277 p. dj. VG. B3. $17.50

JACKSON, Shirley. *Come Along With Me.* 1968. Viking. 1st ed. dj. EX. B13. $65.00

JACKSON, Shirley. *Witchcraft of Salem Village.* 1956. 2nd print. VG. C1. $9.50

JACKSON, W.H. *Description Catalog of Photographs of US Geol Survey...* 1875. GPO. wrp. VG. A5. $75.00

JACKSON, W.H. *Time Exposure.* 1940. NY. 1st ed. dj. VG. B3. $45.00

JACKSON, W.R. *MO Democracy.* 1935. Clarke. 2796 p. VG. $100.00

JACKSON, W.T. *Anatomy of Love.* 1971. NY/London. 1st ed. dj. EX. C1. $14.00

JACKSON. *Topeka Pen & Camera Sketches.* 1890. Topeka. 1st ed. 192 p. VG. B3. $37.50

JACOB. *Plantae Favershamienses.* 1777. London. 1st ed. C2. $275.00

JACOBI, Carl. *Portraits in Moonlight.* 1964. Arkham House. 1st ed. dj. EX. R3. $45.00

JACOBI, Carl. *Revelations in Blk.* 1947. Arkham House. 1st ed. dj. EX. R3. $85.00

JACOBI, Carl. *Revelations in Blk.* 1974. Spearman. 1st Eng ed. dj. EX. R3. $35.00

JACOBS, F.G. *World of Doll Houses.* 1965. NY. 8vo. dj. EX. $20.00

JACOBS, Frank. *Mad World of William M Gaines.* 1972. Lyle Stuart. 1st ed. dj. VG. R3. $35.00

JACOBS, Joseph. *Celtic Fairy Tales.* 1968. Dover. facsimile of 1892 1st ed. PB. VG. C1. $6.00

JACOBS, T.C.H. *Documents of Murder.* 1933. Macaulay. VG. P1. $17.50

JACOBS, T.C.H. *Scorpion's Trail.* 1934. Macaulay. xl. P1. $7.50

JACOBS, W.W. *Captains All.* nd. McKinlay Stone. VG. P1. $10.00

JACOBS, W.W. *Skipper's Wooing.* nd. Thomas Nelson. VG. P1. $10.00

JACOBS & JONES. *Beaver Papers: Story of the Lost Season.* 1983. Crown. 1st ed. B4. $8.00

JACOBS & NEVILLE. *Bridges, Canals, & Tunnels.* 1968. Am Heritage/Smithsonian. 140 p. VG. T5. $15.00

JACOBSEN & ROHWER. *Decisive Battles of WWII: The German View.* 1965. NY. 1st Am ed. 509 p. T5. $42.50

JACQUEMARD, Simonne. *Night Watchman.* 1964. Holt Rinehart Winston. 1st ed. P1. $12.50

JACQUEMARD & SENECAL. *Body Vanishes.* 1980. Dodd Mead. 1st ed. dj. VG. P1. $12.50

JACQUEMART, A. *Hist du Mobilier.* 1876. Paris. Lib Hachette. 4to. TEG. VG. $150.00

JAFFE, Al. *Mad Book of Magic & Other Dirty Tricks.* 1970. Signet. 3rd print. 192 p. EX. J3. $5.00

JAFFE, I.B. *Sculpture of Leonard Baskin.* 1980. NY. 1st ed. inscr. dj. EX. G1. $25.00

JAFFE, R. *Mazes & Monsters.* 1981. NY. 1st ed. dj. M. $10.00

JAFFE, Sherril. *Scars Make Your Body More Interesting.* 1975. Blk Sparrow. Ltd HrdCvr ed. 1/200. sgn. H3. $40.00

JAFFE, Sherril. *This Flower Only Blooms Every Hundred Years.* 1979. Blk Sparrow. Ltd HrdCvr ed. 1/200. sgn. glassine wrp. H3. $30.00

JAFFEE, Bernard. *Crucibles: Lives & Achievements of Great Chemists.* 1932. Newton, NY. B10. $4.50

JAFFRAY, M.E. *Man of Plain Speech.* 1897. London. Headley. 16mo. 136 p. TEG. VG. V1. $12.00

JAFFREY, Sheldon. *Arkham House Companion.* 1989. Starmont House. 1st ed. M. R3. $34.95

JAGODA, Robert. *Friend in Deed.* 1977. Norton. 1st ed. 218 p. dj. EX. B10. $4.50

JAHNS, P. *Frontier World of Doc Holliday: Faro Dealer...* 1957. NY. 1st ed. dj. VG. $25.00

JAKES, John. *And So to Bed.* 1962. Monarch 231. 1st ed. wrp. VG. T9. $15.00

JAKES, John. *Secrets of Stardeep.* 1969. Westminster Pr. 1st ed. dj. EX. R3. $25.00

JAMES, Beauregard. *Road to Birmingham.* 1964. Soc for Racial Peace. dj. EX. K2. $85.00

JAMES, G.W. *In & Around the Grand Canyon.* 1913. Boston. presentation. 352 p. VG. B3. $65.00

JAMES, G.W. *Indian Blankets & Their Makers.* 1937. NY. Ils. 208 p. VG. B3. $100.00

JAMES, Henry. *Am Scene.* 1907. NY. 1st ed. as issued. B3. $40.00

JAMES, Henry. *Ambassadors.* 1903. NY. 1st Am ed. EX. $175.00

JAMES, Henry. *Art of Fiction & Other Essays.* 1947. Oxford. 1st ed. dj. EX. C4. $20.00

JAMES, Henry. *Awkward Age.* 1899. Harper. 1st Am ed. 1st issue. 12mo. VG. C4. $75.00

JAMES, Henry. *Awkward Age.* 1948. Novel Lib. 8vo. dj. B10. $7.50

JAMES, Henry. *Bostonians.* 1886. London. 1st 1 vol ed. EX. $90.00

JAMES, Henry. *Ivory Tower.* 1917. London. 1st ed. EX. $45.00

JAMES, Henry. *Middle Years.* 1917. NY. 1st Am ed. EX. $60.00

JAMES, Henry. *Most Unholy Trade.* 1923. 1st book by Scarab Pr. 1/100. 16mo. G. V1. $100.00

JAMES, Henry. *Notebooks of Henry James.* 1947. Oxford. 1st ed. dj. EX. C4. $35.00

JAMES, Henry. *Notes of a Son & Brother.* 1914. NY. 1st ed. 1st issue. variant bdg. T5. $125.00

JAMES, Henry. *Novels & Tales.* 1907-1920. Scribner. NY ed. 28 vols. plum bdg. H3. $4500.00

JAMES, Henry. *Turn of the Screw.* 1947. Zephyr. dj. EX. P1. $35.00

JAMES, Henry. *What Maisie Knew.* 1897. Chicago/NY. Stone. 1st ed. 470 p. VG. T5. $75.00

JAMES, Jesse Jr. *Jesse James, My Father.* 1906. Cleveland. 2nd print. wrp. VG. C2. $75.00

JAMES, P.D. *Innocent Blood.* nd. BOMC. dj. VG. P1. $7.50

JAMES, P.D. *Innocent Blood.* nd. Scribner. 2nd ed. dj. VG. P1. $10.00

JAMES, P.D. *Innocent Blood.* nd. Scribner. 3rd ed. dj. VG. P1. $7.50

JAMES, P.D. *Skull Beneath the Skin.* 1982. Lester/Orpen Denys. 1st ed. dj. VG. P1. $16.95

JAMES, P.D. *Skull Beneath the Skin.* 1982. Scribner. UP. wrp. EX. B13. $125.00

JAMES, P.D. *Taste for Death.* nd. BOMC. dj. VG. P1. $7.50

JAMES, P.D. *Taste for Death.* 1986. Knopf. UP of 1st Am ed. wrp. EX. C4. $40.00

JAMES, P.D. *Taste for Death.* 1986. Knopf. 1st ed. dj. EX. P1. $18.95

JAMES, Peter. *Possession.* 1988. Doubleday. 1st ed. dj. EX. F5. $16.00

JAMES, Philip. *Children's Books of Yesterday.* 1933. London. Studio. 1st ed. dj. VG. $60.00

JAMES, R.R. *Churchill, Study in Failure 1900-1939.* 1970. NY. 1st ed. 400 p. dj. VG. T5. $25.00

JAMES, S.V. *People Among Peoples.* 1963. Harvard U. 1st ed. 8vo. 397 p. dj. VG. V1. $15.00

JAMES, Stewart. *Abbott's Encyclopedia of Rope Tricks Vol 1 & Vol 2.* nd. Abbott. 2 vols. J3. $30.00

JAMES, Stewart. *Magine Mine No 1: Orig Tricks.* 1957. Royal Oak, MI. 28 p. SftCvr. EX. J3. $4.00

JAMES, Stewart. *Stewart James in Print: 1st 50 Years.* 1989. Toronto. Jogestja. 1st ed. 991 p. EX. J3. $11.00

JAMES, Stewart. *1st Call to Cards.* 1954. Royal Oak, MI. 1st ed. 24 p. SftCvr. NM. J3. $5.00

JAMES, Will. *Lone Cowboy.* 1947. Scribner. Ils Classics Series. EX. $45.00

JAMES, Will. *Lone Cowboy: My Life Story.* 1930. Scribner. inscr/sgn. gilt gr bdg. H3. $350.00

JAMES, Will. *Smoky the Cow Horse.* 1929. Scribner. Ils Classics Ed. $45.00

JAMES, Will. *Smoky the Cow Horse.* 1929. Scribner. sgn. H3. $250.00

JAMES & CRITCHLEY. *Maul & the Pear Tree.* 1986. Mysterious Pr. 1st ed. dj. VG. P1. $17.95

JAMES & STOTZ. *Drums in the Forest.* 1958. Pittsburgh. Ils. 227 p. dj. VG. T5. $22.50

JAMESON, Malcolm. *Tarnished Utopia.* Galaxy Novel 27. 1st ed. wrp. EX. R3. $10.00

JANIFER, L.M. *Knave & the Game.* 1987. Doubleday. 1st ed. dj. EX. F5. $16.00

JANIFER, Laurence. *Reel.* 1983. Doubleday. 1st ed. dj. RS. P1. $20.00

JANIFER, Laurence. *Reel.* 1983. Doubleday. 1st ed. RS. M. R3. $15.00

JANIS, Sidney. *Abstract & Surrealist Art in Am.* 1944. NY. 1st ed. 146 p. G. T5. $17.50

JANNEY, Russell. *So Long As Love Remembers.* 1953. NY. 1st ed. dj. EX. $15.00

JANNEY, S.M. *Conversations on Religious Subjects Between Father...Sons.* 1860. Phil. Friends Book Assn. 16mo. 216 p. VG. V1. $12.50

JANNEY, S.M. *Examination of Causes Which Led to Separation...of Friends.* 1868. Phil. Ellwood Zell. 12mo. 347 p. V1. $16.00

JANNEY, S.M. *Life of William Penn With Selections From Correspondence.* 1852. Phil. Hogan Perkins. 8vo. 560 p. V1. $35.00

JANNEY, S.M. *Memoirs.* 1881. Friends Book Assn. 12mo. 309 p. VG. V1. $14.00

JANNEY, S.M. *Peace Principles Exemplified in Early Hist of PA.* 1876. Friends Book Assn. 16mo. 169 p. G. V1. $20.00

JANVIER, Thomas. *Legends of the City of Mexico.* 1910. Harper. 1st ed. 165 p. F2. $35.00

JAPRISOT, Sebastien. *1 Deadly Summer.* 1982. Secker Warburg. 1st Eng ed. dj. EX. T9. $25.00

JAPRISOT, Sebastien. *10:30 From Marseille.* 1963. Doubleday Crime Club. 1st Am ed. dj. VG. T9. $20.00

JARDIN, Rex. *Devil's Mansion.* 1931. Fiction League. VG. P1. $10.00

JARRELL, Randall. *Bat Poet.* 1964. Macmillan. Ils Maurice Sendak. 1st ed. dj. EX. C4. $40.00

JARRELL, Randall. *Losses: Poems.* 1948. Harcourt Brace. 1st ed. sgn. dj. EX. C4. $275.00

JARRELL, Randall. *Pictures From an Institution.* 1954. Knopf. 1st ed. inscr. dj. EX. K2. $450.00

JARRELL, Randall. *Selected Poems.* 1956. London. Faber. 1st UK ed. dj. EX. C4. $40.00

JARRELL, Randall. *Woman at the WA Zoo.* 1960. Atheneum. 1st ed. dj. EX. C4. $35.00

JARRELL, Randall. *7-League Crutches.* 1951. Harcourt Brace. ARC. dj. RS. EX. K2. $150.00

JARRELL, Randall. *7-League Crutches.* 1951. Harcourt Brace. 1st ed. sgn. dj. EX. C4. $225.00

JARROW, Emil. *Rope Magic: How To Do Rope Tricks.* 1941. Plymouth Cordage. 1st ed. 19 p. SftCvr. EX. J3. $11.00

JARVIS, Charles. *Don Quixote.* 1809. London. Oddy. 15 pls. fld map. 2 vols. 8vo. VG. J2. $120.00

JARVIS, F.G. *Murder at the Met.* 1971. Coward McCann. dj. xl. P1. $5.00

JASEN, D.A. *PG Wodehouse Portrait of Master.* 1974. Mason Lipscomb. 1st ed. dj. VG. P1. $35.00

JASEN, D.A. *PG Wodehouse Portrait of Master.* 1981. Continuum. dj. EX. P1. $25.00

JASPER, Theodore. *Birds of N Am.* 1881. NY. Studer. clr pls. rebound. T3. $450.00

JAY, Allen. *Autobiography of Allen Jay.* 1910. Phil. Winston. 8vo. 421 p. V1. $12.00

JAY, Charlotte. *Man Who Walked Away.* 1958. Crime Club. dj. VG. P1. $20.00

JAYNE, C.F. *String Figures & How To Make Them.* 1962. Dover. 407 p. NM. J3. $3.00

JEAN, Marcel. *Autobiography of Surrealism.* 1980. NY. Viking. sm 4to. VG. $20.00

JEFFERIES, Richard. *Open Air.* 1948. London. Lutterworth. Ils AM Parker. 1st ed. 12mo. 299 p. dj. $22.00

JEFFERIES, Richard. *Story of My Heart.* 1912. London. Ils Waite. 1/160. B7. $215.00

JEFFERIS, Edith. *Memoir of Edith Jefferis.* 1849. Phil. Kite Walton. 16mo. 76 p. G. V1. $9.50

JEFFERS, H.P. *Adventure of the Stewart Companions.* 1978. Harper Row. 1st ed. dj. EX. F5. $18.00

JEFFERS, H.P. *Murder on Mike.* 1984. St Martin. 1st ed. dj. EX. P1. $15.00

JEFFERS, H.P. *Rub Out at the Onyx.* 1981. Ticknor Fields. 1st ed. dj. VG. P1. $15.00

JEFFERS, Robinson. *Be Angry at the Sun.* 1941. Random House. sgn. H3. $125.00

JEFFERS, Robinson. *Californians.* 1916. Macmillan. ARC. EX. K2. $325.00

JEFFERS, Robinson. *Cawdor & Other Poems.* 1928. Liveright. 1st ed. 1/350. sgn. boxed. H3. $275.00

JEFFERS, Robinson. *Dear Judas.* 1929. Liveright. Ltd 1st ed. 1/350. sgn. boxed. EX. H3. $300.00

JEFFERS, Robinson. *Dear Judas.* 1929. Liveright. 1st ed. 2nd print. inscr. H3. $175.00

JEFFERS, Robinson. *Descent to the Dead.* 1931. Random House. Ltd 1st ed. 1/500. sgn. boxed. EX. H3/K2. $300.00

JEFFERS, Robinson. *Flagons & Apples.* 1912. Los Angeles. 1st ed. 1/500. VG. H3. $850.00

JEFFERS, Robinson. *Loving Shepherdess.* 1956. Random House. Ils Kellogg. Ltd ed. 1/115. sgns. boxed. V1. $750.00

JEFFERS, Robinson. *Poems.* 1928. CA Book Club. Ltd ed. 1/310. sgn author/Adams. boxed. H3. $1250.00

JEFFERS, Robinson. *Solstice & Other Poems.* 1935. Random House. 1st ed. inscr. VG. H3. $125.00

JEFFERS, Robinson. *Such Counsels You Gave to Me & Other Poems.* 1937. Random House. Ltd ed. 1/300. sgn. boxed. EX. H3. $300.00

JEFFERS, Robinson. *Such Counsels You Gave to Me & Other Poems.* 1937. Random House. 1st ed. inscr. H3. $125.00

JEFFERSON, Thomas. *Life & Morals of Jesus of Nazareth.* nd. (1902) St Louis. Thompson. Ils. 168 p. VG. B3. $27.50

JEFFERSON, Thomas. *Life & Selected Writings.* 1944. Modern Lib. 756 p. dj. VG. B10. $3.50

JEFFERSON. *Wheeling Glass.* 1947. Colum. 1st ed. dj. VG. C2. $35.00

JEFFREYS, J.G. *Thistlewood Plot.* 1987. Walker. 1st ed. dj. EX. F5. $11.00

JEHL. *Menlo Park Reminiscences.* 1937. Dearborn. 3 vols. VG. B3. $47.50

JEKYLL, Gertrude. *Wall & Water Gardens.* 1901. Scribner. Ils. bl bdg. VG. $50.00

JENKINS, C.F. *Quaker Poems.* 1893. Phil. Winston. 12mo. 269 p. VG. V1. $8.50

JENKINS, Dan. *Semi-Tough.* 1972. Atheneum. 5th ed. 307 p. dj. VG. B10. $4.00

JENKINS, Elizabeth. *Mystery of King Arthur.* 1987. (1st 1975) dj. M. C1. $12.50

JENKINS, Herbert. *Malcolm Sage Detective.* nd. Roy. dj. VG. P1. $15.00

JENKINS, J. *I'm Frank Hamer.* 1968. Austin. 1st ed. dj. VG. B3. $45.00

JENKINS, J.S. *Hist of the War Between the US & Mexico.* 1851. Derby Miller. G. C1. $34.50

JENKINS, J.S. *Voyages of US Exploring Expeditions...1838-1841 & 1843.* 1853. Detroit. Ils. pls. rebound. T1. $45.00

JENKINS, Sara. *We Gather Together.* nd. Crowell. 1st ed? 243 p. dj. VG. B10. $3.50

JENKINS, W.F. *Outlaw Sheriff.* 1934. King. 1st ed. VG. P1. $40.00

JENKINS, Will. *Murder of the USA.* 1946. Crown. 1st ed. dj. EX. R3. $35.00

JENNINGS, Gary. *March of the Demons.* 1977. Assn Pr. dj. VG. P1. $10.00

JENNINGS, P. *Book of Trout Flies.* 1935. Crown. 1st Trade ed. boxed. VG. B3. $60.00

JENNINGS, Robert. *Horse Training Made Easy.* 1866. Phil. Ils. 192 p. G. T5. $32.50

JENNINGS & NORBECK. *Prehistoric in the New World.* 1965. Chicago U. 3rd print. 633 p. dj. F2. $20.00

JENSEN, Johannes. *Long Journey.* nd. McKinlay Stone. 2 vols. VG. R3. $25.00

JEPPSON, J.O. *Mysterious Cure & Others.* 1985. Doubleday. 1st ed. dj. EX. F5. $15.00

JEPSON, Edgar. *Emerald Tiger.* 1928. Macy Masius. 1st ed. VG. R3. $20.00

JEPSON, Edgar. *Horned Shepherd.* 1927. Macy Masius. 1st ed. 1/2000. EX. R3. $35.00

JEPSON, Selwyn. *Golden Dart.* 1949. Crime Club. 1st ed. P1. $15.00

JEPSON, Selwyn. *Man Dead.* 1951. Crime Club. 1st ed. dj. xl. P1. $7.50

JEPSON, Selwyn. *Man Dead.* 1951. Doubleday. VG. P1. $17.50

JEPSON, Selwyn. *Rogues & Diamonds.* 1925. Lincoln Macveagh Dial. 1st ed. VG. P1. $35.00

JEROME, J.K. *Observations of Henry.* 1901. Dodd. 1st ed. 182 p. VG. B10. $15.00

JEROME, J.K. *Passing of the 3rd Floor Back.* 1907. Tauchnitz. VG. R3. $15.00

JEROME, J.K. *Stage Land.* 1889. Chatto Windus. 2nd ed. 80 p. G. H3. $75.00

JEROME, O.F. *Corpse Awaits.* 1946. Mystery House. 1st ed. xl. P1. $5.00

JEROME, O.F. *5 Assassins.* 1958. Mystery House. 1st ed. dj. xl. P1. $6.00

JEROME, V.J. *Negro in Hollywood Films.* 1950. Masses Mainstream. 1st ed. 12mo. 64 p. bl wrp. H3. $75.00

JERROLD, Douglas. *Mrs Caudle's Curtain Lectures & Etc.* 1895. London. Million Lib. VG. C1. $8.50

JERROLD, Douglas. *Works.* c 1850. Phil/London. 5 vols. gilt gr morocco. VG. $100.00

JESS, E. *Anecdotes of Dogs.* 1846. London. 1st ed. EX. $195.00

JESSE, Capt. *Life of Beau Brummell.* 1886. London. 1/150. 2 vols. TEG. VG. $150.00

JESSUP, Richard. *Hot Bl Sea.* 1974. Doubleday. 1st ed. dj. xl. P1. $5.00

JESSUP, Richard. *Quiet Voyage Home.* 1970. Boston. 1st ed. dj. EX. $12.00

JESSUP, Richard. *Sailor.* 1969. Boston. 1st ed. dj. EX. $15.00

JETER, K.W. *Death Arms.* 1987. Morrigan. 1st ed. dj. EX. P1. $30.00

JETER, K.W. *Infernal Devices.* 1987. St Martin. dj. EX. P1. $25.00

JETER, K.W. *Morlock Night.* 1979. DAW Books. 1st ed. sgn. VG. C1. $11.00

JETT, D.C. *Minor Sketches of Major Folk & Where They Sleep...* 1928. Richmond, VA. Ils 1st ed. 128 p. VG. T5. $22.50

JETTER, K.W. *Death Arms.* 1989. St Martin. 1st Am ed. dj. EX. F5. $15.00

JETTER, K.W. *Farewell Horizontal.* 1989. St Martin. 1st ed. dj. EX. F5. $15.00

JETTER, K.W. *In the Land of the Dead.* 1989. Onyx. 1st ed. wrp. EX. F5. $6.50

JEWELL, Derek. *Duke: Portrait of Duke Ellington.* 1977. Norton. 1st ed. 264 p. dj. NM. B10. $12.95

JEWELL, E.A. *Wht Kami.* 1922. Knopf. 1st ed. VG. R3. $12.50

JEWETT, E.M. *Hidden Treasure of Glaston.* 1960. (1st 1946) PB. rare juvenile. VG. C1. $14.00

JEWETT, S.O. *Country of the Pointed Firs.* 1968. Norton. Ils Shirley Burke. 1st ed. dj. EX. C4. $20.00

JEWETT, S.O. *Play Days: Book of Stories for Children.* 1906. Houghton Mifflin. 8vo. 213 p. R4. $50.00

JILLSON, W.R. *Early KY Distillers 1783-1800.* 1940. Louisville, KY. 1/350. 630 p. VG. T5. $65.00

JOBE, J. *Extended Travels in Romantic Am.* 1966. Luasanne. 1st ed. gilt red leather. boxed. EX. K1. $100.00

JOBSON, Hamilton. *Shadow That Caught Fire.* 1972. Scribner. 1st ed. dj. EX. P1. $15.00

JOHN, Evan. *Atlantic Impact 1861.* 1952. Heinemann. 296 p. VG. S1. $7.00

JOHN, Owen. *Sabotage.* 1973. Doubleday Book Club. VG. P1. $7.50

JOHNS, Foster. *Victory Murders.* nd. Economy Book League. VG. P1. $12.50

JOHNS, W.E. *Biggles Flies Again.* nd. Dean. dj. VG. P1. $12.00

JOHNS, W.E. *Biggles Flies to Work.* nd. Dean. VG. P1. $7.50

JOHNS, W.E. *Biggles Hunts Big Game.* nd. Hampton Lib. dj. VG. P1. $10.00

JOHNS, W.E. *Biggles in Africa.* 1946. Oxford. dj. VG. P1. $10.00

JOHNS, W.E. *Biggles in the Jungle.* 1946. Oxford. VG. P1. $10.00

JOHNS, W.E. *Biggles' Air Detective Omnibus.* 1959. Hodder Stoughton. 2nd ed. VG. P1. $10.00

JOHNS, W.E. *Now to the Stars.* 1956. Hodder Stoughton. 1st ed. decor brd. VG. P1. $15.00

JOHNS, W.E. *Worlds of Wonder.* 1962. Hodder Stoughton. 1st ed. decor brd. VG. P1. $12.00

JOHNS, W.E. *Worrals Goes E.* 1946. Musson. VG. P1. $10.00

JOHNSON, Barbara. *Lady of Fashion: Album Styles & Fabrics.* 1987. Thames Hudson. 1st Am ed. giant folio. dj. EX. $80.00

JOHNSON, Charles. *Middle Passage.* 1990. Atheneum. sgn. dj. EX. K2. $100.00

JOHNSON, Charles. *Sorcerer's Apprentice.* 1986. NY. 1st ed. sgn. dj. EX. T9. $55.00

JOHNSON, Clifton. *Land of Heather.* 1903. NY. 1st ed. inscr. EX. $20.00

JOHNSON, Clifton. *Tale of a Blk Cat.* 1917. Dodge. Ils Frank Nankivell. VG. $35.00

JOHNSON, D. *Nudists.* 1959. NY. 1st ed. 180 p. dj. VG. B3. $22.50

JOHNSON, D.M. *Indian Country.* 1953. Ballantine. dj. EX. K2. $65.00

JOHNSON, Denis. *Angels.* 1983. NY. 1st ed. sgn. dj. EX. T9. $45.00

JOHNSON, Denis. *Resuscitation of a Hanged Man.* 1990. Farrar Straus. UP/galley. 1/500. sgn. wrp. fld box. M. C4. $60.00

JOHNSON, Denis. *Stars at Noon.* 1986. Knopf. 1st ed. sgn. dj. EX. C4. $40.00

JOHNSON, Diane. *Dashiell Hammett: A Life.* 1983. Random House. 1st ed. dj. EX. P1. $15.00

JOHNSON, E.C. *Dean Bond of Swarthmore: Quaker Humanist.* 1928. Lippincott. 8vo. 239 p. VG. V1. $12.50

JOHNSON, E.C. *Under Quaker Appointment: Life of Jane Rushmore.* 1953. Phil. 1st ed. 8vo. 211 p. VG. V1. $12.00

JOHNSON, E.R. *Judas.* 1971. Harper Row. 1st ed. dj. xl. P1. $5.00

JOHNSON, E.R. *Mongo's Back in Town.* 1969. Harper Row. 1st ed. inscr/sgn. dj. EX. T9. $35.00

JOHNSON, E.R. *Mongo's Back in Town.* 1970. Macmillan. 1st ed. dj. EX. P1. $20.00

JOHNSON, G. *Colters Hell.* 1938. Los Angeles. 1st ed. sgn. 398 p. dj. VG. B3. $22.50

JOHNSON, G.D. *Autumn Love Circle.* 1928. NY. Harold Vinal. 1st ed. dj. EX. B13. $350.00

JOHNSON, G.W. *Cottage Gardener; or, Amateur & Cottager's Guide...* 1846. London. 2 vols. VG. $85.00

JOHNSON, George. *Peru From the Air.* 1930. Am Geog Soc. 1st ed. 159 p. F2. $30.00

JOHNSON, George. *60 Sleights.* 1925. London. Johnson. 1st ed. 92 p. EX. J3. $16.00

JOHNSON, H.S. *Bl Eagle From Egg to Earth.* 1935. Doubleday. 1st ed. EX. B10. $7.50

JOHNSON, Harold. *Who's Who in Major League Baseball.* 1933. Chicago. Buxton Pub. 1st ed. folio. 544 p. red bdg. VG. K1. $60.00

JOHNSON, Jane. *Talks With the Children...for Family Use or 1st Day Schools.* 1867. Friends Book Assn. 3rd ed. 108 p. V1. $6.00

JOHNSON, Josephine. *Jordanstown.* 1937. NY. 1st ed. dj. VG. B3. $25.00

JOHNSON, Joyce. *Minor Characters.* 1983. Houghton Mifflin. galley sheets. EX. K2. $125.00

JOHNSON, L.B. *Vantage Point.* 1971. Holt. 1st ed. 636 p. dj. B10. $10.00

JOHNSON, Mary. *Long Roll.* 1911. Houghton Mifflin. 683 p. VG. S1. $14.00

JOHNSON, Mary. *Sir Mortimer.* 1904. NY. 1st ed. dj. EX. $12.00

JOHNSON, Mary. *To Have & To Hold.* 1900. Boston. EX. $15.00

JOHNSON, Merle. *Am 1st Eds.* 1947. NY. 4th ed. G. B3. $45.00

JOHNSON, Oliver. *Abolitionists Vindicated in Review of Eli Thayer's Paper.* 1887. Worcester, MA. 1st ed. wrp. EX. $30.00

JOHNSON, Otta. *Picture Book of Houses Around the World.* 1934. Cleveland. 1st ed? 4to. stiff wrp. VG. B10. $4.00

JOHNSON, P.H. *Good Listener.* 1975. NY. 1st ed. dj. M. $12.00

JOHNSON, P.H. *Impossible Marriage.* 1954. Harcourt Brace. 1st Am ed. dj. EX. C4. $25.00

JOHNSON, R.U. *Battles & Leaders of Civil War by...Officers.* 1887-1889. NY. Century. 1st issue. 4to. 4 vols. VG. T1. $165.00

JOHNSON, Robert. *We: Understanding the Psychology of Romantic Love.* 1983. San Francisco. 1st ed. dj. scarce. C1. $16.50

JOHNSON, Rossiter. *Campfires & Battlefields: Pictorial Hist of Civil War.* 1967. Civil War Pr. 532 p. dj. VG. S1. $22.50

JOHNSON, Roy. *Final Call.* 1979. Goodliffe. 68 p. dj. NM. J3. $9.00

JOHNSON, Roy. *2nd Time Around.* 1971. Goodliffe. 84 p. dj. NM. J3. $8.00

JOHNSON, Roy. *3rd Dimension.* 1977. Goodliffe. 89 p. dj. NM. J3. $8.00

JOHNSON, Ryerson. *Trail of the Moaning Ghost.* 1963. Collier. 1st ed. wrp. EX. F5. $10.00

JOHNSON, Samuel. *New Year's Gift.* 1709. London. 12mo. contemporary calf. H3. $25000.00

JOHNSON, Samuel. *Plan of a Dictionary of the Eng Language.* 1747. London. 1st ed. 4to. Sangorski/Sutcliffe bdg. H3. $5000.00

JOHNSON, Samuel. *Works.* 1824. London. Tegg. New ed. 12 vols. octavo. VG. H3. $1000.00

JOHNSON, Samuel. *Works.* 1903. Pafraets Book Co. Literary Club ed. 1/774. 16 vols. H3. $6000.00

JOHNSON, Stanley. *Doomsday Deposit.* 1980. Dutton. dj. EX. P1. $12.50

JOHNSON, Stowers. *Mundane Tree.* 1947. London. Fortune. presentation. dj. w/sgn letter. H3. $50.00

JOHNSON, T.C. *Life & Letters of Robert Lewis Dabney.* 1903. Richmond. TEG. EX. $60.00

JOHNSON, U.E. *20th-Century Drawings 1900-1940.* 1964. Shorewood. slipcase. EX. D4. $20.00

JOHNSON, U.E. *20th-Century Drawings 1940 to the Present.* 1964. Shorewood. slipcase. EX. D4. $20.00

JOHNSON, V.E. *Chemical Magic.* 1920. London. Pearson. 1st ed. 118 p. EX. J3. $22.00

JOHNSON, W.F. *Life of James G Blaine.* 1893. Atlantic Pub. apparent 1st ed. 578 p. G. B10. $4.00

JOHNSON, W.F. *Life of Sitting Bull.* 1891. Edgewood Pub. 545 p. $45.00

JOHNSON, W.F. *Life of William Tecumseh Sherman.* 1891. Edgewood Pub. 607 p. rebound. S1. $42.50

JOHNSON, W.F. *Life of William Tecumseh Sherman.* 1891. np. 12mo. 607 p. G4. $39.00

JOHNSON & COFFIN. *Charles F Coffin.* 1923. Richmond. Nicholson. 8vo. 213 p. VG. V1. $8.00

JOHNSON. *Parker, Am's Finest Shotgun.* 1963. Harrisburg. 2nd ed. dj. EX. C2. $45.00

JOHNSTON, A. *Case of Erle Stanley Gardner.* 1947. NY. 1st ed. 87 p. dj. VG. B3. $45.00

JOHNSTON, A.F. *Land of the Little Colonel.* 1929. Boston. 1st ed. 133 p. VG. B3. $60.00

JOHNSTON, Anna. *Gordon Johnston.* 1947. Baltimore. private print. 8vo. $25.00

JOHNSTON, H.P. *Storming of Stony Point.* 1900. NY. 1st ed. 231 p. TEG. G. T5. $25.00

JOHNSTON, H.P. *Yorktown Campaign & Surrender of Cornwallis, 1781.* 1975. NY. reprint of 1881 ed. dj. VG. T5. $9.50

JOHNSTON, Mary. *Audrey.* 1902. Houghton Mifflin. 1st ed. G. B10. $5.25

JOHNSTON, Mary. *Sweet Rocket.* 1920. Harper. 1st ed. VG. R3. $17.50

JOHNSTON, Mary. *To Have & To Hold.* 1931. Houghton Mifflin. 1st ed. 331 p. VG. B10. $4.00

JOHNSTON, Velda. *Along a Dark Path.* 1967. Dodd Mead. 1st ed. dj. VG. P1. $15.00

JOHNSTON, Velda. *Crystal Cat.* nd. Book Club. dj. EX. P1. $4.50

JOHNSTON, Velda. *Etruscan Smile.* nd. Book Club. dj. VG. P1. $4.50

JOHNSTON, Velda. *Frenchman.* nd. Book Club. dj. VG. P1. $4.50

JOHNSTON, Velda. *Frenchman.* 1976. Doubleday Book Club. VG. P1. $7.50

JOHNSTON, Velda. *I Came to a Castle.* 1969. Dodd Mead. 1st ed. dj. VG. P1. $20.00

JOHNSTON, Velda. *Late Mrs Fonsell.* nd. Book Club. dj. VG. P1. $4.50

JOHNSTON, Velda. *People on the Hill.* 1971. Dodd Mead. 2nd ed. dj. VG. P1. $7.50

JOHNSTON, Velda. *Phantom Cottage.* 1970. Dodd Mead. dj. xl. P1. $6.00

JOHNSTON, Velda. *Presence in an Empty Room.* nd. Book Club. dj. VG. P1. $5.00

JOHNSTON, Velda. *Room With Dark Mirrors.* nd. Book Club. dj. VG. P1. $4.50

JOHNSTON, Velda. *Stone Maiden.* nd. Book Club. dj. VG. P1. $4.50

JOHNSTON, Velda. *Voice in the Night.* nd. Book Club. dj. VG. P1. $4.50

JOHNSTON, Velda. *Voice in the Night.* 1984. Dodd Mead. 1st ed. dj. EX. P1. $12.95

JOHNSTON, William. *Barney.* 1970. Random House. 1st ed. dj. VG. P1. $12.50

JOHNSTON, William. *Bewitched the Opposite Uncle.* 1970. Whitman. VG. P1. $7.50

JOHNSTON, William. *Dr Kildare & the Magic Key.* 1964. Whitman. VG. P1. $7.50

JOHNSTON, William. *Great Camera Caper.* 1965. Whitman. HrdCvr. VG. P1. $10.00

JOHNSTON, William. *Great Indian Uprising.* 1967. Whitman. VG. P1. $7.50

JOHNSTON, William. *Picture Frame Frame-Up.* 1969. Whitman. VG. P1. $7.50

JOHNSTON, William. *Picture Frame Frame-Up.* 1969. Whitman. 1st ed. no dj issued. EX. F5. $8.00

JOHNSTON, William. *Who's Got the Button?* 1968. Whitman. VG. P1. $12.50

JOLAS, Eugene. *Secession in Astropolis.* 1929. Blk Sun. 1st ed. 1/100. wrp/glassine. EX. H3. $250.00

JOLAS, Eugene. *Transition Workshop.* 1949. Vanguard. 1st ed. dj. VG. H3. $40.00

JOLAS & SAGE. *Transition Stories.* 1929. NY. 1st ed. G. $10.00

JOLLEY, Elizabeth. *Foxybaby.* 1985. Viking. 1st ed. inscr. dj. EX. K2. $45.00

JOLLEY, Elizabeth. *Palomino.* 1987. Persea. UP. wrp. EX. B13. $25.00

JOLLY, David. *Antique Map Price Guide.* 1984. Brookline, MA. 288 p. M. $40.00

JOLLY, David. *Antique Maps, Sea Charts, City Views...* 1990. Brookline, MA. M. A5. $40.00

JOLLY, David. *Maps of Am in Periodicals Before 1800.* 1989. Brookline, MA. M. A5. $20.00

JON, Finn. *Magic of Finn Jon.* 1984. Paris. 40 p. VG. J3. $17.00

JONAS, Klaus. *Blbliography of Somerset Maugham.* 1950. S Hadley. 1/700. VG. G1. $25.00

JONES, B. *Design for Death.* 1967. Indianapolis. 1st Am ed. lg 8vo. dj. EX. $30.00

JONES, Bobby. *Rights & Wrongs of Golf.* 1935. NY. 1st ed. VG. B3. $50.00

JONES, C.A. *Bay Area Figurative Art 1950-1965.* 1990. Berkley. D4. $28.00

JONES, C.C. *Life & Services of Hon Maj-Gen Samuel Ebert of GA.* 1887. Cambridge. 1st ed. later wrp. EX. $95.00

JONES, C.K. *Bibliography of Latin Am Bibliographies.* Greenwood. reprint of 1942 ed. F2. $12.50

JONES, C.R. *Hypnotic Experiment of Dr Reeves.* 1894. Brentano. 1st ed. inscr. VG. R3. $35.00

JONES, D.F. *Colossus & the Crab.* 1977. Berkley. 1st ed. wrp. EX. F5. $10.00

JONES, D.W. *Archer's Goon.* 1984. Greenwillow. 1st ed. dj. EX. P1. $15.00

JONES, D.W. *Fire & Hemlock.* 1985. Greenwillow. 1st ed. dj. EX. P1. $15.00

JONES, D.W. *Howl's Moving Castle.* 1986. Greenwillow. 1st ed. clipped dj. EX. F5. $14.00

JONES, D.W. *Howl's Moving Castle.* 1986. Greenwillow. 1st ed. dj. EX. P1. $15.00

JONES, D.W. *Lives of Christopher Chant.* 1988. Greenwillow. 1st ed. dj. EX. P1. $11.95

JONES, D.W. *Witch Week.* 1982. Greenwillow. 1st ed. dj. VG. P1. $20.00

JONES, D.W. *8 Days of Luke.* 1988. Greenwillow. 1st ed. dj. EX. P1. $11.95

JONES, Edward. *Bardic Mus of Primitive Literature...* 1802. London. folio. 112 p. VG. H3. $300.00

JONES, Elwyn. *Barlow Comes to Judgement.* nd. Book Club. dj. VG. P1. $5.00

JONES, Howard. *Logan & Logan Elm.* 1922. Circleville. 12 p. wrp. T5. $12.50

JONES, J.G. *Amityville Horror II.* 1982. Warner. 1st HrdCvr ed. dj. EX. F5. $12.00

JONES, J.P. *India: Its Life & Thought.* 1908. NY. Ils. TEG. VG. T1. $35.00

JONES, James. *From Here to Eternity.* 1951. Scribner. 1st ed. presentation. dj. H3. $300.00

JONES, James. *From Here to Eternity.* 1952. London. Collins. 1st Eng ed. dj. H3. $100.00

JONES, James. *Go to the Widow-Maker.* 1967. Delacorte. 1st ed. dj. EX. H3. $75.00

JONES, James. *Ice Cream Headache.* 1968. Delacorte. 1st ed. dj. EX. H3. $45.00

JONES, James. *Merry Month of May.* 1971. Delacorte. 1st ed. dj. EX. H3. $40.00

JONES, James. *Pistol.* 1958. Scribner. 1st ed. dj. EX. H3. $50.00

JONES, James. *Some Came Running.* 1957. Scribner. 1st ed. presentation. H3. $125.00

JONES, James. *Touch of Danger.* 1973. Doubleday. 1st ed. dj. EX. H3. $50.00

JONES, James. *Whistle.* 1974. Bruccoli Clark. 1st ed. 1/350. sgn. wrp. EX. B13. $60.00

JONES, James. *Whistle.* 1978. Delacorte. 1st Trade ed. dj. EX. H3. $50.00

JONES, Julie. *Art of Empire: Inca of Peru.* 1964. MPA. Ils. 4to. F2. $15.00

JONES, Julie. *Pre-Columbian Art in NY: Selections of Private Collections.* 1969. MPA. Ils. 4to. wrp. F2. $11.00

JONES, K.M. *Plantation S.* 1957. Indianapolis. 1st ed. dj. EX. $50.00

JONES, Ken. *Destroyer Squadron 23.* 1959. Phil/NY. 1st ed. G. $20.00

JONES, L.C. *Things That Go Bump in the Night.* nd. (1959) Hill Wang. 1st ed. 208 p. dj. VG. B10. $6.50

JONES, L.E. *Dime & Penny.* 1977. Jones. 2nd print. SftCvr. M. J3. $1.50

JONES, L.M. *Quakers in Action: Recent Humanitarian & Reform Activities.* 1929. Macmillan. 1st ed. 12mo. 226 p. VG. V1. $9.00

JONES, L.R. *Home: Social Essays.* 1966. NY. 1st ed. dj. EX. $25.00

JONES, L.R. *Preface to a 20-Vol Suicide Note.* 1961. Totem Pr. EX. B4. $20.00

JONES, Langdon. *Eye of the Lens.* 1972. Macmillan. 1st ed. dj. VG. P1/R3. $15.00

JONES, Laurence. *Piney Woods & Its Story.* 1922. NY. 1st ed. inscr. EX. $32.00

JONES, Leroi. *Moderns: Anthology of New Writing in Am.* 1965. MacGibbon Kee. 1st ed. 351 p. dj. R4. $30.00

JONES, M.H. *Swords Into Plowshares.* 1937. Macmillan. 1st print. 12mo. 374 p. dj. VG. V1. $12.00

JONES, Madison. *Buried Land.* 1963. Viking. 1st ed. dj. EX. B13. $75.00

JONES, Paul. *Coronado & Quivira.* 1937. Lyons, KS. private print. A6. $30.00

JONES, R.A. *Early Jackson.* 1942. Columbus. 1st ed. sgn. 70 p. VG. T5. $32.50

JONES, R.F. *Cybernetic Brains.* 1962. Avalon. 1st ed. dj. EX. R3. $17.50

JONES, R.F. *Deviates.* 1959. Beacon. 1st ed. wrp. VG. R3. $15.00

JONES, R.F. *Renaissance.* 1951. Gnome. 1st ed. dj. VG. R3. $20.00

JONES, R.F. *Stories of Great Physicians.* 1963. Whitman. VG. P1. $7.50

JONES, R.F. *This Island Earth.* 1952. Shasta. 1st ed. sgn. dj. EX. R3. $75.00

JONES, R.F. *Toymaker.* 1951. Fantasy. 1st ed. dj. EX. R3. $10.00

JONES, R.F. *Voyage to the Bottom of the Sea.* 1965. Whitman. VG. P1. $10.00

JONES, R.K. *Lure of Adventure.* 1989. Starmont. 1st ed. wrp. M. R3. $9.95

JONES, R.K. *Shudder Pulps.* 1975. Starmont. 1st ed. dj. EX. R3. $20.00

JONES, R.K. *Shudder Pulps.* 1978. New Am Lib. wrp. EX. R3. $10.00

JONES, Rufus. *Boy Jesus & His Companions.* 1924. NY. Macmillan. 12mo. 189 p. G. V1. $7.50

JONES, Rufus. *Call To What Is Vital.* 1948. Macmillan. 12 mo. 143 p. dj. G. V1. $8.00

JONES, Rufus. *Eli & Sibyl Jones: Their Life & Work.* 1889. Porter Coates. 12mo. 316 p. G. V1. $8.50

JONES, Rufus. *Finding the Trail of Life.* 1926. Macmillan. 1st ed. 12mo. 148 p. G. V1. $7.00

JONES, Rufus. *Fundamental Ends of Life.* 1930. Macmillan. 12mo. 144 p. VG. V1. $8.00

JONES, Rufus. *George Fox: Seeker & Friend.* 1930. London. Allen Unwin. 12mo. 221 p. dj. VG. V1. $10.00

JONES, Rufus. *Haverford College: Hist & Interpretation.* 1933. Macmillan. 8vo. 244 p. VG. V1. $14.00

JONES, Rufus. *Inner Life.* 1917. Macmillan. 12mo. 194 p. VG. V1. $8.00

JONES, Rufus. *Life & Message of George Fox, 1624-1924.* 1924. Macmillan. 16mo. 31 p. dj. VG. V1. $7.50

JONES, Rufus. *Luminous Trail.* 1947. Macmillan. 2nd ed. 12mo. 165 p. dj. V1. $8.00

JONES, Rufus. *New Eyes for Invisibles.* 1943. Macmillan. 12mo. 185 p. reading copy. V1. $6.50

JONES, Rufus. *New Quest.* 1929. Macmillan. 4th print. 12mo. 202 p. G. V1. $8.00

JONES, Rufus. *New Studies in Mystical Religion.* 1928. Macmillan. 12mo. 205 p. G. V1. $22.00

JONES, Rufus. *Pathways to the Reality of God.* 1931. Macmillan. 1st ed. 12mo. 253 p. V1. $7.00

JONES, Rufus. *Quakerism: Spiritual Movement.* 1963. Phil Yearly Meeting. 8vo. 205 p. dj. VG. V1. $12.00

JONES, Rufus. *Quakers in the Am Colonies.* 1911. London. Macmillan. 1st ed. 603 p. EX. $85.00

JONES, Rufus. *Religious Foundations.* 1923. Macmillan. 5th print. 12mo. 144 p. G. V1. $8.00

JONES, Rufus. *Rufus Jones Speaks to Our Time.* 1951. Macmillan. 1st print. 8vo. 289 p. dj. VG. V1. $12.00

JONES, Rufus. *Sm-Town Boy.* 1941. Macmillan. 8vo. 154 p. xl. V1. $15.00

JONES, Rufus. *Stories of Hebrew Heroes.* 1928. London. Allen Unwin. 2nd ed. 12mo. 160 p. G. V1. $8.00

JONES, Rufus. *Story of George Fox.* 1919. Macmillan. 1st print. 12mo. 169 p. G. V1. $8.00

JONES, Rufus. *Testimony of the Soul.* 1937. Macmillan. 4th print. 215 p. G. V1. $8.00

JONES, T. *Fantasticks.* 1964. Drama Book Shop. 1st ed. dj. EX. K2. $125.00

JONES, T. *Once Upon a Lake.* 1957. Minneapolis. Ltd 1st ed. sgn. 285 p. dj. VG. B3. $30.00

JONES, V.C. *Gray Ghosts & Rebel Raiders.* 1956. Holt. 431 p. dj. VG. S1. $17.50

JONES, V.C. *8 Hours Before Richmond.* 1957. Holt. 180 p. G. S1. $10.00

JONES, W.L. *King Arthur in Hist & Legend.* 1911. Cambridge. 1st ed. VG. C1. $34.50

JONES, William. *Quaker Campaigns in Peace & War.* 1899. London. Headley. 8vo. 412 p. V1. $14.00

JONES & JONES. *There Was a Little Man.* 1948. Random House. 1st ed. dj. EX. F5. $25.00

JONES & WILLIAMS. *Household Elegancies.* 1877. NY. 5th ed. G. $45.00

JONES. *Destroyer Squadron 23.* 1949. Phil. 1st ed. dj. C2. $27.00

JONG, Erica. *Fanny.* 1980. NY. 1st ed. dj. M. $15.00

JONG, Erica. *Megan's Book of Divorce.* 1984. New Am Lib. 1st ed. dj. EX. B13. $35.00

JONG, Erica. *Parachutes & Kisses.* 1984. New Am Lib. UP. G. $20.00

JONNSON, D. *Angels.* 1983. NY. 1st Am ed. dj. EX. $20.00

JONSON, Ben. *Works of Ben Jonson.* 1857. Phillips Sampson. octavo. 944 p. contemporary sheep. VG. H3. $45.00

JONSON, Ben. *Works.* 1875. London. Bickers. 9 vols. octavo. H3. $850.00

JONSON, Wilfrid. *Let's Pretend.* 1937. London. Johnson. 1st ed. SftCvr. EX. J3. $6.00

JONSON, Wilfrid. *Magic Tricks & Card Tricks.* 1957. Dover. photos. 96 p. NM. J3. $3.00

JORALEMON, Donald. *Symbolic Space & Ritual Time in Peruvian Healing Ceremony.* 1984. San Diego. 1st ed. 24 p. wrp. F2. $10.00

JORDAN, D.S. *Fishes.* 1907. NY. Holt. clr pls. VG. T3. $90.00

JORDAN, D.S. *Fishes.* 1925. NY. Ils Revised ed. 773 p. G. T5. $125.00

JORDAN, David. *Nile Gr.* 1973. John Day. 1st ed. dj. VG. P1. $12.50

JORDAN, Lee. *Cat's Eyes.* 1982. New Am Lib. 1st HrdCvr ed. dj. EX. F5. $15.00

JORDAN, Neil. *Dream of a Beast.* 1983. Random House. 1st Am ed. dj. EX. F5. $17.00

JORDANOFF, Assen. *Safety in Flight.* 1941. Funk Wagnall. 1st ed. sm folio. $40.00

JORDON, C.T. *30 Card Mysteries.* 1920. Penngrove, CA. 2nd Revised ed. 80 p. EX. J3. $6.00

JORDON, C.T. *4 Full Hands.* 1947. Oakland. 40 p. SftCvr. J3. $3.00

JORDON, P. *Nat Road.* 1948. Indianapolis. Am Trail Series. 1st ed. dj. VG. B3. $30.00

JORDON, Richard. *Journal of Life & Religious Labors.* 1877. Friends Bookstore. 16mo. 218 p. EX. V1. $12.00

JORNS, Auguste. *Quakers As Pioneers in Social Work.* 1931. Macmillan. 1st ed. 12mo. 269 p. dj. VG. V1. $12.00

JOSCELYN, Archie. *Golden Bowl.* 1931. Internat Fiction Lib. VG. P1. $10.00

JOSEPH, Eddie. *Premonition.* 1948. Colon. Abbott. 1st ed. 14 p. EX. J3. $4.00

JOSEPH, Franz. *Star Fleet Technical Manual.* 1975. Ballantine. EX. P1. $50.00

JOSEPHSON, E. *Rockefeller, Internationalist.* 1952. NY. 1st ed. dj. VG. B3. $20.00

JOSEPHSON, H. *Golden Threads.* 1949. NY. 1st ed. 325 p. dj. VG. B3. $27.50

JOSEPHUS THE GREAT. *Card Trickery.* nd. NY. Wehman Bros. 130 p. EX. J3. $5.00

JOSEPHUS. *Wonderful & Most Deplorable Hist of Latter Times of Jews.* 1819. Bellows Falls. 12mo. full leather. C1. $75.00

JOSHI, S.T. *HP Lovecraft Annotated Bibliography.* 1981. Kent State. no dj issued. P1. $30.00

JOWETT, George. *Drama of the Lost Disciples.* 1980. London. 10th ed. dj. EX. C1. $11.00

JOYCE, James. *Anna Livia Plurabelle.* 1928. Crosby Gaige. 1st ed. 1/800. sgn. EX. $1250.00

JOYCE, James. *Anna Livia Plurabelle.* 1928. NY. Warde Rudge. 1/50. printer copy. orig bdg. H3. $3500.00

JOYCE, James. *Chamber Music.* 1918. Huebsch. 1st Authorized ed. VG. B10. $55.00

JOYCE, James. *Collected Poems.* 1936. Blk Sun. 1st ed. 1/750. VG. H3. $400.00

JOYCE, James. *Dubliners.* 1914. London. 1st ed. orig bdg. VG. H3. $1500.00

JOYCE, James. *Dubliners.* 1969. Modern Lib. dj. VG. P1. $15.00

JOYCE, James. *Giacomo Joyce.* 1968. London. 1st ed. dj. EX. $45.00

JOYCE, James. *Giacomo Joyce.* 1968. NY. 1st ed. slipcase. EX. $25.00

JOYCE, James. *Letters.* 1957. Viking. 1st Am ed. dj. VG. $20.00

JOYCE, James. *Portrait of Artist As a Young Man.* 1917. NY. Huebesch. 1st ed. VG. $295.00

JOYCE, James. *Portrait of Artist As a Young Man.* 1928. Modern Lib. 299 p. gr cloth. VG. B10. $3.50

JOYCE, James. *Stephen Hero.* 1945. New Directions. 2nd ed. dj. VG. H3. $50.00

JOYCE, James. *Tales Told of Shem & Shaun.* 1929. Blk Sun. 1/500 on Van Gelder Zonen. slipcase. EX. H3. $750.00

JOYCE, James. *Tales Told of Shem & Shaun.* 1929. Blk Sun. 1st ed. 1/100. sgn. slipcase. EX. H3. $2500.00

JOYCE, James. *Ulysses.* 1922. Paris. Shakespeare Co. 1/150. sgn. gilt morocco. wrp. H3. $25000.00

JOYCE, Stanislaus. *My Brother's Keeper.* 1958. Viking. 1st ed. 8vo. dj. EX. $20.00

JUDD, Cyril. *Gunner Cade.* 1952. Simon Schuster. 1st ed. dj. VG. R3. $17.50

JUDD, Cyril. *Sin in Space.* 1961. Beacon. 1st ed. wrp. VG. R3. $15.00

JUDD, Denis. *Eclipse of Kings.* 1976. Stein Day. 1st ed. 223 p. EX. T4. $8.50

JUDD, H.P. *Intro to the HI Language.* 1943. Honolulu. 1st ed. 16mo. 314 p. VG. T1. $45.00

JUDD, L.F. *Honolulu: Sketches of Life in HI Islands 1828-1861.* 1966. Lakeside Classic. 379 p. T5. $22.50

JUDGE, Hugh. *Memoirs & Journal of Hugh Judge.* 1841. Comly. 12mo. 396 p. leather. G. V1. $15.00

JUDSON, C.I. *Mary Jane: Her Visit.* 1918. Barse. Ils. VG. B10. $3.75

JUKES, Mavis. *No One Is Going to Nashville.* 1983. Knopf. 1st ed. dj. EX. B13. $45.00

JULIAN, Philippe. *Symbolists.* 1973. Phaidon. 1st Am ed. 4to. 240 p. EX. R4. $50.00

JULIAN, Philippe. *Triumph of Art Nouveau Paris Exhibition 1900.* 1974. NY. Larousse. 1st Am ed. 4to. dj. EX. R4. $40.00

JUNOT, Madame. *Memoirs of Napoleon: His Court & Family.* 1984. NY. 2 vols. VG. T1. $25.00

JUST, Ward. *Soldier of the Revolution.* 1970. NY. 1st ed. sgn. dj. EX. T9. $50.00

KACHUR, Thomas. *Mecca.* c 1950s. np. Ils. 189 p. wrp. VG. T5. $19.50

KAEL, Pauline. *Citizen Kane Book.* 1971. Boston. 1st ed. 4to. dj. EX. T1. $40.00

KAEMMERER, Ludwig. *Hubert & Jan Van Eyck.* 1898. Bielefeld. Velhagen Klasing. TEG. D4. $20.00

KAFKA, Franz. *Franz Kafka Miscellany. Pre-Fascist Exile.* 1940. NY. Twice a Year. 1st ed. dj. EX. scarce. K2. $85.00

KAFKA, Franz. *Letters to Milena.* 1990. Schocken. UP. K2. $45.00

KAGAN, H.H. *Am Heritage Pictorial Atlas of US Hist.* 1966. NY. Ils. 424 p. dj. VG. T5. $25.00

KAHN, A.E. *Days With Ulanova.* 1962. Simon Schuster. 1st ed. 1/100. sgns. 235 p. H3. $450.00

KAHN, David. *Code Breakers.* 1967. NY. 1st ed. dj. EX. $45.00

KAHN, James. *Timefall.* 1987. St Martin. 1st ed. dj. EX. P1. $16.95

KAHN, Joan. *Edge of the Chair.* nd. BOMC. dj. VG. P1. $7.50

KAHN, Joan. *Some Things Strange & Sinister.* nd. Ellery Queen Mystery Club. VG. P1. $4.50

KAHN, Roger. *Boys of Summer.* 1972. Harper. 1st ed. dj. EX. K1. $45.00

KAHN, Roger. *How the Weather Was.* 1973. Harper. 1st ed. 317 p. dj. VG. B10. $7.00

KAHN. *Big Drink.* 1960. NY. 1st ed. dj. VG. B3. $17.50

KAJAR. *Magic Secrets.* 1971. Brn Book Co. 3rd ed. 48 p. SftCvr. J3. $3.00

KALLEN, Lucille. *No Lady in the House.* nd. Book Club. dj. VG. P1. $4.50

KALLEN, Lucille. *Tanglewood Murder.* 1980. Wyndham. 1st ed. dj. EX. P1. $15.00

KAMARCK, Lawrence. *Dinosaur.* 1968. Random House. 2nd ed. dj. EX. P1. $10.00

KAMINSKY, S.M. *Down for the Count.* 1985. St Martin. 1st ed. dj. EX. F5. $11.00

KAMINSKY, S.M. *Fala Factor.* 1984. St Martin. 1st ed. dj. VG. P1. $12.50

KAMINSKY, S.M. *Fine Red Rain.* 1987. Scribner. 1st ed. dj. EX. P1. $14.95

KAMINSKY, S.M. *Smart Moves.* 1986. St Martin. 1st ed. dj. EX. F5. $15.00

KAMSTRA, Jerry. *Weed: Adventures of a Dope Smuggler.* 1974. Harper Row. 1st ed. dj. EX. B4. $15.00

KAN, Michael. *Notes on a Polished Greenstone Figure From Guerrero, Mexico.* 1968-1969. Brooklyn Mus. reprint. wrp. F2. $7.50

KAN, Michael. *Sculpture of Ancient W Mexico.* 1989. NM U. Ils. 4to. wrp. F2. $25.00

KANE, E.K. *Arctic Explorations in Years 1853-1855.* 1856. Phil. Childs Peterson. 2 vols. A5. $90.00

KANE, Frank. *Grave Danger.* 1954. Washburn. 1st ed. dj. VG. P1. $12.50

KANE, H.T. *Bayous of LA.* 1944. NY. Ils. 12mo. 341 p. VG. G4. $14.00

KANE, H.T. *Dear Dorothy Dix.* 1952. Doubleday. Ils 1st ed. 314 p. G. S1. $6.00

KANE, H.T. *Gentlemen, Swords, & Pistols.* 1951. NY. 1st ed. EX. $15.00

KANE, H.T. *Gone Are the Days.* 1960. Bramhall House. 344 p. G. S1. $12.00

KANE, H.T. *Smiling Rebel.* 1955. NY. 1st ed. dj. EX. $15.00

KANE, Henry. *Conceal & Disguise.* 1966. Macmillan. 1st ed. dj. EX. P1. $20.00

KANE, Henry. *Hang By Your Neck.* nd. Book Club. dj. VG. P1. $4.50

KANE, Henry. *Hang By Your Neck.* 1949. Simon Schuster. 1st ed. dj. VG. P1. $20.00

KANE, Henry. *Report for a Corpse.* 1948. Simon Schuster. 1st ed. dj. VG. P1. $15.00

KANE, William. *In Warm Desire.* 1966. Corinth. 1st ed. wrp. EX. F5. $8.00

KANER, H. *Sun Queen.* 1946. Kaner. dj. VG. P1. $30.00

KANTOR, MacKinlay. *Cuba Libre.* 1940. NY. 1st ed. inscr. 136 p. dj. VG. T5. $45.00

KANTOR, MacKinlay. *Gentle Annie.* 1942. NY. 2nd imp. inscr. 249 p. G. T5. $25.00

KANTOR, MacKinlay. *Glory for Me.* 1942. NY. 1st ed. inscr. dj. VG. T5. $45.00

KANTOR, MacKinlay. *Happy Land.* 1943. NY. 1st ed. inscr. 92 p. dj. VG. T5. $45.00

KANTOR, MacKinlay. *Here Lies Holly Springs.* 1938. private print. Ils McKay. sgn. H3. $50.00

KANTOR, MacKinlay. *Valedictory.* 1939. NY. 1st ed. inscr. 92 p. G. T5. $35.00

KANTOR, MacKinley. *Romance of Rosy Ridge.* 1937. NY. 1st ed. dj. EX. $28.00

KANTOROWICZ, Hermann. *Spirit of British Policy...* 1931. London. 1st Eng ed. 541 p. dj. T5. $42.50

KAPLAN, G.G. *Fine Art of Magic.* 1948. York, PA. Fleming. 1st ed. 341 p. dj. EX. J3. $18.00

KAPLAN, Howard. *Chopin Express.* 1978. Dutton. 1st ed. dj. EX. F5. $13.00

KAPLAN, Justin. *Mark Twain & His World.* 1974. Simon Schuster. dj. VG. $17.00

KARDYRO, Tony. *Kardyro's Kard Konjuring.* 1955. Kardyro. 1st print. 34 p. SftCvr. EX. J3. $3.00

KARDYRO, Tony. *Routine Supreme.* nd. Regow House. 1st ed. sgn. 12 p. SftCvr. NM. J3. $3.00

KAREN, Ruth. *Song of the Quail. Wondrous World of the Maya.* 1972. 4 Winds Pr. 1st ed. 222 p. dj. F2. $20.00

KARFELD, Kurt. *Versunkene Culturen Lebendige Volker: Inka, Maya, & Azteken.* nd. Berlin. Ils. 4to. 80 p. dj. F2. $25.00

KARIG, Walter. *Zotz!* 1947. Rinehart. dj. VG. P1. $10.00

KARLINS & ANDREWS. *Gomorrah.* 1974. Doubleday. 1st ed. dj. EX. P1. $12.50

KARLOFF, Boris. *And the Darkness Falls.* 1946. World. 1st ed. dj. VG. R3. $25.00

KARLOFF, Boris. *Tales of Terror.* 1943. Tower. dj. VG. R3. $10.00

KARLOFF & LINDSAY. *Dear Boris.* 1975. Knopf. 1st ed. dj. EX. R3. $25.00

KARPINSKI, L.C. *Bibliography of Printed Maps of MI 1804-1880.* 1931. Lansing, MI. 1st ed. VG. $75.00

KARPINSKI, L.C. *Hist of Arithmetic.* 1925. Chicago. 1st ed. 200 p. VG. B3. $60.00

KARPOV, I.M. *Widow Cremated Alive.* 1984. NY. 1st ed. dj. M. $12.00

KARR, C. *Remington Handguns.* 1951. Harrisburg. 2nd ed. dj. EX. B3. $30.00

KARR, Phyllis. *King Arthur Companion.* 1983. Reston, VA. 1st ed. dj. C1. $24.50

KARR & KARR. *Remington Handguns.* 1947. Harrisburg. 1st ed. dj. VG. $30.00

KARSON, Joe. *World's Fastest Card Trick.* 1948. Karson Exclusives. 1st ed. sgn. 8 p. SftCvr. NM. J3. $3.00

KASSELL, Leo. *Land of Shuambrana.* 1935. Viking. 1st ed. VG. R3. $15.00

KASTLE, Herbert. *Edward Berner Is Alive Again!* 1975. Prentice Hall. 1st ed. dj. EX. P1. $15.00

KATCHER, Philip. *Army of the Potomac.* 1975. Osprey. 40 p. M. S1. $9.95

KATCHER, Philip. *Confederate Artillery, Cavalry, & Infantry.* 1986. Osprey. 48 p. M. S1. $9.95

KATZ, Friedrich. *Ancient Am Civilizations.* 1972. Praeger. 1st Eng ed. 386 p. dj. F2. $30.00

KATZ, Irving. *Jewish Soldier From MI in the Civil War.* 1962. Wayne State U. 62 p. pamphlet. VG. S1. $6.00

KATZ, Mickey. *Papa, Pray for Me.* 1977. Simon Schuster. 1st ed. 223 p. dj. NM. B10. $6.25

KATZ, Robert. *Ziggurat.* 1977. Houghton Mifflin. 1st ed. dj. VG. P1. $15.00

KATZ, Welwyn. *3rd Magic.* 1988. Vancouver/Toronto. 1st ed. dj. M. C1. $16.50

KATZ, William. *Facemaker.* 1988. McGraw Hill. 1st ed. dj. VG. P1. $16.95

KATZ, William. *Open House.* nd. Book Club. dj. VG. P1. $4.50

KATZ & SMITH. *2 Friends.* 1988. Birch Brook Pr. B4. $10.00

KATZMAN, L. *Photography in CA 1945-1980.* 1984. NY. Hudson Hills Pr. 1st ed. dj. EX. $55.00

KAUFFMAN, H.J. *Early Am Gunsmiths 1650-1850.* 1952. Harrisburg. 1st ed. dj. VG. B3. $65.00

KAUFFMAN, H.J. *PA-KY Rifle.* 1960. Stackpole. Ils. 4to. 376 p. VG. $35.00

KAUFMAN, Bob. *Golden Sardine.* 1967. City Lights. 1st print. EX. B4. $12.00

KAUFMAN, Bob. *Solitudes Crowded With Loneliness.* 1965. New Directions. 1st print. pb. B4. $5.00

KAUFMAN, G.L. *How's Tricks? 125 Tricks & Stunts.* 1939. Stokes. 3rd print. 133 p. dj. EX. J3. $10.00

KAUFMAN, Richard. *Balls! Lessons in Side-Arm Snookery.* 1977. Tannen. 56 p. NM. J3. $12.00

KAUFMAN, Richard. *Card Magic.* 1979. Brooklyn. Robbins. 1st ed. 2nd print. 183 p. dj. NM. J3. $22.00

KAUFMAN, Richard. *Card Magic.* 1979. Kaufman/Greenberg. 1st ed. 183 p. NM. J3. $18.00

KAUFMAN, Richard. *Card Works.* 1981. Kaufman/Greenberg. 1st ed. 164 p. dj. NM. J3. $18.00

KAUFMAN, Richard. *Coin Magic.* 1981. Kaufman/Greenberg. 1st ed. 266 p. dj. NM. J3. $30.00

KAUFMAN, Richard. *Complete Works of Derek Dingle.* 1982. Kaufman/Greenberg. 1st ed. 219 p. dj. NM. J3. $32.00

KAUFMAN, Richard. *Gene Maze Card Book.* 1980. Kaufman/Maze/Greenberg. 1st ed. 93 p. NM. J3. $11.00

KAUFMAN, Richard. *NY Magic Symposium: Close-Up & Stage Collection 2.* 1983. NY Magic Symposium. 1st ed. 133 p. NM. J3. $21.00

KAUFMAN, Richard. *Richard's Almanac Vol 1.* 1983. Kaufman/Greenberg. 1st HrdCvr ed. 112 p. dj. NM. J3. $27.00

KAUFMAN, Richard. *Sawa's Lib of Magic Vol 1.* 1988. Kaufman/Greenberg. 1st ed. 179 p. NM. J3. $33.00

KAUFMAN, Richard. *Secrets of Brother John Hamman.* 1989. Kaufman/Greenberg. 1st ed. dj. NM. J3. $31.00

KAUFMAN, Richard. *Uncanny Scot, Ron Wilson.* 1987. Kaufman/Greenberg. 1st ed. 157 p. dj. NM. J3. $29.00

KAUFMAN, Richard. *Williamson's Wonders.* 1989. Kaufman/Greenberg. 1st ed. dj. NM. J3. $29.00

KAUFMAN, Walter. *What Is Man?* 1988. Readers Digest. 192 p. SftCvr. $5.00

KAUFMAN, Wolfe. *I Hate Blonds.* 1946. Simon Schuster. 1st ed. dj. VG. P1. $10.00

KAUFMAN & HART. *Am Way.* 1939. Random House. 1st ed. dj. EX. H3. $125.00

KAUFMAN & HART. *I'd Rather Be Right.* 1937. Random House. 1st ed. dj. EX. H3. $100.00

KAUFMAN & HART. *Man Who Came to Dinner.* 1939. Random House. 1st ed. dj. VG. H3. $100.00

KAUFMAN & HART. *Once in a Lifetime/Merrily We Roll Along/You Can't Take...* 1942. Random House. 1st Collected ed. dj. EX. H3. $75.00

KAUFMAN & RAEBURN. *Frank Lloyd Wright: Writings & Buildings.* 1960. Horizon. 1st ed. 8vo. 346 p. dj. EX. R4. $100.00

KAUS, Gina. *Catherine: Portrait of an Empress.* 1935. NY. 1st Eng text ed. VG. $15.00

KAVANAGH, Dan. *Duffy.* 1980. London. 1st ed. dj. M. C4. $75.00

KAVANAGH, Dan. *Duffy.* 1980. London. Cape. 1st ed. sgn. dj. EX. B13. $125.00

KAVANAGH, Dan. *Flaubert's Parrot.* 1984. London. Cape. 1st ed. sgn. dj. EX. K2. $500.00

KAVANAGH, Dan. *Going to the Dogs.* 1987. Pantheon. 1st Am ed. dj. EX. T9. $20.00

KAVANAGH-PRIEST, Anne. *Memoirs of a Gothic Am.* 1929. Macmillan. 1st ed. EX. B10. $6.75

KAVANAUGH, James. *Wilderness Homesteaders.* 1951. Caldwell. 303 p. dj. VG. B3. $20.00

KAVANAUGH, James. *Winter Has Lasted Too Long.* 1977. NY. 1st ed. dj. M. $15.00

KAVANAUGH, Marcus. *You Be the Judge.* 1929. Reilly. apparent 1st ed. 316 p. EX. B10. $4.50

KAWAKAMI, K.K. *Manchoukuo, Child of Conflict.* 1933. 1st Am ed. VG. C1. $8.50

KAY, G.G. *Darkest Road.* 1986. Arbor House. 1st ed. dj. EX. P1. $16.95

KAY, G.G. *Summer Tree.* 1985. Arbor House. 1st ed. dj. EX. P1. $15.95

KAY, G.G. *Wandering Fire.* 1st Canadian ed. dj. M. C1. $15.00

KAYE, Marvin. *Amorous Umbrella.* 1981. Doubleday. 1st ed. dj. EX. R3. $15.00

KAYE, Marvin. *Death in Cyprus.* 1984. St Martin. 1st ed. dj. VG. P1. $15.00

KAYE, Marvin. *Devils & Demons.* 1987. Doubleday. dj. EX. P1. $15.95

KAYE, Marvin. *Handbook of Mental Magic.* 1975. Stein Day. 1st ed. 324 p. dj. NM. J3. $17.00

KAYE, Marvin. *Handbook of Mental Magic.* 1985. Stein Day. inscr. wrp. w/letter. EX. R3. $15.00

KAYE, Marvin. *Masterpieces of Terror & Supernatural.* 1985. Doubleday. 2nd ed. dj. VG. P1. $15.95

KAYE & GODWIN. *Masters of Solitude.* 1978. Doubleday. 1st ed. dj. EX. R3. $27.50

KAYE & GODWIN. *Masters of Solitude.* 1978. Doubleday. 1st ed. dj. VG. P1. $20.00

KAYE & GODWIN. *Wintermind.* 1982. Doubleday. 1st ed. dj. EX. P1. $15.00

KAYSER, Jacques. *Dreyfus Affair.* 1931. Heinemann. 1st ed. blk bdg. VG. B10. $10.00

KAZAN, Elia. *Acts of Love.* 1978. NY. 1st ed. dj. EX. $12.00

KAZAN, Elia. *Assassins.* 1972. NY. 1st ed. dj. EX. $12.00

KAZAN, Elia. *Playing With Fire.* nd. London. Delvin. 1st ed. 13 p. SftCvr. EX. J3. $8.00

KAZANTZAKIS, Nikos. *Last Temptation of Christ.* 1960. Simon Schuster. Trans Bien. 1st Am ed. dj. EX. C4. $75.00

KAZANTZAKIS, Nikos. *Zorba the Greek.* 1953. NY. 1st ed. dj. EX. $75.00

KAZANTZAKIS, Nikos. *3 Plays: Christopher Columbus/Melissa/Kouros.* 1969. Simon Schuster. Trans Dallas. 1st Am ed. M. H3. $45.00

KEARNEY, Patrick. *Man's Man: Comedy of Life Under the L.* 1925. NY. Brentano. inscr. G. H3. $75.00

KEATING, H.R.F. *Filmi Filmi Inspector Ghote.* 1977. Crime Club. 1st ed. dj. xl. P1. $5.00

KEATING, H.R.F. *Inspector Ghote Hunts the Peacock.* 1968. Dutton. 1st ed. dj. EX. P1. $20.00

KEATS, John. *Complete Works.* 1904. London. Virtue. Memorial ed. 1/50. 4 vols. lg octavo. H3. $750.00

KEATS, John. *Endymion: A Poetic Romance.* 1927. London. Oxford. facsimile of 1st ed. dj. EX. C4. $45.00

KEATS, John. *Poems of John Keats.* 1966. Cambridge. Ltd Ed Club. Ils/sgn David Gentleman. 1/1500. slipcase. C4. $90.00

KEATS, John. *Poetical Works & Other Writings.* 1938. Scribner. Hampstead ed. 1/1050. 8 vols. slipcases. H3. $1000.00

KEATS, John. *You Might As Well Live.* 1970. NY. 1st ed. dj. VG. $15.00

KEEBLE, John. *Crab Canon.* 1971. Grossman. 1st ed. dj. EX. C4. $40.00

KEEGAN, John. *6 Armies in Normandy From D-Day to Liberation of Paris.* 1983. Penguin. 1st PB ed. 8vo. wrp. B10. $4.00

KEELER, H.S. *Box From Japan.* nd. AL Burt. xl. VG. R3. $17.50

KEELER, H.S. *Spectacles of Mr Cagliostro.* nd. AL Burt. EX. R3. $17.50

KEEN, R.H. *Little Ape.* 1921. London. Hendersons. Ils John Austen. 1st ed. sgns. dj. EX. R4. $200.00

KEENE, Carolyn. *Bungalow Mystery.* nd. Grosset Dunlap. decor brd. VG. P1. $4.00

KEENE, Carolyn. *By Light of the Study Lamp.* nd. Grosset Dunlap. VG. P1. $7.50

KEENE, Carolyn. *Clue in the Jewel Box.* nd. Grosset Dunlap. decor brd. VG. P1. $4.00

KEENE, Carolyn. *Clue of Tapping Heels.* nd. Grosset Dunlap. decor brd. EX. P1. $4.00

KEENE, Carolyn. *Clue of the Whistling Bagpipes.* nd. Grosset Dunlap. decor brd. VG. P1. $4.00

KEENE, Carolyn. *Ghost of Blackwood Hall.* nd. Grosset Dunlap. EX. P1. $4.00

KEENE, Carolyn. *Message in the Hollow Oak.* nd. Grosset Dunlap. decor brd. EX. P1. $4.00

KEENE, Carolyn. *Moonstone Castle Mystery.* nd. Grosset Dunlap. EX. P1. $4.00

KEENE, Carolyn. *Mystery at Lilac Inn.* nd. Grosset Dunlap. decor brd. VG. P1. $4.00

KEENE, Carolyn. *Mystery of Brass-Bound Trunk.* nd. Grosset Dunlap. decor brd. VG. P1. $4.00

KEENE, Carolyn. *Mystery of the Fire Dragon.* nd. Grosset Dunlap. EX. P1. $4.00

KEENE, Carolyn. *Mystery of the Tolling Bell.* nd. Grosset Dunlap. decor brd. VG. P1. $4.00

KEENE, Carolyn. *Password to Larkspur Lane.* nd. Grosset Dunlap. VG. P1. $7.50

KEENE, Carolyn. *Portrait in the Sand.* 1943. Grosset Dunlap. 216 p. VG. B10. $3.75

KEENE, Carolyn. *Quest of the Missing Map.* nd. Grosset Dunlap. decor brd. VG. P1. $4.00

KEENE, Carolyn. *Secret in the Old Attic.* nd. Grosset Dunlap. decor brd. VG. P1. $4.00

KEENE, Carolyn. *Secret of the Red Gate Farm.* nd. Grosset Dunlap. decor brd. VG. P1. $4.00

KEENE, Carolyn. *Sierra Gold Mystery.* nd. Grosset Dunlap. decor brd. EX. P1. $7.50

KEENE, Carolyn. *Sign of the Twisted Candles.* nd. Grosset Dunlap. decor brd. VG. P1. $4.00

KEENE, Day. *Big Kiss-Off.* 1954. Graphic. 1st ed. VG. F5. $10.00

KEENE, Day. *Seed of Doubt.* 1961. Simon Schuster. 1st ed. dj. EX. F5. $20.00

KEIM, D.B.R. *Sheridan's Troopers on the Border.* 1870. Phil. 308 p. A5. $70.00

KEIM, S.L. *Quakers & Indians: Story of William Penn...* 1932. Phil. Winston. 8vo. 47 p. dj. VG. V1. $10.00

KEITH, Brandon. *Affair of the Gentle Saboteur.* 1966. Whitman. VG. P1. $12.50

KEITH, Brandon. *Affair of the Gunrunner's Gold.* 1967. Whitman. VG. P1. $12.50

KEITH, Brandon. *Message From Moscow.* 1966. Whitman. VG. P1. $7.50

KEITH, Brandon. *Uses of Globes.* 1811. NY. 1st Am ed. full leather. C2. $35.00

KEITH, Carlton. *Taste of Sangria.* 1968. Crime Club. 1st ed. VG. P1. $10.00

KEITH, Elmer. *Autobiography.* 1974. NY. Book Club ed. dj. VG. B3. $25.00

KEITH, Elmer. *Big Game Hunting.* 1954. Boston. photos. 410 p. dj. VG. B3. $50.00

KEITH, Elmer. *Big Game Rifles & Cartridges.* 1936. Plantersville. 1st ed. VG. B3. $87.50

KEITH, Elmer. *Guns & Ammo for Big Game Hunting.* 1965. Los Angeles. 1st ed. dj. VG. B3. $100.00

KEITH, Elmer. *Shotguns.* 1950. Harrisburg. 1st ed. dj. VG. B3. $55.00

KEITH, Elmer. *6-Gun Cartridges & Loads.* 1936. Harrisburg. 2nd ed. VG. $50.00

KEITH, Elmer. *6-Gun Cartridges & Loads.* 1936. Plantersville. 1st ed. dj. VG. B3. $100.00

KEITH, Elmer. *6-Guns.* 1955. Harrisburg. 1st ed. dj. VG. B3. $90.00

KELEMEN, Pal. *Art of Am: Ancient & Hispanic.* 1969. Crowell. 1st ed. 402 p. dj. F2. $25.00

KELEMEN, Pal. *Folk Baroque in Mexico: Mestizo Architecture.* 1974. Smithsonian. Ils. 50 p. wrp. F2. $12.50

KELEMEN, Pal. *Medieval Am Art.* 1956. Macmillan. 1st 1 vol ed. 4to. F2. $45.00

KELEMEN, Pal. *Vanishing Art of Am.* 1977. Walker. 1st ed. 4to. F2. $20.00

KELLAND, C.B. *Into His Own: Story of an Airdale.* 1915. Phil. 1st ed. EX. $15.00

KELLAND, C.B. *Key Man.* 1952. Doubleday Book Club. VG. P1. $7.50

KELLAND, C.B. *Nameless Corpse.* 1957. Doubleday Book Club. VG. P1. $7.50

KELLEAM, J.E. *Hunters of Space.* 1960. Avalon. dj. xl. P1. $6.00

KELLEAM, J.E. *Little Men.* 1960. Avalon. dj. xl. P1. $5.00

KELLEAM, J.E. *When the Red King Woke.* 1966. Avalon. 1st ed. dj. EX. P1. $20.00

KELLER, Alan. *Morgan's Raid.* 1961. Indianapolis. 1st ed. 271 p. dj. VG. B3. $25.00

KELLER, D.H. *Folson Flint.* 1969. Arkham House. 1st ed. dj. EX. P1/R3. $30.00

KELLER, D.H. *Homunculus.* 1949. Prime Pr. Ltd ed. 1/112. sgn. dj. EX. R3. $125.00

KELLER, D.H. *Homunculus.* 1949. Prime Pr. 1st ed. dj. EX. R3. $25.00

KELLER, D.H. *Life Everlasting.* 1947. Avalon. 1st ed. dj. VG. R3. $30.00

KELLER, D.H. *Solitary Hunters & the Abyss.* 1948. New Era Pub. 1st ed. sgn. dj. EX. R3. $70.00

KELLER, D.H. *Tales From Underwood.* 1974. Spearman. 1st Eng ed. dj. EX. R3. $25.00

KELLER, H.S. *Mystery of the Fiddling Cracksman.* 1938. Triangle. 4th ed. dj. VG. P1. $30.00

KELLER, Harry. *Official Detective Omnibus.* 1948. Duell Sloan Pierce. 1st ed. VG. P1. $20.00

KELLER, Helen. *Helen Keller's Journal 1936-1937.* 1938. Doubleday Doran. sgn. slipcase. H3. $200.00

KELLER, Helen. *Story of My Life.* 1903. NY. 1st ed. pls. VG. $45.00

KELLER, James. *Men of Maryknoll.* 1943. Grosset Dunlap. 191 p. dj. VG. B10. $3.50

KELLERMAN, Jonathan. *Over the Edge.* 1987. Atheneum. UP. inscr. K2. $75.00

KELLEY, C.F. *Chinese Bronzed From the Buckingham Collection.* 1946. Chicago Art Inst. 1st ed. 4to. 164 p. EX. R4. $60.00

KELLEY, David. *Astronomical Identities of Mesoamerican Gods.* 1980. Miami. 1st ed. 8vo. 54 p. F2. $15.00

KELLEY, Francis. *Blood-Drenched Altars.* 1935. Bruce Pub. 1st ed. 502 p. F2. $15.00

KELLEY, L.P. *Luke Sutton: Outrider.* 1984. Doubleday. 1st ed. dj. RS. EX. P1. $12.50

KELLEY, L.P. *Luke Sutton: Outrider.* 1984. Doubleday. 1st ed. RS. M. R3. $15.00

KELLEY, L.P. *Time 110100.* 1972. Walker. 1st ed. dj. EX. P1/R3. $15.00

KELLEY, Thomas. *I Found Cleopatra.* 1977. Starmont. 1st ed. wrp. EX. R3. $7.50

KELLEY, W.M. *Different Drummer.* 1962. NY. 1st ed. dj. EX. T9. $85.00

KELLIHER, D.T. *Cottonwood Law.* 1946. Phoenix Pr. 1st ed. dj. VG. F5. $15.00

KELLNER, Bruce. *Bibliography of Carl Van Vechten.* 1980. Westport. 1st ed. EX. G1. $15.00

KELLOCK, Harold. *Houdini: His Life Story.* 1931. Bl Ribbon. 6th print. 384 p. VG. J3. $11.00

KELLOGG, Marjorie. *Like the Lion's Tooth.* 1972. NY. 1st ed. presentation. dj. EX. $16.00

KELLY, Anne. *Cuna.* 1966. NY. Barnes. 1st ed. 440 p. dj. xl. P1. $10.00

KELLY, F.K. *Star Ship Invincible.* 1979. Capra. ARC. wrp. EX. F5. $20.00

KELLY, F.K. *Star Ship Invincible.* 1979. Capra. 1st ed. wrp. M. R3. $35.00

KELLY, George. *Reflected Glory.* 1937. NY. French. 1st ed. dj. EX. H3. $50.00

KELLY, George. *Reflected Glory.* 1937. NY. French. 1st ed. presentation. 235 p. dj. H3. $175.00

KELLY, Judith. *Mark of Clover.* 1953. Charlottesville. Ltd ed. inscr. EX. $35.00

KELLY, Mary. *Dead Corpse.* 1966. Michael Joseph. 1st ed. dj. xl. P1. $6.00

KELLY, Mary. *Dead Man's Riddle.* 1967. Walker. dj. VG. P1. $17.50

KELLY, Mary. *Spoilt Kill.* 1962. Michael Joseph. 5th ed. dj. xl. P1. $6.00

KELLY, Robert. *Kill the Messenger Who Brings Bad News.* 1979. Blk Sparrow. HrdCvr ed. 1/50. sgn. H3. $50.00

KELLY, Walt. *I'd Rather Be President.* 1956. Simon Schuster. 1st ed. dj. EX. F5. $40.00

KELLY, Walt. *Pogo a la Sundae.* 1961. NY. 1st ed. wrp. VG. B3. $25.00

KELLY, Walt. *Pogo.* 1951. NY. later print. wrp. VG. $10.00

KELLY & KELLY. *Dancing Diplomats.* 1950. NM U. Ils Gustave Baumann. 1st ed. 254 p. dj. F2. $20.00

KELSEY, D.M. *Life & Public Services of William E Gladstone.* 1898. WA. Ils. EX. $35.00

KELSEY, R.W. *Centennial Hist of Moses Brn School 1819-1919.* 1919. Providence. 1st ed. TEG. EX. T1. $35.00

KELSEY, Vera. *Red River Runs N.* 1951. NY. 1st ed. 298 p. dj. VG. B3. $25.00

KELSEY, Vera. *Whisper Murder.* 1946. Crime Club. 1st ed. xl. VG. P1. $12.50

KELSEY, Vera. *7 Keys to Brazil.* 1940. Funk Wagnall. Revised ed. 314 p. F2. $10.00

KELSEY, Vera. *7 Keys to Brazil.* 1940. NY. 1st ed. dj. EX. T1. $20.00

KELSEY & DE JONGH OSBORNE. *4 Keys to Guatemala.* 1948. Funk Wagnall. Ils. 332 p. dj. F2. $15.00

KELTON, Gerald. *Dolores.* 1934. Eldon. 1st ed. dj. VG. P1. $15.00

KEMBLE, E.W. *Blackberries & Their Adventures.* 1897. NY. 1st ed. pls. VG. T1. $225.00

KEMELMAN, Harry. *Someday the Rabbi Will Leave.* 1985. Morrow. 1st ed. dj. EX. P1. $16.00

KEMLER, E. *Irreverent Mr Mencken.* 1950. Boston. 1st ed. dj. VG. B3. $20.00

KENDALL, Aubyn. *Art & Archaeology of Pre-Columbian Middle Am.* 1977. Boston. Hall. 324 p. F2. $35.00

KENDALL, B.J. *Doctor at Home: Diseases of Man & Horse.* 1887. (1st 1882) VT. Ils. 96 p. $12.50

KENDALL, D.S. *Gentilz: Artist of the Old SW.* 1974. TX U. Ils. 127 p. dj. D4. $40.00

KENDALL, E. *Crested Wren.* 1799. London. Newberry. 1st ed. VG. $250.00

KENDALL, G.W. *Narrative of TX, Santa Fe Expedition.* 1844. Harper. 1st ed. 2 vols. A5. $475.00

KENDALL, John. *Letters on Religious Subjects Written by Diverse Friends...* 1831. Phil. Thomas Kite. 12mo. 2 vols in 1. full leather. VG. V1. $16.00

KENDALL, Jonathan. *Passage Through El Dorado.* 1984. Morrow. 1st ed. 312 p. dj. F2. $15.00

KENDALL, L.B. *Ship's Organization Book, USS Nourmahal, US Coast Guard.* c 1944. np. T5. $95.00

KENDRICK, Baynard. *Blind Man's Bluff.* 1946. Triangle. dj. EX. P1. $15.00

KENDRICK, Baynard. *Out of Control.* 1945. Doubleday Book Club. VG. P1. $10.00

KENNAN, George. *Siberia & the Exile System.* 1891. NY. 1st ed. 2 vols. VG. T1. $35.00

KENNAWAY, James. *Cost of Living Like This.* 1969. NY. 1st ed. dj. EX. $12.00

KENNAWAY, James. *Kennaway Papers.* 1981. London. 1st ed. dj. M. $15.00

KENNAWAY, James. *Tunes of Glory.* 1957. NY. 1st ed. dj. M. $22.00

KENNEALY, Jerry. *Polo Anyone?* 1988. St Martin. 1st ed. dj. EX. F5. $15.00

KENNEALY, Patricia. *Throne of Scone.* 1986. 1st ed. dj. EX. C1. $12.50

KENNEDY, Adam. *Just Like Humphrey Bogart.* 1978. Viking. 1st ed. dj. VG. P1. $15.00

KENNEDY, J.F. *Profiles in Courage.* 1956. NY. 1st ed. 2 djs. EX. $80.00

KENNEDY, J.F. *While Eng Slept.* 1940. London/Melbourne. 1st Eng ed. 256 p. red bdg. scarce. $125.00

KENNEDY, R.E. *More Mellows.* 1931. Dodd Mead. 1st ed. quarto. 179 p. dj. H3. $60.00

KENNEDY, R.F. *Times To Remember.* 1974. 1st Am ed. dj. EX. C1. $6.50

KENNEDY, W.S. *Plan of Union; or, Hist of Presbyterian...Churches...* 1856. Hudson, OH. 1st ed. 262 p. rebacked. T5. $195.00

KENNEDY, William. *Ink Truck.* 1969. London. 1st Eng ed. as issued. EX. K2. $125.00

KENNEDY, William. *Ironweed.* 1983. Viking. UP. EX. K2. $450.00

KENNEDY, William. *Legs.* 1975. Coward McCann. UP. sgn. wrp. EX. B13. $850.00

KENNEDY, William. *Legs.* 1975. Coward McCann. 1st ed. dj. EX. C4. $75.00

KENNEDY, William. *Legs.* 1975. Coward McCann. 1st ed. dj. VG. B3. $45.00

KENNEDY, William. *Quinn's Book.* 1988. Viking. ARC. sgn. dj. EX. K2. $100.00

KENNEDY, William. *Quinn's Book.* 1988. Viking. UP. inscr. wrp. EX. K2. $150.00

KENNEDY & COPPOLA. *Cotton Club.* 1986. St Martin. 1st ed. wrp. EX. B13. $75.00

KENNEDY & LOPEZ. *Semana Santa in Sierra Tarahumara: Comparative Study...* 1981. Los Angeles. 1st ed. 78 p. wrp. F2. $15.00

KENNEDY. *Principles of Aeroplane Construction.* 1911. NY. 137 p. VG. scarce. $85.00

KENNELL, R.E. *Vanya of the Streets.* 1931. Harper. 1st ed. 208 p. B10. $3.50

KENNER, Hugh. *Portrait of an Artist (James Joyce) As a Young Man.* 1968. Ltd Ed Club. Ils/sgn Brian Keogh. 1/1500. slipcase. EX. C4. $150.00

KENNEY, G.C. *General Kenney Reports.* 1949. NY. 1st ed. 594 p. dj. T5. $25.00

KENRICK, Tony. *Faraday's Flowers.* 1985. Doubleday. 1st ed. dj. EX. P1. $14.95

KENT, Alexander. *Enemy in Sight!* 1970. Putnam. 1st Am ed. dj. EX. F5. $22.00

KENT, Alexander. *Inshore Squadron.* 1979. Putnam. 1st Am ed. dj. EX. F5. $15.00

KENT, Alexander. *To Glory We Steer.* 1968. Putnam. 1st Am ed. dj. VG. F5. $25.00

KENT, Alexander. *Tradition of Victory.* 1982. Putnam. 1st Am ed. dj. EX. F5. $17.50

KENT, Charles. *Wellerisms From Pickwick/Master Humphrey's Clock.* 1886. London. Redway. 1st ed. 16mo. violet bdg. H3. $75.00

KENT, H.S. *Poems.* 1908. Phil. Ferris Leach. 16mo. 104 p. VG. V1. $9.50

KENT, Rockwell. *Candide.* 1928. Random House. 1/95 on French rag. sgn. TEG. quarto. H3. $1500.00

KENT, Rockwell. *Journal of Quiet Adventure in AK.* 1920. Putnam. 1st ed. 1st state. 4to. 217 p. TEG. VG. $120.00

KENT, Rockwell. *N by E.* 1930. Brewer Warren. 1st Trade ed. presentation. dj. H3. $175.00

KENT, Rockwell. *N Christmas.* 1941. NY. 1st ed. dj. VG. B3. $25.00

KENT, Rockwell. *Rockwellkentiana.* 1933. Harcourt Brace. 1st ed. VG. $65.00

KENT, Rockwell. *To Thee!* 1946. Manitowoc, WI. Rahr Malting Co. 1st ed. 4to. EX. R4. $100.00

KENT, Rockwell. *World-Famous Paintings.* 1939. Wise. 100 pl. VG. $50.00

KENT, W.W. *Rare Hooked Rugs.* 1941. Springfield. 1st ed. sgn. VG. B3. $40.00

KENWORTHY, L.S. *Introducing Children & Youth to Life of the Spirit.* 1960. Indianapolis. John Woolman. 12mo. 13 p. pamphlet. VG. V1. $4.50

KENYON, Michael. *May You Die in Ireland.* 1965. Morrow. 2nd ed. dj. EX. P1. $12.00

KENYON, Michael. *100,000 Welcomes.* 1970. Coward McCann. 1st ed. dj. EX. F5. $13.00

KEPPLER, Victor. *Man & Camera: Photographic Autobiography.* 1970. NY. 1st ed. slipcase. EX. G1. $35.00

KERBEY, J.O. *Boy Spy in Dixie.* 1897. WA. wrp. VG. $20.00

KERBEY, J.O. *Further Adventures of the Boy Spy in Dixie.* 1897. WA. wrp. VG. $40.00

KERNODLE, G.R. *From Art to Theatre.* 1947. Chicago. 3rd imp. quarto. 255 p. dj. VG. H3. $75.00

KEROUAC, Jack. *Book of Dreams.* 1961. City Lights. 1st ed. wrp. VG. K2. $100.00

KEROUAC, Jack. *Dharma Bums.* 1958. Viking. 1st ed. dj. EX. K2. $185.00

KEROUAC, Jack. *Dr Sax.* 1959. NY. 1st ed. 1/26. sgn. orig brd. EX. H3. $2500.00

KEROUAC, Jack. *Kerouac's Town.* 1973. Capra. Chapbook Series. 1/125. sgn. EX. K2. $45.00

KEROUAC, Jack. *Lonesome Traveler.* 1960. NY. 1st ed. dj. VG. B3. $80.00

KEROUAC, Jack. *Lonesome Traveler.* 1962. London. Deutsch. 1st ed. dj. VG. $75.00

KEROUAC, Jack. *Maggie Cassidy.* 1959. Avon. PB Orig. 1st issue. VG. B13. $50.00

KEROUAC, Jack. *Maggie Cassidy.* 1960. London. 1st UK/PB Orig ed. wrp. VG. scarce. T9. $55.00

KEROUAC, Jack. *Mexico City Bls.* 1959. Grove Evergreen. 1st ed. 3rd print. B4. $5.00

KEROUAC, Jack. *On the Road.* 1957. Viking. 1st ed. dj. EX. C4. $450.00

KEROUAC, Jack. *On the Road.* 1958. London. Deutsch. 1st UK ed. dj. EX. K2. $475.00

KEROUAC, Jack. *Pull My Daisy.* 1961. NY. 1st ed. wrp. K2. $90.00

KEROUAC, Jack. *Sartori in Paris.* 1966. Grove Pr. 1st ed. dj. EX. C4. $100.00

KEROUAC, Jack. *Satori in Paris.* 1967. London. Deutsch. 1st UK ed. dj. K2. $65.00

KEROUAC, Jack. *Satori in Paris.* 1988. Grove Evergreen. EX. B4. $7.95

KEROUAC, Jack. *Vanity of Duluoz.* 1968. NY. 1st ed. as issued. K2. $75.00

KEROUAC, Jack. *Visions of Cody.* 1972. McGraw Hill. ARC. dj. w/promotional sheet. EX. K2. $125.00

KEROUAC, Jack. *Visions of Gerard.* 1963. Farrar Straus. 1st ed. dj. VG. K2. $85.00

KEROUAC, Jan. *Baby Driver.* 1981. St Martin. UP. EX. B4. $40.00

KEROUAC, Jan. *Baby Driver.* 1981. St Martin. 1st ed. inscr. dj. B4. $35.00

KEROUAC, Jan. *Train Song.* 1988. Holt. 1st ed. dj. EX. B4. $15.95

KERR, E.M. *Yoknapatawpha.* 1969. NY. 1st ed. 284 p. dj. VG. B3. $30.00

KERR, Jean. *Please Don't Eat the Daisies.* 1957. NY. 1st ed. dj. EX. $16.00

KERR, Jean. *Snake Has All the Lines.* 1960. NY. 1st ed. dj. EX. $10.00

KERR, Justin. *Maya Vase Book.* 1989. NY. 1/1200. sgn. oblong 4to. F2. $45.00

KERR, Katharine. *Darkspell.* 1987. Doubleday. 1st ed. dj. EX. P1. $17.95

KERR, Walter. *How Not To Write a Play.* 1955. Simon Schuster. 1st ed. 244 p. G. B10. $4.00

KERRICK, H.S. *Military & Naval Am.* 1916. Doubleday Page. 8vo. 404 p. G. $55.00

KERSEY, Jesse. *Narrative of Early Life, Travels, & Gospel Labors.* 1851. Phil. Chapman. 1st ed. 16mo. 288 p. fair. V1. $12.00

KERSEY, Jesse. *Treatise on Fundamental Doctrines of Christian Religion.* 1815. Phil. Kimber. 16mo. 118 p. G. V1. $20.00

KERSH, Gerald. *Night & the City.* 1946. Simon Schuster. 1st ed. dj. EX. F5. $45.00

KERSH, Gerald. *Prelude to a Certain Midnight.* 1947. Doubleday. 1st ed. dj. EX. F5. $45.00

KERSH, Gerald. *Prelude to a Certain Midnight.* 1947. Heinemann. 1st ed. VG. P1. $30.00

KERSH, Gerald. *Secret Masters.* 1953. Ballantine. 1st ed. dj. EX. R3. $75.00

KERSH, Gerald. *Sergeant Nelson of the Guards.* 1945. Winston. VG. P1. $20.00

KERSH, Gerald. *Song of the Flea.* 1948. Heinemann. 1st Canadian ed. VG. P1. $20.00

KERSH, Gerald. *Song of the Flea.* 1948. Heinemann. 2nd ed. VG. P1. $15.00

KERSH, Gerald. *Weak & the Strong.* 1946. Simon Schuster. 1st ed. dj. VG. P1. $25.00

KERSHAW & TEMPLE. *Richard Aldington: An Intimate Portrait.* 1965. IL U. 1st ed. sm 8vo. dj. EX. R4. $20.00

KERSHNER, H.E. *Quaker Service in Modern War: Spain & France 1939-1940.* 1950. Prentice Hall. 1st ed. 8vo. 195 p. dj. VG. V1. $10.00

KERSTEN, Peter. *How To Do Magic for Children.* 1979. Berlin. Kersten. 1st ed. sgn. NM. J3. $9.00

KERTESZ, Andre. *Distortions.* 1976. NY. 1st ed. dj. EX. C2. $37.00

KESEﻨ, Ken. *Day After Superman Died.* 1980. Northridge. Lord John. 1/50. sgn. EX. K2. $250.00

KESEY, Ken. *Day After Superman Died.* 1980. Northridge. Lord John. 1st ed. 1/300. sgn. EX. B13. $85.00

KESEY, Ken. *Demon Box.* 1986. NY. 1st ed. inscr. dj. EX. C4. $85.00

KESEY, Ken. *Demon Box.* 1986. Viking. dj. M. H3. $75.00

KESEY, Ken. *Further Inquiry.* 1990. Viking. UP. wrp. EX. K2. $50.00

KESEY, Ken. *Kesey.* 1977. NW Review Books. 1st HrdCvr ed. dj. EX. K2. $100.00

KESEY, Ken. *Kesey.* 1977. NW Review Books. 2nd ed. stiff wrp. w/inscr card. H3. $125.00

KESEY, Ken. *Little Tricker the Squirrel Meets Big-Double the Bear.* 1990. Viking. Ils/sgn Barry Moser. 1st ed. dj. EX. K2. $45.00

KESEY, Ken. *Sometimes a Great Notion.* 1964. Viking. 1st ed. 1st issue. dj. EX. K2. $150.00

KESEY, Ken. *1 Flew Over the Cuckoo's Nest.* c 1962. Viking. 1st ed. orig bdg. dj. EX. H3. $400.00

KESEY, Ken. *1 Flew Over the Cuckoo's Nest.* 1962. London. 1st UK ed. dj. VG. T9. $150.00

KESEY, Ken. *1 Flew Over the Cuckoo's Nest.* 1962. NY. 1st ed. dj. VG. K2. $225.00

KESSEL, Joseph. *Lion.* 1959. NY. 1st ed. dj. EX. $40.00

KESSLER, Jasha. *Whatever Love Declares.* 1969. Los Angeles. Ltd ed. 1/500. inscr. H3. $40.00

KESSLER, Milton. *Road Came Once.* 1963. OH U. inscr. gray bdg. dj. H3. $40.00

KESTAVAN, G.R. *Pale Invaders.* 1974. Atheneum. 1st ed. dj. EX. F5. $17.00

KETTERER, Bernadine. *Manderley Mystery.* 1937. Eldon. 1st ed. VG. P1. $20.00

KEY, Alexander. *Red Eagle: Adventurous Tale of 2 Young Flyers.* 1930. Wise Parslow. Ils. 120 p. G. T5. $17.50

KEYES, A.M. *5 Senses.* 1911. NY. Ils JW Smith. 12mo. VG. A4. $50.00

KEYES, F.P. *Cookbook.* 1955. Garden City. 1st ed. dj. VG. B3. $32.50

KEYES, F.P. *Frances Parkinson Keyes Cookbook.* 1955. NY. 1st ed. dj. VG. B3. $42.50

KEYES, F.P. *Once on Esplanade.* 1947. Dodd Mead. Apparent 1st ed. 202 p. VG. B10. $5.50

KEYES, F.P. *Sublime Shepherdess: Life of St Bernadette of Lourdes.* 1947. Messner. 4th ed. 182 p. dj. VG. B10. $4.25

KEYES, R.S. *Japanese Woodblock Prints.* 1984. Oberlin College. 270 p. D4. $45.00

KEYES, R.S. *Male Journey in Japanese Prints.* 1989. Berkley. 189 p. dj. D4. $45.00

KEYHOE, D.E. *Flying the Lindbergh.* 1928. NY. 1st ed. 299 p. G. T5. $22.50

KEYSER, Leander. *Birds of the Rockies.* 1902. McClurg. VG. T3. $45.00

KHAYYAM, Omar;   see Fitzgerald, Edward.

KHERDIAN, David. *Homage to Adana.* 1971. Gresno. Giligia Pr. sgn. M. H3. $45.00

KHERDIAN, David. *Taking the Soundings on 3rd Ave.* 1981. Woodstock, NY. 1/50. sgn. gilt bdg. H3. $35.00

KICKNOSWAY, Faye. *O You Can Walk on the Sky.* 1972. Capra. Chapbook Series. 1/50. sgn. G. K2. $20.00

KIDD, J.H. *Personal Recollections of a Cavalryman.* 1908. Ionia. 1st ed. G. B3. $150.00

KIDD, Virginia. *Millenial Women.* 1978. Delacorte. 1st ed. dj. EX. P1. $20.00

KIDDER, Tracy. *Road to Yuba City.* 1974. Doubleday. 1st ed. sgn. dj. EX. B13. $100.00

KIDDER & CHINCHILLA. *Art of the Ancient Maya.* 1959. Crowell. 1st ed. 124 p. dj. F2. $50.00

KIDDER & FLETCHER. *Brazil & the Brazilians.* 1857. Childs Peterson. 1st ed. maps. 630 p. F2. $125.00

KIENZLE, W.X. *Deathbed.* 1986. Andrews McKeel Parker. 1st ed. dj. VG. P1. $15.00

KIENZLE, W.X. *Shadow of Death.* 1983. Andrews McKeel Parker. 1st ed. dj. VG. P1. $15.00

KIERAN, John. *Intro to Birds.* 1950. Doubleday. Ils Don Eckelberry. 77 p. VG. B10. $5.25

KIERAN, John. *Not Under Oath: Recollections & Reflections.* nd. (1964) Houghton. 3rd ed. 282 p. dj. EX. B10. $4.00

KIERNAN, Thomas. *Wht Hound of the Mt & Other Irish Folk Tales.* 1962. NY. 1st ed. dj. EX. C1. $7.50

KILGALLEN, Dorothy. *Girl Around the World.* nd. (1936) McKay. 1st ed. 219 p. VG. B10. $5.75

KILGORE, Trout;   see Farmer, Phillip Jose.

KILIAN, Crawford. *Icequake.* 1979. Douglas McIntyre. 1st ed. dj. VG. P1. $20.00

KILIAN, Crawford. *Tsunami.* 1983. Douglas McIntyre. 1st ed. dj. EX. P1. $20.00

KILLENS, J.O. *And Then We Heart Thunder.* 1963. Knopf. 1st ed. dj. EX. K2. $55.00

KILLENS, J.O. *Youngblood.* 1966. Trident. 2nd ed. dj. EX. K2. $35.00

KILMAN & WRIGHT. *Story of Am Opportunity.* 1954. Prentice Hall. Ils Eggenhoffer. 1st ed. dj. VG. $10.00

KILMER, Joyce. *Circus & Other Essays.* 1916. NY. 1st ed. dj. EX. $65.00

KILWORTH, Garry. *In Solitary.* 1977. Faber. 1st UK ed. dj. EX. F5. $20.00

KIM, R.E. *Martyred.* 1964. Braziller. ARC. wrp. EX. scarce. K2. $150.00

KIMBALL, G.H. *Tropical Africa.* 1960. NY. lg 8vo. 2 vols. dj. EX. $12.50

KIMBALL, Marie. *Jefferson: Road to Glory 1743-1776.* 1943. NY. dj. VG. $15.00

KIMMEL. *Mad Booths of MD.* 1940. Indianapolis. 1st ed. VG. C2. $40.00

KIMMENS, A.C. *Tales of Hashish.* 1977. Morrow. 1st ed. dj. EX. F5. $20.00

KINCAID, Jamaica. *At the Bottom of the River.* 1983. Farrar Straus. UP. wrp. EX. B13. $125.00

KINCAID, Jamaica. *At the Bottom of the River.* 1983. NY. 1st ed. presentation. dj. EX. T9. $50.00

KINCAID, Jamaica. *Lucy.* 1990. Farrar Straus. ARC. glossy wrp. EX. B13. $45.00

KING, E.T. *Memoir With Extracts From Her Letters & Journal.* 1859. Baltimore. Armstrong Berry. 12mo. 128 p. VG. V1. $18.50

KING, Florence. *S Ladies & Gentlemen.* 1975. NY. 1st ed. dj. VG. B3. $27.50

KING, Florence. *Wasp Where Is Thy Sting?* 1977. NY. 1st ed. dj. VG. B3. $25.00

KING, Grace. *La Dame de Sainte Hermine.* 1924. NY. Macmillan. 1st ed. 296 p. dj. VG. B10. $13.00

KING, M.E. *Ancient Peruvian Textiles From Collection of Textile Mus.* 1965. MPA. 1st ed. 4to. wrp. F2. $15.00

KING, M.L. *Where Do We Go From Here: Chaos or Community?* 1967. Harper. 1st ed. sgn. EX. H3. $650.00

KING, O.B. *5 Million in Cash.* 1932. Doubleday Doran. VG. P1. $10.00

KING, R.H. *George Fox & the Light Within, 1650-1660.* 1940. Phil. Friends Bookstore. 1st print. 12mo. 177 p. VG. V1. $7.50

KING, Rosa. *Tempest Over Mexico.* 1935. Little Brn. 1st ed. 319 p. dj. F2. $20.00

KING, Rufus. *Case of the Dowager's Etchings.* 1944. Crime Club. 1st ed. VG. P1. $15.00

KING, Rufus. *Murder Masks Miami.* 1940. Sun Dial. VG. P1. $12.50

KING, Rufus. *Secret Beyond the Door.* 1947. Triangle. dj. VG. P1. $15.00

KING, Rufus. *Variety of Weapons.* 1943. Crime Club. dj. VG. P1. $20.00

KING, Stephen. *Bachman Books.* 1985. New Am Lib. Book Club ed. dj. EX. R3. $12.50

KING, Stephen. *Bachman Books.* 1985. New Am Lib. 2nd ed. dj. EX. P1. $20.00

KING, Stephen. *Carrie.* 1974. Doubleday. 1st ed. dj. M. R3. $500.00

KING, Stephen. *Christine.* 1983. Donald Grant. Ltd 1st ed. sgn. dj. boxed. EX. R3. $350.00

KING, Stephen. *Christine.* 1983. Viking. 1st ed. dj. EX. R3. $25.00

KING, Stephen. *Creep Show.* 1982. New Am Lib. Book Club ed. wrp. EX. $10.00

KING, Stephen. *Cujo.* 1981. Viking. 1st ed. dj. VG. P1. $25.00

KING, Stephen. *Cycle of the Werewolf.* 1983. Land of Enchantment. 1st ed. dj. EX. R3. $125.00

KING, Stephen. *Danse Macabre.* 1981. Everest House. 1st ed. dj. EX. R3. $75.00

KING, Stephen. *Danse Macabre.* 1981. Everest House. 1st ed. Special Pub issue. 1/35. slipcase. EX. C4. $375.00

KING, Stephen. *Danse Macabre.* 1982. Berkley. VG. P1. $15.00

KING, Stephen. *Dark Half.* 1989. Viking. 1st ed. dj. EX. P1. $21.95

KING, Stephen. *Dark Tower 2: Drawing of the 3.* 1983. Donald Grant. Ltd ed. 1/850. sgn. boxed. M. R3. $450.00

KING, Stephen. *Dark Tower 2: Drawing of the 3.* 1983. Donald Grant. 1st ed. dj. EX. R3. $75.00

KING, Stephen. *Dark Tower: Gunslinger.* 1982. Donald Grant. 1st ed. dj. EX. R3. $650.00

KING, Stephen. *Dark Tower: Gunslinger.* 1982. Donald Grant. 1st ed. inscr. dj. EX. R3. $750.00

KING, Stephen. *Dead Zone.* 1981. Viking. 1st ed. dj. EX. R3. $75.00

KING, Stephen. *Different Seasons.* 1982. Viking. UP. inscr. wrp. B13. $575.00

KING, Stephen. *Different Seasons.* 1982. Viking. UP. inscr/dtd 1982. wrp. K2. $750.00

KING, Stephen. *Different Seasons.* 1982. Viking. UP. wrp. EX. K2. $150.00

KING, Stephen. *Different Seasons.* 1982. Viking. 1st ed. dj. EX. R3. $60.00

KING, Stephen. *Eyes of the Dragon.* 1984. Philtrum Pr. 1st ed. 1/1250. sgn. slipcase. EX. R3. $750.00

KING, Stephen. *Eyes of the Dragon.* 1987. Viking. 1st ed. dj. EX. P1. $20.00

KING, Stephen. *Firestarter.* 1980. Donald Grant. 1st ed. 1/725. sgn. boxed. M. R3. $450.00

KING, Stephen. *Firestarter.* 1980. Phantasia. 1st ed. 1/725. sgn. dj. slipcase. EX. B13. $450.00

KING, Stephen. *Firestarter.* 1980. Viking. 1st ed. dj. G. $15.00

KING, Stephen. *It.* 1986. Viking. 1st ed. dj. EX. R3. $22.50

KING, Stephen. *It.* 1986. Viking. 1st ed. dj. VG. P1. $20.00

KING, Stephen. *Misery.* 1987. Viking. ARC. dj. EX. K2. $50.00

KING, Stephen. *Misery.* 1987. Viking. 1st ed. dj. EX. P1. $20.00

KING, Stephen. *Misery.* 1987. Viking. 2nd ed. EX. P1. $10.00

KING, Stephen. *Night Shift.* 1978. Doubleday. 1st ed. dj. EX. R3. $400.00

KING, Stephen. *Pet Sematary.* nd. Book Club. dj. VG. $10.00

KING, Stephen. *Pet Sematary.* 1983. Doubleday. dj. G. R3. $15.00

KING, Stephen. *Pet Sematary.* 1983. Doubleday. 1st ed. dj. EX. P1. $35.00

KING, Stephen. *Pet Sematary.* 1984. GK Hall. Lg Print ed. dj. EX. P1. $25.00

KING, Stephen. *Rage.* 1983. New Eng Lib 53792. PB Orig/1st ed. wrp. EX. T9. $35.00

KING, Stephen. *Reign of Fear.* 1988. Underwood Miller. 1st ed. 1/500. sgn. slipcase. M. R3. $150.00

KING, Stephen. *Roadwork.* 1983. New Eng Lib. PB Orig/1st ed. wrp. EX. T9. $45.00

KING, Stephen. *Running Man.* 1986. Barcelona. Ediciones Martinez Roca. 1st ed. lg wrp. EX. T9. $30.00

KING, Stephen. *Salem's Lot*. 1976. New Eng Lib. 1st Eng ed. dj. EX. R3. $400.00

KING, Stephen. *Shining*. 1977. Doubleday. 1st ed. dj. EX. C4/R3. $225.00

KING, Stephen. *Shining/Salem's Lot/Night Shift/Car*. 1984. Octopus. 4th ed. dj. EX. P1. $15.00

KING, Stephen. *Skeleton Crew*. 1985. Putnam. 1st ed. M. R3. $25.00

KING, Stephen. *Skeleton Crew*. 1985. Scream Pr. 1st ed. 1/1000. sgn. boxed. M. R3. $300.00

KING, Stephen. *Stand*. 1978. Doubleday. 1st ed. dj. VG. P1. $125.00

KING, Stephen. *Stand*. 1985. Doubleday. 1st ed. inscr. dj. NM. R3. $375.00

KING, Stephen. *Thinner*. nd. Book Club. dj. VG. P1. $4.50

KING, Stephen. *Thinner*. nd. New Am Lib. 5th ed. dj. EX. P1. $12.95

KING, Stephen. *Tommyknockers*. 1987. Putnam. 1st ed. dj. VG. P1. $20.00

KING, Stoddard. *Grand Right & Left*. 1927. Doran. sgn. dj. H3. $50.00

KING, Stoddard. *What the Queen Said & Further Facetious Fragments*. 1926. Doran. sgn. dj. H3. $50.00

KING, Tabitha. *Caretakers*. 1983. Macmillan. ARC. sgn. EX. P1. $150.00

KING, Vincent. *Candy Man*. 1972. British SF Book Club. dj. EX. P1. $7.50

KING & STRAUB. *Talisman*. 1984. Donald Grant. 1st ed. 1/1200. sgn. 2 vols. boxed. M. R3. $400.00

KING & STRAUB. *Talisman*. 1984. Viking. 1st ed. dj. VG. P1. $25.00

KING. *Wht Hills*. 1860. Boston. Crosby. Ils Wheelock. 403 p. A5. $75.00

KINGMAN, Dong. *Watercolors*. 1958. Crowell. 1st ed. inscr. dj. w/2 sgn letters. B13. $85.00

KINGSBURY, Donald. *Courtship Rite*. nd. Book Club. dj. VG. P1. $4.50

KINGSBURY, Donald. *Courtship Rite*. 1982. Timescape. 1st ed. wrp. M. R3. $12.50

KINGSFORD-SMITH, Charles. *My Flying Life: Authentic Biography*. 1937. Phil. Ils 1st Am ed. 284 p. dj. G. T5. $22.50

KINGSLEY, Charles. *Water Babies*. 1909. London. Ils Goble/Warwick. Deluxe ed. 1/250. EX. H3. $1250.00

KINGSLEY, Charles. *Westward Ho!* 1920. Scribner. Ils Classics Series. VG. $35.00

KINGSLEY, F.M. *Transfiguration of Miss Philura*. 1911. Funk Wagnall. 1st ed. gilt gr bdg. VG. $15.00

KINGSLEY, Vera. *Satan Has 6 Fingers*. 1943. Crime Club. 1st ed. 276 p. dj. VG. B10. $5.00

KINGSMILL, Hugh. *Return of William Shakespeare*. 1929. Bobbs Merrill. 1st ed. dj. VG. R3. $20.00

KINGSTON, M.H. *China Men*. 1980. Knopf. 1st ed. sgn. dj. EX. B13. $60.00

KINGSTON, M.H. *Tripmaster Monkey: His Fake Book*. 1989. Knopf. UP. wrp. EX. C4. $35.00

KINGSTON, M.H. *Woman Warrior*. 1976. Knopf. 1st ed. dj. EX. B13. $85.00

KINGSTON, William. *Marmaduke Merry the Midshipman; or, My Early Days at Sea*. 1864. Crosby Nichols. VG. C1. $19.00

KINNAIRD, Clark. *This Must Not Happen Again!* 1945. Pilot Pr. dj. VG. P1. $20.00

KINNELL, Galway. *Book of Nightmares*. 1971. Houghton Mifflin. sgn. dj. M. H3. $75.00

KINNELL, Galway. *Fundamental Project of Technology*. 1983. Ewert. Ltd ed. 1/154. sgn. wrp. H3. $75.00

KINNELL, Galway. *Mortal Acts, Mortal Words*. 1980. Houghton Mifflin. sgn. dj. EX. H3. $50.00

KINNELL, Galway. *Selected Poems*. 1982. Houghton Mifflin. Ltd ed. 1/200. sgn. slipcase. M. H3. $75.00

KINNELL, Galway. *What a Kingdom It Was*. 1960. Houghton Mifflin. 1st ed. dj. EX. C4. $60.00

KINNELL, Galway. *When 1 Has Lived a Long Time Alone*. 1990. Knopf. UP. wrp. EX. B13. $45.00

KINNELL, Galway. *2 Poems*. 1979. Janus Pr. Ils Van Vliet. Ltd ed. 1/185. sgns. H3. $60.00

KINNELL & WAKOSKI. *2 Poems*. 1981. Red Ozier Pr. Ils Barry Moser. sgns. wrp. H3. $35.00

KINNEY, Thomas. *Devil Take the Foremost*. 1947. Crime Club. 1st ed. VG. P1. $10.00

KINSELLA, W.P. *Born Indian*. 1981. Oberon. 1st Canadian ed. sgn. wrp. EX. K2. $85.00

KINSELLA, W.P. *Dance Me Outside*. 1985. Godine. 1st Am ed. sgn. dj. EX. K2. $75.00

KINSELLA, W.P. *Fencepost Chronicles*. 1987. Houghton Mifflin. 1st Am ed. sgn. dj. EX. $45.00

KINSELLA, W.P. *IA Baseball Confederacy*. 1986. Boston. 1st ed. dj. M. $20.00

KINSELLA, W.P. *IA Baseball Confederacy*. 1986. Houghton Mifflin. 1st ed. dj. EX. P1. $16.95

KINSELLA, W.P. *Miss Hobbema Pageant*. 1989. Toronto. Harper Collins. 1st ed. inscr. wrp. K2. $85.00

KINSELLA, W.P. *Moccasin Telegraph*. 1984. Godine. 1st Am ed. sgn. dj. EX. K2. $75.00

KINSELLA, W.P. *Red Wolf Red Wolf*. 1987. Toronto. Collins. 1st ed. sgn. dj. EX. K2. $75.00

KINSELLA, W.P. *Scars*. 1978. Overon. 1st Canadian ed. sgn. dj. EX. K2. $375.00

KINSELLA, W.P. *Shoeless Joe Jackson Comes to IA*. nd. (1980) Oberon Pr. 1st ed. sgn. wrp. EX. K2. $100.00

KINSELLA, W.P. *Shoeless Joe*. 1982. Houghton Mifflin. 1st ed. sgn. dj. EX. B13/K2. $250.00

KINSELLA, W.P. *Thrill of the Grass*. 1988. Vancouver. Ltd ed. sgn. stapled wrp. EX. K2. $85.00

KINSELLA & KNIGHT. *Rainbow Warehouse*. 1989. Nova Scotia. Pottersfield. 1st ed. sgns. wrp. K2. $75.00

KINVIG, R.H. *Hist of the Isle of Man*. 1950. Liverpool. 2nd ed. dj. VG. C1. $12.50

KIPLING, Rudyard. *Book of Words*. 1928. London. 1st ed. dj. EX. $45.00

KIPLING, Rudyard. *Brazilian Sketches*. 1940. Doubleday. 1st ed. 115 p. dj. F2. $35.00

KIPLING, Rudyard. *Butterfly That Stamped*. 1947. Garden City. Just-So Stories Series. 8vo. 28 p. dj. VG. $20.00

KIPLING, Rudyard. *Capt Courageous*. 1897. NY. 1st Am ed. decor brd. VG. $75.00

KIPLING, Rudyard. *Courting of Dinah Shadd & Other Stories*. nd. Sears. 230 p. VG. B10. $3.25

KIPLING, Rudyard. *Jungle Book/2nd Jungle Book*. 1894-1895. London. 1st ed. 2 vols. orig bdg. EX. H3. $750.00

KIPLING, Rudyard. *Jungle Books Vol 1*. nd. BOMC. dj. VG. P1. $5.00

KIPLING, Rudyard. *Limits & Renewals*. 1932. London. 1st ed. dj. EX. $55.00

KIPLING, Rudyard. *Many Inventions.* 1893. London. 1st ed. 8vo. bl cloth. VG. $75.00

KIPLING, Rudyard. *Phantom Ricksaw.* 1898. Altemus. G. R3. $12.50

KIPLING, Rudyard. *Puck of Pook's Hill.* 1906. NY. Ils Rackham. 1st Am ed. VG. C1. $79.00

KIPLING, Rudyard. *Sea & Sussex.* 1926. Garden City. 1/150. sgn. EX. H3. $400.00

KIPLING, Rudyard. *Soldiers 3.* c 1920. AL Burt. 366 p. gr bdg. EX. B10. $3.25

KIPLING, Rudyard. *Song of the Eng.* 1909. London. Ils/sgn WH Robinson. 1/500. 30 clr pls. EX. H3. $1750.00

KIPLING, Rudyard. *Song of the Eng.* 1909. NY. Doubleday Page. Ils WH Robinson. 4to. VG. $250.00

KIPLING, Rudyard. *Stalky & Co.* 1899. London. 1st ed. VG. B3. $50.00

KIPLING, Rudyard. *Traffics & Discoveries.* 1904. London. 1st ed. EX. $35.00

KIPLING, Rudyard. *Under the Deodars.* nd. Internat. dj. EX. R3. $15.00

KIPLING, Rudyard. *With the Night Mail.* 1909. NY. 1st ed. dj. EX. $100.00

KIPLING, Rudyard. *Writings in Prose & Verse.* 1907. Scribner. 36 vols. octavo. TEG. gilt mulberry bdg. H3. $750.00

KIPLING, Rudyard. *Years Between.* 1919. London. Ltd ed. 1/200. $75.00

KIPLING, Rudyard. *2nd Jungle Book.* 1895. NY. 1st Am ed. VG. $100.00

KIPLING, Rudyard. *7 Seas.* 1896. Appleton. 1st Am ed. VG. C1. $37.50

KIPLING & BALISTER. *Naulahka: Story of W & E.* 1892. Macmillan. New ed. 379 p. B10. $8.50

KIPPELKAMM, Stefan. *Glass Houses & Winter Gardens of the 19th Century.* 1981. NY. 1st Am ed. VG. G1. $25.00

KIRBY, Helen. *Filly: Niece of Martingale.* 1938. Dutton. 1st ed. 4to. 56 p. dj. VG. $30.00

KIRBY, Michael. *Happenings.* 1966. Dutton. 1st PB ed. B4. $6.00

KIRCHHOFF, Herbert. *Peru.* 1951. Buenos Aires. Ltd ed. 1/3000. 4to. F2. $25.00

KIRK, Betty. *Covering the Mexican Front.* 1942. OK U. 1st ed. sgn. 367 p. F2. $12.50

KIRK, M.L. *Story of the Canterbury Pilgrims.* 1941. Stokes. 4to. 310 p. gilt blk bdg. VG. $55.00

KIRK, Michael. *Cut in Diamonds.* 1986. Doubleday Crime Club. 1st ed. dj. EX. P1. $12.50

KIRK, Michael. *Mayday From Malaga.* 1983. Crime Club. 1st ed. dj. VG. P1. $15.00

KIRK, Russell. *Creature of the Twilight.* 1966. Fleet. 1st ed. dj. EX. R3. $25.00

KIRK, Russell. *Princess of All Lands.* 1979. Arkham House. 1st ed. M. R3. $40.00

KIRKBRIDGE, Ronald. *Only the Unafraid.* 1953. Duell Sloan Pearce. 8vo. 268 p. dj. VG. V1. $6.00

KIRKHAM, Samuel. *Eng Grammar in Familiar Lectures.* 1840. Baltimore. 228 p. T5. $25.00

KIRKPATRICK, B.J. *Bibliography of EM Forster.* 1985. Clarendon Pr. 2nd ed. dj. EX. K2. $45.00

KIRKPATRICK, Sidney. *Cast of Killers.* 1986. Dutton Book Club. 301 p. dj. NM. B10. $5.00

KIRKWOOD, James. *Hit Me With a Rainbow.* 1980. NY. 1st ed. dj. M. $20.00

KIRKWOOD, James. *Some Kind of Hero.* 1975. Crowell. 1st ed. sgn. dj. EX. K2. $45.00

KIRNGOLD, Ralph. *Thaddeus Stevens.* 1955. NY. 1st ed. 460 p. dj. G. T5. $12.50

KIRST, H.H. *No Fatherland.* 1970. Coward McCann. 1st ed. dj. VG. P1. $12.50

KITE, Thomas. *Memoirs & Letters of Thomas Kite.* 1883. Phil. Friends Bookstore. 12mo. 479 p. VG. V1. $15.00

KITTO, John. *Hist of Palestine to the Present Time.* 1852. Boston. Ils. 432 p. VG. $65.00

KITTREDGE, Waiter. *Tenting on the Old Camp Ground.* 1891. Nims Night. G. S1. $27.50

KITZMILLER, H.H. *100 Years of W Reserve.* 1926. Hudson, OH. Ils. 52 p. T5. $15.00

KIZER, Carolyn. *Ungrateful Garden.* 1961. IN U. 1st ed. inscr. dj. EX. C4. $125.00

KIZILOS, A.P. *Dwarf's Legacy.* 1977. Ashley. 1st ed. sgn. dj. w/promotional letter. EX. F5. $25.00

KLAIN, Zora. *Educational Activities of New England Quakers.* 1928. Phil. Westbrook. 1st ed. 8vo. 228 p. VG. V1. $20.00

KLEIN, Charles. *Lion & the Mouse.* 1906. Grosset Dunlap. Photoplay ed. 399 p. VG. B10. $3.50

KLEIN, Gerard. *Overlords of War.* nd. Book Club. VG. P1. $2.00

KLEIN, Robin. *Games.* 1987. Viking Kestrel. 1st ed. dj. EX. F5. $14.00

KLEIN, T.E.D. *Ceremonies.* 1984. Viking. 1st ed. dj. EX. R3. $25.00

KLEIN, William. *Photographs.* 1981. Aperature. dj. EX. $30.00

KLEIN & STARK. *S Am Indian Languages: Retrospect & Prospect.* 1985. Austin. 1st ed. 863 p. dj. F2. $30.00

KLEMIN, Diana. *Ils Book.* 1970. NY. pls. dj. EX. T1. $25.00

KLINE, O.A. *Call of the Savage.* 1937. Clode. 1st ed. dj. EX. R3. $350.00

KLINE, O.A. *Maza of the Moon.* 1930. McClurg. 1st ed. VG. R3. $50.00

KLINE, O.A. *Outlaws of Mars.* 1961. Avalon. 1st ed. dj. EX. R3. $30.00

KLINE, O.A. *Planet of Peril.* 1929. McClurg. 1st ed. VG. R3. $50.00

KLINE, O.A. *Port of Peril.* 1949. Grant. 1st ed. dj. EX. R3. $50.00

KLINE, O.A. *Prince of Peril.* 1962. Avalon. dj. xl. P1. $7.50

KLINE, O.A. *Prince of Peril.* 1962. Avalon. 1st ed. dj. EX. R3. $30.00

KLINE, O.A. *Swordsman of Mars.* 1960. Avalon. 1st ed. dj. EX. R3. $35.00

KLINE, O.A. *Tam, Son of Tiger.* 1962. Avalon. 1st ed. dj. EX. R3. $30.00

KLYVER, R.D. *We Proudly Hail: Collection of Biographies...* 1982. np. Ils. inscr. 88 p. G. T5. $6.50

KNACKFUSS, Hermann. *Durer: Kunstler-Monographien.* 1895. Klassing. 3rd ed. TEG. D4. $20.00

KNACKFUSS, Hermann. *Menzel.* 1895. Bielefeld. 2nd ed. TEG. D4. $25.00

KNAPTON, E.J. *Empress Josephine.* 1963. Cambridge. 1st ed. VG. $12.00

KNEALE, Nigel. *Year of the Sex Olympics.* 1976. Ferret Fantasy. 1st ed. dj. EX. P1. $20.00

KNEBEL, Fletcher. *Night of Camp David.* 1965. NY. 1st ed. dj. EX. $40.00

KNEBEL, Fletcher. *Sabotage.* 1968. NY. 1st ed. dj. EX. $30.00

KNEBEL, Fletcher. *7 Days in May.* 1962. NY. 1st ed. dj. M. $35.00

KNEBEL & BAILEY. *No High Ground.* 1960. Harper. 1st ed. dj. VG. P1. $22.50

KNEE, Ernest. *Mexico: Laredo to Guadalajara.* 1951. Hastings House. 1st ed. dj. F2. $17.50

KNIFFIN, G.C. *Assault & Capture of Lookout Mt.* 1895. WA. 16 p. wrp. T5. $12.50

KNIGHT, Charles. *Old Printer & the Modern Pr.* 1854. London. Murray. 1st ed. 8vo. gilt brn bdg. VG. H3. $250.00

KNIGHT, Clifford. *Affair of the Limping Sailor.* 1942. Dodd Mead. VG. P1. $20.00

KNIGHT, Clifford. *Affair of the Scarlet Crab.* 1937. Dodd Mead. 1st ed. dj. VG. P1. $20.00

KNIGHT, Clifford. *Affair of the Splintered Heart.* 1942. Doubleday Book Club. VG. P1. $12.00

KNIGHT, Clifford. *Death of a Big Shot.* 1951. Dutton. 1st ed. dj. VG. P1. $15.00

KNIGHT, Damon. *Best From Orbit.* 1975. Berkley Putnam. 1st ed. dj. VG. P1. $15.00

KNIGHT, Damon. *Beyond the Barrier.* 1964. Doubleday. 1st ed. dj. xl. P1. $5.00

KNIGHT, Damon. *Beyond Tomorrow.* 1965. Harper Row. 1st ed. dj. VG. P1. $20.00

KNIGHT, Damon. *Charles Ft, Prophet of the Unexplained.* 1970. Doubleday. 1st ed. dj. EX. R3. $20.00

KNIGHT, Damon. *Golden Road.* 1973. Simon Schuster. 1st ed. dj. EX. R3. $15.00

KNIGHT, Damon. *Hell's Pavement.* 1955. Lion. 1st ed. wrp. EX. R3. $17.50

KNIGHT, Damon. *Nebula Award Stories 1965.* nd. Book Club. dj. VG. P1. $4.50

KNIGHT, Damon. *Orbit 10.* 1972. Putnam. 1st ed. dj. VG. P1. $20.00

KNIGHT, Damon. *Orbit 12.* nd. Book Club. dj. VG. P1. $4.50

KNIGHT, Damon. *Orbit 4.* 1968. Putnam. 1st ed. dj. EX. P1. $20.00

KNIGHT, Damon. *Pocketful of Stars.* 1971. Doubleday. 1st ed. dj. EX. R3. $15.00

KNIGHT, Damon. *SF Argosy.* 1972. Simon Schuster. 1st ed. dj. EX. R3. $10.00

KNIGHT, Damon. *SF of the '30s.* nd. Book Club. dj. VG. P1. $5.00

KNIGHT, Damon. *SF of the '30s.* 1977. Avon. 2nd ed. 468 p. wrp. EX. B10. $6.00

KNIGHT, Damon. *Tomorrow & Tomorrow.* nd. Simon Schuster. 2nd ed. VG. P1. $10.00

KNIGHT, Damon. *Toward Infinity.* 1968. Simon Schuster. 1st ed. dj. VG. R3. $15.00

KNIGHT, Damon. *Westerns of the 1940s.* 1977. Bobbs Merrill. 1st ed. dj. VG. P1. $17.50

KNIGHT, Damon. *World & Thorinn.* 1980. Berkley. 1st ed. M. R3. $17.50

KNIGHT, Damon. *100 Years of SF.* 1968. Simon Schuster. 1st ed. dj. EX. R3. $15.00

KNIGHT, Damon. *3 Novels.* nd. Book Club. dj. VG. P1. $4.50

KNIGHT, Damon. *3 Novels.* 1967. Doubleday. 1st ed. dj. xl. VG. R3. $25.00

KNIGHT, David. *Nat Science Books in Eng 1600-1900.* 1972. NY. Praeger. Ils. dj. EX. $55.00

KNIGHT, Eric. *Flying Yorkshireman.* 1938. Harper. 1st ed. dj. VG. P1. $15.00

KNIGHT, Eric. *Sam Sm Flies Again.* 1942. Harper. 1st ed. VG. P1. $15.00

KNIGHT, H.A. *Fungus.* 1985. Star. 1st ed. wrp. EX. F5. $9.00

KNIGHT, J.A. *Woodcock.* 1944. NY. 1st ed. dj. EX. B3. $65.00

KNIGHT, K.M. *Akin to Murder.* 1953. Crime Club. 1st ed. xl. P1. $7.50

KNIGHT, K.M. *Bass Derby Murder.* 1949. Crime Club. 1st ed. dj. EX. F5. $18.00

KNIGHT, K.M. *Bass Derby Murder.* 1949. Crime Club. 1st ed. xl. VG. P1. $7.50

KNIGHT, K.M. *Intrigue for Empire.* 1944. Crime Club. 1st ed. VG. P1. $15.00

KNIGHT, K.M. *Port of 7 Strangers.* 1945. Doubleday Book Club. VG. P1. $10.00

KNIGHT, K.M. *Trademark of a Traitor.* 1943. Crime Club. 1st ed. xl. P1. $6.00

KNIGHT, K.M. *7 Were Veiled.* 1937. Crime Club. 1st ed. VG. P1. $17.50

KNIGHT, Mrs. S.G. *Titbits.* 1965. Boston. VG. P4. $90.00

KNIGHT, Oliver. *Following the Indian Wars.* 1960. Norman. 1st ed. 348 p. dj. A5. $30.00

KNIGHT, Oliver. *Life & Manners in the Frontier Army.* 1978. Norman. dj. A5. $25.00

KNIGHT & ELISOFON. *Hollywood Style.* 1969. Macmillan. 1st ed. folio. 216 p. dj. VG. H3. $60.00

KNIGHT. *Modern Seamanship.* 1917. NY. Ils. 8vo. 712 p. G4. $24.00

KNIGHT. *Pipe & Pouch: Smoker's Own Book of Poetry.* 1894. Boston. 1st ed. 182 p. gilt brn bdg. EX. $50.00

KNIGHTLY, Phillip. *1st Casualty.* 1975. Harcourt. Book Club ed. dj. EX. B10. $6.50

KNOPF, M. *Cook My Darling Daughter.* 1962. NY. dj. VG. B3. $25.00

KNOTT & COOPER. *Gone Away With O'Malley.* 1944. Garden City. Ils 1st ed. 280 p. dj. G. T5. $22.50

KNOWLES, John. *Phineas.* 1968. NY. 1st ed. dj. VG. $12.00

KNOWLES, John. *Stolen Past.* 1983. NY. 1st ed. dj. EX. $12.00

KNOWLES, John. *Vein of Riches.* 1978. Boston. 1st ed. dj. EX. $10.00

KNOWLES, R.S. *1st Pictorial Hist of Am Oil & Gas Industry 1858-1983.* 1983. Athens, OH. 171 p. M. T5. $9.50

KNOWLES, Roderic. *Great Bank of Am Telex Heist.* 1973. Putnam. 1st ed. dj. VG. P1. $12.50

KNOX, Bill. *Draw Batons!* 1973. Doubleday Crime Club. 1st ed. dj. EX. P1. $15.00

KNOX, Bill. *Gray Sentinels.* nd. Book Club. dj. VG. P1. $4.50

KNOX, Bill. *Pilot Error.* 1977. John Long. xl. VG. P1. $5.00

KNOX, Bill. *Sanctuary Isle.* 1962. John Long. 1st ed. dj. VG. P1. $22.50

KNOX, Bill. *Storm Tide.* 1973. Crime Club. 1st ed. dj. VG. P1. $10.00

KNOX, Calvin M.; see Silverberg, Robert.

KNOX, R.A. *Memories of the Future.* 1923. Doran. 1st Am ed. VG. R3. $25.00

KNOX, R.B. *Footlights Afloat.* 1937. Garden City. Ils 1st ed. 300 p. G. T5. $22.50

KNOX, T.W. *Capt John Crane.* 1899. Werner 1st ed. pictorial bdg. VG. F5. $30.00

KNYVETON, John. *Diary of a Surgeon in the Year 1751-1752.* 1937. Appleton Century. 1st ed. dj. G. $45.00

KOBER, Arthur. *Having Wonderful Time.* 1937. Random House. 1st ed. VG. H3. $20.00

KOBER, Arthur. *Having Wonderful Time.* 1937. Random House. 1st ed. sgn. VG. H3. $50.00

KOBLER, John. *Ardent Spirits: Rise & Fall of Prohibition.* nd. Book Club. dj. VG. C1. $5.00

KOBLER, John. *Capone.* 1971. Putnam. VG P1. $7.50

KOCH, C.J. *Doubleman.* 1985. NY. 1st ed. dj M. $10.00

KOCH, F.H. *Am Folk Plays.* 1939. Appleton. 1st ed. dj. EX. C4. $50.00

KOCH, Howard. *Panic Broadcast.* nd. Avon. 6th print. VG. P1. $4.00

KOCH, Kenneth. *Sleeping With Woman.* 1969. Plantin Pr. Ltd HrdCvr ed. 1/150. sgn. dj. H3. $40.00

KOCH, T.W. *Tales for Bibliophiles.* 1929. Caxton. 1/300. VG. $35.00

KOCHER, P.H. *Master of Middle-Earth: Fiction of JRR Tolkien.* 1971. Boston. 1st print. dj. VG. T1. $35.00

KOERBER, Roger. *Zeppelin Posts.* 1978. Southfield. Ils. 140 p. wrp. VG. T5. $17.50

KOESTLER, Arthur. *Roots of Coincidence.* 1972. NY. 1st ed. dj. EX. $12.00

KOHAN, Rhea. *Hand-Me-Downs.* 1980. Random House. 1st ed. 373 p. dj. EX. B10. $3.75

KOHLER. *Hist of Costume.* c 1940. Phil. 16 clr pls. dj. EX. J2. $35.00

KOHN, H.E. *Reflections.* 1963. Eerdmans, MI. Ils. dj. B10. $3.25

KOLB, Ken. *Getting Straight.* 1967. Chilton Books. 1st ed. sgn. dj. EX. B4. $20.00

KOLB, Leon. *Woodcuts of Jacob Steinhardt.* 1962. Jewish Pub Soc. 4to. dj. EX. $30.00

KOLB & LACKEY. *Pot for All Reasons: Ceramic Ecology Revisited.* 1988. Phil. Temple U. 1st ed. 261 p. wrp. F2. $30.00

KOLLWITZ, Kathe. *Graphische Kunst Kathe Kollwitz.* 1932. Berlin. pls. 32 p. stiff wrp. dj. VG. C2. $27.00

KOLUPAEV, Victor. *Hermit's Swing.* 1980. Macmillan. 1st ed. M. R3. $15.00

KOONTZ, D.R. *Checklist of 1st Eds.* 1989. Pandora. VG. P1. $3.00

KOONTZ, D.R. *Cold Fire.* 1991. Putnam. UP. wrp. EX. K2. $75.00

KOONTZ, D.R. *Dark of the Woods/Soft Come the Dragons.* 1970. NY. Ace. PB Orig. wrp. M. w/sgn label. T9. $45.00

KOONTZ, D.R. *Darkfall.* nd. Book Club. dj. VG. P1. $7.50

KOONTZ, D.R. *Darkness Comes.* 1990. Headline. dj. EX. P1. $30.00

KOONTZ, D.R. *Dragonfly.* 1975. Random House. 1st ed. dj. EX. F5. $80.00

KOONTZ, D.R. *Dragonfly.* 1975. Random House. 1st ed. dj. xl. P1. $25.00

KOONTZ, D.R. *Eyes of Darkness.* 1989. Dark Harvest. Ltd 1st ed. 1/400. sgn. slipcase. M. R3. $75.00

KOONTZ, D.R. *Funhouse.* nd. Book Club. dj. G. P1. $7.50

KOONTZ, D.R. *Hanging On.* 1973. Evans. 1st ed. dj. EX. B13. $150.00

KOONTZ, D.R. *Lightning.* nd. Book Club. dj. VG. P1. $7.50

KOONTZ, D.R. *Lightning.* 1988. Putnam. 1st ed. dj. EX. R3. $17.50

KOONTZ, D.R. *Mask.* 1981. Jove. ARC. wrp. EX. F5. $50.00

KOONTZ, D.R. *Midnight.* 1989. Putnam. 1st ed. dj. VG. P1. $19.95

KOONTZ, D.R. *Night Chills.* 1976. Atheneum. 1st ed. dj. VG. R3. $45.00

KOONTZ, D.R. *Night Chills.* 1976. Atheneum. 1st ed. dj. EX. K2. $50.00

KOONTZ, D.R. *Nightmare Journey.* 1975. Berkley Putnam. 1st ed. dj. EX. P1. $175.00

KOONTZ, D.R. *Servants of the Twilight.* 1988. Dark Harvest. Ltd 1st ed. 1/450. sgn. M. R3. $100.00

KOONTZ, D.R. *Shattered.* nd. Book Club. dj. VG. P1. $7.50

KOONTZ, D.R. *Shattered.* 1973. Random House. 2nd print. dj. EX. B13. $35.00

KOONTZ, D.R. *Strangers.* 1986. Putnam. 1st ed. M. R3. $25.00

KOONTZ, D.R. *Surrounded.* 1974. Bobbs Merrill. 1st ed. dj. EX. F5. $20.00

KOONTZ, D.R. *Twilight Eyes.* 1987. London. 1st Eng ed. wrp. VG. R3. $80.00

KOONTZ, D.R. *Vision.* nd. Book Club. dj. VG. P1. $7.50

KOONTZ, D.R. *Vision.* 1977. Putnam. 1st ed. dj. EX. F5. $50.00

KOONTZ, D.R. *Watchers.* nd. Book Club. dj. EX. P1. $7.50

KOONTZ, D.R. *Watchers.* 1987. Putnam. 1st ed. dj. VG. P1. $35.00

KOONTZ, D.R. *Watchers.* 1987. Putnam. 1st ed. inscr/sgn. dj. EX. $65.00

KOONTZ, D.R. *Whispers.* 1980. Putnam. dj. VG. P1. $75.00

KOONTZ, L.K. *Robert Dinwiddie: His Career in Am Colonial Government.* 1941. Glendale, CA. Clark. 1st ed. dj. EX. $45.00

KOOP, T.F. *Weapon of Silence.* 1946. Chicago. 1st ed. 304 p. dj. VG. T5. $25.00

KOPAY, David. *David Kopay Story.* nd. (1977) Arbor House. apparent 1st ed. 247 p. dj. EX. B10. $5.00

KORABIEWICZ, Waclaw. *Matto Grosso.* 1956. Roy Pub. 238 p. dj. F2. $15.00

KOREM, Danny. *Korem Without Limits.* 1985. Brooklyn. Robbins. 1st ed. 181 p. dj. NM. J3. $30.00

KORN, Arthur. *Glass in Modern Architecture of the Bauhaus Period.* 1968. NY. 1st Am ed. VG. G1. $30.00

KORNBLUTH, C.M. *Best of CM Kornbluth.* nd. Book Club. dj. EX. P1. $5.00

KORNBLUTH, C.M. *Best of CM Kornbluth.* 1976. Doubleday. 1st ed. dj. EX. F5. $10.00

KORNBLUTH, C.M. *Mile Beyond the Moon.* 1958. Doubleday. 1st ed. dj. EX. R3. $40.00

KORNBLUTH, C.M. *Syndic.* 1953. Doubleday. 1st ed. dj. VG. R3. $40.00

KORNBLUTH, C.M. *Syndic.* 1953. Doubleday. 1st ed. xl. P1. $12.50

KORNBLUTH, C.M. *Takeoff.* 1952. Doubleday. 1st ed. dj. EX. R3. $55.00

KORNBLUTH, C.M. *Takeoff.* 1952. Doubleday. 1st ed. dj. VG. P1. $30.00

KORSON, George. *Minstrels of the Mine Patch: Songs & Stories...* 1938. PA U. 2nd print. VG. $35.00

KORSON, George. *PA Songs & Legends.* 1949. Phil. 1st ed. 474 p. dj. VG. T5. $15.00

KOSINSKI, Jerzy. *Art of the Self.* 1968. Scientia-Factum. 1st ed. inscr. w/sgn letter. K2. $125.00

KOSINSKI, Jerzy. *Being There.* 1970. Harcourt Brace. sgn. dj. H3. $125.00

KOSINSKI, Jerzy. *Being There.* 1971. London. Bodley Head. 1st ed. dj. EX. K2. $40.00

KOSINSKI, Jerzy. *Blind Date.* 1977. Houghton Mifflin. 1st ed. inscr/sgn. dj. EX. B13. $150.00

KOSINSKI, Jerzy. *Blind Faith.* 1977. 1st ed. dj. EX. C1. $19.50

KOSINSKI, Jerzy. *Cockpit.* 1975. Houghton Mifflin. inscr. dj. w/photo. H3. $75.00

KOSINSKI, Jerzy. *Passion Play.* 1979. NY. 1st ed. dj. M. $12.00

KOSINSKI, Jerzy. *Passion Play.* 1979. St Martin. sgn. glassine dj. M. H3. $75.00

KOSINSKI, Jerzy. *Passion Play.* 1979. St Martin. 1st ed. inscr/sgn. dj. EX. B13. $100.00

KOSINSKI, Jerzy. *Socjologia Amerykanski Wybor Pract.* nd. NY. 1st Polish text ed. sgn. wrp. VG. T9. $300.00

KOSKY, Gerald. *Magic of Gerald Kosky.* 1975. Oakland. Magic Ltd. Ltd Collector ed. 1/500. sgn. dj. NM. J3. $32.00

KOTZWINKLE, W.E.T. *Extra-Terrestrial.* 1987. Putnam. 1st ed. dj. EX. R3. $30.00

KOTZWINKLE, William. *Christmas at Fontaine's.* 1982. Putnam. 1st ed. dj. EX. F5. $15.00

KOTZWINKLE, William. *Dr Rat.* 1976. NY. 1st ed. dj. EX. $25.00

KOTZWINKLE, William. *Fata Morgana.* 1977. London. 1st ed. dj. M. $25.00

KOTZWINKLE, William. *Great World Circus.* 1983. Putnam. 1st ed. dj. VG. P1. $17.50

KOTZWINKLE, William. *Jack-in-the-Box.* 1980. Putnam. 1st ed. dj. VG. P1. $12.50

KOTZWINKLE, William. *Superman III.* 1983. NY. 1st ed. wrp. M. $12.00

KOTZWINKLE, William. *Superman III.* 1983. Warner. UP. wrp. EX. B13. $45.00

KOUFAX, Sandy. *Koufax.* 1966. NY. 1st ed. dj. VG. B3. $15.00

KOUWENHOVEN, J.A. *Adventures in Am 1857-1900.* 1938. NY. lg 4to. VG. $25.00

KOVACS, Ernie. *Zoomar.* 1957. Garden City. 1st ed. dj. VG. $35.00

KOVALEVSKY, Olga. *Studies in Movement of Doris Niles & Serge Leslie.* 1951. Los Angeles. Ltd ed. 1/250. inscr. portfolio w/ties. EX. H3. $75.00

KOWALIK, E.E. *Alone & Unarmed.* 1968. NY. 1st ed. sgn. 317 p. dj. EX. T5. $32.50

KOYAMA. *Japanese Ceramics.* 1961. Oakland. 1st ed. sm folio. pls. dj. VG. C2. $175.00

KRAKEL, Dean. *S Platte Co, Hist of Old Weld Co, CO.* 1954. Powder River Pub. Ils. wrp. A5. $60.00

KRAMER, Daniel. *Bob Dylan.* 1968. Pocket Books. 1st print. PB. B4. $3.00

KRAMER, J. *Allen Ginsberg in Am.* 1969. NY. 1st ed. dj. VG. B3. $15.00

KRAMER, Jerry. *Farewell to Football.* 1969. World. 1st ed. 202 p. dj. EX. B10. $4.50

KRAMER & STERNER. *Wht House Gardens: Hist & Pictorial Record.* 1973. NY. 1st ed. dj. VG. $20.00

KRAMM, Joseph. *Shrike.* 1952. Fireside Book Club. 198 p. dj. EX. B10. $5.00

KRAUSE, Fedor. *Surgery of the Brain & Spinal Cord...* 1909. NY. Rebman. 2 vols. EX. $300.00

KRAUSS, Ruth. *Hole Is To Dig: 1st Book of 1st Definitions.* 1952. Harper. Ils Sendak. VG. B7. $53.00

KREDEL, Fritz. *Anderson's Life & Stories.* 1942. Ltd Ed Club. 2 vols. slipcase. EX. $40.00

KREHBIEL, H.E. *Afro-Am Folk Songs: Study in Racial & Nat Music.* 1914. NY. 1st ed. EX. $80.00

KREIG, Margaret. *Gr Medicine.* 1964. Rand McNally. 1st ed. dj. F2. $20.00

KREISLER, Fritz. *4 Weeks in the Trenches.* 1915. Boston. 1st ed. dj. VG. $35.00

KRESS, Nancy. *Trinity & Other Stories.* 1985. Bluejay. 1st ed. dj. EX. F5. $15.00

KREYMBORG, Alfred. *Mushrooms: A Book of Free Forms.* 1916. NY. Marshall. sgn. H3. $75.00

KRICH, John. *Bump City.* 1979. Berkley. City Miner. 1st ed. wrp. K2. $30.00

KRICK, R.K. *Parker's VA Battery CSA.* 1989. Broadfoot Pub. 487 p. M. S1. $30.00

KRIEG, Wendell. *Functional Neuroanatomy.* 1945. Phil. Blakiston. 1st print. lg quarto. 553 p. EX. $125.00

KRISSDOITTIR, Morine. *John Cowper Powys & the Magical Quest.* 1980. London. 1st ed. dj. NM. C1. $12.50

KROEBER, Alfred. *Archaeological Explorations in Peru.* 1926. Chicago. Field Mus. wrp. F2. $25.00

KROLL, H.H. *Fury in the Earth.* 1945. Bobbs Merrill. 1st ed. dj. EX. F5. $20.00

KROLL, H.W. *Their Ancient Grudge.* 1946. Bobbs Merrill. 1st ed. dj. EX. F5. $18.00

KROSS, Ford. *It Ain't Body Building. Suggestive Mentalism Part II.* c 1990. M. J3. $12.00

KRUGER, Paul. *Finish Line.* 1968. Simon Schuster. 1st ed. dj. VG. P1. $20.00

KRUGER. *Ballon und Luftschiffbau.* 1911. Berlin. Ils 1st ed. German text. 104 p. EX. $110.00

KRUPP, E.C. *Echoes of the Ancient Skies.* 1983. Harper Row. 1st ed. 386 p. F2. $15.00

KRUPP, E.C. *In Search of Ancient Astronomies.* 1978. Doubleday. 1st ed. 300 p. dj. F2. $20.00

KRUTCH, J.W. *Henry David Thoreau by Joseph Wood Krutch.* 1948. Wm Sloane. 1st ed. dj. EX. C4. $35.00

KRUTCH, J.W. *Was Europe a Success?* 1934. NY. 1st ed. dj. VG. B13. $100.00

KUBE-MCDOWELL, Michael. *Alternitives.* 1988. Ace. 1st HrdCvr ed. dj. EX. F5. $10.00

KUBLER, G.A. *Era of Charles Mahon...Stereotyper 1750-1825.* 1938. NY. 1st ed. EX. $30.00

KUBLER, G.A. *Hist Treatises, Abstracts, & Papers on Stereotyping.* 1936. NY. 1st ed. EX. $35.00

KUBLER, G.A. *L&W Arensberg Collection: Pre-Columbian Sculpture.* 1954. MPA. 1st ed. 4to. F2. $30.00

KUBLER, G.A. *New Hist of Stereotyping.* 1941. NY. 1st ed. EX. $40.00

KUBLER, G.A. *Pre-Columbian Art of Mexico & Central Am.* 1986. New Haven. 1st ed. wrp. F2. $35.00

KUBLER, G.A. *Studies in Ancient Am & European Art.* 1985. New Haven. 1st ed. 449 p. F2. $60.00

KUEBLER, Harold. *Treasury of SF Classics.* nd. Book Club. VG. P1. $5.00

KUMMER, F.A. *Ladies in Hades.* nd. Grosset Dunlap. VG. P1. $7.50

KUMMER, F.A. *Song of Sixpence.* 1913. Watt. 1st ed. VG. P1. $15.00

KUMMER, F.A. *1st Days of Knowledge.* 1923. Doran. 1st ed. decor brd. VG. P1. $20.00

KUNDERA, Milan. *Art of the Novel.* 1986. Grove Pr. UP. wrp. EX. C4. $75.00

KUNDERA, Milan. *Book of Laughter & Forgetting.* 1980. Knopf. 1st ed. dj. EX. B13. $50.00

KUNDERA, Milan. *Farewell Pary.* 1976. Knopf. 1st ed. dj. EX. K2. $45.00

KUNDERA, Milan. *Immortality.* 1991. Grove Pr. UP. 1/125. sgn. wrp. EX. C4. $125.00

KUNDERA, Milan. *Joke.* 1969. Coward McCann. 1st ed. dj. C4. $100.00

KUNDERA, Milan. *Joke.* 1969. NY. 1st ed. as issued. K2. $75.00

KUNDERA, Milan. *Joke.* 1982. Harper Row. UP. wrp. EX. K2. $75.00

KUNDERA, Milan. *Joke.* 1982. Harper Row. 1st ed. dj. EX. K2. $30.00

KUNDERA, Milan. *Laughable Loves: Stories.* 1974. Knopf. 1st Am ed. dj. EX. C4. $60.00

KUNDERA, Milan. *Life Is Elsewhere.* 1974. Knopf. 1st Am ed. dj. EX. K2. $55.00

KUNETKA, J.W. *City of Fire Los Alamos.* 1978. Prentice Hall. 1st ed. dj. VG. P1. $15.00

KUNHARDT, Philip. *Life Smiles Back.* 1987. Simon Schuster. 1st ed. 224 p. dj. M. B10. $5.00

KUNKEL, Fritz. *Psychology of Personal Crisis.* 1966. Easton, PA. 8vo. 52 p. SftCvr. VG. V1. $6.00

KUNZ, G.F. *Curious Lore of Precious Stones.* 1913. Phil. 1st ed. EX. $80.00

KUNZ, G.F. *Magic of Jewels & Charms.* 1915. Phil. 1st ed. EX. $95.00

KUPFERBERG & BASHLOW. *1001 Ways To Beat the Draft.* 1967. Blk Cat/Grove Pr. 1st ed. EX. B4. $5.00

KURTZ, Katherine. *Bishop's Heir.* 1984. Del Rey. 1st ed. dj. EX. P1. $14.95

KURTZ, Katherine. *Camber of Culdi.* 1979. Del Rey. 1st HrdCvr ed. M. R3. $15.00

KURTZ, Katherine. *Harrowing of Gwynedd.* 1989. Del Rey. 1st ed. dj. EX. P1. $17.95

KURTZ, Katherine. *King's Justice.* 1985. Del Rey. 1st ed. dj. EX. P1. $17.50

KURTZ, Katherine. *Quest for St Camber.* 1986. Del Rey. 1st ed. dj. EX. P1. $16.95

KURTZ, Katherine. *St Camber.* 1978. Del Rey. dj. EX. P1/R3. $15.00

KUSHNER, Ellen. *Swordpoint.* 1987. Arbor House. 1st ed. dj. EX. F5. $15.00

KUTTNER, Henry. *Best of Henry Kuttner.* 1975. Doubleday. 1st HrdCvr ed. dj. EX. F5. $12.00

KUTTNER, Henry. *Brass Ring.* 1946. Duell Sloan. 1st ed. VG. R3. $35.00

KUTTNER, Henry. *Destination Infinity.* 1975. Garland. 1st HrdCvr ed. M. R3. $20.00

KUTTNER, Henry. *Fury.* 1950. Grosset Dunlap. dj. VG. P1. $60.00

KUTTNER, Henry. *Fury.* 1954. London. 1st Eng ed. inscr. dj. EX. R3. $250.00

KUTTNER, Henry. *Gnome There Was.* 1950. Simon Schuster. 1st ed. dj. VG. R3. $85.00

KUTTNER, Henry. *Man Drowning.* 1952. Harper. 1st ed. dj. VG. P1. $25.00

KUTTNER, Henry. *Mutant.* 1950. Gnome. 1st ed. dj. EX. R3. $95.00

KUTTNER, Henry. *Mutant.* 1954. London. 1st UK ed. inscr/sgn. dj. EX. R3. $250.00

KUTTNER, Henry. *Mutant.* 1954. Weidenfeld Nicolson. dj. VG. P1. $60.00

KUTTNER, Henry. *Robots Have No Tails.* 1952. Gnome. 1st ed. dj. EX. R3. $95.00

KWITNY, Jonathan. *Mullendore Murder Case.* 1975. NY. dj. VG. B3. $35.00

KWITNY, Jonathan. *Shakedown.* 1977. Putnam. 1st ed. dj. VG. P1. $15.00

KYGER, Joanne. *Places To Go.* 1970. Blk Sparrow. 1st ed. 1/200. sgn. EX. $45.00

KYLE, Barry. *Sylvia Plath: A Dramatic Portrait.* 1976. London. Faber. 1st ed. wrp. EX. K2. $55.00

KYLE, Duncan. *Blk Camelot.* 1978. Collins. 1st ed. dj. EX. P1. $15.00

KYLE, Duncan. *Blk Camelot.* 1978. St Martin. 1st ed. dj. VG. P1. $17.50

KYLE, Duncan. *Stalking Point.* 1981. St Martin. 1st ed. dj. EX. P1. $12.50

KYLE, Duncan. *Terror's Cradle.* 1975. Collins. 1st ed. dj. VG. P1. $10.00

KYNE, P.E. *Enchanted Hill.* 1924. Cosmopolitan. VG. P1. $25.00

KYNETT, H.H. *Past Is Prologue.* 1954. np. Ils FW Lane. 189 p. G. T5. $15.00

L'ABBE. *Jerusalem et la Terre-Sainte.* c 1840s. Paris. 4to. French text. 399 p. AEG. EX. $250.00

L'AMOUR, Louis. *Flint.* nd. Bantam. EX. P1. $15.00

L'AMOUR, Louis. *Haunted Mesa.* 1987. Bantam. dj. VG. P1. $19.00

L'AMOUR, Louis. *How the W Was Won.* 1962. Random House. Photoplay/1st ed. EX. F5. $12.00

L'ENGLE, Madeleine. *And Both Were Young.* 1983. Delacorte. 1st ed. dj. EX. P1. $14.00

L'ENGLE, Madeleine. *Swiftly Tilting Planet.* 1978. Farrar Straus. 1st ed. dj. EX. F5. $35.00

L'ENGLE, Madeline. *Severed Wasp.* 1982. Farrar Straus. UP. gray wrp. EX. K2. $30.00

LA BREE, Benjamin. *Confederate Soldier in the Civil War.* 1959. Paterson, NJ. Pageant Books. 480 p. dj. EX. $60.00

LA FARGE, Oliver. *Pause in the Desert.* 1957. Boston. 1st ed. dj. VG. B3. $25.00

LA FOLLETTE, George. *Lightning Changes & Illusion Transformations.* c 1930. Baltimore. 1st ed. stapled manuscript. VG. J3. $5.00

LA FOUNTAINE, George. *Long Walk.* 1986. Putnam. 1st ed. dj. RS. EX. $15.00

LA ORDEN MIRABLE, Ernesto. *Elogio de Quito.* 1950. Madrid. 1st ed. 4to. 122 p. F2. $45.00

LA SPINA, Greye. *Invaders From the Dark.* 1960. Arkham House. 1st ed. dj. EX. R3. $85.00

LA VARRE, William. *Southward Ho! Treasure Hunter in S Am.* 1940. Doubleday. Ils. 301 p. dj. F2. $15.00

LA VARRE, William. *Southward Ho! Treasure Hunter in S Am.* 1940. Nat Travel Club. Ils. 301 p. F2. $12.50

LABAN, Rudolf. *Mastery of Movement.* 1960. London. 2nd ed. octavo. 186 p. dj. EX. H3. $75.00

LABARRE, E.J. *Dictionary of Paper & Papermaking Terms...* 1937. Amsterdam. 45 samples. 315 p. dj. G. T5. $150.00

LABBE, Armand. *Colombia Before Columbus.* 1986. Rizzoli. Ltd HrdCvr ed. 1/200. 4to. 207 p. F2. $100.00

LACEY, P.A. *Death of the Man Upstairs: Critical Appraisal...* 1966. Owensboro. 12mo. 36 p. SftCvr. VG. V1. $7.00

LACHMUND, Margarethe. *With Thine Adversary in the Way.* 1979. Wallingford. Pendle Hill. 12mo. 26 p. pamphlet. G. V1. $2.50

LACKEY, Louana. *Pottery of Acatlan.* 1982. OK U. 1st ed. 164 p. dj. F2. $25.00

LACKLAND, William. *Meteors, Aerolites, Storms, Atmospheric Phenomena.* 1874. NY. 1st Am ed. 12mo. EX. T1. $35.00

LACROIX, Paul. *Manners, Customs, & Dress During the Middle Ages...* 1874. Chapman Hall. 1st Eng ed. octavo. 554 p. VG. H3. $350.00

LAFFERTY, R.A. *Apocalypses.* 1977. Pinnacle. 1st ed. sgn. wrp. EX. F5. $14.00

LAFFERTY, R.A. *Archipelago.* nd. Manuscript Pr. dj. EX. P1. $20.00

LAFFERTY, R.A. *Does Anyone Else Have Something Further To Add?* 1974. Scribner. 1st ed. dj. EX. P1/R3. $20.00

LAFFERTY, R.A. *Flame Is Gr.* 1971. Walker. 1st ed. dj. EX. P1. $30.00

LAFFERTY, R.A. *Golden Gate.* 1982. Corroboree Pr. 1st ed. 1/1000. sgn. M. R3. $32.50

LAFFERTY, R.A. *Not To Mention the Camels.* 1976. Bobbs Merrill. 1st ed. dj. EX. P1. $20.00

LAGERKVIST, Par. *Sibyl.* 1958. Random House. ARC. dj. EX. K2. $55.00

LAHEE, H.C. *Annals of Music in Am.* 1922. Boston. Marshall Jones. 1st ed. octavo. 298 p. VG. H3. $50.00

LAHONTAN, Baron. *Memoires de l'Amerique Septentrionale.* 1715. Hague. 1 vol only. $250.00

LAIDLAW, Marc. *Neon Lotus.* 1988. Bantam. AP. wrp. M. R3. $20.00

LAIGHTON, C. *Letters to Celia.* 1972. Boston. Ltd ed. 1/1000. sgn. dj. VG. B3. $27.50

LAING, Alexander. *Great Ghost Stories of the World.* 1941. Bl Ribbon. VG. P1. $20.00

LAING, Janet. *Honeycombers.* nd. Hodder Stoughton. VG. P1. $8.00

LAIR, M.P. *Collection of Coin Magic.* 1985. 1st ed. 70 p. SftCvr. M. J3. $7.00

LAIT, Jack. *Big House.* nd. Grosset Dunlap. Photoplay ed. VG. P1. $25.00

LAKE, Carolyn. *Under Cover for Wells Fargo.* 1969. Houghton Mifflin. 1st ed. 280 p. dj. EX. B10. $15.00

LAKES, Arthur. *Prospecting for Gold & Silver.* 1896. Scranton. 2nd ed. G. $65.00

LALANNE, Maxime. *Treatise on Etching.* 1890. Boston. Trans Koehler. 10 pls. 79 p. G. T5. $35.00

LAMARTINE. *Pilgrimage to the Holy Land...1832-1833.* 1835. London. 1st Eng ed. 8vo. 3 vols. gilt bdg. VG. $150.00

LAMB, Charles. *Life & Works.* 1899-1900. London. Macmillan. Deluxe ed. 1/600. 12 vols. H3. $1250.00

LAMB, Charles. *Old China.* 1912. Houghton Mifflin. 1/540. 16mo. EX. $75.00

LAMB, Charles. *Works.* 1840. London. Moxin. New ed. VG. $95.00

LAMB, Charles. *Works.* 1903. London. Dent. 12 vols. sm octavo. VG. H3. $1500.00

LAMB, D.I. *Incurable Filibuster.* 1934. Farrar Rinehart. Ils Paul Brn. 1st ed. 298 p. F2. $20.00

LAMB, Edward. *No Lamb for Slaughter.* 1963. Harcourt. 1st ed. 248 p. dj. VG. B10. $5.75

LAMB, F.B. *Rio Tigre & Beyond.* 1985. N Atlantic Books. 1st ed. 227 p. wrp. F2. $15.00

LAMB, F.B. *Wizard of the Upper Amazon.* 1974. N Atlantic Books. 3rd print. 200 p. F2. $12.50

LAMB, Harold. *Durandal.* 1981. Grant. 1st ed. dj. EX. F5. $20.00

LAMB, Harold. *Nur Mahal.* 1935. Doubleday Doran. VG. P1. $25.00

LAMB, Hugh. *Taste of Fear.* 1976. Taplinger. 1st ed. dj. EX. P1. $25.00

LAMB, Hugh. *Victorian Tales of Terror.* 1975. Taplinger. 1st Am ed. dj. EX. R3. $15.00

LAMB, W.K. *Journals & Letters of Sir Alexander Mackenzie.* 1970. Hakluyt Soc. 1st ed. 8vo. 6 maps. 551 p. EX. T1. $65.00

LAMB & LAMB. *Quest for the Lost City.* 1951. Harper. Ils. 340 p. dj. F2. $15.00

LAMB & LAMB. *Quest for the Lost City.* 1951. NY. sgn. dj. VG. B3. $17.50

LAMB & LAMB. *Tales From Shakespeare.* 1909. London. Ils Rackham. 1st ed. 8vo. 304 p. TEG. EX. $85.00

LAMBERT, Derek. *Red Dove.* 1983. Stein Day. 1st ed. dj. VG. P1. $15.00

LAMBERT & MARX. *Eng Popular Art.* 1951. London. Batsford Ltd. 1st ed. 8vo. 120 p. dj. EX. R4. $20.00

LAMBERTON, W.M. *Reconnaissance & Bomber Aircraft of the 1914-1918 War.* 1962. Los Angeles. 1st ed. dj. EX. $55.00

LAMOUR, Dorothy. *My Side of the Road.* 1980. Prentice Hall. 1st ed. sgn. 244 p. dj. EX. H3. $45.00

LAMPITT, Dinah. *Fortune's Soldier.* 1985. Muller. 1st UK ed. dj. EX. F5. $15.00

LAMPSON, Mrs. G.L. *Quaker Post-Bag: Letters to Sir John Rodes to John Gratton.* 1910. Longman Gr. 8vo. 203 p. V1. $18.00

LANCASTER, Clay. *Japanese Influence in Am.* 1963. NY. Ils FL Wright. 1st Am ed. 4to. VG. ES. R5. $90.00

LANCASTER, Graham. *Nuclear Letters.* 1979. Atheneum. 1st ed. dj. VG. P1. $15.00

LANCASTER, Osbert. *Saracen's Head.* 1949. Boston. 1st Am ed. dj. VG. C1. $15.00

LANCHESTER, Elsa. *Charles Laughton & I.* 1938. Harcourt Brace. 1st Am ed. presentation. 296 p. dj. G. H3. $45.00

LANCOUR, Gene. *Globes of Llarum.* 1980. Doubleday. 1st ed. dj. VG. P1. $15.00

LANCOUR, Gene. *Sword for the Empire.* 1978. Doubleday. 1st ed. dj. EX. P1. $17.50

LANCOUR, Gene. *War Machines of Kalinth.* 1977. Doubleday. dj. EX. P1. $17.50

LANDIS, C.S. *Woodchucks & Woodchuck Rifles.* 1951. NY. 1st ed. 402 p. VG. T1. $50.00

LANDIS, C.S. *22-Caliber Varmint Rifles.* 1947. Plantersville. 1st ed. dj. VG. B3. $47.50

LANDON, Christopher. *Ice Cold in Alex.* nd. Popular Book Club. Photoplay ed. VG. P1. $7.50

LANDON, Christopher. *Unseen Enemy.* nd. Book Club. dj. VG. P1. $4.50

LANDOR, A.H.S. *In the Forbidden Land.* 1899. Harper. Ils. 2 vols. EX. B3. $145.00

LANDOR, W.S. *Imaginary Conversations.* 1891. London. Dent. 8vo. 6 vols. VG. $50.00

LANE, Arthur. *Greek Pottery.* 1953. London. 2nd imp. 8vo. 62 p. reprint dj. VG. $45.00

LANE, Eleanor. *Point Sight.* 1913. Althea Pr. 1st ed. 4to. 60 p. EX. R4. $85.00

LANE, Frank. *Funny Talk for Magicians.* 1942. Chicago. Nelmar. 2nd reprint ed. 239 p. EX. J3. $24.00

LANE, Frank. *Help Yourself.* 1931. Lane. 1st ed. 97 p. EX. J3. $8.00

LANE, Frank. *Here's How.* 1934. Springfield, MA. David Brn. 1st print. EX. J3. $3.00

LANE, Hermann. *Air Battle.* 1972. Cornmarket. reprint of 1859 ed. M. R3. $25.00

LANE, R.W. *He Was a Man.* 1925. NY. VG. B3. $22.50

LANE, Sarah. *Batz'L K'Op: True Speech. Yol: Offerings of the Maya.* 1988. Chicago. 1st ed. wrp. F2. $15.00

LANEY. *Gold Hill Mining District of NC.* 1910. Raleigh. 1st ed. fld pl. maps. wrp. VG. C2. $85.00

LANG, Allen Kim. *Wild & Outside.* 1965. Chilton. dj. VG. P1. $20.00

LANG, Andrew. *Angling Sketches.* 1891. Longman Gr. 1st ed. VG. $80.00

LANG, Andrew. *Animal Storybook.* 1896. Longman Gr. Ils HJ Ford. 1st ed. 12mo. 400 p. AEG. VG. $70.00

LANG, Andrew. *Aucassin & Nicolette.* 1896. Portland. Mosher. Ltd 2nd ed. EX. $25.00

LANG, Andrew. *Aucassin & Nicolette.* 1922. Portland. Mosher. Ltd ed. 1/500. 12mo. TEG. C1. $22.50

LANG, Andrew. *Bl Poetry Book.* 1896. Longman Gr. Ils Ford/Speed. 2nd ed. 348 p. AEG. VG. $50.00

LANG, Andrew. *Book of Romance.* 1909. Longman Gr. Ils Ford. 8vo. AEG. VG. $30.00

LANG, Andrew. *Chronicles of Pantouflia.* 1981. Godine. dj. VG. P1. $12.95

LANG, Andrew. *Euterpe: Being 2nd Book of Famous Hist of Herodotus.* 1888. London. 1/550. wrp. ES. fair. T5. $25.00

LANG, Andrew. *Gr Fairy Book.* 1964. Longman Gr. 6th ed. dj. xl. P1. $5.00

LANG, Andrew. *Hist of Whittington.* 1890. London. Longman Gr. 1st ed. 160 p. VG. B10. $7.25

LANG, Andrew. *King Arthur.* 1967. facsimile of 1902 ed. PB. VG. C1. $4.00

LANG, Andrew. *King Arthur: Tales of the Round Table.* c 1980. reprint of 1902 ed. C1. $12.00

LANG, Andrew. *Miracles of Madame St Katherine of Fierbois.* 1897. Way Williams. 1st ed. 1/50. red vellum. w/5 sgn letters. T5. $650.00

LANG, Andrew. *Myth, Ritual, & Religion.* 1887. Longman Gr. 1st ed. 8vo. VG. scarce. $225.00

LANG, Andrew. *Prince Prigio & Prince Ricardo.* 1961. Dent Dutton. dj. EX. P1. $22.50

LANG, Andrew. *Puzzle of Dicken's Last Plot.* 1905. Chapman Hall. 1st ed. sm octavo. 100 p. H3. $45.00

LANG, Andrew. *Red Book of Heroes.* 1909. London. Ils AW Mills. 1st ed. 12mo. EX. $60.00

LANG, Andrew. *True Storybook.* 1910. Longman Gr. Ils Ford/others. AEG. VG. $30.00

LANGART, D.T. *Anything You Can Do.* nd. Book Club. dj. VG. P1. $7.50

LANGART, D.T. *Anything You Can Do.* 1963. Doubleday. 1st ed. dj. VG. R3. $17.50

LANGE, Dorothea. *Photographs of a Lifetime.* 1982. Aperature. 4to. dj. EX. $30.00

LANGE, F.W. *Ancient Treasures of Costa Rica.* 1990. Boulder. 1st ed. lg 8vo. F2. $12.50

LANGE, F.W. *Costa Rican Art & Archaeology.* 1988. Boulder. 1st ed. 336 p. F2. $35.00

LANGE, John. *Binary.* 1972. Knopf. 3rd ed. dj. VG. P1. $10.00

LANGE, Oliver. *Vandenburg.* 1971. Stein Day. dj. VG. P1. $15.00

LANGFORD, G. *Murder of Stanford Wht.* 1962. Indianapolis. 1st ed. dj. VG. B3. $17.50

LANGFORD, N.P. *Discovery of Yellowstone Park.* 1870. St Paul. Haynes. 2nd ed. 188 p. VG. $95.00

LANGFORD, T. *Plain & Full Instruction to Raise All Sorts of Fruit Trees.* 1696. London. Clifwell. rebound. $275.00

LANGLAND, William. *Vision of William Concerning Piers the Plowman...* 1886. Clarendon. 1st ed. 2 vols. EX. C4. $100.00

LANGLEY, Bob. *War Lords.* 1981. Morrow. 1st ed. dj. VG. P1. $15.00

LANGLEY, Lester. *Struggle for the Am Mediterranean.* 1976. GA U. 1st ed. 226 p. dj. F2. $10.00

LANGLEY, Noel. *There's a Porpoise Close Behind Us.* 1953. Arthur Barker. 12th print. dj. VG. P1. $12.00

LANGTON, Jane. *Dark Nantucket Moon.* 1975. NY. 1st ed. dj. VG. B3. $22.50

LANGTON, Jane. *Paper Chains.* 1977. Harper Row. 1st ed. dj. VG. P1. $20.00

LANHAM, Edwin. *Death of a Corinthian.* 1953. Harcourt Brace. 1st ed. dj. VG. P1. $15.00

LANKS, Herbert. *By Pan Am Highway Through S Am.* 1942. Appleton. 1st ed. F2. $15.00

LANMAN, Charles. *Summer in the Wilderness.* 1847. NY. 1st ed. VG. $100.00

LANSDALE, J.R. *Act of Love.* 1989. Kinnell. sgn. dj. EX. P1. $35.00

LANSDALE, J.R. *By Bizarre Hands.* 1989. Mark Ziesing. sgn. dj. EX. P1. $35.00

LANSDALE, J.R. *Cold in July.* 1989. Bantam 28020-1. 1st ed. wrp. EX. T9. $25.00

LANSDALE, J.R. *Cold in July.* 1990. Mark Ziesing. sgn. dj. EX. P1. $35.00

LANSDALE, J.R. *Dead in the W.* 1990. Kinnell. sgn. dj. EX. P1. $35.00

LANSDALE, J.R. *Drive In.* 1989. Kinnell. sgn. dj. EX. P1. $35.00

LANSDALE, J.R. *Savage Season.* 1990. Mark Ziesing. sgn. dj. EX. P1. $35.00

LANSFORD, William. *Pancho Villa.* 1965. Herbourne Pr. 1st ed. 283 p. dj. F2. $20.00

LANTZ & LANE. *Pageant of Pattern for Needlepoint Canvas.* 1973. NY. 1st ed. dj. EX. $85.00

LAPINER, Alan. *Ancient Peruvian Sculpture.* 1967. NY. 2nd print. 4to. F2. $12.50

LAPINER, Alan. *Sun Gods & Saints.* 1969. Andre Emmerich. Ils. 4to. wrp. F2. $12.50

LARCO HOYLE, Rafael. *Checan.* 1965. Geneva. Nagel Pub. Ltd 1st ed. 1/3000. sm folio. 147 p. EX. F2. $60.00

LARCO HOYLE, Rafael. *Peru.* 1966. World. 1st ed. 243 p. F2. $25.00

LARDNER, Dionysius. *Treatise on Heat.* 1833. London. 1st Eng ed. 12mo. VG. T1. $100.00

LARDNER, Ring. *Bib Ballads.* 1915. Volland. 1st ed. EX. B13. $250.00

LARDNER, Ring. *Love Nest.* 1926. NY. 1st ed. VG. A6. $20.00

LARDNER, Ring. *Treat 'Em Rough.* 1918. IN. Ils Carrie. G. $12.00

LARDNER, Ring. *Young Immigrants.* 1920. Indianapolis. 1st ed. dj. VG. B3. $100.00

LARDNER, Ring. *1st & Last.* 1934. NY. 1st ed. dj. VG. B3. $35.00

LARIAR, Lawrence. *Man With the Lumpy Nose.* 1944. Dodd Mead. 1st ed. dj. VG. P1. $15.00

LARKIN, David. *Giants.* 1979. Abrams. 1st ed. dj. EX. F5. $20.00

LARKIN, David. *Once Upon a Time.* 1976. Peacock Pr. 1st ed. P1. $12.50

LARKIN, Philip. *High Windows.* 1974. NY. 1st ed. wrp. M. $12.00

LARNED, J.N. *Hist of the World.* 1915. NY City. Revised Enlarged ed. 5 vols. VG. B10. $25.00

LARREY, D.J. *Memoirs of Military Surgery & Campaigns of French Armies.* 1814. Baltimore. 1st Am ed. 2 vols. P4. $850.00

LARRICK, Nancy. *Parent's Guide to Children's Reading.* 1958. Cardinal. P1. $3.75

LARSEN & PELLATON. *Behind the Lianas.* 1958. London. 1st ed. 211 p. dj. F2. $25.00

LARSON, Ross. *Fantasy & Imagination in Mexican Narrative.* 1977. ASU. 1st ed. 154 p. wrp. F2. $12.50

LARSON, W.H. *7 Great Detective Stories.* 1968. Whitman. VG. P1. $5.00

LARSON & GOULART. *Die, Chameleon!* 1986. Berkley. 1st ed. wrp. EX. F5. $7.00

LARSON & GOULART. *Experiment Terra.* 1984. Berkley. 1st ed. wrp. EX. F5. $7.00

LARSSON, Gosta. *Ships in the River.* 1946. Whittlesy House. 1st ed. dj. EX. F5. $20.00

LARTIGUE, J.H. *Boyhood Photos...Family Album of the Gilded Age.* 1966. Switzerland. 126 p. EX. T5. $300.00

LARTIGUE, J.H. *Diary of a Century.* 1970. NY. dj. metallic dj. EX. $100.00

LARTIGUE, J.H. *Family Album of a Gilded Age.* 1966. Guichard. 4to. EX. $225.00

LASDUN, James. *Delirium Eclipse.* 1985. Harper. 1st ed. dj. EX. F5. $14.00

LASKY, M.J. *Hungarian Revolution.* 1957. NY. 1st Am ed. 318 p. G. T5. $35.00

LASKY, Victor. *It Didn't Start Watergate.* 1977. Dial. inscr. dj. EX. $12.00

LASS. *Steamboating on the Upper MO.* 1962. Lincoln, NE. 1st ed. 215 p. dj. VG. B3. $30.00

LASSAIGNE, Jacques. *Daumier.* 1938. Paris. Hyperion. 1st ed. dj. VG. G1. $40.00

LASSAIGNE, Jacques. *Spanish Painting: Catalian to El Greco.* 1952. Geneva. Skira. 1st ed. folio. boxed. EX. B3. $37.50

LASSER, J.K. *How To Run a Sm Business.* 1950. NY. 1st ed. EX. $10.00

LASSWELL, Mary. *Bread for the Living.* 1948. NY. 1st ed. dj. VG. B3. $40.00

LASSWELL, Mary. *High Time.* 1944. Boston. 1st ed. VG. C1. $9.50

LASSWELL, Mary. *Let's Go for Broke.* 1962. Boston. 1st ed. dj. VG. J2. $12.50

LASSWELL, Mary. *Mrs Rasmussen's Book of 1-Arm Cookery.* 1946. Boston. 1st ed. dj. VG. B3. $35.00

LATH, J.A. *Lost City of the Aztecs.* 1934. Cupples Leon. 1st ed. dj. VG. F5. $22.00

LATHAM, Philip. *Missing Men of Saturn.* 1958. Winston. dj. VG. R3. $25.00

LATHAM, R.M. *Complete Book of the Wild Turkey.* 1956. Harrisburg. 1st ed. dj. EX. $65.00

LATHAM, R.M. *Complete Book of the Wild Turkey.* 1977. Stackpole. dj. EX. $10.00

LATHEN, Emma. *Ashes to Ashes.* Simon Schuster. 2nd ed. dj. EX. P1. $10.00

LATHEN, Emma. *Ashes to Ashes.* 1971. Simon Schuster. 1st ed. dj. VG. P1. $15.00

LATHEN, Emma. *Going for the Gold.* nd. Simon Schuster. 2nd ed. dj. VG. P1. $10.00

LATHEN, Emma. *Longer the Thread.* nd. Book Club. dj. VG. P1. $4.50

LATHEN, Emma. *Longer the Thread.* 1971. Simon Schuster. 1st ed. dj. VG. P1. $15.00

LATHEN, Emma. *Sweet & Low.* nd. Book Club. dj. VG. P1. $4.50

LATIMER, Jonathan. *Blk Is the Fashion for Dying.* 1959. Random House. 1st ed. VG. P1. $20.00

LATIMER, Jonathan. *Headed for a Hearse.* nd. Sun Dial. VG. P1. $12.50

LATIMER, Jonathan. *Lady in the Morgue.* nd. Book Club. dj. VG. P1. $4.50

LATIMER, Jonathan. *Lady in the Morgue.* 1937. Sun Dial. VG. P1. $15.00

LATORRE & LATORRE. *Mexican Kicapoo Indians.* 1976. TX U. 1st ed. 401 p. F2. $15.00

LATOURETTE, Kenneth. *Chinese: Their Hist & Culture.* 1967. Macmillan. Revised 4th ed. 2 vols in 1. dj. EX. T4. $10.00

LATROBE, Benjamin. *Engineering Drawings.* 1980. New Haven. 1st ed. oblong folio. dj. EX. G1. $50.00

LAUBENTHAL, S.A. *Excalibur.* 1977. Ballantine. 1st ed. 2nd print. VG. C1. $11.50

LAUDER, Estee. *Estee.* 1985. NY. 1st ed. dj. EX. B3. $17.50

LAUGHLIN, James. *Sm Book of Poems.* 1948. Milan. 1/500. bl wrp. EX. H3. $200.00

LAUGHLIN, Robert. *Great Tzotzil Dictionary of Santo Domingo, Zinacantan.* 1988. Smithsonian. Tzotzil/Eng/Spanish text. 3 vols. F2. $35.00

LAUGHLIN, Robert. *Of Cabbages & Kings.* 1977. Smithsonian. Contribution to Anthropology Series. 427 p. F2. $25.00

LAUGHLIN, Robert. *Of Shoes & Ships & Sealing Wax.* 1980. Smithsonian. Contribution to Anthropology Series. wrp. F2. $25.00

LAUGHLIN, Robert. *Of Wonders Wild & New.* 1976. Smithsonian. Contribution to Anthropology Series. wrp. F2. $25.00

LAUMER, Keith. *Bolo.* 1976. Berkley. 1st ed. dj. EX. R3. $30.00

LAUMER, Keith. *Catastrophe Planet.* 1970. Dobson. dj. VG. P1. $10.00

LAUMER, Keith. *Deadfall.* 1971. Doubleday. 1st ed. dj. xl. P1. $10.00

LAUMER, Keith. *Glory Game.* 1973. Doubleday. not 1st ed. dj. EX. P1. $10.00

LAUMER, Keith. *Night of Delusions.* 1972. Putnam. 1st ed. dj. VG. P1. $20.00

LAUMER, Keith. *Once There Was a Giant.* 1971. Doubleday. dj. VG. P1. $15.00

LAUMER, Keith. *Other Side of Time.* 1968. Dobson. dj. xl. P1. $10.00

LAUMER, Keith. *Other Side of Time.* 1971. Walker. 1st ed. dj. xl. P1. $7.50

LAUMER, Keith. *Relief's Ransom.* 1975. Dobson. 1st ed. dj. EX. P1. $20.00

LAUMER, Keith. *Shape Changer.* 1972. Putnam. 1st ed. dj. xl. P1. $7.50

LAUMER, Keith. *Time Trap.* 1970. Putnam. 1st ed. dj. xl. P1. $7.50

LAUMER, Keith. *Ultimax Man.* nd. Book Club. dj. VG. P1. $4.50

LAUMER, Keith. *Ultimax Man.* 1978. St Martin. 1st ed. dj. xl. P1. $7.50

LAUMER, Keith. *World Shuffler.* 1970. Putnam. 1st ed. dj. VG. P1. $20.00

LAUMER & DICKSON. *Planet Run.* 1967. Doubleday. 1st ed. dj. VG. R3. $85.00

LAUNAY, Andre. *Harlequin's Son.* 1986. St Martin. 1st Am/HrdCvr ed. dj. EX. F5. $15.00

LAURENCE, W.L. *Dawn Over Zero.* 1947. Knopf. 2nd ed. VG. P1. $12.00

LAURENTS, Arthur. *Clearing in the Woods.* 1957. NY. 1st ed. dj. VG. $10.00

LAURIE, Peter. *Joy of Computers.* 1983. Little Brn. 1st ed. dj. VG. P1. $15.00

LAURVIK, J.N. *Is It Art? Post-Impressionism, Futurism, Cubism.* 1913. Internat Pr. D4. $95.00

LAUTS, Jan. *Carpaccio: Paintings & Drawings.* 1962. Greenwich. 1st Am ed. dj. VG. G1. $35.00

LAVATER, J.C. *Essays on Physiognomy.* 1789, 1792, & 1798. London. Murray. 1st ed. 3 vols in 5. H3. $1850.00

LAVENDER, David. *Bents Ft.* 1954. Doubleday. 1st ed. sgn. dj. A5. $50.00

LAVER, James. *Macrocosmos: A Poem.* 1929. Heinemann. Ltd ed. 1/775. sgn. glassine dj. slipcase. H3. $75.00

LAWES, Lewis. *20-Thousand Years in Sing Sing.* 1932. Long Smith. 1st ed. 412 p. dj. VG. B10. $4.75

LAWHEAD, Stephen. *Merlin.* 1988. 2nd print. M. C1. $11.00

LAWLER, L.B. *Dance in Ancient Greece.* 1965. Wesleyan U. octavo. 160 p. dj. EX. H3. $35.00

LAWLER, T.G. *70 Years of TB Pub: Hist of Ginn & Co 1867-1937.* 1938. Ginn. VG. $20.00

LAWRENCE, D.H. *Aaron's Rod.* 1922. NY. Thomas Seltzer. 1st ed. VG. $27.00

LAWRENCE, D.H. *Birds, Beasts, & Flowers.* 1923. NY. 1st ed. VG. $150.00

LAWRENCE, D.H. *David: A Play.* 1926. Knopf. 1st Am ed. dj. EX. K2. $85.00

LAWRENCE, D.H. *Erotic Works of DH Lawrence.* 1989. Avenel. dj. EX. P1. $12.50

LAWRENCE, D.H. *Escaped Cock.* 1929. Blk Sun. 1st ed. 1/450. wrp/glassine. slipcase. H3. $450.00

LAWRENCE, D.H. *Lady Chatterly's Lover.* nd. private print. Pirate ed. 1/500. 8vo. VG. $175.00

LAWRENCE, D.H. *My Skirmish With Jolly Roger.* 1929. NY. 1st ed. 1/600. M. $85.00

LAWRENCE, D.H. *Pansies.* 1929. London. private print. 1/500. sgn. dj. H3. $500.00

LAWRENCE, D.H. *Pansies.* 1929. London. Martin Secker. 1st Trade ed. VG. $75.00

LAWRENCE, D.H. *Sea & Sardinia.* 1923. London. Secker. 1st Eng ed. H3. $75.00

LAWRENCE, D.H. *Sex: Literature & Censorship.* 1953. NY. 1st ed. dj. EX. $15.00

LAWRENCE, D.H. *Sun: Being the Unexpurgated Version of This Story.* nd. private print. Pirate ed. 1/500. EX. C4. $100.00

LAWRENCE, D.H. *Touch & Go.* 1920. London. Daniel. 1st ed. 96 p. stiff wrp. H3. $75.00

LAWRENCE, D.H. *Touch & Go.* 1920. NY. Seltzer. 1st Am ed. tan brds. H3. $60.00

LAWRENCE, D.H. *Widowing of Mrs Holyrod.* 1914. 1st Am ed. 1/500. VG. B2. $85.00

LAWRENCE, D.H. *Woman Who Rode Away.* 1956. Berkley. B4. $8.00

LAWRENCE, D.H. *Women in Love.* 1930. Boni. 1st Uniform ed. VG. B10. $5.00

LAWRENCE, Frieda. *Not I, But the Wind.* 1934. Rydal Pr. 1st ed. 1/1000. sgn. H3. $250.00

LAWRENCE, Hilda. *Blood Upon the Snow.* 1944. Doubleday Book Club. VG. P1. $10.00

LAWRENCE, Hilda. *Time To Die.* 1947. Pocketbook. 1st ed. PB. VG. B10. $2.00

LAWRENCE, Josephine. *Next Door Neighbors.* 1926. Cupples. 1st ed. 311 p. VG. B10. $4.25

LAWRENCE, Kelly. *Gone Shots.* 1987. Watts. 1st ed. dj. EX. F5. $15.00

LAWRENCE, Louise. *Moonwind.* 1986. Harper Row. 1st ed. dj. RS. EX. P1. $15.00

LAWRENCE, T.E. *Crusader Castles.* 1936. Golden Cockerel. 1st ed. 2 vols. TEG. G. K2. $2000.00

LAWRENCE, T.E. *Essay on Flecker.* 1937. Doubleday Doran. 1st Am ed. 1/56. clamshell box. very rare. K2. $3000.00

LAWRENCE, T.E. *Essential TE Lawrence.* 1951. London. Cape. 1st ed. dj. EX. C4. $40.00

LAWRENCE, T.E. *Home Letters of TE Lawrence & His Brothers.* 1954. London. Blackwell. 1st ed. 4to. 731 p. dj. EX. C4. $75.00

LAWRENCE, T.E. *Home Letters of TE Lawrence & His Brothers.* 1954. Macmillan. 1st ed. dj. EX. K2. $225.00

LAWRENCE, T.E. *Minorities.* 1971. London. Cape. 1st ed. dj. EX. C4. $40.00

LAWRENCE, T.E. *Mint.* 1955. Doubleday Doran. 1st ed. 1/1000. gilt bl buckram. EX. K2. $850.00

LAWRENCE, T.E. *Mint.* 1955. London. 1st Trade ed. dj. VG. $65.00

LAWRENCE, T.E. *Mint.* 1955. London. Cape. 1st Eng ed. 1/2000. slipcase. EX. K2. $500.00

LAWRENCE, T.E. *Odyssey of Homer.* 1932. NY. Oxford. 1st Am Trade ed. 1st print. TEG. G. K2. $75.00

LAWRENCE, T.E. *Oriental Assembly.* 1939. Williams Norgate. 1st ed. gilt brn buckram. dj. EX. K2. $350.00

LAWRENCE, T.E. *Oriental Assembly.* 1940. Dutton. 1st ed. gilt red-brn buckram. dj. EX. K2. $200.00

LAWRENCE, T.E. *Secret Dispatches From Arabia.* 1939. Golden Cockerel. 1st ed. 1/1000. TEG. EX. K2. $850.00

LAWRENCE, T.E. *TE Lawrence by His Friends.* 1937. Doubleday Doran. 1st Am ed. dj. K2. $125.00

LAWRENCE, T.E. *TE Lawrence by His Friends.* 1937. London. Cape. 1st Eng ed. red buckram. dj. EX. K2. $125.00

LAWRENCE, T.E. *TE Lawrence Letters to ET Leeds.* 1988. Whittington Pr. 1st ed. 1/650. cardboard slipcase. M. K2. $350.00

LAWRENCE, T.E. *TE Lawrence to His Biographers, R Graves & L Hart.* 1963. London. Cassell. 1st Combined ed. dj. EX. C4. $45.00

LAWRENCE, T.E. *7 Pillars of Widsom.* 1935. London. Cape. 1st ed. 1/750. quarto. VG. scarce. B13. $1000.00

LAWRENCE, T.E. *7 Pillars of Wisdom.* 1966. Doubleday. not Book Club ed. 622 p. dj. EX. B10. $4.00

LAWRENCE, William. *Roger Wilcott.* 1902. Houghton Mifflin. 1st ed. B10. $7.00

LAWRENCE & WOOLLEY. *Carchemish: Report on Excavations at Djerabis...Part 1.* 1917. British Mus. 1st ed. 4to. VG. rare. K2. $3750.00

LAWRENCE & WOOLLEY. *Wilderness of Zin.* 1914. London. Palestine Exploration Fund. VG. K2. $2250.00

LAWRENSON, T. *French Stage in the 17th Century.* 1957. Manchester. 1st ed. 25 pls. 209 p. dj. EX. H3. $65.00

LAWSON, J.H. *Processional.* 1925. Seltzer. 1st ed. inscr. H3. $40.00

LAWSON, Joan. *Hist of Ballet & Its Makers.* 1964. London. 1st ed. 32 pls. dj. EX. H3. $50.00

LAWSON, Will. *Pacific Steamers.* 1927. Brn Ferguson. 8vo. 244 p. VG. $95.00

LAWTON & FLYNN. *Summary of Doctrine & Testimonies of...Friends.* nd. Phil. Stuckey. 16mo. 106 p. G. V1. $14.00

LAY, Beirne. *I Wanted Wings.* nd. Grosset Dunlap. dj. VG. P1. $15.00

LAYMAN, Richard. *Shadow Man: The Life of Dashiell Hammett.* 1981. Harcourt Brace/Bruccoli Clark. sgn. dj. EX. T9. $45.00

LAYTON, E.T. *And I Was There.* 1985. NY. 1st ed. 596 p. dj. T5. $12.50

LAZARUS, W.C. *Wings in the Sun: Annals of Aviation in FL.* 1951. Orlando, FL. Ils 1st ed. 310 p. dj. xl. T5. $25.00

LAZELL, J.A. *AK Apostle: Life Story of Sheldon Jackson.* 1960. NY. 1st ed. VG. T1. $30.00

LAZZARI, Pietro. *Walking Cross.* 1956. Blk Sun. 1st ed. wrp. EX. H3. $100.00

LE BLANC, M. *Arsen Lupin Verses Herlock Sholmes.* 1910. Chicago. 1st ed. VG. B3. $25.00

LE BOSSU, Adam. *Jeu de Robin et Marion.* 1913. Paris. Trans Langlois. orig wrp. very scarce. C1. $10.00

LE CARRE, John. *Call for the Dead.* 1962. Walker. 1st Am ed. dj. EX. C4. $650.00

LE CARRE, John. *Clandestine Muse.* 1986. Janus Pr. Ltd ed. 1/260. sgn. stiff dj. M. H3. $125.00

LE CARRE, John. *Honorable Schoolboy.* 1977. Hodder Stoughton. 1st ed. dj. VG. P1. $35.00

LE CARRE, John. *Honorable Schoolboy.* 1977. Knopf. 1st Am Trade ed. dj. EX. T9. $35.00

LE CARRE, John. *Little Drummer Girl.* 1983. Hodder Stoughton. 1st ed. dj. EX. P1. $25.00

LE CARRE, John. *Little Drummer Girl.* 1983. Hodder Stoughton. 1st UK Trade ed. dj. EX. T9. $40.00

LE CARRE, John. *Looking Glass War.* nd. Book Club. dj. VG. P1. $4.50

LE CARRE, John. *Perfect Spy.* 1986. NY. 1st ed. dj. EX. T1. $25.00

LE CARRE, John. *Russia House.* 1989. London. 1st ed. 1/250. sgn. K2. $175.00

LE CARRE, John. *Secret Pilgrim.* 1991. 1st Eng ed. sgn. dj. EX. K2. $125.00

LE CARRE, John. *Secret Pilgrim.* 1991. Knopf. UP of 1st Am ed. wrp. EX. K2. $125.00

LE CARRE, John. *Sm Town in Germany.* 1968. Coward McCann. Ltd ed. 1/500. presentation. H3. $300.00

LE CARRE, John. *Sm Town in Germany.* 1968. Coward McCann. 4th print. dj. EX. P1. $15.00

LE CARRE, John. *Sm Town in Germany.* 1968. Heinemann. VG. P1. $20.00

LE CARRE, John. *Smiley's People.* 1980. Hodder Stoughton. 1st ed. dj. VG. P1. $25.00

LE CARRE, John. *Smiley's People.* 1980. Knopf. 1st Am Trade ed. dj. EX. T9. $30.00

LE CARRE, John. *Spy Who Came in From the Cold.* nd. Book Club. dj. VG. P1. $4.50

LE CARRE, John. *Spy Who Came in From the Cold.* nd. Coward McCann. 3rd ed. dj. xl. P1. $10.00

LE CARRE, John. *Spy Who Came in From the Cold.* 1964. Gollancz. 16th print. VG. P1. $10.00

LE CARRE, John. *Tinker Tailor Soldier Spy.* 1974. Hodder Stoughton. UP. wrp. dj. VG. scarce. K2. $225.00

LE CLERCQ, Jacques. *Burnt Offering.* 1930. Brentano. 1st Am ed. 265 p. VG. B10. $4.00

LE CORBEAU, Adrian. *Forest Giant.* 1924. London. Cape. 1st Eng ed. 8vo. G. K2. $175.00

LE CORBEAU, Adrian. *Forest Giant.* 1924. NY. Harper. Trans Ross. 1st Am ed. sgn Wilson. G. K2. $275.00

LE FANU, J.S. *Gr Tea.* 1945. Arkham House. 1st ed. dj. EX. R3. $185.00

LE FANU, J.S. *In a Glass Darkly.* 1929. Peter Davies. VG. P1. $75.00

LE FANU, J.S. *Purcell Papers.* 1975. Arkham House. 1st ed. dj. EX. P1. $15.00

LE GALLIENNE, Richard. *Odes From the Divan of Hafiz.* 1903. private print. Sm Paper ed. 1/300. sgn. 194 p. TEG. VG. V1. $125.00

LE GUIN, U.K. *Adventure of Cobbler's Rune.* 1982. Cheap Street. 1st ed. 1/250. sgns. wrp. M. R3. $70.00

LE GUIN, U.K. *Beginning Place.* 1980. Harper Row. UP. wrp. VG. K2. $125.00

LE GUIN, U.K. *Beginning Place.* 1980. Harper Row. 1st ed. dj. EX. R3. $20.00

LE GUIN, U.K. *Compass Rose.* 1982. Harper Row. UP. wrp. EX. K2. $50.00

LE GUIN, U.K. *Compass Rose*. 1982. Harper Row. 1st Am ed. dj. EX. P1. $30.00

LE GUIN, U.K. *Compass Rose*. 1983. Gollancz. 1st UK ed. dj. EX. F5. $20.00

LE GUIN, U.K. *Eye of the Heron*. 1983. Harper Row. UP of 1st separate ed. EX. K2. $50.00

LE GUIN, U.K. *Eye of the Heron*. 1983. Harper Row. 1st ed. dj. EX. R3. $17.50

LE GUIN, U.K. *Farthest Shore*. 1974. Atheneum. 3rd ed. dj. EX. P1. $15.00

LE GUIN, U.K. *Language of the Night*. 1979. Putnam. 1st ed. dj. EX. R3. $20.00

LE GUIN, U.K. *Language of the Night*. 1980. Perigee. VG. P1. $7.50

LE GUIN, U.K. *Left Hand of Darkness*. 1969. Ace. 1st ed. wrp. VG. R3. $20.00

LE GUIN, U.K. *Left Hand of Darkness*. 1969. Walker. 1st ed. dj. xl. P1. $7.50

LE GUIN, U.K. *Left Hand of Darkness*. 1980. Harper. 1st ed. dj. EX. R3. $20.00

LE GUIN, U.K. *Malafrena*. nd. Putnam. 2nd ed. dj. EX. P1. $15.00

LE GUIN, U.K. *Ones Who Walked Away From Omelas*. 1976. Alternate World Records. 1st ed. M. R3. $20.00

LE GUIN, U.K. *Orsinian Tales*. 1976. Harper. 1st ed. dj. VG. R3. $12.50

LE GUIN, U.K. *Solomon Leviathan's 931st Trip Around the World*. 1983. Philomel. 1st ed. dj. M. $10.00

LE GUIN, U.K. *Tombs of Atuan*. 1976. Atheneum. 5th ed. dj. EX. P1. $15.00

LE GUIN, U.K. *Wild Angels*. 1975. Capra. Chapbook Series. 1/200. sgn. EX. K2. $85.00

LE MAY & KANTOR. *Mission With Le May*. 1965. NY. 1st ed. inscr. dj. EX. $30.00

LE PAUL, Paul. *Card Magic of Brother John Mamman...* 1958. St Louis. Don Lawton. 2nd ed. 47 p. SftCvr. NM. J3. $6.00

LE PAUL, Paul. *Card Magic of Le Paul*. 1949. Danville, IL. Interstate Printers. 2nd ed. sgn. EX. J3. $39.00

LE PLONGEON, Augustus. *Sacred Mysteries Among Mayas & Quiches 11,500 Years Ago*. 1909. NY. Robert Macoy. 3rd ed. 163 p. F2. $55.00

LE QUEUX, William. *Behind the Bronze Door*. nd. Goldsmith. VG. P1. $10.00

LE QUEUX, William. *Closed Book*. 1908. Dodge. G. R3. $12.50

LE QUEUX, William. *Crystal Claw*. 1924. Macaulay. 1st ed. dj. VG. P1. $15.00

LE QUEUX, William. *Elusive 4*. 1930. Cassell. 3rd ed. VG. P1. $13.75

LE QUEUX, William. *Golden 3*. 1931. Fiction League. VG. P1. $20.00

LE QUEUX, William. *Great God Gold*. 1910. Richard Badger. 1st ed. VG. R3. $17.50

LE QUEUX, William. *Man From Downing St*. nd. Hurst Blackett. VG. P1. $15.00

LE QUEUX, William. *Valrose Mystery*. 1928. Wark Lock. VG. P1. $10.00

LE ROY, Arthur. *Futuristic Fantasies...* nd. Cornwall, Canada. Ovette. 1st ed. sgn. SftCvr. EX. J3. $5.00

LE SAGE. *Adventures of Gil Blas*. 1896. London. Ltd ed. 3 vols. VG. $15.00

LEA, Tom. *Hands of Cantu*. 1964. Boston. 1st ed. dj. VG. B3. $40.00

LEA, Tom. *Hands of Cantu*. 1964. Little Brn. 8vo. 244 p. xl. VG. $15.00

LEA, Tom. *King Ranch*. 1957. Boston. 1st ed. 2 vols. boxed. VG. B3. $65.00

LEA, Tom. *Primal Yoke*. 1960. Little Brn. 1st ed. dj. VG. $22.00

LEA, Tom. *Wonderful Country*. nd. Little Brn. 1st ed. dj. VG. $35.00

LEACH, Christopher. *Send Off*. 1973. Scribner. 1st ed. dj. EX. $14.00

LEACH, D.E. *Arms for Empire*. 1973. Macmillan. 1st ed. 8vo. 566 p. VG. B10. $5.50

LEACH, MacEdward. *Book of Ballads*. 1967. Ltd Ed Club. Ils/sgn Fritz Kredel. 1/1500. slipcase. EX. C4. $100.00

LEACH, P.R. *That Man Dawes*. 1930. Reilly Lee. Ils. 4to. dj. VG. $20.00

LEACOCK, Stephen. *Boy I Left Behind Me*. 1946. NY. 1st ed. dj. VG. B3. $17.50

LEACOCK, Stephen. *Nonsense Novels*. nd. London. VG. R3. $15.00

LEAD, Brian. *Laughing at Locksmiths: Legend & Legacy of Harry Houdini*. 1988. Lead. Ltd 1st ed. cbdg. M. J3. $7.50

LEADER, Mary. *Salem's Children*. 1979. Coward McCann. 1st ed. clipped dj. EX. F5. $18.50

LEAF, Munro. *Munro Leaf's Fun Book*. 1941. NY. 1st ed. 4to. dj. VG. $22.00

LEAF, Munro. *Story of Ferdinand*. 1937. NY. Ils Robert Lawson. 7th print. dj. G. T1. $30.00

LEAHY, John. *Drome*. 1952. Fantasy. 1st ed. 1st bdg. dj. EX. R3. $35.00

LEAKEY, L.S.B. *Mau Mau & the Kikuyu*. 1954. London. 115 p. dj. VG. T5. $25.00

LEAKEY, Richard. *Making of Mankind*. 1981. Dutton. 1st ed. 256 p. dj. F2. $15.00

LEAKEY & LEWIN. *Origins*. 1978. Dutton. Ils. 264 p. dj. F2. $15.00

LEAKEY & LEWIN. *People of the Lake*. 1978. Doubleday. Ils. 298 p. dj. F2. $10.00

LEAN, V.S. *Lean's Collectanea*. 1902. Bristol. Arrowsmith. 5 vols. lg octavo. H3. $250.00

LEAR, Peter. *Spider Girl*. 1980. Viking. 1st ed. dj. VG. P1. $15.00

LEARMONT, James. *Master in Sail*. 1954. London. Marshall. 2nd ed. 288 p. dj. VG. B10. $12.00

LEASOR, James. *Love All*. 1971. Heinemann. 1st ed. dj. xl. P1. $5.00

LEASOR, James. *Monday Story*. 1958. Oxford. 2nd ed. dj. xl. P1. $6.00

LEASOR, James. *Spylight*. 1966. Lippincott. dj. VG. P1. $8.00

LEASOR, James. *They Don't Make Them Like Any More*. 1969. Doubleday. 1st ed. dj. VG. P1. $17.50

LEASOR & BURT. *1 That Got Away*. 1956. Collins. 1st ed. dj. VG. P1. $15.00

LEAT, Harry. *Thoughtful Magic*. 1923. London. Leat. 1st ed. 107 p. NM. J3. $5.00

LEAVITT, David. *Equal Affections*. 1989. NY. ARC. wrp. M. $15.00

LEAVITT, David. *Family Dancing: Stories*. 1984. Knopf. 1st ed. dj. EX. C4. $50.00

LEAVITT, R.F. *World of TN Williams*. 1978. Putnam. Ltd ed. 1/250. sgns. dj. boxed. H3. $150.00

LECKIE, R. *Conflict*. 1962. NY. 1st ed. dj. VG. B3. $20.00

LECKY, Walter. *Birds & Books*. 1899. Angel Guardian Pr. 1st ed. 243 p. VG. B10. $6.25

LECUNA & BIERCH. *Selected Writings of Bolivar*. 1951. Colonial Pr. 1st ed. 2 vols. F2. $30.00

LEDERER & BURDICK. *Ugly Am*. 1959. NY. 1st ed. 1st issue. very scarce. K2. $100.00

LEE, Andrew. *Indifferent Children*. 1947. Prentice Hall. 1st ed. dj. EX. B13. $250.00

LEE, Austin. *Miss Hogg & the Bronte Murders*. 1956. Jonathan Cape. 1st ed. dj. EX. P1. $20.00

LEE, Edward. *Needle's Eye.* 1944. Crime Club. 1st ed. VG. P1. $12.50

LEE, G.R. *G-String Murders.* 1942. Tower. 2nd ed. VG. P1. $10.00

LEE, Harper. *To Kill a Mockingbird.* 1960. Lippincott. 1st ed. dj. EX. K2. $950.00

LEE, Harper. *To Kill a Mockingbird.* 1960. Phil. 36th print. presentation. VG. B3. $90.00

LEE, Howard. *Superstition.* 1973. Warner. 1st ed. wrp. EX. F5. $10.00

LEE, Howard. *Way of the Tiger, Sgn of the Dragon.* 1973. Warner. 1st ed. wrp. EX. F5. $10.00

LEE, J.M. *Artilleryman.* 1920. KS City. Ils 1st ed. T5. $95.00

LEE, Jeanette. *Happy Island.* 1911. Century. 1st ed? VG. B10. $4.00

LEE, John. *9th Man.* 1976. Doubleday. dj. EX. P1. $15.00

LEE, Josephine. *Fabulous Manticora.* 1976. John Day. dj. VG. P1. $10.00

LEE, M.A. *Mother Lee's Experience in 15 Years' Rescue Work.* 1906. Omaha. photos. 260 p. G. S1. $9.50

LEE, R.W. *Hist of Valentines.* 1952. Wellesley Hills. dj. EX. $20.00

LEE, Sherman. *Hist of Far E Art.* 1964. Englewood Cliffs. Probably 1st ed. VG. G1. $35.00

LEE, Stan. *Dunn's Conundrum.* 1984. Harper Row. 1st ed. dj. EX. P1. $15.00

LEE, Sydney. *Seigneurs & Sovereigns of Medieval Exeter.* c 1930s. Sydney Lee. Ils. wrp. VG. C1. $12.50

LEE, Tanith. *Dreams of Dark & Light.* 1986. Arkham House. 1st ed. M. R3. $21.95

LEE, Tanith. *E of Midnight.* 1978. St Martin. 1st ed. dj. EX. P1. $30.00

LEE, Tanith. *Electric Forest.* nd. Book Club. dj. VG. P1. $6.00

LEE, Tanith. *Madame 2 Swords.* 1988. Grant. 1st ed. 1/600. sgn. M. R3. $50.00

LEE, Tanith. *Night's Master.* 1984. Highland Pr. 1st ed. 1/500. sgn. M. R3. $50.00

LEE, Vincent. *Buildings of Sacsayhuaman & Other Papers.* 1987-1988. Wilson, WY. sgn. wrp. F2. $20.00

LEE, Vincent. *Chanasuyu: Ruins of Inca Vilcabamba.* 1989. Wilson, WY. 3rd print. sgn. sm 4to. F2. $15.00

LEE, W.C. *Bat Masterson.* 1960. Whitman. VG. P1. $7.50

LEE, W.S. *Stagecoach N.* 1941. NY. 1st ed. dj. VG. B3. $15.00

LEE, Walt. *Reference Guide to Fantastic Films.* 1975. Chelsea Lee. 2nd print. 3 vols. M. R3. $50.00

LEE & LEE. *Illuminated Book of Days.* 1979. Putnam. Ils Greenaway/Grasset. 4to. 213 p. dj. VG. $22.00

LEECH, John. *Annotated Christmas Carol of Charles Dickens.* 1976. Potter. 1st ed. dj. VG. B7. $33.00

LEECH, John. *Pictures of Life & Character.* 1857-1869. London. Bradbury Evans. 5 vols in 1. 480 p. H3. $400.00

LEECH, Margaret. *Reveille in WA.* 1941. Harper. 481 p. G. S1. $9.50

LEEMING, David. *Mythology: Voyage of the Hero.* c 1982. 2nd ed. stiff wrp. VG. C1. $11.00

LEEMING, Joseph. *Fun With Magic.* 1943. Lippincott. 5th imp. 86 p. EX. J3. $16.00

LEEMING, Joseph. *Magic for Everybody.* 1934. Doubleday. 260 p. VG. J3. $6.00

LEEMING, Joseph. *New Book of Magic.* 1939. Doubleday Doran. 197 p. VG. J3. $6.00

LEER, Edward. *Book of Limericks.* nd. (1888) Little Brn. dj. G. B10. $4.00

LEES, J.A. *Peaks & Pines.* 1899. London/NY/Bombay. Ils 1st ed. EX. $45.00

LEES, Walt. *Art of Grafter.* 1983. London. Breese. 25 p. SftCvr. J3. $7.00

LEES, Walt. *More Money Magic of Mike Bornstein.* 1984. Magico Magazine. 35 p. SftCvr. EX. J3. $5.00

LEFFINGWELL, W.B. *Shooting on Upland, Marsh, & Stream.* 1890. Chicago. 1st ed. VG. K1. $90.00

LEGARET, Jean. *Tightrope.* 1968. Little Brn. 1st ed. dj. EX. F5. $14.00

LEGARET, Jean. *Tightrope.* 1968. Little Brn. 1st ed. dj. xl. P1. $5.00

LEGGE, Ronald. *Hawk.* 1909. McBride. 1st ed. VG. R3. $25.00

LEGGETT, B.F. *Sheaf of a Song.* 1887. Alden. 1st ed. 154 p. VG. B10. $7.25

LEGMAN, G. *Art of Mahlon Blaine.* 1982. Peregrine. 1st ed. wrp. M. R3. $13.95

LEGMAN, G. *Fake Revolt.* 1967. Breaking Point. B4. $6.00

LEHMAN, Ernest. *French Atlantic Affair.* 1977. Atheneum. 1st ed. dj. EX. P1. $15.00

LEHMANN, Henri. *Guide to the Ruins of Mixco Viejo.* nd. Guatemala. 8vo. 53 p. wrp. F2. $8.00

LEHMANN, Henri. *Pre-Columbian Ceramics.* 1962. Viking. 1st Am ed. 128 p. F2. $25.00

LEHMANN, Lilli. *How To Sing (Meine Gesangskunst).* 1924. Macmillan. Trans Aldrich. New Revised ed. 304 p. H3. $75.00

LEHMANN, Rosamond. *Ballad & the Source.* 1945. Reynal Book Club. 312 p. gr bdg. VG. B10. $3.00

LEHMANN-HAUPT, Hellmut. *Book in Am: Hist of Making, Selling, & Collecting.* 1939. 1st ed. VG. $50.00

LEHNER & LEHNER. *How They Saw the New World.* 1966. NY. Tudor. 4to. 160 p. dj. F2. $25.00

LEIBER, Fritz. *Best of Fritz Leiber.* 1974. Doubleday. 1st HrdCvr ed. dj. EX. F5. $12.00

LEIBER, Fritz. *Best of Fritz Leiber.* 1974. Doubleday. 1st HrdCvr ed. sgn. dj. EX. F5. $18.00

LEIBER, Fritz. *Best of Fritz Lieber.* nd. Book Club. dj. EX. P1. $7.50

LEIBER, Fritz. *Big Time.* 1976. Ace. 1st ed. wrp. EX. R3. $35.00

LEIBER, Fritz. *Big Time.* 1976. Severn House. 1st ed. dj. EX. P1. $25.00

LEIBER, Fritz. *Ervool.* 1981. Cheap Street. 1st ed. 1/226. sgn. wrp. M. R3. $30.00

LEIBER, Fritz. *Gather Darkness.* 1951. Grosset Dunlap. 1st ed. sgn. dj. VG. P1. $45.00

LEIBER, Fritz. *Girl With the Hungry Eyes.* 1949. Avon. 1st ed. wrp. EX. R3. $35.00

LEIBER, Fritz. *Gr Millenium.* 1977. Severn House. 1st ed. dj. EX. P1. $25.00

LEIBER, Fritz. *Gr Millenium.* 1977. Severn House. 1st ed. sgn. dj. VG. P1. $45.00

LEIBER, Fritz. *Knight & Knave of Swords.* 1988. Morrow. 1st ed. inscr. dj. EX. F5. $25.00

LEIBER, Fritz. *Night's Blk Agents.* 1975. London. 1st ed. dj. EX. R3. $30.00

LEIBER, Fritz. *Night's Blk Agents.* 1980. Gregg Pr. 1st ed. P1. $25.00

LEIBER, Fritz. *Quicks Around the Zodiac.* 1983. Cheap Street. 1st ed. 1/98. sgn. wrp. M. R3. $25.00

LEIBER, Fritz. *Wanderer.* 1967. London. 1st HrdCvr ed. dj. VG. R3. $85.00

LEIBER, Fritz. *2 Sought Adventure.* 1957. Gnome. 1st ed. dj. M. R3. $150.00

LEIBER, Fritz. *3 Swords.* 1988. Nelson Doubleday. 1st HrdCvr ed. dj. EX. F5. $13.00

LEIGHTON, Clara. *Glimpses of S America. A Log.* 1924. Ye Cloister Print Shop. 1st ed. 61 p. VG. F2. $12.50

LEIGHTON, Clare. *Give Us This Day.* 1943. NY. Ils 1st ed. 86 p. dj. VG. T5. $12.50

LEINSTER, Murray. *Forgotten Planet.* 1954. Gnome. 1st ed. dj. EX. R3. $35.00

LEINSTER, Murray. *Forgotten Planet.* 1984. Crown. 1st ed. dj. EX. P1. $12.50

LEINSTER, Murray. *Great Stories of SF.* nd. Random House. 3rd ed. dj. VG. P1. $20.00

LEINSTER, Murray. *Last Spaceship.* nd. Book Club. dj. VG. P1. $6.00

LEINSTER, Murray. *Last Spaceship.* 1949. Fell. 1st ed. dj. EX. R3. $60.00

LEINSTER, Murray. *Men Into Space.* 1960. Berkley. 1st ed. wrp. EX. F5. $10.00

LEINSTER, Murray. *Out of This World.* 1958. Avalon. 1st ed. dj. VG. R3. $25.00

LEINSTER, Murray. *Sidewise in Time.* 1950. Shasta. 1st ed. dj. EX. R3. $135.00

LEINSTER, Murray. *4 From Planet 5.* 1974. Wht Lion. 1st ed. dj. VG. P1. $25.00

LEIPZIGER, Hugo. *Architectonic City of Am.* 1944. TX U. 1st ed. 4to. xl. F2. $25.00

LEITFRED, R.H. *Man Who Was Murdered Twice.* 1937. Gr Circle. xl. P1. $12.50

LEITHAUSER, Brad. *Cats of the Temple.* 1986. Knopf. 1st ed. dj. EX. C4. $20.00

LEITHAUSER, Joachim. *World Beyond the Horizon.* 1955. Knopf. 1st ed. 412 p. dj. F2. $15.00

LEJARD, Andre. *Art of the French Book.* 1947. Paris. Ils 1st ed. 4to. dj. VG. T1. $75.00

LELONG & JAVAL. *Stars Weep.* 1956. Hutchinson. 1st ed. 198 p. dj. F2. $15.00

LEM, Stanislaw. *Chain of Chance.* 1978. Harcourt. 1st ed. dj. EX. R3. $20.00

LEM, Stanislaw. *Imaginary Magnitude.* 1984. Harcourt Brace. 1st ed. dj. EX. P1. $15.95

LEM, Stanislaw. *Investigation.* 1974. Seabury. 1st ed. dj. EX. R3. $30.00

LEM, Stanislaw. *Memoirs of a Space Traveler.* 1982. Harcourt Brace. 1st ed. dj. EX. P1. $15.00

LEM, Stanislaw. *Microworlds.* 1984. Harcourt. 1st ed. dj. EX. F5. $15.00

LEM, Stanislaw. *Mortal Engines.* 1977. Seabury. 1st ed. dj. EX. R3. $20.00

LEM, Stanislaw. *Return From the Stars.* 1980. Harcourt Brace. dj. EX. P1. $15.00

LEM, Stanislaw. *Return From the Stars.* 1980. Harcourt. 1st ed. sgn. dj. EX. $17.50

LEMARCHAND, Elizabeth. *Nothing To Do With the Case.* nd. Book Club. dj. VG. P1. $5.00

LEMARCHAND, Elizabeth. *Troubled Waters.* 1982. Walker. 1st ed. dj. VG. P1. $15.00

LEMARCHAND, Elizabeth. *Unhappy Returns.* 1977. Walker. 1st ed. dj. xl. P1. $5.00

LEMMON, Robert. *Flowers of the World.* nd. (1958) Doubleday. 280 p. VG. B10. $3.75

LEMON, Mark. *Jest Book.* 1864. London. 16mo. VG. T1. $145.00

LENANTON, Carola. *Mrs Barrett's Elopement.* 1930. Grosset. dj. B10. $4.75

LENGYEL, Comel. *Atom Clock.* 1951. Fantasy. 1st ed. dj. EX. F3. $10.00

LENNON, John. *In His Own Write/Spaniard in the Works.* 1967. Signet. 1st PB ed. EX. B4. $5.00

LENSKI, Lois. *Bound Girl of Cobble Hill.* 1966. Lippincott. reprint. 8vo. 291 p. dj. VG. $10.00

LENSKI, Lois. *Journey Into Childhood.* 1972. Lippincott. 1st ed. 208 p. dj. EX. B10. $12.50

LENSKI, Lois. *Living With Others.* 1950. Hartford. wrp. EX. $40.00

LENSKI, Lois. *Ocean-Born Mary.* 1939. Stokes. VG. B7. $48.00

LENSKI, Lois. *Skipping Village.* 1927. Stokes. 1st ed. 4to. 179 p. EX. $75.00

LEONARD, C.L. *Secret of the Spa.* nd. Book Club. dj. VG. P1. $6.00

LEONARD, C.L. *Sinister Shelter.* 1949. Crime Club. VG. P1. $10.00

LEONARD, C.L. *Treachery in Trieste.* 1951. Crime Club. 1st ed. dj. VG. P1. $10.00

LEONARD, Elmore. *Bandits.* nd. Book Club. dj. VG. P1. $5.00

LEONARD, Elmore. *Bandits.* 1987. Arbor House. 1st ed. dj. VG. P1. $17.95

LEONARD, Elmore. *Bandits.* 1987. Arbor House. 1st ed. inscr/sgn. dj. EX. K2. $60.00

LEONARD, Elmore. *Cat Chaser.* 1982. Arbor House. 1st ed. dj. EX. P1. $25.00

LEONARD, Elmore. *Cat Chaser.* 1986. Hall. Lg Print ed. dj. VG. P1. $16.95

LEONARD, Elmore. *City Primeval.* 1986. Hall. Lg Print ed. dj. VG. P1. $16.95

LEONARD, Elmore. *Dutch Treat.* 1977. Arbor House. Ltd ed. 1/350. sgn. slipcase. M. H3. $100.00

LEONARD, Elmore. *Dutch Treat.* 1985. Arbor House. 1st ed. dj. VG. P1. $17.95

LEONARD, Elmore. *Elmore Leonard's Double-Dutch Treat.* nd. Arbor House. sgn. dj. NM. T9. $55.00

LEONARD, Elmore. *Glitz.* 1985. Arbor House. dj. EX. P1. $15.00

LEONARD, Elmore. *Glitz.* 1985. Mysterious Pr. Ltd ed. 1/500. sgn. slipcase. M. H3. $125.00

LEONARD, Elmore. *Gold Coast.* 1983. London. Star. 1st UK ed. sgn. wrp. EX. B13. $50.00

LEONARD, Elmore. *Split Images.* 1981. Arbor House. 1st ed. dj. EX. T9. $30.00

LEONARD, Elmore. *Split Images.* 1986. Hall. Lg Print ed. dj. VG. P1. $16.95

LEONARD, Elmore. *Stick.* 1983. Arbor House. 1st ed. sgn. dj. EX. T9. $40.00

LEONARD, Elmore. *Swag.* 1976. NY. 1st ed. dj. EX. C4. $60.00

LEONARD, Elmore. *Touch.* 1987. Arbor House. 1st ed. dj. EX. P1. $17.95

LEONARD, Elmore. *40 Lashes Less 1.* 1972. Bantam S6928. PB Orig. wrp. NM. T9. $50.00

LEONARD, George. *Shoulder the Sky.* 1959. McDowell. 1st ed. 310 p. VG. B10. $4.00

LEONARD, J. *Flies.* 1950. NY. Ils. 340 p. dj. VG. B3. $60.00

LEONARD, J.L. *Care & Handling of Dogs.* 1928. Doubleday. 374 p. VG. B10. $4.00

LEONARD, Jonathan. *Ancient Am.* 1967. Time. 1st ed. 4to. 192 p. F2. $12.50

LEONHARD, Pat. *Balloons, Everything You Always Wanted To Know...* 1988. Vienna. Leonhard. German/Eng text. EX. J3. $25.00

LEOPOLD, Aldo. *Game Management.* 1933. Scribner. 481 p. VG. $25.00

LEOPOLD. *Robert Dale Owen: A Biography.* 1940. Cambridge. 1st ed. 470 p. VG. B3. $35.00

LERNER & GUNTHER. *Epidemic 9.* 1980. Morrow. 1st ed. dj. EX. F5. $16.00

LEROUX, Gaston. *Double Life.* 1909. Kearney. 1st ed. VG. R3. $20.00

LEROUX, Gaston. *Nomads of the Night.* 1925. Macaulay. decor brd. VG. P1. $30.00

LESAGE, A.R. *Asmodeus.* 1881. London. 1/100. Lauriat bdg. VG. $60.00

LESLEY, Craig. *Winterkill.* 1984. Houghton Mifflin. 1st ed. dj. EX. K2. $35.00

LESLEY, Ted. *Ted Lesley's Working Performer's Marked Deck Manual.* 1987. London. Breese. 2nd ed. 42 p. SftCvr. NM. J3. $11.00

LESLIE, JAMESON, & MURRAY. *Discovery & Adventure in Polar Seas & Regions...* 1831. NY. 16mo. 373 p. G. A6. $60.00

LESLIE, Jean. *Darling Sin.* 1951. Crime Club. 1st ed. dj. VG. P1. $10.00

LESLIE, Jean. *Intimate Journal of Warren Winslow.* 1952. Crime Club. 1st ed. sgn. dj. VG. P1. $30.00

LESLIE, R. *Bears & I.* 1968. NY. 1st ed. 224 p. dj. VG. B3. $20.00

LESLIE, Serge. *7 Leagues of a Dancer.* 1958. London. Beaumont. 1st ed. presentation. 234 p. dj. VG. H3. $50.00

LESSAC, Frane. *Caribbean Canvas.* 1989. Lippincott. 1st ed. dj. EX. B13. $50.00

LESSER, Milton. *Star Seekers.* 1953. Winston. 1st ed. dj. VG. R3. $35.00

LESSING, Doris. *African Stories.* 1965. Simon Schuster. 1st Am ed. dj. EX. C4. $30.00

LESSING, Doris. *Briefing for a Descent Into Hell.* 1971. Knopf. dj. EX. K2. $25.00

LESSING, Doris. *Diary of a Good Neighbor.* 1983. Knopf. UP. EX. K2. $200.00

LESSING, Doris. *Golden Notebook.* 1962. Simon Schuster. 1st Am ed. dj. VG. K2. $75.00

LESSING, Doris. *Good Terrorist.* 1985. NY. 1st ed. dj. M. $12.00

LESSING, Doris. *Marriages Between Zones 3, 4, & 5.* 1980. NY. 1st ed. dj. EX. $20.00

LESSING, Doris. *Prisons We Choose To Live Inside.* 1987. Cape. 1st UK ed. inscr/sgn. dj. EX. K2. $150.00

LESSING, Doris. *Prisons We Choose To Live Inside.* 1987. Harper Row. 1st Am ed. dj. EX. K2. $25.00

LESSING, Doris. *Sirian Experiments.* 1980. Knopf. UP of 1st Am ed. wrp. EX. C4. $25.00

LESSING, Doris. *Summer Before the Dark.* 1973. London. Cape. UP. scarce. B13. $175.00

LESSING, Doris. *5th Child.* 1988. NY. 1st ed. dj. M. $20.00

LESTER, A.J. *OH State Hist of Daughters of Am Revolution.* 1928. Dayton, OH. Ils. 640 p. VG. T5. $15.00

LESTER, C.E. *Life & Voyages of Am Vespucius.* 1853. New Haven. 431 p. G. $65.00

LESTER, Julius. *Revolutionary Notes.* 1970. Blk Cat. PB Orig. VG. B4. $4.00

LESTER, Julius. *To Be a Slave.* 1982. Dial. 1st ed. later print. inscr. dj. EX. K2. $35.00

LESTER & GAHR. *Who I Am.* 1974. Dial. 1st ed. inscr Lester. dj. EX. K2. $50.00

LEUCI, Bob. *Capt Butterfly.* 1989. New Am Lib. ARC. wrp. EX. F5. $17.00

LEVANT, Oscar. *Smattering of Ignorance.* 1940. Doubleday Doran. 1st ed. octavo. 267 p. dj. H3. $50.00

LEVANT, Oscar. *Unimportance of Being Oscar.* 1968. NY. 1st ed. sgn. dj. VG. B3. $25.00

LEVARIE, Norma. *Art & Hist of Books.* 1968. NY. 4to. dj. EX. $35.00

LEVEL, Maurice. *Those Who Return.* 1923. McBride. 1st ed. VG. P1. $20.00

LEVENE, Malcolm. *Carder's Paradise.* 1969. Walker. 1st ed. dj. EX. P1. $15.00

LEVENTHAL. *War.* c 1973. Chicago. 4to. 252 p. dj. EX. $14.00

LEVER, Derek. *Ken Brooke & Friends Vol 1.* 1986. Lancashire, Eng. 1st ed. 298 p. dj. NM. J3. $42.00

LEVERIDGE, Mark. *Mark Leveridge Lecture Experience.* 1990. Leveridge Magic Pub. 1st ed. 82 p. cbdg. M. J3. $25.00

LEVERTOV, Denise. *Candles in Babylon.* 1982. New Directions. long galleys. EX. B13. $85.00

LEVI, Peter. *Grave Witness.* nd. BOMC. dj. VG. P1. $5.00

LEVI, Peter. *Grave Witness.* 1985. St Martin. 1st ed. dj. EX. P1. $12.50

LEVI, Peter. *Light Garden of the Angel King. Journeys in Afghanistan.* 1972. London. Collins. Ils Chatwin. 1st ed. dj. EX. K2. $375.00

LEVI, W.M. *Pigeon.* 1963. Sumter. inscr. 4to. A4. $65.00

LEVI-STRAUSS, C. *World on the Wane.* 1906. Citerion Books. 1st Am ed. 404 p. F2. $25.00

LEVICK, S.J. *Life of Samuel J Levick.* 1896. Phil. WH Pile's Sons. 8vo. 423 p. VG. V1. $10.50

LEVIN, Bob. *Best Ride to NY.* 1978. NY. 1st ed. dj. M. $12.00

LEVIN, Harry. *Power of Blackness: Hawthorne, Poe, Melville.* 1958. Knopf. 1st ed. dj. EX. C4. $25.00

LEVIN, Harry. *Toward Stendhal: An Essay.* 1945. np. Pharos No 3. wrp. EX. C4. $25.00

LEVIN, Ira. *Rosemary's Baby.* 1967. Book Club. 245 p. dj. EX. B10. $3.50

LEVIN, Ira. *Rosemary's Baby.* 1967. Random House. 1st ed. dj. EX. C4. $40.00

LEVIN, Ira. *Stepford Wives.* 1972. Random House. UP. 1st ed. wrp. EX. F5. $50.00

LEVIN, Ira. *Stepford Wives.* 1972. Random House. 1st ed. dj. EX. $15.00

LEVIN, Ira. *Stepford Wives.* 1972. Random House. 1st ed. dj. xl. P1. $5.00

LEVINE, David. *Pens & Needles.* 1969. Gambit. Ltd ed. 1/300. sgn Levine/Updike. dj. EX. K2. $250.00

LEVINE, David. *Pens & Needles.* 1969. Gambit. 1st Trade ed. dj. EX. K2. $60.00

LEVINE, J.E. *Bridge Too Far: Notes From a Film Maker.* 1977. NY. 1st ed. inscr. dj. M. $18.00

LEVINE, P. *5 Detroits.* 1970. Unicorn. 1/1000. EX. B4. $8.00

LEVINREW, Will. *For Sale: Murder.* 1932. Mystery League. 1st ed. VG. P1. $20.00

LEVINTON, Sonia. *Sound To Remember.* 1979. NY. Ils 1st ed. dj. M. $12.00

LEVY, Ed. *Richard Himber: Man & His Magic.* 1980. Magico Magazine. 1st ed. 128 p. NM. J3. $25.00

LEVY, H. *Chinese Footbinding: Hist of a Curious Erotic Custom.* 1966. NY. 1st ed. dj. EX. $20.00

LEVY, Julien. *Surrealism.* 1936. Blk Sun. presentation. dj. VG. H3. $600.00

LEWELLEN, T.C. *Billikin Courier.* 1968. Random House. 2nd ed. dj. EX. P1. $7.50

LEWIN, M.Z. *Missing Woman.* 1981. Knopf. 2nd ed. dj. EX. P1. $10.00

LEWIN, M.Z. *Outside In.* 1980. Knopf. 1st ed. dj. EX. P1. $15.00

LEWIN, W.H. *Up Stream.* nd. London. Authors Club. private print. 1/100. VG. B10. $12.00

LEWIS, A. *Lament for the Molly Maguires.* 1964. NY. 1st ed. dj. VG. B3. $17.50

LEWIS, C.D. *Gate & Other Poems.* 1962. London. 1st ed. dj. EX. $15.00

LEWIS, C.D. *Requiem for the Living.* 1964. NY. 1st ed. dj. EX. $15.00

LEWIS, C.S. *Beyond Personality.* 1945. Macmillan. 1st ed. dj. EX. B13. $50.00

LEWIS, C.S. *Eng Literature in the 16th Century.* 1954. NY. Oxford. 1st Am ed. dj. EX. C4. $45.00

LEWIS, C.S. *Experiment in Criticism.* 1961. Cambridge. 1st ed. dj. EX. $16.00

LEWIS, C.S. *Letters to Children.* 1985. London. 1st ed. dj. EX. $35.00

LEWIS, C.S. *Narrative Poems.* 1972. 1st Am ed. dj. EX. scarce. C1. $14.50

LEWIS, C.S. *Perelandra.* 1905. Avon. wrp. EX. R3. $35.00

LEWIS, C.S. *Perelandra.* 1944. NY. 1st ed. dj. VG. scarce. C1. $34.50

LEWIS, C.S. *Screwtape Letters.* 1945. Reginald Saunders. 1st Canadian ed. VG. P1. $17.50

LEWIS, C.S. *Weight of Glory.* 1949. NY. 1st Am ed. dj. VG. B3. $30.00

LEWIS, Cecil. *Farewell to Wings.* 1964. London. 1st ed. 84 p. VG. T5. $12.50

LEWIS, Charles. *Cain Factor.* 1975. Harwood Smart. 1st ed. dj. EX. P1. $12.50

LEWIS, E.C. *Choice of Miracles.* 1980. Magical Pub. 1st ed. sgn. 213 p. dj. NM. J3. $30.00

LEWIS, E.C. *Further Studies in Mystery.* 1944. London. Davenport. Studies Series. 43 p. SftCvr. EX. J3. $4.00

LEWIS, E.C. *Modus Operandi.* 1944. London. Davenport. 2 vols. SftCvr. EX. J3. $12.00

LEWIS, E.W. *Motor Memories.* 1947. Detroit. Ils 1st ed. dj. VG. T5. $25.00

LEWIS, Enoch. *Dissertation on Oaths.* 1838. Uriah Hunt. 16mo. 100 p. xl. fair. V1. $16.00

LEWIS, F.C. *Scenery of the River Dart.* 1821. London. 1st ed. 36 clr aquatint pls. slipcase. EX. H3. $2500.00

LEWIS, F.J. *Climax.* 1946. Books Inc. 3rd/Photoplay ed. dj. VG. P1. $10.00

LEWIS, Franklin. *Cleveland Indians.* 1949. NY. sgn. 276 p. G. T5. $15.00

LEWIS, G.G. *Practical Book of Oriental Rugs.* 1920. Phil. 5th ed. 8vo. TEG. EX. $45.00

LEWIS, G.K. *Elizabeth Fry.* 1912. London. Headley. 12mo. 176 p. G. V1. $12.00

LEWIS, J. *20th-Century Book: Its Ils & Design.* c 1967. Studio Vista. Ils. dj. EX. $45.00

LEWIS, Jerry. *Jerry Lewis in Person.* 1982. Atheneum. 1st ed. sgn. 310 p. dj. EX. H3. $35.00

LEWIS, Lloyd. *Capt Sam Grant.* 1950. Little Brn. 1st ed. 512 p. G. S1. $15.00

LEWIS, Lloyd. *Sherman: Fighting Prophet.* 1932. Harcourt Brace. 690 p. G. S1. $22.50

LEWIS, Lynn. *Art at Auction. Year at Sotheby Park-Bernet 1977-1978.* 1978. NY. 1st ed. dj. M. $25.00

LEWIS, M.G. *Monk.* c 1900. London. 1/300. 2 vols. VG. R3. $150.00

LEWIS, Oscar. *Pedro Martinez.* 1964. Random House. 1st ed. 507 p. dj. F2. $10.00

LEWIS, Oscar. *Town That Died Laughing.* 1955. Boston. 1st ed. presentation. dj. VG. B3. $22.50

LEWIS, R.H. *Antiquarian Books.* 1978. NY. 1st ed. dj. M. $18.00

LEWIS, Roy. *Error of Judgment.* 1971. Collins Crime Club. 1st ed. dj. EX. P1. $30.00

LEWIS, Sinclair. *Ann Vickers.* 1933. Doubleday. 1st ed. 1/2350. wht dj. slipcase. EX. B13. $200.00

LEWIS, Sinclair. *Arrowsmith.* 1925. Harcourt Brace. Lg Paper ed. 1/500. sgn. boxed. H3. $450.00

LEWIS, Sinclair. *Babbitt.* 1922. np. AP. bl/wht dj. EX. B2. $90.00

LEWIS, Sinclair. *Babbitt.* 1922. Toronto. 1st Canadian ed. 2nd state. dj. EX. B2. $50.00

LEWIS, Sinclair. *Cass Timberlane.* 1945. NY. 1st ed. dj. EX. $45.00

LEWIS, Sinclair. *Elmer Gantry.* 1927. Harcourt Brace. sgn. G. H3. $250.00

LEWIS, Sinclair. *Kingsblood Royal.* 1947. Random House. Ltd ed. 1/1050. sgn. slipcase. EX. H3. $200.00

LEWIS, Sinclair. *Prodigal Parents.* 1939. Mercury Book. EX. B4. $20.00

LEWIS, Sinclair. *Yale Verse 1898-1908.* 1909. New Haven. gilt bl bdg. EX. B2. $175.00

LEWIS, Sinclair. *4 Days on the Webutuck River by CW Benton. Intro by S Lewis.* 1925. Troutbeck Pr. 1/200. EX. B2. $175.00

LEWIS, Trevor. *Children's Magic.* nd. Gwynedd, Wales. Lewis. 22 p. SftCvr. NM. J3. $3.00

LEWIS, Wyndham. *Apes of God.* 1930. London. Arthur Pr. Ltd ed. 1/750. sgn. VG. H3. $150.00

LEWIS, Wyndham. *Enemy.* 1929. London. Arthur Pr. orig wrp. EX. H3. $100.00

LEWIS, Wyndham. *Letters of Wyndham Lewis.* 1963. New Directions. 1st ed. dj. EX. H3. $40.00

LEWIS, Wyndham. *Red Priest.* 1956. Methuen. 1st ed. 298 p. dj. EX. R4. $85.00

LEWIS & CLARK. *Hist of Expedition...Sources of MO...* 1814. Phil. 1st ed. 2 vols. octavo. contemporary sheep. H3. $6000.00

LEWIS & HURWITZ. *Magic for Non-Magicians.* 1975. Los Angeles. Tarcher. 154 p. sgn. dj. NM. J3. $12.00

LEWIS & PARGELLIS. *Granger Country: A Pictorial Social Hist of Burlington RR.* 1949. Boston. Ils Russell Lee. 4to. dj. EX. $30.00

LEWISOHN, Richard. *Mystery Man of Europe: Sir Basil Zaharoff.* 1929. London. 1st ed. VG. $15.00

LEY, Willy. *Willy Ley's Exotic Zoology.* 1959. Viking. 1st ed. dj. RS. EX. P1. $30.00

LHEVINNE, Isadore. *Enchanted Jungle.* 1933. Literary Guild. 1st ed. 310 p. F2. $15.00

LICHTEN. *Decorative Arts of Victoria's Era.* 1950. Scribner. Ils. 274 p. A5. $25.00

LICHTENBERG, Jacqueline. *Mahogany Trinrose.* 1981. Doubleday. 1st ed. dj. EX. P1. $20.00

LIDDELL, C.H.; see Kuttner, Henry.

LIDDY, G.G. *Will.* 1980. NY. 1st ed. dj. M. $15.00

LIEBERMAN, Herbert. *City of the Dead.* 1976. Simon Schuster. 1st ed. dj. EX. P1. $16.00

LIEBLING, A.J. *Chicago: The 2nd City.* 1952. Knopf. 1st ed. dj. EX. H3. $30.00

LIEBLING, A.J. *Honest Rainmaker.* 1953. NY. 1st ed. dj. VG. B3. $40.00

LIEBLING, A.J. *Normandy Revisited.* 1958. NY. 1st ed. dj. VG. B3. $20.00

LIEURE, J. *Gravure Dans le Livre et l'Ornement.* 1927. Paris. Ils. 4to. TEG. EX. $200.00

LIFE. *Great Dinners From Life.* 1969. NY. 1st ed. 239 p. dj. VG. B3. $27.50

LIFSHIN, Lyn. *Old House Poems.* 1975. Capra. Chapbook Series. 1/100. sgn. EX. K2. $20.00

LIGHTFOOT, R.B. *Sikorsky Helicopters: Singular Success.* nd. (1957) Shatford, CT. Ils. wrp. G. T5. $27.50

LIGHTNER, A.M. *Day of the Drones.* 1969. Norton. 1st ed. dj. EX. F5. $18.50

LIGHTNER, A.M. *Space Olympics.* 1967. Norton. 1st ed. decor brd. VG. P1. $15.00

LILJENCRANZ, Oftilie. *Ward of King Canute: Romance of the Danish Conquest.* 1903. Boston. 1st ed. VG. C1. $5.00

LILLY, J. *Mind of the Dolphin.* 1967. NY. 1st ed. sgn. dj. VG. B3. $30.00

LILLY, Lambert. *Early Hist S States.* 1842. Boston. 16mo. VG. G1. $22.00

LILLY LIBRARY. *Bernardo Mendel Collection.* 1964. Bloomington, IN. 4to. wrp. F2. $15.00

LIMBACH, Russell. *Am Trees.* 1942. NY. 4to. 15 clr pls. dj. VG. $20.00

LIMNELIUS, George. *Medbury Ft Murder.* 1939. Crime Club. 1st ed. VG. P1. $15.00

LINARES DE SAPIR, Olga. *Cultural Chronology of the Gulf of Chiriqui, Panama.* 1968. Smithsonian. 4to. F2. $25.00

LINCOLN, Abraham. *Complete Works.* 1920s. Lincoln Memorial U. New Enlarged ed. 12 vols. H3. $200.00

LINCOLN, Abraham. *Writings.* 1905. Putnam. Collector Federal ed. 1/1000. 8 vols. H3. $2750.00

LINCOLN, J.C. *Cape Cod Ballads & Other Verse.* 1902. Brandt. inscr. H3. $200.00

LINCOLN, Joseph. *Thankfuls' Inheritance.* 1915. AL Burt. 382 p. VG. B10. $3.50

LINCOLN, W.B. *In War's Dark Shadow.* 1983. Dial Book Club. tall 8vo. 557 p. dj. EX. B10. $7.00

LINCOLN & LINCOLN. *Ownley Inn.* 1939. Grosset. VG. B10. $3.75

LINCOLN ELECTRIC CO. *Lessons in Arc Welding.* 1943. OH. 2nd ed. 176 p. VG. B10. $3.50

LINDBERGH, A.M. *Bring Me A Unicorn.* 1972. Harcourt. 2nd ed. 258 p. dj. EX. B10. $4.00

LINDBERGH, A.M. *Gift From the Sea.* Pantheon. 20th Anniversary ed. 142 p. dj. NM. B10. $4.25

LINDBERGH, C.A. *Spirit of St Louis.* 1952. NY. 1st/A ed. dj. VG. B3. $25.00

LINDBERGH, C.A. *Spirit of St Louis.* 1952. NY. 1st ed. inscr/sgn. dj. VG. H3. $1000.00

LINDBERGH, C.A. *We.* 1927. NY. 1st ed. dj. EX. B3. $40.00

LINDBERGH, C.A. *We.* 1927. NY. 7th imp. VG. $13.00

LINDBERGH, C.A. *We.* 1927. Putnam. not 1st ed. 318 p. G. B10. $4.00

LINDLEY, Charles. *Lord Halifax's Ghost Book.* 1944. Didier. dj. EX. R3. $12.50

LINDLEY, H. *Capt Cushing in the War of 1812.* 1944. Columbus. 1st ed. EX. $30.00

LINDLEY, Harlow. *Hist of Ordinance of 1787 & Old NW Territory.* 1937. Marietta. Ils. 95 p. wrp. VG. T5. $12.50

LINDLEY, R.A. *Account of Ruth Anna Lindley.* 1893. Friends Bookstore. 16mo. 35 p. SftCvr. EX. V1. $8.00

LINDLEY & WIDNEY. *CA of the S.* 1888. NY. 1st ed. VG. $50.00

LINDOP, A.E. *Singer Not the Song.* 1953. London. 1st ed. dj. EX. $15.00

LINDSAY, C.F. *India: Past & Present.* 1903. Phil. 1st ed. 2 vols. djs. VG. T1. $55.00

LINDSAY, Forbes. *Panama & the Canal Today.* 1912. Boston. Page. Revised ed. 474 p. gilt bdg. F2. $15.00

LINDSAY, M. *New Eng Gun: 1st 200 Years.* 1975. New Haven. 1st ed. dj. VG. B3. $60.00

LINDSAY, Vachel. *Every Soul Is a Circus.* 1929. Macmillan. sgn. dj. H3. $100.00

LINDSAY, Vachel. *Golden Book of Springfield.* 1920. Macmillan. sgn. dj. H3. $100.00

LINDSAY, Vachel. *Golden Whales of CA & Other Rhymes in the Am Language.* 1920. Macmillan. sgn. sm octavo. G. H3. $50.00

LINDSAY, Vachel. *Litany of WA St.* 1929. Macmillan. 1st print. dj. EX. $40.00

LINDSEY, D.L. *In the Lake of the Moon.* 1988. Atheneum. 1st ed. dj. VG. P1. $17.95

LINDSEY, D.L. *Spiral.* 1986. Atheneum. 1st ed. dj. EX. B13. $35.00

LINDSEY, T.J. *OH at Shiloh.* 1903. Cincinnati. Ils. fld maps. 226 p. T5. $55.00

LINDSTRAND, Doug. *AK Sketchbook.* 1982. 5th ed. folio. dj. EX. C1. $24.50

LINDSTRAND & LINDSTRAND. *AK Sketchbook 2.* 1984. 1st ed. sgn. stiff wrp. VG. C1. $19.50

LINGLEY, C.R. *Since the Civil War.* 1921. Century. 635 p. VG. S1. $7.00

LININGTON, Elizabeth. *Consequence of Crime.* nd. Book Club. dj. VG. P1. $5.00

LININGTON, Elizabeth. *Date With Death.* nd. Book Club. dj. VG. P1. $5.00

LININGTON, Elizabeth. *Felony Report.* nd. Book Club. dj. VG. P1. $5.00

LININGTON, Elizabeth. *Policeman's Lot.* nd. Book Club. dj. VG. P1. $5.00

LININGTON, Elizabeth. *Proud Man.* 1955. Viking. 1st ed. dj. VG. P1. $30.00

LININGTON, Elizabeth. *Skeletons in the Closet.* nd. Book Club. dj. VG. P1. $5.00

LININGTON, Elizabeth. *Strange Felony.* nd. Book Club. dj. VG. P1. $5.00

LININGTON, Elizabeth. *Strange Felony.* 1987. Doubleday. 1st Lg Print ed. dj. VG. P1. $16.95

LINKLATER, Eric. *Wind on the Moon.* 1944. Macmillan. Canadian ed. VG. P1. $15.00

LINKS & COLEMAN. *Medical Support of Army Air Forces in WWII.* 1955. WA. Ils. 1027 p. G. T5. $18.50

LINSENMAIER, Walter. *Insects of the World.* nd. (1972) McGraw. 1st Am ed? 392 p. dj. VG. B10. $8.50

LIPMAN, Jean. *Am Folk Art in Wood, Metal, & Stone.* nd. (1948) Pantheon. Ils. 4to. VG. B10. $35.00

LIPPINCOTT, David. *Voice of Armageddon.* 1974. Putnam. 1st ed. dj. VG. P1. $12.50

LIPPINCOTT, J.W. *Red Roan Pony.* 1951. NY. Ils CW Anderson. dj. VG. B3. $27.50

LIPPINCOTT, Mary. *Life & Letters...* 1893. William Pile's Sons. 8vo. 284 p. VG. V1. $12.00

LIPSEY, J.J. *Life of JJ Hagerman, Builder of CO Midland Railway.* 1968. Golden Bell Pr. Ils. 282 p. dj. A5. $40.00

LIPTON, Lawrence. *Holy Barbarians.* 1959. Messner. HrdCvr ed. dj. EX. B4. $12.00

LIPTON, Lawrence. *Holy Barbarians.* 1959. Messner. Review PB ed. wrp. dj. G. B4. $30.00

LISI, Albert. *Machaquila.* 1968. Hasting House. 1st ed. dj. xl. F2. $12.50

LISSNER, Ivar. *Living Past.* 1957. Putnam. 1st ed. 444 p. dj. F2. $10.00

LISTON, Robert. *Pros.* nd. Platt. 275 p. dj. VG. B10. $4.50

LITCHFIELD, Mary. *Spenser's Britomart.* 1896. Boston. 1st ed. VG. C1. $6.50

LITCHFIELD, P.W. *Autumn Leaves: Reflections of an Industrial Lieutenant.* 1945. Ils Kent. 1st ed. 2nd print. 8vo. 125 p. dj. $12.50

LITCHFIELD, P.W. *Some Wingfoot Clan Editorials.* c 1920. Akron. 123 p. stiff wrp. VG. T5. $9.50

LITSEY, E.C. *Beast.* 1959. Mystery House. dj. xl. P1. $5.00

LITT & STAMBAUGH. *Classic Clowning.* nd. Litt/Stambaugh. 1st ed. SftCvr. M. J3. $2.00

LITTAUER, V.S. *Be a Better Horseman.* 1941. Derrydale. 1/1500. 251 p. T5. $35.00

LITTLE & LITTLE. *Blk Shrouds.* 1942. Triangle. dj. VG. P1. $20.00

LITTLE GOLDEN BOOK. *Prayers for Children.* 1942. Simon Schuster. Ils Dixon. 39 p. B10. $5.00

LITTLEHALES, Lillian. *Pablo Casals.* 1929. Norton. 1st ed. 1/150. sgn Casals. scarce. H3. $225.00

LITVINOV, Ivy. *His Master's Voice.* 1973. Gollancz. dj. xl. P1. $5.00

LIVELY, Penelope. *Stitch in Time.* 1976. London. 1st ed. sgn. dj. EX. $55.00

LIVERANI, Giuseppe. *5 Centuries of Italian Majolica.* 1960. NY. 1st Am ed. inscr. VG. G1. $50.00

LIVINGSTON, Armstrong. *Murder Is Easy!* 1936. Robert Speller. 1st ed. VG. P1. $20.00

LIVINGSTON, Jack. *Die Again, MacReady.* nd. Book Club. dj. VG. P1. $4.50

LIVINGSTON, Nancy. *Incidents at Parga.* 1987. St Martin. 1st ed. dj. EX. F5. $12.00

LIVINGSTON, William. *Livingstone's Hist of Republican Party.* 1900. Detroit. 1st ed. 2 vols. VG. B3. $95.00

LIVSEY, C. *Manson Women.* 1980. NY. 1st ed. dj. VG. B3. $22.50

LLEWELLYN, Richard. *Hill of Many Dreams.* 1974. Doubleday. 1st ed. 262 p. xl. B10. $4.00

LLEWELLYN, Richard. *None But the Lonely Heart.* 1943. NY. 1st ed. dj. EX. $28.00

LLOYD, Anne. *Sight & Sound: Book of Poems.* nd. Fine Ed. apparent 1st ed. 56 p. dj. VG. B10. $6.25

LLOYD, Henry. *Cry of Oppression & Cruelty Inflicted Upon...Quakers.* 1677. np. 12mo. 8 p. wrp. V1. $50.00

LLOYD, N. *Hist of Eng House From Primitive Times to Victorian Period.* 1975. London/NY. 1st Am ed. VG. G1. $35.00

LOBAUGH, E.K. *Shadows in Succession.* 1946. Crime Club. 1st ed. dj. VG. P1. $17.50

LOCH, E.E. *Fever, Famine, & Gold.* 1938. Putnam. 1st ed. 257 p. dj. F2. $20.00

LOCHER, A. *With Sword & Crescent.* 1889. Phil. Ils. EX. $50.00

LOCHRIDGE, Richard. *Dead Run.* nd. Book Club. dj. VG. P1. $6.00

LOCHRIDGE, Richard. *Death on the Hour.* nd. Book Club. dj. VG. P1. $6.00

LOCHRIDGE, Richard. *Death on the Hour.* 1974. Lippincott. 1st ed. dj. VG. P1. $7.50

LOCHRIDGE, Richard. *Murder Roundabout.* 1966. Lippincott. 1st ed. dj. xl. P1. $7.50

LOCHRIDGE, Richard. *Not I, Said the Sparrow.* nd. Lippincott. 2nd ed. dj. xl. P1. $5.00

LOCHRIDGE, Richard. *Or Was He Pushed?* nd. Book Club. dj. VG. P1. $6.00

LOCHRIDGE, Richard. *Preach No More.* nd. Book Club. dj. VG. P1. $6.00

LOCHRIDGE, Richard. *Something Up a Sleeve.* nd. Book Club. dj. VG. P1. $6.00

LOCHRIDGE, Richard. *Something Up a Sleeve.* 1972. Lippincott. 1st ed. dj. EX. P1. $15.00

LOCHRIDGE, Richard. *Something Up a Sleeve.* 1972. Lippincott. 2nd ed. dj. VG. P1. $7.50

LOCHRIDGE, Richard. *Squire of Death.* nd. Book Club. dj. VG. P1. $6.00

LOCHRIDGE, Richard. *Streak of Light.* nd. Book Club. dj. VG. P1. $6.00

LOCHRIDGE, Richard. *Twice Retired.* nd. Book Club. dj. xl. P1. $4.00

LOCHRIDGE, Richard. *Write Murder Down.* nd. Book Club. dj. VG. P1. $6.00

LOCHRIDGE, Richard. *10th Life.* 1977. Doubleday Book Club. VG. P1. $7.50

LOCHRIDGE & LOCHRIDGE. *And Left for Dead.* nd. Book Club. dj. VG. P1. $6.00

LOCHRIDGE & LOCHRIDGE. *Catch As Catch Can.* nd. Book Club. dj. VG. P1. $6.00

LOCHRIDGE & LOCHRIDGE. *Curtain for a Jester.* nd. Book Club. VG. P1. $4.00

LOCHRIDGE & LOCHRIDGE. *Dead As a Dinosaur.* nd. Book Club. dj. VG. P1. $6.00

LOCHRIDGE & LOCHRIDGE. *Death of an Angel.* nd. Book Club. dj. VG. P1. $6.00

LOCHRIDGE & LOCHRIDGE. *Death on the Aisle.* 1942. Lippincott. 1st ed. VG. P1. $20.00

LOCHRIDGE & LOCHRIDGE. *Death Takes a Bow.* 1943. Doubleday Book Club. VG. P1. $7.50

LOCHRIDGE & LOCHRIDGE. *Devious 1.* nd. Book Club. dj. VG. P1. $6.00

LOCHRIDGE & LOCHRIDGE. *Distant Clue.* nd. Book Club. dj. VG. P1. $6.00

LOCHRIDGE & LOCHRIDGE. *Drill Is Death.* nd. Book Club. dj. VG. P1. $6.00

LOCHRIDGE & LOCHRIDGE. *Judge Is Reversed.* nd. Book Club. dj. VG. P1. $6.00

LOCHRIDGE & LOCHRIDGE. *Judge Is Reversed.* 1960. Lippincott. 1st ed. dj. xl. P1. $7.50

LOCHRIDGE & LOCHRIDGE. *Key to Death.* nd. Book Club. dj. VG. P1. $6.00

LOCHRIDGE & LOCHRIDGE. *Murder by the Book.* nd. Book Club. dj. VG. P1. $6.00

LOCHRIDGE & LOCHRIDGE. *Murder Has Its Points.* nd. Book Club. dj. VG. P1. $6.00

LOCHRIDGE & LOCHRIDGE. *Murder in a Hurry.* nd. Book Club. dj. VG. P1. $6.00

LOCHRIDGE & LOCHRIDGE. *Murder Is Suggested.* nd. Book Club. dj. VG. P1. $6.00

LOCHRIDGE & LOCHRIDGE. *Murder Within Murder.* nd. Collier. VG. P1. $10.00

LOCHRIDGE & LOCHRIDGE. *Nameless Cat.* 1954. Lippincott. Ils Bacon. sm 8vo. 78 p. VG. $12.00

LOCHRIDGE & LOCHRIDGE. *Night of Shadows.* nd. Book Club. dj. VG. P1. $5.00

LOCHRIDGE & LOCHRIDGE. *Tangled Cord.* nd. Book Club. dj. VG. P1. $6.00

LOCHRIDGE & LOCHRIDGE. *Voyage Into Violence.* nd. Book Club. dj. VG. P1. $5.00

LOCHRIDGE & LOCHRIDGE. *1st Come, 1st Kill.* nd. Book Club. dj. VG. P1. $6.00

LOCHTE, Dick. *Laughing Dog.* nd. Book Club. dj. EX. P1. $4.50

LOCKE, D.R. *Nashby in Exile; or, 6 Months of Travel.* 1882. Toledo/Boston. Locke. 8vo. R4. $85.00

LOCKE, John. *Some Thoughts Concerning Education.* 1738. London. 16mo. 331 p. G4. $27.00

LOCKE, John. *Works.* 1801. London. Johnson Robinson. 10th ed. 10 vols. octavo. H3. $750.00

LOCKE, William. *Lengthening Shadow.* 1923. Dodd. apparent 1st ed. 372 p. VG. B10. $10.00

LOCKHART, J.G. *Life of Sir Walter Scott.* nd. (1903) London/Boston. Ltd ed. 10 vols. TEG. EX. T1. $120.00

LOCKHART, J.G. *Memoirs of Sir Walter Scott.* 1914. London. Macmillan. Lib of Eng Classics. 5 vols. octavo. H3. $125.00

LOCKLEY, R.M. *Islands Round Britain.* 1945. London. 1st ed. dj. VG. C1. $8.00

LOCKWOOD, Mary. *Historic Homes in WA.* 1889. NY. 1st ed. VG. T1. $30.00

LOCKWOOD, S.M. *Antiques.* 1928. Doubleday Doran. Ils Ernest Stock. VG. C1. $24.50

LOCKWOOD, S.M. *NY: Not So Little & Not So Old.* 1926. Doubleday. 197 p. VG. $20.00

LOCKWOOD & ADAMSON. *Hellcats of the Sea.* 1955. NY. 1st ed. dj. VG. B3. $20.00

LOCKWOOD. *Practical Information for Telephonists.* 1893. NY. 16mo. 192 p. G4. $28.00

LODER, Vernon. *Vasy Mystery.* nd. Detective Club. dj. VG. P1. $20.00

LODGE, Edmund. *Portraits of Illustrious Personages of Great Britain.* 1902. Boston. Estes. Ed Magnifique. 1/26. 12 vols. lg octavo. H3. $500.00

LODWICK, John. *1st Steps Inside the Zoo.* 1950. Heinemann. 1st ed. dj. VG. P1. $25.00

LOEB, Edwin. *Sumatra: Its Hist & People...Art & Archaeology.* 1935. Vienna. 8vo. red wrp. VG. $55.00

LOEB, Harold. *Professors Like Vodka.* 1927. Boni Liveright. 1st ed. dj. VG. H3. $35.00

LOEHR, R.C. *MN Farmers' Diaries... 1939.* MN Hist Soc. fld map. 247 p. G. T5. $19.50

LOENING, Grover. *Our Wings Grow Faster.* 1935. NY. 1st ed. lg 8vo. A6. $30.00

LOESSER, A. *Men, Women, & Pianos.* 1954. NY. 1st ed. dj. VG. B3. $30.00

LOFTIE, W.J. *Hist of London.* 1883. London. 2 vols. VG. $75.00

LOFTING, Hugh. *Dr Dolittle's Caravan.* 1926. NY. 1st ed. dj. EX. P4. $60.00

LOFTING, Hugh. *Dr Dolittle's Garden.* nd. Lippincott. decor brd. VG. P1. $7.50

LOFTING, Hugh. *Dr Doolittle's Circus.* nd. Lippincott. decor brd. VG. P1. $7.50

LOFTING & LOFTING. *Dr Doolittle & the Secret Lake.* 1948. Lippincott. 1st ed. 8vo. 366 p. VG. $28.00

LOFTS, Norah. *Gad's Hall.* 1977. Doubleday. 1st ed. dj. EX. F5. $15.00

LOFTS, Norah. *Golden Fleece.* 1944. Knopf. 1st Am ed. 249 p. VG. B10. $4.00

LOFTS, Norah. *Haunting of Gad's Hall.* 1979. Doubleday. 1st ed. dj. EX. F5. $18.00

LOFTS, Norah. *Knights Acre.* c 1975. Book Club. dj. VG. C1. $5.00

LOGAN, H.C. *Cartridges Pictorial Digest of Sm Arms.* 1948. Huntington. 1st ed. dj. VG. B3. $50.00

LOGAN, H.C. *Pictorial Hist of Under-Hammer Gun.* 1960. NY. 4to. dj. EX. G1. $20.00

LOGAN, Olive. *Before the Footlights & Behind the Scenes.* 1870. Phil. Parmelee. 1st ed. octavo. VG. H3. $75.00

LOGAN & STORY. *Correspondence of James Logan & Thomas Story 1724-1741.* 1927. Phil. Friends Hist Assn. 8vo. 100 p. EX. V1. $18.00

LOGGINS, Vernon. *2 Romantics & Their Ideal Life.* 1946. Odyssey. 1st ed. dj. VG. B10. $5.00

LOGOZ, Michel. *Wine Label Design.* 1984. Rizzoli. 154 p. folio. dj. EX. $45.00

LOMAX, Alan. *Mr Jelly Roll.* 1950. Duell Sloan Pearce. 1st ed. octavo. 318 p. dj. EX. H3. $60.00

LOMAX, J.A. *Adventures of a Ballad Hunter.* 1947. Macmillan. 1st ed. octavo. 302 p. VG. H3. $50.00

LOMAX, Louis. *When the Word Is Given.* 1963. Cleveland. 1st ed. dj. VG. B3. $40.00

LOMBARD, N. *Grinning Pig.* 1943. Simon Schuster. 1st ed. rebound. xl. P1. $5.00

LOMBARDI, Mary. *Brazilian Serial Documents: Selective & Annotated Guide.* 1974. Bloomington, IN. 1st ed. 445 p. F2. $15.00

LONDON, Jack. *Abysmal Brute.* 1913. NY. 1st ed. orig bdg. dj. VG. H3. $1250.00

LONDON, Jack. *Acorn Planter.* 1915. Macmillan. 1st ed. wht dj. EX. rare. B13. $3850.00

LONDON, Jack. *Acorn Planter.* 1915. NY. 1st ed. orig cloth. VG. H3. $1250.00

LONDON, Jack. *Before Adam.* 1907. NY. Ils Bull. 1st ed. VG. B3. $60.00

LONDON, Jack. *Call of the Wild.* nd. Grosset Dunlap. dj. VG. P1. $10.00

LONDON, Jack. *Cruise of the Snark.* 1971. Seafarer Books. dj. EX. P1. $12.50

LONDON, Jack. *Iron Heel.* 1908. NY. 1st ed. pictorial bdg. VG. T1. $55.00

LONDON, Jack. *Iron Heel.* 1908. Wilshire Book Co. 354 p. T5. $95.00

LONDON, Jack. *Jack London's Stories for Boys.* 1936. Cupples. apparent 1st ed. 121 p. VG. B10. $4.50

LONDON, Jack. *John Barleycorn.* 1913. NY. Century. 1st ed. G. $25.00

LONDON, Jack. *Lost Face.* 1910. NY. 1st ed. 3rd print. pictorial bdg. VG. T1. $35.00

LONDON, Jack. *Martin Eden.* nd. Armed Services Ed. B4. $15.00

LONDON, Jack. *Martin Eden.* 1946. Penguin. 1st ed. B4. $4.00

LONDON, Jack. *On the Makaloa Mat.* 1920. Macmillan. Later ed. dj. EX. scarce. K2. $125.00

LONDON, Jack. *S Sea Tales.* 1961. Pyramid. 2nd print. EX. B4. $6.00

LONDON, Jack. *Sea Wolf.* 1904. Macmillan. 1st ed. VG. $80.00

LONDON, Jack. *Selected Works of Jack London.* 1964. Parents Inst. VG. P1. $10.00

LONDON, Jack. *Smoke Bellew.* 1912. NY. 1st ed. VG. B3. $65.00

LONDON, Jack. *Tales of Ships & Seas.* nd. Little Bl Book. B4. $10.00

LONDON, Jack. *Was Sie Nie Vergessen.* 1962. Fischer Bucherei. VG. B4. $6.00

LONDON, Jack. *Wht Fang.* 1906. NY. Ils Charles Bull. 1st pub ed. G. T1. $80.00

LONDON ROYAL ACADEMY. *Commemorative Catalog of Exhibition of Dutch Art.* 1929. Burlington House. TEG. D4. $155.00

LONDON YEARLY MEETING. *Collection of Epistles From 1675-1805.* 1806. Baltimore. Cole Hewes. 8vo. 412 p. leather. V1. $28.00

LONDON YEARLY MEETING. *Epistles From the Yearly Meeting...From 1675-1759 Inclusive.* 1760. London. Clark. 4to. 275 p. V1. $130.00

LONDON YEARLY MEETING. *Rules of Discipline With Advices.* 1834. London. Darton Harvey. 3rd ed. 355 p. VG. V1. $60.00

LONDON YEARLY MEETING. *Salutation in the Love of Christ.* 1857. London. Newman. 8vo. 15 p. wrp. VG. V1. $15.00

LONDON YEARLY MEETING. *Summary of Hist, Doctrines, & Discipline of Friends...* 1882. Phil. Friends Bookstore. reprint of 3rd ed. 16mo. 31 p. wrp. G. V1. $12.00

LONG, A.R. *Murder by Magic.* 1947. Phoenix Pr. 1st ed. dj. G. F5. $12.00

LONG, Charles. *Infinite Brain.* 1957. Avalon. 1st ed. dj. EX. R3. $12.50

LONG, Frank Belknap. *Autobiographical Memoir.* 1985. Necromonicon Pr. 1st ed. wrp. EX. F5. $12.00

LONG, Frank Belknap. *Hounds of Tindalos.* 1946. Arkham House. 1st ed. dj. EX. R3. $125.00

LONG, Frank Belknap. *Rehearsal Night.* 1981. private print. 1st ed. 1/250. sgn. wrp. EX. R3. $27.50

LONG, Frank Belknap. *Rim of the Unknown.* 1972. Arkham House. 1st ed. dj. EX. R3. $35.00

LONG, Frank Belknap. *Witch Tree.* 1971. Magnum. 1st ed. wrp. EX. F5. $11.00

LONG, Harold. *Make-Up for Magicians.* 1982. Devon, England. Supreme Magic. SftCvr. M. J3. $10.00

LONG, Huey. *Every Man a King.* 1933. New Orleans. 1st ed. VG. B3. $37.50

LONG, Huey. *My 1st Days in the Wht House.* 1935. Harrisburg. 1st ed. dj. VG. B3. $65.00

LONG, Lyda Belknap; see, Long, Frank Belknap.

LONG, T.A. *Rugged Breed.* 1965. NY. 1st ed. dj. VG. $15.00

LONG, W.J. *Fowls of the Air.* nd. (1901) Athenaeum. gilt gr bdg. VG. B10. $12.00

LONG, W.J. *Fowls of the Air.* nd. Atheneum. 1st ed? TEG. gilt gr bdg. B10. $8.00

LONG & HUGHES. *Atlas of Classical Geog.* 1856. Phil. tall 8vo. VG. $75.00

LONGFELLOW, H.W. *Aftermath.* 1873. Boston. 1st ed. EX. $35.00

LONGFELLOW, H.W. *Complete Writings.* 1904. Houghton Mifflin. Deluxe ed. 1/750. 11 vols. H3. $3000.00

LONGFELLOW, H.W. *Divine Comedy of Dante Alighieri.* nd. (1895) Houghton. 759 p. TEG. G. B10. $5.00

LONGFELLOW, H.W. *Divine Tragedy.* 1871. Boston. Lg Paper ed. EX. $32.00

LONGFELLOW, H.W. *Divine Tragedy.* 1871. Boston. 1st ed. EX. $40.00

LONGFELLOW, H.W. *Masque of Flora.* 1875. Boston. Osgood. 1st ed. dj. VG. B13. $85.00

LONGFELLOW, H.W. *New Eng Tragedies.* 1868. Boston. 1st ed. dj. VG. B13. $85.00

LONGFELLOW, H.W. *Tales of a Wayside Inn.* 1863. Boston. 1st ed. VG. B3. $70.00

LONGFELLOW, H.W. *Tales of a Wayside Inn.* 1864. Boston. 2nd print. EX. $38.00

LONGLEY, P.D. *Rebirth of Venkata Reddi.* 1946. Judson Pr. 2nd ed. P1. $8.00

LONGMATE, Norman. *Air Raid: Bombing of Coventry, 1940.* 1978. NY. 1st Am ed. 302 p. dj. T5. $9.50

LONGSHORE, T.E. *George Fox Interpreted: Religion, Revelations, Motives...* 1881. Phil. Longshore. 16mo. 289 p. G. V1. $16.00

LONGSTRETH, M.A. *Old Pupil.* 1886. Phil. Lippincott. 12mo. 224 p. V1. $12.50

LONGUS. *Daphnis & Chloe.* 1977. NY. Braziller. Trans George Moore. dj. EX. T5. $125.00

LONGWORTH, A.R. *Princess Alice.* 1975. Book Club. 338 p. dj. VG. B10. $3.50

LONGYEAR, B.B. *Circus World.* nd. Book Club. dj. VG. P1. $4.00

LONGYEAR, B.B. *City of Baraboo.* 1980. Berkley Putnam. 1st ed. dj. VG. P1. $15.00

LONGYEAR, B.B. *Sea of Glass.* 1987. St Martin. 1st ed. sgn. dj. EX. P1. $25.00

LONGYEAR, John. *Archaeological Investigations in El Salvador.* 1944. Peabody Mus. lg 4to. wrp. F2. $100.00

LONSDALE, Kathleen. *Peaceful Co-Existence; Christian Obligation.* 1955. London. sgn. 12mo. SftCvr. V1. $7.00

LOOMIS, Andrew. *Eye of the Painter.* 1961. NY. 1st ed. dj. VG. B3. $50.00

LOOMIS, Andrew. *Fun With a Pencil.* 1970. NY. dj. VG. B3. $27.50

LOOMIS, George. *Progressive Glee & Chorus Book.* nd. Ivison Blake. 1st ed. 255 p. G. B10. $6.50

LOOMIS, Noel. *Murder Goes to Pr.* 1937. Phoenix Pr. 1st ed. dj. G. F5. $10.00

LOOMIS, R.S. *Arthurian Literature in the Middle Ages: Collaborative Hist.* 1959. Oxford. 1st ed. dj. VG. C1. $95.00

LOOMIS & LOOMIS. *Medieval Romances.* 1957. Modern Lib. 1st ed. dj. VG. C1. $12.50

LOOS, Anita. *Girl Like I.* 1966. NY. dj. VG. $10.00

LOOS, Anita. *Kiss Hollywood Goodbye.* 1974. London. 1st ed. dj. EX. $18.00

LOOSBROCK & SKINNER. *Wild Bl: Story of Am Air Power.* 1961. NY. dj. VG. $20.00

LOPATE, Phillip. *In Coyoacan.* 1971. NY. Swollen Magpie Pr. 1st ed. 1/300. wrp. B13. $100.00

LOPEZ, Barry. *Arctic Dreams.* 1986. Scribner. 1st ed. dj. EX. B13. $45.00

LOPEZ, Barry. *Coyote Love.* 1989. Coyote Love Pr. Ils/sgn Gary Guch. 1/99. sgn. K2. $125.00

LOPEZ, Barry. *Crow & Weasel.* 1990. N Point Pr. 1st ed. quarto. dj. EX. B13. $50.00

LOPEZ, Barry. *Desert Notes: Reflections in the Eye of a Raven.* 1976. Sheed Andrews/McMeel. 1st ed. dj. EX. K2. $150.00

LOPEZ, Barry. *Giving Birth to Thunder, Sleeping With His Daughter.* 1977. Sheed Andrews/McMeel. ARC. dj. EX. w/promotional material. K2. $150.00

LOPEZ, Barry. *Of Wolves & Men.* 1978. Scribner. reprint. dj. EX. B13. $30.00

LOPEZ, Barry. *River Notes.* 1979. Sheed Andrews/McMeel. 1st ed. dj. EX. K2. $65.00

LOPEZ, Barry. *River Notes.* 1979. Sheed Andrews/McMeel. 1st ed. sgn. clipped dj. EX. B13. $75.00

LOPEZ, Barry. *Winter Count.* 1981. Scribner. UP. wrp. EX. K2. $100.00

LOPEZ, Barry. *Winter Count.* 1981. Scribner. 1st ed. clipped dj. EX. B13. $65.00

LORAC, E.C.R. *Last Escape.* nd. Book Club. dj. VG. P1. $5.00

LORAC, E.C.R. *Screen for Murder.* nd. Book Club. dj. VG. P1. $5.00

LORAC, E.C.R. *Shroud of Darkness.* nd. Book Club. dj. VG. P1. $5.00

LORAC, E.C.R. *Speak Justly of the Dead.* nd. Book Club. dj. VG. P1. $6.00

LORAINE, Philip. *Lions' Ransom.* 1980. Collins Crime Club. 1st ed. dj. xl. P1. $5.00

LORAINE, Philip. *WIL-1 to Curtis.* 1967. Random House. 1st ed. dj. EX. P1. $15.00

LORAINE, W. *Head Wind.* c 1940. NY. Ils. 390 p. dj. VG. B3. $25.00

LORANT, Stefan. *New World.* 1946. Duell Sloan. 1st ed. 292 p. F2. $30.00

LORAYNE, Harry. *Best of Friends.* 1982. NY. Lorayne. 1st ed. 559 p. dj. NM. J3. $37.00

LORAYNE, Harry. *Dingle's Deceptions With Cards & Coins.* nd. Haines House Cards. 1st ed. inscr. SftCvr. NM. J3. $7.50

LORAYNE, Harry. *Magic Book.* 1977. Putnam. 1st ed. 306 p. dj. NM. J3. $10.00

LORAYNE, Harry. *My Favorite Card Tricks.* 1965. Tannen. 1st ed. sgn. 68 p. EX. J3. $6.00

LORAYNE, Harry. *Quantum Leaps.* 1979. NY. Lorayne. 1st ed. 248 p. dj. EX. J3. $35.00

LORAYNE, Harry. *Reputation Makers.* 1971. NY. Lorayne. 1st ed. 287 p. NM. J3. $30.00

LORAYNE, Harry. *Star Quality: Magic of David Regal.* 1987. NY. Lorayne. 1st ed. 279 p. dj. NM. J3. $29.00

LORAYNE, Harry. *Teach-In Lecture.* 1979. NY. Lorayne. 1st ed. 41 p. NM. J3. $5.00

LORAYNE & LUCAS. *Memory Book.* 1974. Stein Day. Book Club ed. dj. EX. J3. $6.00

LORD, A.B. *Singer of Tales.* 1981. Harvard. 4th print. VG. P1. $7.50

LORD, F.A. *Uniforms of the Civil War.* 1970. NY. dj. EX. $20.00

LORD, J. *Frontier Dust.* 1926. Hartford. 1st ed. 1/1000. dj. VG. $30.00

LORD, Sheldon; see Block, Lawrence.

LORD, Walter. *Fremantle Diary.* 1954. Boston. 1st ed. dj. VG. B3. $22.50

LORD, Walter. *Lonely Vigil.* 1977. NY. 1st ed. dj. M. $12.00

LORD, Walter. *Time To Stand.* 1961. NY. 1st ed. sgn. dj. EX. B3. $22.50

LORD, Walter. *Titanic: Night To Remember.* 1976. NY. 1st Ils ed. dj. VG. B3. $35.00

LORENTO, Professor. *Amateur Amusements.* 1878. Hurst. 376 p. G. J3. $37.00

LORRAH, Jean. *Vulcan Academy Murders.* nd. Book Club. dj. VG. P1. $7.50

LORRAIN, Claude. *Selected Drawings.* nd. PA State U. folio. dj. EX. $65.00

LORRAINE, Sid. *Patter...* 1941. Colon, MI. Abbott. 2nd ed. 64 p. SftCvr. EX. J3. $5.00

LOTHROP, Samuel. *Inca Treasure As Depicted by Spanish Historians.* 1964. SW Mus. reprint of 1938 ed. wrp. F2. $15.00

LOTHROP, Samuel. *Polychrome Guanaco Cloaks of Patagonia.* 1929. Mus Am Indian. 1st ed. 30 p. wrp. F2. $15.00

LOTHROP, Samuel. *Treasures of Ancient Am: Arts of Pre-Columbian Civilization.* 1964. Skira. 1st ed. folio. 229 p. F2. $75.00

LOTI, Pierre. *Carmen Sylva.* 1912. NY. 1st ed. EX. $16.00

LOTI, Pierre. *Pecheur D'Islande.* 1893. Paris. Ed Grand Deluxe. 1/150. 4to. VG. T1. $125.00

LOTT, A.S. *Most Dangerous Sea.* 1959. Annapolis. Ils. 322 p. dj. T5. $15.00

LOTT, Bret. *Dream of Old Leaves.* 1989. Viking. 1st ed. dj. RS. M. $12.00

LOUNSBERRY, Lionel. *Quaker Spy: Tale of Revolutionary War.* 1889. Phil. McKay. 12mo. 238 p. G. V1. $8.50

LOUYS, Pierre. *Collected Tales.* 1930. Peacock Pr/Argus Books. 1/2000. 293 p. TEG. dj. slipcase. EX. T5. $125.00

LOUYS, Pierre. *Twilight of the Nymphs.* nd. (1928) London. Fortune Pr. Ils Beaton. Ltd ed. 8vo. dj. EX. R4. $75.00

LOUYS, Pierre. *Twilight of the Nymphs.* 1927. private print. Ils Clara Tice. 1/1250. A4. $50.00

LOVE, E.G. *Situation in Flushing.* 1965. Harper. 1st ed. dj. EX. $12.00

LOVE, R. *Rise & Fall of Jesse James.* 1929. NY. Ils. 446 p. VG. B3. $25.00

LOVE, R.H. *Theodore Earl Butler: Emergence From Monet's.* 1985. Haase Mumm. 1st Am ed. dj. D4. $50.00

LOVECRAFT, H.P. *Dark Brotherhood.* 1966. Arkham House. 1st ed. dj. EX. R3. $90.00

LOVECRAFT, H.P. *Dream Quest of Unknown Kadath.* 1955. Shroud Krueger. 1st ed. wrp/dj. EX. R3. $40.00

LOVECRAFT, H.P. *Dreams & Fancies.* 1962. Arkham House. 1st ed. dj. EX. R3. $125.00

LOVECRAFT, H.P. *Ec'H-Pi-El Speaks.* 1972. De La Ree. 1st ed. wrp. EX. R3. $50.00

LOVECRAFT, H.P. *Horror in the Mus.* 1970. Arkham House. 1st ed. dj. EX. R3. $50.00

LOVECRAFT, H.P. *Lurker at the Threshold.* 1945. Arkham House. 1st ed. dj. VG. B3. $55.00

LOVECRAFT, H.P. *Marginalia.* 1944. Arkham House. 1st ed. dj. EX. R3. $275.00

LOVECRAFT, H.P. *Shuttered Room.* 1959. Arkham House. 1st ed. dj. EX. R3. $90.00

LOVECRAFT, H.P. *Something About Cats.* 1949. Arkham House. 1st ed. dj. VG. R3. $125.00

LOVECRAFT, H.P. *Supernatural Horror in Literature.* 1945. Abramson. 1st ed. VG. R3. $30.00

LOVECRAFT, H.P. *Survivors & Others.* 1957. Arkham House. 1st ed. dj. EX. R3. $65.00

LOVECRAFT, H.P. *Watchers Out of Time.* 1974. Arkham House. 1st ed. dj. EX. R3. $35.00

LOVECRAFT, H.P. *Weird Shadow Over Insmouth.* 1945. Bart House. 1st ed. wrp. VG. R3. $37.50

LOVECRAFT & CONOVER. *Lovecraft at Last.* 1975. Carrolton Clark. 1st ed. 1/1000. dj. slipcase. VG. R3. $100.00

LOVECRAFT & RAVEN. *Occult Lovecraft.* 1975. Gerry De la Ree. 1st wrp. EX. R3. $25.00

LOVELL, C.G. *Golden Isles of GA.* 1939. Boston. Ils. 300 p. dj. VG. B3. $30.00

LOVELL, Marc. *Apple Spy in the Sky.* 1983. Crime Club. 1st ed. dj. VG. P1. $15.00

LOVELL, Marc. *Ethel & the Naked Spy.* 1989. Crime Club. 1st ed. dj. EX. F5. $13.00

LOVELL, Marc. *Imitation Thieves.* 1971. Crime Club. 1st ed. dj. VG. P1. $15.00

LOVELL, Marc. *Spy With His Head in the Clouds.* 1982. Doubleday. 1st ed. dj. xl. P1. $5.00

LOVESEY, Peter. *Bertie & the Tinman.* 1988. Mysterious Pr. 1st ed. dj. EX. F5. $14.00

LOVETT, Robert. *Hist of the Novel in Eng.* nd. (1932) Houghton. 495 p. G. B10. $4.50

LOVISI, Gary. *SF Detective Tales.* 1986. Gryphon. EX. P1. $7.95

LOW, A.M. *Adrift in the Stratosphere.* nd. Blackie. dj. VG. P1. $17.50

LOW, A.M. *What's the World Coming To?* 1950. Lippincott. 1st ed. dj. EX. R3. $35.00

LOWE, Alfred. *6 Cartoons by Alfred Lowe.* 1930. London. W&G Foyle Ltd. Intro O'Flaherty. Ltd ed. 1/750. EX. R4. $50.00

LOWE, Kenneth. *No Tears for Shirley Minton.* 1956. Doubleday Book Club. VG. P1. $7.50

LOWE, Samuel. *Boy Knight.* c 1922. Whitman. scarce juvenile. VG. C1. $8.50

LOWELL, Amy. *Can Grande's Castle.* 1918. NY. 1st ed. EX. $12.00

LOWELL, E.J. *Eve of the French Revolution.* nd. Houghton. 408 p. bl bdg. B10. $10.00

LOWELL, J.R. *Among My Books.* 1870. Boston. 1st ed. xl. EX. $15.00

LOWELL, J.R. *Among My Books. 2nd Series.* 1876. Boston. 1st ed. 1st state. 12mo. VG. T1. $40.00

LOWELL, J.R. *Function of the Poet & Other Essays.* 1920. Boston. 1/575. VG. $12.00

LOWELL, J.R. *Poetical Works.* 1877. Boston. Osgood. Household ed. VG. C1. $34.50

LOWELL, J.R. *Vision of Sir Launfal.* 1900. Ivy/Boston. 1st ed. red leather. VG. C1. $6.00

LOWELL, J.R. *Works.* 1892. Houghton Mifflin. Standard Lib ed. 11 vols. octavo. H3. $250.00

LOWELL, John. *Cradle of the Deep.* 1929. Simon Schuster. 1st ed. 261 p. VG. B10. $4.75

LOWELL, Robert. *Day by Day.* 1977. NY. 1st ed. dj. M. $15.00

LOWELL, Robert. *Dolphin.* 1973. NY. 1st ed. dj. M. $17.00

LOWELL, Robert. *Hist.* 1973. NY. 1st ed. dj. M. $15.00

LOWELL, Robert. *Old Glory.* 1965. NY. Ils 1st ed. 193 p. dj. VG. T5. $25.00

LOWELL, Robert. *Oresteia of Aeschylus.* 1978. NY. 1st ed. dj. M. $12.00

LOWELL, Robert. *Prometheus Bound.* 1969. Farrar Straus Giroux. 1st ed. sgn. dj. EX. K2. $175.00

LOWENSTEIN, Carole. *Festival of Jewish Cooking.* 1971. Herder. 8vo. 53 p. dj. VG. $15.00

LOWNDES, M.B. *And Call It Accident.* 1936. Longman Gr. 1st ed. xl. P1. $10.00

LOWNDES, R.A.W. *Believers' World.* 1961. Avalon. 1st ed. dj. VG. P1. $15.00

LOWRY, Malcolm. *Hear Us O Lord From Heaven Thy Dwelling Place.* 1961. Lippincott. 1st ed. 2nd print. dj. EX. H3. $125.00

LOWRY, Malcolm. *Under the Volcano.* 1965. Lippincott. reprint of 1947 ed. dj. EX. H3. $75.00

LOWRY, Robert. *Fine Me in Fire.* 1948. Doubleday. 1st ed. dj. VG. F5. $20.00

LUBRANT, Boleslaw. *Novel Magic.* 1946. Kanter's Magic Shop. 2nd ed. sgn. SftCvr. M. J3. $3.00

LUBRANT, Boleslaw. *15 Star-Card Effects.* 1956. Kanter's Magic Shop. 1st ed. SftCvr. M. J3. $3.00

LUCAS, Cary. *Unfinished Business.* 1947. Simon Schuster. 1st ed. VG. P1. $10.00

LUCAS, E.V. *Saunterer's Rewards.* 1933. Methuen. 8vo. 208 p. dj. EX. R4. $20.00

LUCAS, E.V. *Selected Essays.* 1954. London. 1st ed. dj. EX. $10.00

LUCAS, Jerry. *Championship Card Tricks.* 1973. Grosset Dunlap. 81 p. VG. J3. $7.50

LUCAS, Margaret. *Account of the Convincement & Call to the Ministry.* nd. Phil. Friends Bookstore. 3rd ed. 92 p. EX. V1. $10.00

LUCAS, Peter. *Prolegomena of Immanuel Kant.* nd. Manchester. 155 p. dj. EX. B10. $6.50

LUCAS, Sidney. *Quaker Story.* 1949. Harper. 12mo. 144 p. dj. VG. V1. $8.00

LUDLOW, F. *Hasheesh Eater.* 1857. NY. 1st ed. G. $150.00

LUDLOW & CLYDE. *Hist of Cleveland Presbyterianism...* 1896. Cleveland. 280 p. T5. $17.50

LUDLUM, Robert. *Chancellor Manuscript.* 1977. Dial. 4th print. dj. VG. P1. $12.50

LUDLUM, Robert. *Chancellor Manuscript.* 1977. NY. 1st ed. dj. VG. B3. $17.50

LUDLUM, Robert. *Gemini Contenders.* 1976. Dial. 1st ed. 402 p. dj. EX. B10. $7.00

LUDLUM, Robert. *Matlock Paper.* 1973. NY. 1st ed. dj. EX. B3. $47.50

LUDLUM, Robert. *Rhinemann Exchange.* 1974. Dial. 2nd ed. dj. VG. P1. $15.00

LUDLUM, Robert. *Road to Gadolfo.* 1975. Dial. 1st ed. dj. EX. P1. $45.00

LUDLUM, Robert. *Road to Gandolfo.* 1975. Dial. 1st ed. 3 variant djs. EX. scarce. B13. $125.00

LUDWIG, Coy. *Maxfield Parrish.* 1973. Watson Guptill. 1st ed. dj. EX. $45.00

LUFF, Joseph. *Autobiography of Elder Joseph Luff.* 1894. Lamoni. inscr Elder Luff. P4. $245.00

LUHR, William. *Raymond Chandler & Film.* 1982. NY. Ungar. 1st ed. dj. EX. T9. $20.00

LUKEMAN, Tim. *Koren.* 1981. Doubleday. 1st ed. dj. EX. F5. $14.00

LUKEMAN, Tim. *Rajan.* 1979. Doubleday. 1st ed. dj. EX. P1. $15.00

LUKEMAN, Tim. *Witchwood.* 1983. Timescape. 1st ed. dj. EX. R3. $20.00

LUKENS, Adam. *Alien World.* 1963. Avalon. dj. EX. P1. $15.00

LUKENS, Adam. *Glass Cage.* 1962. Avalon. 1st ed. dj. EX. R3. $10.00

LUKENS, Adam. *World Within.* 1962. Avalon. 1st ed. dj. EX. R3. $12.50

LUKENS, E.C. *Bl Ridge Memoir.* 1922. Baltimore. Ils. 152 p. T5. $45.00

LUKENS, Susan. *Gleanings at 75.* 1883. Phil. Longstreth. 12mo. 216 p. VG. V1. $10.00

LUMHOLTZ, Carl. *New Trails in Mexico.* 1912. Scribner. 1st ed. 412 p. TEG. F2. $75.00

LUMLEY, Brian. *Burrowers Beneath.* 1988. Ganley. dj. EX. P1. $22.50

LUMLEY, Brian. *Burrowers Beneath.* 1988. Ganley. 1st ed. 1/300. sgn. M. R3. $45.00

LUMLEY, Brian. *Compleat Crow.* 1987. Ganley. Ltd ed. 1/300. sgn. slipcase. M. R3. $45.00

LUMLEY, Brian. *Compleat Crow.* 1987. Ganley. 1st ed. wrp. M. R3. $7.50

LUMLEY, Brian. *Elysia.* 1989. Ganley. Ltd ed. 1/300. sgn. slipcase. M. R3. $50.00

LUMLEY, Brian. *Elysia.* 1989. Ganley. 1st ed. wrp. M. R3. $8.50

LUMLEY, Brian. *Hero of Dreams.* 1986. Ganley. 1st ed. wrp. M. R3. $10.00

LUMLEY, Brian. *Hero of Dreams.* 1986. Ganley. 1st HrdCvr ed. M. R3. $25.00

LUMLEY, Brian. *Mad Moon of Dreams.* 1987. Ganley. Ltd 1st ed. 1/250. sgn. M. R3. $45.00

LUMLEY, Brian. *Mad Moon of Dreams.* 1987. Ganley. 1st ed. dj. EX. P1. $21.00

LUMLEY, Brian. *Necroscope 4: Deadspeak.* 1990. Kinnell. 1st ed. sgn. dj. EX. P1. $40.00

LUMLEY, Brian. *Ship of Dreams.* 1986. Ganley. 1st ed. dj. EX. P1. $21.00

LUMLEY, Brian. *Ship of Dreams.* 1987. Ganley. Ltd ed. 1/250. sgn. M. R3. $45.00

LUMMIS, Charles. *Broncho Pegasus.* 1928. Boston. 1st ed. 150 p. VG. B3. $17.50

LUMSDEN, E.S. *Art of Etching.* 1924. Phil. Lippincott. Ils. 8vo. VG. $30.00

LUNA ARROYO, Antonio. *Chamizal Ya Es Mexicano.* 1964. Mexico. 12mo. 208 p. wrp. F2. $15.00

LUNDWALL, S.J. *SF: What It's All About.* 1971. Ace. VG. P1. $3.50

LUNDY MEMORIAL COMMITTEE. *Memorial to Benjamin Lundy: Pioneer Quaker Abolitionist.* 1939. Putnam, IL. 4to. SftCvr. w/2 p pamphlet. VG. V1. $9.00

LUNT, George. *Origin of the Late War.* 1866. NY. 1st ed. rebound. EX. $50.00

LUPACK, Alan. *Arthur the Greatest King.* 1988. NY/London. 1st ed. sgn. no dj issued. M. C1. $39.00

LUPACK, Alan. *Dream of Camelot.* 1990. Gr Chapel Pr. Ils McWilliams. 1st ed. sgn. C1. $17.50

LUPICA, Mike. *Dead Air.* 1986. Villard. 1st ed. dj. EX. P1. $15.95

LUPOFF, R.A. *ER Burroughs: Master of Adventure.* 1968. Ace. EX. P1. $6.00

LUPOFF, R.A. *Space War Blues.* 1980. Gregg Pr. P1. $15.00

LUPOFF, R.A. *Sword of the Demon.* 1977. Harper Row. 1st ed. inscr/sgn. dj. EX. F5. $35.00

LUPOFF, R.A. *Sword of the Demon.* 1977. Harper Row. 1st ed. dj. EX. P1. $17.50

LUPOFF, R.A. *Triune Man.* 1976. Berkley Putnam. 1st ed. dj. EX. P1. $15.00

LUSK, W.T. *War Letters...* 1911. NY. Ils 1st ed. 304 p. T5. $95.00

LUSKA, Sidney. *As It Was Written.* 1885. Cassell. 1st ed. VG. R3. $35.00

LUTHER, M.L. *Sovereign Power.* 1911. Macmillan. 1st ed. EX. R3. $20.00

LUTTRELL, Claude. *Creation of 1st Arthurian Romance: A Quest.* 1974. London. 1st ed. dj. EX. C1. $18.50

LUTZ, John. *Ride the Lightening.* 1987. St Martin. 1st ed. dj. EX. F5. $14.00

LUTZ, John. *Right To Sing the Blues.* 1986. St Martin. 1st ed. sgn. dj. EX. T9. $20.00

LUXEMBURG, Rosa. *Die Krise der Sozizialdemokratie.* 1919. Berlin. German text. 100 p. wrp. VG. $75.00

LYALL, Gavin. *Blame the Dead.* 1973. Viking. 1st ed. dj. VG. P1. $20.00

LYALL, Gavin. *Conduct of Maj Maxim.* 1983. Viking. 1st ed. dj. VG. P1. $15.00

LYALL, Gavin. *Crocus List.* 1985. Hodder Stoughton. 1st ed. dj. EX. P1. $17.50

LYALL, Gavin. *War in the Air.* 1969. NY. 1st Am ed. dj. T5. $17.50

LYDE, M.J. *Edith Wharton: Convention & Morality in Work of Novelist.* 1959. OK U. 1st ed. dj. VG. K2. $40.00

LYFORD, C.A. *Ojibwa Crafts.* 1953. Indian School Print Shop. 2nd ed. 216 p. $45.00

LYLE, Mel. *Mystery of the Million-Dollar Penny.* 1965. Whitman. VG. P1. $5.00

LYMINGTON, John. *Froomb!* nd. Book Club. dj. VG. P1. $4.50

LYMINGTON, John. *Nowhere Place.* 1971. Doubleday. 1st ed. dj. xl. P1. $5.00

LYMINGTON, Lord. *Spring Song of Iscariot.* 1929. Blk Sun. 1/25. wrp/glassine. EX. H3. $200.00

LYNCH, Jeremiah. *3 Years in the Klondike.* 1967. Lakeside Classic. 375 p. EX. T5. $22.50

LYNCH, Lawrence. *Diamond Coterie.* 1885. Donnelley. G. R3. $15.00

LYNDS, Dennis. *Another Way To Die.* 1972. Random House. 1st ed. dj. EX. F5. $25.00

LYNDS, Dennis. *Circle of Fire.* 1973. Random House. ARC. dj. RS. EX. F5. $25.00

LYNDS, Dennis. *Deadly Innocents.* 1986. Walker. 1st ed. dj. EX. F5/P1. $15.00

LYNDS, Dennis. *Falling Man.* 1970. Random House. 1st ed. dj. EX. F5. $20.00

LYNDS, Dennis. *Falling Man.* 1970. Random House. 1st ed. dj. xl. P1. $5.00

LYNDS, Dennis. *Mirror Image.* 1972. Random House. 1st ed. dj. EX. F5. $20.00

LYNDS, Dennis. *Touch of Darkness.* 1972. Random House. 1st ed. dj. EX. F5. $25.00

LYNES, Russell. *Cadwallader Diversion.* 1959. Harper. dj. EX. P1. $10.00

LYNN, E.A. *Dancers of Arun.* 1979. Berkley Putnam. 1st ed. dj. EX. P1. $17.50

LYNN, E.A. *Dancers of Arun.* 1979. Berkley Putnam. 1st ed. sgn. dj. EX. $22.50

LYNN, E.A. *Different Light.* 1980. British SF Book Club. dj. EX. P1. $10.00

LYNN, E.A. *Torner Trilogy (Watchtower/ Dancers of Arun/N Girl).* 1979-1980. Berkley. 1st ed. 3 vols. djs. EX. R3. $65.00

LYNN, Escott. *Knights in the Air.* 1918. London. Chambers. Ils Earnshaw. 384 p. B10. $7.00

LYNN, Jack. *Factory.* 1983. Harper Row. 1st ed. dj. EX. P1. $15.00

LYON, N.W. *Drama of Early Wyalusing.* 1938. Rainbow Club. 98 p. w/supplement. V1. $15.00

LYON, W.E. *In My Opinion.* 1931. NY. 4th print. VG. $10.00

LYTLE, Andrew. *At the Moon's Inn.* 1941. Indianapolis. 1st ed. inscr. dj. VG. B13. $450.00

LYTLE, Andrew. *Wake for the Living: A Family Chronicle.* 1975. NY. 1st ed. sgn. dj. VG. T9. $85.00

LYTLE, Horace. *No Hunting?* 1928. Dayton, OH. Ils Love. 1st ed. G. T5. $35.00

LYTTON, E.B. *Poetical & Dramatic Works.* 1852-1854. London. 1st ed. 5 vols. C1. $44.50

MAAS, Peter. *Serpico: Cop Who Defied the System*. 1963. Viking. lg 8vo. 314 p. dj. EX. $12.00

MAASS, John. *Gingerbread Age*. 1957. NY. 1st ed. 4to. VG. R5. $25.00

MAASS, John. *Victorian Home in Am*. 1972. Hawthorn. 1st ed. 4to. 235 p. dj. EX. R4. $30.00

MABIE, H.W. *Under the Trees*. 1902. Dodd Mead. Ils Hinton. 1st ed. TEG. VG. $25.00

MABILLE, Victor. *Cigarettes Poesies*. 1853. Paris. 1st ed. French text. 12mo. 149 p. scarce. $60.00

MACARTHUR, C.G. *Bug's-Eye-View of the War*. 1919. Oak Park, IL. 1st ed. 122 p. VG. T5. $125.00

MACARTHUR, Douglas. *Reminiscences*. 1964. NY. 1/1750. sgn. orig bdg. slipcase. H3. $550.00

MACARTHUR, William. *Adventures of Kathlyn*. 1914. Bobbs Merrill. 1st ed? EX. R3. $25.00

MACAULAY, Rose. *Crewe Train*. 1926. Boni. 1st ed. 319 p. dj. EX. B10. $4.00

MACAULAY, T.B. *Hist of Eng From the Accession of James II*. 1849. Harper. 4 vols. lg octavo. H3. $250.00

MACAULAY, T.B. *Works*. nd. 20th C ed. 10 vols. TEG. VG. $45.00

MACBETH, George. *Samurai*. 1975. Harcourt. 1st ed. dj. EX. F5. $15.00

MACBETH, George. *7 Witches*. 1978. Allen. 1st ed. dj. VG. P1. $15.00

MACBETH, George. *7 Witches*. 1978. Harcourt Brace. dj. EX. P1. $15.00

MACCURDY, G.B. *Human Origins. A Manual of Prehistory*. 1924. Appleton. 1st ed. 2 vols. F2. $30.00

MACDONALD, Aeneas. *Whisky*. 1930. Henry Longwell. 1/307. sgn. H3. $85.00

MACDONALD, Anson; see Heinlein, Robert.

MACDONALD, J.D. *Barrier Island*. 1986. Knopf. 1st ed. dj. VG. P1. $17.50

MACDONALD, J.D. *Cinnamon Skin*. 1982. Harper Row. 1st ed. dj. EX. F5/P1. $20.00

MACDONALD, J.D. *Condominium*. nd. BOMC. dj. VG. P1. $7.50

MACDONALD, J.D. *Darker Than Amber*. nd. BOMC. dj. VG. P1. $7.50

MACDONALD, J.D. *Deadly Shade of Gold*. nd. BOMC. dj. VG. P1. $8.00

MACDONALD, J.D. *Deadly Shade of Gold*. 1965. Greenwich. ARC of PB Orig. w/pub slip. EX. rare. T9. $235.00

MACDONALD, J.D. *Deadly Shade of Gold*. 1974. Lippincott. 1st ed. dj. EX. F5. $25.00

MACDONALD, J.D. *Deadly Shade of Gold*. 1974. Lippincott. 1st ed. 336 p. dj. VG. B10. $6.25

MACDONALD, J.D. *Drowner*. 1963. Gold Medal. PB Orig. wrp. NM. T9. $35.00

MACDONALD, J.D. *Empty Copper Sea*. 1978. Lippincott. 1st ed. dj. EX. F5/P1/T9. $30.00

MACDONALD, J.D. *Executioners*. 1958. Simon Schuster. 1st ed. dj. VG. T9. $55.00

MACDONALD, J.D. *Free Fall in Crimson*. 1981. Harper Row. 1st ed. dj. EX. F5/T9. $20.00

MACDONALD, J.D. *Girl, the Gold Watch, & Everything*. 1974. Robert Hale. dj. EX. P1. $45.00

MACDONALD, J.D. *Girl in the Plain Brn Wrp*. 1973. Book Club. dj. VG. P1. $5.00

MACDONALD, J.D. *Good Old Stuff*. nd. Book Club. dj. VG. P1. $5.00

MACDONALD, J.D. *Gr Ripper*. 1979. Lippincott. 1st ed. dj. EX. P1. $25.00

MACDONALD, J.D. *Key to the Suite*. 1968. Robert Hale. dj. VG. P1. $50.00

MACDONALD, J.D. *Last 1 Left*. nd. Book Club. dj. VG. P1. $7.50

MACDONALD, J.D. *Lonely Silver Rain*. 1985. Knopf. 1st ed. dj. VG. P1. $17.50

MACDONALD, J.D. *Long Lavender Look*. 1972. Robert Hale. 1st ed. dj. EX. P1. $40.00

MACDONALD, J.D. *More Good Old Stuff*. 1984. Knopf. 2nd ed. dj. VG. P1. $10.00

MACDONALD, J.D. *Murder for Money*. 1982. Harper Row. UP. gr printed wrp. EX. T9. $35.00

MACDONALD, J.D. *Nightmare in Pink*. nd. BOMC. dj. VG. P1. $7.50

MACDONALD, J.D. *No Deadly Drug*. 1968. Doubleday. dj. NM. T9. $45.00

MACDONALD, J.D. *Please Write for Details*. 1959. NY. 1st ed. as issued. K2. $100.00

MACDONALD, J.D. *Quick Red Fox*. 1974. Lippincott. 4th ed. 206 p. dj. VG. B10. $4.00

MACDONALD, J.D. *Scarlet Rose & 2 Others*. 1973. Lippincott/Crowell. 1st Compilation ed. dj. EX. F5. $10.00

MACDONALD, J.D. *Scarlet Rose*. 1975. Robert Hale. 1st ed. dj. EX. P1. $40.00

MACDONALD, J.D. *Slam the Big Door*. 1960. Gold Medal. PB Orig. wrp. T9. $40.00

MACDONALD, J.D. *Slam the Big Door*. 1987. Mysterious Pr. 1st HrdCvr ed. dj. EX. F5. $15.00

MACDONALD, J.D. *You Live Once*. 1976. London. Hale. 1st ed. dj. T9. $35.00

MACDONALD, J.D. *1 More Sunday*. 1984. Knopf. Book Club ed. 311 p. dj. VG. B10. $3.75

MACDONALD, J.D. *1 More Sunday*. 1984. Knopf. 1st ed. dj. VG. P1. $20.00

MACDONALD, Malcolm. *Tessa d'Arblay*. 1988. St Martin. 1st ed. dj. EX. F5. $15.00

MACDONALD, Philip. *Choice*. 1931. Collins. VG. P1. $30.00

MACDONALD, Philip. *Polerry Mystery*. 1932. Collins. 5th ed. dj. VG. P1. $20.00

MACDONALD, Philip. *Warrant for X*. nd. Doubleday. VG. P1. $10.00

MACDONALD, Philip. *3 for Midnight*. nd. Book Club. dj. VG. P1. $7.50

MACDONALD, Ross. *Archer in Hollywood*. nd. Book Club. dj. VG. P1. $7.50

MACDONALD, Ross. *Bl Hammer*. 1976. Knopf. 1st ed. 270 p. dj. EX. B10. $8.25

MACDONALD, Ross. *Blk Money*. 1966. Knopf. 1st ed. dj. xl. P1. $10.00

MACDONALD, Ross. *Chill*. nd. Book Club. dj. VG. P1. $4.50

MACDONALD, Ross. *Crime Writing*. 1973. Capra. Chapbook Series. 1/250. sgn. EX. K2. $125.00

MACDONALD, Ross. *Far Side of the Dollar*. 1965. Knopf. 1st ed. dj. xl. P1. $10.00

MACDONALD, Ross. *Galton Case*. 1959. Knopf. inscr. dj. H3. $500.00

MACDONALD, Ross. *Goodbye Look*. 1969. Knopf. 1st ed. dj. EX. T9. $40.00

MACDONALD, Ross. *Instant Enemy*. 1968. Knopf. 1st ed. dj. xl. P1. $10.00

MACDONALD, Ross. *Lew Archer Private Investigator.* 1977. Mysterious Pr. Ltd ed. 1/250. sgn. slipcase. M. H3. $175.00

MACDONALD, Ross. *On Crime Writing.* 1973. Santa Barbara, CA. 1/250. sgn. sans dj. EX. T9. $125.00

MACDONALD, Ross. *Sleeping Beauty.* 1973. Knopf. 1st ed. dj. EX. T9. $35.00

MACDONALD, Ross. *Underground Man.* 1971. Knopf. 5th ed. dj. xl. P1. $5.00

MACDONALD, Ross. *Zebra-Striped Hearse.* nd. Book Club. dj. VG. P1. $4.50

MACDONALD, William. *Digging for Gold: Papers on Archaeology for Profit.* 1976. Ann Arbor. Technical Reports No 5. 86 p. wrp. $7.50

MACDONELL, A.G. *Napoleon & His Marshals.* 1934. NY. 1st ed. VG. $15.00

MACDOUGALL, Arthur. *Dud Dean & His Country.* 1946. NY. 1st ed. dj. VG. B3. $27.50

MACDOUGALL, Arthur. *Under a Willow Tree.* 1946. NY. Ils Milton Weiler. 199 p. VG. T5. $22.50

MACDOUGALL, James. *Folk Tale & Fairy Lore in Gaelic & Eng.* 1910. Edinburgh. EX. $50.00

MACE, Elisabeth. *Out There.* 1977. Greenwillow. dj. VG. P1. $12.50

MACE, Thomas. *Musick's Monument...* 1676. London. 1st ed. folio. H3. $6500.00

MACFADDEN, Bernarr. *MacFadden's Encyclopedia of Physical Culture.* 1928. NY. 5 vols. VG. $35.00

MACFADDEN, Bernarr. *Vitality Supreme.* nd. (1915) Physical Culture Co. apparent 1st ed. G. B10. $4.50

MACFARLANE, James. *Am Geol Railway Guide...Geol Formation of Railway Station.* 1879. Appleton. Ils. 224 p. A5. $30.00

MACFARLANE & THOMPSON. *Comprehensive Hist of Eng.* 1861. London. 4 vols. 4to. VG. $100.00

MACGOVERN, William. *Jungle Paths & Inca Ruins.* nd. (1927) Grosset Dunlap. F2. $15.00

MACGOVERN, William. *Jungle Paths & Inca Ruins.* 1927. Century. 1st ed. 526 p. F2. $20.00

MACGRATH, Harold. *Half a Rouge.* 1906. Bobbs Merrill. Apparent 1st ed. 448 p. G. B10. $3.50

MACGRATH, Harold. *Man on the Box.* 1904. Bobbs Merrill. Apparent 1st ed? 361 p. VG. B10. $4.50

MACGREGOR, Ellen. *Miss Pickerel on the Moon.* nd. Weekly Reader. decor brd. P1. $1.75

MACHARG & BALMER. *Blind Man's Eyes.* 1916. Little Brn. 8th print. VG. P1. $15.00

MACHEN, Arthur. *Canning Wonder.* 1926. NY. dj. EX. $35.00

MACHEN, Arthur. *Dog & Duck.* 1924. NY. 1st Am ed. VG. C1. $9.50

MACHEN, Arthur. *Dreads & Drolls.* 1926. London. 1st ed. dj. VG. R3. $60.00

MACHEN, Arthur. *Great God Pan & the Inmost Light.* 1894. London. John Lane. 1st ed. EX. B13. $250.00

MACHEN, Arthur. *Hieroglyphics: Note on Ecstasy in Literature.* 1923. NY. 1st Am ed. VG. C1. $9.50

MACHEN, Arthur. *House of Souls.* 1920. Knopf. VG. R3. $12.50

MACHEN, Arthur. *Secret Glory.* 1923. NY. VG. C1. $12.00

MACHEN, Arthur. *Terror.* 1965. Norton. dj. VG. P1. $30.00

MACHEN, Arthur. *Things Near & Far.* 1923. NY. 1st Am ed. VG. C1. $9.50

MACHEN, Arthur. *Way To Attain.* 1923. Carbonnek. private print. 1st ed. 1/1050. sgn. EX. R3. $75.00

MACHEN, Arthur. *3 Imposters.* 1923. Knopf. 1st ed. dj. VG. R3. $50.00

MACINNES, Helen. *Agent in Place.* nd. Harcourt Brace. 2nd ed. dj. EX. P1. $12.50

MACINNES, Helen. *Assignment in Brittany.* 1942. Little Brn. VG. P1. $13.75

MACINNES, Helen. *Cloak of Darkness.* 1982. Harcourt Brace. 1st ed. dj. VG. P1. $12.00

MACINNES, Helen. *Venetian Affair.* 1963. Harcourt Brace World. 1st ed. dj. VG. P1. $22.50

MACINTOSH, M.T. *Joseph Wright Taylor: Founder of Bryn Mawr College.* 1936. Haverford. CS Taylor. 8vo. sgn. 211 p. G. V1. $18.00

MACISAAC, Fred. *Hothouse World.* 1965. Avalon. 1st ed. dj. EX. R3. $15.00

MACISAC, Fred. *Mental Marvel.* 1930. McClurg. 1st ed. VG. R3. $50.00

MACISAC, Fred. *Vanishing Professor.* 1927. Waterson. 1st ed. dj. xl. VG. R3. $30.00

MACK, Gerstle. *Land Divided.* 1944. NY. Ils. maps. 684 p. T5. $45.00

MACKAYE, H.S. *Panhronicon.* 1904. Scribner. 1st ed. EX. R3. $50.00

MACKENZIE, Compton. *My Record of Music.* nd. (c 1955) Putnam. 1st Am ed. octavo. 280 p. dj. EX. H3. $45.00

MACKENZIE, Compton. *Rival Monster.* 1952. Chatto Windus. dj. VG. P1. $9.25

MACKENZIE, Donald. *Death Is a Friend.* 1967. Houghton Mifflin. 1st ed. dj. EX. F5. $13.00

MACKENZIE, Donald. *Raven After Dark.* 1979. Houghton Mifflin. 1st ed. dj. EX. P1. $7.50

MACKENZIE, Donald. *Raven's Longest Night.* 1983. Crime Club. 1st ed. dj. EX. F5. $15.00

MACKENZIE, Donald. *Raven's Shadow.* 1985. Crime Club. 1st ed. dj. VG. P1. $15.00

MACKENZIE, Donald. *Sleep Is for the Rich.* 1971. Macmillan. 1st ed. dj. VG. P1. $17.50

MACKENZIE, Donald. *Spreewald Collection.* 1975. Macmillan. 2nd ed. dj. xl. P1. $5.00

MACKENZIE & MACKENZIE. *HG Wells: A Biography.* 1973. Simon Schuster. 1st ed. dj. EX. R3. $15.00

MACKEY, CLEGG, & HAYWOOD. *Encyclopedia of Freemasonry.* 1946. Chicago. Revised Enlarged ed. 2 vols. EX. $145.00

MACKEY, Mary. *Immersion.* 1972. San Lorenzo. Ils Mady Sklar. 1st ed. inscr. wrp. VG. T9. $45.00

MACKEY & SOOY. *Early CA Costumes, 1769-1847, & Hist Flags of CA.* 1932. Stanford. 1st ed. octavo. 136 p. dj. EX. H3. $75.00

MACKINSTRY, Elizabeth. *Puck in Pasture.* 1925. Doubleday. 1st/only ed. G. rare. C1. $29.50

MACLAY, E.S. *Hist of Am Privateers.* 1924. Appleton. Ils. 8vo. VG. $85.00

MACLAY, E.S. *Reminiscences of the Old Navy.* 1898. NY. 1st ed. 1/750. EX. $80.00

MACLEAN, Alistair. *Athabasca.* 1980. Collins. 1st ed. dj. EX. P1. $15.00

MACLEAN, Alistair. *Bear Island.* 1971. Doubleday. 1st ed. dj. VG. P1. $15.00

MACLEAN, Alistair. *Capt Cook.* 1972. Doubleday. 1st ed. dj. inscr. dj. EX. B13. $30.00

MACLEAN, Alistair. *Floodgate.* 1983. Doubleday. dj. VG. P1. $12.00

MACLEAN, Alistair. *Floodgate.* 1983. Doubleday. UP. wrp. VG. F5. $17.00

MACLEAN, Alistair. *Ice Station Zebra.* 1963. Doubleday. 1st ed. dj. EX. F5. $25.00

MACLEAN, Alistair. *Lonely Sea.* 1985. Doubleday. 1st ed. dj. EX. F5. $15.00

MACLEAN, Alistair. *Partisans.* 1983. Doubleday. dj. VG. P1. $12.00

MACLEAN, Alistair. *Seawitch.* 1977. Doubleday. 1st ed. dj. EX. F5. $14.00

MACLEAN, Alistair. *Seawitch.* 1977. Doubleday. 1st ed. dj. VG. P1. $10.00

MACLEAN, D.G. *Gene Stratton-Porter: Short Biography & Collector's Guide...* 1987. Decatur, IN. Ils. wrp. T5. $3.95

MACLEAN, J.P. *Journal of Michael Waters...* 1899. Cleveland. Ils. 8vo. printed wrp. G. T5. $32.50

MACLEAN, Katherine. *Missing Man.* nd. Book Club. dj. VG. P1. $4.50

MACLEAN, Katherine. *Missing Man.* 1975. Berkley Putnam. 1st ed. dj. EX. P1. $15.00

MACLEAN, Norman. *River Runs Through It.* 1976. Chicago U. 1st ed. dj. EX. B13. $325.00

MACLEAN, Norman. *River Runs Through It.* 1990. London. Picador. 1st Eng ed. dj. M. B13. $50.00

MACLEAN, Robinson. *Baited Blond.* nd. Book Club. dj. VG. P1. $4.50

MACLEAN & WEST. *Dark Wing.* 1979. Atheneum. 1st ed. dj. EX. P1. $15.00

MACLEISH, Archibald. *Einstein.* 1929. Blk Sun. 1st Separate ed. 1/100. wrp/glassine/slipcase. H3. $450.00

MACLEISH, Archibald. *New Found Land.* 1930. Blk Sun. 1st ed. 1/10 hors commerce. wrp/glassine. EX. H3. $200.00

MACLEOD, Charlotte. *Convivial Codfish.* nd. Book Club. dj. VG. P1. $5.00

MACLEOD, Charlotte. *Corpse in Oozak's Pond.* nd. Book Club. dj. VG. P1. $4.50

MACLEOD, Charlotte. *Curse of the Giant Hogweed.* 1985. Crime Club. 1st ed. dj. VG. P1. $15.00

MACLEOD, Charlotte. *Palace Guard.* nd. Book Club. dj. VG. P1. $5.00

MACLEOD, Charlotte. *Plain Old Man.* nd. Book Club. dj. VG. P1. $4.50

MACLEOD, Charlotte. *Plain Old Man.* 1985. Crime Club. 1st ed. dj. VG. P1. $15.00

MACLEOD, Charlotte. *Recycled Citizen.* nd. Book Club. dj. VG. P1. $5.00

MACLEOD, Charlotte. *Withdrawing Room.* nd. Book Club. dj. VG. P1. $4.50

MACLEOD, Fiona. *Silence of Amor.* 1903. Portland, ME. 1st Am ed. 1/400. VG. C1. $12.50

MACLEOD, Mary. *King Arthur & His Knights.* c 1950. World. Ils Alexander Dobkin. VG. C1. $6.00

MACLEOD, Mary. *King Arthur.* 1970. 3rd ed. VG. C1. $7.50

MACLEOD & BOULTON. *Songs of the N.* c 1895. London. 2 vols. A4. $75.00

MACLYSAGHT, Edward. *Irish Families: Their Names, Arms, & Origins.* 1957. Dublin. Ils. 4to. 366 p. $65.00

MACMAHON & MACPHERSON. *10 Commandments.* nd. Grosset Dunlap. Photoplay ed. VG. P1. $15.00

MACMULLEN, Ramsay. *Soldier & Civilian in Later Roman Empire.* 1963. Cambridge. Ils. 217 p. dj. VG. T5. $19.50

MACNEICE, Louis. *Christopher Columbus.* 1944. London. Faber. 1st ed. H3. $40.00

MACNEICE, Louis. *Mad Islands/ Administrator.* 1964. London. Faber. 1st ed. dj. EX. H3. $40.00

MACNEIL, Robert. *Eudora Welty Seeing Blk & Wht.* 1990. MS U. wrp. dj. EX. K2. $30.00

MACOUN, John. *Manitoba & the Great NW.* 1883. London. 1st ed. fld map/pl. VG. $150.00

MACOUN & MACOUN. *Catalog of Canadian Birds.* 1909. Ottawa. 761 p. wrp. VG. $40.00

MACPHERSON. *Covenanters Under Persecution.* 1923. Edinburgh. 1st ed. 156 p. VG. B3. $20.00

MACQUARRIE, Hector. *Over Here: Impressions of Am by a British Officer.* 1918. Lippincott. 1st ed. 243 p. fair. B10. $3.25

MACSHANE, Frank. *Life of Raymond Chandler.* 1976. Dutton. 1st ed. dj. EX. C4. $25.00

MACTYRE, Paul. *Fish on a Hook.* 1963. Hodder Stoughton. dj. EX. P1. $8.00

MACVICAR, Angus. *Atom Chasers in Tibet.* 1960. Burke. dj. VG. P1. $12.50

MACVICAR, Angus. *Lost Planet.* 1960. Burke. dj. VG. P1. $10.00

MACVICAR, Angus. *Satellite 7.* 1961. Burke. dj. VG. P1. $12.50

MACVICAR, Angus. *Secret of the Lost Planet.* 1959. Burke. 3rd ed. dj. VG. P1. $10.00

MADDEN, David. *Beautiful Greed.* 1961. NY. 1st ed. inscr. dj. VG. T9. $70.00

MADDEN, David. *Cain's Craft.* 1985. Metuchen, NJ. Scarecrow. inscr. gr bdg. no dj issued. EX. T9. $40.00

MADDEN, David. *Wright Morris by David Madden.* 1964. Twayne. 1st ed. sgn. dj. EX. C4. $30.00

MADDEROM, Gary. *4-Chambered Villain.* 1971. Macmillan. 1st ed. dj. EX. P1. $12.50

MADDOCK, Reginald. *Time Maze.* 1960. Thomas Nelson. 1st ed. dj. VG. P1. $15.00

MADDOCK, Stephen. *Danger After Dark.* 1934. Collins. 1st ed. VG. P1. $7.50

MADDOCK, Stephen. *E of Piccadilly.* 1948. Collins. 1st ed. VG. P1. $6.00

MADIS, George. *Winchester Book.* 1971. Lancaster, TX. 1st ed. sgn. $80.00

MADSEN, Bill. *New Jinx.* 1987. Kaufman/Greenberg. 1st HrdCvr ed. 296 p. dj. NM. J3. $32.00

MADSION, L.F. *Maid at King Alfred's Court.* 1900. Penn. 1st ed. VG. R3. $15.00

MAETERLINK, Maurice. *Bl Bird: Fairy Play in 6 Acts.* 1914. Dodd Mead. TEG. EX. $85.00

MAETERLINK, Maurice. *Life of the Bee.* 1902. Dodd Mead. 1st ed. TEG. EX. $125.00

MAETERLINK, Maurice. *Wisdom & Destiny.* 1898. Dodd Mead. 1st ed. TEG. G. $55.00

MAETERLINK, Maurice. *Wisdom & Destiny.* 1898. Dodd Mead. 1st ed. TEG. VG. $85.00

MAGEE, J.D. *Bordentown 1682-1932.* 1932. Bordentown, NJ. Ils Magee. 1st ed. sgns. G. T5. $35.00

MAGEE, M. *Champions.* c 1980. NY. 1st Am ed. 4to. 191 p. EX. $21.50

MAGGIN, E.S. *Superman: Last Son of Krypton.* 1978. Warner. 1st HrdCvr ed. dj. VG. F5. $10.00

MAGIDOFF & MAGIDOFF. *Russian SF 1968.* 1968. NY U. 1st ed. inscr. dj. EX. F5. $24.00

MAGILL, E.H. *Educational Instit in Religious Soc of Friends.* 1893. WB Conkey. 8vo. wrp. V1. $8.00

MAGILL, Marcus. *Murder in Full Flight.* 1933. Lippincott. 1st ed. VG. P1. $15.00

MAGISTRALE, Anthony. *Moral Voyages of Stephen King.* 1986. Starmont. 1st ed. wrp. M. R3. $9.95

MAGNER, D. *Taming & Educating Horses.* 1886. Battle Creek. Ils. 1088 p. EX. $85.00

MAGRIEL, P. *Backgammon.* 1973. NY. 1st ed. dj. EX. B3. $37.50

MAGRIEL, Paul. *Chronicles of the Am Dance.* 1948. Holt. 1st ed. octavo. 268 p. dj. VG. H3. $75.00

MAGUS, Jim. *Astro Disks I: Dark Side of the Moon.* 1989. Exclusive Magical Pub. 1st ed. SftCvr. M. J3. $15.00

MAHAN, A.T. *Admiral Farragut.* 1895. NY. Ils. 333 p. TEG. T5. $29.50

MAHAN, A.T. *Gulf & Inland Waters.* 1883. NY. 267 p. VG. T5. $39.50

MAHER, J.T. *Twilight of Splendor.* 1975. Boston. 1st ed. 453 p. dj. VG. B3. $35.00

MAHFOUZ, Naguib. *Beginning & the End.* 1989. Doubleday. UP. sgn. wrp. EX. B13. $175.00

MAHFOUZ, Naguib. *Palace Walk.* 1990. Doubleday. 1st ed. sgn. dj. M. B13. $175.00

MAHONEY & WHITNEY. *Contemporary Ils of Children's Books.* 1930. Boston. Ils 1st ed. 134 p. B3. $45.00

MAILER, Norman. *Ancient Evenings.* 1983. Little Brn. Ltd ed. 1/350. sgn. slipcase. M. H3. $150.00

MAILER, Norman. *Barbary Shore.* 1951. Rinehart. 1st ed. dj. EX. H3. $50.00

MAILER, Norman. *Deer Park.* 1955. Putnam. 1st ed. dj. VG. H3. $50.00

MAILER, Norman. *Executioner's Song.* 1979. Little Brn. Review ed. sgn. dj. w/photo. H3. $100.00

MAILER, Norman. *Idol & the Octopus.* 1968. Dell. PB Orig. EX. K2. $35.00

MAILER, Norman. *Maidstone: A Mystery.* 1971. Signet Film Series W4782. 1st ed. wrp. NM. T9. $25.00

MAILER, Norman. *Marilyn: A Biography.* 1973. Grosset Dunlap. sgns. boxed. H3. $200.00

MAILER, Norman. *Marilyn: A Biography.* 1973. NY. Ltd ed. 2nd print. sgn Mailer/Schiller. wht moire bdg. EX. T9. $65.00

MAILER, Norman. *Marilyn: A Biography.* 1973. NY. 1st ed. 1st print. sm 4to. 270 p. beige bdg. VG. T1. $125.00

MAILER, Norman. *Naked & the Dead.* nd. np. 1st ed author's 1st book. dj. H3. $200.00

MAILER, Norman. *Naked & the Dead.* 1949. London. 1st UK ed. dj. RS. K2. $100.00

MAILER, Norman. *Of a Sm & Modest Malignancy, Wicked & Bristing With Dots.* 1980. Lord John. 1/300. sgn. slipcase. M. H3. $100.00

MAILER, Norman. *Prisoner of Sex.* 1971. Little Brn. 1st ed. dj. EX. K2. $20.00

MAILER, Norman. *Tough Guys Don't Dance.* 1984. Random House. Ltd ed. 1/350. sgn. boxed. M. H3. $125.00

MAILER, Norman. *Tough Guys Don't Dance.* 1984. Random House. 1st ed. sgn. dj. M. H3. $65.00

MAILER, Norman. *Wht Negro.* nd. City Lights. 1st ed. 2nd issue. wrp. EX. K2. $25.00

MAILING, Arthur. *Koberg Link.* 1979. Harper Row. 1st ed. dj. VG. P1. $15.00

MAILING, Arthur. *Schroeder's Game.* 1977. Harper Row. 1st ed. dj. xl. P1. $5.00

MAILS, Thomas. *Mystic Warriors of the Plains.* 1972. Doubleday. 2nd ed. dj. VG. B3. $45.00

MAINE, C.E. *Alph.* nd. Book Club. 1st ed. dj. EX. P1. $4.50

MAINE, C.E. *Count-Down.* nd. Hodder Stoughton. VG. P1. $8.00

MAINE, C.E. *Darkest of Nights.* 1962. Hodder Stoughton. 1st ed. dj. xl. P1. $7.00

MAINE, C.E. *Isotope Man.* nd. Book Club. dj. VG. P1. $4.50

MAINE, C.E. *Man Who Couldn't Sleep.* nd. Book Club. dj. VG. P1. $4.50

MAINE, C.E. *Timeliner.* 1955. Hodder Stoughton. dj. VG. P1. $20.00

MAINE, C.E. *Timeliner.* 1955. Rinehart. 1st ed. dj. EX. R3. $25.00

MAINE, Charles. *He Owned the World.* 1960. Avalon. 1st ed. dj. EX. R3. $15.00

MAIR, G.B. *Day Kruschev Panicked.* 1961. Cassell. 1st ed. dj. VG. P1. $10.00

MAIR, G.B. *Miss Turquoise.* 1965. Random House. 1st ed. dj. VG. P1. $15.00

MAIR, G.B. *Wreath of Camellias.* 1970. Jarrolds. dj. xl. P1. $5.00

MAJAX, Gerald. *Carre Magique.* 1982. Paris. Dell Arte. French text. 63 p. NM. J3. $11.00

MAJAX, Gerald. *Magie des Thimble Magic...* 1979. Strasbourg, France. French/Eng text. sgn. SftCvr. EX. J3. $20.00

MAJAX, Gerald. *Pouvoir de la Magie.* 1986. Paris. Table Ronde. sgn. French text. 208 p. NM. J3. $15.00

MAJOR, Charles. *When Knighthood Was in Flower.* nd. Grosset Dunlap. Photoplay ed. VG. P1. $20.00

MAJOR, Clarence. *All-Night Visitors.* 1969. Olympia. ARC. dj. RS. VG. K2. $125.00

MAJOR, Clarence. *All-Night Visitors.* 1969. Olympia. 1st ed. dj. EX. K2. $85.00

MAJOR, Clarence. *My Amputations.* 1986. Fiction Collective. 1st ed. sgn. xl. K2. $25.00

MAJOR, Clarence. *Swallow the Lake.* 1970. Middletown. 1st ed. dj. EX. K2. $35.00

MAJOR, R.H. *Hist of Medicine.* 1954. Springfield. Ils. 2 vols. $90.00

MAJOR. *Popular Prints of Am.* 1973. Crown. Ils. 183 p. A5. $35.00

MAJORS, Alexander. *70 Years on the Frontier.* 1893. Rand McNally. Ils. 325 p. A5. $70.00

MALAMUD, Bernard. *Assistant.* 1957. Farrar Straus Cudahy. 1st print. dj. EX. H3. $250.00

MALAMUD, Bernard. *Fixer.* 1966. Farrar Straus Giroux. 1st ed. dj. EX. H3. $60.00

MALAMUD, Bernard. *Idiots 1st.* 1963. Farrar Straus. 1st ed. dj. EX. H3. $60.00

MALAMUD, Bernard. *Magic Barrel.* 1958. Farrar Straus Giroux. ARC. dj. RS. EX. B13. $125.00

MALAMUD, Bernard. *Magic Barrel.* 1958. Farrar Straus Giroux. 1st ed. dj. VG. H3. $100.00

MALAMUD, Bernard. *Natural.* 1952. Harcourt Brace. 1st ed. dj. G. H3. $650.00

MALAMUD, Bernard. *Natural.* 1952. Harcourt Brace. 1st ed. dj. NM. K2. $1000.00

MALAMUD, Bernard. *Natural.* 1953. Eyre Spottiswoode. 1st UK ed. dj. EX. K2. $250.00

MALAMUD, Bernard. *New Life.* 1961. Farrar Straus Cudahy. 1st ed. dj. VG. H3. $75.00

MALAMUD, Bernard. *Pictures of Fidelman: An Exhibition.* 1969. Farrar Straus Giroux. 1st ed. dj. EX. H3. $60.00

MALAMUD, Bernard. *Rembrandt's Hat.* 1973. Farrar Straus. 1st ed. sgn. dj. EX. B13. $100.00

MALAMUD, Bernard. *Stories of Bernard Malamud.* 1983. Farrar Straus. UP. wrp. EX. B13. $100.00

MALAMUD, Bernard. *Stories of Bernard Malamud.* 1983. Farrar Straus. 1/225. sgn. slipcase. EX. T5. $65.00

MALAMUD, Bernard. *Tenants.* 1971. Farrar Straus Giroux. 1st ed. dj. EX. H3. $60.00

MALAMUD, Bernard. *Tenants.* 1971. Farrar Straus Giroux. 1st ed. dj. G. $35.00

MALAN, A.H. *Famous Homes of Great Britain.* 1900. NY. 1st Am ed. 4to. TEG. VG. T1. $45.00

MALANGA, Gerard. *10 Poems for 10 Poets.* 1970. Blk Sparrow. 1st ed. 1/200. sgn. dj. EX. $20.00

MALCOLM, Janet. *In the Freud Archives.* 1984. Knopf. AP. EX. K2. $25.00

MALCOLM, John. *Back Room in Somers Town.* 1985. Scribner. EX. P1. $12.95

MALCOLM-SMITH, George. *Come Out, Come Out.* 1965. Crime Club. 1st ed. dj. xl. P1. $5.00

MALDINEY, Henri. *Foundation Marguerite et Aime Maeght.* 1964. Paris. EX. P4. $245.00

MALET, Lucas. *Far Horizon.* 1907. Dodd Mead. 1st ed. dj. VG. F5. $12.00

MALIN, P.M. *Design for Living.* 1935. Phil. Book Committee. 12mo. 22 p. pamphlet. V1. $6.00

MALLARD, R.Q. *Plantation Life Before Emancipation.* 1892. Richmond. 1st ed. 237 p. G. T1. $40.00

MALLET, Jacqueline. *They Can't Hang Me!* 1974. Harper Row. 1st ed. dj. EX. P1. $12.50

MALLET, Thierry. *Glimpses of the Barren Lands.* 1930. NY. private print. Ils. 142 p. EX. $30.00

MALLEY. *Graven by Fishermen Themselves.* 1983. Mystic. pictorial wrp. VG. C2. $22.00

MALLORY, Drew. *Target Manhattan.* 1975. Putnam. 1st ed. dj. VG. P1. $15.00

MALLOY, Fred. *Devil's Holiday.* 1952. Woodford Pr. 1st ed. dj. EX. F5. $22.00

MALONE, Kemp. *10 Old Eng Poems Put Into Modern Eng Alliterative Verse.* 1951. Baltimore. 2nd print. VG. C1. $11.00

MALONE, Robert. *Robot Book.* 1978. Harvest. VG. P1. $10.00

MALORY, Thomas. *Arthur Pendragon of Britain.* 1943. Doubleday. 1st/only ed. VG. C1. $85.00

MALORY, Thomas. *Morte d'Arthur.* 1910-1911. London. Warner. 1/500. 4 vols. slipcase. H3. $1500.00

MALORY, Thomas. *Morte d'Arthur.* 1920. London. Ils Flint. 2 vols. VG. T5. $125.00

MALORY, Thomas. *Morte d'Arthur.* 1982. Scribner. Ltd ed. AEG. slipcase. M. H3. $150.00

MALORY, Thomas. *Noble & Joyous Book Entytled le Morte d'Arthur.* 1914. Ashendene Pr. 1/145. folio. EX. B10. $45.00

MALOUF, David. *Child's Play.* 1982. London. 1st ed. sgn. dj. EX. B13. $125.00

MALZBERG, Barry. *Beyond Apollo.* 1972. Random House. 1st ed. dj. EX. R3. $40.00

MALZBERG, Barry. *Down Here in the Dream Quarter.* 1976. Doubleday. 1st ed. dj. EX. R3. $30.00

MALZBERG, Barry. *Galaxies.* 1980. Gregg Pr. 1st ed. M. R3. $30.00

MALZBERG, Barry. *Galaxies.* 1980. Gregg Pr. 1st ed. no dj issued. EX. P1. $20.00

MALZBERG, Barry. *Guernica Night.* 1974. Bobbs Merrill. 1st ed. dj. EX. F5/P1/R3. $20.00

MALZBERG, Barry. *Herovit's World.* 1973. Random House. 1st ed. dj. EX. R3. $17.50

MALZBERG, Barry. *Man Who Loved the Midnight Lady.* 1980. Doubleday. 1st ed. dj. xl. P1. $5.00

MALZBERG & PRONZINI. *Dark Sins, Dark Dreams.* 1978. Doubleday. 1st ed. dj. RS. EX. P1. $20.00

MAMET, David. *Am Buffalo: A Play.* 1977. NY. Correct 1st ed. wrp. EX. T9. $75.00

MANCHESTER, H.A. *Matches Were Made in Heaven & in Barberton, OH.* 1977. Barberton. Ils. 108 p. EX. T5. $15.00

MANCINI, Giambattista. *Practical Reflection on Figurative Art of Singing.* 1912. Gorham Pr. octavo. 194 p. VG. H3. $40.00

MANDEL, George. *Flee the Angry Strangers.* 1952. Bobbs Merrill. 1st ed. dj. B4. $15.00

MANGIONE, J. *Dream & the Deal: Federal Writer's Project 1935-1943.* c 1972. Little Brn. 1st ed. dj. EX. $20.00

MANJE, J.M. *Unknown AZ & Sonora 1693-1721.* 1954. Tucson. dj. VG. $40.00

MANKIEWICZ, Don. *Trial.* 1955. Harper. Ltd ed. sgn. H3. $75.00

MANKIEWICZ, Don. *Trial.* 1955. Harper. 1st ed. presentation. H3. $50.00

MANN, Al. *Scorpio's Curve: Occult Business With a Business Card.* nd. Great Cacapon, NJ. M. J3. $25.00

MANN, E.B. *Killers' Range.* 1943. Triangle. dj. VG. P1. $6.00

MANN, E.B. *Stampede.* 1943. Triangle. VG. P1. $4.00

MANN, E.B. *Thirsty Range.* 1945. Blakiston. 281 p. dj. VG. B10. $3.50

MANN, E.B. *Thirsty Range.* 1945. Triangle. VG. P1. $10.00

MANN, Erika. *School for Barbarians.* 1938. Modern Age. SftCvr. VG. $22.00

MANN, Graciela. *12 Prophets of Aleijadinho.* 1967. Austin. 1st ed. 4to. dj. F2. $30.00

MANN, Heinrich. *Little Town.* 1931. Houghton Mifflin. 1st ed. dj. EX. scarce. B13. $250.00

MANN, Horace. *Slavery: Letters & Speeches.* 1851. Mussey. 1st ed. 564 p. G. S1. $75.00

MANN, Jack. *Her Ways Are Death.* 1981. Bookfinger. reprint of 1941 ed. EX. R3. $25.00

MANN, James. *Wallace Collection Catalogs: European Arms & Armor.* 1962. London. 2 vols. EX. $50.00

MANN, Thomas. *Beloved Returns Lotte in Weimar.* 1940. Knopf. Ltd ed. dj. boxed. H3. $250.00

MANN, Thomas. *Death in Venice & Other Stories.* 1925. Knopf. 1st Eng text ed. dj. EX. B13. $1250.00

MANN, Thomas. *Dr Faustus.* 1948. Knopf Book Club. 510 p. VG. B10. $3.50

MANN, Thomas. *Exchange of Letters.* 1938. Overbrook Pr. 1st ed. 1/350. sgn. wrp. VG. B13. $350.00

MANN, Thomas. *Joseph & His Brothers.* 1938. Knopf. 1st ed. later print. sgn dj. K2. $125.00

MANN, Thomas. *Listen, Germany!* 1943. Knopf. 1st ed. dj. EX. scarce. B13. $50.00

MANN, Thomas. *Nocturnes.* 1934. Equinox. Ils Lynd Ward. 1st ed. 1/1000. sgn. boxed. H3. $250.00

MANN, Thomas. *Order of the Day.* 1942. Knopf. 1st ed. dj. EX. B13. $65.00

MANN, Thomas. *Sketch of My Life.* 1930. Harrison of Paris. 1/695. EX. B13. $125.00

MANN, Thomas. *Transposed Heads.* 1941. Knopf. ARC. dj. EX. K2. $100.00

MANN, W.A. *Roster of the Rainbow Division.* 1917. NY. 1st ed. 541 p. G. T5. $32.50

MANNERS, D.X. *Dead to the World.* 1947. David McKay. dj. xl. P1. $5.00

MANNES, Marya. *Message From a Stranger.* 1948. Viking. 1st ed. VG. P1. $10.00

MANNING, Olivia. *My Husband, Cartwright.* 1956. London. Ils Len Deighton. 1st ed. dj. EX. $70.00

MANNING, Samuel. *Palestine Ils.* nd. Hurst. Ils. purple bdg. VG. B10. $10.00

MANNIX, D.P. *Killers.* 1968. Dutton. 1st ed. dj. VG. P1. $20.00

MANO, D.K. *Take 5.* 1982. Doubleday. 1st ed. inscr. dj. EX. K2. $40.00

MANOR, Jason. *Pawns of Fear.* 1955. Viking. 1st ed. dj. xl. P1. $6.00

MANOR, Jason. *Too Dead To Run.* 1953. Viking. 1st ed. dj. VG. P1. $17.50

MANSFIELD, Harold. *Vision: Saga of the Sky.* 1956. NY. Ils. 389 p. dj. VG. T5. $17.50

MANSFIELD, J.C. *Kit Carson.* 1933. World Syndicate. VG. P1. $11.50

MANTLEY, John. *27th Day.* nd. Book Club. VG. P1. $3.00

MANVELL, Roger. *Dreamers.* 1957. Simon Schuster. 1st ed. clipped dj. EX. F5. $35.00

MAPPLETHORPE, Robert. *Lady Lisa Lyons.* 1983. Viking. HrdCvr ed. dj. EX. K2. $350.00

MAPPLETHORPE, Robert. *Lady Lisa Lyons.* 1983. Viking. 1st HrdCvr ed. inscr/sgn. dj. EX. B13. $1250.00

MAPPLETHORPE, Robert. *Power of Theatrical Madness.* nd. (1986) np. photos. dj. EX. K2. $125.00

MARAINI, Fosco. *Meeting With Japan.* 1959. Viking. 467 p. dj. EX. B10. $6.25

MARAT, J.P. *Polish Letters.* 1904. Boston. Bibliophile Soc. 1/461. 8vo. VG. T6. $55.00

MARBLE, M.S. *Lady Forgot.* 1947. Harper. 1st ed. dj. EX. F5. $16.00

MARCH, Carl. *Magic Made Easy.* 1953. Croydon Pub. 1st ed. 96 p. EX. J3. $4.00

MARCH, J.M. *Set-Up.* 1928. Covici Friede. Ltd ed. 1/275. sgn. H3. $75.00

MARCONICK. *Orig Magic 3.* nd. Amsterdam. Mephisto Huis. 1st ed. dj. NM. J3. $11.00

MARCONICK. *Orig Magic.* 1967. Brussels. Klingsor. 1st ed. 200 p. dj. NM. J3. $22.00

MARCOSSON, I.F. *Autobiography of a Clown.* 1910. NY. Moffat Yard. 1st ed. sm octavo. 102 p. G. H3. $85.00

MARCOSSON, Isaac. *Copper Heritage.* 1955. Dodd. 254 p. dj. EX. B10. $7.25

MARCOSSON, Isaac. *Industrial Main St.* 1953. Dodd Mead. apparent 1st ed. 220 p. dj. EX. B10. $5.00

MARCUS, Joyce. *Debating Oaxaca Archaeology.* 1990. Ann Arbor. Mus Antropology No 84. 270 p. wrp. F2. $25.00

MARCUS, Joyce. *Inscr of Calakmul.* 1987. Ann Arbor. Ils. 4to. 205 p. wrp. F2. $20.00

MARCUS, Joyce. *Later Intermediate Occupation at Cerro Azul, Peru.* 1987. Anthro Mus. 1st ed. 4to. 112 p. wrp. F2. $20.00

MARDEN, William. *Exile of Ellendon.* 1974. Doubleday. 1st ed. dj. EX. R3. $20.00

MARETT, Robert. *Peru.* 1969. Praeger. 1st ed. dj. xl. F2. $10.00

MARGOLIES, Joseph. *Strange & Fantastic Stories.* 1946. Whittlesey House. 1st ed. dj. EX. R3. $35.00

MARGOLIS, W.J. *Eucalyptus Poems.* 1974. Croupier. EX. B4. $10.00

MARGUERITE, Henry. *Album of Dogs.* 1970. Rand McNally. Ils Wesley Dennis. 4to. 64 p. VG. $22.00

MARGULIES, Leo. *Master Mystery Stories.* 1945. Hampton. VG. P1. $25.00

MARINARO, V.C. *Modern Dry-Fly Code.* 1950. Putnam. Ils Pearce Bates. dj. VG. $75.00

MARK, Jan. *Ennead.* 1978. Crowell. 1st ed. dj. EX. P1. $10.00

MARKHAM, Beryl. *W With the Night.* 1942. Boston. 1st ed. dj. VG. B3. $45.00

MARKHAM, C.R. *Incas of Peru.* 1912. London. 3rd imp. 443 p. F2. $40.00

MARKHAM, Charles. *Pre-Hispanic Settlement Dynamics in Central Oaxaca, Mexico.* 1981. Vanderbilt U. wrp. F2. $15.00

MARKHAM, Edwin. *Lincoln & Other Poems.* 1908. McClure. early ed. sgn. TEG. gilt gr bdg. H3. $125.00

MARKHAM, Edwin. *Man With the How & Other Poems.* 1913. Doubleday Page. early ed. inscr. G. H3. $50.00

MARKHAM, Edwin. *New Poems: 80 Songs at 80/5th Book of Verse.* 1932. Doubleday Doran. sgn. H3. $20.00

MARKHAM, Edwin. *Shoes of Happiness & Other Poems.* 1915. Doubleday Page. inscr. VG. H3. $40.00

MARKHAM, Robert. *Colonel Sun.* 1968. Harper Row. 1st ed. dj. VG. P1. $35.00

MARKHAM, Robert. *Colonel Sun.* 1968. Jonathan Cape. 1st ed. dj. EX. P1. $35.00

MARKHAM, Sidney. *Colonial Architecture of Antigua, Guatemala.* 1966. Am Philosophical Soc. Ltd 1st ed. lg 4to. dj. F2. $50.00

MARKHAM, Sidney. *Colonial Central Am: A Bibliography.* 1977. Tempe. 1st ed. 245 p. F2. $30.00

MARKHAM, Virgil. *Inspector Rusby's Finale.* 1933. Farrar Rinehart. 1st ed. xl. P1. $7.50

MARKS, Alexander. *Jubilee Vol.* 1950. NY. octavo. 667 p. EX. $45.00

MARKS, Jamake; see Highwater, Jamake.

MARKS, Jeanette. *Willow Pollen.* 1921. Boston. 4 Seas. 1st ed. 90 p. B10. $7.50

MARKS, Percy. *Dead Man Dies.* 1929. Century. 351 p. dj. VG. B10. $3.25

MARKS-HIGHWATER, Jamake; see Highwater, Jamake.

MARKSTEIN, George. *Chance Awakening.* 1978. Ballantine. 1st ed. dj. EX. P1. $20.00

MARKUS, Julia. *La Mora.* 1976. Decatur House. 1st ed. 1/1000. wrp. EX. K2. $30.00

MARKUS, Julia. *Patron of the Arts in 2 Novellas.* 1977. Cambridge. Apple Wood Pr. 1st ed. wrp. EX. K2. $25.00

MARLO, Ed. *Cardician.* 1977. Chicago. Magic Inc. 5th print. 199 p. VG. J3. $8.00

MARLO, Ed. *Deck Decetpion.* 1942. Chicago. Ireland. 1st ed. 24 p. SftCvr. EX. J3. $7.00

MARLO, Ed. *Ed Marlo on the Acrobatic Cards.* 1968. Magic Inc. 1st ed. sgn. SftCvr. EX. J3. $8.00

MARLO, Ed. *Ed Marlo on the Acrobatic Cards.* 1981. Magic Inc. 3rd print. SftCvr. M. J3. $4.50

MARLO, Ed. *Faro Controlled Miracles.* 1964. Chicago. Marlo. Ltd ed. inscr. 71 p. NM. J3. $50.00

MARLO, Ed. *Magic 7.* 1954. Chicago. Ireland. 1st print. 23 p. SftCvr. NM. J3. $7.00

MARLOW, Lewis. *Welsh Ambassadors.* 1975. (1st 1936) Quality PB. NM. C1. $6.50

MARLOWE, Derek. *Echoes of Celandine.* 1970. Viking. dj. xl. P1. $5.00

MARLOWE, Piers. *Knife for Your Heart.* 1966. John Gifford. dj. VG. P1. $12.50

MARLOWE, Piers. *Men in Her Death.* 1964. Thriller Book Club. xl. P1. $4.00

MARLOWE, Stephen. *Cawthorn Journals.* 1975. Prentice Hall. 1st ed. dj. xl. P1. $5.00

MARLOWE, Stephen. *Man With No Shadow.* nd. Prentice Hall. 2nd ed. dj. EX. P1. $15.00

MARLOWE, Stephen. *Search for Bruno Heidler.* 1966. Macmillan. 3rd ed. dj. VG. P1. $12.50

MARLOWE, Stephen. *Search for Bruno Heidler.* 1967. Boardman. 1st ed. dj. EX. P1. $20.00

MARLOWE, Stephen. *1956.* 1981. Arbor House. 1st ed. dj. VG. P1. $15.00

MARPLES, Richard. *Encyclopedia of the Dog.* 1985. London. 1st ed. 192 p. B10. $8.50

MARQUAND, J.P. *Mr Moto Is So Sorry.* 1938. Little Brn. 1st ed. dj. EX. $85.00

MARQUAND, J.P. *Thank You Mr Moto.* nd. Herbert Jenkins. 3rd ed. dj. VG. P1. $17.50

MARQUEZ, G.G. *El Amor en los Tiempos del Colera.* 1985. Bogota. True 1st ed. Spanish text. dj. EX. T9. $65.00

MARQUEZ LOPEZ, J.M. *Mused Arqueologico de Tikal.* 1988. Guatemala. 4to. 18 p. wrp. F2. $15.00

MARQUIS, Don. *Dreams & Dust.* 1915. NY. 1st ed. VG. $20.00

MARQUIS, Don. *Out of the Sea.* 1927. 1st ed. scarce. C1. $22.50

MARQUIS, Don. *Sun Dial Time.* 1936. Doubleday Doran. 1st ed. dj. G. $40.00

MARRIC, J.J. *Gideon's Lot.* nd. Book Club. dj. VG. P1. $4.50

MARRIC, J.J. *Gideon's Power.* nd. Book Club. dj. VG. P1. $4.50

MARRIC, J.J. *Gideon's River.* 1968. Harper Book Club. dj. B10. $3.25

MARRIC, J.J. *Gideon's River.* 1968. Harper Row. 1st ed. dj. VG. P1. $15.00

MARRIC, J.J. *Gideon's Staff.* nd. Book Club. dj. VG. P1. $4.50

MARRIC, J.J. *Gideon's Vote.* nd. Book Club. dj. VG. P1. $4.50

MARRIC, J.J. *Gideon's Wrath.* nd. Book Club. dj. VG. P1. $4.50

MARRIOTT, Crittenden. *Isle of Dead Ships.* 1925. Lippincott. dj. VG. P1/R3. $30.00

MARRYAT, Frank. *Diary in Am.* 1839. London. Longman. 3 vols. VG. A5. $75.00

MARRYAT, Frank. *Mts & Molehills; or, Reflections of a Burnt Journal...* 1855. London. 1st ed. 8 pls not in Am ed. EX. H3. $850.00

MARRYAT, Frank. *Pacha of Many Tales.* 1873. Appleton. VG. R3. $25.00

MARSH, Howard. *Adventure's a Wench.* 1934. NY. 1st ed. 340 p. VG. T5. $32.50

MARSH, J.B.T. *Story of the Jubilee Singers.* 1892. Cleveland Print. octavo. 311 p. VG. H3. $85.00

MARSH, J.R. *4 Years in the Rockies; or, Adventures of Isaac P Rose.* 1884. New Castle, PA. 1st ed. 12mo. 262 p. VG. T1. $325.00

MARSH, John. *Brain of Paul Menoloff.* 1953. Forbes Robertson. 1st ed. xl. P1. $5.00

MARSH, Ngaio. *Artists in Crime.* 1938. Geoffrey Bles. 1st ed. VG. P1. $40.00

MARSH, Ngaio. *Blk As He's Painted.* 1974. Collins Crime Club. 1st ed. dj. VG. P1. $15.00

MARSH, Ngaio. *Clr Scheme.* 1943. Collins. 1st ed. VG. P1. $12.50

MARSH, Ngaio. *Death in a Wht Tie.* 1938. Geoffrey Bles. VG. P1. $35.00

MARSH, Ngaio. *Final Curtain.* 1947. Little Brn. 1st ed. VG. P1. $25.00

MARSH, Ngaio. *Grave Mistake.* 1978. Little Brn. 693 p. dj. NM. B10. $3.50

MARSH, Ngaio. *Hand in Glove.* 1962. Collins Crime Club. dj. VG. P1. $25.00

MARSH, Ngaio. *Man Lay Dead.* 1934. Geoffrey Bles. 1st ed. VG. P1. $45.00

MARSH, Ngaio. *Off With His Head.* 1957. Collins Crime Club. dj. VG. P1. $30.00

MARSH, Ngaio. *Singing in the Shrouds.* 1959. Collins Crime Club. dj. VG. P1. $25.00

MARSH, Ngaio. *Spinsters in Jeopardy.* 1980. Collins Crime Club. 2nd ed. dj. EX. P1. $12.50

MARSH, Ngaio. *Tied Up in Tinsel.* 1972. Collins Crime Club. 1st ed. dj. VG. P1. $20.00

MARSH, Ngaio. *Vintage Murder.* 1972. Little Brn. 1st Am ed. dj. EX. T9. $35.00

MARSH, T.W. *Early Friends in Surrey & Sussex.* 1886. London. S Harris. 8vo. 162 p. V1. $18.00

MARSHAL, Edison. *W With the Vikings.* 1961. 1st ed. dj. EX. C1. $8.50

MARSHALL, Donald; see Westlake, D.E.

MARSHALL, Edison. *Deadfall.* 1927. Cosmopolitan. 1st ed. dj. EX. R3. $20.00

MARSHALL, Edison. *Deadfall.* 1927. Cosmopolitan. 1st ed. EX. F5. $15.00

MARSHALL, Edison. *Earth Giant.* 1960. Doubleday. 1st ed. dj. EX. R3. $37.50

MARSHALL, Edison. *Ogden's Strange Secret.* nd. AL Burt. dj. VG. R3. $25.00

MARSHALL, Edison. *Ogden's Strange Secret.* 1934. Kinsey. 1st ed. VG. R3. $25.00

MARSHALL, Edison. *Pagan King.* nd. Book Club. dj. VG. C1. $10.00

MARSHALL, Edison. *Viking.* 1951. Farrar. 1st ed. dj. VG. F5. $16.00

MARSHALL, Edison. *Yankee Pasha.* nd. Book Club. dj. EX. P1. $3.75

MARSHALL, Frances. *Bunny Book for Magicians.* 1985. Magic Inc. 2nd print. 125 p. cbdg. M. J3. $10.00

MARSHALL, Paule. *Praise Song for the Widow.* 1983. Putnam. UP. inscr. wrp. VG. $250.00

MARSHALL, Raymond. *In a Vain Shadow.* 1951. Jarrolds. 1st ed. dj. VG. P1. $25.00

MARSHALL, S.L.A. *Bastogne: Story of 1st 8 Days.* 1946. WA. Ils 1st ed. inscr. 261 p. G. T5. $37.50

MARSHALL, William. *Far Away Man.* 1984. Holt Rinehart Winston. 1st ed. dj. VG. P1. $14.95

MARSHALL, William. *Head 1st.* 1986. Holt. 1st ed. dj. VG. P1. $14.95

MARSHALL, William. *Out of Nowhere.* 1988. Mysterious Pr. 1st ed. dj. EX. F5/P1. $16.00

MARSHALL, William. *Road Show.* 1985. Holt Rinehart Winston. 1st ed. dj. EX. P1. $15.00

MARSHALL, William. *SF.* 1981. Holt Rinehart Winston. 1st ed. dj. EX. P1. $17.50

MARSHALL, William. *Thin Air.* 1977. Hamish Hamilton. 1st ed. dj. RS. EX. P1. $30.00

MARSHALL, William. *Thin Air.* 1977. Hamish Hamilton. 1st Eng ed. dj. EX. T9. $25.00

MARSHALL & MARSHALL. *Success Book Vol 4.* 1984. Magic Inc. 1st print. 233 p. NM. J3. $16.00

MARSHALL & STOCK. *Ira Aldridge.* 1958. Macmillan. 1st ed. octavo. 355 p. dj. EX. H3. $75.00

MARSHALL. *My 50 Years of Chess.* 1942. NY. Ltd ed. inscr. VG. C2. $65.00

MARSHE, Richard. *Panama Apassionata.* 1951. Woodford Pr. 1st ed. dj. EX. F5. $20.00

MARSHE, Richard. *Wicked Woman.* 1950. Woodford Pr. 1st ed. dj. EX. F5. $22.00

MARSON, G.F. *Ghosts, Ghouls, & Gallows.* 1946. Rider. 1st ed. dj. VG. P1. $25.00

MARSTALLER, L.S. *Ebb & Flow.* 1935. Nicholson. sgn. 77 p. VG. B10. $5.75

MARSTEN, Richard. *Rocket to Luna.* 1953. Winston. 1st ed. VG. R3. $10.00

MARSTEN, Richard. *Spiked Heel.* 1956. Holt. 1st ed. VG. P1. $25.00

MARTEL, Suzanne. *City Under Ground.* 1964. Viking. 1st ed. dj. VG. P1. $20.00

MARTENS, F.H. *Violin Mastery.* 1919. Stokes. 1st ed. 282 p. H3. $50.00

MARTIN, A.E. *Sinners Never Die.* 1944. Simon Schuster. VG. P1. $10.00

MARTIN, E.S. *Luxury of Children & Some Other Luxuries.* 1904. NY. Ils Stilwell. TEG. VG. A4. $30.00

MARTIN, Edgar. *Boots & the Mystery of Unlucky Vas.* 1943. Whitman. VG. P1. $7.00

MARTIN, Franklin. *S Am From a Surgeon's Point of View.* 1922. NY. Revell. 1st ed. 325 p. F2. $25.00

MARTIN, G.R.R. *Armageddon Rag.* 1983. Nemo Pr. Ltd ed. 1/500. sgn. slipcase. M. R3. $50.00

MARTIN, G.R.R. *Armageddon Rag.* 1983. Poseidon. 1st ed. dj. EX. P1. $20.00

MARTIN, G.R.R. *Dying of the Light.* 1978. London. 1st Eng ed. sgn. dj. EX. R3. $50.00

MARTIN, G.R.R. *New Voices in SF.* 1977. Macmillan. 1st ed. dj. xl. P1. $5.00

MARTIN, H.T. *Castorologia: Hist & Traditions of Canadian Beaver.* 1892. London. Stanford. VG. T3. $85.00

MARTIN, Isaac. *Journal of Life, Travels, Labors, & Religious Exercises.* 1834. Phil. WP Gibbons. 12mo. 160 p. leather. V1. $26.00

MARTIN, J.S. *General Manpower.* 1938. Simon Schuster. 1st ed. dj. EX. R3. $22.50

MARTIN, Malachi. *3 Popes & the Cardinal.* 1972. NY. 1st print. dj. VG. $15.00

MARTIN, Percy. *Mexico's Treasure House (Guanajuato).* 1906. Cheltenham Pr. 1st ed. pls. 259 p. F2. $45.00

MARTIN, Pete. *Marilyn Monroe.* 1956. London. 1st ed. photos. 110 p. VG. $50.00

MARTIN, Pete. *Will Acting Spoil Marilyn Monroe?* 1956. Doubleday. 1st ed. dj. K1. $30.00

MARTIN, Pete. *Will Acting Spoil Marilyn Monroe?* 1956. NY. 1st ed. dj. EX. B3. $50.00

MARTIN, Steve. *Cruel Shoes.* 1979. Putnam. presentation. 128 p. dj. EX. H3. $75.00

MARTIN, Stuart. *Hangman's Guests.* 1931. Harper. 1st ed. xl. G. P1. $4.00

MARTIN, Stuart. *Trial of Scotland Yard.* 1930. Harper. VG. P1. $6.00

MARTIN, Stuart. *15 Cells.* 1928. Harper. 3rd ed. G. P1. $4.00

MARTIN & TUTTLE. *Windhaven.* 1981. Timescape. 1st ed. dj. EX. P1. $20.00

MARTIN. *50 Years of Am Golf.* 1936. NY. 1st ed. 423 p. VG. C2. $195.00

MARTIN. *50 Years of Lawn Tennis in the US.* 1931. NY. Ltd ed. 1/3000. 256 p. VG. C2. $125.00

MARTINEAU, Harriet. *Life in the Wilds; or, The S African Settlement.* 1843. Hartford. 24mo. 177 p. V1. $45.00

MARTINEK, F.V. *Don Winslow & Scorpion's Stronghold.* 1946. Whitman. Ils. VG. P1. $7.50

MARTINENGO-CESARESCO, Evelyn. *Essays in Study of Folk Songs.* 1886. George Redway. 1st ed. octavo. 395 p. H3. $75.00

MARTINEZ, Al. *Jigsaw John.* 1975. Tarcher. 1st ed. dj. EX. P1. $15.00

MARTINEZ, Daryl. *Daryl's Rope Routine.* 1987. Anaheim. Martinez. 1st ed. SftCvr. NM. J3. $8.00

MARTYN, Wyndham. *Return of Anthony Trent.* 1925. Barse Hopkins. VG. P1. $15.00

MARTYN, Wyndham. *Secret of the Silver Car.* nd. Grosset. dj. B10. $4.25

MARVEL, I. *Dream Life.* 1852. NY. TEG. EX. $35.00

MARVEL, Ike. *Dream Life.* c 1910. Hurst. 265 p. VG. B10. $3.50

MARVIN, C. *Training the Trotting Horse.* 1892. NY. 4th ed. VG. scarce. K1. $75.00

MARWUIS, Don. *Out of the Sea.* 1927. NY. 1st ed. VG. C1. $19.00

MARX, Groucho. *Many Happy Returns.* 1942. NY. 1st ed. VG. B3. $25.00

MARX, Groucho. *Memoirs of a Mangy Lover.* 1963. NY. 1st ed. dj. VG. B3. $25.00

MARX & BARBER. *Harpo Speaks!* 1961. Geis. 1st ed. 475 p. VG. H3. $50.00

MARZIO. *Demographic Art.* 1979. Godine. Ils. 358 p. A5. $60.00

MASARIK, Al. *Invitation to a Dying.* 1972. Vagabond. 1/1000. B4. $5.00

MASEFIELD, John. *Book of Discoveries.* nd. Stokes. Ils Gordon Browne. TEG. VG. $25.00

MASEFIELD, John. *Chaucer.* 1931. Cambridge. inscr. H3. $100.00

MASEFIELD, John. *Coming of Christ.* 1928. Macmillan. 1st ed. 1/350. sgn. boxed. H3. $35.00

MASEFIELD, John. *Esther & Berenice.* 1922. NY. 1st ed. VG. $10.00

MASEFIELD, John. *Jim Davis.* 1932. Nelson. 1st ed. 242 p. EX. B10. $20.00

MASEFIELD, John. *Melloney Holtspur; or, The Pangs of Love.* 1922. Macmillan. 1/1000. sgn. H3. $15.00

MASEFIELD, John. *Midnight Folk.* 1927. London. 1st ed. VG. C1. $12.50

MASEFIELD, John. *Midnight Folk.* 1959. Heinemann. 2nd ed. xl. VG. P1. $10.00

MASEFIELD, John. *Midsummer Night.* 1928. NY. 1st Am ed. VG. C1. $12.50

MASEFIELD, John. *Minnie Maylow's Story.* 1931. London. 1st UK ed. dj. EX. C1. $12.50

MASEFIELD, John. *Minnie Maylow's Story.* 1931. NY. 1st Am ed. xl. C1. $5.00

MASEFIELD, John. *Odtaa.* 1926. Macmillan. 2nd ed. 416 p. dj. EX. B10. $10.00

MASEFIELD, John. *Reynard the Fox.* 1919. Macmillan. 1st ed. 166 p. VG. B10. $10.00

MASEFIELD, John. *Sara Harker.* 1924. Macmillan. 1st ed. 412 p. red bdg. VG. B10. $6.50

MASEFIELD, John. *Taking of Helen.* 1923. NY. Ltd ed. sgn. boxed. EX. $45.00

MASEFIELD, John. *Tristan & Isolt.* 1927. NY. 1st Am ed. xl. G. C1. $7.50

MASKELYNE & DEVANT. *Our Magic.* 1911. Dutton. 1st ed. 487 p. EX. J3. $80.00

MASKELYNE & DEVANT. *Our Magic.* 1946. Fleming Book. 2nd ed. 318 p. EX. J3. $14.00

MASON, A.E.W. *Courtship of Morrice Buckler.* nd. Grayson. VG. P1. $7.50

MASON, A.E.W. *Courtship of Morrice Buckler.* 1973. Tom Stacey. dj. EX. P1. $12.50

MASON, A.E.W. *House in Lordship Lane.* 1946. Dodd Mead. xl. P1. $10.00

MASON, A.E.W. *Truants.* 1904. Harper. 1st ed. 378 p. B10. $6.00

MASON, A.E.W. *3 Gentlemen.* 1932. Doubleday. 1st ed. VG. R3. $20.00

MASON, A.E.W. *3 Gentlemen.* 1946. Dodd Mead. VG. P1. $10.00

MASON, A.L. *Romance & Tragedy of Pioneer Life.* 1883. Cincinnati. 1st ed. 1032 p. T5. $95.00

MASON, A.T. *Brandeis: A Free Man's Life.* 1946. Viking. 1st ed. tall 8vo. VG. B10. $7.50

MASON, B.A. *In Country.* 1985. Harper Row. ARC. inscr. dj. RS. EX. K2. $85.00

MASON, B.A. *Love Life.* 1989. Chatto Windus. 1st Eng ed. sgn. dj. EX. K2. $50.00

MASON, B.A. *Nabokov's Garden.* 1974. Ann Arbor. Ardis. 1st HrdCvr ed. dj. EX. K2. $125.00

MASON, B.A. *Shiloh & Other Stories.* 1982. Harper Row. 1st ed. dj. EX. B13. $75.00

MASON, B.A. *Shiloh & Other Stories.* 1982. Harper Row. 1st ed. K2. $60.00

MASON, B.A. *Spence & Lila.* 1988. Chatto Windus. 1st Eng ed. sgn. dj. EX. K2. $50.00

MASON, B.S. *Dances & Stories of the Am Indian.* 1944. NY. 1st ed. dj. VG. $40.00

MASON, Bernard. *Active Games & Contests.* 1937. Barnes. tall 8vo. VG. B10. $4.00

MASON, Charles. *Uncle Tom & Andy Bill.* 1908. NY. 1st ed. VG. B3. $42.50

MASON, D.R. *Phaeton Condition.* 1973. Putnam. 1st ed. dj. EX. P1. $15.00

MASON, Eugene. *Arthurian Chronicles Represented by Wace & Layamon.* c 1910. Everymans ed. C1. $12.00

MASON, F.V.W. *Armored Giants.* 1980. Little Brn. 1st ed. dj. VG. S1. $7.00

MASON, F.V.W. *Cutlass Empire.* 1949. Doubleday. not Book Club ed. 396 p. dj. VG. B10. $3.75

MASON, Gregory. *Columbus Came Late.* 1931. Century. 1st ed. 341 p. F2. $25.00

MASON, Gregory. *S of Yesterday.* 1940. Holt. 1st ed. 401 p. F2. $30.00

MASON, H.M. *Lafayette Escadrille.* 1964. NY. 1st ed. dj. VG. $20.00

MASON, Hilary. *Morisco.* 1979. Atheneum. 1st ed. dj. EX. F5. $16.00

MASON, J.A. *Tepecano: Piman Language of W Mexico.* 1917. NY Academy of Science. wrp. F2. $20.00

MASON, Jackie. *Jackie Mason From Birth to Rebirth.* 1988. Little Brn. 1st ed. dj. NM. J3. $12.00

MASON, James. *Art of Chess.* 1905. London. Ils 3rd ed. 459 p. G. T5. $35.00

MASON, John. *Treatise on Self-Knowledge.* 1813. Montpelier. 24mo. 194 p. G. G4. $21.00

MASON, O.T. *Aboriginal Am Basketry: Studies in Textile Art...* 1904. WA. 1st ed. 248 pls. NM. $100.00

MASON, V.W. *Bl Hurricane.* nd. Book Club. dj. VG. P1. $4.50

MASON, V.W. *Bl Hurricane.* 1955. Jarrolds. 1st ed. dj. VG. P1. $7.50

MASON, V.W. *Budapest Parade Murders.* 1935. Crime Club. 1st ed. VG. P1. $22.50

MASON, V.W. *Saigon Singer.* nd. Book Club. dj. VG. P1. $4.50

MASON, V.W. *Saigon Singer.* 1946. Doubleday. 1st ed. VG. P1. $7.50

MASON, V.W. *Seeds of Murder.* 1930. Crime Club. 1st ed. VG. P1. $15.00

MASON, V.W. *Spider House.* 1932. Mystery League. 1st ed. VG. P1. $12.50

MASON, V.W. *Trouble in Burma.* 1962. Doubleday. 1st ed. VG. P1. $7.50

MASON, V.W. *Trouble in Burma.* 1963. Robert Hale. 1st ed. dj. VG. P1. $12.50

MASON, V.W. *WA Legation Murders.* 1936. Crime Club. VG. P1. $20.00

MASON, William. *Spiritual Treasury for Children of God. Vol 1.* 1819. New Brunswick. Terhune. 4th Am ed. 384 p. G. B10. $7.75

MASON & GIPSON. *Castle Island Case.* 1938. Reynal Hitchcock. 1st ed. VG. P1. $30.00

MASON. *Primitive Travel & Transportation.* 1894. US Nat Mus. 300 p. A5. $50.00

MASSEY, E.M. *New & Orig Magic.* 1922. Spon Chamberlain. 1st ed. 200 p. EX. J3. $50.00

MASSIE, Chris. *Gr Circle.* 1944. Tower. xl. P1. $5.00

MASSINGER, Philip. *Plays of Philip Massinger With Notes...* 1857. NY. Mahn. New Complete 1-vol ed. contemporary sheep. H3. $45.00

MASTERMAN, W.S. *Gr Toad.* 1929. Dutton. 1st ed. VG. P1. $25.00

MASTERMAN, W.S. *Mystery of 52.* nd. Dutton Clue Mystery. 286 p. G. B10. $3.50

MASTERMAN, W.S. *2 L O.* nd. Mckinley Stone/Mackenzie. VG. P1. $7.00

MASTERS, E.L. *Songs & Satires.* 1916. 1st reprint ed. VG. C1. $4.50

MASTERS, E.L. *Spoon River Anthology.* 1918. Macmillan. Ils. VG. $55.00

MASTERS, John. *Bugles & a Tiger.* 1956. Viking Book Club. Ils. 312 p. dj. VG. B10. $4.00

MASTERSON, Whit. *Evil Come, Evil Go.* nd. Book Club. dj. VG. P1. $4.50

MASTERSON, Whit. *Evil Come, Evil Go.* 1961. Dodd Mead. 1st ed. dj. EX. F5. $20.00

MASTERSON, Whit. *Evil Come, Evil Go.* 1961. Dodd Mead. 1st ed. dj. xl. P1. $7.50

MASTERSON, Whit. *Last 1 Kills.* 1969. Dodd Mead. dj. VG. P1. $20.00

MASTERSON, Whit. *Man on a Nylon String.* 1963. Dodd Mead. 1st ed. dj. xl. P1. $7.50

MASTERTON, Graham. *Mirror.* 1988. Tor Books. 1st ed. dj. EX. F5. $16.00

MASUR, H.Q. *Broker.* 1981. Souvenir Pr. 1st ed. dj. EX. P1. $15.00

MATEAUX, Clara. *Noble Lives & Brave Deeds.* c 1900-1910. McLoughlin. 148 p. G. B10. $5.25

MATHER, Arthur. *Mind Breaker.* 1980. Delacorte. 1st Am ed. dj. VG. F5. $11.00

MATHER, Berkley. *Road & the Star.* 1965. Scribner. 1st ed. dj. EX. F5. $15.00

MATHERS, E.P. *Red Wise.* 1926. Golden Cockerel. Ils Robert Gibbings. 1/500. dj. EX. C4. $75.00

MATHERS, E.P. *7 Voyages of Sinbad the Sailor.* 1949. Heritage Pr. Ils Edward Wilson. slipcase. T1. $20.00

MATHES, W.M. *Conquistador in CA.* 1973. Dawson Bookshop. Ltd ed. 1/500. 123 p. F2. $35.00

MATHESON, John. *Needle in the Haystack.* 1930. Jr Literary Guild. Ils D'Aulaire. 4to. EX. scarce. $50.00

MATHESON, R.C. *Scars.* 1987. Scream. 1st ed. sgn. M. R3. $30.00

MATHESON, Richard. *Beardless Warriors.* 1960. Little Brn. 1st ed. later state. dj. EX. F5. $20.00

MATHESON, Richard. *Born of Man & Woman.* 1954. Chamberlain. 1st ed. dj. EX. R3. $175.00

MATHESON, Richard. *Earthbound.* 1989. Robinson. dj. EX. P1. $30.00

MATHESON, Richard. *Hell House.* 1971. Viking. 1st ed. dj. VG. R3. $150.00

MATHESON, Richard. *I Am Legend.* nd. Book Club. dj. EX. P1. $10.00

MATHESON, Richard. *I Am Legend.* 1954. Fawcett. 1st ed. wrp. VG. R3. $25.00

MATHESON, Richard. *I Am Legend.* 1954. Gold Medal 417. 1st ed. wrp. VG. T9. $55.00

MATHESON, Richard. *I Am Legend.* 1954. NY. PB Orig. sgn. EX. T9. $65.00

MATHESON, Richard. *I Am Legend.* 1970. Walker. 1st HrdCvr ed. dj. xl. EX. R3. $50.00

MATHESON, Richard. *Ride the Nightmare.* 1959. Ballantine 301K. 1st ed. sgn. wrp. VG. T9. $40.00

MATHESON, Richard. *Stir of Echoes.* 1958. Lippincott. 1st ed. G. R3. $25.00

MATHESON, Richard. *What Dreams May Come.* 1978. Putnam. 1st ed. dj. VG. P1. $75.00

MATHESON, Richard. *What Dreams May Come.* 1978. Putnam. 1st ed. dj. xl. P1. $25.00

MATHEWS, D.L. *Very Welcome Death.* 1961. Holt Rinehart Winston. 1st ed. P1. $7.50

MATHEWS, J. *Talking to the Moon.* 1945. Chicago. 1st ed. dj. VG. B3. $17.50

MATHEWS, J.J. *Wah'Kon-Tah, Osage & Wht Man's Road.* 1932. OK U. 1st ed. 8vo. VG. B10. $5.50

MATHIAS, Fred. *Amazing Bob Davis.* 1944. NY. Longman. 1st ed. 326 p. dj. F2. $15.00

MATHIS, Edward. *Natural Prey.* 1987. Scribner. 1st ed. dj. EX. P1. $15.95

MATNARD, Theodore. *Too Sm a World: Life of Francesca Cabrini.* nd. (1945) Bruce. Probably 1st ed. B10. $5.25

MATOS MOCTEZUMA, Eduardo. *Great Temple of the Aztecs.* 1988. Thames Hudson. 1st ed. sm 4to. dj. F2. $32.50

MATOS MOCTEZUMA, Eduardo. *Teotihacan.* 1990. Rizzoli. 1st ed. lg 4to. dj. F2. $75.00

MATOS MOCTEZUMA, Eduardo. *Treasures of the Great Temple.* 1990. La Jolla. 1st ed. lg 4to. 180 p. F2. $40.00

MATSCHAT, C.H. *Murder at the Blk Crook.* 1943. Farrar Rinehart. 1st ed. xl. P1. $10.00

MATSCHAT, Cecile. *7 Grass Huts.* 1939. Literary Guild. Ils. 281 p. F2. $12.50

MATTES, Merrill. *Indians, Infants, & Infantry.* 1960. Denver. Ils. 304 p. A5. $40.00

MATTHEW, J.E. *Literature of Music.* 1896. London. Stock. 1st ed. octavo. 281 p. VG. H3. $25.00

MATTHEWS, Brander. *Tales of Fantasy & Fact.* 1896. Harper. 1st ed. VG. R3. $30.00

MATTHEWS, Caitlin. *Arthur & the Sovereignty of Britain.* nd. Arkana. 1st ed. PB. M. C1. $10.00

MATTHEWS, Caitlin. *Elements of the Goddess.* Eng PB. True 1st ed. M. C1. $10.00

MATTHEWS, Cornelius. *Poems on Man in His Various Aspects Under Am Republic.* 1843. Wiley Putnam. inscr. G. C4. $150.00

MATTHEWS, Cornelius. *Various Writings of Cornelius Matthews. Complete in 1 Vol.* 1843. Harper. 1st ed. 8vo. inscr. VG. C4. $150.00

MATTHEWS, Harry. *Sinking of the Odradek Stadium.* 1975. Harper. 1st ed. dj. EX. R3. $20.00

MATTHEWS, Jack. *Bitter Knowledge.* 1964. NY. 1st ed. sgn. dj. EX. T9. $45.00

MATTHEWS, John. *Arthurian Reader.* 1988. London. 1st ed. sgn. dj. M. C1. $22.00

MATTHEWS, John. *Gawain: Knight of the Goddess, Restoring an Archtype.* 1990. London. 1st ed. dj. M. C1. $20.00

MATTHEWS, John. *Merlin in Calydon.* 1981. Hunting Raven Pr. 1/300. sgn. M. C1. $27.50

MATTHEWS & CLAYTON. *Midnight Whispers.* nd. Book Club. dj. VG. P1. $4.50

MATTHEWS & POLLACK. *Tarot Tales.* 1989. London. 1st ed. sgn. M. C1. $15.00

MATTHEWS & STEWART. *Warriors of Arthur.* 1987. London. 1st ed. dj. M. C1. $19.00

MATTHIESSEN, F.O. *Henry James: Stories of Writers & Artists.* nd. New Directions. 346 p. EX. B10. $4.50

MATTHIESSEN, F.O. *Trans: An Elizabethan Art.* 1931. Cambridge. Harvard. 1st ed. dj. EX. C4. $30.00

MATTHIESSEN, Peter. *At Play in the Fields of the Lord.* 1965. Random House. ARC. EX. C4. $85.00

MATTHIESSEN, Peter. *At Play in the Fields of the Lord.* 1965. Random House. 1st ed. dj. EX. K2. $65.00

MATTHIESSEN, Peter. *At Play in the Fields of the Lord.* 1965. Random House. 1st ed. sgn. dj. EX. K2. $125.00

MATTHIESSEN, Peter. *Cloud Forest.* 1961. NY. 1st ed. dj. EX. $85.00

MATTHIESSEN, Peter. *Cloud Forest.* 1962. London. Deutsch. 1st ed. sgn. dj. EX. B13. $100.00

MATTHIESSEN, Peter. *Far Tortuga.* 1975. Random House. 1st ed. dj. EX. K2. $40.00

MATTHIESSEN, Peter. *In the Spirit of Crazy Horse.* 1983. NY. 1st ed. dj. EX. B3. $105.00

MATTHIESSEN, Peter. *In the Spirit of Crazy Horse.* 1983. NY. 1st ed. dj. VG. B3. $85.00

MATTHIESSEN, Peter. *In the Spirit of Crazy Horse.* 1983. Viking. UP of 1st ed. wrp. EX. very scarce. K2. $450.00

MATTHIESSEN, Peter. *Indian Country.* 1984. Viking. AP. K2. $150.00

MATTHIESSEN, Peter. *Indian Country.* 1984. Viking. UP. wrp. EX. C4. $125.00

MATTHIESSEN, Peter. *Indian Country.* 1984. Viking. 1st ed. dj. EX. K2. $45.00

MATTHIESSEN, Peter. *Indian Country.* 1985. London. Collins Harvill. 1st Eng ed. dj. EX. K2. $45.00

MATTHIESSEN, Peter. *Killing Mr Watson.* 1989. Viking. UP. wrp. EX. C4. $125.00

MATTHIESSEN, Peter. *Killing Mr Watson.* 1990. Random House. 1st ed. sgn. dj. EX. K2. $75.00

MATTHIESSEN, Peter. *Men's Lives: The Surfmen & Baymen of the S Fork.* 1986. Random House. 1st ed. dj. EX. K2. $40.00

MATTHIESSEN, Peter. *Midnight Turning Gray.* 1984. Bristol, RI. Ampersand. 1st ed. wrp. EX. K2. $50.00

MATTHIESSEN, Peter. *On the River Styx & Other Stories.* 1989. Random House. 1st ed. dj. EX. K2. $30.00

MATTHIESSEN, Peter. *Oomingmak.* 1967. Hastings. 1st ed. sgn. dj. EX. B13. $85.00

MATTHIESSEN, Peter. *Oomingmak.* 1967. NY. 1st ed. dj. EX. T9. $45.00

MATTHIESSEN, Peter. *Partisans.* 1955. Viking. 1st ed. inscr. dj. EX. K2. $250.00

MATTHIESSEN, Peter. *Partisans.* 1956. Secker Warburg. ARC. dj. RS. EX. K2. $200.00

MATTHIESSEN, Peter. *Profile: Cesar Chavez.* 1969. UAW W Regional 6. reprint. EX. K2. $200.00

MATTHIESSEN, Peter. *Raditzer.* 1962. London. Heinemann. 1st Eng ed. dj. EX. K2. $85.00

MATTHIESSEN, Peter. *Sal Si Puedes: Cesar Chavez & the New Am Revolution.* 1969. NY. 1st ed. dj. EX. $55.00

MATTHIESSEN, Peter. *Seal Pool.* 1972. Doubleday Doran. Ils William Pene du Bois. 1st ed. dj. EX. K2. $250.00

MATTHIESSEN, Peter. *Shorebirds of N Am.* 1967. Viking. ARC. dj. RS. EX. K2. $275.00

MATTHIESSEN, Peter. *Shorebirds of N Am.* 1967. Viking. Ils RV Clem. 1st ed. folio. dj. EX. K2. $150.00

MATTHIESSEN, Peter. *Snow Leopard.* 1978. Viking. Ltd ed. 1/199. TEG. acetate dj. EX. K2. $275.00

MATTHIESSEN, Peter. *Snow Leopard.* 1978. Viking. 5th print. inscr. dj. VG. $37.00

MATTHIESSEN, Peter. *Under the Mt Wall.* 1962. Viking. 1st ed. dj. VG. $30.00

MATTHIESSEN, Peter. *Wildlife in Am.* 1987. Viking. ARC of revised reissue. dj. EX. K2. $45.00

MATTHIESSEN, Peter. *Wind Birds.* 1973. Viking. 1st ed. sm quarto. dj. EX. K2. $85.00

MAUDE, F.M. *Evolution of Modern Strategy From 18th Century to Present.* 1905. London. 1st ed. 135 p. xl. T5. $65.00

MAUGHAM, R.C.F. *Africa As I Have Known It, Nyasaland.* 1929. London. John Murray. 1st ed. VG. $50.00

MAUGHAM, W.S. *Andalusia, Land of the Blessed Virgin.* 1935. Borzoi Books. PB. dj. EX. B4. $25.00

MAUGHAM, W.S. *Ashenden; or, The British Agent.* 1938. Doubleday. 1st Am ed. EX. B13. $40.00

MAUGHAM, W.S. *Caesar's Wife.* 1922. Heinemann. 1st ed. red buckram. H3. $150.00

MAUGHAM, W.S. *Cakes & Ale; or, Skeleton in the Cupboard.* nd. Heinemann. Ltd ed. 1/1000. sgns. boxed. H3. $400.00

MAUGHAM, W.S. *Cakes & Ale; or, Skeleton in the Cupboard.* 1930. London. Heinemann. 1st print. VG. $65.00

MAUGHAM, W.S. *Circle.* 1921. Heinemann. 1st ed. brn printed wrp. H3. $50.00

MAUGHAM, W.S. *Circle.* 1921. London. Ltd ed. 1/500. cloth bdg. EX. B2. $250.00

MAUGHAM, W.S. *Don Fernando.* 1935. London. 1st ed. dj. EX. B2. $45.00

MAUGHAM, W.S. *For Service's Rendered.* 1932. Heinemann. 1st ed. dj. VG. H3. $75.00

MAUGHAM, W.S. *Gentleman in the Parlor.* 1930. London. 1st ed. dj. EX. B2. $50.00

MAUGHAM, W.S. *Home & Beauty.* 1923. Heinemann. 1st ed. red buckram. EX. H3. $150.00

MAUGHAM, W.S. *Jack & Straw.* 1912. Heinemann. 1st ed. yel printed wrp. H3. $125.00

MAUGHAM, W.S. *Judgement Seat.* 1934. London. Centaur. Ltd 1st ed. 1/150. sgns. H3. $250.00

MAUGHAM, W.S. *Letter.* 1925. NY. Special Souvenir issue. orange wrp. EX. B2. $135.00

MAUGHAM, W.S. *Letter.* 1927. Heinemann. 1st ed. red buckram. H3. $150.00

MAUGHAM, W.S. *Liza of Lambeth.* 1947. Heinemann. Jubilee ed. 1/1000. sgn. dj. H3. $250.00

MAUGHAM, W.S. *Loaves & Fishes.* 1924. Heinemann. 1st ed. brn printed wrp. scarce. H3. $100.00

MAUGHAM, W.S. *Loaves & Fishes.* 1924. Heinemann. 1st ed. red buckram. H3. $125.00

MAUGHAM, W.S. *Making of a Saint.* 1976. Harper. 1st ed. VG. B2. $35.00

MAUGHAM, W.S. *Moon & Sixpence.* 1919. Doran. 1st ed. 314 p. VG. B10. $12.00

MAUGHAM, W.S. *Narrow Corner.* 1932. London. 1st ed. dj. EX. B2. $75.00

MAUGHAM, W.S. *Of Human Bondage.* 1939. New Haven. Ltd Ed Club. Ils/sgn John Sloan. 2 vols. slipcase. EX. C4. $400.00

MAUGHAM, W.S. *Of Human Bondage. With Digression on Art of Fiction.* 1946. Lib of Congress. 1/500. sgn. VG. K2. $125.00

MAUGHAM, W.S. *Our Betters.* 1923. London. 1st ed. VG. B3. $60.00

MAUGHAM, W.S. *Our Betters.* 1924. Heinemann. early reprint. VG. H3. $25.00

MAUGHAM, W.S. *Points of View.* 1958. London. 1st ed. dj. VG. B3. $35.00

MAUGHAM, W.S. *Razor's Edge.* 1944. Doubleday Doran. Ltd ed. 1/750. sgn. slipcase. EX. H3. $175.00

MAUGHAM, W.S. *Razor's Edge.* 1944. Garden City. 1st ed. dj. EX. B2. $35.00

MAUGHAM, W.S. *Razor's Edge.* 1944. Heinemann. 1st UK ed. dj. EX. scarce. K2. $500.00

MAUGHAM, W.S. *Razor's Edge.* 1972. Heinemann. not 1st ed. 303 p. red bdg. EX. $10.00

MAUGHAM, W.S. *Sacred Flame.* 1928. Doubleday Doran. 1st ed. VG. H3. $100.00

MAUGHAM, W.S. *Sheppey.* 1933. Heinemann. 1st ed. dj. EX. H3. $150.00

MAUGHAM, W.S. *Unattainable.* 1923. Heinemann. 1st ed. red buckram. EX. H3. $150.00

MAUGHAM, W.S. *Unknown.* 1920. Heinemann. 1st ed. 1st issue. brn print wrp. VG. H3. $75.00

MAUGHAM, W.S. *Writer's Notebook.* 1949. Doubleday. Ltd ed. 1/1000. sgn. TEG. boxed. H3. $300.00

MAUGHAM, W.S. *Writer's Notebook.* 1949. Heinemann. Ltd ed. 1/1000. sgn. H3. $250.00

MAULDIN, Bill. *Bill Mauldin in Korea.* 1952. NY. 1st ed. dj. VG. B3. $35.00

MAULDIN, Bill. *Up Front.* 1945. Holt. 1st ed. tall 8vo. VG. B10. $6.00

MAUREL, Andre. *Fortnight in Naples.* 1921. Putnam. 1st ed. 385 p. EX. B10. $5.00

MAUREY, E.B. *When the W Began: Story of Coraopolis & OH Valley.* 1930. Coraopolis. 75 p. wrp. G. T5. $25.00

MAURIAC, Francois. *2nd Thoughts: Reflections on Life & Literature.* 1961. World. 191 p. dj. EX. B10. $4.75

MAUROIS, Andre. *Chelsea Way.* 1930. Mathews Marrot. Ltd ed. 1/530. sgn. dj. H3. $125.00

MAUROIS, Andre. *Silence of Col Bramble.* 1930. Appleton. Trans Wilfrid Jackson. sgn. EX. H3. $75.00

MAUROIS, Andre. *Weigher of Souls.* 1931. Appleton. 1st ed. 192 p. VG. B10. $10.00

MAURY, D.H. *Recollections of Virginian in Mexican, Indian, & Civil War.* 1894. NY. 1st ed. inscr. VG. $65.00

MAURY, M.F. *Resources of WV.* 1876. Wheeling WV. 1st ed. wrp. $80.00

MAUS, C.P. *World's Great Madonna Anthology of Pictures, Poetry...* nd. (1947) Harper. Book Club ed? VG. B10. $6.25

MAVITY, N.B. *Tule Marsh Murder.* 1929. Crime Club. 1st ed. VG. P1. $20.00

MAVOR, William. *Catechism of Animated Nature.* 1821. NY. Wood. 12mo. wrp. EX. $75.00

MAWE, Thomas. *Every Man His Own Gardener.* 1779. London. 8th print. rebound. VG. R5. $210.00

MAXWELL, J.C. *World Makers.* 1969. Arcadia. 1st Am ed. dj. EX. F5. $15.00

MAXWELL, Kurt. *Equinox.* 1987. Arbor House. 1st ed. dj. EX. F5. $14.00

MAXWELL, Mike. *Commercial Magic of JC Wagner.* 1987. Tahoma, CA. L&L Pub. 1st ed. 164 p. dj. NM. J3. $30.00

MAXWELL, Mike. *Louis Falanga's Lake Tahoe Card Magic.* 1985. Tahoma, CA. 2nd ed. SftCvr. M. J3. $12.50

MAXWELL, Mike. *Louis Falanga's Lake Tahoe Magic.* 1985. Louis Falanga. 1st ed. 77 p. SftCvr. NM. J3. $9.00

MAXWELL, Spencer. *Collecting Abbey.* 1991. Santa Fe. Vinegar Tom Pr. 1st ed. 1/125. wrp. EX. K2. $25.00

MAXWELL, Spencer. *Collecting Abbey.* 1991. Santa Fe. Vinegar Tom Pr. Ltd ed. 1/26. sgn. EX. K2. $125.00

MAXWELL, W. *Atlas of the Great Barrier Reef.* 1968. Amsterdam. Elsevier. Ils. dj. EX. $25.00

MAXWELL, William. *Old Man at the Railroad Crossing & Other Tales.* 1966. Knopf. 1st ed. sgn. dj. EX. K2. $100.00

MAXWELL, William. *They Came Like Swallows.* 1937. Harper. 1st ed. dj. scarce wraparound band. K2. $125.00

MAXWELL, William. *They Came Like Swallows.* 1937. NY. 1st ed. sgn. dj. EX. T9. $70.00

MAXWELL, William. *Writer As Illusionist.* 1955. np. self-pub offprint. 1st ed. EX. K2. $125.00

MAXXE, Robert; see Rosenblum, Robert.

MAY, E.L. *Souvenir Hist of Camp Sheridan.* 1918. Montgomery, AL. 122 p. wrp. T5. $15.00

MAY, Earl. *2000 Miles Through Chile.* 1924. Century. 1st ed. 462 p. F2. $25.00

MAY, John. *Hawks of N Am.* 1935. Nat Audubon Soc. clr pls. VG. T3. $65.00

MAY, Julian. *Many Clr Land.* 1981. Houghton Mifflin. 1st ed. dj. EX. R3. $20.00

MAY, Julian. *Saga of the Pliocene Exile.* 1981-1984. Houghton Mifflin. 1st ed. 1/500. 5 vols. djs. M. $100.00

MAY, Robert. *Rudolph the Red-Nosed Reindeer.* 1939. Maxton. VG. B7. $28.00

MAYER, K.H. *Maya Monuments: Sculptures of Unknown Provence in Europe.* 1978. Acoma Books. 1st ed. 4to. wrp. F2. $15.00

MAYER, K.H. *Maya Monuments: Sculptures of Unknown Provence in US.* 1980. Acoma Books. 1st ed. 4to. wrp. F2. $20.00

MAYER, K.H. *Mushroom Stones of Mesoamerica.* 1977. Ramona. Acoma Books. 1st ed. 46 p. wrp. F2. $15.00

MAYER & IMMOOS. *Japanese Theatre.* 1977. Rizzoli. 1st Am ed. 194 p. dj. EX. H3. $75.00

MAYHAR, Ardath. *Exile on Vlahil.* 1984. Doubleday. ARC. dj. RS. EX. F5. $20.00

MAYHAR, Ardath. *Lords of the Triple Moons.* 1983. Atheneum. 1st ed. dj. EX. F5. $18.00

MAYHAR, Ardath. *Soul-Singer of Tyrnos.* 1981. Atheneum. 1st ed. dj. EX. P1. $17.50

MAYHAR, Ardath. *World Ends in Hickory Hollow.* 1985. Doubleday. 1st ed. RS. M. R3. $17.50

MAYHEW, Edward. *Ils Horse Doctor.* 1865. NY. Ils. 8vo. 536 p. G. G4. $22.00

MAYHEW, Edward. *Ils Horse Management.* 1864. Phil. 1st ed. 8vo. 548 p. G. G4. $49.00

MAYHEW & LONG. *Fireball.* 1977. Methuen. 1st ed. dj. VG. P1. $15.00

MAYHEW & MAYHEW. *Acting Charades; or, Deeds Not Words.* ca 1850. London. Bogue. 1st ed. 134 p. VG. H3. $150.00

MAYNARD, C.J. *Eggs of N Am Birds.* 1890. Boston. De Wolfe Fiske. clr pls. VG. T3. $45.00

MAYNARD, Theodore. *St Benedict & His Monks.* nd. (1954) Kennedy. probably 1st ed. 241 p. dj. VG. B10. $5.00

MAYNE, William. *Hill Road.* 1969. Dutton. 1st ed. dj. xl. P1. $5.00

MAYO, Charles. *Story of My Family & Career.* 1968. NY. ARC. 351 p. dj. EX. B3. $17.50

MAYO, James. *Shamelady.* 1966. Heinemann. 1st ed. VG. P1. $10.00

MAYO, Jim; see L'amour, Louis.

MAYOH, William. *Magic by Ho Yam.* 1949. S Bend, IN. Peterson. 1st ed. 137 p. EX. J3. $20.00

MAZIERE, Francis. *Expedition Tumuc-Humac.* 1955. Doubleday. 1st ed. 249 p. dj. F2. $15.00

MCALLISTER, Callista. *Pornella.* 1975. Capra. Chapbook Series. 1/100. sgn. EX. K2. $20.00

MCALLISTER, Hugh. *Sea Gold.* nd. Saafield. VG. P1. $10.00

MCALLISTER, Mary. *Report of Friend's Boarding Home.* 1892. Concord Quarterly Meeting. 32mo. VG. V1. $7.00

MCBAIN, Ed. *Another Part of the City.* 1986. Mysterious Pr. 1st ed. dj. VG. P1. $15.95

MCBAIN, Ed. *Blood Relatives.* nd. Book Club. dj. VG. P1. $4.50

MCBAIN, Ed. *Calypso.* 1979. Viking. 1st ed. dj. EX. F5. $22.00

MCBAIN, Ed. *Cinderella.* 1986. Holt. 1st ed. dj. VG. P1. $14.95

MCBAIN, Ed. *Cop Hater.* 1958. London. TV Boardman. 1st HrdCvr ed. inscr. orange bdg. VG. T9. $65.00

MCBAIN, Ed. *Goldilocks.* 1977. Arbor House. 1st ed. dj. EX. F5. $20.00

MCBAIN, Ed. *Guns.* 1976. Random House. 1st ed. dj. EX. P1. $20.00

MCBAIN, Ed. *Jack & the Beanstalk.* 1984. Holt. 1st ed. dj. EX. F5. $17.00

MCBAIN, Ed. *Jungle Kids.* 1956. Pocket Book 1126. 1st ed. wrp. EX. T9. $35.00

MCBAIN, Ed. *Let's Hear It for the Deaf Man.* nd. Book Club. dj. EX. P1. $4.50

MCBAIN, Ed. *Let's Hear It for the Deaf Man.* 1973. Doubleday. VG. P1. $7.50

MCBAIN, Ed. *Let's Hear It for the Deaf Man.* 1973. Doubleday. 2nd ed. dj. EX. P1. $15.00

MCBAIN, Ed. *Long Time No See.* nd. Book Club. dj. VG. P1. $4.50

MCBAIN, Ed. *Lullaby.* 1989. Morrow. 2nd ed. dj. EX. P1. $16.00

MCBAIN, Ed. *Rumpelstiltskin.* 1981. Viking. 1st ed. dj. EX. F5. $18.00

MCBAIN, Ed. *Snow Wht & Rose Red.* 1985. Holt Rinehart Winston. 1st ed. dj. EX. F5/P1. $15.00

MCBAIN, Ed. *Vespers.* 1990. Morrow. 1st ed. dj. EX. P1. $18.95

MCBAIN, Ed. *Where There's Smoke.* 1975. Random House. 1st ed. dj. EX. F5. $22.00

MCBAIN, Ed. *3 From the 87th.* nd. Book Club. dj. EX. P1. $10.00

MCBAIN, Ed. *8 Blk Horses.* nd. Book Club. dj. EX. P1. $5.00

MCBRIDE, Chris. *Wht Lions of Timbavati.* 1977. London. Paddington. 1st ed. pls. EX. $10.00

MCBRIDE, George. *Chile: Land & Soc.* 1936. Am Geog Soc. Research Series No 19. 408 p. F2. $25.00

MCCABE, J.D. *Hist of War Between Germany & France.* 1871. Nat Pub Co. Ils. VG. $45.00

MCCAFFREY, Anne. *Coelura.* 1987. Tor Books. 1st ed. dj. EX. P1. $15.00

MCCAFFREY, Anne. *Dragon Drums.* 1979. Atheneum. 1st ed. dj. EX. F5. $20.00

MCCAFFREY, Anne. *Dragon Quest.* 1978. Del Rey. 1st Am ed. dj. EX. R3. $25.00

MCCAFFREY, Anne. *Girl Who Heard Dragons.* 1985. Cheap Street. 1st ed. 1/137. sgn. slipcase. M. R3. $200.00

MCCAFFREY, Anne. *Ireta Adventure.* 1984. Del Rey. 1st HrdCvr ed. dj. EX. F5. $12.00

MCCAFFREY, Anne. *Killashandra.* 1985. Del Rey. 1st ed. dj. P1/R3. $16.95

MCCAFFREY, Anne. *Lady.* 1987. Ballantine. 1st ed. dj. VG. P1. $17.50

MCCAFFREY, Anne. *Moreta, Dragonlady of Pern.* 1983. Del Rey. 1st ed. dj. P1/R3. $15.00

MCCAFFREY, Anne. *Rowan.* 1990. Ace Putnam. 1st ed. dj. EX. F5. $16.00

MCCAFFREY, Anne. *Stitch in Snow.* 1985. Tor Books. 2nd ed. dj. EX. P1. $14.95

MCCAFFREY, Anne. *Wht Dragon.* 1978. Del Rey. 1st ed. dj. EX. F5. $20.00

MCCAFFREY, Anne. *Wht Dragon.* 1978. Del Rey. 1st ed. inscr/sgn. dj. EX. R3. $32.50

MCCAFFREY, Anne. *Year of the Lucy.* 1986. Tor Books. dj. VG. P1. $14.95

MCCAGUE. *Cumberland. Rivers of Am Series.* 1973. NY. 1st ed. dj. VG. B3. $27.50

MCCAMMON, R.R. *Bethany's Sin.* 1989. Kinnell. dj. EX. P1. $30.00

MCCAMMON, R.R. *Mystery Walk.* 1983. Holt Rinehart Winston. dj. VG. P1. $35.00

MCCAMMON, R.R. *Night Boat.* 1990. Kinnell. dj. EX. P1. $30.00

MCCAMMON, R.R. *Stinger.* nd. Book Club. dj. VG. P1. $5.00

MCCAMMON, R.R. *Stinger.* 1988. Kinnell. dj. EX. P1. $30.00

MCCAMMON, R.R. *They Thirst.* 1990. Kinnell. dj. EX. P1. $30.00

MCCAMMON, R.R. *Usher's Passing.* 1984. Holt Rinehart Winston. 1st ed. dj. VG. P1. $20.00

MCCANN, Edson; seé Del Rey, Lester.

MCCARTER, M.H. *Corner Stone.* 1915. McClurg. 1st ed. stiff wrp. VG. R3. $50.00

MCCARTHY, Carlton. *Detailed Minutiae of Soldier Life in Army of N VA.* Time Life. reprint. EX. S1. $17.50

MCCARTHY, Cormac. *Blood Meridan.* 1985. Random House. ARC. dj. RS. w/photo. B13. $85.00

MCCARTHY, Cormac. *Child of God.* 1973. Random House. 1st ed. clipped dj. EX. B13. $85.00

MCCARTHY, Cormac. *Child of God.* 1975. London. Chatto Windus. 1st UK ed. dj. EX. B13. $75.00

MCCARTHY, Cormac. *Suttree.* 1979. Random House. UP. wrp. EX. B13. $185.00

MCCARTHY, Cormac. *Suttree.* 1979. Random House. 1st ed. dj. EX. B13. $50.00

MCCARTHY, Mary. *Cannibals & Missionaries.* 1979. Harcourt Brace. 1st ed. dj. VG. P1. $15.00

MCCARTHY, Mary. *Ideas & the Novel.* 1980. NY. 1st ed. sgn. dj. EX. T9. $55.00

MCCARTHY, Mary. *Memoirs of a Catholic Girlhood.* 1957. NY. 1st ed. dj. VG. B3. $15.00

MCCARTHY, Mary. *Memoirs of a Catholic Girlhood.* 1963. Berkley. 1st PB ed. EX. B4. $5.00

MCCARTHY, Mary. *Vietnam.* 1967. Harcourt Brace World. 1st ed. 8vo. stiff wrp. EX. R4. $25.00

MCCARTHY, Shawna. *Isaac Asimov's Fantasy!* 1985. Dial. dj. RS. EX. P1. $15.00

MCCAULEY, Kirby. *Dark Forces.* nd. Book Club. dj. VG. P1. $7.50

MCCAULEY, Kirby. *Dark Forces.* 1980. Viking. 1st ed. sgn by 8 contributors. dj. scarce. EX. F5. $75.00

MCCAULEY, Kirby. *Frights.* 1976. St Martin. 1st ed. dj. xl. P1. $7.50

MCCAY, W. *Little Nemo in Slumberland.* 1941. Chicago. Ils. VG. B3. $47.50

MCCLANAHAN, Ed. *Famous People I Have Known.* 1985. Farrar Straus. 1st ed. sgn. dj. EX. C4. $25.00

MCCLANAHAN, Ed. *Natural Man.* 1983. Farrar Straus. UP. wrp. EX. B13. $150.00

MCCLANAHAN, Ed. *Natural Man.* 1983. Farrar Straus. 1st ed. sgn. dj. EX. C4. $35.00

MCCLAREN, Ian. *Beside the Bonnie Briar Bush.* 1895. Chicago. Sergel. brn bdg. VG. C1. $9.00

MCCLARY, Thomas. *3,000 Years.* 1954. Fantasy. Ltd ed. 1/300. sgn. dj. EX. R3. $75.00

MCCLARY, Thomas. *3,000 Years.* 1954. Fantasy. 1st ed. 2nd bdg. EX. R3. $7.50

MCCLELLAN, G.B. *Manual of Bayonet Exercise...for Army of US.* 1862. Phil. 12mo. 24 pls. 118 p. VG. scarce. G4. $74.00

MCCLELLAN, G.B. *Report on the Organization & Campaigns of Army of Potomac.* 1864. NY. 1st ed. 8vo. 480 p. VG. G4. $59.00

MCCLELLAND, N. *Young Decorators.* 1928. NY. 1st ed. VG. $15.00

MCCLINTOCK, Alexander. *Best of Luck.* 1917. Doran. VG. B10. $8.75

MCCLOY, Helen. *Burn This.* 1980. Dodd Mead. 1st ed. dj. xl. P1. $7.50

MCCLOY, Helen. *Changeling Conspiracy.* 1976. Dodd Mead. 1st ed. dj. EX. P1. $22.50

MCCLOY, Helen. *Do Not Disturb.* 1945. Tower. VG. P1. $15.00

MCCLOY, Helen. *Man in the Moonlight.* 1940. Morrow. 1st ed. dj. VG. P1. $15.00

MCCLOY, Helen. *Question of Time.* 1971. Dodd Mead. 1st ed. dj. EX. P1. $20.00

MCCLURE, J.B. *Stories & Sketches of General Grant at Home & Abroad.* 1880. Chicago. Ils. sm 8vo. 215 p. gilt red bdg. VG. G4. $30.00

MCCLURE, James. *Cop World.* 1984. Pantheon. 1st ed. dj. EX. P1. $16.95

MCCLURE, James. *Gooseberry Fool.* 1974. Harper Row. 1st ed. clipped dj. EX. T9. $25.00

MCCLURE, James. *Snake.* 1976. Harper Row. 1st ed. dj. EX. P1. $20.00

MCCLURE, K.M. *Lincoln's Own Yarns & Stories.* nd. (1920s?) Winston. G. B10. $4.00

MCCLURE, Michael. *Beard.* 1967. Coyote. Ils Wes Wilson. EX. B4. $4.00

MCCLURE, Michael. *Grabbing of the Fairy.* 1978. Truck Pr. Ils Stewart Brand. inscr. EX. B4. $20.00

MCCLURE, Michael. *Little Odes & the Raptors.* 1969. Blk Sparrow. 1st ed. 1/200. sgn. dj. EX. $20.00

MCCLURE, Michael. *Love Lion Book.* 1966. 4 Seasons. 2nd print. sgn. EX. B4. $15.00

MCCLURE, Michael. *Rare Angel.* 1975. Blk Sparrow. 2nd print. B4. $10.00

MCCLURE, Michael. *Surge.* 1969. Frontier Pr. pamphlet. sgn. B4. $20.00

MCCLURE & MORRIS. *Authentic Life of William McKinley.* 1901. np. Memorial ed. 503 p. VG. T5. $9.50

MCCOLLEY, Sutherland. *Pre-Columbian Art: Collectors' Choices.* 1973. Hudson River Mus. Ils. 4to. wrp. F2. $10.00

MCCOMB, William. *1st Book of William.* 1947. Birmingham, Eng. Goodliffe. 1st ed. NM. J3. $4.00

MCCONKEY, H.E.B. *Dakota War Whoop.* 1965. Lakeside Classic. 395 p. TEG. EX. T5. $22.50

MCCONNELL, Frank. *Blood Lake.* nd. Book Club. dj. EX. P1. $4.50

MCCONNELL, J.R. *Flying for France.* 1919. NY. VG. $20.00

MCCORD, David. *About Boston.* 1973. Boston. Little Brn. PB. stiff wrp. VG. B10. $2.25

MCCORD, W.B. *Souvenir Hist of Ye Old Town of Salem, OH...* nd. (1906) Salem, OH. 128 p. G. T5. $35.00

MCCORKLE, Jill. *Ferris Beach.* 1990. Algonquin Books. ARC. wrp. EX. C4. $30.00

MCCORMICK, R.R. *War Without Grant.* 1950. NY. 1st ed. 14 maps. 245 p. T5. $32.50

MCCORMICK, V.T. *Charcoal & Chalk.* 1926. Norfolk. 1st ed. VG. $45.00

MCCOUBREY, J.W. *Am Tradition in Painting.* 1970. Braziller. 2nd print. D4. $20.00

MCCOY, A. *Politics of Heroin in SE Asia.* 1972. NY. 464 p. dj. VG. B3. $35.00

MCCOY, Horace. *I Should Have Stayed Home.* 1938. Knopf. 1st ed. dj. H3. $100.00

MCCOY, Horace. *I Should Have Stayed Home.* 1938. Knopf. 1st ed. yel bdg. T9. $25.00

MCCOY, Horace. *Kiss Tomorrow Goodbye.* 1948. Random House. 1st ed. dj. VG. T9. $45.00

MCCOY, Horace. *No Pockets in a Shroud.* 1943. Signet 690. 1st Am ed. wrp. EX. T9. $30.00

MCCOY, J.G. *Hist Sketches of Cattle Trade of W & SW...* 1874. KS City. Ramsey Millett Hudson. 1st ed. VG. H3. $1500.00

MCCOY, M.H. *10 Escape From Tojo.* 1944. Farrar Rinehart. 1st ed. dj. EX. P1. $25.00

MCCOY, Richard. *Rites of Knighthood.* 1989. 1st ed. dj. EX. C1. $17.50

MCCRACKEN, Harold. *AK Bear Trails.* 1931. NY. 1st ed. dj. EX. B3. $90.00

MCCRACKEN, Harold. *Very Soon Now, Joe.* 1947. NY. 1st ed. dj. VG. C2. $25.00

MCCRUM, Robert. *In the Secret State.* 1980. Simon Schuster. 1st ed. dj. VG. P1. $15.00

MCCULLERS, Carson. *Ballad of the Sad Cafe.* 1951. Houghton Mifflin. 1st ed. dj. H3. $60.00

MCCULLERS, Carson. *Clock Without Hands.* 1961. Houghton Mifflin. 1st ed. dj. EX. H3. $50.00

MCCULLERS, Carson. *Member of the Wedding.* 1946. Houghton Mifflin. 1st ed. dj. EX. H3. $150.00

MCCULLERS, Carson. *Member of the Wedding.* 1951. New Directions. 1st ed. dj. EX. H3. $100.00

MCCULLERS, Carson. *Reflections in the Golden Eye.* 1941. Houghton Mifflin. 1st ed. sgn. dj. VG. B13. $87.50

MCCULLERS, Carson. *Reflections in the Golden Eye.* 1950. New Directions. 1st ed. dj. EX. B13. $45.00

MCCULLERS, Carson. *Square Root of Wonderful.* 1958. Houghton Mifflin. 1st ed. dj. EX. B13. $65.00

MCCULLERS, Carson. *Sweet As a Pickle & Clean As a Pig.* 1964. Houghton Mifflin. 1st ed. dj. EX. H3. $75.00

MCCULLEY, Johnston. *Blk Star's Return.* nd. Hutchinson. VG. P1. $20.00

MCCULLEY, Johnston. *Scarlet Scourge.* 1925. Chelsea House. 1st ed. VG. P1. $35.00

MCCULLEY, Walbridge. *Blood on Nassau's Moon.* nd. Book Club. dj. VG. P1. $4.00

MCCULLOUGH, Colleen. *Creed for the 3rd Millennium.* 1985. Harper Row. 1st ed. dj. VG. $12.00

MCCULLOUGH, Colleen. *Indecent Obsession.* 1981. Harper Row. dj. VG. $12.00

MCCULLOUGH, Colleen. *Thorn Birds.* 1977. Harper Row. 1st ed. dj. VG. $15.00

MCCULLOUGH & LEUBA. *PA Main Line Canal.* 1973. York, PA. Ils. 184 p. wrp. VG. T5. $15.00

MCCUTCHAN, G.B. *Brewster's Millions.* nd. Grosset Dunlap. Photoplay ed. VG. P1. $12.50

MCCUTCHAN, Philip. *Halfhyde & the Flag Capt.* 1980. St Martin. 1st ed. dj. EX. F5. $16.00

MCCUTCHAN, Philip. *Poulter's Passage.* 1967. Harrap. 1st ed. dj. EX. P1. $17.50

MCCUTCHEON, G.B. *Books Once Were Men.* 1931. NY. 1/1000. 8vo. slipcase. EX. $25.00

MCCUTCHEON, G.B. *Cowardice Court.* 1906. Dodd Mead. Ils Fisher. 1st ed. VG. B10. $7.00

MCCUTCHEON, G.B. *Oliver October.* 1923. Dodd Mead. 1st ed? 337 p. G. B10. $3.50

MCDARRAH, Fred. *Greenwich Village.* 1963. Corinth Books. VG. B4. $10.00

MCDARRAH, Fred. *Kerouac & Friends.* 1985. NY. 1st ed. dj. M. $10.00

MCDERMID, Finaly. *Ghost Wanted.* 1945. Tower. 1st ed. dj. VG. P1. $12.50

MCDERMOTT, F.J. *Seth Eastman: Pictorial Hist of the Indian.* 1962. OK U. 1st ed. dj. VG. $25.00

MCDONALD, Frank. *Provenance.* 1979. Atlantic/Little Brn. 1st ed. dj. VG. P1. $15.00

MCDONALD, Philip. *Rasp.* 1936. NY. 1st ed. dj. VG. B3. $45.00

MCDONALD, W.N. *Hist of Laurel Brigade, Orig the Asby Cavalry.* 1907. Baltimore. 1st ed. $300.00

MCDONELL, Gordon. *Intruder From the Sea.* nd. Book Club. dj. VG. P1. $4.50

MCDONOUGH, J.L. *Chattanooga: Death Grip on the Confederacy.* 1984. Knoxville. Ils. 298 p. dj. M. S1. $20.00

MCDOWELL, Rider. *Mercy Man.* 1987. St Martin. 1st ed. dj. EX. F5. $15.00

MCELROY, Joseph. *Ancient Hist: A Paraphase.* 1971. NY. 1st ed. dj. EX. C4. $50.00

MCEWAN, Ian. *Comfort of Strangers.* 1981. Simon Schuster. 1st ed. dj. EX. B13. $45.00

MCEWAN, Ian. *In Between the Sheets.* 1978. Simon Schuster. 1st Am ed. sgn. dj. EX. K2. $55.00

MCEWAN, Ian. *Innocent.* 1990. Doubleday. ARC of 1st Am ed. wrp. EX. K2. $25.00

MCEWAN, Ian. *Panama.* 1978. Farrar Straus. 1st ed. dj. EX. K2. $25.00

MCEWAN, Ian. *To Skin a Cat.* 1986. Dutton. 1st ed. dj. EX. K2. $25.00

MCFARLAND, Dennis. *Music Room.* 1990. Houghton Mifflin. ARC. wrp. EX. .C4. $45.00

MCFEE, Inez. *Story of the Idylls of the King.* 1912. Ils Kirk. 1st ed. C1. $18.00

MCFEE, William. *Casuals of the Sea.* 1935. Literary Guild. 481 p. gr/wht bdg. VG. B10. $5.00

MCFEE, William. *Harbor Master.* 1931. Doubleday Doran. Ltd ed. 1/377. sgn. slipcase. H3. $100.00

MCFEE, William. *N of Suez.* 1930. Doubleday Doran. Ltd ed. 1/350. sgn. boxed. H3. $100.00

MCFEE, William. *Watch Below.* 1940. Random House. Ltd ed. 1/250. sgn. boxed. H3. $125.00

MCFEE, William. *6-Hour Shift.* 1920. Doubleday Page. Ltd ed. 1/375. sgn. H3. $85.00

MCGARRY, Mary. *Great Folk Tales of Ireland.* c 1972. NY. dj. VG. C1. $7.50

MCGARTH, Patrick. *Spider.* 1990. Poseidon. UP. wrp. EX. B13. $35.00

MCGEE, T.D. *Hist of Irish Settlers in N Am.* 1852. Boston. 5th Am ed. VG. $50.00

MCGERR, Patricia. *Murder Is Absurd.* 1967. Crime Club. 1st ed. Lib bdg. xl. P1. $5.00

MCGILL, Ormond. *Real Mental Magic.* 1989. Chicago. Ireland. 1st ed. 143 p. NM. J3. $21.00

MCGINLEY, Patrick. *Devil's Diary.* 1988. St Martin. 1st ed. dj. EX. F5. $13.00

MCGINNIS, Joe. *Fatal Vision.* 1983. Putnam. 663 p. dj. $12.00

MCGIVERN, W.P. *Choice of Assassins.* 1974. Collins. dj. VG. P1. $15.00

MCGIVERN, W.P. *Matter of Honor.* 1984. Arbor House. dj. EX. P1. $16.50

MCGIVERN, W.P. *Police Special.* 1962. Dodd Mead. 1st ed. dj. EX. T9. $20.00

MCGIVERN, W.P. *Savage Streets.* 1973. Collins. 2nd ed. dj. EX. P1. $10.00

MCGRATH, Patrick. *Blood & Water & Other Tales.* 1988. Poseidon. 1st ed. sgn. dj. EX. K2. $30.00

MCGRAW, Eloise. *Joel & the Great Merlin.* nd. Book Club. VG. C1. $4.00

MCGREGOR, R.R. *Heritage of the Commonwealth & Other Papers.* 1916. Doubleday. 1st ed. 344 p. TEG. B10. $12.00

MCGREW, C.B. *Italian Doorways.* 1929. Cleveland. 1st ed. folio. VG. G1. $100.00

MCGREW, Fenn. *Taste of Death.* 1953. Rinehart. 1st ed. VG. P1. $10.00

MCGUANE, Thomas. *Bushwacked Piano.* 1971. Simon Schuster. 1st ed. dj. EX. B13. $65.00

MCGUANE, Thomas. *Keep the Change.* 1989. Houghton Mifflin. Special ed. 1/150. sgn. slipcase. M. C4. $100.00

MCGUANE, Thomas. *Keep the Change.* 1989. Houghton Mifflin. 1st ed. sgn. dj. EX. B13. $75.00

MCGUANE, Thomas. *Nobody's Angel.* 1981. Farrar Straus. 1st ed. sgn. dj. M. C4. $75.00

MCGUANE, Thomas. *Outside Chance.* 1990. Boston. AP. revised reissue. K2. $50.00

MCGUANE, Thomas. *Panama.* 1978. Farrar Straus. 1st ed. dj. EX. B13. $35.00

MCGUANE, Thomas. *Panama.* 1978. NY. AP. 1st issue. tall gr wrp. K2. $250.00

MCGUANE, Thomas. *Sporting Club.* 1968. Simon Schuster. 1st ed. sgn. dj. EX. C4. $125.00

MCGUANE, Thomas. *To Skin a Cat.* 1986. Dutton. 1st ed. sgn. dj. EX. K2. $50.00

MCGUANE, Thomas. *To Skin a Cat.* 1986. NY. AP. K2. $35.00

MCGUANE, Thomas. *92 in the Shade.* 1973. Farrar Straus. 1st ed. dj. EX. B13. $75.00

MCGUANE, Thomas. *92 in the Shade.* 1974. Collins. 1st UK ed. sgn. dj. EX. B13. $75.00

MCGUANE, Thomas. *92 in the Shade.* 1974. London. Collins. 1st UK ed. dj. EX. C4. $30.00

MCGUIGAN, Dorothy. *Hapsburgs.* 1966. NY. 1st ed. VG. $10.00

MCGUINN & BAZELON. *Am Military Button Makers & Dealers.* 1984. Chelsea, MI. Ils Revised ed. sgns. 120 p. EX. T5. $25.00

MCGUIRE, J.W. *Diary of S Refugee During the War.* 1986. Salem, NH. reprint of 1862. 360 p. VG. T5. $27.50

MCGURK, Slater. *Grand Central Murders.* 1964. Macmillan. 1st ed. dj. xl. P1. $5.00

MCHARGUE, Georges. *Hot & Cold Running Cities.* 1974. Holt. 1st ed. dj. EX. P1. $15.00

MCHENRY & ROPER. *Smith & Wesson Handguns.* 1947. Huntington. dj. VG. B3. $60.00

MCHUGH, Tom. *Time of the Buffalo.* 1972. NY. 1st ed. 339 p. dj. EX. T5. $22.50

MCHUGH, Vincent. *I Am Thinking of My Darling.* 1943. Simon Schuster. 1st ed. dj. EX. R3. $25.00

MCILVAINE, C. *Autobiography of Gordon Saltonstall Hubbard.* nd. (1969) Citadel. 182 p. dj. M. B10. $8.50

MCILWRAITH, Thomas. *Birds of Ontario.* 1894. William Briggs. VG. T3. $45.00

MCINDOE, K.G. *Rubber Tree in Liberia.* 1968. private print. inscr. 76 p. wrp. VG. T5. $12.50

MCINERNEY, Jay. *Ransom.* 1985. Vintage. ARC. EX. K2. $30.00

MCINERNY, Ralph. *Death of Cold.* 1977. Vanguard. 1st ed. dj. EX. P1. $20.00

MCINERNY, Ralph. *Priest.* nd. Book Club. dj. VG. P1. $4.50

MCINERNY, Ralph. *2nd Vespers.* 1980. Vanguard. 1st ed. dj. EX. P1. $17.50

MCINTOSH, J.T. *Born Leader.* nd. Book Club. dj. xl. P1. $4.00

MCINTOSH, J.T. *Time for a Change.* 1967. Michael Joseph. dj. VG. P1. $20.00

MCINTOSH, J.T. *1 in 300.* 1954. Doubleday. 1st ed. dj. EX. R3. $50.00

MCINTOSH, Jane. *Practical Archaeologist.* 1986. Facts on File. 1st ed. 4to. 192 p. dj. F2. $12.50

MCINTYRE, Loren. *Incredible Incas & Their Timeless Land.* 1975. WA. 1st ed. 199 p. dj. $10.00

MCINTYRE, V.N. *Barbary.* 1986. Houghton Mifflin. 1st ed. dj. EX. F5. $15.00

MCINTYRE, V.N. *Fireflood & Other Stories.* 1979. Houghton Mifflin. 1st ed. dj. EX. F5. $20.00

MCINTYRE, V.N. *Fireflood & Other Stories.* 1979. Houghton Mifflin. 1st ed. inscr/sgn. dj. EX. R3. $40.00

MCINTYRE, V.N. *Superluminal.* 1983. Houghton Mifflin. 1st ed. dj. VG. R3. $30.00

MCKAY, Claude. *Banjo.* 1929. NY. 1st ed. dj. VG. H3. $400.00

MCKAY, Claude. *Long Way From Home.* 1937. Furman. 1st ed. dj. VG. K2. $300.00

MCKEAN, W.B. *Ribbon Creek.* 1958. NY. 1st ed. presentation. dj. VG. B3. $27.50

MCKENNA, H.D. *House in the City: Guide to Buying & Renovating Row Houses.* 1971. NY. 1st ed. VG. G1. $20.00

MCKENNA, Maurice. *Hist of Fond du Lac County, WI. Vol 2.* 1912. Clarke. 715 p. G. B10. $30.00

MCKENNA, Richard. *Casey Agnistes.* 1973. Harper Row. 1st ed. dj. EX. P1. $20.00

MCKENNEY, Ruth. *Loud Red Patrick.* 1949. London. 1st Eng ed. inscr. dj. T5. $19.50

MCKENNEY, Ruth. *Love Story.* 1951. London. later print. 285 p. VG. T5. $15.00

MCKIERNAN, D.L. *Darkest Day.* 1984. Doubleday. 1st ed. dj. VG. P1. $15.00

MCKIERNAN, D.L. *Shadows of Doom.* 1984. Doubleday. 1st ed. dj. VG. P1. $15.00

MCKILLIP, P.A. *Harpist in the Wind.* 1979. Atheneum. 1st ed. dj. F5. $40.00

MCKILLIP, P.A. *Heir of Sea & Fire.* 1977. Atheneum. 1st ed. dj. EX. F5. $65.00

MCKILLIP, P.A. *Heir of Sea & Fire.* 1977. Atheneum. 2nd ed. dj. EX. P1. $12.50

MCKILLIP, P.A. *Moon-Flash.* 1984. Atheneum. 1st ed. dj. EX. F5. $20.00

MCKILLIP, P.A. *Stepping From the Shadows.* 1982. Atheneum. 1st ed. inscr. dj. EX. R3. $35.00

MCKISHNIE, A.P. *Dwellers of the Marsh Realm.* 1937. Donohue. Ils Franz Johnston. dj. NM. A4. $30.00

MCKUEN, Rod. *In Someone's Shadow.* 1969. Random House. 1st ed. 107 p. dj. G. B10. $3.50

MCKUEN, Rod. *Stanyon St & Other Sorrows.* 1966. Random House. sgn. dj. H3. $15.00

MCLACHLAN, Ian. *7th Hexagram.* nd. BOMC. dj. VG. P1. $5.00

MCLACHLAN, Ian. *7th Hexagram.* 1976. Macmillan. 1st ed. dj. EX. P1. $15.00

MCLEAN, A.C. *Death on All Hallows.* 1958. Washburn. 1st Am ed. 191 p. dj. VG. B10. $4.25

MCLEAN, E.W. *Father Struck It Rich.* 1936. Boston. 1st ed. 316 p. dj. VG. B3. $25.00

MCLEAN, Katherine. *Missing Man.* 1975. Berkley. 1st ed. dj. EX. R3. $10.00

MCLELLAN, M.E. *Expedition to Revillagigedo Islands, Mexico, in 1925.* 1926. Academy of Sciences. wrp. F2. $10.00

MCLEOD & MACK. *Ethnic Sculpture.* 1985. Harvard. 1st ed. 72 p. wrp. F2. $12.50

MCLOUGHLIN, J.C. *Helix & the Sword.* 1983. Doubleday. 1st ed. dj. RS. EX. P1. $20.00

MCLOUGHLIN BROTHERS. *Frisky the Squirrel.* 1904. Christmas Eve Series. sm 4to. EX. $50.00

MCLOUGHLIN BROTHERS. *Linen ABC Book: 1st Steps.* 1899. 12mo. linen p/wrp. G. $40.00

MCLOUGHLIN BROTHERS. *Little Bo Peep.* 1903. Mother Goose Series. 4to. 14 p. wrp. VG. $22.00

MCLOUGHLIN BROTHERS. *Little Ones ABC.* 1907. 12mo. linen p/wrp. VG. $40.00

MCLOUGHLIN BROTHERS. *Little Tots' Pastime.* nd. Little Chatterwell Series. 8vo. G. $20.00

MCLOUGHLIN BROTHERS. *Merry Christmas ABC.* 1899. 8vo. wrp. EX. $55.00

MCLOUGHLIN BROTHERS. *Picture Land Stories.* 1906. Ils Nast. VG. $50.00

MCLOUGHLIN BROTHERS. *Red Riding Hood.* c 1880. NY. Aunt Kate's Series. 16 p. VG. $30.00

MCLUHAN, H.M. *Mechanical Bride: Folklore of Industrial Man.* 1951. NY. Vanguard. 1st ed. inscr. EX. K2. $475.00

MCLUHAN & WATSON. *From Cliche to Archetype.* 1970. Viking. 1st ed. dj. EX. K2. $45.00

MCMAHAN, Anna. *Florence in the Poetry of the Brownings.* 1904. McClurg. 1st ed. 225 p. EX. B10. $8.25

MCMAHON, Jo. *Deenie Folks & Friends of Theirs.* c 1928. Volland. Ils 4th ed. G. $15.00

MCMAHON, T.P. *Cornered at 6.* 1972. Simon Schuster. 1st ed. P1. $6.00

MCMASTER, J.B. *US in the World War.* 1920. NY. 1st ed. VG. $12.00

MCMERRELL, John. *Grammar of the Carnataca Language.* 1820. Madras. 4to. $75.00

MCMILLAN, Terry. *Mama.* 1987. Houghton Mifflin. 1st ed. dj. EX. B13. $85.00

MCMULLEN, Mary. *But Nellie Was So Nice.* nd. Book Club. dj. VG. P1. $4.50

MCMULLEN, Mary. *But Nellie Was So Nice.* 1979. Crime Club. dj. VG. P1. $15.00

MCMULLEN, Mary. *Death by Bequest.* 1977. Crime Club. dj. VG. P1. $15.00

MCMULLEN, Mary. *Man With 50 Complaints.* 1978. Crime Club. 1st ed. dj. VG. P1. $15.00

MCMULLEN, Mary. *My Cousin Death.* nd. Book Club. dj. VG. P1. $4.50

MCMULLEN, Mary. *Strangle Hold.* nd. Book Club. dj. VG. P1. $4.00

MCMURTRIE, D.C. *Book: Story of Printing & Bookmaking.* 1937. NY. Ils 1st ed. 676 p. dj. VG. T5. $45.00

MCMURTRIE, D.C. *Book: Story of Printing & Bookmaking.* 1965. Oxford U. 8th print. 8vo. EX. $25.00

MCMURTRIE, D.C. *Golden Book.* 1927. Pascal Covici. 1st ed. 1/2000. 4to. EX. $100.00

MCMURTRY, Larry. *Affair in Arcady.* 1959. Reynal. 1st ed. dj. EX. B13. $100.00

MCMURTRY, Larry. *All My Friends Are Going To Be Strangers.* 1972. Simon Schuster. UP. tall wrp. EX. B13. $750.00

MCMURTRY, Larry. *All My Friends Are Going To Be Strangers.* 1972. Simon Schuster. 1st ed. inscr. dj. EX. K2. $200.00

MCMURTRY, Larry. *Anything for Billy.* 1988. Simon Schuster. AP. EX. K2. $125.00

MCMURTRY, Larry. *Booked Up Catalog 1.* 1971. Booked Up. 1st ed. EX. K2. $50.00

MCMURTRY, Larry. *Buffalo Girls.* 1990. NY. UP. K2. $125.00

MCMURTRY, Larry. *Buffalo Girls.* 1990. Simon Schuster. UP. printed wrp. EX. C4. $125.00

MCMURTRY, Larry. *Buffalo Girls.* 1990. Simon Schuster. 1st ed. sgn. dj. EX. K2. $65.00

MCMURTRY, Larry. *Desert Rose.* 1983. Simon Schuster. Ltd ed. 1/250. sgn. slipcase. M. H3. $275.00

MCMURTRY, Larry. *Desert Rose.* 1983. Simon Schuster. UP. wrp. EX. B13. $175.00

MCMURTRY, Larry. *Horseman, Pass By.* 1961. Harper. 1st ed. inscr/sgn. dj. EX. K2. $1250.00

MCMURTRY, Larry. *In a Narrow Grave.* 1968. Austin. Encino. 1st ed. 1/250. sgn. slipcase. EX. scarce. K2. $1200.00

MCMURTRY, Larry. *In a Narrow Grave.* 1971. Touchstone. 1st PB ed. inscr/sgn. wrp. EX. K2. $100.00

MCMURTRY, Larry. *Last Picture Show.* 1966. Dial. 1st ed. dj. EX. H3. $200.00

MCMURTRY, Larry. *Leaving Cheyenne.* 1963. Harper Row. 1st ed. EX. H3. $125.00

MCMURTRY, Larry. *Lonesome Dove.* 1985. NY. 1st ed. dj. EX. B3. $175.00

MCMURTRY, Larry. *Moving On.* 1970. Simon Schuster. 1st Trade ed. inscr. dj. EX. K2. $200.00

MCMURTRY, Larry. *Moving On.* 1971. London. 1st UK ed. sgn. dj. EX. B13. $150.00

MCMURTRY, Larry. *Somebody's Darling.* 1978. NY. 1st ed. dj. EX. $45.00

MCMURTRY, Larry. *Terms of Endearment.* 1975. Simon Schuster. ARC. dj. RS. scarce. K2. $75.00

MCMURTRY, Larry. *Terms of Endearment.* 1975. Simon Schuster. UP. sgn. wrp. EX. B13. $750.00

MCNALLY, Dennis. *Desolate Angel: Biography Jack Kerouac.* 1979. Random House. 1st ed. 2nd print. dj. B4. $15.00

MCNALLY, Francis. *Improved Stystem of Geog.* 1866. NY. Barnes. 4to. 35 maps. VG. C1. $100.00

MCNALLY & MCNALLY. *This Is Mexico.* 1947. NY. Dodd. 1st ed. sm 4to. 216 p. dj. F2. $15.00

MCNASPY, C.J. *At Face Value.* 1978. Loyola. wrp. EX. K2. $75.00

MCNEIL, John. *Spy Game.* 1980. Coward McCann Geoghegan. 1st ed. dj. VG. P1. $15.00

MCNEIL, M.L. *Round the Mulberry Bush.* 1938. Saalfield. Ils FB Peat. 1st ed. 4to. VG. $35.00

MCNEILE, H.C. *Bulldog Drummond Returns.* nd. Book Club. dj. VG. P1. $4.50

MCNEILE, H.C. *Bulldog Drummond's 3rd Round.* nd. Grosset Dunlap. VG. P1. $7.50

MCNEILL, Don. *Moving Through Here.* 1970. Knopf. dj. VG. B4. $10.00

MCNEILL, J.C. *Lyrics From Cotton Land.* 1922. Charlotte, NC. 1st ed. 187 p. VG. B3. $45.00

MCNELIS. *Copper King at War.* 1969. Missoula. 230 p. dj. VG. B3. $20.00

MCPHEE, John. *Basin & Range.* 1981. Farrar Straus. 1st ed. dj. EX. $20.00

MCPHEE, John. *Coming Into the Country.* 1977. Farrar Straus. UP. VG. K2. $85.00

MCPHEE, John. *Coming Into the Country.* 1978. London. 1st Eng ed. inscr. dj. EX. $40.00

MCPHEE, John. *Control of Nature.* 1989. Farrar Straus. UP. wrp. EX. C4. $75.00

MCPHEE, John. *Crofter & the Laird.* 1970. Farrar Straus. 1st ed. dj. EX. K2. $100.00

MCPHEE, John. *Deltoid Pumpkin Seed.* 1973. NY. 1st ed. dj. EX. $40.00

MCPHEE, John. *Giving Good Weight.* 1979. Farrar Straus. 1st ed. dj. VG. $15.00

MCPHEE, John. *Levels of the Game.* 1975. Farrar Straus. 1st ed. dj. EX. C4. $50.00

MCPHEE, John. *Looking for a Ship.* 1990. Farrar Straus. 1st ed. sgn. dj. EX. K2. $50.00

MCPHEE, John. *Oranges.* 1967. Farrar Straus. 1st ed. dj. EX. C4. $50.00

MCPHEE, John. *Pieces of the Frame.* 1975. Farrar Straus. 1st ed. dj. EX. K2. $65.00

MCPHEE, John. *Pine Barrens.* 1981. NY. Ils Curtsinger. 1st ed. dj. EX. $35.00

MCPHEE, John. *Place de la Concorde Suisse.* 1984. Farrar Straus. AP. EX. K2. $65.00

MCPHEE, John. *Survival of the Bark Canoe.* 1975. Farrar Straus. 1st ed. dj. EX. C4. $60.00

MCPHEE, William. *Reflections of Marsyas.* 1933. Slide Mt Pr. 1/300. sgn. EX. B2. $65.00

MCPHERSON, J.A. *Elbow Room.* 1977. Little Brn. 1st ed. dj. EX. C4. $35.00

MCPHERSON, J.M. *Battle Cry of Freedom.* 1988. NY. 1st ed. dj. M. $25.00

MCPHERSON, James. *Poems of Ossian.* 1847. Leipzig. VG. C1. $59.50

MCPHERSON & WILLIAMS. *Railroad: Trains & Train People in Am Culture.* 1976. NY. 1st ed. sgns. dj. EX. T9. $60.00

MCSHANE, Mark. *Lashed But Not Leashed.* 1976. Crime Club. 1st ed. dj. VG. P1. $15.00

MCSHANE, Mark. *Seance.* 1962. Crime Club. 1st ed. VG. P1. $10.00

MCSHERRY, Frank. *Civil War Women.* 1988. August House. 175 p. PB. M. S1. $9.95

MCSPADDEN, J.W. *Famous Ghost Stories.* nd. Cadmus Books. VG. P1. $15.00

MCVICKAR, H.W. *Greatest Show on Earth: Soc.* 1892. Harper. 20 pls. gilt blk bdg. VG. H3. $250.00

MEAD, Charles. *Mississippian Scenery: Poem Descriptive of Interior N Am.* 1819. Phil. S Potter Co. 12mo. 113 p. full leather. $175.00

MEAD, Charles. *Old Civilizations of Inca Land.* 1932. NY. 2nd ed. 141 p. F2. $20.00

MEAD, Clifford. *Thomas Pynchon: Bibliography.* 1989. Dalkey Archive Pr. 1st ed. dj. EX. K2. $39.95

MEAD, D.W. *Water Power Engineering.* 1908. McGraw. 1st ed. 787 p. B10. $5.00

MEAD, Margaret. *Blackberry Winter.* 1972. Morrow. 1st ed. dj. EX. $10.00

MEAD, Margaret. *Culture & Commitment.* 1970. Nat Hist Pr. Special Members ed. dj. VG. $10.00

MEAD, Shepherd. *Big Ball of Wax.* 1954. Simon Schuster. 1st ed. dj. VG. R3. $27.50

MEAD & BUNZEL. *Golden Age of Am Anthropology.* 1960. Braziller. 1st ed. 4to. 630 p. F2. $15.00

MEADE, L.T. *Beautiful Palace.* c 1910-1920. Donahue. 473 p. VG. B10. $3.25

MEADE, L.T. *Rebels of the School.* c 1920s. Hurst. 342 p. dj. G. B10. $3.50

MEADOW BROOK ART GALLERY. *Art of Pre-Columbian Am.* 1976. Rochester, MI. Ils. 4to. wrp. F2. $10.00

MEAGHER, Maude. *Gr Scamander.* 1933. Houghton. 1st ed. VG. F5. $25.00

MEAGHER, S. *Accessories After the Fact.* 1976. NY. 1st ed. 477 p. wrp. B3. $25.00

MEANS, P.A. *Fall of Inca Empire & Spanish Rule in Peru 1530-1780.* 1932. Scribner. 1st ed. 351 p. F2. $30.00

MEANY, Tom. *Milwaukee's Miracle Braves.* 1954. NY. 1st ed. dj. VG. B3. $20.00

MEARNS, D.C. *Lincoln Papers.* 1948. NY. Intro Carl Sandburg. 2 vols. djs. slipcase. T1. $40.00

MEARNS, Hughes. *Richard Richard.* 1916. Penn. 1st ed. 446 p. VG. B10. $3.50

MECKEN, H.L. *Selected Prejudices.* 1927. Knopf. 1st ed. dj. VG. K2. $135.00

MECKEN & NATHAN. *Heliogabalus.* 1920. Knopf. Ltd ed. 1/2000. dj. EX. K2. $150.00

MEDGHER, S. *Accessories After the Fact.* 1967. Indianapolis. 1st ed. 477 p. dj. VG. B3. $45.00

MEDRINGTON, A.C.P. *Dozen of Magic.* 1917. Medrington. 1st ed. 32 p. VG. J3. $4.00

MEE, Margaret. *In Search of Flowers of the Amazon Forests.* 1989. Nonesuch. Ils. 4to. dj. F2. $50.00

MEEHAN, J.P. *Lady of the Limberlost.* 1928. Doubleday. 1st ed. VG. $125.00

MEEK, M.R.D. *In Remembrance of Rose.* 1987. Scribner. 1st ed. dj. EX. P1. $14.95

MEEK, S.P. *Drums of Tapajos.* 1961. Avalon. xl. P1. $7.50

MEEK, S.P. *Frog the Horse That Knew No Master.* 1965. Knopf. 13th print. decor brd. VG. P1. $4.00

MEEKER, Ezra. *Busy Life of 85 Years of Ezra Meeker.* 1916. Seattle. Ils. 399 p. A5. $35.00

MEEKER, Ezra. *Kate Mulhall. Romance of OR Trail.* 1926. NY. 1st ed. sgn. dj. VG. B3. $30.00

MEETING FOR SUFFERINGS. *Memorials of Deceased Friends of New Eng Yearly Meeting.* 1857. Providence. Knowles. 16mo. 78 p. G. V1. $10.00

MEGGS, B. *Saturday Games.* 1974. Random House. 1st ed. dj. EX. T9. $20.00

MEGRUE, R.C. *Under Cover.* 1914. Little Brn. 1st ed. VG. P1. $20.00

MEIER, Richard. *Richard Meier, Architect: Buildings & Projects 1966-1976.* 1976. NY. 1st ed. VG. G1. $20.00

MEIER-GRAEFE, Julius. *Vincent Van Gogh: Biographical Study.* 1933. Literary Guild. Revised ed. 2 vols. D4. $25.00

MEIGHAN, Clement. *Archaeology of Amapa, Nayarit.* 1976. UCLA. 1st ed. 4to. dj. F2. $40.00

MEINERTZHAGEN, R. *Birds of Arabia.* 1954. London. 1st ed. 624 p. VG. B3. $275.00

MEINHOLD, William. *Sidonia the Sorceress.* 1893. Hammersmith. Trans Wilde. 1/300. orig vellum. H3. $1250.00

MEISS, Milard. *Visconti Hours.* 1972. NY. 1st ed. 8vo. 262 p. EX. T1. $50.00

MEJIA DE RODAS, Idalma. *Change in Colotenango: Costume, Migration, & Hierarchy.* 1989. Ixchel Mus. 1st ed. Eng text. 142 p. F2. $35.00

MEKEEL, A.J. *Quakerism & a Creed.* 1936. Friends Bookstore. 12mo. 171 p. VG. V1. $8.00

MELINE, J.F. *2,000 Miles on Horseback...in Year 1866.* 1967. NY. 317 p. lacks frontis map. T5. $50.00

MELLEN, Grenville. *Book of the US.* 1842. Hartford. 8vo. 847 p. G. G4. $30.00

MELLEN. *Lonely Warrior.* 1949. NY. 1st ed. 177 p. dj. VG. B3. $15.00

MELLIZK, A.D. *Story of an Old Farm; or, Life in NJ in 18th Century.* 1889. Somerville, NJ. Ils. 743 p. G. T5. $95.00

MELNICK, J.C. *Gr Cathedral: Hist of Mill Creek Park, Youngstown, OH.* 1976. Youngstown. 1st ed. 446 p. T5. $27.50

MELOY, A.S. *Theatres & Motion Picture Houses.* 1916. NY. Architects Supply. 1st ed. 1/2000. 120 p. scarce. H3. $200.00

MELTZER, David. *Bark, a Polemic.* 1973. Capra. Chapbook Series. 1/75. sgn. EX. K2. $20.00

MELTZER, David. *San Francisco Poets.* 1971. Ballantine. PB Orig. sgn. EX. T9. $35.00

MELTZER, Milton. *Voices From the Civil War.* 1898. Crowell. Stated 1st ed. 203 p. M. S1. $13.95

MELVILLE, Herman. *Moby Dick.* 1851. NY. 1st ed. orig bdg. EX. H3. $30000.00

MELVILLE, Herman. *Moby Dick; or, The Whale.* 1855. NY. 1st Am ed. 2nd print. orig cloth. VG. rare. H3. $5000.00

MELVILLE, Herman. *Redburn: His 1st Voyage.* 1948. London. Cape. 1st ed. 12mo. dj. EX. C4. $25.00

MELVILLE, Herman. *Selected Poems.* 1944. New Directions. 1st ed. dj. slipcase. EX. K2. $65.00

MELVILLE, Herman. *Typee.* nd. Avon. Red/Gold ed. NM. B4. $15.00

MELVILLE, Herman. *Wht Jacket.* 1850. NY. 1st Am ed. 1st print. 1st bdg. VG. $1350.00

MELVILLE, Herman. *Works.* 1922. London. Constable. Standard ed. 1/750. 16 vols. octavo. H3. $3000.00

MELVILLE, Lewis. *Lady Mary Wortley Montagu: Her Life & Letters 1689-1762.* c1920s. Houghton. 8vo. 312 p. VG. B10. $10.00

MELVILLE, Lewis. *More Stage Favorites of 18th Century.* 1929. Hutchinson. 1st ed. 286 p. dj. EX. H3. $75.00

MELVILLE-ROSS, Antony. *Blindfold.* 1978. Harper Row. 1st ed. dj. EX. P1. $12.50

MENABONI & MENABONI. *Menaboni's Birds.* 1950. NY. Rinehart. 1st ed. dj. EX. $50.00

MENCKEN, H.L. *Artist.* 1912. Boston. John Luce. 1st ed. EX. B13. $150.00

MENCKEN, H.L. *Christmas Story.* 1946. NY. 1st ed. dj. VG. B3. $22.50

MENCKEN, H.L. *Gang of Pecksmiths.* 1975. New Rochelle. 1st ed. dj. VG. B3. $17.50

MENCKEN, H.L. *Meckeniana: A Schimpflexikon.* 1928. Knopf. Ltd ed. 1/230. sgn. boxed. H3. $350.00

MENCKEN, H.L. *Notes on Democracy.* 1926. Knopf. Ltd ed. 1/235. sgn. boxed. H3. $225.00

MENCONI, S.E. *Uncommon Spirit: Sculpture in Am 1800-1940.* 1989. Hirschl/Adler Gallery. 107 p. D4. $20.00

MENDE, Robert. *Spit & the Stars.* 1949. Rinehart. 1st ed. dj. EX. F5. $17.50

MENDELSOHN, Jack. *Forest Calls Back.* 1965. Little Brn. 1st ed. sgn. 267 p. dj. F2. $15.00

MENDELSON, Drew. *Pilgrimage.* 1981. DAW. 1st ed. wrp. EX. F5. $7.00

MENDOZA, J.F. *Book of John.* 1978. Mendoza. 1st ed. 138 p. NM. J3. $18.00

MENDOZA, J.F. *Close-Up Presentation.* 1979. Presto Place. 1st ed. 107 p. NM. J3. $14.00

MENDOZA, J.F. *John: Verse 2.* 1980. Viking. 1st ed. 137 p. NM. J3. $18.00

MENDOZA, J.F. *Magician Tested, Audience Approved.* 1985. Dan Fleshman. 1st ed. 66 p. cbdg. M. J3. $15.00

MENDOZA, J.F. *Mendoza Cups & Balls.* 1972. Toronto. Morrisey. 2nd print. SftCvr. NM. J3. $3.00

MENINGTON. *Custer Story.* 1950. NY. 1st ed. 339 p. dj. VG. B3. $35.00

MENJOU & MUSSELMAN. *It Took 9 Tailors.* 1948. McGraw Hill. 1st ed. presentation. dj. EX. H3. $75.00

MENJOU & MUSSELMAN. *It Took 9 Tailors.* 1948. NY. 1st ed. presentation. dj. VG. B3. $20.00

MENTZER, Jerry. *Another Close-Up Cavalcade.* 1975. Mentzer. 1st ed. 159 p. NM. J3. $15.00

MENTZER, Jerry. *Card Cavalcade 2.* 1974. Mentzer. 1st ed. 225 p. NM. J3. $15.00

MENTZER, Jerry. *Cards & Cases.* 1975. Mentzer. 1st ed. 50 p. NM. J3. $6.00

MENTZER, Jerry. *Close-Up Cavalcade Finale.* 1977. Mentzer. 1st ed. 197 p. NM. J3. $15.00

MENTZER, Jerry. *Counts, Cuts, Moves, & Subtlety.* 1985. Mentzer. 8th print. 73 p. NM. J3. $4.00

MENTZER, Jerry. *Magic of Paul Harris.* 1976. Mentzer. 1st reprint. 67 p. NM. J3. $8.00

MENTZER, Jerry. *New & Novel Knowledge.* 1975. Mentzer. 1st ed. 59 p. NM. J3. $6.00

MENTZER, Jerry. *Rick Johnson's Strike 1.* 1973. Mentzer. 1st ed. 11 p. SftCvr. VG. J3. $2.00

MENTZER, Michael. *World of Owen Gromme.* 1983. Stanton Lee. 1st ed. lg oblong folio. 240 p. slipcase. EX. R4. $100.00

MENZEL & BOYD. *World of Flying Saucers.* nd. Book Club. dj. VG. P1. $4.50

MERCHANT, Elizabeth. *King Arthur & His Knights.* 1927. Winston. Ils Godwin. 1st ed. dj. VG. R3. $10.00

MEREDITH, R.C. *Storm Over Sumter: Opening Engagement of Civil War.* 1957. Simon Schuster. 214 p. dj. S1. $8.00

MEREDITH, R.C. *This Was Andersonville.* 1957. NY. 1st ed. dj. VG. B3. $35.00

MEREDITH, R.C. *Vestiges of Time.* 1978. Doubleday. 1st ed. dj. xl. P1. $5.00

MEREJCOVXKI, Dmitri. *Romance of Leonardo Da Vinci.* nd. Heritage. reprint. 580 p. G. B10. $6.00

MERIDITH, Owen. *Lucile.* c 1895. NY. Lupton. 12mo. floral gr bdg. VG. C1. $7.50

MERILLAT, L.A. *Veterinary Military Hist.* 1935. KS City. Ils. 2 vols. 1172 p. VG. T5. $55.00

MERIMEE, Prosper. *Carmen.* 1941. NY. Ltd Ed Club. Ils/sgn Jean Charlot. 1/1500. slipcase. EX. C4. $75.00

MERLIN, Jack. *And a Pack of Cards.* 1964. Tannen. Revised ed. 93 p. NM. J3. $4.00

MERLIN, Jean. *Entertaining: Balloons.* 1986. Paris. 1st ed. inscr. 120 p. J3. $32.50

MERRICK, Leonard. *Quaint Companions.* nd. Hodder Stoughton. VG. P1. $15.00

MERRICK, William. *Packard Case.* 1961. Random House. 1st ed. dj. VG. P1. $10.00

MERRIL, Judith. *5th Annual of Year's Best SF.* 1960. Simon Schuster. 1st ed. dj. EX. F5. $20.00

MERRILD, Knud. *Poet & 2 Painters: Memoir of DH Lawrence.* 1939. Viking. inscr. dj. D4. $200.00

MERRILL, James. *Braving the Elements.* 1973. Chatto Windus. 1st ed. dj. EX. B13. $65.00

MERRILL, James. *Country of a Thousand Years of Peace.* 1959. Knopf. 1st ed. dj. EX. B13. $100.00

MERRILL, James. *Fire Screen.* 1970. Chattow Windus. 1st ed. clipped dj. EX. B13. $75.00

MERRILL, James. *Souvenirs.* 1984. Nadja Pr. 1/226. sgn. wrp. H3. $60.00

MERRILL, James. *Yel Pages.* 1974. Cambridge, MA. 1/800. wrp. EX. T9. $55.00

MERRILL, Judith. *Beyond Human Ken.* 1952. Random House. 1st ed. dj. EX. R3. $25.00

MERRILL, Judith. *Beyond Human Ken.* 1954. Pennant. 1st ed. wrp. EX. R3. $20.00

MERRILL, Judith. *Beyond the Barriers of Space & Time.* nd. Book Club. dj. VG. P1. $6.00

MERRILL, Judith. *Beyond the Barriers of Space & Time.* 1954. Random House. 1st ed. dj. EX. R3. $25.00

MERRILL, Judith. *Path Into the Unknown.* 1968. Delacorte. dj. VG. P1. $10.00

MERRILL, Judith. *SF 57.* 1957. Gnome. 1st ed. dj. VG. P1. $25.00

MERRILL, Judith. *SF 59.* 1959. Gnome. 1st ed. dj. VG. P1. $30.00

MERRILL, Judith. *Shadow on the Hearth.* 1950. Doubleday. 1st ed. dj. EX. R3. $45.00

MERRILL, Judith. *Shadow on the Hearth.* 1950. Doubleday. 1st ed. dj. VG. P1. $30.00

MERRILL, Judith. *Shadow on the Hearth.* 1953. Sidgwick Jackson. ARC. dj. RS. VG. P1. $30.00

MERRILL, Judith. *Shot in the Dark.* 1950. Bantam. 1st ed. wrp. G. R3. $35.00

MERRILL. *Sketches of Hist Bennington.* 1898. Cambridge. 1st ed. 99 p. G. B3. $22.50

MERRIMAN, J.D. *Flower of Kings: Study of Arthurian Legend in Eng.* 1973. KS U. 1st ed. dj. VG. C1. $75.00

MERRITT, A. *Burn, Witch, Burn.* 1951. Avon. wrp. EX. R3. $25.00

MERRITT, A. *Creep, Shadow.* nd. Avon. wrp. EX. R3. $35.00

MERRITT, A. *Dwellers in the Mirage/Face in Abyss.* 1953. Liveright. dj. VG. P1. $75.00

MERRITT, A. *Face in the Abyss.* 1943. Avon. wrp. G. R3. $7.50

MERRITT, A. *Fox Woman.* 1949. Avon. 1st ed. wrp. VG. R3. $17.50

MERRITT, A. *Fox Woman.* 1949. Avon/Eshbach. Special 1st ed. 1/300. wht dj. EX. R3. $300.00

MERRITT, A. *Fox Woman/Bl Pagoda.* 1946. NY. 1st ed. 1/1000. 109 p. VG. T5. $35.00

MERRITT, A. *Mental Monster.* 1946. Avon Murder Mystery. 1st ed. VG. R3. $10.00

MERRITT, A. *Moon Pool.* 1951. Avon. wrp. VG. R3. $15.00

MERRITT, A. *Reflections in the Moon Pool.* 1985. Oswald Train. 1st ed. dj. EX. P1. $20.00

MERRITT, A. *Ship of Ishtar.* nd. Borden. Ils Finlay. Memorial ed. dj. EX. R3. $35.00

MERRITT, A. *Ship of Ishtar.* 1951. Avon. wrp. EX. R3. $35.00

MERRITT, A. *7 Footprints to Satan.* 1942. Avon. wrp. VG. R3. $20.00

MERRYMAN, Richard. *Andrew Wyeth.* 1968. Boston. 1st ed. dj. VG. B3. $205.00

MERRYMAN, William. *Yankee Caballero.* 1940. Nat Travel Club. 1st ed. 317 p. F2. $15.00

MERTEN, George. *Marionette.* 1957. Toronto. Nelson. 1st ed. 152 p. dj. EX. H3. $60.00

MERTON, Thomas. *Spiritual Direction & Meditation.* nd. (1960) Liturgical Pr. Apparent 1st ed. dj. VG. B10. $7.50

MERTON, Thomas. *Waters of Siloe.* nd. Random House. Book Club ed. dj. EX. B10. $3.75

MERTON & ANDREWS. *Monastic Journey.* 1977. KS City. 1st Am ed. 185 p. dj. EX. B10. $7.00

MERTON & SUZUKI. *Encounter.* 1988. Larkspur. 1st ed. 1/1060. M. K2. $65.00

MERULLO, Roland. *Leaving Losapas.* 1991. Houghton Mifflin. 1st ed. sgn. dj. EX. K2. $40.00

MERWIN, Mrs. George. *3 Years in Chile.* 1966. S IL U Pr. reprint of 1863 ed. F2. $15.00

MERWIN, Sam. *House of Many Worlds.* 1951. Doubleday. 1st ed. dj. EX. R3. $30.00

MERWIN, Sam. *Murder in Mini.* 1940. Crime Club. 1st ed. VG. P1. $30.00

MERWIN, Sam. *Wht Widows.* 1953. Doubleday. 1st ed. dj. EX. R3. $35.00

MERWIN, W.S. *Dancing Bears.* 1954. New Haven. Yale. 1st ed. dj. VG. B13. $100.00

MERWIN, W.S. *W Wind: Supplement of Am Poetry.* 1961. London. Poetry Book Soc. 12mo. 11 p. wrp. EX. C4. $75.00

MESERVE. *Photographs of Abraham Lincoln.* 1944. NY. 1st ed. dj. VG. C2. $45.00

MESNY, Rene. *Television et Transmission des Images.* 1933. Paris. Lib Armand Colin. presentation. VG. H3. $125.00

MESSENGER, Phyllis. *Ethics of Collecting Cultural Property.* 1990. NM U. 4to. 266 p. dj. F2. $35.00

MESSICK, Dale. *Brenda Starr, Girl Reporter.* 1943. Whitman. dj. VG. P1. $15.00

METALIOUS, G. *Peyton Place.* 1956. NY. 1st ed. dj. VG. B3. $45.00

METCALF, Paul. *Genoa.* 1965. Highlands, NC. 1st ed. sgn. dj. EX. T9. $95.00

METCALFE, John. *Smoking Leg.* 1926. Doubleday. 1st ed. VG. R3. $45.00

METRAUX, Alfred. *Hist of the Incas.* 1969. Pantheon. 1st Am ed. 205 p. dj. F2. $20.00

METROPOLITAN MUSEUM OF ART. *Art of Africa, Pacific Islands, & Am.* 1981.Ils Boltin. 4to. wrp. F2. $7.50

METROPOLITAN MUSEUM OF ART. *Houses for the Hereafter.* 1987.Ils. 4to. wrp. F2. $15.00

METROPOLITAN MUSEUM OF ART. *Mexico: Splendors of 30 Centuries.* 1990. Little Brn. 1st ed. 4to. dj. F2. $75.00

METZ, Jerred. *Temperate Voluptuary.* 1975. Capra. Chapbook Series. 1/50. sgn. EX. K2. $20.00

METZGER, Albert. *Origines Orientales du Christianisme Textes & Documents.* 1906. Paris. 12mo. G1. $45.00

MEYER, David. *Wizard Exposed.* 1987. Glenwood, IL. 2nd print. 175 p. M. J3. $24.50

MEYER, Franz. *Mac Chagall.* nd. (1963) Abrams. 1st ed. 4to. 775 p. EX. R4. $85.00

MEYER, J.J. *Try Another World.* 1942. Business Bourse. 1st ed. dj. EX. R3. $10.00

MEYER, Karl. *Plundered Past.* 1973. Atheneum. 1st ed. 353 p. dj. F2. $20.00

MEYER, L. *Off the Sauce.* 1967. NY. 1st ed. dj. VG. B3. $20.00

MEYER, Nicholas. *W-End Horror.* nd. Book Club. dj. EX. P1. $4.50

MEYERS, Alfred. *Murder Ends the Song.* 1941. Reynal Hitchcock. xl. VG. P1. $7.50

MEYERS, Barlow. *Adventure at 2 Rivers.* 1961. Whitman. EX. P1. $15.00

MEYERS, Barlow. *Have Gun Will Travel.* 1959. Whitman. VG. P1. $6.00

MEYERS, Barlow. *Janet Lennon at Camp Calamity.* 1962. Whitman. VG. P1. $8.50

MEYERS, Barlow. *Mystery at Medicine Wheel.* 1964. Whitman. VG. P1. $5.00

MEYNELL, Alice. *Rhythm of Life.* 1893. London. 1/550. G. $20.00

MEYNELL, Alice. *Spirit of the Place.* 1899. London. VG. $15.00

MEYNELL, Laurence. *Hooky & the Crock of Gold.* 1975. Macmillan. 1st ed. dj. xl. P1. $5.00

MEYNELL, Laurence. *Hooky & the Prancing Horse.* 1980. Macmillan. 1st ed. dj. EX. P1. $15.00

MEYRINK, Gustav. *Golem.* 1928. Houghton Mifflin. 1st Am ed. VG. R3. $30.00

MIALL, Robert. *UFO 2: Sporting Blood.* 1973. Warner. 1st Am ed. wrp. EX. F5. $8.00

MICHAEL, D.J. *Death Tour.* 1978. Bobbs Merrill. 1st ed. dj. EX. F5. $20.00

MICHAELS, Barbara. *Into the Darkness.* 1990. Simon Schuster. 1st ed. dj. EX. P1. $18.95

MICHAELS, Barbara. *Shattered Silk.* 1986. Atheneum. 1st ed. dj. EX. P1. $15.95

MICHAELS, Leonard. *I Would Have Saved Them If I Could.* 1975. Farrar Straus. 1st ed. dj. EX. B13. $45.00

MICHAUD, Stephen. *Only Living Witness: True Account of Homicidal Insanity.* 1983. Linden Pr. Book Club ed? 332 p. dj. VG. B10. $4.00

MICHEL, Genevieve. *Rules of Tikal.* 1989. Guatemala. 1st ed. wrp. F2. $15.00

MICHEL, P.H. *Romanesque Wall Paintings in France.* 1949. Paris. Ils. clr pls. EX. $50.00

MICHELL, E.B. *Art & Practice of Hawking.* 1971. Newton, MA. Ils. 291 p. dj. VG. B3. $30.00

MICHELMAN, Joseph. *Violin Varnish.* 1946. Cincinnati. Michelman. 1st ed. presentation. 185 p. EX. H3. $45.00

MICHENER, Carroll. *Heirs of the Incas.* 1924. Minton Balch. 1st ed. 287 p. F2. $20.00

MICHENER, Ezra. *Autobiographical Notes From Life & Letters.* 1893. Friends Book Assn. 12mo. 202 p. VG. V1. $15.00

MICHENER, Ezra. *Obituary Memoir of Mary S Michener.* 1885. Friends Book Assn. 18mo. 29 p. SftCvr. EX. V1. $8.00

MICHENER, Ezra. *Retrospect of Early Quakerism...Phil Yearly Meeting.* 1860. Phil. Ellwood Zell. 1st print. 8vo. 434 p. G. V1. $32.00

MICHENER, J.A. *Bridge at Andau.* 1957. Random House. 1st ed. 270 p. VG. $25.00

MICHENER, J.A. *Centennial.* 1974. Random House. 1st ed. 1/500. sgn. slipcase. EX. K2. $125.00

MICHENER, J.A. *Chesapeake.* 1978. Random House. sgn. dj. H3. $100.00

MICHENER, J.A. *Chesapeake.* 1978. Random House. UP. wrp. VG. B13. $125.00

MICHENER, J.A. *Drifters.* 1971. Random House. 1st ed. 1/500. sgn. slipcase. EX. K2. $125.00

MICHENER, J.A. *Floating World.* 1954. NY. 1st ed. dj. VG. B3. $85.00

MICHENER, J.A. *Floating World.* 1954. NY. 2nd print. dj. VG. $30.00

MICHENER, J.A. *Iberia: Spanish Travels & Reflections.* 1968. Random House. Ltd ed. 1/500. sgn. dj. boxed. H3. $225.00

MICHENER, J.A. *Michener Miscellany.* 1973. NY. 1st ed. dj. VG. B3. $45.00

MICHENER, J.A. *Poland.* 1983. Random House. UP. wrp. VG. B13. $100.00

MICHENER, J.A. *Presidential Lottery.* 1969. NY. 1st ed. dj. VG. B3. $25.00

MICHENER, J.A. *Sayonara.* 1954. NY. 1st ed. 243 p. dj. VG. T5. $25.00

MICHENER, J.A. *Source.* 1965. NY. 1st ed. dj. VG. B3. $40.00

MICHENER, J.A. *Space.* 1982. Random House. UP. wrp. EX. B13. $100.00

MICHENER, J.A. *Sports in Am.* nd. Random House. UP. red wrp. VG. B13. $125.00

MICHENER, J.A. *Tales of the S Pacific.* 1950. NY. Special Ltd ed. 1/1500. VG. B3. $100.00

MICHENER, J.A. *Tales of the S Pacific.* 1951. London. Collins. 1st UK ed. dj. EX. B13. $275.00

MICHENER, J.A. *USA.* 1981. Crown. 1st ed. clipped dj. EX. B13. $75.00

MICK, A.H. *With the 102 Infantry Divsion Through Germany.* 1947. WA. 1st ed. 541 p. T5. $125.00

MIDDLETON, Don. *Roy Rogers & the Gopher Creek Gunman.* 1945. Whitman. dj. VG. P1. $20.00

MIDDLETON, Richard. *Ghost Ship.* 1912. London. 1st ed. VG. R3. $30.00

MIDDLETON, Thomas. *Hengist, King of Kent; or, Mayor of Queens Borough.* 1838. Scribner. 1st ed. VG. rare. C1. $120.00

MIDDLETON, W.D. *S Shore, Last Interurban.* 1973. San Marino. Ils. 176 p. dj. VG. T5. $22.50

MIDLER, Bette. *View From a Broad.* 1980. NY. presentation. dj. VG. B3. $35.00

MIERS, E.S. *General Who Marched to Hell.* 1951. NY. 1st ed. 349 p. VG. T5. $19.50

MIGEOD, F.W.H. *Languages of W Africa.* 1911. London. 1st ed. 2 vols. xl. VG. $60.00

MIGHELS, P.V. *Crystal Sceptre.* 1906. Harper. decor brd. VG. P1. $20.00

MILES, Beryl. *Spirit of Mexico.* 1966. London. Murray. Ils. 208 p. dj. F2. $12.50

MILES, Carlota. *Almada of Alamos.* 1962. Tucson. Ltd ed. 1/50. 197 p. full leather. F2. $65.00

MILES, Lowell. *As It Was & As It Is.* 1845. Lowell. 1st ed. map. 234 p. rare. $150.00

MILL, H.R. *Siege of the S Pole.* 1905. NY. 1st ed. VG. T1. $22.00

MILL, J.S. *On Liberty.* 1891. NY. VG. $12.00

MILLAR, Margaret. *Devil Loves Me.* nd. Collier. VG. P1. $15.00

MILLAR, Margaret. *Devil Loves Me.* nd. Grosset Dunlap. dj. VG. P1. $10.00

MILLAR, Margaret. *Fire Will Freeze.* nd. Book Club. VG. P1. $3.00

MILLAR, Margaret. *Fire Will Freeze.* 1944. Tower. dj. VG. P1. $15.00

MILLAR, Margaret. *Wives & Lovers.* 1954. Random House. 1st ed. clipped dj. EX. F5. $20.00

MILLAR & BANKART. *Plastering, Plain & Decor.* nd. NY. Ils 4th ed. dj. VG. T5. $95.00

MILLARD, Tex. *Cuttin' the Corners.* 1966. Barnes. apparent 1st ed. 176 p. dj. VG. B10. $5.00

MILLAY, E.S.V. *Buck in the Snow & Other Poems.* 1928. Harper. Ltd ed. 1/515. sgn. boxed. EX. H3. $200.00

MILLAY, E.S.V. *Buck in the Snow.* 1928. NY. Ltd ed. 1/515. sgn. VG. H3. $90.00

MILLAY, E.S.V. *Conversations at Midnight.* 1937. Harper. 1st ed. glassine dj. boxed. EX. B13. $75.00

MILLAY, E.S.V. *Huntsman, What Quarry?* 1939. Harper. 1st ed. tissue dj. boxed. EX. B13. $75.00

MILLAY, E.S.V. *King's Henchman.* 1927. Harper. early ed. dj. VG. H3. $50.00

MILLAY, E.S.V. *Lamp & the Bell.* 1921. Harper. early ed. dj. EX. H3. $50.00

MILLAY, E.S.V. *Lamp & the Bell.* 1921. NY. Frank Shay. 1st ed. stiff wrp. morocco slipcase. H3. $150.00

MILLAY, E.S.V. *Make Bright the Arrows.* 1940. Harper. 1st ed. dj. boxed. EX. B13. $75.00

MILLAY, E.S.V. *Wine From These Grapes.* 1934. Harper. 1st ed. tissue dj. slipcase. EX. B13. $75.00

MILLAY, E.S.V. *2 Slatterns & a King.* 1924. Cincinnati. Stewart Kidd. pamphlet. EX. H3. $20.00

MILLAY, E.S.V. *2nd April.* 1921. Harper. 112 p. VG. $18.00

MILLER, Arthur. *After the Fall.* 1964. Viking. Sgn Ltd ed. 1/999. slipcase. EX. H3. $250.00

MILLER, Arthur. *After the Fall.* 1964. Viking. 1st ed. sgn. dj. EX. H3. $75.00

MILLER, Arthur. *After the Fall: A Play by Arthur Miller.* 1964. Viking. Ltd ed. 1/999. sgn. boxed. M. H3. $250.00

MILLER, Arthur. *Creation of the World & Other Business.* 1973. Viking. 1st ed. dj. EX. H3. $40.00

MILLER, Arthur. *Death of a Salesman.* 1939. NY. 1st ed. dj. VG. $125.00

MILLER, Arthur. *Death of a Salesman.* 1949. Stockholm. Forlag. 1st Swedish ed. wrp. VG. H3. $40.00

MILLER, Arthur. *Death of a Salesman.* 1949. Viking. 1st ed. dj. EX. H3. $200.00

MILLER, Arthur. *Death of a Salesman.* 1981. Viking. Ltd Ils ed. 1/500. sgn. slipcase. H3. $125.00

MILLER, Arthur. *Focus.* 1958. PB Orig. VG. B4. $5.00

MILLER, Arthur. *Incident at Vichy.* 1965. Viking. 1st ed. dj. EX. H3. $45.00

MILLER, Arthur. *Maya Rulers of Time.* 1986. Phil. 1st ed. 4to. wrp. F2. $25.00

MILLER, Arthur. *Misfits.* 1961. Dell. PB Orig. sgn. wrp. EX. T9. $60.00

MILLER, Arthur. *Misfits.* 1961. Viking. 1st ed. dj. EX. H3. $75.00

MILLER, Arthur. *Mural Paintings of Teotihuacan.* 1973. Dumbarton Oaks. 1st ed. 4to. dj. F2. $15.00

MILLER, Arthur. *On the Edge of the Sea: Mural Painting at Tanch-Tulum.* 1983. Dumbarton Oaks. 1st ed. 133 p. F2. $35.00

MILLER, Arthur. *Price.* 1968. London. Secker Warburg. 1st UK ed. dj. EX. H3. $35.00

MILLER, Arthur. *Price.* 1968. Viking. 1st ed. dj. EX. H3. $45.00

MILLER, Arthur. *Situation Normal.* 1944. Reynal Hitchcock. sgn. H3. $150.00

MILLER, D.S. *Drum Taps in Dixie: Memories of a Drummer Boy 1861-1865.* 1905. Watertown, NY. 1st ed. EX. $50.00

MILLER, E.D. *Modern Polo.* 1925. London. 5th ed. 8vo. 480 p. VG. $50.00

MILLER, F.F. *Pink Lightning: Collection of Verse.* 1926. Chicago. Seymour. 1st ed. 8vo. 69 p. dj. R4. $15.00

MILLER, Francis. *Photo Hist of the Civil War.* 1911. NY. 1st ed. 10 vols. $265.00

MILLER, Henry. *Air-Conditioned Nightmare.* 1945. New Directions. 1st ed. dj. EX. C4. $75.00

MILLER, Henry. *Big Sur & the Oranges of Hieronymus.* 1957. New Directions. 1st ed. dj. VG. $45.00

MILLER, Henry. *Crazy Cock.* 1991. Grove Pr. UP. pictorial wrp. EX. C4. $50.00

MILLER, Henry. *Joey.* 1979. Capra. Ltd ed. 1/250. sgn. dj. H3. $125.00

MILLER, Henry. *Joey: Vol 3 Book of Friends.* 1979. Santa Barbara. 1/250. sgn. 126 p. dj. T5. $37.50

MILLER, Henry. *Just Wild About Harry.* 1963. New Directions. 1st ed. dj. EX. K2. $65.00

MILLER, Henry. *My Bike & Other Friends.* 1978. Capra. Ltd ed. sgn. dj. EX. H3. $125.00

MILLER, Henry. *My Bike & Other Friends: Vol 2 Book of Friends.* 1978. Capra. sgn. 110 p. dj. T5. $37.50

MILLER, Henry. *Notes on Aaron's Rod.* 1980. Blk Sparrow. 1/276. sgn. M. H3. $75.00

MILLER, Henry. *On Turning 80.* 1972. Capra. Chapbook Series. 1/200. presentation. EX. K2. $85.00

MILLER, Henry. *Order & Chaos.* 1966. Loujon Pr. Leather ed. 1/99. sgn. slipcase. EX. H3. $150.00

MILLER, Henry. *Paintings of Henry Miller: Paint As You Like & Die Happy.* 1982. Capra. 1/250. sgn Durrell. boxed. H3. $100.00

MILLER, Henry. *Reflections on the Maurizius Case.* 1974. Capra. sgn. 62 p. wrp. EX. T5. $25.00

MILLER, Henry. *Theatre & Other Pieces.* 1979. Stoker. inscr. wrp. H3. $100.00

MILLER, Henry. *Tropic of Cancer.* 1934. Paris. Obelisk. 1st ed. inscr. 12mo. slipcase. H3. $1500.00

MILLER, Henry. *Tropique du Cancer.* 1945. Ed Denoel. 1st French ed. inscr. H3. $250.00

MILLER, Hugh. *Art of Eddie Joseph.* 1978. Supreme Magic. 343 p. dj. NM. J3. $22.00

MILLER, Hugh. *Baker's Bonanza.* nd. London. Stanley. 128 p. dj. NM. J3. $16.00

MILLER, Hugh. *Horace Bennett's Prize-Winning Magic.* nd. Supreme Magic. 80 p. dj. NM. J3. $13.00

MILLER, Hugh. *Koran's Legacy.* 1972. London. 1st ed. 180 p. NM. J3. $18.00

MILLER, Hugh. *Magic for Minors.* nd. London. Stanley. 85 p. EX. J3. $9.00

MILLER, Hugh. *Rink's Magic From Holland.* nd. London. Stanley. 1st ed. 255 p. dj. NM. J3. $19.00

MILLER, J.C. *Sam Adams: Pioneer in Propaganda.* 1936. Little Brn. 1st ed. 437 p. VG. B10. $10.00

MILLER, Janet. *Camel Bells of Baghdad.* 1934. Houghton Mifflin. 1st ed. 299 p. VG. J2. $20.00

MILLER, Joaquin. *Building of the City Beautiful.* 1893. Stone Kimball. 1st ed. 1/50. VG. B13. $250.00

MILLER, Kelly. *Kelly Miller's Hist of the W for Human Rights.* 1919. WA. Ils. 495 p. G. T5. $37.50

MILLER, Kelly. *Race Adjustment Essays on the Negro in Am.* 1908. NY. Neale. 1st ed. VG. $95.00

MILLER, Kenneth; see Macdonald, Ross.

MILLER, L. *Wht River Raft.* 1910. Boston. 1st ed. VG. B3. $15.00

MILLER, L.C. *Handsprings for Hamburgers.* 1929. Hollywood. 1st ed. 202 p. VG. B3. $40.00

MILLER, M.E. *Art of Mesoamerica From Olmec to Aztec.* 1990. NY. Ils. 240 p. wrp. F2. $15.00

MILLER, Marc. *Death at the Easel.* 1956. Arcadia. 1st ed. dj. xl. P1. $5.00

MILLER, Marc. *Death Is a Liar.* 1959. Arcadia. 1st ed. dj. VG. P1. $15.00

MILLER, Max. *It's Tomorrow Out Here.* nd. (1945) McGraw. Apparent 1st ed. 186 p. dj. VG. B10. $10.00

MILLER, Merle. *On Being Different.* 1971. Popular Lib. 1st PB ed. inscr. VG. B4. $12.00

MILLER, P.S. *Alicia in Blunderland.* 1983. Oswald Train. 1st ed. dj. EX. P1. $10.00

MILLER, R.J. *USS Akron.* 1932. San Diego. Ils. 31 p. wrp. T5. $50.00

MILLER, Richard. *Brassai: Secret Paris of the 1930s.* 1976. NY. 1st Am ed. VG. G1. $25.00

MILLER, Snowden. *Roy Rogers & the Rimrod Renegades.* 1952. Whitman. dj. VG. P1. $20.00

MILLER, T. *Cactus Air Force.* 1969. NY. 1st ed. 242 p. VG. B3. $37.50

MILLER, W.H. *Boy Explorers & Ape-Man of Sumatra.* 1923. Harper. 1st ed. decor brd. VG. P1. $10.00

MILLER, W.J. *Training of an Army: Camp Curtin & N Civil War.* 1990. Wht Mane. 334 p. dj. M. S1. $27.95

MILLER, W.M. *Canticle for Leibowitz.* 1960. Lippincott. 2nd ed. dj. VG. P1. $30.00

MILLER & FULOP. *Holy Devil.* 1928. Viking. Ils. photos. VG. $12.50

MILLER & PERLES. *What Are You Going To Do About It?* 1971. Turret. Ltd ed. 1/100. sgns. dj. H3. $85.00

MILLER & STRANGE. *Centenary Bibliography of Pickwick Papers.* 1936. London. Argonaut. gr bdg. H3. $45.00

MILLETT, Kate. *Elegy for Sita.* 1979. Targ Ed. 1st ed. 1/350. sgn. H3. $60.00

MILLHISER, Marlys. *Michael's Wife.* 1972. Putnam. 1st ed. dj. EX. F5. $17.50

MILLIGAN, Spike. *Adolf Hitler: My Part in His Downfall.* 1971. London. Michael Joseph. 1st ed. 146 p. dj. EX. B10. $6.25

MILLIS, Mark. *Son of Mystery.* 1939. Saalfield. VG. P1. $10.00

MILLIS, Walter. *Last Phase: Allied Victory in W Europe.* 1946. Boston. 1st ed. VG. $12.00

MILLIS, Walter. *Martial Spirit.* 1931. Literary Guild. Ils. G. B10. $3.75

MILLS, Alfred. *Pictures of Roman Hist in Miniature.* 1811. Phil. 32mo. 96 p. printed brd. EX. $325.00

MILLS, Arthur. *Escapade.* 1933. Collins. 5th ed. P1. $7.00

MILLS, Arthur. *Intrigue Island.* 1930. Collins. 1st ed. dj. VG. P1. $50.00

MILLS, Dorothy. *Arms of the Sun.* 1926. London. VG. R3. $30.00

MILLS, Enos. *Wild Life on the Rockies.* 1909. Boston. Ils 1st ed. 263 p. VG. B3. $27.50

MILLS, J.C. *Our Inland Seas: Their Shipping & Commerce for 3 Centuries.* 1976. Cleveland. reprint of 1910 ed. VG. T5. $12.50

MILLS, J.T. *John Bright.* 1893. London. Hicks. 12mo. 202 p. VG. V1. $12.00

MILLS, James. *Report to the Commissioner.* 1972. Farrar Straus Giroux. 1st ed. dj. VG. P1. $14.00

MILLS, L.S. *Legend of Barkhamsted Lighthouse.* 1952. np. Ils. 141 p. ES. VG. T5. $19.50

MILLS, L.W. *Sagebrush Saga.* 1956. Utah. 1st ed. 4to. inscr. suede wrp. K1. $50.00

MILLS, Osmington. *Sundry Fell Designs.* 1968. Roy. dj. EX. P1. $10.00

MILLS, R.P. *Best From Fantasy & SF: 9th Series.* nd. Book Club. dj. VG. P1. $4.50

MILLS, W.C. *OH Archeological Exhibit of the Jamestown Exposition.* 1907. Columbus. 49 p. TEG. new endpapers. G. T5. $25.00

MILNE, A.A. *By Way of Intro.* 1929. Dutton. 1st Am ed. 1/166. sgn. slipcase. H3. $250.00

MILNE, A.A. *Christopher Robin Storybook.* 1929. Dutton. 1st ed. dj. EX. B13. $300.00

MILNE, A.A. *King's Breakfast & Other Selections.* 1947. Dutton. Ils E Shepard. 1st ed. dj. EX. $20.00

MILNE, A.A. *More Very Young Songs From When We Were Very Young...* 1929. McClelland Stewart. 1st ed. lg quarto. 40 p. VG. H3. $75.00

MILNE, A.A. *Pooh Party Book.* 1971. Dutton. Ils Shepard. 1st ed. 8vo. 146 p. dj. VG. $15.00

MILNE, A.A. *Teddy Bear & Other Songs From When We Were Very Young.* 1926. McClelland Stewart. 1st ed. lg quarto. 43 p. VG. H3. $125.00

MILNE, A.A. *Those Were the Days.* 1929. Methuen. Ltd ed. 1/250. sgn. TEG. H3. $175.00

MILNE, A.A. *Toad of Toad Hall.* 1929. London. 1st ed. dj. EX. $65.00

MILNE, A.A. *When I Was Very Young.* 1930. Fountain Pr. 1st Am ed. 1/842. sgn. slipcase. H3. $250.00

MILNE, A.A. *Winnie the Pooh.* 1926. NY. 1st Am ed. VG. B3. $75.00

MILNE, Jean. *Fiesta Time in Latin Am.* 1965. Ward Ritchie. 1st ed. 236 p. dj. F2. $15.00

MILNE, John. *Moody Man.* 1988. Viking. 1st Am ed. dj. EX. F5. $15.00

MILNER, George. *Leave-Taking.* 1966. Dodd Mead. 1st ed. dj. VG. P1. $12.50

MILTON, C.J. *Landmarks of Old Wheeling.* 1943. Wheeling. 1st ed. folio. B3. $22.50

MILTON, G.F. *Age of Hate: Andrew Johnson & the Radicals.* 1930. Coward McCann. 788 p. G. S1. $9.50

MILTON, John. *Paradise Lost & Paradise Regained.* 1936. Ltd Ed Club. Ils/sgn Carlotta Petrina. 1/1500. VG. C4. $60.00

MILTON, John. *Paradise Lost.* 1669. London. Simmons. 1st ed. 5th state. Sangorski/Sutcliffe bdg. H3. $22500.00

MILTON, John. *Poems in Eng.* 1926. London. 1/90. 2 vols in 1. full vellum. H3. $1000.00

MILTON, John. *Poems...* 1645. London. 1st ed. variant on title p. Zaehnsdorf bdg. H3. $15000.00

MILTON, John. *Poetical Works.* 1890. London. Macmillan. 2nd ed. 3 vols. tall octavo. EX. H3. $600.00

MILTON, John. *Works...in Verse & Prose.* 1863. London. Bickers Bush. 8 vols. octavo. Zaehnsdorf bdg. H3. $850.00

MINCH, Stephen. *Ever So Sleightly: Professional Card Technique of MA Nash.* 1975. Calgary. 1st ed. VG. J3. $14.00

MINCH, Stephen. *NY Magic Symposium Collection 4.* 1985. NY. 1st ed. 119 p. NM. J3. $24.00

MINCH, Stephen. *NY Magic Symposium Collection 5.* 1986. NY. 1st ed. Eng/Japanese text. 140 p. NM. J3. $22.00

MINCH, Stephen. *Secrets of a Puerto Rican Gambler.* 1980. Prime Pr. 1st ed. 115 p. SftCvr. NM. J3. $9.00

MINCH, Stephen. *Spectacle: Compilation of Modern Wonders.* 1990. Tahoma, CA. 1st ed. dj. M. J3. $29.95

MINCH, Stephen. *Vernon Chronicles Vol I: Lost Inner Secrets.* 1987. Tahoma, CA. L&L Pub. 1st ed. 235 p. dj. NM. J3. $31.00

MINCH & FLEISCHER. *NY Magic Symposium Collection 3.* 1984. Magic Symposium. 1st ed. 135 p. NM. J3. $23.00

MINER, L. *Am Political Verse 1783-1788.* 1937. Cedar Rapids. 1st ed. 274 p. dj. VG. B3. $47.50

MINER, Mike. *Civil War Flags.* 1987. pamphlet. sgn. G. S1. $4.50

MINES, Samuel. *Best From Startling Stories.* 1953. Holt. 1st ed. dj. EX. R3. $12.50

MINGAZZINI, Paolino. *Greek Pottery Painting.* 1969. London. sm 8vo. dj. EX. $15.00

MINNIGERODE, Meade. *Some Personal Letters of Herman Melville & a Bibliography.* 1922. NY. 1st ed. 1/1500. VG. $50.00

MINO & TSIANG. *Ice & Gr Clouds: Traditions of Chinese Celedon.* 1987. Indianapolis Mus Art/IU. D4. $25.00

MINOT, Stephen. *Chill of Dusk.* 1964. Doubleday. 1st ed. dj. xl. P1. $7.50

MINOT, Susan. *Lust & Other Stories.* 1989. Houghton Mifflin. UP. EX. K2. $30.00

MINSTER OF STATE. *Australia for the Tourist.* 1914. Melbourne. 1st ed. 174 p. G. B3. $22.50

MIRZA, Rebecca. *Guide to Selected Latin Am Manuscripts in Lilly Lib.* 1974. Bloomington, IN. 4to. 58 p. wrp. F2. $7.50

MISCIATTELLI, Piero. *Piccolomini Lib in Cathedral of Siena.* 1924. Siena, Italy. pls. T5. $75.00

MISHELL, Ed. *Hold-Out Miracles.* 1969. Tannen. 1st ed. 61 p. NM. J3. $3.00

MISHIMA, Yukio. *Madame de Sade.* 1968. London. Peter Owen. 1st ed. dj. VG. B13. $65.00

MISHIMA, Yukio. *5 Modern No Plays.* 1957. Knopf. 1st Am ed. inscr. dj. EX. C4. $750.00

MITCHELL, Carleton. *Islands to Windward.* 1948. NY. 1st ed. maps. gilt bdg. VG. T1. $45.00

MITCHELL, F.H. *Fundamentals of Electronics.* 1959. Addison. 2nd ed. 260 p. VG. B10. $4.50

MITCHELL, Gladys. *Rising of the Moon.* nd. Book Club. dj. VG. P1. $5.00

MITCHELL, Gladys. *Uncoffin'd Clay.* 1982. St Martin. 1st ed. dj. EX. P1. $15.00

MITCHELL, Gladys. *Winking at the Brim.* 1977. McKay/Washburn. dj. EX. P1. $15.00

MITCHELL, J.A. *Cloria Victis.* 1897. Scribner. 1st ed. TEG. gilt bdg. G. B10. $6.25

MITCHELL, J.A. *Drowsy.* 1917. Stokes. 1st ed. VG. R3. $25.00

MITCHELL, J.A. *Silent War.* 1906. Life. 1st ed. dj. EX. R3. $35.00

MITCHELL, J.L. *Cairo Dawns.* 1931. Bobbs Merrill. 1st ed. dj. EX. R3. $35.00

MITCHELL, J.L. *Conquest of the Maya.* 1935. Dutton. 2nd print. 279 p. F2. $20.00

MITCHELL, J.L. *Earth Conquerors.* 1934. Simon Schuster. not 1st ed. peach bdg. VG. B10. $5.00

MITCHELL, J.L. *3 Go Back.* 1932. Bobbs Merrill. 1st ed. G. R3. $30.00

MITCHELL, J.Q. *1st Settlement in OH...* 1888. OH Soc of NY. 8vo. 12 p. wrp. xl. G. T5. $27.50

MITCHELL, James. *Dead Ernest.* 1987. Henry Holt. 1st ed. dj. EX. P1. $15.95

MITCHELL, James. *Death & Bright Water.* 1974. Morrow. 1st ed. dj. VG. P1. $25.00

MITCHELL, Joseph. *Joe Gould's Secret.* 1965. Viking. 1st ed. dj. EX. B13. $50.00

MITCHELL, Margaret. *Gone With the Wind.* June 1936. 1st ed. dj. VG. J2. $60.00

MITCHELL, Margaret. *Gone With the Wind.* May 1936. Macmillan. 1st ed. 1st issue. later issue dj. EX. C4. $1000.00

MITCHELL, Peter. *Great Flower Painters: 4 Centuries of Floral Art.* 1973. Woodstock. Overlook. D4. $95.00

MITCHELL, S.A. *System of Modern Geography...Am, Europe, Asia, Africa...* 1856. Cowperthwait. Ils. 336 p. A5. $40.00

MITCHELL, S.W. *Hugh Wynne: Free Quaker.* 1897. NY. Century. 12mo. 2 vols. V1. $10.00

MITCHELL, S.W. *Red City.* 1908. Century. 1st ed. 421 p. VG. B10. $5.50

MITCHELL, Scott. *Sables Spell Trouble.* 1963. Hammond Hammond. 1st ed. dj. xl. P1. $5.00

MITCHELL, T.C. *How To Become a Ventriloquist.* nd. (1919) London Magical Co. sm octavo. VG. H3. $40.00

MITCHELL. *Mitchell's School Atlas.* 1857. Phil. Cowperthwait. 4to. 18 maps. VG. C1. $65.00

MITCHISON, Naomi. *Blood of the Martyrs.* 1939. London. Constable. 1st ed. dj. EX. B13. $65.00

MITCHISON, Naomi. *Solution 3.* 1975. Dobson. 1st ed. dj. EX. P1. $15.00

MITFORD, Jessica. *Kind & Unusual Punishment.* 1973. Knopf. Book Club ed. dj. VG. $4.50

MITFORD, Jessica. *Poison Penmanship.* 1979. Knopf. 1st ed. inscr. dj. VG. B13. $75.00

MITFORD, Jessica. *Poison Penmanship.* 1979. Knopf. 1st ed. 277 p. dj. EX. $20.00

MITSCHERLICH. *Doctors of Infamy.* 1949. NY. 1st ed. 172 p. dj. VG. B3. $35.00

MO, Timothy. *Insular Possession.* 1968. London. UP. wrp. VG. $45.00

MO, Timothy. *Sour Sweet.* 1982. London. Andre Deutsch. 1st ed. dj. M. C4. $125.00

MOATS, Leone. *Thunder in Their Veins: Memoir of Mexico.* 1932. Century. 1st ed. 279 p. dj. F2. $15.00

MOBERG, Ivar. *Cotton Loomfixer's Manual.* 1942. McGraw. 1st ed. 197 p. VG. B10. $7.25

MODEL, Lisette. *Photographs.* 1979. Aperature. dj. EX. $35.00

MODESSIT, L.E. *Fires of Paratime.* 1982. Timescape. 1st HrdCvr ed. dj. EX. F5. $10.00

MODIGLIANI. *Pencil Portraits.* 1951. Blk Sun. 11 loose sheets in folio. H3. $400.00

MOEHRING, John. *Texan Trixter.* 1986. Panorama Production. 1st ed. 99 p. M. J3. $8.00

MOGELEVER, J. *Death to Traitors.* 1960. NY. 1st ed. dj. VG. B3. $35.00

MOHOLY-NAGY, Laszlo. *Vision in Motion.* 1947. Chicago. 1st ed. dj. M. $200.00

MOHOLY-NAGY, Sibyl. *Architecture of Paul Rudolph.* 1970. NY. 1st ed. EX. G1. $20.00

MOHR, Nicolaus. *Excursion Through Am.* 1973. Chicago. Ils. 398 p. T5. $22.50

MOISE, L.C. *Biography of Isaac Harby With Account of Reformed Soc.* c 1931. Columbia, SC. 1st ed. EX. $75.00

MOJTABAI, A.G. *Mundome.* 1974. NY. 1st ed. sgn. dj. EX. T9. $45.00

MOKIERE. *Dramatic Works.* 1875. Edinburgh. Paterson. 6 vols. lg octavo. G. H3. $200.00

MOKLER, A.J. *Ft Caspar, Platte River Station.* 1939. Prairie Pub. 1st ed. presentation. VG. A5. $60.00

MOLINA SOLIS, J.F. *Hist del Descumbrimiento y Conquista de Yucatan...* 1943. Mexico. 2nd ed. 2 vols. F2. $75.00

MOLLER, Helen. *Dancing With Helen Moller.* 1918. John Lane. 1st ed. quarto. 115 p. VG. H3. $125.00

MOLLOY, Anne. *Lucy's Christmas.* 1950. Boston. 1st ed. dj. VG. B3. $17.50

MOLSON, Francis. *Children's Fantasy.* 1989. Starmont. 1st ed. wrp. M. R3. $9.95

MOMADAY, N.S. *Ancient Child.* 1989. Doubleday. UP. wrp. EX. K2. $25.00

MOMADAY, N.S. *House Made of Dawn.* 1968. Harper Row. galley sheets. EX. rare. K2. $450.00

MOMADAY, N.S. *House Made of Dawn.* 1968. NY. 1st ed. dj. EX. C4. $75.00

MOMADAY, N.S. *Names.* 1978. Harper. 1st ed. sgn. dj. EX. B13. $100.00

MOMADAY, N.S. *Way to Rainy Mt.* 1900. nd. NM U. 1st ed. clipped dj. EX. B13. $65.00

MOMADAY, N.S. *Way to Rainy Mt.* 1969. NM U. 3rd print. inscr. dj. H3. $85.00

MOMADAY & MUENCH. *CO.* 1973. Rand McNally. 1st ed. dj. EX. K2. $75.00

MONACO, Richard. *Broken Stone.* 1985. Ace. 1st ed. PB. EX. C1. $3.50

MONACO, Richard. *Final Quest.* 1980. NY. 1st ed. dj. M. C1. $14.00

MONAGHAN, Jay. *Book of Am W.* 1963. Bonanza. dj. VG. $16.00

MONAGHAN, Jay. *Book of Am W.* 1963. NY. 1st ed. dj. EX. G1. $30.00

MONAGHAN, Jay. *Civil War on the W Border 1854-1865.* 1955. Bonanza. 474 p. dj. VG. S1. $15.00

MONAGHAN, Jay. *Great Rascal: Exploits of Amazing Ned Buntline.* 1951. Bonanza. 1st ed. 353 p. dj. NM. J3. $12.00

MONAGHAN, Jay. *Life of General Custer.* 1959. Boston. 1st ed. 469 p. dj. VG. B3. $40.00

MONAHAN, John; see Burnett, W.R.

MONCREIFF & POTTINGER. *Simple Heraldry Cheerfully Ils.* 1965. London. 11th imp. dj. VG. C1. $12.50

MONCRIEFF, A.R. *Romance & Legend of Chivalry.* 1934. 1st ed. bl bdg. VG. C1. $9.50

MONCRIEFF, C.S. *Song of Roland.* 1938. Ltd Ed Club. Ils/sgn Angelo. TEG. EX. $125.00

MONCRIEFF, Perrine. *New Zealand Birds & How To Identify Them.* nd. Aukland. Whitcomb Tombs Ltd. 2nd ed. VG. T3. $15.00

MONOT, Susan. *Monkeys.* 1986. Dutton/Lawrence. 1st ed. dj. EX. K2. $30.00

MONROE, Lyle; see Heinlein, Robert.

MONROE, Marilyn. *My Story.* 1974. NY. 1st ed. dj. VG. B3. $20.00

MONSARRAT, Nicholas. *HM Corvette.* 1943. Lippincott. 1st ed. 168 p. VG. B10. $10.00

MONSARRAT, Nicholas. *Kappillan of Malta.* 1973. London. 1st ed. sgn. dj. EX. $50.00

MONSARRAT, Nicholas. *Tribe That Lost Its Head.* 1956. Cassell. 1st ed. dj. VG. P1. $25.00

MONTAGNE, Prosper. *Encyclopedia of Food, Wine, & Cookery.* 1966. Crown. 7th print. 1101 p. dj. EX. B10. $18.00

MONTAGU, Ewen. *Beyond Top Secret Ultra.* 1978. Coward McCann. 1st ed. dj. EX. P1. $12.50

MONTAGU. *Studies & Essays in Hist Science in Homage to George Sarton.* 1946. NY. 1st ed. VG. C2. $45.00

MONTAGUE, Frederick. *Westminster Wizardry.* nd. London. Goldston. 95 p. EX. J3. $19.00

MONTAGUE, Joseph. *Ole Jim Bridger.* 1927. Chelsea House. 1st ed. 242 p. G. $5.00

MONTAGUE, Richard. *Oceans, Poles, & Airmen.* 1971. NY. 1st ed. dj. VG. $15.00

MONTGOMERY, F.T. *Billy Whiskers in an Airplane.* 1912. Saalfield. 1st ed. VG. B3. $35.00

MONTGOMERY, F.T. *Billy Whiskers' Painting & Drawing Book.* 1909. Saalfield. 4to. 4 clr pl p. EX. scarce. T1. $75.00

MONTGOMERY, Horace. *Johnny Cobb: Confederate Aristocrat.* 1964. Athens, GA. 1st ed. stiff wrp. $25.00

MONTGOMERY, L.M. *Anne's House of Dreams.* nd. Grosset. 245 p. dj. VG. B10. $3.50

MONTGOMERY, Rutherford. *Living Wilderness.* nd. (1964) Dodd. Ils. 294 p. EX. B10. $5.25

MONTI, Franco. *Pre-Columbian Terracottas.* 1969. London. Hamlyn. 1st ed. dj. F2. $20.00

MONTIAGNE, Michael. *Essays.* 1902-1904. Houghton Mifflin. 1/265. 3 vols. H3. $750.00

MOODY, M.C. *Quakerism.* nd. Lancaster. Brookshire Pub. 8vo. 8 p. wrp. G. V1. $6.00

MOON, Bucklin. *Without Magnolias.* 1949. Doubleday. 1st ed. dj. EX. F5. $20.00

MOON, William Least Heat. *Bl Highways.* 1983. Little Brn. UP. wrp. EX. B13. $250.00

MOONEY, Ted. *Easy Travel to Other Planets.* 1981. Farrar Straus. UP. wrp. EX. B13. $45.00

MOONEY, Ted. *Easy Travel to Other Planets.* 1981. London. Cape. 1st Eng ed. dj. EX. K2. $30.00

MOONEY, Ted. *Traffic & Laughter.* 1990. NY. UP. wrp. EX. C4. $20.00

MOORCOCK, Michael. *Adventures of Una Persson & Catherine Cornelius...* 1976. Quarted. 1st ed. sgn. dj. P1. $35.00

MOORCOCK, Michael. *Alien Heat.* 1973. Harper. dj. VG. P1. $15.00

MOORCOCK, Michael. *Before Armageddon.* 1975. Allen. 1st ed. dj. EX. P1. $20.00

MOORCOCK, Michael. *Breakfast in the Ruins.* 1971. Random House. 1st Am ed. sgn. dj. EX. R3. $27.50

MOORCOCK, Michael. *Breakfast in the Ruins.* 1971. Random House. 1st ed. dj. EX. F5/P1. $15.00

MOORCOCK, Michael. *Byzantium Endures.* 1981. Random House. UP. tall wrps. EX. K2. $25.00

MOORCOCK, Michael. *Byzantium Endures.* 1981. Random House. 1st ed. dj. VG. P1. $17.50

MOORCOCK, Michael. *Chinese Agent.* 1970. Macmillan. 1st ed. dj. EX. R3. $15.00

MOORCOCK, Michael. *City in the Autumn Stars.* 1987. Ace. 1st ed. dj. EX. P1. $16.95

MOORCOCK, Michael. *Elric Saga I.* 1984. Doubleday. 1st Compilation ed. dj. EX. F5. $10.00

MOORCOCK, Michael. *Elric Saga II.* 1984. Doubleday. 1st Compilation ed. dj. EX. F5. $10.00

MOORCOCK, Michael. *End of All Songs.* 1976. Harper. 1st ed. dj. EX. P1/R3. $15.00

MOORCOCK, Michael. *End of All Songs.* 1976. Harper. 1st ed. inscr. dj. EX. R3. $35.00

MOORCOCK, Michael. *Eng Assassin.* 1972. Harper. 1st ed. dj. EX. R3. $20.00

MOORCOCK, Michael. *Entropy Tango.* 1981. New Eng Lib. 1st ed. sgn. dj. EX. P1. $30.00

MOORCOCK, Michael. *Eternal Champion.* 1978. Harper. 1st Revised/HrdCvr ed. dj. EX. F5. $15.00

MOORCOCK, Michael. *Gloriana.* 1978. London. 1st Eng ed. dj. EX. R3. $40.00

MOORCOCK, Michael. *Gloriana.* 1979. Avon. AP. 1st Am ed. VG. R3. $25.00

MOORCOCK, Michael. *Hollow Lands.* nd. Book Club. dj. EX. P1. $4.50

MOORCOCK, Michael. *Hollow Lands.* 1974. Harper Row. 1st ed. dj. EX. P1. $15.00

MOORCOCK, Michael. *Ice Schooner.* 1977. Harper. 1st ed. dj. EX. R3. $17.50

MOORCOCK, Michael. *Land Leviathan.* 1974. Doubleday. 1st ed. dj. EX. P1/R3. $10.00

MOORCOCK, Michael. *Legends From the End of Time.* 1976. Harper. 1st ed. inscr. dj. EX. R3. $35.00

MOORCOCK, Michael. *Nomad of Time.* nd. Book Club. dj. xl. P1. $5.00

MOORCOCK, Michael. *Silver Warriors.* 1973. Dell. 1st ed. wrp. EX. F5. $8.00

MOORCOCK, Michael. *Stormbringer.* 1965. London. 1st ed. dj. EX. R3. $100.00

MOORCOCK, Michael. *Vanishing Tower.* 1981. Archival. 1st ed. M. R3. $35.00

MOORCOCK, Michael. *War Hound & the World's Pain.* 1981. Timescape. dj. EX. P1. $17.50

MOORE, A.C. *My Roads to Childhood.* 1939. NY. 1st ed. VG. $35.00

MOORE, Barbara. *Wolf Whispered Death.* 1986. St Martin. 1st ed. dj. EX. P1. $16.00

MOORE, Brian. *Cold Heaven.* 1983. Holt Rinehart Winston. UP. wrp. EX. K2. $35.00

MOORE, Brian. *Emperor of Ice Cream.* 1965. NY. 1st ed. dj. EX. T9. $45.00

MOORE, Brian. *Great Victorian Collection.* 1975. NY. 1st Am ed. dj. EX. C4. $25.00

MOORE, Brian. *I Am Mary Dunne.* 1968. Viking. 2nd ed. dj. VG. P1. $7.00

MOORE, Brian. *Mangan Inheritance.* 1979. McClelland Stewart. 1st ed. dj. VG. P1. $20.00

MOORE, Brian. *Temptation of Eileen Hughes.* 1981. Farrar Straus. UP. wrp. EX. K2. $35.00

MOORE, C.L. *Doomsday Morning.* nd. Book Club. dj. VG. P1. $7.50

MOORE, C.L. *Judgment Night.* 1952. Gnome. 1st ed. dj. VG. P1. $75.00

MOORE, C.L. *Judgment Night.* 1952. Gnome. 1st ed. VG. R3. $25.00

MOORE, C.L. *NW of Earth.* 1954. Gnome. 1st ed. dj. EX. R3. $150.00

MOORE, C.L. *Scarlet Dream.* 1981. Donald Grant. 1st ed. dj. EX. P1. $20.00

MOORE, C.L. *Shambleau.* 1953. Gnome. 1st ed. dj. EX. R3. $110.00

MOORE, Daniel. *Dawn Visions.* 1964. City Lights. 1/1950. VG. B4. $6.00

MOORE, E.E. *Traveling With Thomas Story.* 1947. Letchworth. 1st print. 8vo. 320 p. dj. M. V1. $12.00

MOORE, F.F. *Castle Omeragh.* 1903. NY. Appleton. 1st ed. 12mo. 404 p. V1. $6.50

MOORE, Frank. *Rebellion Record.* 1861-1868. Putnam. 1st ed. 11 vols. H3. $1000.00

MOORE, George. *Aphrodite in Aulis.* 1930. Heinemann. Ltd ed. 1/825. sgn. H3. $35.00

MOORE, George. *Avowals.* 1919. London. private print. 1/1000. sgn. dj. H3. $35.00

MOORE, George. *Brook Kerith: A Syrian Story.* 1916. Laurie/Riverside. 1st ed. sm quarto. H3. $40.00

MOORE, George. *Brook Kerith: A Syrian Story.* 1929. Heinemann. 1/375. sgns. vellum. EX. H3. $125.00

MOORE, George. *Brook Kerith: A Syrian Story.* 1929. Macmillan. Ils Stephen Gooden. 1/500. sgns. TEG. H3. $75.00

MOORE, George. *Coming of Gabrielle.* 1920. London. 1/1000. sgn. dj. VG. $15.00

MOORE, George. *In Single Strictness.* 1922. Boni Liveright. Ltd ed. 1/1050. sgn. H3. $35.00

MOORE, George. *Making of an Immortal: Play in 1 Act.* 1927. Bowling Gr. Ltd ed. 1/1240. H3. $75.00

MOORE, George. *Passing of the Essenes: Drama in 3 Acts.* 1930. Heinemann. Ltd ed. 1/775. sgn. TEG. boxed. H3. $100.00

MOORE, George. *Peronnick the Fool.* 1933. Harrap. Ils Gooden. 1/525. sgns. TEG. vellum. H3. $200.00

MOORE, George. *Peronnik the Fool.* 1926. Mt Vernon, NY. 1st ed. 1/785. 68 p. VG. T5. $75.00

MOORE, George. *Ulick & Soracha.* 1926. Boni Liveright. Ltd ed. 1/1250. sgn. H3. $40.00

MOORE, H.T. *Intelligent Heart.* 1962. Grove Pr. EX. P1. $2.50

MOORE, J.G. *E Gate: Invitation to Arts of China & Japan.* 1979. Cleveland. Ils 1st ed. sgn. lg 4to. 269 p. dj. EX. T5. $35.00

MOORE, J.T. *Tom's Last Forage.* 1926. Cokesbury Pr. 1st print. orig mail envelope. $100.00

MOORE, Marianne. *Complete Poems.* 1981. Macmillan/Viking. 1st ed. dj. EX. C4. $25.00

MOORE, Marianne. *Fables of Fontaine.* 1954. Viking. Ltd ed. 1/400. sgn. boxed. M. H3. $300.00

MOORE, Merrill. *Case Records From a Sonnetorium.* 1951. NY. Twayne. 1st ed. inscr. dj. EX. B13. $65.00

MOORE, Merrill. *Miscellany 1st Series 1 Through 10.* 1939. Boston. inscr. octavo. 400 p. H3. $225.00

MOORE, Mrs. Bloomfield. *Keely & His Discoveries.* 1893. London. 372 p. ES. VG. T5. $175.00

MOORE, Patrick. *Boys` Book of Atronomy.* 1964. Burke. 4th ed. VG. P1. $10.00

MOORE, Patrick. *Science & Fiction.* 1957. Harrap. 1st ed. dj. EX. P1. $45.00

MOORE, R.A. *Life for the Confederacy.* 1987. Broadfoot Pub. 192 p. dj. M. S1. $20.00

MOORE, R.W. *Weimar, Athens of Germany.* c 1918. Hamilton. Ils. inscr. stiff wrp. VG. B10. $6.00

MOORE, Thomas. *Poetical Works.* 1856. Little Brn. 6 vols. VG. $175.00

MOORE, Thomas. *Utopia.* nd. Easton Pr. leather bdg. M. R3. $25.00

MOORE, Ward. *Greener Than You Think.* 1947. Sloane. 1st ed. dj. EX. R3. $30.00

MOORE, Ward. *Greener Than You Think.* 1947. Sloane. 1st ed. dj. VG. P1. $25.00

MOORE, William. *Bayonets in the Sun.* 1978. St Martin. 1st Am/HrdCvr ed. dj. EX. F5. $20.00

MOOREHEAD. *Stone Ornaments Used by Indians in US & Canada.* 1917. Andover. 448 p. A5. $260.00

MOORMAN, Charles. *Arthurian Triptych.* 1960. CA U. 1st ed. dj. VG. C1. $32.50

MORAN, Richrd. *Dallas Down.* 1988. Arbor House. 1st ed. dj. EX. F5. $16.00

MORAND, Paul. *Blk Magic.* 1929. London. Ils Aaron Douglas. 1st ed. G. T5. $37.50

MORAND, Paul. *Indian Air.* 1933. Cassell. 1st ed. 235 p. dj. F2. $17.50

MORAVIA, Alberto. *1934.* 1982. Farrar Straus. Trans William Weaver. UP. wrp. EX. K2. $30.00

MORE, Hannah. *Search After Happiness.* 1811. Phil. Bailey. 12mo. 72 p. wrp. EX. $125.00

MORE, L.T. *Isaac Newton: A Biography.* 1934. 1st ed. 675 p. VG. B3. $30.00

MORELAND & BANNISTER. *Antique Maps: Collector's Guide.* 1989. Phaiden Christies. 326 p. M. A5. $40.00

MORELLA & EPSTEIN. *It Girl.* 1976. NY. 1st ed. dj. EX. B3. $20.00

MORELY, Christopher. *Ballad of NY.* 1950. Doubleday. 1st ed. dj. EX. $22.00

MORFORD, Henry. *Days of Shoddy: Novel of the Great Rebellion in 1861.* 1963. Phil. 1st ed. 478 p. VG. T5. $45.00

MORGAN, Al. *Essential Man.* 1977. Playboy. 1st ed. dj. EX. P1. $15.00

MORGAN, Barbara. *Martha Graham: 16 Dances in Photographs.* 1941. Duell Sloan Pearce. 1st ed. quarto. 160 p. dj. EX. H3. $125.00

MORGAN, Dale. *Humboldt. Rivers of Am Series.* 1943. NY. 1st ed. dj. VG. B3. $35.00

MORGAN, Dan. *Concrete Horizon.* 1976. Millington. 1st ed. dj. EX. P1. $15.00

MORGAN, Dan. *High Destiny.* 1975. Millington. 1st ed. dj. EX. P1. $15.00

MORGAN, G. *Life of James Monroe.* 1921. Boston. 1st ed. dj. VG. B3. $35.00

MORGAN, L.H. *Am Beaver & His Works.* 1868. Lippincott. rebound. VG. T3. $65.00

MORGAN, M. *1 Man's Gold Rush.* 1967. Seattle. 1st ed. dj. VG. B3. $35.00

MORGAN, Seth. *Homeboy.* 1990. Chatto Windus. ARC. wrp. EX. K2. $45.00

MORGAN & LESTER. *Leica Manual.* 1947. NY. 11th ed. 8vo. dj. EX. $30.00

MORGENSTERN, S. *Silent Gondoliers.* 1983. Del Rey. 1st ed. dj. EX. P1. $17.50

MORHART, H.D. *Zoar Story.* 1969. Dover, OH. Ils. sgn. 137 p. wrp. VG. T5. $9.50

MORICE, Anne. *Murder in Outline.* 1979. St Martin. dj. EX. P1. $15.00

MORICE, Anne. *Pub & Be Killed.* 1986. St Martin. 1st ed. dj. VG. P1. $12.95

MORISON, Frank. *Sunset.* 1932. Century. 1st ed. VG. R3. $15.00

MORISON, S.E. *John Paul Jones: Sailor's Biography.* 1959. Boston. 1st ed. dj. EX. $15.00

MORISON, S.E. *Liberation of the Philippines.* 1959. Boston. Ils. fld map. 338 p. G. T5. $12.50

MORISON, S.E. *Old Bruin.* 1967. Boston. 1st ed. 482 p. dj. VG. $20.00

MORITZ, C.P. *Anton Reiser: Psychological Novel.* 1926. Oxford U. 1st World Classics ed. VG. R4. $10.00

MORLEY, Christopher. *Human Being: A Story.* 1934. Doubleday Doran. early ed. inscr. dj. H3. $85.00

MORLEY, Christopher. *Kitty Foyle.* nd. Grosset Dunlap. Photoplay ed. dj. VG. P1. $15.00

MORLEY, Christopher. *Parnassus on Wheels.* nd. BOMC. dj. VG. P1. $7.50

MORLEY, Christopher. *Shadygaff.* nd. Doubleday. 326 p. VG. B10. $5.50

MORLEY, Christopher. *Streamlines.* 1936. Doubleday. 1st ed. 290 p. VG. B10. $10.00

MORLEY, Christopher. *Thorofare.* 1942. NY. 1st ed. dj. VG. T5. $45.00

MORLEY, Christopher. *Thunder on the Left.* 1925. Doubleday Page. VG. P1. $7.00

MORLEY, Christopher. *Thunder on the Left.* 1926. Heinemann. 2nd ed. VG. P1. $6.00

MORLEY, Christopher. *Trojan Horse.* 1937. Lippincott. 3rd ed. 248 p. VG. B10. $3.75

MORLEY, Christopher. *Where the Bl Begins.* nd. Grosset. Ils. 215 p. dj. VG. B10. $3.75

MORLEY, Christopher. *Where the Bl Begins.* 1923. Doubleday Page. decor brd. VG. P1. $15.00

MORLEY, J.V. *Recollections.* 1917. Macmillan. 2nd ed. 2 vols. G. B10. $17.00

MORLEY, John. *19th-Century British Essays.* 1970. Chicago U. 1st Am ed. dj. EX. C4. $20.00

MORLEY, S.G. *Ancient Maya.* 1976. Stanford. 3rd ed. 507 p. dj. F2. $20.00

MORLEY & MARQUIS. *Pandora Lifts the Lid.* 1924. NY. 1st ed. sgn. VG. $25.00

MORLEY. *Palette Knife.* 1929. Chelsea. Chocorua Pr. 1/450. sm 4to. sgn. G. C2. $65.00

MORRE, C. *Timing a Century.* 1945. Cambridge. 1st ed. 362 p. VG. B3. $32.50

MORRELL, David. *Brotherhood of the Rose.* 1984. St Martin. 1st ed. sgn. dj. EX. P1. $25.00

MORRELL, David. *Covenant of the Flame.* 1991. Warner. ARC. wrp. EX. C4. $20.00

MORRELL, David. *Fireflies.* 1988. Dutton. 1st ed. dj. EX. F5. $16.00

MORRELL, David. *Fraternity of the Stone.* 1985. St Martin. 1st ed. dj. VG. P1. $20.00

MORRELL, David. *League of Night & Fog.* 1987. Dutton. 1st ed. dj. VG. P1. $17.95

MORRELL, David. *Testament.* 1975. Evans. 1st ed. dj. EX. R3. $35.00

MORRELL, David. *Totem.* 1979. Evans. 1st ed. dj. EX. R3. $75.00

MORRELL, David. *1st Blood.* 1972. Evans. dj. EX. C4. $50.00

MORRELL & LLOYD. *New Magical Sleights & Fakes.* 1906. London. Hamley. 50 p. EX. J3. $9.00

MORRESSY, John. *Frostworld & Dreamfire.* 1977. Doubleday. 1st ed. dj. EX. P1. $15.00

MORRESSY, John. *Nail Down the Stars.* 1973. Walker. 1st ed. presentation to Simak. dj. EX. F5. $40.00

MORRESSY, John. *Under a Calculating Star.* 1975. Doubleday. 1st ed. dj. EX. F5. $14.00

MORRESSY, John. *Under a Calculating Star.* 1975. Doubleday. 1st ed. dj. xl. P1. $5.00

MORRIS, Ann. *Digging in Yucatan.* 1934. Doubleday. Ils. 279 p. F2. $15.00

MORRIS, Bud. *More Magic With Electronics.* 1975. Morris Magic. 2nd ed. 59 p. EX. J3. $8.00

MORRIS, Charles. *Story of Mexico.* 1914. np. 1st ed. 404 p. F2. $15.00

MORRIS, Desmond. *Animal Days.* 1979. Jonathan Cape. 1st ed. dj. EX. P1. $15.00

MORRIS, Desmond. *Beyond the Wizardwall.* 1986. Baen. 1st ed. dj. EX. P1. $15.95

MORRIS, Desmond. *Cruiser Dreams.* 1981. Putnam. 1st ed. dj. EX. P1. $15.00

MORRIS, Desmond. *Dream Dancer.* 1980. Berkley Putnam. 1st ed. dj. EX. P1. $15.00

MORRIS, Don. *Close-Up Encounters.* 1981. Camden, SC. 1st ed. 130 p. NM. J3. $10.00

MORRIS, Edwin. *Copper Moon.* nd. (1928) Grosset. VG. B10. $3.50

MORRIS, Gouverneur. *If You Touch Them They Vanish.* 1913. Scribner. 1st ed. EX. R3. $35.00

MORRIS, H.P. *Glimpses of the Life of Samuel Morris.* 1907. Phil. private print. 12mo. 207 p. VG. V1. $10.00

MORRIS, H.S. *Hannah Bye: Eclogue in Prose.* 1920. Phil. Penn Pub. 1st ed. 12mo. 266 p. V1. $6.00

MORRIS, Ivan. *Modern Japanese Stories: An Anthology.* 1962. Rutland. Tuttle. 1st ed. dj. EX. C4. $35.00

MORRIS, J.R. *Diana's Smile.* 1969. Croupier. 1/1000. inscr. B4. $15.00

MORRIS, J.R. *He Has Heard.* nd. Croupier. 1/1000. VG. B4. $6.00

MORRIS, J.R. *Roadrunner's End.* 1984. Croupier/Bowery. 1/100. PB. dj. M. B4. $8.00

MORRIS, James. *Cities.* 1964. Harcourt Brace World. 1st ed. dj. EX. K2. $45.00

MORRIS, Jim. *Sheriff of Purgatory.* 1979. Doubleday. 1st ed. dj. EX. F5. $12.00

MORRIS, John. *Age of Arthur.* c 1973. 2nd print. dj. VG. C1. $16.50

MORRIS, John. *Candywine Development.* 1971. Citadel Pr. 1st ed. dj. VG. P1. $12.50

MORRIS, Mary. *Crossroads.* 1983. Houghton Mifflin. UP. wrp. EX. K2. $75.00

MORRIS, Mary. *Vanishing Animals & Other Stories.* 1979. Godine. UP. wrp. EX. K2. $85.00

MORRIS, Mary. *Vanishing Animals & Other Stories.* 1979. Godine. 1st ed. dj. EX. C4. $35.00

MORRIS, Mary. *Waiting Room.* 1989. Doubleday. ARC. EX. K2. $30.00

MORRIS, Percy. *Field Guide to Shells.* 1958. Houghton Mifflin. Revised ed. 8vo. B10. $4.25

MORRIS, R.A.V. *Lyttleton Case.* nd. Detective Story Club 15. dj. G. P1. $7.50

MORRIS, Rosamund. *Great Suspense Stories.* 1962. Hart. decor brd. VG. P1. $15.00

MORRIS, William. *Earthly Paradise.* 1868-1870. London. 1st ed. 4 vols in 3. inscr. orig bdg. H3. $1500.00

MORRIS, William. *Hist of Over Sea.* 1902. Russell. C1. $9.00

MORRIS, William. *In Defense of Guinevere & Other Poems.* 1900. London. VG. C1. $11.00

MORRIS, William. *Poems by the Way.* 1896. Boston. xl. G. $8.00

MORRIS, Willie. *About Fiction.* 1975. Harper. 1st ed. dj. EX. B13. $45.00

MORRIS, Willie. *Courting of Marcus Dupree.* 1983. Doubleday. 1st ed. dj. EX. C4. $60.00

MORRIS, Wright. *Deep Sleep.* 1953. Scribner. dj. EX. C4. $100.00

MORRIS, Wright. *Fire Sermon.* nd. Harper. unbound galley sheets. 2nd state. EX. B13. $100.00

MORRIS, Wright. *God's Country & My People.* 1968. Harper. 1st ed. lg quarto. dj. EX. B13. $75.00

MORRIS, Wright. *Love Among the Cannibals.* 1957. Harcourt Brace. inscr. dj. H3. $100.00

MORRIS, Wright. *War Games.* 1972. Blk Sparrow. Ltd ed. 1/300. sgn. EX. H3. $75.00

MORRIS & HENDERSON. *WWII in Pictures.* 1945-1946. NY. 3 vols. VG. $30.00

MORRIS & PHILLIPS. *How To Operate Financially Successful Haunted House.* 1980. Morris Costumes. 101 p. VG. J3. $6.00

MORRIS & THOMPSON. *Huanuco Pampa.* 1985. Thames Hudson. 1st ed. 181 p. dj. F2. $30.00

MORRIS. *How We Treat Wounds Today.* 1886. NY. 12mo. 162 p. C2. $65.00

MORRISON, Arthur. *Gr Diamond.* 1908. Wessels. 2nd Am ed. EX. F5. $8.00

MORRISON, P.G. *Index of Printers, Pub, & Booksellers in Pollard & Redgrave.* 1950. Charlottesville. xl. VG. G1. $35.00

MORRISON, Toni. *Bluest Eye.* 1979. London. 1st UK ed. dj. EX. T9. $85.00

MORRISON, Toni. *Pathways to the Gods.* 1978. Harper. 1st ed. 208 p. dj. F2. $20.00

MORRISON, Toni. *Sula.* 1974. NY. 2nd ed. presentation. dj. VG. B3. $60.00

MORRISON, Toni. *Sula.* 1980. London. 2nd UK ed. dj. EX. K2. $25.00

MORRISON, Toni. *Tar Baby.* 1981. Knopf. UP. wrp. EX. K2. $200.00

MORRISON, Toni. *Tar Baby.* 1981. Knopf. 1st ed. sgn. dj. EX. B13. $125.00

MORRISON, Toni. *Tar Baby.* 1981. Knopf. 2nd print. inscr/sgn. dj. H3. $125.00

MORRISON, Tony. *Lizzie: A Victorian Lady's Amazon Adventure.* 1986. London. Ils. 160 p. dj. F2. $17.50

MORRISON, William. *Mel Oliver & Space Rover on Mars.* 1954. Gnome. 1st ed. dj. EX. R3. $25.00

MORROW, James. *Continent of Lies.* 1984. Holt. 1st ed. RS. M. R3. $25.00

MORROW, James. *This Is the Way the World Ends.* 1986. Holt. 1st ed. sgn. dj. EX. R3. $30.00

MORSE, A.R. *Works of MP Shiel.* 1948. Fantasy. 1st ed. dj. EX. R3. $35.00

MORSE, Donald. *Fantastic in World Literature & the Arts.* 1987. Greenwood. 1st ed. RS. M. R3. $45.00

MORSE, Peter. *John Sloan's Prints.* 1969. New Haven/London. Ils 1st Trade ed. 401 p. dj. VG. T5. $250.00

MORSE, S. *Siege of U City.* 1912. St Louis. 1st ed. G. B3. $25.00

MORTENSEN, William. *Model.* 1937. San Francisco. 1st ed. dj. VG. B3. $27.50

MORTENSEN, William. *Outdoor Portraiture.* 1951. Camera Craft. 2nd ed. 208 p. dj. VG. $7.50

MORTIMER, John. *Wrong Side of the Park.* 1960. London. 1st ed. dj. EX. $70.00

MORTIMER, W.G. *Hist of Coca: Divine Plant of the Incas.* 1901. NY. Vail. 1st ed. EX. scarce. $235.00

MORTON, Anthony. *Blame the Baron.* 1951. Duell Sloan Pearce. 1st ed. xl. VG. P1. $7.50

MORTON, David. *Sonnet Today & Yesterday.* 1926. Putnam. 1st ed. 71 p. TEG. B10. $27.00

MORTON, Eleanor. *Josiah Wht: Prince of Pioneers.* 1946. NY. Stephen Daye. 1st ed. 8vo. 300 p. dj. VG. V1. $10.00

MORTON, Stanley. *Yankee Trader.* 1947. Sheridan House. 1st ed. dj. EX. F5. $22.00

MOSCONI, Willie. *On Pocket Billiards.* 1972. Crown. 27th print. inscr. wrp. EX. B13. $85.00

MOSELEY & DAY. *Chan Chan: Andean Desert City.* 1982. NM U. 1st ed. 373 p. dj. F2. $25.00

MOSER, Don. *Central Am Jungles.* 1975. Time Life. 1st ed. 184 p. F2. $15.00

MOSES, Bernard. *S Am on the Eve of Emancipation.* 1908. Putnam. 1st ed. 356 p. F2. $10.00

MOSES, Henry. *Goethe's Faust by M Retzsch.* 1843. London. Tilt Bogue. 26 pls. G. R5. $125.00

MOSES & PHILLIPS. *Rhythmic Action Plays & Dances.* 1916. Milton Bradley. 4to. 164 p. VG. $22.00

MOSKOWITZ, Anthony. *Hist of the Movement.* 1980. Donald Grant. 1st ed. dj. EX. P1. $15.00

MOSKOWITZ, Sam. *Editor's Choice in SF.* 1954. World. 1st ed. dj. EX. R3. $25.00

MOSKOWITZ, Sam. *Explorers of the Infinite.* 1974. Hyperion. EX. R3. $12.50

MOSKOWITZ, Sam. *Explorers of the Infinite.* 1963. World. 1st ed. inscr. dj. EX. R3. $30.00

MOSKOWITZ, Sam. *Horrors Unknown.* 1971. World. 1st ed. dj. EX. R3. $15.00

MOSKOWITZ, Sam. *Immortal Storm.* 1951. Burnwell. 1st ed. wrp. EX. $125.00

MOSKOWITZ, Sam. *Immortal Storm.* 1974. Hyperion. reprint of 1954 ed. wrp. EX. R3. $25.00

MOSKOWITZ, Sam. *Modern Masterpieces of SF.* 1965. World. 1st ed. dj. EX. R3. $17.50

MOSKOWITZ, Sam. *Seekers of Tomorrow.* 1966. World. 1st ed. sgn. dj. EX. R3. $25.00

MOSKOWITZ, Sam. *Under the Moons of Mars.* 1970. Holt Rinehart Winston. 1st ed. dj. G. P1. $25.00

MOSLEY, Leonard. *On Borrowed Time: How WWII Began.* 1969. NY. BOMC. dj. VG. $10.00

MOSLEY, Walter. *Devil in a Bl Dress.* 1991. London. Serpent's Tail. 1st ed. wrp. EX. T9. $25.00

MOSS, Howard. *Instant Lives.* 1974. NY. 1st ed. dj. VG. $25.00

MOSTEL, Zero. *Zero by Mostel.* 1965. Horizon. 1/250. sgn. slipcase. w/sgn lithograph. H3. $275.00

MOULE, T. *Heraldry of Fish.* 1842. London. 1st ed. xl. K1. $50.00

MOWAT, Farley. *Whale for the Killing.* 1972. Little Brn. 1st Am ed. dj. EX. C4. $40.00

MOWBRAY, J.H. *Conquest of the Air by Airships & Other Flying Machines...* 1910. np. Ils. 400 p. fair. T5. $35.00

MOWRER, Edgar. *This Am World.* nd. (1928) Sears. 1st ed? 276 p. VG. B10. $5.00

MOYA, V.J. *Maski Meksykanskie.* 1976. Warsaw. sm 4to. F2. $750.00

MOYES, Patricia. *Blk Widower.* 1975. Collins Crime Club. 1st ed. dj. EX. P1. $15.00

MOYES, Patricia. *Death & the Dutch Uncle.* 1968. Collins Crime Club. 1st ed. dj. xl. P1. $7.50

MOYES, Patricia. *Murder Fantastical.* 1967. Collins Crime Club. 1st ed. dj. xl. P1. $7.50

MOYES, Patricia. *Night Ferry to Death.* nd. Book Club. dj. EX. P1. $4.50

MOYES, Patricia. *Night Ferry to Death.* 1985. Holt Rinehart Winston. 1st ed. dj. EX. P1. $13.95

MOYES, Patricia. *To Kill a Coconut.* 1977. Collins Crime Club. 1st ed. dj. VG. P1. $15.00

MOYES, Patricia. *Who Is Simon Warwick?* nd. Holt Rinehart. 2nd ed. dj. VG. P1. $7.50

MOZANS, H.J. *Up the Orinoco & Down the Magdalena.* 1910. Appleton. 1st ed. 439 p. F2. $50.00

MOZART, W.A. *Clavier Auszug von Mozarts Zauberfloete.* c 1793. Bonn. oblong folio. 145 p. contemporary calf. VG. H3. $350.00

MOZART, W.A. *Dom Giovanni.* c 1800. Hambourg. quarto. 2 parts in 1. contemporary calf. H3. $350.00

MOZART, W.A. *Selection From Vocal Compositions...Never Before Pub.* 1816. London. 3 vols. slipcase. VG. H3. $850.00

MRABET, Mohammed. *Big Mirror.* 1989. London. Owen. 1st ed. wrp. EX. K2. $35.00

MRABET, Mohammed. *M'Hashish.* 1988. London. Owen. 1st Eng ed. wrp. EX. K2. $35.00

MUCHA, Jiri. *Alphonse Mucha: Master of Art Nouveau.* 1967. Prague. VG. G1. $20.00

MUELLER, James. *Use of Sampling in Archaeological Survey.* 1974. Menasha, WI. 91 p. wrp. F2. $5.00

MUHLBACH, L. *Queen Hortense.* 1905. NY. Fowle. Ils. 383 p. VG. B10. $3.75

MUIR, Augustus. *Shadow on the Left.* 1928. Methuen. 1st ed. VG. P1. $20.00

MUIR, John. *Mt of CA.* 1921. NY. New Enlarged ed. VG. $25.00

MUIR, John. *Our Nat Parks.* 1901. Boston. 2nd ed. photos. VG. $25.00

MUIR, John. *Our Nat Parks.* 1901. Riverside Pr. 1st ed. $75.00

MUIR, John. *Stickeen.* 1909. Boston/NY. 6th imp. VG. C1. $24.00

MUIR, John. *Thousand-Mile Walk to the Gulf.* 1916. Houghton Mifflin. 1st ed. dj. EX. B13. $175.00

MUIR, John. *Writings.* 1917-1924. Houghton Mifflin. Sierra ed. 10 vols. H3. $1000.00

MUIR, P.H. *Book Collecting As a Hobby.* 1947. Knopf. 1st Am ed. xl. VG. B10. $6.25

MUIR, P.H. *Victorian Ils Books.* 1971. Praeger. sm 4to. dj. EX. $60.00

MULHOLLAND, John. *Art of Illusion: Magic for Men To Do.* 1944. Scribner. 1st ed. 142 p. dj. NM. J3. $13.00

MULHOLLAND, John. *Book of Magic.* 1963. Scribner. 1st ed. dj. EX. J3. $18.00

MULHOLLAND, John. *Book of Magic.* 1963. Scribner. 1st PB print. NM. J3. $6.00

MULHOLLAND, John. *Magic of the World.* 1965. Scribner. 1st ed. dj. EX. J3. $20.00

MULHOLLAND, John. *Our Mysteries.* nd. NY. Flosso Hornmann Magic. NM. J3. $3.00

MULLALLY, Frederic. *Assassins.* 1965. Walker. 1st ed. dj. EX. P1. $10.00

MULLEN, Robert. *Dominican Architecture in 16th-Century Oaxaca.* 1975. Tempe. 1st ed. 260 p. dj. F2. $25.00

MULLEN, Stanley. *Kinsmen of the Dragon.* 1951. Shasta. 1st ed. dj. VG. R3. $50.00

MULLER, Herbert. *Uses of the Past.* 1953. Oxford. apparent 1st ed. 394 p. dj. EX. B10. $8.50

MULLER, Marcia. *Edwin of the Iron Shoes.* nd. Book Club. dj. xl. P1. $4.00

MULLER, Marcia. *Legend of the Slain Soldiers.* 1985. Walker. 1st ed. dj. EX. P1. $13.95

MULLER, V.K. *Eng-Russian Dictionary.* 1977. Moscow. 4to. 877 p. gilt bl bdg. EX. T1. $25.00

MULLGARDT, L.C. *Architecture & Landscape Gardening of Exposition.* 1915. San Francisco. 2nd ed. EX. $75.00

MULLIGAN & HILDRETH. *Hist of 825th Aviation Engineer Battalion...* nd. Munich. in original mailer. T5. $65.00

MULRYAN, Lenore. *Mexican Figural Ceramists & Their Work.* 1982. UCLA. Ils. 4to. 40 p. wrp. F2. $20.00

MULVIHILL, William. *Sands of Kalahari.* nd. Book Club. dj. VG. P1. $4.50

MUMEY, Nolie. *Anselm Holcomb Barker: Pioneer Builder, Early Settler...* 1959. Denver. 1/500. fld map. EX. $50.00

MUMEY, Nolie. *Nathan Addison Baker.* 1965. Denver. 1/500. sgn. EX. $65.00

MUMEY, Nolie. *Pioneer Denver Including Scenes of Central City, CO City...* 1948. Artcraft Pr. 1/240. sgn. A5. $150.00

MUNDELL, E.H. *Erle Stanley Gardner: A Checklist.* 1968. Kent State. no dj issued. EX. P1. $12.50

MUNDELL, E.H. *List of Orig Appearance of Dashiell Hammett's Magazine Work.* nd. np. 60 p. gr bdg. no dj issued. EX. T9. $20.00

MUNDEN & BEERS. *Guide to Federal Archives Relating to Civil War.* 1962. WA. EX. $30.00

MUNDORFF & STEWART. *In an Old HI Garden: Album of HI's Flowers.* 1943. HI. sm 4to. wrp. M. $35.00

MUNDY, Talbot. *Devil's Guard.* 1926. Bobbs Merrill. 1st ed. EX. F5. $30.00

MUNDY, Talbot. *Devil's Guard.* 1945. Oriental Club. 1st ed. dj. EX. R3. $40.00

MUNDY, Talbot. *E & W.* 1937. Appleton. 1st ed. dj. EX. R3. $200.00

MUNDY, Talbot. *Full Moon.* 1935. Appleton. 1st ed. dj. EX. R3. $225.00

MUNDY, Talbot. *Gunga Sahib.* 1934. Appleton. 1st ed. dj. EX. R3. $225.00

MUNDY, Talbot. *Jimgrim & Allah's Peace.* 1936. Appleton. 1t ed. dj. EX. R3. $225.00

MUNDY, Talbot. *Jungle Jest.* 1932. Century. 1st ed. dj. VG. R3. $150.00

MUNDY, Talbot. *King of the Khyber Rifles.* c1940s. Grosset Dunlap. Madison Square ed. dj. VG. F5. $15.00

MUNDY, Talbot. *King of the Khyber Rifles.* 1972. Tom Stacey. dj. xl. P1. $7.50

MUNDY, Talbot. *Old Ugly-Face.* 1940. Appleton. 1st ed. VG. R3. $25.00

MUNDY, Talbot. *Old Ugly-Face.* 1950. Wells Shakespeare. 1st ed. dj. EX. R3. $40.00

MUNDY, Talbot. *Om.* 1924. Bobbs Merrill. 1st ed. VG. R3. $27.50

MUNDY, Talbot. *Thos of Samothrace.* 1958. Gnome. dj. VG. B3. $45.00

MUNDY, Talbot. *Tros of Samothrace.* 1934. NY. 1st Am ed. inscr. pictorial bdg. dj. EX. T5. $195.00

MUNGO, Raymond. *My Life & Hart Times With the Liberation News Service.* 1970. Boston. Beacon. 1st HrdCvr ed. dj. EX. K2. $40.00

MUNHALL, E. *Masterpieces of the Frick Collection.* 1970. NY. 1st ed. fld pls. VG. G1. $20.00

MUNN, H.T. *Tales of the Eskimo.* nd. London. dj. VG. A6. $37.50

MUNN, H.W. *Banner of Joan.* 1975. Ltd 1st ed. 1/975. dj. NM. C1. $12.00

MUNRO, Alice. *Dance of the Happy Shades & Other Stories.* 1973. McGraw Hill. 1st Am ed. dj. EX. C4. $60.00

MUNRO, Alice. *Friend of My Youth: Stories.* 1990. Knopf. ARC. sgn. wht wrp. boxed. EX. C4. $50.00

MUNRO, Alice. *Moons of Jupiter.* 1982. Toronto. Macmillan. 1st ed. dj. EX. C4. $45.00

MUNRO, Alice. *Progress of Love.* 1986. Knopf. 1st ed. inscr. dj. EX. K2. $65.00

MUNRO, Alice. *Something I've Been Meaning To Tell You: 13 Stories.* 1974. Toronto. McGraw Hill. 1st ed. dj. EX. C4. $65.00

MUNRO, D.C. *Middle Ages 395-1272.* 1924. NY. maps. VG. $15.00

MUNRO, Hugh. *Clutha Plays a Hunch.* 1959. Ives Washburn. 1st ed. dj. VG. P1. $15.00

MUNRO, James. *Innocent Bystanders.* 1970. Knopf. 1st ed. dj. xl. P1. $10.00

MUNSEY, Cecil. *Disneyana.* 1974. NY. 1st ed. dj. EX. B3. $60.00

MUNSON, G.B. *Robert Frost.* 1927. Doran. 1st ed. sgn. EX. B13. $225.00

MURBARGER, Nell. *30,000 Miles in Mexico.* 1961. Palm Desert, CA. 1st ed. 310 p. dj. F2. $15.00

MURCHIE, Guy. *Song of the Sky.* 1954. Cambridge. BOMC. dj. VG. $10.00

MURDOCH, Nina. *Tryolean June: Summer Holiday in Austrian Tyrol.* 1936. NY. 1st ed? 279 p. xl. VG. B10. $4.25

MURFIN, J.V. *Gleam of Bayonets.* nd. Bonanza. dj. EX. $20.00

MURIE, O.J. *Elk of N Am.* 1951. WA. 1st ed. dj. EX. B3. $62.50

MURIE, O.J. *2 in the Far N.* 1962. NY. Ils 1st ed. 438 p. dj. VG. B3. $30.00

MURPHY, Arthur. *Life of David Garrick, Esq.* 1801. London. Foot. 1st ed. 2 vols. contemporary calf. H3. $175.00

MURPHY, Audie. *To Hell & Back.* 1949. NY. 1st ed. sgn. dj. EX. $70.00

MURPHY, Francis. *Dragon Mask Temples in Central Am.* 1989. Hong Kong. 1st ed. oblong 4to. dj. F2. $95.00

MURPHY, Gloria. *Playroom.* 1987. Donald Fine. 1st ed. dj. EX. F5. $15.00

MURPHY, Haughton. *Murders & Acquisitions.* 1988. Simon Schuster. 1st ed. dj. EX. P1. $16.95

MURPHY, Marguerite. *Dangerous Legacy.* 1962. Avalon. 1st ed. dj. xl. P1. $5.00

MURPHY, S.R. *Caves of Fires.* 1980. Atheneum. 1st ed. dj. EX. F5. $22.00

MURPHY, S.R. *Flight of the Fox.* 1978. Atheneum. 1st ed. dj. EX. P1. $15.00

MURPHY, S.R. *Ivory Lyre.* 1987. Harper Row. 1st ed. dj. EX. P1. $17.50

MURPHY, S.R. *Soonie & the Dragon.* 1979. Atheneum. 1st ed. dj. EX. P1. $17.50

MURPHY, S.R. *Wolf Bell.* 1979. Atheneum. 1st ed. dj. EX. P1. $15.00

MURPHY, Yannick. *Stories in Another Language.* 1987. Knopf. 1st ed. dj. M. $10.00

MURPHY & COCHRAN. *Temple Dogs.* 1989. New Am Lib. 1st ed. dj. EX. P1. $18.95

MURRAY, Albert. *Hero & the Blues.* 1973. Columbia, MO. 1st ed. sgn. dj. w/card. T9. $50.00

MURRAY, C.S. *Here Come Joe Mungin.* 1942. Putnam. 1st ed. dj. VG. F5. $12.50

MURRAY, Cromwell. *Day of the Dead.* 1946. McKay. VG. P1. $7.00

MURRAY, J.O. *Immortal 600.* 1905. Winchester, VA. 1st ed. VG. $160.00

MURRAY, Lindley. *Intro to the Eng Reader.* 1829. Phil. Probasco. sm 8vo. $20.00

MURRAY, M. *Splendor That Was Egypt.* 1959. NY. Ils. 354 p. dj. VG. B3. $17.50

MURRAY, Max. *King & the Corpse.* 1948. Farrar Straus. dj. VG. P1. $12.50

MURRAY, Max. *Sunshine Corpse.* 1954. Michael Joseph. 1st ed. xl. VG. P1. $8.00

MURRAY, Pauli. *Dark Testament & Other Poems.* 1970. Silvermine. 1st ed. dj. EX. B13. $85.00

MURRAY, W.H.H. *How John Norton the Trapper Kept His Christmas.* 1891. Boston. Ils. 109 p. G. T5. $18.50

MURRAY, William. *Tip on a Dead Crab.* 1984. Viking. 1st ed. inscr. dj. EX. T9. $45.00

MUSCHAMP, Herbert. *File Under Architecture.* 1974. MIT Pr. 117 p. D4. $35.00

MUSEUM OF MODERN ART. *Art in Our Time.* 1939. NY World's Fair ed. 384 p. D4. $75.00

MUSEUM OF MODERN ART. *Henri Rousseau.* 1985.NY Graphic Soc/Little Brn. dj. D4. $40.00

MUSEUM OF MODERN ART. *Latin Am Prints From the MOMA.* 1974. NY. Ils. Eng/Spanish text. wrp. F2. $10.00

MUSEUM OF MODERN ART. *Photographer & the Am Landscape.* 1963. Doubleday. D4. $20.00

MUSEUM OF MODERN ART. *Raymond Wielgus Collection.* 1960. NY. Ils. 4to. 32 p. F2. $10.00

MUSEUM OF MODERN ART. *20 Centuries of Mexican Art.* 1940. NY. 1st ed. 4to. 199 p. F2. $20.00

MUSEUM OF PRIMIIVE ART. *Sculpture From Peru in the MPA.* 1964. NY. Ils. 32 p. F2. $7.50

MUSEUM OF PRIMITIVE ART. *Stone Sculpture From Mexico.* 1959. MPA. 4to. wrp. F2. $15.00

MUSGRAVE & MUSGRAVE. *Waterfowl in IA.* 1947. Des Moines. 2nd ed. pls. G. C2. $25.00

MUSSEY, Barrows. *Magic.* 1942. Barnes. 83 p. dj. NM. J3. $8.00

MUSSOLINI, Benito. *Cardinal's Mistress.* 1928. NY. 1st Am ed. 232 p. G. T5. $25.00

MUSSON, Clettus. *World's Best Clown Gags.* nd. Flosso Hornmann Magic. EX. J3. $3.00

MUSTE, A.J. *Camp of Liberation.* 1954. London. Peace News Ltd. 12mo. 16 p. pamphlet. V1. $6.50

MYERS, A.C. *Quaker Arrivals at Phil 1682-1750.* 1902. Phil. Ferris Leach. 12mo. 131 p. xl. V1. $8.50

MYERS, Gary. *House of the Worm.* 1975. Arkham House. 1st ed. dj. EX. P1. $15.00

MYERS, J.H. *Transfigured Life.* nd. (1900) Eaton Mains. tan bdg. VG. B10. $4.50

MYERS, J.M. *Alamo.* 1948. NY. 1st ed. 240 p. dj. VG. T5. $19.50

MYERS, J.M. *Deaths of the Bravos.* 1962. Boston/Toronto. 1st ed. dj. $15.00

MYERS, J.M. *Out on Any Limb.* 1942. Dutton. 1st ed. G. R3. $12.50

MYERS, J.M. *Print in a Wild Land.* 1967. Doubleday. 1st ed. 274 p. dj. NM. B10. $15.00

MYERS, J.M. *Silverlock.* c 1950s-1960s. PB Orig. VG. C1. $12.00

MYERS, J.M. *Silverlock.* 1949. Dutton. 1st ed. dj. VG. C1. $95.00

MYERS, R.J. *Cross of Frankenstein.* 1975. Lippincott. 1st ed. dj. EX. P1. $25.00

MYERS. *Some Notes on Am Pewterers.* 1926. Garden City. Ils. 96 p. VG. C2. $40.00

MYLONAS, George. *Mycenae & the Mycenaean Age.* 1966. Princeton. 1st ed. sm folio. 250 p. EX. T4. $37.50

MYRICK, Jim. *Life Behind the Chase.* 1964. Licking, MO. 1st ed. inscr. VG. $20.00

NABOKOV, Vladimir. *Ada; or, Ardor.* 1969. McGraw Hill. 1st ed. dj. EX. H3. $45.00

NABOKOV, Vladimir. *Eye.* 1965. Phaedra. 1st ed. 1st issue. dj. EX. $50.00

NABOKOV, Vladimir. *Glory.* 1971. McGraw Hill. 1st Am ed. dj. EX. H3. $50.00

NABOKOV, Vladimir. *King, Queen, Knave.* 1968. McGraw Hill. 1st Am ed. H3. $75.00

NABOKOV, Vladimir. *Laughter in the Dark.* 1938. Bobbs Merrill. 1st ed. VG. $75.00

NABOKOV, Vladimir. *Lectures on Ulysses: Facsimile of the Manuscript.* 1980. Bloomfield Hills. 1st ed. 1/500. quarto. K2. $150.00

NABOKOV, Vladimir. *Look at the Harlequins!* 1974. NY. 1st ed. dj. M. $30.00

NABOKOV, Vladimir. *Pale Fire.* 1962. NY. 2nd imp. dj. EX. $45.00

NABOKOV, Vladimir. *Poems.* 1959. Doubleday. 1st ed. dj. EX. C4. $150.00

NABOKOV, Vladimir. *Real Life of Sebastian Knight.* 1941. New Directions. 1st Trade ed. 1/500. 8vo. VG. $60.00

NABOKOV, Vladimir. *Real Life of Sebastian Knight.* 1959. New Directions. 1st ed. dj. EX. C4. $30.00

NADEAU, Remi. *Ft Laramie & the Sioux Indians.* 1967. Englewood Cliffs. Ils. 335 p. dj. A5. $30.00

NADER, George. *Chrome.* 1978. Putnam. 1st ed. dj. VG. P1. $15.00

NADER & TAYLOR. *Big Boys.* 1986. 1st ed. dj. EX. C1. $8.50

NAGEL, Otto. *Kathe Kollwitz.* 1971. Greenwich. 1st Eng text ed. dj. EX. G1. $35.00

NAIPAUL, Shiva. *Beyond the Dragon's Mouth.* 1985. Viking. UP. wrp. EX. K2. $30.00

NAIPAUL, Shiva. *Journey to Nowhere.* 1980. Simon Schuster. UP. wrp. EX. B13. $55.00

NAIPAUL, V.S. *Area of Darkness.* 1964. London. Deutsch. 1st ed. dj. VG. K2. $125.00

NAIPAUL, V.S. *Area of Darkness.* 1964. Macmillan. 1st ed. dj. VG. K2. $50.00

NAIPAUL, V.S. *Area of Darkness.* 1964. NY. 1st Am ed. dj. EX. C4. $75.00

NAIPAUL, V.S. *Bend in the River.* 1979. London. Andre Deutsch. 1st ed. dj. EX. C4. $75.00

NAIPAUL, V.S. *Congo Diary.* 1980. Los Angeles. 1st ed. 1/330. sgn. sans dj. EX. T9. $85.00

NAIPAUL, V.S. *Congo Diary.* 1980. Sylvester Orphanos. Ltd ed. 1/330. lg octavo. M. H3. $125.00

NAIPAUL, V.S. *Congo Diary.* 1980. Sylvester Orphanos. 1st ed. 1/300. sgn. EX. B13. $125.00

NAIPAUL, V.S. *Finding the Centre.* 1984. London. Deutsch. 1st ed. dj. EX. B13. $50.00

NAIPAUL, V.S. *House for Mr Biswas.* 1961. London. Deutsch. 1st ed. dj. EX. C4. $275.00

NAIPAUL, V.S. *House for Mr Biswas.* 1961. London. Deutsch. 1st ed. dj. VG. scarce. K2. $235.00

NAIPAUL, V.S. *House for Mr Biswas.* 1983. Knopf. UP of 2nd Am ed. wrp. EX. K2. $45.00

NAIPAUL, V.S. *Loss of El Dorado.* 1969. London. Deutsch. 1st ed. dj. EX. K2. $125.00

NAIPAUL, V.S. *Loss of El Dorado.* 1970. Knopf. 1st Am ed. dj. EX. $55.00

NAIPAUL, V.S. *Million Mutinies Now.* 1981. NY. Viking. UP. wrp. EX. K2. $45.00

NAIPAUL, V.S. *Mystic Masseur.* 1959. Vanguard. 1st Am ed. dj. EX. C4. $75.00

NAIPAUL, V.S. *Return of Eva Peron/The Killings in Trinidad.* 1980. London. Deutsch. 1st ed. dj. EX. B13. $75.00

NAIPAUL, V.S. *Turn in the S.* 1989. NY. 1st ed. sgn. dj. EX. $95.00

NANCE, E.C. *Faith of Our Fighters.* 1944. St Louis. Ils. 304 p. VG. T5. $12.50

NAPIER, William. *Eng Battles & Sieges in the Peninsula.* 1910. London. Popular ed. 469 p. G. T5. $25.00

NARA NATIONAL MUSEUM. *Arts of the Lotus Sutra.* 1979. 254 p. ES. D4. $35.00

NARCEJAC, Thomas. *Art of Simenon.* 1952. London. Routledge/Kegan Paul. 1st ed. clipped dj. NM. T9. $40.00

NASBY, Petroleum. *Eckoes From KY.* 1868. Boston. Ils Thomas Nast. 12mo. 324 p. G. G4. $38.00

NASBY, Petroleum. *Swingin' 'Round the Cirkle.* 1867. Boston. Ils Thomas Nast. 12mo. 299 p. G. G4. $40.00

NASH, Anne. *Death by Design.* 1944. Crime Club. 1st ed. xl. VG. P1. $7.50

NASH, Ogden. *Free Wheeling.* 1931. Simon Schuster. sgn. gr bdg. dj. H3. $100.00

NASH, Ogden. *Happy Days.* 1933. Simon Schuster. Ils Soglow. sgn. dj. H3. $100.00

NASH, Ogden. *Hard Lines.* 1931. Simon Schuster. sgn. orange bdg. dj. H3. $75.00

NASH, Ogden. *Many Long Years Ago.* nd. Little Brn. dj. VG. P1. $15.00

NASH, Ogden. *Primrose Path.* 1935. Simon Schuster. sgn. orange bdg. dj. H3. $150.00

NASH, Ogden. *Primrose Path.* 1935. Simon Schuster. 1st ed. dj. EX. B13. $175.00

NASH, Ogden. *Private Dining Room.* nd. Little Brn. dj. VG. P1. $15.00

NASH, Ogden. *Versus.* nd. Little Brn. dj. VG. P1. $15.00

NASH, Ogden. *You Can't Get There From Here.* nd. Little Brn. dj. VG. P1. $15.00

NASH & OFFEN. *Dillinger Dead or Alive.* 1970. Chicago. 1st ed. dj. VG. B3. $27.50

NASH & OFFEN. *Dillinger Dead or Alive.* 1970. Chicago. 1st ed. sgns. dj. VG. B3. $37.50

NASON, E. *Life & Times of Charles Sumner.* 1874. Boston. 1st ed. 12mo. 356 p. G. G4. $19.00

NASTASE, Ilie. *Break Point.* 1986. St Martin. 1st ed. dj. EX. P1. $15.95

NATHAN, G.J. *Art of the Night.* 1928. Knopf. 1st ed. sm octavo. 296 p. dj. EX. H3. $75.00

NATHAN, G.J. *Encyclopedia of the Theatre.* 1940. Knopf. 1st ed. octavo. 449 p. dj. VG. H3. $40.00

NATHAN, G.J. *Entertainment of a Nation; or, 3 Sheets in the Wind.* 1942. Knopf. 1st ed. 290 p. dj. EX. H3. $100.00

NATHAN, G.J. *Morning After the 1st Night.* 1938. Knopf. 1st ed. 281 p. dj. EX. H3. $75.00

NATHAN, G.J. *Popular Theatre.* 1923. Knopf. Popular ed. 236 p. dj. VG. H3. $25.00

NATHAN, G.J. *Testament of a Critic.* 1931. Knopf. 1st ed. wht dj. EX. B13. $50.00

NATHAN, G.J. *Theatre of the Moment.* 1936. Knopf. 1st ed. octavo. 309 p. dj. EX. H3. $75.00

NATHAN, Robert. *But Gently Day.* 1945. Knopf. dj. VG. P1. $17.50

NATHAN, Robert. *Cedar Box & Other Poems.* 1929. Bobbs Merrill. Ltd ed. G. $30.00

NATHAN, Robert. *Elixir.* 1971. NY. 1st Am ed. VG. C1. $12.00

NATHAN, Robert. *Elixir.* 1971. NY. 1st ed. dj. EX. C1. $19.50

NATHAN, Robert. *Heaven & Hell & the Megas Factor.* 1975. Delacorte. 3rd ed. dj. EX. P1. $10.00

NATHAN, Robert. *Mr Whittle & the Morning Star.* 1947. Knopf. 2nd ed. dj. VG. P1. $15.00

NATHAN, Robert. *They Went on Together.* 1941. Knopf. 1st ed. 191 p. dj. G. B10. $5.00

NATHAN, Robert. *Winter Tide.* 1940. Knopf. 1st ed. G. $16.00

NATHAN, Robert. *1 More Spring.* 1933. Knopf. 1st ed. inscr. dj. EX. C4. $50.00

NATHAN-TURNER, John. *Tardis Inside Out.* 1985. Random House. 1st ed. wrp. EX. F5. $9.00

NATHANSON, Leon. *Slydini Encores.* 1966. Slydini Studio. 1st ed. sgn. 145 p. EX. J3. $40.00

NATIONAL GEOGRAPHIC SOCIETY. *Book of Dogs.* 1919. 4to. 96 p. VG. $40.00

NAUMANN, Emil. *Hist of Music.* 1886. Cassell. 2 vols. contemporary calf. H3. $300.00

NAY, CArol. *Timmy Rides the China Clipper.* 1947. Chicago. Ils 94 p. G. T5. $12.50

NAYLOR, Gloria. *Mama Day.* 1988. Ticknor Fields. 1st ed. sgn. dj. EX. K2. $45.00

NAYLOR, Gloria. *Women of Brewster Place.* 1983. NY. Viking. 1st ed. dj. EX. K2. $400.00

NAYLOR, P.R. *Dark of the Tunnel.* 1985. Atheneum. 1st ed. dj. EX. P1. $11.95

NEAL, J.C. *Charcoal Sketches; or, Scenes in a Metropolis.* 1839. Phil. Ils DC Johnston. VG. $150.00

NEALE, C.M. *Index to Pickwick.* 1897. London. Hitchcock. 8vo. 76 p. gr bdg. scarce. H3. $75.00

NEALE, Samuel. *Life & Religious Labors of Samuel Neale.* 1806. Phil. 1st Am ed. 12mo. 97 p. G4. $22.00

NEALE, Samuel. *Some Account of Life & Religious Labors.* 1806. Phil. Parke. 16mo. 97 p. fair. V1. $16.00

NEALE, Tom. *Island to Myself.* 1966. NY. 1st ed. dj. VG. B3. $22.50

NEALE & NEALE. *Some Account of Lives & Religious Labors...* 1845. Friends Bookstore. Stereotype ed. 12mo. 179 p. VG. V1. $12.00

NEARING, H. *Sinister Researches of CP Ransom.* 1954. Doubleday. 1st ed. dj. VG. P1. $35.00

NEEDHAM. *Trout Streams.* 1940. Ithaca. 2nd print. dj. VG. C2. $32.00

NEELEY. *Neeley's Panorama of Our New Possessions.* 1898. NY. 1st ed. oblong 8vo. photos. VG. $75.00

NEELY, Richard. *Shadows From the Past.* 1983. Delacorte. 1st ed. dj. VG. P1. $15.95

NEELY, Richard. *Walter Syndrome.* nd. Book Club. VG. P1. $3.00

NEEPER, Cary. *Place Beyond Man.* 1975. Scribner. 1st ed. dj. EX. P1. $12.50

NEIDECKER, Lorine. *Bl Chicory.* 1976. New Rochelle. Elizabeth Pr. 1st ed. 1/400. slipcase. EX. C4. $100.00

NEIL, C.L. *Modern Conjurer & Drawing Room Entertainer.* 1947. NY. Wehman. 2nd print. 386 p. EX. J3. $25.00

NEILANDS, J.B. *Harvest of Death.* 1972. NY. Ils 1st ed. 304 p. dj. T5. $22.50

NEILL, A.S. *Problem Child.* 1926. London. Jenkins. 1st ed. 8vo. 256 p. VG. R4. $35.00

NEILL, Patrick. *Practical Fruit, Flower, & Vegetable Gardner's Companion.* 1855. NY. 12mo. EX. A4. $100.00

NELMS, Henning. *Magic & Showmanship.* 1969. Dover. 322 p. NM. J3. $3.00

NELSON, C.M. *Barren Harvest.* 1949. Crime Club. 1st ed. VG. P1. $6.50

NELSON, H.L. *Dead Giveaway.* 1950. Rinehart. 1st ed. VG. P1. $12.50

NELSON, L.J. *Rhythm for Rain: Drama & Ancient Culture of Hopi Indians.* 1937. Houghton. dj. VG. $30.00

NELSON, R.F. *Time Quest.* 1985. Tor Books. 1st ed. wrp. EX. F5. $7.00

NELSON, Robert. *Comedy Mentalism Vol 3.* 1971. Calgary. 2nd ed. 48 p. EX. J3. $11.00

NELSON, Robert. *Confessions of a Medium.* 1969. Nelson Enterprises. Revised ed. 27 p. VG. J3. $6.00

NELSON, Robert. *Effective Answers to Questions.* 1963. Nelson Ent. New Revised Enlarged Deluxe ed. 9th print. J3. $9.00

NELSON, Robert. *Miracles in Mentalism & Psychic Experimentation.* 1972. Calgary. 2nd ed. 60 p. NM. J3. $5.00

NELSON, Robert. *More Effective Answers to Questions.* 1948. Nelson Ent. 4th ed. 20 p. NM. J3. $6.00

NELSON, Robert. *Projected Answers.* 1956. Nelson Ent. 30 p. EX. J3. $8.00

NELSON, Robert. *Sensational Effects.* 1975. Calgary. Revised Enlarged ed. NM. J3. $6.00

NELSON, Robert. *Visions of Tomorrow by the Diviner of Destiny.* 1972. Calgary. 2nd ed. 17 p. NM. J3. $6.00

NELSON, Truman. *Old Man: John Brn at Harper's Ferry.* 1973. Holt Rinehart Winston. 394 p. dj. VG. $9.00

NELSON, Walter. *Sm Wonder: Amazing Story of the Volkswagen.* 1970. Little Brn. Revised ed. EX. B10. $4.25

NELSON, William. *Laws of Eng concerning Game of Hunting, Hawking, Fishing...* 1736. London. 282 p. full old calf w/leather label. T5. $195.00

NELSON & DE LAWRENCE. *Answers to Questions.* 1958. Nelson Ent. Revised ed. 27 p. VG. J3. $6.00

NELSON & GRANT. *Brain Busters.* 1974. Calgary. 6 p. stapled manuscript. NM. J3. $4.00

NELSON & MOORE. *Super Prediction Tricks.* 1975. Calgary. 1st ed. 42 p. NM. J3. $8.00

NEMOTO, Takeshi. *Tokyo Trickery.* 1977. Magic Inc. 2nd print. 87 p. NM. J3. $5.00

NERUDA, Pablo. *Memoirs.* 1977. Farrar Straus. UP. EX. K2. $50.00

NERUDA, Pablo. *New Poems 1968-1970.* 1972. Grove Pr. UP of bilingual ed. tall wrp. EX. K2. $85.00

NERUDA, Pablo. *Passions & Impressions.* 1982. Farrar Straus. UP. wrp. EX. B13. $45.00

NERUDA, Pablo. *Song of Protest.* 1976. Morrow. AP of 1st Am ed. EX. K2. $75.00

NERUDA, Pablo. *Splendor & Death of Joaquin Murieta.* 1972. Farrar Straus. UP. tall wrp. Trade dj. scarce. K2. $100.00

NERUDA, Pablo. *Toward the Splendid City.* 1974. Farrar Straus. UP of bilingual ed. tall wrp. EX. scarce. K2. $85.00

NERUDA, Pablo. *We Are Many.* 1967. London. Cape Goliard. Ltd ed. 1/100. sgns. dj. H3. $125.00

NESBIT, R.C. *Strike Wings: Special Anti-Shipping Squadrons 1942-1945.* 1984. London. Ils 1st ed. 288 p. T5. $15.00

NESS, Eliot. *Untouchables.* 1957. NY. 1st ed. dj. VG. B3. $27.50

NESS & ORWIG. *IA Artists of the 1st Hundred Years.* 1939. Wallace Homestead. Intro Grant Wood. 1st ed. 253 p. EX. scarce. R4. $65.00

NESVADBA, Josef. *Lost Face.* 1971. Taplinger. 1st ed. dj. VG. P1. $15.00

NEUHAUS, Eugen. *Art of the Exposition.* 1915. San Francisco. Paul Elder. 89 p. G. T5. $22.50

NEUTRA, Richard. *Life & Human Habitat.* 1956. Stuttgart. EX. G1. $100.00

NEUTRA, Richard. *Richard Neutra: 1950-1960 Buildings & Projects.* 1959. NY. 1st ed. VG. G1. $100.00

NEUTRA, Richard. *World & Dwelling.* 1962. NY. 1st Am ed. VG. G1. $85.00

NEVILLE, Kris. *SF of Kris Neville.* 1984. S IL U. 1st ed. dj. EX. R3. $10.00

NEVILLE, Margot. *Murder of the Nymph.* 1950. Crime Club. 1st ed. dj. EX. P1. $15.00

NEVINS, Allan. *Ordeal of the Union.* 1973. Scribner. 500 p. dj. VG. S1. $12.00

NEVINS, Allan. *Study in Power, John D Rockefeller...* 1953. NY. 1st ed. 2 vols. slipcase. VG. T5. $45.00

NEVINS, Allan. *War for the Union Vol 3.* 1971. NY. Ils 1st ed. 532 p. dj. T5. $17.50

NEVINS, F.J. *Yankee Dared.* 1933. Chicago. 1st ed. dj. G. $16.00

NEVINS, F.M. *1st You Dream, Then You Die.* 1988. Mysterious Pr. 1st ed. sgn. dj. EX. F5. $25.00

NEW YORK YEARLY MEETING. *Discipline of Yearly Meeting...Held in NY.* 1872. NY. Corlies Macy. 8vo. 92 p. G. V1. $15.00

NEW YORK YEARLY MEETING. *Memorials Concerning Deceased Friends.* 1889. NY. Caulon. 16mo. 122 p. VG. V1. $8.00

NEWBERRY, J.S. *Geol Atlas of State of OH.* 1879. OH Geol Survey. folio. scarce. A5. $120.00

NEWBY, Eric. *Big Red Train Ride.* 1978. NY. St Martin. 1st Am ed. dj. VG. $20.00

NEWCOMB. *Savo (Guadalcanal Naval Battle).* 1961. NY. 1st ed. 278 p. dj. VG. B3. $25.00

NEWELL, Mrs. D. *Family Circle & Parlor Annual.* c 1849. NY. 1st ed. VG. $20.00

NEWFIELD, Jack. *Prophetic Minority.* 1967. Signet. VG. B4. $4.00

NEWHALL, Beaumont. *Daguerreotype in Am.* 1968. NY. Ils. 176 p. dj. VG. B3. $65.00

NEWHALL, Beaumont. *Photography: Essays & Images.* 1980. MOMA. 328 p. dj. D4. $40.00

NEWHALL & EDKINS. *William H Jackson.* 1974. Ft Worth. 1st ed. presentation. dj. EX. C2. $39.00

NEWHOUSE, Edward. *Hollow of the Wave.* 1949. Sloane. 1st ed. 318 p. dj. EX. w/sgn letter. B10. $25.00

NEWLAND, C.A. *My Self & I.* 1962. Coward McCann. 1st ed. dj. VG. K2. $50.00

NEWLIN, E.C. *May Rain.* 1948. Dorrance. 2nd ed. dj. VG. B10. $3.50

NEWMAN, Daisy. *Diligence in Love.* 1951. Doubleday. 1st reprint ed. 8vo. 253 p. VG. V1. $7.00

NEWMAN, Ernest. *Study of Wagner.* 1899. London. Bertram Dobell. 1st ed. 401 p. VG. H3. $150.00

NEWMAN, H.S. *Memories of Stanley Pumphrey.* 1883. NY. 12mo. 292 p. VG. V1. $10.00

NEWMAN, P.S. *Invaders' Alien Missile Threat.* 1967. Big Little Book. VG. P1. $5.00

NEWMAN, Robert. *Identity Unknown.* 1945. Ziff Davis. 1st ed. dj. EX. F5. $30.00

NEWMAN, Robert. *Testing of Tertius.* 1973. Atheneum. 1st ed. dj. extremely rare. C1. $45.00

NEWMAN, Sharan. *Guinevere Evermore.* 1985. St Martin. 1st ed. lg wrp. RS. M. R3. $10.00

NEWMAN, Sharan. *Guinevere.* PB Orig. VG. C1. $7.50

NEWPORT, David. *Indices, Hist & Rational, to Revision of Scriptures.* 1871. Lippincott. 1st ed. 16mo. 220 p. VG. V1. $12.00

NEWPORT, Elizabeth. *Memoir of Elizabeth Newport.* 1874. Phil. Comly. 16mo. 423 p. G. V1. $10.00

NEWQUIST, Roy. *Special Kind of Magic.* 1968. Rand McNally. 2nd print. 156 p. dj. EX. H3. $20.00

NEWTON, A.E. *Books & Business.* 1930. Appelicon Pr/Rudge. 1/325. sgn. EX. A4. $50.00

NEWTON, A.E. *Dr Johnson: A Play.* 1923. Boston. 1st ed. G. B3. $25.00

NEWTON, A.E. *Edward Newton on Books & Business.* 1930. Apellicon Pr. 1st ed. 1/325. inscr/sgn. dj. EX. $110.00

NEWTON, A.E. *End Papers.* 1933. Little Brn. Dream Children ed. sgn. slipcase. M. $75.00

NEWTON, A.E. *Format of the Eng Novel.* 1928. Rowfant Club. 1st ed. 1/289. boxed. M. $275.00

NEWTON, A.E. *Magnificent Farce & Other Diversions of a Book Collector.* 1921. Boston. 1st ed. inscr. M. $60.00

NEWTON, A.E. *Newton on Blackstone.* 1937. Phil. 1/2000. sgn. dj. EX. $55.00

NEWTON, A.E. *Thomas Hardy: Novelist or Poet.* 1929. Phil. 1/950. 4to. boxed. NM. A4. $100.00

NEWTON, A.E. *Tourist in Spite of Himself.* 1930. Little Brn. Ltd ed. 1/525. sgn. slipcase. EX. $48.00

NEWTON, C.C. *Once Upon a Time in CT.* nd. (1916) Houghton. Ils. 140 p. VG. B10. $6.50

NEWTON, Norman. *Thomas Gage in Spanish Am.* 1969. Faber Farber. 1st ed. 214 p. dj. F2. $20.00

NEWTON & BOLTIN. *Nelson Rockefeller Collection: Masterpieces of Primitve Art.* 1987. NY. 1st ed. dj. EX. G1. $40.00

NEWTON. *Uses of Globes.* 1854. London. 4th ed. 12mo. 148 p. VG. C2. $40.00

NIATUM, Duane. *Cycle for the Woman in the Field.* 1973. Baltimore. Laughing Man. inscr. VG. K2. $45.00

NIATUM, Duane. *Pieces.* 1981. NY. Strawberry. sm pamphlet. wrp. EX. K2. $30.00

NIATUM, Duane. *Songs for the Harvester of Dreams.* 1981. Seattle. WA U. 1st ed. dj. EX. K2. $40.00

NIATUM, Duane. *Taos Pueblo.* 1973. Greenfield Review. 1st ed. wrp. EX. K2. $30.00

NIATUM, Duane. *Turning to the Rhythms of Her Song.* 1977. Seattle. Jawbone. 1/200. wrp. EX. K2. $35.00

NICHOLLS, Peter. *Science in SF.* 1985. Knopf. 1st ed. wrp. EX. R3. $17.50

NICHOLS, Beverley. *Case of Human Bondage: Tragic Marriage of Somerset Maugham.* 1966. Secker Warburg. 1st ed. dj. EX. C4. $30.00

NICHOLS, Beverly. *Laughter on the Stairs.* 1953. London. Cape. 1st ed. inscr. dj. EX. B13. $75.00

NICHOLS, Bob. *Shotgunner.* 1949. NY. 1st ed. dj. VG. B3. $30.00

NICHOLS, Dale. *2 Years Before the Mast.* 1941. Heritage. VG. B7. $21.00

NICHOLS, Fan. *Be Silent, Love.* 1960. Simon Schuster. 1st ed. dj. EX. F5. $16.00

NICHOLS, Fan. *Pawn.* 1950. Woodford Pr. 1st ed. dj. EX. F5. $20.00

NICHOLS, G.W. *Story of the Great March.* 1865. NY. Ils. 12mo. fld map. 408 p. gr bdg. G4. $32.00

NICHOLS, John. *Magic Journey.* 1978. Holt Rinehart. UP. HrdCvr. very scarce. K2. $300.00

NICHOLS, John. *Milagro Beanfield War.* 1974. NY. 1st ed. dj. EX. C4. $125.00

NICHOLS, Kenny. *All About the Town.* nd. Akron. Danner Pr. 128 p. wrp. VG. T5. $22.50

NICHOLS, Leigh. *Shadow Fires.* nd. Book Club. dj. EX. P1. $7.50

NICHOLS, M.E. *Hist of the Meridian.* 1934. Brooklyn, NY. private print. 117 p. EX. B10. $20.00

NICHOLS, R.F. *Stakes of Power 1845-1977.* 1961. Hill Wang. 241 p. VG. S1. $10.00

NICHOLS, Robert. *Fishbo; or, The Looking Glass Loaned.* 1934. Heinemann. Ltd ed. 1/1000. sgn. dj. H3. $100.00

NICHOLS, Roy. *Battles & Leaders of the Civil War.* 1956. NY. 1st ed. 4 vols. boxed. G. $100.00

NICHOLS, Ruth. *Left-Handed Spirit.* 1978. Macmillan of Canada. dj. VG. P1. $12.50

NICHOLS, Ruth. *Song of the Pearl.* 1976. Macmillan. 1st Canadian ed. dj. EX. P1. $20.00

NICHOLS, T.L. *40 Years of Am Life.* 1937. NY. dj. EX. $60.00

NICHOLSON, Elizabeth. *Home Manual; or, Economical Cook & House Book.* c 1880. Phil. 16mo. 160 p. G. G4. $39.00

NICHOLSON, Irene. *Mexican & Central Am Mythology.* 1967. London. Hamlyn. 1st ed. dj. F2. $20.00

NICHOLSON, Kenyon. *Barker.* nd. Grosset Dunlap. Photoplay ed. VG. P1. $25.00

NICHOLSON, Margaret. *Am-Eng Usage.* 1957. Oxford. 1st ed. 671 p. VG. B10. $5.00

NICHOLSON, Norman. *HG Wells.* 1957. Novelists Series 4. VG. P1. $7.50

NICHOLSON & CORDY-COLLINS. *Pre-Columbian Art From the Land Collection.* 1979. CA Academy of Sciences. 1st ed. 272 p. wrp. F2. $25.00

NICHOLSON. *Mechanics Companion.* 1831. NY. 1st Am ed. full leather. C2. $95.00

NICKLAUS, Frederick. *Man Who Bit the Sun.* 1964. New Directions. dj. B4. $10.00

NICKLAUS, Thelma. *Harlequin.* 1956. Braziller. 1st Am ed. 259 p. dj. EX. H3. $75.00

NICKOLAUS, Paul. *Tanzerinnen.* 1919. Delphin Verlag. sm octavo. 89 p. VG. H3. $125.00

NICKOLAY, J.G. *Outbreak of War.* nd. NY. Brussel. PB. VG. S1. $6.00

NICKOLAY, Michael. *Brother & Sister.* 1979. Lippincott. 1st ed. dj. EX. F5. $14.00

NICOL, Eric. *Say Uncle.* 1961. Harper. dj. VG. P1. $10.00

NICOL, Eric. *Space Age Go Home!* 1964. Ryerson. 3rd ed. dj. VG. P1. $10.00

NICOLAY & HAY. *Abraham Lincoln: A Hist.* 1890. Century. 1st ed. 10 vols. octavo. H3. $4000.00

NICOLE, Christopher. *Caribee.* 1974. St Martin. 1st ed. dj. EX. P1. $12.50

NICOLLS, W.J. *Daughters of Suffolk.* 1910. Lippincott. 1st ed. sgn. 332 p. B10. $20.00

NICOLSON, Harold. *Dwight Morrow.* 1935. Harcourt. 1st ed. B10. $7.00

NICOLSON, J.U. *King of Blk Isles.* 1924. 3rd print. VG. C1. $5.00

NICOLSON, J.U. *King of Blk Isles.* 1925. Chicago. Covici. Revised ed. dj. VG. B10. $10.00

NIELSEN, Helen. *Verdict Suspended.* 1964. Morrow. 1st ed. dj. xl. P1. $6.00

NIELSON, Norm. *Magic Castle Walls of Fame.* 1988. Nielsen Magic. Ltd ed. 1/500. 557 p. dj. M. J3. $45.00

NIELSON, Norm. *Magic Castle Walls of Fame.* 1988. Nielsen Magic. 1st ed. 557 p. M. J3. $24.50

NIEMEYER, E.V. *General Bernardo Reyes.* 1966. Monterrey, Mexico. 1st ed. 1/1000. 261 p. wrp. F2. $12.50

NIETSCHMANN, Bernard. *Caribbean Edge.* 1979. Bobbs Merrill. 1st ed. dj. F2. $15.00

NIETZ, J. *Old TBs.* 1961. Pittsburgh. dj. EX. $40.00

NIJINSKY, Romola. *Nijinsky.* 1936. Simon Schuster. 1st ed presentation. dj. VG. H3. $100.00

NIKOLA, Louis. *Nikola Card System.* 1937. NY. Holden. 2nd ed. 28 p. SftCvr. NM. J3. $4.00

NILES, Blair. *Colombia: Land of Miracles.* 1939. Appleton. Ils. 398 p. dj. F2. $10.00

NILES, Blair. *Peruvian Pageant.* 1937. Bobbs Merrill. 1st ed. 311 p. dj. F2. $20.00

NILES, J.J. *Singing Soldiers.* 1927. NY. Ils Williamson. 1st ed. dj. VG. B3. $45.00

NILSEN, Vladimir. *Cinema As a Graphic Art.* nd. (1937) London. Newnes. 1st ed. 226 p. dj. VG. H3. $75.00

NIN, Anais. *Celebration.* 1973. Magic Circle. 1/55. sgns. purple bdg. H3. $250.00

NIN, Anais. *Child Born Out of the Fog.* c1947. Gemor Pr. inscr. sm octavo. peach wrp. H3. $125.00

NIN, Anais. *Children of the Albatross.* 1959. Peter Owen. inscr. sm octavo. dj. H3. $150.00

NIN, Anais. *Cities of the Interior.* 1959. private print. Ils Ian Hugo. inscr. wrp. H3. $100.00

NIN, Anais. *Collages.* 1964. London. Peter Owen. 1st ed. inscr. dj. EX. K2. $100.00

NIN, Anais. *Delta of Venus.* 1977. Harcourt Brace. UP. tall wrp. EX. K2. $100.00

NIN, Anais. *Diary of Anais Nin 1947-1955.* 1974. Harcourt Brace. sgn. dj. M. H3. $75.00

NIN, Anais. *House of Incest.* 1936. Paris. Siana Ed. 1/249 sgn. quarto. sewn wrp. VG. H3. $300.00

NIN, Anais. *Novel of the Future.* 1968. Macmillan. 1st ed. 8vo. 214 p. dj. EX. R4. $50.00

NIN, Anais. *Nuances.* 1970. Sans Souci Pr. 1/99. sgn. Indian raw silk bdg. M. H3. $250.00

NIN, Anais. *Paris Revisited.* 1972. Capra. Chapbook Series. 1/250. sgn. EX. K2. $100.00

NIN, Anais. *Spy in the House of Love.* nd. Paris/NY. British Book Centre. 1st ed. inscr. dj. EX. K2. $100.00

NIN, Anais. *Under a Glass Bell & Other Stories.* 1948. Dutton. 1st ed. 8vo. 221 p. dj. R4. $50.00

NIN, Anais. *Under a Glass Bell.* 1944. Gemor Pr. 1/300. inscr. H3. $350.00

NIN, Anais. *Winter of Artifice.* c 1942. 1/500. sgn. glassine dj. slipcase. H3. $300.00

NIN, Anais. *Winter of Artifice.* 1942. NY. Ils Ian Hugo. inscr. EX. C4. $300.00

NISOT, E.H. *Sleepless Men.* 1959. Crime Club. 1st ed. dj. VG. P1. $15.00

NISSENSON, Hugh. *Tree of Life.* 1985. NY. 1st ed. 159 p. EX. T5. $12.50

NIVEN, David. *Once Over Lightly.* 1951. Prentice Hall. 1st ed. 276 p. dj. EX. H3. $60.00

NIVEN, Larry. *Integral Trees.* 1984. Del Rey. 1st ed. dj. VG. P1. $15.00

NIVEN, Larry. *Magic Goes Away.* 1978. Ace. Ltd HrdCvr ed. 1/1000. sgn. dj. EX. R3. $35.00

NIVEN, Larry. *Magic Goes Away.* 1978. Grosset Dunlap. 1st ed. sgn. dj. EX. P1. $30.00

NIVEN, Larry. *Ringworld.* 1973. British SF Book Club. dj. VG. P1. $7.50

NIVEN, Larry. *Smoke Ring.* 1987. Del Rey. 1st ed. dj. EX. P1. $17.50

NIVEN, Larry. *World Out of Time.* nd. Holt Rinehart. 2nd ed. dj. EX. P1. $12.50

NIVEN, Larry. *World Out of Time.* 1976. Holt Rinehart. dj. EX. P1. $30.00

NIVEN, POURNELLE, & BARNES. *Legacy of Heorot.* 1987. Simon Schuster. 1st ed. sgns. dj. EX. R3. $37.50

NIVEN, POURNELLE, & BARNES. *Oath of Fealty.* 1981. Timescape. 1st ed. dj. EX. R3. $17.50

NIVEN & BARNES. *Achilles' Choice.* 1991. Tor Books. 1st ed. dj. EX. F5. $16.00

NIVEN & BARNES. *Dream Park.* 1981. Phantasia. 1st ed. 1/600. sgn. M. R3. $75.00

NIVEN & POURNELLE. *Footfall.* 1985. Del Rey. 1st ed. dj. EX. P1. $17.95

NIVEN & POURNELLE. *Legacy of Heorot.* 1987. Simon & Schuster. 1st ed. dj. EX. P1. $17.95

NIVEN & POURNELLE. *Lucifer's Hammer.* 1977. Playboy. 1st ed. dj. VG. P1. $30.00

NIXON, Alan. *Attack on Vienna.* 1972. St Martin. 1st ed. dj. EX. P1. $12.50

NIXON, Alan. *Item 7.* 1970. Simon Schuster. 1st ed. dj. EX. P1. $12.50

NIXON, H. *Lower Piedmont Country.* 1946. NY. 1st ed. dj. VG. B3. $17.50

NIXON, Richard. *Real War.* 1980. Warner. sgn. boxed. M. $55.00

NIXON, Richard. *6 Crises.* 1962. NY. 1st ed. inscr. dj. VG. $125.00

NIXON, W.O. *How Marcus Whitman Saved OR.* 1895. Star Pub. 1st ed. VG. $18.00

NOAKES, E.E. *Magical Orig...* 1914. London. Bell. 1st ed. 151 p. EX. J3. $20.00

NOBILE, Umberto. *L'Aviazione.* 1918. Roma. Ils. 186 p. printed wrp. T5. $150.00

NOCK, O.S. *Railways at the Zenith of Steam 1920-1940.* 1970. London. dj. VG. $9.00

NOEL, Bernard. *Art Mexicain.* 1968. Paris. French text. 4 vols. 12mo. F2. $25.00

NOEL, Ruth. *Mythology of Middle Earth.* 1977. 1st ed. dj. EX. C1. $11.50

NOEL, Theophilus. *Autobiography & Reminiscences.* 1904. Chicago. 1st ed. 349 p. VG. B3. $135.00

NOEL-HUME, I. *Martin's Hundred.* 1982. NY. 1st ed. 343 p. dj. VG. B3. $35.00

NOLAN, W.F. *Hammett: A Life at the Edge.* 1982. Congdon Weed. inscr. dj. EX. T9. $45.00

NOLAN, W.F. *Hemingway: Last Days of the Lion.* 1974. Capra. Chapbook Series. 1/75. sgn. K2. $50.00

NOLAN, W.F. *Logan: A Trilogy.* 1986. Maclay. 1st ed. dj. EX. R3. $17.50

NOLAN & JOHNSON. *Logan's Run.* 1967. Dial. 1st ed. inscr Nolan. dj. VG. F5. $60.00

NOLL, Arthur. *From Empire to Republic.* 1903. McClurg. 1st ed. 336 p. F2. $15.00

NORMAN, Albert. *Operation Overlord.* 1952. Military Pub. 1st ed. 230 p. VG. B10. $17.00

NORMAN, Barry. *Matter of Mandrake.* 1968. Walker. 1st ed. dj. VG. P1. $12.50

NORMAN, Earl. *Kill Me in Tokyo.* 1958. Berkley. 1st ed. wrp. EX. F5. $12.00

NORMAN, James. *Murder Chop Chop.* 1942. Morrow. dj. VG. P1. $15.00

NORMAN, Marsha. *'Night, Mother.* 1983. Hill Wang. UP. EX. B13. $65.00

NORRIS, C.G. *Guest of Robin Hood.* 1954. Grabhorn. NM. C1. $15.00

NORRIS, Frank. *Nutro 29.* 1950. Rinehart. 1st ed. dj. VG. R3. $25.00

NORRIS, Kathleen. *Works.* 1920. Doubleday Page. Autograph ed. 1/277. 11 vols. octavo. H3. $375.00

NORSE, Harold. *Karma Circuit.* 1967. Nothing Doing in London Pr. B4. $10.00

NORTH, Eric. *Ant Men.* 1960. Winston. 1st ed. dj. VG. R3. $20.00

NORTH, Ingoldsby. *Book of Love Letters.* c1867. NY. 12mo. 156 p. G. $12.50

NORTH, Joseph. *Men in the Ranks.* 1938. Friends of Lincoln Brigade. pamphlet. M. H3. $100.00

NORTH, Sterling. *Night Outlasts the Whippoorwill.* 1936. Macmillan. inscr. dj. H3. $50.00

NORTH, Sterling. *Rascal.* 1963. Dutton. 1st ed. dj. EX. C4. $35.00

NORTH & BOUTELL. *Speak of the Devil.* nd. Book Club. VG. P1. $6.00

NORTHEND. *Speeches...Upon Political Subjects From 1860 to 1869.* 1869. Salem. 12mo. 268 p. G. G4. $12.00

NORTHROP, H.D. *Popular Hist of Am...Together With Graphic Account...HI.* c 1898. Springfield. Ils. 8vo. 480 p. G. $18.00

NORTHURP, Solomon. *12 Years a Slave.* 1854. Auburn. Ils. 336 p. G. $250.00

NORTON, Andre. *Catseye.* 1961. Harcourt Brace. 1st ed. xl. P1. $12.50

NORTON, Andre. *Cross-Time Agent.* 1975. Gollancz. dj. xl. P1. $7.50

NORTON, Andre. *Crossroads of Time.* 1978. Gregg Pr. 1st HrdCvr ed. dj. EX. R3. $25.00

NORTON, Andre. *Dragon Magic.* 1973. PB Orig. VG. C1. $2.50

NORTON, Andre. *Galactic Derelict.* 1967. World. 3rd ed. dj. xl. P1. $10.00

NORTON, Andre. *Horn Crown.* nd. Book Club. 1st ed. dj. VG. P1. $5.00

NORTON, Andre. *Ice Crown.* 1970. Viking. 1st ed. dj. VG. P1. $15.00

NORTON, Andre. *Ice Crown.* 1971. Longman Young. 1st ed. dj. VG. P1. $35.00

NORTON, Andre. *Iron Cage.* 1974. Viking. 1st ed. dj. EX. P1. $35.00

NORTON, Andre. *Key Out of Time.* 1963. World. 1st ed. dj. xl. P1. $15.00

NORTON, Andre. *Night of Masks.* 1964. Harcourt. 1st ed. dj. EX. R3. $65.00

NORTON, Andre. *Opal-Eyed Fan.* 1977. Dutton. 1st ed. dj. VG. P1. $20.00

NORTON, Andre. *Operation Time Search.* nd. Harcourt Brace. dj. EX. P1. $15.00

NORTON, Andre. *Ordeal in Otherwhere.* 1964. World. 1st ed. dj. EX. R3. $85.00

NORTON, Andre. *Ordeal in Otherwhere.* 1964. World. 1st ed. dj. xl. P1. $20.00

NORTON, Andre. *Ordeal in Otherwhere.* 1965. World. 2nd ed. dj. xl. P1. $10.00

NORTON, Andre. *Outside.* 1976. Blackie. dj. xl. P1. $7.50

NORTON, Andre. *Quest Crosstime.* 1965. Viking. 1st ed. dj. EX. R3. $65.00

NORTON, Andre. *Red Hart Magic.* 1976. Crowell. 1st ed. dj. VG. P1. $22.50

NORTON, Andre. *Scarface.* 1963. Harcourt/World. 8th print. dj. xl. P1. $10.00

NORTON, Andre. *Secret of the Lost Race.* 1978. Gregg Pr. 1st HrdCvr ed. dj. EX. R3. $25.00

NORTON, Andre. *Shadow Hawk.* 1960. Harcourt. 1st ed. dj. EX. R3. $90.00

NORTON, Andre. *Sioux Spaceman.* 1978. Gregg Pr. 1st HrdCvr ed. dj. EX. R3. $25.00

NORTON, Andre. *Sm Shadows Creep.* 1974. Dutton. 1st ed. dj. EX. P1. $15.00

NORTON, Andre. *Space Service World.* 1953. World. 1st ed. dj. EX. R3. $200.00

NORTON, Andre. *Star Hunter.* 1961. Ace. 1st ed. wrp. EX. R3. $10.00

NORTON, Andre. *Star Man's Son 2250 AD.* nd. Harcourt/World. 8th print. xl. P1. $12.50

NORTON, Andre. *Star Man's Son.* 1980. Gregg Pr. 1st ed. M. R3. $20.00

NORTON, Andre. *Tales of the Witch World.* 1987. Tor Books. 1st ed. dj. VG. P1. $15.95

NORTON, Andre. *Time Traders.* 1979. Gregg Pr. 1st ed. 4 vols. djs. VG. R3. $50.00

NORTON, Andre. *Voorloper.* nd. Book Club. dj. EX. P1. $4.50

NORTON, Andre. *Voorloper.* 1980. Doubleday. 1st HrdCvr ed. dj. EX. F5. $10.00

NORTON, Andre. *Witch World.* 1963. Ace. 1st ed. wrp. EX. R3. $15.00

NORTON, Andre. *Wraiths of Time.* 1976. Atheneum. 2nd ed. dj. EX. P1. $15.00

NORTON, Andre. *Wraiths of Time.* 1977. Atheneum. 3rd ed. dj. EX. P1. $10.00

NORTON, C.A. *Melville Davisson Post.* 1973. Popular. EX. P1. $12.50

NORTON, Carol. *Bobs: Girl Detective.* 1928. Burton. VG. B10. $3.75

NORTON, Mary. *Bed Knob & Broomstick.* 1966. Harcourt/World. 9th print. xl. P1. $5.00

NORTON, Mary. *Borrowers Afield.* 1955. Harcourt Brace. Ils Kush. 1st Am ed. dj. EX. C4. $30.00

NORTON, Mary. *Borrowers.* nd. Harcourt Brace. dj. EX. P1. $12.50

NORTON & CRISPIN. *Cryphon's Eyrie.* 1984. Tor Books. 1st ed. dj. EX. P1. $12.95

NORTON & MADLEE. *Star Ka'at at World.* 1978. Walker. dj. EX. P1. $20.00

NORTON & MADLEE. *Star Ka'at.* nd. Weekly Reader. decor brd. EX. P1. $5.00

NORTON & SCHWARTZ. *Imperial Lady.* 1989. Tor Books. 1st ed. dj. EX. F5. $15.00

NOURSE, A.E. *Intern.* nd. Book Club. dj. VG. P1. $4.00

NOURSE, J.E. *Am Explorations in the Ice Zones.* c 1884. Boston. 8vo. 624 p. brn cloth. xl. G. G4. $29.00

NOVAK, Joseph; see Kosinski, Jerzy.

NOVO, Salvador. *NM Grandeur.* 1967. Mexico. 1st ed. 1/6000. dj. F2. $15.00

NOVOTNY, F. *Toulouse-Lautrec.* 1969. Phaidon. 1st ed. dj. EX. G1. $40.00

NOWELL, Elizabeth. *Thomas Wolfe: A Biography.* 1960. Doubleday. 1st ed. dj. EX. C4. $25.00

NOWELL-SMITH, Simon. *Letters to Macmillan.* 1967. London. Macmillan. 1st ed. 8vo. 384 p. dj. EX. R4. $20.00

NOWLAN, P.F. *Armageddon 2419 AD.* 1962. Avalon. 1st ed. dj. EX. R3. $35.00

NOWLAN, P.F. *Armageddon 2419 AD.* 1962. Avalon. dj. xl. P1. $7.50

NOWLAN & CALKINS. *Adventures of Buck Rogers.* 1934. Whitman. 1st ed. VG. R3. $85.00

NOYES, Alfred. *Flower of Old Japan.* 1914. NY. 12mo. gilt leather. VG. T1. $20.00

NOYES, Alfred. *Sherwood; or, Robin Hood & the 3 Kings.* c 1911. NY. 1st ed? xl. C1. $11.00

NOYES, P.B. *Goodly Heritage.* 1958. Rinehart. 1st ed. 275 p. VG. B10. $5.75

NOYES, P.B. *My Father's House.* 1937. NY. 1st ed. 312 p. dj. VG. B3. $27.50

NOYES, P.B. *Pallid Giant.* 1927. Revell. 2nd ed. 300 p. VG. B10. $4.00

NUETZEL, Charles. *Last Call for the Stars.* 1970. Lenox Hill. dj. xl. P1. $7.50

NUNIS, D.B. *Hudson's Bay Co's 1st Fur Brigade to Sacramento Valley.* 1968. Fair Oaks. sm 4to. 59 p. VG. T5. $85.00

NUTCHUK. *Back to the Smokey Sea.* 1944. Messner. 5th print. 225 p. dj. VG. B10. $3.25

NUTCHUK. *Son of the Smokey Sea.* 1958. Messner. 17th print. 243 p. dj. VG. B10. $3.25

NUTID, F.F.T. *Mexikansk Konst.* 1952. Stockholm. Swedish/Eng/Spanish text. F2. $20.00

NUTINI, Hugo. *Essays on Mexican Kinship.* 1976. Pittsburgh U. 1st ed. 256 p. F2. $30.00

NUTTING, Wallace. *Clock Book.* 1924. Framingham. 1st ed. 250 pls. 312 p. VG. B3. $60.00

NUTTING, Wallace. *CT Beautiful.* 1935. Garden City. dj. VG. B3. $20.00

NWEEYA, Samuel. *Persia the Land of the Magi.* c 1920. np. Nweeya. VG. J2. $10.00

NYE, Bill. *Bill Nye & Boomerang.* 1881. Belford Clarke. VG. A5. $80.00

NYE, Bill. *Bill Nye's Remarks.* 1891. Chicago. Thompson Thomas. 389 p. A5. $40.00

NYE, Bill. *Bill Nye's Remarks.* 1901. Chicago. Ils. 8vo. 504 p. gilt olive-gr bdg. G4. $26.00

NYE, Bill. *Hist of Eng.* 1904. Phil. VG. C1. $11.00

NYE, Robert. *Beowulf.* 1968. Hill Wang. 1st ed. dj. VG. C1. $6.00

NYE, Robert. *Falstaff.* 1976. London. Hamish Hamilton. 1st ed. dj. EX. C4. $65.00

NYE, Robert. *Merlin.* 1979. NY. 1st Am ed. dj. EX. C1. $18.00

NYE, Robert. *Merlin.* 1981. Bantam. 1st Am PB ed. EX. C1. $3.50

NYE, W.H. *Wharf Rats...& Other People.* 1948. Cleveland. Ils Jack R Allen. 1/300. inscr. 67 p. T5. $19.50

NYE, W.S. *Here Come the Rebels.* 1965. Baton Rouge. 1st ed. sgn. dj. VG. B3. $65.00

O'BRIAN, Patrick. *Last Pool.* 1950. London. 1st ed. dj. VG. $35.00

O'BRIEN, Edna. *Fanatic Heart.* 1984. Farrar Straus. AP. EX. K2. $30.00

O'BRIEN, Edna. *James & Nora. Portrait of Joyce's Marriage.* 1981. Lord John. Ltd ed. 1/276. sgn. M. H3. $100.00

O'BRIEN, Geoffrey. *Dream Time: Chapters From the '60s.* 1988. Viking. dj. M. B4. $15.95

O'BRIEN, Geoffrey. *Hard-Boiled Am.* 1981. Van Nostrand Reinhold. 1st ed. wrp. EX. T9. $30.00

O'BRIEN, J.J. *How To Run a Lathe.* 1941. S Bend Lathe Works. 41st ed. VG. B10. $4.25

O'BRIEN, Pat. *Outwitting the Hun: My Escape From a German Prison Camp.* 1918. NY. 1st ed. inscr. VG. $30.00

O'BRIEN, Tim. *Going After Cacciato.* 1978. Delacorte. 1st ed. dj. EX. B13. $65.00

O'BRIEN, Tim. *Going After Cacciato.* 1978. Delacorte. 1st ed. sgn. dj. EX. K2. $150.00

O'BRIEN, Tim. *Going After Cacciato.* 1979. London. Cape. 1st ed. sgn. dj. EX. K2. $85.00

O'BRIEN, Tim. *If I Die in a Combat Zone.* 1973. Delacorte. 1st ed. dj. EX. very scarce. K2. $450.00

O'BRIEN, Tim. *If I Die in a Combat Zone.* 1973. Delacorte. 1st ed. sgn. dj. EX. K2. $750.00

O'BRIEN, Tim. *If I Die in a Combat Zone.* 1973. London. Calder Boyars. 1st ed. sgn. dj. EX. K2. $200.00

O'BRIEN, Tim. *If I Die in a Combat Zone.* 1973. London. Calder Boyars. 1st UK ed. dj. EX. T9. $70.00

O'BRIEN, Tim. *N Lights.* 1976. London. 1st UK ed. 1/900. as issued. EX. K2. $50.00

O'BRIEN, Tim. *N Lights.* 1976. London. Calder Boyars. 1st UK ed. sgn. dj. EX. K2. $200.00

O'BRIEN, Tim. *Nuclear Age.* 1985. Knopf. UP. wrp. EX. B13. $85.00

O'BRIEN, Tim. *Nuclear Age.* 1985. Knopf. 1st ed. sgn. dj. EX. C4. $50.00

O'BRIEN, Tim. *Speaking of Courage.* 1980. Santa Barbara. Neville. Ltd ed. 1/326. sgn. dj. EX. K2. $75.00

O'BRIEN, Tim. *Things They Carried.* 1990. Houghton Mifflin. 1st ed. sgn. dj. M. C4/K2. $50.00

O'CASEY, Sean. *Behind Gr Curtains/Figure in Night/Moon Shines on Kylenamoe.* 1961. St Martin. 1st ed. dj. H3. $50.00

O'CASEY, Sean. *Bishop's Bonfire.* 1955. Macmillan. 1st ed. dj. EX. H3. $45.00

O'CASEY, Sean. *Drums of Father Ned.* 1960. St Martin. 1st ed. dj. EX. H3. $60.00

O'CASEY, Sean. *Oak Leaves & Lavender.* 1946. Macmillan. 1st ed. dj. RS. VG. H3. $75.00

O'CASEY, Sean. *Plough & the Stars.* 1926. Macmillan. 1st Am ed. dj. EX. H3. $75.00

O'CASEY, Sean. *Purple Dust.* 1940. Macmillan. 1st ed. H3. $60.00

O'CASEY, Sean. *Silver Tassie.* 1928. Macmillan. 1st Am ed. dj. EX. H3. $45.00

O'CASEY, Sean. *2 Plays: Juno & the Paycock/Shadow of a Gunman.* 1925. Macmillan. 1st Am ed. dj. EX. H3. $60.00

O'CONNELL, Nicholas. *At the Field's End: Interviews With 20 Pacific NW Writers.* 1987. Seattle. Madrona. 1st HrdCvr ed. dj. EX. K2. $45.00

O'CONNOR, Flannery. *Complete Stories.* 1971. Farrar Straus. UP. wrp. EX. scarce. C4. $325.00

O'CONNOR, Flannery. *Complete Stories.* 1971. Farrar Straus. 1st ed. dj. EX. C4. $125.00

O'CONNOR, Flannery. *Conquest.* 1930. Grosset. VG. B3. $65.00

O'CONNOR, Flannery. *Everything That Rises Must Converge.* 1965. London. Faber. UP of 1st Eng ed. wrp. EX. K2. $450.00

O'CONNOR, Flannery. *Everything That Rises Must Converge.* 1966. London. UP of 1st UK ed. wrp. EX. B13. $550.00

O'CONNOR, Flannery. *Good Man Is Hard To Find.* 1955. Harcourt Brace. 1st ed. dj. EX. C4. $350.00

O'CONNOR, Flannery. *Habit of Being: Letters of Flannery O'Connor.* 1979. Farrar Straus. 1st ed. dj. EX. C4. $50.00

O'CONNOR, Flannery. *Mystery & Manners: Occasional Prose.* 1969. Farrar Straus. 1st ed. dj. EX. C4. $125.00

O'CONNOR, Flannery. *Various Lives of Keats & Chapman & the Brother.* 1976. London. 1st ed. dj. EX. B13. $50.00

O'CONNOR, Flannery. *Violent Bear It Away.* 1960. Farrar Straus. 1st ed. dj. EX. C4. $275.00

O'CONNOR, Flannery. *Wise Blood.* 1952. Harcourt. 1st ed. dj. VG. B3. $300.00

O'CONNOR, Frank. *Midnight Court.* 1945. London/Dublin. Fridberg. dj. VG. K2. $85.00

O'CONNOR, Frank. *Road to Stratford.* 1948. London. Metheun. dj. VG. K2. $75.00

O'CONNOR, Frank. *Traveler's Samples.* 1951. London. Macmillan. dj. EX. K2. $65.00

O'CONNOR, Jack. *Arms & Ammunitions Manual.* 1965. NY. 1st ed. inscr. dj. VG. $12.50

O'CONNOR, Jack. *Big Game Rifle.* 1952. NY. 1st ed. dj. VG. B3. $125.00

O'CONNOR, Jack. *Boomtown.* 1938. NY. 1st ed. G. B3. $17.50

O'CONNOR, Jack. *Horse & Buggy W.* 1969. NY. 2nd ed. dj. VG. B3. $45.00

O'CONNOR, Jack. *Hunting in Rockies.* 1947. NY. 1st ed. VG. B3. $70.00

O'CONNOR, Jack. *Hunting in the SW.* 1945. Knopf. 1st Trade ed. 279 p. VG. B3. $70.00

O'CONNOR, Jack. *Hunting Rifle.* 1970. NY. 1st ed. dj. VG. B3. $35.00

O'CONNOR, P.F. *Season for Unnatural Causes.* 1975. Urbana, IL. 1st ed. sgn. wrp. EX. T9. $35.00

O'CONNOR, Philip. *Selected Poems: 1936-1966.* 1968. London. Cape. 1st ed. dj. EX. C4. $25.00

O'COTTER, Pat. *Rhymes of a Roughneck.* 1918. Seward, AL. 1st ed. presentation. 92 p. R4. $25.00

O'DONNEL, Peter. *Modesty Blaise.* 1965. London. 1st ed. dj. VG. B3. $40.00

O'DONNELL, E.P. *Gr Margins.* 1936. Houghton Mifflin. 1st ed. 499 p. VG. $15.00

O'DONNELL, Elliott. *Casebook of Ghosts.* 1969. Taplinger. dj. xl. P1. $7.00

O'DONNELL, Elliott. *Phantoms of the Night.* 1956. Rider. 1st ed. dj. EX. P1. $30.00

O'DONNELL, Lawrence; see Kuttner, Henry.

O'DONNELL, Lillian. *Aftershock.* 1977. Doubleday Book Club. VG. P1. $7.50

O'DONNELL, Lillian. *Casual Affairs.* 1985. Putnam. 1st ed. dj. EX. P1. $16.95

O'DONNELL, Lillian. *Children's Zoo.* nd. Book Club. dj. VG. P1. $4.50

O'DONNELL, Lillian. *Falling Star.* nd. Book Club. dj. VG. P1. $5.00

O'DONNELL, Lillian. *Falling Star.* 1979. Putnam. dj. EX. P1. $20.00

O'DONNELL, Lillian. *Good Night To Kill.* 1989. Putnam. 1st ed. dj. EX. P1. $17.95

O'DONNELL, Lillian. *Ladykiller.* nd. Book Club. dj. VG. P1. $4.50

O'DONNELL, Lillian. *No Business Being a Cop.* nd. Book Club. dj. VG. P1. $5.00

O'DONNELL, Lillian. *Wicked Designs.* 1980. Putnam. 1st ed. dj. VG. P1. $12.50

O'DONNELL, Peter. *Dragon's Claw.* 1985. Mysterious Pr. 1st ed. dj. EX. P1. $15.95

O'DONNELL, Peter. *Modesty Blaise.* 1965. Doubleday. 1st ed. dj. xl. P1. $6.00

O'DONNELL, Peter. *Modesty Blaise.* 1965. Souvenir Pr. 1st ed. dj. P1. $30.00

O'DONNELL, Peter. *Modesty Blaise.* 1965. Souvenir Pr. 1st ed. dj. xl. P1. $7.50

O'DONNELL, Peter. *Modesty Blaise.* 1984. Pierce. 1st ed. wrp. EX. R3. $10.00

O'DONNELL, Peter. *Xanadu Talisman.* 1981. Mysterious Pr. dj. EX. P1. $15.00

O'DUFFY, Eimar. *Spacious Adventures of Man in St.* 1929. Macmillan. 2nd ed. VG. P1. $31.75

O'FAOLAIN, Sean. *Bird Alone.* 1936. London. Cape. 1st ed. dj. EX. C4. $30.00

O'FAOLAIN, Sean. *Born Genius: A Short Story.* 1936. Detroit. Schuman. 1/250. sgn. slipcase. EX. C4. $60.00

O'FAOLAIN, Sean. *King of the Beggars.* 1938. NY. 1st Am ed. 338 p. dj. VG. T5. $65.00

O'FARRELL, William. *Snakes of St Cyr.* 1951. Duell Sloan Pearce. dj. xl. P1. $5.00

O'FLAHERTY, Liam. *Assassin.* 1928. Jonathan Cape. 1/150. sgn. dj. H3. $150.00

O'FLAHERTY, Liam. *Ecstasy of Angus.* 1931. Joiner Steele. 1/350. sgn. TEG. H3. $100.00

O'FLAHERTY, Liam. *House of Gold.* 1929. Jonathan Cape. sgn. orange bdg. dj. H3. $75.00

O'FLAHERTY, Liam. *Mr Gilholey.* 1936. Jonathan Cape. inscr. dj. H3. $125.00

O'FLAHERTY, Liam. *Tourist's Guide to Ireland.* nd. London. Mandrake. sgn. H3. $75.00

O'FLAHERTY, Liam. *2 Years.* 1930. Jonathan Cape. inscr. dj. H3. $100.00

O'HARA, Frank. *City in Winter & Other Poems.* 1951. Ed Tibor de Nagy Gallery. Ils Larry Rivers. 1/150. inscr. wrp. C4. $1250.00

O'HARA, Frank. *Jackson Pollock.* 1959. Braziller. Ils Pollock. dj. VG. K2. $85.00

O'HARA, Frank. *Meditations in an Emergency.* 1957. Grove Pr. wrp. EX. K2. $45.00

O'HARA, John. *And Other Stories.* 1968. Random House. 1st ed. 1/300. sgn. slipcase. EX. B13. $185.00

O'HARA, John. *Files on Parade.* 1939. NY. 1st ed. as issued. scarce. K2. $300.00

O'HARA, John. *Good Samaritan & Other Stories.* nd. (1974) Random House. 2nd ed. dj. VG. B10. $3.75

O'HARA, John. *Hellbox.* 1947. Random House. 1st ed. dj. VG. P1. $35.00

O'HARA, John. *Horse Knows the Way.* 1964. Random House. Ltd ed. 1/250. sgn. EX. H3. $100.00

O'HARA, John. *Instrument.* 1967. Random House. Ltd ed. 1/300. sgn. acetate dj. EX. K2. $150.00

O'HARA, John. *Lockwood Concern.* 1965. Random House. 1/300. sgn. boxed. H3. $125.00

O'HARA, John. *Lovey Childs.* 1969. Random House. Ltd ed. 1/200. sgn. slipcase. EX. K2. $150.00

O'HARA, John. *Sermons & Soda Water.* 1961. London. Cresset. 1/525. sgn. 3 vols. slipcase. M. H3. $150.00

O'HARA, Kane. *Tom Thumb: A Burletta Altered From Henry Fielding.* 1830. London. Ils Cruikshank. 16mo. wrp. V1. $100.00

O'HARA, MACKINALY, & STONE. *3 Views of the Novel.* 1957. Lib of Congress. 1st ed. wrp. VG. B13. $35.00

O'KEEFE, Bernard. *Trapdoor.* 1988. Houghton. 1st ed. dj. EX. F5. $12.00

O'KEEFE, C. *Georgia O'Keefe.* 1976. NY. 1st Trade ed. fld pl. EX. G1. $100.00

O'MEARA, Walter. *Daughters of the Country: Women of Fur Traders & Mt Men.* 1968. NY. 1st ed. dj. VG. $10.00

O'MEARA, Walter. *Duke of War.* 1966. 1st ed. dj. xl. scarce. C1. $25.00

O'NEALE, Lila. *Textile Periods in Ancient Peru 3: Gauze Weaves.* 1948. Berkley. Ils. 4to. wrp. F2. $30.00

O'NEILL, C. *Wild Train.* 1956. NY. presentation. 492 p. dj. VG. B3. $32.50

O'NEILL, Eugene. *Ah, Wilderness!* 1933. Random House. 1st ed. dj. EX. H3. $150.00

O'NEILL, Eugene. *Ah, Wilderness!* 1936. Stockholm. Forlag. 1st Swedish ed. pictoral wrp. VG. H3. $40.00

O'NEILL, Eugene. *All God's Chillun Got Wings & Welded.* 1924. Boni Liveright. 1st ed. dj. G. H3. $25.00

O'NEILL, Eugene. *Beyond the Horizon.* 1920. Boni Liveright. 1st ed. VG. H3. $100.00

O'NEILL, Eugene. *Complete Works.* 1924. Boni Liveright. Ltd ed. 1/1200. sgn. 2 vols. H3. $450.00

O'NEILL, Eugene. *Days Without End.* 1934. Random House. 1st ed. dj. EX. H3. $100.00

O'NEILL, Eugene. *Days Without End.* 1934. Random House. 1st ed. presentation. dj. VG. H3. $850.00

O'NEILL, Eugene. *Dynamo.* 1929. Liveright. Ltd ed. 1/775. sgn. slipcase. w/photo. VG. H3. $200.00

O'NEILL, Eugene. *Emperor Jones.* 1928. Boni Liveright. Special Ltd ed. 1/775. sgn. dj. H3. $225.00

O'NEILL, Eugene. *Ett Stycke Poet (A Touch of the Poet).* 1957. Raben & Sjogren. 1st Swedish ed. printed wrp. VG. H3. $30.00

O'NEILL, Eugene. *Gold.* 1920. Boni Liveright. 1st ed. sgn. dj. EX. H3. $950.00

O'NEILL, Eugene. *Great God Brn/Fountain/Dreamy Kid/Before Breakfast.* 1926. Jonathan Cape. 1st Eng ed. dj. H3. $125.00

O'NEILL, Eugene. *Great God Brn/Fountain/Moon of the Caribees/6 Other Plays...* 1926. Boni Liveright. 1st ed. dj. EX. B13. $225.00

O'NEILL, Eugene. *Lazarus Laughed.* 1927. Boni Liveright. 1st Am ed. Trade print. dj. H3. $125.00

O'NEILL, Eugene. *Lazarus Laughed.* 1927. Boni Liveright. 1st Am ed. 1/775. sgn. slipcase. H3. $150.00

O'NEILL, Eugene. *Long Day's Journey Into Night.* 1956. Yale. 1st ed. EX. H3. $75.00

O'NEILL, Eugene. *Marco Millions.* 1927. Boni Liveright. Ltd ed. 1/450. sgn. EX. H3. $200.00

O'NEILL, Eugene. *Marco Millions.* 1927. Boni Liveright. 1st ed. dj. H3. $75.00

O'NEILL, Eugene. *Moon for the Misbegotton.* 1952. Random House. 1st ed. dj. EX. H3. $75.00

O'NEILL, Eugene. *Mourning Becomes Electra: A Trilogy.* 1931. Horace Liveright. 1st ed. dj. EX. H3. $75.00

O'NEILL, Eugene. *Plays.* 1934. Scribner. Wilderness ed. 1/770. sgn. 12 vols. TEG. EX. H3. $1500.00

O'NEILL, Eugene. *Strange Interlude.* 1928. Boni Liveright. Ltd ed. 1/775. sgn. slipcase. EX. H3. $300.00

O'NEILL, Eugene. *Touch of the Poet.* 1957. Yale. 1st ed. dj. EX. H3. $75.00

O'NEILL, J.P. *Metropolitan Cats.* 1981. Abrams. sm folio. dj. EX. $35.00

O'NEILL, John. *Drunkard: A Poem.* 1842. London. Tilt Bogue. Ils Cruikshank. V1. $85.00

O'NEILL, John. *Prodigal Genius.* 1944. NY. presentation. 326 p. VG. B3. $32.50

O'NEILL, Rose. *Loves of Edwy Kewpie.* 1904. Boston. 1st ed. VG. B3. $52.50

O'ROURKE, P.J. *Parliament of Whores.* 1991. Atlantic. 1st ed. sgn. dj. M. B13. $50.00

O'SHAUGHNESSY, Edith. *Diplomat's Wife in Mexico.* 1916. Harper. 1st ed. 356 p. F2. $15.00

O'SULLIVAN, T.H. *Am Frontiers.* 1981. Aperature. oblong 4to. dj. EX. $25.00

OATES, J.C. *All the Good People I've Left Behind.* 1979. Blk Sparrow. Ltd ed. 1/300. sgn. M. H3. $50.00

OATES, J.C. *Am Appetites.* 1989. Dutton. UP. wrp. EX. K2. $40.00

OATES, J.C. *Cybele.* 1979. Blk Sparrow. 1/300. sgn. M. H3. $50.00

OATES, J.C. *Cybele.* 1979. Blk Sparrow. 1st Trade ed. wrp. VG. K2. $15.00

OATES, J.C. *Do With Me What You Will.* 1973. Vanguard. AP. wrp. EX. K2. $175.00

OATES, J.C. *Heat & Other Stories.* 1991. Dutton. UP. wrp. EX. K2. $45.00

OATES, J.C. *Hostile Sun.* 1973. Blk Sparrow. Ltd ed. 1/300. sgn. M. H3. $60.00

OATES, J.C. *Invisible Woman: New & Selected Poems 1972-1982.* 1982. Princeton. 1st ed. 1/300. sgn. slipcase. EX. $75.00

OATES, J.C. *Luxury of Sin.* 1984. Lord John. 1/125. sgn. wrp. EX. K2. $45.00

OATES, J.C. *Marriages & Infidelities.* 1972. Vanguard. UP. wrp. VG. K2. $125.00

OATES, J.C. *Miracle Play.* 1974. Blk Sparrow. Ltd ed. 1/350. sgn. EX. H3. $50.00

OATES, J.C. *Mysteries of Winterthurn.* 1984. Franklin Lib. Ltd 1st ed. sgn. EX. K2. $65.00

OATES, J.C. *On Boxing.* 1987. NY. 1st ed. presentation. dj. EX. T9. $55.00

OATES, J.C. *Queen of the Night.* 1979. Lord John. Ltd ed. 1/300. sgn. EX. H3. $75.00

OATES, J.C. *Seduction & Other Stories.* 1975. Blk Sparrow. Ltd ed. 1/350. sgn. EX. H3. $100.00

OATES, J.C. *Soul/Mate.* 1989. Dutton. ARC. wrp. EX. K2. $35.00

OATES, J.C. *Soul/Mate.* 1989. Dutton. 1st ed. dj. EX. F5. $14.00

OATES, J.C. *Stepfather.* 1978. Lord John. Ltd ed. 1/300. sgn. EX. H3. $75.00

OATES, J.C. *Them.* 1969. Vanguard. 1st ed. dj. EX. C4. $45.00

OATES, J.C. *Triumph of the Spider Monkey.* 1976. Blk Sparrow. 1st ed. 1/50. sgn. dj. slipcase. EX. K2. $150.00

OATES, J.C. *Women Whose Lives Are Food, Men Whose Lives Are Money.* 1978. Baton Rouge. 1st ed. dj. EX. K2. $55.00

OATES, J.C. *Writer.* 1988. Dutton. UP. EX. K2. $40.00

OATES, J.C. *You Must Remember This.* 1987. Dutton. ARC. printed wrp. EX. K2. $30.00

OBER, Frederick. *Young Folks' Hist of Mexico.* 1895. Chicago. Weeks. Revised Enlarged ed. 558 p. F2. $25.00

OBERDORFER, Don. *Tet!* 1971. NY. Ils 1st ed. sgn. 385 p. dj. VG. T5. $35.00

ODELL, Samuel. *Sampson: Hist Romance.* 1891. Cincinnati/NY. 1st ed. VG. C1. $9.50

ODETS, Clifford. *Clash by Night.* 1942. Random House. 1st ed. dj. VG. H3. $60.00

ODETS, Clifford. *Country Girl.* 1951. Viking. 1st ed. dj. VG. H3. $50.00

ODETS, Clifford. *Golden Boy.* 1937. Random House. 1st ed. dj. EX. B13. $150.00

ODETS, Clifford. *Night Music.* 1940. Random House. 1st ed. dj. EX. H3. $125.00

ODETS, Clifford. *Paradise Lost.* 1936. Random House. 1st ed. dj. VG. H3. $100.00

ODETS, Clifford. *Rocket to the Moon.* 1939. Random House. 1st ed. dj. VG. H3. $100.00

ODETS, Clifford. *3 Plays.* 1935. Covici Freide. 1st ed. dj. EX. B13. $125.00

ODUM & JOHNSON. *Negro & His Songs.* 1925. NC U. 1st ed. 306 p. EX. H3. $200.00

OFFUT, A. *Blk Sorceror of Blk Castle.* 1976. Hall. 1st ed. wrp. EX. R3. $10.00

OGDEN, G.W. *Claim No 1.* 1922. Grosset Dunlap. dj. EX. R3. $50.00

OGILVIE, E. *My World Is an Island.* 1950. NY. 1st ed. dj. VG. B3. $17.50

OGLESBY, Carl. *New Left Reader.* 1969. Blk Cat. PB Orig. VG. B4. $4.00

OHARA, Houn. *Ikebana: Creative Tradition.* 1970. Tokyo. 1st ed. dj. G1. $100.00

OHLSON, Hereward. *Thunderbolt & the Rebel Planet.* 1954. Lutterworth. 1st ed. dj. VG. P1. $15.00

OHNET, Georges. *Poison Dealer.* 1922. Greening. VG. P1. $20.00

OKAMOTO & WILLIAMS. *Urban Design Manhattan: Regional Plan Assn.* 1969. Viking. Studio Book. dj. D4. $45.00

OLANDER & GREENBERG. *Time of Passage.* 1978. Taplinger. 1st ed. dj. EX. P1. $15.00

OLDENBURG, Claes. *Photo Log & Pr Log, May 1974-August 1976.* 1976. Stuttgart. Hansjorg Mayer. 2 vols. slipcase. EX. $75.00

OLDS, A.F. *Diseases of the Horse & Their Treatment.* 1891. Chicago. Ils. 55 p. wrp. VG. T5. $12.50

OLECK, H.L. *Singular Fury.* 1968. World. 1st ed. dj. xl. P1. $7.50

OLIPHANT, Laurence. *Land of Gilead With Excursions in Lebanon.* 1881. NY. Ils. maps. 430 p. VG. $75.00

OLIPHANT, Mrs. M.O.W. *Hist Characters of Reign of Queen Anne.* 1894. NY. Ils 1st Am ed. TEG. T5. $95.00

OLIPHANT, Mrs. M.O.W. *Makers of Florence.* 1891. London. 422 p. VG. $35.00

OLIVER, Chad. *Edge of Forever.* 1971. Shelbourne. 1st ed. dj. VG. R3. $15.00

OLIVER, Chad. *Edge of Forever.* 1971. Sherbourne. 1st ed. dj. EX. P1. $17.50

OLIVER, Chad. *Mists of Dawn.* 1979. reprint of 1960 ed. dj. EX. R3. $25.00

OLIVER, Chad. *Shadows in the Sun.* 1985. Crown. 1st ed. dj. EX. P1. $12.50

OLIVER, Chad. *Winds of Time.* nd. Book Club. dj. VG. P1. $4.50

OLIVER, Mary. *Provincetown.* 1987. Bucknell U. Ils Barnard Taylor. 1/185. sgn. EX. H3. $50.00

OLIVIERI, David; see Wharton, Edith.

OLLIVANT, Alfred. *Tomorrow.* 1927. Doubleday. 1st Am ed. G. R3. $12.50

OLMSTED, L.A. *Set Up for Murder.* 1962. Avalon. 1st ed. dj. xl. P1. $5.00

OLNEY, R.R. *Tales of Time & Space.* 1969. Whitman. VG. P1. $5.00

OLSCHKI, Leonardo. *Grail Castle & Its Mysteries.* 1966. CA U. 1st ed. dj. VG. C1. $22.50

OLSEN, Austin. *Corcho Bliss.* 1972. Simon Schuster. 1st ed. dj. EX. F5. $15.00

OLSEN, Tillie. *Tell Me a Riddle.* 1978. Delacorte. 1/100. sgn. EX. H3. $75.00

OLSHAKER, Mark. *Einstein's Brain.* 1981. Evans. 1st ed. dj. EX. P1. $15.00

OLSON, Charles. *Call Me Ishmael.* 1947. Reynal Hitchcock. 1st ed. dj. EX. C4. $200.00

OLSON, Charles. *Causal Mythology.* 1969. 4 Seasons. EX. B4. $10.00

OLSON, Charles. *Maximus Poems.* London. Jargon/Corinth. 1st HrdCvr ed. dj. EX. K2. $50.00

OLSON, Charles. *Selected Writings.* 1966. New Directions. Intro Robert Creeley. 1st ed. dj. EX. C4. $35.00

OLSON, Charles. *Stocking Cap: A Story.* 1966. Grabhorn Hoyem. 1/100. wrp. EX. C4. $200.00

OLSON, Charles. *Y & X.* 1948. Blk Sun. Ils Corrado Cagli. EX. H3. $350.00

OLSON, Robert. *Carl Rosini: His Life & His Magic.* 1966. Magic Inc. 1st ed. 100 p. NM. J3. $10.00

OLSON, Robert. *Illusion Builder to Fu Manchu (David Bamberg)...* 1986. Morris Costumes. 1st ed. 219 p. dj. NM. J3. $30.00

OLSON, Robert. *World's Greatest Magician: Tribute to Howard Thurston.* 1981. Calgary. 1st ed. 301 p. NM. J3. $30.00

OMAN, Carola. *Napoleon at the Channel.* 1942. NY. 1st Am ed. 316 p. dj. VG. T5. $22.50

ONDAATJE, Michael. *Collected Works of Billy the Kid.* 1981. London. Calder Boyars. 1st UK ed. sgn. dj. EX. K2. $85.00

ONDAATJE, Michael. *In the Skin of the Lion.* 1987. Knopf. 1st Am ed. sgn. dj. EX. C4. $45.00

ONDAATJE, Michael. *There's a Trick With a Knife I'm Learning To Do.* 1979. Norton. 1st HrdCvr ed. dj. EX. B13. $45.00

ONDRICEK & MITTELMANN. *Meistertechnik des Violinspiels.* c 1909. Leipzig. quarto. G. H3. $50.00

ONEAL, C.M. *Gardens & Homes of Mexico.* 1947. Dallas. Ils. 221 p. dj. T5. $22.50

ONWHYN, Thomas. *32 Ils to Pickwick by Onwhyn & Other Eminent Artists.* c 1848. London. Newman. VG. H3. $125.00

OOSTENS-WITTAMER, Yolande. *Belle Epoque: Belgian Posters, Watercolors, & Drawings.* 1970. Grossman Pub. 1st ed. oblong 4to. 94 p. dj. EX. R4. $50.00

OPIE & OPIE. *Oxford Dictionary of Nursery Rhymes.* 1952. Oxford. Ils. 467 p. dj. xl. G. B3. $27.50

OPPEN, Mary. *Meaning a Life: An Autobiography.* 1978. Blk Sparrow. 1/200. sgn. EX. H3. $40.00

OPPENHEIM, E.P. *Battle of Basinghall St.* 1935. McClellan Stuart. 1st Canadian ed. dj. VG. P1. $30.00

OPPENHEIM, E.P. *Betrayal.* nd. McKinlay Stone. VG. P1. $7.50

OPPENHEIM, E.P. *Betrayal.* 1904. Dodd Mead. 1st ed. VG. P1. $20.00

OPPENHEIM, E.P. *Dumb Gods Speak.* 1937. Little Brn. VG. P1. $12.50

OPPENHEIM, E.P. *Dumb Gods Speak.* 1937. McClelland Stewart. 1st Canadian ed. dj. VG. P1. $30.00

OPPENHEIM, E.P. *Envoy Extraordinary.* 1937. Little Brn. 1st ed. VG. P1. $20.00

OPPENHEIM, E.P. *Envoy Extraordinary.* 1937. McClelland Stewart. dj. VG. P1. $20.00

OPPENHEIM, E.P. *Exit a Dictator.* 1939. Little Brn. 1st ed. VG. P1. $12.50

OPPENHEIM, E.P. *Floating Peril.* 1939. Little Brn. 3rd ed. VG. P1. $12.50

OPPENHEIM, E.P. *Glenlitten Murder.* nd. Review of Reviews. VG. P1. $10.00

OPPENHEIM, E.P. *Golden Beast.* 1926. Little Brn. 1st ed. VG. P1. $20.00

OPPENHEIM, E.P. *Great Impersonation.* nd. Hodder Soughton. VG. P1. $7.50

OPPENHEIM, E.P. *Great Impersonation.* 1920. Little Brn. 1st ed. VG. P1. $10.00

OPPENHEIM, E.P. *Great Secret.* nd. McKinlay Stone. VG. P1. $7.50

OPPENHEIM, E.P. *Harvey Garrard's Crime.* nd. AL Burt. dj. VG. P1. $8.00

OPPENHEIM, E.P. *Havoc.* nd. McKinlay Stone. VG. P1. $7.50

OPPENHEIM, E.P. *Illustrious Prince.* nd. McKinlay Stone. VG. P1. $7.50

OPPENHEIM, E.P. *Last Train Out.* nd. Collier. VG. P1. $10.00

OPPENHEIM, E.P. *Lighted Way.* nd. AL Burt. VG. P1. $5.00

OPPENHEIM, E.P. *Lighted Way.* nd. McKinlay Stone. VG. P1. $7.50

OPPENHEIM, E.P. *Lost Leader.* 1909. Little Brn. 1st ed. VG. R3. $25.00

OPPENHEIM, E.P. *Magnificent Hoax.* 1936. McClelland Stewart. VG. P1. $7.50

OPPENHEIM, E.P. *Maker of Hist.* nd. McKinlay Stone. VG. P1. $7.50

OPPENHEIM, E.P. *Maker of Hist.* 1919. Ward Lock. VG. P1. $7.50

OPPENHEIM, E.P. *Man From Sing Sing.* 1944. Tower. 2nd ed. dj. VG. P1. $15.00

OPPENHEIM, E.P. *Man From Sing Sing.* 1944. Tower. 2nd ed. VG. P1. $7.00

OPPENHEIM, E.P. *Matorni's Vineyard.* 1928. Little Brn. VG. P1. $12.50

OPPENHEIM, E.P. *Matorni's Vineyard.* 1928. McClelland Stewart. 1st ed. VG. P1. $7.50

OPPENHEIM, E.P. *Million-Pound Deposit.* 1930. Little Brn. VG. P1. $20.00

OPPENHEIM, E.P. *Mischief-Maker.* nd. McKinlay Stone. VG. P1. $7.50

OPPENHEIM, E.P. *Mysterious Mr Sabin.* nd. McKinlay Stone. VG. P1. $7.50

OPPENHEIM, E.P. *Nicholas Goade, Detective.* nd. Review of Reviews. VG. P1. $10.00

OPPENHEIM, E.P. *Ostrekoff Jewels.* 1932. McClelland Stewart. P1. $15.00

OPPENHEIM, E.P. *Ostrekoff Jewels.* 1932. McClelland Stewart. 1st Canadian ed. dj. VG. P1. $30.00

OPPENHEIM, E.P. *Passionate Quest.* 1924. McClelland Stewart. 1st Canadian ed. VG. P1. $10.00

OPPENHEIM, E.P. *Pawns Count.* 1918. McClelland Goodchild. VG. P1. $20.00

OPPENHEIM, E.P. *People's Man.* nd. McKinlay Stone. VG. P1. $7.50

OPPENHEIM, E.P. *Peter Ruff & the Double 4.* nd. McKinlay Stone. VG. P1. $5.00

OPPENHEIM, E.P. *Prince of Sinners*. nd. McKinlay Stone. VG. P1. $7.50

OPPENHEIM, E.P. *Pulpit in the Grill Room*. 1939. Little Brn. 1st ed. VG. P1. $20.00

OPPENHEIM, E.P. *Secret*. nd. Ward Lock. VG. P1. $10.00

OPPENHEIM, E.P. *Spy Paramount*. 1935. McClelland Stewart. VG. P1. $10.00

OPPENHEIM, E.P. *Spymaster*. 1938. Little Brn. 1st ed. VG. P1. $20.00

OPPENHEIM, E.P. *Spymaster*. 1938. Little Brn. 2nd ed. VG. P1. $12.00

OPPENHEIM, E.P. *Stranger's Gate*. 1939. Little Brn. 1st ed. VG. P1. $15.00

OPPENHEIM, E.P. *Stranger's Gate*. 1939. McClelland Stewart. dj. EX. P1. $25.00

OPPENHEIM, E.P. *Survivor*. nd. Ward Lock. VG. P1. $10.00

OPPENHEIM, E.P. *Tempting of Tavernake*. 1912. Little Brn. 1st ed. VG. P1. $15.00

OPPENHEIM, E.P. *Traitors*. nd. McKinlay Stone. VG. P1. $7.50

OPPENHEIM, E.P. *Up the Ladder of Gold*. 1931. Little Brn. VG. P1. $20.00

OPPENHEIM, E.P. *What Happened to Forester?* 1930. Little Brn. 5th print. VG. P1. $8.50

OPPENHEIM, E.P. *Yel Crayon*. nd. McKinlay Stone. VG. P1. $7.50

OPPENHEIM, E.P. *Yel House*. nd. Collier. VG. P1. $10.00

OPPENHEIM, E.P. *Zeppelin's Passenger*. 1918. McClelland Goodchild. 1st Canadian ed. VG. P1. $20.00

OPTIC, Oliver. *Oliver Optic's New Storybook*. 1920. Hurst. 4to. EX. $40.00

OPTIC, Oliver. *Our Standard Bearer; or, The Life of Gen Ulysses S Grant*. 1868. Boston. Ils Nast. 12mo. 348 p. G. G4. $28.00

ORBEN, Robert. *Encyclopedia of Patter*. 1946. NY. Orben. 1st ed. 40 p. SftCvr. VG. $30.00

ORBEN, Robert. *Encyclopedia of Patter*. 1946. Orben. 4th ed. wrp. VG. H3. $25.00

ORBEN, Robert. *Orben's Current Comedy Vol 3*. 1961. Orben. 60 p. VG. J3. $10.00

ORCUTT, W.D. *Balance*. nd. (1922) Stokes. 351 p. VG. $6.00

ORCUTT, W.D. *Daggers & Jewels*. 1931. Benvenuto Cellini. 1st ed. inscr. VG. $12.00

ORCUTT, W.D. *Moth*. 1912. Harper. 1st ed. 335 p. VG. B10. $8.50

ORCZY, Baroness. *Beau Brocade*. 1953. Hodder Stoughton. 36th print. dj. VG. P1. $15.00

ORCZY, Baroness. *Beau Brocade*. 1953. Hodder Stoughton. 36th print. dj. xl. P1. $5.00

ORCZY, Baroness. *Bride of the Plains*. nd. Hutchinson. VG. P1. $12.00

ORCZY, Baroness. *Bronze Eagle*. nd. Hodder Stoughton. VG. P1. $10.00

ORCZY, Baroness. *Leatherface*. 1916. Hodder Stoughton. decor brd. VG. P1. $22.75

ORCZY, Baroness. *Scarlet Pimpernel*. 1946. Musson. VG. P1. $15.00

ORCZY, Baroness. *Uncrowned King*. 1937. Hodder Stoughton. 3rd ed. VG. P1. $18.00

ORCZY, Baroness. *Under Caesar*. 1914. Hodder Stoughton. decor brd. P1. $27.25

ORDE & MICHAELS. *Night They Stole Manhattan*. 1980. Putnam. 1st ed. dj. EX. P1. $15.00

ORDWAY & SHARPE. *Rocket Team*. 1979. NY. Ils 1st ed. 462 p. dj. VG. T5. $15.00

ORLOVITZ, Gil. *Diary of Dr Eric Zeno*. 1953. Inferno Pr. 1st ed. EX. B13. $65.00

ORMOND, Clyde. *Hunting Our Medium-Sized Game*. 1958. Harrisburg. 1st ed. dj. EX. $15.00

ORMSBEE, T.H. *Field Guide to Early Am Furniture*. nd. Bonanza. gr bdg. EX. $12.50

OROZCO, J.C. *Artist in NY*. 1974. TX U. 1st ed. dj. F2. $20.00

OROZCO, J.C. *Autobiography*. 1962. TX U. 1st ed. 171 p. dj. F2. $25.00

ORR, A. *In the Ice King's Palace*. 1986. Little Brn. 1st ed. M. R3. $15.95

ORR, A. *World in Amber*. 1985. Bluejay. 1st ed. dj. M. C1. $12.00

ORR, J.L. *Smithville Days...* 1922. Smithville, OH. Ils 1st ed. 128 p. VG. T5. $25.00

ORRIN, J.F. *Conjurer's Vade Mecum*. nd. Phil. McKay. 159 p. VG. J3. $10.00

ORTIZ, Darwin. *Darwin Ortiz at the Card Table*. 1988. Kaufman/Greenberg. 1st ed. dj. NM. J3. $29.00

ORTIZ, R.D. *Great Sioux Nation*. 1977. Moon Books. 1st ed. quarto. wrp. EX. K2. $50.00

ORTIZ, S.J. *Fight Back: For the Sake of People for Sake of Land*. nd. Albuquerque. sgn. wrp. EX. K2. $45.00

ORTIZ, S.J. *Going for the Rain*. 1976. Harper Row. 1st ed. dj. EX. K2. $85.00

ORTIZ, S.J. *Good Journey*. 1977. Turtle Island. 1/100. VG. scarce. K2. $50.00

ORVIS, Kenneth. *Night Without Darkness*. 1965. McClelland Stewart. VG. P1. $7.50

ORWELL, George. *Animal Farm*. nd. BOMC. VG. P1. $3.00

ORWELL, George. *Eng Your Eng*. 1953. London. 1st ed. dj. EX. $65.00

ORWELL, George. *James Burnham & the Managerial Revolution*. 1946. London. Socialist Book Centre. 1st Separate ed. EX. K2. $950.00

ORWELL, George. *1984*. nd. BOMC. VG. P1. $3.75

ORY & CHAMAGNE. *Technique de la Radiodiffusion et de la Television...* 1937. Paris. 2 vols. orange wrp. VG. H3. $150.00

OSBORN, Robert. *Vulgarians*. c 1960. Greenwich, CT. Ils. dj. VG. T5. $12.50

OSBORNE, Harold. *Indians of the Andes*. 1952. London. Routledge. 1st ed. 266 p. dj. F2. $25.00

OSBORNE, Harold. *S Am Mythology*. 1968. London. Hamlyn. 1st ed. dj. F2. $20.00

OSBORNE, John. *Plays for Eng: Blood of Bambergs/Under Plain Cover*. 1963. London. Faber. 1st ed. dj. EX. H3. $30.00

OSBORNE, Lilly de Jongh. *4 Keys to El Salvador*. 1956. Funk Wagnal. 1st ed. 221 p. dj. F2. $15.00

OSBORNE, Tom. *Coin Tricks Vol 1: Classics of Magic*. 1945. Phil. Osborne. 1st ed. 30 p. SftCvr. EX. J3. $3.00

OSBORNE, Tom. *Cups & Balls Magic*. 1937. Phil. Kanter. 1st ed. 48 p. SftCvr. NM. J3. $4.00

OSBORNE, Tom. *Tom Osborne Lecture*. 1953. Magician Guild Am. 10 p. stapled manuscript. J3. $5.00

OSBORNE, Tom. *3-Shell Game*. 1938. Phil. Kanter. 1st ed. 58 p. SftCvr. EX. J3. $5.00

OSGOOD, Henry. *So This Is Jazz*. 1926. Boston. 1st ed. 8vo. 258 p. orange bdg. VG. scarce. $125.00

OSKISON, J.M. *Tecumseh & His Times*. 1938. Putnam. 1st ed. dj. EX. K2. $175.00

OSMOND, Andrw. *Saladin!* 1976. Doubleday. dj. VG. P1. $10.00

OSOFSKY, G. *Harlem: Making of a Ghetto.* 1966. NY. 1st ed. 259 p. dj. VG. B3. $25.00

OSSIPENKO, Paulina. *Soviet Far E.* c 1939. USSR. Ils. wrp. VG. T5. $35.00

OSTER, Jerry. *Club Dead.* 1988. Harper Row. 1st ed. dj. EX. F5/P1. $15.95

OSTER, Jerry. *Rancho Maria.* 1986. Harper Row. 1st ed. dj. EX. P1. $14.95

OSTER, Jerry. *Sweet Justice.* 1985. Harper Row. 1st ed. dj. EX. F5. $14.00

OSTIN, Bob. *Fingertip Fantasies.* 1968. Goodliffe. 1st ed. 88 p. EX. J3. $3.00

OSTIN, Bob. *Fingertip Fantasies.* 1976. Devon, Eng. Supreme Magic. 2nd print. dj. NM. J3. $6.00

OSTRANDER, Isabel. *Annihilation.* 1924. McBride. 1st ed. VG. R3. $12.50

OTERO, M.A. *My 9 Years As Governor of NM.* 1940. NM U. Deluxe ed. 1/400. dj. VG. A5. $100.00

OTIS, C.H. *MI Trees.* 1926. Ann Arbor. VG. T3. $15.00

OTIS, James. *How the Twins Captured a Hessian.* nd. (1902) Crowell. Ils. VG. B10. $4.50

OTIS, James. *Mr Stubb's Bother.* nd. (1910) Harper. Ils. VG. B10. $4.00

OTIS, James. *Toby Tyler; or, 10 Weeks With the Circus.* 1923. Harper. dj. VG. P1. $15.00

OTTUM, Bob. *See the Kid Run.* 1978. Simon Schuster. 1st ed. dj. EX. P1. $15.00

OUELLETT, Gary. *Finger on the Card: Masters of Magic Vol 1 No 1.* nd. Sillery, Canada. 1st ed. 22 p. SftCvr. NM. J3. $5.00

OUELLETT, Gary. *Pro-Control.* 1988. Sillery, Canada. Revised ed. 53 p. dj. NM. J3. $15.00

OUELLETT, Gary. *Silver Passage: Masters of Magic Vol 1 No 3.* 1982. Sillery, Canada. 25 p. SftCvr. NM. J3. $7.00

OUELLETT, Gary. *Threshold: Masters of Magic Vol 1 No 5.* 1981. Sillery, Canada. sgn. NM. J3. $12.00

OURSLER, Will. *Trial of Vincent Doon.* 1941. Simon Schuster. 2nd ed. P1. $12.00

OUSPENSKY & LOSSKY. *Meaning of Icons.* 1955. Boston. 1st ed. 222 p. dj. VG. B3. $75.00

OVERBECK, Alicia. *Living High.* 1935. Appleton. 1st ed. 382 p. F2. $15.00

OVERSTREET, Bob. *Comic Book Price Guide No 11.* 1981. Overstreet. VG. P1. $12.50

OVERSTREET, Bob. *Comic Book Price Guide.* 1984. Harmony. VG. P1. $10.00

OVERSTREET, H.A. *Enduring Quest.* 1931. Norton. 1st ed. 277 p. VG. B10. $4.50

OVERTON, Grant. *Am Nights Entertainment.* 1923. Appleton Doran. 1st ed. dj. VG. P1. $35.00

OVERTON, Grant. *When Winter Came to Main St.* 1922. Doran. 1st ed. VG. B10. $9.00

OVERTON, R.C. *Gulf to Rockies.* 1963. Austin, TX. 410 p. decor buckram. VG. T5. $22.50

OVERTON. *Burlington W.* 1941. Cambridge. 1st ed. dj. EX. C2. $45.00

OVETTE, Joseph. *Advanced Magic.* 1919. Dundee Lake, NJ. 1st ed. 60 p. VG. J3. $6.00

OVETTE, Joseph. *Bargain Magic.* c 1921. Heaney Magic. 1st ed. 48 p. EX. J3. $6.00

OVETTE, Joseph. *Eggstraordinary Ways of Eggshibiting With Eggs.* c 1934. Cornwall, Canada. 1st ed. sgn. SftCvr. EX. J3. $12.00

OVETTE, Joseph. *Magician's New Field.* 1916. Dundee Lake, NJ. 1st ed. 30 p. SftCvr. EX. J3. $5.00

OVETTE, Joseph. *Practical Telepathy.* 1924. Reilly. 1st ed. 125 p. G. J3. $12.00

OVETTE, Joseph. *Publicity Miracles.* 1928. Cornwall, Canada. 1st ed. G. J3. $3.00

OVETTE, Joseph. *Silk Creations.* 1931. Cornwall, Canada. 1st ed. EX. J3. $5.00

OVETTE, Joseph. *Tricks & Illusionettes, Ovette's.* 1944. Robbins. 32p. NM. J3. $2.00

OVINGTON, M.W. *Walls Came Tumbling Down.* 1947. Harcourt. 1st ed. sgn. dj. EX. $15.00

OVINGTON, Ray. *Fresh-Water Fishing.* 1976. Hawthorn. 2nd/PB ed. 152 p. wrp. VG. B10. $2.25

OWEN, D.D.R. *Authurian Romance: 7 Essays.* 1972. Barnes Noble. dj. VG. C1. $25.00

OWEN, David. *Fantastic Planets.* 1979. Reed Books. dj. VG. P1. $15.00

OWEN, Frank. *Husband for Kutani.* 1928. Furman. 1st ed. sgn. dj. VG. R3. $50.00

OWEN, Frank. *Murder for the Millions.* 1946. Fell. 1st ed. dj. EX. R3. $20.00

OWEN, Frank. *Porcelain Magician.* 1948. Gnome. 1st ed. VG. R3. $15.00

OWEN, Frank. *Rare Earth.* 1931. Lantern Pr. 1st ed. sgn. dj. EX. R3. $40.00

OWEN, Frank. *Scarlet Hill.* 1941. Carlyle House. 1st ed. G. R3. $25.00

OWEN, G.B. *Long, Long Trail.* 1923. Chelsea House. 1st ed. 320 p. VG. B10. $4.75

OWEN, Guy. *Flim-Flam Man & the Apprentice Grifter.* 1972. Crown. 1st ed. dj. EX. F5. $20.00

OWENS, H.J. *Scandalous Adventures of Reynard the Fox: Modern Version.* 1945. Knopf. Stated 1st ed. B7. $45.00

OWINGS & CHALKER. *Revised Lovecraft Bibliography.* 1973. Mirage. 1st ed. wrp. EX. R3. $10.00

OXENHAM, John. *Hidden Years.* 1952. McKay. Family Classic Series. 244 p. EX. B10. $3.75

OZICK, Cynthia. *Bloodshed & 3 Novellas.* 1976. Knopf. 1st ed. dj. EX. B13. $45.00

OZICK, Cynthia. *Messiah of Stockholm.* 1987. Knopf. 1st ed. 8vo. dj. EX. $15.00

OZICK, Cynthia. *Pagan Rabbi & Other Stories.* 1971. Knopf. 1st ed. dj. EX. C4. $50.00

PABEL, Reinhold. *Enemies Are Human.* 1953. Phil. 1st ed. 248 p. dj. T5. $45.00

PACE, Tom. *Fisherman's Luck.* nd. Book Club. dj. EX. P1. $4.50

PACKARD, F.L. *Broken Waters.* 1925. Copp/Clarke. VG. P1. $20.00

PACKARD, F.L. *Doors of the Night.* 1922. Copp/Clarke. VG. P1. $25.00

PACKARD, F.L. *Jimmie Dale & Bl Envelope Murder.* 1930. Copp/Clarke. VG. P1. $20.00

PACKARD, F.L. *Locked Book.* 1924. Copp/Clarke. VG. P1. $12.50

PACKARD, F.L. *Miracle Man.* 1914. Copp/Clarke. VG. P1. $15.00

PACKARD, F.L. *Night Operator.* 1919. Copp/Clarke. VG. P1. $15.00

PACKARD, F.L. *Tiger Claws.* nd. Collier. G. P1. $15.00

PACKARD, F.L. *Tiger Claws.* 1928. Copp/Clarke. 1st ed. VG. P1. $25.00

PACKARD, J.F. *Grant's Tour Around the World.* 1880. Forshee McMakin. VG. S1. $16.00

PACKARD, William. *To Peel an Apple.* 1963. NY. 1st ed. sgn. wrp. EX. T9. $35.00

PACKER, E.L. *Day With Our Gang.* 1929. Whitman. VG. T5. $150.00

PADDLEFORD. *How Am Eats.* 1960. NY. 1st ed. sgn. dj. VG. B3. $40.00

PADEN, I.D. *Wake of the Prairie Schooner.* 1943. NY. Ils 1st ed. 514 p. G. T5. $15.00

PADGETT, Lewis; see Kuttner, Henry.

PAGE, C.H. *Chief Am Poets.* 1905. Houghton Mifflin. B10. $5.00

PAGE, Francis. *Confucious Comes to Broadway.* 1940. Wisdom House. 1st ed. dj. K. R3. $35.00

PAGE, H.S. *Between the Flags.* 1929. Derrydale. 1/850. M. $100.00

PAGE, H.S. *Over the Open.* 1925. NY. Ils 1st ed. 155 p. VG. T5. $22.50

PAGE, J.M. *True Story of Andersonville Prison.* 1908. Neale. 1st ed. VG. B3. $110.00

PAGE, Patrick. *Bell's Book of Tricks.* 1974. NY. Bell. 2nd print. dj. EX. J3. $3.00

PAGE, Patrick. *Big Book of Magic.* 1976. Cal. 1st Am print. 235 p. dj. xl. EX. J3. $5.00

PAGE, Patrick. *Pull Book.* 1987. London. Breese. 1st ed. 54 p. NM. J3. $10.00

PAGE, Patrick. *150 Comedy Props: How To Make & Use.* 1977. Page. 1st ed. 160 p. EX. J3. $10.00

PAGE, T.N. *Coast of Bohemia.* 1906. NY. 1st Am ed. VG. C1. $19.50

PAGE, T.N. *Gordon Keith.* 1903. Scribner. 1st ed. 548 p. VG. B10. $6.50

PAGE, V.W. *How To Run an Automobile.* 1917. NY. 171 p. G. T5. $35.00

PAINE, A.B. *Adventures of Mark Twain.* 1944. Grosset Dunlap. 353 p. tan bdg. VG. B10. $3.50

PAINE, A.B. *AR Bear: Tale of Fanciful Adventure.* nd. Parents Inst. 1st ed? $12.00

PAINE, A.B. *Hollow Tree Deep Woods Book.* 1938. NY. dj. VG. B3. $27.50

PAINE, A.B. *Hollow Tree Snowed-In Book.* 1938. NY. dj. VG. B3. $27.50

PAINE, A.B. *Mark Twain's Notebook.* 1935. NY. 1st ed. 413 p. T5. $50.00

PAINE, A.B. *Ship Dwellers.* 1910. Harper. 1st ed. 393 p. VG. B10. $15.00

PAINE, Lauran. *Horseman.* 1986. Walker. 1st ed. dj. EX. F5. $11.00

PAINE, Thomas. *Centenary Memorial Ed of Life & Writings.* 1915. NY. Vincent Parke. 10 vols. octavo. H3. $350.00

PAINE, Thomas. *Life & Works.* 1925. Paine Hist Assn. 10 vols. octavo. H3. $300.00

PAINE & KLAUSER. *Famous Composers & Their Works.* 1891. Boston. Millet. 7 vols. G. H3. $250.00

PAINTER, Charlotte. *Seeing Things.* 1976. Random House. 1st ed. dj. EX. B13. $65.00

PAINTER. G.D. *Marcel Proust Letters to His Mother.* 1956. London. Rider. 1st ed. 8vo. 238 p. dj. EX. R4. $15.00

PAKULA, M.H. *Centennial Album of the Civil War.* c 1960. NY. Ils Yoseloff. dj. VG. $25.00

PAL, George. *Wonderful World of the Brothers Grimm.* 1962. MGM. 1st ed. no dj issued. EX. F5. $15.00

PALADILHE & PIERRE. *Gustave Moreau.* 1972. London. Thames Hudson. 1st ed. 4to. 176 p. dj. EX. R4. $30.00

PALEN, L.S. *Water & Gold.* 1930. Dutton. 1st ed. 268 p. VG. B10. $7.00

PALETTE, Peter. *Ils to Nicholas Nickleby Part 2.* 1838. London. Grattan. 1st ed. 4 pl. wrp. H3. $100.00

PALEY, Grace. *Later the Same Day.* 1985. Farrar Straus. UP. wrp. EX. C4. $75.00

PALEY, Grace. *Leaning Forward.* 1985. Granite Pr. Ltd ed. 1/125. sgn. Creighton/Blinn bdg. K2. $125.00

PALEY, Grace. *Leaning Forward: Poems.* 1985. Granite Pr. 1st ed. 1/125. sgn. B13/K2. $125.00

PALEY, Grace. *Little Disturbances of Man.* 1959. Doubleday. 1st ed. K2. $125.00

PALGRAVE, F.T. *Golden Treasury.* nd. London. Frowde. 12mo. gilt gr calf/cloth. EX. $150.00

PALLEN, C.B. *Meaning of the Idylls of the King.* 1904.1st ed. VG. C1. $17.50

PALMER, Frederick. *Am in France.* 1918. Dodd. 1st ed. red bdg. VG. B10. $4.25

PALMER, J.W. *New & Old; or, CA & India.* 1859. London. Sampson Low. 1st ed. 433 p. VG. $85.00

PALMER, Michael. *Circular Gates.* 1974. Blk Sparrow. 1st ed. 1/175. sgn. dj. EX. $20.00

PALMER, Michael. *Sisterhood.* nd. Book Club. dj. VG. P1. $4.50

PALMER, Ray. *Poetical Works of Ray Palmer.* 1876. Barnes. Complete ed. AEG. B10. $7.00

PALMER, Tony. *Trials of Oz.* 1971. Manchester. 1st PB ed. B4. $9.00

PANATI, Charles. *Pleasure of Rory Malone.* 1982. St Martin. 1st ed. dj. EX. F5. $15.00

PANCAKE, Breece D'J. *Stories of Breece D'J Pancake.* nd. Boston. Posthumous ed. dj. EX. T9. $55.00

PANGBORN, Edgar. *Davy.* 1967. London. 1st Eng ed. dj. EX. R3. $30.00

PANGBORN, Edgar. *Davy.* 1967. St Martin. 1st ed. dj. EX. R3. $85.00

PANGBORN, Edgar. *Judgment of Eve.* 1966. Simon Schuster. 1st ed. dj. EX. R3. $50.00

PANGBORN, Edgar. *Mirror for Observers.* 1954. Doubleday. 1st ed. dj. EX. R3. $150.00

PANGBORN, Edgar. *W of the Sun.* 1953. Doubleday. 1st ed. dj. EX. R3. $50.00

PANOFSKY, Erwin. *Early Netherlandish Painting: Its Orig & Character.* 1966. Cambridge. 2 vols. djs. D4. $250.00

PANSHIN, Alexei. *Farewell to Yesterday's Tomorrow.* 1975. Berkley Putnam. 1st ed. dj. VG. P1. $17.50

PANSHIN, Alexei. *Transmutations.* 1982. Elephant Books. 1st ed. 1/150. sgn. M. R3. $30.00

PANSHIN, Alexei. *World Beyond the Hill.* 1989. Tarcher. 1st ed. sgn. M. R3. $50.00

PAPE & ASPLER. *Chain Reaction.* 1978. Viking. 1st ed. dj. EX. P1. $15.00

PAPINI, Giovanni. *Life of Christ.* nd. (1923) Harcourt. 416 p. VG. B10. $3.50

PAPOLOS, Janice. *Performing Artist's Handbook.* 1984. Cincinnati. 1st ed. 219 p. dj. NM. J3. $9.00

PAPP, Desiderius. *Creation's Doom.* 1934. Appleton. 1st ed. dj. VG. R3. $50.00

PARCHER, Emily. *Shady Gardens: How To Plan & Grow.* 1955. Prentice Book Club. 292 p. dj. EX. B10. $4.50

PARK, Paul. *Soldiers of Paradise.* 1987. Arbor House. 1st ed. dj. EX. P1. $17.95

PARK, R.B. *Book Shops: How To Run Them.* 1929. Doubleday Doran. 1st ed. 152 p. dj. VG. T5. $17.50

PARKER, A. *Ping-Pong: The Game & How To Play It.* 1902. NY. 1st ed. 8vo. VG. $20.00

PARKER, Dorothy. *Death & Taxes: New Poems.* 1931. Viking. 1st ed. dj. EX. C4. $60.00

PARKER, Dorothy. *Not So Deep As a Well.* 1936. Viking. Ltd 1st ed. 1/485. sgn. H3. $100.00

PARKER, Dorothy. *Sunset Gun.* 1940. Pocket Book 76. paper wrp. VG. B10. $2.50

PARKER, F.A. *Naval Howitzer Ashore.* 1865. NY. 1st ed. rebound. EX. $165.00

PARKER, Gilbert. *Right of Way.* 1901. Grosset. 418 p. VG. B10. $3.50

PARKER, Gilbert. *Weavers: Tale of Eng & Egypt 50 Years Ago.* 1907. Harper. 1st ed. 529 p. VG. B10. $6.50

PARKER, John. *Tidings Out of Brazil.* 1957. NM U. 1st ed. 1/1000. 48 p. F2. $40.00

PARKER, K.T. *Drawings of Hans Holbein at Windsor Castle.* 1983. NY. 4to. dj. A4. $50.00

PARKER, M.J. *Children's Party Book.* 1923. np. Rogers. Ils FT Hunter. 12mo. wrp. VG. $22.00

PARKER, Maude. *Intriguer.* 1952. Rinehart. 1st ed. dj. xl. P1. $7.50

PARKER, Maude. *Which Mrs Torr?* 1951. Rinehart. 1st ed. dj. VG. P1. $10.00

PARKER, R.B. *Catskill Eagle.* 1985. NY. Delacorte/Lawrence. 1st ed. sgn. dj. EX. T9. $30.00

PARKER, R.B. *Crimson Joy.* 1988. Delacorte. 1st ed. dj. EX. $20.00

PARKER, R.B. *Early Autumn.* 1981. Delacorte. 1st print. orange brd. dj. EX. $25.00

PARKER, R.B. *Godwulf Manuscript.* c 1973. Book Club. dj. VG. C1. $4.00

PARKER, R.B. *Godwulf Manuscript.* 1974. Houghton Mifflin. 1st ed. dj. EX. C4. $200.00

PARKER, R.B. *Pale Kings & Princes.* 1987. Delacorte. 1st ed. dj. EX. P1. $15.95

PARKER, R.B. *Taming a Sea Horse.* 1986. Delacorte. 1st ed. dj. EX. P1. $15.95

PARKER, R.B. *Taming a Sea Horse.* 1986. NY. 1st ed. sgn. dj. EX. C4. $50.00

PARKER, R.B. *Valediction.* 1984. Delacorte. 1st ed. dj. EX. F5. $18.00

PARKER, T.J. *Laguna Head.* nd. Book Club. dj. VG. P1. $4.50

PARKER, T.J. *Little Saigon.* 1988. St Martin. 1st ed. dj. EX. P1. $18.95

PARKER, T.V. *Cherokee Indians.* 1907. NY. 1st ed. 107 p. VG. B3. $50.00

PARKER-SCHLEY, J. *Sampson & Cervera.* 1910. WA. Neale. 1st ed. 333 p. VG. B3. $65.00

PARKINSON, John. *Paradisi in Sole Paradisus Terrestris...* 1656. London. 2nd ed. folio. contemporary calf. H3. $2000.00

PARKMAN, Francis. *CA & OR Trail...* 1849. NY. 1st ed. 1st print. orig bdg. H3. $3000.00

PARKMAN, Francis. *Conspiracy of Pontiac & Indian War After Conquest of Canada.* 1883. Boston. 10th ed. 2 vols. T5. $65.00

PARKMAN, Francis. *Hist of Conspiracy of Pontiac.* 1868. Little Brn. A5. $40.00

PARKMAN, Francis. *Montcalm & Wolfe.* 1899. Boston. Ils Holiday ed. EX. $60.00

PARKMAN, Francis. *OR Trail.* 1943. Ltd Ed Club. Ils/sgn Maynard Dixon. 1/1500. 4to. slipcase. C4. $125.00

PARKMAN, Francis. *Works.* 1915. Scribner. Fontenae ed. 16 vols. octavo. VG. H3. $300.00

PARKS, Gordon. *Born Blk.* 1970. Lippincott. UP. wrp. EX. K2. $45.00

PARKS, Tim. *Family Planing.* 1989. Grove Weidenfeld. ARC. dj. w/pub material. M. B13. $25.00

PARMENTER, Christine. *Golden Age.* nd. (1942) Crowell. 343 p. VG. B10. $3.75

PARMENTER, Ross. *Lawrence in Oazaca: Quest for the Novelist in Mexico.* 1984. Peregrine Smith Books. 1st ed. 384 p. dj. F2. $20.00

PARRIS, John. *My Mts, My People.* 1957. Asheville. 1st ed. sgn. dj. VG. B3. $35.00

PARRISH, Anne. *All Kneeling.* 1928. Harper. 1st ed. 322 p. dj. VG. B10. $3.50

PARRISH, Edward. *Education in Soc of Friends Past, Present...* 1865. Lippincott. 16mo. 80 p. G. V1. $20.00

PARRISH, Edward. *Essay on Education in Soc of Friends...* 1866. Lippincott. 16mo. 99 p. G. V1. $20.00

PARRISH, Frank. *Bird in the Net.* 1988. Harper Row. 1st ed. dj. VG. P1. $15.95

PARRISH, Frank. *Fly in the Cobweb.* 1986. Harper Row. dj. EX. P1. $15.00

PARRISH, Maxfield. *Arabian Nights: Their Best-Known Tales.* 1942. Scribner. 4to. 339 p. VG. $45.00

PARRISH, Maxfield. *Golden Treasury of Songs & Lyrics.* 1911. NY. 1st ed. EX. $150.00

PARRISH, Randall. *Red Mist.* 1914. McClurg. 1st ed. 401 p. VG. B10. $6.25

PARRISH, Robert. *Bert Allerton's Close-Up Magician.* 1958. Chicago. Ireland. 2nd print. 72 p. EX. J3. $6.00

PARRISH, Robert. *For Magicians Only.* 1944. NY. Ackerman. Perpetua ed. 240 p. EX. J3. $12.00

PARRISH, Robert. *New Ways To Mystify.* 1945. NY. Ackerman. 1st ed. 124 p. dj. EX. J3. $12.00

PARRISH, W.W. *Who's Who in World Aviation.* 1955. WA. 345 p. xl. T5. $19.50

PARRISH & CROSSLAND. *Mammoth Book of Thrillers, Ghosts...* 1936. Odhams. G. P1. $20.00

PARRY, David. *Scarlet Empire.* 1906. Bobbs Merrill. 1st ed. VG. R3. $35.00

PARRY, Michel. *Savage Heroes.* 1980. Taplinger. 1st ed. dj. EX. P1. $15.00

PARRY, Michel. *Supernatural Solution.* 1976. Taplinger. dj. VG. P1. $17.50

PARRY, W.E. *Journal of 2nd Voyage for Discovery of NW Passage 1821-1823.* 1969. NY. reprint of London 1824 ed. EX. A4. $100.00

PARRY, W.E. *Journals of Voyage for Discovery of NW Passage 1819-1820.* 1968. NY. reprint of London 1821 ed. 4to. EX. A4. $100.00

PARSONS, C.M. *Quaker Cross: Story of the Old Browne House.* 1911. Nat Am Soc. 12mo. 342 p. VG. V1. $10.00

PARSONS, J.E. *Henry Deringer's Pocket Pistol.* 1952. NY. 1st ed. dj. VG. B3. $45.00

PARSONS, J.E. *Peace Maker & Its Rivals.* 1950. NY. dj. VG. B3. $50.00

PARSONS, J.E. *Smith & Wesson Revolvers.* 1957. NY. 1st ed. dj. VG. B3. $60.00

PARSONS, Jeffrey. *Miscellaneous Studies in Mexican Prehistory.* 1972. Ann Arbor. Ils. 170 p. F2. $15.00

PARSONS, Lee. *Bilbao, Guatemala: Archaeological Study of Pacific Coast...* 1974. Milwaukee Public Mus. 2nd print. wrp. F2. $25.00

PARSONS, Lee. *Pre-Columbian Am.* 1974. Milwaukee Public Mus. 1st ed. 1/3000. wrp. F2. $20.00

PARSONS & PARSONS. *Maguey Utilization in Highland Central Mexico.* 1990. Ann Arbor. Mus of Anthropology Papers No 82. wrp. M. F2. $25.00

PARTCH, Virgil. *Man the Beast.* 1953. Duell. 1st ed. tall 8vo. VG. B10. $4.25

PARTINGTON, Wilfred. *Forging Ahead: True Story of Upward Progress of TJ Wise.* 1939. NY. 8vo. dj. VG. T6. $35.00

PARTON, James. *Life & Times of Aaron Burr.* 1892. Boston. Enlarged ed. 2 vols. EX. $35.00

PASTERNAK, Boris. *Dr Zhivago.* 1958. Pantheon Book Club. 558 p. VG. B10. $3.50

PASZTORY, Esther. *Aztec Stone Sculpture.* 1977. NY. Ils. wrp. F2. $10.00

PATCHEN, Kenneth. *Dark Kingdom.* 1942. NY. Harriss Givens. sgn. cream wrp. slipcase. H3. $500.00

PATCHEN, Kenneth. *Famous Boating Party & Other Poems in Prose.* 1954. New Directions. Special Painted 1st ed. 1/50. sgn. scarce. H3. $400.00

PATCHEN, Kenneth. *First Will & Testament.* 1939. New Directions. Ltd 1st ed. 1/800. inscr. H3. $125.00

PATCHEN, Kenneth. *Journal of Albion Moonlight.* 1941. NY. Patchen. Subscriber ed. 1/50. 1st issue. sgn. VG. H3. $650.00

PATCHEN, Kenneth. *Memoirs of a Shy Pornographer.* 1945. New Directions. 1st ed. sgn. G. scarce. $100.00

PATCHEN, Kenneth. *Poem-Scapes.* 1958. Jonathan Williams. Special Painted ed. 1/75. sgn. H3. $450.00

PATCHEN, Kenneth. *Poem-Scapes.* 1958. Jonathan Williams. 1st ed. 1/42. sgn. H3. $350.00

PATCHEN, Kenneth. *Poems of Humor & Protest.* nd. City Lights. 12th print. B4. $3.00

PATCHEN, Kenneth. *Red Wine & Yel Hair.* 1949. New Direction. Special Painted ed. 1/108. sgn. H3. $600.00

PATCHEN, Kenneth. *Sleepers Awake on the Precipice.* 1946. NY. Blk Paper ed. 1/148. sgn. gilt red bdg. H3. $275.00

PATCHEN, Kenneth. *Teeth of the Lion.* 1942. New Directions. 1st ed. wrp. EX. $65.00

PATCHEN, Kenneth. *To Say If You Love Someone...* 1948. Prairie City, IL. 1st ed. 1/6. hand painted/bound. slipcase. H3. $1250.00

PATCHEN, Kenneth. *When We Were Here Together.* 1957. New Directions. Special Painted 1st ed. 1/75. sgn. H3. $500.00

PATCHEN, Kenneth. *1st Will & Testament.* 1948. New Directions. Ltd ed. 1/126. sgn. H3. $225.00

PATCHETT, M.E. *Adam Troy, Astroman.* 1954. Lutterworth. dj. VG. P1. $15.00

PATCHETT, M.E. *Kidnappers of Space.* 1953. Lutterworth. 1st ed. dj. VG. P1. $15.00

PATCHIN, F.G. *Pony Rider Boys With TX Rangers.* nd. Saalfield. dj. VG. P1. $15.00

PATER, Walter. *Works.* 1913. London. Macmillan. Lib ed. 10 vols. TEG. EX. H3. $500.00

PATON, L.A. *Les Prophecies be Merlin.* 1966. reprint of 1926 ed. French text. 2 vols. C1. $24.00

PATRI, Giacoma. *Stronger Than Death: Short Stories of the Russians at War.* 1944. Grabhorn/Am-Russian Inst. 1/1500. 81 p. VG. $25.00

PATRICK, William. *Spirals.* nd. Houghton Mifflin. 2nd ed. dj. VG. P1. $10.00

PATRICK, William. *Spirals.* 1983. Houghton Mifflin. 1st ed. dj. RS. EX. P1. $15.00

PATROUCH, J.F. *SF of Isaac Asimov.* 1976. Panther. VG. P1. $4.00

PATTEE, F.L. *Feminine '50s.* 1940. NY. VG. $25.00

PATTEN, G.W. *Voices of the Border.* 1867. NY. 1st ed. VG. $25.00

PATTERSON, Harry. *Valhalla Exchange.* nd. BOMC. dj. VG. P1. $7.50

PATTERSON, Innis. *Eppworth Case.* 1930. Farrar Rinehart. 1st ed. dj. VG. P1. $30.00

PATTERSON, J.B. *Life of Ma-Ka-Tai-Me-She-Kia-Kiak; or, Blk Hawk.* 1934. Boston. 155 p. rebound. VG. T5. $95.00

PATTERSON, J.H. *Man-Eaters of Tsavo.* 1908. London. 4th ed. 338 p. rebound. $35.00

PATTERSON, James. *Virgin.* 1980. McGraw Hill. 1st ed. dj. VG. P1. $15.00

PATTERSON, M.C. *Author Newsletters & Journals.* 1979. Gale Research. HrdCvr ed. P1. $23.75

PATTERSON, Stella. *Dear Mad'm.* 1956. NY. 1st ed. 261 p. dj. VG. B3. $25.00

PATTIE, J.O. *Personal Narrative of James O Pattie of KY.* 1930. Lakeside Classic. Ils. 428 p. VG. T5. $45.00

PATTISON, Barrie. *Seal of Dracula.* nd. Bounty. dj. VG. P1. $12.50

PATTY, V.C. *Hats & How To Make Them.* 1925. Chicago. Ils. 194 p. VG. T5. $25.00

PAUL, Barbara. *But He Was Already Dead...* 1986. Scribner. 1st ed. dj. EX. P1. $13.95

PAUL, Barbara. *17th Stair.* 1975. St Martin. 1st ed. dj. EX. P1. $15.00

PAUL, Elliot. *Concert Pitch.* 1938. Random House. inscr. dj. H3. $75.00

PAUL, Virginia. *This Was Cattle Ranching Yesterday & Today.* 1973. Bonanza. dj. VG. $12.00

PAUL & HAMALIAN. *Naked I.* 1971. Fawcett. PB Orig. B4. $6.00

PAYNE, David. *Early From the Dance.* 1989. Doubleday. ARC. wrp. EX. K2. $25.00

PAYNE, E.F. *Charity of Charles Dickens.* 1929. Bibliophile Soc. 1/425. 8vo. full polished calf. T6. $50.00

PAYNE, Laurence. *Malice in Camera.* 1983. Crime Club. 1st ed. dj. EX. P1. $15.00

PAYNE, Laurence. *Nose on My Face.* nd. Book Club. dj. VG. P1. $4.50

PAYNE, Robert. *Life & Death of Adolf Hitler.* 1973. NY. BOMC. dj. VG. $8.00

PAYNE. *Art Metal Work.* 1914. Peoria. 1st ed. G. C2. $35.00

PAZ, Octavio. *Conjunctions & Disjunctions.* 1973. Seaver/Viking. UP. wrp. EX. K2. $75.00

PAZ, Octavio. *New Poetry of Mexico. Selected, With Notes, by Octavio Paz.* 1972. Secker Warburg. Bilingual/1st UK ed. dj. EX. C4. $25.00

PAZ, Octavio. *Other Mexico: Critique of the Pyramid.* 1972. Grove Pr. UP. tall wrp. EX. K2. $125.00

PAZ. *Life of Joaquin Murrietta.* 1937. Chicago. 174 p. dj. VG. A5. $30.00

PEABODY, G.A. *S Am Journals 1858-1859.* 1937. Peabody Mus. 1/581. 209 p. slipcase. F2. $75.00

PEACOCK, T.L. *Misfortunes of Elphin.* 1924. Oxford. gr bdg. VG. C1. $14.50

PEARE, C.O. *Herbert Hoover Story.* 1965. NY. Crowell. 8vo. 247 p. xl. V1. $7.50

PEARE, Catherine. *Helen Keller Story.* 1959. Crowell. 1st ed. 183 p. dj. VG. B10. $4.50

PEARL, Jack. *Dam of Death.* 1967. Whitman. VG. P1. $7.50

PEARL, Jack. *Fear Formula.* 1968. Whitman. EX. P1. $12.50

PEARL, Jack. *Garrison's Gorillas & the Fear Formula.* 1968. Whitman. 1st ed. no dj issued. EX. F5. $10.00

PEARLMAN, Moshe. *Army of Israel.* 1950. NY. 1st ed. 256 p. VG. T5. $25.00

PEARLSTEIN, Philip. *Lithographs & Etchings.* 1978. Springfield Art Mus. 1st ed. 4to. sgn. wrp. EX. B13. $75.00

PEARSON, Edmund. *Studies in Murder.* 1938. Mod Lib. 333 p. dj. EX. $11.00

PEARSON, F.S. *Butchered Baseball.* nd. Barnes. Apparent 1st ed. 88 p. xl. VG. B10. $3.75

PEARSON, G.W. *Records of the MA Volunteer Militia.* 1913. Boston. 4to. 448 p. gilt blk bdg. EX. G4. $47.00

PEARSON, Hayden. *New Eng Year.* 1966. Norton. 1st ed. 255 p. dj. EX. B10. $4.50

PEARSON, Hesketh. *Conan Doyle.* 1946. London. Guild Books. 1st Biography ed. B4. $8.00

PEARSON, John. *Kindness of Dr Avicenna.* 1982. Holt Rinehart. 1st ed. dj. EX. P1. $15.00

PEARSON, Preston. *Hearing the Noise: My Life in NFL.* 1985. Morrow. 1st ed. 303 p. dj. M. B10. $6.25

PEARSON, Ridley. *Seizing of Yankee Gr Mall.* 1987. St Martin. 1st ed. dj. EX. P1. $18.95

PEARSON, Virginia. *Everything But Elephants.* 1947. Whittlesey House. 1st ed. 211 p. F2. $10.00

PEARSON, William. *Hunt the Man Down.* nd. Book Club. dj. VG. P1. $4.50

PEARSON, William. *Trial of Honor.* 1967. New Am Lib. 1st ed. dj. xl. P1. $5.00

PEARY, Robert. *N Pole.* 1910. NY. Stokes. 1st Trade ed. fld map. VG. $80.00

PEASE, Howard. *Secret Cargo.* nd. (1931) Doubleday. Book Club ed? 272 p. G. B10. $3.50

PEATTIE, L.R. *Pan's Parish.* 1931. Century. inscr. dj. H3. $85.00

PECK, C.H. *State of NY Annual Report of State Botanist 1895.* 1897. Albany. Lyon. VG. T3. $125.00

PECK, Graham. *2 Kinds of Time.* 1950. Houghton Mifflin. 1st ed. sgn. dj. B10. $25.00

PECK, Herbert. *Book of Rookwood Pottery.* nd. (1968) Bonanza. later print. quarto. 184 p. dj. R4. $65.00

PECK, Paula. *Art of Fine Baking.* 1961. Book Club. Ils. 320 p. dj. NM. B10. $4.50

PECK, S.M. *Maybloom & Myrtle.* 1910. Dana Estes. 1st ed. inscr. dj. EX. B13. $85.00

PECKHAM, H.H. *Narratives of Colonial Am 1704-1765.* 1971. Lakeside Classic. Ils. 314 p. EX. T5. $22.50

PECKHAM, H.H. *Pontiac & the Indian Uprising.* 1947. Princeton, NJ. Ils 1st ed. 346 p. dj. G. T5. $22.50

PECKHAM, Richard. *Murder in Strange Houses.* 1929. Minton Balch. VG. P1. $12.50

PEDLER, Margaret. *Yesterdays Harvest.* 1926. Doran. 1st ed. 303 p. VG. B10. $3.50

PEDLER & DAVIS. *Dynostar Menace.* 1975. Scribner. 1st ed. dj. EX. P1. $10.00

PEDLER & DAVIS. *Mutant 59: The Plastic-Eaters.* nd. Book Club. dj. VG. P1. $4.50

PEEL, C.D. *Hell Seed.* 1979. St Martin. 1st Am ed. dj. EX. F5. $15.00

PEEL, John. *End of the Affair.* 1987. Borgo Pr. EX. P1. $17.50

PEEL, John. *Girl From UNCLE Part 1.* 1987. Borgo Pr. EX. P1. $17.50

PEEL, John. *Girl From UNCLE Part 2.* 1987. Borgo Pr. EX. P1. $17.50

PEIRCE, Josephine. *Fire on the Hearth: Evolution & Romance of Heating Stove.* 1951. Springfield. Ils. EX. $30.00

PEISSEL, Michel. *Lost World of Quintana Roo.* 1963. Dutton. 1st ed. 306 p. dj. F2. $20.00

PEKIN, L.B. *Darwin.* 1938. Stackpole. 1st ed. 109 p. dj. VG. B10. $3.50

PELLOWE, William. *Royal Road to Mexico.* 1937. Watergate Pub. 1st ed. sgn, 168 p. F2. $15.00

PELRINE & PELRINE. *Ian Fleming: Man With the Golden Pen.* 1966. Swan 112. VG. P1. $6.00

PELTON, B.W. *Furniture Making & Cabinet Work, a Handbook.* 1949. NY. Ils. 596 p. G. T5. $22.50

PELTZ, Edith. *Bland But Grand.* nd. (1929) Doubleday. 140 p. dj. VG. B10. $3.00

PELZER, L. *Cattlemen's Frontier.* 1939. AC Clark. 1st ed. inscr. VG. K1. $175.00

PEMBERTON, T.E. *John Hare, Comedian, 1865-1895.* 1895. Routledge. 1st ed. 202 p. VG. H3. $100.00

PENCE, Raymond. *Essays by Present-Day Writers.* 1925. Macmillan. not 1st ed. 360 p. VG. B10. $3.50

PENDERGAST, David. *Palenque.* 1967. OK U. 1st ed. 213 p. dj. F2. $30.00

PENDLETON, Victor. *Assyrian Tents.* 1904. Jewish Pub Soc. 1st ed. VG. R3. $37.50

PENDLETON, Victor. *Lost Prince Almon.* 1898. Jewish Pub Soc. 1st ed. EX. R3. $42.50

PENDLETON, W.F. *Confederate Memoirs: Early Life & Family Hist.* 1958. Bryn Athyn. 1st ed. EX. $85.00

PENDO, Stephen. *Raymond Chandler on Screen: His Novels Into Film.* 1976. Metuchen, NJ. Scarecrow. 1st ed. no dj issued. EX. T9. $20.00

PENDRY, Eric. *Way To Go Home.* 1977. Norton. 1st ed. dj. EX. F5. $15.00

PENFIELD, F.C. *Present-Day Egypt.* 1903. Century. 396 p. TEG. EX. J2. $20.00

PENINGTON, Isaac. *Brief Extracts From the Works of Isaac Penington.* 1819. Phil. Rakestraw. 16mo. 62 p. V1. $16.00

PENINGTON, Isaac. *Letters of Isaac Penington, an Eminent Minister of Gospel.* 1859. Assn Friends Diffusion Knowledge 125 p. xl. V1. $12.00

PENINGTON, Isaac. *Selections From Isaac Penington.* 1892. Boston. Roberts Bros 1st print. 113 p. AEG. G. V1. $8.50

PENINGTON, Mary. *Experiences in the Life of Mary Penington.* nd. Phil. Biddle Pr 16mo. 116 p. V1. $8.00

PENMAN, Sharon. *Falls the Shadow.* 1988 UP. EX. C1. $8.50

PENN, John. *Ad for Murder.* 1982. Scribner 1st ed. dj. EX. P1. $15.00

PENN, John. *Deadly Sickness.* 1985. Scribner. 1st ed. dj. EX. P1. $13.95

PENN, William. *Brief Account of Rise & Progress of People Called Quakers.* 1916. Phil. Rakestraw. 12mo. 95 p. xl. G. V1. $22.00

PENN, William. *Fruits of Solitude.* 1906. Chicago. Lakeside Classic. 1st ed. VG. scarce. K1. $125.00

PENN, William. *Harmony of Divine & Heavenly Doctrines.* 1822. NY. Refine Weeks. 16mo. 155 p. V1. $28.00

PENN, William. *My Irish Journal 1669-1670.* 1952. Longman Gr. 1st print. 8vo. 103 p. dj. VG. V1. $15.00

PENN, William. *No Cross, No Crown.* nd. Friends Bookstore. 12mo. 408 p. VG. V1. $12.50

PENN, William. *No Cross, No Crown.* 1953. Phil. Collins. 12mo. 426 p. full leather. G. V1. $9.50

PENN, William. *Passages From the Life & Writings of William Penn.* nd. Friends Bookstore. 12mo. 512 p. VG. V1. $8.00

PENN, William. *Rise & Progress of People Called Quakers.* 1855. Phil. Chapman. 16mo. VG. V1. $12.00

PENN, William. *Select Works With a Journal of His Life.* 1771. London. folio. 862 p. V1. $160.00

PENN & WHITEHEAD. *Christian Quaker & His Divine Testimony Stated & Vindicated.* 1824. Phil. Rakestraw. 12mo. 555 p. V1. $60.00

PENN TERENTENARY COMMITTEE. *Remember William Penn With More Fruits of Solitude.* 1944. Phil. 8vo. VG. V1. $16.00

PENNEBAKER, D.A. *Bob Dylan: Don't Look Back.* 1968. Ballantine. VB. B4. $5.00

PENNELL, Joseph. *Adventures of an Ils.* 1925. Boston. 1st Trade ed. M. $50.00

PENNELL, Joseph. *Etchers & Etching.* 1920. London. 1/100. sgn. very scarce. $200.00

PENNELL, Joseph. *Little Book of London.* c 1925. London. Ils. wrp. w/newspaper article. VG. A4. $30.00

PENNINGTON, Campbell. *Tepehuan of Chihuahua.* 1969. UT U. 1st ed. 413 p. dj. F2. $30.00

PENNY, F.E. *Magic in the Air.* 1935. Hodder Stoughton. 2nd ed. VG. P1. $7.50

PENROSE, Margaret. *Motor Girls on the Coast.* 1913. Cupples. Ils. dj. VG. B10. $3.25

PENTECOST, Hugh. *Death by Fire.* 1986. Dodd Mead. 1st ed. dj. EX. P1. $15.95

PENTECOST, Hugh. *Girl Watcher's Funeral.* 1969. Dodd Mead. dj. VG. P1. $7.50

PENTECOST, Hugh. *Judas Freak.* 1974. Dodd Mead. dj. VG. P1. $15.00

PENTECOST, Hugh. *Murder in Luxury.* 1981. Dodd Mead. 1st ed. dj. xl. P1. $7.50

PENTECOST, Hugh. *Plague of Violence.* 1970. Dodd Mead. 1st ed. dj. EX. F5. $15.00

PENTECOST, Hugh. *Sniper.* 1965. Dodd Mead. dj. xl. P1. $6.00

PENTECOST, Hugh. *Sow Death, Reap Death.* 1981. Dodd Mead. 1st ed. dj. VG. P1. $15.00

PENTECOST, Hugh. *Substitute Victim.* 1984. Dodd Mead. 1st ed. dj. VG. P1. $15.00

PENTECOST, Hugh. *Where the Snow Was Red.* nd. Book Club. dj. VG. P1. $5.00

PENZLER, Otto. *Great Detectives.* 1978. Little Brn. 1st ed. dj. VG. P1. $20.00

PEPPER, Charles. *Panama to Patagonia.* 1906. McClurg. 1st ed. 398 p. VG. F2. $25.00

PEPYS, Samuel. *Diary & Correspondence.* 1875. London. Bell. New ed. 4 vols. sm octavo. H3. $225.00

PEPYS, Samuel. *Diary of Pepys.* nd. Boston. Brainard. 1/1000. 18 vols. TEG. VG. $60.00

PEPYS, Samuel. *Diary.* 1892. NY. Croscup. Autograph ed. 1/125. 18 vols. octavo. H3. $1750.00

PEPYS, Samuel. *Diary.* 1892. Wheatley Ed. 1/1000. 18 vols. tall 8vo. VG. $100.00

PERCY, Bishop. *Ballads & Romances.* 1867 & 1868. London. Turbner. 1st ed. 4 vols. EX. C1. $250.00

PERCY, W.A. *Lanterns on the Levee.* 1941. NY. 1st ed. dj. VG. B3. $55.00

PERCY, W.A. *Lanterns on the Levee.* 1941. NY. 5th print. dj. VG. $35.00

PERCY, Walker. *Diagnosing the Modern Malaise.* 1985. Faust Pub. Ltd ed. 1/250. sgn. M. H3. $85.00

PERCY, Walker. *Lancelot.* 1977. Farrar Straus Giroux. UP. wrp. EX. K2. $150.00

PERCY, Walker. *Lancelot.* 1977. Farrar Straus Giroux. 1st ed. dj. EX. H3. $50.00

PERCY, Walker. *Last Gentlemen.* 1966. Farrar Straus Giroux. 1st ed. dj. VG. H3. $60.00

PERCY, Walker. *Lost in the Cosmos.* 1983. Farrar Straus Giroux. 1st ed. dj. EX. H3. $40.00

PERCY, Walker. *Love in the Ruins.* 1971. Farrar Straus Giroux. 1st ed. dj. EX. H3. $75.00

PERCY, Walker. *Message in the Bottle.* 1975. Farrar Straus Giroux. presentation. dj. EX. H3. $125.00

PERCY, Walker. *Message in the Bottle.* 1975. Farrar Straus Giroux. 1st ed. dj. EX. H3. $50.00

PERCY, Walker. *Moviegoer.* 1961. Knopf. 1st ed. dj. EX. H3. $400.00

PERCY, Walker. *Novel Writing in an Apocalyptic Time.* 1986. Faust Pub. 1/300. sgn. H3. $150.00

PERCY, Walker. *Symbol As Need.* 1954. Fordham U Quarterly. sgn. wrp. fld cloth slipcase. H3. $500.00

PERCY, Walker. *Thanatos Syndrome.* 1987. Farrar Straus. dj. VG. P1. $15.00

PERCY, Walker. *2nd Coming.* 1980. Farrar Straus Giroux. 1st Trade ed. dj. EX. H3. $50.00

PERCY, Walker. *2nd Coming.* 1981. Farrar Straus. Ltd ed. 1/450. sgn. slipcase. EX. K2. $125.00

PERCY, William Alexander. *Little Shepherd's Song.* 1922. NY. Ricordi. 1st ed. VG. B13. $45.00

PEREC, G.W. *Memory of Childhood.* 1988. London. Collins. 1st ed. dj. EX. B13. $45.00

PERELMAN, S.J. *Best of SJ Perelman.* 1947. Modern Lib. dj. VG. P1. $15.00

PERELMAN, S.J. *Most of SJ Perelman.* nd. BOMC. dj. VG. P1. $7.50

PERELMAN, S.J. *Vinegar Puss.* 1975. Simon Schuster. inscr. dj. H3. $500.00

PERERA, Victor. *Loch Ness Monster Watches.* 1974. Capra. Chapbook Series. 1/75. sgn. EX. K2. $20.00

PERERA & BRUCE. *Last Lord of Palenque.* 1982. Little Brn. 1st ed. 311 p. dj. F2. $25.00

PEREY, Lucien. *Roman du Grand Roi.* 1894. Paris. 5th ed. sgn. TEG. G. R5. $25.00

PEREZ MALDONADO, Raul. *Tales From Chichicastenago.* 1989. Guatemala. 72 p. wrp. F2. $10.00

PERKERSON, Medora. *Wht Columns in GA.* 1952. NY. sgn. dj. VG. B3. $20.00

PERKINS, Eli. *Saratoga.* 1901. NY. Ils Arthur Lumley. 8vo. gilt bdg. VG. $50.00

PERKINS, F.B. *Picture & the Men.* 1867. NY. 1st ed. 190 p. T5. $15.00

PERKINS, Wilma. *Fannie Farmer Jr Cookbook.* 1942. 1st ed. dj. VG. $15.00

PERKINS & TANIS. *Native Am of N Am.* 1975. Scarecrow. 558 p. F2. $25.00

PERKINS. *Tuscan Sculptors: Their Lives, Works, & Times.* 1864. Longman. 2 vols. A5. $65.00

PERKOFF, S.Z. *Alphabet.* 1973. Red Hill Pr. 1/672. M. B4. $10.00

PERKOFF, S.Z. *Gathering Tribe.* 1983. Blk Ace/Croupier. 1/350. dj. M. B4. $15.00

PERKOFF, S.Z. *Visions for the Tribe.* 1976. Blk Ace. 1/300. B4. $7.00

PERKS, Sydney. *Essays on Old London.* 1927. Cambridge. 78 p. EX. $25.00

PERLES, Alfred. *Great True Spy Adventures.* 1974. Bobbs Merrill. 1st ed. dj. EX. P1. $15.00

PERLES, Alfred. *My Friend Lawrence Durrell.* 1961. Scorpion Pr. 1st ed. 1/50. sgn. dj. EX. H3. $100.00

PEROWNE, Barry. *Singular Conspiracy.* 1974. Bobbs Merrill. 1st ed. dj. EX. P1. $15.00

PERRY, Bliss. *Carlyle: How To Know Him.* nd. (1915) Bobbs Merrill. 267 p. xl. G. B10. $3.75

PERRY, Charles. *Brief Expositions & Vindication of...Doctrines...Friends.* 1885. Riverside. 8vo. 43 p. VG. V1. $18.00

PERRY, Fred. *Perry on Tennis.* 1937. Phil. 1st ed. 155 p. dj. VG. B3. $30.00

PERRY, Stella. *Angel of Christmas.* 1917. Stokes. dj. VG. B7. $48.00

PERRY & PERRY. *Maya Missions...Spanish Colonial Churches of Yucatan.* 1988. Espandana Pr. 1st ed. sgn. 249 p. dj. F2. $15.00

PERSE, St.-John. *Letters.* 1979. Princeton. 1st ed. dj. EX. C4. $25.00

PERSHING, J.J. *My Experiences in the World War.* Author's ed. 2 vols. TEG. djs. T5. $250.00

PERSICO, J.E. *Piercing of the Reich.* 1979. Viking. 1st ed. dj. VG. P1. $17.50

PERSICO, J.E. *Spider Web.* 1979. Crown. 1st ed. dj. VG. P1. $15.00

PERTCHIK & PERTCHIK. *Flowering Trees of the Caribbean.* 1951. Rinehart. 1st ed. 4to. 125 p. F2. $35.00

PERTWEE, Roland. *Hell's Loose.* 1929. Houghton Mifflin. VG. P1. $7.50

PERTWEE, Roland. *Interference.* nd. Readers Lib. VG. P1. $10.00

PERTWEE, Roland. *MX – XX 3.* 1929. Heinemann. 2nd ed. Lib bdg. xl. P1. $5.00

PERUCHO, Joan. *Nat Hist.* 1988. Knopf. 1st ed. dj. EX. F5. $16.00

PERUGINI, M.E. *Art of Ballet.* 1915. London. Secker. 1st ed. 339 p. VG. H3. $60.00

PESETSKY, Bette. *Stories Up to a Point.* 1981. Knopf. AP. K2. $35.00

PETAJA, Emil. *As Dream & Shadow.* 1972. SISU Pub. 1st ed. sgn. dj. EX. R3. $25.00

PETAJA, Emil. *Stardrift.* 1971. Fantasy. 1st ed. dj. M. R3. $25.00

PETERKIN, Julia. *Scarlet Sister Mary.* 1928. Indianapolis. Airplane ed. sgn. EX. C4. $85.00

PETERKIN & ULMANN. *Roll, Jordan, Roll.* 1933. NY. Ballou. 1st ed. dj. VG. B13. $225.00

PETERS, Charles. *Autobiography.* 1915. Sacramento. Ils 231 p. wrp. A5. $40.00

PETERS, Daniel. *Tikal: Novel About Maya.* 1983. Random House. 1st ed. 422 p. dj. NM. B10. $4.50

PETERS, Elizabeth. *Legend in Gr Velvet.* 1976. Dodd Mead. 1st ed. dj. EX. P1. $50.00

PETERS, Elizabeth. *Lion in the Valley.* 1986. Atheneum. 1st ed. dj. EX. P1. $20.00

PETERS, Elizabeth. *Mummy Case.* 1985. Congdon Weed. 1st ed. dj. EX. P1. $20.00

PETERS, Ellis. *Blk Is Clr of True-Love's Heart.* nd. Book Club. dj. VG. P1. $7.50

PETERS, Ellis. *Heretic's Apprentice.* 1989. Stoddart. 1st ed. dj. VG. P1. $17.50

PETERS, Ellis. *Hermit of Eyton Forest.* 1988. Mysterious Pr. 1st ed. dj. EX. F5. $14.00

PETERS, Ellis. *House of Gr Turf.* nd. Morrow. dj. xl. P1. $7.50

PETERS, Ellis. *Raven in the Foregate.* 1986. Morrow. 1st ed. dj. VG. P1. $15.95

PETERS, Harry. *Currier & Ives: Printmakers of Am.* 1942. Doubleday. Special ed. 192 p. VG. B10. $10.00

PETERS, Ludovic. *2 After Malic.* 1966. Walker. 1st ed. dj. VG. P1. $12.50

PETERS, W.E. *Ride Around Athens Co & Where & How To Find.* 1940. Athens, OH. Ils 2nd ed. 72 p. T5. $15.00

PETERS, Zach. *10 Dreams.* 1927. Winston. 1st ed. dj. EX. R3. $20.00

PETERS & BURLEIGH. *Birds of Newfoundland.* 1951. St Johns. Ils Peterson. dj. VG. C2. $35.00

PETERSEN, Carl. *On the Track of the Dixie Limited.* 1979. La Grange, IL. 1/1000. orange wrp. VG. $25.00

PETERSEN, Carmen. *Maya of Guatemala.* 1976. WA U. 1st ed. lg 4to. dj. F2. $45.00

PETERSEN, Clarence. *Bantam Story.* 1970. Bantam. EX. P1. $4.50

PETERSEN & ELVIN. *Sunday News Family Cookbook.* 1962. NY. Rowman. Book Club ed? 4to. VG. B10. $7.00

PETERSHAM & PETERSHAM. *Auntie.* 1936. Doubleday. Ils. VG. B7. $25.00

PETERSHAM & PETERSHAM. *Christ Child As Told by Matthew & Luke.* 1931. Doubleday. VG. B7. $33.00

PETERSHAM & PETERSHAM. *Miki.* 1929. Doubleday Doran. 1st ed. 4to. 63 p. VG. $35.00

PETERSON, Frederick. *Ancient Mexico.* 1959. London. George Allen. 1st ed. 313 p. dj. F2. $25.00

PETERSON, Frederick. *Ancient Mexico.* 1959. NY. Putnam. dj. F2. $20.00

PETERSON, H.L. *Am Knives.* 1958. NY. 178 p. dj. VG. B3. $30.00

PETERSON, Henry. *Pemberton; or, 100 Years Ago.* 1898. Phil. HJ Coates. 12mo. 393 p. reading copy. V1. $8.50

PETERSON, Houseon. *Treasury of World's Great Speeches.* 1954. Simon Schuster. 2nd ed. 856 p. dj. VG. B10. $7.50

PETERSON, Jeannette. *Pre-Columbian Flora & Fauna.* 1990. La Jolla. Mingei Mus. 1st ed. 4to. wrp. M. F2. $35.00

PETERSON & HANSON. *Pilot Knob. Thermopylae of the W.* 1964. Cape Girardeau reprint of 1914 ed. T5. $19.50

PETIEVICH, Gerald. *Shakedown.* 1988. Simon Schuster. 1st ed. dj. EX. P1. $16.95

PETRIE, Sidney. *Reduce & Control Weight Through Self-Hypnotism.* 1966. Prentice. 4th ed. dj. VG. B10. $3.00

PETRY, Anne. *Country Place.* 1947. Houghton Mifflin. 1st ed. dj. VG. K2. $55.00

PETTIGREW, Thomas. *Biographical Memoirs of Most Celebrated Physicians.* 1840. London. 4 vols in 2. $475.00

PEVSNER, Nikolaus. *Studies in Art, Architecture, & Design. Vol 1 & Vol 2.* 1968. NY. Walker. 1st Am ed. 4to. 2 vols. djs. R4. $125.00

PEYROU, Manuel. *Thunder of the Roses.* 1972. NY. Herder. dj. EX. K2. $65.00

PHELAN, J.T. *Phelan, Malone, Kevill, Stutz, & Flaes Families.* 1985. Gateway Pr. 1st ed. 158 p. EX. B10. $15.00

PHELPS, Gilbert. *Gr Horizons: Travels in Brazil.* 1964. Simon Schuster. 1st ed. 255 p. dj. F2. $15.00

PHELPS, R.H. *Newgate of CT: Its Origin & Early Hist...Simsbury Mines...* 1876. Hartford. Ils. A5. $55.00

PHELPS, Robert. *Earthly Paradise.* 1966. Farrar Book Club. 505 p. dj. EX. B10. $4.00

PHELPS, W.L. *As I Like It. 2nd Series.* 1924. Scribner. 1st ed. 282 p. B10. $7.25

PHELPS & HOWELLS. *Bryant & Other Essays.* 1924. NY. 1st ed. inscr. dj. VG. $20.00

PHELPS & WATSON. *Hist & Military Map of Border & S States.* 1863. NY. wrp. T5. $150.00

PHIFER, Charles. *Diaz the Dictator.* 1913. Menace Pub. 2nd ed. 8vo. 143 p. F2. $15.00

PHILADELPHIA YEARLY MEETING. *Brief Narrative...Phil Yearly Meeting of Friends.* 1873. Phil. Friends Bookstore. 16mo. 40 p. wrp. G. V1. $12.50

PHILADELPHIA YEARLY MEETING. *Christian Advices.* 1808. Kimber Conrad. 24mo. 112 p. leather. V1. $15.00

PHILADELPHIA YEARLY MEETING. *Christian Advices.* 1859. Phil. Friends Bookstore. 16mo. 130 p. V1. $12.00

PHILADELPHIA YEARLY MEETING. *Collection of Memorials...PA, NJ, etc.* 1787. Phil. 12mo. 439 p. V1. $45.00

PHILADELPHIA YEARLY MEETING. *Friends' Meeting House, 4th & Arch St, Phil.* 1904. Phi. Winston. 12mo. 141 p. G. V1. $20.00

PHILADELPHIA YEARLY MEETING. *Memorials Concerning Deceased Friends...1788-1819.* 1821. Phil. SW Conrad. 16mo. 184 p. G. V1. $18.00

PHILADELPHIA YEARLY MEETING. *Memorials Concerning Deceased Friends...1854.* 1955. Phil. TE Chapman. 16mo. 24 p. wrp. G. V1. $12.00

PHILADELPHIA YEARLY MEETING. *On the Right Authority & Qualification for Religious Labor.* 1886. Friends Bookstore. 16mo. 19 p. EX. V1. $8.00

PHILADELPHIA YEARLY MEETING. *Plymouth Meeting Controversy.* 1957. Phil. 8vo. SftCvr. VG. V1. $8.00

PHILADELPHIA YEARLY MEETING. *Proceedings of the Yearly Meeting.* 1940. Phil. Friends Bookstore. 12mo. 212 p. G. V1. $6.00

PHILADELPHIA YEARLY MEETING. *Report of Yearly Meeting on Burials & Marriages.* 1840. Phil. 16mo. V1. $10.00

PHILADELPHIA YEARLY MEETING. *Rules of Discipline of Yearly Meeting of Friends.* 1838. Joseph Painter. 24mo. 109 p. full leather. V1. $12.50

PHILADELPHIA YEARLY MEETING. *Rules of Discipline of Yearly Meeting of Friends.* 1843. Phil. John Richards. 12mo. 108 p. full leather. V1. $20.00

PHILIPPE, C.L. *Bubu of Montparnasse.* 1932. Blk Sun. Preface Eliot. wrp. H3. $75.00

PHILIPS, Benjamin. *Scrofula: Its Nature, Causes, Prevalence, & Treatment.* 1846. Lea Blanchard. J2. $50.00

PHILIPS, Judson. *Wings of Madness.* 1966. Dodd Mead. 1st ed. dj. EX. F5. $15.00

PHILLIPPE, Julian. *Symbolists.* 1973. London. 1st ed. VG. G1. $25.00

PHILLIPS, A.A. *Nuevo Arte Poetico y Pablo Neruda.* 1936. Santiago, Chile. Nascimento. wrp. EX. K2. $85.00

PHILLIPS, A.M. *Mislaid Charm.* 1947. Prime Pr. 1st ed. 1st state dj. VG. P1. $25.00

PHILLIPS, A.M. *Mislaid Charm.* 1947. Prime Pr. 1st ed. 2nd state dj. VG. P1. $25.00

PHILLIPS, Catherine. *Memoirs of Life of Catherine Phillips...* 1797. London. James Phillips. 12mo. 392 p. leather. V1. $28.00

PHILLIPS, Conrad. *Unrepentant.* 1958. Roy. dj. VG. P1. $12.50

PHILLIPS, D.G. *Worth of a Woman.* 1908. Appleton. 1st ed. gilt gr bdg. VG. H3. $25.00

PHILLIPS, E.C. *Little Sally Waters.* 1926. Houghton Mifflin. 1st ed. dj. VG. B10. $7.50

PHILLIPS, J.A. *Blk Tickets.* 1979. Delacorte. UP. wrp. EX. C4. $200.00

PHILLIPS, J.A. *Fast Lanes.* 1984. NY. 1st ed. 1/26. sgns. as issued. K2. $175.00

PHILLIPS, J.A. *Fast Lanes.* 1987. Dutton. ARC. dj. RS. w/promotional material. K2. $35.00

PHILLIPS, J.A. *How Mickey Made It.* 1981. Bookslinger. 1st ed. 1/150. sgn. EX. B13/K2. $100.00

PHILLIPS, J.A. *Sweethearts.* 1976. Carrboro. Truck Pr. 1st ed. 1/400. inscr. wrp. EX. B13. $300.00

PHILLIPS, J.A. *Sweethearts.* 1976. Carrboro. Truck Pr. 1st ed. 1/400. sm quarto. wrp. VG. K2. $125.00

PHILLIPS, R. *Involuntary Immortals.* 1959. Avalon. 1st ed. dj. EX. R3. $30.00

PHILLIPS, R. *Time Trap.* 1949. Century. 1st ed. wrp. EX. R3. $20.00

PHILLIPS, R. *World of If.* 1951. Merit Books. 1st ed. wrp. EX. R3. $8.00

PHILLIPS, Robert. *Louis L'Amour.* 1989. Paperjacks. VG. P1. $3.75

PHILLIPS, Stephen. *Ulysses.* 1902. Macmillan. 1st Am ed. 1/100. NM. C1. $12.50

PHILLIPS, W. *Qataban & Sheba.* 1955. NY. 1st ed. inscr. dj. EX. $30.00

PHILLIPS, W.B. *Life & Labor in the Old S.* 1929. Phil. 375 p. G. S1. $8.00

PHILLIPS, W.S. *Indian Tales for Little Folks.* 1928. Platt Munk. oblong 4to. VG. $50.00

PHILLIPS, Wendell. *US Constitution & It's Pro-Slavery Comprimises.* 1856. NY. 208 p. G. S1. $35.00

PHILLIPS, Wendell. *US Constitution: Pro-Slavery Compact.* 1856. Phil. Am Anti-Slavery Soc. G. S1. $50.00

PHILLPOTTS, Eden. *Circe's Island/Girl & the Faun.* 1926. NY. 1st Am ed. presentation. G. $45.00

PHILLPOTTS, Eden. *Daniel Sweetland.* 1906. Authors News. Probably 1st ed. 320 p. VG. B10. $5.00

PHILLPOTTS, Eden. *Dish of Apples.* 1921. London. Ils/sgn Rackham. 1/500. EX. $350.00

PHILLPOTTS, Eden. *Widecombe Ed of Eden Phillpott's Dartmoor Novels.* 1927. London. Macmillan. Ltd ed. 1/1500. sgn. 20 vols. H3. $350.00

PHILLPOTTS, Eden. *100 Sonnets.* 1929. London. Benn. 1st ed. 1/54. sgn. TEG. EX. H3. $100.00

PHIPPS, Joseph. *True Christian Baptism & Communion.* nd. Phil. Friends Bookstore. 16mo. 48 p. VG. V1. $14.00

PHISTERER, Frederick. *Statistical Record of Armies of the US.* nd. Jack Brussel. 343 p. G. S1. $9.00

PIAGET, H.F. *Watch: Its Construction, Merits, Defects.* 1877. 3rd ed. VG. $80.00

PIATIGORSKY, Gregor. *Cellist.* 1965. Doubleday. 1st ed. presentation. dj. H3. $100.00

PICARD, Nancy. *Dead Crazy.* nd. Book Club. dj. EX. P1. $5.00

PICARD, Nancy. *Marriage Is Murder.* 1987. Scribner. 1st ed. dj. EX. P1. $15.00

PICARD, Nancy. *No Body.* 1986. Scribner. 1st ed. dj. EX. P1. $13.95

PICASSO, Pablo. *Hunk of Skin.* 1968. City Lights. 1st print. B4. $10.00

PICCARD, Auguste. *In Ballonn & Bathyscaphe.* 1956. London. Cassell. 1st ed. 8vo. 192 p. dj. EX. R4. $25.00

PICCHU & BINGHAM. *Lost City of the Incas.* 1962. NY. Ils. 263 p. dj. VG. B3. $30.00

PICK, Robert. *Empress Maria Theresa.* 1966. NY. 1st ed. EX. $12.00

PICKETT, C.E. *For More Than Bread.* 1953. Little Brn. 8vo. 433 p. dj. G. V1. $9.00

PICKETT, C.E. *Internat Responsibility of Friends.* 1959. High Point, NC. 12mo. 11 p. VG. V1. $5.00

PICKFORD, Mary. *Demi-Widow.* 1935. Bobbs Merrill. 1st ed. 272 p. EX. H3. $75.00

PICKFORD, Mary. *My Rendezvous With Life.* 1935. NY. Kinsey. 1st ed. 12mo. 37 p. EX. H3. $40.00

PICKFORD & LAST. *Arthurian Bibliography.* 1981. London. Brewer. 1st ed. dj. VG. C1. $59.00

PICO, Laurence. *Beyond the Horizon.* 1989. St. Martin. 1st ed. dj. B10. $4.50

PIERCE. *Memoir & Letters of Charles Sumner.* 1877. Boston. 2 vols. xl. G4. $17.00

PIERCEY, Marge. *Braided Lives.* 1982. Summit. 2nd ed. dj. VG. P1. $12.50

PIERCY, Marge. *Gone to Soldiers.* 1987. Summit. ARC. EX. K2. $25.00

PIERSON, Donald. *Cruz das Almas: A Brazilian Village.* 1951. GPO. 4to. 226 p. wrp. F2. $15.00

PIESSEL, Michel. *Lost World of Quintana Roo.* 1963. Dutton. 1st ed. dj. EX. R3. $15.00

PIGGOT, Stuart. *Druids.* 1975. (1st 1968) NM. C1. $14.50

PIGOTT, Stuart. *Druids.* 1981. (1st 1968) Eng PB. Ils. VG. C1. $4.00

PIKE, J.S. *Prostrate State: SC Under Negro Government.* 1935. NY. EX. $30.00

PIKE, Z.M. *SW Expedition of Zebulon M Pike.* 1925. Lakeside Classic. 239 p. T5. $35.00

PIKE. *Scout & Ranger.* 1865. Cincinnati. Hawley. Ils. 394 p. G. A5. $600.00

PILLSBURY, Ann. *100 Prize-Winning Recipes.* 1950-1959. MN. Ils. 10 vols. VG. T5. $95.00

PINCANO, Felice. *Eyes.* nd. Book Club. dj. VG. P1. $4.50

PINCHER, Chapman. *Not With a Bang.* nd. Book Club. dj. VG. P1. $4.50

PINCHER, Chapman. *Not With a Bang.* 1965. New Am Lib. 1st ed. dj. EX. R3. $10.00

PINCHER, Chapman. *Not With a Bang.* 1965. New Am Lib. 1st ed. VG. P1. $4.75

PINCHER, Chapman. *Not With a Bang.* 1965. Weidenfeld Nicolson. dj. G. P1. $10.00

PINEDA, Rafael. *Tierra Doctorada.* 1978. Caracas. 1st ed. 4to. 622 p. dj. F2. $45.00

PINI & PINI. *Complete Elfquest.* 1985. Donning. Ltd HrdCvr ed. sgns. 4 vols. slipcase. M. R3. $75.00

PINI & PINI. *Elfquest Book 1.* 1981. Donning. Ltd 1st ed. sgn. boxed. EX. P1. $225.00

PINI & PINI. *Elfquest Book 2.* 1982. Donning. Ltd 1st ed. sgn. boxed. EX. P1. $150.00

PINI & PINI. *Elfquest Book 3.* 1983. Donning. Ltd 1st ed. sgn. boxed. EX. P1. $100.00

PINI & PINI. *Elquest Book 4.* 1984. Donning. Ltd 1st ed. sgn. boxed. EX. P1. $75.00

PINKERTON, Allan. *Detective & the Somnambulist.* 1877. Belord. 1st Canadian ed. G. P1. $40.00

PINKERTON, Allan. *Spy of the Rebellion.* 1883. Boston. 1st ed. 688 p. VG. $50.00

PINKERTON, R.E. *Test of Donald Norton.* 1924. Grosset Dunlap. dj. EX. R3. $40.00

PINNER, David. *Ritual.* 1967. New Authors Ltd. 1st ed. dj. EX. P1. $12.50

PINO SAAVEDRA, Yolando. *Cuentos Folkloricos de Chile.* 1963. Santiago. 1st ed. sm 4to. 408 p. wrp. F2. $20.00

PINO SAAVEDRA, Yolando. *Folk Tales of Chile.* 1968. Routledge. 1st Eng ed. 317 p. dj. F2. $20.00

PINTER, Harold. *French Lieutenant's Woman: A Screenplay.* 1981. Little Brn. UP. dj. EX. K2. $75.00

PINTER, Harold. *Poems.* 1971. Enitharmon Pr. 2nd ed. 1/100. sgn. H3. $75.00

PINTER & FOWLES. *French Lieutenant's Woman.* 1981. Little Brn. 1st ed. sgns. slipcase. EX. H3. $100.00

PIPER, Evelyn. *Nanny.* nd. Book Club. dj. VG. P1. $4.50

PIPER, Evelyn. *Stand-In.* nd. Book Club. dj. VG. P1. $4.50

PIPER, Evelyn. *Stand-In.* 1970. McKay Washburn. 1st ed. dj. xl. P1. $5.00

PIPER, H.B. *Space Viking.* 1975. Garland. 1st HrdCvr ed. EX. R3. $100.00

PIPER, Watty. *Famous Fairy Tales.* nd. (1928) Platt Munk. 2nd ed? B10. $5.00

PIRSIG, R.M. *Zen & the Art of Motorcycle Maintenance.* 1974. Morrow. 1st ed. dj. VG. K2. $65.00

PIRTLE, Alfred. *Battle of Tippecanoe.* 1900. Louisville, KY. 158 p. T5. $150.00

PISERCHIA, Doris. *Spaceling.* nd. Book Club. 1st ed. dj. EX. P1. $4.50

PITTENGER, William. *Daring & Suffering: Hist of Great Railroad Adventure.* 1982. Time Life. reprint of 1863 ed. S1. $17.50

PITTENGER, William. *In Pursuit of the General.* 1965. San Marino, CA. Ils. dj. VG. T5. $25.00

PITTS, John. *Faith Healing: Fact or Fiction?* 1961. Hawthorn. 1st ed. 159 p. PB. NM. B10. $3.50

PITTS, Zasu. *Candy Hits.* 1964. NY. dj. VG. B3. $15.00

PIZOR & COMP. *Man in the Moon.* 1971. Praeger. 1st ed. dj. EX. R3. $10.00

PLAGMAN, Bentz. *Boxwood Maze.* 1972. Sat Review Pr. 1st ed. dj. EX. F5. $14.00

PLANCHE, F.D.A. *Evening Amusements for Everyone.* nd. Phil. Coates. 282 p. gilt red bdg. J3. $42.00

PLANTE, David. *Ghost of Henry James.* 1970. Boston. 1st Am ed. inscr/sgn. dj. EX. T9. $135.00

PLANTE, David. *Ghost of Henry James.* 1970. Boston. Gambit. 1st ed. dj. EX. B13. $85.00

PLANTE, David. *Slides.* 1971. London. MacDonald. 1st ed. dj. EX. C4. $60.00

PLATH, Sylvia. *Child.* 1971. Exeter. Rougemont Pr. Ltd ed. 1/325. wrp/dj. EX. K2. $125.00

PLATH, Sylvia. *Colossus & Other Poems.* 1960. London. Heinemann. 1st ed/pub display copy. dj. EX. K2. $1000.00

PLATH, Sylvia. *Journals of Sylvia Plath.* 1982. NY. Dial. UP. wrp. EX. K2. $75.00

PLATH, Sylvia. *Surgeon at 2 AM & Other Poems.* 1971. Portland. 1st Collected ed. 1/100. inscr. wrp. H3. $500.00

PLATO. *Dialogues.* 1892. Oxford. Clarendon. 3rd ed. 5 vols. octavo. H3. $750.00

PLATO. *Republic.* 1944. Ltd Ed Club. 1/1200. 2 vols. slipcase. EX. C4. $100.00

PLATT, Kin. *Body Beautiful Murder.* 1976. Random House. 1st ed. dj. VG. P1. $17.50

PLATT, Kin. *Giant Kill.* 1974. Random House. 1st ed. sgn. dj. RS. EX. F5. $35.00

PLATT, Kin. *Kissing Gourami.* 1970. Random House. 1st ed. presentation. dj. EX. F5. $40.00

PLATT, Kin. *Screwball King Murder.* 1978. Random House. 1st ed. dj. VG. P1. $15.00

PLEASANTS, W.S. *Stingaree Murders.* 1932. Mystery League. 1st ed. VG. P1. $15.00

PLINY. *Epistles.* 1925. Bibliophile Soc. 1/405. 3 vols. lg octavo. slipcases. H3. $150.00

PLOMER, William. *Celebrations.* 1972. London. Cape. 1st ed. dj. EX. B13. $45.00

PLOMER, William. *Collected Poems.* 1960. London. Cape. 1st ed. dj. EX. B13. $85.00

PLOMER, William. *Dorking Thigh.* 1945. London. Cape. 1st ed. dj. EX. B13. $85.00

PLOMER, William. *George Gissing Exhibition.* 1971. London. Enitharmon Pr. 1st ed. 1/195. sgn. ES. EX. B13. $85.00

PLOMER, William. *Shot in the Dark.* 1955. London. Cape. 1st ed. dj. EX. B13. $65.00

PLOMER, William. *Taste & Remember.* 1966. London. Cape. 1st ed. dj. EX. B13. $45.00

PLOWMAN, G.T. *Etching & Other Graphic Arts.* 1914. NY. 1st ed. 154 p. T5. $35.00

PLOWRIGHT, Teresa. *Dreams of an Unseen Planet.* 1986. Arbor House. 1st ed. dj. RS. EX. P1. $17.50

PLUMMER, W. *Holy Goof.* 1981. Prentice Hall. 1st ed. dj. M. $40.00

PLUMMER & MCCALLA. *Public Discussion on Doctrine of Trinity.* 1842. Phil. Kay. 1st ed. 288 p. VG. B10. $8.25

PLUMPELLY. *Across Am & Asia.* 1870. Leypoldt Holt. 3rd ed. xl. A5. $50.00

PLUTARCH OF CHAERONEA. *Lives of Noble Grecians & Romans, Compared Together.* 1928. Houghton Mifflin. 1/500. 8 vols. lg octavo. Riverside bdg. H3. $900.00

PLUTARCH OF CHAERONEA. *Lives of Noble Grecians & Romans.* 1579. London. Trans 1st ed. folio. Riviere bdg. H3. $15000.00

POE, E.A. *Complete Works.* 1902. Putnam/Knickerbocker. Tamerlane ed. 1/300. 10 vols. EX. H3. $5000.00

POE, E.A. *Gold Bug (Az Aranybogar).* 1965. Budapest. Szepirodalmi Konyvkiado. 1st Hungarian ed. T9. $35.00

POE, E.A. *Murders in Rue Morgue.* 1958. Antibes. Allen. 1/150. EX. $175.00

POE, E.A. *Narrative of Arthur Gordon Pym.* 1930. Ltd Ed Club. 1/1500. slipcase. EX. C4. $60.00

POE, E.A. *Prose Tales of EA Poe.* 1883. Armstrong. 508 p. VG. $125.00

POE, E.A. *Raven & Other Poems.* 1942. Columbia U. ARC facsimile of 1845 ed. gilt brn bdg. VG. T9. $145.00

POE, E.A. *Selected Stories of Edgar Allen Poe.* nd. Armed Services Ed. PB. G. B4. $8.00

POE, E.A. *Tales & Poems.* c 1900. NY. Hall. Buckner Lib ed. 6 vols. octavo. H3. $200.00

POE, E.A. *Tales & Poems.* c 1900. Phil. Barrie. Lib ed. 1/250. 6 vols. lg octavo. H3. $250.00

POE, E.A. *Tales of Edgar Allan Poe.* 1965. Whitman. VG. P1. $5.00

POE, E.A. *Tales of Mystery & Imagination.* 1933. NY. Ils Clarke. dj. EX. $90.00

POE, E.A. *Tales of Mystery & Imagination.* 1941. Ltd Ed Club. Ils/sgn Wm Sharp. 1/1500. 4to. slipcase. EX. C4. $100.00

POE, E.A. *Works of the Late EA Poe.* 1850. NY. 2nd print. 2 vols. fair. T5. $65.00

POE, E.A. *Works.* 1902. Scribner. 10 vols. sm octavo. TEG. gr buckram. H3. $300.00

POE, E.A. *Works.* 1908. Lippincott. 8 vols. sm octavo. VG. H3. $275.00

POE, O.M. *Report of Transcontinental Railways.* 1883. Corps Army Engineers. fld map. 64 p. A5. $50.00

POGANY, Willy. *100 Years of W Reserve.* 1926. Hudson, OH. 8vo. wrp. $35.00

POGUE, F.C. *George C Marshall...1880-1939.* 1963. NY. 1st ed. 421 p. dj. VG. T5. $12.50

POHL, Frederick. *Assignment in Tomorrow.* nd. Book Club. VG. P1. $3.00

POHL, Frederick. *Best of Frederik Pohl.* nd. Book Club. dj. VG. P1. $4.50

POHL, Frederick. *Chernobyl.* 1987. Bantam. AP. EX. R3. $25.00

POHL, Frederick. *Cool War.* 1981. Del Rey. 1st ed. dj. VG. P1. $15.00

POHL, Frederick. *Digits & Dastards.* 1968. London. 1st HrdCvr ed. M. R3. $25.00

POHL, Frederick. *Galaxy 30 Years of SF.* nd. Book Club. dj. VG. P1. $6.00

POHL, Frederick. *Gateway Trip.* 1990. Del Rey. 1st ed. dj. EX. F5. $15.00

POHL, Frederick. *Gateway.* nd. Book Club. dj. VG. P1. $4.50

POHL, Frederick. *Heechee Rendezvous.* nd. Del Rey. 2nd ed. dj. EX. P1. $20.00

POHL, Frederick. *Jem.* 1978. St Martin. 1st ed. dj. EX. P1. $20.00

POHL, Frederick. *Man Plus.* 1976. Random House. 1st ed. sgn. dj. EX. F5. $50.00

POHL, Frederick. *Man Plus.* 1976. SF Book Club. inscr. dj. EX. R3. $15.00

POHL, Frederick. *Midas World.* 1983. St Martin. 1st ed. dj. EX. R3. $15.00

POHL, Frederick. *Nebula Winners 14.* 1980. Harper. 1st ed. dj. EX. P1. $15.00

POHL, Frederick. *SF Roll of Honor.* 1975. Random House. 1st ed. dj. EX. P1. $15.00

POHL, Frederick. *Starburst.* 1982. Del Rey. 1st ed. dj. VG. P1. $15.00

POHL, Frederick. *Tales From the Planet Earth.* 1986. St Martin. 1st ed. dj. VG. P1. $16.00

POHL, Frederick. *Way the Future Was.* nd. Book Club. dj. VG. P1. $5.00

POHL, Frederick. *Way the Future Was.* 1978. Del Rey. dj. VG. P1. $15.00

POHL, Frederick. *Way the Future Was.* 1979. Del Rey. VG. P1. $3.25

POHL, Frederick. *Years of the City.* 1984. Timescape. 1st ed. dj. VG. P1. $15.00

POHL, Frederick. *7th Galaxy Reader.* 1964. Doubleday. 2nd ed. dj. VG. P1. $15.00

POHL & KORNBLUTH. *Presidential Year.* 1956. Ballantine. HrdCvr/1st ed. dj. VG. scarce. B13. $200.00

POHL & KORNBLUTH. *Space Merchants.* 1953. Ballantine. 1st ed. dj. EX. R3. $250.00

POHL & KORNBLUTH. *Venus, Inc.* nd. Book Club. dj. EX. P1. $4.50

POHL & KORNBLUTH. *11th Galazy Reader.* 1969. Doubleday. 1st ed. dj. EX. R3. $15.00

POHL & WILLIAMSON. *Starchild Trilogy.* nd. Book Club. dj. VG. P1. $7.00

POHL & WILLIAMSON. *Undersea City.* 1958. Gnome. 1st ed. dj. EX. R3. $35.00

POHL & WILLIAMSON. *Undersea Quest.* 1954. Gnome. 1st ed. sgn Williamson. dj. EX. F5. $60.00

POHLMAN. *Vietnam II: Hist of 3rd Brigade, 82nd Airborne Division...* nd. (1969) np. 4to. photos. 141 p. orig mailer. C2. $85.00

POINC, Eugene. *Imagination: Illusions of Eugene Poinc.* 1981. Calgary. 1st ed. 101 p. NM. J3. $20.00

POINDEXTER. *Ayer Incas.* 1930. NY. 1st ed. 2 vols. VG. C2. $125.00

POLAK, Max. *Beeldtelegrafie en Televisie.* 1928. Kosmos. 1st ed. sm octavo. 72 p. wrp. scarce. H3. $175.00

POLL & LOTHAR. *Szene 1988 Mockba. Vier Kunstler, Vier Positionen...* 1988. Berlin. D4. $20.00

POLLARD, Alfred. *Romance of King Arthur & His Knights.* 1917. Macmillan. Ils Rackham. 1st ed. 1/250. VG. C1. $650.00

POLLARD, E.A. *Life of Jefferson Davis, Secret of Hist of S Confederacy.* 1869. Atlanta. 1st ed. 536 p. G. T5. $42.50

POLLARD, E.A. *Lost Cause: New S Hist of War of Confederates.* 1867. NY. Treat. 752 p. dj. VG. S1. $20.00

POLLARD, E.A. *S Hist of the War: Last Year of the War.* 1866. NY. Ils. 8vo. 363 p. blk bdg. G. G4. $29.00

POLLARD, E.A. *S Hist of the War: 2nd Year of the War.* 1866. NY. Ils. 8vo. 386 p. dk gr bdg. G. G4. $46.00

POLLARD, J.A. *John Greenleaf Whittier: Friend of Man.* 1949. Houghton Mifflin. 1st ed. 615 p. dj. V1. $9.00

POLLEY, R.L. *Lincoln: His Words & His World.* c 1965. NY. 1st ed. 4to. 98 p. dj. VG. G4. $8.00

POLLOCK, Channing. *Fool.* nd. Grosset Dunlap. Photoplay ed. VG. P1. $10.00

POLLOCK, H.E.D. *Architectural Survey Hill Country of Yucatan & N Campeche.* 1980. Peabody Mus. 1st ed. 4to. wrp. F2. $50.00

POLLOCK, J.C. *Mission MIA.* 1982. Crown. 1st ed. dj. EX. P1. $12.95

POLLOCK, Robert. *Course of Time: Poem.* 1834. Concord, NH. Eastman Webster. V1. $100.00

POLLOCK, W.H. *Imp of Henry Irving.* 1908. NY. Longman Gr. 1st ed. presentation. 140 p. VG. H3. $50.00

POLSKY, Thomas. *Cugel.* 1950. Dutton. 1st ed. G. P1. $12.50

POMERANTZ, Charlotte. *Chalk Doll.* 1989. Lippincott. Ils Frane Lessac. 1st ed. dj. EX. B13. $35.00

POND, G.E. *Shenandoah Valley.* nd. NY. Brussel. 287 p. PB. VG. S1. $6.00

POND. *Sportsman's Directory & Yearbook.* 1892. Pond Godley. Ils. 205 p. VG. A5. $125.00

PONIATOWSKA, Elena. *Dear Diego.* 1986. Pantheon. 1st ed. dj. EX. K2. $25.00

PONICSAN, Daryl. *Cinderella Liberty.* 1973. NY. 1st ed. dj. EX. $22.00

PONICSAN, Daryl. *Ringmaster.* 1978. NY. ARC. dj. M. $16.00

PONICSAN, Daryl. *Unmarried Man.* 1980. NY. 1st ed. dj. M. $12.00

POORE, B.P. *Life of US Grant.* nd. Donohue. 594 p. G. S1. $15.00

POORE, B.P. *60 Years in the Nat Metropolis.* c 1886. Phil. 2 vols. tan bdg. $75.00

POPE, Alexander. *Poetical Works.* 1785. Glasgow. Foulis Pr. 3 vols. VG. H3. $750.00

POPE, Alexander. *Works.* 1769. London. Bathurst. 5 vols. VG. H3. $900.00

POPE, Alexander. *Works.* 1835. London. Valpy. 4 vols. sm octavo. TEG. VG. H3. $300.00

POPE, C.H. *Giant Snakes.* 1961. NY. 1st ed. dj. VG. B3. $30.00

POPE, Gustavus. *Journey to Mars.* 1974. Hyperion. reprint of 1894 ed. EX. R3. $15.00

POPE, Jessie. *3 Jolly Anglers.* nd. London. Blackie. Ils. 4to. EX. R4. $75.00

POPE, Saxton. *Bows & Arrows.* c 1915. Berkley. 1st ed. 20 pls. dj. VG. B3. $135.00

POPE, Saxton. *Hunting With the Bow & Arrow.* 1925. Putnam. 1st ed. VG. K1. $45.00

POPE & POPE. *Antoinette Pope School Cookbook.* 1948. NY. 1st ed. dj. VG. B3. $22.50

POPENOE, Dorothy. *Santiago de Los Caballeros de Guatemala.* 1933. Harvard U. 1st ed. 74 p. F2. $20.00

POPHAM, Hugh. *Into Wind: Hist of British Naval Flying.* 1969. London. Ils 1st ed. 307 p. dj. VG. T5. $12.50

POPKIN, Zelda. *Death of Innocence.* 1971. Lippincott. 1st ed. dj. xl. P1. $5.00

POPKIN, Zelda. *Journey Home.* nd. Book Club. dj. VG. P1. $4.50

PORGES, Irwin. *Edgar Rice Burroughs.* 1976. Brigham Young U. 3rd ed. dj. EX. P1. $30.00

PORTER, B.P. *Old Canal Days.* 1942. Columbus. Premiere ed. sgn. 469 p. VG. T5. $42.50

PORTER, D.B. *N Am Negro Poets.* 1945. Hattiesburg, MS. 1st ed. wht wrp. VG. B13. $100.00

PORTER, D.D. *Naval Hist of the Civil War.* 1886. NY. 1st ed. 4to. 843 p. VG. scarce. G4. $79.00

PORTER, G.S. *At the Foot of the Rainbow.* nd. Grosset. 258 p. G. B10. $4.50

PORTER, G.S. *Daughter of the Land.* 1918. Doubleday. 1st ed. EX. $30.00

PORTER, G.S. *Freckles.* 1904. Grosset Dunlap. 433 p. A5. $60.00

PORTER, G.S. *Freckles.* 1965. Golden Pr. decor brd. VG. P1. $7.50

PORTER, G.S. *Girl of the Limberlost.* Aug 1909. Doubleday. 1st ed. EX. $45.00

PORTER, G.S. *Girl of the Limberlost.* 1909. Doubleday. 1st ed. G. $25.00

PORTER, G.S. *Homing With the Birds.* 1920. Doubleday. 2nd ed. H3. $200.00

PORTER, G.S. *Jesus of the Emerald.* 1923. Doubleday. 1st ed. glassine dj. EX. B3. $600.00

PORTER, G.S. *Laddie.* 1915. Doubleday. 1st ed. VG. $15.00

PORTER, G.S. *Magic Garden.* 1927. Garden City. 1st ed. 272 p. T5. $27.50

PORTER, G.S. *Michael O'Halloran.* 1915. Doubleday. Delft Series. VG. $50.00

PORTER, G.S. *Michael O'Halloran.* 1915. Doubleday. 1st ed. gr bdg. VG. $18.00

PORTER, G.S. *Moths of the Limberlost.* 1912. Doubleday. 1st ed. boxed. EX. $150.00

PORTER, G.S. *Music of the Wild.* 1910. NY. VG. $120.00

PORTER, G.S. *Song of the Cardinal.* 1903. Bobbs Merrill. 1st ed. VG. $90.00

PORTER, G.S. *Song of the Cardinal.* 1906. Indianapolis. New ed. VG. $50.00

PORTER, G.S. *What I Have Done With Birds.* 1907. Bobbs Merrill. Ils. 257 p. scarce. A5. $220.00

PORTER, Horace. *Campaigning With Grant.* 1982. Time Life. reprint of 1897 ed. S1. $17.50

PORTER, Joyce. *Package Included Murder.* 1976. Bobbs Merrill. 1st ed. dj. VG. P1. $20.00

PORTER, K.A. *Collected Essays & Occasional Writings.* 1970. Delacorte. Ltd ed. 1/250. sgn. TEG. boxed. H3. $125.00

PORTER, K.A. *Defense of Circe.* 1954. NY. Ltd 1st ed. EX. $40.00

PORTER, K.A. *French Song Book.* 1933. Paris. Harrison. 1/595 on Van Gelder. sgn. dj. VG. H3. $175.00

PORTER, K.A. *Hacienda.* 1934. NY. Harrison of Paris. Ltd ed. 1/895. inscr. boxed. H3. $200.00

PORTER, K.A. *Leaning Tower.* 1944. NY. 1st ed. dj. EX. $75.00

PORTER, K.A. *Never-Ending Wrong.* 1977. Boston. 1st ed. dj. M. $12.00

PORTER, K.A. *Never-Ending Wrong.* 1977. Little Brn. UP. wrp. EX. B13. $95.00

PORTER, K.A. *Ship of Fools.* 1962. Boston. 1st ed. dj. M. $30.00

PORTER & AUERBACH. *Mexican Churches.* 1988. NM U. 4to. 109 p. F2. $30.00

PORTER & SUNDER. *Matt Field on the Santa Fe Trail.* 1960. OK. 1st ed. 315 p. dj. A5. $40.00

PORTIS, Charles. *True Grit.* 1968. NY. 1st ed. dj. EX. $12.00

PORZIO. *Lithography: 200 Years of Art, Hist, & Technique.* 1982. Abrams. Ils. 280 p. A5. $60.00

POST, C.C. *10 Years a Cowboy.* 1895. Rhodes McClure. VG. $16.00

POST, M.D. *Strange Schemes of Randoph Mason.* 1973. Oswald Train. 1st ed. dj. EX. P1. $15.00

POST, M.D. *Uncle Abner.* 1918. Appleton. 1st ed. G. F5. $55.00

POST, Wiley. *Around the World in 8 Days.* 1931. Chicago. 1st ed. dj. VG. B3. $40.00

POTOK, Chaim. *Book of Lights.* 1981. NY. 1st ed. dj. EX. $25.00

POTOK, Chaim. *Wanderings.* 1978. NY. Ltd ed. sgn. slipcase. EX. $95.00

POTTER, Beatrix. *Tale of Benjamin Bunny.* 1904. London. 1st ed. orig brd. VG. H3. $600.00

POTTER, Beatrix. *Tale of Jemima Puddle Duck.* 1908. London. 1st ed. H3. $300.00

POTTER, D.M. *Impending Crisis 1848-1861.* 1976. Harper Row. 638 p. VG. S1. $7.00

POTTER, Dennis. *Sufficient Carbohydrate.* 1983. London. 1st ed. inscr. wrp. EX. T9. $60.00

POTTER, J. *Treasure Diver's Guide.* 1972. NY. Revised 1st ed. 567 p. dj. B3. $35.00

POTTER, Stephen. *Anti-Woo.* 1965. NY. 1st ed. dj. EX. $12.00

POTTER, Stephen. *Gamesmanship.* nd. NY. Holt. 128 p. dj. EX. J3. $7.00

POTTER, Stephen. *Lifemanship.* 1951. NY. 1st ed. dj. EX. $18.00

POTTS, Jean. *Affair of the Heart.* 1970. Gollancz. 1st ed. dj. xl. P1. $5.00

POTTS, Jean. *Lightning Strikes Twice.* 1958. Scribner. 1st ed. dj. xl. P1. $5.00

POTTS, Jean. *Man With the Cane.* 1957. Doubleday Book Club. VG. P1. $7.50

POUND, Ezra. *Cantos (1-95).* 1956. New Directions. 1st ed. dj. EX. C4. $100.00

POUND, Ezra. *Imaginary Letters.* 1930. Blk Sun. 1st ed. 1/300. wrp/glassine/slipcase. EX. H3. $350.00

POUND, Ezra. *Lume Spento.* 1965. New Directions. 1st ed. glassine dj. M. $28.00

POUND, Ezra. *Selected Cantos of Ezra Pound.* 1967. London. Faber. Trade PB ed. presentation. wrp. slipcase. H3. $500.00

POUND, Ezra. *Ta Hio.* 1928. WA U. 1st ed. 1/575. wrp. EX. $110.00

POUND & MIA. *Discussion of the Arts, Their Use & Future in Am.* 1950. (1st 1913) Chicago. dj. VG. $50.00

POURNELLE, Jerry. *King David's Spaceship.* nd. Book Club. dj. VG. P1. $4.50

POURNELLE, Jerry. *King David's Spaceship.* 1980. Simon Schuster. 1st ed. dj. EX. R3. $12.50

POURNELLE, Jerry. *Storms of Victory.* 1987. Ace. 1st ed. dj. VG. P1. $16.95

POURNELLE, Jerry. *That Buck Rogers Stuff.* 1977. Extequer Pr. 1st ed. 1/500. sgn. dj. EX. R3. $35.00

POURNELLE, Jerry. *War World Vol I: The Burning Eye.* 1988. Baen. 1st ed. wrp. EX. F5. $7.00

POWELL, A.M. *Personal Reminiscences of the Anti-Slavery...Reformers.* 1899. Plainfield, NJ. AR Powell. 1st ed. 8vo. 279 p. V1. $18.00

POWELL, E.A. *End of the Trail.* 1924. NY. 1st ed. VG. $30.00

POWELL, E.A. *In Barbary: Tunisia, Algeria, Morocco, & Sahara.* 1926. Century. 483 p. VG. J2. $15.00

POWELL, E.A. *Vive la France!* 1915. Scribner. 1st ed. 254 p. VG. B10. $8.25

POWELL, H.M.T. *Santa Fe Trail.* 1931. Grabhorn. 1/300. folio. EX. H3. $2500.00

POWELL, J.W. *Exploration of the CO River.* 1957. Chicago. Intro Wallace Stegner. 1st ed. dj. EX. B13. $65.00

POWELL, J.W. *2nd Annual Report of US Geol Survey 1880-1881.* 1882. GPO. Ils. 4to. 588 p. VG. T1. $90.00

POWELL, L.C. *Profiles of People & Places of the SW & Beyond.* 1976. Northland. Ltd ed. 1/100. sgns. boxed. H3. $125.00

POWELL, Lester. *Spot the Lady.* 1950. Collins Crime Club. 1st ed. dj. VG. P1. $15.00

POWELL, Nicolas. *Sacred Spring: Arts in Vienna 1898-1918.* 1974. NY Graphic Soc. 1st Am ed. 4to. 224 p. dj. EX. R4. $50.00

POWELL, Padgett. *Typical.* 1991. Farrar Straus. UP. wrp. EX. C4. $40.00

POWELL, Padgett. *Typical.* 1991. Farrar Straus. 1st ed. sgn. dj. M. C4. $35.00

POWELL, Padgett. *Woman Named Drown.* 1987. Farrar Straus. UP. wrp. EX. C4. $45.00

POWELL, Richard. *False Clrs.* nd. Book Club. dj. VG. P1. $5.00

POWELL, Talmage. *Priceless Particle.* 1969. Whitman. VG. P1. $7.50

POWELL, Talmage. *Smasher.* 1959. Macmillan. 1st ed. dj. w/sgn label. P1. $35.00

POWELL, Talmage. *Thing in B-3.* 1969. Whitman. VG. P1. $5.00

POWELL, Van. *Haunted Hanger.* 1932. Saalfied. VG. P1. $7.50

POWELL, Watson. *Elmos Scott: Professor Goes W.* 1954. IL U. 134 p. A5. $45.00

POWERS, J.F. *Prince of Darkness & Other Stories.* 1948. NY. 1st ed. sgn. dj. VG. T9. $125.00

POWERS, J.L. *Blk Abyss.* 1966. Arcadia. dj. VG. P1. $12.50

POWERS, Thomas. *War at Home.* 1973. Grossman. 1st ed. 348 p. dj. NM. B10. $7.00

POWERS, Tim. *Anubis Gates.* 1989. Zeising. 1st HrdCvr ed. M. R3. $25.00

POWERS, Tim. *Dinner at Deviant's Palace.* nd. Book Club. dj. VG. P1. $7.50

POWERS, Tim. *On Stranger Tides.* 1987. Ultramarine. 1st ed. 1/150. sgn. M. R3. $200.00

POWERS, Tom. *Horror Movies.* 1989. Lerner. 1st ed. VG. P1. $15.00

POWYS, J.C. *Autobiography.* 1934. NY. 1st Am ed. C1. $7.50

POWYS, J.C. *Suspended Judgments. Essays on Books & Sensations.* 1916. NY. Shaw. sgn. H3. $100.00

POWYS, J.C. *Wood & Stone: A Romance.* 1915. NY. Shaw. inscr. dj. H3. $250.00

POWYS, Llewelyn. *Earth Memories.* 1938. NY. 1st ed. dj. EX. $38.00

POWYS, Llewelyn. *Skin for Skin.* 1926. London. 1st ed. 1/900. 151 p. w/sgn note. T5. $75.00

POWYS, Llewelyn. *Verdict of Bridlegoose.* 1927. London. 1st ed. 1/900. 143 p. G. T5. $25.00

POWYS & POWYS. *Tithe Barn/Dover & the Eagle.* 1932. London. Bhat. sgns. blk bdg. H3. $75.00

POYER, Joe. *Contract.* 1978. Atheneum. 1st ed. VG. P1. $10.00

POYER, Joe. *N Cape.* 1969. Doubleday. 1st ed. dj. xl. P1. $5.00

POYER, Joe. *Operation Malacca.* 1968. Doubleday. 1st ed. dj. EX. F5. $16.00

PRADA, Renato. *Breach.* 1971. Doubleday. 1st ed. dj. EX. K2. $35.00

PRAGER, Emily. *Clea & Zeus Divorce.* 1987. Vintage. PB Orig/1st ed. inscr. wrp. EX. C4. $25.00

PRAGER, Emily. *Visit From the Footbinder.* 1982. Wyndham. UP. EX. K2. $65.00

PRAGNELL, Festus. *Gr Man of Graypec.* 1950. Greenburg. 1st ed. dj. EX. R3. $30.00

PRANGBORN, Edgar. *Davy.* 1967. Dobson. dj. EX. P1. $35.00

PRANGBORN, Edgar. *Judgment of Eve.* 1966. Simon Schuster. 1st ed. dj. xl. P1. $12.50

PRANGBORN, Edgar. *W of the Sun.* 1953. Doubleday. 1st ed. dj. VG. P1. $35.00

PRANTERA, Amanda. *Strange Loop.* 1984. Dutton. 1st ed. dj. EX. F5. $15.00

PRASSE, L.E. *Lyonel Feininger: Difinitive Catalog of His Graphic Work.* 1972. Cleveland Mus of Art. 1st ed. 4to. 304 p. dj. EX. R4. $275.00

PRATCHETT, Terry. *Strata.* 1981. St Martin. 1st ed. dj. EX. R3. $13.50

PRATHER, R.S. *Amber Effect.* 1986. Tor Books. 1st ed. dj. EX. P1. $12.95

PRATHER, R.S. *Kubla Khan Caper.* 1966. Trident Pr. 1st ed. dj. EX. F5. $32.00

PRATO, Piero. *Caproni Reggiane Fighters 1938-1945.* 1971. Genoa. Ils. 64 p. T5. $8.50

PRATT, Fletcher. *Civil War in Pictures.* 1955. Garden City. 256 p. G. S1. $5.00

PRATT, Fletcher. *Marines War.* 1948. NY. 1st ed. 456 p. dj. VG. B3. $30.00

PRATT, Fletcher. *Night Work.* 1946. NY. 1st ed. 267 p. dj. VG. B3. $22.50

PRATT, Fletcher. *Secret & Urgent: Story of Codes & Ciphers.* 1942. Bl Ribbon. 282 p. VG. B10. $4.50

PRATT, Fletcher. *Undying Fire.* 1953. Ballantine. 1st ed. dj. EX. R3. $40.00

PRATT, Fletcher. *World of Wonder.* 1951. Twayne. 1st ed. dj. EX. R3. $30.00

PRATT, PIPER, & MERRILL. *Petrified Planet.* 1952. Twayne. 1st ed. dj. EX. R3. $50.00

PRATT, R.K. *You Tell My Son.* 1958. NY. 1st ed. dj. EX. $15.00

PRATT, Samuel. *Paternal Present.* 1802. London. 1st ed. G. $95.00

PRATT, Samuel. *Scriptural Stories for Very Young Children.* 1814. Phil. 12mo. 68 p. wrp. $100.00

PRATT, Theodore. *Murder Goes to the World's Fair.* nd. Eldon. VG. P1. $25.00

PRATT, Theodore. *Valley Boy.* 1946. Duell. 1st ed. dj. EX. F5. $12.00

PRATT & WHITNEY AIRCRAFT CO. *Overhaul Manual, Twin Wasp, C-Series Engines.* 1940. E Hartford. Ils. T5. $95.00

PREDMORE, R.L. *Cervantes by Richard L Predmore.* 1973. Dodd Mead. 1st Am ed. 4to. 224 p. dj. EX. C4. $25.00

PREISS, Byron. *Raymond Chandler's Philip Marlowe.* 1988. Knopf. 1st ed. dj. EX. P1. $18.95

PRESCOTT, W.H. *Conquest of Mexico.* 1844. Paris. 1st French ed in Eng text. 3 vols. F2. $125.00

PRESCOTT, W.H. *Conquest of Peru.* 1890. Internat Book Co. 2 vols. VG. $35.00

PRESCOTT, W.H. *Hist of Conquest of Peru.* nd. Heritage. Ils Everett Gee Jackson. 504 p. F2. $15.00

PRESCOTT, W.H. *Works.* 1851. Harper. 8 vols. VG. H3. $400.00

PRESCOTT, W.H. *Works.* 1878. London. Routledge. 12 vols. octavo. H3. $550.00

PREUSS, Paul. *Starfire.* 1988. Tor Books. 1st ed. dj. EX. P1. $17.95

PREVOST, Abbe. *Manon Lescaut.* 1928. London/NY. Ils Alastair. Ltd ed. 1/1850. EX. R4. $125.00

PRICE, Anthony. *Col Butler's Wolf.* 1973. Crime Club. 1st ed. dj. xl. P1. $6.00

PRICE, Anthony. *Gummer Kelly.* 1984. Doubleday Crime Club. 1st ed. dj. VG. P1. $11.95

PRICE, Anthony. *October Men.* 1974. Crime Club. 1st ed. dj. xl. P1. $5.00

PRICE, C. *Memories of Old MT.* 1945. Pasadena. 7th print. 154 p. dj. VG. B3. $27.50

PRICE, C.M. *Poster Design.* 1922. NY. New Enlarged ed. $150.00

PRICE, E.H. *Far Lands, Other Days.* 1975. Carcosa. Ils Evans. Ltd 1st ed. 1/2000. dj. EX. C1. $32.50

PRICE, E.L. *Hist of E Cleveland.* 1970. np. Ils. sgn. 93 p. VG. T5. $35.00

PRICE, H.A. *Memoir of Hannah A Price.* 1889. Norristown. Wills. 12mo. 157 p. VG. V1. $9.00

PRICE, M.E. *Angora Twinnies.* c 1915. Rochester, NY. Stecher Litho Co. EX. $35.00

PRICE, Pattie. *Bantu Tales.* 1938. NY. Ils Desmond Smith. 1st ed. dj. T5. $25.00

PRICE, Reynolds. *Country Mouse, City Mouse.* 1981. NC Wesleyan College. 1st Separate ed. sgn. wrp. EX. K2. $85.00

PRICE, Reynolds. *Kate Vaiden.* 1986. Atheneum. UP. wrp. EX. C4. $60.00

PRICE, Reynolds. *Nativity From the Apocryphal of James.* 1974. private print. 1/225. sgn. K2. $75.00

PRICE, Reynolds. *Palpable God: 30 Stories Trans From the Bible...* 1978. Atheneum. 1st ed. inscr. dj. EX. C4. $50.00

PRICE, Reynolds. *Presence & Absence: Versions From the Bible.* 1973. Bruccoli Clark. Ltd ed. 1/300. sgn. slipcase. H3. $75.00

PRICE, Reynolds. *Real Copies: Will Price, Crichton Davis, Phyllis Peacock...* 1988. NC Wesleyan Pr. 1/26. sgn. wrp. w/photo. EX. C4. $175.00

PRICE, Reynolds. *Surface of Earth.* 1975. Atheneum. 1st ed. dj. EX. B13. $50.00

PRICE, Reynolds. *Thing Itself.* 1966. Friend of Duke U Lib. pamphlet. 1/750. EX. K2. $100.00

PRICE, Richard. *Wanderers.* 1974. Boston. 1st ed. dj. M. $26.00

PRICE, Richard. *Wanderers.* 1974. NY. 1st ed. sgn. dj. EX. T9. $45.00

PRICE, Uvedale. *Essays on the Picturesque.* 1810. London. 3 vols. H3. $1000.00

PRICE, Vincent. *I Like What I Know: Visual Autobiography.* 1959. NY. 1st ed. dj. VG. $20.00

PRICE, Willard. *Roving S.* 1948. John Day. 1st ed. 373 p. dj. F2. $15.00

PRICE & PRICE. *Treasury of Great Recipes.* 1965. Ampersand. 1st ed. padded leather. glassine dj. EX. B3. $60.00

PRICHARD, Anita. *Fondue Magic.* nd. (1969) Hearthside. apparent 1st ed. 192 p. dj. EX. B10. $4.50

PRIESS, Byron. *Planets.* 1985. Bantam. 1st ed. inscr. M. R3. $30.00

PRIESS, Byron. *Universe.* 1987. Bantam. 1st ed. inscr. dj. EX. R3. $27.50

PRIEST, Christopher. *Darkening Island.* 1972. Harper. 1st Am ed. dj. EX. R3. $8.50

PRIEST, Christopher. *Dream of Wessex.* 1977. Faber Faber. 1st ed. dj. EX. F5. $25.00

PRIEST, Christopher. *Glamour.* 1985. Doubleday. 1st ed. dj. EX. P1. $15.95

PRIEST, Christopher. *Indoctrinaire.* 1970. Harper. 1st Am ed. dj. EX. R3. $15.00

PRIEST, Christopher. *Infinite Summer.* 1979. Scribner. 1st ed. dj. EX. P1. $15.00

PRIEST, J.C. *Forbidden.* 1952. Woodford Pr. 1st ed. dj. EX. F5. $20.00

PRIEST, J.M. *Antietam: Soldiers' Battle.* 1989. Wht Mane. 437 p. dj. M. S1. $34.95

PRIESTLEY, J.B. *Angel Pavement.* nd. Dent. 4th ed. VG. P1. $15.00

PRIESTLEY, J.B. *Blackout in Gretley.* 1943. Clipper Books. dj. EX. P1. $30.00

PRIESTLEY, J.B. *Carfitt Crisis.* 1976. NY. 1st ed. dj. M. $14.00

PRIESTLEY, J.B. *Daylight on Saturday.* 1943. Harper. 3rd ed. 280 p. dj. VG. B10. $3.50

PRIESTLEY, J.B. *Daylight on Saturday.* 1943. NY. 1st ed. dj. EX. $17.00

PRIESTLEY, J.B. *Faraway.* 1932. Macmillan. 1st ed. VG. P1. $25.00

PRIESTLEY, J.B. *Festival at Farbridge.* 1951. Heinemann. 1st ed. VG. P1. $30.00

PRIESTLEY, J.B. *Good Companions.* 1929. Harper. 1st ed. VG. P1. $35.00

PRIESTLEY, J.B. *Good Companions.* 1929. Harper. 1st ed. 639 p. G. B10. $4.50

PRIESTLEY, J.B. *Good Companions.* 1930. Musson. VG. P1. $25.00

PRIESTLEY, J.B. *It's an Old Country.* nd. Atlantic/Little Brn. 2nd ed. dj. EX. P1. $17.50

PRIESTLEY, J.B. *Lost Empires.* 1966. Reprint Soc. dj. VG. P1. $7.50

PRIESTLEY, J.B. *Saturn Over the Water.* 1961. Heinemann. 1st ed. dj. VG. P1. $25.00

PRIESTLEY, J.B. *Shapes of Sleep.* 1962. Heinemann. 1st ed. dj. VG. P1. $25.00

PRIESTLEY, J.B. *31st of June: Tale of True Love, Enterprise, Progress...* 1962. 1st Am ed. dj. VG. C1. $27.50

PRIME, W.C. *Among the N Hills.* 1895. NY. 1st ed. 209 p. VG. B3. $15.00

PRINCE, H.A. *Grandma's Album Quilt.* 1936. Portland, ME. 1st ed. dj. VG. B3. $30.00

PRINCHON, Edgcumb. *Dan Sickles, Hero of Gettysburg & Yankee King of Spain.* 1945. Garden City. 1st ed. 280 p. dj. T5. $17.50

PRINGLE, Cyrus. *Record of a Quaker Conscience.* 1918. Macmillan. 1st ed. 16mo. V1. $12.00

PROCTER, Maurice. *Body To Spare.* nd. Book Club. dj. VG. P1. $4.50

PROCTER, Maurice. *Hideaway.* 1968. Harper Row. 1st ed. dj. xl. P1. $5.00

PROCTER, Maurice. *His Weight in Gold.* nd. Book Club. dj. VG. P1. $4.50

PROCTER, Maurice. *His Weight in Gold.* 1966. Harper Row. 1st ed. dj. EX. P1. $17.50

PROCTER, Maurice. *Homicide Blond.* 1965. Harper Row. 1st ed. dj. VG. P1. $15.00

PROCTER, Maurice. *Killer at Lg.* 1976. John Long. dj. VG. P1. $15.00

PROCTER, Maurice. *Rogue Running.* 1966. Harper Row. 1st ed. dj. EX. P1. $17.50

PROCTER, Maurice. *2 Men in 20.* nd. Book Club. dj. VG. P1. $4.50

PRODGES, C.H. *Adventures in Bolivia.* 1922. Dodd Mead. 1st ed. 232 p. dj. F2. $40.00

PROKOSCH, Frederic. *Strom & Echo.* 1948. Doubleday. sgn. gilt blk bdg. lavender slipcase. H3. $125.00

PRONZINI, Bill. *Arbor House Treasury of Horror.* 1981. Arbor House. 1st ed. dj. EX. P1. $30.00

PRONZINI, Bill. *Gun in Cheek.* 1982. Coward McCann. 1st ed. dj. EX. F5. $16.00

PRONZINI, Bill. *Mummy!* 1980. Arbor House. 1st ed. dj. EX. R3. $15.00

PRONZINI, Bill. *Quicksilver.* nd. Book Club. dj. VG. P1. $4.50

PRONZINI, Bill. *Scatter-Shot.* 1982. St Martin. 1st ed. dj. EX. F5. $17.50

PRONZINI, Bill. *Shackles.* 1988. St Martin. 1st ed. dj. VG. P1. $16.95

PRONZINI, Bill. *Sm Felonies.* 1988. St Martin. 1st ed. dj. EX. F5. $15.00

PRONZINI, Bill. *Specter!* 1982. Arbor House. 1st ed. dj. EX. P1. $15.00

PRONZINI, Bill. *Voodoo!* 1980. Arbor House. 1st ed. dj. EX. R3. $15.00

PRONZINI, Bill. *Werewolf!* nd. SF Book Club. dj. EX. R3. $8.50

PRONZINI & MALZBERG. *Prose Bowl.* 1980. St Martin. 1st ed. dj. EX. F5. $20.00

PRONZINI & MULLER. *Deadly Arts.* 1985. Arbor House. 1st ed. dj. VG. P1. $15.95

PROPPER, M.M. *Ticker Tape Murder.* 1930. Harper. 4th ed. VG. P1. $15.00

PROSCHOWSKY, Frantz. *Way To Sing.* 1923. Boston. Birchard. octavo. 131 p. VG. H3. $35.00

PROSKAUER, J.J. *How'd Ja Do That?...* 1934. NY. Popper Co. 1st ed. sgn. 92 p. EX. J3. $14.00

PROSKOURIAKOFF, Titiana. *Jades From the Cenote of Sacrifice, Chichen Itza.* 1974. Peabody Mus. 4to. 216 p. wrp. F2. $75.00

PROTESTANT EPISCOPAL CHURCH. *Book of Common Prayer.* nd. (1935) Nelson. crown 8vo. 1000 p. AEG. boxed. B10. $5.00

PROTTER & PROTTER. *Folk & Fairy Tales of Far-Off Lands.* 1965. Duell. Ils Rosenwasser. dj. EX. B10. $6.50

PROUST, Marcel. *Recherche du Temps Perdu.* c 1919. Paris. Gallimard. 16 vols. octavo. H3. $375.00

PROUTY, Amy. *Mexico & I.* 1951. Dorrance. 1st ed. 258 p. F2. $10.00

PRYOR & PRYOR. *Airplane Book.* 1935. Harcourt Brace. Ils. 98 p. probably rebound. G. T5. $12.50

PSEUDOMAN, Akkad. To 80. 1937. Scientific Pub. 1st ed. dj. VG. P1. $35.00

PSEUDOMAN, Akkad. To 80. 1937. Scientific Pub. 1st ed. VG. R3. $25.00

PUGIN & PUGIN. *Gothic Architecture Selected...Ancient Edifices in Eng.* 1923. Cleveland. 5 vols in 1. portfolio-style bdg. G. T5. $65.00

PULLAN, Mrs. *Lady's Manual of Fancy Work.* 1859. NY. Ils. VG. C2. $75.00

PULLEN, J.J. *Shower of Stars.* 1966. Lippincott. 1st ed. presentation. $45.00

PULLEN, J.J. *20th ME.* 1957. Phil. 1st ed. dj. VG. B3. $45.00

PULLINGER, Kate. *When the Moster Dies.* 1989. Jonathan Cape. 1st UK ed. dj. EX. F5. $15.00

PULS, Herta. *Textiles of the Kuna, Indians of Panama.* 1988. Aylesbury. 72 p. wrp. F2. $10.00

PURCELL, L.H. *Miracle in MS.* nd. (1965) Comet Pr. 1st ed? 252 p. dj. VG. B10. $12.00

PURSER, Philip. *4 Days to the Fireworks.* 1965. Walker. 1st ed. dj. VG. P1. $12.50

PURSH, Frederick. *Journal of Botanical Excursion NE Parts...PA & NY in 1807.* 1923. Syracuse. reprint of 1869 ed. 113 p. wrp. T5. $35.00

PURTILL, Richard. *JRR Toklien: Myth, Morality, & Religion.* 1984. Harper. 1st ed. RS. M. R3. $12.95

PUSHKIN, Alexander. *Captain's Daughter.* 1928. Viking. 1st Complete Eng Trans ed. dj. scarce. VG. B13. $85.00

PUSHKIN, Alexander. *Eugene Onegin: A Novel in Verse.* 1964. Bollingen/Pantheon. 1st ed. 4 vols. djs. slipcase. EX. C4. $275.00

PUSHKIN, Alexander. *4 Stories...* 1987. Greenbrae. Allen Pr. Ils John De Pol. 1/145. EX. H3. $375.00

PUTNAM, Ruth. *Alsace & Lorraine.* 1915. Putnam. 2nd ed. VG. B10. $10.00

PUTNAM, S.B. *Richmond During the War.* 1982. Time Life. reprint of 1867 ed. EX. S1. $17.50

PUZO, Mario. *Dark Arena.* 1955. NY. 1st ed. dj. VG. B3. $25.00

PUZO, Mario. *Fools Die.* 1978. Putnam. Ltd ed. 1/350. sgn. H3. $50.00

PUZO, Mario. *Fools Die.* 1978. Putnam. 1st ed. presentation. dj. EX. H3. $125.00

PUZO, Mario. *Fortunate Pilgrim.* 1965. Heinemann. 1st Eng ed. presentation. dj. EX. H3. $125.00

PUZO, Mario. *Godfather.* 1969. Putnam. ARC. presentation. wrp. EX. H3. $400.00

PUZO, Mario. *Sicilian.* 1984. Linden Pr. 1st ed. dj. VG. P1. $17.95

PYEN, J.B. *Lake Scenery of Eng.* 1859. London. 25 lithos. gilt embossed gr cloth. recased. VG. T5. $125.00

PYLE, Ernie. *Brave Men.* nd. (1944) Holt. Book Club ed? VG. B10. $3.75

PYLE, Howard. *Merry Adventures of Robin Hood.* 1908. NY. Scribner. G. $20.00

PYLE, Howard. *Merry Adventures of Robin Hood.* 1968. Dover. 1st ed. VG. C1. $4.50

PYLE, Howard. *Story of Champions of the Round Table.* 1905. NY. 1st ed. EX. $50.00

PYLE, Howard. *Story of Champions of the Round Table.* 1922. Scribner. C1. $16.00

PYLE, Howard. *Story of Champions of the Round Table.* 1968. Dover. PB. VG. C1. $5.00

PYM, Barbara. *Unsuitable Attachment.* 1982. London. Macmillan. UP. wrp. VG. K2. $65.00

PYM, Horace. *Memories of Old Friends.* 1882. Lippincott. apparent 1st ed? 378 p. VG. B10. $15.00

PYNCHON, Thomas. *Crying of Lot 49.* 1966. Lippincott. 1st ed. dj. C4. $275.00

PYNCHON, Thomas. *Crying of Lot 49.* 1966. Lippincott. 1st ed. dj. EX. K2. $285.00

PYNCHON, Thomas. *Gravity's Rainbow.* 1973. Viking. ARC. dj. VG. RS. rare. K2. $750.00

PYNCHON, Thomas. *Low Lands.* 1978. Aloes Books. Pirate pamphlet. 1/1500. wrp. EX. K2. $45.00

PYNCHON, Thomas. *Lowlands.* 1978. Aloes Books. 2nd print. 1/500. M. B4. $10.00

PYNCHON, Thomas. *Secret Integration.* 1980. London. Aloes Books. Pirate ed. wrp. EX. K2. $40.00

PYNCHON, Thomas. *Secret Integration.* 1980. London. Aloes Books. 1st ed. wrp. EX. B13. $40.00

PYNCHON, Thomas. *Slow Learner.* 1984. Boston. 1st ed. dj. EX. $45.00

PYNCHON, Thomas. *Sm Rain.* nd. London. Aloes Books. 1st ed. wrp. EX. B13. $40.00

PYNCHON, Thomas. *V.* 1963. Lippincott. ARC. dj. RS. scarce. K2. $1250.00

PYNCHON, Thomas. *V.* 1963. Lippincott. 1st ed. dj. EX. C4. $375.00

PYNE, H.R. *Hist of 1st NJ Cavalry.* 1871. Trenton. 1st ed. 350 p. VG. $95.00

QUAIFE, M.M. *Siege of Detroit in 1763: Journal of Pontiac's Conspiracy...* 1958. Lakeside Classic. 293 p. VG. T5. $25.00

QUARLES, Francis. *Argalus & Parthenia.* 1656. London. Last Corrected ed. sm quarto. Riviere bdg. H3. $3500.00

QUARRY, Nick; see Albert, Marvin H.

QUEEN, Ellery. *Brn Fox Mystery.* 1955. Little Brn. 4th ed. dj. VG. P1. $15.00

QUEEN, Ellery. *Case Book of Ellery Queen.* 1945. Bestseller Mystery B59. 1st ed. G. T9. $30.00

QUEEN, Ellery. *Cherished Classics.* 1978. Davis Pub. 351 p. AEG. EX. B10. $4.25

QUEEN, Ellery. *Chinese Orange Mystery.* 1934. Stokes. 1st ed. xl. P1. $12.50

QUEEN, Ellery. *Chinese Orange Mystery.* 1941. Triangle. dj. VG. P1. $10.00

QUEEN, Ellery. *Devil To Pay.* 1941. Triangle. dj. VG. P1. $10.00

QUEEN, Ellery. *Devil To Pay.* 1946. Tower. VG. P1. $10.00

QUEEN, Ellery. *Door Between.* 1941. Triangle. VG. P1. $10.00

QUEEN, Ellery. *Egyptian Cross Mystery.* 1941. Triangle. 4th ed. dj. VG. P1. $12.00

QUEEN, Ellery. *Fine & Private Place.* 1973. Doubleday Book Club. EX. P1. $7.50

QUEEN, Ellery. *Halfway House.* Triangle. dj. VG. P1. $10.00

QUEEN, Ellery. *Literature of Crime.* 1952. Cassell. 1st ed. dj. VG. P1. $20.00

QUEEN, Ellery. *Multitude of Sins.* 1978. Dial. 1st ed. dj. VG. P1. $15.00

QUEEN, Ellery. *New Adventures of Ellery Queen.* nd. Triangle. dj. VG. P1. $10.00

QUEEN, Ellery. *Player on the Other Side.* nd. Book Club. dj. VG. P1. $4.00

QUEEN, Ellery. *Queen's Awards 1946.* 1946. Little Brn. 1st ed. P1. $12.50

QUEEN, Ellery. *Red Chipmunk Mystery.* 1946. Lippincott. 1st ed. dj. EX. P1. $45.00

QUEEN, Ellery. *Rogues Gallery: Great Criminals of Modern Fiction.* 1945. Little Brn. 1st ed. 562 p. VG. B10. $10.00

QUEEN, Ellery. *Roman Hat Mystery.* 1948. Tower. P1. $10.00

QUEEN, Ellery. *Siamese Twin Mystery.* 1946. Triangle. dj. VG. P1. $12.50

QUEEN, Ellery. *There Was an Old Woman.* 1943. Little Brn. 1st ed. VG. P1. $30.00

QUEEN, Ellery. *To the Queen's Taste.* 1946. Little Brn. 1st ed. VG. P1. $30.00

QUEEN, Ellery. *Tragedy of X.* nd. Grosset Dunlap. dj. VG. P1. $10.00

QUEEN, Ellery. *Tragedy of X.* 1978. CA U. VG. P1. $10.00

QUEEN, Ellery. *10 Days' Wonder.* 1948. Little Brn. VG. P1. $10.00

QUEEN, Ellery. *4 of Hearts.* 1941. Triangle. dj. VG. P1. $12.50

QUEEN, Ellery. *4 of Hearts.* 1946. Tower. 1st ed. VG. P1. $10.00

QUEEN, Ellery. *4th Side of the Triangle.* nd. Book Club. VG. P1. $3.00

QUEEN & SULLIVAN. *Blighted Dwellings.* 1986. Longmeadow. 2nd ed. 288 p. dj. NM. B10. $4.25

QUENNELL, C.H.B. *Modern Suburban Houses.* 1906. London. 1st ed. G. R5. $60.00

QUENNELL, Peter. *Inscr on a Fountainhead.* 1929. London. Faber. Ltd ed. 1/300. sgn. H3. $25.00

QUENNELL, Peter. *Samuel Johnson: His Friends & Enemies.* 1973. Am Heritage Pr. 1st Am ed. 4to. 272 p. dj. EX. C4. $20.00

QUENNELL, Peter. *Sgn of the Fish.* nd. (1960) Viking. Book Club ed? 255 p. VG. B10. $4.50

QUENTIN, Patrick. *Follower.* nd. Book Club. dj. VG. P1. $4.50

QUENTIN, Patrick. *Follower.* 1950. Simon Schuster. 1st ed. dj. VG. P1. $15.00

QUENTIN, Patrick. *Gr-Eyed Monster.* 1960. Gollancz. 1st ed. dj. VG. P1. $20.00

QUENTIN, Patrick. *Man With 2 Wives.* 1955. Gollancz. 1st ed. dj. VG. P1. $20.00

QUENTIN, Patrick. *Puzzle for Fiends.* 1946. Simon Schuster. dj. xl. P1. $5.00

QUENTIN, Patrick. *Puzzle for Players.* nd. Simon Schuster. xl. P1. $5.00

QUENTIN, Patrick. *Run to Death.* 1948. Simon Schuster. VG. P1. $10.00

QUICK, Dorothy. *Something Evil.* 1958. Arcadia. 1st ed. dj. G. R3. $17.50

QUICK, Herbert. *Double Hero.* 1906. Bobbs Merrill. 1st ed. 319 p. G. B10. $4.00

QUICK, Herbert. *VA of the Airlines.* 1909. Bobbs Merrill. 1st ed. VG. R3. $30.00

QUILLER-COUCH, A.T. *Oxford Book of Ballads.* 1910. Oxford. 1st ed. AEG. EX. T1. $25.00

QUILLER-COUCH, A.T. *Oxford Book of Eng Verse 1250-1900.* 1908. Oxford. 1st ed. AEG. EX. $25.00

QUILLER-COUCH & DU MAURIER. *Castle Dor.* c 1962. Book Club. dj. VG. C1. $3.50

QUILLER-COUCH & DU MAURIER. *Castle Dor.* nd. Book Club. dj. EX. P1. $4.50

QUINN, Carey. *Daffodils.* nd. (1950) Hearthside Pr. 1st ed? 204 p. dj. VG. B10. $4.00

QUINN, E.B. *Death Is a Restless Sleeper.* 1941. Mystery House. 1st ed. dj. VG. F5. $22.00

QUINN, Seabury. *Alien Flesh.* 1977. Oswald Train. 1st ed. dj. EX. P1. $20.00

QUINN, Seabury. *Phantom Fighter.* 1966. Mycroft Moran. 1st ed. dj. VG. P1. $60.00

QUINTANILLA, Luis. *All the Brave.* 1939. Modern Age Books. 1st Trade ed. red wrp. H3. $40.00

QUINTON, J.A. *Heaven's Antidote.* nd. Phil. Challen. 155 p. VG. B10. $12.00

RABBIT, Peter. *Drop City.* 1971. Olympia. 1st PB ed. VG. B4. $10.00

RABE, Peter. *Anatomy of a Killer.* 1960. Abelard Schuman. 1st ed. dj. xl. P1. $12.50

RABE, Peter. *House in Naples.* 1956. Gold Medal 547. 1st ed. wrp. VG. T9. $25.00

RABE, Peter. *Out Is Death.* 1959. London. Muller. 1st ed. wrp. NM. T9. $30.00

RABE, Peter. *Stop This Man!* 1955. Gold Medal 506. 1st ed. wrp. VG. T9. $30.00

RABELAIS, Francois. *Gargantua & Pantagruel.* 1942. Heritage. Ils Lynd Ward. slipcase. EX. T1. $20.00

RABKIN, E.S. *Fantastic in Literature.* 1977. Princeton PB. VG. P1. $3.25

RABOFF, Peyser. *How To Beat Those Cordon Bleus.* 1974. Pasadena. 1st ed. dj. VG. B3. $22.50

RACHERBAUMER, Jon. *Arch Triumphs.* 1978. Magic Ltd. 1st ed. 44 p. EX. J3. $11.00

RACHERBAUMER, Jon. *Card Finesse.* 1982. Danny Korem. 1st ed. 202 p. dj. NM. J3. $22.00

RACHERBAUMER, Jon. *Good Turns.* 1977. Magic Ltd. 1st ed. 21 p. NM. J3. $4.00

RACHERBAUMER, Jon. *Lecture Notes 1.* 1976. Magic Ltd. 1st ed. 29 p. NM. J3. $4.00

RACHERBAUMER, Jon. *Universal Card.* 1975. NY. Tannen. Yod Series. 1st ed. 35 p. NM. J3. $12.00

RACINA, Thomas. *Great Los Angeles Blizzard.* 1977. Putnam. 1st ed. dj. VG. P1. $15.00

RACKHAM, Arthur. *Ondine.* 1913. Paris. French text. 15 pls w/tissue guards. G. C2. $65.00

RACKHAM, Arthur. *Ring of the Nibelung.* 1939. Garden City. 48 clr pls. dj. EX. $130.00

RACKHAM, Arthur. *Rip Van Winkle.* 1905. London/NY. 1st ed. 4to. TEG. VG. $160.00

RACKHAM, Arthur. *Romance of King Arthur & His Knights of Round Table.* 1917. Macmillan. 1st Am ed. 8vo. 517 p. VG. $155.00

RACKHAM, Arthur. *Undine.* 1909. London. 1/1000. sgn. Bayntun bdg. EX. H3. $950.00

RADCLIFFE, Garnett. *Lady From Venus.* 1947. London. 1st ed. dj. EX. R3. $35.00

RADCLIFFE, William. *Fishing From the Earliest Times.* 1921. Dutton. 478 p. VG. $50.00

RADFORD & SWANSTON. *Arthurian Sites in the W.* 1979. Exeter U. 4th imp. stiff wrp. VG. C1. $11.50

RADIGUET, Raymond. *Devil in the Flesh.* 1932. Black Sun. Intro Huxley. wrp. VG. H3. $100.00

RADIN, E. *Lizzie Borden, the Untold Story.* 1961. NY. 1st ed. 266 p. dj. VG. B3. $20.00

RADIN, Paul. *Story of the Am Indian.* nd. (1927) Boni. Ils. VG. B10. $10.00

RADLEY, Shelia. *Fate Worse Than Death.* 1986. Scribner. 1st ed. dj. EX. P1. $13.95

RADLEY, Shelia. *Quiet Road to Death.* 1984. Scribner. 1st ed. dj. EX. P1. $17.50

RADLEY, Shelia. *Who Saw Him Die?* 1987. Scribner. 1st ed. dj. VG. P1. $14.95

RADNER, S.H. *Magic for Fun...* 1956. Padell Book. 1st ed. 93 p. EX. J3. $3.00

RADNOTI, Mikios. *Clouded Sky.* 1972. Harper. Stated 1st ed. 112 p. glossy wrp. EX. B10. $4.00

RADOT, J.V. *French Drawings...15th-19th Centuries.* 1964. Shorewood. slipcase. EX. D4. $20.00

RAGOZIN, Zenaide. *Chaldea From the Earliest Times to Rise of Assyria.* 1889. London. 8vo. 381 p. VG. $27.50

RAINE, J.W. *Land of the Saddlebags: Mt People of Appalachia.* 1924. NY. VG. J2. $20.00

RAINE, William Macleod. *Border Breed.* 1944. Triangle. 4th ed. VG. P1. $6.00

RAINE, William Macleod. *CO.* nd. Grosset Dunlap. dj. VG. P1. $20.00

RAINE, William Macleod. *CO.* 1929. Grosset Dunlap. 316 p. A5. $30.00

RAINE, William Macleod. *Gunsight Pass.* 1921. Houghton Mifflin. 1st ed. 331 p. dj. G. B10. $5.75

RAINE, William Macleod. *Gunsight Pass.* 1946. Triangle. VG. P1. $7.50

RAINE, William Macleod. *To Ride the River With.* 1936. Houghton Mifflin. VG. P1. $12.50

RAINE, William Macleod. *Troubled Waters.* 1925. McBride. 1st ed. 12mo. dj. EX. C4. $60.00

RAINE, William Macleod. *TX Man.* 1928. Doubleday Doran. VG. P1. $11.50

RAINE, William Macleod. *Yukon Trail.* 1942. Triangle. 7th ed. dj. VG. P1. $10.00

RAINES, C.W. *Bibliography of TX.* 1955. Frontier Pr. reprint of 1896 ed. boxed. VG. $75.00

RAINWATER, Dorothy. *Encyclopedia of Am Silver Manufacturers.* 1975. Crown. Ils. 8vo. 222 p. xl. EX. B10. $6.00

RAMAYNE, Korda. *Do the Dead Return?* 1974. Calgary. 16 p. stapled manuscript. J3. $4.00

RAMSAY, Allan. *Gentle Shepherd: Pastoral Comedy.* 1899. London. Blk. 1st ed. 176 p. R4. $15.00

RAMSAY, David. *Hist of SC From Its 1st Settlement in 1670 to Year 1808.* 1809. Charleston. 1st ed. 478 p. G. T1. $50.00

RAMSAY, Diana. *Dark Descends.* 1975. Harper. 1st Am ed. dj. EX. F5. $20.00

RAMSAY, J. *Am Potters & Pottery.* 1939. NY. 1st ed. 304 p. G. B3. $60.00

RAMSAYE, Terry. *Million & 1 Nights.* 1926. Simon Schuster. 1st ed. 2 vols. octavo. VG. H3. $200.00

RAMSEY, Frederic Jr. *Been Here & Gone.* 1969. Rutgers. octavo. 177 p. dj. VG. H3. $40.00

RAMSEY, Leonidas. *Time Out for Adventure: Let's Go to Mexico.* 1934. Doubleday. 1st ed. 315 p. dj. F2. $15.00

RAND, Ayn. *Atlas Shurgged.* 1957. Random House. 1st ed. dj. VG. B13. $150.00

RAND, Ayn. *For the New Intellectual.* 1961. NY. 1st ed. dj. VG. B3. $35.00

RAND, Ayn. *We the Living.* 1936. London. 1/1000. sgn. orig bl bdg. dj. EX. H3. $2250.00

RAND MCNALLY. *Rand McNally Standard Atlas of the World.* 1886. Chicago. Continental Pub. sm folio. 192 p. VG. C1. $100.00

RANDAL, Jason. *Psychology of Deception (Why Magic Works).* 1982. Venice, CA. 1st ed. 209 p. dj. NM. J3. $20.00

RANDALL, D.A. *Ham-Mishkan: The Wonderful Tent.* 1886. Cincinnati. 420 p. G. T5. $19.50

RANDALL, E.O. *Masterpieces of OH Mound Builders.* 1908. Columbus. Ils 1st ed. inscr. 126 p. VG. T5. $47.50

RANDALL, F.E. *Haldane Station.* 1973. Harcourt. 1st ed. dj. EX. F5. $20.00

RANDALL, J.D. *Jihad Ultimatum.* 1988. Saybrook. 1st ed. dj. EX. F5. $14.00

RANDALL, J.G. *Civil War & Reconstruction.* 1937. Boston. Heath. 959 p. S1. $9.00

RANDALL, J.G. *Divided Union.* 1961. Little Brn. dj. G. S1. $8.50

RANDALL, J.G. *Lincoln the President: Midstream.* 1953. Dodd Mead. dj. VG. S1. $10.00

RANDALL, R.P. *Mary Lincoln: Biography of a Marriage.* 1953. Little Brn. 1st ed. 555 p. dj. VG. $12.00

RANDALL, R.P. *Mary Lincoln: Biography of a Marriage.* 1953. Little Brn. 1st ed. 555 p. G. S1. $7.00

RANDALL, Robert. *Dawning Light.* 1959. Gnome. 1st ed. dj. EX. R3. $20.00

RANDALL, Robert. *Dawning Light.* 1959. Gnome. 1st ed. dj. xl. P1. $15.00

RANDELL, Jack. *I'm Alone.* 1930. Bobbs Merrill. 1st ed. 317 p. xl. VG. B10. $5.00

RANDISI, R.J. *Full Contact.* 1984. St Martin. 1st ed. dj. VG. P1. $13.95

RANDISI, Robert. *Eyes Have It.* 1984. Mysterious Pr. 1st ed. dj. EX. F5. $15.00

RANDOLPH, Vance. *Ozark Anthology.* 1940. Caldwell. Caxton. 1st ed. dj. EX. B13. $65.00

RANDOLPH, Vance. *We Always Lie to Strangers.* 1951. Columbia. 1st ed. dj. EX. B13. $60.00

RANKINE, John. *Never the Same Door.* 1967. Dobson. 1st ed. dj. EX. P1. $20.00

RANSOME, Stephen. *Frazer Acquittal.* 1955. Crime Club. 1st ed. dj. VG. P1. $20.00

RAPHAEL, F. *List of Books.* 1981. Harmony. 1st Am ed. 159 p. dj. M. B10. $6.25

RAPHAEL, Rick. *President Must Die.* 1981. Norton. 1st ed. dj. EX. F5. $18.00

RAPPAPORT, B. *Complete Guide to Collecting Antique Pipes.* 1979. Exton, PA. lg 8vo. dj. EX. $25.00

RASCOE, Burton. *Prometheans: Ancient & Modern.* 1933. Putnam. Ltd ed. 1/125. inscr. dj. H3. $75.00

RASMUSSON, R.M. *UFO Literature.* 1985. McFarland. 1st ed. M. R3. $15.00

RASPE, R.E. *Travels of Baron Munchausen.* 1929. Ltd Ed Club. Ils/sgn John Held. 1/1500. slipcase. EX. C4. $100.00

RATH, Virginia. *Posted for Murder.* 1942. Crime Club. 1st ed. dj. VG. P1. $22.50

RATHBONE, Basil. *In & Out of Character.* 1962. Doubleday. 1st ed. octavo. 278 p. dj. EX. H3. $175.00

RATHBONE, Basil. *In & Out of Character.* 1962. NY. dj. VG. B3. $50.00

RATHBONE, Julian. *Carnival!* 1976. Michael Joseph. 1st ed. dj. VG. P1. $20.00

RATHBONE, Julian. *Euro-Killers.* 1979. Pantheon. 1st ed. dj. VG. P1. $15.00

RATHBONE, Julian. *Watching the Detectives.* 1983. Pantheon. 1st ed. dj. VG. P1. $13.95

RATHER, Dan. *Camera Never Blinks.* 1977. Morrow Book Club. 320 p. dj. EX. B10. $3.75

RATHJEN, C.H. *Treasures.* 1975. Whitman. VG. P1. $8.00

RATTIGAN, T.M. *French Without Tears.* 1938. Farrar Rinehart. 1st ed. dj. EX. H3. $40.00

RAUM, G.B. *Existing Conflict...Republican Government & S Oligarchy.* 1884. Cleveland. 1st ed. 479 p. G. T5. $65.00

RAUSCHER, W.V. *John Calvert Magic & Adventures Around the World.* 1987. Baton Rouge. Claitor. 1st ed. 305 p. dj. NM. J3. $20.00

RAUSCHER, W.V. *Marco the Magi: Wise Man of Magic.* 1983. Woodbury, NJ. 1st ed. 34 p. NM. J3. $10.00

RAUSCHER, W.V. *Wand: Story & Symbol.* 1983. Rauscher. 1st ed. EX. J3. $8.00

RAWICZ. *Long Walk.* 1956. London. 1st ed. dj. VG. B3. $20.00

RAWLINGS, M.K. *Cross Creek Cookery.* 1942. NY. 1st ed. dj. VG. B3. $35.00

RAWLINGS, M.K. *Cross Creek.* 1942. Scribner. 1st ed. dj. VG. B13. $5.00

RAWLINGS, M.K. *Marjorie Kinnan Rawlings Cookbook.* 1960. London. Hamond. 1st UK ed. dj. EX. B13. $85.00

RAWLINGS, M.K. *Marjorie Rawlings Reader.* 1956. Scribner. 1st ed. dj. VG. K2. $50.00

RAWLINGS, M.K. *Sojourner.* 1953. NY. 1st ed. dj. VG. B3. $45.00

RAWLINGS, M.K. *Sojourner.* 1953. Scribner Book Club. 313 p. VG. B10. $3.50

RAWLINGS, M.K. *Yearling.* 1938. NY. 1st ed. dj. VG. B3. $32.50

RAWLINSON, A. *Adventures in Near E 1918-1922.* 1924. London. 3rd print. 375 p. VG. $20.00

RAWLINSON, George. *5 Great Monarchies of the Ancient E World.* 1862-1867. London. Murray. 1st ed. 4 vols. H3. $350.00

RAWSON, Clayton. *Golden Book of Magic.* 1964. Golden Pr. 104 p. VG. J3. $6.00

RAWSON, Clayton. *How To Entertain Children With Magic You Can Do.* 1962. Simon Schuster. 1st print. NM. J3. $10.00

RAY, Frederick. *Gettysburg Sketches.* 1939. Gettysburg. PB. G. S1. $5.00

RAY, G.W. *Through 5 Republics on Horseback.* 1921. Hauser Pub. 21st Revised ed. sgn. 305 p. F2. $25.00

RAY, Jimmy. *Between the Acts.* nd. Royal House Magic. 1st ed. 31 p. SftCvr. EX. J3. $3.00

RAY, Jospeh. *Primary Lessons & Tables in Arithmetic.* 1857. Cincinnati. 80 p. G. T5. $12.50

RAY, Man. *Self-Portrait.* 1963. Boston/Toronto. 1st ed. dj. VG. $75.00

RAY, Michele. *2 Shores of Hell.* 1968. NY. K2. $35.00

RAY, Ophelia. *Daughter of the Tejas.* 1965. Greenwich. NY Graphic Soc. 1st ed. dj. EX. K2. $150.00

RAY, R.J. *Merry Christmas, Murdock.* 1989. Delacorte. 1st ed. dj. VG. P1. $16.95

RAY. *Legends of Red River Valleys.* 1941. San Antonio. 1st ed. dj. VG. C2. $30.00

RAYER, F.G. *Tomorrow Sometimes Comes.* 1951. Home/Van Thal. 1st ed. VG. P1. $15.00

RAYMOND, Alex. *Flash Gordon Escapes to Arboria.* 1977. Nostalgia. 1st ed. lg wrp. EX. R3. $12.50

RAYMOND, Alex. *Flash Gordon in the Caverns of Mongo.* 1936. Grosset Dunlap. 1st ed. repro dj. VG. R3. $50.00

RAYMOND, Alex. *Flash Gordon in the Planet Mongo.* 1974. Nostalgia. 1st ed. dj. EX. R3. $27.50

RAYMOND, H.J. *Life & Public Services of Abraham Lincoln.* 1865. Derby Miller. 808 p. rebound. G. S1. $45.00

RAYMOND, John. *Simenon in Court.* 1968. Hamish Hamilton. 1st ed. dj. VG. T9. $20.00

RAYMOND, L.R. *Child's Story of the Nativity.* 1934. Random House. Ils. VG. B10. $12.00

RAYMOND, M. *God Goes to Murderer's Row.* 1951. Bruce. dj. VG. P1. $10.00

RAYMOND, Nancy. *Smoky, Little Kitten Who Didn't Want To.* nd. Fideler Co. Ils Dirk. 4to. 26 p. dj. VG. $25.00

RAYMOND, Wayte. *Silver Dollars of N & S Am.* 1964. Whitman. Ils. 125 p. F2. $15.00

RAYNAUD, Georges. *Anales de los Zahil de los Indios Cakchiqueles.* 1937. Guatemala. Segunda ed. 71 p. wrp. xl. F2. $25.00

RAYTER, Joe. *Stab in the Dark.* 1955. Mill Morrow. 1st ed. dj. VG. P1. $15.00

READ, John. *Prelude to Chemistry.* 1937. NY. 1st ed. 328 p. dj. VG. B3. $27.50

READ, Opie. *Gold Gause Veil.* 1927. Chicago. Canterbury. 1st ed. sgn. 383 p. VG. B10. $15.00

READ, R.W. *Calostro Mind Reading Act.* 1945. Calostro. 1st ed. sgn. 31 p. VG. J3. $5.00

READ & GAINES. *Journals, Drawings, & Papers of JG Bruff 1849-1851.* 1949. NY. CA Century ed. dj. EX. A4. $75.00

READE, Amye. *Slaves of the Sawdust.* 1892. NY. Hovendon. 1st Am ed. octavo. 312 p. H3. $60.00

READE, Hamish. *Comeback for Stark.* 1968. Putnam. dj. EX. P1. $10.00

READER'S DIGEST. *World's Last Mysteries.* 1978. NY. 1st ed. 4to. 319 p. F2. $12.50

READY, William. *Understanding Tolkien & Lotr.* nd. PB Lib. VG. P1. $4.00

REAGAN, Ronald. *Where's the Rest of Me?* 1965. NY. 1st ed. sgn. EX. $125.00

REAM, Lamont. *Coin Creations.* 1981. Magical Pub. 1st ed. 51 p. SftCvr. NM. J3. $4.00

REAMY, Tom. *Blind Voices.* 1978. Berkley. 1st ed. M. R3. $25.00

REAMY, Tom. *San Diego Lightfoot Sue.* 1979. Earthlight. 1st ed. dj. EX. R3. $22.50

RECINOS, Adrian. *Popol Vuh.* 1961. Norman, OK. 5th print. dj. F2. $17.50

RECORD, Paul. *Tropical Frontier.* 1969. Knopf. 1st ed. 325 p. F2. $15.00

REDDALL, H.F. *Songs That Never Die.* nd. (1890) Moore Co. 1st ed? 615 p. G. B10. $17.00

REDDING, Saunders. *Am in India.* 1954. Indianapolis. 1st ed. dj. VG. B3. $20.00

REDESDALE, Lord. *Memories.* nd. Dutton. 2 vols. TEG. VG. R5. $30.00

REDFIELD, Robert. *Folk Culture of Yucatan.* 1941. Chicago U. 1st ed. 416 p. F2. $25.00

REDFIELD, Robert. *Village That Chose Progress. Chan Kom Revisited.* 1950. Chicago U. 1st ed. 187 p. dj. F2. $25.00

REDGATE, John. *Killing Season.* nd. Book Club. VG. P1. $3.00

REDMON, Anne. *2nd Sight.* 1987. Dutton. 1st ed. dj. EX. F5. $15.00

REDPATH. *Public Life of Capt Brn.* 1860. Boston. 1st ed. 2mo. 407 p. G. G4. $26.00

REECE, B.H. *Bow Down in Jericho.* 1950. NY. 1st ed. dj. VG. B3. $35.00

REED, Alma. *Ancient Past of Mexico.* 1966. Crown. 1st ed. 388 p. dj. F2. $20.00

REED, Alma. *Mexican Muralists.* 1960. Crown. 1st ed. 191 p. dj. F2. $35.00

REED, G.I. *Bench & Bar of OH.* 1897. Chicago. 2 vols. VG. T5. $195.00

REED, Ishmael. *Flight to Canada.* 1976. Random House. UP. wrp. EX. B13. $85.00

REED, Ishmael. *Flight to Canada.* 1976. Random House. 1st ed. dj. EX. $35.00

REED, Ishmael. *Last Days of LA Red.* 1974. NY. 1st ed. sgn. dj. EX. T9. $55.00

REED, Kit. *At War As Children.* 1964. Farrar Straus. 1st ed. dj. xl. P1. $7.50

REED, Myrtle. *Master of Vineyard.* 1910. NY. 12mo. NM. A4. $25.00

REED, Robert. *Hormone Jungle.* 1987. Donald Fine. 1st ed. dj. EX. P1. $17.95

REED & MATHESON. *Narrative Visit: Am Churches.* 1835. NY. 1st Am ed. 2 vols. VG. scarce. G1. $75.00

REED & REED. *Ils in Am 1880-1980.* 1984. Soc of Ils Ltd ed. 1/2750. VG. $55.00

REEP, Diana. *Rescue & Romance.* 1982. Popular. HrdCvr ed. VG. P1. $15.00

REEVE, A.B. *Craig Kennedy Listens In.* nd. McKinlay Stone MacKenzie. VG. P1. $10.00

REEVE, A.B. *Craig Kennedy Listens In.* 1923. Harper. 1st ed. dj. EX. R3. $50.00

REEVE, A.B. *Craig Kennedy on the Farm.* nd. McKinlay Stone MacKenzie. P1. $12.50

REEVE, A.B. *Ear in the Wall.* nd. Hodder Stoughton. VG. P1. $10.00

REEVE, A.B. *Gold of Gods.* 1915. McClelland Goodchild Stewart. 1st Canadian ed. P1. $11.00

REEVE, A.B. *Master Mystery.* 1919. Grosset Dunlap. Photoplay ed. dj. G. R3. $25.00

REEVE, A.B. *Perils of Elaine.* 1915. Harper. Photoplay ed. G. R3. $15.00

REEVE, A.B. *Radio Detective.* 1926. Grosset Dunlap. Photoplay ed. VG. R3. $15.00

REEVE, A.B. *War Terror.* 1915. Harper. VG. P1. $15.00

REEVE, Christopher. *Murder Steps Out.* 1951. Doubleday Book Club. VG. P1. $7.50

REEVES, James. *Story of Jackie Thimble.* 1964. Dutton. Ils Ardizzone. 1st ed. 16mo. 31 p. VG. $18.00

REEVES, John. *Murder Before Matins.* 1984. Doubleday. 1st ed. dj. EX. P1. $12.95

REEVES-STEVEN, Garfield. *Dream Land.* 1991. Warner. 1st ed. dj. EX. F5. $6.50

REGLER, Gustave. *Great Crusade.* 1940. Longman Gr. 1st ed. dj. EX. H3. $100.00

REICHE, Maria. *Mystery on the Desert.* 1987. Stuttgart. 6th print. sgn. 92 p. F2. $25.00

REICHEL-DOLMATOFF, Gerardo. *Amazonian Cosmos.* 1971. Chicago U. 1st ed. 290 p. dj. F2. $25.00

REICHEL-DOLMATOFF, Gerardo. *People of Aritama.* 1970. Chicago U. Ils. 483 p. dj. F2. $15.00

REICHENBACH, W. *Automatic Pistol Marksmanship.* 1937. Onslow Co, NC. 1st ed. dj. VG. B3. $50.00

REICHMANN, Felix. *Sugar, Gold, & Coffee.* 1959. Cornell U. 1st ed. 160 p. F2. $25.00

REID, Alexander. *Paris.* nd. Barnes. Ils. 76 p. dj. VG. B10. $4.00

REID, M.J.C. *Arthurian Legend: Comparison of Treatment...Literature.* 1970. London/NY. VG. C1. $39.50

REID, Mayne. *Giraffe Hunters.* 1880. NY. Ils. sgn. gilt gr bdg. VG. $50.00

REID, Mayne. *Odd People.* 1860. NY. Ils. fair. T5. $9.50

REID, Mayne. *Plant Hunters; or, Adventures Among the Himalaya Mts.* 1844. Ticknor Field. Ils. G. $65.00

REID, P.R. *Colditz Story.* 1953. Lippincott. 2nd ed. 288 p. VG. B10. $4.00

REID, T.B.W. *Tristan of Beroul: Textual Commentary.* 1972. Oxford. 1st ed. dj. VG. C1. $7.50

REID, W.M. *Story of Old Ft Johnson.* 1906. Putnam. 240 p. xl. A5. $30.00

REID, Wally. *Magic on Stage.* 1980. Magic Ltd. 1st ed. 124 p. dj. NM. J3. $16.00

REIGER, G. *Zane Grey: Outdoorsman.* 1972. Englewood Cliffs. dj. VG. B3. $27.50

REILLY, Helen. *File on Fufus Ray.* 1937. NY. 1st Am ed. wrp. VG. $60.00

REILLY, Helen. *Follow Me*. 1960. Random House. 1st ed. dj. EX. P1. $25.00

REILLY, Helen. *Mr Smith's Hat*. 1936. Crime Club. 1st ed. xl. VG. P1. $15.00

REILLY, Helen. *Murder at Arroways*. 1950. Random House. 1st ed. dj. xl. P1. $7.50

REILLY, Helen. *Name Your Poison*. 1942. Doubleday Book Club. VG. P1. $12.50

REILLY, Helen. *31st Bullfinch*. 1930. Crime Club. 1st ed. VG. P1. $25.00

REILLY, J.M. *Velot, the Lion Hunter*. 1910. NY/Baltimore/Atlanta. 1st ed. EX. $50.00

REILLY, R.T. *Red Hugh, Prince of Donegal*. 1957. Farrar. 1st ed. dj. VG. F5. $10.00

REINACH, S. *Apollo*. nd. Scribner. Revised ed. 350 p. VG. B10. $8.00

REINFELD, Fred. *British Chess Masters Past & Present*. 1947. London. Bell. apparent 1st ed. 92 p. dj. VG. B10. $4.25

REINHARD, J.R.R. *Medieval Pagent*. 1970. Haskel House. reprint of 1939 ed. EX. C1. $16.50

REINHARTZ & COLLEY. *Mapping of the Am SW*. nd. A&M U. 88 p. M. A5. $30.00

REISNER, R. *Bird: Legend of Charlie Parker*. 1962. NY. 1st ed. VG. B3. $42.50

REISZNER, J.C. *ABC, Buchstabir und Lesebuch...* c 1950. Cleveland. 144 p. fair. T5. $27.50

REMAN. *Norse Discoveries & Explorations in Am*. 1949. CA U. 1st ed. dj. EX. $25.00

REMARQUE, E.M. *All Quiet on the W Front*. 1929. Little Brn. 3rd print. VG. $10.00

REMARQUE, E.M. *Spark of Life*. 1952. Appleton Century. dj. VG. $12.00

REMARQUE, E.M. *Time To Love & Time To Die*. 1954. Harcourt. 1st ed. 378 p. EX. B10. $17.50

REMENTHAM, John. *Lurking Shadow*. nd. MacDonald. dj. xl. P1. $5.00

REMENTHAM, John. *Peacemaker*. 1947. MacDonald. 1st ed. dj. VG. P1. $7.00

REMINGTON, Frederic. *Bigelow: Borderland of Czar & Kaiser*. 1895. Harper. Ils. VG. B3. $40.00

REMINGTON, Frederic. *Collected Writings*. 1979. Doubleday. 1st ed. 649 p. dj. VG. RS. B3. $40.00

REMINGTON, Frederic. *Drawings*. 1898. NY. Russell. oblong folio. G. B3. $395.00

REMINGTON, Frederic. *Men With the Bark On*. 1900. 1st ed. 1st issue. EX. B2. $165.00

RENDELL, Ruth. *Bridesmaid*. 1989. Doubleday. dj. EX. P1. $17.95

RENDELL, Ruth. *Heartstones*. 1987. Harper Row. 1st ed. dj. EX. P1. $10.95

RENDELL, Ruth. *Killing Doll*. nd. BOMC. dj. VG. P1. $5.00

RENDELL, Ruth. *Killing Doll*. 1984. Pantheon. 1st ed. dj. EX. F5. $15.00

RENDELL, Ruth. *Live Flesh*. nd. Book Club. dj. VG. P1. $4.50

RENDELL, Ruth. *New Girlfriend*. nd. BOMC. dj. EX. P1. $5.00

RENDELL, Ruth. *Talking to Strange Men*. 1987. Hutchinson. 1st ed. dj. VG. P1. $15.00

RENDELL, Ruth. *Talking to Strange Men*. 1987. Pantheon. 1st ed. dj. EX. P1. $16.95

RENNER, F.G. *Paper Talk*. 1962. Ft Worth. 1st ed. glassine dj. VG. B3. $80.00

RENO, M.R. *Final Proof*. 1976. Harper Row. 1st ed. dj. xl. P1. $5.00

REPP, E.E. *Radium Pool*. 1949. Fantasy. 1st ed. dj. EX. R3. $15.00

REPP, E.E. *Stellar Missiles*. 1949. Fantasy. 1st bdg. dj. EX. R3. $20.00

REPPLIER, Agnes. *Counter Currents*. 1916. Boston. 3rd imp. inscr. G. $30.00

REPPLIER, Agnes. *Fireside Sphinx*. 1901. Boston/NY. 1st ed. $20.00

REPS, Paul. *Unwrinkling Plays*. 1965. Japan. Tuttle. 1st ed. B4. $10.00

RESNICK, Michael. *Eros Ascending*. 1984. Phantasia. Ltd ed. 1/300. sgn. M. R3. $40.00

RESNICK, Michael. *Eros Ascending*. 1984. Phantasia. 1st ed. M. R3. $17.00

RESNICK, Michael. *Eros at Zenith*. 1984. Phantasia. Ltd ed. 1/300. sgn. dj. slipcase. EX. P1. $50.00

RESNICK, Michael. *Eros at Zenith*. 1984. Phantasia. 1st ed. M. R3. $17.00

RESNICK, Michael. *Goddess of Ganymede*. 1967. Donald Grant. 1st ed. 1/750. dj. EX. F5. $35.00

RESNICK, Michael. *Official Guide to the Fantastics*. 1976. House of Collectibles. 1st ed. wrp. EX. R3. $7.50

RESNIK, Mike. *Ivory*. 1988. Tor Books. 1st ed. dj. EX. F5. $20.00

REVERE, W.J. *Keel & Saddle; or, 40 Years of Military & Naval Service*. 1872. Osgood. 1st ed. VG. $65.00

REVKIN, Andrew. *Burning Season*. 1990. Houghton Mifflin. 1st ed. 317 p. dj. F2. $20.00

REXROTH, Kenneth. *Excerpts From a Life*. 1981. Santa Barbara. 1st ed. 1/350. sgn. dj. H3. $45.00

REXROTH, Kenneth. *Heart's Garden*. 1967. Cambridge. 1st ed. 1/75. sgn Eng/Japanese. dj. EX. $115.00

REXROTH, Kenneth. *20 Times in Same Place...Anthology of Santa Barbara Poetry*. 1973. Painted Cave Books. Ltd ed. 1/85. sgn. H3. $75.00

REYES, Carlos. *Prisoner*. 1973. Capra. Chapbook Series. 1/100. sgn. EX. K2. $20.00

REYNOLDS, Don. *Champion of Champions: Story of Nornay Saddler*. 1950. NY. 1st ed. VG. $25.00

REYNOLDS, Frank. *Mr Pickwick*. nd. (1910) Hodder Stoughton. quarto. H3. $350.00

REYNOLDS, H. *World's Oldest Writings*. 1938. Chicago. 1st ed. presentation. 328 p. dj. VG. B3. $30.00

REYNOLDS, J.E. *In French Creek Valley*. 1938. Meadville, PA. Ils. 352 p. T5. $45.00

REYNOLDS, Mack. *Case of the Little Gr Men*. 1951. Phoenix Pr. 1st ed. dj. VG. R3. $60.00

REYNOLDS, Quentin. *Curtain Rises*. 1944. Random House Book Club. 353 p. dj. VG. B10. $3.50

REYNOLDS, Quentin. *Curtain Rises*. 1944. Random House. 5th ed. 353 p. dj. EX. H3. $4.00

REYNOLDS, Quentin. *Headquarters*. 1955. Harper. 1st ed. 339 p. dj. VG. B10. $5.25

REYNOLDS, Reginald. *Wisdom of John Woolman With Selection of His Writings...* 1948. London. Allen Unwin. 1st ed. 12mo. 178 p. VG. V1. $12.00

REZIKOFF, Charles. *Jews of Charleston: Hist of Am Jewish Community*. 1950. Phil. Ils 1st ed. dj. VG. $30.00

REZNIKOFF, Charles. *By the Waters of Manhattan*. 1930. Boni. pb. VG. B4. $12.00

RHEAD, Louis. *Fisherman's Lures*. 1920. Scribner. 1st ed. VG. C1. $15.00

RHEAD. *Earthenware Collector*. 1920. London. 1st ed. VG. C2. $40.00

RHODE, John. *Death of an Author.* 1948. Dodd Mead. 1st ed. dj. G. F5. $18.00

RHODES, W.B. *Crest of Little Wolf: Tale of Young Lovell & Wars of Roses.* 1904. Cincinnati. 1st ed. gr bdg. EX. C1. $9.50

RHODIUS, Appollonius. *Argonautica.* 1957. Athens. 1/1500. sgn Tassos. boxed. EX. $30.00

RHYS, Ernest. *Noble & Joyous Hist of King Arthur/Book of...Adventures.* c 1895-1900. London. 2 vols. VG. C1. $16.00

RICARDO, David. *Works & Correspondence.* 1951. Cambridge U. 1st ed. 10 vols. octavo. H3. $650.00

RICE, A.H. *Lovey Mary.* 1903. Century. Ils Shinn. sm 8vo. VG. $20.00

RICE, A.H. *Mrs Wiggs' Cabbage Patch.* 1902. Century. 12mo. 153 p. VG. $20.00

RICE, Anne. *Cry to Heaven.* 1982. Knopf. UP. w/reviewer's notes. EX. K2. $175.00

RICE, Anne. *Feast of All Saints.* 1979. NY. 1st ed. sgn. dj. VG. B3. $50.00

RICE, Anne. *Interview With the Vampire.* 1976. Knopf. sgn. dj. H3. $450.00

RICE, Anne. *Interview With the Vampire.* 1976. Knopf. UP. wrp. EX. K2. $1250.00

RICE, Anne. *Interview With the Vampire.* 1976. NY. 1st ed. dj. EX. $395.00

RICE, Anne. *Queen of the Damned.* 1988. Knopf. Ltd ed. 1/150. sgn. H3. $350.00

RICE, Anne. *Queen of the Damned.* 1988. NY. UP. K2. $90.00

RICE, Anne. *Queen of the Damned.* 1988. NY. 1st ed. dj. EX. $75.00

RICE, Anne. *Vampire Lestat.* 1985. Knopf. 1st ed/complimentary copy. dj. EX. C4. $150.00

RICE, Anne. *Witching Hour.* 1990. Knopf. UP. wrp. EX. C4. $100.00

RICE, Craig. *Corpse Steps Out.* 1945. Tower. VG. P1. $10.00

RICE, Craig. *Having Wonderful Crime.* 1944. Nicholson Watson. VG. P1. $12.50

RICE, Craig. *Having Wonderful Crime.* 1944. Simon Schuster. 2nd ed. VG. P1. $15.00

RICE, Craig. *Having Wonderful Life.* 1944. Tower. Photoplay/2nd ed. dj. VG. P1. $17.50

RICE, Craig. *Home Sweet Homicide.* 1946. Tower. 1st/Photoplay ed. dj. EX. F5. $22.00

RICE, Craig. *Knocked for a Loop.* 1957. Simon Schuster. 1st ed. VG. P1. $15.00

RICE, Craig. *Lucky Stiff.* 1947. Tower. dj. VG. P1. $20.00

RICE, Craig. *Thursday Turkey Murders.* 1946. Tower. dj. VG. P1. $20.00

RICE, Elmer. *Dream Girl.* 1946. Coward McCann. 1st ed. dj. EX. B13. $65.00

RICE, Elmer. *Voyage to Purilia.* 1930. Cosmopolitan. 1st ed. dj. RS. EX. R3. $60.00

RICE, Elmer. *Winner.* 1954. Dramatists Play Service. 1st ed. dj. EX. B13. $45.00

RICE, Harold. *Capers With Clr.* 1943. Silk King Studio. 20 p. NM. J3. $4.00

RICE, Harold. *Exclusive Magic.* 1970. Calgary. 2nd ed. 38 p. EX. J3. $6.00

RICE, L. *Character Reading From Handwriting.* 1927. NY. 1st ed. 374 p. VG. B3. $27.50

RICE, Robert. *Business of Crime.* 1956. Farrar Straus Cudahy. 1st ed. dj. VG. P1. $15.00

RICE, Talbot. *Great Palace of the Byzantine Emperors.* 1958. Edinburgh. Ils. 4to. TEG. EX. $200.00

RICE & MCBAIN. *April Robin Murders.* nd. Book Club. dj. VG. P1. $5.00

RICE & RICE. *Little Book of Lullabies.* nd. (1910) Reilly Britton. 63 p. G. B10. $4.00

RICE & STOUDT. *Shenandoah Pottery.* 1929. Strasberg, VA. 1st ed. sgn. VG. J2. $65.00

RICH, Adrienne. *Necessities of Life.* 1966. Norton. 1st ed. dj. EX. C4. $40.00

RICH, G.E. *Artistic Horseshoeing: Practical & Scientific Treatise.* 1907. Akron. Ils. 233 p. recased. T5. $35.00

RICH, John. *Face of S Am: An Aerial Traverse.* 1942. Am Geog Soc. 1st ed. 299 p. dj. F2. $30.00

RICH, L.D. *Only Parent.* 1953. Peoples Book Club. 1st ed. 245 p. dj. B10. $3.75

RICHARD, Mark. *Ice at the Bottom of the World.* 1989. Knopf. 1st ed. sgn. dj. EX. K2. $35.00

RICHARDS, Allen. *To Market to Market.* 1961. Macmillan. 1st ed. dj. VG. P1. $15.00

RICHARDS, E.C. *They Refuse To Be Criminals.* 1946. W Chester. Nur Mahal. 12mo. 48 p. SftCvr. VG. V1. $6.00

RICHARDS, L.E. *Capt January.* 1898. Estes Lauriat. 12mo. 64 p. $18.00

RICHARDS, L.E. *Capt January.* 1916. Page VG. $16.00

RICHARDS, L.E. *Elizabeth Fry: The Angel of the Prisons.* 1916. NY. Appleton. 1st ed 12mo. 206 p. G. V1. $12.50

RICHARDS, L.E. *Mrs Tree.* 1902. Dana Estes. Ils Merrill. 12mo. VG. $18.00

RICHARDS, L.E. *Tirra Lirra: Rhymes Old & New.* 9132. Little Brn. 1st ed. 4to. $20.00

RICHARDS, Louis. *11 Days in the Militia During the War of the Rebellion.* 1883. Phil. private print. 1st ed. $60.00

RICHARDS, Milton. *Tom Blake's Mysterious Adventure.* 1929. Saalfied. VG. P1. $5.00

RICHARDSON, A.D. *Beyond the MS 1857-1867.* 1867. Hartford. Ils 1st ed. 8vo. EX. T1. $45.00

RICHARDSON, A.D. *Secret Service: Field, Dungeon, & Escape.* 1897. WA. wrp. VG. $50.00

RICHARDSON, D.M. *Quakers Past & Present.* c 1914. NY. Dodge. 16mo. 96 p. VG. V1. $9.00

RICHARDSON, Frederick. *Folk Tales From Far E.* 1927. Winston. 1st ed. 254 p. VG. $25.00

RICHARDSON, H.H. *Ultima Thule.* 1929. Norton. 1st ed. 314 p. VG. B10. $5.00

RICHARDSON, J.D. *Messages & Papers of Jefferson Davis & the Confederacy.* 1983. Chelsea House. 2 vols. PB. VG. S1. $15.00

RICHARDSON, J.M.R. *6 Generations of Friends in Ireland 1655-1890.* 1894. London. Hicks. 2nd ed. 12mo. VG. V1. $12.00

RICHARDSON, John. *Account of Life, Ministry, & Travels.* 1774. London. Mary Hinde. 3rd ed. 8vo. 242 p. rebound. VG. V1. $85.00

RICHARDSON, John. *Account of Life, Ministry, & Travels.* 1867. Phil. TW Stuckey. 12mo. 196 p. G. V1. $25.00

RICHARDSON, M.R. *Sheep Wagon Family.* 1954. Dodd Mead. Ils Wilkin. 217 p. dj. EX. $15.00

RICHARDSON, Norval. *Lead of Honor.* 1910. Boston. Page. 2nd ed. 341 p. G. B10. $3.50

RICHARDSON, R.H. *Tilton Territory: Hist Narrative, Warren Township...OH.* 1977. Phil. Ils. 300 p. dj. T5. $8.50

RICHARDSON, William. *Wound*. 1974. Capra. Chapbook Series. 1/75. sgn. EX. K2. $20.00

RICHARDSON. *Medicology; or, Home Encyclopedia of Health*. 1902. NY. Ils. 1400 p. VG. $90.00

RICHARDSON. *Motion Picture Handbook*. 1912. NY. 2nd print. 432 p. G. C2. $40.00

RICHARDSON. *You Should Have Been Here Yesterday*. 1974. Beaverton. Ltd ed. 1/1200. sgn. pls. dj. EX. C2. $75.00

RICHLER, Mordecai. *Acrobats*. 1954. Putnam. 1st ed. dj. EX. C4. $45.00

RICHMOND, Grace. *Red Pepper Burns*. 1920. AL Burt. 229 p. VG. B10. $2.25

RICHMOND, Grace. *Red Pepper Returns*. 1931. Doubldeday. 1st Canadian ed. scarce? B10. $6.25

RICHMOND, Mary. *Shaker Literature: A Bibliography*. 1977. Shaker Community. 2 vols. EX. $45.00

RICKENBACKER, Eddie. *Fighting the Flying Circus*. 1919. NY. presentation. 371 p. B3. $75.00

RICKMAN, Gregg. *Philip K Dick: The Last Testament*. 1985. Fragments W. EX. P1. $9.95

RIDEOUT, Mrs. Grant. *Ancestors & Descendants of Morris A Bradley*. 1948. Cleveland. Ils. 169 p. VG. T5. $25.00

RIDER, H.H. *She*. 1887. London. 1st ed. 1st issue. orig cloth. EX. H3. $850.00

RIDER, J.W. *Hot Tickets*. 1987. Arbor House. 1st ed. dj. EX. F5. $14.00

RIDGE, J.R. *Poems*. 1868. San Francisco. Henry Payot. VG. K2. $500.00

RIDGWAY, Robert. *Birds of N & Middle Am*. 1907. US Nat Mus. 105 pls. 973 p. VG. A5. $40.00

RIDGWAY, Robert. *Ornithology of IL*. 1913. Bloomington, IL. reprint of 1898 ed. 2 vols. VG. T3. $125.00

RIDGWAY, Robert. *Scientific Ils*. 1938. Stanford. Ils. sm 4to. 173 p. dj. EX. C2. $55.00

RIDING, Laura. *Description of Life*. 1980. Targ Ed. Ltd 1st ed. 1/350. sgn. H3. $75.00

RIDPATH, Ian. *Ils Encyclopedia of Astronomy & Space*. 1976. Crowell. 1st ed. dj. EX. R3. $20.00

RIDPATH & BUEL. *Am Reference Library*. nd. np. Deluxe ed. 1/500. 8vo. 6 vols. EX. T1. $125.00

RIEFENSTAHL, Leni. *Last of the Nuba*. 1974. Harper Row. 1st ed. photos. dj. EX. K2. $150.00

RIEGEL, R.E. *Crown of Glory*. 1935. New Haven. 1st ed. 281 p. dj. VG. B3. $55.00

RIEGEL, R.E. *Story of the W Railroads*. 1926. NY. 1st ed. 345 p. VG. B3. $27.50

RIEMAN, Terry. *Vamp Till Ready*. 1954. Harper. 1st ed. dj. EX. P1. $15.00

RIESENBERG, Felix. *Early Steamships*. 1933. NY. 1st ed. xl. G. B3. $95.00

RIESENBERG, Felix. *Sea War*. 1956. NY. Ils. 320 p. VG. T5. $25.00

RIESS, Curt. *Story of WWII*. 1945. Garden City. 1st ed. 670 p. VG. B10. $4.75

RIFKIN, Shepard. *Murderer Vine*. 1970. Dodd Mead. 1st ed. dj. VG. P1. $15.00

RIGGS, S.R. *Mary & I: 40 Years With the Sioux*. 1880. Chicago. 1st ed. A5. $65.00

RIGGS, S.R. *Mary & I: 40 Years With the Sioux*. 1887. Boston. 437 p. VG. B3. $50.00

RIGNEY & DOUGLAS. *Real Bohemia*. 1961. Basic Books. dj. EX. B4. $17.50

RIIS, Jacob. *Neighbors: Life Stories of the Other Half*. 1914. NY. 1st ed. 8vo. VG. $25.00

RILEY, C.V. *Noxious & Beneficial Insects of MO 1869-1872 & 1873-1876*. 2 vols. VG. T3. $45.00

RILEY, J.W. *An Old Sweetheart*. 1891. Bowen Merrill. G. T5. $35.00

RILEY, J.W. *Child Rhymes. With Hoosier Pictures by Will Vawter*. 1898. Indianapolis. 1st ed. VG. C1. $14.50

RILEY, J.W. *Complete Works*. c 1913. New Castle, PA. Randall. Elizabeth Marine Riley ed. 1/150. H3. $1500.00

RILEY, J.W. *Flying Islands of the Night*. 1892. Bowen Merrill. sgn. TEG. stiff cream wrp. boxed. VG. H3. $200.00

RILEY, J.W. *His Pa's* 1903. Bobbs Merrill. 1st ed. TEG. B10. $3.75

RILEY, J.W. *Old Sweetheart of Mine*. nd. (1903) Bobbs Merrill. Ils Christy. 1st ed. VG. B10. $7.00

RILEY, J.W. *Raggedy Man*. 1907. Indianapolis. 1st ed. 8 pls. G. T5. $45.00

RILEY, J.W. *Rubaiyat of Doc Sifers*. 1897. NY. 1st ed. 12mo. EX. A4. $50.00

RINEHART, Luke. *Long Voyage Back*. 1983. Delacorte. 1st ed. dj. EX. P1. $17.50

RINEHART, M.R. *After House*. 1914. Boston/NY. Ils MW Preson. 1st ed. 280 p. T5. $9.50

RINEHART, M.R. *Breaking Point*. nd. AL Burt. VG. P1. $7.50

RINEHART, M.R. *Breaking Point*. 1922. Doran. VG. P1. $10.00

RINEHART, M.R. *Circular Staircase*. 1943. Triangle. 6th ed. dj. VG. P1. $7.00

RINEHART, M.R. *Frightened Wife*. nd. Blk. dj. VG. P1. $4.00

RINEHART, M.R. *Great Mistake*. 1946. Triangle. dj. VG. P1. $15.00

RINEHART, M.R. *K*. nd. Grosset Dunlap. dj. VG. P1. $15.00

RINEHART, M.R. *Long Live the King*. 1917. Thomas Allen/Houghton Mifflin. 1st ed. V G. P1. $15.00

RINEHART, M.R. *Lost Ecstasy*. nd. Grosset Dunlap. Photoplay ed. VG. P1. $20.00

RINEHART, M.R. *Lost Ecstasy*. 1927. Doran. 1st ed. VG. P1. $15.00

RINEHART, M.R. *Love Ecstasy*. 1944. Tower. 2nd ed. dj. VG. P1. $10.00

RINEHART, M.R. *Man in Lower 10*. nd. Grosset Dunlap. clr pl tipped onto front brd. VG. P1. $10.00

RINEHART, M.R. *Red Lamp*. 1925. Doran. 1st ed. VG. P1. $8.50

RINEHART, M.R. *Street of 7 Stars*. nd. Grosset Dunlap. VG. P1. $7.50

RINEHART, M.R. *Tempermental People*. 1924. Doran. sgn. TEG. rebound morocco. H3. $200.00

RINEHART, M.R. *Tish*. 1916. Houghton Mifflin. inscr. orange cloth. H3. $100.00

RINEHART, M.R. *Tish*. 1938. Triangle. VG. P1. $10.00

RINEHART, M.R. *When a Man Marries*. nd. (1910) NY. Grosset Dunlap. reprint. EX. $15.00

RINEHART, M.R. *Yel Room*. 1945. Farrar Rinehart. 1st ed. VG. P1. $15.00

RING, Adam. *Killers Play Rough*. 1946. Crown. 1st ed. dj. VG. P1. $15.00

RIPLEY, W. *Main Street & Wall Street*. 1927. Little Brn. not 1st ed. 360 p. VG. B10. $4.00

RIPLEY & DANA. *New Am Cyclopaedia. Vol 2*. 1863. NY. lg 8vo. 786 p. G4. $14.00

RISK, Salom. *Syrian Yankee*. 1944. (1st 1943) Doubleday. sgn. 317 p. dj. VG. B10. $5.00

RISLEY, Eleanor. *Abandoned Orchard.* 1932. Little Brn. 1st ed. 284 p. VG. B10. $4.75

RITCHIE, Jack. *Little Boxed of Bewilderment.* 1989. St Martin. 1st ed. dj. EX. T9. $20.00

RITCHIE. *Modern Ivory Carving.* 1972. S Brunswick. dj. VG. C2. $30.00

RITTENHOUSE, Jack. *Am Horse-Drawn Vehicles.* 1948. Bonanza. not 1st ed. 99 p. dj. VG. B10. $6.00

RITTENHOUSE, Jessie. *Little Book of Am Poets.* 1915. Houghton Mifflin. 1st ed. 306 p. TEG. B10. $4.50

RITTENHOUSE, Jessie. *Little Book of Modern Verse.* nd. (1913) Houghton. 211 p. fair. B10. $4.00

RIVES, Amelie. *Quick or the Dead?* 1888. Lippincott. VG. R3. $25.00

RIVET, Paul. *Maya Cities.* 1960. Elek Books. 1st ed. 234 p. dj. F2. $20.00

ROBBE-GRILLET, Alain. *Maison de Rendezvous.* 1966. Grove Pr. 1st ed. dj. EX. $25.00

ROBBINS, Harold. *Descent From Xanadu.* 1984. Simon Schuster. 1st ed. 335 p. dj. EX. B10. $4.00

ROBBINS, Harold. *Memories of Another Day.* 1979. Simon Schuster. 1st ed. dj. EX. B10. $5.00

ROBBINS, Tom. *Another Roadside Attraction.* 1971. Doubleday. 1st ed. dj. EX. H3. $150.00

ROBBINS, Tom. *Another Roadside Attraction.* 1973. London. Allen. 1st UK ed. inscr. dj. EX. B13. $75.00

ROBBINS, Tom. *Even Cowgirls Get the Blues.* 1976. Houghton Mifflin. UP. presentation. bl wrp. H3. $200.00

ROBBINS, Tom. *Even Cowgirls Get the Blues.* 1976. Houghton Mifflin. 1st ed. inscr. wrp. H3. $150.00

ROBBINS, Tom. *Jitterbug Perfume.* 1984. Bantam. 1st ed. dj. RS. EX. P1. $20.00

ROBBINS, Tom. *Still Life With Woodpecker.* 1980. Bantam. 1st HrdCvr ed. dj. EX. B13/K2. $65.00

ROBERT, Les. *Pepper Pike.* 1988. St Martin. 1st ed. dj. EX. F5. $16.00

ROBERT-HOUDIN, J.E. *Memoirs.* 1944. Minneapolis. Jones. 1st ed. 457 p. EX. J3. $17.00

ROBERTS, Daniel. *Some Memoirs of the Life of John Roberts.* nd. Phil. Longstreth. 16mo. 108 p. V1. $10.00

ROBERTS, Ellwood. *Lyrics of Quakerism.* 1895. Norristown. Wills. 8vo. 273 p. VG. V1. $8.00

ROBERTS, K. *It Must Be Your Tonsils.* 1936. NY. dj. VG. B3. $27.50

ROBERTS, Keith. *Kiteworld.* nd. Book Club. dj. VG. P1. $4.50

ROBERTS, Kenneth. *Antiquamania...* 1928. NY. Ils 1st ed. 260 p. G. T5. $25.00

ROBERTS, Kenneth. *Boon Island.* 1956. Doubleday. sgn. dj. H3. $75.00

ROBERTS, Kenneth. *Boon Island.* 1956. NY. presentation. G. T5. $25.00

ROBERTS, Kenneth. *Capt Caution: Chronicle of Arundel.* 1934. Doubleday Doran. inscr. dj. H3. $150.00

ROBERTS, Kenneth. *Cowpens: Great Morale-Builder.* 1957. Westholm Pub. 1st ed. 1/400. VG. T5. $25.00

ROBERTS, Kenneth. *Henry Gross & His Dowsing Rod.* 1951. Doubleday. 1st ed. sgn. dj. EX. B13. $85.00

ROBERTS, Kenneth. *I Wanted To Write.* 1949. Garden City. 1st ed. 471 p. G. T5. $12.50

ROBERTS, Kenneth. *Lydia Bailey.* 1947. Doubleday. Ltd ed. sgn. slipcase. ES. H3. $175.00

ROBERTS, Kenneth. *Lydia Bailey.* 1947. Doubleday. 1st ed. 488 p. xl. G. B10. $4.00

ROBERTS, Kenneth. *March to Quebec.* 1938. NY. 1st ed. dj. VG. B3. $45.00

ROBERTS, Kenneth. *March to Quebec.* 1947. Garden City. 720 p. G. T5. $17.50

ROBERTS, Kenneth. *Oliver Wiswell.* 1940. Doubleday Doran. sgn. 2 vols. TEG. slipcase. H3. $175.00

ROBERTS, Kenneth. *Oliver Wiswell.* 1940. NY. 1st ed. dj. VG. B3. $35.00

ROBERTS, Kenneth. *Our Cornell.* 1939. Ithaca. Ils MB Wht. 1st ed. VG. B3. $50.00

ROBERTS, Kenneth. *Our Cornell.* 1939. Ithaca. 1st ed. VG. B3. $65.00

ROBERTS, Kenneth. *Rabble in Arms.* 1936. NY. inscr. 870 p. T5. $95.00

ROBERTS, Kenneth. *Sun Hunting.* 1922. Bobbs Merrill. 1st ed. 2nd issue bdg. dj. EX. B13. $200.00

ROBERTS, Kenneth. *Sun Hunting.* 1922. Indianapolis. 1st ed. VG. P4. $60.00

ROBERTS, Kenneth. *Trending Into ME.* 1938. Boston. Ils Wyeth. 1st ed. dj. EX. B3. $65.00

ROBERTS, Kenneth. *Trending Into ME.* 1938. Boston. Ils Wyeth. 1st Trade ed. 394 p. G. T5. $37.50

ROBERTS, Kenneth. *Water Unlimited.* 1957. NY. 1st ed. dj. VG. B3. $32.50

ROBERTS, L.J. *Biographical Sketch With Extracts From Her Journal...* 1895. Phil. Ferris. 12mo. 286 p. VG. V1. $12.00

ROBERTS, Les. *Infinite No of Monkeys.* 1987. St Martin. 1st ed. dj. EX. F5. $20.00

ROBERTS, Les. *Not Enough Horses.* 1988. St Martin. 1st ed. dj. EX. F5. $15.00

ROBERTS, Lionel. *In-World.* 1968. Arcadia. 1st ed. dj. xl. P1. $5.00

ROBERTS, Mary. *Conchologist's Companion.* 1824. London. 8vo. rebound. VG. $50.00

ROBERTS, Mary. *Ruins & Old Trees Associated With Memorable Events...* c 1840. London. Ils Gilbert. 8vo. EX. $90.00

ROBERTS, Orlando. *Narrative of Voyages & Excursions on E Coast...Central Am.* 1965. FL U. facsimile of 1827 ed. 12mo. F2. $15.00

ROBERTS, Patricia. *Tender Prey.* 1983. Doubleday. 1st ed. dj. VG. P1. $15.00

ROBERTS, S.C. *Dr Johnson in Cambridge. Essays in Boswellian Imitation.* 1922. London. 1st ed. VG. $40.00

ROBERTS, W.F. *Wheatley: His Life & Works.* 1910. London. 4to. wrp. $50.00

ROBERTS & GOODCHILD. *Dear Old Gentleman.* 1954. Macmillan. 1st Am ed. dj. EX. F5. $24.00

ROBERTS & MOUNTFORD. *Dream-Time Book: Australian Aboriginal Myths in Paintings...* 1973. Englewood Cliffs. 1st ed. lg folio. dj. EX. $75.00

ROBERTSON, F. *Ram in the Thicket: Story of Roaming Homesteader Family...* 1959. NY. Ils dj. VG. $20.00

ROBERTSON, J.H. *Sandy Township Hist...* c 1910. Magnolia, OH. Sandy Valley Pr. 16 p. wrp. fragile. T5. $22.50

ROBERTSON, J.I. *Stonewall Brigade.* 1977. Baton Rouge. dj. M. $40.00

ROBERTSON, L.M. *Frederika & the Convict.* 1965. Crime Club. 1st ed. dj. xl. P1. $5.00

ROBERTSON, M.G. *Sculpture of Palenque Vol 2.* 1985. Princeton. 1st ed. 4to. 350 p. dj. F2. $125.00

ROBERTSON, M.G. *3rd Palenque Round Table.* 1978. Austin. 1st ed. 226 p. dj. F2. $35.00

ROBERTSON, Martin. *Greek Painting.* 1959. Luasanne. Great Centuries of Painting Series. 100 pls. T5. $65.00

ROBERTSON, R.B. *Of Whales & Men: 1st-Hand Account of Antarctic Whaling.* 1954. Book Club. 299 p. dj. VG. B10. $4.25

ROBERTSON, Thomas. *SW Utopia.* 1964. Ward Ritchie. Ils. 266 p. dj. F2. $15.00

ROBERTSON, William. *Annual Report of Am Hist Assn for Year 1907.* 1908. GPO. F2. $25.00

ROBERTSON, William. *Works.* 1822. London. octavo. 12 vols. EX. $400.00

ROBERTSON & HARRIS. *Soapy Smith: King of Frontier Conmen.* 1961. NY. 1st ed. 244 p. dj. VG. B3. $25.00

ROBESON, Kenneth; see Goulart, Ron.

ROBESON, Paul. *Here I Stand.* 1958. Othello Assn. HrdCvr ed. sgn. dj. EX. scarce. K2. $300.00

ROBICSEK & HALES. *Maya Ceramic Vases From the Classic Period.* 1982. VA U Mus. 1st ed. 4to. wrp. F2. $20.00

ROBICSK, F. *Smoking God: Tobacco in Maya Art, Hist, & Religion.* 1978. Norman. 1st Am ed. dj. EX. $35.00

ROBINS. *Elizabethway Stations.* 1913. Dodd Mead. 1st ed. xl. G. R5. $25.00

ROBINSON, Alvan Jr. *MA Collection of Martial Music.* 1820. Exeter, NH. 72 p. wrp. B3. $250.00

ROBINSON, C.N. *British Tar in Fact & Fiction.* 1909. Harper. Ils. 8vo. VG. $65.00

ROBINSON, E.A. *Amaranth.* 1934. Macmillan. inscr. gilt bl bdg. H3. $35.00

ROBINSON, E.A. *Glory of the Nightingales.* 1930. Macmillan. inscr. gilt gr bdg. gr dj. H3. $40.00

ROBINSON, E.A. *Glory of the Nightingales.* 1930. Macmillan. Ltd ed. 1/500. sgn. bl bdg. slipcase. H3. $50.00

ROBINSON, E.A. *Lancelot.* 1920. NY. Review 1st ed. VG. C1. $44.50

ROBINSON, E.A. *Lancelot.* 1920. NY. Seltzer. Special ed. 1/450. VG. C1. $65.00

ROBINSON, E.A. *Roman Bartholow.* 1923. Macmillan. Ltd ed. 1/750. sgn. TEG. H3. $35.00

ROBINSON, E.A. *Talifer.* 1933. Macmillan. Ltd ed. 1/273. sgn. boxed. VG. $60.00

ROBINSON, E.A. *Tristram.* 1927. later print. VG. C1. $3.00

ROBINSON, E.F. *Houses in Am.* 1936. NY. Ils TP Robinson. A4. $40.00

ROBINSON, Edith. *Little Puritan.* 1901. Page. Ils Schmidt. Cosy Corner Series. VG. $7.00

ROBINSON, Gil. *Old Wagon Days.* 1925. Brockwell. 1st ed. octavo. 250 p. VG. H3. $75.00

ROBINSON, Henry. *Stout Cortez.* 1931. Century. 1st ed. 347 p. F2. $15.00

ROBINSON, John. *Ferns in Their Homes & Ours.* 1883. Boston. 4th ed. 8 clr pls. gilt bdg. EX. $45.00

ROBINSON, K.S. *Memory of Whiteness.* 1985. Tor Books. dj. VG. P1. $17.50

ROBINSON, Marilynne. *Housekeeping.* 1980. NY. Farrar Straus. 1st ed. inscr. dj. EX. B13. $100.00

ROBINSON, Marilynne. *Mother Country.* 1989. London. Faber. 1st Eng ed. sgn. dj. EX. K2. $50.00

ROBINSON, Roger. *Ken Bulmer: A Bibliography.* 1983. Beccon. EX. P1. $3.50

ROBINSON, Roger. *SF & Fantasy Magazine Checklist.* 1984. Beccon. EX. P1. $3.50

ROBINSON, Sara. *KS: Its Interior & Exterior Life.* 1856. Boston. Ils. G. T1. $30.00

ROBINSON, Ted. *Life, Love, & the Weather.* 1945. Cleveland. 1/212. EX. $20.00

ROBINSON, W. *Story of AZ.* 1919. Berryhill. VG. $37.00

ROBINSON, W.M. *Confederate Privateers.* 1928. New Haven. 1st ed. dj. EX. $50.00

ROBINSON, William. *Friends of a Half Century.* 1891. London. Hicks. 1st ed. 8vo. 330 p. VG. V1. $26.00

ROBISON, Mary. *Oh!* 1981. Knopf. UP. wrp. EX. C4. $35.00

ROBISON, Mary. *Subtraction.* 1991. Knopf. UP. wrp. EX. C4. $25.00

ROBSON, William. *Old Play-Goer.* 1854. Longman Brn Gr Longman. octavo. 252 p. slipcase. H3. $125.00

ROBYNS, Gwen. *Light of a Star.* 1970. NY. 1st ed. dj. VG. B3. $35.00

ROBYNS, Gwen. *Mystery of Agatha Christie.* 1978. NY. 1st ed. dj. VG. $12.00

ROCKNE, Mrs. Knute. *Autobiography of Knute Rockne.* 1931. Notre Dame. Ltd ed. sgn. boxed. VG. B3. $50.00

ROCKWELL, Carey. *Danger in Deep Space.* nd. Grosset Dunlap. dj. EX. P1. $20.00

ROCKWELL, Carey. *On the Trail of the Space Pirates.* nd. Grosset Dunlap. decor brd. VG. P1. $15.00

ROCKWELL, Carey. *Stand By for Mars!* nd. Grosset Dunlap. decor brd. VG. P1. $10.00

ROCKWELL, F.F. *Gardening Under Glass.* 1923. NY. Ils. VG. $30.00

ROCKWELL, F.F. *Home Vegetable Gardening.* 1918. Burpee Co. Ils. VG. B10. $4.75

ROCKWELL, Norman. *My Adventures As an Ils.* 1960. Stated 1st ed. dj. EX. $30.00

ROCKWELL, W.F. *Rebellious Colonel Speaks.* 1964. McGraw. Stated 1st ed. 277 p. dj. VG. B10. $5.00

ROCKWOOD, Roy. *Bomba & the Giant Cataract.* nd. Clover. VG. P1. $5.00

ROCKWOOD, Roy. *Bomba & the Hostile Chieftain.* nd. Cupples Leon. dj. VG. P1. $10.00

ROCKWOOD, Roy. *Bomba at the Moving Mt.* nd. Cupples Leon. dj. VG. P1. $11.50

ROCKWOOD, Roy. *Bomba at the Moving Mt.* nd. Grosset Dunlap. dj. VG. P1. $7.50

ROCKWOOD, Roy. *Bomba in the Abandoned City.* nd. Cupples Leon. VG. P1. $7.50

ROCKWOOD, Roy. *Bomba in the Swamp of Death.* nd. Grosset Dunlap. VG. P1. $5.00

ROCKWOOD, Roy. *Bomba on Terror Trail.* nd. Clover. decor brd. VG. P1. $5.00

ROCKWOOD, Roy. *Bomba on Terror Trail.* nd. Cupples Leon. VG. P1. $7.00

ROCKWOOD, Roy. *By Air Express to Venus.* 1929. Cupples Leon. VG. R3. $15.00

ROCKWOOD, Roy. *By Spaceship to Saturn.* 1935. Cupples Leon. VG. R3. $15.00

ROCKWOOD, Roy. *Lost on the Moon.* nd. Whitman. dj. VG. P1. $20.00

ROCKWOOD, Roy. *Through Space to Mars.* 1935. Cupples Leon. VG. R3. $15.00

RODD, Ralph. *Midnight Murder.* 1931. Collins Crime Club. 1st ed. VG. P1. $20.00

RODEN, H.W. *Too Busy To Die.* 1944. Doubleday Book Club. VG. P1. $10.00

RODEN, H.W. *Too Busy To Die.* 1944. Morrow. xl. VG. P1. $5.00

RODEN, H.W. *Wake for a Lady.* 1946. Morrow. 1st ed. dj. VG. F5. $20.00

RODEN, H.W. *You Only Hang Once.* 1945. Triangle. 4th ed. dj. VG. P1. $10.00

RODGERS & HAMMERSTEIN. *Me & Juliet.* 1953. Random House. 1st ed. dj. VG. H3. $50.00

RODGERS & HAMMERSTEIN. *OK!* 1943. Random House. 1st ed. dj. VG. H3. $100.00

RODITI, Edouard. *Disorderly Poet.* 1975. Capra. Chapbook Series. 1/100. sgn. EX. K2. $20.00

RODMAN, H.A. *Destiny Express.* 1990. Atheneum. UP. wrp. w/promotional sheet. K2. $50.00

RODMAN, O.H.P. *Handbook of Salt-Water Fishing.* 1950. NY. Ils 1st ed. inscr. 274 p. T5. $9.50

RODMAN, Selden. *Artists in Tune With Their World.* 1985. New Haven. 1st ed. wrp. F2. $10.00

RODMAN, Selden. *Caribbean.* 1968. Hawthorn Books. 1st ed. 4to. 320 p. dj. F2. $15.00

RODMAN, Selden. *Colombia Traveler.* 1971. Hawthorn Books. 1st ed. 173 p. dj. F2. $15.00

RODMAN, Selden. *Guatemala Traveler.* 1967. Meredith Pr. 1st ed. 127 p. dj. F2. $15.00

RODMAN, Selden. *Mexican Traveler.* 1969. Meredith Pr. 1st ed. 264 p. dj. F2. $15.00

RODNEY. *Kootenai Brn.* 1969. Sidney, British Columbia. 1st Canadian ed. dj. VG. C2. $37.00

RODRIQUEZ, Mario. *Cadiz Experiment in Central Am 1808-1826.* 1978. CA U. 1st ed. 316 p. dj. F2. $20.00

ROE, E.P. *Orig Belle.* nd. (1885) Dodd. 533 p. VG. B10. $3.75

ROEBURT, John. *Hollow Man.* 1954. Simon Schuster. 1st ed. dj. EX. F5. $20.00

ROEBURT, John. *Lunatic Time.* 1956. Simon Schuster. 1st ed. dj. VG. F5. $22.50

ROEBURT, John. *Ruby MacLaine.* 1964. MacFadden. 1st ed. wrp. EX. F5. $8.00

ROEBURT, John. *Seneca – USA.* 1947. Samuel Curl. 1st ed. dj. VG. F5. $17.00

ROEDER, Ralph. *Juarez & His Mexico.* 1947. Viking. 761 p. F2. $10.00

ROEDER, Ralph. *Men of the Renaissance.* 1933. NY. 1st ed. VG. $10.00

ROEHRENBECK, W.J. *Regiment That Saved the Capital.* 1961. NY. sgn. dj. EX. $30.00

ROETHKE, Theodore. *Lost Son & Other Poems.* 1948. Doubleday. dj. w/sgn leaf. H3. $350.00

ROFFMAN, Jan. *Walk in the Dark.* 1970. Crime Club. 1st ed. dj. VG. P1. $15.00

ROGERS, George. *Memorandum Travels of Universalist Preacher.* 1845. Cincinnati. VG. G1. $60.00

ROGERS, Mike. *Complete Mike Rogers.* 1975. Chicago. Magic Inc. 1st ed. 250 p. NM. J3. $14.00

ROGERS, Mike. *New Wave Rambling Ace.* 1988. Bali-Sterling Magic. NM. J3. $6.00

ROGERS, Samuel. *Recollections of the Table Talk of Samuel Rogers.* 1856. London. Ils. AEG. full leather. M. $250.00

ROGERS, Spender. *Case of Surgical Amputation From Aboriginal Peru.* 1973. San Diego. 1st ed. 4to. wrp. F2. $7.50

ROGERS, Terri. *Secrets: Orig Magic of Terri Rogers.* 1986. London. Breese. 1st ed. 81 p. dj. NM. J3. $18.00

ROGERS, Terri. *Word of Mind.* 1986. London. Breese. 1st ed. 13 p. SftCvr. NM. J3. $8.00

ROGERS & HAMMERSTEIN. *Carousel.* 1946. Knopf. 1st ed. dj. EX. B13. $100.00

ROHMER, Richard. *Exodus UK.* 1975. McClelland Stewart. 1st ed. dj. EX. P1. $10.00

ROHMER, Sax. *Bimbashi Barouk of Egypt.* 1944. McBride. 1st ed. dj. EX. R3. $100.00

ROHMER, Sax. *Bimbashi Barouk of Egypt.* 1970. Bookfinger. M. R3. $10.00

ROHMER, Sax. *Brood of the Witch Queen.* nd. Collier. VG. P1. $20.00

ROHMER, Sax. *Brood of the Witch Queen.* 1924. Doubleday Page. 1st ed. VG. P1. $45.00

ROHMER, Sax. *Daughter of Fu Manchu.* nd. Collier. EX. R3. $10.00

ROHMER, Sax. *Daughter of Fu Manchu.* 1931. Doubleday Doran. 1st ed. G. P1. $15.00

ROHMER, Sax. *Day the World Ended.* 1930. Crime Club. 1st ed. xl. G. R3. $10.00

ROHMER, Sax. *Devil Doctor.* 1973. Tom Stacey. dj. EX. P1. $20.00

ROHMER, Sax. *Dope.* 1919. NY. McBride. 2nd print. gilt gr bdg. VG. $50.00

ROHMER, Sax. *Dream Detective.* nd. AL Burt. VG. P1. $20.00

ROHMER, Sax. *Drums of Fu Manchu.* nd. Collier. EX. R3. $10.00

ROHMER, Sax. *Emperor Fu Manchu.* 1954. London. 1st ed. dj. EX. R3. $50.00

ROHMER, Sax. *Emperor of Am.* nd. Collier. G. R3. $10.00

ROHMER, Sax. *Fire Tongue.* nd. McKinlay. VG. R3. $10.00

ROHMER, Sax. *Fu Manchu's Bride.* nd. Collier. VG. R3. $10.00

ROHMER, Sax. *Golden Scorpion.* 1932. Methuen. 11th print. VG. P1. $25.00

ROHMER, Sax. *Golden Scorpion.* 1920. McBride. 1st ed. fair. $10.00

ROHMER, Sax. *Golden Scorpion.* 1972. Tom Stacey. dj. EX. P1. $20.00

ROHMER, Sax. *Gr Eyes of Bast.* 1920. McBride. 1st ed. VG. P1. $75.00

ROHMER, Sax. *Hand of Fu Manchu.* nd. AL Burt. G. R3. $10.00

ROHMER, Sax. *Insidious Fu Manchu.* nd. AL Burt. dj. VG. P1. $40.00

ROHMER, Sax. *Insidious Fu Manchu.* nd. Grosset Dunlap. dj. EX. R3. $25.00

ROHMER, Sax. *Island of Fu Manchu.* 1941. Crime Club. 1st ed. dj. EX. R3. $100.00

ROHMER, Sax. *Mask of Fu Manchu.* nd. AL Burt. dj. VG. R3. $22.50

ROHMER, Sax. *Mask of Fu Manchu.* nd. Collier. EX. R3. $10.00

ROHMER, Sax. *Mask of Fu Manchu.* 1955. Cassell. VG. P1. $15.00

ROHMER, Sax. *Moon of Madness.* nd. AL Burt. VG. P1. $25.00

ROHMER, Sax. *Mystery of Fu Manchu.* nd. Methuen. 2nd ed. G. P1. $20.00

ROHMER, Sax. *Mystery of Fu Manchu.* 1972. Tom Stacey. dj. EX. P1. $20.00

ROHMER, Sax. *Orchard of Tears.* 1969. Bookfinger. 1st Am ed. EX. R3. $15.00

ROHMER, Sax. *President Fu Manchu.* nd. Collier. EX. R3. $10.00

ROHMER, Sax. *Quest of the Sacred Slipper.* nd. AL Burt. dj. VG. P1. $50.00

ROHMER, Sax. *Quest of the Sacred Slipper.* nd. Collier. VG. R3. $10.00

ROHMER, Sax. *Re-Enter Fu Manchu.* 1957. London. 1st ed. dj. EX. R3. $50.00

ROHMER, Sax. *Return of Fu Manchu.* nd. McKinlay Stone MacKenzie. VG. P1. $10.00

ROHMER, Sax. *Return of Fu Manchu.* nd. AL Burt. VG. P1. $7.50

ROHMER, Sax. *Shadow of Fu Manchu.* 1948. Crime Club. 1st ed. dj. EX. R3. $100.00

ROHMER, Sax. *Sins of Severac Babylon.* 1928. Cassell. 7th ed. xl. G. P1. $12.00

ROHMER, Sax. *Sins of Severac Babylon.* 1967. Bookfinger. 1st Am ed. EX. R3. $15.00

ROHMER, Sax. *Tales of E & W.* nd. AL Burt. VG. R3. $12.50

ROHMER, Sax. *Tales of E & W.* 1933. Doubleday. 1st ed. VG. R3. $30.00

ROHMER, Sax. *Trail of Fu Manchu.* nd. Collier. VG. R3. $10.00

ROHMER, Sax. *Yel Claw.* nd. McKinlay Stone MacKenzie. VG. P1. $20.00

ROHMER, Sax. *Yel Claw.* nd. AL Burt. dj. VG. R3. $27.50

ROHMER, Sax. *Yel Claw.* 1924. Methuen. 11th ed. dj. VG. P1. $25.00

ROHMER, Sax. *Yu'an Hee See Laughs.* 1932. Crime Club. 1st ed. EX. R3. $27.50

ROHMER, Sax. *Yu'an Hee See Laughs.* 1932. NY. 1st ed. dj. VG. B3. $65.00

ROHMER, Sax. *7 Sins.* 1943. McBride. 1st ed. dj. EX. R3. $100.00

ROIS & SCIBELLA. *2 for Her.* 1989. Blk Ace. 2nd ed. 1/100. PB. B4. $6.00

ROITER, Fulvio. *Mexique.* 1970. Zurich. Atlantis. 1st ed. 4to. 175 p. F2. $20.00

ROJANKOVSKY, F. *Tall Book of Nursery Tales.* nd. NY/Evanston. Harper Row. 120 p. VG. $18.00

ROJAS, Pedro. *Art & Architecture of Mexico.* 1968. London. Hamlyn. 1st ed. dj. F2. $25.00

ROLFE, Lionell. *Last Train N.* 1987. Panjandrum. sgn. EX. B4. $10.00

ROLFE, Lionell. *Literary LA.* 1981. Chronicle Books. wrp. EX. B4. $8.00

ROLFE, William. *Shakespeare's King Richard the 2nd.* nd. (1918) Am Book. Ils. VG. B10. $4.25

ROLLINS. *Cowboy.* 1922. NY. 1st ed. VG. C2. $35.00

ROLPH, C.H. *Trail of Lady Chatterley.* 1961. private print. Ils Hogarth. 1st ed. EX. $55.00

ROLVAAG, O.E. *Giants in the Earth.* 1927. Harper. 1st ed. dj. EX. C4. $40.00

ROLVAAG, O.E. *Peder Victorious.* 1929. Harper. 1st ed. VG. $11.00

ROMANO, Deane. *Flight From Time 1.* 1972. Walker. 1st ed. dj. VG. P1. $12.50

ROMBAUER, Irma. *Cookbook for Girls & Boys.* 1952. Bobbs Merrill. 1st ed. 243 p. dj. EX. $15.00

ROMBAUER, Irma. *Joy of Cooking.* 1946. Indianapolis. 6th print. sgn. G. B3. $35.00

ROMERO & SPARROW. *Martin.* 1977. Stein Day. 1st ed. dj. EX. F5. $30.00

ROMSEY, Peter. *Lidless Eye.* nd. Roy. dj. VG. P1. $7.50

RONALD, James. *This Way Out.* 1939. Lippincott. 1st ed. dj. xl. P1. $10.00

ROOKE, Leon. *Fat Woman.* 1981. Knopf. UP. wrp. EX. C4. $25.00

ROOKE, Leon. *Good Baby.* 1990. Knopf. AP. EX. K2. $15.00

ROOKWOOD, Roy. *Bomba, Jungle Boy/Swamp of Death.* 1929. Cupples. tan bdg. G. B10. $3.00

ROOKWOOD, Roy. *Bomba/Jaguar Island.* 1953. Grosset. VG. B10. $3.00

ROOKWOOD. *OR State Documents: Checklist 1843-1925.* 1925? OR Hist Soc. 283 p. A5. $35.00

ROONEY & HARTWELL. *Off the Record: Best Stories of Foreign Correspondents.* 1952. NY. 1st Am ed. 42 sgns. VG. C1. $149.00

ROOS, Kelley. *Who Saw Maggie Brn?* 1967. Dodd Mead. 1st ed. dj. xl. P1. $5.00

ROOSEVELT, Anna. *Parmana.* 1980. Academic Pr. 1st ed. 320 p. F2. $35.00

ROOSEVELT, Eleanor. *Christmas: A Story.* 1940. Knopf. Ils Kredel. 1st ed. dj. VG. $22.00

ROOSEVELT, Eleanor. *This I Remember.* 1949. NY. 1st ed. 1/1000. sgn. EX. $95.00

ROOSEVELT, Kermit. *Long Trail.* 1921. Review of Reviews. sgn. 12mo. VG. H3. $75.00

ROOSEVELT, Nicholas. *Venezuela's Place in the Sun.* 1940. Round Table. 1st ed. 88 p. F2. $10.00

ROOSEVELT, Theodore. *African Game Trails.* 1910. NY. 1st ed. G. $35.00

ROOSEVELT, Theodore. *African Game Trails.* 1910. NY. 1st ed. VG. K1. $100.00

ROOSEVELT, Theodore. *Naval War of 1812.* 1882. NY. 1st ed. EX. G1. $80.00

ROOSEVELT, Theodore. *Outdoor Pastimes of an Am Hunter.* 1905. NY. 1st ed. VG. $65.00

ROOSEVELT, Theodore. *Ranch Life & Hunting Trail.* 1897. NY. Century. Ils Remington. 186 p. VG. B3. $75.00

ROOSEVELT, Theodore. *Rank & File.* 1928. NY. Ils JW Thomason. 1st ed. VG. T5. $32.50

ROOSEVELT, Theodore. *Rough Riders.* 1899. NY. 1st ed. 298 p. TEG. T5. $225.00

ROOSEVELT, Theodore. *Through the Brazilian Wilderness.* 1914. Scribner. 1st ed. 382 p. F2. $60.00

ROOSEVELT, Theodore. *Winning of the W.* 1889. NY. Presidential ed. 4 vols. VG. T1. $70.00

ROOSEVELT, Theodore. *Works.* 1923. Scribner. Memorial ed. 1/1050. 24 vols. H3. $850.00

ROPES, J.C. *Army Under Pope.* nd. NY. Brussel. 229 p. PB. VG. S1. $6.00

ROPS, Felicien. *Felicien Rops: l'Art et la Vie.* 1928. np. (Paris) Eds Marcel Seheur. 1st ed. 298 p. R4. $125.00

ROQUELAURE, A.N. see Rice, Ann.

RORIMER, James. *Ultra-Violet Rays & Use in Examination of Works of Art.* 1931. Met Mus Art. 1/1000. VG. $45.00

ROSCOE, Theodore. *Grave Must Be Deep.* 1988. Starmont. 1st ed. wrp. M. R3. $9.95

ROSCOE, Theodore. *Toughest in the Legion.* 1989. Starmont. 1st ed. wrp. M. R3. $9.95

ROSCOE, Theodore. *US Submarine Operations in WWII.* 1950. Annapolis. Ils. fld maps. 577 p. T5. $25.00

ROSCOE, Theodore. *Web of Conspiracy.* 1959. Prentice Hall. 1st ed. dj. VG. B3. $32.50

ROSCOE, Theodore. *Web of Conspiracy.* 1960. Englewood Cliffs. 2nd ed. dj. EX. B3. $25.00

ROSCOE, Theodore. *Z Is for Zombie.* 1989. Starmont. 1st ed. wrp. M. R3. $9.95

ROSE, R.R. *Advocates & Adversaries.* 1977. Chicago. Ils. TEG. 328 p. VG. T5. $22.50

ROSE, Thomas. *Westmoreland, Cumberland, Durham, & Northumberland, Ils.* 1833. London. 4to. 3 vols. AEG. gilt bdg. T5. $175.00

ROSE, Wendy. *Hopi Roadrunner Dancing.* 1973. Greenfield Review. 1st ed. K2. $55.00

ROSE & BACON. *Day of the Cid.* 1919. CA U. 130 p. VG. C1. $9.50

ROSE & CARLESS. *Manual of Surgery for Students & Practioners.* 1904. Wood. 5th ed. 1200 p. gilt bl bdg. VG. $60.00

ROSE & ROSE. *Shattered Ring.* 1970. John Knox Pr. VG. P1. $7.50

ROSE & SOUCHON. *New Orleans Jazz: A Family Album.* 1967. Baton Rouge. Ils 1st ed. 4to. 232 p. dj. EX. T1. $50.00

ROSENBACH, A.S.W. *Biography of Edwin Wolf.* 1960. Cleveland. 1st ed. dj. $75.00

ROSENBACH, A.S.W. *Book Hunter's Holiday.* 1936. Houghton Mifflin. Ltd ed. 1/760. sgn. boxed. H3. $250.00

ROSENBACH, A.S.W. *Books & Bidders.* 1927. Boston. Ils. EX. T1. $30.00

ROSENBERG, J.D. *Fall of Camelot: Study of Tennyson's Idylls of the King.* 1973. Harvard U. 1st ed. M. C1. $19.50

ROSENBLUM, Robert. *Arcade.* 1984. Doubleday. 1st ed. dj. EX. F5. $15.00

ROSENBLUM, Robert. *Sweetheart Deal.* nd. Book Club. dj. VG. P1. $5.00

ROSENBLUM, Robert. *Sweetheart Deal.* 1976. Putnam. 1st ed. dj. EX. P1. $15.00

ROSENDAHL, C.E. *Up Ship!* 1931. NY. Ils. sgn. 311 p. VG. T5. $150.00

ROSENFELD, Paul. *Port of NY.* 1924. Harcourt Brace. 1st ed. wht dj. EX. B13. $300.00

ROSHWALD, Mordecai. *Level 7.* nd. Signet D2659. 2nd ed. xl. rebound. VG. P1. $3.00

ROSINE ASSOCIATION. *Annual Report of the Managers.* 1860. Phil. Diament. 16mo. 12 p. wrp. VG. V1. $15.00

ROSS, Alexander. *Fur Hunters of the Far W...* 1855. London. Smith Elder. 1st ed. 1st issue. 2 vols. orig bdg. VG. H3. $750.00

ROSS, Barnaby. *Tragedy of Y.* 1932. Viking. 1st ed. VG. P1. $50.00

ROSS, Colin. *Eleanor.* 1953. Woodford Pr. 1st ed. dj. EX. F5. $20.00

ROSS, Colin. *To Take a Wife.* 1952. Woodford Pr. 1st ed. dj. EX. F5. $25.00

ROSS, Edward. *S of Panama.* 1921. Century. 396 p. F2. $10.00

ROSS, Ishbel. *Angel of the Battlefield: Life of Clara Barton.* 1956. Harper. 305 p. dj. xl. G. S1. $8.50

ROSS, Ishbel. *Through the Lich-Gate: Biography of Little Church...* 1931. Payson. TEG. dj. EX. $30.00

ROSS, J.H. *What I Saw in NY.* 1852. Derby Miller. 2nd ed. sgn. VG. $40.00

ROSS, M. *W of Alfred Jacob Miller.* 1951. Norman. 1st ed. 4to. 200 pls. dj. VG. $65.00

ROSS, Mrs. W.P. *Life & Times of Hon William P Ross.* nd. Ft Smith, AR. 1st ed. VG. $95.00

ROSS, Norman. *Epic of Man.* 1961. Time Inc. 1st ed. folio. 307 p. F2. $10.00

ROSS, Philip. *Talley's Truth.* 1987. Tor Books. 1st ed. dj. EX. F5. $12.00

ROSS, Sam. *He Ran All the Way.* 1947. Farrar Straus. 1st ed. dj. VG. T9. $30.00

ROSSETTI, D.G. *Ballads & Narrative Poems.* 1893. Kelmscott Pr. 1/310. orig limp vellum. H3. $850.00

ROSSHANDLER, Leo. *Man-Eaters & Pretty Ladies.* 1972. NY. 2nd print. wrp. F2. $20.00

ROSSI, Jean-Baptiste; see Japrisot, Sebastien.

ROSSITER, Oscar. *Tetrasomy 2.* 1974. Doubleday. 1st ed. dj. EX. P1. $12.50

ROSSKAM, E. *Towboat River.* 1948. NY. 1st ed. 295 p. dj. VG. B3. $35.00

ROSTAND, Edmund. *Cyrano de Bergerac.* 1898. Paris. 1st ed. 1/50 on Japan. red morocco. H3. $3500.00

ROSTAND, Robert. *D'Artagnan Signature.* 1976. Putnam. 1st ed. dj. VG. P1. $12.50

ROSTRON, Arthur. *Home From the Sea.* 1931. NY. 1st ed. G. B3. $42.50

ROSTRON, Arthur. *Home From the Sea.* 1931. NY. 1st ed. 259 p. VG. B3. $55.00

ROSZAK, Theodore. *Dreamwatcher.* 1985. Doubleday. 1st ed. dj. RS. EX. P1. $15.00

ROTERBERG, A. *Card Tricks: How To Do Them, Sleight of Hand.* 1902. Chicago. Drake. 168 p. VG. J3. $10.00

ROTH, Holly. *Content Assignment.* nd. Book Club. VG. P1. $3.00

ROTH, Holly. *Mask of Glass.* nd. Book Club. VG. P1. $3.00

ROTH, Holly. *Sleeper.* 1955. Simon Schuster. 1st ed. dj. VG. P1. $10.00

ROTH, Joseph. *Job: Story of a Simple Man.* 1931. Viking. 1st Am ed. dj. EX. B13. $50.00

ROTH, Philip. *Anatomy Lesson.* 1983. Farrar Straus. UP. wrp. ES. EX. B13. $65.00

ROTH, Philip. *Facts: Novelist's Autobiography.* 1988. Farrar Straus. UP. wrp. EX. C4. $45.00

ROTH, Philip. *Goodbye Columbus & 5 Short Stories.* 1966. Modern Lib. 1st ed. sgn. wht dj. EX. T9. $55.00

ROTH, Philip. *Great Am Novel.* 1973. Holt Rinehart Winston. 1st ed. dj. VG. H3. $40.00

ROTH, Philip. *Letting Go.* 1962. Random House. 1st ed. dj. EX. H3. $75.00

ROTH, Philip. *My Life As a Man.* 1974. Holt Rinehart Winston. 3rd print. dj. EX. H3. $35.00

ROTH, Philip. *On the Air.* nd. New Am Review. 1/1500. wrp. EX. K2. $65.00

ROTH, Philip. *Our Gang.* 1971. Random House. 1st ed. dj. EX. H3. $60.00

ROTH, Philip. *Portnoy's Complaint.* 1969. Random House. 1st ed. dj. EX. H3. $85.00

ROTH, Philip. *Professor of Desire.* 1977. Farrar Straus Giroux. 1st ed. dj. EX. H3. $60.00

ROTH, Philip. *Reading Myself & Others.* 1975. Farrar Straus Giroux. 1st ed. dj. EX. H3. $30.00

ROTH, Philip. *When She Was Good.* 1967. Random House. 1st ed. dj. EX. H3. $50.00

ROTH, Philip. *Zuckerman Bound.* 1985. Farrar Straus. 1st ed. dj. EX. B13. $200.00

ROTH, Philip. *Zuckerman Unbound.* 1981. Farrar Straus Giroux. Ltd 1st ed. 1/350. sgn. slipcase. B13/H3. $75.00

ROTHENBERG, Jerome. *Seneca Journal.* 1978. New Directions. inscr. wrp. EX. K2. $50.00

ROTHENSTEIN & CECIL. *Men of the RAF.* 1942. London. 1st ed. 134 p. dj. T5. $75.00

ROTHERY, Agnes. *Images of Earth: Guatemala.* 1937. Viking. 2nd print. 206 p. F2. $15.00

ROTHWELL, H.T. *Dive Deep for Danger.* 1966. Roy. VG. P1. $10.00

ROTHWELL, H.T. *Duet for 3 Spies.* 1967. Roy. 1st ed. dj. EX. P1. $10.00

ROTSLER, William. *Blackhawk.* 1982. Warner. 1st ed. wrp. EX. F5. $7.50

ROTSLER, William. *Mr Merlin: Episode 1.* 1st/only ed. pb. VG. C1. $5.00

ROTTENSTEINER, Franz. *SF Book.* 1975. New Am Lib. EX. P1. $15.00

ROTTENSTEINER, Franz. *SF Book.* 1975. Seabury. dj. EX. P1. $15.00

ROTTENSTEINER, Franz. *View From Another Shore.* 1973. Seabury. VG. P1. $7.50

ROUCHAUD, Martin. *Time of Our Lives.* nd. (1946) Pantheon. 1st Am ed. 322 p. dj. xl. B10. $4.25

ROUECHE, Berton. *Feral.* nd. Book Club. dj. VG. P1. $3.00

ROUGHEAD, William. *Murderer's Companion.* 1941. Readers Club. VG. P1. $20.00

ROUNDS, Glen. *Ol' Paul the Mighty Logger.* 1936. Holiday House. sq 8vo. dj. EX. $25.00

ROURKE, Thomas. *Gomez, Tyrant of the Andes*. 1936. Morrow. 1st ed. 320 p. dj. F2. $15.00

ROUSE & CRUXENT. *Venezuelan Archaeology*. 1969. New Haven. 2nd print. 179 p. dj. F2. $25.00

ROUSSEAU, J.J. *Confessions*. 1902. Phil. Gebbie. Astral ed. 1/56. 12 vols. quarto. H3. $750.00

ROUSSEAU, J.J. *Nouvelle Heloise, Lettres de Deux Amans...* 1794. Paris. Chez Le Prieur. Nouvelle ed. 6 vols. 12mo. VG. H3. $300.00

ROUSSEAU, J.J. *Oeuvres Completes*. 1835. Paris. Libraire-Editeur. 4 vols. tall octavo. H3. $400.00

ROUSSEAU, Victor. *Messiah of the Cylinder*. 1974. Hyperion. reprint of 1917 ed. EX. R3. $15.00

ROUSSEAU, Victor. *Sea Demons*. 1974. Hyperion. reprint of 1924 ed. EX. R3. $15.00

ROWE, Ann. *Century of Change in Guatemalan Textiles*. 1981. NY. 1st ed. 4to. wrp. F2. $22.00

ROWE, Ann. *Junius B Bird Conference on Andean Textiles*. 1968. WA. Textile Mus. 1st ed. 4to. wrp. F2. $35.00

ROWE, C.A. *Quaker Boy Growing Up*. 1961. NY. Exposition Pr. 1st ed. sgn. 12mo. 170 p. dj. V1. $9.00

ROWE, John. *Long Live the King*. 1984. Stein Day. dj. VG. P1. $15.00

ROWENA. *Fantastic Art of Rowena*. 1983. Pocket Books. 1st ed. sgn. lg wrp. M. R3. $20.00

ROWLEY, John. *Taxidermy & Mus Exhibition*. 1925. NY. 1st ed. VG. G1. $22.00

ROWNTREE, J.W. *Man's Relation to God & Other Addresses*. 1919. Friends Bookstore. Pennsbury Series 3. 8vo. 191 p. VG. V1. $10.00

ROWNTREE, J.W. *Social Service: Its Place in the Soc of Friends*. 1913. London. Headley. 12mo. 127 p. G. V1. $10.00

ROWSE. *Cousin Jacks (Cornish in Am)*. 1969. NY. 1st ed. VG. B3. $40.00

ROY, L.E. *Polly in the SW*. 1925. Grosset. Ils Barbour. dj. VG. B10. $4.25

ROY, L.E. *Prince of Atlantis*. 1929. Educational Pr. 1st ed. EX. R3. $35.00

ROYKE, Mike. *Up Against It*. 1967. Chicago. Regnery. 1st ed. 8vo. 214 p. dj. EX. R4. $25.00

RUARK, Robert. *Horn of the Hunter*. 1953. Doubleday. 1st ed. EX. $50.00

RUARK, Robert. *Horn of the Hunter*. 1953. Garden City. dj. VG. B3. $70.00

RUARK, Robert. *Old Man Grows Older*. 1961. NY. 1st ed. dj. VG. B3. $47.50

RUARK, Robert. *Old Man's Boy Grows Older*. 1961. NY. 1st ed. dj. EX. B3. $65.00

RUARK, Robert. *Something of Value*. 1955. London. Hamond Hamond. 1st UK ed. inscr. dj. VG. B13. $50.00

RUARK, Robert. *Use Enough Gun*. 1966. NY. 1st ed. dj. VG. P1. $30.00

RUARK, Robert. *Use Enough Gun*. 1966. NY. 1st print. dj. EX. T1. $40.00

RUARK, Robert. *1 for the Road*. 1949. NY. Ils Taylor. 1st ed. dj. EX. $35.00

RUAS, Charles. *Conversations With Am Writers*. 1984. London. Quartet Books. 1st Eng ed. dj. EX. K2. $40.00

RUBEN ROMERO, J. *Anticipacion a la Muerte*. 1939. Mexico. Ruben Romero. 1st ed. sgn. wrp. EX. K2. $50.00

RUBENSTEIN, Arthur. *My Many Years*. 1980. NY. 1st ed. dj. VG. B3. $25.00

RUBER, Peter. *Last Bookman*. 1968. NY. 1st ed. 1/2500. dj. EX. $35.00

RUBIN, Jerry. *Do It!* 1970. Ballantine. 1st PB ed. VG. B4. $5.00

RUBIN, William. *Cezanne: Late Work*. 1977. MOMA. 416 p. D4. $35.00

RUBY, J.S. *Bl & Gray: Georgetown U & Civil War*. 1961. WA. dj. EX. $40.00

RUCK, Berta. *Spice of Life*. 1952. Dodd. 1st ed. dj. VG. B10. $4.50

RUDAUX & VAUCOULEURS. *Larousse Encyclopedia of Astronomy*. 1967. Prometheus. 2nd ed. dj. xl. P1. $15.00

RUDKIN, Margaret. *Margaret Rudkin Pepperidge Farm Cookbook*. 1963. Atheneum. 1st ed. 440 p. VG. B10. $12.00

RUDOFSKY, B. *Are Clothes Modern?* 1947. Chicago. 1st ed. 4to. dj. EX. $40.00

RUDOFSKY, B. *Streets for People*. 1969. NY. 1st ed. 8vo. dj. EX. $30.00

RUDORFF, Raymond. *House of the Brandersons*. 1973. Arbor house. dj. VG. P1. $20.00

RUEGAMER, Lana. *Hist of IN Hist Soc 1830-1980*. 1980. IN. 1st ed. 383 p. wht buckram. VG. B10. $10.00

RUELL, Patrick. *Castle of the Demon*. 1971. Hawthorn. 1st ed. dj. EX. P1. $20.00

RUELL, Patrick. *Long Kill*. nd. BOMC. dj. EX. P1. $7.50

RUELL, Patrick. *Red Christmas*. 1972. John Long. 1st ed. VG. P1. $12.50

RUFF, Ivan. *Dark Red Star*. 1985. Pluto Pr. 1st HrdCvr ed. dj. EX. F5. $16.00

RUFZ, E. *Enquete Sur le Serpent de la Martinque*. 1860. Paris. 2nd ed. 8vo. 402 p. gr wrp. G. rare. T1. $650.00

RUGGLES, R.G. *1 Rose (O'Neill)*. 1964. Oakland. 1st ed. sgn. dj. VG. B3. $95.00

RUHL, Arthur. *Central Am*. 1928. Scribner. 1st ed. 284 p. F2. $15.00

RUHL, Arthur. *Other Am*. 1909. Scribner. Ils. 321 p. F2. $15.00

RUINI, Carlo. *Anatomia del Cavallo, Infermita et Suoi Rimedii*. 1618. Venice. Prati. 4th ed? 2 vols in 1. folio. rare. H3. $10000.00

RUKEYSER, Muriel. *Beast in View*. 1944. Garden City. 1st ed. dj. EX. $20.00

RUKEYSER, Muriel. *Willard Gibbs*. 1945. Garden City. 1st ed. dj. VG. C2. $35.00

RULE, Ann. *Sm Sacrifices: True Story of Passion & Murder*. 1987. New Am Lib. 1st print. dj. VG. $17.00

RUMBELOW, Donald. *Complete Jack the Ripper*. 1975. Book Club. dj. VG. C1. $4.00

RUNDELL, E.R. *Clr of Blood*. 1948. Crowell. 1st ed. clipped dj. EX. F5. $18.00

RUNDLE, Anne. *Moon Branches*. 1986. Macmillan. 1st ed. dj. EX. F5. $15.00

RUNYON, Charles. *Weapon*. 1974. Doubleday. 1st ed. dj. EX. R3. $12.50

RUNYON, Damon. *Take It Easy*. 1938. NY. 1st ed. inscr. orig bdg. VG. H3. $400.00

RUNYON, Damon. *Take It Easy*. 1941. Triangle. VG. P1. $15.00

RUPERT. *Apostle Spoons*. 1929. London. 1st ed. dj. VG. C2. $45.00

RUPERTI, M. *Dogs of Character*. 1957. London. 1st ed. sm 4to. photos. VG. $20.00

RUPP, I.D. *Orig Hist of Religious Denominations at Present in US*. 1844. Phil/Harrisburg. 1st ed. EX. $75.00

RUSBY, Henry. *Jungle Memories*. 1933. Whittlesey House. 1st ed. 388 p. dj. F2. $40.00

RUSCHA, Edward. *26 Gasoline Stations*. 1969. 3rd ed. 1/3000. sgn. B4. $10.00

RUSH, Allison. *Last of Danu's Children*. 1984. PB. VG. C1. $3.00

RUSH, Norman. *Mating.* 1991. Knopf. UP. wrp. EX. C4. $30.00

RUSHDIE, Salman. *Jaguar Smile.* 1987. Viking. 1st ed. 171 p. dj. F2. $20.00

RUSHDIE, Salman. *Satanic Verses.* 1988. London. Viking. 1st ed. sgn. dj. M. C4. $500.00

RUSHDIE, Salman. *Satanic Verses.* 1989. NY. 1st Am ed. dj. EX. T9. $60.00

RUSKIN, John. *King of the Golden River.* 1905. McLoughlin Bros. Ils GA Davis. 8vo. VG. $35.00

RUSKIN, John. *King of the Golden River.* 1932. London. Ils Rackham. 1/550. sgn. boxed. EX. $350.00

RUSKIN, John. *Works.* nd. (1898) Estes. 27 vols. octavo. H3. $2000.00

RUSKIN, John. *Works.* 1903. London. Allen. Lib ed. 1/2062. 39 vols. lg octavo. H3. $6000.00

RUSS, Joanna. *Zanzibar Cat.* 1983. Arkham House. 1st ed. M. R3. $40.00

RUSS, Joanna. *2 of Them.* 1978. Berkley Putnam. 1st ed. dj. EX. P1. $25.00

RUSSELL, Bertrand. *Portraits From Memory & Other Essays.* 1956. Simon Schuster. 1st ed. 246 p. VG. B10. $8.25

RUSSELL, C.M. *Between Us & Evil.* 1950. Crime Club. 1st ed. VG. P1. $10.00

RUSSELL, C.M. *Dreadful Reckoning.* 1941. Crime Club. 1st ed. VG. P1. $22.50

RUSSELL, C.M. *No Time for Crime.* 1945. Crime Club. 1st ed. dj. VG. P1. $20.00

RUSSELL, Don. *103 Fights & Scrimmages.* 1936. WA. 1st ed. stiff wrp. $80.00

RUSSELL, E.F. *Deep Space.* 1954. Fantasy. Ltd ed. 1/300. sgn. dj. EX. R3. $150.00

RUSSELL, E.F. *Deep Space.* 1954. Fantasy. 1st ed. VG. R3. $15.00

RUSSELL, E.F. *Dreadful Sanctuary.* 1951. Fantasy. 1st ed. sgn. dj. EX. F5. $47.50

RUSSELL, E.F. *Dreadful Sanctuary.* 1972. Dobson. dj. EX. P1. $35.00

RUSSELL, E.F. *Great Explosion.* nd. Book Club. dj. VG. P1. $7.50

RUSSELL, E.F. *Great World Mysteries.* 1957. Doubleday. 1st ed. dj. EX. R3. $75.00

RUSSELL, E.F. *Sentinels From Space.* 1953. Bouregy Curl. 1st ed. dj. VG. P1. $45.00

RUSSELL, E.F. *Sinister Barrier.* 1948. Fantasy. Ltd ed. 1/500. sgn. dj. EX. R3. $125.00

RUSSELL, E.F. *Sinister Barrier.* 1948. Fantasy. 1st ed. dj. EX. R3. $55.00

RUSSELL, Elbert. *Hist of Quakerism.* 1942. NY. Macmillan. 8vo. 586 p. V1. $12.50

RUSSELL, Peter. *Ezra Pound.* 1950. London. Nevill. 1st ed. dj. EX. K2. $100.00

RUSSELL, Phillips. *Red Tiger: Adventures in Yucatan & Mexico.* 1929. Brentano. 1st ed. 336 p. F2. $25.00

RUSSELL, Ray. *Case Against Satan.* nd. Catholic Book Club. dj. VG. P1. $5.00

RUSSELL, Ray. *Colony.* 1969. Sherbourne. 1st ed. dj. VG. P1. $20.00

RUSSELL, Ray. *Dirty Money.* 1988. St Martin. 1st ed. dj. EX. F5. $15.00

RUSSELL, Ray. *Holy Horatio!* 1976. Capra. Chapbook Series. 1/100. sgn. EX. K2. $20.00

RUSSELL, Ray. *Incubus.* 1976. Morrow. 1st ed. sgn. dj. EX. F5. $30.00

RUSSELL, Ray. *Little Lexicon of Love.* 1966. Sherbourne. 1st ed. VG. P1. $15.00

RUSSELL, Ray. *Transit of Earth.* 1971. Playboy Pr. 1st ed. wrp. EX. F5. $8.00

RUSSELL, Ross. *Sound.* 1962. McFadden. 1st PB ed. VG. B4. $5.00

RUSSELL, T. *Am's War for Humanity.* c 1919. np. Victoru ed. 8vo. 514 p. G. G4. $19.00

RUSSELL, W.C. *Tragedy of Ida Noble.* 1893. London. 1st Eng ed. G. $35.00

RUSSELL OF LIVERPOOL, Lord. *Knights of Bushido: Hist of Japanese War Atrocities.* 1958. NY. Ils 1st ed. 334 p. dj. G. T5. $42.50

RUSSELL. *Bird Lives.* 1973. NY. dj. VG. B3. $45.00

RUSSO, W.L. *Everett Ruess.* 1983. Peregrine Smith. 1st ed. dj. VG. K2. $35.00

RUST, Art. *Legends: Conversations With Baseball Greats.* 1989. 1st ed. dj. EX. C1. $14.50

RUTHERFORD, Douglas. *Blk Leather Murders.* 1966. Walker. 1st ed. dj. VG. P1. $15.00

RUTHERFORD, Douglas. *Gilt-Edged Cockpit.* 1971. Crime Club. dj. xl. P1. $5.00

RUTHERFORD, Douglas. *Kick Start.* 1974. Walker. 1st ed. dj. xl. P1. $5.00

RUTHERFORD, Douglas. *On Track of Death.* 1959. Abelard Schuman. dj. VG. P1. $15.00

RUTHERFORD, Edward. *Sarum: Novel of Eng.* 1987.1st Am ed. dj. M. C1. $12.50

RUTHERFORD, Ernest. *Radioactive Substances & Their Radiations.* 1913. Cambridge. 1st ed. 699 p. $125.00

RUTHERFORD, W.D.J. *165 Days. Story of 25th Division on Luzon.* 1945. np. Ils. T5. $32.50

RUTLEDGE, Archibald. *Am Hunter.* 1937. Phil. dj. VG. B3. $40.00

RUTLEDGE, Archibald. *Hunters' Choice.* 1946. NY. 1st ed. dj. VG. B3. $70.00

RUTLEDGE, Maryse. *Silver Peril.* 1931. Fiction League. G. P1. $5.00

RUTLEDGE, Nancy. *Preying Mantis.* 1947. Crime Club. 1st ed. dj. VG. P1. $20.00

RYAN, A.J. *Poems: Patriotic, Religious, Miscellaneous.* 1904. NY. Household ed. 473 p. AEG. T5. $35.00

RYAN, Alan. *Bones Wizard.* 1988. Doubleday. ARC. dj. RS. EX. F5. $18.00

RYAN, Alan. *Cast a Cold Eye.* 1984. Dark Harvest. 1st ed. dj. EX. F5/R3. $25.00

RYAN, Alan. *Quadriphobia.* 1986. Doubleday. 1st ed. dj. RS. EX. P1. $17.50

RYAN, C.C. *Starry Messenger.* 1979. St Martin. 1st ed. dj. RS. EX. P1. $20.00

RYAN, Cornelius. *Bridge Too Far.* nd. Simon Schuster. 2nd ed. dj. VG. P1. $12.50

RYAN, Cornelius. *Last Battle.* nd. Book Club. 8vo. 571 p. dj. EX. B10. $5.00

RYAN, M.E. *For the Soul of Rafael.* 1907. McClurg. lg 8vo. VG. $30.00

RYAN, Patrick. *How I Won the War.* 1967. Ballantine. 1st PB ed. VG. B4. $4.00

RYDELL, Forbes. *Annalisa.* 1960. Gollancz. 1st ed. dj. VG. P1. $12.00

RYDELL & GILBERT. *Great Book of Magic.* 1976. Abrams. 1st ed. 271 p. silver wrp. NM. J3. $10.00

RYDER, Edward. *Elizabeth Fry: Life & Labors...* 1884. NY. E Walker's Son. 3rd ed. 8vo. 389 p. V1. $18.00

RYDER, Jonathan; see Ludlum, Robert.

RYLANDS, George. *Poems.* 1931. Hogarth. Ltd ed. 1/350. inscr. H3. $200.00

RYS, Ernest. *Leaf Burners.* 1918. London. 1st ed. sgn. VG. C1. $49.50

RYWELL, M. *Smith & Wesson: Story of the Revolver.* 1953. Harriman, TN. 1st ed. dj. VG. B3. $60.00

RYWELL, M. *Trail of Samuel Colt.* 1953. Harriman, TN. 1st ed. 1/1000. dj. VG. $60.00

SABATINI, Rafael. *Banner of the Bull.* c 1920s. Houghton Mifflin. 254 p. VG. B10. $3.50

SABATINI, Rafael. *Bellarion.* 1926. Houghton Mifflin. 1st ed. dj. EX. R3. $50.00

SABATINI, Rafael. *Hounds of God.* nd. Houghton Mifflin. dj. EX. R3. $20.00

SABATINI, Rafael. *Scaramouche: King Maker.* nd. Houghton Mifflin. dj. EX. R3. $20.00

SABATINI, Rafael. *Scaramouche: King Maker.* 1923. Grosset Dunlap. Photoplay ed. dj. EX. F5. $25.00

SABERHAGEN, F. *Dominion.* 1982. 1st ed. PB. VG. C1. $2.50

SABLOFF, Jeremy. *Cities of Ancient Mexico: Reconstructing a Lost World.* 1989. Thames Hudson. 1st ed. 224 p. wrp. F2. $15.00

SABRETACHE. *Monarchy & the Chase.* 1948. London. 1st ed. dj. VG. $25.00

SACHS, E.T. *Sleight of Hand.* 1884. London. Upcott Gill. 2nd/Enlarged ed. 408 p. EX. J3. $51.00

SACHS, E.T. *Sleight of Hand.* 1946. Fleming Book. 4th ed. 400 p. EX. J3. $11.00

SACHS. *Modern Prints & Drawings.* 1954. Knopf. Ils. 262 p. A5. $25.00

SACKETT. *Modern Battles of Trenton.* 1914. Crowell. 1st ed. G. C2. $25.00

SACKS, Janet. *Best of SF Monthly.* 1975. London. 1st ed. dj. EX. R3. $10.00

SACKVILLE-WEST, V. *Garden.* 1946. London. Michael Joseph. ARC. Ltd ed. 1/750. sgn. TEG. H3. $175.00

SADE, D.A.F. *Idee sur les Romans.* 1878. Paris. Rouveyre. 1st ed. 1/10. 12mo. wrp. R4. $100.00

SADLER, Mark; see Lynd, Dennis.

SAFFORD, W.H. *Life of Harman Blennerhassett.* 1850. Chillicothe. 1st ed. VG. T5. $125.00

SAFIRE, William. *Full Disclosure.* 1977. Doubleday. 1st ed. dj. VG. P1. $15.00

SAGAN, Francoise. *Heart-Keeper.* 1968. Dutton. 1st ed. dj. VG. P1. $8.00

SAGE, Dana. *22 Brothers.* 1950. Simon Schuster. dj. VG. P1. $7.50

SAHHON, Dell. *With a Vengeance.* 1966. Morrow. 1st ed. dj. EX. $18.00

SAINSBURY, Noel. *Billy Smith, Secret Service Ace.* 1932. Cupples Leon. VG. P1. $10.00

SAINT-EXUPERY, Antoine. *Night Flight.* 1932. NY. 1st Am ed. dj. EX. $90.00

SAINT-LAURENT, Cecil. *Cautious Maiden.* 1955. Crown. dj. xl. P1. $5.00

SAJER, Guy. *Forgotten Soldier.* 1971. NY. 1st ed. dj. VG. B3. $47.50

SALAMAN, M.C. *London Past & Present.* 1916. London. Studio. Ils. 4to. A4. $60.00

SALE, E.T. *Manors of VA in Colonial Times.* 1909. Lippincott. 1/1000. lg octavo. VG. $75.00

SALE, Richard. *Benefit Performance.* 1946. Simon Schuster. 1st ed. xl. P1. $7.00

SALE, Richard. *Not Too Narrow...Not Too Deep.* 1943. Tower. dj. VG. P1. $20.00

SALE, Richard. *Wht Buffalo.* 1975. Simon Schuster. 1st ed. dj. VG. P1. $15.00

SALINAS PEDRAZA, Jesus. *Otomi: Geography & Fauna.* 1978. NM U. 1st ed. 248 p. dj. F2. $15.00

SALINGER, J.D. *Catcher in the Rye.* nd. Random House. Modern Lib. 1st ed. dj. EX. H3. $10.00

SALINGER, J.D. *Catcher in the Rye.* 1951. Boston. 1st ed. EX. G1. $200.00

SALINGER, J.D. *Catcher in the Rye.* 1953. Paris. Robert Laffont. Trans Jean-Baptiste Rossi. 1st ed. wrp. NM. T9. $250.00

SALINGER, J.D. *Franny & Zooey.* 1961. Little Brn. 1st ed. dj. EX. H3. $150.00

SALINGER, J.D. *Kit Book for Soldiers, Sailors, & Marines.* 1942. Chicago. Con Book Pub. 1st ed. 12mo. pub mailing box. EX. B13. $850.00

SALINGER, J.D. *Raise High the Roof Beam, Carpenters/Catcher in the Rye.* 1965. Moscow. Central Committee. scarce. H3. $250.00

SALINGER, J.D. *Raise High the Roof Beam, Carpenters/Seymour.* 1959. Little Brn. 1st ed. dj. VG. H3. $60.00

SALINGER, J.D. *9 Stories.* 1953. Little Brn. 1st ed. dj. VG. M. $250.00

SALINGER, Pierre. *On Instructions of My Government.* 1971. Doubleday. 1st ed. dj. VG. P1. $15.00

SALISBURY & SALISBURY. *2 Captains W.* 1950. NY. 2nd print. dj. VG. $15.00

SALLASKA, Georgia. *3 Ships & 3 Kings.* 1969.1st Am ed. dj. VG. C1. $6.00

SALMONSON, J.A. *Swordswoman.* nd. Book Club. dj. EX. P1. $4.50

SALTER, James. *Arm of Flesh.* 1961. Harper. 1st ed. dj. EX. H3. $100.00

SALTER, James. *Dusk & Other Stories.* 1988. N Point Pr. UP. sgn. wrp. EX. C4. $75.00

SALTER, James. *Dusk & Other Stories.* 1988. N Point Pr. 1st ed. sgn. dj. EX. C4. $45.00

SALTER, James. *Hunter.* 1956. Harper. 1st ed. inscr. dj. EX. H3. $125.00

SALTER, James. *Light Years.* 1975. Random House. UP. sgn. wrp. EX. C4. $225.00

SALTER, James. *Light Years.* 1975. Random House. 1st ed. dj. EX. H3. $75.00

SALTER, James. *Light Years.* 1975. Random House. 1st ed. sgn. dj. EX. C4. $100.00

SALTER, James. *Solo Faces.* 1979. Little Brn. 1st ed. sgn. dj. EX. C4. $75.00

SALTER, James. *Sport & a Pastime.* 1967. Doubleday. Paris Review. 1st ed. dj. EX. H3. $75.00

SALTER, James. *Sport & a Pastime.* 1987. London. 1st UK ed. sgn. dj. EX. C4. $65.00

SALTER, James. *Sport & a Pastime.* 1987. London. Cape. UP. sgn. wrp. EX. C4. $125.00

SALZ, Beate. *Human Element in Industrialization.* 1955. Am Anthropologist. 265 p. wrp. F2. $15.00

SAMACHSON & SAMACHSON. *Good Digging.* 1960. Rand McNally. Ils. 224 p. dj. F2. $7.50

SAMUELS, Ernest. *Bernard Berenson: Making of a Connoisseur.* 1979. Belknap Pr. 477 p. dj. D4. $25.00

SANCEAU, Elaine. *Land of Prester John.* 1944. Knopf. 1st ed. clipped dj. EX. B13. $45.00

SANCHEZ, Thomas. *Mile Zero.* 1989. Knopf. ARC. sgn. wrp. boxed. EX. C4. $50.00

SANCHEZ, Thomas. *Mile Zero.* 1989. Knopf. 1st ed. dj. EX. B13. $35.00

SANCHEZ, Thomas. *Mile Zero.* 1990. NY. AP. sgn. wrp. K2. $45.00

SANCHEZ, Thomas. *Zoot-Suit Murders.* 1978. NY. 1st ed. sgn. dj. EX. T9. $45.00

SANCHEZ, Thomas. *4 Visions of Am.* 1977. Capra. Ltd ed. 1/225. sgns. dj. EX. scarce. K2. $175.00

SAND, Algo. *Senor Bum in the Jungle.* 1932. Nat Travel Club. Ils Robert Rotter. 1st ed. 319 p. F2. $25.00

SAND, George. *IN.* 1902. Phil. Barrie. 6 double pls. G. R5. $20.00

SAND, George. *Masterpieces.* 1902. Phil. Barrie. 1/1000. 20 vols. octavo. H3. $6000.00

SAND, George. *Mauprat.* 1902. Phil. Barrie. 9 double pls. G. R5. $20.00

SANDBURG, Carl. *Abraham Lincoln: The War Years.* 1939. Harcourt Brace. 4 vols. gray linen. VG. S1. $60.00

SANDBURG, Carl. *Always the Young Strangers.* 1953. Harcourt Brace. Autographed ed. dj. H3. $50.00

SANDBURG, Carl. *Am Song Bag.* 1927. Harcourt Brace. sgn. dj. H3. $75.00

SANDBURG, Carl. *Cornhuskers.* 1918. Holt. 1st ed. 2nd state. inscr. H3. $125.00

SANDBURG, Carl. *Good Morning Am.* 1928. Grosby Gaige. Ltd ed. 1/811. sgn. H3. $200.00

SANDBURG, Carl. *People, Yes.* 1942. Harcourt Brace. 6th print. inscr. dj. H3. $125.00

SANDBURG, Carl. *Poems of the Midwest.* 1946. Cleveland/NY. World. 1/950. EX. $125.00

SANDBURG, Carl. *Prairie Years.* 1926. Harcourt Brace. 2 vols. boxed. G. S1. $26.00

SANDBURG, Carl. *Remembrance Rock.* 1948. Harcourt Brace. Ltd ed. 1/1000. 2 vols. slipcase. H3. $150.00

SANDBURG, Carl. *Remembrance Rock.* 1948. NY. 1st ed. dj. VG. B3. $20.00

SANDBURG, Carl. *Slabs of the Sunburnt W.* 1922. Harcourt Brace. 1st ed. sgn. sm octavo. H3. $40.00

SANDBURG, Carl. *Smoke & Steel.* 1920. Harcourt Brace. inscr. H3. $125.00

SANDBURG, Carl. *Storm Over the Land.* 1939. Harcourt Brace. 1st ed. 440 p. G. S1. $10.00

SANDBURG, Carl. *Storm Over the Land.* 1944. Alden Pr. 250 p. VG. S1. $7.00

SANDERS, A.H. *At the Sgn of the Stockyard Inn.* 1915. Chicago. Breeders Gazette. 322 p. A5. $50.00

SANDERS, C.W. *Man From MI.* 1924. Chelsea House. dj. VG. R3. $15.00

SANDERS, Dori. *Clover.* 1990. Algonquin Books. ARC. sgn. dj. RS. EX. B13. $85.00

SANDERS, Dori. *Clover.* 1990. Algonquin Books. 1st ed. sgn. dj. B13. $55.00

SANDERS, Ed. *Poem From Jail.* 1963. City Lights. 3rd print. B4. $3.00

SANDERS, Ed. *Shards of God.* 1971. Blk Cat. PB Orig. VG. B4. $4.00

SANDERS, George. *Crime on My Hands.* 1944. Simon Schuster. 1st ed. dj. xl. P1. $15.00

SANDERS, George. *Stranger at Home.* 1947. Pilot Pr. 1st ed. VG. P1. $20.00

SANDERS, Lawrence. *Anderson Tapes.* 1970. Putnam. 1st ed. dj. VG. T9. $60.00

SANDERS, Lawrence. *Case of Lucy Bending.* 1982. Putnam. 4to. dj. EX. $16.00

SANDERS, Lawrence. *Passion of Molly T.* 1984. Putnam. 1st ed. dj. VG. P1. $16.95

SANDERS, Lawrence. *Tangent Objective.* 1976. Putnam. 1st ed. dj. VG. P1. $20.00

SANDERS, Lawrence. *Timothy's Game.* 1988. Putnam. 1st ed. dj. VG. P1. $18.95

SANDERS, Toby. *How To Be a Compleat Clown.* 1980. Stein Day. 1st Scarborough Books ed. EX. J3. $7.00

SANDERS, W.B. *Negro Child Welfare in NC.* 1933. Chapel Hill. 1st ed. 326 p. VG. $30.00

SANDERS, Winston P.; see Anderson, Poul.

SANDERS. *Talks of Beatnik Glory.* 1975. NY. 1st ed. dj. VG. B3. $22.50

SANDERSON, G.P. *Concealed Art of Magic.* 1972. Goodliffe. 1st ed. 174 p. dj. NM. J3. $15.00

SANDERSON, Ivan. *Ivan Sanderson's Book of Great Jungles.* 1965. Messner. 1st ed. 480 p. F2. $15.00

SANDFORD & MERTEN. *Words of 1 Syllable.* 1881. NY/London. Cassell. 96 p. VG. $25.00

SANDO, J.S. *Pueblo Indians.* 1982. San Francisco. Indian Hist. 2nd ed. dj. EX. K2. $45.00

SANDOZ, Mari. *Buffalo Hunters: Story of the Hide Men.* 1954. Hastings. 2nd print. VG. $10.00

SANDOZ, Mari. *Capitol City.* 1939. Little Brn. 1st Stated ed. tan bdg. VG. $10.00

SANDOZ, Mari. *Horse Catcher.* 1957. Phil. 1st ed. dj. VG. B3. $30.00

SANDOZ, Mari. *Old Jules.* 1935. Little Brn 1st ed. dj. VG. $10.00

SANDOZ, Mari. *Old Jules' Country.* 1965 Hastings House. 1st ed. 319 p. EX. B10 $5.75

SANDOZ, Maurice. *Pleasures of Mexico* 1955. London. Guilford Pr. 1st ed. 4to. dj F2. $20.00

SANDS, David. *Journal of Life & Gospel Labors of David Sands.* 1848. Collins. 12mo 286 p. VG. V1. $40.00

SANDS, George. *Sansational (sic) Rope.* 1972. Pierre Ent. 2nd print. NM. J3. $3.00

SANDS, Leo. *Guide to Mobile Radio.* 1967. Chilton. 1st ed. 210 p. EX. B10. $3.50

SANDSTROM, Alan. *Traditional Curing & Crop Fertility Rituals Among Otomi...* 1981. Bloomington, IN. Ils. 104 p. wrp. F2. $20.00

SANDSTROM & SANDSTROM. *Traditional Papermaking & Paper Cult Figures of Mexico.* 1986. OK U. 1st ed. 327 p. dj. F2. $25.00

SANFORD, John. *Man Without Shoes.* 1982. Blk Sparrow. 1/2000. sgn. 452 p. dj. EX. T5. $45.00

SANFORD, Mrs. D.P. *Little Brn House & Children Who Lived in It.* 1878. NY. Ils. 212 p. TEG. G. T5. $25.00

SANFORD, Trent. *Story of Architecture in Mexico.* 1947. Norton. 1st ed. 363 p. F2. $30.00

SANGER, George. *70 Years a Showman.* 1926. Dutton. 1st Am ed. octavo. 249 p. VG. H3. $60.00

SANGER, Joan. *Case of the Missing Corpse.* 1936. Gr Circle. VG. P1. $12.50

SANGER, Margaret. *Autobiography.* 1938. NY. 1st ed. 504 p. dj. VG. B3. $37.50

SANGER, Margaret. *Autobiography.* 1939. NY. 1st ed. dj. w/sgn letter. B3. $50.00

SANGSTER, Jimmy. *Foreign Exchange.* 1968. Norton. 1st ed. dj. VG. P1. $15.00

SANGSTER, Margaret. *Cross Roads.* nd. (1919) Bible House. 159 p. VG. B10. $4.50

SANKKEY, Jay. *When Creators Collide.* 1987. Brisvane. Harris Magic. 1st ed. 77 p. EX. J3. $12.00

SANTAYANA, George. *Little Essays Drawn From Writings of George Satayana.* 1920. London. 1st ed. EX. $50.00

SANTAYANA, George. *Works.* 1936-1937. Scribner. Triton ed. 1/940. 14 vols. slipcases. H3. $650.00

SANTEE, Ross. *Bubbling Spring*. 1949. NY. Scribner. 1st ed. 2nd state. w/inscr drawing. H3. $500.00

SANTEE, Ross. *Cowboy*. 1928. Cosmopolitan. VG. $55.00

SANTEE, Ross. *Lost Pony Tracks*. 1953. NY. 1st ed. dj. VG. B3. $25.00

SANTEE, Ross. *Rummy Kid Goes Home & Other Stories of the SW*. 1965. NY. 1st ed. dj. EX. $20.00

SANTESSON, H.S. *Fantastic Universe Omnibus*. nd. Book Club. dj. VG. P1. $4.50

SANTESSON, H.S. *Fantastic Universe Omnibus*. 1960. Prentice Hall. 1st ed. dj. EX. F5. $20.00

SANTIAGO, Danny. *Famous All Over Town*. 1983. Simon Schuster. UP. wrp. EX. K2. $65.00

SANTINI. *Primera Guia Cinematografica Mexicana*. 1934. Mexico. quarto. VG. H3. $150.00

SANTMEYER, H.H. *And Ladies of the Club*. 1983. OH U. 1st ed. dj. M. $50.00

SAPIO MARTINO, Raul. *Guatemala: Maya Land of Eternal Spring*. 1959. Guatemala. 1st ed. 95 p. F2. $15.00

SAPIO MARTINO, Raul. *Guide to Mexico*. 1942. np. Ils. maps. 180 p. dj. F2. $10.00

SAPPER. *John Walters*. nd. Hodder Stoughton. dj. VG. P1. $17.50

SAPPER. *Lieutenant & Others*. 1916. Hodder Stoughton. VG. P1. $20.00

SAPPER. *Man in Ratcatcher*. nd. Hodder Stoughton. VG. P1. $15.00

SAPPER. *Tiny Carteret*. 1932. Musson/Hodder Stoughton. VG. P1. $15.00

SARABIA VIEJO, M.J. *Juego de Gallos en Nueva Espana*. 1972. Seville. 1st ed. 149 p. wrp. F2. $25.00

SARAVIA, Carlos. *Magica Della Voce: La Ventriloquia*. 1983. Saravia. Italian text. 79 p. EX. J3. $5.00

SARAVIA, Carlos. *Magic of Rezvani*. 1949. Raphael House. 1st Eng ed. 89 p. NM. J3. $5.00

SARAZEN, Gene. *Golf Magazines: Your Long Game*. nd. (1964) Harper. not Book Club ed. 188 p. dj. VG. B10. $5.00

SARG, Tony. *Tony Sarg's Book of Animals*. 1925. Greenberg Pub. 4to. VG. $35.00

SARG, Tony. *Tony Sarg's Marionette Book*. 1921. NY. 1st ed. 12mo. 58 p. VG. $18.00

SARGENT, F.W. *Eng, the US, & the S Confederacy*. 1969. Negro U. 194 p. EX. S1. $9.50

SARGENT, George. *Busted Bibliophile*. 1928. Boston. 1st ed. 1/600. inscr. EX. $120.00

SARGENT, M.P. *Pioneer Sketches: Scenes & Incidents of Former Days*. 1891. Erie, PA. A4. $55.00

SARGENT, Pamela. *Alien Upstairs*. 1983. Doubleday. 1st ed. dj. EX. P1. $15.00

SARGENT, Pamela. *Golden Space*. 1982. Timescape. 1st ed. dj. EX. P1. $15.50

SARGENT, Pamela. *Mt Cage*. 1983. Cheap Street. 1st ed. 1/99. sgn. wrp. M. R3. $25.00

SARGENT, Pamela. *Shore of Women*. 1986. Crown. 1st ed. dj. EX. P1. $16.95

SARGENT, Pamela. *Watchstar*. nd. Book Club. dj. VG. P1. $4.50

SARNOFF, David. *Biographical Sketch...* c 1961. Radio Corp Am. presentation. 48 p. VG. H3. $60.00

SAROYAN, William. *Dogs; or, Paris Comedy & 2 Other Plays*. 1969. Phaedra. 1st ed. dj. EX. H3. $40.00

SAROYAN, William. *Don't Go Away Mad & 2 Other Plays*. 1949. Harcourt Brace. 1st ed. dj. VG. H3. $100.00

SAROYAN, William. *Get Away Old Man*. 1944. Harcourt Brace. 1st ed. dj. EX. H3. $75.00

SAROYAN, William. *Get Away Old Man*. 1946. London. Faber. 1st UK ed. dj. VG. H3. $60.00

SAROYAN, William. *Human Comedy*. 1943. Harcourt Book Club. 291 p. dj. VG. B10. $3.50

SAROYAN, William. *My Heart's in the Highlands*. 1939. Harcourt Brace. 1st ed. dj. scarce. H3. $125.00

SAROYAN, William. *Native Am*. 1938. San Francisco. Fields. Ltd ed. 1/450. inscr. dj. H3. $275.00

SAROYAN, William. *Peace: It's Wonderful & 26 Other Stories*. 1939. Modern Age. 1st ed. wrp. VG. $20.00

SAROYAN, William. *Razzle-Dazzle; or, Human Ballet, Opera, & Circus...* 1942. Harcourt Brace. 1st ed. dj. EX. H3. $85.00

SAROYAN, William. *Saroyan's Fables*. 1941. Harcourt Brace. Ltd ed. 1/1000. sgn. boxed. H3. $150.00

SAROYAN, William. *Special Announcement*. 1940. House of Books. Ltd ed. 1/250. sgn. H3. $150.00

SAROYAN, William. *Time of Your Life*. 1941. London. French. Acting ed. orange wrp. EX. H3. $45.00

SAROYAN, William. *Trouble With Tigers*. 1938. Harcourt Brace. inscr. beige bdg. dj. H3. $150.00

SARRANTINO, Al. *Campbell Wood*. 1986. Doubleday. 1st ed. dj. RS. EX. P1. $17.50

SARTON, May. *Cloud Stone Sun Vine*. 1961. NY. 1st ed. dj. VG. B3. $25.00

SARTON, May. *Poet & the Donkey*. 1969. Norton. 1st ed. dj. EX. C4. $25.00

SARTON, May. *Poet & the Donkey*. 1969. Norton. 1st ed. sgn. dj. H3. $50.00

SARTON, May. *World of Light*. 1976. Norton. gr bdg. dj. w/sgn card. H3. $60.00

SARTORIS, Ramon. *3 Plays*. 1944. Blk Sun. Ils Tanning. dj. slipcase. H3. $300.00

SARTRE, J.P. *Chips Are Down*. 1951. London. Rider. 1st Trans ed. dj. EX. H3. $50.00

SARTRE, J.P. *Words*. 1966. Crest. 1st PB ed. EX. B4. $5.00

SASOWSKY, Norman. *Reginald Marsh: Catalog Raisonne of His Prints*. 1976. NY. square 8vo. dj. EX. $25.00

SASSOON, Siegfried. *Old Century & 7 More Years*. 1939. Viking. 1st ed. 267 p. gr bdg. EX. B10. $10.00

SASSOON, Siegfried. *Sherston's Progress*. 1936. London. Faber. 1st ed. 1/300. sgn. TEG. H3. $100.00

SASSOON, Siegfried. *Wealth of Youth*. 1942. Viking. 1st ed. 259 p. EX. B10. $20.00

SATIVA, Mary. *Acid Temple Ball*. 1969. Travelers Companion. 1st PB ed. B4. $20.00

SATRE, J.P. *Portrait of the Anti-Semite*. 1946. Partisan Review Series. wrp. EX. scarce. $40.00

SAUL, Frank. *Human Skeletal Remains of Altar de Sacrificios*. nd. Peabody Mus. sm 4to. 123 p. wrp. F2. $15.00

SAUNDBY, Robert. *Air Bombardment: Story of Its Development*. 1961. London. Ils. 176 p. dj. VG. T5. $22.50

SAUNDERS, Caleb; see Heinlein, Robert.

SAVAGE, Blake. *Rip Foster Rides the Gray Planet*. 1952. Whitman. xl. P1. $5.00

SAVAGE, C.C. *World Geog, Hist, & Statistical...* 1855. NY. Ensign Bridgman Fanning. 8vo. maps. 500 p. C1. $115.00

SAVAGE, Henry. *Seeds of Time: Background of S Thinking.* 1959. Holt. 1st ed. 312 p. VG. B10. $4.50

SAVAGE. *Hist Republic Co, KS.* 1901. Beliot. Enlarged ed. VG. C2. $55.00

SAVAONAROLA, D.J. *Facts & Figures From Italy.* 1847. London. Bentley. 1st ed. 8vo. yel bdg. H3. $150.00

SAVCHENKO, Vladimir. *Self-Discovery.* 1979. Macmillan. 1st ed. dj. EX. F5. $14.00

SAVERY, William. *Journal of Life, Travels, & Religious Labors.* nd. Friends Bookstore. Stereotype ed. 12mo. 485 p. VG. V1. $10.00

SAVILLE, Marshall. *Bibliographic Notes on Xochicalco, Mexico.* 1928. NY. Mus Am Indian. 1st ed. 12mo. wrp. F2. $12.50

SAVOY, Gene. *Antisuyo: Search for the Lost Cities of the Amazon.* 1970. Simon Schuster. 1st ed. 220 p. dj. F2. $30.00

SAVOY, Gene. *On the Trail of the Feathered Serpent.* 1974. Bobbs Merrill. 1st ed. 217 p. dj. F2. $20.00

SAWYER, Alan. *Ancient Peruvian Ceramics.* 1966. NY. Ltd 1st ed. 144 p. F2. $30.00

SAWYER, Alan. *Ancient Peruvian Ceramics.* 1975. PA U Mus Art. Ils. 4to. wrp. F2. $15.00

SAWYER, Alan. *Animal Sculpture in Pre-Columbian Art.* 1957. Art Inst Chicago. 1st ed. sq 4to. wrp. F2. $15.00

SAWYER, G.S. *S Institutes; or, Inquiry Into Origin...Slavery.* 1859. Phil. 8vo. 393 p. VG. $65.00

SAWYER, J.A. *Wagon Road From Niobara to VA City.* 1866. WA. 8vo. 32 p. disbound. $50.00

SAXON, Peter. *Killing Bone.* 1970. Howard Baker. dj. xl. P1. $5.00

SAXON & DREYER. *Friends of Joe Gilmore & Some Friends of Lyle Saxon.* 1948. Hastings House. VG. $17.50

SAY, Thomas. *Am Entomology: Insects of N Am.* 1869. NY. Bouton. clr pls. 2 vols. rebound. VG. T3. $175.00

SAYCE, A.H. *Egypt of the Hebrews & Herodotos.* 1895. NY. Macmillan. 358 p. G. $45.00

SAYER, Chloe. *Arts & Crafts of Mexico.* 1990. Chronicle Books. 1st ed. 4to. dj. F2. $35.00

SAYER, Chloe. *Mexican Textile Techniques.* 1988. Aylesbury. 1st ed. wrp. F2. $10.00

SAYERS, D.L. *Gaudy Night.* 1947. Albatross. dj. VG. P1. $35.00

SAYERS, D.L. *Great Short Stores.* 1954. Gollancz. 16th ed. P1. $20.00

SAYERS, D.L. *Omnibus of Crime.* nd. Book Club. VG. P1. $3.50

SAYERS, D.L. *Omnibus of Crime.* 1929. Payson Clarke. 1st ed. VG. P1. $30.00

SAYERS, D.L. *Story of Easter.* 1955. London. Ils. EX. $45.00

SAYERS, D.L. *Strong Poison.* 1930. Brewer Warren. 2nd ed. xl. P1. $10.00

SAYERS, D.L. *Treasury of Sayers Stories.* 1958. Gollancz. dj. VG. P1. $35.00

SAYERS, D.L. *Zeal of Thy House.* 1937. Gollancz. 1st ed. dj. VG. K2. $65.00

SAYERS, D.L. *3 Great Lord Peter Novels.* 1978. Gollancz. dj. EX. P1. $25.00

SAYERS, D.L. *9 Tailors.* 1939. Gollancz. 11th ed. dj. VG. P1. $20.00

SAYERS, John. *Anarchist's Convention.* 1979. Little Brn. 1st ed. dj. EX. K2. $50.00

SAYERS, John. *Union Dues.* 1978. Little Brn. 1st ed. inscr. dj. EX. K2. $125.00

SAYLE, W.D. *Trip to the Land of Romance.* 1921. np. Sayle. Ils. 95 p. gilt bdg. F2. $15.00

SAYLER, O.M. *Max Reinhardt & His Theatre.* 1924. NY. Ils 1st ed. pls. VG. scarce. $125.00

SAYLER, O.M. *Max Reinhardt & His Theatre.* 1926. Brentano. Miracle ed. octavo. 381 p. VG. H3. $150.00

SAYLES, John. *Clan of the Cave Bear.* 1983. Universal City. screenplay. studio wrp. EX. K2. $275.00

SAYLES, John. *Los Gusanos.* 1991. Harper Collins. ARC. wrp. EX. C4. $35.00

SAYLES, John. *Pride of the Bimbos.* 1975. NY. 1st ed. dj. EX. T9. $125.00

SAYLES, John. *Union Dues.* 1977. Little Brn. UP. sgn. wrp. EX. K2. $275.00

SAYLES, John. *Valley of Horses.* 1983. Universal City. screenplay. EX. K2. $350.00

SAYLOR, H.H. *Architectural Styles of Country Houses.* 1912. NY. 1st ed. VG. R5. $95.00

SAYLOR, H.H. *Bungalows: Design & Construction.* 1913. NY. Revised ed. xl. G. R5. $50.00

SAYRE, Joel. *Persian Gulf Command.* 1945. NY. 1st ed. dj. VG. $35.00

SCADUTO, A. *Scapegoat.* 1976. NY. Putnam. 1st ed. 512 p. dj. VG. B3/P1. $17.50

SCARBOROUGH, Dorothy. *Wind.* 1925. Harper. 1st ed. dj. EX. B13. $650.00

SCARBOROUGH, E.A. *Healer's War.* 1988. Doubleday. 1st ed. dj. EX. P1. $17.95

SCARBOROUGH. *Homes of the Cavaliers.* 1930. NY. 1st ed. photos. 392 p. VG. B3. $25.00

SCARLETT, Roger. *Back Bay Murders.* nd. Crime Club. VG. P1. $7.50

SCARLETT, Roger. *Murder Among the Angels.* 1932. Crime Club. VG. P1. $15.00

SCARNE, John. *Scarne on Card Tricks.* 1950. Crown. 1st print. 308 p. VG. J3. $11.00

SCARNE, John. *Scarne's Magic Tricks.* 1951. Crown. 1st print. 256 p. EX. J3. $9.00

SCARTH-DIXON, William. *Hertfordshire Hunt.* 1932. London. 12mo. wrp. EX. A4. $20.00

SCATTERGOOD, Thomas. *Journal of Life & Religious Labors of Thomas Scattergood.* nd. Friends Bookstore. 8vo. 496 p. xl. V1. $12.00

SCATTERGOOD, Thomas. *Journal of Life & Religious Labors of Thomas Scattergood.* nd. Phil. Stereotype ed. 8vo. 496 p. rebound. VG. V1. $16.00

SCHACHNER, Nat. *Space Lawyer.* 1953. Gnome. 1st ed. VG. R3. $12.50

SCHADEWALDT, Hans. *Polish Acts of Atrocity Against German Minority in Poland.* 1940. Berlin/NY. 2nd ed. 259 p. wrp. T5. $27.50

SCHAEFER, Jack. *Shane.* 1949. Boston. 1st ed. dj. VG. B3. $75.00

SCHAFF, Morris. *Jefferson Davis: His Life & Personality.* 1922. Boston. 1st ed. VG. $35.00

SCHALDACH, William. *Path to Enchantment.* 1963. NY. 1st ed. dj. VG. B3. $22.50

SCHALDACH, William. *Wind on Your Cheek.* 1972. Rockville Center. 1st ed. dj. VG. B3. $27.50

SCHALLER, G.B. *Golden Shadows, Flying Hooves.* 1973. Knopf. 1st ed. dj. EX. K2. $35.00

SCHALLER, G.B. *Year of the Gorilla.* 1964. Chicago U. 1st ed. clipped dj. EX. B13. $40.00

SCHARF, J. *Hist of Confederate States' Navy From Its Organization...* 1887. NY. Ils. 8vo. 824 p. rebound. scarce. G4. $75.00

SCHAUFFLER, E.T. *Parnell.* 1936. NY. French. 1st ed. H3. $45.00

SCHEINER, Olive. *Dreams.* 1901. Roycroft. VG. C1. $34.00

SCHELE & MILLER. *Blood of Kings.* 1986. Kimball Art Mus. 1st Corrected ed. sgn. dj. F2. $60.00

SCHELL, W.G. *Is the Negro a Beast?* 1901. Moundsville, WV. 1st ed. 238 p. G. B3. $47.50

SCHEM, A.J. *War in the E Between Russia & Turkey.* 1878. NY. 1st ed. full leather. T1. $35.00

SCHERER, J.L. *Magic Handbook.* 1968. Science/Mechanics Pub. 112 p. NM. J3. $7.00

SCHERF, Margaret. *Beautiful Birthday Cake.* 1971. Crime Club. dj. xl. P1. $6.00

SCHERF, Margaret. *Don't Wake Me Up While I'm Driving.* 1977. Crime Club. 1st ed. dj. VG. P1. $15.00

SCHERF, Margaret. *If You Want a Murder Well Done.* 1974. Crime Club. dj. xl. P1. $6.00

SCHERF, Margaret. *Judicial Body.* 1957. Crime Club. 1st ed. dj. VG. P1. $20.00

SCHEZEN, Roberto. *Visions of Ancient Am.* 1990. Rizzoli. 1st ed. 216 p. dj. F2. $50.00

SCHIAPARELLI. *Shocking Life.* 1954. NY. 1st ed. dj. EX. B3. $20.00

SCHIFF & LEIBER. *World Fantasy Awards Vol 2.* 1980. Doubleday. 1st ed. dj. EX. R3. $20.00

SCHIFF & LEIBER. *World Fantasy Awards Vol 2.* 1980. Doubleday. 1st ed. dj. VG. P1. $17.50

SCHILLER, Fredrich. *Gesammelte Werke.* 1923. Verlag. 1st ed. German text. 5 vols. TEG. VG. R5. $75.00

SCHILPP, Arthur. *Albert Einstein: Philosopher-Scientist.* 1949. Evanston, IL. 1/750. sgn Einstein. orig cloth. EX. H3. $2000.00

SCHISGALL, Oscar. *Devil's Daughter.* 1932. Fiction League. 1st ed. VG. P1. $25.00

SCHLEMMER, Tut. *Letters & Diaries of Oskar Schlemmer.* 1972. Wesleyan U. Ils. dj. D4. $40.00

SCHLESINGER, Arthur Jr. *1000 Days: JF Kennedy in Wht House.* 1965. Houghton Mifflin. apparent 1st ed. 8vo. dj. VG. B10. $15.00

SCHLESINGER, Kathleen. *Instruments of Modern Orchestra & Early Records...Vol 2.* 1910. Scribner. VG. H3. $50.00

SCHLEY, W.S. *45 Years Under the Flag.* 1904. NY. 1st ed. 1/100. sgn. EX. $140.00

SCHLINGER, Peter. *Select Guide to Chilean Lib & Archives.* 1979. Bloomington, IN. 4to. wrp. F2. $10.00

SCHLOBIN, Roger. *Aesthetics of Fantasy Literature.* 1982. Notre Dame. 1st ed. dj. VG. P1. $25.00

SCHLOBIN, Roger. *Literature of Fantasy.* 1979. Garland. 1st ed. EX. P1. $35.00

SCHMIDT, Harold. *Syrian Yankee.* 1935. private print. 64 p. stiff wrp. dj. VG. B10. $3.50

SCHMIDT, M.M. *400 Outstanding Women of World & Costumology of Their Time.* 1933. Chicago. 1st ed. EX. $25.00

SCHMIDT, P.W. *127th Infantry in World War.* 1919. Sheboygan, WI. 1st ed. 189 p. VG. T5. $65.00

SCHMIDT, Stanley. *Analog: Writer's Choice Vol 2.* 1984. Dial. 1st ed. RS. M. R3. $12.95

SCHMIDT, Stanley. *From Mind to Mind.* 1984. Doubleday. 1st ed. dj. RS. EX. P1. $15.00

SCHMIDT, W.S. *Doberman Pinscher in Am.* 1940. Milwaukee. 1st ed. EX. $35.00

SCHMIDT-PAULI, E.V. *We Indians: Passing of a Great Race.* 1931. Dutton. 1st ed. 256 p. A5. $40.00

SCHMITT & BROWN. *Fighting Indians of the W.* 1948. NY. 1st ed. dj. VG. $50.00

SCHMITZ, J.H. *Pride of Monsters.* 1970. Macmillan. 1st ed. dj. EX. P1. $25.00

SCHMITZ, J.H. *Tale of 2 Clocks.* nd. Book Club. dj. VG. P1. $7.50

SCHMITZ, James. *Agent of Vega.* 1960. Gnome. 1st ed. dj. EX. R3. $27.50

SCHMITZ, James. *Witches of Karres.* 1968. Chilton. dj. EX. R3. $35.00

SCHMUTZLER, Robert. *Art Nouveau.* nd. (c 1964) Abrams. 1st Am ed. 4to. 322 p. dj. EX. R4. $165.00

SCHNACKENBERG, Gjertrud. *Lamplit Answer.* 1985. Farrar Straus. AP. K2. $15.00

SCHNEIDER, Al. *Al Schneider on Coins.* 1975. Schneider. 1st ed. 95 p. NM. J3. $11.00

SCHNEIDER, Al. *Matrix.* 1980. Schneider. 4th ed. sgn. NM. J3. $5.00

SCHNEIDER, Bruno. *Renoir.* nd. Crown. 94 p. dj. EX. B10. $6.75

SCHNEIDER, N.F. *Y-Bridge City: Story of Zanesville & Muskingham Co, OH.* 1950. Cleveland. Ils. 414 p. dj. VG. T5. $35.00

SCHNEIDERMAN, Steven. *Meir Yedid's Stage Stuff.* 1986. NY. 1st ed. sgn Meir Yedid. dj. NM. J3. $18.00

SCHOENER, A. *Harlem on My Mind.* 1968. NY. Ils. 255 p. SftCvr. VG. B3. $27.50

SCHOFIELD, Hugh. *Those Incredible Christians.* 1968. NY. 1st ed. dj. VG. B3. $20.00

SCHOLES & ROYS. *Maya Contal Indians of Acalan-Tixchel.* 1948. WA. 1st ed. 565 p. F2. $75.00

SCHOLES & ROYS. *Maya Contal Indians of Acalan-Tixchel.* 1968. OK U. 2nd print. dj. F2. $25.00

SCHOLL, William. *Elementary Course in Practipedics.* nd. Chicago. 143 p. VG. B10. $4.50

SCHOLZ, Janos. *Baroque & Romantic Stage Design.* 1955. Beechhurst Pr. Bittner Art Book. quarto. 24 p. dj. EX. H3. $65.00

SCHONS, Dorothy. *Book Censorship in New Spain.* 1949. Austin, TX. Ltd ed. 1/200. 4to. F2. $20.00

SCHONS, Dorothy. *Notes From Spanish Archives.* 1946. Austin, TX. 1/200. 4to. wrp. F2. $15.00

SCHOOLCRAFT. *Travels in Central Portion of MS Valley.* 1825. NY. Collins. 459 p. A5. $250.00

SCHORER, Mark. *Sinclair Lewis: An Am Life.* 1961. McGraw Hill. 1st ed. inscr. dj. VG. B13. $85.00

SCHOTTER, Roni. *Efan the Great.* 1986. Lothrop. Ils Rodney Pate. 1st ed. dj. EX. B13. $45.00

SCHOW, D.J. *Kill Riff.* 1988. Tor Books. AP. Special Ltd ed. dj. M. R3. $25.00

SCHOW, D.J. *Silver Scream.* 1988. Dark Harvest. 1st ed. M. R3. $35.00

SCHRADER, O. *Prehistoric Antiquities of Aryan Peoples.* 1890. London. 8vo. 486 p. VG. T6. $30.00

SCHRADER & BROOKS. *Preliminary Report on Cape Nome Gold Region, AK.* 1900. Ils. 56 p. A5. $60.00

SCHREIBER & SCHREIBER. *Exploring the Amazon.* 1970. WA. 1st ed. 207 p. dj. F2. $12.50

SCHREIBER & SCHREIBER. *Vanished Cities.* 1957. Knopf. 1st Am ed. 344 p. dj. F2. $15.00

SCHREINER, Olive. *Trooper Peter Halket of Mashonaland.* 1897. Boston. 1st ed. EX. $25.00

SCHROEDER, Doris. *Annette & Mystery at Moonstone Bay.* 1962. Whitman. VG. P1. $10.00

SCHROEDER, Doris. *Annette Sierra Summer.* 1960. Whitman. VG. P1. $6.00

SCHROEDER, Doris. *Desert Inn Mystery.* 1961. Whitman. VG. P1. $10.00

SCHROEDER, Doris. *Gunsmoke.* 1958. Big Little Book. VG. P1. $7.50

SCHROEDER, Doris. *Saga of Wildcat Creek.* 1963. Whitman. VG. P1. $7.50

SCHRYER, Frans. *Rancheros of Pisaflores.* 1980. Toronto U. 1st ed. 210 p. F2. $15.00

SCHUCK & SOHLMAN. *Alfred Nobel.* 1929. London. 1/100. inscr. quarto. VG. H3. $600.00

SCHULBERG, Budd. *Harder They Fall.* 1947. NY. 1st ed. inscr/dtd 1947. dj. EX. $165.00

SCHULBERG, Budd. *On the Waterfront.* 1980. Carbondale, IL. 1st ed. dj. EX. T9. $65.00

SCHULBERG, Budd. *What Makes Sammy Run?* 1978. Penguin. inscr. PB. H3. $50.00

SCHULTZ, J.W. *Quest of Fishdog Skin.* 1913. Boston. VG. B3. $40.00

SCHUSTER, Hal. *Files Magazine Spotlight on Monkees.* 1987. Borgo Pr. EX. P1. $17.50

SCHUTZ, B.M. *All the Old Bargains.* 1985. Bluejay. 1st ed. sgn. dj. EX. P1. $25.00

SCHUTZ, B.M. *Embrace the Wolf.* 1985. Bluejay. 1st ed. dj. EX. P1. $13.95

SCHUYLER, Eugene. *Turkistan: Notes of Journey in Russian Turkistan.* 1885. Scribner. 3rd Am ed. 2 vols. VG. $35.00

SCHUYLER, G.S. *Blk & Conservative.* 1966. New Rochelle. Arlington House. 1st ed. dj. EX. B13. $30.00

SCHUYLER, HARTLEY, & GRAHAM. *Ils Catalog of Civil War Military Goods.* 1985. Dover. 142 p. PB. S1. $10.95

SCHUYLER, James. *Alfred & Guinevere.* 1958. Harcourt Brace. 1st ed. inscr twice. dj. EX. C4. $300.00

SCHUYLER, James. *What's for Dinner?* 1978. Blk Sparrow. Ltd ed. 1/226. sgn. H3. $45.00

SCHWARTZ, Delmore. *Poet's Pack of George WA High School.* 1932. NY. Rudge. 1st ed. dj. VG. K2. $90.00

SCHWARTZ, Delmore. *Shenandoah.* 1941. New Directions. 1st HrdCvr ed. dj. EX. K2. $160.00

SCHWARTZ, Delmore. *Summer Knowledge.* 1959. Doubleday. 1st ed. dj. EX. K2. $100.00

SCHWARTZ, Delmore. *Vaudeville for a Princess.* 1950. New Directions. 1st ed. dj. EX. B13. $75.00

SCHWARTZ, L.S. *Leaving Brooklyn.* 1989. Boston. 1st ed. sgn. dj. M. $15.00

SCHWARTZ & WOLFE. *Hist of Am Art Porcelain.* 1967. NY. 1st ed. sm folio. $25.00

SCHWARTZ-NOBEL, Loretta. *Engaged to Murder.* 1987. Viking. 2nd ed. dj. EX. P1. $15.00

SCHWATKA, F. *Summer in AK.* 1893. St Louis. Ils. 8vo. 418 p. VG. T6. $40.00

SCHWED, Fred. *Pleasure Was All Mine.* 1951. NY. 1st ed. dj. EX. $30.00

SCHWED, Peter. *Great Stories From World of Sports.* 1958. Simon Schuster. 1st ed. 3 vols. VG. B10. $12.00

SCHWEITZER, Albert. *JS Bach.* 1911. London. Beietkopf Hartel. 1st ed. 2 vols. stiff cream wrp. EX. H3. $400.00

SCHWEITZER, Albert. *Mystery of the Kingdom of God.* 1914. NY. 1st ed. 275 p. VG. B3. $25.00

SCHWEITZER, Darrell. *Discovering HP Lovecraft.* 1987. Starmont. 1st ed. wrp. M. R3. $9.95

SCHWEITZER, Darrell. *Discovering Modern Horror Fiction 1.* 1985. Starmont. 1st ed. wrp. M. R3. $9.95

SCHWEITZER, Darrell. *Discovering Stephen King.* 1988. Starmont. 1st ed. wrp. M. R3. $9.95

SCHWEITZER, Darrell. *Shattered Goddess.* 1988. Starmont. wrp. M. R3. $9.95

SCHWIMMER, Rosika. *Tisza Tales.* nd. np. Ils Willy Pogany. 1st ed. 4to. 225 p. VG. $50.00

SCOFIELD, Mrs. L.T. *Roster of Union Soldiers & Sailors...Cuyahoga Co, OH....* 1889. Cleveland. 40 p. wrp. T5. $25.00

SCORTIA, Thomas. *Best of Thomas N Scortia.* 1981. Doubleday. 1st ed. dj. EX. F5/R3. $12.50

SCORTIA, Thomas. *Strange Bedfellows.* 1972. Random House. 1st ed. dj. VG. R3. $15.00

SCORTIA & ROBINSON. *Glass Inferno.* nd. Book Club. dj. VG. P1. $4.50

SCORTIA & ROBINSON. *Nightmare Factor.* 1978. Doubleday. 1st ed. dj. VG. P1. $10.00

SCORTIA & ROBINSON. *Prometheus Crisis.* nd. Book Club. dj. EX. P1. $4.50

SCOTLAND, John. *Talkies.* 1930. London. Lockwood. 1st ed. 194 p. VG. H3. $75.00

SCOTT, A.C. *Flower & the Willow World. Story of the Geisha.* 1960. NY. 1st print. dj. EX. T1. $20.00

SCOTT, E.H. *AK Days.* 1923. Chicago. 1st ed. EX. scarce. K1. $50.00

SCOTT, Edward. *Dancing As an Art & Pastime.* 1892. London. Bell. 1st ed. 214 p. rebound by CF Fox. slipcase. H3. $250.00

SCOTT, Fred. *What To See & How To See It in Honolulu.* 1901. Honolulu. 12mo. photos. G. P1. $45.00

SCOTT, G.R. *Into Whose Hands.* 1945. London. Swan. 1st ed. 236 p. VG. B10. $12.00

SCOTT, J.A. *Geog Dictionary of US of Am.* 1805. Phil. Armstrong. Revised Enlarged 1st ed. 8vo. fld map. G. C1. $100.00

SCOTT, J.R. *Beatrix of Clare.* 1907. Lippincott. 1st ed. 365 p. G. B10. $3.50

SCOTT, J.R. *Colonel of the Red Huzzars.* nd. Grosset Dunlap. 341 p. VG. B10. $3.50

SCOTT, Jeremy. *Mandrake Root.* 1946. Jarrolds. VG. P1. $30.00

SCOTT, Job. *Works of Job Scott.* 1831. Phil. Comly. 8vo. V1. $80.00

SCOTT, John. *Ancient Mesoamerica: Selections From U Gallery Collections.* 1987. Gainesville. 1st ed. wrp. F2. $15.00

SCOTT, John. *Duke of Oblivion.* 1914. Lippincott. 1st ed. VG. R3. $35.00

SCOTT, Justin. *Normandie Triangle.* 1981. Arbor House. 1st ed. dj. VG. P1. $15.00

SCOTT, Justin. *Rampage.* nd. Book Club. dj. VG. P1. $4.50

SCOTT, L.B. *Mrs Scott's N Am Seasonal Cookbook.* 1921. Winston. 4to. 252 p. EX. $25.00

SCOTT, Leroy. *Children of the Whirlwind.* 1921. Internat Fiction Ed. dj. VG. F5. $10.00

SCOTT, Melissa. *Kindly Ones.* 1987. Baen. 1st HrdCvr ed. dj. EX. F5. $11.00

SCOTT, Mrs. C. *Old Days in Bohemian London.* c 1910-1920. Stokes. 272 p. fair. B10. $5.00

SCOTT, Peter. *Observations of Wildlife.* 1980. Phaidon. Ils. 112 p. dj. EX. $30.00

SCOTT, Richenda. *Elizabeth Cadbury, 1858-1951.* 1956. London. Harrap. 2nd print. 200 p. dj. VG. V1. $9.50

SCOTT, Robert. *God Is Still My Copilot.* 1967. Phoenix. 1st ed. dj. VG. B3. $22.50

SCOTT, Robert. *War of the Rebellion.* 1985. Broadfoot Pub. reprint. EX. S1. $15.00

SCOTT, Samuel. *Diary of Some Religious Exercises & Experience of S Scott...* 1811. Phil. Kimber Conrad. 12mo. 264 p. fair. V1. $10.00

SCOTT, Walter. *Antiquary.* 1816. Edinburgh. 1st ed. 3 vols. VG. $100.00

SCOTT, Walter. *Ivanhoe.* 1951. Ltd Ed Club. Ils/sgn Edward A Wilson. 2 vols. slipcase. EX. C4. $60.00

SCOTT, Walter. *Ivanhoe: A Romance.* 1940. Ltd Ed Club. Ils/sgn Allen Lewis. 4to. 2 vols. slipcase. C4. $75.00

SCOTT, Walter. *Journal From Orig Manuscript at Abbotsford.* 1891. NY. Ils. 2 vols. TEG. VG. $35.00

SCOTT, Walter. *Rokeby: A Poem.* 1813. Edinburgh. 2nd ed. VG. T1. $45.00

SCOTT, Walter. *Tales of Grandfather.* 1828. Paris. Galignani. 12mo. 2 vols. VG. C1. $95.00

SCOTT, Walter. *Talisman.* 1968. Ipswich. 1/1500. sgn Castellon. boxed. EX. $25.00

SCOTT, Walter. *Waverley.* 1901. Edinburgh. Edinburgh ed. 1/1040. 48 vols. H3. $6000.00

SCOTT, Walter. *Waverley; or, 'Tis 60 Years Since.* 1961. Ltd Ed Club. Ils/sgn Robert Ball. 1/1500. slipcase. EX. C4. $50.00

SCOTT-HERON, Gil. *Vulture.* 1970. World. 1st ed. dj. EX. B13. $95.00

SCOTT-KILVERT, Ian. *British Writers Vol 6.* 1983. NY. 1st ed. 460 p. dj. M. C1. $12.50

SCUDDER, H.E. *Bodleys on Wheels.* 1879. Boston. 222 p. G. T5. $22.50

SCUDDER, J.M. *Specific Medication & Specific Medicines.* 1871. Cincinnati. 1st ed. sm octavo. 253 p. VG. $150.00

SCUDDER, S.H. *Everyday Butterflies.* 1899. Houghton Mifflin. clr pls. VG. T3. $25.00

SCULATTI, G. *Catalog of Cool.* 1982. Warner. 1st print. M. B4. $10.00

SCULL, David. *Union With God in Thought & Faith.* 1908. Phil. Winston. 8vo. 98 p. VG. V1. $12.50

SEABROOK, William. *Witchcraft.* 1940. Harcourt. 1st ed. dj. VG. R3. $27.50

SEABROOKE, Terry. *Around the World in a Baking Tin.* 1986. Magical Pub. 1st ed. 112 p. dj. NM. J3. $21.00

SEAGRAVE, A.D. *Golf Retold: Story of Golf in Cleveland.* 1940. Cleveland. 1st ed. 148 p. VG. B3. $95.00

SEALE, Bobby. *Trial of Bobby Seale.* 1970. Blk Cat. 1st print. EX. B4. $8.00

SEARLE, Ronald. *Those Daring Young Men in Their Jaunty Jalopies.* 1969. Putnam. 1st ed. quarto. dj. EX. B13. $75.00

SEARLE, Ronald. *Those Magnificent Men in Their Flying Machines.* 1965. Norton. 1st ed. quarto. dj. EX. B13. $85.00

SEARLES, Lynn. *Ultimate Aces.* 1958. Chicago. Ireland. 1st ed. SftCvr. EX. J3. $5.00

SEARLS, Hank. *Pilgrim Project.* nd. Book Club. dj. VG. P1. $4.50

SEARS, A.B. *Thomas Worthington.* 1958. Columbus. Ils. 260 p. dj. VG. T5. $12.50

SEARS, John Van Der Zee. *My Friends at Brook Farm.* 1912. NY. 1st ed. 172 p. VG. T5. $27.50

SEARS, S.W. *George B McClellan: The Young Napoleon.* 1988. Ticknor Fields. 492 p. dj. EX. S1. $17.50

SEAVER, B.E. *Doylestown 1827-1952.* 1952. Rittman. 100 p. VG. T5. $19.50

SEDGWICK, H.D. *Cortes the Conqueror.* 1926. Bobbs Merrill. 390 p. F2. $12.50

SEEBOHM, Caroline. *Man Who Was Vogue: Life & Times of Conde Nast.* 1982. NY. 1st ed. dj. VG. $15.00

SEELEY, Mabel. *Chuckling Fingers.* 1941. Crime Club. dj. VG. P1. $15.00

SEELEY, Mabel. *Crying Sisters.* 1944. Triangle. dj. VG. P1. $15.00

SEELEY, Mabel. *11 Came Back.* nd. Book Club. dj. VG. P1. $6.00

SEINGALT, Jacques; see Casanova De Seingalt, Jacques.

SEITZ, D.C. *Dreadful Decade 1869-1879.* 1926. Indianapolis. xl. G. $10.00

SEITZ, D.C. *Trial of William Penn & William Mead...in 1719.* 1919. Boston. Marshall Jones. 1st ed. 12mo. VG. V1. $10.00

SELA, Owen. *Bearer Plot.* 1972. Pantheon. 1st Am ed. dj. EX. T9. $40.00

SELA, Owen. *Exchange of Eagles.* 1977. Pantheon. 1st ed. dj. VG. P1. $15.00

SELBY, Hubert. *Last Exit to Brooklyn.* 1964. NY. UP. scarce. K2. $250.00

SELDEN, Elizabeth. *Dancer's Quest.* 1935. CA U. 1st ed. quarto. 215 p. VG. H3. $125.00

SELF, M.C. *Chitter-Chat Stories.* 1946. Dutton. Ils Grilley. 1st ed. 8vo. $15.00

SELF, M.C. *Fun on Horseback.* 1945. Barnes. 4th ed. 229 p. VG. B10. $3.50

SELL & WEYBRIGHT. *Buffalo Bill & the Old W.* 1955. NY. 1st ed. dj. VG. G1. $25.00

SELLER, Eduard. *Observations & Studies in Ruins of Palenque.* 1976. CA. 1st ed. 4to. F2. $40.00

SELLERS, Tom. *Tom Sellers' Magical Mixture.* 1943. London. Davenport. 31 p. SftCvr. EX. J3. $3.00

SELLINGS, Arthur. *Quy Effect.* 1966. Dobson. 1st ed. dj. VG. P1. $15.00

SELLON, Edward. *Ups & Downs of Life.* 1987. Dennis McMillan. reprint of 1867 ed. M. R3. $50.00

SELOUS, F.C. *Travel & Adventure in SE Africa.* 1893. London. 1st ed. VG. $80.00

SELTZER, C.A. *Council of 3.* 1900. NY. 1st ed. 177 p. G. T5. $17.50

SELTZER, C.A. *Raider.* 1929. NY. 1st ed. dj. VG. B3. $27.50

SELTZER, C.A. *Silverspurs.* nd. Grosset Dunlap. VG. P1. $7.50

SELZ, Peter. *Work of Jean Dubuffet.* 1962. Doubleday. dj. D4. $30.00

SEMMES, H. *Portrait of Patton.* 1955. NY. 1st ed. dj. RS. VG. B3. $32.50

SEMMES, Raphael. *Memoirs of Service Afloat During the War Between the States.* 1869. Baltimore. 1st Am ed. 8vo. 833 p. G4. $49.00

SENDAK, Maurice. *Outside Over There.* 1981. Harper Row. sgn. gilt red cloth. dj. EX. H3. $60.00

SENDAK, Maurice. *Tale of Mme D'Aulnoy.* 1974. Frank Hallman. Ils Sendak. Ltd ed. 1/326. sgns. wrp. H3. $175.00

SENNETT, Mack. *King of Comedy.* 1954. Doubleday. 1st ed. octavo. 284 p. dj. EX. H3. $50.00

SENSING, Thurman. *Champ Ferguson: Confederate Guerilla.* 1942. Nashville. 1st ed. inscr. VG. $75.00

SERANNE. *Am Cooks.* 1967. 1st ed. 796 p. VG. B3. $27.50

SERLING, Rod. *From the Twilight Zone.* nd. Book Club. dj. VG. P1. $7.50

SERVER, James. *Collecting of Guns.* 1964. Harrisburg. 1st ed. 4to. dj. EX. G1. $20.00

SERVICE, R.W. *Ballads of a Cheechako.* 1933. Toronto. Ryerson. sgn. gilt bl bdg. dj. H3. $225.00

SERVICE, R.W. *Complete Poems of Robert Service.* 1945. Dodd Mead. later print. sgn. dj. VG. H3. $225.00

SERVICE, R.W. *Master of the Microbe.* nd. AL Burt. dj. VG. R3. $25.00

SERVICE, R.W. *Master of the Microbe.* 1926. Barse Hopkins. 1st ed. VG. R3. $15.00

SERVICE, R.W. *Rhymes of a Red Cross Man.* 1933. Toronto. Ryerson. later print. sgn. dj. H3. $200.00

SERVISS, G.P. *Columbus of Space.* 1974. Hyperion. reprint of 1894 ed. EX. R3. $20.00

SERVISS, G.P. *Edison's Conquest of Mars.* 1947. Carcosa. 1st ed. EX. R3. $35.00

SERVISS, G.P. *Moon Metal.* 1900. Harper. 1st ed. VG. $65.00

SERVISS, G.P. *Moon Metal.* 1972. Starmont. EX. R3. $15.00

SERVISS, G.P. *2nd Deluge.* 1974. Hyperion. reprint of 1912 ed. EX. R3. $15.00

SETON, Anya. *Avalon.* c 1965. Avalon. dj. VG. C1. $3.50

SETON, E.T. *Biography of a Grizzly.* 1900. NY. 1st ed. VG. B3. $45.00

SETON, E.T. *Birch Bark Roll.* 1927. NY. VG. B3. $40.00

SETON, E.T. *Gospel of the Redman.* 1938. NY. sgns. dj. VG. B3. $70.00

SETON, E.T. *Lives of the Hunted.* 1901. NY. 1st ed. no dj issued. VG. B3. $35.00

SETTERINGTON, Arthur. *Straight-Line Mysteries.* 1972. Calgary. 1st ed. 48 p. NM. J3. $6.00

SETTLE, M.L. *Blood Tie.* 1977. Houghton Mifflin. UP. EX. B13. $75.00

SETTLE, M.L. *Killing Ground.* 1982. Farrar Straus. ARC. glossy wrp. EX. B13. $35.00

SETTLE, M.L. *Killing Ground.* 1982. Farrar Straus. Ltd ed. 1/150. sgn. slipcase. EX. K2. $65.00

SETTLE, M.L. *Know Nothing.* 1960. Viking. 1st ed. dj. EX. B13. $75.00

SETTLE, M.L. *O Beulah Land.* 1956. Viking. 1st ed. dj. EX. $25.00

SETTLE, R.W. *March of the Mounted Riflemen...* 1940. Glendale. Clark. Ils. 380 p. A5. $120.00

SETTLE & SETTLE. *Saddles & Spurs: Saga of the Pony Express.* 1955. Stackpole. Ils 217 p. dj. A5. $30.00

SETTNER, Irving. *If a Poet Is.* 1974. Twin Angel. inscr. EX. B4. $6.00

SEUSS, Dr. *Marvin K Mooney Will You Please Go Now!* 1976. Random House. tall 8vo. dj. B10. $3.50

SEUSS, Dr. *500 Hats of Bartholomew Cubbins.* 1938. Vanguard. 1st ed. dj. EX. K1. $40.00

SEVERIN, Gregory. *Paris Codex: Decoding an Astromical Ephemeris.* 1981. Am Philosophical Soc. 4to. 101 p. wrp. F2. $25.00

SEVERN, Bill. *Big Book of Magic.* 1974. McKay. 1st ed. 248 p. dj. NM. J3. $12.00

SEVERN, Bill. *Magic Fun for Everyone.* 1986. Dutton. 1st ed. sgns. dj. NM. J3. $12.00

SEVERN, Bill. *Magic in Your Pockets.* 1964. McKay. 1st ed. 147 p. dj. EX. J3. $11.00

SEVERN, Bill. *Packs of Fun.* 1967. McKay. 2nd print. dj. EX. J3. $10.00

SEVERN, Merlyn. *Ballet in Action.* 1938. Bodley Head. 1st ed. quarto. 128 p. VG. H3. $75.00

SEVIGNE, Madame. *Letters.* 1927. London. Spurr Swift. 1/1000. 10 vols. TEG. VG. $45.00

SEWEL, William. *Hist of Rise, Increase, & Progress of...Quakers.* 1774. Burlington. Collins. 3rd Corrected ed. 4to. 812 p. V1. $135.00

SEWEL, William. *Hist of Rise, Increase, & Progress of...Quakers.* 1844. NY. Baker Crane. 8vo. 2 vols in 1. V1. $30.00

SEWELL, Elizabeth. *Orphic Voice: Poetry & Nat Hist.* 1960. New Haven. ARC. dj. RS. EX. C4. $60.00

SEXTON, Anne. *Book of Folly.* 1972. Boston. 1st ed. 1/500. sgn. boxed. K2. $85.00

SEXTON, W.T. *Soldiers in the Sun: Adventure in Imperialism.* 1939. Harrisburg. Ils. 297 p. xl. G. T5. $25.00

SEYMOUR, Gerald. *Song in the Morning.* 1987. Norton. 1st ed. dj. VG. P1. $17.95

SEYMOUR, Henry. *Infernal Idol.* 1967. Thriller Book Club. dj. VG. P1. $7.50

SEYMOUR, Henry. *Intrigue in Tangier.* 1958. John Gifford. 1st ed. dj. VG. P1. $15.00

SEYMOUR, Maurice. *Seymour on Ballet: 101 Photographs.* 1947. Pellegrini Cudahy. 1st ed. quarto. dj. EX. H3. $85.00

SEYMOUR, R.F. *Across the Gulf: Journey Through Parts of Yucatan...* 1928. Alderbrink Pr. 1/475. sgn. VG. $45.00

SEYOUR-SMITH, M. *Who's Who in 20th-Century Literature.* 1976. Holt Book Club. 573 p. dj. EX. B10. $5.00

SHAARA, Michael. *Killer Angels.* 1974. McKay. 2nd ed. dj. VG. B3. $27.50

SHACKELTON, E.H. *Heart of the Antarctic.* 1909. Phil. 1st Am ed. 2 vols. VG. T1. $30.00

SHACOCHIS, Bob. *Easy in the Islands.* 1985. NY. ARC. sgn. dj. w/pub slip. T9. $60.00

SHADWELL, Arthur. *Industrial Efficiency.* 1906. London. 2 vols. xl. $50.00

SHADWELL, Thomas. *Complete Works.* 1927. London. Fortune. 1/90 on Kelmscott. 5 vols. lg octavo. H3. $1250.00

SHAGAN, Steve. *Discovery.* nd. Book Club. dj. VG. P1. $4.50

SHAH, Sirdar Ali. *Book of Oriental Literature.* nd. (1938) Garden City. 1st Am ed? 404 p. gilt blk cloth. VG. B10. $8.50

SHAKESPEARE, Nicholas. *Vision of Elena Silves.* 1990. Knopf. UP. wrp. EX. B13. $30.00

SHAKESPEARE, William. *Poems. Edited by FS Ellis.* 1893. London. Kelmscott Pr. 1/500. stiff wrp/ties. NM. A4. $1000.00

SHAKESPEARE, William. *Tempest.* 1908. London. Ils Paul Woodroffe. 129 p. G. T5. $45.00

SHAKESPEARE, William. *Tragic Hist of Hamlet, Prince of Denmark.* 1909. Hammersmith. 1/250. orig vellum. EX. H3. $600.00

SHAKESPEARE, William. *Works.* 1723-1725. London. 1st ed. 6 vols. H3. $2750.00

SHAKESPEARE, William. *Works.* 1880-1881. London. Bickers. 10 vols. Ramage bdg. H3. $1750.00

SHAKESPEARE, William. *Works.* 1920s. London. Macmillan. 9 vols. octavo. Bayntun bdg. H3. $1250.00

SHAKESPEARE, William. *Works.* 1747. London. Knapton. Warburton ed. 8 vols. octavo. H3. $2000.00

SHAKESPEARE, William. *Works.* 1863. Cambridge. Macmillan. 9 vols. octavo. Bayntun bdg. H3. $2000.00

SHAKESPEARE, William. *Works.* 1922. London. Gresham. 8 vols. lg octavo. VG. H3. $400.00

SHAKESPEARE, William. *Works.* 1929. Nonesuch. 1/1600. 7 vols. octavo. H3. $1250.00

SHALETT, Sidney. *Old Nameless: Epic of a US Battlewagon.* 1943. Appleton. 1st ed. VG. B10. $6.50

SHALHOPE, R.E. *Sterling Price: Portrait of a Southerner.* 1971. Columbia, MO. 1st ed. dj. EX. $25.00

SHAND, William. *Tempest in a Teacup.* 1958. Roy. 1st ed. dj. xl. P1. $5.00

SHANGE, Ntosake. *Girls Who Have Considered Suicide.* 1975. San Lorenzo. 1st ed. VG. very scarce. B13. $150.00

SHANGE, Ntosake. *Sassafrass, Cypress, & Indigo.* 1982. St Martin. UP. wrp. EX. scarce. B13. $85.00

SHANKLAND, F.N. *Birds.* 1936. Saalfield. Ils FB Peat. 4to. fair. B10. $3.50

SHANNON, Dell. *Appearances of Death.* nd. Book Club. dj. VG. P1. $5.00

SHANNON, Dell. *Blood Count.* nd. Book Club. dj. VG. P1. $5.00

SHANNON, Dell. *Blood Count.* 1986. Morrow. 1st ed. dj. EX. F5. $13.00

SHANNON, Dell. *Cold Trail.* nd. Book Club. dj. VG. P1. $5.00

SHANNON, Dell. *Crime File.* nd. Book Club. dj. VG. P1. $5.00

SHANNON, Dell. *Death of a Busybody.* nd. Book Club. dj. VG. P1. $5.00

SHANNON, Dell. *Double Bluff.* nd. Book Club. dj. VG. P1. $5.00

SHANNON, Dell. *Felony at Random.* nd. Book Club. dj. VG. P1. $5.00

SHANNON, Dell. *Felony at Random.* 1979. Morrow. 1st ed. dj. VG. P1. $15.00

SHANNON, Dell. *Mark of Murder.* nd. Book Club. dj. VG. P1. $5.00

SHANNON, Dell. *Schooled To Kill.* 1969. Morrow. 1st ed. dj. xl. P1. $7.50

SHANNON, Dell. *Spring of Violence.* nd. Book Club. dj. VG. P1. $5.00

SHANNON, Dell. *With Intent To Kill.* nd. Book Club. dj. VG. P1. $5.00

SHAO, Paul. *Orig of Ancient Am Cultures.* 1983. IA U. 1st ed. oblong 4to. F2. $40.00

SHAPIRO, Karl. *Adam & Eve.* 1986. Bucknell U. Ltd ed. 1/125. sgn. H3. $150.00

SHAPIRO, Karl. *Person, Place, & Thing.* 1942. Reynall Hitchcock. inscr. lg octavo. dj. H3. $75.00

SHAPIRO, Karl. *Poems 1940-1953.* 1953. Random House. inscr. dj. H3. $40.00

SHAPIRO, Stanley. *Simon's Soul.* 1977. Putnam. 1st ed. clipped dj. EX. F5. $18.50

SHARER, Robert. *Prehistory of Chalchuapa, El Salvador.* 1978. PA U. 1st ed. 4to. 3 vols. wrp. F2. $45.00

SHARKEY, Don. *Woman Shall Conquer.* nd. (1952) Bruce. Probably 1st ed. 306 p. dj. VG. B10. $4.00

SHARKEY, Jack. *Murder Maestro Please.* 1960. Abelard Schuman. 1st ed. dj. xl. P1. $8.00

SHARMAN, Mirian. *Face of Danger.* 1967. Gollancz. 1st ed. dj. xl. P1. $5.00

SHARP, Marilyn. *Masterstroke.* 1981. Marek. 1st ed. dj. VG. P1. $15.00

SHARP, Marilyn. *Sunflower.* 1979. Marek. 1st ed. dj. EX. P1. $15.00

SHARP, William. *Life of Percy Bysshe Shelley.* 1887. London. 8vo. VG. $35.00

SHARP & OPPE. *Dance: Hist Survey of Dancing in Europe.* 1924. London/NY. Probable 1st ed. VG. G1. $60.00

SHARP. *Hist of Diocese of Brooklyn 1853-1953.* 1954. NY. 1st ed. 2 vols. slipcase. VG. C2. $45.00

SHARPE, Alton. *Expert Card Conjuring.* 1968. Sharpe. Ltd Deluxe 1st ed. 141 p. NM. J3. $70.00

SHARPE, Alton. *Expert Card Conjuring/Expert Card Chicanery.* 1976. NY. Robbins. 2 vols. EX. J3. $10.00

SHARPE, Alton. *Expert Card Mysteries.* 1975. NY. Tannen. 1st ed. 2nd print. 195 p. VG. J3. $8.00

SHARPE, Alton. *Expert Hocus-Pocus.* 1973. NY. Tannen. 2nd print. 173 p. NM. J3. $10.00

SHARPE, S.G. *Tobe.* 1945. NC U. 5th print. 4to. 121 p. dj. $22.00

SHARPLES, E.S. *Little Friends.* 1914. Phil. Biddle Pr. 12mo. 129 p. VG. V1. $8.00

SHARPLESS, Isaac. *Hist of Quaker Government in PA: Quakers in the Revolution.* 1899. Phil. TS Leach. 12mo. 255 p. G. V1. $10.00

SHARPLESS, Isaac. *Political Leaders of Provincial PA.* 1919. Macmillan. 8vo. 248 p. dj. VG. V1. $10.00

SHARPLESS, Isaac. *Quaker Boy on the Farm & at School.* 1908. Biddle Pr. 8vo. 38 p. VG. V1. $10.00

SHARPLESS, Isaac. *Story of a Sm College.* 1918. Phil. Winston. 1st ed. 8vo. 237 p. VG. V1. $12.50

SHARPLESS, Jack. *Presences of Mind: Collected Books of Jack Sharpless.* 1989. Frankfort. Gnomon. 1/26. sgns. no dj issued. M. C4. $75.00

SHARPS, Les. *Sharp Sorcery.* 1977. Supreme Magic. 76 p. dj. NM. J3. $10.00

SHATNER, William. *Tekwar.* 1989. Phantasia. 1st ed. 1/475. sgn. M. R3. $175.00

SHAW, Artie. *Trouble With Cinderella.* 1952. NY. 1st ed. dj. VG. B3. $30.00

SHAW, Bernard. *Adventures of the Blk Girl.* 1932. Constable. 6th ed. decor brd. VG. P1. $7.50

SHAW, Bernard. *Apple Cart.* 1930. London. Constable. 1st ed. dj. EX. H3. $75.00

SHAW, Bernard. *Apple Cart.* 1931. Brentano. 1st Am ed. dj. VG. H3. $60.00

SHAW, Bernard. *Back to Methuselah (A Metabiological Pentateuch).* 1939. Ltd Ed Club. Ils John Farleigh. 1/1500. slipcase. EX. C4. $50.00

SHAW, Bernard. *Back to Methuselah.* 1921. London. Constable. 1st ed. dj. H3. $85.00

SHAW, Bernard. *Collected Works.* 1930. NY. Wise. Ayot St Lawrence ed. 1/1790. 30 vols. H3. $600.00

SHAW, Bernard. *In Good King Charles' Golden Days.* 1939. London. Constable. 1st ed. dj. EX. H3. $50.00

SHAW, Bernard. *Intelligent Woman's Guide to Socialism & Capitalism.* 1928. NY. Brentano. 1st ed. G. R5. $15.00

SHAW, Bernard. *Misalliance/Dark Lady of Sonnets/Fanny's 1st Play.* 1914. London. Constable. 1st ed. TEG. gr bdg. H3. $75.00

SHAW, Bernard. *Plays.* 1929. London. Constable. 12 vols. 12mo. fld case. H3. $300.00

SHAW, Bernard. *Simpleton/Six/Millionairess.* 1936. London. Constable. 1st ed. dj. H3. $75.00

SHAW, Bernard. *St Joan.* 1924. London. Constable. 1st ed. inscr. w/cast-sgn playbill. H3. $200.00

SHAW, Bernard. *St Joan.* 1924. NY. Brentano. 1st Am ed. VG. $20.00

SHAW, Bernard. *Trans & Tomfooleries.* 1926. Brentano. 1st Am ed. 276 p. EX. B10. $22.50

SHAW, Bernard. *Widower's House.* 1893. London. 1st Am ed. VG. $100.00

SHAW, Bernard. *Widower's House.* 1908. London. VG. $8.00

SHAW, Bernard. *Works.* 1920s. Brentano. 20 vols. sm octavo. H3. $1250.00

SHAW, Bob. *Cosmic Kaleidoscope.* 1976. Gollancz. 1st ed. dj. EX. P1. $25.00

SHAW, Bob. *Cosmic Kaleidoscope.* 1977. Doubleday. 1st ed. dj. VG. P1. $20.00

SHAW, Bob. *Medusa's Children.* nd. Book Club. dj. VG. P1. $4.50

SHAW, Bob. *Orbitsville Judgement.* 1990. Gollancz. 1st ed. dj. EX. P1. $25.00

SHAW, Bob. *Ragged Astronauts.* 1986. Baen. 1st ed. dj. VG. P1. $15.95

SHAW, Bob. *Wooden Spaceships.* 1988. Baen. 1st ed. dj. EX. F5/P1. $15.00

SHAW, Bob. *Wreath of Stars.* 1976. Gollancz. 1st ed. dj. EX. P1. $20.00

SHAW, C.G. *Low-Down.* 1928. NY. Holt. Ils Peter Arno. 1st ed. 8vo. dj. EX. R4. $35.00

SHAW, G.B. *London Music in 1888-1889 As Heard by Corno di Bassetto.* 1937. Constable. octavo. 420 p. dj. EX. H3. $75.00

SHAW, H.K. *Budkeye Disciples.* 1952. St Louis. 504 p. dj. VG. T5. $17.50

SHAW, Irwin. *Beggar-Man, Thief.* nd. (1977) Delacorte. 1st ed. 436 p. dj. NM. B10. $7.50

SHAW, Irwin. *Bread Upon the Waters.* 1981. Delacorte. 1st ed. 1/500. sgn. AEG. slipcase. H3. $60.00

SHAW, Irwin. *In the Company of Dolphins.* 1964. NY. Geis. 1st ed. dj. EX. K2. $65.00

SHAW, Irwin. *Nightwork.* 1975. Delacorte. UP. EX. B13. $60.00

SHAW, Irwin. *Young Lions.* 1948. Random House. ARC. 1/813. presentation. EX. K2. $75.00

SHAW, Joseph. *Hard-Boiled Omnibus.* 1946. NY. 1st ed. dj. VG. B3. $35.00

SHAW, Luella. *True Hist of Some of the Pioneers of CO.* 1909. Hotchiss, CO. 269 p. wrp. A5. $45.00

SHAW, S.C. *Sketches of Wood Co.* 1878. Parkesburg, WV. 1st ed. gray wrp. $45.00

SHAXTON, Alan. *My Kind of Magic.* 1970. Goodliffe. 1st ed. 77 p. dj. NM. J3. $9.00

SHAY, Frank. *Deep Sea Chanties.* 1925. London. Ils Edward Wilson. 4to. A4. $85.00

SHAY, Gene. *Secrets of Magic Revealed...* 1977. Running Pr. 1st ed. EX. J3. $5.00

SHEA, J.G. *Child's Hist of the US.* 1872. NY. Ils. sm 4to. AEG. VG. T1. $60.00

SHEA, J.G. *Hist of Catholic Church Within the Limits of US.* 1886-1892. NY. 1st ed. 4 vols. xl. G. T5. $195.00

SHEA, Micheal. *Quest for Simbilis.* 1974. DAW Books. 1st ed. wrp. EX. scarce. F5. $11.00

SHEA. *It's All in the Game (Milton Bradley).* 1960. NY. 1st ed. sgn President M Bradley. dj. VG. B3. $22.50

SHEAHAN, J.W. *Life of Stephen A Douglas.* 1860. NY. 1st ed. 528 p. fair. T5. $15.00

SHECKLEY, Robert. *Calibre .50.* 1961. Bantam A2216. 1st ed. wrp. NM. T9. $35.00

SHECKLEY, Robert. *Futuropolis.* 1978. A&W Visual Lib. 1st ed. wrp. EX. R3. $12.50

SHECKLEY, Robert. *Is That What People Do?* 1984. Holt. 1st ed. dj. EX. F5. $20.00

SHECKLEY, Robert. *Mindswap.* nd. Book Club. dj. VG. P1. $4.50

SHECKLEY, Robert. *Mindswap.* 1966. Delacorte. 1st ed. dj. EX. F5. $30.00

SHECKLEY, Robert. *Victim Prime.* 1987. Methuen. 1st ed. dj. EX. P1. $20.00

SHECKLEY, Robert. *10th Victim.* 1965. Ballantine U5050. 1st ed. wrp. EX. T9. $35.00

SHEED, Wilfred. *Baseball & Lesser Sports.* 1991. Harper Collins. UP. wrp. EX. K2. $35.00

SHEED, Wilfred. *Clare Boothe Luce.* 1982. Dutton. 1st ed. 183 p. dj. NM. B10. $5.00

SHEEHAN, Murray. *Eden.* 1928. Dutton. 3rd ed. VG. P1. $6.00

SHEEHAN, Neil. *Bright Shining Lie.* 1988. Random House. 1st ed. dj. M. $30.00

SHEEHAN, P.P. *1 Gift.* 1974. Shroud Krueger. 1st ed. wrp. EX. R3. $10.00

SHEEHAN, Perley. *Abyss of Wonders.* 1953. Fantasy. 1/1500. boxed. EX. R3. $30.00

SHEFFIELD, Charles. *Between the Strokes of Night.* 1985. Baen. 1st ed. wrp. EX. F5. $6.00

SHEFFIELD, Charles. *McAndrew Chronicles.* nd. Tor Books. 1st ed. wrp. EX. F5. $10.00

SHEFFIELD, Charles. *Nimrod Hunt.* 1986. Baen. 1st ed. wrp. EX. F5. $6.00

SHEFFIELD & BISCHOFF. *Selke.* 1982. Macmillan. 1st ed. dj. EX. R3. $15.00

SHELDON, Charles. *Wilderness of Denali.* 1960. NY. dj. EX. A6. $38.50

SHELDON, Lee. *Doomed Planet.* 1967. Avalon. 1st ed. dj. EX. R3. $10.00

SHELDON, Richard. *Poor Prisoner's Defense.* 1949. Simon Schuster. VG. P1. $10.00

SHELDON, Roy. *Atoms in Action.* 1953. Hamilton Panther. dj. VG. P1. $35.00

SHELDON, Roy. *House of Entropy.* 1953. Hamilton Panther. dj. VG. P1. $35.00

SHELDON, Sidney. *Master of the Game.* 1982. Morrow. 1st ed. 495 p. dj. M. B10. $5.00

SHELDON, Sidney. *Naked Face.* nd. Book Club. dj. VG. P1. $4.00

SHELDON, W. *Book of the Am Woodcock.* 1971. MA U. 2nd ed. dj. VG. B3. $27.50

SHELLABARGER, Samuel. *Capt From Castile.* 1945. Little Brn. 1st ed. EX. F5. $10.00

SHELLEY, E.M. *Hunting Big Game With Dogs in Africa.* 1924. Columbus, MS. 1st ed. sgn. photos. EX. $100.00

SHELLEY, Mary. *Frankenstein.* 1953. Lion Book 146. 1st print. wrp. VG. T9. $35.00

SHELLEY, P.B. *Complete Poetical Works.* 1892. Riverside. Lg Paper ed. 1/250. 8 vols. octavo. H3. $450.00

SHELLEY, P.B. *Complete Works.* 1906. London. Virtue. 1/26. 8 vols. octavo. H3. $1500.00

SHELLEY, P.B. *Complete Works.* 1927. London. Julian Ed/Benn. 10 vols. octavo. TEG. djs. slipcase. H3. $1250.00

SHELLEY, P.B. *Notebooks of Percy Bysshe Shelley.* 1911. Boston. 1/465. 3 vols. G. T5. $195.00

SHELLEY, P.B. *Poems. Selected, Edited, & Intro by Stephen Spender.* 1971. Ltd Ed Club. Ils/sgn Richard S Smith. slipcase. EX. C4. $100.00

SHELLEY, P.B. *Poetical Works.* 1888. Chatto Windus. 5 vols. sm octavo. TEG. VG. H3. $350.00

SHELLEY, P.B. *Posthumous Poems.* 1924. London. 1st ed. rebacked. morocco slipcase. H3. $1500.00

SHELLEY, P.B. *Works...in Verse & Prose.* 1880. London. Reeves Turner. 8 vols. octavo. EX. H3. $1500.00

SHEPARD, Irving. *Jack London's Tales of Adventure.* 1956. NY. 1st ed. VG. T1. $45.00

SHEPARD, Leslie. *Dracula Book of Great Vampire Stories*. 1977. Citadel. 1st ed. dj. EX. R3. $12.50

SHEPARD, Lucius. *Jaguar Hunter*. 1987. Arkham House. 2nd ed. sgn author/Ils. M. R3. $35.00

SHEPARD, Lucius. *Scalehunter's Beautiful Daughter*. 1988. Ziesing. 1st ed. dj. P1/R3. $16.95

SHEPARD, Sam. *Fool for Love*. 1984. London. Faber. 1st Eng ed. wrp. EX. K2. $55.00

SHEPARD, Sam. *Motel Chronicles & Hawk Moon*. 1985. London. Faber. UP of 1st Eng ed. EX. K2. $100.00

SHEPARD, Sam. *5 Plays*. 1967. Bobbs Merrill. ARC. dj. RS. B13. $350.00

SHEPHERD, Jean. *Ferrair in the Bedroom*. 1972. Dodd Mead. 1st ed. dj. EX. K2. $35.00

SHEPHERD, Jim. *Flights*. 1983. Knopf. UP. wrp. EX. C4. $50.00

SHEPHERD, Michael; see Ludlum, Robert.

SHERATON, Mimi. *Visions of Sugarplums*. 1968. Random House. Book Club ed. 8vo. 205 p. dj. $12.00

SHERBONDY, Jeannette. *Weaving & Symbolism in the Andes*. 1985. Bloomington. Andean Studies Occasional Papers 2. 72 p. wrp. F2. $12.50

SHERIDAN, Jeff. *Nothing's Impossible: Stunts To Entertain & Amaze*. 1982. NY. 1st ed. dj. NM. J3. $12.00

SHERIDAN, R.B. *Rivals*. 1907. NY. Crowell. Ils Margaret Armstrong. 8vo. TEG. EX. R4. $30.00

SHERMAN, Dan. *Dynasty of Spies*. 1980. Arbor House. 1st ed. dj. VG. P1. $15.00

SHERMAN, Harold. *Among African Tribes*. 1933. Goldsmith. 1st ed. dj. EX. R3. $25.00

SHERMAN, Harold. *Gr Man*. 1946. Century. 1st ed. wrp. EX. R3. $10.00

SHERMAN, Harold. *Tahara, Boy King of the Desert*. 1933. Goldsmith. VG. P1. $12.50

SHERMAN, S.P. *Poetical Works of Joaquin Miller*. 1923. Putnam/Knickerbocker. sgn. TEG. w/sgn letter. VG. H3. $125.00

SHERMAN, W.T. *Memoirs*. 1891. NY. 1st ed. 2 vols. VG. B3. $75.00

SHERMAN, W.T. *Memorial in Art, Oratory, & Literature...Army of TN*. 1904. WA. EX. $50.00

SHERMER, Matt. *You Must Run the World!* 1959. Blk Sun. wrp. EX. H3. $200.00

SHERMER, Matt. *You Must Run the World!* 1959. Blk Sun. wrp. w/sgn note. EX. H3. $325.00

SHERREL, Carl. *Raum*. 1977. Avon. 1st ed. PB. VG. C1. $4.00

SHERRY, Edna. *Survival of the Fittest*. 1960. Dodd Mead. 1st ed. dj. VG. P1. $12.50

SHERWOOD, E.W. *Rainbow Hoosier*. c1920. Indianapolis. 1st ed. 211 p. T5. $60.00

SHERWOOD, Martin. *Maxwell's Demon*. 1976. New Eng Lib. 1st ed. dj. EX. P1. $15.00

SHERWOOD, Martin. *Survival*. 1975. New Eng Lib. 1st ed. dj. EX. P1. $15.00

SHERWOOD, R.E. *Abe Lincoln in IL*. 1939. Scribner. 1st ed. dj. VG. H3. $75.00

SHERWOOD, R.E. *Reunion in Vienna*. 1932. Scribner. 1st ed. dj. VG. H3. $100.00

SHETRONE, H.C. *Primer of OH Archaeology*. 1945. Columbus. Ils 4th ed. wrp. VG. T5. $12.50

SHIEL, M.P. *Children of the Wind*. 1923. Knopf. 1st ed. VG. P1. $45.00

SHIEL, M.P. *How the Old Woman Got Home*. 1928. Macy Masius. 1st ed. VG. R3. $20.00

SHIEL, M.P. *Invisible Voices*. 1935. London. 1st ed. VG. R3. $85.00

SHIEL, M.P. *Purple Cloud*. 1930. Vanguard. 1st ed. chipped dj. EX. F5. $60.00

SHIEL, M.P. *Purple Cloud*. 1930. Vanguard. 1st ed. Tower dj. VG. R3. $40.00

SHIEL, M.P. *Purple Cloud*. 1946. World. dj. VG. P1. $30.00

SHIEL, M.P. *Purple Coud*. 1963. Gollancz. dj. VG. P1. $25.00

SHIEL, M.P. *Xelucha & Others*. 1975. Arkham House. 1st ed. M. R3. $25.00

SHIELDS, G.O. *Big Game of N Am*. 1890. Chicago. 1st ed. EX. K1. $125.00

SHIELDS, G.O. *Cruising in the Cascades*. 1889. Rand McNally. 1st ed. VG. $45.00

SHINER, Lewis. *Deserted Cities of the Heart*. 1988. Doubleday. 1st ed. dj. EX. P1. $17.95

SHINNO, Tat. *Flower Arranging To Copy*. 1966. Doubleday. 1st ed. 246 p. dj. EX. $25.00

SHIRAS, W.H. *Children of the Atom*. 1953. Gnome. 1st ed. dj. VG. P1. $65.00

SHIRAS, W.H. *Children of the Atom*. 1978. Pennyfarthing. dj. EX. P1. $15.00

SHIRER, W.L. *Berlin Diary: Journal of Foreign Correspondent 1934-1941*. 1941. NY. 1st ed. 605 p. dj. T5. $15.00

SHIRER, W.L. *Rise & Fall of 3rd Reich: Hist of Nazi Germany*. 1960. Simon Schuster Book Club. 1245 p. dj. VG. B10. $7.00

SHIREY, O.C. *America: Story of the 442nd Comabat Team*. 1946. WA. 1st ed. 151 p. xl. T5. $75.00

SHIRLEY, Glen. *Buckskin & Spurs: Gallery of Frontier Rogues & Heroes*. 1958. NY. 1st ed. dj. EX. $15.00

SHIRLEY, John. *Transmaniacon*. 1979. Zebra. 1st ed. wrp. EX. F5. $20.00

SHIRLEY, R.W. *Mapping of the World: Early Printed World Maps 1492-1700*. 1989. London. Holland Pr. 2nd ed. M. A5. $150.00

SHOBIN, David. *Seeding*. 1982. Linden Pr. 1st ed. dj. EX. P1. $17.50

SHOLOKHOV, Mikhail. *Harvest on the Don*. 1961. NY. Knopf. 1st Am ed. dj. EX. $35.00

SHORES, Louis. *Highways in the Sky: Story of the AACS*. 1947. NY. Ils. sgn. 269 p. T5. $19.50

SHORT, Ernest. *Hist of Sculpture*. 1907. London. Heinemann. 1st ed. 327 p. G. B10. $6.00

SHORT, Luke. *Saddle by Starlight*. 1952. Houghton. 1st ed. 169 p. dj. VG. B10. $25.00

SHORT, Luke. *Sunset Graze*. 1942. Doubleday Doran. 1st ed. xl. P1. $5.00

SHORT, Wayne. *This Raw Land*. 1968. NY. 1st ed. dj. VG. B3. $22.50

SHORTT & DOUGHTY. *Canada & Its Provinces*. 1913-1914. Toronto. Pub Assn Canada Ltd. 1/875. 22 vols. H3. $2250.00

SHORTT & DOUGHTY. *Canada & Its Provinces*. 1914-1917. Edinboro ed. 1/875. 23 vols. xl. A4. $1200.00

SHOUMATOFF, Alex. *Capital of Hope*. 1980. Coward McCann. 1st ed. 209 p. dj. F2. $15.00

SHOUMATOFF, Alex. *In S Light*. 1986. Simon Schuster. 1st ed. 239 p. dj. F2. $15.00

SHOUMATOFF, Alex. *World Is Burning*. 1990. Little Brn. 1st ed. 377 p. dj. M. F2. $20.00

SHURE, David. *Hester Bateman: Queen of Eng Silversmiths*. 1959. Doubleday. dj. VG. $25.00

SHURTER, E.D.B. *Orations & Speeches of Henry W Grady.* 1910. TX U. EX. $30.00

SHUTE, H.A. *Real Diary of a Real Boy.* 1902. Everett Pr. inscr. slipcase. H3. $150.00

SHUTE, H.A. *Real Diary of a Real Boy.* 1911. Everett Pr. 200 p. G. B10. $4.25

SHUTE, H.A. *Sequil; or, Things Whitch Ain't Finished in the 1st.* 1904. Everett Pr. scarce. H3. $150.00

SHUTE, Nevil. *In the Wet.* 1953. London. 1st ed. dj. VG. $40.00

SHUTE, Nevil. *In the Wet.* 1975. Heinemann. 7th ed. dj. EX. P1. $17.50

SHUTE, Nevil. *No Highway.* 1949. Morrow. 1st ed. dj. EX. B13. $40.00

SHUTE, Nevil. *No Highway.* 1951. Heinemann. 7th ed. VG. P1. $10.00

SHUTE, Nevil. *On the Beach.* 1957. Melbourne. Heinemann. 1st ed. dj. EX. B13. $75.00

SHUTE, Nevil. *Pastoral.* 1944. Morrow. dj. VG. P1. $17.50

SHUTE, Nevil. *Trustee From the Toolroom.* 1960. Morrow. VG. P1. $15.00

SIAN-TEK, Lim. *Folk Tales From China.* nd. (1944) Day. 1st ed? VG. B10. $10.00

SIBLEY, Celestine. *Malignant Heart.* 1958. Crime Club. 1st ed. dj. VG. P1. $12.50

SIBSON, Thomas. *Sketches of Expeditions From the Pickwick Club.* 1838. London. Sherwood Gilbert Piper. 1st ed. H3. $125.00

SICHEL, P. *Jersey Lily.* 1958. NY. 1st ed. dj. VG. B3. $20.00

SICHEL, Walter. *Sheridan by Walter Sichel.* 1909. Houghton Mifflin. 1st ed. 2 vols. EX. C4. $50.00

SICK, Helmut. *Tukani.* 1960. NY. Eriksson-Taplinger. 1st Am ed. 240 p. dj. F2. $20.00

SIDNEY, Philip. *Astrophel & Stella.* 1931. np. Nonesuch. 1st ed. 1/725. slipcase. EX. $125.00

SIDNEY, Philip. *Countess of Pembroke's Arcadia.* 1662. London. Lloyd. 11th ed. V1. $325.00

SIDRYS, Raymond. *Archaeological Excavations in N Belize, Central Am.* 1983. UCLA. 1st ed. 4to. wrp. F2. $25.00

SIEBER, Roy. *Sculptures of Blk Africa.* 1968. Los Angeles. 1st ed. 4to. wrp. EX. T1. $40.00

SIEBERT, W.H. *Quaker Section of Underground Railroad in N OH.* 1930. Columbus. reprint. wrp. VG. T5. $25.00

SIEGEL, P.J. *Mentalism a la Mode.* 1974. Siegel. 1st ed. sgn. 55 p. NM. J3. $8.00

SIEGEL, Robert. *Alpha Centauri.* 1980. Cornerstone. 2nd ed. dj. EX. P1. $10.00

SIEGFRIED, Andre. *Impressions of S Am.* 1933. Harcourt. 1st ed. 192 p. dj. F2. $25.00

SIEYES, E.J. *What Is the 3rd Estate?* 1964. Praeger. 1st ed. 214 p. VG. B10. $7.50

SIGAUD, L.A. *Belle Boyd: Confederate Spy.* 1944. Richmond. VG. $32.00

SIKO, L.M. *Ceremony.* 1977. NY. 1st ed. inscr. dj. EX. T9. $135.00

SIKORSKY, Igor. *Invisible Encounter.* 1947. NY. 1st ed. sgn. dj. VG. B3. $50.00

SILBERER, Victor. *Grundzuge der Praktichen Luftschiffahrt.* 1910. Berlin. Schmidt. 248 p. w/2 ads. T5. $125.00

SILKO, L.M. *Ceremony.* 1977. Viking. 1st ed. dj. VG. B13. $100.00

SILKO, L.M. *Storyteller.* 1981. Seaver. 1st HrdCvr ed. dj. EX. K2. $85.00

SILL, E.R. *Around the Horn: Journal, Dec 10, 1861 to March 25, 1862.* 1944. New Haven. Ils 1st ed. 79 p. dj. EX. T5. $35.00

SILLITOE, Alan. *Shaman & Other Poems.* 1968. Turret. Ltd ed. 1/100. sgn. dj. H3. $50.00

SILVERBERG, Robert. *Chains of the Sea.* 1973. Thomas Nelson. 1st ed. dj. EX. P1/R3. $10.00

SILVERBERG, Robert. *Conglomeroid Cocktail Party.* 1984. Arbor House. 1st ed. dj. EX. P1. $14.95

SILVERBERG, Robert. *Deep Space.* nd. Book Club. dj. VG. P1. $4.50

SILVERBERG, Robert. *Downward to the Earth.* nd. Book Club. dj. VG. P1. $4.00

SILVERBERG, Robert. *Downward to the Earth.* 1970. SF Book Club. 1st ed. Frazetta dj. EX. R3. $10.00

SILVERBERG, Robert. *Dying Inside.* 1972. Scribner. 1st ed. dj. EX. R3. $15.00

SILVERBERG, Robert. *Earthmen & Strangers.* 1966. Duell Sloan. 1st ed. dj. EX. R3. $10.00

SILVERBERG, Robert. *Edge of Space.* 1979. Elsevier/Nelson. 1st ed. dj. EX. P1. $15.00

SILVERBERG, Robert. *Ends of Time.* 1973. Hawthorn. 1st ed. dj. EX. R3. $8.50

SILVERBERG, Robert. *Feast of St Dioysus.* 1975. Scribner. 1st ed. dj. EX. F5. $16.00

SILVERBERG, Robert. *Galactic Dreamers.* 1977. Random House. 1st ed. dj. EX. P1. $15.00

SILVERBERG, Robert. *Gate of Worlds.* 1978. Gollancz. dj. EX. P1. $20.00

SILVERBERG, Robert. *Gilgamesh the King.* 1984. Arbor House. 1st ed. dj. EX. P1. $16.95

SILVERBERG, Robert. *Great Adventures in Archaeology.* 1964. Dial. 1st ed. 402 p. dj. F2. $10.00

SILVERBERG, Robert. *Homefaring.* 1983. Phantasia. 1st ed. 1/450. sgn. M. R3. $50.00

SILVERBERG, Robert. *Hotrod Sinners.* 1962. Bedside Book. 1st ed. wrp. EX. scarce F5. $10.00

SILVERBERG, Robert. *Infinite Jests.* 1974. Chilton. 1st ed. dj. EX. P1. $17.50

SILVERBERG, Robert. *Lion Time in Timbuctoo.* 1990. Axototl. 1st Trade ed. sgn. stiff wrp. EX. C1. $12.50

SILVERBERG, Robert. *Lord of Darkness.* 1983. Arbor House. 1st ed. dj. EX. P1. $17.50

SILVERBERG, Robert. *Lord Valentine's Castle.* 1980. NY. 1st ed. 1/250. sgn. 444 p. slipcase. EX. T5. $70.00

SILVERBERG, Robert. *Lost Cities & Vanished Civilizations.* 1962. Chilton. 1st ed. dj. VG. F5. $28.00

SILVERBERG, Robert. *Mutants.* nd. Book Club. dj. VG. P1. $4.50

SILVERBERG, Robert. *New Atlantis.* nd. Book Club. dj. EX. P1. $4.50

SILVERBERG, Robert. *New Dimensions 10.* 1980. Harper Row. 1st ed. dj. EX. P1. $20.00

SILVERBERG, Robert. *New Dimensions 5.* 1975. Harper Row. 1st ed. dj. EX. P1. $15.00

SILVERBERG, Robert. *New Dimensions 7.* 1977. Harper Row. 1st ed. dj. EX. P1. $20.00

SILVERBERG, Robert. *New Dimensions.* 1978. Harper. 1st ed. dj. EX. F5. $8.00

SILVERBERG, Robert. *Other Dimensions.* 1973. Hawthorn. 1st ed. dj. EX. R3. $8.50

SILVERBERG, Robert. *Parsecs & Parables.* 1970. Doubleday. 1st ed. dj. EX. R3. $17.50

SILVERBERG, Robert. *Regan's Planet.* 1964. Pyramid. 1st ed. wrp. EX. F5. $10.00

SILVERBERG, Robert. *Shadrach in the Furnace.* 1976. Bobbs Merrill. 1st ed. sgn. dj. EX. R3. $35.00

SILVERBERG, Robert. *Sunrise on Mercury.* 1975. Nelson. 1st ed. dj. EX. R3. $15.00

SILVERBERG, Robert. *Threads of Time.* nd. Book Club. dj. VG. P1. $4.50

SILVERBERG, Robert. *Threads of Time.* 1974. Nelson. 1st ed. dj. EX. R3. $12.50

SILVERBERG, Robert. *To the Stars.* 1971. Hawthorn. 1st ed. dj. EX. P1. $20.00

SILVERBERG, Robert. *Tom O'Bedlam.* 1985. Donald Fine. 1st ed. dj. EX. P1. $16.95

SILVERBERG, Robert. *Tom O'Bedlam.* 1985. Donald Fine. 1st ed. dj. EX. R3. $16.95

SILVERBERG, Robert. *Tower of Glass.* 1970. Scribner. 1st ed. sgn. dj. VG. R3. $35.00

SILVERBERG, Robert. *Unfamiliar Territory.* 1973. Scribner. 1st ed. dj. EX. F5. $18.00

SILVERBERG, Robert. *Valentine Pontifex.* 1975. Arbor House. 1st ed. dj. RS. EX. R3. $15.00

SILVERBERG, Robert. *World Inside.* 1976. Millington. dj. EX. P1. $15.00

SILVERBERG, Robert. *World of a Thousand Clrs.* 1982. Arbor House. 1st ed. dj. EX. P1. $14.95

SILVERBERG, Robert. *Worlds of Maybe.* 1970. Nelson. 1st ed. dj. EX. R3. $20.00

SILVERBERG & GREENBERG. *Arbor House Treasury of Modern SF.* 1980. Priam. wrp. EX. R3. $15.00

SILVERMAN. *Violin Hunter.* 1957. NY. 1st ed. dj. VG. B3. $27.50

SILVERS & SAFFRON. *This Laugh Is on Me.* 1973. Prentice Hall. 1st ed. dj. VG. P1. $15.00

SIMAK, C.D. *All the Traps of Earth.* nd. Book Club. dj. VG. P1. $6.00

SIMAK, C.D. *Best SF Stories.* 1965. Doubleday. dj. EX. R3. $15.00

SIMAK, C.D. *Cemetery World.* 1973. SF Book Club. inscr. dj. EX. R3. $15.00

SIMAK, C.D. *Cemetery World.* nd. Book Club. dj. EX. P1. $4.50

SIMAK, C.D. *Cosmic Engineers.* 1950. Gnome. 1st ed. dj. VG. P1. $100.00

SIMAK, C.D. *Creator.* 1946. Fantasy Crawford. 1st ed. wrp. VG. R3. $75.00

SIMAK, C.D. *Enchanted Pilgrimage.* nd. Book Club. dj. VG. P1. $4.50

SIMAK, C.D. *Fellowship of the Talisman.* 1978. Book Club. dj. VG. C1. $3.50

SIMAK, C.D. *Fellowship of the Talisman.* 1978. Del Rey. 1st ed. dj. EX. P1. $20.00

SIMAK, C.D. *Heritage of Stars.* nd. Book Club. dj. VG. P1. $4.50

SIMAK, C.D. *March of Science.* 1969. Harper Row. VG. P1. $20.00

SIMAK, C.D. *Mastodonia.* nd. Book Club. dj. EX. P1. $4.50

SIMAK, C.D. *Mastodonia.* 1978. Del Rey. 1st ed. dj. EX. P1. $20.00

SIMAK, C.D. *Our Children's Children.* 1974. Putnam. 1st ed. sgn. clipped dj. EX. F5. $28.00

SIMAK, C.D. *Out of Their Minds.* 1970. Putnam. 1st ed. sgn. clipped dj. EX. F5. $25.00

SIMAK, C.D. *Project Pope.* nd. Book Club. dj. VG. P1. $4.50

SIMAK, C.D. *Ring Around the Sun.* 1953. Simon Schuster. 1st ed. dj. EX. R3. $75.00

SIMAK, C.D. *Special Deliverance.* 1953. Simon Schuster. 1st ed. dj. EX. R3. $15.00

SIMAK, C.D. *Special Deliverance.* 1982. Del Rey. 1st ed. dj. EX. P1. $20.00

SIMAK, C.D. *Strangers in the Universe.* nd. Book Club. dj. VG. P1. $6.00

SIMAK, C.D. *Time & Again.* 1951. Simon Schuster. 1st ed. dj. EX. R3. $65.00

SIMAK, C.D. *Time Is the Simplest Thing.* nd. Book Club. dj. VG. P1. $5.00

SIMAK, C.D. *Time Is the Simplest Thing.* 1961. Doubleday. 1st ed. dj. EX. F5. $60.00

SIMAK, C.D. *Visitors.* nd. Book Club. dj. VG. P1. $4.50

SIMAK, C.D. *Visitors.* 1980. Del Rey. 1st ed. dj. EX. P1. $20.00

SIMAK, C.D. *Where the Evil Dwells.* 1982. Del Rey. 1st ed. dj. EX. P1. $20.00

SIMAK, C.D. *Where the Evil Dwells.* 1982. Del Rey. 1st ed. sgn. dj. EX. F5. $27.00

SIMENON, Georges. *African Trio.* 1979. Harcourt Brace. 1st ed. dj. VG. P1. $20.00

SIMENON, Georges. *Cat.* 1967. Harcourt Brace World. 1st ed. dj. xl. P1. $5.00

SIMENON, Georges. *Cat.* 1972. Hamish Hamilton. 1st ed. dj. xl. P1. $5.00

SIMENON, Georges. *Delivery.* 1981. Harcourt Brace. dj. xl. P1. $5.00

SIMENON, Georges. *Dissappearance of Odile.* nd. Harcourt Brace. 2nd ed. dj. VG. P1. $10.00

SIMENON, Georges. *Girl in His Past.* 1952. Prentice Hall. 1st ed. VG. P1. $17.50

SIMENON, Georges. *Glass Cage.* 1971. Harcourt Brace. 1st ed. 148 p. dj. EX. B10. $4.00

SIMENON, Georges. *Hatter's Phantoms.* 1976. Doubleday Book Club. VG. P1. $7.50

SIMENON, Georges. *Hatter's Phantoms.* 1976. Harcourt Brace. dj. EX. P1. $15.00

SIMENON, Georges. *Innocents.* 1973. Harcourt. 1st Am ed. dj. EX. F5. $16.00

SIMENON, Georges. *Inspector Maigret & the Dead Girl.* 1955. Doubleday Book Club. VG. P1. $7.50

SIMENON, Georges. *Little Saint.* 1965. Harcourt Brace World. 1st Eng-language ed. dj. NM. T9. $80.00

SIMENON, Georges. *Maigret & the Apparition.* 1977. Hall. Lg Print ed. dj. VG. P1. $10.00

SIMENON, Georges. *Maigret & the Blk Sheep.* 1976. Harcourt Brace. 1st ed. dj. VG. P1. $15.00

SIMENON, Georges. *Maigret & the Headless Corpse.* 1968. Doubleday Book Club. VG. P1. $7.50

SIMENON, Georges. *Maigret Afraid.* 1983. Harcourt Brace. dj. VG. P1. $15.00

SIMENON, Georges. *Maigret's War of Nerves.* 1986. Harcourt Brace. 2nd ed. dj. VG. P1. $6.00

SIMENON, Georges. *Move.* 1968. Harcourt Brace World. 1st ed. dj. xl. P1. $6.00

SIMENON, Georges. *November.* 1970. Harcourt Brace. 1st ed. dj. EX. $15.00

SIMENON, Georges. *Prison.* 1969. Harcourt Brace. 1st ed. dj. xl. P1. $5.00

SIMENON, Georges. *When I Was Old.* 1971. Harcourt Brace. 1st Eng-language ed. dj. VG. w/sgn bookplate. T9. $30.00

SIMENON, Georges. *5 Times Maigret.* 1964. Harcourt Brace World. 1st ed. dj. VG. P1. $17.50

SIMKINS, F.B. *S, Old & New: A Hist 1820-1947.* 1951. Knopf. 4th ed. VG. B10. $7.00

SIMMONS, Dan. *Carrion Comfort.* 1990. Headline. dj. EX. P1. $45.00

SIMMONS, Dan. *Hyperion.* 1989. Bantam. 1st ed. M. R3. $50.00

SIMMONS, Dan. *Hyperion.* 1990. Headline. dj. EX. P1. $45.00

SIMMONS, Dan. *Song of Kali.* 1985. London. 1st Eng ed. dj. EX. $50.00

SIMMONS, Geoffrey. *Adam Experiment.* 1978. Arbor House. 1st ed. dj. EX. P1. $15.00

SIMMONS, H.E. *Concise Encyclopedia of the Civil War.* 1965. Bonanza. dj. VG. S1. $6.00

SIMMONS, Roger. *Palca & Pucara: Study of Effects of Revolution.* 1974. CA U. wrp. F2. $15.00

SIMMONS, William. *Hist of Nat Assn of Naval Veterans.* 1895. Phil. Ils. 161 p. G. T5. $25.00

SIMMONS & BOAL. *Best of the Diners' Club Magazine.* 1962. Regents Am. dj. VG. P1. $20.00

SIMMS, W.G. *Beauchampe; or, KY Tragedy.* 1856. NY. xl. $35.00

SIMMS, W.G. *Border Eagles.* 1840. Phil. 2 vols. xl. $225.00

SIMMS, W.G. *Cassique of Kiawah.* 1859. NY. $40.00

SIMMS, W.G. *Charleston Book.* 1845. Charleston. 404 p. $60.00

SIMMS, W.G. *Damsel of Darien.* 1839. Phil. 2 vols. EX. $250.00

SIMMS, W.G. *Eutaw.* 1856. NY. Review ed. 582 p. $50.00

SIMMS, W.G. *Guy Rivers.* 1834. NY. 2 vols. $180.00

SIMMS, W.G. *Helen Halsey.* 1845. NY. $350.00

SIMMS, W.G. *Katharine Walton; or, Rebel of Dorchester.* 1854. NY. xl. $35.00

SIMMS, W.G. *Katherine Walton; or, Rebel of Dorchester.* 1851. Phil. 1st ed. 186 p. wrp. $350.00

SIMMS, W.G. *Kinsman.* 1841. Phil. 2 vols. 1275 p. $40.00

SIMMS, W.G. *Life of Capt John Smith.* 1846. NY. Ils. rebound. $35.00

SIMMS, W.G. *Life of Chevalier Bayard.* 1847. NY. 401 p. G. $35.00

SIMMS, W.G. *Life of Francis Marion.* 1844. NY. Ils. 347 p. $50.00

SIMMS, W.G. *Lily & the Totem.* 1850. Baker Scribner. 2nd ed. G. B3. $45.00

SIMMS, W.G. *Little Journeys to the Homes of Am Authors: WC Bryant.* 1896. NY. wrp. $40.00

SIMMS, W.G. *Martin Faber.* 1833. NY. G. $60.00

SIMMS, W.G. *Mellichampe.* 1836. NY. $180.00

SIMMS, W.G. *Murder Will Out.* 1841. Phil. 1st ed. 42 p. $125.00

SIMMS, W.G. *Partisan.* 1835. NY. $40.00

SIMMS, W.G. *Pelayo.* 1838. NY. 2 vols. $200.00

SIMMS, W.G. *Views & Reviews in Am Literature.* 1845. NY. $120.00

SIMMS, W.G. *Wigwam & the Cabin.* 1845. NY. 1st/2nd Series. 2 vols. $120.00

SIMON, A.L. *Wines of the World.* 1967. McGraw Hill. 719 p. VG. $75.00

SIMON, Bill. *Controlled Miracles.* 1963. Chicago. Ireland. 2nd print. 36 p. EX. J3. $4.00

SIMON, Bill. *Effective Card Magic.* 1952. NY. Tannen. 1st ed. later print. 181 p. EX. J3. $6.00

SIMON, Bill. *Sleightly Sensational.* 1954. NY. Tannen. 1st ed. 39 p. SftCvr. EX. J3. $3.00

SIMON, J.M. *Guatemala: Eternal Spring, Eternal Tyranny.* 1987. Norton. 4to. 256 p. F2. $22.50

SIMON, J.S. *Sgn of the Fool.* 1971. Ace. EX. B4. $35.00

SIMON, Neil. *Last of the Red-Hot Lovers.* 1970. Random House. 1st ed. dj. EX. B13. $35.00

SIMON, Neil. *Plaza Suite.* 1969. Random House. 1st ed. dj. EX. B13. $45.00

SIMON, Neil. *Prisoner of 2nd Ave.* 1972. Random House. 1st ed. dj. EX. H3. $40.00

SIMON, Neil. *Simon Says.* 1971. Arlington House. 1st ed. dj. VG. B3. $27.50

SIMON, Roger. *Big Fix.* 1973. Straight Arrow. 1st ed. wrp. NM. T9. $20.00

SIMONDS, Frank. *Hist of the World War.* 1917-1920. NY. Ils. VG. A6. $65.00

SIMONS, Roger. *Bullet for a Beast.* 1964. Roy. dj. xl. P1. $5.00

SIMONS, Roger. *Irving Solution.* 1977. Arbor House. 1st ed. dj. EX. P1. $15.00

SIMONSON, G.R. *Hist of the Am Aircraft Industry.* 1968. Cambridge. 1st ed. dj. VG. T5. $25.00

SIMPSON, C.T. *In Lower FL Wilds.* 1920. NY. 1st ed. dj. EX. $40.00

SIMPSON, Dorothy. *Last Seen Alive.* 1985. Scribner. 1st ed. dj. EX. P1. $13.95

SIMPSON, E.B. *Robert Louis Stevenson's Edinburgh Days.* 1914. London. 1st ed. gilt red bdg. VG. $20.00

SIMPSON, George. *Attending Marvels Patagonia Journal.* 1934. Macmillan. 1st ed. 295 p. F2. $15.00

SIMPSON, Mona. *Anywhere But Here.* 1983. Knopf. UP. wrp. EX. C4. $50.00

SIMPSON, Mona. *Anywhere But Here.* 1987. Knopf. 1st ed. sgn. dj. EX. K2. $65.00

SINCLAIR, Andrew. *Project.* 1960. Simon Schuster. 1st ed. dj. EX. P1. $10.00

SINCLAIR, Harold. *Music Out of Dixie.* 1952. Rinehart. 1st ed. dj. EX. C4. $25.00

SINCLAIR, May. *Uncanny Stories.* 1923. Macmillan. VG. R3. $20.00

SINCLAIR, Upton. *Brass Check.* 1920. Pasadena. Sinclair. presentation. VG. H3. $75.00

SINCLAIR, Upton. *Manassar: Novel of the War.* 1904. Macmillan. 1st ed. 412 p. VG. B10. $5.00

SINGER, Bant. *Don't Slip Delaney.* 1964. Collins. 1st ed. dj. VG. P1. $15.00

SINGER, I.B. *Collected Stories of Isaac Bashevis Singer.* 1981. Farrar Straus. UP. wrp. EX. B13. $85.00

SINGER, I.B. *Collected Stories.* 1982. Farrar Straus Giroux. Ltd ed. 1/450. sgn. slipcase. H3. $125.00

SINGER, I.B. *Golem.* 1982. Farrar Straus Giroux. Ltd ed. 1/450. sgn. slipcase. H3. $125.00

SINGER, I.B. *Golem.* 1982. NY. Ils/sgn Uri Sholevitz. 1st ed. slipcase. EX. $145.00

SINGER, I.B. *Image.* 1985. NY. Ltd ed. 1/450. sgn. slipcase. EX. $135.00

SINGER, I.B. *Lost in Am.* 1981. Doubleday. Ils Soyer. Ltd ed. 1/500. sgns. slipcase. H3. $125.00

SINGER, I.B. *Love & Exile.* 1984. Doubleday. 1st ed. sgn. dj. EX. C4. $60.00

SINGER, I.B. *Shosha.* 1978. Farrar Straus Giroux. sgn. dj. H3. $65.00

SINGER, I.B. *Yentl the Yeshiva Boy.* 1983. Farrar Straus Giroux. Ils Frasconi. 1/450. sgns. slipcase. H3. $125.00

SINGER, I.J. *Sinner (Yoshe Kalb).* 1933. Liveright. 1st ed. dj. EX. B13. $125.00

SINGER, Kurt. *More Spy Stories.* 1955. Allen. dj. xl. P1. $10.00

SINGER, Kurt. *Tales From the Unknown.* 1970. London. 1st ed. dj. EX. R3. $15.00

SINGER, Kurt. *Tales of the Uncanny.* 1968. London. 1st ed. dj. EX. R3. $15.00

SINGLETON, Esther. *Guide to Opera.* 1910. Dodd. Ils. TEG. VG. B10. $8.25

SINGMASTER, E. *Gettysburg.* 1913. Boston. 1st ed. 190 p. VG. B3. $30.00

SINSABAUGH, Chris. *Who, Me? 40 Years of Automobile Hist.* 1940. Detroit. Ils 1st ed. 377 p. dj. G. T5. $65.00

SIODMAK, Curt. *City in the Sky.* 1974. Putnam. 1st ed. dj. xl. P1. $5.00

SIODMAK, Curt. *City in the Sky.* 1975. Barrie Jenkins. 1st ed. dj. xl. P1. $10.00

SIODMAK, Curt. *Donovan's Brain.* 1944. Triangle. dj. VG. R3. $10.00

SIODMAK, Curt. *Hauser's Memory.* nd. Book Club. dj. EX. P1. $4.50

SIODMAK, Curt. *3rd Ear.* 1971. Putnam. 1st ed. dj. EX. P1. $12.50

SIPE, C.H. *Mt Vernon & the WA Family.* 1924. Pittsburgh, PA. 1st ed. wrp. xl. B10. $2.50

SIPLE, Paul. *Boy Scout With Byrd.* 1931. NY. 1st ed. 165 p. VG. T5. $35.00

SIPLE, Paul. *Exploring at Home.* 1932. Putnam. 1st ed. 216 p. VG. B10. $7.00

SIRINGO, C.A. *Riata & Spurs.* 1931. Boston. VG. K1. $30.00

SIRINGO, C.A. *TX Cowboy With Intro by Dobie.* 1950. Sloan Assn. dj. EX. $55.00

SISKIND, Janet. *To Hunt in the Morning.* 1973. Oxford U. 1st ed. 214 p. dj. F2. $15.00

SISKING, Aaron. *Places.* 1976. Light Gallery. 4to. dj. EX. $25.00

SITWELL, Edith. *Gardeners & Astronomers: New Poems.* 1953. NY. 1st ed. inscr. dj. EX. $95.00

SITWELL, Edith. *Popular Song.* 1928. Faber Gwyer. Lg Paper ed. 1/500. sgn. H3. $125.00

SITWELL, Edith. *Song of the Cold.* 1948. NY. Vintage. inscr. 8vo. 113 p. dj. VG. V1. $75.00

SITWELL, Edith. *5 Variations on a Theme.* 1933. Duckworth. inscr. octavo. H3. $150.00

SITWELL, H.D.W. *Crown Jewels & Other Regalia in Tower of London.* 1953. London. Dropmore Pr. 1st ed. 4to. 116 p. dj. EX. R4. $125.00

SITWELL, Osbert. *Dickens.* 1932. Chatto Windus. Ltd ed. 1/110. sgn. TEG. H3. $100.00

SITWELL, Osbert. *Eng Reclaimed.* 1927. Duckworth. Ltd ed. 1/165. sgn. H3. $125.00

SITWELL, Osbert. *Great Morning.* 1947. Little Brn. 1st ed. 360 p. dj. VG. B10. $10.00

SITWELL, Sacheverell. *Cyder Feast & Other Poems.* 1927. Duckworth. Ltd ed. 1/165. sgn. H3. $125.00

SITWELL, Sacheverell. *Gold Wall & Mirror.* 1961. World. 1st ed. 286 p. dj. F2. $20.00

SITWELL, Sacheverell. *Monks, Nuns, & Monasteries.* 1965. NY. 1st ed. 4to. dj. EX. G1. $27.00

SITWELL, Sacheverell. *Old-Fashioned Flowers.* 1948. London. 4to. VG. G1. $22.00

SITWELL. *Audubon's Am Birds.* 1949. London. Batsford. 1st ed. 16 clr pls. dj. VG. C2. $25.00

SITWELL. *Theatrical Figures in Porcelain.* 1949. London. pls. VG. C1. $45.00

SJOWALL & WAHLOO. *Man Who Went Up in Smoke.* 1966. Norstedts. 1st Swedish ed. wrp. NM. T9. $125.00

SJOWALL & WAHLOO. *Man Who Went Up in Smoke.* 1969. Pantheon. 1st ed. dj. EX. F5. $14.00

SJOWALL & WAHLOO. *Terrorists.* 1976. Pantheon. ARC. dj. EX. T9. $30.00

SKEAPING, John. *Big Tree of Mexico.* 1953. IU U. 1st ed. 234 p. dj. F2. $15.00

SKEELS, Dell. *Romance of Perceval in Prose.* 1961. Seattle. 1st ed. dj. EX. C1. $32.50

SKEETERS, Paul. *Sidney H Sime: Master of Fantasy.* 1978. Ward Ritchie. 1st ed. lg wrp. M. R3. $15.00

SKELDING, S.B. *Flowers From Here & There.* 1885. NY. 1st ed. VG. $35.00

SKELTON, Red. *Gertrude & Heathcliffe.* 1974. NY. 1st Am ed. dj. EX. C1. $7.50

SKINNER, Ainslie. *Harrowing.* 1980. Rawson Wade. 1st Am ed. dj. EX. R3. $12.50

SKIPP & SPECTOR. *Book of the Dead.* 1989. Ziesing. 1st ed. dj. P1/R3. $22.00

SKUTCH, Alexander. *Naturalist on a Tropical Farm.* 1980. CA U. 1st ed. 397 p. wrp. F2. $12.50

SKUTCH, Alexander. *Nature Through Tropical Windows.* 1983. CA U. Ils Dana Gardner. 1st ed. 374 p. dj. F2. $20.00

SLADEK, John. *Bugs.* 1989. Macmillan. 1st ed. dj. EX. P1. $22.50

SLADEK, John. *Invisible Gr.* 1979. Walker. 1st ed. dj. VG. P1. $25.00

SLADEK, John. *Muller-Fokker Effect.* 1971. Morrow. 1st ed. sgn. dj. EX. F5. $50.00

SLADEK, John. *Red Noise.* 1982. Cheap Street. 1st ed. 1/99. sgn. wrp. M. R3. $30.00

SLADEN, Douglas. *Younger Am Poets 1830-1890.* 1891. London. Griffith. 1st ed. 8vo. 666 p. VG. B10. $15.00

SLATER, Nigel. *Falcon.* 1979. Atheneum. 1st ed. dj. EX. P1. $15.00

SLATER, Philip. *How I Saved the World.* 1985. Dutton. dj. VG. P1. $16.95

SLAUGHTER, Frank. *Thorn of Arimathea.* c 1960. 1st PB ed. VG. C1. $3.50

SLAVIN, Neal. *Britons.* 1986. Aperature. folio. dj. EX. $30.00

SLAVITT, D.R. *Eclogues of Virgil.* 1971. Doubleday. Ils Davidson. Ltd ed. sgn. slipcase. H3. $35.00

SLESAR, Henry. *Thing at the Door.* 1974. Random House. 1st ed. dj. xl. P1. $7.50

SLESAR, Henry. *Thing at the Door.* 1975. Hamish Hamilton. dj. EX. P1. $22.50

SLESAR, Henry. *Thing at the Door.* 1975. Hamish Hamilton. 1st UK ed. dj. NM. T9. $50.00

SLICK, S.E. *William Trent & the W.* 1947. Harrisburg. 188 p. dj. T5. $19.50

SLIM, Field Marshal. *Defeat Into Victory.* 1961. NY. 468 p. dj. T5. $22.50

SLOAN, Benjamin. *Merrimac & the Monitor.* 1926. Columbia, SC. 1st ed. wrp. EX. $25.00

SLOANE, Eric. *Age of Barns.* 1967. NY. 1st ed. dj. VG. B3. $40.00

SLOANE, Eric. *Diary of an Early Am Boy, Eric Sloane: 1805.* 1962. NY. dj. VG. $15.00

SLOANE, Eric. *Spirit of 76.* 1973. NY. 1st ed. presentation w/sketch. VG. $35.00

SLOANE, W.M. *Life of Napoleon Bonaparte.* 1896. Century. 28 vols. Bayntun bdg. clamshell slipcases. H3. $20000.00

SLOANE, William. *Edge of Running Water.* 1939. Farrar Rinehart. 1st ed. VG. P1. $12.50

SLOANE, William. *To Walk the Night.* 1946. Tower. dj. EX. P1. $25.00

SLOCUM, D.B. *Atlas of Amputations.* 1949. Mosby. Ils. lg quarto. 562 p. EX. $95.00

SLOCUM & CAHOON. *Bibliography of James Joyce 1882-1941.* 1953. New Haven. 1st ed. dj. VG. G1. $22.00

SLUSSER, George. *Bridges to Fantasy.* 1982. S IL U. 1st ed. dj. VG. P1. $25.00

SMALL, A.J. *Avenging Ray.* 1930. Crime Club. VG. P1. $15.00

SMALL, A.J. *Mystery Maker.* 1930. Crime Club. 1st ed. VG. P1. $15.00

SMALL, A.J. *Vantine Diamonds.* 1930. Crime Club. 1st ed. VG. P1. $20.00

SMALL, S.H. *Sword & Candle.* 1927. Bobbs Merrill. 1st ed. dj. EX. F5. $22.00

SMALLEY, E.V. *Hist of N Pacific RR.* 1881. NY. Putnam. ARC. 437 p. EX. $95.00

SMART. *Makers of Surveying Instruments in Am Since 1700.* 1972. Troy. VG. C2. $65.00

SMELTZER, Gerald. *Canals Along the Lower Susquehanna (1796-1900).* 1963. York, PA. 140 p. wrp. VG. T5. $25.00

SMILEY, Jane. *Age of Grief.* 1987. Knopf. 1st ed. dj. M. $10.00

SMILEY, Jane. *Catskill Crafts.* 1988. Crown. 1st ed. sm quarto. dj. EX. B13. $45.00

SMITH, A.D.H. *Wastrel.* 1911. Duffield. 1st ed. VG. F5. $16.00

SMITH, Adam. *Inquiry Into the Nature & Causes of Wealth of Nations.* 1870. London. Nelson. 429 p. VG. $65.00

SMITH, Al. *Cards on Demand.* 1980. Smith. 1st ed. 40 p. SftCvr. EX. J3. $12.00

SMITH, B.E. *Century Atlas of the World.* 1897. Century. 4to. 117 maps. lacks front cover. C1. $110.00

SMITH, B.T. *Private Smith's Journal...* 1963. Lakeside Classic. Ils 253 p. T5. $25.00

SMITH, Bradley. *Mexico: Hist in Art.* 1968. Gemini Smith. 1st ed. sm folio. dj. F2. $30.00

SMITH, C.A. *Genius Loci.* 1948. Arkham House. 1st ed. dj. EX. R3. $175.00

SMITH, C.A. *Grotesques & Fantastiques.* 1973. Gerry De La Ree. 1st ed. wrp. EX. R3. $50.00

SMITH, C.A. *Hill of Dionysus.* 1962. Squires Beck. 1st ed. 1/175. no dj issued. EX. R3. $400.00

SMITH, C.A. *Lost Worlds.* 1944. Arkham House. 1st ed. dj. VG. R3. $125.00

SMITH, C.A. *Other Dimensions.* 1970. Arkham House. 1st ed. dj. EX. R3. $60.00

SMITH, C.A. *Star Treader & Other Poems.* 1912. Robertson. 1st ed. VG. R3. $100.00

SMITH, C.R. *Theatre Crafts: Book of Make-Up, Masks, & Wigs.* 1977. Rodale Pr. 2nd print. 248 p. EX. J3. $5.00

SMITH, C.W. *OH: The Buckeye State.* 1946. Haldeman Julius. 32 p. wrp. T5. $12.50

SMITH, C.W. *Red Ryder & Secret of the Lost Mine.* 1947. Whitman. dj. VG. P1. $17.50

SMITH, Captain. *Asiatic Costumes.* 1828. Ackermann. 1st ed. 12mo. 88 p. VG. H3. $275.00

SMITH, Charlie. *Canaan.* 1984. Simon Schuster. UP. sgn. wrp. EX. C4. $75.00

SMITH, Charlie. *Shine Hawk.* 1988. Paris Review Ed. UP. sgn. wrp. EX. C4. $50.00

SMITH, Cordwainer. *Atomsk.* 1949. Duell Sloan. 1st ed. VG. R3. $35.00

SMITH, Cordwainer. *Best of Cordwainer.* 1964. SF Book Club. 1st ed. dj. EX. R3. $10.00

SMITH, Cordwainer. *Norstrilia.* 1988. Gollancz. dj. EX. P1. $22.50

SMITH, Cordwainer. *Ria.* 1947. Duell Sloan. 1st ed. dj. EX. R3. $100.00

SMITH, Cordwainer. *Underpeople.* 1975. Sphere. 1st UK ed. wrp. EX. F5. $7.50

SMITH, Cordwainer. *You Will Never Be the Same.* 1963. Regency. 1st ed. wrp. EX. R3. $20.00

SMITH, D. *Martyrs of Oblong & Little.* 1948. Caldwell. 1st ed. 310 p. dj. VG. B3. $30.00

SMITH, D. *24th MI.* 1962. Harrisburg. 1st ed. dj. EX. B3. $50.00

SMITH, Dennis. *Glitter & Ash.* 1980. Dutton. 1st ed. dj. VG. P1. $12.50

SMITH, E.E. *Children of the Lens.* 1954. Fantasy. 1st ed. later bdg. dj. EX. R3. $100.00

SMITH, E.E. *Copy Shop.* 1985. Doubleday. 1st ed. dj. EX. F5. $14.00

SMITH, E.E. *Copy Shop.* 1985. Doubleday. 1st ed. dj. RS. EX. P1. $17.50

SMITH, E.E. *Galactic Patrol.* 1950. Fantasy. 1st ed. dj. EX. R3. $100.00

SMITH, E.E. *Gray Lensman.* nd. Gnome. 1st ed. dj. VG. P1. $25.00

SMITH, E.E. *Gray Lensman.* 1951. Fantasy. 1st ed. dj. EX. R3. $80.00

SMITH, E.E. *Gray Lensman.* 1951. Fantasy. 1st ed. dj. VG. P1. $25.00

SMITH, E.E. *Perfect Planet.* 1962. Avalon. 1st ed. dj. G. P1. $7.50

SMITH, E.E. *Skylark of Valeron.* 1949. Fantasy. 1st ed. dj. VG. P1. $45.00

SMITH, E.E. *Skylark of Valeron.* 1949. Fantasy. 1st ed. sgn. dj. EX. R3. $100.00

SMITH, E.E. *Skylark 3.* 1948. Fantasy. 1st ed. dj. VG. R3. $65.00

SMITH, E.E. *Skylark 3.* 1948. Fantasy. 1st ed. VG. P1. $25.00

SMITH, E.E. *Triplanetary.* 1948. Fantasy. 1st ed. dj. VG. R3. $50.00

SMITH, E.E. *Vortex Blaster.* 1960. Gnome. 1st ed. dj. EX. R3. $30.00

SMITH, E.E. *1st Lensman.* 1950. Fantasy. Ltd ed. 1/500. sgn. dj. VG. R3. $150.00

SMITH, E.E. *2nd-Stage Lensman.* 1953. Fantasy. Ltd ed. 1/500. sgn. dj. EX. R3. $200.00

SMITH, E.E. *2nd-Stage Lensman.* 1953. Fantasy. 1st ed. dj. VG. R3. $85.00

SMITH, E.W. *Up River & Down.* 1966. NY. 2nd ed. dj. VG. B3. $20.00

SMITH, F.A. *Corpse in Handcuffs.* 1969. Macmillan. 1st ed. dj. EX. P1. $12.50

SMITH, F.H. *Col Carter's Christmas.* 1903. Scribner. 1st ed. B10. $10.00

SMITH, F.H. *In Dicken's London.* 1914. Scribner. 1st ed. 31 pl. 8vo. H3. $50.00

SMITH, G.H. *Ancient Costumes of Great Britain & Ireland From Druids...* 1898. oversized. dj. M. C1. $24.50

SMITH, G.H. *Doomsday Wing.* 1963. Monarch. 1st ed. sgn. wrp. EX. F5. $17.00

SMITH, G.H. *Druids' World.* 1967. Avalon. 1st ed. dj. xl. P1. $6.00

SMITH, G.H. *Flames of Desire.* 1963. France. 1st ed. sgn. wrp. EX. F5. $22.00

SMITH, G.H. *Forgotten Planet.* 1965. Avalon. 1st ed. dj. EX. P1. $15.00

SMITH, G.O. *Between Worlds.* 1929. Stellar. wrp. EX. R3. $35.00

SMITH, G.O. *Hellflower.* 1953. Abelard Schuman. 1st ed. dj. VG. P1. $20.00

SMITH, G.O. *Nomad.* 1950. Prime Pr. 1st ed. dj. EX. R3. $45.00

SMITH, G.O. *Operation Interstellar.* 1950. Century. 1st ed. EX. R3. $10.00

SMITH, G.O. *Pattern of Conquest.* 1949. Gnome. 1st ed. dj. EX. R3. $37.50

SMITH, G.O. *Troubled Star.* 1957. Avalon. 1st ed. dj. EX. R3. $30.00

SMITH, G.O. *Troubled Star.* 1959. Beacon. 1st ed. wrp. EX. R3. $10.00

SMITH, G.O. *Venus Equilateral.* 1947. Prime Pr. 1st ed. dj. EX. R3. $40.00

SMITH, H. *Ethno-Botany of the Menomini Indians.* 1923. Milwaukee. 1st ed. 4to. 36 pls. VG. $50.00

SMITH, H.A. *Great Chili Confrontation.* 1969. Trident. 1st ed. inscr. dj. EX. B13. $100.00

SMITH, H.A. *How To Write Without Knowing Nothing.* 1961. Little Brn. 1st ed. inscr. dj. EX. K2. $50.00

SMITH, H.A. *Mr Kleiri's Kampf.* 1939. Stackpole. 1st ed. inscr. dj. VG. very scarce. K2. $125.00

SMITH, H.A. *People Named Smith.* 1950. Doubleday. 1st ed. inscr. dj. EX. B13. $65.00

SMITH, H.A. *Rebel Yell.* 1954. Doubleday. s/inscr Leo Hirshfield. 1st ed. dj. EX. B13. $45.00

SMITH, H.A. *Short Hist of Fingers.* 1963. Little Brn. 1st ed. inscr. dj. EX. K2. $50.00

SMITH, H.A. *Son of Rhubarb.* 1967. Trident. 1st ed. sgn. dj. EX. B13. $50.00

SMITH, H.A. *To Hell in a Handbasket.* 1962. Doubleday. 1st ed. inscr. dj. EX. K2. $50.00

SMITH, H.A. *Waikiki Beachnick.* 1960. Little Brn. 1st ed. inscr. dj. EX. B13. $65.00

SMITH, H.A. *We Went Thataway.* 1949. Doubleday. later print. inscr. dj. VG. B13. $45.00

SMITH, H.C. *Sulgrave Manor & WA.* 1933. London. 1st ed. sm 4to. dj. M. T1. $35.00

SMITH, H.J. *Chicago: A Portrait.* 1931. Chicago. EX. A4. $35.00

SMITH, H.L. *Airways: Hist of Commercial Aviation in US.* 1942. NY. 1st ed. fld chart. 30 p. G. T5. $25.00

SMITH, H.M. *Inspector Frost in Crevenna Cove.* 1933. Minton Balch. 1st ed. xl. P1. $10.00

SMITH, H.M. *Inspector Frost in the City.* 1930. Doubleday. 1st ed. VG. P1. $17.50

SMITH, H.W. *John M Whitall: Story of His Life.* 1879. Phil. private print. 12mo. 338 p. V1. $12.00

SMITH, Janet. *Annotated Bibliography of & about Ernesto Cardenal.* 1979. Tempe. 1st ed. p. wrp. F2. $10.00

SMITH, Jeffrey. *New Perspectives on the Art of Renaissance Nuremberg.* 1985. TX U. 102 p. D4. $15.00

SMITH, Joseph. *Book of Mormon.* 1830. Palmyra. 1st ed. lacks 1 leaf preliminaries. VG. H3. $4500.00

SMITH, Joseph. *Descriptive Catalog of Friends' Books.* 1867. London. 1st ed. 2 vols. 1 rebound. VG. V1. $120.00

SMITH, K.N. *Catching Fire.* 1982. Doubleday Book Club. VG. P1. $7.50

SMITH, L.A. *Music of the Waters.* 1888. London. 1st ed. 363 p. VG. $75.00

SMITH, L.N. *Crystal Empire.* 1986. Tor Books. 1st ed. dj. EX. P1. $17.95

SMITH, L.N. *Lando Calrissian & the Flamewind of Oseon.* 1983. Del Rey. 1st HrdCvr ed. dj. EX. F5. $10.00

SMITH, L.P. *Phil Quaker: Hannah Whitall Smith.* 1950. Harcourt Brace. 1st ed. 8vo. 234 p. dj. VG. V1. $9.00

SMITH, L.P. *Songs & Sonnets.* 1909. London. 1st ed. dj. EX. $55.00

SMITH, L.P. *Treasury of Eng Prose.* 1919. London. 1st ed. G. $25.00

SMITH, L.P. *Unforgotten Years.* nd. Little Brn. Probably Book Club ed. 295 p. VG. B10. $3.50

SMITH, L.P. *Unforgotten Years.* 1939. Little Brn. 1st ed. 8vo. 296 p. VG. V1. $6.00

SMITH, Lee. *Cakewalk.* 1981. Putnam. UP. wrp. EX. B13. $125.00

SMITH, M.C. *Gorky Park.* 1981. NY. Special Readers ed. presentation. wrp. EX. T9. $55.00

SMITH, M.C. *Nightwing.* nd. Norton. 3rd ed. dj. VG. P1. $10.00

SMITH, M.C. *Nightwing.* 1977. Norton. 1st ed. dj. EX. $15.00

SMITH, Mark. *Death of the Detective.* 1974. Knopf. 1st ed. dj. EX. T9. $30.00

SMITH, Martin Cruz. *Gorky Park.* 1981. Random House. 1st ed. inscr. printed wrp. EX. T9. $55.00

SMITH, Nicol. *Bush Master: Into the Jungles of Dutch Guiana.* 1941. Bobbs Merrill. 1st ed. 315 p. dj. F2. $20.00

SMITH, Nicol. *Rain Forest Corridors: Transamazon Colonization Scheme.* 1982. CA U. 1st ed. 248 p. dj. F2. $20.00

SMITH, Norman. *Descartes: Philosophical Writings.* nd. (1958) Modern Lib. dj. B10. $4.50

SMITH, Patti. *Ha! Ha! Houdini!* 1977. Gotham Book Mart. 1st ed. 1/26. sgn. wrp. EX. B13. $85.00

SMITH, R.C. *In & Out of Town.* 1970. Boston. Branden Pr. 1st ed. dj. VG. w/sgn letter. B10. $15.00

SMITH, Red. *Views of Sport.* 1954. NY. 1st ed. dj. VG. B3. $15.00

SMITH, Rosamond; see Oates, J.C.

SMITH, Roswell. *Smith's Quarto or 2nd Book of Geog.* 1857. Lippincott. 4to. 25 maps. C1. $125.00

SMITH, S.K. *Susan Spray.* 1931. Harper. 1st ed. 385 p. dj. VG. B10. $4.00

SMITH, Shelley. *Afternoon To Kill.* 1953. Collins Crime Club. 1st ed. dj. xl. P1. $7.50

SMITH, Southwood. *Treatise on Fever.* 1835. Phil. 8vo. 326 p. G. G4. $43.00

SMITH, Stephen. *Handbook of Surgical Operations.* 1983. Baltimore. 273 p. PB. EX. S1. $17.00

SMITH, Stevie. *Me Again: Uncollected Writings of Stevie Smith.* 1981. Farrar Straus. UP. wrp. EX. B13. $45.00

SMITH, Stewart. *Retrievers & How To Break Them for Sport & Field Trials.* nd. London. Field Pr Ltd. 4th ed. 16mo. 62 p. $18.00

SMITH, Thorne. *Biltmore Oswald: Diary of a Hapless Recruit.* 1918. Stokes. 1st ed. dj. EX. R3. $150.00

SMITH, Thorne. *Bishop's Jaegars.* 1933. Doubleday Doran. VG. P1. $12.00

SMITH, Thorne. *Bishop's Jaegers.* nd. Sun Dial. VG. P1. $6.00

SMITH, Thorne. *Did She Fall?* nd. Sun Dial. dj. VG. P1. $10.00

SMITH, Thorne. *Lazy Bear Lane.* 1931. NY. 1st ed. VG. B3. $60.00

SMITH, Thorne. *Night Life of the Gods.* 1939. Sun Dial. Photoplay ed. dj. VG. P1. $35.00

SMITH, Thorne. *Rain in the Doorway.* 1933. Doubleday Doran. 1st ed. VG. P1. $20.00

SMITH, Thorne. *Rain in the Doorway.* 1933. Doubleday. 1st ed. 304 p. G. B10. $3.75

SMITH, Thorne. *Rain in the Doorway.* 1937. Sun Dial. dj. VG. P1. $15.00

SMITH, Thorne. *Stray Lamb.* nd. Sun Dial. dj. VG. P1. $7.50

SMITH, Thorne. *Stray Lamb.* 1940. Triangle. dj. VG. P1. $12.00

SMITH, Thorne. *Topper Takes a Trip.* nd. Sun Dial. dj. VG. P1. $8.00

SMITH, Thorne. *Topper.* 1942. Sun Dial. dj. VG. P1. $25.00

SMITH, Thorne. *Turnabout.* 1931. Doubleday Doran. 1st ed. VG. P1. $17.50

SMITH, Uriah. *US in Light of Prophecy; or, Exposition of Revelation 8...* 1876. Battle Creek. 3rd ed. 200 p. fair. T5. $19.50

SMITH, W.B. *Clr Line: Brief in Behalf of the Unborn.* 1905. NY. 1st ed. 261 p. VG. $45.00

SMITH, W.E. *Master of the Photographic Essay.* 1981. Aperature. 4to. dj. EX. $30.00

SMITH, W.E. *Minamata: Life – Sacred & Profane.* c 1973. portfolio of 12 photos. sgn. EX. K2. $375.00

SMITH, W.P. *My Indian Friends. Mis Amigos Indigenas.* 1960. Mexico. 1st ed. 123 p. F2. $15.00

SMITH, Watson. *Kiva Mural Decor at Awatovi & Kawaika-a.* 1952. Cambridge, MA. wrp. $75.00

SMITH, Wilbur. *Shout at the Devil.* 1968. Coward McCann. 1st ed. dj. EX. F5. $25.00

SMITH & FINLAY. *Klarkash-Ton & Monstro Ligriv.* 1974. De La Ree. 1st ed. wrp. EX. R3. $30.00

SMITH COLLEGE. *25th-Reunion Book Smith College Class of 1919.* 1944. Ils. sbdg. A5. $25.00

SMITH. *Anatomical Atlas, Ils of the Structure of the Human Body.* 1847. Phil. not 1st ed. 4to. 200 p. G. $165.00

SMITH. *Hist of IN.* 1897. Indianapolis. Blair. 1st ed. 2 vols. xl. VG. A5. $75.00

SMITHSONIAN. *Art of John Held Jr.* c 1970s. 28 p. D4. $10.00

SMITHSONIAN. *Smithsonian Book of Invention.* 1978. Norton, NY. 3rd ed. 4to. dj. B10. $7.00

SMOLLETT, Tobias. *Adventures of Peregrine Pickle.* 1929. NY. Ltd ed. 1/950. TEG. M. T1. $50.00

SMOLLETT, Tobias. *Expedition of Humphry Clinker.* 1771. London. 1st ed. 12mo. 3 vols. contemporary calf. H3. $1100.00

SMOLLETT, Tobias. *Novels.* 1926. Houghton Mifflin/Blackwell. 1/500. 11 vols. H3. $1000.00

SMOLLETT, Tobias. *Works.* 1797. London. Law Johnson. 8 vols. VG. H3. $600.00

SMOLLETT, Tobias. *Works.* 1905. Jenson Soc. 1/1000. 12 vols. TEG. H3. $125.00

SMYTH, H.D. *Atomic Energy for Military Purposes.* 1947. Princeton. 7th ed. dj. VG. P1. $10.00

SMYTHE, RUTLEDGE, & HAYWARD. *Carolina Low Country.* 1931. NY. 1st ed. 327 p. VG. B3. $45.00

SNAITH, J.C. *Araminta.* 1923. McLeod. 1st ed. VG. P1. $8.00

SNAITH, J.C. *Council of 7.* nd. Collins. VG. P1. $8.00

SNAITH, S. *Grips With Everest.* 1938. NY. 1st ed. 258 p. dj. VG. B3. $35.00

SNEDEKER, C.D. *Uncharted Ways.* 1936. Doubleday Doran. 12mo. 340 p. VG. V1. $6.00

SNELL, Edmund. *Wht Owl.* 1930. Lippincott. 1st ed. dj. EX. R3. $50.00

SNELL, R.J. *Jane Withers & the Phantom Violin.* nd. Whitman. dj. VG. P1. $10.00

SNELL, R.J. *Whispering Isles.* 1927. Reilly Lee. VG. P1. $10.00

SNODGRASS, Melinda. *Very Lg Array: NM SF.* 1987. NM U. 1st ed. RS. M. R3. $16.95

SNODGRASS, W.D. *Heart's Needle.* 1983. NY. ARC. sgn. wrp. w/pub slip. EX. T9. $45.00

SNOW, C.H. *Lakeside Murder.* nd. Wright Brn. VG. P1. $15.00

SNOW, Dorothea. *Secret of the Summer.* 1958. Whitman. VG. P1. $6.00

SNOW, E.R. *Amazing Sea Stories Never Told Before.* 1955. Dodd. 2nd ed. VG. B10. $4.25

SNOW, E.R. *Boston Bay Mysteries & Other Tales.* 1977. NY. 1st ed. dj. EX. $20.00

SNOW, E.R. *Ghosts, Gales, & Gold.* 1972. NY. 1st ed. dj. EX. $20.00

SNOW, E.R. *Great Atlantic Adventures.* 1970. NY. 1st ed. dj. EX. $20.00

SNOW, E.R. *Marine Mysteries & Dramatic Disasters of New Eng.* 1976. NY. 1st ed. dj. EX. $20.00

SNOW, E.R. *Pilgrim Returns to Cape Cod.* 1946. Boston. 1st ed. dj. EX. $25.00

SNOW, E.R. *Supernatural Mysteries & Other Tales.* 1974. NY. 1st ed. dj. EX. $20.00

SNOW, Edgar. *People on Our Side.* nd. (1944) Random House. Book Club ed? 324 p. VG. B10. $3.50

SNOW, Glenna. *Glenna Snow's Cookbook.* 1938. Akron. 1st ed. inscr. 396 p. fair. T5. $30.00

SNOW, Glenna. *Glenna Snow's Cookbook.* 1947. Akron. 3rd ed. 396 p. T5. $17.50

SNOW, Jack. *Dark Music & Other Spectral Tales.* 1947. Herald. 1st ed. dj. VG. P1. $45.00

SNYDER, C.M. *Flaw in the Sapphire.* nd. McLeod Allen. decor brd. VG. P1. $9.00

SNYDER, C.M. *Flaw in the Sapphire.* 1909. Metropolitan. 1st ed. pictorial bdg. F5. $25.00

SNYDER, Gary. *Myths & Texts.* 1960. Totem Pr/Corinth Books. 1st ed. sgn. wrp. EX. C4. $125.00

SNYDER, H. *Book of Big Game Hunting.* 1950. NY. 1st ed. dj. EX. B3. $35.00

SNYDER & VALENTINO. *In th' Olde Dayes of the Kyng Arthur.* 1987. Scott Pr. 1st ed. stiff wrp. NM. C1. $11.00

SOARES, John. *Loaded Dice, True Story of a Casino Cheat.* 1985. Taylor. 1st ed. 217 p. dj. M. J3. $10.00

SOBY, J.T. *Rene Magritte.* 1965. MOMA. dj. D4. $30.00

SOHL, Jerry. *Altered Ego.* nd. Book Club. dj. VG. P1. $3.00

SOHL, Jerry. *Altered Ego.* 1954. Rinehart. 1st ed. VG. P1. $12.50

SOHL, Jerry. *Costigan's Needle.* nd. Book Club. VG. P1. $3.00

SOHL, Jerry. *Prelude to Peril.* 1957. Rinehart. 1st ed. dj. VG. P1. $30.00

SOHL, Jerry. *Resurrection of Frank Borchard.* 1973. Simon Schuster. 1st ed. dj. EX. P1. $10.00

SOHL, Jerry. *Spun Sugar Hole.* 1971. Simon Schuster. 1st ed. dj. VG. P1. $10.00

SOLEY, J.R. *Blockade & the Cruisers.* nd. NY. Brussel. 257 p. PB. S1. $6.00

SOLEY, J.R. *Blockade & the Cruisers.* 1883. NY. 1st ed. 12mo. 257 p. G. G4. $26.00

SOLEY, J.R. *Blockade & the Cruisers.* 1883. Scribner. Civil War Series 1. 257 p. VG. T5. $39.50

SOLOMON, Brad. *Gone Man.* 1977. Random House. 1st ed. dj. EX. F5. $13.00

SOLOMON, Brad. *Open Shadow.* 1978. Summit. 1st ed. dj. EX. P1. $15.00

SOLOMON, C. *Slam Bidding & Point Count.* 1951. Macrae. 1st ed? 281 p. VG. B10. $7.50

SOLTERA, Maria. *Lady's Ride Across Spanish Honduras.* 1964. FL U. facsimile of 1884 ed. 319 p. F2. $20.00

SOMERS, Jane; see Lessing, Doris.

SOMMERS, Jim. *Build Your Own Illusions.* 1974. Chiago. Magic Inc. 1st ed. 88 p. NM. 3. $8.00

SONDERN, Frederic. *Brotherhood of Evil: The Mafia.* 1959. Farrar Straus Cudahy. dj. VG. P1. $7.50

SONDHEIM & LAPINE. *Sunday in the Park With George.* 1986. Dodd Mead. 1/250. sgns. slipcase. EX. B13. $250.00

SONDLEY, F.A. *Indian's Curse: Legend of the Cherokees.* nd. Asheville? 1st ed. orig wrp. $30.00

SONNECK, O.G.T. *Bibliography of Early Secular Am Music (18th Century).* 1964. Da Capo. reprint of 1945 ed. 617 p. dj. EX. H3. $45.00

SONNICHSEN, C.L. *Cowboys & Cattle Kings.* 1950. OK U. 1st ed. dj. VG. C2. $35.00

SONREL, Pierre. *Traite de Scenographie.* 1943. Paris. Odette Lieutier. octavo. 301 p. H3. $75.00

SONTAG, R.J. *Germany & Eng: Background of Conflict 1848-1894.* 1938. NY. 1st ed. 25.00

SONTAG, Susan. *Benefactor.* 1963. NY. 1st d. sgn. dj. EX. T9. $50.00

SONTAG, Susan. *Susan Sontag Reader.* 1982. Farrar Straus. Ltd ed. 1/350. sgn. slipcase. EX. K2. $65.00

SONTAG, Susan. *Under the Sgn of Saturn.* 1980. Farrar Straus. UP. wrp. VG. B13. 55.00

SORENSEN, Lorin. *Classy Ford V8.* 1982. Helena, CA. Ils 1st ed. EX. T5. $45.00

SORENSON, Alfred. *Hist of Omaha From Pioneer Days to Present Time.* 1889. Omaha. nd ed. EX. $85.00

SORRELL, Walter. *Dance Has Many Faces.* 1951. Cleveland. World. 1st ed. octavo. 88 p. dj. H3. $50.00

SORRENTINO, Gilbert. *Blk & Wht.* 1964. otem Pr. VG. B4. $6.00

SORRENTINO, Gilbert. *Something Said.* 984. Berkley. UP. EX. scarce. K2. $50.00

SOTHERN, E.H. *Julia Marlowe's Story.* 954. Rinehart. 1st ed. 237 p. dj. VG. B10. 0.00

SOUSA, J.P. *Marching Along.* 1928. Boston. t ed. sgn Sousa's granddaughter. dj. VG. 3. $70.00

SOUSA, J.P. *5th String.* 1902. Bowen errill. Ils Christy. gilt gr bdg. VG. $15.00

SOUSA, J.P. *5th String.* 1903. Ward Lock. presentation. gilt burgundy bdg. VG. H3. $300.00

SOUSTELLE, Jacques. *Daily Life of the Aztecs.* 1961. London. 1st ed. 319 p. F2. $15.00

SOUSTELLE, Jacques. *Mexico.* 1967. World. 1st ed. 285 p. dj. F2. $10.00

SOUSTELLE, Jacques. *4 Sins.* 1971. NY. Grossman. 1st ed. 256 p. dj. F2. $15.00

SOUTHALL, Eliza. *Brief Memoir With Portions of Diary, Letters...* 1869. Assn Diffusion of Knowledge. 16mo. VG. V1. $10.00

SOUTHARD, S.L. *Argument in Case of Decow & Hendrickson Versus Shotwell.* 1834. Phil. Weaver. 8vo. 279 p. V1. $40.00

SOUTHWORTH, Mrs. *Hidden Hand.* nd. (1930s) Grosset. 487 p. VG. B10. $3.50

SOUTHWORTH & WILKE. *Certain Young Man of Assisi.* 1934. John Henry Nash. 4to. sgns. EX. P4. $145.00

SOUZA, Raymond. *Major Cuban Novelists.* 1976. MO U. 1st ed. dj. F2. $15.00

SOYER, Nicholas. *Soyer's Paper Bag Cookery.* 1911. Strugis Walton. 2nd ed. 8vo. 130 p. VG. B10. $6.25

SOYER, Raphael. *Self-Revealment: A Memoir.* 1969. NY. 1st ed. 4to. dj. EX. G1. $22.00

SOYINKA, Wole. *Interpreters.* 1965. London. Deutsch. sgn. dj. H3. $75.00

SPAETH, Sigmund. *Facts of Life in Popular Song.* 1934. Whittesey House. 1st ed. octavo. 148 p. VG. H3. $45.00

SPALDING, H. *Encyclopedia of Blk Humor & Folklore.* 1972. Middle Village, NY. 1st ed. 489 p. dj. VG. B3. $22.50

SPARK, Muriel. *Bang-Bang Your'e Dead.* 1982. London. PB Orig. presentation. wrp. EX. T9. $40.00

SPARK, Muriel. *Comforters.* 1957. Lippincott. 1st Am ed. dj. VG. B13. $100.00

SPARK, Muriel. *Loitering With Intent.* 1981. Coward. UP. wrp. EX. B13. $65.00

SPARKES-MOORE. *Hetty Gr: Woman Who Loved Money.* 1930. Doubleday. 1st ed. EX. B3. $45.00

SPARKS, Jared. *Life of George WA.* 1844. Boston. Tappan Dennet. Ils. G. $40.00

SPARKS, Jared. *Life of George WA.* 1854. np. 12mo. 344 p. xl. G4. $18.00

SPARLING, H.H. *Kelmscott Pr & William Morris, Master Craftsmen.* 1924. Macmillan. 1st ed. rebound. EX. $95.00

SPARROW, W.S. *British Sporting Artists.* 1922. London/NY. 4to. EX. $85.00

SPEAKMAN, T.H. *Divisions in the Soc of Friends.* 1869. Lippincott. 1st ed. 12mo. SftCvr. G. V1. $15.00

SPEAKMAN, T.H. *Divisions in the Soc of Friends.* 1896. Lippincott. Enlarged 3rd ed. 12mo. 127 p. G. V1. $14.00

SPEARMAN, F.H. *Whispering Smith.* nd. Hodder Stoughton. VG. P1. $7.50

SPEED, James. *Opinion on Constitutional Power of the Military...* 1865. WA. 1st ed. 8vo. 16 p. missing wrp. VG. rare. T1. $150.00

SPEER, Albert. *Inside the 3rd Reich.* 1970. NY. BOMC. dj. VG. $10.00

SPENCE, Lewis. *Encyclopedia of Occultism.* 1960. NY. U Books. 1st Am ed. slipcase. VG. C1. $19.50

SPENCE, Lewis. *Legends & Romances of Brittany.* c 1920. Stokes. B10. $6.25

SPENCE, Lewis. *Legends & Romances of Brittany.* nd. NY. 423 p. VG. C1. $19.50

SPENCER, Elizabeth. *Snare.* 1972. McGraw Hill. 1st ed. dj. EX. B13. $50.00

SPENCER, Elizabeth. *This Crooked Way.* 1952. NY. 1st ed. sgn. dj. K2. $45.00

SPENCER, I. *Walter Crane.* 1975. Macmillan. 1st Am ed. 4to. 208 p. EX. R4. $45.00

SPENCER, J.A. *Hist of US From Earliest Period to Administration Buchanan.* 1858. NY. 1st ed. 3 vols. 4to. VG. T1. $60.00

SPENDER, Stephen. *Generous Days.* 1971. Random House. 1st Am ed. sgn. gray bdg. dj. H3. $75.00

SPENDER, Stephen. *Letters to Christopher.* 1980. Blk Sparrow. 1/50. sgn. 219 p. slipcase. T5. $75.00

SPENDER, Stephen. *Making of a Poem.* 1955. Hamish Hamilton. sgn. dj. H3. $75.00

SPENDER, Stephen. *Poems of Dedication.* 1947. NY. 1st ed. 60 p. T5. $15.00

SPENSER, Edmund. *Faerie Queen Book 1.* 1958. Cambridge. 8th ed. VG. P1. $5.00

SPENSER, Edmund. *Faerie Queene.* 1953. Heritage. 1st ed. slipcase. EX. C1. $15.00

SPERLICH & SPERLICH. *Guatemala Backstrap Weaving.* 1980. OK U. 1st ed. 176 p. dj. F2. $35.00

SPEWACK, Samuel. *Skyscraper Murder*. 1928. Macaulay. 2nd ed. VG. P1. $15.00

SPICER, Bart. *Burned Man*. 1966. Atheneum. 1st ed. xl. VG. P1. $5.00

SPICER, Bart. *Long Gr*. nd. Book Club. dj. VG. P1. $4.00

SPICER, Bart. *Taming of Carney Wilde*. nd. Book Club. dj. VG. P1. $5.00

SPICER, Jack. *Book of Magazine Verse*. c1966. Wht Rabbit. 2nd print. B4. $8.00

SPICER & DUNCAN. *Ode & Arcadia*. 1974. Ark Pr. 1/1000. EX. B4. $20.00

SPIDEN, Herbert. *Maya Art & Civilization*. 1957. Indian Hills, CO. Revised Enlarged ed. 432 p. F2. $45.00

SPIEGELMAN, Art. *Maus: A Survivor's Tale*. 1986. NY. 1st ed. wrp. w/sgn drawing. T9. $200.00

SPIELMANN, M.H. *Hist of Punch*. 1895. London. Cassell. 1st ed. 4to. TEG. EX. $50.00

SPILLANE, Mickey. *By-Pass Control*. 1966. Dutton. 1st ed. xl. P1. $10.00

SPILLANE, Mickey. *Deep*. 1961. Dutton. 1st ed. VG. P1. $15.00

SPILLANE, Mickey. *Flier*. 1964. Corgi Book. PB Orig. wrp. VG. w/sgn bookplate. T9. $50.00

SPILLANE, Mickey. *Girl Hunters*. 1962. Dutton. 1st ed. dj. VG. P1. $30.00

SPILLANE, Mickey. *I the Jury*. 1947. NY. 1st ed. EX. G1. $90.00

SPILLANE, Mickey. *I the Jury*. 1949. Paris. 1st French ed. wrp. VG. T9. $75.00

SPILLANE, Mickey. *Last Cop Out*. 1973. Dutton. 1st ed. dj. VG. P1. $20.00

SPILLANE, Mickey. *Last Cop Out*. 1973. Dutton. 1st ed. dj. xl. P1. $7.50

SPILLANE, Mickey. *Long Wait*. 1951. Dutton. 1st ed. dj. EX. F5. $55.00

SPILLANE, Mickey. *Twisted Thing*. 1966. Dutton. 1st ed. dj. xl. P1. $10.00

SPILLER, B.L. *Drummer in the Woods*. 1962. Princeton. 1st ed. dj. VG. B3. $60.00

SPILLER, B.L. *Grouse Feathers*. 1972. NY. Ltd ed. sgn. dj. VG. B3. $45.00

SPILLER, B.L. *More Grouse Feathers*. 1972. NY. Ltd ed. sgn. dj. VG. B3. $45.00

SPILLMAN, Louis. *So This Is S Am*. 1962. Waynesboro Pub. 1st ed. inscr. 140 p. dj. F2. $15.00

SPILSBURY, A. *Tourmaline Expedition*. 1906. London. Dent. Ils. fld map. rebound. VG. $22.00

SPINDEN, H.J. *Ancient Civilization of Mexico & Central Am*. 1928. NY. Revised 3rd ed. 270 p. F2. $25.00

SPINDEN, H.J. *Maya Art & Civilization*. 1957. Falcon Wing Pr. Revised Enlarged ed. 432 p. dj. F2. $50.00

SPINRAD, Norman. *Bug Jack Barron*. 1969. Walker. 1st ed. dj. xl. G. R3. $50.00

SPINRAD, Norman. *Child of Fortune*. 1985. Bantam. AP. 1st ed. wrp. EX. R3. $20.00

SPINRAD, Norman. *Last Hurrah of the Golden Horde*. nd. Book Club. dj. VG. P1. $5.00

SPINRAD, Norman. *Little Heroes*. 1987. Bantam. 1st ed. dj. EX. P1. $18.95

SPINRAD, Norman. *Men in the Jungle*. 1967. Doubleday. 1st ed. dj. VG. P1. $50.00

SPINRAD, Norman. *Songs From the Stars*. 1980. Simon Schuster. 1st ed. dj. EX. P1. $15.00

SPLINT, Sarah. *Art of Cooking & Serving*. nd. (1930) Procter Gamble. 252 p. VG. B10. $4.25

SPONSEL, Heinz. *Timeless Trail*. 1971. McKay. 1st ed. 150 p. dj. F2. $10.00

SPOONER, Bill. *Choice or Chance? Magical Spoonerism No 1*. 1977. Raleigh, NC. 1st ed. SftCvr. w/cards & dice. NM. J3. $5.00

SPOONER, W. *Back Woodsmen; or, Tales of the Borders*. 1883. Dibble. VG. $50.00

SPRAGUE, Marshall. *Great Gates: Story of Rocky Mt Passes*. 1964. Boston. 1st ed. 468 p. VG. T5. $17.50

SPRECHMAN, J.R. *Caribe*. 1986. Dutton. 1st ed. dj. EX. F5. $10.00

SPREIRGEN, P.D. *Urban Design & Architecture of Towns & Cities*. 1969. NY. 1st ed. 243 p. dj. VG. B3. $35.00

SPRING, A.W. *Caspar Collins: Life & Exploits of Indian Fighter of 1860s*. 1927. NY. 197 p. A5. $50.00

SPRING, A.W. *Cheyenne & Blk Hills Sage & Express Routes*. 1949. Glendale. Clark. Ils. 418 p. A5. $80.00

SPRINGER, Anton. *Raffael Und Michelangelo*. 1895. Leipzig. 2 vols. EX. T1. $100.00

SPRINGER, J.S. *Forest Life & Forest Trees*. 1851. NY. gilt bdg. EX. $150.00

SPRINGER, Nancy. *Wht Hart*. nd. Book Club. dj. VG. P1. $4.50

SPRINGS, E.W. *War Birds: Diary of an Unknown Aviator*. 1926. NY. Ils Clayton Knight. 277 p. G. T5. $32.50

SPROAT, Iain. *Wodehouse at War*. 1981. Ticknor Fields. 1st ed. dj. EX. P1. $20.00

SPRUILL, Steven. *Keepers of the Gate*. 1977. Doubleday. 1st ed. dj. EX. R3. $10.00

SPRUILL, Steven. *Paradox Planet*. 1988. Doubleday. 1st ed. dj. EX. R3. $10.00

SPURGEON, C.H. *Speakers' Complete Program for Schools...Entertainment*. c1892-1893. Ziegler. 1st ed? 496 p. G. B10. $7.50

SPYRI, Johanna. *Mazli*. 1923. Lippincott. Ils Kirk. Gift ed. 4to. 320 p. TEG. EX. $40.00

SQUAREY, C. *Popular Treatise on Agricultural Chemistry*. 1842. London. 1st ed. NM. $60.00

SQUIER, E.G. *Waikna; or, Adventures on the Mosquito Shore*. 1965. FL U. reprint of 1855. F2. $20.00

SQUIER, E.L. *Gringa: Am Woman in Mexico*. 1934. Houghton Mifflin. 1st ed. 282 p. F2. $15.00

SQUIRE, E.S. *Tricks & Magic Made Easy*. 1919. NY. Clode. 1st ed. 188 p. dj. NM. J3. $13.00

SQUIRES, W.H.T. *Unleashed at Long Last Reconstruction in VA*. 1939. Portsmouth, VA. 1st ed. sgn. VG. $40.00

ST. JOHN, Nicole. *Guinevere's Gift*. nd. Book Club. dj. EX. C1. $3.00

ST. JOHN, Philip. *Rocket Jockey*. 1957. Winston. dj. VG. R3. $20.00

ST. LOUIS & LUBIN. *Panorama de la Poesie Haitienne*. 1950. Haiti. Deschamps. 1st ed. 8vo. 635 p. VG. R4. $125.00

ST. PAUL, John. *Hist of Soc of Sons of Am Revolution*. 1962. Pelican. apparent 1st ed. 256 p. dj. VG. B10. $12.00

STABLEFORD, B.M. *Journey to the Center*. 1982. Doubleday. 1st HrdCvr ed. dj. EX. F5. $10.00

STABLEFORD, B.M. *Man in a Cage*. 1975. John Day. 1st ed. dj. VG. P1. $20.00

STABLEFORD, B.M. *Mysteries of Modern Science*. 1980. Littlefield. VG. P1. $7.50

STABLEFORD, B.M. *Paradise Game*. 1976. Dent. 1st ed. sgn. dj. EX. P1. $25.00

STABLEFORD, B.M. *Promised Land*. 1975. Dent. 1st ed. sgn. dj. EX. P1. $25.00

STABLER, William. *Memoir of Life of Edward Stabler With Collection of Letters.* 1846. Phil. John Richards. 12mo. 312 p. full leather. V1. $14.00

STACEY, C.P. *Victory Campaign: Operations in NW Europe 1944-1945, Vol 3.* 1960. Ottawa. Ils. 770 p. T5. $45.00

STACKPOLE, E.J. *They Met at Gettysburg.* 1956. Bonanza. 342 p. dj. VG. S1. $10.00

STACKPOLE, H.D.V. *Garden of God.* nd. Jacobsen. dj. EX. R3. $25.00

STACKPOLE. *Scrimshaw at Mystic Seaport.* 1966. Mystic. 2nd print. dj. VG. C2. $30.00

STACTON, David; see Clifton, Bud.

STACY-JUDD, R.B. *Ancient Mayas.* 1934. Haskell Travers. 1st ed. 277 p. F2. $45.00

STACY-JUDD, R.B. *Atlantis: Mother of Empires.* 1939. Los Angeles. 1/1500. folio. 6. $65.00

STAFFORD, Jean. *Boston Adventure.* c 1944. Harcourt Brace. 1st ed. VG. $15.00

STAGG, Albert. *Almadas & Alamos 1783-1867.* 1978. AZ U. 1st ed. 173 p. dj. F2. 20.00

STAGGE, Jonathan. *Death My Darling Daughters.* 1945. Crime Club. VG. P1. $20.00

STAHL, David. *Don't Stall, Stahl!* 1978. Eagle Magic. 1st ed. 29 p. SftCvr. NM. J3. 7.00

STAMM, Russell. *Invisible Scarlet O'Neil.* 1943. Whitman. VG. P1. $5.00

STAMP, C. *Dudley Stamp Lost in Rocky Mts.* 1913. Chicago. 151 p. VG. B3. $45.00

STANARD, M.N. *Story of VA's 1st Century.* 1928. Phil. 1st ed. A6. $30.00

STANDISH, M.E. *My Little Son & Other Poems.* nd. np. 39 p. VG. B10. $4.50

STANG, Ragna. *Art of Gustav Vigeland.* 1948. Oslo. dj. VG. B10. $5.50

STANGE, Alfred. *German Painting 14th-5th Centuries.* 1950. London. 1st ed. folio. EX. G1. $35.00

STANILAND, Medburn. *Back to the Future.* 1947. London. 1st ed. dj. EX. R3. $25.00

STANISLAVSKY, Konstantin. *Stanislavsky Art of the Stage.* 1950. London. Faber. 1st ed. 311 p. VG. H3. $50.00

STANISLAVSKY, Konstantin. *Stanislavsky Produces Othello.* 1948. London. Bles. Trans Nowak. 1st ed. 244 p. dj. EX. H3. $75.00

STANLEY, A.P. *Sinai & Palestine.* 1877. Scribner. 590 p. G. $45.00

STANLEY, H.M. *In Darkest Africa.* 1890. NY. 1st Am ed. 2 vols. G. T5. $75.00

STANLEY, H.M. *In Darkest Africa.* 1890. Scribner. 1st Am ed. 2 vols. pocket maps. VG. K1. $100.00

STANLEY, H.M. *Through the Dark Continent.* 1879. NY. 2 vols. VG. B3. $85.00

STANSBERRY, Domenic. *Spoiler.* 1987. Atlantic Monthly. 1st ed. dj. EX. F5. $12.00

STANTON, Frank. *Up From GA.* 1902. NY. 1st ed. VG. B3. $25.00

STANWOOD, Brooks. *7th Child.* 1981. Linden Pr. dj. EX. P1. $10.00

STANWOOD, D.A. *Memory of Eva Ryker.* nd. BOMC. dj. VG. P1. $4.50

STANYON, Ellis. *Conjuring for Amateurs.* 1905. London. Upcott Gill. 1st ed. 98 p. J3. $20.00

STANYON, Ellis. *Magic.* 1906. London. Gay Bird. 244 p. VG. J3. $16.00

STANYON, Ellis. *Magic.* 1910. Phil. Penn. 244 p. VG. J3. $21.00

STAPLEDON, Olaf. *Far Future Calling.* 1979. Oswald Train. 1st ed. dj. EX. P1. $15.00

STAPLEDON, Olaf. *Flames.* 1947. London. 1st ed. dj. EX. R3. $60.00

STAPLEDON, Olaf. *Last & 1st Men.* 1931. NY. Cape/Smith. 1st Am ed. dj. EX. K2. $175.00

STAPLEDON, Olaf. *Last & 1st Men.* 1934. London. dj. EX. R3. $17.50

STAPLEDON, Olaf. *Odd John.* 1936. Dutton. 1st Am ed. dj. EX. K2. $175.00

STAPLEDON, Olaf. *Star Maker.* 1937. London. 1st ed. VG. R3. $32.50

STAPP, William. *Prisoners of Perote.* 1977. TX U. reprint of 1845 ed. F2. $25.00

STARBEL, Thelma. *Caribee.* 1957. Harper. Book Club ed. 312 p. dj. EX. B10. $3.75

STARCHEY, Lytton. *Portraits in Miniature & Other Essays.* 1931. Chatto Windus. Ltd ed. 1/260. sgn. TEG. EX. H3. $200.00

STARK, J.H. *Stark's Ils Bermuda Guide.* 1902. Boston/London/Bermuda. 1st ed. EX. $45.00

STARK, Richard; see Westlake, D.E.

STARKEY, Lycurgus. *James Bond: World of Values.* 1966. Abingdon. PB. stiff wrp. VG. B10. $3.75

STARNES, Richard. *Another Mug for the Bier.* 1950. Lippincott. 1st ed. VG. P1. $8.00

STARR, Ida. *Gardens of the Caribbees.* 1904. Page. 2 vols. F2. $45.00

STARR, Kara. *Merlin's Journal of Time: Camelot Adventure.* 1989. Solana Beach, CA. sgn. PB. M. C1. $11.50

STARR, L.M. *Bohemian Brigade, Civil War Newsman in Action.* 1954. NY. Ils 1st ed. 367 p. G. T5. $15.00

STARR, S.Z. *Col Grenfell's Wars: Life of a Soldier of Fortune.* 1971. Baton Rouge. sgn. EX. $25.00

STARRETT, Vincent. *Ebony Flame.* 1922. Chicago. Ltd 1st ed. 1/350. $75.00

STARRETT, Vincent. *Ebony Flame.* 1922. Covici McGee. Ltd ed. 1/350. sgn. H3. $125.00

STARRETT, Vincent. *Jimmy Lavender.* 1973. Bookfinger. VG. P1. $12.00

STARRETT, Vincent. *Last Bookman.* 1968. Candlelight. Ltd ed. 1/2500. 4to. 115 p. dj. VG. V1. $30.00

STARRETT, Vincent. *Murder in Peking.* nd. Collier. VG. P1. $15.00

STARRETT, Vincent. *Murder on B Deck.* 1929. Crime Club. 1st ed. VG. P1. $20.00

STARRETT, Vincent. *Seaports in the Moon.* 1928. Garden City. 1st ed. VG. C1. $24.50

STARRETT, Vincent. *221B: Studies in Sherlock Holmes.* 1940. NY. 1st ed. dj. VG. T1. $90.00

STASHEFF, Christopher. *Warlock Enlarged.* 1985. Doubleday. 1st HrdCvr ed. dj. EX. F5. $12.00

STASHEFF, Christopher. *Warlock in Spite of Himself.* 1975. Garland. 1st HrdCvr ed. EX. R3. $25.00

STATTEN, Vargo. *Cataclysm.* nd. London. Scion. 1st ed. wrp. VG. R3. $10.00

STATTEN, Vargo. *Catalyst.* 1951. London. 1st ed. wrp. VG. R3. $10.00

STATTEN, Vargo. *Devouring Fire.* 1951. London. 1st ed. wrp. EX. R3. $10.00

STATTEN, Vargo. *New Satellite.* 1951. London. Scion. 1st ed. wrp. VG. R3. $10.00

STATTEN, Vargo. *Time Trap.* 1952. London. 1st ed. wrp. G. R3. $10.00

STATTEN, Vargo. *2,000 Years On.* nd. London. Scion. 1st ed. wrp. VG. R3. $10.00

STAUTON, Schuyler. *Daughters of Destiny.* 1906. Reilly Britton. 1st ed. EX. F5. $18.00

STEAD, Christina. *Salzburg Tales.* 1934. NY. 1st ed. dj. EX. B2. $150.00

STEALEY, O.O. *130 Pen Pictures of Live Men.* 1910. WA. 1st ed. 473 p. TEG. VG. B10. $8.25

STED, Richard. *They All Bleed Red.* 1954. Simon Schuster. 1st ed. dj. VG. P1. $8.00

STEDMAN, E.C. *Poetical Works.* 1888. Boston. Household ed. inscr. G. $35.00

STEEGMULLER, Francis. *Selected Letters of Flaubert.* 1953. Farrar. 1st ed. 281 p. dj. EX. B10. $5.50

STEEL, F.A. *Law of the Threshold.* 1924. Macmillan. 1st Am ed. dj. EX. R3. $22.50

STEEL, Kurt. *Ambush House.* 1943. Harcourt Brace. 1st ed. VG. P1. $15.00

STEEL, Kurt. *Crooked Shadow.* 1939. Little Brn. 1st ed. 311 p. VG. B10. $10.00

STEEL, Kurt. *Imposter.* 1945. Tower. VG. P1. $10.00

STEEL, Max. *Where She Brushed Her Hair & Other Stories.* 1968. Harper. 1st ed. sgn. dj. EX. F5. $16.00

STEELE, Curtis. *Blood Reign of the Dictator.* 1966. Corinth. 1st ed. wrp. EX. F5. $15.00

STEELE, Curtis. *Invasion of the Yel Warlords.* 1966. Corinth. 1st ed. wrp. EX. F5. $18.00

STEELE, M.F. *Am Campaigns.* 1943. WA. 2 vols. G. T5. $65.00

STEELE, W.F. *Last Word on Cards.* 1952. Chicago. Steele. 1st ed. 63 p. SftCvr. VG. J3. $6.00

STEELE, W.F. *50 Tricks You Can Do, You Will Do, Easy To Do.* nd. NY. Tannen. 64 p. SftCvr. EX. J3. $4.00

STEELE, W.F. *52 Amazing Card Tricks.* 1949. Chicago. Steele. 1st ed. 64 p. EX. J3. $5.00

STEELE, W.F. *52 Amazing Card Tricks.* 1972. Phil. Lee Gray. 64 p. SftCvr. NM. J3. $2.00

STEELE. *City That Is.* 1909. San Francisco. Ils. 101 p. A5. $50.00

STEELE. *New Guide to the Pacific Coast, Santa Fe Route.* 1890. Rand McNally. Ils. 211 p. A5. $50.00

STEEMAN, Andre. *6 Dead Men.* 1932. Farrar Rinehart. 1st ed. VG. P1. $17.50

STEFANSSON, Vilhjalmur. *Unsolved Mysteries of the Arctic.* 1938. Macmillan. Ils/sgn Kent. 1/200. sgn. boxed. H3. $350.00

STEFFENS, Lincoln. *Autobiography of Lincoln Steffens.* 1931. London. 1st ed. 2 vols. EX. $30.00

STEGNER, Wallace. *All the Little Live Things.* 1967. Viking. 1st ed. sgn. dj. EX. B13. $100.00

STEGNER, Wallace. *Angel of Repose.* 1971. Doubleday Doran. 1st Trade ed. EX. K2. $50.00

STEGNER, Wallace. *Central NW.* 1947. Houghton Mifflin. Look at Am Series. sgn. dj. VG. K2. $100.00

STEGNER, Wallace. *City of the Living.* 1955. Houghton Mifflin. 1st ed. inscr. dj. EX. B13. $125.00

STEGNER, Wallace. *Crossing to Safety.* 1987. Random House. UP. wrp. EX. K2. $45.00

STEGNER, Wallace. *Gathering of Zion.* 1964. McGraw Hill. galley sheets. very scarce. K2. $475.00

STEGNER, Wallace. *Mormon Country.* 1942. NY. 362 p. dj. VG. T5. $37.50

STEGNER, Wallace. *On the Teaching of Creative Writing.* 1988. Hanover, NH. sgn. K2. $85.00

STEGNER, Wallace. *On the Writing of Hist.* 1989. np. 1st ed. 1/100. sgn. lg wrp. EX. B13. $175.00

STEGNER, Wallace. *Preacher & the Slave.* 1950. Houghton Mifflin. 1st ed. dj. EX. B13. $135.00

STEGNER, Wallace. *Spectator Bird.* 1976. Franklin Lib. 1st ed. EX. K2. $65.00

STEGNER, Wallace. *Wolf Willow.* 1962. Viking. 1st ed. dj. EX. B13. $50.00

STEGNER, Wallace. *Women on the Wall.* 1948. Boston. 1st ed. dj. VG. B3. $45.00

STEGNER, Wallace. *Women on the Wall.* 1950. Houghton Mifflin. 1st ed. dj. EX. B13. $265.00

STEGNER, Wallace. *1 Way To Spell Man: Essays With a W Bias.* 1982. Doubleday. 1st ed. dj. EX. C4. $40.00

STEICHEN, Edward. *Life in Photography.* 1963. NY. Ils 1st ed. 4to. dj. EX. $55.00

STEIN, A.M. *Alp Murder.* 1970. Crime Club. 1st ed. dj. xl. P1. $5.00

STEIN, A.M. *Blood on the Stars.* 1964. Crime Club. 1st ed. dj. xl. P1. $5.00

STEIN, A.M. *Chill Factor.* 1978. Crime Club. dj. VG. P1. $15.00

STEIN, A.M. *Death Meets 400 Rabbits.* 1953. Crime Club. 1st ed. xl. VG. P1. $7.50

STEIN, A.M. *Garbage Collector.* 1984. Crime Club. 1st ed. dj. EX. F5. $15.00

STEIN, A.M. *Kill Is a 4-Letter Word.* 1968. Crime Club. 1st ed. dj. xl. P1. $5.00

STEIN, A.M. *Lock & Key.* 1973. Crime Club. 1st ed. dj. VG. P1. $12.50

STEIN, A.M. *Nose for It.* 1980. Crime Club. 1st ed. dj. VG. P1. $15.00

STEIN, A.M. *Sitting Up Dead.* 1958. Crime Club. dj. xl. P1. $5.00

STEIN, Ben. *Croesus Conspiracy.* 1978. Simon Schuster. 1st ed. dj. EX. P1. $10.00

STEIN, Ben. *Manhattan Gambit.* 1983. Doubleday. 1st ed. dj. VG. P1. $12.50

STEIN, Gertrude. *Acquaintance With Description.* 1929. London. Seizin. Ltd ed. 1/225. glassine wrp. H3. $450.00

STEIN, Gertrude. *Composition As Explanation.* 1926. London. 1st ed. glassine dj. VG. $145.00

STEIN, Gertrude. *Geography & Plays.* 1922. Boston. 4 Seasons. 1st ed. 1st issue bdg/dj. EX. B13. $750.00

STEIN, Gertrude. *Lectures in Am.* 1935. Random House. 1st ed. dj. M. $100.00

STEIN, Gertrude. *Portraits & Prayers.* 1934. NY. not 1st ed. sgn. VG. B3. $150.00

STEIN, Gertrude. *World Is Round.* 1939. NY. Scott. Ils Hurd. sgns. boxed. H3. $550.00

STEIN, Ralph. *Treasury of the Automobile.* nd. (1961) Golden Pr. Probable 1st ed 248 p. dj. VG. B10. $6.50

STEIN, Solomon. *Magic Maestro Please.* 1941. NY. Stein. 1st ed. 47 p. SftCvr. EX. J3. $4.00

STEIN, Solomon. *Touch of Treason.* 1985. St Martin. 1st ed. dj. VG. P1. $15.00

STEIN, William. *Haulcan: Life in the Highlands of Peru.* 1961. Ithaca. 1st ed. 383 p. F2. $25.00

STEINBECK, John. *Acts of King Arthur & His Noble Knights.* 1976. Farrar Straus Giroux. 1st ed. dj. EX. H3. $50.00

STEINBECK, John. *Bombs Away.* nd. np. 1st ed. John Swope photos. dj. VG. H3. $60.00

STEINBECK, John. *Burning Bright.* 1950. NY. 1st ed. dj. VG. B3. $45.00

STEINBECK, John. *Burning Bright.* 1951. Heinemann. 1st UK ed. dj. VG. B13. $45.00

STEINBECK, John. *Cannery Row.* 1945. Viking. 1st ed. 2nd state bdg. dj. VG. H3. $100.00

TEINBECK, John. *Chapter 34 From the ovel E of Eden.* 1952. Bronxville, NY. alenti Angelo. 1st/A ed. 1/125. wrp. B13. 250.00

TEINBECK, John. *Cup of Gold.* nd. opular Lib. B4. $15.00

TEINBECK, John. *Cup of Gold.* 1936. ovici Friede. 2nd ed. dj. VG. H3. $100.00

TEINBECK, John. *E of Eden.* 1952. Viking. td ed. 1/1500. sgn. slipcase. EX. K2. 000.00

TEINBECK, John. *E of Eden.* 1952. Viking. t ed. dj. VG. H3. $50.00

TEINBECK, John. *E of Eden.* 1952. Viking. t ed. 1/1500. sgn. boxed. H3. $1000.00

TEINBECK, John. *E of Eden.* 1954. antam. 1st PB ed. B4. $6.00

TEINBECK, John. *Forgotten Village.* 1941. king. 1st ed. dj. EX. H3. $125.00

TEINBECK, John. *Grapes of Wrath.* nd. rmed Services Ed. VG. B4. $15.00

TEINBECK, John. *Grapes of Wrath.* 1939. einemann. 1st UK ed. dj. EX. H3. $150.00

TEINBECK, John. *Grapes of Wrath.* 1939. king. 1st ed. dj. VG. H3. $500.00

TEINBECK, John. *Grapes of Wrath.* 1939. king. 1st ed. orig bdg. dj. EX. H3. 250.00

EINBECK, John. *Grapes of Wrath.* 1939. king. 1st ed. dj. EX. extremely rare. K2. 200.00

EINBECK, John. *Grapes of Wrath.* 1940. d Ed Club. 2 vols. slipcase. M. H3. 75.00

EINBECK, John. *In Dubious Battle.* 1936. vici Friede. 1st ed. 2nd print. dj. RS. VG. . $300.00

EINBECK, John. *In Dubious Battle.* 1936. vici Friede. 1st ed. sgn. orange bdg. dj. . $1000.00

EINBECK, John. *Journal of a Novel, E of n Letters.* 1969. NY. 1st Trade ed. dj. VG. $25.00

EINBECK, John. *Journal of a Novel.* 1969. . 1st ed. dj. VG. B3. $35.00

EINBECK, John. *Journal of a Novel.* 1970. inemann. 1st UK ed. dj. EX. B13. $50.00

EINBECK, John. *Journal of a Novel: E of n Letters.* 1969. Viking. 1st Trade ed. dj. . H3. $75.00

EINBECK, John. *Log From the Sea of tez.* 1951. Viking. 2nd ed. EX. H3. $50.00

STEINBECK, John. *Long Valley.* 1938. Viking. 1st ed. dj. VG. H3. $150.00

STEINBECK, John. *Long Valley.* 1939. Viking. 4th ed. 303 p. VG. B10. $4.25

STEINBECK, John. *Moon Is Down.* 1942. Viking. ARC. 1/700. wrp. VG. K2. $275.00

STEINBECK, John. *Moon Is Down.* 1942. Viking. 1st ed. 2nd state. bl bdg. dj. VG. $45.00

STEINBECK, John. *Moon Is Down.* 1942. Viking/Haddon Craftsmen. 1st ed. dj. VG. H3. $75.00

STEINBECK, John. *Of Mice & Men.* 1937. Covici Friede. Play ed. dj. EX. scarce. K2. $500.00

STEINBECK, John. *Of Mice & Men.* 1937. Covici Friede. 1st ed. 1st issue. dj. EX. H3. $225.00

STEINBECK, John. *Of Mice & Men.* 1937. NY. 1st ed. 2nd state. dj. VG. $135.00

STEINBECK, John. *Of Mice & Men.* 1947. World. dj. EX. $20.00

STEINBECK, John. *Once There Was a War.* 1958. Viking. 1st ed. dj. EX. H3. $100.00

STEINBECK, John. *Pastures of Heaven.* 1951. Bantam. 1st print. VG. P1. $6.00

STEINBECK, John. *Pearl.* 1947. Viking. Ils Jose Clemente Orozco. 2nd print. 123 p. F2. $20.00

STEINBECK, John. *Pearl.* 1947. Viking. Ils Orozco. 1st ed. dj. M. H3. $100.00

STEINBECK, John. *Pearl.* 1948. London. 1st ed. dj. EX. $85.00

STEINBECK, John. *Red Pony.* nd. Viking. Ils Wesley Dennis. slipcase. VG. $15.00

STEINBECK, John. *Red Pony.* 1945. Viking. 1st ed. boxed. J2. $12.50

STEINBECK, John. *Red Pony.* 1945. Viking. 1st Ils ed. slipcase. H3. $60.00

STEINBECK, John. *Russian Journal.* 1948. Viking. Ils Robert Capa. dj. VG. K2. $60.00

STEINBECK, John. *Russian Journal.* 1948. Viking. Ils Robert Capa. 1st ed. dj. EX. H3. $125.00

STEINBECK, John. *Sea of Cortez.* 1941. NY. 1st ed. VG. B3. $90.00

STEINBECK, John. *Sea of Cortez.* 1941. Viking. 1st ed. dj. VG. H3. $250.00

STEINBECK, John. *Short Reign of Pippin 4.* 1957. Viking. 1st ed. H3. $50.00

STEINBECK, John. *Sweet Thursday.* 1954. Viking. 1st ed. dj. EX. B13. $50.00

STEINBECK, John. *Sweet Thursday.* 1954. Viking. 1st ed. dj. H3. $75.00

STEINBECK, John. *Sweet Thursday.* 1956. Bantam. 1st PB ed. EX. B4. $8.00

STEINBECK, John. *Their Blood Is Strong.* 1938. Simon J Lubin Soc of CA. 4th print. G. $50.00

STEINBECK, John. *To a God Uknown.* 1933. NY. Ballou. 1st ed. 1st issue. 1/598. dj. EX. B13. $2250.00

STEINBECK, John. *Tortilla Flat.* 1947. Ils Peggy Worthington. 1st ed. dj. EX. B2. $175.00

STEINBECK, John. *Travels With Charley: In Search of Am.* 1962. Viking. dj. VG. $12.00

STEINBECK, John. *Viking Portable Steinbeck.* 1943. Viking. 1st ed. dj. EX. B13. $85.00

STEINBECK, John. *Wayward Bus.* 1950. Bantam. 1st PB ed. VG. B4. $5.00

STEINBECK, John. *Winter of Our Discontent.* 1957. London. dj. EX. B2. $35.00

STEINBECK, John. *Winter of Our Discontent.* 1961. Viking. Ltd 1st ed. 1/500. EX. H3. $300.00

STEINBECK, John. *Working Days. Journals of Grapes of Wrath.* 1989. Viking. UP. wrp. EX. K2. $100.00

STEINBECK, John. *2-in-1.* 1947. London. Reprint Soc. 1st ed? dj. EX. B13. $50.00

STEINBERG, M.B. *Hist of the 14th St Theatre.* 1931. NY. Ils 1st ed. EX. $35.00

STEINHOUSE. *Tell It All.* 1874. Cincinnati. 1st ed. 623 p. G. B3. $35.00

STEININGER & VAN DE VELDE. *3 Dollars a Year.* 1935. Delphic Studios. 1st ed. 121 p. dj. F2. $25.00

STEINMEYER, Jim. *1st Law of Byro-No-Monics: An Ils Lecture.* 1988. Steinmeyer. M. J3. $7.50

STEJNEGER, Leonhard. *Land Reptiles of HI Islands.* 1899. WA. 1st ed. 8vo. gray wrp. VG. T1. $125.00

STELTZER, Ulli. *Health in the Guatemalan Highlands.* 1983. WA U. 1st ed. 80 p. dj. F2. $20.00

STENHOUSE, Mrs. T.B.H. *Tell It All: Story of Life's Experience in Mormonism.* 1875. Hartford. Ils. 8vo. VG. T1. $40.00

STENSON, P. *Odyssey of CH Lightoller.* 1984. NY. 1st ed. 325 p. dj. VG. B3. $35.00

STEPHAN, Enno. *Spies in Ireland.* 1965. Harrisburg. 1st Am ed. dj. EX. $20.00

STEPHAN, Leslie. *Reprise.* 1988. St Martin. 1st ed. dj. EX. F5. $12.00

STEPHEN, C.E. *Quaker Stronghold.* 1981. Phil. Longstreth. 12mo. 211 p. VG. V1. $8.50

STEPHEN, David. *Bodach the Badger.* 1983. St Martin. 1st ed. dj. VG. P1. $10.95

STEPHENS, C.A. *Busy Year at the Squires.* nd. (1922) Mason Co. 313 p. VG. B10. $4.00

STEPHENS, C.A. *When Life Was Young.* nd. (1918) Old Squires Bookstore. xl. VG. B10. $5.00

STEPHENS, Frank. *CA Mammals.* 1906. San Diego. w/sgn letter. VG. T3. $40.00

STEPHENS, H.B. *Jacques Cartier & Hist of 4 Voyages to Canada.* 1890. Montreal. 8vo. VG. A4. $100.00

STEPHENS, J.L. *Incidents of Travel in Central Am, Chiapas, & Yucatan.* 1841. NY. 1st ed. xl. $75.00

STEPHENS, J.L. *Incidents of Travel in Central Am, Chiapas, & Yucatan.* 1841. NY. Harper. 2 vols. EX. $300.00

STEPHENS, J.L. *Incidents of Travel in Central Am, Chiapas, & Yucatan.* 1949. Rutgers. 1st ed. 2 vols in 1. dj. F2. $30.00

STEPHENS, J.L. *Incidents of Travel in Yucatan.* 1962. OK U. 1st ed. 2 vols. F2. $50.00

STEPHENS, James. *Crock of Gold.* 1912. Macmillan. inscr. sm octavo. H3. $250.00

STEPHENS, James. *Etched in Moonlight.* 1928. Macmillan. Ltd ed. 1/750. sgn. boxed. H3. $75.00

STEPHENS, James. *On Prose & Verse.* 1928. NY. Rudge Warde. 1/1000. 41 p. VG. T5. $25.00

STEPHENS, James. *Theme & Variations.* 1930. Fountain Pr. Ltd ed. 1/850. sgn. boxed. H3. $125.00

STEPHENS, R.N. *Capt Ravenshaw.* 1901. Page. Ils Goodman/Pyle. 1st ed. EX. F5. $15.00

STEPHENS, Roger. *Down That Pan Am Highway.* 1948. NY. Stephens. 1st ed. 4to. 352 p. F2. $15.00

STEPHENSON, Sarah. *Memoirs of Life & Travels in Service of the Gospel.* 1807. Phil. Kimber Conrad. 12mo. 233 p. full leather. rebacked spine. V1. $35.00

STEPTOE, John. *Baby Says.* 1988. Lathrop. 1st ed. dj. EX. B13. $35.00

STERANKO, John. *Steranko on Cards Vol 1.* 1974. Magic Inc. 2nd print. 102 p. EX. J3. $6.00

STERLING, George. *Caged Eagle & Other Poems.* 1916. San Francisco. Robertson. 1st ed. inscr. VG. $45.00

STERLING, George. *Wine of Wizardry & Other Poems.* 1909. San Francisco. 1st ed? VG. B3. $45.00

STERLING, Robert. *Probable Cause.* 1960. NY. 1st ed. dj. VG. B3. $20.00

STERLING, Rod. *Patterns.* 1957. Simon Schuster. 1st ed. dj. EX. H3. $65.00

STERLING, S.H. *Lady of King Arthur's Court.* 1907. NY. 1st ed. very scarce. C1. $29.50

STERLING, S.H. *Shakespeare's Sweetheart.* 1905. np. VG. C1. $11.50

STERLING, S.H. *Shakespeare's Sweetheart.* 1905. Phil. Ils Clara Peck. dj. boxed. M. A4. $60.00

STERLING, Stewart. *Body in the Bed.* 1959. Lippincott. 1st ed. xl. VG. P1. $5.00

STERLING, Stewart. *Dead of Night.* 1950. Dutton. 1st ed. dj. VG. P1. $25.00

STERLING, Stewart. *Dead Wrong.* 1947. Lippincott. 1st ed. dj. xl. P1. $10.00

STERLING, Stewart. *Too Hot To Handle.* nd. Book Club. dj. VG. P1. $4.50

STERLING, Stewart. *Too Hot To Handle.* 1961. Random House. 1st ed. VG. P1. $10.00

STERLING, Thomas. *Silent Siren.* 1958. Gollancz. 1st ed. dj. xl. P1. $7.50

STERLING, Tom. *Amazon.* 1974. Time Life. Ils. 183 p. F2. $10.00

STERN, Laurence. *Sentimental Journey Through France & Italy.* 1910. London. Williams Norgate. Ils/sgn Hopkins. Deluxe ed. 1/500. 4to. TEG. R4. $175.00

STERN, Leopold. *Easy Marks.* c 1928. NJ. sgn. 282 p. G. B10. $17.00

STERN, P.V.D. *Pocket Book of Modern Am Short Stories.* 1943. Pocket Books. EX. B4. $15.00

STERN, P.V.D. *Secret Missions of the Civil War.* 1959. Bonanza. 320 p. dj. EX. S1. $12.00

STERN, R.M. *I Hide We Seek.* nd. Book Club. dj. VG. P1. $4.50

STERNBERG, Jacques. *Future Without Future.* 1971. Seabury. 1st Am ed. dj. VG. R3. $15.00

STERNE, Laurence. *Life & Opinions Tristam Shandy.* 1935. Heritage. Ils TN Cleland. slipcase. M. T1. $20.00

STERNE, Laurence. *Sentimental Journe Through France & Italy.* 1768. London. 1 ed. 2 vols. Riviere bdg. H3. $1500.00

STERNE, Laurence. *Sentimental Journe Through France & Italy.* 1929. Blk Sun. 1/33 on Arches. wrp/glassine/slipcase. H3 $150.00

STERNE, Laurence. *Sentimental Journe Through France & Italy.* 1941. Heritage. Sylvain Sauvage. slipcase. EX. T1. $20.00

STERNE, Laurence. *Works.* 1783. Londo 7 vols. 12mo. fore-edge painting H3. $2500.00

STERNE, Laurence. *Works.* 192 Shakespeare Head. Lg Paper ed. 1/50 7 vols. TEG. EX. H3. $650.00

STERNHEIM, Carl. *Fairfax.* 1923. Knop Trans Kathner. 1/950. 66 p. G. T5. $15.00

STEUBEN, J. *Strike Strategy.* 1950. NY. 1 ed. dj. VG. B3. $17.50

STEUSSY, Martin. *Dreams of Dawn.* 198 Del Rey. 1st HrdCvr ed. dj. EX. F5. $10.00

STEVENS, C.A. *Bordan's US Sharpshoote in Army of the Potomac.* 1892. St Paul. A $150.00

STEVENS, Francis. *Claimed.* 1966. Avalo 1st ed. dj. EX. R3. $20.00

STEVENS, Francis. *Heads of Cerberus.* 195 Fantasy. 1st ed. 1/1500. boxed. EX. R $30.00

STEVENS, G.E. *Wicked City.* 1906. Chicag 304 p. P4. $25.00

STEVENS, G.R. *Hist of the Canadian N Railways.* 1973. Macmillan. 1st print. 582 dj. EX. $35.00

STEVENS, Ruth. *Hi Ya Neighbor: Intim Glimpses of FDR at Warm Springs...* 194 Tupper Love. 1st ed. dj. VG. $15.00

STEVENS. *Picturesque HI.* 1894. Ph oblong 4to. 126 p. VG. $120.00

STEVENSON, B.E. *King in Babylon.* 191 Sm Maynard. 1st ed. VG. R3. $25.00

STEVENSON, D.A. *World's Lighthous Before 1820.* 1959. London. Oxford U. 1st 4to. 310 p. dj. EX. R4. $150.00

STEVENSON, D.E. *House on the Cliff.* 19 Holt. 3rd ed. 282 p. dj. EX. B10. $3.75

STEVENSON, Mrs. M.I. *Letters Fr Samoa 1891-1895.* 1906. NY. 1st ed. TEG. T1. $35.00

STEVENSON, Mrs. R.L. *Cruise of the Janet Nichol Among the S Sea Islands: A Diary.* 1914. NY. 1st ed. EX. $95.00

STEVENSON, P.E. *Race for the Emperor's Cup.* 1907. NY. 1st ed. 8vo. presentation. TEG. T1. $95.00

STEVENSON, R.L. *Child's Garden of Verses.* 1929. Platt Munk. VG. B7. $43.00

STEVENSON, R.L. *Child's Garden of Verses.* 1944. Ltd Ed Club. Ils/sgn Roger Duvoisin. slipcase. EX. $50.00

STEVENSON, R.L. *Confessions of a Unionist.* 1920. Cambridge, MA. private print. 8vo. 20 p. wrp. VG. V1. $60.00

STEVENSON, R.L. *Dr Jekyll & Mr Hyde.* nd. Books Inc. P1. $7.50

STEVENSON, R.L. *Dr Jekyll & Mr Hyde.* nd. Grosset Dunlap. Photoplay ed. dj. VG. P1. $60.00

STEVENSON, R.L. *Dr Jekyll & Mr Hyde.* nd. London. Kangaroo Books. 1st issue. wrp. VG. T9. $40.00

STEVENSON, R.L. *Dr Jekyll & Mr Hyde.* 1886. London. 1st UK ed. orig buff wrp. VG. H3. $2000.00

STEVENSON, R.L. *Dr Jekyll & Mr Hyde.* 1945. Random House. 1st Canadian ed. VG. P1. $8.00

STEVENSON, R.L. *Dr Jekyll & Mr Hyde/Inland Voyage.* 1912. Tauchnitz. wrp. EX. R3. $25.00

STEVENSON, R.L. *Footnote on Hist: 8 Years of Trouble in Samoa.* 1892. Scribner. 1st ed. 322 p. EX. $65.00

STEVENSON, R.L. *Hist of Moses.* 1919. Oak Knoll, PA. Newton. 1st ed. 16mo. wrp. A4. $100.00

STEVENSON, R.L. *Kidnapped.* 1886. London. Cassell. 1st ed. 2nd issue. $250.00

STEVENSON, R.L. *Kidnapped: Being the Adventures of David Balfour in 1751.* 1938. Ltd Ed Club. Ils/sgn HA Miller. 1/1500. slipcase. EX. C4. $60.00

STEVENSON, R.L. *Letters to Family & Friends.* 1906. London. Methuen. 7th ed. 2 vols. EX. $65.00

STEVENSON, R.L. *Novels & Tales.* 1902. Scribner. 26 vols. octavo. TEG. H3. $2500.00

STEVENSON, R.L. *Novels & Tales.* 1905. Scribner. 26 vols. TEG. Lauriat bdg. EX. H3. $3000.00

STEVENSON, R.L. *Novels & Tales.* 1909. Scribner. 26 vols. octavo. TEG. VG. H3. $1500.00

STEVENSON, R.L. *Silverado Squatters.* 1952. Grabhorn. 1st ed. 8vo. M. $60.00

STEVENSON, R.L. *Treasure Island.* 1938. Rand McNally. EX. P1. $20.00

STEVENSON, R.L. *Treasure Island.* 1941. Ltd Ed Club. Ils/sgn Edward A Wilson. 1/1500. slipcase. EX. C4. $90.00

STEVENSON, R.L. *Virginibus Puerisque.* 1893. Ltd ed. 1/212. gr cloth/vellum. EX. B2. $75.00

STEVENSON, R.L. *Virginibus Puerisque.* 1903. Roycroft. EX. $40.00

STEVENSON, R.L. *When the Devil Was Well.* 1921. Bibliophile Soc. 1/450. 8vo. T6. $45.00

STEVENSON, R.L. *Works.* 1921. Scribner. Vailima ed. 26 vols. octavo. slipcases. H3. $1250.00

STEVENSON, R.R. *Mind of Robert Louis Stevenson.* nd. Yoseloff. slipcase. VG. R3. $20.00

STEVENSON, Violet. *Modern Herbal: How To Grow, Cook, & Use Herbs.* 1974. 144 p. dj. M. C1. $7.00

STEVENSON & CRAWFORD. *Songs With Music From a Child's Garden of Verses.* nd. London. Ils MW Tarrant. VG. $20.00

STEVERS & PENDLEBURY. *Sea Lanes.* 1935. NY. inscr. VG. $17.50

STEWART, C.W. *Official Records of Union & Confederate Navies in War...* 1914. WA. Ils. 915 p. G. T5. $19.50

STEWART, D.C. *Setts of the Scottish Tartans With Descriptive/Hist Notes.* 1950. Edinburgh. Oliver Boyd. 1st ed. sm 4to. 125 p. dj. EX. R4. $30.00

STEWART, F.E. *Compend of Pharmacy.* 1900. Phil. 5th Revised ed. 187 p. G. T5. $22.50

STEWART, F.H. *Notes on Old Gloucester Co.* 1977. Baltimore. 2nd issue. 2 vols. gilt red bdg. EX. T1. $45.00

STEWART, F.M. *Mephisto Waltz.* nd. Coward McCann. 3rd ed. dj. EX. P1. $7.00

STEWART, F.M. *Methuselah Enzyme.* 1970. Arbor House. 1st ed. dj. EX. P1. $10.00

STEWART, G.R. *US 40: Cross Section of USA.* 1953. Boston. Ils 1st ed. 311 p. G. T5. $12.50

STEWART, George. *NA 1: The N – S Continental Highway Looking S.* 1957. Houghton Mifflin. 1st ed. 230 p. F2. $10.00

STEWART, Ian. *Peking Payoff.* 1975. Macmillan. 1st ed. dj. EX. P1. $10.00

STEWART, J.L. *Goddess of Mercy.* 1927. McClelland Stewart. xl. VG. P1. $7.50

STEWART, Mary. *Crystal Cave.* 1970. London. 1st UK ed. dj. EX. $30.00

STEWART, Mary. *Hollow Hills.* 1973. Hodder Stoughton. 1st ed. dj. EX. P1. $25.00

STEWART, Mary. *Last Enchantment.* 1979. 1st UK ed. dj. EX. C1. $9.50

STEWART, Mary. *Last Enchantment.* 1979. Morrow Book Club. 439 p. dj. EX. B10. $3.50

STEWART, Mary. *My Brother Michael.* 1960. London. 1st ed. inscr. VG. B13. $65.00

STEWART, Mary. *Wicked Day.* 1983. NY. 1st Am ed. dj. VG. C1. $7.50

STEWART, Michael. *Blindsight.* 1987. St Martin. ARC. RS. M. R3. $16.95

STEWART, Michael. *Blindsight.* 1987. St Martin. 1st ed. dj. EX. F5. $16.00

STEWART, Robert. *Book of Merlin.* 1987. 1st Am ed. dj. EX. C1. $17.50

STEWART, T.D. *Bibliography of Physical Anthropology in Latin Am 1937-1948.* nd. NY. sm 4to. 59 p. wrp. F2. $10.00

STEWART, Virginia. *45 Contemporary Mexican Artists.* 1952. Stanford. 2nd print. 167 p. dj. T5. $35.00

STEWART, W.A.C. *Quakers & Education As Seen in Their Schools in Eng.* 1971. Kennikat Pr. 2nd ed. 8vo. 310 p. VG. V1. $10.00

STICKGOLD & NOBLE. *Glory Hits.* nd. BOMC. dj. VG. P1. $4.50

STIEFF, P. *Drink & Be Merry in MD.* 1932. NY. 6th print. dj. VG. B3. $25.00

STIEGLITZ, Alfred. *Georgia O'Keefe: A Portrait.* 1978. NY. 1st ed. slipcase. EX. G1. $95.00

STIEGLITZ, Julius. *Chemistry in Medicine.* 1928. Chemical Foundation. 1st ed. 758 p. VG. B10. $6.50

STILES, George. *Dragoman.* 1913. Harper. 1st ed. 311 p. VG. B10. $4.00

STILES, J.C. *Modern Reform Examined.* 1858. Phil. brn bdg. G. G4. $30.00

STILL, James. *Rusties & Riddles & Gee-Haw Whimmy-Diddles.* 1989. Lexington. 1st ed. sgn. dj. M. B13. $35.00

STILLMAN, Jacob. *1850 Voyage, San Francisco by Sea & by Land.* 1967. Palo Alto. Ltd ed. 1/2350. VG. G1. $22.00

STILLSON, Blanche. *Wings: Insects, Birds, Men.* 1954. Indianapolis. Ils 1st ed. 299 p. dj. T5. $17.50

STILSON, Charles. *Ace of Blades.* nd. Grosset Dunlap. dj. EX. R3. $20.00

STILSON, Charles. *Cavalier of Navarre.* nd. Grosset Dunlap. G. R3. $12.50

STILSON, Charles. *Minos of Sardanes.* 1966. Avalon. 1st ed. dj. EX. R3. $15.00

STILSON, Charles. *Polaris & the Immortals.* 1968. Avalon. 1st ed. dj. EX. R3. $15.00

STILSON, Charles. *Polaris of the Snows.* 1965. Avalon. 1st ed. dj. EX. R3. $15.00

STIMSON & BUNDY. *On Active Service in Peace & War.* 1948. NY. 1st ed. 698 p. T5. $19.50

STINETORF, L.A. *Cina Problana.* 1960. Bobbs Merrill. 1st ed. 256 p. dj. F2. $15.00

STINSON, Jim. *Low Angles.* 1986. Scribner. 1st ed. dj. EX. F5. $12.50

STITH, J.E. *Redshift Rendezvous.* 1990. Ace. UP. wrp. w/promotional letter. EX. F5. $25.00

STOAN, Stephen. *Pablo Morillo & Venezuela, 1815-1820.* 1974. OH State U. 1st ed. 249 p. dj. F2. $15.00

STOCKMAN, D.A. *Triumph of Politics: Why the Reagan Revolution Failed.* 1986. NY. 1st ed. dj. EX. T1. $22.00

STOCKRIDGE, Frank. *FL in the Making.* nd. Bower Pub. 1st ed. 351 p. VG. B10. $7.00

STOCKTON, F.R. *Buccaneers & Pirates of Our Coasts.* 1898. NY. 1st ed. 325 p. VG. B3. $45.00

STOCKTON, F.R. *Captain's Toll Gate.* 1903. Appleton. 1/160. sgn. G. H3. $50.00

STOCKTON, F.R. *Great Stone of Sardis.* 1898. Harper. Ils Peter Newell. 230 p. VG. $40.00

STOCKTON, F.R. *Great Stone of Sardis.* 1899. Harper. VG. R3. $25.00

STOCKTON, F.R. *Novels & Stories.* 1899. Scribner. 18 vols. octavo. TEG. H3. $300.00

STOCKTON, F.R. *Storyteller's Pack.* 1897. NY. Ils Newell/Kemble. 1st ed. VG. B3. $45.00

STOCKTON, F.R. *Vizier of the 2-Horned Alexander.* 1899. Century. 1st ed. VG. R3. $25.00

STODDARD, Elizabeth. *Poems.* 1895. Houghton. 1st ed. 1/1000. TEG. dj. EX. B10. $25.00

STODDARD, H.L. *Bobwhite Quail.* 1931. Scribner. 1st ed. VG. $60.00

STODDARD, H.L. *Bobwhite Quail.* 1941. NY. 2nd ed. VG. $30.00

STODDARD, R.H. *Personal Reminiscences of Chorley, Planche, & Young.* 1875. Scribner/Armstrong. G. B10. $8.00

STOKER, Bram. *Dracula.* nd. Grosset Dunlap. Photoplay ed. VG. P1. $50.00

STOKER, Bram. *Jewel of 7 Stars.* 1904. Harper. 1st ed. VG. R3. $65.00

STOKER, Bram. *Mystery of the Sea.* 1903. Heinemann. sgn. H3. $300.00

STOKER, Bram. *Personal Reminiscences of Henry Irving.* 1906. NY. 1st Am ed. 2 vols. EX. $50.00

STOKER, Bram. *Watter's Mou.* 1895. Westminster. 1st ed. 12mo. VG. $85.00

STOKER, Robert. *Legacy of Arthur's Chester.* 1965. 1st ed. dj. VG. C1. $15.00

STOKES, Cedric. *Staffordshire Assassins.* nd. Macdonald. VG. P1. $10.00

STOKES, Geoffrey. *Starmaking Machinery: Odyssey of an Album.* 1976. Bobbs Merrill. dj. EX. B4. $25.00

STOKES, J.S. *Memoirs of John S Stokes.* 1893. Friends Bookstore. 12mo. 433 p. VG. V1. $8.00

STOKES, Katherine. *Motor Maids at Sunrise Camp.* 1914. Hurst. 1st ed. 311 p. VG. B10. $3.50

STOKES, M.L. *Iron Tiger.* 1958. Arcadia. 1st ed. dj. xl. P1. $6.00

STOKES, William. *Honduras.* 1950. WI U. 1st ed. dj. F2. $25.00

STOLBOV, Bruce. *Last Fall.* 1987. Doubleday. 1st ed. dj. EX. P1. $12.95

STOLK, H.N.; see Marconick.

STOLPE, D.O. *Images & Myths.* 1982. Aptos, CA. 1st ed. K2. $35.00

STONE, Andy. *Song of the Kingdom.* 1979. Doubleday. 1st ed. dj. EX. P1. $15.00

STONE, Doris. *Arqueologia de la Costa Norte de Honduras.* 1975. Peabody Mus. 103 p. wrp. F2. $25.00

STONE, Doris. *Pre-Columbian Man Finds Central Am.* 1976. Peabody Mus. 2nd print. wrp. F2. $20.00

STONE, Doris. *Pre-Columbian Man in Costa Rica.* 1977. Peabody Mus. 1st ed. 238 p. wrp. F2. $20.00

STONE, Doris. *Pre-Columbian Plant Migration.* 1984. Cambridge. 1st ed. 4to. 183 p. wrp. F2. $30.00

STONE, E.A. *Unita Co, Its Place in Hist.* 1924. Glendale. Clark. Ils. 276 p. A5. $75.00

STONE, E.D. *Recent & Future Architecture.* 1967. NY. 1st ed. sgn. dj. EX. T1. $50.00

STONE, Eugenia. *Robin Hood's Arrow.* 1949. Chicago. 1st ed. dj. EX. C1. $14.00

STONE, Eugenia. *Squire for King Arthur.* 1955. Chicago. Follet. 1st ed. dj. scarce. juvenile. C1. $29.50

STONE, Fred. *Rolling Stone.* 1945. Whittlesey House. 1st ed. octavo. 246 p. dj. EX. H3. $35.00

STONE, Hampton. *Kid Was Last Seen Hanging 10.* 1966. Simon Schuster. 1st ed. dj. xl. P1. $5.00

STONE, Hampton. *Kid Who Came Home With a Corpse.* 1972. Simon Schuster. 1st ed. dj. xl. P1. $5.00

STONE, Hampton. *Swinger Who Swung by the Neck.* 1970. Simon Schuster. 1st ed. dj. xl. P1. $5.00

STONE, I. *Passions of the Mind.* 1971. Doubleday. dj. VG. $40.00

STONE, Irving. *Adversary in the House.* 1947. Doubleday. sgn. dj. H3. $100.00

STONE, Irving. *Clarence Darrow for the Defense.* 1941. NY. dj. T1. $30.00

STONE, Irving. *Those Who Love: Biographical Novel of Abigail & John Adams.* 1965. Doubleday. inscr. dj. H3. $100.00

STONE, L.F. *Out of the Void.* 1967. Avalon. dj. xl. P1. $5.00

STONE, L.F. *Out of the Void.* 1967. Avalon. 1st ed. dj. EX. R3. $20.00

STONE, Lloyd. *HI Net.* 1945. Honolulu. private print. dj. G. A6. $35.00

STONE, Martha. *At the Sgn of the Midnight.* 1975. Tucson. 1st ed. 262 p. dj. F2. $20.00

STONE, Robert. *Best Am Short Stories.* 1988. Houghton Mifflin. sgn. dj. EX. K2. $55.00

STONE, Robert. *Children of Light.* 1986. Knopf. sgn. dj. H3. $75.00

STONE, Robert. *Children of Light.* 1986. London. Deutsch. 1st UK ed. dj. EX. K2. $65.00

STONE, Robert. *Children of Light.* 1986. London. Deutsch. 1st UK ed. 1/4500. sgn. dj. EX. K2. $125.00

STONE, Robert. *Dog Soldiers.* 1974. Boston. UP. 1st issue. sgn. K2. $350.00

STONE, Robert. *Dog Soldiers.* 1974. Houghton Mifflin. UP. EX. K2. $225.00

STONE, Robert. *Dog Soldiers.* 1974. Houghton Mifflin. 1st ed. dj. w/pub letter. EX. C4. $150.00

STONE, Robert. *Dog Soldiers.* 1974. Houghton Mifflin. 1st ed. sgn. dj. EX. K2. $125.00

STONE, Robert. *Dog Soldiers.* 1975. Secker Warburg. 1st UK ed. dj. EX. very scarce. K2. $150.00

STONE, Robert. *Flag for Sunrise.* 1981. Knopf. UP. wrp. EX. C4. $100.00

STONE, Robert. *Flag for Sunrise.* 1981. Secker Warburg. 1st UK ed. dj. EX. K2. $65.00

STONE, Robert. *Hall of Mirrors.* 1967. Boston. 1st ed. sgn. as issued. K2. $350.00

STONE, Robert. *Hall of Mirrors.* 1967. Boston. 1st ed. 1st issue dj. VG. T9. $250.00

STONE, Robert. *Hall of Mirrors.* 1967. Houghton Mifflin. 1st ed. inscr/sgn. dj. EX. C4. $375.00

STONE, Robert. *Hall of Mirrors.* 1968. Fawcett. 1st PB ed. wrp. RS. EX. C4. $50.00

STONE, Ted. *13 Canadian Ghost Stories.* 1988. Prairie Books. 1st ed. sgn. dj. EX. P1. $25.00

STONE, W.S. *Teri Taro From Bora Bora.* 1940. Knopf. 1st ed. 133 p. B10. $4.50

STONE & CRAM. *Am Animals.* 1910. Doubleday Page. clr pls. VG. T3. $65.00

STONEBRAKER, J.C. *Puritan & the Cavalier.* 1915. Hagerstown. EX. $50.00

STONEHAM, C.T. *Lion's Way.* 1932. Stokes. 1st ed. dj. EX. R3. $25.00

STONEY, S.G. *Plantations of the Carolina Low Country.* 1939. Charleston. 1st ed. sgn. dj. EX. $150.00

STONEY, S.G. *Plantations of the Carolina Low Country.* 1939. Charleston. 2nd ed. dj. boxed. VG. $100.00

STONEY, S.G. *Plantations of the Carolina Low Country.* 1955. Carolina Art Assn. Ltd ed. 1/2000. dj. EX. T1. $65.00

STOREY, David. *This Sporting Life.* 1960. Macmillan. 1st Am ed. dj. EX. C4. $45.00

STORKE, E.G. *Complete Hist of the Great Am Rebellion.* 1863. Auburn. rebound. VG. S1. $30.00

STORM, Barry. *Thunder God's Gold.* 1945. Tortilla, AZ. 1st ed. photos. 166 p. VG. B3. $25.00

STORM, Barry. *Thunder God's Gold.* 1946. Phoenix. Treasure Trail ed. 167 p. VG. B3. $30.00

STORM, Colton. *Invitation to Book Collecting: Its Pleasures & Practices.* 1947. NY. 1st ed. dj. G. $35.00

STORY, J.T. *Mix Me a Person.* 1960. Macmillan. 1st ed. dj. VG. P1. $15.00

STORY, Thomas. *Doctrines of Soc of Friends...* nd. Phil. Book Assn Friends. 16mo. 195 p. V1. $14.50

STOTZ, C.M. *Early Architecture of W PA.* 1936. NY. 1/1000. fld map. 290 p. G. T5. $175.00

STOUGHTON, John. *William Penn: Founder of PA.* 1882. Hodder Stoughton. 12mo. 364 p. xl. VG. V1. $10.50

STOUT, Carol. *San Blas Cuna Acculturation: An Introduction.* 1947. Viking. 124 p. stiff wrp. F2. $25.00

STOUT, J.W. *Autobiography & Poems.* 1938 & 1947. 2 vols. wrp. scarce. A6. $45.00

STOUT, Rex. *All Aces.* nd. Book Club. dj. VG. P1. $7.50

STOUT, Rex. *And Be a Villain.* nd. Book Club. dj. VG. P1. $5.00

STOUT, Rex. *Before Midnight.* 1956. Collins Crime Club. 1st ed. dj. VG. P1. $40.00

STOUT, Rex. *Death of a Doxy.* 1966. Viking. 1st ed. dj. VG. P1. $15.00

STOUT, Rex. *Doorbell Rang.* nd. Book Club. dj. VG. P1. $4.50

STOUT, Rex. *Doorbell Rang.* 1965. Viking. 3rd ed. dj. VG. P1. $15.00

STOUT, Rex. *Double for Death.* 1939. Farrar Rinehart. 1st ed. VG. P1. $75.00

STOUT, Rex. *Family Affair.* nd. Book Club. dj. EX. P1. $5.00

STOUT, Rex. *Family Affair.* 1975. NY. 1st ed. dj. EX. $30.00

STOUT, Rex. *Gambit.* nd. Book Club. dj. EX. P1. $6.00

STOUT, Rex. *Illustrious Dunderheads.* 1942. Knopf. 1st ed. VG. P1. $45.00

STOUT, Rex. *In the Best Families.* nd. Book Club. dj. VG. P1. $5.00

STOUT, Rex. *Might As Well Be Dead.* nd. Book Club. dj. VG. P1. $6.00

STOUT, Rex. *Mother Hunt.* nd. Book Club. dj. VG. P1. $4.00

STOUT, Rex. *Mt Cat.* 1939. Farrar Rinehart. 1st ed. VG. C1. $25.00

STOUT, Rex. *Nero Wolfe Omnibus.* 1944. Cleveland. 1st ed. dj. VG. $30.00

STOUT, Rex. *Right To Die.* nd. Book Club. dj. VG. P1. $6.00

STOUT, Rex. *Silent Speaker.* 1946. Viking. 1st ed. dj. EX. very scarce. B13. $375.00

STOUT, Rex. *Trio for Blunt Instruments.* nd. Book Club. dj. EX. P1. $6.00

STOUT, Rex. *Trouble in Triplicate.* nd. Book Club. dj. VG. P1. $5.00

STOUT, Rex. *2nd Confession.* 1973. Tom Stacey. dj. EX. P1. $15.00

STOUT, Rex. *3 for the Chair.* nd. Book Club. dj. VG. P1. $6.00

STOUT, Rex. *3 Men Out.* nd. Book Club. dj. EX. P1. $6.00

STOUT, W.W. *Tanks Are Mighty Fine Things.* 1946. Detroit. Ils. 144 p. T5. $19.50

STOVER, Ronald. *Brains for Janes.* 1948. Pirate Pr. 1st ed. 1/200. EX. R3. $75.00

STOW, Randolph. *Visitants.* 1981. Taplinger. 1st ed. dj. EX. F5. $14.00

STOWE, H.B. *Dread: Tale of Great Dismal Swamp.* 1856. Boston. 1st ed. 2 vols. EX. $80.00

STOWE, H.B. *Key to Uncle Tom's Cabin: Presenting the Orig Facts...* 1853. Boston. Jewett. 1st ed. 262 p. VG. $90.00

STOWE, H.B. *Men of Our Times.* 1868. Hartford. 1st ed. G. C1. $17.50

STOWE, H.B. *Old-Town Folks.* 1874. Osgood. 608 p. xl. B10. $3.50

STOWE, H.B. *Uncle Tom's Cabin.* 1852. Boston. 1st ed. 1st issue. orig gilt brn bdg. EX. H3. $6750.00

STOWE, H.B. *Uncle Tom's Cabin.* 1852. London. Ils Cruikshank. 1st UK ed. orig parts. wrp. VG. rare. H3. $5000.00

STOWE, H.B. *Uncle Tom's Cabin.* 1852. London. 1st ed. 12mo. Sangorski/Sutcliff bdg. slipcase. A4. $600.00

STOWE, H.B. *Uncle Tom's Cabin; or, Life Among the Lowly.* 1852. Boston. 3rd ed. 2 vols. very scarce. $300.00

STOWE, H.B. *Uncle Tom's Cabin; or, Life Among the Lowly.* 1938. Ltd Ed Club. Ils/sgn Covarrubias. 4to. slipcase. EX. C4. $250.00

STOWE, H.B. *We & Our Neighbors.* 1875. NY. 1st ed. EX. $35.00

STOWE, J.L. *Winter Stalk.* 1979. Simon Schuster. 1st ed. dj. EX. F5. $18.00

STOWE, L.B. *Saints, Sinners, & Beechers.* 1934. Indianapolis. 1st ed. 450 p. dj. VG. B3. $22.50

STRACHEY, Edward. *Morte d'Arthur.* 1899. (1st 1868) London. gilt gr bdg. VG. C1. $9.50

STRACHEY, Lionel. *Love Letters of Famous Royalties & Commanders.* 1909. NY. 1st ed. VG. T1. $22.00

STRACHEY, Lytton. *Ermyntrude & Esmeralda.* 1969. Stein Day. Ils Erte. 1st ed. 8vo. 77 p. dj. EX. R4. $25.00

STRAHAN, K.C. *Death Traps.* nd. Grosset Dunlap. VG. P1. $7.50

STRAHL, Paul. *Quarrel.* 1947. Duell Sloane Pearce. 1st ed. dj. G. S1. $6.00

STRANG, Herbert. *Boys of the Light Brigade.* 1905. London. Ils Rainey. 12mo. VG. A4. $35.00

STRANGE, J.S. *Catch the Gold Ring.* nd. Book Club. dj. VG. P1. $4.50

STRANGE, J.S. *Silent Witnesses.* 1938. Crime Club. 1st ed. VG. P1. $17.50

STRANGE, J.S. *Unquiet Grave.* 1949. Crime Club. 1st ed. dj. VG. P1. $20.00

STRATTON, R.B. *Captivity of Oatman Girls.* 1960. Carlton Porter. 290 p. A5. $160.00

STRAUB, Peter. *Floating Dragon.* 1983. Collins. 1st ed. dj. EX. P1. $35.00

STRAUB, Peter. *Floating Dragon.* 1983. Putnam. 1st ed. dj. VG. P1. $25.00

STRAUB, Peter. *Ghost Story.* 1979. Coward McCann. 1st ed. sgn. clipped dj. EX. F5. $50.00

STRAUB, Peter. *Koko.* 1988. Dutton. ARC. wrp. EX. K2. $35.00

STRAUB, Peter. *Shadow Land.* 1960. Coward McCann. ARC. wrp. EX. $50.00

STRAUB, Peter. *Shadow Land.* 1980. Coward McCann. 1st ed. dj. VG. P1. $25.00

STRAYER, HUNTER, & DAVIS. *Behind the Wht Mask of the Ku Klux Klan.* c 1929. McKeesport, PA. Ils. 237 p. VG. T5. $42.50

STRAYER, HUNTER, & DAVIS. *Famous Suit of Knights of the Ku Klux Klan in Equity.* 1927. McKeesport, PA. 63 p. wrp. VG. T5. $35.00

STREATFIELD, R.A. *Life Stories of Great Composers.* nd. (1910) Presser. 1st ed? 584 p. VG. B10. $5.00

STREET, James. *Gauntlet.* 1945. Doubleday. 1st ed. 311 p. dj. VG. B10. $15.00

STREET, James. *Goodbye My Lady.* 1954. Phil. 1st ed. dj. VG. B3. $22.50

STREET, James. *Oh Promised Land.* 1940. NY. 1st ed. dj. VG. B3. $30.00

STREET, Julian. *Abroad at Home: Am Ramblings, Observations, & Adventures.* 1914. Century. 1st ed. 517 p. TEG. VG. B10. $11.50

STREETER, Burnett. *Adventure.* 1928. Macmillan. 1st ed. 247 p. dj. VG. B10. $7.50

STREETER, E. *That's Me All Over, Mabel.* c 1919. NY. 12mo. 69 p. G. G4. $19.00

STRETE, C.K. *Paint Your Face on a Drowning in the River.* 1978. Greenwillow. 1st ed. clipped dj. EX. B13. $100.00

STRIBLING, T.S. *Sound Wagon.* 1936. Literary Guild. dj. B10. $4.50

STRIBLING, T.S. *Unfinished Cathedral.* 1934. Literary Guild. 383 p. VG. B10. $3.50

STRICKLAND, A.B. *Roger Williams.* 1919. Boston. 1st ed. VG. B3. $22.50

STRICKLAND, Agnes. *Lives of the Queens of Eng From the Norman Conquest.* 1902. Phil. Barrie. Royal ed. 1/39. 16 vols. lg octavo. H3. $1250.00

STRICKLAND, Agnes. *Lives of the Queens of Scotland & Eng Princesses.* 1852-1859. Edinburgh. Blackwood. 8 vols. TEG. H3. $300.00

STRIEBER, Whitley. *Billy.* 1990. Putnam. UP. wrp. EX. B13. $30.00

STRIEBER, Whitley. *Blk Magic.* 1982. Morrow. 1st ed. dj. EX. R3. $30.00

STRIEBER, Whitley. *Communion.* 1987. Beech Tree. 1st ed. sgn. dj. EX. P1. $20.00

STRIEBER, Whitley. *Communion.* 1987. Morrow. 1st ed. dj. EX. R3. $17.95

STRIEBER, Whitley. *Night Church.* nd. Book Club. dj. VG. P1. $4.50

STRIEBER & KUNETKA. *War Day.* nd. BOMC. dj. VG. P1. $7.50

STRIEBER & KUNETKA. *War Day.* 1984. Holt. 1st ed. dj. EX. R3. $15.00

STRIKER, Fran. *Lone Ranger & the Gold Robbery.* nd. Grosset Dunlap. VG. P1. $7.50

STRIKER, Fran. *Lone Ranger & the Mystery Ranch.* nd. Grosset Dunlap. VG. P1. $10.00

STRIKER, Fran. *Lone Ranger & the Outlaw Stronghold.* nd. Grosset Dunlap. G. P1. $7.50

STRIKER, Fran. *Lone Ranger & the Silver Bullet.* nd. Grosset Dunlap. dj. VG. P1. $15.00

STRIKER, Fran. *Lone Ranger at the Haunted Gulch.* nd. Grosset Dunlap. VG. P1. $10.00

STRIKER, Fran. *Lone Ranger on Powderhorn Trail.* nd. Grosset Dunlap. dj. VG. P1. $12.50

STRIKER, Fran. *Lone Ranger Traps the Smugglers.* nd. Grosset Dunlap. VG. P1. $10.00

STRIKER, Fran. *Lone Ranger W of Maverick Pass.* nd. Grosset Dunlap. VG. P1. $15.00

STRIKER, Fran. *Telltale Scar.* 1947. Grosset. 216 p. dj. VG. B10. $4.00

STRINGER, Arthur. *City of Peril.* nd. AL Burt. VG. P1. $7.50

STRIPPEL, Dick. *Amelia Earhart: Myth & Reality.* 1972. NY. 1st ed. dj. VG. $12.00

STRONG, L.A.G. *Corporal Tune.* 1934. Gollancz. VG. P1. $15.00

STRONG, Paul. *Young Settler.* 1938. NY. Ils Wiese. 1st ed. VG. $12.50

STROSS, Brian. *Tzeltal Tales of Demons & Monsters.* 1978. MO U. 4to. 40 p. wrp. F2. $10.00

STRUGATSKY & ARKADY. *Aliens, Travelers, & Other Strangers.* 1984. Macmillan. 1st ed. RS. M. R3. $20.00

STRUGATSKY & ARKADY. *Noon: 22nd C.* 1978. Macmillan. 1st ed. dj. EX. R3. $20.00

STRUGATSKY & ARKADY. *Ugly Swans.* 1979. Macmillan. 1st ed. dj. VG. P1. $15.00

STRYPE, John. *Life of the Learned Sir John Cheke.* 1821. Clarendon. 8vo. 218 p. V1. $45.00

STUART, Alexander. *War Zone.* 1989. Doubleday. 1st ed. M. R3. $16.95

STUART, Brian. *Mysterious Monsieur Moray.* 1950. Ward Lock. 1st ed. xl. VG. P1. $7.50

STUART, Gene. *Discovering Man's Past in Am.* 1969. Nat Geog. 1st ed. 210 p. dj. F2. $15.00

STUART, Gene. *Mighty Aztecs.* 1981. Nat Geog. 1st ed. 4to. dj. F2. $15.00

STUART, Gene. *Mysterious Maya.* 1977. Nat Geog. 1st ed. 4to. repaired dj. F2. $15.00

STUART, Jesse. *Album of Destiny.* 1944. NY. 1st ed. dj. VG. $55.00

STUART, Jesse. *Beyond Dark Hills.* 1938. NY. 1st ed. EX. $55.00

STUART, Jesse. *Foretaste of Glory.* 1946. NY. 1st ed. dj. VG. A4. $35.00

STUART, Jesse. *God's Oddling.* 1960. NY/Toronto/London. 1st ed. dj. VG. $20.00

STUART, Jesse. *Hold April.* 1962. NY. 1st ed. inscr. dj. w/sgn letter. EX. A4. $375.00

STUART, Jesse. *Plowshare in Heaven.* 1958. NY. 1st ed. dj. VG. B3. $45.00

STUART, Jesse. *Save Every Lamb.* 1964. NY. 1st ed. dj. VG. B3. $45.00

STUART, Jesse. *Thread That Runs So True.* 1949. NY. sgn. 293 p. dj. VG. T5. $32.50

STUBBS, Jean. *Dear Laura.* 1973. Macmillan. 1st ed. dj. xl. P1. $7.50

STUBBS, Jean. *Travelers.* 1963. Macmillan. xl. VG. P1. $5.00

STUCHL, Vladimir. *Am Fairy Tales.* 1979. London. Octopus. 1st ed. sm 4to. B10. $14.00

STUCK, H. *10,000 Miles With a Dog Sled.* 1914. NY. 1st ed. VG. $50.00

STUCKEN, Edward. *Great Wht Gods.* 1934. Farrar. 1st ed. 712 p. VG. F2. $12.50

STUCLIFFE, R. *Sword at Sunset.* 1963. Hodder Stoughton. 2nd imp. dj. EX. scarce. C1. $9.50

STUDER, J.H. *Studer's Birds of N Am.* 1881. NY/Columbus. 119 clr pls. G. B3. $500.00

STUDER, J.H. *Studer's Popular Ornithology.* 1977. Harrison House. reprint of 1881 ed. gilt full leather. EX. T1. $95.00

STURGEON, L.M. *Theodore Sturgeon.* 1981. Unger. 1st ed. M. R3. $10.95

STURGEON, Theodore. *Dreaming Jewels.* 1953. Farrar. 1st ed. dj. EX. R3. $50.00

STURGEON, Theodore. *E Pluribus Unicorn.* 1953. Abelard. 1st ed. dj. EX. R3. $125.00

STURGEON, Theodore. *Godbody.* 1986. Donald Fine. 1st ed. dj. VG. P1. $15.00

STURGEON, Theodore. *Golden Helix.* 1979. Doubleday. 1st HrdCvr ed. dj. EX. F5. $12.00

STURGEON, Theodore. *Maturity.* 1977. Rune Pr. 1st ed. 1/700. sgn. dj. EX. R3. $50.00

STURGEON, Theodore. *More Than Human.* 1953. Farrar. 1st ed. dj. EX. R3. $200.00

STURGEON, Theodore. *Touch of Strange.* nd. Book Club. dj. VG. P1. $7.50

STURGEON, Theodore. *Touch of Strange.* 1958. Doubleday. 1st ed. dj. EX. R3. $100.00

STURGEON, Theodore. *Way Home.* 1955. Funk Wagnall. 1st ed. dj. EX. R3. $125.00

STURGEON, Theodore. *Without Sorery.* 1948. Prime Pr. 1st ed. dj. EX. R3. $90.00

STURGEON & WARD. *Sturgeon's W.* 1973. Doubleday. 1st ed. sgn. dj. EX. F5. $65.00

STUYVESANT, M.S. *How the US Ship Cumberland Went Down.* 1887. St Louis. 1st ed. EX. $25.00

STYLES, Showell. *Tiger Patrol.* 1957. Collins. 1st ed. VG. P1. $10.00

STYRON, William. *Admiral Robert Penn Warren & the Snows of Winter.* 1981. Palaemon. Ltd ed. 1/150. sgn. H3. $125.00

STYRON, William. *Admiral Robert Penn Warren & the Snows of Winter: Tribute.* 1978. Palaemon. 1/26. sgn. wrp. C4. $100.00

STYRON, William. *As He Lay Dead, a Bitter Grief.* 1981. Albondocani. 1/300. sgn. marbled wrp. EX. C4. $75.00

STYRON, William. *Blankenship.* 1988. Pr de la Warr. 1/100. sgn. EX. K2. $65.00

STYRON, William. *Confessions of Nat Turner.* 1967. Random House. 1st ed. 8vo. dj. EX. $20.00

STYRON, William. *Confessions of Nat Turner.* 1979. Franklin Lib. reissue. sgn. AEG. EX. K2. $85.00

STYRON, William. *Darkness Visible: A Memoir of Madness.* 1990. Random House. UP. sgn. wrp. EX. C4/K2. $100.00

STYRON, William. *In the Clap Shack.* 1973. Random House. 1st ed. dj. EX. H3. $75.00

STYRON, William. *Lie Down in Darkness.* 1951. Bobbs Merrill. 1st ed. dj. EX. K2. $175.00

STYRON, William. *Long March.* 1952. NY. ARC. sgn. dj. EX. T9. $90.00

STYRON, William. *Long March.* 1962. Hamish Hamilton. 1st UK/1st HrdCvr ed. inscr. dj. EX. C4. $125.00

STYRON, William. *Long March.* 1968. NY. 1st HrdCvr ed. VG. B2. $50.00

STYRON, William. *Quiet Dust & Other Writings.* 1982. Random House. UP. sgn. wrp. EX. C4. $100.00

STYRON, William. *Set This House on Fire.* 1960. Random House. 1st ed. gilt blk bdg. EX. $55.00

STYRON, William. *Set This House on Fire.* 1960. Random House. 1st ed. sgn. advance dj. EX. B13. $600.00

STYRON, William. *Shadrach.* 1979. Sylvester Orphanos. Ltd ed. 1/300. sgn. EX. K2. $65.00

STYRON, William. *Sophie's Choice.* 1979. Random House. UP. sgn. wrp. EX. C4. $150.00

STYRON, William. *Sophie's Choice.* 1979. Random House. 1st ed. sgn. dj. H3. $75.00

STYRON, William. *Sophie's Choice.* 1979. Random House. 1st Trade ed. gilt red cloth. dj. EX. $30.00

STYRON, William. *This Quiet Dust & Other Writings.* 1982. NY. Ltd ed. 1/250. sgn. 305 p. slipcase. EX. T5. $75.00

STYRON, William. *This Quiet Dust & Other Writings.* 1982. Random House. 1st ed. gilt blk bdg. dj. EX. $15.00

SUBLETTE, C.M. *Bright Face of Danger.* 1926. Little Brn. 2nd ed. 321 p. dj. B10. $4.50

SUDEK, Josef. *Fotografie.* 1956. Prague. lg 8vo. 232 p. dj. EX. $525.00

SUDHALTER. *Bix: Man & Legend.* 1974. New Rochelle. 1st ed. dj. VG. B3. $45.00

SUDWORTH, G.B. *Forest Trees of the Pacific Slope.* 1908. US Dept Agriculture. rebound. VG. T3. $30.00

SUE, Eugene. *Wandering Jew.* 1844. London. 1st ed. rebound. VG. R3. $350.00

SUJAN, Lee. *Fine Art of Chinese Cooking.* 1962. Gramercy. 1st ed. 234 p. dj. EX. B10. $3.25

SUKENICK, Lynn. *Houdini.* 1973. Capra. Chapbook Series. 1/100. sgn. EX. K2. $20.00

SULLIVAN, George. *Discover Archaeology.* 1980. Doubleday. 1st ed. 273 p. dj. F2. $10.00

SULLIVAN & TUCKER. *Hist of 105th Regiment of Engineers.* 1919. NY. Ils. 466 p. T5. $42.50

SULLY, D.C. *Memoirs.* 1827. Paris. Nouvelle ed. 6 vols. VG. $100.00

SULZBERGER, C.L. *Tooth Merchant.* 1973. Quadrangle. 1st ed. dj. VG. P1. $10.00

SUMMERS, Gerald. *African Bestiary.* 1974. Simon Schuster. 1st ed. 222 p. dj. EX. B10. $5.00

SUMMERS, Ian. *Tomorrow & Tomorrow.* 1978. Workman. 1st ed. dj. VG. P1. $25.00

SUMMERS, Montague. *Bibliography of Restoration Drama.* nd. (1935) Fortune Pr. 1st ed. dj. EX. H3. $50.00

SUMMERS, Montague. *Vampire in Europe.* 1929. Dutton. 1st Am ed. VG. R3. $50.00

SUMMERS, Montague. *Vampire: His Kith & Kin.* 1929. NY. 1st Am ed. 356 p. VG. B3. $45.00

SUMMERSBY, Kay. *Eisnehower Was My Boss.* 1948. NY. Ils 1st ed. 302 p. dj. VG. T5. $17.50

SUPER, C.W. *Study of Rural Community.* 1922. Oberlin. 1st ed. stiff wrp. T5. $15.00

SURTEES, R.S. *Handly Cross.* 1903. Appleton. Ils John Leech. VG. C1. $34.50

SUSANNE. *Famous Saddle Horses.* 1936. Louisville. VG. G1. $30.00

SUSS, M.H. *Stage Magic: Illusions, 6 Complete Plans.* 1951. np. 1st ed. SftCvr. VG. J3. $12.00

SUTCLIFF, Rosemary. *Capricorn Bracelet.* 1973. 1st ed. dj. xl. C1. $8.50

SUTCLIFF, Rosemary. *Hound of Ulster.* 1st Am ed. dj. scarce. EX. C1. $21.50

SUTCLIFF, Rosemary. *Rider on a Wht Horse.* 1959. 1st Am ed. dj. scarce. C1. $12.00

SUTCLIFF, Rosemary. *Silver Branch.* 1963. London. Ils Charles Keeping. dj. EX. C1. $16.00

SUTCLIFF, Rosemary. *Sword at Sunset.* nd. Book Club. HrdCvr ed. VG. C1. $4.00

SUTCLIFF, Rosemary. *Sword at Sunset.* 1964. 1st PB ed. VG. C1. $3.00

SUTHERLAND, Edwin. *Principles of Criminology.* 1939. Lippincott. not 1st ed. 651 p. VG. B10. $4.50

SUTHERLAND, Graham. *Complete Graphic Work.* 1978. Rizzoli. 4to. dj. EX. $40.00

SUTPHEN, V.T. *Doomsman.* 1906. Harper. 1st ed. VG. R3. $27.50

SUTPHEN, V.T. *King's Champion.* 1927. Harper. 1st ed. EX. R3. $15.00

SUTTON, G.M. *At the Bend in the Mexican River.* 1972. NY. Paul Eriksson. 1st ed. 12 clr pls. 184 p. F2. $35.00

SUTTON, Henry. *Vector.* 1970. Bernard Geis. 3rd ed. dj. VG. P1. $10.00

SUTTON, Jeff. *Apollo at Go.* nd. Book Club. dj. xl. P1. $3.00

SUTTON, Jeff. *Atom Conspiracy.* 1963. Avalon. dj. EX. P1. $15.00

SUTTON, Jeff. *Beyond Apollo.* 1967. Gollancz. dj. VG. P1. $17.50

SUTTON, Margaret. *Haunted Attic.* nd. Grosset Dunlap. dj. VG. P1. $7.50

SUTTON, Margaret. *Mysterious Half Cat.* nd. Grosset Dunlap. VG. P1. $7.50

SUTTON, Margaret. *Name on the Bracelet.* nd. Grosset Dunlap. dj. VG. P1. $15.00

SUTTON, Margaret. *Unfinished House.* nd. Grosset Dunlap. VG. P1. $10.00

SUTTON, Margaret. *Vanishing Shadow.* nd. Grosset Dunlap. dj. VG. P1. $7.50

SUTTON, Margaret. *Voice in the Suitcase.* 1935. Grosset Dunlap. G. P1. $10.00

SUTTON, Margaret. *7 Strange Clues.* 1932. Grosset Dunlap. VG. P1. $15.00

SUTTON, R.L. *Silver Kings of AR Pass & Other Stories.* 1937. KS City. sgn. 352 p. dj. EX. scarce. $75.00

SUTTON, S.P. *More Tales To Tremble By.* 1968. Whitman. VG. P1. $7.50

SUYIN, Han. *Enchantress.* 1985. Bantam. 1st ed. dj. M. R3. $16.95

SVETLOFF, Valerian. *Anna Pavlova.* 1922. Paris. De Brunoff. 1st French ed. 1/325. sgn. VG. H3. $750.00

SWADOS, Harvey. *Am Writer & the Great Depression.* 1966. Indianapolis. dj. EX. K2. $35.00

SWAN, Michael. *British Guiana: Land of 6 Peoples.* 1957. London. 1st ed. 235 p. dj. F2. $25.00

SWAN, Michael. *Marches of El Dorado.* 1958. London. Jonathan Cape. 1st ed. dj. F2. $20.00

SWAN, T.B. *Gr Phoenix.* 1972. DAW Books. 1st ed. wrp. EX. F5. $8.00

SWAN, T.B. *Queens Walk in the Dusk.* 1977. Heritage Pr. 1st ed. 1/2000. acetate dj. EX. F5. $35.00

SWANBERG, W.A. *1st Blood.* 1957. Scribner. dj. VG. S1. $7.00

SWANN, T.B. *Forest of Forever.* 1971. PB. VG. C1. $3.50

SWANN, T.B. *Queens Walk in the Dusk.* 1977. Heritage. 1st ed. M. R3. $50.00

SWANSON, N.H. *1st Rebel.* 1937. NY. 1st ed. sgn. VG. $40.00

SWANSON. *Hist of Jefferson Parish.* 1975. Gretna. lg 4to. dj. VG. C2. $35.00

SWARTHMORE COLLEGE FACULTY. *Adventure in Education: Swarthmore College Under Aydelotte.* 1941. Macmillan. 1st ed. 8vo. 236 p. VG. V1. $12.50

SWARTHMORE COLLEGE FACULTY. *Laws of Swarthmore College Relating to Students.* 1883. Lippincott. 24mo. 20 p. pamphlet. VG. V1. $15.00

SWARTHMORE COLLEGE. *Minutes of Proceedings of 2nd Annual Meeting of Corp.* 1866. Phil. Merrihew. 12mo. 12 p. wrp. fair. V1. $12.00

SWARTHMORE COLLEGE. *Minutes of Proceedings of 3rd Annual Meeting of Corp.* 1867. Phil. Merrihew. 12mo. 15 p. wrp. fair. V1. $12.00

SWARTHMORE COLLEGE. *Minutes of Proceedings of 5th Annual Meeting of Corp.* 1869. Phil. Merrihew. 12mo. 15 p. wrp. fair. V1. $12.00

SWARTHMORE COLLEGE. *15th Annual Catalog.* 1883. Friends Bookstore. 8vo. 69 p. wrp. V1. $10.00

SWARTHMORE CONFERENCES. *Proceedings.* 1896. Phil. Franklin Printing. 8vo. 72 p. VG. V1. $16.00

SWARTHOUT, Paul. *Hills Beyond the Hills.* nd. (1971) N Country. 1st ed? 327 p. dj. EX. B10. $7.00

SWEDENBORG, Emanuel. *Works.* c 1900. Houghton Mifflin. Roth ed. 32 vols. octavo. H3. $850.00

SWEET, F.H. *Story of Puss in Boots.* nd. (c 1930s) np. Ils FB Comstock. VG. $45.00

SWEETSER, M.F. *King's Handbook of Boston Harbor.* 1882. Cambridge. Ils Copeland. 12mo. VG. A4. $60.00

SWEETSER, M.F. *King's Handbook of the US.* c 1891. Buffalo, NY. 12mo. 51 clr maps. 939 p. G. G4. $29.00

SWENSON, John. *Beatles Yesterday & Today.* 1977. Zebra. PB. VG. B4. $3.50

SWIFT, Jonathan. *Gulliver's Travels.* nd. (1910) Chicago. Young Folks Classic Series. 175 p. VG. $40.00

SWIFT, Jonathan. *Gulliver's Travels.* 1909. London/NY. Ils/sgn Rackham. Lg Paper ed. TEG. rebound. EX. $425.00

SWIFT, Jonathan. *Gulliver's Travels.* 1979. Franklin Lib. Ils Morten. M. C1. $19.50

SWIFT, Jonathan. *Modest Proposal.* 1969. NY. Ils Baskin. EX. $30.00

SWIGGETT, Howard. *Extraordinary Mr Morris.* 1952. NY. 1st ed. EX. $12.00

SWINBURNE, A.C. *Note of an Eng Republican.* 1876. London. 1st ed. orig wrp. EX. $50.00

SWINBURNE, A.C. *Posthumous Poems.* 1918. London/NY. 1st ed. dj. EX. scarce. C1. $17.00

SWINBURNE, A.C. *Tale of Balen.* 1896. London. 1st ed. VG. C1. $89.00

SWINFORD, Paul. *Faro Fantasy/More Faro Fantasy.* 1968 & 1971. Haley Pr. 1st ed. 2 vols. w/cards. NM. J3. $8.00

SWINFORD, Paul. *Lecture Notes.* 1971. Oakland, CA. Busby. 2nd ed. 12 p. NM. J3. $4.00

SWINTON, William. *Campaigns of the Army of the Potomac.* 1866. NY. 1st ed. VG. $45.00

SWISHER, J.A. *IA Department of Grand Army of the Republic.* 1936. IA City. 194 p. VG. S1. $25.00

SWORD, W. *Shiloh Bloody April.* 1974. NY. 1st ed. dj. VG. B3. $45.00

SYLVA, Carmen. *Letters & Poems of Queen Elizabeth.* 1920. Bibliophile Soc. 2 vols. 8vo. VG. T6. $45.00

SYLVESTER, Martin. *Lethal Vintage.* 1988. Villard. 1st ed. dj. EX. F5. $12.00

SYLVESTER, S.H. *Taxidermist's Manual.* 1865. Middleboro, MA. 3rd ed. VG. $15.00

SYLVESTER, W.A. *Modern House: Carpenter's Companion & Building Guide.* c1883. Boston. 8vo. 210 p. VG. $40.00

SYMONDS, J.A. *Problem in Greek Ethics.* 1901. London. private print. 1st ed. 1/100. EX. B13. $100.00

SYMONDS, J.A. *Problem in Modern Ethics.* 1896. London. private print. 1st ed. 1/100. EX. B13. $100.00

SYMONDS, J.A. *Shelley.* 1884. London. 8vo. $40.00

SYMONDS, R.W. *Thomas Tompion: Life & Work.* 1951. London. 1st ed. 320 p. dj. VG. B3. $70.00

SYMONDS & WHINERAY. *Victorian Furniture.* 1965. London. Country Life. 2nd print. 4to. 232 p. dj. EX. $25.00

SYMONS, A.J.A. *Emin: Governor of Equatoria.* 1928. London. Fleuron. Ltd ed. 1/300. sgn. H3. $100.00

SYMONS, A.J.A. *Episode in the Life of the Queen of Sheba.* 1929. private print. 1st ed. 1/125. inscr. scarce. H3. $175.00

SYMONS, A.J.A. *Quest for Corvo.* 1934. Macmillan. 1st ed. dj. EX. H3. $50.00

SYMONS, Arthur. *Knave of Hearts.* 1913. NY. Lane. 1st ed. dj. EX. B13. $75.00

SYMONS, Arthur. *Toy Cart.* 1919. Dublin/London. 1st ed. dj. EX. H3. $30.00

SYMONS, Arthur. *Tristan & Iseult: Play in 4 Acts.* 1917. NY. 1st Am ed. VG. C1. $49.50

SYMONS, Julian. *Criminal Acts.* nd. BOMC. dj. VG. P1. $10.00

SYMONS, Julian. *End of Solomon Grundy?* 1964. Collins Crime Club. 1st ed. dj. EX. P1. $20.00

SYMONS, Julian. *Man Whose Dreams Came True.* 1968. Harper Row. 1st ed. dj. VG. P1. $17.50

SYMONS, Julian. *Verdict of 13.* 1979. Harper Row. 1st ed. dj. EX. P1. $15.00

SYMONS, T.W. *Report of Examination of Upper Columbia River...* 1882. GPO. 133 p. A5. $120.00

SZARKOWSKI, John. *Irving Penn.* nd. MOMA. 4to. dj. EX. $40.00

SZARKOWSKI, John. *Winogrand: Figments From the Real World.* 1988. MOMA. D4. $30.00

SZEWCZYK, David. *Calendar of Peruvian & Other S Am Manuscripts...* 1977. Phil. 1st ed. 4to. 190 p. F2. $35.00

SZEWCZYK, David. *Viceroyalty of New Spain & Early Independent Mexico.* 1980. Phil. 1st ed. 4to. 139 p. F2. $30.00

SZIGETI, Joseph. *With Strings Attached.* 1949. Cassell. 1st ed. 323 p. dj. EX. B10. $6.50

SZOLNOKI, Rose. *Namath: My Son Joe.* 1975. Oxmoor House. sgn. 131 p. $35.00

TABER, Gladys. *Evergreen Tree.* 1937. Phil. 1st ed. dj. VG. B3. $95.00

TABER, Gladys. *Mrs Daffodil.* 1957. Phil. 1st ed. dj. VG. B3. $60.00

TABER, Gladys. *Stillmeadow Cookbook.* 1965. Phil. 1st ed. dj. VG. B3. $35.00

TABER, Gladys. *What Cooks at Stillmeadow.* 1958. Phil. 1st ed. dj. G. B3. $45.00

TABER, Gladys. *1st Book of Dogs.* 1949. NY. dj. VG. B3. $40.00

TACK, Alfred. *Spy Who Wasn't Exchanged.* 1970. Mystery Book Guild. dj. VG. P1. $5.00

TAFT, Lorado. *Hist of Am Sculpture.* 1924. NY. New Revised/1st ed. 8vo. 604 p. dj. EX. T1. $45.00

TAFT, R. *Artists & Ils of the Old W.* 1975. Bonanza. reprint. dj. EX. $20.00

TAGGART. *Hist of 3rd Infantry Division WWII.* 1947. WA. 1st ed. 574 p. G. B3. $105.00

TAGORE, Rabindranath. *Crescent Moon.* 1920. Child Poems. 1st ed. sgn. G. B13. $35.00

TAINE, H.A. *Hist of Eng Literature.* 1877. Chatto Windus. Trans Von Laun. New ed. A4. $50.00

TAINE, John. *Cosmic Geoids.* 1950. Fantasy. 1st bdg. dj. VG. R3. $17.50

TAINE, John. *Crystal Horde.* 1952. Fantasy. Ltd ed. 1/300. sgn. dj. EX. R3. $70.00

TAINE, John. *Crystal Horde.* 1952. Fantasy. 1st ed. dj. P1/R3. $25.00

TAINE, John. *Forbidden Garden.* 1947. Fantasy. Ltd ed. 1/500. sgn. dj. EX. R3. $60.00

TAINE, John. *Forbidden Garden.* 1947. Fantasy. 1st ed. dj. EX. R3. $25.00

TAINE, John. *Forbidden Garden.* 1947. Fantasy. 1st ed. VG. P1. $17.50

TAINE, John. *Gold Tooth.* 1927. Dutton. 1st ed. dj. VG. R3. $100.00

TAINE, John. *Gr Fire.* 1928. Dutton. 1st ed. VG. R3. $40.00

TAINE, John. *Gr Fire.* 1952. Fantasy. 1st bdg. dj. EX. R3. $27.50

TAINE, John. *Iron Star.* 1951. Fantasy. 1st bdg. 2 djs as issued. VG. R3. $30.00

TAINE, John. *Iron Star.* 1976. Hyperion. reprint of 1930 ed. M. R3. $15.00

TAINE, John. *Queen of the Sciences.* 1931. Williams. 1st ed. dj. EX. R3. $40.00

TAINE, John. *Seeds of Life.* 1951. Fantasy. Ltd ed. 1/300. sgn. dj. EX. R3. $70.00

TAINE, John. *Seeds of Life.* 1951. Fantasy. 1st ed. dj. VG. P1. $35.00

TAIPEI, Taiwan. *Chinese Cultural Art Treasures Ils Handbook.* 1976. Republic of China. 10th ed. Eng text. D4. $20.00

TAKI, Seiichi. *Japanese Fine Art.* 1931. Tokyo. 1st ed. dj. EX. G1. $50.00

TALBERT, Ernest. *Old Countries Discovered Anew.* nd. (1913) Boston. Estes. apparent 1st ed. 396 p. VG. B10. $8.25

TALBOT, E. *My People of the Plains.* 1906. Harper. Ils. 265 p. A5. $40.00

TALBOT, F.A. *Motion Pictures: How They Are Made & Worked.* 1912. Phil/London. Ils. 340 p. VG. $100.00

TALBOT, F.A. *Moving Pictures: How They Are Made & Worked.* 1923. Phil. Ils. 429 p. $50.00

TALBOT, F.A. *Practical Cinematography & Its Applications.* 1913. Lippincott. 1st ed. sm octavo. 262 p. VG. H3. $125.00

TALBOT, Michael. *Bog.* 1986. Morrow. 1st ed. dj. EX. F5. $20.00

TALESE, Gay. *Honor Thy Father.* nd. Book Club. dj. VG. P1. $4.50

TALLMADGE, T. *Architecture in Old Chicago.* 1941. Chicago. 1st ed. 218 p. dj. VG. B3. $45.00

TALMAN, W.B. *Normal Lovecraft.* 1973. De La Ree. 1st ed. wrp. EX. R3. $20.00

TAMARIZ, Juan. *Magic Way.* 1988. Madrid. 1st ed. 187 p. dj. M. J3. $45.00

TAMAYO, Rufino. *Works on Paper 1926 to Present.* 1979. NY. Ils. wrp. F2. $5.00

TAMAYO, Rufino. *50 Years of Paintings.* 1978. NY. 1st ed. sm 4to. wrp. F2. $20.00

TAN, Amy. *Joy Luck Club.* 1989. Putnam. 1st ed. 1st print. inscr. dj. EX. B13. $150.00

TAN, Amy. *Kitchen God's Wife.* 1991. NY. 1st ed. sgn. dj. M. C4. $50.00

TANAKA, Yusaku. *No Costumes of Japan 1573-1829.* nd. np. 95 pls. portfolio. VG. H3. $250.00

TANIZAKI, Junichiro. *Cat, a Man, & 2 Women.* 1990. Tokyo/NY. Kodansha. ARC. glossy wrp. EX. B13. $45.00

TANIZAKI, Junichiro. *Diary of an Old Man.* 1965. Knopf. 1st ed. clipped dj. EX. B13. $50.00

TARBELL, Harlan. *Tarbell Course in Magic Vol 1.* 1941. NY. Revised ed. 408 p. VG. T1. $40.00

TARBELL, Harlan. *Tarbell Course in Magic Vol 1.* 1942. NL Magic Co. Revised ed. 2nd print. 408 p. EX. J3. $12.00

TARBELL, Harlan. *Tarbell Course in Magic Vol 1.* 1971. NY. Tannen. Revised ed. 9th print. dj. NM. J3. $16.00

TARBELL, Harlan. *Tarbell Course in Magic Vol 2.* 1942. NY. NL Magic Co. 1st HrdCvr ed. 407 p. dj. NM. J3. $16.00

TARBELL, Harlan. *Tarbell Course in Magic Vol 2.* 1946. NY. Tannen. 3rd print. 407 p. EX. J3. $12.00

TARBELL, Harlan. *Tarbell Course in Magic Vol 5.* 1948. NY. Tannen. Revised ed. 2nd print. VG. J3. $12.00

TARBELL, Harlan. *Tarbell Course in Magic Vol 6.* 1954. NY. Tannen. 1st ed. 3rd print. 409 p. dj. NM. J3. $16.00

TARBELL, I.M. *In the Footsteps of the Lincolns.* 1924. Harper. 418 p. G. S1. $22.50

TARBELL, I.M. *Lincoln's Chair.* 1920. Macmillan. 1st ed. 55 p. dj. VG. B10. $5.50

TARG, William. *Bibliophile in the Nursery.* 1957. Cleveland. 1st ed. dj. EX. $60.00

TARKINGTON, Booth. *Gentle Julia.* 1922. Doubleday. early ed. inscr. dj. H3. $200.00

TARKINGTON, Booth. *Gentleman From IN.* 1899. Doubleday McClure. 1st ed. 1st issue. sgn. gr morocco slipcase. H3. $350.00

TARKINGTON, Booth. *Gentleman From IN.* 1935. NY. 1-By-1 ed. presentation. EX. $85.00

TARKINGTON, Booth. *Guest of Quesnay.* 1908. McClurg. 1st ed. 335 p. VG. B10. $10.00

TARKINGTON, Booth. *Image of Josephine.* 1945. Garden City. 1st ed. presentation. G. $75.00

TARKINGTON, Booth. *Penrod & Sam.* 1916. Doubleday Page. 1st ed. later state. sgn. TEG. H3. $250.00

TARKINGTON, Booth. *Seventeen.* nd. Grosset Dunlap. VG. P1. $5.00

TARKINGTON, Booth. *Some Old Portraits.* 1939. Doubleday. 1/247. inscr. boxed. VG. $100.00

TARKINGTON, Booth. *2 Vanrevels.* 1902. London. 1st UK ed. G. $45.00

TARKINGTON, Booth. *2 Vanrevels.* 1902. McClure Phillips. Deluxe Ltd ed. 1/500. sgn. TEG. H3. $125.00

TARR, Bill. *Now You See It, Now You Don't...* 1976. Vintage Books. 224 p. EX. J3. $9.00

TARR, Judith. *Dagger & the Cross.* 1991. Doubleday. 1st ed. dj. EX. F5. $15.00

TARR, Judith. *Golden Horn.* 1985. Bluejay. 1st ed. dj. EX. R3. $17.50

TARRANT, John. *Clauberg Trigger.* 1979. Atheneum. 1st ed. dj. EX. P1. $15.00

TATE, Allen. *Fathers.* 1938. Putnam. 1st ed. dj. VG. $50.00

TATE, Allen. *Jefferson Davis: His Rise & Fall.* 1929. NY. 1st ed. VG. B3. $32.50

TATE, Allen. *Jefferson Davis: His Rise & Fall.* 1929. NY. 1st ed. 1st state. dj. EX. $70.00

TATE, Peter. *Country Love & Poison Rain.* 1973. Doubleday. 1st ed. dj. EX. R3. $10.00

TATE, Peter. *Faces in the Flames.* 1976. Doubleday. 1st ed. dj. VG. P1. $12.50

TATE, Peter. *Greencomber.* 1979. Doubleday. 1st ed. dj. EX. P1. $12.50

TATE, Peter. *Moon on an Iron Meadow.* 1974. Doubleday. 1st ed. dj. VG. P1. $12.50

TATE & AGAR. *Who Owns America?* 1936. Houghton Mifflin. 1st ed. sgns. dj. EX. B13. $1850.00

TATHAM, Julie. *Cherry Ames, Country Doctor's Nurse.* nd. Grosset Dunlap. dj. VG. P1. $6.00

TATHAM, Julie. *Cherry Ames, Dude Ranch Nurse.* nd. Grosset Dunlap. dj. VG. P1. $6.00

TATHAM, Julie. *Cherry Ames, Rest Home Nurse.* nd. Grosset Dunlap. dj. VG. P1. $6.00

TATHAM, Julie. *Cherry Ames at Spencer.* nd. Grosset Dunlap. dj. VG. P1. $6.00

TATLOCK & MACKAYE. *Complete Poetical Works of Geoffrey Chaucer.* 1912. NY. 1st ed. sm 4to. VG. T1. $90.00

TATUM, F.C. *Old Westtown.* 1888. Phil. Ferris Bros. 8vo. 151 p. G. V1. $22.00

TAUB, Jacob. *Doc & His Deck.* 1976. NY. Tannen. 2nd print. dj. NM. J3. $13.00

TAUBE, Karl. *Albers Collection of Pre-Columbian Art.* 1988. Hudson Hills. 1st ed. 176 p. dj. F2. $35.00

TAUSSIG, C.W. *Philip Kappel.* 1929. Hutson/Colnaghi. spine missing. D4. $35.00

TAVERNER, H.T. *Charles Dickens: Story of His Life.* 1870. Harper. 1st Am ed. 8vo. H3. $75.00

TAYLOR, Anna. *Drustan the Wanderer.* 1971. NY. 1st ed. dj. EX. scarce. C1. $17.00

TAYLOR, B.C. *Annals...of Bergen of Reformed Dutch Church...* 1857. NY. Ils. 479 p. G. A5. $45.00

TAYLOR, B.F. *Pictures of Life in Camp & Field.* 1875. Chicago. 2nd ed. T5. $45.00

TAYLOR, Bayard. *Travels in Arabia.* 1883. Scribner. VG. J2. $10.00

TAYLOR, Bernard. *Kindness of Strangers.* 1985. St Martin. 1st ed. dj. EX. F5. $16.00

TAYLOR, Bernard. *Moorstone Sickness.* 1982. St Martin. 1st ed. dj. EX. F5. $20.00

TAYLOR, Charles. *Samuel Tuke: His Life, Work, & Thoughts.* 1909. London. Headley. 12mo. 283 p. G. V1. $9.00

TAYLOR, Deems. *Treasury of Stephen Foster.* 1946. Random House Book Club. Ils William Sharp. 222 p. G. B10. $7.00

TAYLOR, E.E. *Cameos From the Life of George Fox.* nd. London. Headley. 12mo. 119 p. G. V1. $12.50

TAYLOR, F.R. *Life of William Savery of Phil 1750-1804.* 1925. Macmillan. 1st print. 474 p. dj. VG. V1. $9.00

TAYLOR, Gerald. *Classical Technique of Fire Eating.* 1980. Calgary. 43 p. SftCvr. EX. J3. $7.00

TAYLOR, H.O. *Medieval Mind.* 1949. Harvard. 4th ed. 5th print. 2 vols. VG. C1. $15.00

TAYLOR, Isaac. *Orig of the Aryans.* 1890. NY. xl. fair. $8.00

TAYLOR, Jane; see Taylor, Anna.

TAYLOR, John. *African Rifles & Cartridges.* 1948. Georgetown, SC. 1st ed. G. B3. $80.00

TAYLOR, M.I. *Rebellion of the Princess.* 1903. McClure Phillips. 1st ed. B10. $6.50

TAYLOR, Norman. *Clr in the Garden.* 1953. Van Nostrand. Book Club ed. dj. EX. B10. $4.00

TAYLOR, P.A. *Going, Going, Gone.* nd. Norton. 1st ed. dj. VG. P1. $25.00

TAYLOR, P.A. *3 Plots for Asey Mayo.* 1942. Norton. 1st ed. dj. VG. P1. $25.00

TAYLOR, Peter. *Collected Stories.* 1969. Farrar Straus Giroux. 1st ed. sgn. dj. EX. K2. $150.00

TAYLOR, Peter. *Collected Stories.* 1969. NY. ARC. presentation. dj. w/pub slip. EX. T9. $175.00

TAYLOR, Peter. *Fugitives, Agrarians, & Other 20th-Century S Writers.* 1985. Charlottesville. sm pamphlet. wrp. EX. K2. $20.00

TAYLOR, Peter. *Happy Families Are All Alike.* 1959. McDowell Obolensky. 1st ed. sgn. dj. EX. K2. $125.00

TAYLOR, Peter. *In the Miro District & Other Stories.* 1977. Chatto Windus. 1st UK ed. sgn. dj. H3. $65.00

TAYLOR, Peter. *In the Miro District.* 1977. Knopf. 1st ed. dj. EX. B13. $65.00

TAYLOR, Peter. *Miss Leonora When Last Seen.* 1963. Obolensky. ARC. sgn. dj. RS. EX. B13. $400.00

TAYLOR, Peter. *Old Forest & Other Stories.* 1985. Dial Doubleday. UP. wrp. VG. K2. $75.00

TAYLOR, Peter. *Summons to Memphis.* 1986. Knopf. 1st ed. sgn. dj. EX. K2. $100.00

TAYLOR, Peter. *Summons to Memphis.* 1986. NY. Knopf. UP. sgn. wrp. EX. K2. $200.00

TAYLOR, Peter. *TN Day in St Louis.* 1957. NY. 1st ed. inscr. as issued. K2. $175.00

TAYLOR, R.L. *WC Fields: His Follies & Fortunes.* 1949. NY. 1st ed. dj. VG. $18.00

TAYLOR, Richard. *Destruction & Reconstruction: Personal Experiences...* 1879. NY. 1st ed. 8vo. 274 p. G. G4. $55.00

TAYLOR, Robert. *Indians of Middle Am: Intro to Ethnology of Mexico...* 1989. Lifeway Books. 1st ed. 304 p. F2. $25.00

TAYLOR, T. *Magnificent Mitscher.* 1954. NY. 1st ed. dj. VG. B3. $50.00

TAYLOR, Tony. *Spotlight on 101 Great Magic Acts.* 1964. Calgary. 1st ed. 88 p. VG. J3. $7.00

TAYLOR, Valerie. *Girls in 3B.* 1965. Gold Medal. EX. B4. $12.00

TAYLOR, William. *Landlord & Peasant in Colonial Oaxaca.* 1972. Stanford. 1st ed. 287 p. dj. F2. $20.00

TAYLOR, William. *Our S Am Cousins.* 1878. Nelson Phillips. 1st ed. 12mo. 318 p. F2. $30.00

TAYLOR & TAYLOR. *OH Statesmen & Annals of Progress 1788-1900.* 1899. Columbus. 2 vols in 1. T5. $22.50

TEAGUE, E.H. *Henry Moore: Bibliography & Reproductions Index.* 1981. McFarland. 165 p. dj. EX. D4. $15.00

TEALE, E.W. *Journey Into Summer*. 1960. Dodd Mead. 3rd ed. 366 p. dj. VG. B10. $3.75

TEASDALE, Sara. *Rainbow Gold: Poems Old & New*. 1923. Macmillan. Ils Dugland Walker. 8vo. 267 p. VG. $18.00

TEBBEL, John. *George WA's Am*. 1954. Dutton. 1st ed. 478 p. dj. VG. B10. $6.50

TEECE, Henry. *Red Queen, Wht Queen*. 1958. 1st Am ed. dj. EX. C1. $14.00

TEED, G.H. *Shadow Crook*. 1956. Miller. 1st ed. dj. VG. P1. $17.50

TEGNER, Esaias. *Frithiof's Saga*. 1953. Ltd Ed Club. Ils/sgn Eric Palmquist. 4to. slipcase. EX. C4. $40.00

TEICHMANN, Howard. *George S Kaufman: Intimate Portrait*. 1972. NY. 1st ed. VG. $10.00

TEMIANKA, Henri. *Facing the Music*. 1973. McKay. octavo. 272 p. dj. EX. H3. $20.00

TEMPLE, Lynn. *Navajo Escapade*. 1974. NY. Vantage. 1st ed. dj. EX. K2. $45.00

TEMPLE, W.F. *4-Sided Triangle*. nd. London. 1st ed. sgn. dj. EX. R3. $25.00

TEMPLETON, R.H. *Quick Brn Fox*. 1945. Chicago. 1st ed. 1/450. EX. $20.00

TENN, William. *Children of Wonder*. nd. Book Club. dj. VG. P1. $7.50

TENN & WESTLAKE. *Once Against the Law*. 1968. Macmillan. 1st ed. dj. EX. P1. $25.00

TENNYSON, Alfred. *Enoch Arden*. 1865. Ticknor Fields. 9th ed. 204 p. VG. B10. $12.50

TENNYSON, Alfred. *Geraint & Enid*. nd. London. Ils Shaw. 1st ed. EX. $85.00

TENNYSON, Alfred. *Holy Grail & Other Poems*. 1870. Boston. 1st Am ed. VG. $35.00

TENNYSON, Alfred. *Holy Grail & Other Poems*. 1870. London. 1st ed. C1. $8.50

TENNYSON, Alfred. *In Memoriam*. nd. Altemus. 12mo. 182 p. decor gr bdg. VG. $7.50

TENNYSON, Alfred. *In Memoriam*. 1933. London. Nonesuch. 1/2000. slipcase. EX. $75.00

TENNYSON, Alfred. *Maud*. 1855. Boston. 1st Am ed. VG. $95.00

TENNYSON, Alfred. *Poems: Selected & Intro by John D Rosenberg*. 1974. Cambridge. Ltd Ed Club. Ils/sgn Reynolds Stone. 1/2000. slipcase. EX. C4. $75.00

TENNYSON, Alfred. *Poetical Works*. 1885. Chicago. Arundel Poets Series. B10. $5.50

TENNYSON, Alfred. *Works*. 1907-1908. London. Eversley ed. 12mo. 9 vols. EX. T1. $175.00

TEPPER, S.S. *Northshore: Awakeners Vol 1*. 1987. Tor Books. 1st ed. dj. EX. P1. $14.95

TERHUNE, A.P. *Real Tales of Real Dogs*. 1935. Akron, OH/NY. Ils Thorne. 1st ed. lg 4to. VG. $40.00

TERHUNE, A.P. *Runaway Bag*. nd. AL Burt. G. P1. $5.00

TERHUNE, A.P. *Story of Damon & Pythias*. 1915. Grosset Dunlap. Photoplay ed. dj. VG. P1. $35.00

TERHUNE, A.P. *Syria From the Saddle*. 1896. NY. 1st ed. 318 p. VG. B3. $65.00

TERHUNE, A.P. *True Dog Stories*. 1936. Akron, OH/NY. Ils Thorne. 1st ed. VG. $20.00

TERKEL, Studs. *Good War*. 1984. NY. 1st ed. inscr. dj. EX. $35.00

TERMAN, Douglas. *Free Flight*. 1980. Scribner. 1st ed. dj. EX. F5. $16.00

TERMAN, Douglas. *1st Strike*. 1979. Scribner. UP. wrp. EX. F5. $20.00

TERMAN, Douglas. *1st Strike*. 1979. Scribner. 1st ed. dj. EX. F5. $13.00

TERRALL, Robert. *They Deal in Death*. 1944. Books Inc. VG. P1. $12.50

TERRANOVA, Elaine. *Cult of the Right Hand*. 1991. Doubleday. ARC. dj. M. B13. $25.00

TERRELL, J.U. *Bunkhouse Papers*. 1971. NY. 1st ed. 251 p. dj. VG. B3. $25.00

TERRELL, J.U. *War for the CO River*. 1965. Glendale, CA. Clarke. 1st ed. 2 vols. VG. T5. $65.00

TERRES, J.K. *Audubon Book of True Nature Stories*. 1958. NY. 1st ed. dj. VG. $8.00

TERRES, J.K. *Songbirds in Your Garden*. 1968. NY. Ils Kalmenoff. dj. VG. $8.00

TERRY, Edward. *Artists & Writers in the Evolution of Latin Am*. 1971. AL U. 2nd print. 191 p. dj. F2. $15.00

TERRY, Ellen. *Russian Ballet*. 1913. Bobbs Merrill. 1st Am ed. octavo. 52 p. EX. H3. $125.00

TERRY, Ellen. *Story of My Life*. 1908. McClure. 1st ed. octavo. 407 p. VG. H3. $50.00

TERWILLIGER, C. *Horolovar 400-Day Clock Repair Guide*. 1965. Bronxville. 5th ed. dj. VG. $20.00

TESSIER, Thomas. *Finishing Touches*. 1986. Atheneum. 1st ed. dj. EX. F5. $35.00

TEVETH, S. *Banks of Tammuz*. 1969. Viking. dj. VG. J2. $12.00

TEVIS, Walter. *Man Who Fell to Earth*. 1963. Fawcett. 1st ed. wrp. EX. F5. $25.00

TEVIS, Walter. *Steps of the Sun*. 1983. Doubleday. 1st ed. dj. RS. EX. P1. $20.00

TEY, Josephine. *Franchise Affair*. 1959. Peter Davis. 4th print. dj. VG. P1. $7.50

TEY, Josephine. *Miss Pym Disposes*. 1946. London. Peter Davis. 1st ed. VG. T9. $25.00

TEY, Josephine. *Shilling for Candles*. 1954. Macmillan. 2nd print. VG. P1. $12.00

THACKERAY, W.M. *Complete Works*. 1904. Harper. 26 vols. octavo. VG. H3. $350.00

THACKERAY, W.M. *Rose & the Ring*. 1942. NY. Ltd Ed Club. Ils Titmarsh/Kredel. 1/1500. folio. slipcase. C4. $40.00

THACKERAY, W.M. *Thackeray Alphabet*. 1930. Harper. 1st ed.d 16mo. dj. VG. $25.00

THACKERAY, W.M. *Thackerayana*. 1875. London. 8vo. VG. $50.00

THACKERAY, W.M. *Vanity Fair*. 1847-1848. London. 1st ed. 40 pls. orig wrp. w/orig drawings. H3. $4500.00

THACKERAY, W.M. *Works*. 1869. London. Smith Elder. 22 vols. H3. $1000.00

THACKERAY, W.M. *Works*. 1901. London. Smith Elder. 1/1000. 26 vols. octavo. H3. $1250.00

THANE, Elswyth. *Homing*. 1957. Duell. 1st ed. 272 p. dj. VG. B10. $4.00

THANE, Elswyth. *Yankee Stranger*. 1944. Peoples Book Club. 306 p. dj. B10. $6.25

THANET, Octave. *Stories of a W Town*. 1893. NY. Ils Frost. 1st ed. VG. B3. $45.00

THATCHER, B.B. *Memoir of Phillis Wheatley: Native African & Slave*. 1834. Boston. 2nd ed. 16mo. A4. $125.00

THAW, H.K. *Traitor*. 1926. Phil. Dorance. 8vo. 271 p. dj. EX. $25.00

THAYER, Eli. *Hist of the KS Crusade: Its Friends & Foes*. 1889. NY. 1st ed. VG. $80.00

THAYER, J.S. *Hess Cross*. 1977. Putnam. 1st ed. dj. EX. P1. $15.00

THAYER, J.S. *Pursuit*. 1986. Crown. 1st ed. dj. VG. P1. $12.50

THAYER, Theodore. *Israel Pemberton: King of the Quakers.* 1943. Hist Soc PA. 1st ed. 8vo. 260 p. VG. V1. $14.00

THAYER, W.M. *Marvels of the New W.* 1889. Norwich, CT. Ils. 715 p. VG. A5. $80.00

THAYER, W.R. *Life & Letters of John Hay.* nd. (1915) Houghton. 5th impression. 2 vols. VG. B10. $11.50

THEIRS, M.A. *Hist of French Revolution.* 1838. London. Ils. 8vo. 5 vols. gilt half leather. VG. T1. $80.00

THELWELL, Norman. *Thelwell.* 1989. London. Chris Beetles. D4. $15.00

THEOCRITOS. *Complete Poems.* 1929. London. Fanfrolico. Ils/sgn Lionel Ellis. 1/30. full vellum. EX. H3. $850.00

THEROUX, Alexander. *3 Wogs.* 1972. Gambit. 1st ed. dj. EX. C4. $75.00

THEROUX, Paul. *Blk House.* 1974. Houghton Mifflin. 1st Am ed. dj. H3. $75.00

THEROUX, Paul. *Blk House.* 1974. London. 1st UK ed. dj. EX. K2. $85.00

THEROUX, Paul. *Christmas Card.* 1978. Houghton Mifflin. 1st ed. dj. EX. B13. $85.00

THEROUX, Paul. *Family Arsenal.* 1976. Houghton Mifflin. 1st Am ed. sgn. dj. H3. $60.00

THEROUX, Paul. *Girls at Play.* 1969. Boston. 1st ed. dj. EX. $35.00

THEROUX, Paul. *Girls at Play.* 1969. Houghton Mifflin. 1st ed. 209 p. dj. VG. B10. $10.00

THEROUX, Paul. *Half Moon St.* 1984. Houghton Mifflin. sgn. dj. H3. $75.00

THEROUX, Paul. *Jungle Lovers.* 1971. Boston. 1st ed. dj. EX. $35.00

THEROUX, Paul. *Kingdom by the Sea.* 1983. Houghton Mifflin. 1st Am ed. dj. H3. $75.00

THEROUX, Paul. *London Snow: A Christmas Story.* 1979. Salisbury. Russell. Ltd Sgn ed. 1/450. glassine wrp. H3. $100.00

THEROUX, Paul. *London Snow: A Christmas Story.* 1979. Salisbury. Russell. 1st ed. 1/450. sgn. w/pub prospectus. K2. $75.00

THEROUX, Paul. *Mosquito Coast.* 1982. Houghton Mifflin. Book Club ed. 374 p. F2. $10.00

THEROUX, Paul. *Mosquito Coast.* 1982. Houghton Mifflin. Ltd ed. 1/350. sgn. boxed. H3. $100.00

THEROUX, Paul. *Mosquito Coast.* 1982. Houghton Mifflin. 1st Am ed. dj. H3. $50.00

THEROUX, Paul. *My Secret Hist.* 1989. London. 1st ed. as issued. EX. K2. $30.00

THEROUX, Paul. *My Secret Hist.* 1989. London. Hamond. 1st ed. sgn. dj. EX. B13. $95.00

THEROUX, Paul. *Old Patagonian Express.* 1979. Houghton Mifflin. Book Club ed. 404 p. F2. $10.00

THEROUX, Paul. *Old Patagonian Express.* 1979. Houghton Mifflin. 1st Am ed. dj. H3. $75.00

THEROUX, Paul. *Ozone.* 1986. Putnam. 1st ed. dj. EX. P1. $19.95

THEROUX, Paul. *Sailing Through China.* 1984. Houghton Mifflin. 1st ed. dj. EX. K2. $20.00

THEROUX, Paul. *St Jack.* 1973. Boston. 1st ed. dj. VG. B3. $35.00

THEROUX, Paul. *Waldo.* 1967. NY. 1st ed. dj. EX. T9. $60.00

THEROUX & CHATWIN. *Patagonia Revisited.* 1985. Salisbury. Russell. Ltd ed. 1/250. sgns. glassine dj. H3. $125.00

THEROUX & CHATWIN. *Patagonia Revisited.* 1986. Houghton Mifflin. 1st ed. sgn. dj. EX. K2. $45.00

THESLEFF, Holger. *Farewell Windjammer.* 1951. London. Thames Hudson. 1st ed. 240 p. dj. EX. B10. $15.00

THETARD, Henry. *Merveilleuse Hist du Cirque.* 1947. Paris. Prisma. 2 vols. (vol 2 in dj) scarce. H3. $250.00

THIESSEN, Grant. *SF Collector Vol 1.* 1980. Pandora. Ltd HrdCvr ed. 1/140. sgn. EX. P1. $25.00

THIGPEN & CLECKLEY. *3 Faces of Eve.* 1957. Secker Warburg. presentation. dj. H3. $125.00

THOMAS, A.B. *Richard H Thomas, MD: Life & Letters.* 1905. Phil. Winston. 12mo. 438 p. G. V1. $10.00

THOMAS, A.B. *St Stephen's House: Friends' Emergency Work in Eng...1920.* nd. London. Emergency Com. 8vo. 151 p. glassine dj. EX. V1. $10.00

THOMAS, A.B. *Story of Baltimore Yearly Meeting From 1672 to 1938.* nd. Baltimore. Weant Pr. 12mo. 142 p. G. V1. $15.00

THOMAS, A.C. *Edward Lawrence Scull: A Brief Memoir...* 1891. Riverside. 8vo. 156 p. VG. V1. $14.00

THOMAS, A.L.B. *Nancy Lloyd: Journal of Quaker Pioneer.* 1927. Frank Maurice Inc. 8vo. 192 p. VG. V1. $10.00

THOMAS, Abel. *Brief Memoir Concerning Abel Thomas.* 1824. Benjamin/Kite. 12mo. 51 p. xl. V1. $15.00

THOMAS, Augustus. *Witching Hour.* 1908. Harper. 1st ed. inscr. EX. F5. $60.00

THOMAS, Bertram. *Alarms & Excursions in Arabia.* 1931. Bobbs Merrill. 1st ed. 296 p. VG. J2. $20.00

THOMAS, Bob. *King Cohn: Life & Times of Harry Cohn.* 1967. London. Barrie. 1st ed. 381 p. dj. NM. B10. $8.25

THOMAS, Craig. *Firefox Down.* 1983. Bantam. 1st ed. dj. EX. P1. $20.00

THOMAS, Craig. *Firefox.* 1977. Holt Rinehart Winston. 1st ed. dj. EX. P1. $25.00

THOMAS, Craig. *Sea Leopard.* 1981. Viking. 1st ed. dj. EX. F5. $16.00

THOMAS, Craig. *Winter Hawk.* 1987. Collins. 1st ed. dj. EX. P1. $20.00

THOMAS, Donald. *Mad Hatter Summer.* 1983. 1st ed. dj. VG. C1. $8.50

THOMAS, Dylan. *Adventures in the Skin Trade.* 1968. New Directions. 1st ed. dj. EX. H3. $50.00

THOMAS, Dylan. *Child's Christmas in Wales.* c 1954. New Directions. 1st Separate ed. dj. EX. $40.00

THOMAS, Dylan. *Map of Love. Verse & Prose.* 1939. London. Dent. sgn. dj. H3. $750.00

THOMAS, Dylan. *Me & My Bike.* 1965. NY. Ils Leonora Box. 1st Trade ed. dj. T5. $47.50

THOMAS, Dylan. *Notebooks of Dylan Thomas.* 1967. New Directions. 1st ed. dj. EX. C4. $50.00

THOMAS, Dylan. *Under Milk Wood.* 1954. New Directions. 1st Am ed. dj. EX. H3. $75.00

THOMAS, E.M. *Confederate Nation 1861-1865.* 1977. NY. 1st ed. dj. EX. $25.00

THOMAS, E.M. *Selected Poems.* 1926. London/NY. Harper. Stated 1st ed. EX. $35.00

THOMAS, Edward. *Quaker Adventures.* 1928. NY. Revell. 8vo. 221 p. VG. V1. $9.00

THOMAS, F.P. *Aircraft Construction.* 1928. US Naval Inst. 1st ed. 232 p. T5. $45.00

THOMAS, Henry. *Short-Title Catalogs of Spanish, Spanish-Am, & Portuguese...* 1966. London. British Mus. 1st ed. dj. F2. $25.00

THOMAS, Howard. *Road to 60.* 1966. Prospect Books. 1st ed. 336 p. EX. H3. $9.50

THOMAS, Howard. *Tales From the Adirondack Foothills.* 1980. NY. Prospect. 2nd print. dj. EX. B10. $6.25

THOMAS, Jean. *Bl Ridge Country.* 1942. NY. 1st ed. 338 p. dj. VG. B3. $25.00

THOMAS, Jean. *Devil's Ditties: Stories of KY Mt People With Songs...* 1931. Chicago. Hatfield. Ils Cyril Mullen. quarto. 180 p. VG. $25.00

THOMAS, L.B. *New Secret.* 1946. Thomas Allen. VG. P1. $5.00

THOMAS, Leslie. *Man With the Power.* 1973. Eyre Methuen. dj. VG. P1. $15.00

THOMAS, Louis. *Good Children Don't Kill.* 1968. Dodd Mead. 1st ed. dj. EX. P1. $10.00

THOMAS, Lowell. *Good Evening Everybody.* 1976. Morrow. not 1st ed. 349 p. dj. B10. $5.25

THOMAS, Lowell. *Hero of Vincennes.* 1929. Boston. 1st ed. dj. VG. B3. $35.00

THOMAS, Lowell. *Old Gimlet Eye.* 1933. NY. 1st ed. inscr. dj. VG. T5. $35.00

THOMAS, P.P. *Dissertation on the Ancient Chinese Vases of Shang Dynasty.* 1851. London. 1st ed. EX. $65.00

THOMAS, R. *Authentic Account of Most Remarkable Events...* nd. NY. Ils. 2 vols in 1. G4. $29.00

THOMAS, R.H. *Penelve; or, Among the Quakers.* 1898. London. Headley. 12mo. 366 p. VG. V1. $8.00

THOMAS, Ross. *Backup Men.* 1971. Morrow. 1st ed. dj. xl. P1. $12.50

THOMAS, Ross. *Brass Go-Between.* nd. Book Club. dj. VG. P1. $4.50

THOMAS, Ross. *Briarpatch.* 1984. Simon Schuster. ARC. inscr. dj. EX. K2. $100.00

THOMAS, Ross. *Briarpatch.* 1984. Simon Schuster. 1st ed. dj. EX. P1. $15.95

THOMAS, Ross. *Cast a Yel Shadow.* 1967. Morrow. 1st ed. dj. EX. K2. $125.00

THOMAS, Ross. *Cold War Swap.* 1966. Morrow. 1st ed. dj. EX. B13. $350.00

THOMAS, Ross. *Fools in Town Are on Our Side.* 1970. Hodder Stoughton. 1st UK ed. inscr. dj. NM. T9. $225.00

THOMAS, Ross. *Highbinders.* 1974. Morrow. 1st ed. dj. EX. F5. $25.00

THOMAS, Ross. *If You Can't Be Good.* 1973. Morrow. 1st ed. dj. EX. T9. $35.00

THOMAS, Ross. *If You Can't Be Good.* 1973. Morrow. 1st ed. dj. xl. P1. $10.00

THOMAS, Ross. *Missionary Stew.* 1983. Simon Schuster. inscr. dj. EX. K2. $60.00

THOMAS, Ross. *Money Harvest.* 1975. Morrow. 1st ed. dj. VG. P1. $35.00

THOMAS, Ross. *Out on the Rim.* 1987. Mysterious Pr. ARC. EX. K2. $25.00

THOMAS, Ross. *Out on the Rim.* 1987. Mysterious Pr. 1st ed. dj. EX. P1. $17.95

THOMAS, Ross. *Porkchoppers.* 1972. Morrow. 1st ed. dj. EX. T9. $40.00

THOMAS, Ross. *Procane Chronicle.* 1972. Morrow. 1st ed. dj. xl. F5. $20.00

THOMAS, Ross. *Spies, Thumbsuckers, etc.* 1989. Lord John. 1st ed. 1/250. sgn. gilt bdg. no dj issued. T9. $65.00

THOMAS, Ross. *4th Durango.* 1989. Mysterious Pr. ARC. sgn. wrp. EX. K2. $45.00

THOMAS, Ruth. *Flint & Fireflies.* nd. (1942) Boston. Manthorne. 64 p. dj. VG. B10. $5.00

THOMAS, Wilbur. *Gen George H Thomas.* 1964. NY. 1st ed. 649 p. T5. $42.50

THOMAS & THOMAS. *Hist of Friends in Am.* 1905. Phil. Winston. 4th ed. 12mo. 246 p. VG. V1. $10.50

THOMASON, J.W. *Fix Bayonets!* 1926. NY. 3rd print. 245 p. T5. $12.50

THOMASON, J.W. *Jeb Stuart.* 1946. NY. dj. VG. B3. $35.00

THOMASON, J.W. *Jeb Stuart.* 1953. NY. Ils. 512 p. dj. G. T5. $12.50

THOMPSON, Ames. *Strange Adventure Stories for Boys.* 1935. Cupples Leon. dj. VG. P1. $15.00

THOMPSON, C.W. *Fiery Epoch 1830-1877.* 1931. Indianapolis. 1st ed. dj. VG. $20.00

THOMPSON, Charles. *Sketches of Old Bristol.* 1942. Providence. 1st ed. sgn. tall 8vo. B10. $17.50

THOMPSON, E.T. *Lives of the Hunted.* 1901. NY. 1st imp. VG. T1. $30.00

THOMPSON, Edward. *In Araby Orion.* 1930. NY. Ils Harry Brown. G. $30.00

THOMPSON, Edward. *People of the Serpent.* 1932. Houghton Mifflin. 1st ed. 301 p. F2. $25.00

THOMPSON, George. *Great Thompson's Orig Comedy Medicine Pitch.* c 1946. Town House Magic. stapled manuscript. EX. J3. $4.00

THOMPSON, Gunnar. *Nu Sun: Asian-Am Voyages 500 BC.* 1989. Pioneer Pub. 1st ed. 4to. 231 p. dj. F2. $25.00

THOMPSON, H.S. *Curse of Lono.* 1983. Bantam. ARC. wrp. EX. w/promotional material. K2. $100.00

THOMPSON, H.S. *Fear & Loathing in Las Vegas.* 1971. NY. Ils Steadman. 1st ed. 206 p. dj. VG. T5. $27.50

THOMPSON, H.S. *Fear & Loathing in Las Vegas.* 1971. Random House. 1st ed. dj. as issued. K2. $75.00

THOMPSON, H.S. *Fear & Loathing on the Campaign Trail 1972.* 1973. San Francisco. 1st ed. dj. VG. B3. $30.00

THOMPSON, H.S. *Fear & Loathing on the Campaign Trail 1972.* 1973. Straight Arrow. 1st ed. dj. K2. $40.00

THOMPSON, H.S. *Hell's Angels.* 1967. NY. 1st ed. dj. EX. $100.00

THOMPSON, J.E. *Civilization of the Mayas.* 1958. Chicago. Field Mus. reprint of 1927 ed. wrp. F2. $15.00

THOMPSON, J.E. *Mexico Before Cortez.* 1933. Scribner. 1st ed. 298 p. F2. $30.00

THOMPSON, J.E. *Rise & Fall of the Maya Civilization.* 1956. Norman. 287 p. dj. F2. $20.00

THOMPSON, J.G. *Miracle Makers.* 1975. Magic Ltd. 1st ed. 306 p. dj. NM. J3. $15.00

THOMPSON, J.G. *My Best.* 1945. Hopkins. 1st ed. 384 p. G. J3. $12.00

THOMPSON, J.G. *My Best.* 1945. Phil. Hopkins. 1st ed. 384 p. EX. J3. $16.00

THOMPSON, J.G. *Sleight Intended.* 1973. Omaha. Modern Litho. 65 p. SftCvr. EX. J3. $5.00

THOMPSON, Jim. *Getaway.* 1959. Signet 1584. PB Orig. wrp. VG. T9. $70.00

THOMPSON, Jim. *Hell of a Woman.* 1954. Lion. PB Orig. 16mo. wrp. EX. C4. $500.00

THOMPSON, Jim. *Kill-Off.* 1957. Lion Lib 142. 1st ed. VG. T9. $45.00

THOMPSON, Jim. *Kill-Off.* 1957. NY. Lion. PB Orig. wrp. EX. K2. $150.00

THOMPSON, Jim. *Killer Inside Me.* 1984. Quill. UP of reissue. wrp. EX. K2. $35.00

THOMPSON, Jim. *Now & on Earth.* 1986. Belen, NM. Dennis McMillan. 1/400. dj. EX. T9. $195.00

THOMPSON, Jim. *Now & on Earth.* 1986. Macmillan. Intro Stephen King. reprint. dj. M. P1. $75.00

THOMPSON, Jim. *Savage Night.* 1953. NY. PB Orig. VG. T9. $150.00

THOMPSON, Jim. *TX by the Tail.* 1965. Gold Medal. PB Orig. wrp. T9. $135.00

THOMPSON, Jim. *Wild Town.* 1957. Signet 1461. PB Orig. VG. T9. $40.00

THOMPSON, Joyce. *Conscience Place.* 1984. Doubleday. 1st ed. RS. M. R3. $13.95

THOMPSON, Kay. *Eloise in Moscow.* 1959. NY. 1st ed. VG. B3. $60.00

THOMPSON, Kay. *Eloise in Paris.* 1957. NY. presentation. dj. VG. B3. $225.00

THOMPSON, Kay. *Eloise in Paris.* 1957. NY. 3rd ed. dj. VG. B3. $40.00

THOMPSON, Kay. *Eloise.* 1955. NY. 1st ed. dj. VG. B3. $95.00

THOMPSON, Lawrence. *Essays in Hispanic Bibliography.* 1970. Shoe String Pr. 1st ed. 117 p. F2. $20.00

THOMPSON, Paul. *Work of William Morris.* 1967. Viking. 1st Am ed. dj. EX. C4. $30.00

THOMPSON, R.P. *Princess of Cozytown.* 1922. Volland. 1st ed. VG. B3. $60.00

THOMPSON, R.P. *Wishing Horse of Oz.* Reilly Lee. later issue. rust cloth. VG. $40.00

THOMPSON, Randall. *Peaceable Kingdom.* c 1936. Boston. Schirmer Music Co. 8vo. 94 p. G. V1. $14.00

THOMPSON, S.L. *Recovery.* 1980. Warner. dj. VG. P1. $15.00

THOMPSON, T.S. *Thompson's Coast Pilot.* 1869. Detroit. 5th ed. 175 p. ES. T5. $250.00

THOMPSON, Vance. *Gr Ray.* 1924. Bobbs Merrill. 1st ed. VG. R3. $20.00

THOMPSON, Vance. *Pointed Tower.* nd. AL Burt. VG. P1. $6.00

THOMPSON, W.C. *On the Road With a Circus.* 1903. np. octavo. 259 p. VG. H3. $125.00

THOMPSON, W.C. *On the Road With a Circus.* 1905. New Amsterdam Book Co. octavo. 259 p. VG. H3. $60.00

THOMPSON, W.I. *Island Out of Time.* 1985. Dial. 1st ed. dj. RS. EX. P1. $17.50

THOMPSON, Wallace. *Rainbow Countries of Central Am.* 1927. Chautauqua Pr. 284 p. F2. $15.00

THOMPSON. *Short Hist of Am Railways.* 1925. NY. Ils. 473 p. VG. C2. $45.00

THOMSON, Basil. *PC Richardson's 1st Case.* nd. AL Burt. VG. P1. $7.50

THOMSON, H.D. *Great Book of Thrillers.* 1935. Odhams. VG. P1. $25.00

THOMSON, June. *Dark Stream.* 1986. Crime Club. 1st ed. dj. VG. P1. $15.00

THOMSON, June. *Question of Identity.* 1977. Crime Club. 1st ed. dj. EX. P1. $20.00

THOREAU, H.D. *Cape Cod.* 1896. Boston/NY. Ils Amelia Watson. 1st ed. $50.00

THOREAU, H.D. *Journals.* 1962. Dover. 2 vols. djs. boxed. B3. $95.00

THOREAU, H.D. *Letters to Various Persons.* 1865. Ticknor Fields. 1st ed. $195.00

THOREAU, H.D. *Walden & the ME Woods.* 1882. Houghton Mifflin. 2 vols. G. R5. $75.00

THORN, Ismay. *Little Sisters of Pity: Dunce of the Village.* 1892. London. VG. C1. $17.50

THORN, R.S. *Twin Serpents.* nd. Book Club. dj. VG. P1. $4.50

THORNBURG, Newton. *Knockover.* 1968. Gold Medal D1933. 1st ed. wrp. VG. T9. $25.00

THORNDIKE, Joseph. *Discovery of Lost Worlds.* 1979. Am Heritage. 1st ed. 4to. 352 p. slipcase. F2. $20.00

THORNE, Anthony. *Venice.* 1960. Studio Book. 1st UK ed. 24 clr pls. sm 4to. $15.00

THORNE, Guy. *Ravenscroft Affair.* nd. Grosset Dunlap. dj. VG. P1. $12.50

THORNE, Guy. *When It Was Dark.* 1905. William Briggs. VG. P1. $7.50

THORNELL, J.H. *Bill of the Play.* nd. (1881) London. Pictorial World. 1st ed. 115 p. VG. H3. $125.00

THORP, John. *Letters of Late John Thorp...Prefixed (With) Memoir.* 1821. NY. Wood. 16mo. 252 p. G. V1. $18.00

THORP, N.H. *Cowboy Songs.* 1908. Estancia, NM. 1st ed. wrp. M. $60.00

THORP, Raymond. *Bowie Knife.* 1948. Albuquerque. 1st ed. dj. VG. $30.00

THORP, Roderick. *Detective.* nd. Book Club. dj. VG. P1. $4.50

THORP, Roderick. *Detective.* 1966. Dial. 1st ed. dj. VG. P1. $7.50

THORP, Roderick. *Nothing Lasts Forever.* 1979. Morrow. dj. EX. P1. $15.00

THORP, Roderick. *Rainbow Drive.* 1986. Summit. 1st ed. dj. EX. F5. $14.00

THRASHER, M.B. *Tuskegee.* 1901. Boston. 2nd ed. 215 p. xl. VG. $45.00

THRASHER, M.B. *Tuskegee.* 1900. Boston. 1st ed. 215 p. VG. B3. $55.00

THRUELSEN. *Grumman Story.* 1976. NY. 1st ed. dj. VG. C2. $25.00

THUNBERG, C.P. *Flora Japonica.* 1975. Oriole. facsimile. dj. EX. $55.00

THURBER, James. *Further Fables for Our Time.* 1956. NY. 1st ed. VG. C1. $9.50

THURBER, James. *Men, Women, & Dogs.* 1943. NY. dj. VG. B3. $22.50

THURBER, James. *My World & Welcome to It.* 1942. 3rd print. VG. C1. $3.50

THURBER, James. *O My Omar: Musical Comedy.* 1921. Columbus. 4to. string-tied wrp. VG. scarce. $250.00

THURBER, James. *Thurber Carnival.* nd. (1945) Harper. Ils. 369 p. G. $12.50

THURBER, James. *Thurber on Humor.* 1954. Ohioana Lib. pamphlet. 8vo. EX. $150.00

THURBER, James. *Wonderful O.* nd. Simon Schuster. 2nd ed. dj. xl. P1. $10.00

THURBER, James. *13 Clocks.* 1950. Simon Schuster. 3rd print. dj. VG. B7. $38.00

THURSTON, C.B. *New Story of Little Blk Sambo.* 1926. Racine. 24mo. 10 clr pls. dj. EX. T1. $55.00

THURSTON, Howard. *My Life of Magic.* 1929. Phil. Dorrance. 1st print. 273 p. EX. J3. $110.00

THURSTON, Howard. *Tricks With Cards.* 1903. Morris. 83 p. EX. J3. $6.00

THURSTON, Howard. *200 Tricks You Can Do.* 1926. Sully. 1st ed. HrdCvr. EX. J3. $15.00

THURSTON, Howard. *300 Tricks You Can Do.* 1948. Comet. 1st print. 239 p. VG. J3. $2.00

THURSTON, Howard. *400 Tricks You Can Do.* 1948. Garden City. 2 vols in 1. VG. J3. $5.00

THURSTON, Joseph. *Toilette. In 3 Books.* 1730. London. 2nd ed. rebound. VG. $100.00

THURSTON, K.C. *Mystics.* 1907. Harper. 1st ed. VG. R3. $15.00

THURSTON, Robert. *Alicia II.* 1978. Putnam. 1st ed. dj. EX. P1. $10.00

THWAITE, Anthony. *Larkin at 60.* 1982. London. Faber. 1st ed. sgn Heaney. dj. EX. K2. $75.00

THWAITE, Mary. *From Primer to Pleasure in Reading.* 1972. Boston. 1st Am ed. dj. EX. $45.00

THWAITES, R.G. *On the Storied OH: Historical Pilgrimage...* 1903. Chicago. 1st ed. 334 p. T5. $35.00

THWING, Eugene. *World's Best 100 Detective Stories 8.* 1929. Funk Wagnall. G. P1. $10.00

THYSSEN, F. *I Paid Hitler.* 1941. NY. 1st ed. dj. VG. B3. $22.50

TIBBLES, T.H. *Buckskin & Blanket Days...* 1957. Garden City. 1st ed. dj. VG. T5. $15.00

TIBOL, Raquel. *Prints of the Mexican Masters.* 1987. Chicago. 1st ed. lg 4to. F2. $15.00

TILGHMAN, Christopher. *In a Father's Place.* 1990. NY. 1st ed. sgn. K2. $55.00

TILLEY, Patrick. *Fade-Out.* 1975. Morrow. 1st ed. dj. EX. F5. $16.00

TILT, Edward. *Handbook of Uterine Therapeutics & Diseases of Women.* 1881. NY. Wood. 4th ed. VG. J2. $15.00

TIMBRES & TIMBRES. *We Didn't Ask Utopia.* 1943. Prentice Hall. 1st Canadian ed. 8vo. 290 p. G. V1. $10.00

TIME LIFE. *Brother Against Brother.* 1990. Prentice Hall. 431 p. dj. M. S1. $39.95

TIME LIFE. *Epic of Flight.* 1983. Chicago. 20 vols. EX. B3. $175.00

TIME LIFE. *Wines & Spirits.* 1968. Ils. 208 p. sbdg. VG. B10. $6.00

TIMERMAN, Jacobo. *Chile: Death in the S.* 1987. Knopf. 1st ed. 134 p. dj. F2. $15.00

TIMERMAN, Jacobo. *Prisoner Without a Name, Cell Without a Number.* 1981. Knopf. 1st ed. 164 p. dj. F2. $15.00

TIMMONS, Wilbert. *John F Finerty Reports Porfirian Mexico.* 1879. TX W Pr. 1st ed. 334 p. dj. F2. $20.00

TIMMONS, Wilbert. *Tadeo Ortiz: Mexican Colonizer & Reformer.* 1974. El Paso. Ils Jose Cisneros. 82 p. wrp. F2. $15.00

TINAYRE, Marcelle. *Madame De Pompadour.* 1926. Putnam. 1st Am ed? 220 p. xl. VG. B10. $5.00

TINKER, Ben. *Mexican Wilderness & Wildlife.* 1978. TX U. 1st ed. 315 p. dj. F2. $20.00

TINLEY, HUMPHREYS, & IRVING. *Clr Planning of the Garden.* 1924. London. Ils Walters. 8vo. VG. $90.00

TIONG, P.Y. *Phoa Yan Tiong.* nd. Amsterdam. Tiong. 1st ed. SftCvr. EX. J3. $4.00

TIPTREE, James Jr. *Byte Beautiful.* 1985. Doubleday. 1st ed. dj. EX. F5. $15.00

TITCOMB, Timothy. *Titcomb's Letters to Young People.* 1861. Scribner. 26th ed. 251 p. VG. B10. $10.00

TITIEV, Mischa. *Araucanian Culture in Transition.* 1951. Ann Arbor. Ils. 164 p. wrp. F2. $15.00

TOBACK, James. *Jim.* 1971. Doubleday. 1st ed. 133 p. dj. EX. B10. $5.00

TODD, J.A. *Banks of the Nile.* 1913. London. Blk. 1st ed. 282 p. TEG. T5. $47.50

TODD, R.L. *Picturesque Wooster.* 1907. Wooster. Ils. 28 p. wrp. T5. $27.50

TODD, W.E. *Birds of W PA.* 1940. Pittsburgh. 1st ed. VG. $75.00

TODD & WHEELER. *Utopia.* 1978. Harmony Books. VG. P1. $15.00

TODISH, Timothy. *Am's 1st World War: French & Indian War 1754-1763.* 1982. Grand Rapids, MI. Ils. 1/2000. sgn. 115 p. T5. $12.50

TOFTE, Arthur. *Survival Planet.* 1977. Bobbs Merrill. 1st ed. dj. EX. R3. $15.00

TOKLAS, A.B. *Staying Alone: Letters of Alice B Toklas.* 1973. Liveright. 1st Am ed. dj. EX. C4. $25.00

TOLAND, John. *Dillinger Days.* 1963. NY. 1st ed. 371 p. dj. VG. B3. $22.50

TOLIVER & CONSTABLE. *Blond Knight of Germany.* 1970. Garden City. Ils. 318 p. xl. G. T5. $15.00

TOLKIEN, J.R.R. *Book of Lost Tales, Part 2.* 1984. Book Club. dj. EX. C1. $4.00

TOLKIEN, J.R.R. *Hobbit.* 1938. Boston. 1st Am ed. orig bdg. dj. VG. H3. $2000.00

TOLKIEN, J.R.R. *Hobbit.* 1938. Boston. 1st Am ed. VG. H3. $500.00

TOLKIEN, J.R.R. *Hobbit's Journal.* 1985. Exley. 1st ed. wrp. EX. F5. $10.00

TOLKIEN, J.R.R. *Mr Bliss.* 1983. Houghton Mifflin. 1st ed. dj. VG. P1. $17.50

TOLKIEN, J.R.R. *Silmarillion.* 1977. Allen Unwin. 1st ed. dj. EX. P1. $25.00

TOLKIEN, J.R.R. *Silmarillion.* 1977. Allen Unwin. 2nd ed. dj. VG. P1. $12.50

TOLKIEN, J.R.R. *Silmarillion.* 1977. Houghton Mifflin. 1st ed. dj. EX. R3. $15.00

TOLKIEN, J.R.R. *Silmarillion.* 1977. Houghton Mifflin. 1st ed. dj. VG. P1. $12.50

TOLKIEN, J.R.R. *Sir Gawain, Pearl, & Sor Orfeo.* 1975. Boston. 1st ed. EX. C1. $7.50

TOLKIEN, J.R.R. *Sir Gawain & the Gr Knight.* 1955. Oxford. VG. C1. $10.00

TOLKIEN, J.R.R. *Sir Gawain & the Gr Knight.* 1975. Houghton Mifflin. 1st Am ed. M. R3. $50.00

TOLKIEN, J.R.R. *Smith of Wooton Major.* 1967. Boston. Ils Baynes. 1st ed. dj. EX. $50.00

TOLKIEN, J.R.R. *Smith of Wooton Major.* 1967. Houghton Mifflin. 1st ed. VG. P1. $30.00

TOLKIEN, J.R.R. *Treason of Isengard.* 1989. Boston. UP. K2. $45.00

TOLKIEN, J.R.R. *2 Towers.* nd. Houghton Mifflin. dj. EX. R3. $50.00

TOLKIEN & SWAN. *Road Goes Ever On.* 1967. Boston. 1st ed. dj. EX. $50.00

TOLLES, F.B. *George Logan, Agrarian Democrat: Survey of His Writings.* 1951. offprint. 8vo. 20 p. wrp. VG. V1. $6.00

TOLLES, F.B. *George Logan of Phil.* 1953. Oxford. 1st ed. 8vo. 362 p. dj. VG. V1. $9.50

TOLLES, F.B. *Of the Best Sort But Plain: The Quaker Esthetic.* 1959. reprint. 12mo. 19 p. disbound. VG. V1. $6.00

TOLLES, F.B. *PA's 1st Scientist, James Logan.* 1951. offprint. 8vo. 20 p. wrp. VG. V1. $6.00

TOLLES, F.B. *Quaker Reaction to Leaves of Grass.* 1947. Reprint. 8vo. G. V1. $6.00

TOLSTOY, L.N. *Anna Karenina.* 1933. Ltd Ed Club. Ils/sgn Nikolas Piskariov. 2 vols. slipcase. C4. $75.00

TOLSTOY, L.N. *Anna Karenina.* 1951. Ltd Ed Club. Ils/sgn Barnett Freedman. 2 vols. slipcase. C4. $50.00

TOLSTOY, L.N. *Complete Works.* 1898. NY. Dumont. Emancipation ed. 24 vols. TEG. VG. H3. $375.00

TOLSTOY, L.N. *Life.* c 1895. NY. Crowell. Trans Hapgood. VG. C1. $17.50

TOLSTOY, L.N. *LN Tolstoy: His Writings.* 1904. Cambridge. Estes. 1/210. 28 vols. TEG. EX. H3. $3500.00

TOLSTOY, L.N. *War & Peace.* 1886-1887. NY. Gottgerger. 1st Am ed. 6 vols. EX. H3. $3000.00

TOLSTOY, Nikolai. *Coming of the King: Novel of Merlin.* 1989. 1st ed. dj. NM. C1. $12.00

TOMALIN, Claire. *Life & Death of Mary Wollstonecraft.* 1974. NY/London. 1st ed. dj. EX. C1. $12.00

TOMES, Robert. *War in the S: Hist of Great Am Rebellion.* c 1867. NY. 3 vols. VG. G4. $95.00

TOMKINS, Calvin. *Living Well Is the Best Revenge.* 1971. Viking. 1st ed. dj. EX. B13. $65.00

TOMKINS & PLANCHE. *12 Designs for the Costume of Shakespeare's Richard the 3rd.* 1830. London. Colnaghi. 1st ed. 20 p. clamshell slipcase. H3. $650.00

TOMLINSON, Edward. *New Road to Riches.* 1939. Scribner. 1st ed. 438 p. F2. $10.00

TOMLINSON, Everett. *Jack Stone of Tait School.* 1917. Barse. 1st ed. 252 p. VG. B10. $3.75

TOMLINSON, H.M. *All Our Yesterdays.* 1930. Harper. 1/350. sgn. gray bdg. H3. $85.00

TOMLINSON, H.M. *Face of the Earth.* c 1950. Bobbs Merrill. 1st Am ed? 246 p. VG. B10. $4.50

TOMPKINS, Peter. *Mysteries of the Mexican Pyramids.* 1976. Harper. 1st ed. 427 p. F2. $20.00

TOMPKINS, W.A. *Roy Rogers & Ghost of Mystery Rancho.* nd. Whitman. dj. VG. P1. $15.00

TOMS, Agnes. *Joy of Eating Natural Foods.* 1971. Devin, CT. not 1st ed. dj. EX. B10. $3.75

TONKIN, Peter. *Journal of Edwin Underhill.* nd. Hodder Stoughton. 2nd ed. dj. VG. P1. $15.00

TOOHEY, J.L. *Hist of Pulitzer Prize Plays.* 1967. Citadel. 1st ed. quarto. 344 p. dj. EX. H3. $25.00

TOOKER, Richard. *Day of the Brn Horde.* 1929. Payson Clarke. 1st ed. VG. R3. $20.00

TOOLE, J.K. *Confederacy of Dunces.* 1980. Baton Rouge. 1st ed. dj. EX. K2. $300.00

TOOLE, J.K. *Neon Bible.* 1989. Grove Pr. UP. wrp. EX. C4. $25.00

TOOMER, Jean. *Flavor of Man.* 1949. Young Friends Movement. sm octavo. wrp. EX. rare. B13. $850.00

TOOR, Frances. *New Guide to Mexico.* 1944. Mexico. 1st ed. 350 p. dj. F2. $10.00

TOOR, Frances. *Treasury of Mexican Folkways.* 1947. Crown. 1st ed. 566 p. F2. $25.00

TOPLIFF, S. *Topliff's Travels: Letters From Abroad 1828-1829.* 1906. Boston. fld map. 246 p. VG. $30.00

TOPOL & NEZNANSKY. *Deadly Games.* 1983. London. Quartet Books. 1st ed. 235 p. dj. EX. B10. $4.25

TORCHIA, Joseph. *Kryptonite Kid.* 1979. Holt Rinehart Winston. inscr. dj. H3. $75.00

TORCHIA, Joseph. *Kryptonite Kid.* 1979. Holt Rinehart Winston. UP of 1st ed. wrp. EX. F5. $20.00

TORIBIO MEDINA, Jose. *Bibliografia de las Lenguas Quecha y Aymara.* 1930. Mus Am Indian. 1st ed. Spanish text. wrp. F2. $20.00

TORRES LANZAS, Pedro. *Catalogo de Documentos Conservados Archivo...Indias Sevilla.* 1912. Madrid. Primera Serie. 584 p. F2. $15.00

TORREY, John. *Nat Hist of NY: Botany.* 1843. Appleton/Wiley Putnam. 2 vols. clr pls. VG. T3. $450.00

TOURGE, A.W. *Fool's Errand & the Invisible Empire.* c 1885. Ils ed. gilt brn bdg. VG. C1. $24.50

TOURNEY, Leonard. *Old Saxon Blood.* 1988. St Martin. 1st ed. dj. EX. F5. $13.00

TOUSSAINT, Manuel. *Arte Colonial en Mexico.* 1962. Mexico. UNAM. 2nd ed. 303 p. dj. F2. $100.00

TOWNE, Robert. *Chinatown.* 1983. Santa Barbara. Neville. Ltd ed. EX. H3. $400.00

TOWNLEY, Houghton. *Bishop's Emeralds.* 1908. Watt. apparent 1st ed. 424 p. G. B10. $3.50

TOWNSEND, A.N. *Chronology of the Soc of Friends.* 1895. Friends Book Assn. 12mo. 51 p. xl. G. V1. $12.50

TOWNSEND, F.H. *Punch Drawings.* c 1920. NY. lg 4to. dj. EX. $45.00

TOWNSEND, W.P. *Brief Narrative of Life of Jacob Lindley.* nd. Friends Bookstore. 16mo. 95 p. V1. $12.00

TOWNSEND. *Lincoln & His Wife's Hometown.* 1929. Indianapolis. 1st ed. dj. VG. B3. $42.50

TOY, Sidney. *Castles of Great Britain.* 1953. London/Melbourne/Toronto. xl. VG. $35.00

TOYNBEE, Philip. *Prothalamium: Cycle of the Holy Grail.* 1970. Greenwood Pr. VG. C1. $7.50

TRACHTMAN, Paula. *Disturb Not the Dream.* 1981. Crown. 1st ed. dj. EX. F5. $15.00

TRACY, C.R. *Directory of Magicians.* 1951. Sioux City. Tracy. 1st print. 312 p. VG. J3. $10.00

TRACY, Don. *Last Boat Out of Cincinnati.* 1970. Trident Pr. 1st ed. dj. xl. P1. $5.00

TRACY, Louis. *Lastingham Murder.* 1928. Clode. VG. P1. $18.25

TRACY, Louis. *Wings of the Morning.* nd. Winston. Ils. 319 p. VG. B10. $4.50

TRACY, R.M. *32 Impromptu Card Tricks.* nd. Chicago. Felsman. 1st ed. 24 p. SftCvr. NM. J3. $4.00

TRACY, R.W. *Sword of Desire.* 1952. Arco. 1st ed. dj. EX. F5. $20.00

TRAGER, Philip. *Wesleyan Photographs by Philip Trager.* 1982. NC Wesleyan U. 1/70. sgn. slipcase. w/photo. EX. B13. $275.00

TRAIN, Arthur. *His Children's Children.* 1923. Scribner. VG. P1. $7.50

TRAIN, Arthur. *Lost Gospel.* 1925. Scribner. 1st ed. VG. R3. $20.00

TRAIN, Arthur. *Mr Tutt Finds a Way.* 1945. Scribner. 1st ed. VG. P1. $12.50

TRAIN, Arthur. *Tutt & Mr Tutt.* 1943. Triangle. VG. P1. $10.00

TRAPROCK, Walter. *Cruise of the Kawa.* nd. (1921) Putnam. gray bdg. VG. B10. $5.00

TRAUBEL, H. *With Walt Whitman in Camden.* 1915. NY. 3 vols. VG. B3. $90.00

TRAVEN, B. *Bridge in the Jungle.* 1967. Hill Wang. dj. xl. P1. $5.00

TRAVEN, B. *Man Nobody Knows.* 1961. Regency. 1st ed. EX. B4. $30.00

TRAVEN, B. *March to the Monteria.* 1964. Dell. 1st print. VG. B4. $6.00

TRAVERS, Hugh. *Madame Aubry Dines With Death.* 1967. Harper Row. 1st ed. dj. VG. P1. $10.00

TRAVIS, Gerry. *Big Bite.* 1957. Mystery House. 1st ed. dj. VG. P1. $9.00

TRAYER, G. *Wood in Aircraft Construction.* 1930. WA. 1st ed. 276 p. dj. VG. B3. $45.00

TREAT, Lawrence. *H As in Hangman.* 1942. Duell Sloan Pearce. 1st ed. VG. P1. $20.00

TREAT, Lawrence. *H As in Hunted.* nd. Collier. VG. P1. $10.00

TREAT, Lawrence. *O As in Omen.* 1943. Duell Sloan Pearce. 1st ed. G. P1. $12.50

TREAT, Lawrence. *Q As in Quicksand.* 1947. Duell Sloan Pearce. 1st ed. Lib bdg. xl. P1. $6.00

TREECE, Henry. *Carnival King.* 1955. London. Faber. 1st ed. dj. EX. H3. $35.00

TREECE, Henry. *Castles & Kings.* 1959. London. 1st ed. dj. EX. C1. $24.00

TREECE, Henry. *Dark Island.* 1952. 1st Am ed. dj. VG. C1. $18.00

TREECE, Henry. *Eagle King.* 1st Am ed. dj. VG. C1. $12.50

TREECE, Henry. *Man With a Sword.* 1964. Pantheon. 1st ed. dj. xl. F5. $8.00

TREECE, Henry. *Man With a Sword.* 1979. (1st 1962) Oxford. EX. C1. $7.50

TREECE, Henry. *Men of the Hills.* 1958. 1st Am ed. dj. EX. C1. $12.00

TREECE, Henry. *Queen's Broach.* 1967.1st Am ed. dj. EX. C1. $17.50

TREECE, Henry. *Ride Into Danger.* 1961. (1st 1959) 2nd print. dj. EX. C1. $9.00

TREECE, Henry. *Ride Into Danger.* 1961. Citerion. 2nd ed. dj. VG. P1. $15.00

TREECE, Henry. *Splintered Sword.* 1970. Brockhampton Pr. dj. xl. P1. $5.00

TREECE, Henry. *Windswept City.* 1967. 1st Am ed. EX. C1. $9.00

TREECE, Henry. *Windswept City.* 1967. Hamish Hamilton. xl. P1. $5.00

TREGOLD, Thomas. *Practical Treatise on Railroads & Carriages.* 1838. London. 2nd ed. G. $85.00

TREHARNE, R.F. *Glastonbury Legends.* 1974. PB. VG. C1. $7.50

TRELEASE, A.W. *Reconstruction: Great Experiment.* 1971. NY. 1st ed. dj. EX. $13.00

TREMAYNE, Peter. *Fires of Lan-Kern.* 1980. St Martin. 1st ed. dj. EX. F5/P1. $20.00

TREMEARNE, A.J.N. *Ban of the Bori: Demons & Demon Dancing in W & N Africa.* c 1914. London. Heath Cranton Ouseley. 504 p. VG. H3. $100.00

TRENHOLM, Virginia. *Footprints on the Frontier.* 1945. Douglas. 1/1000. sgn. A5. $80.00

TRENT, W.P. *Stevenson's Workshop.* 1921. Bibliophile Soc. 1/450. 8vo. T6. $40.00

TREVANIAN. *Loo Sanction.* nd. Book Club. dj. VG. P1. $4.50

TREVANIAN. *Summer of Katya.* 1983. Crown. 1st ed. dj. VG. P1. $15.00

TREVANIAN. *Summer of Katya.* 1983. Granada. 1st ed. dj. VG. P1. $17.50

TREVELYAN, G.M. *Life of John Bright.* 1913. Boston. 3rd ed. 480 p. VG. V1. $12.00

TREVELYAN, Marie. *Land of Arthur: Its Heroes & Heroines.* c 1895. decor bdg. VG. C1. $49.50

TREVOR, Elleston. *Bury Him Among Kings.* nd. Book Club. dj. VG. P1. $4.50

TREVOR, Elleston. *Forbidden Kingdom.* 1955. Lutterworth. VG. P1. $20.00

TREVOR, William. *Elizabeth Alone.* 1973. Viking. 1st Am ed. dj. EX. K2. $40.00

TREVOR-ROPER, H.R. *Last Days of Hitler.* 1947. NY. 1st ed. VG. $12.00

TRIETSCH, J.H. *Printer & the Prince.* 1955. NY. 1st ed. dj. EX. $15.00

TRILBY, G.D.M. *Trilby.* 1894. Harper. 1st Am ed. VG. B10. $7.00

TRIPLETT, Frank. *Conquering the Wilderness.* 1890. np. Ils Nast/Darley. 8vo. 742 p. G. G4. $33.00

TRIPLETT, June. *Salt-Water Taffy.* 1929. Putnam. 1st ed. 206 p. G. B10. $6.25

TRIPP, Miles. *Some Predators Are Male.* 1985. St Martin. 1st ed. dj. EX. P1. $12.95

TROCCHI, Alex. *Cain's Book.* 1979. Grove Pr. 3rd print. B4. $4.00

TROLLOPE, Anthony. *Autobiography.* 1883. Edinburgh/London. 1st ed. 2 vols. VG. H3. $600.00

TROLLOPE, Anthony. *Barsetshire Novels.* 1929. Houghton Mifflin. 14 vols. lg octavo. Riverside bdg. EX. H3. $3000.00

TROLLOPE, Anthony. *He Knew He Was Right.* 1868-1869. London. 1st ed. pub slipcase. rare. H3. $7500.00

TROLLOPE, Anthony. *Lady Anna.* 1874. London. Chapman Hall. 2 vols. orig bdg. H3. $6000.00

TROLLOPE, Anthony. *Last Chronicle of Barset.* 1867. London. Smith Elder. 1st ed. 2 vols. contemporary bdg. VG. R5. $1000.00

TROLLOPE, Anthony. *Struggles of Brn, Jones, & Robinson.* 1862. Harper. 1st ed. A4. $200.00

TROLLOPE, Anthony. *Writings.* 1900. Phil. Gebbie. Collector ed. 1/250. 30 vols. TEG. H3. $2750.00

TROLLOPE, Frances. *Domestic Manners of Am.* 1832. London. 2nd ed. 2 vols. 12mo. T1. $90.00

TROLLOPE, Frances. *Widow Barnaby.* 1840. London. 1st 1 vol ed. 12mo. VG. T1. $40.00

TROST, Nick. *Gambling Tricks With Dice.* 1975. Columbus. Trost. 1st ed. SftCvr. NM. J3. $6.00

TROTT, H. *Santa Claus in Santa Land.* 1943. NY. 1st ed. dj. VG. $22.00

TROTTA, Geri. *Veronica Died Monday.* 1952. Dodd Mead. 1st ed. xl. P1. $5.00

TROUT, Kilgore; see Vonnegut, Kurt.

TROWBRIDGE, W.R.H. *Cagliostro.* 1926. NY. dj. VG. $30.00

TROYAT, Henri. *Tolstoy.* 1968. np. Pirate ed. 322 p. dj. VG. B10. $4.25

TRUAX, Sarah. *Woman of Parts: Memories of Life on Stage.* 1949. London. Longman. 1st ed. 247 p. EX. B10. $6.50

TRUEBLOOD, D.E. *Company of the Committed.* 1961. Harper. 12mo. 113 p. dj. VG. V1. $7.50

TRUEBLOOD, D.E. *Declaration of Freedom.* 1955. Harper. 1st ed. 12mo. inscr. 124 p. VG. V1. $7.50

TRUEBLOOD, D.E. *Foundations for Reconstruction.* 1946. NY. Harper. 12mo. 109 p. dj. VG. V1. $7.50

TRUEBLOOD, D.E. *Friends World Conference, 1937: Advance Study Outlines.* 1936. Phil. 8vo. 64 p. V1. $6.50

TRUEBLOOD, D.E. *Humor of Christ.* 1964. Harper. 12mo. 125 p. dj. G. V1. $7.50

TRUEBLOOD, D.E. *Incendiary Fellowship.* 1967. Harper. 8vo. 121 p. dj. VG. V1. $7.50

TRUEBLOOD, D.E. *Predicament of Modern Man.* 1944. Harper. 4th ed. 12mo. 105 p. dj. VG. V1. $7.50

TRUEBLOOD, D.E. *Your Other Vocation.* 1952. Harper. 12mo. 125 p. G. V1. $7.50

TRUEBLOOD & TRUEBLOOD. *Recovery of Family Life.* 1953. Harper. dj. G. V1. $7.50

TRUETT, V.S. *On the Hoof in NV.* 1950. Los Angeles. 1st ed. 613 p. VG. B3. $95.00

TRUMAN, H.S. *Year of Decisions.* 1955. Doubleday. 1st ed. inscr. 2 vols. djs. EX. B13. $475.00

TRUMAN, Margaret. *Murder at the Kennedy Center.* 1989. Random House. 1st ed. dj. EX. P1. $17.50

TRUMBO, Dalton. *Devil in the Book.* 1956. CA Emergency Defense. Ltd ed. 1/750. sgn. wrp. EX. H3. $85.00

TRUMBO, Dalton. *Night of the Aurochs.* nd. Viking. UP. wrp. EX. B13. $85.00

TRUSS, Seldon. *Doctor Was a Dame.* 1953. Crime Club. 1st ed. dj. VG. P1. $20.00

TRUSS, Seldon. *Sweeter for His Going.* 1950. Hodder Stoughton. 1st ed. G. P1. $10.00

TRUSS, Seldon. *Technique for Treachery.* 1963. Crime Club. 1st ed. dj. xl. P1. $5.00

TRUSS, Seldon. *Turmoil at Brede.* 1931. Mystery League. 1st ed. VG. P1. $12.50

TUBB, E.C. *Alien Seed.* 1976. Arthur Barker. 1st ed. dj. VG. P1. $17.50

TUBB, E.C. *Rogue Planet.* 1977. Arthur Barker. 1st ed. dj. VG. P1. $17.50

TUBB, E.C. *Scatter of Stardust.* 1976. Dobson. 1st ed. dj. EX. P1. $20.00

TUCHMAN, Barbara. *Guns of August.* 1962. NY. BOMC. dj. VG. $6.00

TUCHMAN, Barbara. *March of Folly.* 1984. Knopf. 1st ed. 447 p. dj. EX. B10. $5.35

TUCHMAN, Barbara. *Stilwell & the Am Experience in China 1911-1945.* 1971. NY. Ils. 621 p. dj. G. T5. $35.00

TUCK, D.H. *Encyclopedia of SF & Fantasy Vol 3.* 1982. Advent. 1st ed. no dj issued. EX. P1. $30.00

TUCKER, G.F. *Quaker Home.* 1891. Boston. Reed. 12mo. 426 p. VG. V1. $8.00

TUCKER, Glenn. *High Tide at Gettysburg.* 1982. Morningside. 462 p. PB. G. S1. $7.50

TUCKER, Glenn. *Poltroons & Patriots.* 1954. Indianapolis. 1st ed. 2 vols. djs. VG. B3. $30.00

TUCKER, Glenn. *Tecumseh: Vision of Glory.* 1956. Indianapolis. 1st ed. 399 p. dj. VG. B3. $47.50

TUCKER, Glenn. *Zeb Vance.* 1965. Indianapolis. 1st ed. dj. VG. B3. $30.00

TUCKER, Sophie. *Some of These Days.* 1945. NY. 1st ed. inscr/sgn. VG. $45.00

TUCKER, Wilson. *Chinese Doll.* 1946. Rinehart. 1st ed. inscr. dj. EX. R3. $200.00

TUCKER, Wilson. *City in the Sea.* Galaxy Novel 11. EX. R3. $10.00

TUCKER, Wilson. *City in the Sea.* 1951. Rinehart. 1st ed. inscr/sgn. dj. EX. R3. $150.00

TUCKER, Wilson. *Dove.* 1948. Rinehart. 1st ed. dj. VG. P1. $50.00

TUCKER, Wilson. *Dove.* 1948. Rinehart. 1st ed. inscr/sgn. dj. EX. R3. $150.00

TUCKER, Wilson. *Ice & Iron.* 1974. Doubleday. 1st ed. dj. EX. R3. $15.00

TUCKER, Wilson. *Ice & Iron.* 1974. SF Book Club. inscr. dj. EX. R3. $15.00

TUCKER, Wilson. *Lincoln Hunters.* nd. Book Club. dj. VG. P1. $4.50

TUCKER, Wilson. *Long Loud Silence.* nd. Book Club. dj. VG. P1. $7.50

TUCKER, Wilson. *Procession of the Damned.* 1965. Crime Club. 1st ed. dj. VG. P1. $20.00

TUCKER, Wilson. *Red Herring.* 1951. Rinehart. 1st ed. inscr. dj. EX. R3. $125.00

TUCKER, Wilson. *Stalking Man.* 1949. Rinehart. 1st ed. inscr. EX. R3. $125.00

TUCKER, Wilson. *This Witch.* 1971. Doubleday. 1st ed. dj. xl. P1. $7.50

TUCKER, Wilson. *Time Masters.* 1953. Rinehart. 1st ed. dj. EX. R3. $75.00

TUCKER, Wilson. *To Keep or Kill.* 1947. Rinehart. 1st ed. inscr. dj. EX. R3. $150.00

TUCKER, Wilson. *Warlock.* 1967. Crime Club. 1st ed. dj. xl. P1. $10.00

TUDOR, Tasha. *Take Joy: The Tasha Tudor Christmas Book.* 1966. Cleveland. 1st ed. oblong 4to. dj. VG. $40.00

TUKE, Henry. *On Public Worship & Appropriation of 1 Day in the Week...* nd. Phil. Tract Assn of Friends. 16mo. V1. $7.00

TUKE, Henry. *Repentance Towards God/Faith Towards Our Lord Jesus Christ.* nd. Phil. Tract Assn Friends 127. 16mo. 4 p. G. V1. $7.00

TULLY, Andrew. *Supreme Court.* nd. Book Club. dj. VG. P1. $4.50

TULLY, Jim. *Emmett Lawler.* 1922. NY. 1st ed. VG. A6. $50.00

TUNISON, J.S. *Grail Problem.* 1904. 1st ed. 134 p. VG. C1. $39.50

TUNNAH, W.F.; see Amalfi.

TUPPER, Harmon. *To the Great Ocean: Taming of Siberia.* 1965. Little Brn. 1st ed. 536 p. dj. EX. T4. $20.00

TURCHI, Peter. *Magician.* 1991. Dutton. 1st ed. sgn. dj. M. C4. $20.00

TURGENIEFF, Ivan. *Novels & Stories.* 1903. Scribner. Ruisdael ed. 1/204. 16 vols. Stikeman bdg. H3. $3500.00

TURNBULL, A.D. *Hist of US Naval Aviation.* 1949. New Haven. Ils 1st ed. inscr. 345 p. VG. T5. $45.00

TURNBULL, Margaret. *Handsome Man.* 1928. Reilly Lee. 1st ed. 361 p. dj. G. B10. $3.50

TURNBULL, Peter. *Claws of the Gryphon.* 1986. St Martin. 1st ed. dj. EX. F5. $11.00

TURNER, C.C. *Aerial Navigation of Today.* 1910. London. Ils 2nd ed. 326 p. G. T5. $42.50

TURNER, F.S. *Quakers: A Study Hist & Critical.* 1889. London. Swan Sonnenschein. 12mo. 408 p. G. V1. $9.00

TURNER, George. *Drowning Towers.* 1987. Arbor House. 1st ed. dj. EX. F5. $15.00

TURNER, Henry. *Internat Incident.* 1956. London. Wingate. 1st ed. 205 p. dj. EX. B10. $4.25

TURNER, James. *4th Ghost Book.* 1965. Barrie Rockliff. dj. VG. P1. $17.50

TURNER, W.P. *Circle of Squares.* 1968. Walker. dj. VG. P1. $10.00

TURNER & HARRISON. *Pulltrouser Swamp.* 1983. TX U. 1st ed. 310 p. dj. F2. $25.00

TURNEY, I.V. *Paul Bunyan Comes W.* 1928. Boston. Ils Rhodes. 1st ed. dj. VG. B3. $17.50

TUROLLA, Pina. *Beyond the Andes.* 1980. Harper. 1st ed. 364 p. dj. F2. $15.00

TUROW, Scott. *Burden of Proof.* 1990. Farrar Straus. 1st ed. sgn. dj. EX. B13. $85.00

TUROW, Scott. *Presumed Innocent.* 1987. Farrar Straus Giroux. 1st ed. dj. EX. K2. $65.00

TUROW, Scott. *Presumed Innocent.* 1987. Farrar Straus Giroux. 5th print. dj. VG. P1. $18.95

TUSHINGHAM, A.D. *Gold for the Gods.* 1976. Toronto. 1st ed. 146 p. wrp. F2. $15.00

TUTTLE, C.R. *General Hist of State of MI.* 1874. Detroit. 730 p. EX. $50.00

TUTTLE, W.C. *Mission River Justice.* 1955. Avalon. dj. xl. P1. $6.00

TUTUOLA, Amos. *Palm-Wine Drunkard.* 1954. Grove Pr. 1st Am ed. dj. EX. K2. $50.00

TWAIN, Mark. *Adventures of Huckleberry Finn.* nd. NY/London. Harper. Ils Juvenile Series. VG. $20.00

TWAIN, Mark. *Adventures of Huckleberry Finn.* 1885. NY. Orig Pub Prospectus to 1st Am ed. VG. H3. $7500.00

TWAIN, Mark. *Adventures of Huckleberry Finn.* 1885. NY. Webster. Ils Kemble. 1st Am ed. later state. 366 p. D4. $625.00

TWAIN, Mark. *Adventures of Huckleberry Finn.* 1885. Webster. 1st ed. 1st issue. gilt gr bdg. EX. K2. $2500.00

TWAIN, Mark. *Adventures of Huckleberry Finn.* 1885. Webster. 1st ed. 1st issue. gilt gr bdg. VG. K2. $1250.00

TWAIN, Mark. *Adventures of Huckleberry Finn.* 1942. Ltd Ed Club. Ils/sgn Thomas Hart Benton. slipcase. VG. C4. $200.00

TWAIN, Mark. *Adventures of Tom Sawyer.* c 1930. World. 317 p. VG. $20.00

TWAIN, Mark. *Adventures of Tom Sawyer.* nd. Donohue. dj. VG. P1. $15.00

TWAIN, Mark. *Adventures of Tom Sawyer.* nd. NY/London. Ils Juvenile Series. VG. $20.00

TWAIN, Mark. *Adventures of Tom Sawyer.* 1939. Ltd Ed Club. Ils/sgn Thomas Hart Benton. slipcase. EX. C4. $275.00

TWAIN, Mark. *Am Claimant.* 1892. NY. Webster. 1st ed. gr bdg. VG. C1. $95.00

TWAIN, Mark. *CT Yankee in King Arthur's Court.* nd. Book League. orig tissue wrp. P1. $10.00

TWAIN, Mark. *CT Yankee in King Arthur's Court.* nd. Grosset Dunlap. dj. VG. P1. $7.50

TWAIN, Mark. *CT Yankee in King Arthur's Court.* 1889. NY. uncut copy of 1st ed. contemporary sheep. EX. H3. $7500.00

TWAIN, Mark. *CT Yankee in King Arthur's Court.* 1889. Webster. 1st ed. later state. EX. K2. $350.00

TWAIN, Mark. *CT Yankee in King Arthur's Court.* 1942. Heritage Pr. Ils Warren Chappell. slipcase. M. $20.00

TWAIN, Mark. *Double-Barreled Detective Story.* 1902. NY. 1st ed. reg/gold bdg. VG. B3. $95.00

TWAIN, Mark. *Editorial Wild Oats.* 1905. NY/London. 1st ed. scarce. $60.00

TWAIN, Mark. *Eng As She Is Taught.* 1887. London. Unwin. True 1st ed. EX. K2. $385.00

TWAIN, Mark. *Extracts From Adam's Diary.* 1950. Whitcombe Gilmour. VG. P1. $7.50

TWAIN, Mark. *Following the Equator.* 1897. Hartford. Am Pub. 1st ed. 8vo. 712 p. G. V1. $70.00

TWAIN, Mark. *Gilded Age.* 1873. Am Pub Co. 1st ed. 1st issue. full calf. repaired spine. EX. H3. $2500.00

TWAIN, Mark. *Innocents Abroad.* 1869. Hartford. 1st ed. 3rd issue. gilt blk bdg. $125.00

TWAIN, Mark. *Innocents Abroad.* 1871. Hartford. Orig Pub Prospectus to 1st Am ed. VG. H3. $3000.00

TWAIN, Mark. *Life of the MS.* 1883. Boston. Osgood. 1st ed. 2nd state. VG. $100.00

TWAIN, Mark. *Life on the MS.* 1883. Boston. 1st Am ed. 1st issue. pub sheep bdg. rebacked. VG. H3. $500.00

TWAIN, Mark. *Life on the MS.* 1944. Heritage. Ils/sgn TH Benton. slipcase. VG. $200.00

TWAIN, Mark. *Life on the MS.* 1944. Ltd Ed Club. Ils/sgn TH Benton. slipcase. EX. C4. $350.00

TWAIN, Mark. *Tom Sawyer Abroad.* nd. Grosset Dunlap. dj. VG. P1. $17.50

TWAIN, Mark. *Tom Sawyer Detective.* nd. Grosset Dunlap. dj. VG. P1. $17.50

TWAIN, Mark. *Tramp Abroad.* 1880. Hartford. 1st ed. 1st state. orig bdg. VG. H3. $450.00

TWAIN, Mark. *Writings.* nd. (1907) Harper. Hillcrest ed. 25 vols. Bayntun bdg. H3. $5000.00

TWAIN, Mark. *Writings.* 1929. Harper. Stormfield ed. 1/1024. 37 vols. djs. H3. $4150.00

TWAIN, Mark. *Yankee at the Court of King Arthur.* nd. Musson. VG. P1. $7.50

TWAIN, Mark. *Yankee in King Arthur's Court.* 1890. Charles L Webster. G. P1. $75.00

TWAIN & WARNER. *Gilded Age.* 1884. Hartford. later ed. inscr to US Grant Jr. H3. $4000.00

TWILFORD, W.R. *Sown in the Darkness.* 1940. Tremayne. 1st ed. dj. EX. R3. $75.00

TWOPENY, William. *Eng Metalwork: 93 Drawings.* 1904. London. 4to. T1. $125.00

TYAS, Robert. *Language of Flowers; or, Foral Emblems of Thoughts...* 1869. London. 1st ed. 12 clr pls. 223 p. AEG. G. T5. $125.00

TYLER, Anne. *Accidental Tourist.* 1985. Knopf. 1st ed. sgn. dj. EX. K2. $100.00

TYLER, Anne. *Breathing Lessons.* 1988. Franklin Lib. 1st ed. sgn. EX. K2. $125.00

TYLER, Anne. *Breathing Lessons.* 1988. Knopf. UP. wrp. EX. B13. $85.00

TYLER, Anne. *Breathing Lessons.* 1988. Knopf. 1st ed. dj. EX. K2. $35.00

TYLER, Anne. *Breathing Lessons.* 1988. Toronto. Viking. 1st Canadian ed. dj. EX. K2. $50.00

TYLER, Anne. *Celestial Navigation.* 1974. Knopf. 1st ed. sgn. dj. EX. B13. $275.00

TYLER, Anne. *Dinner at the Homesick Restaurant.* 1982. Knopf. 1st ed. dj. EX. B13. $65.00

TYLER, Anne. *Dinner at the Homesick Restuarant.* 1982. London. 1st ed. dj. EX. $55.00

TYLER, Anne. *If Morning Ever Comes.* 1972. Knopf. Book Club ed. dj. EX. B13. $65.00

TYLER, Anne. *Searching for Caleb.* 1976. Knopf. 1st ed. sgn. dj. EX. B13. $250.00

TYLER, Anne. *Visit With Eudora Welty.* 1980. Chicago. Pressworks. 1st ed. 1/100. wrp. EX. B13. $150.00

TYLER, J.E.A. *Tolkien Companion.* 1976. St Martin. M. R3. $12.95

TYLER, M.P. *Grandmother Tyler's Book.* 1925. NY. 1st ed. VG. $25.00

TYLER, Wilfred. *Playing With Magic.* 1953. London. Armstrong. 1st ed. 107 p. dj. EX. J3. $8.00

TYLER & FURNAS. *Whatever Goes Up.* 1934. Bobbs Merrill. 1st ed. octavo. 317 p. VG. H3. $60.00

TYMN, Marshall. *Am Fantasy & SF 1948-1973.* 1979. Starmont. 1st ed. wrp. EX. R3. $15.00

TYMN, Marshall. *SF Reference Book.* 1980. Starmont. wrp. M. R3. $25.00

TYMN, Marshall. *SF: A Teacher's Guide.* 1988. Starmont. 1st ed. wrp. M. R3. $15.95

TYMN & SCHLOBIN. *Year's Scholarship in SF 1972-1975.* 1979. Kent State. no dj issued. P1/R3. $15.00

TYNAN, Katherine. *Daughter of the Fields.* 1901. Chicago. McClurg. 1st ed. EX. B13. $45.00

TYNAN, Kathleen. *Agatha.* 1978. Ballantine. 2nd ed. dj. VG. P1. $17.50

TYRRELL, J.W. *Across the Sub-Arctic of Canada.* 1897. Toronto. Briggs. VG. $150.00

UBELAKER, Douglas. *Ayalan Cemetery.* 1981. Smithsonian. 1st ed. sm 4to. 175 p. F2. $20.00

UHNAK, Dorothy. *False Witness.* 1981. Simon Schuster. 1st ed. dj. VG. P1. $10.00

UHNAK, Dorothy. *Investigation.* nd. Simon Schuster. 4th ed. dj. VG. P1. $12.50

UHNAK, Dorothy. *Law & Order.* 1973. Simon Schuster. 1st ed. dj. VG. P1. $17.50

UHNAK, Dorothy. *Victims.* 1985. Simon Schuster. 1st ed. dj. VG. P1. $12.50

UKERS, William. *Romance of Tea.* 1936. NY. 1st ed. 276 p. VG. B3. $30.00

ULANOV, Barry. *Duke Ellington.* 1946. NY. Creative Age. 1st ed. 322 p. dj. RS. EX. H3. $85.00

ULLMAN, Betty. *Voluptuaries.* 1978. Putnam. 1st ed. dj. EX. F5. $17.00

ULLMAN, J.M. *Neon Haystack.* nd. Book Club. dj. VG. P1. $4.50

ULLMAN, J.R. *Day on Fire.* 1958. World. 1st ed. 701 p. VG. B10. $5.50

ULLMAN, J.R. *River of the Sun.* 1951. Lippincott Book Club. 444 p. VG. B10. $3.50

ULLMAN, James. *Other Side of the Mt.* 1938. NY. Carrick Evans. 1st ed. 336 p. F2. $15.00

ULLMAN, S.G. *Valentino As I Kew Him.* 1926. Macy Masius. 3rd print. presentation. 218 p. VG. H3. $150.00

UNDERWOOD, C.F. *Famous Love Songs: Old & New.* c 1908. Bobbs Merrill. 18 pls. EX. $90.00

UNDERWOOD, Michael. *Murder on Trial.* 1975. Ian Henry. VG. P1. $12.50

UNDERWOOD, Michael. *Trout in the Milk.* 1971. NY. 1st ed. dj. VG. B3. $25.00

UNDERWOOD, P.K. *Karloff.* 1972. NY. 1st Am ed. dj. EX. $25.00

UNDERWOOD & MILLER. *Bare Bones.* 1988. Underwood Miller. 1st ed. 1/1000. boxed. M. R3. $175.00

UNDERWOOD & MILLER. *Jack Vance: Writers of the 21st Century.* 1980. Taplinger. 1st ed. dj. EX. $15.00

UNGERER, Tomi. *Poster Art of Tomi Ungerer.* 1971. NY. 1st ed. folio. dj. EX. G1. $20.00

UNKELBACH, K. *Love on a Leash.* 1964. NJ. Ils Bob Bugg. 1st ed. dj. EX. $15.00

UNRAU, W.E. *Tending the Talking Wire.* 1979. Salt Lake City. Ils. dj. A5. $30.00

UNTERMEYER, Louis. *Poems of John Greenleaf Whittier.* 1945. Heritage. Ils RJ Holden. slipcase. EX. T1. $20.00

UNTERMEYER, Louis. *Poems of William Cullen Bryant.* 1947. Heritage. Ils Thomas Nason. slipcase. EX. T1. $20.00

UNTERMEYER, Louis. *Wonderful Adventures of Paul Bunyan.* 1945. Ltd Ed Club. Ils/sgn Everett Jackson. slipcase. EX. $40.00

UNWIN, Frances. *Etcher & Draughtsman.* 1928. London. Fleuron Ltd. 1/300. 4to. VG. $25.00

UP DE GRAFF, F.W. *Head Hunters of the Amazon.* 1923. Duffield. 1st ed. 337 p. F2. $40.00

UP DE GRAFF, F.W. *Head Hunters of the Amazon.* 1923. Garden City. 337 p. dj. F2. $15.00

UPDIKE, D.B. *Updike: Am Printer & His Merrymount Pr.* 1947. 1st ed. dj. EX. $50.00

UPDIKE, James; see Burnett, W.R.

UPDIKE, John. *Afterlife.* 1987. 6th Chamber. 1/175. sgn. EX. K2. $175.00

UPDIKE, John. *Assorted Prose.* 1965. Knopf. 1st ed. dj. w/sgn tipped-in sheet. EX. K2. $225.00

UPDIKE, John. *Assorted Prose.* 1966. Fawcett. 1st PB ed. EX. K2. $20.00

UPDIKE, John. *Bath After Sailing.* 1968. Country Squires. Ltd ed. 1/125. sgn. wrp. EX. K2. $750.00

UPDIKE, John. *Bech Is Back.* 1982. Knopf. ARC. sgn. dj. w/promotional post card. B13. $125.00

UPDIKE, John. *Bech Is Back.* 1982. Knopf. Ltd ed. 1/500. sgn. dj. H3. $150.00

UPDIKE, John. *Bech Is Back.* 1982. Knopf. 1st ed. sgn. dj. EX. C4. $60.00

UPDIKE, John. *Bech Is Back.* 1982. Knopf. 1st ed. 1/500. sgn. dj. slipcase. EX. B13. $175.00

UPDIKE, John. *Bech: A Book.* 1970. Knopf. Ltd ed. 1/500. sgn. dj. boxed. H3. $175.00

UPDIKE, John. *Bech: A Book.* 1970. Knopf. Ltd ed. 1/500. sgn. dj. slipcase. EX. B13. $225.00

UPDIKE, John. *Bech: A Book.* 1970. Knopf. 1st ed. sgn. dj. EX. B13. $65.00

UPDIKE, John. *Beloved.* 1982. Lord John. Deluxe ed. 1/100. sgn. no dj issued. EX. K2. $200.00

UPDIKE, John. *Beloved.* 1982. Lord John. Ltd ed. 1/300. sgn. EX. K2. $100.00

UPDIKE, John. *Bottom's Dream.* 1969. Knopf. 1st Trade ed. dj. EX. K2. $100.00

UPDIKE, John. *Buchanan Dying.* 1974. London. Deutsch. 1st UK ed. sgn. dj. EX. B13. $100.00

UPDIKE, John. *Carpentered Hen & Other Creatures.* 1982. Knopf. ARC/reissue. sgn. dj. EX. B13. $85.00

UPDIKE, John. *Carpentered Hen & Other Tame Creatures.* 1958. Harper. 1st ed. dj. EX. H3. $450.00

UPDIKE, John. *Centaur.* 1963. Knopf. 1st ed. dj. w/sgn label on half title. EX. C4. $175.00

UPDIKE, John. *Centaur.* 1964. Fawcett. 1st ed. EX. K2. $20.00

UPDIKE, John. *Centaur.* 1983. Ballantine. 1st PB ed. VG. K2. $15.00

UPDIKE, John. *Chaste Planet.* 1980. Worcester. Metacom. Ltd ed. 1/300. sgn. wrp. EX. H3. $75.00

UPDIKE, John. *Child's Calendar.* 1965. Knopf. 1st Trade ed. sgn. dj. EX. K2. $275.00

UPDIKE, John. *Corre, Conejo (Rabbit, Run).* 1979. Bruguera. 1st Spanish ed. wrp. VG. K2. $45.00

UPDIKE, John. *Coup.* 1978. Knopf. Ltd ed. 1/350. sgn. dj. slipcase. EX. B13. $250.00

UPDIKE, John. *Coup.* 1978. Knopf. 1st ed. sgn. dj. EX. B13. $85.00

UPDIKE, John. *Coup.* 1978. Knopf. 2nd ed. 298 p. VG. B10. $5.00

UPDIKE, John. *Couples.* 1968. NY. 1st ed. dj. EX. $35.00

UPDIKE, John. *Couples: Short Story.* 1976. Halty Ferguson. Ltd ed. 1/250. sgn. wrp. dj. H3. $125.00

UPDIKE, John. *Cunts.* 1974. NY. Frank Hallman. 1/250. sgn. no dj issued. EX. K2. $250.00

UPDIKE, John. *Ego & Art in Walt Whitman.* 1980. Targ Ed. Ltd ed. 1/350. sgn. dj. K2. $85.00

UPDIKE, John. *From the Journal of a Leper.* 1978. Lord John. Ltd ed. 1/300. sgn. H3. $75.00

UPDIKE, John. *Getting Older.* 1986. Helsinki. Eurographica. 1st ed. 1/350. sgn. stiff wrp. dj. EX. B13. $175.00

UPDIKE, John. *Getting the Words Out.* 1988. Lord John. Deluxe ed. 1/50. sgn. EX. K2. $125.00

UPDIKE, John. *Getting the Words Out.* 1988. Lord John. Ltd ed. 1/250. sgn. EX. K2. $85.00

UPDIKE, John. *Hoping for a Hoopoe.* 1959. London. Gollancz. 1st UK ed. sgn. dj. EX. B13. $250.00

UPDIKE, John. *Hugging the Shore.* 1984. Vintage. 1st Trade PB ed. EX. K2. $20.00

UPDIKE, John. *Impressions.* 1985. Sylvester Orphanos. 1/330. sgn. slipcase. EX. K2. $250.00

UPDIKE, John. *Jester's Dozen.* 1984. Lord John. Ltd ed. 1/150. sgn. H3. $125.00

UPDIKE, John. *Just Looking.* 1989. Knopf. Ltd ed. 1/350. sgn. slipcase. EX. B13. $200.00

UPDIKE, John. *Just Looking.* 1989. Knopf. UP. wrp. EX. K2. $150.00

UPDIKE, John. *Just Looking.* 1989. Knopf. 1st ed. sgn. dj. EX. B13. $85.00

UPDIKE, John. *Marry Me.* 1976. Franklin Lib. 1st ed. EX. K2. $65.00

UPDIKE, John. *Marry Me.* 1976. Knopf. Ltd ed. 1/300. sgn. dj. slipcase. EX. B13. $250.00

UPDIKE, John. *Marry Me.* 1976. Knopf. 1st ed. sgn. dj. EX. B13. $75.00

UPDIKE, John. *Midpoint & Other Poems.* 1969. Knopf. ARC. sgn. dj. RS. EX. B13. $150.00

UPDIKE, John. *Midpoint & Other Poems.* 1969. Knopf. 1st ed. 1/350. sgn. dj. slipcase. EX. B13. $175.00

UPDIKE, John. *Month of Sundays.* 1975. Knopf. ARC of 1st Trade ed. dj. EX. K2. $85.00

UPDIKE, John. *Month of Sundays.* 1975. Knopf. Book Club ed. 228 p. EX. B10. $4.50

UPDIKE, John. *Month of Sundays.* 1975. Knopf. Ltd ed. 1/450. sgn. dj. slipcase. B13/H3. $175.00

UPDIKE, John. *Month of Sundays.* 1975. Knopf. Ltd ed. 1/450. sgn. dj. slipcase. K2. $125.00

UPDIKE, John. *Month of Sundays.* 1975. Knopf. 1st ed. sgn. dj. EX. B13. $100.00

UPDIKE, John. *Museums & Women.* 1972. Knopf. Ltd ed. 1/350. sgn. slipcase. EX. B13. $150.00

UPDIKE, John. *Museums & Women.* 1972. Knopf. 1st ed. sgn. dj. EX. B13. $85.00

UPDIKE, John. *Music School.* 1966. Knopf. 1st ed. 1st issue. inscr. dj. EX. K2. $275.00

UPDIKE, John. *Music School.* 1966. Knopf. 2nd issue. sgn. dj. EX. B13. $150.00

UPDIKE, John. *Music School.* 1967. Fawcett. 1st ed. EX. K2. $20.00

UPDIKE, John. *Music School.* 1980. Vintage. 1st ed. EX. K2. $15.00

UPDIKE, John. *Of the Farm.* 1965. NY. 1st ed. dj. EX. $45.00

UPDIKE, John. *Of the Farm.* 1967. Fawcett. 1st ed. EX. K2. $20.00

UPDIKE, John. *Olinger Stories: A Selection.* 1964. NY. PB Orig. sgn. EX. T9. $50.00

UPDIKE, John. *Olinger Stories: A Selection.* 1964. Vintage. PB Orig. wrp. EX. K2. $45.00

UPDIKE, John. *People 1 Knows.* 1980. Lord John. Deluxe ed. 1/100. sgn. slipcase. EX. K2. $175.00

UPDIKE, John. *People 1 Knows.* 1980. Lord John. Ltd ed. 1/300. sgn. slipcase. EX. K2. $100.00

UPDIKE, John. *People 1 Knows. Interviews With Insufficiently Famous Am.* 1980. Lord John. Deluxe Ltd ed. 1/100. sgn. slipcase. H3. $125.00

UPDIKE, John. *Picked-Up Pieces.* 1975. Knopf. Ltd ed. 1/250. sgn. dj. boxed. H3. $150.00

UPDIKE, John. *Picked-Up Pieces.* 1975. Knopf. 1st Trade ed. sgn. clipped dj. EX. B13. $75.00

UPDIKE, John. *Pigeon Feathers & Other Stories.* 1981. Franklin Lib. Ltd ed. sgn. full leather. EX. B13. $150.00

UPDIKE, John. *Pigeon Feathers.* 1962. Knopf. 1st ed. later print. sgn. dj. EX. $45.00

UPDIKE, John. *Pigeon Feathers.* 1963. Fawcett. 1st PB ed. sgn. EX. K2. $50.00

UPDIKE, John. *Plumes du Pigeon.* 1964. Paris. Ed de Seuil. 1st French ed. wrp. EX. K2. $85.00

UPDIKE, John. *Poorhouse Fair.* 1959. Knopf. 1st ed. dj. EX. B13. $250.00

UPDIKE, John. *Poorhouse Fair.* 1959. Knopf. 1st ed. sgn. dj. H3. $450.00

UPDIKE, John. *Poorhouse Fair.* 1959. London. Gollancz. 1st UK ed. sgn. dj. EX. K2. $650.00

UPDIKE, John. *Poorhouse Fair.* 1964. Fawcett. 1st PB ed. sgn. EX. K2. $50.00

UPDIKE, John. *Problems.* 1979. Knopf. 1/350. sgn. dj. slipcase. EX. B13. $150.00

UPDIKE, John. *Rabbit, Run.* 1960. Knopf. 1st ed. sgn. dj. EX. K2. $650.00

UPDIKE, John. *Rabbit, Run.* 1962. Fawcett. 1st PB ed. VG. K2. $30.00

UPDIKE, John. *Rabbit at Rest.* 1990. Knopf. 1st ed. yel wrp. EX. K2. $150.00

UPDIKE, John. *Rabbit at Rest.* 1990. London. Deutsch. 1st ed. dj. EX. B13. $45.00

UPDIKE, John. *Rabbit at Rest.* 1990. NY. UCP. EX. K2. $150.00

UPDIKE, John. *Rabbit Is Rich.* 1981. Knopf. UP. wrp. EX. C4. $150.00

UPDIKE, John. *Rabbit Is Rich.* 1981. Knopf. 1st ed. sgn. dj. EX. B13. $100.00

UPDIKE, John. *Rabbit Is Rich.* 1982. London. Deutsch. 1st ed. dj. EX. B13. $75.00

UPDIKE, John. *Rabbit Is Rich/Rabbit Redux/Rabbit Run.* 1981. Knopf. 1st ed. wrp. EX. C4. $20.00

UPDIKE, John. *Rabbit Redux.* 1971. Knopf. 1/350. sgn. Special bdg. slipcase. B13/C4. $350.00

UPDIKE, John. *Rabbit Redux.* 1971. Knopf. 1st ed. sgn. dj. EX. B13. $125.00

UPDIKE, John. *Rabbit Redux.* 1972. London. Deutsch. 1st UK ed. dj. EX. B13. $85.00

UPDIKE, John. *Rabbit Run.* 1960. Knopf. 1st ed. dj. VG. B13. $275.00

UPDIKE, John. *Rabbit Run.* 1961. London. Deutsch. 1st UK ed. dj. EX. scarce. B13. $300.00

UPDIKE, John. *Ring.* 1964. Knopf. 1st ed. sgn Updike/Chappell. Gibraltar Lib bdg. B13. $300.00

UPDIKE, John. *Roger's Version.* 1986. Knopf. Ltd ed. 1/350. sgn. dj. slipcase. EX. B13. $200.00

UPDIKE, John. *Roger's Version.* 1986. Knopf. 1st ed. inscr. dj. EX. B13. $85.00

UPDIKE, John. *Roger's Version.* 1986. Knopf. 1/350. sgn. Special bdg. acetate dj. slipcase. EX. C4. $150.00

UPDIKE, John. *S.* 1988. Knopf. 1st ed. sgn. dj. EX. B13. $65.00

UPDIKE, John. *S.* 1988. Knopf. 1st ed. 1/350. sgn. dj. slipcase. EX. B13. $200.00

UPDIKE, John. *S.* 1988. London. Deutsch. 1st UK ed. 1/97. sgn. slipcase. EX. K2. $650.00

UPDIKE, John. *S.* 1988. NY. 1st ed. 1/350. sgn. slipcase. EX. $145.00

UPDIKE, John. *Self-Consciousness.* 1989. Knopf. 1st ed. 1/350. sgn. dj. slipcase. EX. B13. $175.00

UPDIKE, John. *Self-Consciousness.* 1989. Knopf. 1st Trade ed. M. K2. $25.00

UPDIKE, John. *Self-Consciousness.* 1989. NY. 1st Trade ed. sgn. dj. EX. $45.00

UPDIKE, John. *Soft Spring Night in Shillington.* 1986. Lord John. Ltd ed. 1/250. sgn. EX. K2. $85.00

UPDIKE, John. *Soft Spring Night in Shillington.* 1986. Lord John. Deluxe ed. 1/50. sgn. slipcase. EX. K2. $175.00

UPDIKE, John. *Talk From the '50s.* 1979. Lord John. Deluxe Ltd ed. 1/75. sgn. H3. $125.00

UPDIKE, John. *Talk From the '50s.* 1979. Lord John. Ltd ed. 1/300. sgn. EX. K2. $75.00

UPDIKE, John. *Telephone Poles & Other Poems.* 1963. Adams House. 1st ed. dj. EX. K2. $45.00

UPDIKE, John. *Telephone Poles.* 1964. London. Deutsch. 1st ed. sgn. clipped dj. EX. B13. $85.00

UPDIKE, John. *Tossing & Turning.* 1978. Knopf. 1/350. sgn. Special bdg. dj. slipcase. EX. C4. $175.00

UPDIKE, John. *Trust Me.* 1987. Knopf. 1st ed. 1/350. sgn. dj. slipcase. EX. B13. $225.00

UPDIKE, John. *Verse.* 1965. Crest. 1st ed. wrp. EX. B13. $45.00

UPDIKE, John. *Witches of Eastwick.* 1984. Franklin Lib. Ltd 1st ed. sgn. EX. K2. $85.00

UPDIKE, John. *Witches of Eastwick.* 1984. Knopf. 1st ed. 1/350. sgn. dj. slipcase. EX. B13. $250.00

UPDIKE, John. *3 Illuminations in Life of Am Author.* 1979. NY. 1/350. sgn. tissue wrp. VG. T5. $95.00

UPDIKE, John. *3 Illuminations in Life of Am Author.* 1979. Targ Ed. Ltd ed. sgn. dj. EX. K2. $100.00

UPDIKE, John. *5 Poems.* 1980. Cleveland. Bits. 1/185. sgn. wrp. orig envelope. EX. K2. $100.00

UPFIELD, A.W. *Bachelors of Broken Hill.* 1950. Crime Club. 1st ed. G. P1. $10.00

UPFIELD, A.W. *Bone Is Pointed.* 1966. Angus Robertson. dj. xl. P1. $10.00

UPFIELD, A.W. *Bony & the Kelly Gang.* 1976. Am Reprint Co. VG. P1. $10.00

UPFIELD, A.W. *Death of a Swagman.* 1945. Crime Club. 1st ed. xl. P1. $15.00

UPFIELD, A.W. *Death of a Swagman.* 1962. Angus Robertson. dj. xl. P1. $12.50

UPFIELD, A.W. *Devil's Steps.* 1965. Angus Robertson. xl. P1. $10.00

UPFIELD, A.W. *Gripped by Drought.* 1990. Macmillan. dj. EX. P1. $30.00

UPFIELD, A.W. *House of Cain.* 1983. Macmillan. dj. EX. P1. $40.00

UPFIELD, A.W. *Journey to the Hangman.* 1959. Crime Club. 1st ed. dj. xl. P1. $15.00

UPFIELD, A.W. *Mr Jelly's Business.* 1964. Angus Robertson. dj. xl. P1. $10.00

UPFIELD, A.W. *Murchison Murders.* 1987. Dennis McMillan. reprint of 1867 ed. M. R3. $50.00

UPFIELD, A.W. *Murchison Murders.* 1987. Dennis McMillan. 1st ed. dj. EX. P1. $15.00

UPFIELD, A.W. *New Shoe.* nd. CA U. 2nd ed. EX. P1. $10.00

UPFIELD, A.W. *Royal Abduction.* 1984. Dennis McMillan. reprint of 1932 ed. M. R3. $50.00

UPFIELD, A.W. *Venom House.* 1952. Doubleday. 1st ed. dj. VG. P1. $25.00

UPFIELD, A.W. *Widows of Broome.* nd. Book Club. dj. VG. P1. $6.00

UPFIELD, A.W. *Winds of Evil.* 1961. Angus Robertson. dj. VG. P1. $20.00

UPSON, W.H. *Keep 'Em Crawling.* 1942. NY. 1st ed. sgn. dj. VG. B3. $30.00

UPSON, W.H. *Piano Movers.* 1927. St Charles. 1st ed. VG. B3. $35.00

UPTON, Charles. *Panic Grass.* 1968. City Lights. 1st ed. EX. B4. $8.00

UPTON, G.P. *Musical Pastels With Ils From Rare Prints & Facsimiles.* 1902. McClurg. 1st ed. 12mo. TEG. EX. R4. $25.00

UPTON, Mark. *Dark Summer.* 1979. Coward McCann. 1st ed. dj. EX. F5. $15.00

UPTON, Richard. *Ft Custer on the Big Horn 1877-1898.* 1973. Glendale. Clark. Ils. presentation. 308 p. A5. $40.00

UPTON, Robert. *Fade Out.* 1984. Viking. 1st ed. dj. EX. F5. $15.00

UPTON, Robert. *Golden Fleecing.* 1979. St Martin. 1st ed. dj. EX. P1. $12.50

URIS, Leon. *Exodus.* 1958. Doubleday. 1st ed. inscr. clipped dj. VG. B13. $85.00

URQUHART, R.E. *Arnhem.* 1958. NY. Ils 1st ed. 238 p. dj. VG. T5. $42.50

URTEAGA, Horacio. *Imperio Incaico.* 1931. Lima. Ils. 269 p. F2. $35.00

USSHER, USSHER, & USSHER. *Extracts From Letters...Later of City of Waterford, Ireland.* 1884. Phil. Friends Bookstore. 16mo. 148 p. V1. $14.00

USTINOV, Peter. *Dear Me.* 1977. Little Brn. 1st ed. 374 p. dj. EX. B10. $5.00

USTINOV, Peter. *5 Plays.* nd. (1965) Little Brn. 317 p. B10. $3.50

UTTLEY, Alison. *Country Things.* 1946. London. Faber. 1st ed. EX. B10. $15.00

UTTLEY, Alison. *Traveler in Time.* 1958. Faber Faber. dj. xl. P1. $7.50

VACHSS, Andrew. *Blossom.* 1990. Knopf. UP. sgn. wrp. EX. K2. $45.00

VACHSS, Andrew. *Flood.* 1985. Donald Fine. Special Advance Reader ed. sgn. dj. NM. T9. $55.00

VACHSS, Andrew. *Strega.* 1987. Knopf. 1st ed. dj. VG. P1. $18.95

VAIL, Sharon. *4 Poems.* 1942. Blk Sun. wrp. EX. H3. $150.00

VAILLANT, George. *Artists & Craftsmen in Ancient Central Am.* 1935. Am Mus Nat Hist. Ils. 102 p. 4to. wrp. F2. $15.00

VAILLANT, George. *Aztecs of Mexico.* 1941. Doubleday. 1st ed. 340 p. F2. $20.00

VALCARCEL, L.E. *Cuzco.* 1942. Lima, Peru. 3rd ed. sm 4to. 37 p. stiff wrp. F2. $15.00

VALCARCEL, L.E. *Indians of Peru.* 1950. Pocahontas Pr. Ils Pierre Verger. 1st ed. dj. F2. $30.00

VALDES, A.P. *4th Estate.* 1901. Brentano. 1st ed. 461 p. G. B10. $4.50

VALENTINE, D.T. *Manual of...the City of NY 1865.* 1865. NY. Ils. 12mo. pls. 879 p. VG. G4. $45.00

VALENTINE, D.T. *Obsequies of Abraham Lincoln in City of NY.* 1866. NY. 1st ed. 8vo. 254 p. gilt blk bdg. xl. T1. $125.00

VALENZUELA, Luisa. *Lizard's Tail.* 1983. Farrar Straus. UP. wrp. EX. K2. $40.00

VALERY, Paul. *Fragments des Memories d'un Poeme.* 1938. Paris. Grasset. sgn. wrp. H3. $100.00

VALERY, Paul. *Poesies.* 1930. Paris. Gallimard. presentation. cream wrp. glassine dj. H3. $150.00

VALERY, Paul. *Souvenir de Paul Souday.* 1929. Abbeville. Paillart. 1/200. inscr. gray wrp. glassine dj. H3. $100.00

VALERY, Paul. *Une Conquete Methodique.* 1924. Paillart. Ltd ed. 1/238. sgn. wrp. glassine dj. H3. $100.00

VALK, Melvin. *World Index to Gottfried's Tristan.* 1958. WI U. 1st ed. EX. C1. $9.00

VALLEJO, Boris. *Fantastic Art of Vallejo.* 1978. Del Rey. 1st ed. wrp. EX. R3. $10.00

VAN ASH, Cay. *Fires of Fu Manchu.* 1987. Harper Row. 1st ed. dj. EX. P1. $15.95

VAN ATTA, Winfred. *Shock Treatment.* nd. Book Club. dj. VG. P1. $4.50

VAN BRUGH, John. *Complete Works of Sir John Van Brugh.* 1927-1928. Nonesuch. 1/410. 4to. 4 vols. EX. C4. $100.00

VAN CLEVE, C. *3 Score Years & 10.* 1888. Ft Snelling, MN. 1st ed. G. B3. $65.00

VAN DE POLL, Willem. *Surinam: Country & Its People.* 1951. Hauge, Netherlands. 1st ed. 4to. 199 p. F2. $25.00

VAN DE WALLE, B. *Transmission des Textes Littaires Egyptiens.* 1948. Bruxelles. xl. VG. G1. $25.00

VAN DE WATER, F.F. *Plunder.* 1933. Canadian Crime Club. dj. VG. P1. $15.00

VAN DE WATERING, Janwillem. *Empty Mirror: Experiences in Japanese Monastery.* 1974. Houghton Mifflin. 1st Am ed. 145 p. dj. VG. $15.00

VAN DE WETERING, Janwillem. *Inspector Saito's Sm Satori.* 1985. Putnam. 1st ed. inscr. dj. EX. K2. $45.00

VAN DER MEER, Ron. *Pop-Up Book of Magic Tricks.* 1983. Viking. 1st ed. NM. J3. $10.00

VAN DER ZEE, James. *Harlem Book of the Dead.* 1978. Dobbs Ferry, NY. 1st ed. dj. EX. $125.00

VAN DINE, S.S. *Bishop Murder Case.* 1929. Scribner. 1st ed. VG. P1. $20.00

VAN DINE, S.S. *Dragon Murder Case.* 1933. Scribner. 1st ed. dj. EX. F5. $120.00

VAN DINE, S.S. *Garden Murder Case.* 1935. Scribner. 1st ed. VG. P1. $35.00

VAN DINE, S.S. *Greene Murder Case.* 1928. Scribner. 1st ed. VG. P1. $25.00

VAN DINE, S.S. *Scarab Murder Case.* 1945. Tower. dj. VG. P1. $17.50

VAN DIVER. *Their Tattered Flags.* 1970. NY. 1st ed. 362 p. dj. VG. B3. $27.50

VAN DOREN, Carl. *Great Rehearsal: Story...Constitution of US.* 1948. Viking. 1st ed? 336 p. VG. B10. $4.25

VAN DOREN, Carl. *James Branch Cabell.* 1932. Literary Guild. VG. P1. $15.00

VAN DOREN, Carl. *Literary Works of Abraham Lincoln.* 1942. Readers Club. 302 p. dj. VG. S1. $10.00

VAN DYKE, Henry. *Bl Flower.* 1902. Scribner. 1st ed. 298 p. TEG. EX. B10. $10.00

VAN DYKE, Henry. *Dead Piano.* 1971. NY. 1st ed. sgn. dj. EX. T9. $45.00

VAN DYKE, Henry. *Lost World: Christmas Legend of Long Ago.* 1899. Scribner. 1st ed. VG. C1. $12.50

VAN DYKE, Henry. *Poetry of Nature.* 1914. NY. Ils. 12mo. w/sgn letter. A4. $35.00

VAN DYKE, Henry. *Story of the Other Wise Man.* 1896. Harper. 1st ed. VG. C1. $19.50

VAN DYKE, Roy. *Fun With Balloons.* 1959. Colon. Abbotts. 1st ed. 14 p. SftCvr. EX. J3. $3.00

VAN EVERY, Dale. *Final Challenge: Am Frontier 1808-1845.* 1964. NY. 1st ed. 378 p. dj. T5. $15.00

VAN EVRIE, J.H. *Negroes & Negro Slavery.* 1861. NY. 1st ed. 339 p. VG. $110.00

VAN GELDER, R. *Am Legend: Treasury of Our Country's Yesterdays.* 1946. Appleton. 1st ed. 535 p. VG. B10. $6.00

VAN GULIK, Robert. *Given Day.* 1984. Dennis McMillan. dj. EX. P1. $40.00

VAN GULIK, Robert. *Given Day.* 1984. Dennis McMillan. 1st Am ed. M. R3. $50.00

VAN GULIK, Robert. *Murder in Canton.* 1967. Scribner. 1st ed. dj. VG. P1. $75.00

VAN LHIN, Erik. *Battle on Mercury.* 1953. Winston. 1st ed. VG. R3. $12.50

VAN LHIN, Erik. *Battle on Mercury.* 1958. Winston. 2nd ed. dj. VG. P1. $25.00

VAN LOON, H.W. *Adventures & Escapes of Gustavus Vasa.* 1945. NY. 1st ed. dj. VG. $17.50

VAN LOON, H.W. *Ancient Man.* 1920. Boni Liveright. 1st ed. 20 pls. 16 maps. 109 p. VG. $22.00

VAN LOON, H.W. *Arts.* 1937. Simon Schuster. 675 p. dj. VG. B10. $6.50

VAN LOON, H.W. *How To Look at Pictures.* 1938. Nat Com for Art. 1st ed. VG. $7.50

VAN LUSTBADER, Eric. *Beneath an Opal Moon.* 1980. Doubleday. 1st ed. dj. EX. R3. $20.00

VAN LUSTBADER, Eric. *Dai-San.* 1978. Doubleday. 1st ed. dj. EX. P1. $22.50

VAN LUSTBADER, Eric. *Shallows of Night.* 1978. Doubleday. 1st ed. dj. EX. R3. $20.00

VAN LUSTBADER, Eric. *Sirens.* 1981. Evans. 1st ed. dj. VG. P1. $15.00

VAN LUSTBADER, Eric. *Sunset Warrior.* 1977. Doubleday. 1st ed. dj. EX. R3. $20.00

VAN MARLE, Raimond. *Development of Italian Schools of Painting.* 1970. NY. Hacker Art Books. reprint of 1923 ed. 19 vols. EX. H3. $350.00

VAN NOPPEN, I.W. *Stoneman's Last Raid.* 1961. Raleigh. 1st ed. 112 p. EX. $45.00

VAN PAASSEN, Pierre. *Time Is Now.* 1941. NY. 1st ed. VG. $12.00

VAN PEEBLES, Mario. *Bear for the FBI.* nd. np. 1st Am ed. sgn. dj. EX. T9. $55.00

VAN RENSSELAER, Alexander. *Fun With Magic.* 1957. Doubleday. 56 p. dj. NM. J3. $17.00

VAN SCHAACK, H.C. *Memoirs of the Life of Henry Van Schaack.* 1892. Chicago. 1st ed. 233 p. EX. $65.00

VAN SCYOC, S.J. *Cloud Cry.* 1977. Berkley. dj. EX. P1. $15.00

VAN SCYOC, S.J. *Star Mother.* nd. Book Club. dj. VG. P1. $4.50

VAN SCYOC, S.J. *Star Mother.* 1976. Berkley Putnam. 1st ed. dj. xl. P1. $7.50

VAN SCYOC, S.J. *Sun Waifs.* 1981. Berkley Putnam. 1st HrdCvr ed. dj. EX. F5. $10.00

VAN STAN, Ina. *Peruvian Textiles & Artifacts.* 1971. Gainesville. Ils. map. wrp. F2. $10.00

VAN STAN, Ina. *Textiles From Beneath the Temple of Pachacamac, Peru.* 1967. Phil. 1st ed. 4to. wrp. F2. $25.00

VAN VECHTEN, Carl. *Firecrackers: A Realistic Novel.* 1925. Knopf. 1/195. sgn. boxed. H3. $150.00

VAN VOGT, A.E. *Away & Beyond.* 1952. Payson Clarke. 1st ed. dj. EX. R3. $10.00

VAN VOGT, A.E. *Battle of Forever.* 1978. Authors Co-Op. 1st ed. dj. EX. R3. $20.00

VAN VOGT, A.E. *Book of Ptath.* 1947. Fantasy. Ltd ed. 1/500. sgn. dj. EX. R3. $125.00

VAN VOGT, A.E. *Book of Ptath.* 1947. Fantasy. 1st ed. dj. EX. R3. $55.00

VAN VOGT, A.E. *House That Stood Still.* 1950. Greenberg. 2nd ed. dj. EX. R3. $15.00

VAN VOGT, A.E. *Masters of Time.* 1950. Fantasy. 1st ed. dj. VG. P1. $75.00

VAN VOGT, A.E. *Mind Cage.* nd. Book Club. dj. VG. P1. $4.50

VAN VOGT, A.E. *Mind Cage.* 1957. Simon Schuster. 1st ed. dj. EX. F5. $45.00

VAN VOGT, A.E. *Mixed Men.* 1952. Gnome. 1st ed. clipped dj. EX. F5. $45.00

VAN VOGT, A.E. *Mixed Men.* 1952. Gnome. 1st ed. VG. R3. $20.00

VAN VOGT, A.E. *Rogue Ship.* nd. Book Club. dj. VG. P1. $4.50

VAN VOGT, A.E. *Slan.* 1946. Arkham House. 1st ed. dj. VG. R3. $150.00

VAN VOGT, A.E. *Slan.* 1951. Simon Schuster. dj. G. P1. $20.00

VAN VOGT, A.E. *Slan.* 1951. Simon Schuster. 1st ed. dj. EX. R3. $25.00

VAN VOGT, A.E. *Slan.* 1953. London. 1st UK ed. dj. VG. R3. $25.00

VAN VOGT, A.E. *Van Vogt Omnibus 2.* 1971. Sidgwick Jackson. 1st ed. dj. EX. P1. $12.50

VAN VOGT, A.E. *World of Null-A.* 1950. Grosset Dunlap. dj. VG. P1. $35.00

VAN VOGT & HULL. *Out of the Unknown.* 1948. Fantasy. 2nd print. dj. EX. R3. $22.50

VAN VORST, Marie. *1st Love.* nd. Grosset Dunlap. 330 p. VG. B10. $3.50

VAN YOUNG, Eric. *Hacienda & Market in 18th-Century Mexico.* 1981. Berkley, CA. 1st ed. 388 p. dj. F2. $20.00

VAN ZANTWIJK, Rudolph. *Aztec Arrangement.* 1985. OK U. 1st ed. 345 p. dj. F2. $25.00

VANBRUCH, John. *Complete Works.* 1927. Nonesuch. 1/1300. 4 vols. EX. H3. $375.00

VANCE, Jack. *Araminta Station.* 1988. Tor Books. 1st ed. Boris Vallejo dj. EX. F5. $16.00

VANCE, Jack. *City of the Chasch.* 1975. London. 1st ed. dj. EX. R3. $22.50

VANCE, Jack. *Cugel's Saga.* 1983. Timescape. 1st ed. dj. EX. R3. $20.00

VANCE, Jack. *Dirdir.* 1980. Underwood Miller. 1st ed. sgn. no dj issued. EX. P1. $30.00

VANCE, Jack. *Dying Earth.* 1950. Hillman. 1st ed. wrp. VG. F5. $135.00

VANCE, Jack. *Fox Valley Murders.* 1966. Bobbs Merrill. 1st ed. dj. xl. P1. $15.00

VANCE, Jack. *Gray Prince.* 1974. Bobbs Merrill. 1st ed. dj. EX. R3. $20.00

VANCE, Jack. *Killing Machine.* 1964. Berkley. 1st ed. wrp. EX. F5. $15.00

VANCE, Jack. *Lost Moons.* 1982. Underwood Miller. 1st ed. dj. EX. F5. $20.00

VANCE, Jack. *Masks: Thaery.* 1976. Berkley. 1st ed. dj. EX. R3. $15.00

VANCE, Jack. *Moon Moth.* 1975. London. 1st HrdCvr ed. dj. EX. R3. $20.00

VANCE, Jack. *Planets of Adventure.* 1975. London. 1st HrdCvr ed. 4 vols. djs. EX. R3. $20.00

VANCE, Jack. *Pleasant Grove Murders.* 1967. Bobbs Merrill. 1st ed. dj. EX. F5. $110.00

VANCE, Jack. *Space Pirate.* 1953. Toby Books. 1st ed. wrp. EX. F5. $30.00

VANCE, Jack. *Star King.* 1964. Berkley. 1st ed. wrp. EX. F5. $15.00

VANCE, Jack. *To Live Forever.* 1956. Ballantine. 1st ed. wrp. EX. R3. $35.00

VANCE, Jack. *Vandals of the Void.* 1979. Gregg Pr. Revised 1st ed. sgn. dj. EX. F5. $50.00

VANCE, L.J. *Brass Bowl.* nd. AL Burt. G. P1. $6.00

VANCE, L.J. *Dead Ride Hard.* 1926. Copp Clarke. 1st ed. VG. P1. $17.50

VANCE, L.J. *Detective.* 1932. Lippincott. VG. T9. $20.00

VANCE, L.J. *Fortune Hunter.* nd. Grosset Dunlap. VG. P1. $10.00

VANCE, L.J. *Lone Wolf's Last Prowl.* nd. AL Burt. G. P1. $6.00

VANCE, L.J. *Pool of Flame.* 1909. Dodd Mead. 1st ed. dj. VG. F5. $30.00

VANCE, L.J. *Red Masquerade.* 1921. Doubleday Page. VG. P1. $17.50

VANCE, L.J. *Wht Fire.* nd. Grosset Dunlap. P1. $7.50

VANCE, Marguerite. *Song for a Lute.* 1961. (1st 1958) Ils Pellicer. 2nd print. xl. VG. C1. $5.00

VANDER VAT, Dan. *Gentlemen of War.* 1984. Morrow. 1st Am ed. 205 p. dj. M. B10. $7.00

VANDERBILT, Cornelius Jr. *Living Past of Am: Pictorial Treasury of Hist Houses...* 1959. Crown. 4th ed. 234 p. dj. EX. B10. $8.25

VANDERBILT, Gloria. *Blk Knight/Wht Knight.* 1987. Knopf. 1st ed. 299 p. dj. NM. B10. $7.00

VANDERCOOK, J.W. *Blk Majesty: Life of Christophe, King of Haiti.* 1928. NY. 1st ed. 207 p. slipcase. VG. T5. $35.00

VANDERCOOK, J.W. *Murder in Haiti.* nd. Book Club. dj. VG. P1. $4.50

VANDERCOOK, J.W. *Murder in Trinadad.* nd. Grosset Dunlap. P1. $6.00

VANDERCOOK, J.W. *Murder in Trinidad.* 1941. Triangle. 2nd ed. G. P1. $5.00

VANDIVER. *Their Tattered Flags.* 1970. NY. 1st ed. dj. VG. B3. $35.00

VANN, R.T. *Social Development of Eng Quakerism 1655-1755.* 1969. Cambridge, MA. 8vo. 259 p. VG. V1. $16.00

VANSTTART, Peter. *Lancelot.* 1978. London. Owen. 1st/only ed. dj. VG. C1. $65.00

VARDRE, Leslie. *Nameless Ones.* 1967. John Long. dj. VG. P1. $15.00

VARGAS LLOSA, Mario. *Aunt Julia & the Scriptwriter.* 1982. Farrar Straus. UP. wrp. EX. K2. $65.00

VARGAS LLOSA, Mario. *Gr House.* 1969. Harper Row. 1st ed. dj. EX. K2. $40.00

VARGAS LLOSA, Mario. *Time of the Hero.* 1966. Grove Pr. 1st ed. dj. EX. B13. $45.00

VARGAS LLOSA, Mario. *War at the End of the World.* 1984. Farrar Straus. 1st ed. dj. EX. K2. $35.00

VARGAS LLOSA, Mario. *War of the End of the World.* 1984. Farrar Straus. UP. wrp. EX. K2. $100.00

VARGAS LLOSA, Mario. *Who Killed Palomino Molero?* 1987. Farrar Straus. 1st ed. dj. EX. K2. $25.00

VARLEY, John. *Demon.* nd. Book Club. P1. $4.50

VARLEY, John. *Demon.* 1984. Berkley. 1st Trade ed. wrp. M. R3. $10.00

VARLEY, John. *Millenium.* 1983. Berkley. 1st HrdCvr ed. dj. EX. F5. $13.00

VARLEY, John. *Ophiuchi Hotline.* nd. Book Club. dj. VG. P1. $4.50

VARLEY, John. *Ophiuchi Hotline.* 1977. Dial. 1st ed. dj. EX. R3. $25.00

VARLEY, John. *Titan.* 1979. Berkley Putnam. 1st ed. dj. VG. P1. $22.50

VARLEY, John. *Titan.* 1979. Putnam. 1st ed. dj. EX. R3. $60.00

VARNER & VARNER. *Dogs of the Conquest.* 1983. OK U. 1st ed. 238 p. dj. F2. $20.00

VARNEY, A.C. *Our Homes & Their Adornments.* 1883. Detroit/Cleveland. 1st ed. G. $40.00

VARNEY, Carleton. *Decor With Clr.* nd. (1972) Creative Home Lib. 1st ed? 173 p. dj. B10. $5.50

VARVARO, Alberto. *Beroul's Romance of Tristan.* 1972.1st UK ed. dj. EX. C1. $12.50

VATLET, Jean. *Delirium Magicum: Close-Up Magic of Christian Chelman.* nd. Belgium. Deuxieme ed. French text. EX. J3. $20.00

VAUCAIRE, Michel. *Bolivar the Liberator.* 1929. Houghton Mifflin. 1st ed. 324 p. dj. F2. $15.00

VAUGHN, J.W. *Battle of Platte Bridge.* 1963. Norman. 1st ed. presentation. dj. A5. $40.00

VAUGHN, J.W. *Reynolds Campaign on the Powder River.* 1961. OK U. 1st ed. inscr. dj. A5. $50.00

VAUGHN, J.W. *With Crook on the Rosebut.* 1956. Stackpole. Ils 1st ed. inscr. dj. A5. $65.00

VAUGHT, Elsa. *Diary of an Unknown Soldier: Sept 5, 1862-Dec 7, 1862.* ca 1959. Fayetteville. 1st ed. orig wrp. EX. $25.00

VAUX, Calvert. *Villas & Cottages.* 1857. NY. Ils 1st ed. 318 p. T5. $195.00

VAUX, Roberts. *Memoirs of the Life of Anthony Benezet.* 1817. Phil. Parke. 16mo. 136 p. V1. $15.00

VEECK, Bill. *Hustler's Handbook.* 1965. NY. 1st ed. dj. VG. B3. $15.00

VELIKOVSKY, Immanuel. *Worlds in Collision.* 1950. Doubleday. 1st ed. dj. EX. R3. $15.00

VENABLES, Hubert. *Frankenstein Diaries.* 1980. Viking. 1st ed. dj. EX. P1. $20.00

VENNING, Michael. *Murder Through the Looking Glass.* 1943. Coward McCann. 1st ed. dj. VG. P1. $30.00

VENUS, Brenda. *Dear, Dear Brenda.* 1986. NY. 1st ed. 191 p. dj. EX. T5. $22.50

VENYS, Ladislav. *Hist of Mau Mau Movement in Kenya.* 1970. Prague. 125 p. wrp. G. T5. $12.50

VERCORS. *You Shall Know Them.* 1953. Little Brn. 1st ed. VG. P1. $12.50

VERCORS. *You Shall Know Them.* 1953. McClelland Stewart. 1st ed. dj. VG. P1. $15.00

VERISSIMO, Erico. *Mexico.* 1960. London. MacDonald. 1st ed. 360 p. dj. F2. $15.00

VERNE, Jules. *Caesar Cascabel.* 1890. Cassell. 1st Am ed. VG. R3. $95.00

VERNE, Jules. *Clipper of the Clouds.* 1962. Assn Booksellers. dj. EX. R3. $12.50

VERNE, Jules. *Demon of Cawnpore.* 1959. Arco. dj. EX. R3. $12.50

VERNE, Jules. *Dropped From the Clouds.* 1940. Dent Dutton. 7th print. dj. VG. P1. $15.00

VERNE, Jules. *End of the Journey.* 1965. Arco. dj. EX. R3. $12.50

VERNE, Jules. *Gr Ray & the Blockade Runners.* 1965. Arco. 1st ed. dj. xl. P1. $6.00

VERNE, Jules. *Homeward Bound.* 1965. Arco. dj. EX. R3. $12.50

VERNE, Jules. *Master of the World.* 1962. Assn Booksellers. dj. EX. R3. $12.50

VERNE, Jules. *Masterless Men.* 1962. Arco. dj. EX. R3. $12.50

VERNE, Jules. *Measuring a Meridian.* 1964. Arco. dj. EX. R3. $12.50

VERNE, Jules. *School for Crusoes.* 1966. Arco. dj. EX. R3. $12.50

VERNE, Jules. *Secret of the Island.* 1959. Bernard Hanison. 1st ed. dj. VG. P1. $25.00

VERNE, Jules. *Secret of Wilhelm Storitz.* 1963. Assn Booksellers. dj. EX. R3. $12.50

VERNE, Jules. *Tigers & Traitors.* 1959. Arco. dj. EX. R3. $12.50

VERNE, Jules. *Tour of the World in 80 Days.* nd. Lupton. VG. P1. $12.50

VERNE, Jules. *Traveling Circus.* 1966. Arco. dj. EX. R3. $12.50

VERNE, Jules. *Unwilling Dictator.* 1962. Arco. dj. EX. R3. $12.50

VERNE, Jules. *20,000 Leagues Under the Sea.* nd. Grosset Dunlap. VG. P1. $7.50

VERNER, Gerald. *Murder in Manuscript.* 1963. Wright Brn. dj. xl. P1. $5.00

VERNON & ROSS. *Revelations.* 1984. Magical Pub. 1st ed. 224 p. dj. NM. J3. $25.00

VERRILL, A.H. *Boys' Book of Buccaneers.* 1927. Dodd Mead. G. P1. $12.00

VERRILL, A.H. *Bridge of Light.* 1950. Fantasy. 1st ed. 1/300. sgn. dj. EX. R3. $55.00

VERRILL, A.H. *Carib Gold.* nd. Children's Pr. dj. VG. P1. $15.00

VERRILL, A.H. *Home Radio: How To Make & Use It.* 1922. NY. 116 p. EX. $40.00

VERRILL, A.H. *Old Civilizations of the New World.* 1929. Bobbs Merrill. 1st ed. 393 p. F2. $20.00

VERRILL, A.H. *Panama of Today.* 1937. NY. Dodd Mead. 314 p. dj. F2. $15.00

VERRILL & VERRILL. *Am's Ancient Civilizations.* 1953. Putnam. 334 p. F2. $12.50

VESTER, Bertha. *Flowers of the Holy Land.* 1962. Hallmark. Apparent 1st ed. 62 p. dj. EX. B10. $3.50

VIBERT, Lionel. *Story of the Craft...Development of Freemasonary.* nd. London. Spencer. 88 p. VG. B10. $3.75

VICARY, J.F. *Saga Time.* 1887. London. 1st ed. VG. C1. $27.50

VICKERS, Roy. *Whispering Death.* 1947. Jefferson House. 1st ed. dj. VG. F5. $25.00

VICTOR, Edward. *Further Magic of the Hands.* 1946. NY. Holden. 1st ed. 112 p. EX. J3. $11.00

VICTOR, Edward. *Magic of the Hands.* 1942. NY. Tannen. 2nd ed. 119 p. wrp. EX. J3. $5.00

VIDAL, Gore. *Best Man.* 1960. Little Brn. 1st ed. dj. EX. H3. $85.00

VIDAL, Gore. *Creation.* 1981. Random House. Ltd 1st ed. 1/500. sgn. slipcase. EX. K2. $50.00

VIDAL, Gore. *In a Yel Wood.* 1947. Dutton. 1st ed. sgn. dj. EX. K2. $200.00

VIDAL, Gore. *Julian.* 1981. Franklin Center. 1st ed. sgn. K2. $85.00

VIDAL, Gore. *Kalki.* 1978. Random House. 1st ed. dj. VG. P1. $20.00

VIDAL, Gore. *Messiah.* 1980. Gregg Pr. 1st ed. M. R3. $12.50

VIDAL, Gore. *Thirsty Evil.* 1956. NY. Zero. 1st ed. dj. EX. K2. $45.00

VIDAL, Gore. *Visit to a Sm Planet.* 1956. Little Brn. 1st ed. dj. EX. H3. $75.00

VIDAL, Gore. *2nd Am Revolution.* 1982. Random House. UP. wrp. EX. B13. $65.00

VIERECK & ELDRIDGE. *Invincible Adam.* 1946. Gold Label. P1. $10.00

VIETZEN, R.C. *Yesterday's Ohioans.* 1973. np. Ils. sgn. VG. T5. $32.50

VIGNAU-WILBERG, Peter. *Gemalde Une Skulpturen.* 1973. Zurich. 233 p. D4. $40.00

VILLANO, Anthony. *Brick Agent.* 1977. Quadrangle. 1st ed. dj. EX. P1. $15.00

VILLARD & NAGEL. *Hemingway in Love & War: Lost Diary of Agnes Von Kurowsky...* 1989. Northeastern U. UP. wrp. EX. K2. $200.00

VILLEGAS, V.M. *Hierros Coloniales en Zacatecas.* 1955. Mexico. Ltd ed. 1/1500. 4to. wrp. F2. $60.00

VINCENT, Frank. *In & Out of Central Am & Other Sketches & Studies of Travel.* 1898. Appleton. 246 p. xl. F2. $20.00

VINCENT, George. *Theodore Miller, Rough Rider.* 1899. Akron. Ils 1st ed. 179 p. TEG. VG. T5. $42.50

VINE, Barbara. *Dark-Adapted Eye.* 1986. Viking. 1st ed. dj. VG. P1. $15.00

VINEY, Charles. *Sherlock Holmes in London.* 1989. Houghton Mifflin. 1st ed. dj. EX. P1. $24.95

VINGE, J.D. *Cat's Paw.* 1988. Warner. 1st ed. dj. EX. F5. $16.00

VINGE, J.D. *Fireship.* nd. Book Club. dj. VG. P1. $4.50

VINGE, J.D. *Snow Queen.* 1980. 4th print. dj. VG. C1. $4.50

VINGE, J.D. *Summer Queen.* 1991. Warner. UP. wrp. EX. C4. $50.00

VINGE, J.D. *World's End.* 1984. Bluejay. 1st ed. dj. VG. P1. $20.00

VINGE, J.D. *World's End.* 1984. Bluejay. 1st ed. 1/750. sgn. M. R3. $40.00

VINGE, Venor. *Across Realtime.* nd. Book Club. dj. VG. P1. $7.50

VINGE, Venor. *Marooned in Realtime.* 1986. Bluejay. dj. EX. P1. $17.95

VINGE, Venor. *Peace War.* 1984. Blueday. 1st ed. dj. EX. P1. $16.95

VINGE, Venor. *Witling.* 1976. Dobson. 1st ed. dj. EX. P1. $35.00

VINING, E.G. *Being 70: The Measure of a Year.* 1978. Viking. 1st ed. 8vo. 195 p. dj. G. V1. $8.50

VINING, E.G. *Friend of Life: Biography of Rufus M Jones.* 1958. Lippincott. 8vo. 347 p. VG. V1. $7.00

VINING, E.G. *Quiet Pilgrimage.* 1970. Lippincott. 8vo. 410 p. dj. G. V1. $10.00

VINING, E.G. *Return to Japan.* 1960. Lippincott. 8vo. 285 p. dj. VG. V1. $8.50

VINING, E.G. *Take Heed of Loving Me.* 1964. Lippincott. 8vo. 352 p. dj. VG. V1. $10.00

VINING, E.G. *Taken Girl.* 1972. Viking. 8vo. 190 p. dj. VG. V1. $12.50

VINING, E.G. *VA Exiles.* 1955. Phil. Longstreth. Book Club ed. 8vo. 255 p. dj. VG. V1. $8.00

VINING, E.G. *Windows for the Crown Prince.* 1952. Lippincott. 7th ed. 8vo. 320 p. dj. VG. V1. $9.00

VINING, E.G. *World in Tune.* 1954. Harper. 16mo. 124 p. dj. VG. V1. $7.50

VINZ, Mark. *Letters to the Poetry Editor.* 1975. Capra. Chapbook Series. 1/50. sgn. EX. K2. $20.00

VIPONT, Elfrida. *Story of Quakerism 1652-1952.* 1955. London. Bannisdale Pr. 3rd print. 312 p. 8vo. dj. EX. V1. $12.00

VIRGIL. *Oeuvres.* 1796. Paris. Plassan. Nouvelle ed. 4 vols. octavo. H3. $450.00

VISSCHER, W.L. *Fetch Over the Canoe: Story of a Song.* 1908. Chicago. Atwell. 1st ed. 12mo. 115 p. R4. $25.00

VISSCHER, W.L. *Pony Express.* 1908. Rand McNally. 1st ed. VG. $45.00

VITTORINI, Elio. *Red Carnation.* 1952. New Directions. 1st Am ed. dj. EX. C4. $30.00

VIVIAN, C.E. *City of Wonder.* nd. London. dj. VG. R3. $20.00

VIVIAN, E.C. *Fields of Sleep.* 1980. Donald Grant. 1st ed. dj. VG. P1. $20.00

VIVIAN, Francis. *Dead Opposite the Church.* 1959. Herbert Jenkins. 1st ed. VG. P1. $10.00

VIZENOR, G.R. *Summer in the Spring: Lyric Poems of the Ojibway.* 1965. Minneapolis. Nodin. 1st ed. dj. EX. K2. $85.00

VIZETELLY, Henry. *Hist of Champagne.* 1883. London. Ils. 4to. 263 p. AEG. V1. $250.00

VLIET, R.G. *Rockspring.* 1974. NY. 1st ed. dj. EX. T9. $45.00

VLIET, R.G. *Scorpio Rising.* 1985. Random House. UP. yel wrp. EX. K2. $35.00

VOGT, W.C. *Bait Casting.* 1928. Longman Gr. 1st ed. presentation. EX. $40.00

VOGT & LEVENTHAL. *Prehistoric Settlement Patterns.* 1983. NM U. 1st ed. 519 p. F2. $25.00

VOKINS, Joan. *God's Mighty Power Magnified.* 1871. Cockermouth. D Fidler. New ed. 16mo. 132 p. xl. V1. $25.00

VOLL, Sister Felicia. *Study of Vista Maria School, Detroit, MI.* 1946. Loyola U. sgn. 117 p. R4. $25.00

VOLLARD, Josephine. *Little Pets Pleasure Book.* nd. (c 1910) McLoughlin Bros. Little Chatterwell Series. G. $15.00

VOLLMER & PARKER. *Crime, Crooks, & Cops.* 1937. Funk Wagnall. VG. P1. $15.00

VOLTAIRE. *Age of Louis XIV.* 1770. London. 2 vols. G. $250.00

VOLTAIRE. *Candide.* 1928. NY. Ils/sgn Rockwell Kent. 1/1470. 8vo. VG. $150.00

VOLTAIRE. *Hist of Zadig; or, Destiny an Oriental Tale.* 1952. Paris. Ltd Ed Club. Ils Sauvage. 1/1500. 8vo. slipcase. EX. C4. $50.00

VOLTAIRE. *Philosophical Dictionary.* 1824. London. Hunt. 6 vols. 12mo. slipcases. VG. H3. $450.00

VOLTAIRE. *Works.* c 1901. NY. Ed Pacification. 1/1000. 43 vols. H3. $600.00

VOLWILER, A. *Croghan & the W Movement.* 1926. Cleveland. Clark. 1st ed. 370 p. VG. B3. $50.00

VON ABELE, Rudolph. *Alexander H. Stephens.* 1946. Knopf. dj. VG. S1. $12.00

VON BULOW. *Mein Bericht Zur Marneschlacht.* 1919. Berlin. 7 maps. 85 p. T5. $37.50

VON ESCHENBACH, Wolfram. *Parzival.* 1894. London. David Nutt. Trans Jessie L Weston. 2 vols. VG. T6. $30.00

VON FALKE, J. *Art in the House.* 1879. Boston. Ils Prang. 4to. gilt brn bdg. EX. $165.00

VON FECHHEIMER, Hedwig. *Die Plastic der Agypter.* 1922. Berlin. 168 p. sm 4to. B10. $10.00

VON GOETHE, J.W. *Faust: A Tragedy, the 1st Part.* 1932. Ltd Ed Club. Ils/sgn Rene Clarke. 1/1500. slipcase. EX. C4. $45.00

VON GOETHE, J.W. *Faust: A Tragedy.* 1906. Houghton Mifflin. Lg Paper ed. 1/650. 4 vols. EX. H3. $200.00

VON HAGEN, Victor. *Ancient Sun Kingdoms...Aztec, Maya, Inca.* 1961. World. 1st ed. 618 p. dj. F2. $25.00

VON HAGEN, Victor. *Desert Kingdoms of Peru.* 1965. NY Graphic Soc. 1st Am ed. 191 p. dj. F2. $30.00

VON HAGEN, Victor. *Golden Man: Quest for El Dorado.* 1974. London. Book Club. 1st ed. 346 p. dj. F2. $20.00

VON HAGEN, Victor. *Gr World of the Naturalists.* 1948. NY. Greenberg Pub. 1st ed. 392 p. dj. F2. $25.00

VON HAGEN, Victor. *Highway of the Sun.* 1955. Duell. 1st ed. 320 p. dj. F2. $20.00

VON HAGEN, Victor. *Incas of Pero de Cieza De Leon.* 1959. OK U. 1st ed. 397 p. dj. F2. $25.00

VON HAGEN, Victor. *Maya Explorer* 1948. OK U. Ils. maps. 324 p. F2. $20.00

VON HAGEN, Victor. *Off With Their Heads.* 1937. Macmillan. 1st ed. 220 p. F2. $20.00

VON HAGEN, Victor. *S Am Called Them.* 1949. London. Robert Hale. 1st ed. 401 p. F2. $20.00

VON HAGEN, Victor. *Search for the Maya.* 1973. Saxton House. 1st ed. 365 p. dj. F2. $25.00

VON HAGEN, Victor. *Sun Kingdom of the Aztecs.* 1958. World. 126 p. F2. $12.50

VON HAGEN, Victor. *4 Seasons of Manuela.* 1952. Duell Sloan/Little Brn. 1st ed. 320 p. dj. F2. $20.00

VON HANSTEIN, Otfrid. *World of the Incas.* 1925. Dutton. 189 p. F2. $25.00

VON HARBOU, Thea. *Metropolis.* 1927. London. 1st ed. VG. R3. $75.00

VON HUMBOLDT, Alexander. *Cosmos: Sketch of Physical Description of Universe.* nd. (1844) NY. 12mo. 5 vols. VG. T1. $125.00

VON KOEIGSWALD, G.H.R. *Meeting Prehistoric Man.* 1956. London. Scientific Book Club. 216 p. dj. F2. $7.50

VON KUEHNELT-LEDDIHN, E. & C. *1979 Moscow.* 1940. Sheed Ward. 1st ed. dj. EX. R3. $25.00

VON MANSTEIN, Field Marshall. *Lost Victories.* 1958. Chicago. 1st ed. dj. EX. B3. $40.00

VON WINNING, Hugo. *John Platt Collection of Pre-Columbian Art.* 1986. VA U Art Mus. 1st ed. 4to. wrp. F2. $25.00

VON WUTHENAU, Alexander. *Art of Terra-Cotta Pottery in Pre-Columbian Central & S Am.* 1969. Crown. 1st UK ed. dj. F2. $25.00

VONNEGUT, Kurt. *Bluebeard.* 1987. Delacorte. 1st ed. 1/500. sgn. boxed. R3. $100.00

VONNEGUT, Kurt. *Breakfast of Champions.* 1973. Delacorte. 1st ed. dj. EX. R3. $17.50

VONNEGUT, Kurt. *Breakfast of Champions.* 1973. Delacorte. 5th print. dj. EX. P1. $10.00

VONNEGUT, Kurt. *Dead-Eye Dick.* 1982. Delacorte. dj. EX. R3. $15.00

VONNEGUT, Kurt. *Fates Worse Than Death.* 1982. London. 1st ed. wrp. EX. T9. $25.00

VONNEGUT, Kurt. *Fates Worse Than Death.* 1982. Nottingham. Bertrand Russell. 1st ed. wrp. EX. B13. $50.00

VONNEGUT, Kurt. *Fates Worse Than Death.* 1982. Nottingham. pamphlet. EX. K2. $45.00

VONNEGUT, Kurt. *God Bless You, Mr Rosewater; or, Pearls Before Swine.* 1965. Holt Rinehart Winston. 1st ed. dj. EX. H3. $150.00

VONNEGUT, Kurt. *God Bless You Mr Rosewater.* 1965. London. Cape. 1st ed. dj. VG. B13. $110.00

VONNEGUT, Kurt. *Happy Birthday, Wanda June.* 1971. Delacorte. 1st ed. dj. EX. H3. $50.00

VONNEGUT, Kurt. *Jailbird.* 1979. Delacorte. 1st ed. dj. G. P1. $7.50

VONNEGUT, Kurt. *Jailbird.* 1979. Delacorte/Lawrence. Ltd ed. 1/500. sgn. AEG. boxed. H3. $100.00

VONNEGUT, Kurt. *Mother Night.* 1966. Harper Row. 1st HrdCvr ed. dj. EX. H3. $75.00

VONNEGUT, Kurt. *Mother Night.* 1966. Harper Row. 1st HrdCvr ed. sgn. dj. EX. K2. $175.00

VONNEGUT, Kurt. *Nothing Is Lost Save Honor.* 1984. Nouveau Pr. Ltd ed. 1/300. sgn. H3. $85.00

VONNEGUT, Kurt. *Palm Sunday.* 1981. Delacorte. 1st ed. dj. EX. R3. $15.00

VONNEGUT, Kurt. *Palm Sunday.* 1981. Delacorte. 1st ed. 1/500. sgn. slipcase. K2. $75.00

VONNEGUT, Kurt. *Palm Sunday: Autobiographical Collage.* 1981. Delacorte. Ltd ed. 1/500. sgn. AEG. cloth slipcase. H3. $100.00

VONNEGUT, Kurt. *Player Piano.* nd. Book Club. dj. VG. P1. $4.50

VONNEGUT, Kurt. *Player Piano.* 1952. Scribner. 1st ed. w/sgn label. VG. R3. $75.00

VONNEGUT, Kurt. *Player Piano.* 1952. Scribner. 1st ed. 2nd issue bdg. dj. EX. H3. $75.00

VONNEGUT, Kurt. *Slapstick.* 1976. Delacorte. 1st ed. dj. EX. R3. $17.50

VONNEGUT, Kurt. *Slapstick; or, Lonesome No More!* 1976. Delacorte. UP. wrp. EX. B13. $100.00

VONNEGUT, Kurt. *Slapstick; or, Lonesome No More!* 1976. Delacorte/Lawrence. Ltd ed. 1/250. sgn. AEG. boxed. H3. $125.00

VONNEGUT, Kurt. *Slaughterhouse 5; or, The Children's Crusade.* 1969. Delacorte. 1st ed. dj. H3. $400.00

VONNEGUT, Kurt. *Slaughterhouse 5; or, The Children's Crusade.* 1969. Delacorte. 1st ed. dj. K2. $300.00

VONNEGUT, Kurt. *Wampeters, Foma, & Granfalloons.* 1974. Delacorte. 1st ed. dj. EX. H3. $60.00

VONNEGUT, Kurt. *Wampeters, Foma, & Granfalloons.* 1974. NY. AP. K2. $175.00

VONNEGUT, Kurt. *Welcome to the Monkey House.* 1968. Delacorte. ARC. dj. H3. $100.00

VONNEGUT, Kurt. *Welcome to the Monkey House.* 1968. Delacorte/Lawrence. 1st ed. dj. EX. K2. $185.00

VONNEGUT, Kurt. *Welcome to the Monkey House.* 1969. Jonathan Cape. 1st UK ed. dj. EX. H3. $50.00

VORIS, A.C. *Charleston in the Rebellion.* 1888. Cincinnati. VG. T5. $45.00

VORSE, M.H. *Time & the Town.* 1942. NY. 1st ed. dj. w/letter. VG. B3. $95.00

VOSBURGH, Jack. *Little Miracles.* 1944. Sayre, PA. Vosburgh. 1st ed. EX. J3. $3.00

VYDRA. *Folk Painting on Glass.* nd. Prague. 1st ed. 4to. VG. C2. $40.00

WADDELL, A.M. *Colonial Officer & His Time 1754-1773.* 1890. Raleigh. 1st ed. VG. $40.00

WADE, Henry. *Heir Presumptive.* 1953. Macmillan. 1st ed. dj. VG. P1. $20.00

WADE, Henry. *Litmore Snatch.* 1957. Macmillan. 1st ed. dj. VG. P1. $22.50

WADE, Henry. *Verdict of You All.* 1970. Howard Baker. dj. VG. P1. $10.00

WADE, Jonathan. *Back to Life.* 1961. Pantheon. dj. EX. P1. $12.50

WADE, M. *Margaret Fuller: Whetstone of Genius.* 1940. NY. Ils. 304 p. dj. VG. B3. $22.50

WADE, M.H. *Boy Who Dared: Story of William Penn.* 1929. Appleton. 1st ed. 12mo. 328 p. VG. V1. $10.00

WADE, Robert. *Knave of Eagles.* 1969. Random House. 1st ed. dj. EX. F5. $15.00

WADE. *Titanic: End of a Dream.* 1979. NY. 1st ed. 338 p. dj. VG. B3. $22.50

WADSWORTH, William. *Poetical Works.* c 1910. Crowell. 949 p. VG. B10. $3.50

WAGENKNECHT, Edward. *Lillian Gish.* 1927. WA U. Chapbook 7. 1st ed. 26 p. wrp. H3. $45.00

WAGENKNECHT, Edward. *6 Novels of the Supernatural.* 1944. Viking. 1st ed. VG. P1. $35.00

WAGER, Walter. *Otto's Boy.* 1985. Macmillan. 1st ed. dj. EX. P1. $16.95

WAGER, Walter. *Telefon.* nd. Book Club. dj. VG. P1. $4.50

WAGER, Walter. *Telefon.* 1975. Macmillan. 2nd ed. dj. VG. P1. $10.00

WAGER, Walter. *Time of Reckoning.* 1977. Playboy. 1st ed. dj. VG. P1. $17.50

WAGGONER, Diana. *Hills of Faraway (Guide to Fantasy).* 1978. Atheneum. 1st ed. dj. VG. P1. $25.00

WAGLEY, Charles. *Welcome of Tears.* 1977. Oxford. 1st ed. sm 4to. wrp. F2. $10.00

WAGNER, D. *Upholstery, Drapes, & Silpcovers.* 1955. NY. 1st ed. dj. EX. $18.00

WAGNER, Geoffrey. *Another Am: In Search of Canyons.* 1972. London. 1st ed. dj. EX. $10.00

WAGNER, Jane. *Search for Signs of Intelligent Life in the Universe.* 1986. NY. 1st ed. sgn Wagner/Tomlin. dj. EX. T9. $65.00

WAGNER, K.E. *Book of Kane.* 1985. Donald Grant. 1st ed. dj. P1/R3. $20.00

WAGNER, K.E. *Dark Crusade.* 1976. Warner. 1st ed. wrp. EX. F5. $10.00

WAGNER, K.E. *Why Not You & I?* 1987. Dark Harvest. Ltd ed. 1/52. sgn. leather bdg. boxed. M. R3. $250.00

WAGNER, K.E. *Why Not You & I?* 1987. Dark Harvest. 1st ed. M. R3. $35.00

WAGNER, William. *Continental! Its Motor & Its People.* 1983. CA. 240 p. dj. VG. w/promotional brochure c 1939. T5. $25.00

WAGSTAFF, H.M. *James A Graham Papers 1861-1884.* 1928. Chapel Hill. wrp. VG. G1. $22.00

WAGSTAFF, W.R. *Hist of Soc of Friends Compiled From Standard Records.* 1845. Wiley Putnam. 8vo. 400 p. G. V1. $16.00

WAIN, John. *Wild Track.* 1966. Viking. 1st Am ed. 8vo. dj. EX. R4. $12.50

WAIN & BINGHAM. *More Jingles, Jokes, & Funny Folks.* nd. McLoughlin Bros. New Chimney Corner Series. 8vo. wrp. $60.00

WAINER, Cord; see Dewey, Thomas B.

WAINRIGHT. *Pathways & Abiding Places of Our Lord Ils in Journal...* 1851. NY. 1st ed. 4to. 196 p. VG. $150.00

WAINWRIGHT, John. *Man of Law.* 1980. St Martin. 1st ed. dj. EX. P1. $5.00

WAINWRIGHT, Philip. *Hist of the 101st Machine Gun Battalion.* 1922. Hartford, CT. Ils 1st ed. presentation. 8vo. VG. T1. $60.00

WAISBARD & WAISBARD. *Masks, Mummies, & Magicians.* 1966. Praeger. Ils. maps. 176 p. dj. F2. $15.00

WAITE, A.E. *Lives of Alchemystical Philosophers.* 1888. London. 1st ed. 8vo. gilt brn bdg. VG. T1. $95.00

WAITE, A.E. *Quest of the Golden Stair.* 1974. New Castle. PB. VG. C1. $5.00

WAITE, A.E. *Songs & Poems of Fairyland.* c 1890s. London. VG. scarce. C1. $20.00

WAKEFIELD, Dan. *Addict.* 1963. Gold Medal. 1st ed. EX. B4. $15.00

WAKEFIELD, H.R. *Clock Strikes 12.* 1946. Arkham House. 1st ed. dj. EX. R3. $85.00

WAKEFIELD, H.R. *Hearken To the Evidence.* 1934. Doubleday Doran. G. P1. $15.00

WAKOSKI, Diane. *Abalone.* 1974. Blk Sparrow. Ltd HrdCvr ed. 1/126. sgn. dj. H3. $75.00

WAKOSKI, Diane. *Cap of Darkness: Including Looking for King of Spain...* 1980. Blk Sparrow. Ltd ed. 1/50. sgn. H3. $65.00

WAKOSKI, Diane. *Coins & Coffins.* 1962. Hawk's Well. 1st ed. inscr. EX. K2. $125.00

WAKOSKI, Diane. *Diamond Merchant.* 1968. Sans Souci Pr. sgn. dj. EX. H3. $85.00

WAKOSKI, Diane. *Greed Parts 5 Through 7.* 1971. Blk Sparrow. 1/1000. EX. B4. $8.00

WAKOSKI, Diane. *Lament of the Lady Bank Dick.* 1969. Sans Souci Pr. Ltd ed. 1/99. sgn. glassine wrp. H3. $75.00

WAKOSKI, Diane. *Moon Has a Complicated Geography.* 1969. Odda Tala. sgn. sm folio. wht wrp. H3. $35.00

WAKOSKI, Diane. *Waiting for the King of Spain.* 1976. Blk Sparrow. Ltd HrdCvr ed. 1/50. sgn. w/poem. H3. $60.00

WALCOTT, Derek. *Caribbean Poetry of D Walcott & the Art of Romare Bearden.* 1983. NY. Ltd Ed Club. 1/2000. 4to. sgns. sans dj. EX. T9. $95.00

WALCOTT, Derek. *Fortunate Traveler.* 1981. Farrar Straus. UP. wrp. EX. K2. $50.00

WALCOTT, Derek. *Sea Grapes.* 1976. Farrar Straus. 1st ed. dj. w/photo. EX. C4. $25.00

WALDEN, Walter. *Voodoo Gold Trail.* 1922. Sm Maynard. 1st ed. VG. R3. $12.50

WALDMAN, Anne. *Giant Night.* 1970. Corinth Books. 1/2000. inscr. VG. B4. $15.00

WALDORF. *Kid on the Comstock.* 1970. Palo Alto. 1st ed. 198 p. dj. VG. B3. $20.00

WALDROP, Howard. *Dozen Tough Jobs.* 1989. Ziesing. 1st ed. dj. EX. P1. $16.00

WALDROP, Howard. *Them Bones.* 1989. Ziesing. 1st ed. dj. P1/R3. $20.00

WALDROP, Keith. *To the Sincere Reader.* 1970. Guildford. 2nd print. 1/300. sgns. D4. $75.00

WALDROP, Rosmarie. *When They Have Senses.* 1980. Burning Deck. 1st ed. inscr. wrp. VG. K2. $45.00

WALDSEEMULLER, Martin. *Cosmographiae Intro...4 Voyages of Amerigo Vespucci.* 1907. NY. 1st facsimile ed. EX. $75.00

WALKER, Alice. *Clr Purple.* 1982. Harcourt Brace. inscr. dj. H3. $100.00

WALKER, Alice. *Good Night, Willie Lee, I'll See You in the Morning.* 1979. Dial. 1st ed. dj. EX. K2. $450.00

WALKER, Alice. *Good Night, Willie Lee, I'll See You in the Morning.* 1979. Dial. 1st ed. xl. very scarce. B13. $45.00

WALKER, Alice. *Once.* 1968. Harcourt Brace. ARC. sgn. RS. EX. K2. $850.00

WALKER, Alice. *Once.* 1976. NY. ARC/1st PB ed. wrp. w/pub slip. EX. T9. $35.00

WALKER, Alice. *Temple of My Familiar.* 1989. Harcourt Brace. inscr/sgn. dj. H3. $85.00

WALKER, Alice. *Temple of My Familiar.* 1989. Harcourt Brace. 1st ed. sgn. dj. B13. $65.00

WALKER, Alice. *3rd Life of Grange Copeland.* 1970. Harcourt Brace. 1st ed. dj. EX. K2. $200.00

WALKER, Barbara. *Skeptical Feminist: Discovering the Virgin, Mother, & Crone.* 1987. 1st ed. dj. EX. C1. $9.50

WALKER, Cora. *Cuatemo, Last of the Aztec Emperors.* 1934. Dayton Pr. 1st ed. 348 p. F2. $20.00

WALKER, D.S. *Celebration of 100th Anniversary of Laying of Cornerstone...* 1896. GPO. 4to. 142 p. VG. $30.00

WALKER, David. *Lord's Pink Ocean.* 1972. Collins. 1st UK ed. clipped dj. EX. F5. $21.00

WALKER, David. *Lord's Pink Ocean.* 1972. Houghton Mifflin. 1st ed. dj. EX. P1. $15.00

WALKER, Fred. *Song of the Clyde: Hist of Clyde Shipbuilding.* 1985. Norton. 1st Am ed. 233 p. dj. EX. B10. $7.75

WALKER, Irma. *Lucifer Wine.* 1977. Bobbs Merrill. 1st ed. dj. EX. F5. $16.00

WALKER, J.M. *Life of Capt Joseph Fry, the Cuban Martyr.* 1875. Hartford. Ils. 8vo. G. T1. $50.00

WALKER, P.H. *Wagon Masters.* 1968. OK U. 2nd ed. dj. EX. $20.00

WALKER, Ronald. *Infernal Paradise. Mexico & the Modern Eng Novel.* 1978. CA U. 1st ed. 391 p. dj. F2. $20.00

WALKER, Walter. *Rules of the Knife Fight.* 1986. Harper Row. 1st ed. dj. EX. P1. $17.95

WALKER, Warren. *Erie Canal: Gateway to Empire.* 1963. Boston. 1st ed. 113 p. wrp. $17.50

WALKER & WALKER. *Up-To-Date Conjuring.* nd. London. Routledge. 147 p. VG. J3. $16.00

WALKER. *Wonderful Era of Great Dance Bands.* 1964. Berkeley. 1st ed. dj. VG. B3. $45.00

WALKEY, S. *In Quest of Sheba's Treasure.* nd. London. 1st ed? VG. R3. $35.00

WALL, Bernhardt. *Man's Best Friend: Plea to the Jury by GG Vest...* 1920. NY. AP. 1/125. sgn. EX. $250.00

WALL, Mervyn. *Return of Fursey.* 1948. London. 1st ed. dj. EX. R3. $85.00

WALL, Mervyn. *Unfortunate Fursey.* 1947. Crown. 1st Am ed. dj. VG. R3. $20.00

WALLACE, D.F. *Broom of the System.* 1987. Viking. HrdCvr 1st ed. dj. EX. B13. $95.00

WALLACE, D.F. *Girl With Curious Hair.* 1898. Norton. ARC. EX. K2. $35.00

WALLACE, Edgar. *Again the 3 Just Men.* nd. AL Burt. dj. VG. P1. $10.00

WALLACE, Edgar. *Avenger.* nd. Leisure Lib. dj. VG. P1. $17.50

WALLACE, Edgar. *Big Foot.* nd. John Long. VG. P1. $10.00

WALLACE, Edgar. *Bones.* nd. Ward Lock. dj. VG. P1. $15.00

WALLACE, Edgar. *Bosambo of the River.* 1973. Tom Stacey. dj. VG. P1. $20.00

WALLACE, Edgar. *Crimson Circle.* nd. AL Burt. VG. P1. $7.50

WALLACE, Edgar. *Day of Uniting.* 1930. Mystery League. 1st ed. dj. VG. P1. $25.00

WALLACE, Edgar. *Devil Man.* 1933. Collins Crime Club. 5th ed. VG. P1. $8.00

WALLACE, Edgar. *Diana of Kara-Kar.* nd. AL Burt. VG. P1. $12.50

WALLACE, Edgar. *Double.* nd. Grosset Dunlap. VG. P1. $7.50

WALLACE, Edgar. *Edgar Wallace Reader of Mystery.* 1943. Tower. VG. P1. $15.00

WALLACE, Edgar. *Flying Squad.* nd. Hodder Stoughton. VG. P1. $12.50

WALLACE, Edgar. *Flying Squad.* 1929. Crime Club. 1st ed. VG. P1. $17.50

WALLACE, Edgar. *Frightened Lady.* 1932. Hodder Stoughton. 1st ed? G. P1. $10.00

WALLACE, Edgar. *Frightened Lady.* 1933. Musson. 1st ed. G. P1. $10.00

WALLACE, Edgar. *Governor of Chi-Foo.* 1933. World Syndicate. 1st ed. dj. VG. P1. $35.00

WALLACE, Edgar. *Gr Ribbon.* 1931. Doubleday Doran. G. P1. $6.00

WALLACE, Edgar. *Gunman's Bluff.* 1930. Doubleday Doran. VG. P1. $12.50

WALLACE, Edgar. *Hairy Arm.* 1938. Triangle. VG. P1. $12.00

WALLACE, Edgar. *Hand of Power.* 1930. Mystery League. 1st ed. VG. P1. $15.00

WALLACE, Edgar. *Keepers of the King's Peace.* nd. Ward Lock. VG. P1. $20.00

WALLACE, Edgar. *Keepers of the King's Peace.* 1973. Tom Stacey. dj. VG. P1. $15.00

WALLACE, Edgar. *Lt Bones.* 1972. Tom Stacey. dj. EX. P1. $12.50

WALLACE, Edgar. *Man at the Carlton.* 1931. Musson. 1st Canadian ed. VG. P1. $10.00

WALLACE, Edgar. *Melody of Death.* nd. Readers Lib. dj. VG. P1. $20.00

WALLACE, Edgar. *Mouthpiece.* 1950. Hutchinson. dj. xl. P1. $10.00

WALLACE, Edgar. *Mr Commissioner Sanders.* 1930. Doubleday. 1st ed. EX. F5. $10.00

WALLACE, Edgar. *Northing Tramp.* 1931. Doubleday Doran. VG. P1. $12.00

WALLACE, Edgar. *On the Spot.* 1932. Doubleday Doran. VG. P1. $7.50

WALLACE, Edgar. *On the Spot.* 1955. John Long. dj. xl. P1. $10.00

WALLACE, Edgar. *People: Autobiography of a Mystery Writer.* 1929. Crime Club. 1st ed. 234 p. dj. very scarce. B10. $27.50

WALLACE, Edgar. *Red Aces.* nd. Hodder Stoughton. VG. P1. $10.00

WALLACE, Edgar. *Sanders of the River.* nd. Ward Lock. VG. P1. $20.00

WALLACE, Edgar. *Sanders of the River.* 1972. Tom Stacey. dj. EX. P1. $12.50

WALLACE, Edgar. *Sandi, the King-Maker.* nd. Ward Lock. VG. P1. $20.00

WALLACE, Edgar. *Sinister Man.* nd. AL Burt. VG. P1. $7.50

WALLACE, Edgar. *Sinister Man.* 1938. Triangle. VG. P1. $7.50

WALLACE, Edgar. *Sinister Man.* 1951. Hodder Stoughton. VG. P1. $7.50

WALLACE, Edgar. *Squeaker.* nd. Hodder Stoughton. Cheap ed. VG. P1. $7.50

WALLACE, Edgar. *Squealer.* nd. AL Burt. VG. P1. $7.50

WALLACE, Edgar. *Strange Countess.* 1950. Hodder Stoughton. 28th print. VG. P1. $10.00

WALLACE, Edgar. *Terror Keep*. 1928. Doubleday Doran. VG. P1. $10.00

WALLACE, Edgar. *Twister*. 1930. John Long. G. P1. $7.50

WALLACE, Edgar. *When the Gangs Came to London*. nd. AL Burt. dj. VG. P1. $15.00

WALLACE, Edgar. *When the Gangs Came to London*. 1969. John Long. dj. VG. P1. $10.00

WALLACE, Edgar. *Wht Face*. nd. Crime Club. VG. P1. $10.00

WALLACE, Edgar. *Wht Face*. 1932. Doubleday Doran. G. P1. $7.50

WALLACE, Edgar. *Wht Face*. 1932. Musson. 1st ed. VG. P1. $8.00

WALLACE, Edgar. *Wht Face*. 1932. Musson/Hodder Stoughton. VG. P1. $15.00

WALLACE, Edgar. *Wht Face*. 1952. Hodder Stoughton. VG. P1. $7.50

WALLACE, Edgar. *Yel Snake*. nd. Hodder Stoughton. G. P1. $7.50

WALLACE, Edgar. *4 Just Men*. nd. Hodder Stoughton. VG. P1. $10.00

WALLACE, Edgar. *4 Just Men*. 1905. Tallis Pr. 1st ed. xl. P1. $75.00

WALLACE, Edward. *Destiny & Glory*. 1957. Coward McCann. 1st ed. 320 p. dj. F2. $20.00

WALLACE, F.L. *Address: Centauri*. 1955. Gnome. 1st ed. dj. VG. R3. $15.00

WALLACE, I.S. *Mexico Today*. 1936. Boston. Meador. 1st ed. 364 p. F2. $25.00

WALLACE, Ian. *Deathstar Voyage*. nd. Book Club. dj. VG. P1. $4.50

WALLACE, Ian. *Deathstar Voyage*. 1972. Dobson. 1st ed. dj. EX. P1. $12.50

WALLACE, Ian. *Pan Sagittarius*. 1973. Putnam. dj. EX. P1. $15.00

WALLACE, Ian. *Purloined Prince*. 1971. McCall. 1st ed. dj. VG. P1. $25.00

WALLACE, Irving. *Fabulous Showman: Life of PT Barnum*. 1959. Knopf. 280 p. dj. EX. J3. $8.00

WALLACE, Irving. *Pigeon Project*. 1979. Simon Schuster. 1st ed. dj. EX. P1. $15.00

WALLACE, Irving. *R Document*. 1976. Simon Schuster. 1st ed. dj. EX. P1. $17.50

WALLACE, Irving. *7th Secret*. nd. Book Club. dj. VG. P1. $4.50

WALLACE, Lew. *Ben-Hur: A Tale of the Christ*. 1880. NY. 1st ed. 1st issue. orig bdg. VG. H3. $1000.00

WALLACE, Lew. *Fair God*. nd. Grosset Dunlap. VG. P1. $10.00

WALLACE, Lew. *Prince of India*. 1893. Harper. 1st ed. sgn. 2 vols. VG. R3. $150.00

WALLACE, Lew. *Prince of India*. 1893. Harper. 1st ed. 2 vols. VG. R3. $50.00

WALLACE, Lew. *1st Christmas*. 1902. NY. 1st ed. dj. EX. J2. $12.00

WALLACE, Marie. *Come to the Country*. 1953. Cleveland. Ils Anne Hopkins. 1st ed. sgn. 153 p. T5. $15.00

WALLACE, Marie. *Frog in the Milk Pan*. 1963. Victoria Pub. 1st ed. 184 p. dj. T5. $6.50

WALLACE, Marilyn. *Sister in Crime 2*. 1990. Berkley. 1st HrdCvr ed. dj. EX. F5. $16.00

WALLACE, R.L. *Canary Book*. c 1900. London. 3rd ed. pls. VG. $55.00

WALLACE, Willard. *Appeal to Arms: Military Hist of Am Revolution*. 1951. Harper. 1st ed. 308 p. VG. B10. $6.75

WALLANT, E.L. *Human Season*. 1960. Harcourt Brace. 1st ed. dj. EX. H3. $125.00

WALLING, H.F. *Atlas of the Dominion of Canada*. 1875. Montreal. Tackabury. 1st issue. folio. EX. T1. $450.00

WALLING, R.A.J. *Corpse With the Dirty Face*. 1936. Morrow. 1st ed. 307 p. VG. B10. $5.00

WALLING, R.A.J. *Corpse With the Eerie Eye*. nd. Books Inc. G. P1. $5.00

WALLING, R.A.J. *Stroke of 1*. 1931. Morrow. 2nd ed. G. P1. $12.00

WALLIS, C. *Stories on Stone: Book on Am Epitaphs*. 1954. NY. dj. EX. $30.00

WALLIS, Dave. *Only Lovers Left Alive*. 1964. Dutton. 1st ed. dj. EX. F5. $25.00

WALLIS, Dave. *Only Lovers Left Alive*. 1964. Dutton. 1st ed. dj. VG. P1. $12.50

WALLIS, E.E. *Tariri: My Story*. 1965. Harper. 1st ed. 126 p. dj. F2. $15.00

WALLMANN, J.M. *Judas Cross*. 1974. Random House. 1st ed. dj. EX. P1. $16.00

WALPOLE, Horace. *Works*. 1798. London. Robinson Edwards. 5 vols. quarto. H3. $250.00

WALPOLE, Hugh. *Cathedral*. 1949. London. 1st ed. 531 p. B10. $3.50

WALPOLE, Hugh. *Killer & the Slain*. 1942. Macmillan. 2nd ed. G. P1. $6.00

WALPOLE, Hugh. *Mr Huffam*. 1938. private print. 1/200. VG. P1. $30.00

WALPOLE, Hugh. *Portrait of a Man With Red Hair*. nd. Daily Express. dj. VG. P1. $10.00

WALSH, A.V. *Rackets Are My Racket...* 1952. Am Magician Guild. 1st ed. 12 p. stapled manuscript. J3. $10.00

WALSH, J.M. *Vandals of the Void*. 1976. Hyperion. reprint of 1931 ed. EX. R3. $15.00

WALSH, M.M.B. *4-Clr Hoop*. 1976. Putnam. 1st ed. dj. EX. P1. $12.50

WALSH, R.J. *Burning Shame of Am: Outline Against Tobacco*. 1924. NY. Ils/sgn George Illian. 1st ed. VG. T1. $25.00

WALSH, Thomas. *Action of the Tiger*. 1967. Simon Schuster. 1st ed. dj. xl. P1. $5.00

WALSH, Thomas. *Face of the Enemy*. 1966. Simon Schuster. 1st ed. dj. xl. P1. $5.00

WALSH, Warren. *Readings in Russian Hist*. 1948. Syracuse. 1st ed. 549 p. VG. B10. $7.25

WALT. *Car-Builder's Dictionary*. 1895. Ils 3rd ed. VG. C2. $185.00

WALTER, Barbara. *Mini Mysteries With Cards*. 1980. Magic Ltd. 1st ed. 166 p. dj. NM. J3. $15.00

WALTER, Elizabeth. *Sin Eater*. 1967. Harvill. dj. VG. P1. $20.00

WALTER, G.W. *Stories of Upstate NY*. 1973. Faulkner. 1st ed. 160 p. dj. EX. B10. $6.50

WALTER, George. *Chips & Shavings*. 1966. Faulkner. 1st ed. dj. B10. $6.25

WALTER, Mildred Pitts. *Have a Happy*. 1989. Lathrop. 1st ed. dj. EX. B13. $35.00

WALTER, Mildred Pitts. *Justin & the Best Biscuits in the World*. 1986. Lathrop. Ils Catherine Stock. dj. EX. B13. $40.00

WALTER, Mildred Pitts. *Trouble's Child*. 1985. Lathrop. 1st ed. dj. EX. B13. $45.00

WALTER & HARDING. *Paid in Full*. 1908. Dillingham. 1st ed. 333 p. G. B10. $3.50

WALTER. *Manual for Essence Industry*. 1916. NY. Ltd ed. 1/5000. VG. C2. $75.00

WALTERS, H.B. *Art of the Greeks*. 1906. NY. Ils 1st Am ed. 112 pls. 277 p. G. T5. $95.00

WALTON, Donald. *Rockwell Portrait*. 1978. Sheed. 1st ed. 285 p. dj. EX. B10. $6.75

WALTON, Evangeline. *Sword Is Forged*. 1983. Timescape. 1st ed. dj. EX. P1/R3. $15.00

WALTON, Evangeline. *Witch House.* 1945. Arkham House. 1st ed. dj. EX. R3. $75.00

WALTON, George. *Mineral Springs of US & Canada With Maps, Analysis, & Notes.* 1873. NY. VG. $90.00

WALTON, Izaak. *Compleat Angler.* 1931. London. Ils/sgn Rackham. 1/775. sgn. boxed. EX. $250.00

WALTON, Izaak. *Lives (Donne, Wotton, Hooker, Herbert, & Sanderson).* 1825. London. 8vo. 502 p. VG. $90.00

WALTON, Izaak. *Universal Angler.* 1676. London. Marriott. 5th ed. 19th-Century bdg. H3. $3500.00

WALTON, J.S. *John Kinsey: Speaker of PA Assembly & Justice...* 1900. Friends Book Assn. 16mo. 69 p. EX. V1. $7.50

WALTON, Joseph. *Brief Biographies of Some Members of Soc of Friends.* nd. Friends Bookstore. 16mo. 160 p. G. V1. $10.00

WALTON, Joseph. *Footprints & Waymarks for Help of Christian Traveler.* 1894. Friends Bookstore. 12mo. 515 p. VG. V1. $8.00

WALTON, Joseph. *Incidents, Ils, Doctrines, & Hist of Soc of Friends.* 1897. Phil. Friends Bookstore. 12mo. 766 p. VG. V1. $10.00

WALTON, Roy. *Cardboard Charades.* 1971. London. Davenport. 54 p. SftCvr. EX. J3. $3.00

WALTON, Roy. *Devil's Playthings...* 1969. London. Davenport. 61 p. SftCvr. NM. J3. $5.00

WALTON, Roy. *Some Late Extra Card Tricks.* 1975. London. Davenport. 1st ed. sgn. 26 p. SftCvr. NM. J3. $5.00

WALZEL, Oskar. *Deutsche Dichtung von Gottsched Bis Zur Gegenwart.* 1927. Verlag. 2 vols. EX. $150.00

WAMBAUGH, Joseph. *4 Complete Novels.* nd. Avenel. 1st ed. dj. EX. P1. $15.00

WANDREI, Donald. *Dark Odyssey.* 1931. Webb. 1st ed. 1/400. sgn. dj. EX. R3. $250.00

WANDREI, Donald. *Ecstasy.* 1928. Recluse Pr. 1st ed. 1/322. tissue dj. EX. R3. $350.00

WANDREI, Donald. *Eye & the Finger.* 1944. Arkham House. 1st ed. dj. EX. R3. $225.00

WANDREI, Donald. *Web of Easter Island.* 1948. Arkham House. 1st ed. dj. EX. R3. $80.00

WANGERIN, Walter. *Book of Sorrows.* 1985. Harper Row. 1st ed. dj. EX. P1. $15.95

WANGERIN, Walter. *Book of the Dun Cow.* 1978. Harper Row. 2nd ed. dj. VG. P1. $10.00

WANGERIN, Walter. *Book of the Dun Cow.* 1980. Allen Lane. dj. EX. P1. $25.00

WARD, Christopher. *Strange Adventures of Jonathan Drew.* 1932. Simon Schuster. not 1st ed. 395 p. dj. VG. B10. $4.00

WARD, Christopher. *Twisted Tales.* 1924. Holt. apparent 1st ed. 217 p. G. B10. $5.00

WARD, Julian. *Compass Points to Fear.* nd. Hodder Stoughton. xl. VG. P1. $5.00

WARD, Lynd. *God's Man.* 1929. NY. 1st ed. sgn. VG. B3. $125.00

WARD, Lynd. *Madman's Drum: A Novel in Woodcuts by Lynd Ward.* 1930. Jonathan Cape. presentation. dj. H3. $300.00

WARD, Lynd. *Song Without Words: Book of Engravings on Wood.* 1936. Random House. 1/1250. sgn. slipcase. H3. $250.00

WARD-JACKSON, E. & J.P. *Ward-Jackson's Gymnastics for the Fingers & Wrist.* nd. NY. Fisher. octavo. VG. H3. $25.00

WARDE, Frederick. *Bruce Rogers, Designer of Books.* 1925. Cambridge. Ils. 8vo. xl. VG. T6. $45.00

WARDLAW. *Fundamentals of Baseball.* 1924. NY. 1st ed. 12mo. 111 p. VG. C2. $35.00

WARE, C.F. *Greenwich Village 1920-1930.* 1935. Boston. 1st ed. fld map. 496 p. dj. VG. B3. $45.00

WARE, E.F. *Ward's Hist of Coffee Co.* 1930. Atlanta. 1st ed. VG. $50.00

WARE, R.D. *In the Woods & on the Shore.* 1908. Boston. 1st ed. VG. $55.00

WARHOL, Andy. *A.* 1968. Grove Pr. 1st ed. dj. VG. B3. $45.00

WARHOL, Andy. *Bl Movie.* 1970. NY. 1st/PB Orig ed. photos. EX. T9. $65.00

WARHOL, Andy. *Philosophy of Andy Warhol. From A to B & Back Again.* 1975. Harcourt Brace. sgn. H3. $50.00

WARLOCK, Peter. *Complete Book of Magic.* nd. London. Abbey Lib. reprint. 141 p. dj. NM. J3. $16.00

WARLOCK, Peter. *Peter Warlock's Book of Magic.* 1956. London. Arco. 1st ed. 141 p. EX. J3. $12.00

WARNER, C.D. *Backlog Studies.* 1873. Boston. Osgood. 281 p. VG. B10. $4.25

WARNER, C.D. *In the Levant.* 1879. Boston. 391 p. VG. $40.00

WARNER, Ernest. *Jordans: A Quaker Shrine, Past & Present.* 1921. London. Friends Bookshop. 8vo. 28 p. VG. V1. $12.00

WARNER, Harry. *Wealth of Fable.* 1976. Fanhistorica Pr. 1st ed. wrp. M. R3. $20.00

WARNER, Mignon. *Death in Time.* 1982. Crime Club. 1st ed. dj. EX. P1. $12.50

WARNER, Mignon. *Girl Who Was Clairvoyant.* 1982. Crime Club. 1st ed. dj. VG. P1. $12.50

WARNER, S.T. *Kingdoms of Elfin.* 1957. London. 1st UK ed. dj. EX. R3. $35.00

WARNER, S.T. *Kingdoms of Elfin.* 1977. Viking. 1st ed. dj. VG. P1. $17.50

WARNER, S.T. *Mr Fortune's Maggot.* 1927. Viking. 1st ed. G. $10.00

WARNER, Stanley. *Son of the Ages.* 1914. Doubleday. 1st ed. VG. R3. $35.00

WARNER, Stanley. *Story of the Strange Career.* 1902. Appleton. 1st ed. VG. R3. $25.00

WARNER, WILLIAMS, & MOORE. *Orchid Album...* 1882-1897. London. Ils Fitch. 1st ed. 528 pls. 11 vols. orig bdg. H3. $17500.00

WARNER. *Archbishop Lamy, an Epoch Maker...* 1936. Santa FE. 316 p. VG. A5. $70.00

WARNER-CROZETTI, R. *Widderburn Horror.* 1971. Leisure Books. 1st ed. wrp. EX. F5. $15.00

WARRE, H. *Sketches in N Am & the OR Territory.* 1970. Barre, MA. 1/1750. 71 pls. T5. $75.00

WARREN, B.H. *Report on the Birds of PA.* 1888. Harrisburg. clr pls. VG. T3. $75.00

WARREN, C.E. *Katz Awa: Bismark of Japan.* 1904. NY. Buck. Ils. 16mo. scarce. A5. $45.00

WARREN, E.R. *Beaver: Its Work & Its Ways.* 1927. Baltimore. Williams Wilkins. VG. T3. $20.00

WARREN, Geoffrey. *Royal Souvenirs.* nd. (1977) Orbis. 1st ed. EX. B10. $6.50

WARREN, H.M. *To & From Phil.* 1908. private print. VG. $100.00

WARREN, J.C. *Masodon Giganteus of N Am.* 1852. Boston. Wilson. pls. lg fld pl. VG. T3. $175.00

WARREN, Joseph. *Revenge.* nd. Grosset Dunlap. Photoplay ed. VG. P1. $20.00

WARREN, R.L. *Mary Coffin Starbuck & the Early Hist of Nantucket.* 1987. Andover, NY. Pingry Pr. 1st ed. 8vo. 286 p. VG. V1. $9.50

WARREN, R.P. *All the King's Men.* 1946. NY. 1st ed. VG. B13. $85.00

WARREN, R.P. *At Heaven's Gate.* 1943. NY. later print. sgn. 391 p. G. T5. $25.00

WARREN, R.P. *Audubon: A Vision.* 1969. Random House. Ltd ed. 1/300. boxed. H3. $150.00

WARREN, R.P. *Ballad of a Sweet Dream of Peace: Charade for Easter.* 1980. Pressworks. Ltd ed. 1/350. sgn. no dj issued. w/music score. K2. $75.00

WARREN, R.P. *Band of Angels.* 1955. Random House. inscr. H3. $75.00

WARREN, R.P. *Being Here: Poetry 1977-1980.* 1980. NY. 1st ed. dj. EX. $45.00

WARREN, R.P. *Being Here: Poetry 1977-1980.* 1980. Random House. Ltd ed. 1/250. sgn. boxed. EX. H3. $150.00

WARREN, R.P. *Brother to Dragons.* 1953. NY. 1st ed. dj. EX. $85.00

WARREN, R.P. *Brother to Dragons: Tale in Verse & Voices. New Version.* 1979. Random House. 1st ed. sgn. dj. H3. $85.00

WARREN, R.P. *Cave.* 1959. Random House. 1st print. brn bdg. VG. $20.00

WARREN, R.P. *Chief Joseph of the Nez Perce.* 1983. NY. 1st ed. 1/250. sgn. slipcase. EX. $125.00

WARREN, R.P. *Circus in the Attic.* 1947. NY. 1st ed. clipped dj. EX. B13. $250.00

WARREN, R.P. *Democracy & Poetry.* 1975. Harvard. 1st ed. dj. EX. $40.00

WARREN, R.P. *Incarnations: Poems 1966-1968.* 1968. Random House. Ltd ed. 1/250. sgn. dj. H3. $175.00

WARREN, R.P. *John Greenleaf Whittier's Poetry: Appraisal & Selection.* 1971. Minneapolis U. sgn. H3. $75.00

WARREN, R.P. *Legacy of the Civil War.* 1961. NY. 1st print. dj. EX. $45.00

WARREN, R.P. *Love: 4 Versions.* 1981. Palaemon. 1st ed. 1/200. sgn. EX. H3. $200.00

WARREN, R.P. *Meet Me in the Gr Glen.* 1971. Random House. Ltd ed. 1/300. sgn. boxed. EX. H3. $125.00

WARREN, R.P. *New & Selected Poems 1923-1985.* 1985. NY. 1st ed. 1/350. sgn. slipcase. EX. $125.00

WARREN, R.P. *Night Rider.* 1939. Houghton Mifflin. 1st ed. dj. VG. C4. $45.00

WARREN, R.P. *Now & Then: Poems 1976-1978.* 1978. Random House. Ltd ed. 1/200. sgn. boxed. H3. $150.00

WARREN, R.P. *Or Else Poem/Poems 1968-1974.* 1974. Random House. sgn. dj. H3. $75.00

WARREN, R.P. *Place To Come To.* 1977. Random House. sgn. dj. H3. $75.00

WARREN, R.P. *Place To Come To.* 1977. Random House. 1st ed. dj. VG. $20.00

WARREN, R.P. *Rumor Verified: Poems 1979-1980.* 1981. NY. Ltd ed. 1/250. sgn. slipcase. EX. $115.00

WARREN, R.P. *Rumor Verified: Poems 1979-1980.* 1981. Random House. sgn. dj. H3. $65.00

WARREN, R.P. *Segregation.* 1956. NY. 1st ed. 1st print. dj. EX. $60.00

WARREN, R.P. *Segregation.* 1957. London. 1st ed. dj. EX. $45.00

WARREN, R.P. *Selected Poems 1923-1975.* 1981. Franklin Lib. 1st ed. sgn. K2. $100.00

WARREN, R.P. *Selected Poems: New & Old 1923-1966.* 1954. NY. 1st Trade ed. dj. VG. T5. $37.50

WARREN, R.P. *Selected Poems: New & Old 1923-1966.* 1966. Random House. Ltd ed. 1/250. sgn. dj. slipcase. B13. $175.00

WARREN, R.P. *Selected Poems: New & Old 1923-1966.* 1966. Random House. Ltd 1st ed. 1/250. sgn. dj. boxed. H3. $200.00

WARREN, R.P. *World Enough & Time.* 1950. Random House. inscr/sgn. H3. $75.00

WARREN, R.P. *World Enough & Time.* 1950. Random House. 1st ed. sgn. dj. EX. K2. $125.00

WARREN, Raymond. *Prairie President.* 1930. Reilly Lee. 427 p. G. S1. $9.50

WARREN. *Household Physician for Use of Families, Planters, Seamen...* 1870. Boston. 4to. pls. 799 p. G. $125.00

WARWICK, Sidney. *Silver Basilisk.* nd. Hodder Stoughton. dj. VG. P1. $10.00

WASHBURN, Mark. *Armageddon Game.* 1977. Putnam. 1st ed. dj. VG. P1. $12.50

WASHBURN, O.A. *General Red: True Story of Hound Who Led Pack Against Bear.* 1972. Austin. 1st ed. dj. VG. B3. $22.50

WASS, Verrall. *Magically Yours.* 1953. London. Armstrong. 1st ed. 146 p. VG. J3. $11.00

WASSERSTROM, Robert. *Class & Soc in Central Chiapas.* 1983. CA U. 1st ed. 357 p. dj. F2. $20.00

WATERS, Frank. *CO.* 1946. Rinehart. 1st Trade ed. dj. EX. K2. $65.00

WATERS, Frank. *Masked Gods.* 1950. Albuquerque. dj. EX. $85.00

WATERS, Frank. *Woman at Otowi Crossing.* 1966. Denver. Swallow. 1st ed. dj. EX. K2. $45.00

WATERS, T. *Recollections of a (London) Policeman.* 1857. (1st 1856) Boston. 376 p. G. $44.00

WATERS, T.A. *Lost Victim.* 1973. Random House. 1st ed. 144 p. dj. xl. NM. J3. $22.00

WATERS. *Coca-Cola Ils Hist.* 1978. NY. 1st ed. dj. VG. B3. $35.00

WATERTON, Charles. *Wanderings in S Am.* nd. Dutton. Intro Edmund Selous 12mo. 261 p. F2. $20.00

WATERTON, Charles. *Wanderings in S Am.* 1879. London. New ed. 520 p. gilt cloth bdg. F2. $75.00

WATERTON, Charles. *Wanderings in S Am.* 1909. NY. Ils Charles Livingston Bull 16 pls. 338 p. F2. $30.00

WATKIN, L.E. *Spin & Marty.* 1956 Whitman. G. P1. $4.50

WATKINS, Paul. *Calm at Sunset, Calm a Dawn.* 1989. Houghton Mifflin. UP. wrp EX. K2. $50.00

WATKINS, Paul. *Night Over Day Over Night.* 1988. Knopf. UP. wrp. EX. K2. $75.00

WATKINS, S. *Pleasures of Smoking.* 1948 NY. dj. VG. $15.00

WATKINS & HIERS. *Robert Penn Warren Talking: Interviews 1950-1978.* 1980. Random House. sgn Warren. dj. EX. H3. $75.00

WATKINS & SNYDER. *Litany of Sh'Reev* 1976. Doubleday. 1st ed. dj. EX. P1. $12.50

WATKINS-PITCHFORD, Denys. *Little Gray Men.* nd. Jr Literary Guild. VG. P1 $5.00

WATKINSON, Valerie. *Sped Arrow.* 1964 Scribner. 1st ed. dj. xl. P1. $5.00

WATSON, Colin. *It Shouldn't Happen to Dog.* nd. Book Club. dj. VG. P1. $4.50

WATSON, Colin. *Just What the Docto Ordered.* nd. Book Club. dj. VG. P1. $5.00

WATSON, Colin. *6 Nuns & a Shotgun.* nd Book Club. dj. VG. P1. $4.50

WATSON, Ian. *Books of the Blk Current* 1985. Doubleday. 1st HrdCvr ed. dj. EX. F* $12.00

WATSON, Ian. *Embedding.* 1973. Scribner 1st ed. dj. EX. R3. $35.00

WATSON, Ian. *Queenmagic, Kingmagic.* 1986. Gollancz. 1st ed. sgn. dj. EX. P1. $30.00

WATSON, Ian. *Slow Birds & Other Stories.* 1985. Gollancz. 1st ed. sgn. dj. EX. P1. $30.00

WATSON, Ian. *Sunstroke & Other Stories.* 1982. Gollancz. 1st ed. sgn. dj. EX. P1. $30.00

WATSON, Robert. *Notes on the Early Settlement of Cottage Grove & Vicinity...* 1924. Northfield, MN. 38 p. wrp. T5. $22.50

WATSON, Sally. *Witch of the Glens.* 1963. Viking. 2nd ed. 275 p. dj. VG. B10. $3.50

WATSON, Sydney. *In the Twinkling of an Eye.* nd. Nicholson. VG. P1. $7.50

WATSON, Sydney. *Scarlet & Purple.* 1933. Revell. dj. VG. P1. $8.00

WATSON, William. *Eloping Angel.* 1893. Mathews Lane/Virgo Street. VG. B10. $20.00

WATSON, William. *Muse in Exile.* 1913. VG. scarce. C1. $8.50

WATSON & REES. *Mystery of the Downs.* nd. Grosset Dunlap. VG. P1. $7.50

WATT-EVANS, Lawrence. *Denner's Wreck.* 1988. Avon. 1st HrdCvr ed. dj. EX. F5. $10.00

WAUCHOPE. *Excavations at Zacualpa, Guatemala.* 1948. Tulane. 4to. F2. $35.00

WAUGH, Alec. *Hot Countries With Woodcuts by Lynn Ward.* 1930. NY. VG. $17.00

WAUGH, Evelyn. *Charles Ryder's Schooldays.* 1982. Little Brn. UP. wrp. EX. B13. $65.00

WAUGH, Evelyn. *Handful of Dust.* 1934. Chapman Hall. 1st UK ed. presentation/inscr. dj. VG. K2. $6500.00

WAUGH, Evelyn. *Helena.* 1950. Chapman Hall. 1st UK ed. dj. EX. H3. $125.00

WAUGH, Evelyn. *Helena.* 1950. Little Brn. 1st Am ed. dj. EX. H3. $125.00

WAUGH, Evelyn. *Helena.* 1950. London. 1st ed. dj. VG. $75.00

WAUGH, Evelyn. *Holy Places.* 1953. London. Queen Ann Pr. Ils/sgn R Stone. ltd ed. 1/50. sgn. dj. EX. B13. $1000.00

WAUGH, Evelyn. *Labels. A Mediterranean Journey.* 1930. Duckworth. 1st ed. dj. scarce. H3. $650.00

WAUGH, Evelyn. *Little Learning.* 1964. Chapman Hall. 1st ed. dj. EX. B13. $65.00

WAUGH, Evelyn. *Love Among the Ruins.* 1953. Chapman Hall. 1st ed. dj. EX. H3. $60.00

WAUGH, Evelyn. *Loved Ones.* 1948. Little Brn. 2nd ed. 164 p. EX. $25.00

WAUGH, Evelyn. *Men at Arms.* 1952. Little Brn. 1st Am ed. dj. VG. H3. $40.00

WAUGH, Evelyn. *Mexico: An Object Lesson.* 1939. Little Brn. 1st Am ed. dj. EX. H3. $200.00

WAUGH, Evelyn. *Mr Loveday's Little Outing.* 1936. Chapman Hall. 1st ed. inscr. EX. K2. $1500.00

WAUGH, Evelyn. *Mr Loveday's Little Outing.* 1936. Little Brn. 1/750. dj. EX. K2. $600.00

WAUGH, Evelyn. *Officers & Gentlemen.* 1955. Chapman Hall. 1st ed. dj. EX. H3. $100.00

WAUGH, Evelyn. *Remote People.* 1931. London. Duckworth. 1st ed. inscr to Jane Marston. dj. EX. K2. $2500.00

WAUGH, Evelyn. *Scoop: A Novel About Journalists.* 1933. Chapman Hall. 1st ed. H3. $100.00

WAUGH, Evelyn. *Scott-King's Modern Europe.* 1949. Little Brn. 1st ed. dj. H3. $40.00

WAUGH, Evelyn. *They Were Still Dancing.* 1931. Jonathan Cape/Harrison Smith. 1st Am ed. dj. H3. $250.00

WAUGH, Evelyn. *Tourist in Africa.* 1960. Chapman Hall. 1st UK ed. dj. EX. H3. $100.00

WAUGH, Evelyn. *Tourist in Africa.* 1960. Little Brn. 1st Am ed. dj. EX. H3. $50.00

WAUGH, Hillary. *Con Game.* nd. Book Club. dj. xl. P1. $4.00

WAUGH, Hillary. *Late Mrs D.* nd. Book Club. dj. xl. P1. $4.00

WAUGH, Hillary. *Rich Man, Dead Man.* 1956. Crime Club. 1st ed. dj. G. P1. $15.00

WAUGH, Hillary. *8th Mrs Bluebeard.* nd. Book Club. dj. VG. P1. $4.50

WAUGH, William. *Diseases of the Respiratory Organs.* 1901. Clinic. VG. J2. $15.00

WAUGH. *Collecting Hooked Rugs.* 1927. NY. Ils. 8vo. dj. EX. $50.00

WAY, T.R. *Memories of James McNeill Whistler.* 1912. London. 1st ed. pls. VG. $30.00

WAYLAND, J.W. *John Kagi & John Brn.* 1961. Strasburg, VA. M. $25.00

WAYNE, John. *America, Why I Love Her.* 1977. Simon Schuster. 1st ed. quarto. dj. EX. B13. $35.00

WAYNE, Joseph. *By Gun & Spur.* 1952. Dutton. 1st ed. VG. P1. $10.00

WEARIN. *Political Am.* 1967. Shenand. Ils. 137 p. dj. VG. C2. $27.00

WEATHERWAX, P. *Indian Corn in Old Am.* 1954. Macmillan. 1st ed. 4to. EX. $30.00

WEAVER, M.P. *Aztecs, Maya, & Their Predecessors.* 1973. Seminar Pr. 2nd print. 347 p. F2. $25.00

WEAVER, Ward. *Hang My Wreath.* 1941. Funk Wagnall. 1st ed? 358 p. VG. B10. $4.00

WEAVER, William. *Verdi.* 1977. NY. Thames Hudson. quarto. 256 p. dj. EX. H3. $65.00

WEBB, A.S. *Peninsula: McClellan's Campaign of 1862.* 1881. Scribner. 219 p. blue linen. fair. S1. $15.00

WEBB, A.S. *Peninsula: McClellan's Campaign of 1862.* 1989. Broadfoot Pub. 219 p. dj. M. S1. $25.00

WEBB, Addison. *Beekeeping for Profit & Pleasure.* 1944. NY. 2nd print. dj. VG. C1. $8.50

WEBB, D.B. *Diary & Letters.* 1898. Phil. Friends Bookstore. 12mo. 199 p. VG. V1. $12.50

WEBB, Evelyn. *Something To Die For.* 1991. Morrow. ARC. glossy wrp. EX. B13. $45.00

WEBB, J.W. *Altowman; or, Life & Adventure in Rocky Mts.* 1846. NY. 2 vols. T5. $650.00

WEBB, Jack. *Big Sun.* nd. Rinehart. 2nd ed. dj. G. P1. $15.00

WEBB, Maria. *Fells of Swarthmore Hall & Their Friends.* 1896. Phil. Longstreth. 12mo. 468 p. V1. $16.00

WEBB, Maria. *Penns & Peningtons of the 17th Century...* 1877. Phil. Longstreth. 12mo. 446 p. fair. V1. $18.00

WEBB, Paul. *Comin' 'Round the Mt.* 1938. NY. 1st ed. dj. VG. B3. $20.00

WEBB, Sharon. *Earthchild.* 1982. Atheneum Argo. 1st ed. dj. VG. P1. $15.00

WEBB, W.J. *How To Bat & Run Bases.* 1941. Chicago. 1st ed. wrp. VG. K1. $15.00

WEBBER, Malcolm. *Medicine Show.* 1941. Caxton. Ils Harting. 1st ed. 265 p. dj. H3. $75.00

WEBER, Carl. *Fore-Edge Painting: Hist Survey of Curious Art...* 1966. Irvington-on-Hudson. 1st ed. dj. EX. $200.00

WEBER, Gottfried. *Theory of Music Composition...* 1851. London. Robert Cocks. 1st UK ed. 2 vols. EX. H3. $250.00

WEBER, H.L. *Out of the Spook Cabinet.* 1947. Oakland, CA. Jones. 1st ed. 30 p. SftCvr. NM. J3. $4.00

WEBER, V.F. *Ko-Ji Ho-Ten.* 1965. Hacker Art Books. reprint. 2 vols. D4. $210.00

WEBSTER, F.A.M. *Lord of the Leopards.* nd. Hutchinson. dj. VG. P1. $25.00

WEBSTER, H.K. *Man With the Scarred Hand.* nd. Bobbs Merrill. 1st ed? 285 p. VG. B10. $4.00

WEBSTER, H.K. *Sky-Man.* 1910. Century. 1st ed. VG. R3. $17.50

WEBSTER, Noah. *Legacy From Tenerife.* 1984. Doubleday. 1st ed. dj. EX. P1. $12.50

WEBSTER, Richard. *Aura Reading for Fun & Profit.* 1988. Aukland. Brookfield Pr. 1st ed. 66 p. NM. J3. $22.00

WEBSTER, Richard. *Psychometry From A to Z.* 1987. Aukland. Brookfield Pr. 1st ed. 73 p. NM. J3. $24.00

WECTER, Dixon. *Age of Great Depression 1929-1941.* 1948. NY. 1st ed. dj. EX. $8.00

WEEDEN, Howard. *Old Voices.* 1904. NY. Ils 1st ed. G. T5. $125.00

WEEDEN, Howard. *Shadows on the Wall.* 1899. Huntsville. 1st ed. VG. B3. $90.00

WEEGEE. *Naked City.* 1945. NY. Probably 1st ed. EX. G1. $34.00

WEEKES, Refine. *Life of William Penn & Other Poems...* 1822. NY. Mahlon Day. 16mo. 192 p. V1. $12.00

WEEKS, A.G. *Ils of Diurnal Lepidoptera.* 1905. Boston. Cambridge. 2 vols. clr pls. VG. T3. $250.00

WEEKS, R.K. *Convict B 14.* 1920. Brentano. VG. P1. $20.00

WEEKS, S.B. *S Quakers & Slavery.* 1896. Baltimore. EX. $75.00

WEEMS, M.L. *God's Revenge Against Duelling.* 1816. Phil. 2nd ed. VG. $225.00

WEEMS, M.L. *3 Discourses: Marriage, Drink, & Adultery.* 1929. NY. Ltd ed. 1/1000. VG. $25.00

WEES, F.S. *Country of the Strangers.* 1960. Doubleday. 1st ed. dj. RS. VG. P1. $20.00

WEES, F.S. *M'Lord I Am Not Guilty.* nd. Book Club. dj. VG. P1. $4.50

WEIDMAN, Jerome. *W Somerset Maugham Sampler.* 1943. Garden City. 1st ed. 489 p. VG. $6.00

WEIL, Thomas. *Area Handbook for Chile.* 1969. GPO. 1st ed. 507 p. xl. F2. $10.00

WEINBAUM, Stanley. *Blk Flame.* 1948. Fantasy. 1st ed. dj. EX. R3. $55.00

WEINBAUM, Stanley. *Martian Odyssey.* 1949. Fantasy. 1st ed. dj. EX. R3. $55.00

WEINBAUM, Stanley. *Red Peri.* 1952. Fantasy. 1st ed. dj. EX. R3. $75.00

WEINBAUM, Stanley. *Red Peri.* 1952. Fantasy. 1st ed. Donald Grant bdg. dj. M. P1. $35.00

WEINBERG, George. *Numberland.* 1987. St Martin. 1st ed. dj. EX. P1. $10.00

WEINBERG, Robert. *Far Below & Other Horrors.* 1974. Starmont. 1st ed. dj. EX. R3. $25.00

WEINBERG, Robert. *8th Gr Man.* 1989. Starmont. 1st ed. wrp. M. R3. $9.95

WEINER, Alex; see Aldini.

WEINER, Irv. *Perfected Nest of Boxes...* 1976. Weiner. stapled manuscript. w/boxes. J3. $6.00

WEINERT & ARTHUR. *Defender of the Chesapeake: Story of Ft Monroe.* 1989. Wht Mane. 361 p. dj. M. S1. $19.95

WEINGARTEN, A. *Sky Is Falling.* 1977. NY. 1st ed. 260 p. dj. VG. B3. $17.50

WEINTRAUB, Stanley. *Shaw: Autobiography 1898-1950, the Playwright Years.* nd. (1970) Weybright Talley. 1st ed. dj. EX. B10. $5.75

WEISKOPF, Herman. *On 3: Inside the Sport's Huddle.* 1975. Little Brn. 1st ed. 230 p. dj. EX. B10. $3.75

WEISMANN, Elizabeth. *Art & Time in Mexico.* 1985. Harper. 1st ed. 248 p. dj. F2. $35.00

WEISS, Joe. *Passion Blues.* 1953. Woodford Pr. 1st ed. dj. EX. F5. $25.00

WEISS, Joe. *Way You Make Your Bed.* 1954. Woodford Pr. 1st ed. dj. EX. F5. $22.00

WEISS, Joe. *Wildcat Hunt.* 1959. Toga Books. 1st ed. dj. EX. F5. $27.00

WEISS & GOODGOLD. *To Be Continued.* 1973. Crown. 1st ed. VG. R3. $20.00

WEISS & ZIEGLER. *Thomas Say, Early Am Naturalist.* 1931. Springfield. 1st ed. dj. VG. C2. $75.00

WEISSMULLER, Johnny. *How He Does It* 1930. Grosset Dunlap. 1st ed/reprint c Swimming the Am Crawl. dj. B13. $150.00

WEISZ, Josef. *Alpenblumen.* 1959 Germany. tall 8vo. 95 clr pls. dj. EX. $35.00

WEITLANER-JOHNSON, Irmgard. *Desig Motifs of Mexican Indian Textiles.* 1976. Gra Austria. 2 vols. F2. $125.00

WEIZMAN, Ezer. *On Eagle's Wings.* 1977 2nd print. inscr. dj. xl. VG. C1. $9.50

WELCH, Christopher. *Hist of Boehm Flute.* 1896. NY. Schirmer. 3rd ed. 504 p. G. H3 $125.00

WELCH, Christopher. *6 Lectures o Record...in Relation to Literature.* 1911 Oxford. Ils. music. index. VG. H3. $125.00

WELCH, James. *Death of Jim Loney.* 1979 Harper Row. UP. wrp. EX. K2. $125.00

WELCH, James. *Fools Crow.* 1986. Viking ARC. K2. $50.00

WELCH, James. *Riding the Earthboy 4(* 1976. Harper Row. Revised reissue. sgn. d EX. K2. $85.00

WELCH, James. *Riding the Earthboy 4(* 1981. World. 1st ed. dj. EX. K2. $85.00

WELCH, James. *Winter in the Blood.* 1974 Harper Row. 1st ed. dj. EX. K2. $45.00

WELCH, Ronald. *Hawk.* 1967. Oxford U 1st UK ed. dj. EX. F5. $20.00

WELCH, Ronald. *Nicholas Carey.* 196 Criterion. 1st ed. dj. EX. F5. $20.00

WELCH, Thomas. *Indians of S Am.* 198 WA. 4to. 594 p. wrp. F2. $50.00

WELCH & FIGUERAS. *Travel Accounts Descriptions of Latin Am & Caribbean.* 198 WA. 1st ed. 4to. 293 p. wrp. F2. $30.00

WELCH & GUTIERREZ. *Aztecs.* 1987. W/ 1st ed. 169 p. wrp. F2. $25.00

WELCH & GUTIERREZ. *Incas.* 1987. W/ 1st ed. 145 p. wrp. F2. $25.00

WELDON, Fay. *Cloning of Joanna Ma* 1989. Viking. UP. wrp. EX. K2. $30.00

WELKER, T.D. *Conflicts & Triumphs of Itinerant, Rev John Kiger, DD.* 189 Cincinnati. 1st ed. 301 p. G. T5. $17.50

WELLES, Patricia. *Babyhip.* 1967. Dutto 1st ed. dj. EX. K2. $35.00

WELLMAN, M.W. *After Dark.* nd. Boo Club. dj. VG. P1. $4.50

WELLMAN, M.W. *After Dark.* 1980. Doubleday. 1st ed. dj. VG. P1. $15.00

WELLMAN, M.W. *Dark Destroyers.* 1959. Avalon. dj. xl. P1. $10.00

WELLMAN, M.W. *Lost & the Lurking.* 1981. Doubleday. 1st ed. dj. VG. P1. $25.00

WELLMAN, M.W. *Old Gods Waken.* nd. Book Club. dj. VG. P1. $4.50

WELLMAN, M.W. *Old Gods Waken.* 1979. Doubleday. 1st ed. dj. VG. P1. $25.00

WELLMAN, M.W. *Rebel Boast: 1st at Bethel, Last at Appomattox.* 1956. NY. 1st ed. 317 p. G. T5. $27.50

WELLMAN, M.W. *Rebel Mail Runner.* 1954. Holiday House. 1st ed. dj. EX. R3. $30.00

WELLMAN, M.W. *Rebel Songster.* 1955. Charlotte. tall 8vo. decor wrp. VG. C2. $35.00

WELLMAN, M.W. *School of Darkness.* 1985. Doubleday. 1st ed. M. R3. $20.00

WELLMAN, M.W. *Sojarr of Titan.* 1949. Crestwood. 1st ed. dj. EX. R3. $25.00

WELLMAN, M.W. *Twice in Time.* nd. Avalon. dj. xl. P1. $10.00

WELLMAN, Paul. *Spawn of Evil.* 1964. NY. 1st ed. 350 p. dj. VG. B3. $17.50

WELLMAN, Paul. *Trampling Herd.* 1939. NY. 1st ed. 433 p. dj. VG. B3. $35.00

WELLS, A.W. *Hail to the Jeep: Factual & Pictorial Hist.* 1946. NY. Ils. G. T5. $27.50

WELLS, Basil. *Doorways to Space.* 1951. Fantasy. 1st ed. dj. EX. R3. $15.00

WELLS, Basil. *Planets of Adventure.* 1949. Fantasy. 1st bdg. dj. EX. R3. $20.00

WELLS, Carolyn. *Affair at Flower Acres.* nd. Doubleday Doran. Canadian ed. VG. P1. $15.00

WELLS, Carolyn. *Broken O.* nd. AL Burt. VG. P1. $7.50

WELLS, Carolyn. *Face Cards.* 1925. NY. AL Burt. 334 p. VG. J3. $5.00

WELLS, Carolyn. *Horror House.* 1931. Lippincott. 1st ed. xl. P1. $7.50

WELLS, Carolyn. *Importance of Being Murdered.* 1939. Lippincott. xl. P1. $7.50

WELLS, Carolyn. *Missing Link.* 1939. Triangle. dj. VG. P1. $10.00

WELLS, Carolyn. *Money Musk.* 1936. Lippincott. G. P1. $10.00

WELLS, Carolyn. *Sleeping Dogs.* nd. Collier. G. P1. $7.50

WELLS, Carolyn. *Wht Alley.* nd. Hodder Stoughton. dj. VG. P1. $20.00

WELLS, Carveth. *Panamexico!* 1937. McBride. 1st ed. 343 p. dj. F2. $15.00

WELLS, H.G. *Autocracy of Mr Parham.* 1930. Doubleday Doran. 1st ed. dj. G. P1. $45.00

WELLS, H.G. *Bealby.* 1915. Macmillan. VG. P1. $25.00

WELLS, H.G. *Collector's Book of SF by HG Wells.* 1978. Castle. dj. EX. P1. $10.00

WELLS, H.G. *Complete SF Treasury of HG Wells.* 1978. Avenel. dj. EX. P1. $10.00

WELLS, H.G. *Complete SF Treasury of HG Wells.* 1978. Avenell. facsimile. VG. C1. $6.50

WELLS, H.G. *Croquet Player.* 1937. Viking. dj. VG. P1. $12.50

WELLS, H.G. *Early Writings in Science & SF.* 1975. CA U. 1st ed. 1975. dj. EX. R3. $25.00

WELLS, H.G. *Experiment in Autobiography: Discoveries & Conclusions...* 1934. Macmillan. 1st Am ed. inscr. dj. EX. C4. $350.00

WELLS, H.G. *Famous Short Stories.* 1938. Garden City. VG. R3. $10.00

WELLS, H.G. *Fate of Man.* 1939. Alliance. VG. P1. $30.00

WELLS, H.G. *Floor Games.* 1911. London. Frank Palmer. 1st ed. EX. B13. $200.00

WELLS, H.G. *Food of the Gods.* nd. Thomas Nelson. sgn/dtd 1909. VG. P1. $250.00

WELLS, H.G. *Future in Am.* 1907. Tauchnitz. 1st Continental ed. EX. R3. $20.00

WELLS, H.G. *Happy Turning: Dream of Life.* 1956. Heinemann. presentation. dj. H3. $200.00

WELLS, H.G. *Hist of Mr Polly.* 1957. London. Folio Soc. Ils Ribbons. 1st ed. slilpcase. C1. $14.00

WELLS, H.G. *In the Days of the Comet.* nd. Collins. G. P1. $7.00

WELLS, H.G. *In the Days of the Comet.* 1906. London. 1st ed. Currey state B. VG. R3. $95.00

WELLS, H.G. *Invisible Man.* nd. Thomas Nelson. G. P1. $5.00

WELLS, H.G. *Joan & Peter.* 1918. Macmillan. 1st ed. G. P1. $12.50

WELLS, H.G. *Little Wars: A Game for Boys.* 1913. London. Frank Palmer. 1st ed. EX. very scarce. B13. $400.00

WELLS, H.G. *Meanwhile.* 1927. Doran. 1st ed. VG. P1. $30.00

WELLS, H.G. *Men Like Gods.* 1923. London. 1st ed. VG. R3. $40.00

WELLS, H.G. *Mr Britling Sees It Through.* 1916. Macmillan. not 1st ed. 443 p. VG. B10. $3.50

WELLS, H.G. *Mr Britling Sees It Through.* 1916. Macmillan. 5th print. VG. P1. $10.00

WELLS, H.G. *Research Magnificent.* 1915. Macmillan. 1st ed. G. R3. $15.00

WELLS, H.G. *Salvaging of Civilization.* 1921. Cassell. VG. P1. $20.00

WELLS, H.G. *Sea Lady.* 1902. Appleton. 1st Am ed. VG. R3. $75.00

WELLS, H.G. *Sea Lady.* 1976. Hyperion. reprint of 1902 ed. EX. R3. $15.00

WELLS, H.G. *Secret Places in the Heart.* 1922. Macmillan. 1st ed. 287 p. dj. EX. B10. $12.50

WELLS, H.G. *Tales of Space & Time.* nd. Leipzig. 1st Continental ed. wrp. EX. B13. $45.00

WELLS, H.G. *Tales of the Unexpected.* nd. Collins. VG. P1. $10.00

WELLS, H.G. *Time Machine.* nd. Armed Services Ed. wrp. VG. B4. $15.00

WELLS, H.G. *Time Machine.* nd. Leipzig. Tauchnitz. 1st Continental ed. wrp. EX. B13. $85.00

WELLS, H.G. *Time Machine.* 1931. Random House. Ils Dwiggins. slipcase. EX. R3. $25.00

WELLS, H.G. *Time Machine/Man Who Could Work Miracles.* 1964. London. Pan. 2nd ed. EX. P1. $8.00

WELLS, H.G. *Tono Bungay.* 1959. Collins. dj. VG. P1. $10.00

WELLS, H.G. *Undying Fire.* nd. Cassell. VG. P1. $15.00

WELLS, H.G. *Valley of Spiders.* nd. Novel Lib. dj. G. P1. $25.00

WELLS, H.G. *War in the Air.* nd. George Bell. G. P1. $30.00

WELLS, H.G. *War in the Air.* 1908. London. 1st ed. Currey C bdg. G. R3. $40.00

WELLS, H.G. *War of the Worlds.* 1954. Whitman. VG. P1. $7.50

WELLS, H.G. *Wife of Sir Isaac Harman*. 1914. Macmillan. 1st ed. G. P1. $7.50

WELLS, H.G. *Works*. 1924-1927. Scribner. Atlantic ed. 1/1670. sgn. H3. $2000.00

WELLS, H.G. *1st Men on the Moon*. 1901. London. 1st ed. G. R3. $50.00

WELLS, H.G. *7 Famous Novels*. 1934. Knopf. 1st ed. G. P1. $20.00

WELLS, H.G. *7 SF Novels of HG Wells*. nd. Dover. dj. EX. R3. $15.00

WELLS, Helen. *Cherry Ames, Army Nurse*. nd. Grosset Dunlap. dj. VG. P1. $7.50

WELLS, Helen. *Cherry Ames, Camp Nurse*. 1957. Grosset Dunlap. dj. VG. P1. $6.00

WELLS, Helen. *Cherry Ames, Student Nurse*. nd. Grosset Dunlap. dj. VG. P1. $7.50

WELLS, Helen. *Cherry Ames: Island Nurse*. 1960. Grosset. 184 p. dj. VG. B10. $3.75

WELLS, Helen. *Hidden Valley Mystery*. nd. Grosset Dunlap. dj. VG. P1. $7.50

WELLS, Helen. *Silver Wings for Vicki*. nd. Grosset Dunlap. dj. VG. P1. $7.50

WELLS, Helen. *Vicki Finds an Answer*. nd. Grosset Dunlap. dj. VG. P1. $7.50

WELLS, James. *With Touch of Elbow*. 1909. Phil. 1st ed. 362 p. G. B3. $65.00

WELLS, R.A. *Manners, Culture, & Dress of the Best Am Soc*. 1891. Richardson. Ils. 8vo. 502 p. VG. $25.00

WELLS, Tobias. *Brenda's Murder*. 1973. Crime Club. 1st ed. dj. xl. P1. $5.00

WELTY, Eudora. *Acrobats in a Park*. 1980. Lord John. Ltd ed. 1/300. sgn. H3. $125.00

WELTY, Eudora. *Bride of the Innisfallen*. 1955. Harcourt Brace. 1st ed. dj. EX. B13. $450.00

WELTY, Eudora. *Bride of the Innisfallen*. 1955. Harcourt Brace. 1st ed. sgn. dj. EX. scarce. K2. $550.00

WELTY, Eudora. *Bride of the Innisfallen*. 1955. Harcourt Brace. 1st ed. 2nd issue. sgn. dj. EX. C4. $175.00

WELTY, Eudora. *Bride of the Innisfallen*. 1955. Harcourt Brace. 1st ed. 2nd state. 1st bdg. dj. EX. K2. $75.00

WELTY, Eudora. *Bye-Bye Brevoort*. 1980. Jackson, MS. New Stage Theatre. 1st ed. 1/476. sgn. EX. B13. $135.00

WELTY, Eudora. *Collected Stories of Eudora Welty*. 1980. Harcourt Brace. UP. wrp. EX. very scarce. B13. $950.00

WELTY, Eudora. *Collected Stories*. 1980. NY. 1/500. sgn. slipcase. EX. T9. $200.00

WELTY, Eudora. *Curtain of Gr*. 1941. Doubleday. 1st ed. dj. fair. B13. $400.00

WELTY, Eudora. *Delta Wedding*. 1946. Harcourt Brace. 1st ed. dj. G. H3. $125.00

WELTY, Eudora. *Delta Wedding*. 1946. Harcourt Brace. 1st ed. sgn. dj. EX. C4. $350.00

WELTY, Eudora. *Eye of the Story*. 1977. Random House. Ltd ed. 1/200. sgn. boxed. EX. H3. $200.00

WELTY, Eudora. *Eye of the Story*. 1977. Random House. 1st ed. dj. EX. B13. $45.00

WELTY, Eudora. *Eye of the Story*. 1978. NY. 1st Trade ed. dj. EX. $25.00

WELTY, Eudora. *Eye of the Story*. 1987. Virago. UP of 1st Eng ed. EX. K2. $85.00

WELTY, Eudora. *Flock of Guinea Hens Seen From a Car*. 1970. Albondocani. 1/300. stapled wrp. envelope. EX. B13. $150.00

WELTY, Eudora. *Golden Apples*. 1948. Harcourt Brace. 1st ed. dj. M. C4. $400.00

WELTY, Eudora. *Golden Apples*. 1949. Harcourt Brace. 1st ed. dj. EX. H3. $150.00

WELTY, Eudora. *Henry Gr: Novelist of the Imagination*. 1961. TX Quarterly. 1st ed. sgn. wrp. EX. B13/K2. $450.00

WELTY, Eudora. *Ida M'Toy*. 1979. IL U. Ltd ed. 1/350. sgn. H3. $200.00

WELTY, Eudora. *Ida M'Toy*. 1979. Urbana, IL. IL U. 1st ed. 1/350. sgn. EX. B13. $250.00

WELTY, Eudora. *In Blk & Wht: Photographs of the '30s & '40s*. 1985. Northridge. 1/400. sgn. no dj issued. EX. C4. $150.00

WELTY, Eudora. *Losing Battles*. 1970. Random House. Ltd ed. 1/300. sgn. boxed. H3. $375.00

WELTY, Eudora. *Losing Battles*. 1970. Random House. 1st ed. sgn. dj. H3. $85.00

WELTY, Eudora. *On Short Stories*. 1949. Harcourt Brace. 1st ed. 1/1500. sgn. glassine dj. EX. B13. $300.00

WELTY, Eudora. *Photographs*. 1989. MS U. 1st ed. 1/375. sgn. slipcase. w/sgn post card. EX. B13. $285.00

WELTY, Eudora. *Place in Fiction*. 1957. House of Books. 1st ed. 1/300. sgn. glassine dj. EX. B13. $850.00

WELTY, Eudora. *Ponder Heart*. 1954. Harcourt Brace. 1st ed in book form. dj. VG. H3. $125.00

WELTY, Eudora. *Ponder Heart*. 1954. London. Hamish Hamilton. UP. EX. K2. $425.00

WELTY, Eudora. *Retreat*. 1981. Palaemon. Ltd ed. 1/240. sgn. H3. $175.00

WELTY, Eudora. *Robber Bridegroom*. 1942. Doubleday. 1st ed. dj. EX. scarce. B13. $600.00

WELTY, Eudora. *Robber Bridegroom*. 1987. Pennroyal Pr. Ils/sgn Barry Moser. 1/150. sgn. full leather. C4. $450.00

WELTY, Eudora. *Some Notes on Time in Fiction*. 1973. Jackson, MS. scarce offprint. stapled wrp. EX. B13. $275.00

WELTY, Eudora. *Sweet Devouring*. 1969. Albondocarri Pr. 1st ed in book form. 1/176. $250.00

WELTY, Eudora. *Visit of Charity: Story*. 1941. NY. Decision. 8vo. wrp. EX. $25.00

WELTY, Eudora. *Wide Net & Other Stories*. 1943. Harcourt Brace. 1st ed. dj. EX. K2. $650.00

WELTY, Eudora. *1 Writer's Beginnings*. 1984. Harvard. Ltd ed. 1/350. sgn. cloth slipcase. H3. $200.00

WELTY, Eudora. *3 Papers on Fiction*. 1962. Smith College. pamphlet. wrp. EX. K2. $75.00

WELTY & SHARP. *Norton Book of Friendship*. 1991. Norton. UP. wrp. EX. B13. $100.00

WENDT, Herbert. *Sex Life of the Animals*. 1965. Simon Schuster. 1st ed. 383 p. dj. EX. B10. $5.75

WENDT & KOGAN. *Bet a Million*. 1948. Indianapolis. 1st ed. sgns. 357 p. dj. VG. B3. $32.50

WENK, Timothy. *Insomnia: Impossible Nightmare, Impossible Dream*. 1988. Metempirical Magic. 1st ed. NM. J3. $8.00

WENTWORTH, M.J. *James Tissot: Catalog Raisonne of His Prints*. 1978. Minneapolis. 4to. wrp. $30.00

WENTWORTH, Patricia. *Alington Inheritance*. nd. Book Club. dj. VG. P1. $5.00

WENTWORTH, Patricia. *Ivory Dagger*. 1951. Lippincott. 1st ed. VG. P1. $20.00

WENTWORTH, Patricia. *Ladies' Bane*. 1973. Wht Lion. dj. xl. P1. $7.50

WENTWORTH, Patricia. *Miss Silver Comes To Stay*. 1949. Lippincott. 1st ed. VG. P1. $20.00

WENTWORTH, Patricia. *Pilgrim's Rest*. 1946. Lippincott. 1st ed. VG. P1. $25.00

WENTWORTH, Patricia. *Pilgrim's Rest.* 1948. Hodder Stoughton. 1st ed. G. P1. $15.00

WENTZEL, George. *Lovecraft Collector's Lib.* 1979. Strange Co. 1st ed. lg wrp. M. R3. $100.00

WERFEL, A.M. *And the Bridge Is Love.* 1958. NY. 1st ed. 312 p. dj. VG. B3. $25.00

WERNER, Josef. *Bilder und Radierungen.* c 1984. Munchen. inscr. pls. EX. $25.00

WERPER, Barton. *Tarzan & the Silver Globe.* 1964. Gold Star. 1st ed. wrp. VG. R3. $17.50

WERT, J.D. *From Winchester to Cedar Creek: Shenandoah Campaign of 1864.* 1987. S Mountain Pr. 1st ed. dj. EX. S1. $17.50

WERTHAM. *Seduction of the Innocent.* 1954. NY. dj. VG. B3. $40.00

WESSEL. *Ethnic Survey Woonsocket.* 1931. Chicago. 1st ed. VG. B3. $20.00

WEST, Jerry. *Happy Hollisters.* nd. (1961) Doubleday. dj. B10. $4.25

WEST, Jessamyn. *Love Is Not What You Think.* 1959. Harcourt Brace. 1st ed. 16mo. 38 p. xl. V1. $6.00

WEST, Levoh. *Making an Etching.* 1932. London. Ils. 79 p. T5. $25.00

WEST, Mae. *Goodness Had Nothing To Do With It.* 1959. NY. 1st ed. dj. VG. B3. $22.50

WEST, Mae. *Goodness Had Nothing To Do With It.* 1959. Prentice Hall. 1st ed. presentation. dj. VG. H3. $125.00

WEST, Nathanael. *Cool Million.* 1954. Neville Spearman. 1st UK ed. dj. EX. H3. $100.00

WEST, Nathanael. *Day of the Locust.* 1939. Random House. 1st ed. dj. EX. scarce. K2. $1000.00

WEST, Nathanael. *Day of the Locust.* 1951. Grey Walls. 1st UK ed. dj. EX. H3. $75.00

WEST, Nathanael. *Miss Lonelyhearts.* 1933. NY. Liveright. 1st ed. 1st issue. 1/800. very scarce. K2. $250.00

WEST, Nathanael. *Miss Lonelyhearts.* 1949. Grey Walls. 1st UK ed. H3. $75.00

WEST, Owen; see Koontz, Dean R.

WEST, Paul. *Alley Jaggers.* 1966. London. Hutchinson. 1st UK ed. dj. EX. K2. $45.00

WEST, Paul. *Alley Jaggers.* 1966. NY. 1st ed. sgn. Milton Glaser dj. EX. T9. $45.00

WEST, Paul. *Byron & the Spoiler's Art.* 1960. London. 1st ed. dj. EX. scarce. $50.00

WEST, Paul. *Women of Whitechapel & Jack the Ripper.* 1991. Random House. UP. wrp. EX. K2. $30.00

WEST, R. *Lincoln's Scapegoat General.* 1965. Boston. 1st ed. 462 p. dj. VG. B3. $40.00

WEST, Rebecca. *Harriet Hume.* 1929. Doubleday. 1st ed. dj. EX. B13. $50.00

WEST, Rebecca. *Meaning of Treason.* 1947. Viking. not 1st ed. 307 p. VG. B10. $3.25

WEST, Richard. *Tolkien Criticism: An Annotated Checklist.* 1981. Kent State. Revised Enlarged 1st ed. M. R3. $25.00

WEST, Wallace. *Bird of Time.* 1959. Gnome. 1st ed. dj. VG. P1. $25.00

WEST, Wallace. *Everlasting Exiles.* 1967. Avalon. 1st ed. dj. EX. R3. $15.00

WEST, Wallace. *Memory Bank.* 1961. Avalon. 1st ed. dj. xl. R3. $5.00

WEST, Wallace. *River of Time.* 1963. Avalon. 1st ed. inscr. dj. VG. R3. $17.50

WEST, Wallace. *Time Lockers.* 1964. Avalon. 1st ed. inscr. dj. EX. R3. $12.50

WESTCOTT, Glenway. *Grandmothers: A Family Portrait.* 1927. Harper. 1/250. sgn. Special bdg. EX. C4. $50.00

WESTLAKE, D.E. *Anarchaos.* 1967. Ace F-421. PB Orig. sgn. wrp. EX. T9. $35.00

WESTLAKE, D.E. *Bank Shot.* nd. Book Club. dj. VG. P1. $4.50

WESTLAKE, D.E. *Busy Body.* 1966. Boardman. 1st ed. dj. xl. P1. $10.00

WESTLAKE, D.E. *Curious Facts Preceeding My Execution & Other Fictions.* 1968. Random House. 1st ed. sgn. VG. T9. $45.00

WESTLAKE, D.E. *Damsel.* 1968. Hodder Stoughton. 1st UK ed. dj. NM. T9. $30.00

WESTLAKE, D.E. *Good Behavior.* 1986. Mysterious Pr. 1st ed. dj. VG. P1. $15.95

WESTLAKE, D.E. *High Adventure.* nd. BOMC. dj. VG. P1. $7.50

WESTLAKE, D.E. *Jimmy the Kid.* 1974. Evans. 1st ed. dj. xl. P1. $12.50

WESTLAKE, D.E. *Kahawa.* 1981. Viking. inscr. dj. H3. $60.00

WESTLAKE, D.E. *Levine.* 1984. Mysterious Pr. 1st ed. dj. VG. P1. $15.00

WESTLAKE, D.E. *Levine.* 1984. NY. Ltd ed. 1/250. sgn. slipcase. EX. $55.00

WESTLAKE, D.E. *Likely Story.* 1984. Penzler. 1st ed. dj. VG. P1. $17.50

WESTLAKE, D.E. *Point Blank.* 1984. Allison Busby. 1st ed. dj. EX. P1. $17.50

WESTLAKE, D.E. *Ra'Ivavae: Expedition to Polynesia.* 1961. NY. Ils. dj. VG. $10.00

WESTLAKE, D.E. *Slayground.* 1971. Random House. 1st ed. dj. xl. P1. $10.00

WESTLAKE, D.E. *Trust Me on This.* 1988. Mysterious Pr. 1st ed. dj. VG. P1. $16.95

WESTLAKE, D.E. *Why Me?* 1983. NY. 1st ed. sgn. dj. VG. $45.00

WESTMORE, PERC, WALLY, & BUD. *Westmore Beauty Book.* 1956. Shasta Korshak. 1st ed. dj. EX. R3. $75.00

WESTON, Carolyn. *Poor, Poor Ophelia.* nd. Random House. 3rd ed. dj. xl. P1. $5.00

WESTON, Carolyn. *Rouse the Demon.* nd. Random House. dj. VG. P1. $7.50

WESTON, Carolyn. *Susannah Screaming.* 1975. Random House. 1st ed. dj. xl. P1. $5.00

WESTON, Garnett. *Hidden Portal.* nd. Collier. VG. P1. $10.00

WESTON, Garnett. *Murder in Haste.* 1935. Stokes. G. P1. $8.00

WESTON, J.L. *From Ritual to Romance.* 1941. NY. VG. C1. $21.50

WESTON, J.L. *Quest of the Holy Grail.* 1964. London. Frank Cass. dj. C1. $44.50

WESTON, J.L. *Romance, Vision, & Satire.* 1912. 1st ed. xl. VG. C1. $9.50

WESTON, J.L. *Romance, Vision, & Satire.* 1912. Boston. 1st ed. VG. C1. $17.00

WESTON, J.L. *Sir Gawain & the Gr Knight.* 1905. NY Amsterdam Book Co. 2nd ed. 1/210. rare. C1. $47.50

WESTON, Peter. *Andromeda 1.* 1977. Dobson. 1st ed. dj. EX. P1. $20.00

WESTROPP, Hodder. *Handbook of Archaeology.* 1878. London. 2nd ed. 8vo. 600 p. VG. $35.00

WETANSON & HOOBLER. *Hunters.* 1978. Doubleday. 1st ed. dj. EX. P1. $12.50

WETFISH, Gene. *Origins of Art.* 1953. Bobbs Merrill. 1st ed. 300 p. dj. F2. $25.00

WETHERALD & HICKS. *Sermons.* 1826. Phil. Gould. 1st ed. 312 p. VG. V1. $85.00

WETHERELL, W.D. *Hyannis Boat & Other Stories.* 1989. Little Brn. 1st ed. dj. EX. K2. $15.95

WETHERN, G. *Wayward Angel.* 1978. NY. 1st ed. dj. VG. B3. $35.00

WETMORE, H.C. *Last of the Great Scouts.* 1918. Grosset Dunlap. 1st ed. 8vo. 333 p. dj. R4. $45.00

WETMORE, H.C. *Out of a Fleur-De-Lis...* 1903. Boston. Ils. 432 p. G. T5. $25.00

WETZEL. *Practical Fly Fishing.* 1945. Boston. 2nd ed. dj. VG. C2. $95.00

WEVERKA, Robert. *1 Minute to Eternity.* 1968. Morrow. dj. VG. P1. $12.50

WEXLER, Norman. *Joe.* 1970. Avon. 1st PB ed. VG. B4. $4.00

WEYER, Edward. *Primitive Peoples Today.* nd. (1958) Doubleday. 4to. 288 p. dj. F2. $15.00

WEYGAND, Maxime. *Hist de l'Armee Francaise.* 1938. np. (Paris) 1/385. French text. 4to. A4. $100.00

WEYGANDT, Cornelius. *Red Hills.* 1929. Phil. 4th print. 251 p. VG. B10. $10.00

WEYTH, Andrew. *Helga Pictures.* 1987. Abrams. 1st ed. dj. EX. B3. $35.00

WEYTHERN. *Wayward Angel.* 1978. NY. 1st ed. dj. VG. B3. $25.00

WHARTON, Edith. *Age of Innocence.* 1920. Appleton. 1st ed. VG. B13. $185.00

WHARTON, Edith. *Backward Glance.* 1934. Appleton. 1st ed. dj. EX. K2. $225.00

WHARTON, Edith. *Book of the Homeless.* 1916. NY. 1st Trade ed. 155 p. VG. B3. $45.00

WHARTON, Edith. *Book of the Homeless.* 1916. Scribner. 1st ed. lg quarto. EX. very scarce. K2. $450.00

WHARTON, Edith. *Crucial Instances.* 1901. Scribner. 1st ed. EX. K2. $175.00

WHARTON, Edith. *Ethan Frome.* 1922. Scribner. Special ed. 1/2000. dj. EX. K2. $125.00

WHARTON, Edith. *Ethan Frome.* 1936. Scribner. 1st Play ed. H3. $50.00

WHARTON, Edith. *Ethan Frome.* 1939. Portland. Ltd Ed Club. Ils/sgn Henry Varnum Poor. 1/1500. slipcase. K2. $125.00

WHARTON, Edith. *Fast & Loose: A Novelette.* 1977. Charlottesville, VA. 1st ed. cloth box. EX. scarce. B13. $250.00

WHARTON, Edith. *Fighting France.* 1915. Scribner. 1st ed. EX. K2. $60.00

WHARTON, Edith. *French Ways & Their Meaning.* 1919. Macmillan. 1st UK ed. EX. K2. $65.00

WHARTON, Edith. *Fruit of the Tree.* 1907. Scribner. 1st ed. EX. K2. $85.00

WHARTON, Edith. *Glimpses of the Moon.* 1922. Appleton. 1st ed. VG. K2. $60.00

WHARTON, Edith. *Gods Arrive.* 1932. Appleton. 1st ed. dj. EX. K2. $125.00

WHARTON, Edith. *Gods Arrive.* 1932. Appleton. 1st ed. VG. K2. $45.00

WHARTON, Edith. *Here & Beyond.* 1926. Appleton. 1st ed. dj. EX. B13. $325.00

WHARTON, Edith. *House of Mirth.* 1905. Scribner. 1st ed. G. K2. $65.00

WHARTON, Edith. *Hudson River Bracketed.* 1929. Appleton. 1st ed. VG. K2. $65.00

WHARTON, Edith. *Italian Villas & Their Gardens.* 1904. Century. 1st ed. sm quarto. EX. K2. $375.00

WHARTON, Edith. *Italian Villas & Their Gardens.* 1905. NY. Ils Parrish. 2nd ed. 270 p. EX. T5. $175.00

WHARTON, Edith. *Madame de Treymes.* 1907. NY. Ils 1st ed. VG. B3. $40.00

WHARTON, Edith. *Madame de Treymes.* 1907. Scribner. 1st ed. EX. B13. $100.00

WHARTON, Edith. *Mother's Recompense.* 1925. Appleton. 1st ed. dj. EX. B13. $185.00

WHARTON, Edith. *Reef.* 1912. Appleton Century. 1st ed. VG. K2. $50.00

WHARTON, Edith. *Son at the Front.* 1923. Scribner. 1st ed. dj. VG. K2. $45.00

WHARTON, Edith. *Son at the Front.* 1923. Scribner. 1st ed. 426 p. VG. B10. $15.00

WHARTON, Edith. *Twilight Sleep.* 1927. Appleton. 1st ed. VG. K2. $45.00

WHARTON, Edith. *Valley of Decision. Vol 1 & 2.* 1902. Scribner. 1st ed. 2 vols. TEG. K2. $125.00

WHARTON, Edith. *World Over.* 1936. Appleton. 1st ed. dj. EX. K2. $135.00

WHARTON, Edith. *Writing of Fiction.* 1925. Scribner. 1st ed. dj. EX. B13. $275.00

WHARTON, Edith. *Writing of Fiction.* 1925. Scribner. 1st ed. VG. K2. $75.00

WHARTON, William. *Dad.* 1981. Knopf. UP. tall wrp. EX. K2. $125.00

WHARTON, William. *Pride.* 1985. Knopf. UP. wrp. EX. C4. $30.00

WHEATLEY, Dennis. *Bill for the Use of a Body.* 1964. Hutchinson. 1st ed. dj. G. P1. $15.00

WHEATLEY, Dennis. *Century of Spy Stories.* nd. Hutchinson. G. P1. $15.00

WHEATLEY, Dennis. *Codeword Golden Fleece.* 1947. Universal Book Club. VG. P1. $3.00

WHEATLEY, Dennis. *Codeword Golden Fleece.* 1952. Hutchinson. 3rd ed. G. P1. $7.50

WHEATLEY, Dennis. *Curtain of Fear.* nd. Book Club. dj. G. P1. $3.00

WHEATLEY, Dennis. *Dark Secret of Josephine.* 1955. Hutchinson. 1st ed. dj. VG. P1. $30.00

WHEATLEY, Dennis. *Eunich of Stamboul.* 1935. Little Brn. 1st ed. dj. VG. R3. $35.00

WHEATLEY, Dennis. *Fabulous Valley.* 1954. Hutchinson. 7th print. dj. VG. P1. $15.00

WHEATLEY, Dennis. *Gunmen, Gallants, & Ghosts.* 1955. London. dj. VG. R3. $15.00

WHEATLEY, Dennis. *Haunting of Toby Jugs.* 1951. Hutchinson. 3rd ed. dj. G. P1. $25.00

WHEATLEY, Dennis. *Herewith the Clues.* 1986. Magnolia. EX. P1. $15.00

WHEATLEY, Dennis. *Island Where Time Stands Still.* 1954. Hutchinson. 1st ed. dj. VG. F5. $60.00

WHEATLEY, Dennis. *Malinsay Massacre.* 1986. Magnolia. EX. P1. $15.00

WHEATLEY, Dennis. *Man Who Missed the War.* 1946. Book Club. dj. VG. P1. $7.50

WHEATLEY, Dennis. *Man Who Missed the War.* 1953. Hutchinson. 3rd ed. VG. P1. $12.00

WHEATLEY, Dennis. *Mayhem in Greece.* 1966. Hutchinson. dj. xl. P1. $5.00

WHEATLEY, Dennis. *Old Rowley.* 1934. Dutton. 1st Am ed. dj. VG. R3. $25.00

WHEATLEY, Dennis. *Rising Storm.* nd. Hutchinson. G. P1. $12.50

WHEATLEY, Dennis. *Secret War.* 1954. Hutchinson. 8th print. dj. VG. P1. $10.00

WHEATLEY, Dennis. *Star of Ill-Omen.* 1952. Hutchinson. 1st ed. dj. VG. P1. $40.00

WHEATLEY, Dennis. *Strange Conflict.* 1950. Hutchinson. dj. G. P1. $12.50

WHEATLEY, Dennis. *Strange Conflict.* 1952. Hutchinson. dj. VG. P1. $25.00

WHEATLEY, Dennis. *Strange Conflict.* 1952. Hutchinson. 3rd ed. VG. P1. $7.50

WHEATLEY, Dennis. *Strange Story of Linda Lee.* nd. Book Club. dj. VG. P1. $5.00

WHEATLEY, Dennis. *Such Power Is Dangerous.* 1965. Hutchinson. 10th print. dj. xl. P1. $5.00

WHEATLEY, Dennis. *To the Devil, a Daughter.* 1953. Hutchinson. 2nd ed. dj. VG. P1. $30.00

WHEATLEY, Dennis. *Total War.* 1941. Hutchinson. Trade PB ed. sgn. H3. $30.00

WHEATLEY, Dennis. *V for Vengeance.* 1942. Macmillan. dj. VG. R3. $15.00

WHEATLEY, Dennis. *Vendetta in Spain.* 1961. Hutchinson. dj. VG. P1. $20.00

WHEATLEY, Dennis. *Vendetta in Spain.* 1961. London. 1st ed. dj. EX. R3. $30.00

WHEATLEY, Dennis. *Worlds Far From Here.* 1952. London. 1st ed. dj. EX. R3. $20.00

WHEATLEY, Phyllis. *Poems.* 1909. Phil. 8vo. VG. $35.00

WHEATON, Helen. *Prekaska's Wife: Year in the Aleutians.* 1945. Dodd. 2nd ed. 251 p. VG. B10. $4.25

WHEELER, G.M. *Preliminary Report Concerning Explorations...NV & AR.* 1872. GPO. fld map. 96 p. A5. $160.00

WHEELER, G.M. *Report Upon US Geog Surveys W of the 100th Meridian.* 1889. GPO. gilt brn bdg. VG. T1. $95.00

WHEELER, George. *Pierpont Morgan & Friends: Anatomy of a Myth.* 1973. NJ. 1st ed. dj. M. T1. $25.00

WHEELER, Homer. *Buffalo Days.* 1925. Indianapolis. 1st ed. 369 p. VG. B3. $47.50

WHEELER, Richard. *Sword Over Richmond.* 1986. Fairfax Pr. 371 p. dj. M. S1. $7.99

WHEELER, T.G. *Lost Threshold.* 1968. Phillips. 1st ed. dj. EX. F5. $25.00

WHEELOCK, J.H. *Poems Old & New.* 1956. Scribner. presentation. dj. H3. $40.00

WHEELOCK, J.S. *Boys in Wht.* 1870. Lange Hillman. 274 p. G. S1. $37.50

WHELEN. *Wilderness Hunting & Wildcraft.* 1927. Marshallton. 1st ed. VG. C2. $55.00

WHETTEN, Nathan. *Rural Mexico.* 1948. Chicago. 1st ed. 671 p. F2. $12.50

WHIGHAM, H.J. *How To Play Golf.* 1898. Chicago. Stone. New ed. 335 p. VG. B10. $20.00

WHISHAW, Lorna. *Mexico Unknown.* 1962. London. 1st ed. inscr. 256 p. F2. $15.00

WHITAKER, Alma. *Bacchus Behave! Lost Art of Polite Drinking.* 1933. NY. inscr. P4. $25.00

WHITAKER, Herman. *W Winds.* 1914. San Francisco. Ils. presentation. 219 p. G. A5. $40.00

WHITAKER & BIRD. *Identification & Significance of Cucurbit Materials...* 1949. NY. Am Mus Novitates 1426. wrp. F2. $10.00

WHITAKER & WHITAKER. *Potter's Wheel.* 1978. NM U. 1st ed. 4to. dj. F2. $25.00

WHITE, A.H. *Story of Serapina.* 1951. Jr Literary Guild/Viking. Ils Tony Palazzo. 1st ed. 4to. 128 p. dj. EX. $25.00

WHITE, Brunel. *Modern Master Mysteries.* nd. Llandilo, S Wales. 1st ed. VG. J3. $4.00

WHITE, Brunel. *Orig Mysteries for Magicians.* nd. Llandilo, S Wales. 1st ed. 82 p. EX. J3. $6.00

WHITE, E.B. *Am Opinion of France From Lafayette to Poincare.* 1927. NY. 1st ed. G. $40.00

WHITE, E.B. *Lady Is Cold.* 1929. NY. 1st ed. VG. B3. $45.00

WHITE, E.B. *Letters.* 1976. NY. 1st ed. dj. VG. B3. $32.50

WHITE, E.B. *Poems & Sketches of EB White.* 1981. Harper Row. UP. wrp. EX. K2. $75.00

WHITE, E.B. *Subtreasury of Am Humor.* nd. BOMC. dj. VG. P1. $7.50

WHITE, E.B. *Subtreasury of Am Humor.* nd. Coward McCann. P1. $10.00

WHITE, E.B. *1 Man's Meat.* 1942. Harper. 1st ed. dj. EX. B13. $250.00

WHITE, E.L. *Lukundoo.* 1927. Doran. 1st ed. VG. R3. $35.00

WHITE, E.L. *Lukundoo.* 1927. London. 1st UK ed. G. R3. $17.50

WHITE, E.L. *Song of the Sirens.* 1934. Dutton. Revised 1st ed. dj. EX. R3. $27.50

WHITE, E.L. *Step in the Dark.* 1946. Books Inc. VG. P1. $12.50

WHITE, Edgar. *Omar at Christmas.* 1973. Lathrop. 1st ed. clipped dj. EX. B13. $50.00

WHITE, F.M. *Mystery of the Ravenspurs.* 1916. Hood. wrp. VG. R3. $25.00

WHITE, G.M. *Judy of Rouges Harbor.* 1918. Grosset Dunlap. 357 p. B10. $3.50

WHITE, G.S. *Memoirs of Samuel Slater 1768-1835.* 1836. Phil. 2nd ed. G. $200.00

WHITE, Gilbert. *Nat Hist of Selbourne.* 1854. London. 40 clr pls. VG. $135.00

WHITE, J. *Billie Holiday: Her Life & Times.* 1987. Universe Books. Ils. lg wrp. EX. B4. $10.00

WHITE, J.A. *Facts To Help Make OH Dry.* 1917. np. (Colubmus) 1st ed. 47 p. printed wrp. G. T5. $9.50

WHITE, J.M. *Game of Troy.* 1971. McKay. 1st ed. dj. EX. F5. $16.00

WHITE, James. *All Judgment Fled.* 1968. London. 1st ed. dj. EX. R3. $30.00

WHITE, James. *Watch Below.* 1966. Walker. 1st ed. dj. EX. R3. $10.00

WHITE, Jim. *Crow's Story of Deer.* 1974. Capra. Chapbook Series. 1/75. sgn. EX. K2. $20.00

WHITE, L.B. *So You Want To Be a Magician?* 1972. Addison Wesley. 1st print. 224 p. EX. J3. $12.00

WHITE, Lionel. *Coffin for a Hood.* 1958. Gold Medal 775. 1st ed. wrp. NM. T9. $30.00

WHITE, Lionel. *House Next Door.* 1956. Dutton. 1st ed. dj. VG. B10. $3.50

WHITE, Lionel. *Ransomed Madonna.* 1964. Dutton. 1st ed. dj. EX. T9. $40.00

WHITE, Margaret Bourke; see Bourke-White, Margaret.

WHITE, N.I. *Am Negro Folk Songs.* 1965. Folklore Assn. octavo. 504 p. dj. EX. H3. $75.00

WHITE, P.L. *Beekmantown, NY.* 1979. TX. Ils 1st ed. dj. M. T1. $30.00

WHITE, Patrick. *Burnt Ones.* 1964. Viking. 1st Am ed. dj. EX. C4. $50.00

WHITE, Patrick. *Riders in the Chariot.* 1961. London. 1st UK ed. dj. EX. C4. $60.00

WHITE, R.Y. *We Too Built Columbus.* 1936. Columbus. 1st ed. 480 p. T5. $45.00

WHITE, S.E. *Blazed Trail.* 1902. Grosset Dunlap. 413 p. VG. B10. $3.50

WHITE, S.E. *Gold.* 1913. Doubleday Page. 1st ed. clr pls. pictorial bdg. EX. F5. $28.00

WHITE, S.E. *Leopard Woman.* 1916. Doubleday. 1st ed. VG. R3. $25.00

WHITE, S.E. *Rose Dawn.* 1920. Doubleday. 1st ed. dj. VG. B10. $5.00

WHITE, S.E. *Silent Places.* 1904. McClure Phillips. 6th imp. TEG. B10. $6.00

WHITE, T.H. *Am at Last.* 1965. 1st Am ed. dj. VG. C1. $8.50

WHITE, T.H. *Book of Merlyn.* 1977. TX U. 2nd ed. dj. VG. P1. $15.00

WHITE, T.H. *Breach of Faith: Fall of Richard Nixon.* 1975. NY. 1st ed. VG. $10.00

WHITE, T.H. *Elephant & the Kangaroo.* 1989. (1947 1st) pb. VG. C1. $3.50

WHITE, T.H. *Farewell Victoria.* 1934. Smith Haas. 1st ed. 258 p. dj. EX. B10. $45.00

WHITE, T.H. *Ill-Made Knight.* 1940. Putnam. 1st Am ed. dj. rare. C1. $49.50

WHITE, T.H. *Once & Future King.* nd. Book Club. dj. EX. C1. $7.50

WHITE, T.H. *Sword in the Stone.* 1964. Time Reading Program. 1st ed. PB. VG. C1. $4.50

WHITE, Ted. *Best From Amazing.* 1976. London. 1st ed. dj. EX. R3. $15.00

WHITE, Ted. *Best From Fantastic.* 1976. London. 1st ed. dj. EX. R3. $15.00

WHITE, Ted. *Trouble on Project Ceres.* 1971. Westminster. 1st ed. dj. EX. R3. $20.00

WHITE, Ted. *Trouble on Project Ceres.* 1971. Westminster. 1st ed. dj. xl. P1. $7.50

WHITE, W.A. *God's Puppets.* 1916. Macmillan. inscr. H3. $75.00

WHITE, W.A. *Stratagems & Spoils: Stories of Love & Politics.* 1909. Macmillan. early ed. sgn. H3. $50.00

WHITE, W.H. *View From the 40th Floor.* 1960. Wm Sloane. sgn. dj. EX. C4. $40.00

WHITE, W.L. *Captives of Korea.* 1957. NY. 1st ed. dj. G. T5. $25.00

WHITE, Walter. *Man Called Wht.* 1948. NY. 1st ed. 382 p. dj. VG. $25.00

WHITE, Walter. *Rising Wind.* 1945. NY. 1st ed. 155 p. VG. $18.00

WHITE & ADAMS. *Mystery.* 1907. McClure Philips. Ils Will Crawford. 1st ed. VG. F5. $45.00

WHITE & IGLEHART. *World's Columbian Exposition, Chicago, 1893.* 1893. Boston. Ils. maps. 640 p. G. T5. $22.50

WHITEFIELD, Raoul. *Death in a Bowl.* 1988. London. No Exit Pr. 1st ed. dj. EX. T9. $35.00

WHITEFIELD, Raoul. *Gr Ice.* 1930. Knopf. 1st ed. sans dj. VG. T9. $75.00

WHITEFIELD, Raoul. *Virgin Kills.* 1988. London. No Exit. 1st Eng ed. dj. EX. K2. $30.00

WHITEHEAD, A.N. *Aims of Education.* 1929. NY. 1st ed. dj. VG. B3. $17.50

WHITEHEAD, A.N. *Vampire in Europe.* 1961. NY. 329 p. dj. VG. B3. $45.00

WHITEHEAD, Don. *FBI Story.* 1956. Random House. inscr/sgn. dj. M. $50.00

WHITEHEAD, Henry. *Jumbee & Other Uncanny Tales.* 1944. Arkham House. 1st ed. dj. EX. R3. $200.00

WHITEHEAD, L. *New House That Jack Built.* 1865. NY. Beadle. Ils Stephens. wrp. $100.00

WHITEHEAD, Richard. *Our Faith Moved Mts!* 1944. Princeton U. 1st ed. 1/725. inscr. 84 p. F2. $45.00

WHITEHILL, W.M. *Boston in the Age of Kennedy.* 1966. OK U. 1st ed. 208 p. B10. $3.50

WHITELOCK, W.W. *Literary Guillotine.* 1903. John Lane. 1st ed. 12mo. C4. $75.00

WHITESON, Leon. *Scanners.* 1980. Tower. 1st ed. wrp. EX. F5. $8.50

WHITFIELD, David. *Clone Wars.* 1987. Vantage. 1st ed. dj. EX. F5. $16.00

WHITFIELD, Raoul. *Gr Ice.* 1930. NY. 1st ed. sans dj. VG. T9. $60.00

WHITING, Frederick. *Modern Mastoid Operation.* 1905. Phil. lg 8vo. 353 p. VG. $85.00

WHITING, Lilian. *Kate Field: A Record.* 1899. Little Brn. 610 p. TEG. EX. $30.00

WHITING, Nathan. *Buffalo Poem.* 1970. Pym Randall. Ltd ed. 1/90. sgn. dj. H3. $40.00

WHITING, Nathan. *Wht Courting the Sergeant's Daughter.* 1969. Pym Randall. 1/90. sgn. dj. H3. $40.00

WHITLOCK, Brand. *Turn of the Balance.* 1970. Bobbs Merrill. inscr. brn bdg. H3. $50.00

WHITMAN, S.H. *Edgar A Poe & His Critics.* 1860. NY. 1st ed. gilt bdg. EX. $100.00

WHITMAN, Walt. *Am Band.* 1982. Viking. Ils/sgn William Everson. sgn. dj. H3. $75.00

WHITMAN, Walt. *Complete Prose Works.* 1907. Boston. 1st reprint of Ltd ed of 1888. uncut. TEG. VG. T1. $40.00

WHITMAN, Walt. *Drum Taps.* 1865. NY. 1st ed. 1st issue. EX. $350.00

WHITMAN, Walt. *Leaves of Grass.* 1891-1892. McKay. gr bdg. TEG. EX. $200.00

WHITMAN, Walt. *Leaves of Grass.* 1930. Random House/Grabhorn. Ils Angelo. 1/400. inscr/sgn. EX. H3. $2500.00

WHITMAN, Walt. *Wartime Whitman.* nd. Armed Services Ed. wrp. B4. $25.00

WHITNEY, Alec. *Armstrong.* 1977. Crime Club. dj. EX. P1. $12.50

WHITNEY, Alex. *Voices in the Wind.* 1976. McKay. 1st ed. dj. F2. $15.00

WHITNEY, Asa. *Railroad to OR.* 1848. WA. 77 p. disbound. VG. $75.00

WHITNEY, Caspar. *Flowing Road.* 1912. Lippincott. 1st ed. 319 p. F2. $30.00

WHITNEY, Caspar. *Musk Ox, Bison, Sheep, & Goat.* 1904. Macmillan. VG. T3. $75.00

WHITNEY, Daniel. *Family Physician: Theory & Practice of Physic...* 1833. NY. Gilbert. 1st ed. 599 p. full leather. VG. J2. $65.00

WHITNEY, J.H. *Ballads of War & Peace.* 1904. Baraboo, WI. 1st ed. sgn. EX. R4. $35.00

WHITNEY, Janet. *Elizabeth Fry, Quaker Heroine.* 1937. Little Brn. 3rd ed. 338 p. reading copy. V1. $7.50

WHITNEY, Janet. *John Woolman: Am Quaker.* 1942. Little Brn. 1st ed. 8vo. 490 p. dj. VG. V1. $12.50

WHITNEY, Mrs. A.D.T. *Ascutney St.* 1891. Houghton Mifflin. 1st ed. VG. B10. $4.75

WHITNEY, P.A. *Columbella.* nd. Book Club. dj. VG. P1. $4.50

WHITNEY, P.A. *Glass Flame.* nd. Book Club. dj. VG. P1. $4.50

WHITNEY, P.A. *Hunter's Gr.* nd. Book Club. dj. VG. P1. $3.50

WHITNEY, P.A. *Listen for the Whisperer.* nd. Book Club. dj. VG. P1. $4.50

WHITNEY, P.A. *Poinciana.* 1980. Doubleday. 1st ed. dj. G. P1. $12.00

WHITNEY, P.A. *Sea Jade.* 1964. Appleton Century. 1st ed. dj. VG. P1. $15.00

WHITNEY, P.A. *Silverhill.* nd. Book Club. dj. VG. P1. $4.50

WHITNEY, P.A. *Snowfire.* nd. Book Club. dj. VG. P1. $4.50

WHITNEY, P.A. *Stone Bull.* 1977. Doubleday. 1st ed. dj. EX. F5. $12.00

WHITNEY, P.A. *Vermilion.* nd. Book Club. dj. VG. P1. $4.50

WHITNEY, P.A. *Winter People.* nd. Book Club. dj. VG. P1. $4.50

WHITNEY, P.A. *7 Tears for Apollo.* 1963. Better Homes Book Service. 1st ed. dj. G. P1. $10.00

WHITTAKER, F. *Popular Life of General George A Custer.* 1876. NY. Ils 1st ed. EX. K1. $100.00

WHITTAKER, J.C. *We Thought We Heard the Angels Sing.* 1946. NY. later print. sgn. dj. G. T5. $22.50

WHITTEN, L.H. *Progeny of the Adder.* 1966. Hodder Stoughton. 1st ed. dj. VG. P1. $35.00

WHITTEN, Wilfred. *Quaker Pictures 2nd Series.* 1894. London. Hicks. 4to. VG. V1. $15.00

WHITTIER, J.G. *Complete Writings.* c 1892. Houghton Mifflin. Amesbury ed. 7 vols. EX. H3. $450.00

WHITTIER, J.G. *Miriam & Other Poems.* 1871. Fields Osgood. 1st ed. 1st issue. G. $25.00

WHITTIER, J.G. *Poetical Works.* 1887. Boston. Ils. 8vo. VG. $35.00

WHITTIER, J.G. *Poetical Works.* 1888. Boston. Houghton Mifflin. Household ed. 12mo. 478 p. V1. $12.00

WHITTIER, J.G. *Snow Bound.* 1866. Boston. 1st ed. 1st issue. EX. $125.00

WHITTIER, J.G. *Whittier's Poems (Selected).* 1918. Harrogate. Yorkshire. 24mo. SftCvr. V1. $9.00

WHITTIER, J.G. *Works.* 1892-1894. Boston. Author ed. 1/750. 9 vols. EX. A4. $200.00

WHITTINGTON, Dick. *Dick Whittington & His Cat.* 1950. Scribner. Weekly Reader Book Club. 4to. VG. $20.00

WHITTINGTON, Harry. *Devil Has Wings.* 1960. Abelard Schuman. 1st ed. dj. VG. P1. $20.00

WHITTINGTON, Harry. *Mourn the Hangman.* 1952. Graphic. 1st ed. wrp. VG. F5. $13.00

WHITTINGTON, Harry. *Treachery Trail.* 1968. Whitman. VG. P1. $10.00

WHITTLESEY, Charles. *Early Hist of Cleveland, OH...* 1867. Cleveland. Ils. 487 p. T5. $225.00

WHITTLESEY, Charles. *Miscellaneous Papers by Col Charles Whittlesey.* 1886. Cleveland. wrp. G. T5. $145.00

WHITTMAN, George. *Matter of Intelligence.* 1975. Macmillan. 1st ed. dj. EX. P1. $15.00

WHYMPER, Charles. *Egyptian Birds.* 1909. London. Blk. clr pls. VG. T3. $50.00

WHYMPER, Edward. *Travels Amongst the Great Andes of the Equator.* 1949. London. Lehmann. reprint of 1892 ed. dj. F2. $15.00

WHYTE, Bertha. *7 Treasure Cities of Latin Am.* 1964. October House. 1st ed. sm 4to. 286 p. F2. $25.00

WHYTE-MELVILLE, G.J. *Songs & Verses.* 1924. NY. Ils Lionel Edwards. VG. B3. $27.50

WIBBERLEY, Leonard. *Mouse on Wall St.* 1969. Morrow. 1st ed. dj. EX. R3. $20.00

WIBBERLEY, Leonard. *Mouse That Saved the W.* 1981. Morrow. 1st ed. dj. EX. F5. $15.00

WIBBERLEY, Leonard. *1 in 4.* 1976. Morrow. 1st ed. dj. EX. R3. $10.00

WICKENDEN, James. *Claim in the Hills.* 1957. Rinehart. 1st ed. 275 p. dj. F2. $15.00

WICKERSHAM, James. *Old Yukon Tales, Trails, & Trials.* 1938. WA. Ils. 8vo. dj. A5/T6. $50.00

WICKERSHAM, James. *Old Yukon Tales, Trails, & Trials.* 1938. WA. 1st ed. VG. K1. $30.00

WICKSON, E.J. *CA Garden: Flowers, Shrubs, Trees, & Vines.* 1915. Pacific Rural Pr. 1st ed. VG. C1. $14.00

WICKWARE, F.S. *Dangerous Ground.* nd. Doubleday. VG. P1. $7.50

WICKWARE, F.S. *Dangerous Ground.* nd. Literary Guild. dj. VG. P1. $7.00

WIDEMAN, J.E. *Damballah.* 1981. Bard/Avon. PB Orig. wrp. EX. K2. $25.00

WIENER, Jan. *Assassination of Heydrich.* 1969. NY. 1st ed. 177 p. dj. VG. T5. $25.00

WIENER, Willard. *4 Boys & a Gun.* 1944. Dial. 1st ed. dj. EX. F5. $28.00

WIENERS, John. *Selected Poems.* 1972. Grossman. 1st ed. dj. EX. C4. $25.00

WIESEL, Elie. *Accident.* 1968. Hill Wang. 1st ed. inscr. dj. EX. K2. $50.00

WIESEL, Elie. *Beggar in Jerusalem.* 1970. Random House. Trans Edelman/author. sgn. boxed. H3. $125.00

WIESEL, Elie. *Zalmen; or, The Madness of God.* 1974. Random House. 1st ed. dj. H3. $50.00

WIGGAM, A.E. *Next Age of Man.* nd. Bl Riffon. 418 p. VG. B10. $3.50

WIGGIN, K.D. *Birds' Christmas Carol.* nd. Houghton. Ils. 8vo. VG. B10. $5.00

WIGGIN, K.D. *Mother Carey's Chickens.* 1911. Grosset. Ils AB Stephens. 355 p. VG. $20.00

WIGGIN, K.D. *Mother Carey's Chickens.* 1930. Boston. Ils ES Gr. VG. $15.00

WIGGIN, K.D. *Rebecca of Sunnybrook Farm.* nd. Grosset Dunlap. Photoplay ed. VG. P1. $15.00

WIGGIN, K.D. *Susanna & Sue.* 1909. Boston. 1st ed. dj. VG. $30.00

WIGGINS, Marianne. *Went S.* 1980. Delacorte. 1st ed. presentation. clipped dj. scarce. B13. $175.00

WIGHT. *Tobacco: Its Use & Abuse.* 1889. Columbia, SC. Pickett. 3rd ed. 8vo. 232 p. EX. $50.00

WIHLFAHRT, J. *Treatise on Baking.* 1935. Standard Brands. 3rd ed. 468 p. VG. $40.00

WILBER & SCHOENHOLTZ. *Silver Wings.* 1948. Appleton Century. Ils Milt Caniff. dj. VG. P1. $20.00

WILBERT, Johannes. *Navigators of the Orinoco: River Indians of Venezuela.* 1980. Mus Cultural Hist. 1st ed. 4to. wrp. F2. $10.00

WILBUR, H.W. *Job Scott: An 18th-Century Friend.* 1911. Phil. 16mo. 112 p. VG. V1. $14.00

WILBUR, H.W. *Life & Labors of Elias Hicks.* 1910. Phil. 1st ed. 8vo. 242 p. V1. $16.00

WILBUR, H.W. *Study in Doctrine & Discipline.* 1912. Phil. Jenkins. 2nd ed. 16mo. 69 p. VG. V1. $10.00

WILBUR, Homer. *Meliboeus Hippnax. The Bigelow Papers.* 1848. Cambridge. 1st ed. 1st issue. G. T1. $35.00

WILBUR, John. *Journal & Correspondence of John Wilbur.* 1859. Providence. Whitney. 8vo. 596 p. V1. $26.00

WILBUR, John. *Narrative of Late Proceedings of New Eng Yearly Meeting.* 1845. NY. Piercy Reed. 12mo. G. V1. $35.00

WILBUR, John. *Republication of Letters of John Wilbur to George Crosfield.* 1879. Providence. Reid. 1st ed. 12mo. 124 p. VG. V1. $9.00

WILBUR, Richard. *Opposites.* 1973. NY. 1st ed. inscr/drawing. dj. EX. T9. $50.00

WILBUR, Sabyl. *Life of Mary Baker Eddy.* 1918. Boston. Deluxe ed. 422 p. EX. $45.00

WILCOCKE, S.H. *Hist of Vice Royalty of Buenos Ayres...* 1807. London. 1st ed. 2 fld maps. 1 plan. 576 p. 8vo. VG. T1. $200.00

WILCOX, Collin. *Aftershock.* nd. Book Club. VG. P1. $2.50

WILCOX, Collin. *Hiding Place.* 1973. Random House. 1st ed. dj. EX. F5. $16.00

WILCOX, Collin. *Long Way Down.* nd. Book Club. dj. VG. P1. $4.50

WILCOX, Collin. *Power Plays.* 1979. Random House. 1st ed. dj. VG. P1. $17.50

WILCOX, Collin. *3rd Figure.* 1968. Dodd Mead. 1st ed. dj. VG. P1. $17.50

WILCOX, E.W. *Poems of Pleasure.* nd. (1902) Chicago. Whitman. 1st ed. 158 p. EX. B10. $6.50

WILCOX, Frank. *OH Canals: Pictorial Survey of OH Canals...* 1969. Kent, OH. 1st ed. dj. VG. T5. $65.00

WILCOX, James. *Modern Baptists.* nd. np. 1st ed. presentation. dj. EX. T9. $65.00

WILCOX, R.T. *Mode in Footwear.* 1951. NY/London. 1st ed. dj. EX. $40.00

WILCOX, R.T. *Mode in Furs.* 1951. NY/London. 1st ed. dj. EX. $60.00

WILCOX, Richard. *Of Men & Battle.* 1944. NY. Ils David Fredenthal. 124 p. dj. VG. T5. $12.50

WILD, John. *Textiles in Archaeology.* 1988. Aylesbury. 1st ed. 68 p. wrp. F2. $10.00

WILDE, Oscar. *Ballad of Reading Gaol.* 1937. Ltd Ed Club. Ils/sgn Zhenya Gay. boxed. VG. B3. $55.00

WILDE, Oscar. *Ballad of Reading Gaol.* 1937. Ltd Ed Club. Ils/sgn Zhenya Gay. 4to. slipcase. EX. C4. $60.00

WILDE, Oscar. *Birthday of the Infanta.* 1928. Blk Sun. 1st ed. 1/100. wrp/glassine. EX. H3. $600.00

WILDE, Oscar. *Complete Works.* 1923. Doubleday. Patron Deluxe ed. 12 vols. TEG. VG. H3. $1000.00

WILDE, Oscar. *House of Pomegranates.* 1891. London. Ricketts Shannon. 1st ed. VG. H3. $750.00

WILDE, Oscar. *Picture of Dorian Gray.* nd. Internat Collectors Lib. VG. P1. $10.00

WILDE, Oscar. *Picture of Dorian Gray.* 1891. London. 1st ed. 1/250. sgn. orig brd. Ricketts bdg. H3. $3500.00

WILDE, Oscar. *Picture of Dorian Gray.* 1944. Tower. dj. xl. P1. $10.00

WILDE, Oscar. *Salome, With 16 Drawings by Aubrey Beardsley.* 1930. Williams Belasco Meyers. New Classics Lib. VG. $21.00

WILDE, Oscar. *Salome.* 1938. Paris/London. Ltd Ed Club. 2 vols. slipcase. EX. C4. $250.00

WILDER, Alec. *Am Popular Song: Great Innovators 1900-1950.* 1972. Oxford. 1st ed. 536 p. dj. VG. B10. $6.75

WILDER, Cherry. *Luck of Brin's 5.* 1977. Atheneum. 1st ed. dj. EX. R3. $30.00

WILDER, Cherry. *Nearest Fire.* 1980. Atheneum. 1st ed. dj. EX. R3. $30.00

WILDER, Cherry. *Princess of the Chamelin.* 1984. Atheneum. 1st ed. dj. EX. F5. $25.00

WILDER, David. *Hist of Leominster.* 1853. Fitchburg. 1st ed. gilt red cloth. VG. T1. $30.00

WILDER, Thornton. *Angel That Toubled the Waters & Other Plays.* 1928. Coward McCann. Ltd ed. 1/1775. dj. H3. $135.00

WILDER, Thornton. *Angel That Troubled the Waters & Other Plays.* 1928. Coward McCann. 1/775. sgn. dj. EX. B13. $175.00

WILDER, Thornton. *Angel That Troubled the Waters & Other Plays.* 1928. Coward McCann. 2nd ed. 149 p. VG. $20.00

WILDER, Thornton. *Bridge of San Luis Rey.* 1929. Boni/Boni. Ils/sgn Kent. Ltd ed. sgn. boxed. H3. $400.00

WILDER, Thornton. *Cabala.* 1926. Boni/Boni. 1st ed. 1st print. H3. $200.00

WILDER, Thornton. *Heaven's My Destination.* 1935. Harper. 1st ed. tan bdg. VG. $12.00

WILDER, Thornton. *Ides of March.* 1948. Harper. Ltd 1st ed. 1/750. H3. $75.00

WILDER, Thornton. *Lucrece.* 1933. Houghton Mifflin. 1st ed. dj. EX. H3. $100.00

WILDER, Thornton. *Merchant of Yonkers.* 1939. Harper. 1st ed. dj. EX. H3. $150.00

WILDER, Thornton. *Our Town.* 1958. Longman Gr. 3rd ed. VG. P1. $6.00

WILDER, Thornton. *Skin of Our Teeth.* 1942. Harper. 1st ed. dj. reading copy. H3. $60.00

WILDER, Thornton. *Woman of Andros.* 1930. Boni/Boni. inscr. gilt cream bdg. dj. H3. $125.00

WILDER, Thornton. *Women of Andros.* 1930. Boni. 1st ed. 162 p. dj. VG. B10. $45.00

WILDER, Thornton. *8th Day.* 1967. NY. Ltd ed. 1/500. sgn. boxed. VG. B3. $40.00

WILEY, B.I. *Embattled Confederates.* 1964. Bonanza. 290 p. dj. VG. S1. $15.00

WILEY, B.I. *Life of Billy Yank.* 1952. Indianapolis. 1st ed. RS. $40.00

WILHELM, Donald. *How We Make Steel.* 1939. Akron. Saalfield. Ils. 22 p. dj. VG. T5. $15.00

WILHELM, G.P. *Machine Gun Fire Control.* 1917. Cleveland. Ils. 84 p. G. T5. $12.50

WILHELM, J.J. *Later Cantos of Ezra Pound by JJ Wilhelm.* 1977. NY. 1st ed. dj. M. $14.00

WILHELM, Kate. *Abyss.* 1971. Doubleday. 1st ed. dj. xl. P1. $7.50

WILHELM, Kate. *Clewiston Test.* 1976. Farrar Straus Giroux. 1st ed. dj. EX. F5. $20.00

WILHELM, Kate. *Clewiston Test.* 1976. Farrar Straus Giroux. 1st ed. dj. VG. P1. $15.00

WILHELM, Kate. *Clewiston Test.* 1976. Farrar Straus Giroux. 3rd ed. dj. EX. P1. $10.00

WILHELM, Kate. *Crazy Time.* 1988. St Martin. 1st ed. dj. EX. P1. $16.95

WILHELM, Kate. *Downstairs Room.* 1968. Doubleday. 1st ed. dj. EX. R3. $35.00

WILHELM, Kate. *Downstairs Room.* 1968. Doubleday. 1st ed. dj. xl. P1. $7.50

WILHELM, Kate. *Hamlet Trap.* 1987. St Martin. 1st ed. dj. EX. F5. $15.00

WILHELM, Kate. *Infinity Box.* 1975. Harper Row. 1st ed. dj. VG. P1/R3. $17.50

WILHELM, Kate. *Juniper Time.* 1979. Harper Row. 1st ed. dj. EX. P1. $20.00

WILHELM, Kate. *Killer Thing.* nd. Book Club. dj. VG. P1. $4.50

WILHELM, Kate. *Mile-Long Spaceship.* 1980. Gregg Pr. no dj issued. P1. $15.00

WILHELM, Kate. *Somerset Dreams.* 1978. Harper Row. 1st ed. dj. EX. P1. $20.00

WILHELM, Kate. *Welcome, Chaos.* 1983. Houghton Mifflin. 1st ed. dj. EX. P1. $15.00

WILHELM, Kate. *Where Late the Sweet Birds Sang.* 1976. Harper. 1st ed. dj. EX. R3. $50.00

WILHELM & THOMAS. *Year of the Cloud.* nd. Book Club. dj. VG. P1. $4.50

WILKINS, John. *Mathematical & Philosophical Works.* 1708. London. 1st Collected ed. contemporary calf. H3. $850.00

WILKINS, Mary. *Wind in the Rosebush.* 1903. London. 1st ed. VG. R3. $45.00

WILKINS, W.G. *1st & Early Am Eds of Works of Charles Dickens.* 1910. Torch Pr. 1/200. H3. $250.00

WILKINS-FREEMAN, M.E. *Collected Ghost Stories.* 1974. Arkham House. 1st ed. dj. EX. P1. $15.00

WILKINSON, G.K. *Nick the Click.* 1968. Putnam. 1st ed. dj. EX. $15.00

WILKINSON, W.C. *Greek Classics in Eng.* 1900. Funk Wagnall. apparent 1st ed. 2 vols. VG. B10. $6.50

WILLARD, Barbara. *Augustine Came to Kent.* 1963. Book Club. dj. VG. C1. $4.00

WILLARD, Frances. *How To Win.* 1886.13th ed. gilt gr cloth. EX. $15.00

WILLARD, J.H. *Farmer's Wife: Story of Ruth.* nd. (1906) Altemus. Beautiful Stories Series. VG. B10. $3.75

WILLARD, T.A. *City of the Sacred Well.* 1926. Grosset Dunlap. Ils. 293 p. F2. $20.00

WILLARD, T.A. *Wizard of Zacna.* 1939. Stratford Co. 1st ed. dj. VG. R3. $37.50

WILLARD, Theodore. *Lost Empire of the Itzae & Mayas.* 1933. Arthur Clark. 1st ed. 449 p. scarce. F2. $65.00

WILLEFORD, Charles. *Everybody's Metamorphosis.* 1988. Dennis McMillan. 1st ed. 1/400. sgn. M. R3. $50.00

WILLEFORD, Charles. *Kiss Your Ass Goodbye.* 1987. Dennis McMillan. 1st ed. 1/400. sgn. M. R3. $50.00

WILLEFORD, Charles. *Long Saturday Night.* 1962. Gold Medal. PB Orig. EX. T9. $50.00

WILLEFORD, Charles. *Machine in Ward 11.* 1963. Belmont. 1st ed. EX. T9. $40.00

WILLEFORD, Charles. *Miami Blues.* 1984. NY. 1st ed. sgn. dj. EX. T9. $300.00

WILLEFORD, Charles. *New Forms of Ugly.* 1987. Dennis McMillan. 1st ed. 1/350. sgn. M. R3. $50.00

WILLEFORD, Charles. *Off the Wall.* 1980. Montclair. Pegasus Rex. 1st ed. inscr. dj. EX. scarce. K2. $275.00

WILLEFORD, Charles. *Proletarian Laughter.* 1948. Yonkers, NY. Alicat. 1st ed. 1/1000. sgn. tan wrp. NM. T9. $250.00

WILLEFORD, Charles. *Sideswipe.* 1987. St Martin. 1st ed. dj. VG. P1. $22.50

WILLEFORD, Charles. *Sideswipe.* 1988. London. Gollancz. 1st ed. Hoyte dj. T9. $50.00

WILLEFORD, Charles. *Something About a Soldier.* 1986. Random House. 1st ed. sgn. dj. EX. T9. $90.00

WILLEFORD, Charles. *Way We Die Now.* nd. Book Club. dj. VG. P1. $5.00

WILLEFORD, Charles. *Way We Die Now.* 1988. NY. ARC of 1st ed. dj. w/photo. T9. $55.00

WILLEFORD, Charles. *Way We Die Now.* 1988. Random House. 1st ed. dj. EX. P1. $20.00

WILLEFORD, Charles. *Woman Chaser.* 1960. Newsstand Lib. PB Orig. wrp. NM. T9. $135.00

WILLEMS, Emilio. *Buzios Island.* 1966. Seattle. 2nd print. 116 p. F2. $15.00

WILLETTS, Jacob. *Compendious System of Geography.* 1818. Poughkeepsie. 1 pl. 466 p. fair. T5. $25.00

WILLEY, Gordon. *Essays in Maya Archaeology.* 1987. NM U. 1st ed. 245 p. dj. F2. $25.00

WILLEY, Gordon. *Middle Am Anthropology.* 1958. Pan Am Union. 1st ed. 60 p. wrp. F2. $25.00

WILLIAM. *3 Days on the OH River.* 1854. Carlton Porter. 66 p. A5. $85.00

WILLIAMS, Alan. *Shah-Mak.* 1976. Coward McCann Geoghegan. 1st ed. dj. EX. P1. $17.50

WILLIAMS, Alan. *Snake Water.* 1966. Odhams. dj. xl. P1. $10.00

WILLIAMS, AMES, & STARRETT. *Stephen Crane, a Bibliography.* 1970. NY. 8vo. $20.00

WILLIAMS, Archibald. *Conquering the Air.* 1928. NY. Ils. 343 p. G. T5. $17.50

WILLIAMS, B.S. *Orchid Grower's Manual.* 1877. London. 5th ed. 8vo. VG. $85.00

WILLIAMS, Brad. *Well-Dressed Skeleton.* 1963. Herbert Jenkins. VG. P1. $12.50

WILLIAMS, C.H.C. *Horse Owner's Ils Guide.* 1879. Claremont, NH. Ils Revised ed. 280 p. T5. $35.00

WILLIAMS, C.R.A. *Biography of Revolutionary War Heroes.* 1839. Providence. 1st ed. 312 p. T5. $67.50

WILLIAMS, C.W. *Knife of the Times & Other Stories.* 1932. Dragon. 1/500. presentation. H3. $450.00

WILLIAMS, C.W. *Yes, Mrs Williams: Personal Record of My Mother.* 1959. McDowell Obolensky. sgn. dj. H3. $350.00

WILLIAMS, Charles. *Aground.* nd. Book Club. dj. VG. P1. $4.50

WILLIAMS, Charles. *Big City Girl.* 1951. Gold Medal 163. 1st ed. wrp. EX. T9. $35.00

WILLIAMS, Charles. *Dead Calm.* 1963. NY. Viking. 1st ed. dj. VG. T9. $40.00

WILLIAMS, Charles. *Descent Into Hell.* 1949. Pelligrini Cudahy. VG. P1. $25.00

WILLIAMS, Charles. *Don't Just Stand There.* 1967. London. Cassell. 1st ed. dj. EX. T9. $35.00

WILLIAMS, Charles. *Go Home Stranger.* 1954. Gold Medal 371. 1st ed. wrp. VG. T9. $20.00

WILLIAMS, Charles. *Long Saturday Night.* 1962. Gold Medal. 1st ed. wrp. EX. T9. $15.00

WILLIAMS, Charles. *Man on a Leash.* nd. Book Club. dj. VG. P1. $4.50

WILLIAMS, Charles. *Nothing in Her Way.* 1956. Paris. Gallimard. 1st French ed. sans dj. VG. T9. $45.00

WILLIAMS, Charles. *River Girl.* 1961. Gold Medal 207. 1st ed. wrp. NM. T9. $30.00

WILLIAMS, Charles. *Sailcloth Shroud.* nd. Book Club. dj. VG. P1. $4.50

WILLIAMS, David. *Copper, Gold, & Treasure.* 1982. St Martin. 1st ed. dj. VG. P1. $10.00

WILLIAMS, David. *Murder in Advent.* 1985. St Martin. 1st ed. dj. VG. P1. $14.95

WILLIAMS, E.G. *Orderly Book of H Bouquet's Expedition Against OH Indians.* 1960. Pittsburgh. 1st ed. 1/200. presentation. EX. $65.00

WILLIAMS, E.W. *Child of the Sea.* 1905. Harbor Springs. 1st ed. 229 p. VG. B3. $65.00

WILLIAMS, Edward. *Opiate Addiction: Its Handling & Treatment.* 1922. NY. 1st ed. inscr. 194 p. VG. $50.00

WILLIAMS, F.D. *MI Soldiers in Civil War.* 1960. Lansing, MI. 43 p. pamphlet. S1. $5.00

WILLIAMS, G.M. *Siege of Trencher's Farm.* 1969. Secker Warburg. 1st ed. dj. xl. P1. $5.00

WILLIAMS, H.N. *Fair Conspirator: Marie de Rohan Duchesse de Chevreuse.* 1913. NY. EX. $35.00

WILLIAMS, Herbert. *Terror at Night.* 1947. Avon. 1st ed. EX. R3. $27.50

WILLIAMS, Ivor. *Pedeir Keinc y Maginogi.* 1951. (1st 1930) Cardiff. Welsh text. dj. VG. C1. $16.50

WILLIAMS, J.A. *Night Song.* 1961. Farrar Strauss. 1st ed. dj. EX. K2. $85.00

WILLIAMS, J.A. *This Is My Country Too.* 1965. New Am Lib/World. 1st ed. dj. EX. K2. $55.00

WILLIAMS, J.R. *Bull of the Woods.* 1944. NY. VG. $50.00

WILLIAMS, J.R. *Redrawn by Request.* 1945. Garden City. 1st ed. dj. VG. B3. $30.00

WILLIAMS, J.S. *Hist of Invasion & Capture of WA.* 1857. NY. 1st ed. 371 p. T5. $65.00

WILLIAMS, Jay. *AK Adventure.* 1952. Harrisburg. 1st ed. dj. VG. B3. $45.00

WILLIAMS, Joan. *Wintering.* 1971. Harcourt Brace. 1st ed. dj. EX. B13. $45.00

WILLIAMS, John. *Angry Ones.* 1960. NY. 1st PB ed. sgn. EX. T9. $45.00

WILLIAMS, John. *Stoner.* 1965. NY. 1st ed. sgn. dj. EX. T9. $75.00

WILLIAMS, Jonathan. *Empire Finals at Verona.* 1959. Highlands, NC. Complimentary Review copy. wrp. EX. T9. $55.00

WILLIAMS, Jonathan. *Portrait Photographs.* 1979. Gnome Pr. 1/50. sgn. special bdg. slipcase. EX. C4. $175.00

WILLIAMS, Joy. *Changeling.* 1978. Doubleday. 1st ed. dj. EX. F5. $14.00

WILLIAMS, K.P. *Lincoln Finds a General: Military Hist of Civil War.* 1949. Macmillan. 1 vol only. 902 p. VG. S1. $7.00

WILLIAMS, Oscar. *Man Coming Toward You.* 1940. Oxford. inscr. dj. H3. $100.00

WILLIAMS, P.L. *Song of Daniel.* 1989. Atlanta. Peachtree. ARC. dj. EX. K2. $25.00

WILLIAMS, R.J. *Bermudiana. Photos by Walter Rutherford.* 1936. Bermudian Pub. 1st ed. 4to. VG. T1. $45.00

WILLIAMS, Tennessee. *Androgyne, Mon Amour.* 1977. New Directions. 1st ed. sgn. dj. EX. K2. $150.00

WILLIAMS, Tennessee. *Baby Doll.* 1956. New Directions. 1st ed. variant dj. EX. H3. $100.00

WILLIAMS, Tennessee. *Camino Real.* 1970. New Directions. 1st PB ed. sgn. wrp. EX. K2. $85.00

WILLIAMS, Tennessee. *Cat on a Hot Tin Roof.* nd. (1955) New Directions. 1st ed. sgn. dj. EX. K2. $200.00

WILLIAMS, Tennessee. *Eccentricities of the Nightingale/Summer & Smoke.* 1964. New Directions. 1st ed. dj. EX. H3. $45.00

WILLIAMS, Tennessee. *Glass Menagerie.* 1949. New Directions. New Classics ed. dj. EX. H3. $40.00

WILLIAMS, Tennessee. *Gnadiges Fraulein.* 1967. Dramatists Play Service. Acting ed. sgn. wrp. EX. K2. $100.00

WILLIAMS, Tennessee. *Grand.* 1964. House of Books. 1/300. sgn. glassine dj. EX. C4. $300.00

WILLIAMS, Tennessee. *Hard Candy.* 1959. New Directions. 1st Trade ed. sgn. dj. EX. K2. $125.00

WILLIAMS, Tennessee. *In the Winter of Cities.* nd. (1956) New Directions. 1st ed. sgn. dj. EX. K2. $250.00

WILLIAMS, Tennessee. *In the Winter of Cities.* nd. (1964) New Directions. 1st PB ed. sgn. wrp. EX. K2. $85.00

WILLIAMS, Tennessee. *Letters to Donald Windham 1940-1965.* 1976. Verona. Ltd ed. 1/500. wrp/dj/acetate/slipcase. EX. K2. $125.00

WILLIAMS, Tennessee. *Letters to Donald Windham 1940-1965.* 1976. Verona. Ltd ed. 1/500. sgn Williams/Windham. dj. slipcase. EX. K2. $650.00

WILLIAMS, Tennessee. *Memoirs.* 1975. Doubleday. 1st ed. inscr. dj. EX. K2. $200.00

WILLIAMS, Tennessee. *Moise & the World of Reason.* 1975. Simon Schuster. ARC. sgn. dj. EX. K2. $150.00

WILLIAMS, Tennessee. *Moise & the World of Reason.* 1975. Simon Schuster. inscr/sgn. dj. H3. $150.00

WILLIAMS, Tennessee. *Moise & the World of Reason.* 1975. Simon Schuster. 1/350. sgn. full leather. EX. B13. $250.00

WILLIAMS, Tennessee. *Moise & the World of Reason.* 1975. Simon Schuster. 1st ed. inscr/sgn. dj. EX. B13. $185.00

WILLIAMS, Tennessee. *Moise & the World of Reason.* 1975. Simon Schuster. 1st ed. sgn. dj. EX. K2. $85.00

WILLIAMS, Tennessee. *Mutilated.* 1967. Dramatists Play Service. Acting ed. sgn. stapled wrp. EX. K2. $135.00

WILLIAMS, Tennessee. *New Voices in the Am Theater.* 1944. Modern Lib. ARC. sgn. dj. EX. K2. $100.00

WILLIAMS, Tennessee. *Night of the Iguana.* 1962. New Directions. 1st ed. dj. VG. H3. $75.00

WILLIAMS, Tennessee. *Orpheus Descending With Battle of Angels.* 1958. New Directions. 1st ed. dj. VG. H3. $75.00

WILLIAMS, Tennessee. *Out Cry.* 1973. New Directions. ARC. sgn. dj. EX. K2. $200.00

WILLIAMS, Tennessee. *Period of Adjustment: High Point Over a Cavern.* 1960. New Directions. 1st ed. dj. EX. H3. $100.00

WILLIAMS, Tennessee. *Roman Spring of Mrs Stone.* 1950. New Directions. 1st ed. sgn. dj. EX. K2. $225.00

WILLIAMS, Tennessee. *Roman Spring of Mrs Stone.* 1950. NY. 1st ed. dj. VG. B3. $27.50

WILLIAMS, Tennessee. *Rose Tattoo.* 1951. New Directions. 1st ed. 2nd bdg. dj. VG. H3. $50.00

WILLIAMS, Tennessee. *Rose Tattoo.* 1954. Secker Warburg. 1st UK ed. dj. EX. H3. $100.00

WILLIAMS, Tennessee. *Sm Craft Warnings.* 1972. New Directions. ARC. sgn. dj. EX. K2. $175.00

WILLIAMS, Tennessee. *Steps Must Be Gentle: Dramatic Reading for 2 Performers.* 1980. Targ Ed. Ltd 1st ed. 1/350. sgn. H3. $100.00

WILLIAMS, Tennessee. *Streetcar Named Desire.* 1948. New Directions. 1st ed. pictorial brd. dj. H3. $350.00

WILLIAMS, Tennessee. *Suddenly Last Summer.* 1958. New Am Lib. 8th print. inscr. EX. K2. $65.00

WILLIAMS, Tennessee. *Where I Live.* 1977. New Directions. ARC. dj. RS. w/promotional sheet. EX. K2. $65.00

WILLIAMS, Tennessee. *Where I Live.* 1977. New Directions. 1st PB ed. inscr. wrp. EX. K2. $85.00

WILLIAMS, Tennessee. *1 Arm.* nd. (1954) New Directions. 1st Trade ed. sgn. dj. EX. K2. $125.00

WILLIAMS, Tennessee. *27 Wagons Full of Cotton & Other Plays.* 1953. New Directions. 3rd ed. sgn. dj. EX. K2. $125.00

WILLIAMS, Tennessee. *27 Wagons Full of Cotton & Other Plays.* 1966. New Directions. 1st PB ed/taken from 3rd ed. sgn. EX. K2. $75.00

WILLIAMS, Tennessee. *27 Wagons Full of Cotton & Other Plays.* 1953. New Directions. 1st ed. dj. VG. H3. $50.00

WILLIAMS, Thomas. *Whipple's Castle.* 1968. NY. 1st ed. sgn. dj. EX. T9. $55.00

WILLIAMS, Valentine. *Crouching Beast.* 1930. Hodder Stoughton. 8th print. G. P1. $10.00

WILLIAMS, Valentine. *Mr Ramosi.* nd. Collier. G. P1. $7.50

WILLIAMS, Valentine. *Mystery of the Gold Box.* nd. Collier. VG. P1. $10.00

WILLIAMS, Valentine. *Red Mass.* nd. Hodder Stoughton. VG. P1. $15.00

WILLIAMS, Valentine. *Return of Clubfoot.* nd. Thomas Allen. VG. P1. $15.00

WILLIAMS, Valentine. *3 of Clubs.* nd. Hodder Stoughton. VG. P1. $15.00

WILLIAMS, W.C. *Build-Up.* 1952. NY. 1st ed. dj. VG. B3. $45.00

WILLIAMS, W.C. *Collected Later Poems.* 1956. New Directions. Horace Mann ed. 1/52. sgn. slipcase. EX. rare. K2. $1000.00

WILLIAMS, W.C. *In the Money.* 1940. New Directions. 1st ed. inscr. VG. B13. $400.00

WILLIAMS, W.K. *OH Farm Laws & Legal Forms.* 1895. Columbus. 234 p. T5. $7.50

WILLIAMS, W.W. *Hist of Fire Lands...* 1879. Cleveland. Ils 1st ed. 524 p. T5. $175.00

WILLIAMS & GARDNER. *Pairdaeza.* 1975. Dentdale, Cubria. Jargon. 1/75. sgns. EX. very scarce. C4. $750.00

WILLIAMS & UNDERWOOD. *Ted Williams Fishing Big 3.* 1982. NY. 1st ed. dj. VG. B3. $20.00

WILLIAMS & WILLIAMS. *Memoir of Jesse & Hannah Williams, Late of Plymouth, PA.* 1875. Phil. Pile. 12mo. 202 p. V1. $12.00

WILLIAMS & WINDHAM. *You Touched Me!* 1947. NY. Samuel French. Acting ed. sgns. wrp. EX. K2. $200.00

WILLIAMS. *Dawn TN Valley & TN Hist.* 1937. Johnson City. VG. C2. $75.00

WILLIAMS-ELLIS. *Out of This World 4.* 1964. Blackie. dj. VG. P1. $15.00

WILLIAMSON, Chet. *Dreamthorp.* 1989. Dark Harvest. Ltd ed. 1/400. sgn. slipcase. M. R3. $50.00

WILLIAMSON, Chet. *Dreamthorp.* 1989. Dark Harvest. 1st ed. M. R3. $19.95

WILLIAMSON, J.J. *Mosby's Rangers.* 1982. Time Life. reprint. EX. S1. $17.50

WILLIAMSON, J.N. *Masques 2.* 1987. Maclay. 1st ed. 1/300. sgn by editor. M. R3. $75.00

WILLIAMSON, J.N. *Masques.* 1984. Maclay. dj. VG. P1. $12.50

WILLIAMSON, Jack. *Brother to Demons, Brother to Gods.* 1979. Bobbs Merrill. 1st ed. dj. EX. P1. $17.50

WILLIAMSON, Jack. *Cometeers.* 1950. Fantasy. 1st ed. dj. VG. R3. $30.00

WILLIAMSON, Jack. *Cometeers.* 1950. Fantasy. 1st ed. sgn. dj. EX. R3. $50.00

WILLIAMSON, Jack. *Darker Than You Think.* 1975. Garland. 1st ed. M. R3. $20.00

WILLIAMSON, Jack. *Early Williamson.* 1951. Doubleday. 1st ed. dj. VG. R3. $20.00

WILLIAMSON, Jack. *Golden Blood.* 1978. Tamerlane. 1st ed. 1/150. sgn. M. R3. $40.00

WILLIAMSON, Jack. *Gr Girl.* 1950. Avon. 1st ed. wrp. EX. R3. $40.00

WILLIAMSON, Jack. *Humanoid Touch.* nd. Book Club. dj. VG. P1. $4.50

WILLIAMSON, Jack. *Humanoid Touch.* 1980. Phantasia. 1st ed. 1/500. sgn. M. R3. $40.00

WILLIAMSON, Jack. *Humanoids.* 1949. Simon Schuster. 1st ed. dj. EX. R3. $40.00

WILLIAMSON, Jack. *Legion of Space.* 1947. Fantasy. 1st ed. dj. EX. R3. $40.00

WILLIAMSON, Jack. *Legion of Space.* 1975. Garland. 1st ed. M. R3. $15.00

WILLIAMSON, Jack. *Legion of Time.* 1952. Fantasy. 1st ed. dj. EX. R3. $15.00

WILLIAMSON, Jack. *Legion of Time.* 1952. Fantasy. 1st ed. Donald Grant bdg. dj. M. P1. $17.50

WILLIAMSON, Jack. *Life Burst.* 1984. Del Rey. 1st ed. dj. EX. P1. $12.95

WILLIAMSON, Jack. *Manseed.* nd. Book Club. dj. VG. P1. $4.50

WILLIAMSON, Jack. *Moon Children.* 1972. London. 1st Eng ed. dj. EX. R3. $15.00

WILLIAMSON, Jack. *Power of Blackness.* 1976. Berkley. 1st ed. dj. EX. R3. $10.00

WILLIAMSON, John. *Ferns of KY.* 1878. Louisville. Ils. 8vo. VG. $60.00

WILLIAMSON, Mrs. M.L. *Life of Thomas J Stonewall Jackson.* 1899. Richmond, VA. Ils. 12mo. 248 p. G. G4. $27.00

WILLIAMSON, R.W. *Tennis Courts in India.* 1927. Calcutta. Ils. VG. scarce. T1. $65.00

WILLIAMSON, Thames. *Hunky.* 1929. Coward McCann. sgn. dj. H3. $75.00

WILLIAMSON & WILLIAMSON. *Soldier of the Legion.* 1914. Doubleday Page. 1st ed. VG. F5. $24.00

WILLIS, C.M. *Chamois Murder.* 1935. Unicorn Pr. 1st ed. sgn. dj. VG. P1. $25.00

WILLIS, Lionel. *Coastal Trade.* 1975. London. 45 clr pls. oblong folio. dj. slipcase. NM. A4. $80.00

WILLIS, Ted. *Man-Eater.* 1977. Morrow. 1st ed. dj. VG. P1. $15.00

WILLISON, G.F. *Behold VA!* nd. Harcourt. Stated 1st ed. 424 p. dj. VG. B10. $10.00

WILLISON, G.F. *Pilgrim Reader.* 1953. Doubleday. 1st ed. 8vo. 585 p. VG. B10. $6.75

WILLMARTH, P.R. *Magic of Matt Sculien.* 1959. Chicago. Ireland. 1st ed. 169 p. NM. J3. $14.00

WILLMARTH, P.R. *Ring & Rope Book Vol 1.* 1975. Willmarth. 1st ed. 59 p. SftCvr. EX. J3. $6.00

WILLMARTH, P.R. *Trevor Lewis.* 1981. Strandridge Magic. 98 p. NM. J3. $6.00

WILLS, Jesse. *Early & Late: Fugitive Poems & Others.* 1959. Nashville. Vanderbilt. 1st ed. sgn. dj. EX. B13. $100.00

WILLSON, Ann. *Familiar Letters of Ann Willson.* 1850. Phil. Parrish. 12mo. 270 p. G. V1. $15.00

WILLSON, Beckles. *John Sidell & the Confederates in Paris.* 1932. NY. VG. $30.00

WILMERDING, John. *Fitz Hugh Lane.* 1971. NY. 1st ed. 4to. dj. EX. G1. $22.00

WILMERDING, John. *Robert Salmon: Painter of Ship & Shore.* 1971. Peabody Mus. 1st ed. 4to. 123 p. dj. EX. $95.00

WILMINGTON YEARLY MEETING. *Discipline of Wilmington Yearly Meeting of Friends.* 1905. Richmond. Nicholson Pr. 12mo. 98 p. V1. $8.50

WILMOT, J.E. *Life of Right Honorable Sir John Eardley Wilmot.* 1811. London. 8vo. 241 p. xl. G4. $30.00

WILSON, A.E. *King Panto: Story of Pantomine.* 1935. NY. 1st ed. dj. EX. $15.00

WILSON, A.N. *Gentlemen in Eng.* 1985. London. Hamond. 1st ed. dj. EX. B13. $50.00

WILSON, A.N. *Hilaire Belloc.* 1984. Hamish Hamilton. 1st ed. dj. M. C4. $40.00

WILSON, A.N. *How Can We Know?* 1985. London. Hamond. 1st ed. dj. EX. B13. $65.00

WILSON, A.N. *Incline Our Hearts.* 1988. London. Hamond. 1st ed. dj. EX. B13. $45.00

WILSON, A.N. *Kindly Light.* 1979. Secker Warburg. 1st ed. dj. EX. B13. $75.00

WILSON, A.N. *Laird of Abbotsford: View of Sir Walter Scott.* 1980. London. Oxford. 1st ed. dj. M. C4. $60.00

WILSON, A.N. *Love Unknown.* 1986. Hamish Hamilton. 1st ed. dj. M. C4. $40.00

WILSON, A.N. *Pen Friends From Porlock.* 1988. London. Hamond. 1st ed. dj. EX. B13. $45.00

WILSON, A.N. *Scandal.* 1983. Hamish Hamilton. 1st ed. dj. M. C4. $85.00

WILSON, A.N. *Stray.* 1987. London. Walker. 1st ed. dj. EX. B13. $50.00

WILSON, A.N. *Who Was Oswald Fish?* 1981. Secker Warburg. 1st ed. dj. EX. B13. $65.00

WILSON, A.N. *Wise Virgin.* 1982. Secker Warburg. 1st ed. dj. M. C4. $85.00

WILSON, Angus. *Old Men at the Zoo.* 1961. Viking. 1st ed. dj. xl. P1. $5.00

WILSON, B.K. *Legends of the Round Table.* 1968. Ils Calati. 2nd imp. EX. C1. $14.50

WILSON, C. *Picturesque Palestine, Sinai, & Egypt.* c 1880. London. Virtue. folio. 4 vols. rebound. G. $250.00

WILSON, Carter. *Crazy February.* 1966. Lippincott. 1st ed. 250 p. dj. F2. $15.00

WILSON, Colin. *Casebook of Murder.* 1969. Cowles. 1st ed. dj. VG. P1. $25.00

WILSON, Colin. *Mind Parasites.* 1967. Arkham House. 1st ed. dj. EX. R3. $65.00

WILSON, Colin. *Occult: A Hist.* nd. Book Club. dj. VG. P1. $10.00

WILSON, Colin. *Order of Assassins: Psychology of Murder.* 1972. Hart Davis. 1st UK ed. 242 p. dj. EX. R4. $35.00

WILSON, Colin. *Orig Sexual Impulse.* 1963. NY. 1st ed. dj. VG. B3. $25.00

WILSON, Colin. *Outsider.* 1956. Houghton Mifflin. 1st ed. dj. VG. P1. $75.00

WILSON, Colin. *Philosopher's Stone.* 1971. Crown. 1st Am ed. dj. EX. scarce. F5. $55.00

WILSON, Colin. *Rasputin & the Fall of the Romanovs.* 1964. Farrar Straus. 1st ed. 240 p. dj. EX. T4. $7.50

WILSON, Colin. *Religion & the Rebel.* 1957. Boston. 1st ed. 338 p. dj. VG. B3. $17.50

WILSON, Colin. *Ritual in the Dark.* 1960. Houghton Mifflin. 1st ed. dj. VG. P1. $25.00

WILSON, Colin. *Schoolgirl Murder Case.* 1975. Rupert Hart-Davis. 2nd ed. dj. EX. P1. $15.00

WILSON, Colin. *Strindberg.* 1972. Random House. 1st ed. dj. EX. H3. $25.00

WILSON, Colin. *Tree by Tolkien.* 1973. Covent Garden Pr. 1/100. sgn. dj. H3. $125.00

WILSON, Colin. *Tree by Tolkien.* 1974. Capra. Chapbook Series. 1/200. sgn. EX. K2. $45.00

WILSON, E.E. *Wings of Dawn.* 1950. Palm Beach. 175 p. dj. T5. $9.50

WILSON, E.G. *Famous Old Euclid Ave of Cleveland Vol 2.* 1937. np. Ils. 265 p. VG. T5. $45.00

WILSON, E.H. *Aristocrats of the Garden.* 1926. Boston. 1st ed. VG. $45.00

WILSON, E.H. *Lilies of E Asia.* 1929. London/Boston. 2nd imp. quarto. 110 p. EX. $50.00

WILSON, E.H. *More Aristocrats of the Garden.* 1928. Boston. 1st ed. VG. $45.00

WILSON, E.H. *Plant Hunting.* 1927. Boston. 1st ed. 2 vols. xl. $30.00

WILSON, Earl. *Earl Wilson's NY.* 1964. Simon Schuster. 1st ed. 384 p. dj. VG. B10. $5.25

WILSON, Edmund. *Apologies to the Iroquois.* 1960. NY. 1st ed. dj. VG. B3. $25.00

WILSON, Edmund. *Bit Between My Teeth.* 1965. Farrar Straus. 1st ed. dj. EX. K2. $25.00

WILSON, Edmund. *Boys in the Back Room.* 1941. Colt Pr. 1st ed. dj. EX. H3. $150.00

WILSON, Edmund. *Europe Without Baedeker.* 1966. NY. Revised ed. presentation. VG. $65.00

WILSON, Edmund. *Little Bl Light.* 1950. Farrar Straus. 1st ed. dj. VG. K2. $35.00

WILSON, Edmund. *Prelude: Landscapes, Characters, & Conversations...* 1967. Farrar Straus. 1st ed. 278 p. dj. VG. B10. $7.00

WILSON, Edmund. *The '40s: From Notebooks & Diaries of the Period.* 1983. Farrar Straus. UP. wrp. EX. K2. $45.00

WILSON, Edmund. *To the Finland Station.* 1940. Harcourt Brace. 1st ed. dj. EX. K2. $250.00

WILSON, Edmund. *To the Finland Station.* 1940. Harcourt Brace. 1st ed. dj. w/sgn letter. VG. H3. $125.00

WILSON, Edmund. *Triple Thinkers.* 1938. Harcourt Brace. 1st ed. dj. VG. H3. $75.00

WILSON, Edmund. *Triple Thinkers.* 1948. Oxford. Revised 1st ed. clipped dj. EX. B13. $85.00

WILSON, Erasmus. *System of Human Anatomy.* 1849. Phil. 8vo. 576 p. VG. G4. $49.00

WILSON, F.E. *Peace of Mad Anthony.* 1909. Greenville, OH. Ils. 122 p. xl. fair. T5. $12.50

WILSON, F.P. *Healer.* 1984. Doubleday. 1st ed. dj. EX. R3. $15.00

WILSON, F.P. *Keep.* 1981. Morrow. 1st ed. dj. EX. R3. $32.50

WILSON, F.P. *Keep.* 1981. Morrow. 1st ed. dj. VG. P1. $25.00

WILSON, F.P. *Wheels Within Wheels.* 1978. Doubleday. 1st ed. dj. VG. P1. $30.00

WILSON, F.T. *Federal Aid in Domestic Disturbances 1787-1903.* 1903. GPO. 394 p. T5. $19.50

WILSON, Francis. *Eugene Field I Knew.* 1898. Scribner. 1/200. sgn. H3. $100.00

WILSON, Gahan. *Everybody's Favorite Duck.* 1988. Mysterious Pr. 1st ed. dj. VG. P1. $15.95

WILSON, H. *Vishnu Purna: A System of Hindu Mythology & Tradition.* 1840. London. 703 p. G. $80.00

WILSON, H.L. *Oh, Doctor!* 1923. Copp Clarke. VG. P1. $17.50

WILSON, Harris. *Arnold Bennett & HG Wells: Record of...Friendship.* 1960. Hart Davis. 1st ed. 8vo. 290 p. dj. R4. $20.00

WILSON, Hazel. *Herbert's Space Trip.* 1965. Knopf. VG. P1. $15.00

WILSON, J.A. *Adventures of Alf Wilson.* 1897. WA. wrp. VG. $60.00

WILSON, J.C. *3-Wheeling Through Africa.* 1936. Indianapolis. 1st ed. presentation. w/letter. VG. B3. $35.00

WILSON, J.F. *Master Key.* nd. Grosset Dunlap. Photoplay ed. VG. P1. $20.00

WILSON, James. *Memorial Hist of City of NY.* 1892.4 vols. 4to. $175.00

WILSON, John. *Obra Morava en Nicaragua: Trasfondo y Breve Hist.* 1975. San Jose. Ils. inscr. 4to. 337 p. wrp. F2. $15.00

WILSON, Lanford. *Angels Fall.* 1983. Hill Wang. UP. wrp. EX. B13. $85.00

WILSON, Lanford. *Hot L Baltimore.* 1973. NY. 1st HrdCvr ed. dj. EX. K2. $45.00

WILSON, Lanford. *Mound Builders.* 1976. Hill Wang. 1st ed. dj. EX. B13. $85.00

WILSON, Laura. *Good Morning, Mexico.* 1937. Sutton House. 1st ed. 75 p. F2. $10.00

WILSON, Mitchell. *Footsteps Behind Her.* nd. Simon Schuster. 3rd ed. dj. VG. P1. $12.50

WILSON, R.C. *Crooked Tree.* 1980. Putnam. 1st ed. dj. VG. P1. $15.00

WILSON, R.C. *Icefire.* 1984. Putnam. 1st ed. dj. EX. F5. $17.00

WILSON, R.C. *Quaker Relief: Account of Relief Work...1940-1948.* 1952. Allen Unwin. 1st ed. 8vo. 373 p. dj. G. V1. $10.00

WILSON, Robert. *Mexico & Its Religion With Incidents of Travel...* 1855. Harper. 1st ed. 406 p. F2. $45.00

WILSON, Steve. *Dealer's Move.* 1978. Macmillan. 1st ed. dj. EX. P1. $15.00

WILSON, W. *New Dictionary of Music.* nd. (1835) London. 1st ed. 12mo. 290 p. VG. H3. $125.00

WILSON, W.B. *Few Acts & Actors in Tragedy of Civil War.* 1892. Phil. G. T5. $19.50

WILSON, W.H. *Sensational Card Tricks.* 1934. Sewickley, PA. Wilson. 1st ed. sgn. SftCvr. J3. $5.00

WILSON, W.L. *Borderland Confederate.* 1962. Pittsburgh. 1st ed. EX. $25.00

WILSON & EVANS. *Aves Hawaiiensis: Birds of the Sandwich Islands.* 1890-1899. London. 8 orig parts. 64 pls. EX. H3. $10000.00

WILSON & FOX-DAVIES. *Tabitha Stories.* 1988. London. Walker. 1st ed. quarto. dj. EX. B13. $50.00

WILSON. *Drugs & Pharmacy in the Life of GA.* 1959. Atlanta. dj. EX. C2. $35.00

WILSON. *S Pacific Railroad: A Hist.* 1952. NY. 1st ed. 256 p. dj. VG. B3. $37.50

WILTSE, S.E. *Kindergarden Stories & Morning Talks.* 1890. Boston. Ginn. 1st ed. 212 p. G. B10. $4.00

WINANS, W. *Sporting Rifle.* 1908. NY. 1st ed. 217 p. VG. B3. $125.00

WINCHESTER, Mark. *In the Hands of the Lamas.* nd. Queensway Pr. VG. P1. $20.00

WIND, H.W. *World of PG Wodehouse.* 1972. Praeger. dj. VG. P1. $20.00

WIND, Oswald. *40 Days.* 1972. Collins. 1st ed. dj. EX. P1. $15.00

WINDSOR, D.B. *Quaker Enterprise: Friends in Business.* 1980. London. Muller. 1st ed. 8vo. 176 p. dj. EX. V1. $15.00

WINDWARD, Walter. *Fives Wild.* 1976. Atheneum. 1st ed. dj. VG. P1. $15.00

WINFORD, E.C. *Femme Mimics.* 1954. Dallas, TX. 1st ed. 164 p. VG. T5. $150.00

WING, Henry. *Milk & Its Products.* 1915. Macmillan. not 1st ed. 433 p. EX. B10. $4.25

WINKS, R.W. *Modus Operandi: An Excursion Into Detective Fiction.* 1982. Godine. 1st ed. sgn. dj. EX. T9. $35.00

WINN, M.D. *Macadam Trail.* 1931. NY. 319 p. T5. $22.50

WINSOR, Kathleen. *Forever Amber.* 1944. London. 1st ed. dj. EX. $40.00

WINSTON, Robert. *Andrew Johnson.* nd. (1928) Holt. 8vo. 549 p. VG. B10. $7.50

WINTER, Douglas. *Blk Wine.* 1986. Dark Harvest. 1st ed. M. R3. $30.00

WINTER, Douglas. *Prime Evil.* 1988. New Am Lib. 1st ed. sgn. M. R3. $25.00

WINTER, Douglas. *Splatter.* 1987. Footsteps. 1st ed. 1/26. wrp. EX. R3. $75.00

WINTER, Douglas. *Stephen King: Art of Darkness.* nd. New Am Lib. 3rd ed. dj. VG. P1. $12.50

WINTER, Douglas. *Stephen King: Art of Darkness.* 1984. New Am Lib. wrp. EX. R3. $10.00

WINTER, Milo. *Arabian Nights.* nd. Chicago. Rand Windermere Series. 293 p. VG. B10. $15.00

WINTER, William. *Life & Art of Edwin Booth.* 1893. NY. Ils. 8vo. 308 p. G. G4. $19.00

WINTER, William. *Life of David Belasco.* 1925. NY. 2 vols. VG. $60.00

WINTER, William. *Stage Life of Mary Anderson.* 1886. George Coombes. 1st ed. octavo. 151 p. wrp. VG. H3. $60.00

WINTER. *Gold of Freedom.* 1944. Naylor. sgn. 276 p. dj. A5. $40.00

WINTERBOTHAM, F.W. *Nazi Connection.* 1978. Harper Row. 1st ed. dj. VG. P1. $15.00

WINTERBOTHAM, Russ. *Lord of Nardos.* 1966. Avalon. 1st ed. dj. EX. R3. $12.50

WINTERICH, J.T. *Early Am Books & Printing.* 1935. Houghton Mifflin. tall 8vo. VG. $45.00

WINWAR, Frances. *Oscar Wilde & the Yel '90s.* nd. Bl Ribbon. VG. B10. $4.25

WIPPLE, S. *Trial of Bruno Richard Hauptmann.* 1937. NY. 1st ed. dj. VG. B3. $35.00

WIRZ, Paul. *Damonen und Wilde in Neuguinea.* 1928. Stuttgart, Germany. 1st ed. 8vo. ES. VG. $65.00

WISE, H.A. *Los Gringos; or, Inside View of Mexico & CA...* 1849. NY. 1st ed. orig bdg. VG. $95.00

WISE, I.M. *Judaism: Its Doctrine & Duties.* 1872. Cincinnati. VG. $150.00

WISE, J.C. *Long Arm of Lee: Hist of Artillery of Army of N VA.* 1915. Lynchburg. 1st ed. 2 vols. T5. $175.00

WISE, J.C. *Red Man in the New World Drama.* 1931. WA. 1st ed. 4to. red bdg. VG. T1. $40.00

WISE, T.J. *Bibliography of William Woodsworth.* 1916. London. 1/100. sm 4to. xl. G. T6. $200.00

WISE & FRASER. *Great Tales of Terror & the Supernatural.* 1944. Random House. 1st ed. dj. EX. R3. $20.00

WISEMAN, Thomas. *Day Before Sunrise.* 1976. Holt Rinehart Winston. dj. EX. P1. $15.00

WISEMAN, Thomas. *Day Before Sunrise.* 1976. Holt Rinehart Winston. dj. VG. P1. $12.50

WISER, William. *K.* 1971. NY. 1st ed. presentation. dj. EX. T9. $65.00

WISSCHER, W.L. *Pony Express; or, Blazing the Westward Way.* 1946. Chicago. reprint of 1908 ed. A5. $35.00

WISTAR, Caspar. *System of Anatomy for...Students of Medicine.* 1842. Phil. 2 vols. VG. G4. $48.00

WISTAR, I.J. *Autobiography of Issac Jones Wistar 1827-1905.* 1937. Phil. 2nd ed. dj. EX. $100.00

WISTER, Marina. *Helen & Others.* 1924. Macmillan. Ltd ed. 1/350. sgn. boxed. H3. $75.00

WISTER, Owen. *Journey in Search of Christmas.* 1904. NY. Ils Remington. 1st ed. 92 p. TEG. T5. $95.00

WISTER, Owen. *Lin McLean.* nd. AL Burt. G. P1. $6.00

WISTER, Owen. *Red Men & Wht.* nd. Grosset Dunlap. G. P1. $7.50

WISTER, Owen. *Red Men & Wht.* 1896. NY. 1st ed. VG. $75.00

WISTER, Owen. *Roosevelt: Story of Friendship.* 1930. NY. later print. A4. $25.00

WISTER, Owen. *Virginian.* nd. (1930) Grosset. 506 p. dj. VG. B10. $8.25

WISTER, Owen. *When W Was W.* 1928. Macmillan. sgn. bl bdg. H3. $125.00

WITHERSPOON, M.F. *Daddy Dave.* 1887. NY. 116 p. wrp. xl. VG. $35.00

WITTER, Dean. *Shikar.* 1961. San Francisco. 1st ed. VG. B3. $25.00

WITTKE, Carl. *Hist of the State of OH.* 1941-1944. Columbus. Ils. 6 vols. G. T5. $125.00

WITTMER, Margret. *Floreana Adventure.* 1961. Dutton. 1st ed. 239 p. dj. F2. $15.00

WITWER, H.C. *Fighting Back.* nd. Grosset Dunlap. Photoplay ed. VG. P1. $17.50

WITWER, H.C. *Leather Pushers.* nd. Grosset Dunlap. Photoplay ed. VG. P1. $17.50

WITWER, H.C. *Leather Pushers.* nd. Grosset Dunlap. VG. P1. $17.50

WODEHOUSE, P.G. *Author! Author!* 1962. Simon Schuster. 1st ed. dj. VG. P1. $50.00

WODEHOUSE, P.G. *Bachelors Anonymous.* 1974. Simon Schuster. 1st ed. dj. EX. P1. $25.00

WODEHOUSE, P.G. *Biffen's Millions.* 1964. Simon Schuster. 1st ed. VG. P1. $20.00

WODEHOUSE, P.G. *Big Money.* 1931. McClelland Stewart. 1st Canadian ed. VG. P1. $60.00

WODEHOUSE, P.G. *Bill the Conqueror.* nd. Goodchild. 1st Canadian ed. G. P1. $35.00

WODEHOUSE, P.G. *Bill the Conqueror.* 1934. Methuen. 15th print. VG. P1. $30.00

WODEHOUSE, P.G. *Blandings Castle.* nd. Herbert Jenkins. 2nd ed. VG. P1. $35.00

WODEHOUSE, P.G. *Brinkmanship of Galahad Threepwood.* 1964. Simon Schuster. 1st ed. dj. VG. P1. $20.00

WODEHOUSE, P.G. *Carry on Jeeves.* nd. Herbert Jenkins. 3rd ed. VG. P1. $25.00

WODEHOUSE, P.G. *Century of Humor.* 1934. Hutchinson. VG. P1. $40.00

WODEHOUSE, P.G. *Clicking of Cuthbert.* nd. Herbert Jenkins. 13th print. G. P1. $25.00

WODEHOUSE, P.G. *Code of the Woosters.* nd. Herbert Jenkins. 6th print. VG. P1. $25.00

WODEHOUSE, P.G. *Code of the Woosters.* 1939. Sun Dial. VG. P1. $30.00

WODEHOUSE, P.G. *Crime Wave at Blandings.* 1937. Sun Dial. VG. P1. $30.00

WODEHOUSE, P.G. *Eggs, Beans, & Crumpets.* 1940. Longman Gr. 1st ed. dj. VG. P1. $60.00

WODEHOUSE, P.G. *Fore! The Best of Wodehouse on Golf.* 1983. Ticknor Fields. UP. wrp. EX. B13. $125.00

WODEHOUSE, P.G. *Full Moon.* 1947. Doubleday. 1st ed. VG. P1. $40.00

WODEHOUSE, P.G. *Full Moon.* 1947. Herbert Jenkins. 1st ed. VG. P1. $40.00

WODEHOUSE, P.G. *Gold Bat.* 1974. Souvenir Pr. dj. EX. P1. $15.00

WODEHOUSE, P.G. *Golf Without Tears.* 1924. Doran. 1st ed. VG. P1. $60.00

WODEHOUSE, P.G. *Head of Kay's.* 1922. A&C Blk. 4th ed. VG. P1. $40.00

WODEHOUSE, P.G. *Heavy Weather.* nd. AL Burt. VG. P1. $25.00

WODEHOUSE, P.G. *Heavy Weather.* 1933. McClelland Stewart. 1st Canadian ed. VG. P1. $60.00

WODEHOUSE, P.G. *Heavy Weather.* 1960. Herbert Jenkins. dj. xl. P1. $10.00

WODEHOUSE, P.G. *Hot Water.* nd. Herbert Jenkins. 2nd ed. dj. G. P1. $40.00

WODEHOUSE, P.G. *Hot Water.* 1932. McClelland Stewart. 1st Canadian ed. VG. P1. $50.00

WODEHOUSE, P.G. *Ice in the Bedroom.* 1961. Herbert Jenkins. 1st ed. dj. VG. P1. $25.00

WODEHOUSE, P.G. *Jeeves & the Tie That Binds.* 1971. Simon Schuster. 1st ed. dj. EX. P1. $25.00

WODEHOUSE, P.G. *Laughing Gas.* 1936. McClelland Stewart. 1st Canadian ed. VG. P1. $50.00

WODEHOUSE, P.G. *Leave It to Psmith.* nd. AL Burt. VG. P1. $12.00

WODEHOUSE, P.G. *Luck of the Bodkins.* 1935. McClelland Stewart. 1st Canadian ed. dj. VG. P1. $75.00

WODEHOUSE, P.G. *Man Upstairs.* 1924. Methuen. 9th print. VG. P1. $40.00

WODEHOUSE, P.G. *Meet Mr Mulliner.* nd. AL Burt. dj. VG. P1. $30.00

WODEHOUSE, P.G. *Most of PG Wodehouse.* nd. BOMC. dj. VG. P1. $20.00

WODEHOUSE, P.G. *Most of PG Wodehouse.* 1960. Simon Schuster. 1st ed. dj. VG. P1. $30.00

WODEHOUSE, P.G. *Mr Mulliner Speaking.* 1929. McClelland Stewart. 1st Canadian ed. VG. P1. $50.00

WODEHOUSE, P.G. *Mulliner Omnibus.* 1935. Herbert Jenkins. 1st ed. VG. P1. $35.00

WODEHOUSE, P.G. *No Nudes Is Good Nudes.* 1970. NY. 1st ed. dj. EX. B3. $27.50

WODEHOUSE, P.G. *Not George WA.* 1980. Continuum. dj. EX. P1. $12.50

WODEHOUSE, P.G. *Nothing But Wodehouse.* 1946. Doubleday. dj. VG. P1. $35.00

WODEHOUSE, P.G. *Perfect's Uncle.* 1972. Souvenir Pr. dj. EX. P1. $15.00

WODEHOUSE, P.G. *Piccadilly Jim.* nd. Herbert Jenkins. dj. VG. P1. $40.00

WODEHOUSE, P.G. *Pigs Have Wings.* 1952. NY. 1st ed. dj. VG. $60.00

WODEHOUSE, P.G. *Pothunters.* 1972. Souvenir Pr. dj. EX. P1. $12.50

WODEHOUSE, P.G. *Prince & Betty.* 1912. WJ Watts Popular ed. decor brd. VG. P1. $250.00

WODEHOUSE, P.G. *Purloined Paperweight.* 1967. Simon Schuster. 1st ed. dj. VG. $25.00

WODEHOUSE, P.G. *Quick Service.* 1941. Longman Gr. 1st Canadian ed. VG. P1. $40.00

WODEHOUSE, P.G. *Right Ho, Jeeves.* 1934. McClelland Stewart. 1st Canadian ed. VG. P1. $60.00

WODEHOUSE, P.G. *Sam the Sudden.* 1925. Methuen. 1st ed. VG. P1. $75.00

WODEHOUSE, P.G. *Something Fresh.* 1924. Methuen. 9th print. VG. P1. $35.00

WODEHOUSE, P.G. *Spring Fever.* 1964. Herbert Jenkins. 2st ed. VG. P1. $40.00

WODEHOUSE, P.G. *Stiff Upper Lip, Jeeves.* 1963. NY. 1st ed. dj. EX. $55.00

WODEHOUSE, P.G. *Summer Lightning.* nd. Herbert Jenkins. 7th ed. dj. VG. P1. $45.00

WODEHOUSE, P.G. *Summer Moonshine.* nd. Herbert Jenkins. 2nd ed. VG. P1. $25.00

WODEHOUSE, P.G. *Summer Moonshine.* 1937. Doubleday Doran. 1st ed. VG. P1. $50.00

WODEHOUSE, P.G. *Sunset at Blandings.* 1977. Chatto Windus. 1st ed. dj. VG. P1. $20.00

WODEHOUSE, P.G. *Tales of St Austin's.* 1972. Souvenir Pr. dj. EX. P1. $15.00

WODEHOUSE, P.G. *Thank You, Jeeves!* nd. Herbert Jenkins. 3rd ed. VG. P1. $25.00

WODEHOUSE, P.G. *Thank You, Jeeves!* nd. Triangle. VG. P1. $17.50

WODEHOUSE, P.G. *Ukridge.* 1924. Herbert Jenkins. 1st ed. VG. P1. $50.00

WODEHOUSE, P.G. *Uncle Fred in the Springtime.* 1900. nd. Herbert Jenkins. 4th print. VG. P1. $35.00

WODEHOUSE, P.G. *Uncle Fred in the Springtime.* 1939. Herbert Jenkins. 1st ed. VG. P1. $60.00

WODEHOUSE, P.G. *Uncle Fred in the Springtime.* 1939. McClelland Stewart. 1st Canadian ed. dj. VG. P1. $75.00

WODEHOUSE, P.G. *Very Good, Jeeves.* 1930. McClelland Stewart. 1st Canadian ed. VG. P1. $60.00

WODEHOUSE, P.G. *Weekend Wodehouse.* 1940. Garden City. G. P1. $35.00

WODEHOUSE, P.G. *Wht Feather.* 1972. Souvenir Pr. dj. EX. P1. $12.50

WODEHOUSE, P.G. *Wodehouse Nuggets.* 1983. Hutchinson. 1st ed. dj. EX. P1. $17.50

WODEHOUSE, P.G. *Wodehouse on Crime.* 1981. Ellery Queen Mystery Club. 1st ed. dj. EX. P1. $20.00

WODEHOUSE, P.G. *Wodehouse on Crime.* 1981. Ticknor Fields. UP. wrp. EX. B13. $125.00

WODEHOUSE, P.G. *World of Jeeves.* 1976. Barrie Jenkins. 4th print. dj. VG. P1. $25.00

WODEHOUSE, P.G. *World of Mr Mulliner.* 1972. Barrie Jenkins. 1st ed. dj. VG. P1. $25.00

WODEHOUSE, P.G. *Young Men in Spats.* 1936. Herbert Jenkins. 1st ed. xl. VG. P1. $40.00

WODEHOUSE, P.G. *Young Men in Spats.* 1936. McClelland Stewart. 1st Canadian ed. VG. P1. $50.00

WODEHOUSE, P.G. *3 Men & a Maid.* nd. AL Burt. VG. P1. $15.00

WODEHOUSE, P.G. *5 Complete Novels.* 1983. Avenel. 1st ed. dj. EX. P1. $15.00

WODEHOUSE & BOLTON. *Bring on the Girls.* 1953. Simon Schuster. 1st ed. G. P1. $40.00

WOIWODE, Larry. *Even Tide.* 1977. Farrar Straus. UP. B13. $75.00

WOLD, A.L. *Star God.* 1980. St Martin. 1st ed. dj. EX. F5. $14.00

WOLDMAN, A.A. *Lincoln & the Russians.* 1952. World. 311 p. dj. EX. S1. $15.00

WOLF, Bill. *Reveries of an Outdoor Man.* 1946. Putnam. 1st ed. 1/350. tall 8vo. VG. $25.00

WOLF, Blue. *Dwifa's Curse: Tale of the Stone Age.* 1921. Robert Scott. VG. P1. $60.00

WOLF, Eric. *Sons of the Shaking Earth.* 1959. Chicago. 1st ed. 303 p. dj. F2. $20.00

WOLF, Eric. *Valley of Mexico.* 1976. NM U. 1st ed. 337 p. dj. F2. $20.00

WOLF, Gary. *Who Censored Roger Rabbit?* 1981. St Martin. 1st ed. dj. xl. P1. $10.00

WOLF, Leonard. *Wolf's Complete Book of Terror.* 1979. Clarkson N Potter. dj. VG. P1. $20.00

WOLF, Simon. *Am Jew As Patriot, Soldier, & Citizen.* 1895. Phil. 1st ed. 576 p. EX. $65.00

WOLFE, Bertram. *Portrait of Mexico.* 1937. Covici Friede. Ils Rivera. 1st ed. VG. F2. $30.00

WOLFE, C.T. *Of Time & the River.* 1935. Scribner. inscr. dj. H3. $1250.00

WOLFE, Gary. *Generation Removed.* 1977. Doubleday. 1st ed. dj. EX. R3. $15.00

WOLFE, Gene. *Citadel of the Autarch.* nd. Book Club. dj. VG. P1. $4.50

WOLFE, Gene. *Citadel of the Autarch.* 1983. Timescape. 1st ed. dj. VG. P1. $50.00

WOLFE, Gene. *Claw of the Conciliator.* 1981. Timescape. 1st ed. dj. EX. F5. $50.00

WOLFE, Gene. *Devil in the Forest.* 1976. Follett. 1st ed. Lib ed bdg. dj. EX. R3. $35.00

WOLFE, Gene. *Free Live Free.* 1984. Ziesing. 1st ed. 1/750. sgn. dj. EX. R3. $40.00

WOLFE, Gene. *Free Live Free.* 1985. Tor Books. 1st ed. dj. EX. P1. $16.95

WOLFE, Gene. *Gene Wolfe's Book of Days.* 1981. Doubleday. 1st ed. dj. EX. R3. $15.00

WOLFE, Gene. *Pandora by Holly Hollander.* 1990. Tor Books. ARC. dj. w/promotional materials. EX. B13. $35.00

WOLFE, Gene. *Peace.* 1975. Harper Row. 1st ed. dj. EX. P1. $35.00

WOLFE, Gene. *Soldier of the Mist.* 1986. Tor Books. 1st ed. dj. EX. R3. $30.00

WOLFE, Gene. *Sword of the Lictor.* 1982. Timescape. 1st ed. dj. EX. F5/R3. $55.00

WOLFE, Gene. *There Are Doors.* 1988. Tor Books. 1st ed. sgn. dj. EX. F5. $23.00

WOLFE, Gene. *Urth of the New Sun.* 1987. Tor Books. 1st ed. dj. EX. F5. $20.00

WOLFE, Gene. *Urth of the New Sun.* 1987. Ultramarine. 1st ed. 1/250. sgn. M. R3. $150.00

WOLFE, Gene. *Wolfe Archipelago.* 1983. Ziesing. 1st ed. 1/800. M. R3. $40.00

WOLFE, Gene. *5th Head of Cerberus.* 1977. Scribner. 1st ed. dj. EX. P1. $35.00

WOLFE, H.A. *Stories of Immortal Crimes.* c 1930. London. VG. $20.00

WOLFE, Thomas. *Bonfire of the Vanities.* 1987. Farrar Straus. UP. K2. $100.00

WOLFE, Thomas. *Bonfire of the Vanities.* 1987. Farrar Straus. UP. wrp. C4. $150.00

WOLFE, Thomas. *Bonfire of the Vanities.* 1987. Farrar Straus. 1st ed. dj. EX. C4. $50.00

WOLFE, Thomas. *Electric Kool-Aid Acid Test.* 1968. Farrar Straus. 1st ed. dj. EX. C4. $90.00

WOLFE, Thomas. *Face of a Nation.* 1939. Scribner. 1st ed. dj. EX. H3. $125.00

WOLFE, Thomas. *From Bauhaus to Our House.* 1981. Farrar Straus Giroux. Ltd ed. 1/350. sgn. cloth slipcase. H3. $85.00

WOLFE, Thomas. *From Bauhaus to Our House.* 1982. London. UP. wrp. VG. $45.00

WOLFE, Thomas. *From Death to Morning.* 1935. Scribner. 1st ed. dj. VG. H3. $200.00

WOLFE, Thomas. *From Death to Morning.* 1935. Scribner. 1st ed. 1st issue. dj. EX. $300.00

WOLFE, Thomas. *Hills Beyond.* 1941. Harper. 1st ed. dj. VG. H3. $100.00

WOLFE, Thomas. *Kandy-Kolored Tangerine-Flake Streamline Baby.* 1965. NY. 1st ed. dj. VG. $65.00

WOLFE, Thomas. *Look Homeward, Angel: A Play.* 1958. Scribner. 1st ed. dj. EX. H3. $60.00

WOLFE, Thomas. *Look Homeward Angel.* nd. Modern Lib Giant. 626 p. VG. B10. $3.75

WOLFE, Thomas. *Look Homeward Angel.* 1929. Scribner. 1st ed. 1st state. dj. VG. H3. $750.00

WOLFE, Thomas. *Look Homeward Angel.* 1947. NY. Ils Douglas Gorsline. 1st ed. 8vo. EX. T1. $60.00

WOLFE, Thomas. *Mannerhouse.* 1948. Harper. 1st ed. dj. EX. H3. $100.00

WOLFE, Thomas. *Mannerhouse: A Play & a Prologue in 3 Acts.* 1948. Harper. Ltd ed. 1st print. 1/500. dj. slipcase. M. $450.00

WOLFE, Thomas. *Of Time & the River.* 1935. Scribner. 1st ed. dj. H3. $100.00

WOLFE, Thomas. *Of Time & the River.* 1951. Paris. 1st French ed. sgn. orig wrp. EX. R4. $85.00

WOLFE, Thomas. *Radical Chic & Mau-Mauing the Flak Catchers.* 1970. NY. 1st ed. dj. VG. $35.00

WOLFE, Thomas. *Right Stuff.* 1979. Farrar Straus. UP. wrp. VG. C4. $125.00

WOLFE, Thomas. *Story of a Novel.* 1936. Scribner. 1st ed. dj. EX. H3. $100.00

WOLFE, Thomas. *Thomas Wolfe's Letter to His Mother, Julia Elizabeth Wolfe.* 1943. Scribner. 1st ed. 1st issue. dj. M. $250.00

WOLFE, Thomas. *W Journal.* 1951. Pittsburgh. 1st ed. dj. EX. H3. $125.00

WOLFE, Thomas. *Web & the Rock.* 1939. Harper. 1st ed. dj. EX. H3. $150.00

WOLFE, Thomas. *You Can't Go Home Again.* 1940. NY. 1st ed. dj. VG. B3. $45.00

WOLFE, Thomas. *You Can't Go Home Again.* 1942. Dial. 1st ed. 743 p. VG. B10. $4.50

WOLFF, Geoffrey. *Blk Sun: Brief Transit & Violent Eclipse of Harry Crosby.* 1976. Random House. Book Club ed. 400 p. dj. EX. B10. $4.50

WOLFF, Geoffrey. *Sightseer.* 1973. NY. 1st ed. presentation. dj. EX. T9. $40.00

WOLFF, L. *Lockout.* 1965. NY. 1st ed. 297 p. dj. VG. B3. $22.50

WOLFF, R.L. *Strange Stories & Other Explorations in Victorian Fiction.* 1971. Boston. Gambit. 1st ed. 8vo. 378 p. dj. R4. $25.00

WOLLE, M.S. *Stampede to Timberline, Ghost Towns, & Mining Camps of CO.* 1950. Boulder, CO. Ils. sgn. 544 p. VG. T5. $12.50

WOLLHEIM, D.A. *Flight Into Space.* 1950. Fell. 1st ed. dj. EX. R3. $20.00

WOLLHEIM, D.A. *Mike Mars Astronaut.* 1961. Doubleday. 1st ed. dj. EX. R3. $15.00

WOLLHEIM, D.A. *Mike Mars Astronaut.* 1961. Doubleday. 1st ed. dj. VG. P1. $12.00

WOLLHEIM, D.A. *Mike Mars Astronaut.* 1961. Doubleday. 1st ed. sgn. dj. EX. F5. $25.00

WOLLHEIM, D.A. *Mike Mars at Cape Canaveral.* 1961. Doubleday. 1st ed. sgn. dj. VG. P1. $25.00

WOLLHEIM, D.A. *Mike Mars Flies the X-15.* 1961. Doubleday. dj. VG. P1. $10.00

WOLLHEIM, D.A. *Mike Mars in Orbit.* 1961. Doubleday. 1st ed. dj. VG. P1. $12.00

WOLLHEIM, D.A. *Mike Mars in Orbit.* 1961. Doubleday. 1st ed. sgn. dj. VG. P1. $25.00

WOLLHEIM, D.A. *Mike Mars S Pole Spaceman.* 1962. Doubleday. 1st ed. dj. EX. R3. $15.00

WOLLHEIM, D.A. *Secret of Saturn's Rings.* 1954. Winston. 1st ed. VG. P1. $15.00

WOLLHEIM, D.A. *Secret of the 9th Planet.* 1959. Winston. 1st ed. Lib bdg. xl. P1. $7.50

WOLLHEIM, D.A. *1975 Annual World's Best SF.* nd. Book Club. dj. VG. P1. $4.50

WOLLHEIM, D.A. *2-Dozen Dragon Eggs.* 1977. Dobson. 1st UK/HrdCvr ed. sgn. dj. EX. F5. $50.00

WOMACK, Jack. *Ambient.* 1987. Weidenfeld. 1st ed. dj. EX. F5. $22.50

WONG, Jeanyee. *Buddha: Life & Teachings.* c 1950s. Peter Pauper. Ils Wong. slipcase. NM. C1. $10.00

WOOD, Christina. *Safari S Am.* 1973. Taplinger. 1st ed. 224 p. dj. F2. $15.00

WOOD, Clement. *Strange Fires.* 1951. Woodford Pr. 1st ed. dj. EX. F5. $20.00

WOOD, Clement. *Woman Who Was Pope.* 1931. NY. 1st ed. sgn. VG. B3. $25.00

WOOD, F.S. *Roosevelt As We Knew Him.* nd. (1927) Winston. gilt gr bdg. VG. B10. $7.25

WOOD, H.G. *Henry T Hodgkin: A Memoir.* 1937. London. Student Christian Movement. 1st ed. 8vo. V1. $8.50

WOOD, J.P. *Spunkwater, Spunkwater!* nd. (1968) Pantheon. 182 p. VG. B10. $6.50

WOOD, Melusine. *Advanced Hist Dances.* 1960. London. 1st ed. octavo. 189 p. dj. EX. H3. $75.00

WOOD, Melusine. *More Hist Dances.* 1956. London. 1st ed. octavo. 159 p. dj. VG. H3. $50.00

WOOD, Michael. *In Search of the Dark Ages.* 1987. 1st Am ed. dj. EX. C1. $17.50

WOOD, Robert. *Voyage of the Water Witch.* 1984. Labyrinthos. 1st ed. 4to. 106 p. wrp. F2. $20.00

WOOD, Ted. *Live Bait.* 1985. Collier Macmillan Canada. 1st ed. dj. EX. P1. $15.00

WOOD, Ted. *Live Bait.* 1985. Collier Macmillan. 1st Canadian ed. dj. EX. P1. $15.00

WOOD, W.B. *Personal Recollections of the Stage...* 1855. Phil. Baird. 1st ed. octavo. 477 p. G. H3. $50.00

WOOD, W.H.S. *Friends of City of NY in the 19th Century.* 1904. NY. private print. 8vo. 68 p. wrp. G. V1. $12.00

WOOD, Wallace. *Wizard King.* 1978. Wallace Wood. 1st ed. sgn. dj. EX. P1. $45.00

WOOD, William. *Capt of the Civil War.* 1921. New Haven. 424 p. G. S1. $6.00

WOOD & WILLIAMSON. *Soc of Friends Vindicated.* 1832. Trenton. Gray. 8vo. 90 p. G. V1. $40.00

WOOD & WOOD. *Book of Meetings, Times, & Places of Meetings in Am.* 1858. NY. Wood. 18mo. 98 p. V1. $10.00

WOODARD, B.A. *Diamonds in the Salt.* 1967. Pruitt. Ils 200 p. A5. $25.00

WOODARD, Luke. *Morning Star: Treatise on the...Work of Lord Jesus Christ.* 1875. New Vienna. Friends Pub House. 12mo. 395 p. V1. $15.00

WOODBURY, Richard. *Abstracts of New World Archaeology.* 1960. WA. 194 p. wrp. F2. $10.00

WOODCOCK, George. *Ravens & Prophets.* 1952. London. 1st ed. dj. VG. $20.00

WOODFORD & CARTER. *Starved.* 1953. Sgn Pr. 1st ed. dj. EX. F5. $20.00

WOODHOUSE, Martin. *Tree Frog.* nd. Book Club. dj. xl. P1. $3.00

WOODIWISS, J.C. *Some New Ghost Stories.* 1931. Simpkin Marshall. 1st ed. P1. $90.00

WOODIWISS, K.E. *Come Love a Stranger.* nd. Book Club. dj. VG. P1. $4.50

WOODLOCK, T.F. *Thinking It Over.* 1947. McMullen. 1st ed. 292 p. dj. VG. B10. $4.50

WOODMAN, C.M. *Present Day Message of Quakerism.* 1915. Boston. Pilgrim Pr. 12mo. inscr. 106 p. VG. V1. $9.00

WOODMAN, C.M. *Quakers Find a Way.* 1950. Bobbs Merrill. 1st ed. 8vo. 280 p. dj. VG. V1. $8.50

WOODMAN, Jim. *Discovering Yucatan.* 1966. Doubleday. 1st ed. 84 p. dj. F2. $12.50

WOODROW, Mrs. Wilson. *Moonhill Mystery.* 1930. Macaulay. VG. P1. $10.00

WOODS, Frederick. *Young Winston's Wars: Orig Dispatches of WS Churchill...* 1973. NY. Ils. 350 p. dj. T5. $22.50

WOODS, John. *2 Years' Residence on Eng Prairie of IL.* 1968. Lakeside Classic. Ils. 242 p. EX. T5. $22.50

WOODS, Josephine. *High Spots in the Andes.* 1935. Putnam. 1st ed. 320 p. dj. F2. $25.00

WOODS, Leigh. *Gipsy, the Greyhound.* nd. NY. 253 p. VG. T5. $15.00

WOODS, Ralph. *Treasury of the Familiar.* 1942. NY. 1st ed. dj. VG. B3. $40.00

WOODS, Samuel. *Pembina Settlement: Report of Major Woods.* 1850. WA. 8vo. 55 p. disbound. $25.00

WOODS, Sara. *Bloody Instruction.* nd. Book Club. dj. VG. P1. $4.50

WOODS, Sara. *Knives Have Edges.* 1968. Holt Rinehart Winston. 1st ed. dj. VG. P1. $15.00

WOODS, Sara. *Past Praying For.* 1968. Harper Row. 1st ed. dj. xl. P1. $6.00

WOODS, Sara. *Serpent's Tooth.* 1971. Collins Crime Club. 1st ed. dj. EX. P1. $7.50

WOODS, Sara. *Tarry & Be Hanged.* nd. Book Club. dj. VG. P1. $4.50

WOODS, Sara. *Tarry & Be Hanged.* 1971. Holt Rinehart Winston. 1st ed. dj. EX. P1. $15.00

WOODS, Sara. *This Fatal Writ.* nd. Book Club. dj. VG. P1. $4.50

WOODS, Sara. *Though I Know She Lies.* nd. Book Club. dj. VG. P1. $5.00

WOODS, Sara. *Where Should He Die?* 1983. Macmillan. 1st ed. dj. VG. P1. $17.50

WOODS, Sara. *Yet She Must Die.* nd. Book Club. dj. VG. P1. $4.50

WOODWARD, W.E. *Years of Madness.* 1951. NY. EX. $15.00

WOODWORTH. *Kodiak Bear AK Adventure.* 1958. Harrisburg. 1st ed. 204 p. dj. VG. B3. $85.00

WOOLERY. *Bethany Years.* 1941. Huntington. 1st ed. 290 p. dj. VG. B3. $22.50

WOOLEY, Persia. *Child of the N Spring.* nd. np. 1st ed. sgn. dj. EX. C1. $12.50

WOOLEY, Persia. *Child of the N Spring.* 1987. 1st ed. sgn. dj. M. C1. $19.50

WOOLF, Virginia. *Beau Brummell.* 1930. Rimington Hooper. 1/550. sgn. EX. K2. $550.00

WOOLF, Virginia. *Contemporary Writers.* 1965. London. 1st ed. dj. EX. $30.00

WOOLF, Virginia. *Diary of VA Woolf Vol 3: 1925-1930.* 1980. Harcourt Brace. UP. wrp. EX. K2. $45.00

WOOLF, Virginia. *Flush.* 1933. NY. 1st ed. 8vo. EX. T1. $40.00

WOOLF, Virginia. *Fresh-Water.* 1976. Harcourt Brace. 1st ed. M. H3. $40.00

WOOLF, Virginia. *Granite & Rainbow.* 1958. London. 1st ed. dj. VG. B3. $70.00

WOOLF, Virginia. *Haunted House & Other Stories.* 1943. Hogarth. 1st UK ed. EX. H3. $150.00

WOOLF, Virginia. *Room of One's Own.* 1929. Hogarth. 1st Am ed. dj. VG. K2. $75.00

WOOLF, Virginia. *Writer's Diary.* 1954. Harcourt Brace. 1st Am ed. dj. VG. H3. $100.00

WOOLF, Virginia. *Years.* 1937. Hogarth. 1st ed. dj. EX. B13. $400.00

WOOLF, Virginia. *Years.* 1937. Hogarth. 1st ed. dj. VG. H3. $300.00

WOOLF, Virginia. *2nd Common Reader.* 1932. Harcourt Brace. 1st ed. dj. EX. H3. $150.00

WOOLF, Virginia. *2nd Common Reader.* 1932. NY. 1st ed. 395 p. dj. VG. T5. $125.00

WOOLLCOTT, Alexander. *Woollcott Reader: Bypaths in the Realms of Gold.* 1935. Viking. Ltd ed. 1/1500. sgn. boxed. H3. $150.00

WOOLLCOTT, Alexander. *Woollcott's 2nd Reader.* 1937. Viking. Ltd ed. 1/1500. sgn. boxed. H3. $125.00

WOOLLCOTT & KAUFMAN. *Dark Tower: A Melodrama.* 1934. Random House. 1st ed. inscr Woollcott. dj. EX. H3. $125.00

WOOLLEY, Persia. *Child of the N Spring.* 1st ed. sgn. dj. EX. C1. $7.00

WOOLMAN, John. *Journal of John Woolman.* 1871. Houghton Mifflin. 15th print. 12mo. 315 p. VG. V1. $10.00

WOOLMAN, John. *Journal of John Woolman.* 1950. Chicago. Regnery. 8vo. 233 p. dj. VG. V1. $12.00

WOOLMAN, John. *Journal of Life, Gospel Labors, & Christian Experiences.* 1880. Friends Book Assn. 12mo. 256 p. G. V1. $10.00

WOOLRICH, Cornell. *Best of William Irish.* nd. Book Club. dj. VG. P1. $8.00

WOOLRICH, Cornell. *Beyond the Night.* 1959. Avon T-354. 1st ed. wrp. NM. T9. $25.00

WOOLRICH, Cornell. *Children of the Ritz.* 1927. Boni Liveright. 1st ed. VG. T9. $50.00

WOOLRICH, Cornell. *Cover Charge.* 1926. NY. 1st ed. VG. T9. $300.00

WOOLRICH, Cornell. *Deadline at Dawn.* 1944. Lippincott. VG. P1. $30.00

WOOLRICH, Cornell. *Deadline at Dawn.* 1946. 1st Photoplay ed. dj. VG. F5. $25.00

WOOLRICH, Cornell. *Hotel Room.* 1958. Random House. 1st ed. dj. VG. T9. $55.00

WOOLRICH, Cornell. *I Married a Dead Man.* 1948. Lippincott. 1st ed. lavender bdg. VG. T9. $30.00

WOOLRICH, Cornell. *Night Has a Thousand Eyes.* 1949. Penguin. 1st UK ed. wrp. VG. T9. $65.00

WOOLRICH, Cornell. *Phantom Lady.* nd. Collier. VG. P1. $15.00

WOOLRICH, Cornell. *Phantom Lady.* 1944. Tower. Photoplay ed. dj. VG. P1. $25.00

WOOLRICH, Cornell. *Waltz Into Darkness.* 1947. Lippincott. 1st ed. VG. P1. $20.00

WORDSWORTH, William. *Complete Poetical Works.* 1910. Houghton Mifflin. Lg Paper ed. 1/500. 10 vols. lg octavo. H3. $1500.00

WORDSWORTH, William. *Poems. Selected, Edited, & Intro by Jonathan Woodsworth.* 1973. Cambridge. Ltd Ed Club. Ils/sgn John O'Conner. 1/2000. slipcase. EX. C4. $90.00

WORDSWORTH, William. *Poetical Works.* 1905. London. Bell. 7 vols. sm octavo. TEG. VG. H3. $500.00

WORK, J.W. *Folk Song of the Am Negro.* 1915. Nashville. Fisk U. 1st ed. A4. $50.00

WORLEY, William. *My Dead Wife.* 1948. Simon Schuster. 1st ed. dj. EX. F5. $20.00

WORMSER, Richard. *Lonesome Quarter.* nd. Sears Readers Club. VG. P1. $4.50

WORST, Edward. *More Problems in Woodwork.* 1929. Milwaukee. Bruce. 2nd ed. B10. $7.00

WORSTHORNE, S.T. *Venetian Opera in 17th Century.* 1968. Claredon. reprint of 1954 ed. 194 p. dj. EX. H3. $45.00

WORTH, Herman. *Repro of Antique Furniture.* 1924. Bruce Pub. 2nd ed. B10. $7.00

WORTH, Jonathan. *Inaugural Address of Jonathan Worth, Governor of NC.* 1866. Raleigh. 1st ed. orig wrp. VG. $45.00

WORTS, G.F. *Dangerous Young Man.* 1940. Kinsey. 1st ed. dj. EX. F5. $40.00

WOUK, Herman. *Caine Mutiny.* 1952. Doubleday. Ils 1st ed. sgn. dj. H3. $100.00

WOUK, Herman. *Real Diary of a Real Boy.* 1955. Doubleday Book Club. 565 p. dj. VG. B10. $3.75

WPA WRITER'S PROGRAM. *Copper Camp (Butte, MT).* 1943. NY. 1st ed. VG. B3. $35.00

WPA WRITER'S PROGRAM. *Guide to Roanoke.* 1948. Roanoke. 1st ed. 390 p. pocket map. VG. B3. $40.00

WPA WRITER'S PROGRAM. *ID Encyclopedia.* 1938. Caldwell. 1st ed. 452 p. VG. B3. $165.00

WPA WRITER'S PROGRAM. *State Guide to NV.* 1940. Portland. 1st ed. map. VG. B3. $45.00

WPA WRITER'S PROGRAM. *State Guide to OH.* 1940. Oxford. 1st ed. dj. w/pocket map. VG. B3. $45.00

WPA WRITER'S PROGRAM. *State Guide to OR.* 1940. Portland. 1st ed. G. B3. $30.00

WPA WRITER'S PROGRAM. *State Guide to SD.* 1952. NY. 2nd ed. 1st print. dj. VG. B3. $60.00

WRE, E.F. *Indian War of 1864, Being a Fragment of Hist of KS.* 1911. Topeka. 1st ed. $150.00

WREDE, P.C. *Snow Wht & Rose Red.* 1989. Tor Books. 1st ed. sgn. dj. EX. F5. $20.00

WREN, P.C. *Beau Geste.* 1952. John Murray. dj. xl. P1. $7.50

WREN, P.C. *Beau Ideal.* 1952. John Murray. 9th ed. dj. VG. P1. $17.50

WREN, P.C. *Beau Sabreur.* nd. Grosset Dunlap. Photoplay ed. VG. P1. $15.00

WREN, P.C. *Beau Sabreur.* 1953. John Murray. 8th print. dj. VG. P1. $17.50

WREN, P.C. *Sowing Glory.* 1931. Longman Gr. 1st ed. xl. G. P1. $7.50

WREN, P.C. *Stepsons of France.* 1927. Longman Gr. 11th print. VG. P1. $15.00

WREN, P.C. *Uniform of Glory.* 1956. Gryphon. 3rd ed. dj. VG. P1. $17.50

WREN, P.C. *Wages of Virtue.* 1949. John Murray. 26th print. dj. VG. P1. $17.50

WREN & MCKAY. *2nd Baffle Book.* 1929. Crime Club. 1st ed. VG. P1. $20.00

WRIGHT, A.M.R. *Old Ironsides.* nd. Grosset Dunlap. Photoplay ed. G. P1. $12.50

WRIGHT, Austin. *Islandia.* 1942. Farrar Rinehart. dj. R3. $75.00

WRIGHT, Austin. *Islandia.* 1942. NY. 1st ed. dj. orig tissue wrp. EX. B13. $225.00

WRIGHT, Charles. *Bloodlines.* 1975. Middletown, CT. 1st ed. dj. EX. B13. $50.00

WRIGHT, Charles. *China Trace.* 1977. Middeltown, CT. 1st ed. B13. $50.00

WRIGHT, Charles. *Grave of the Right Hand.* 1970. Middletown, CT. 1st ed. sgn. dj. EX. T9. $45.00

WRIGHT, Charles. *Wig.* 1966. Farrar Straus. 1st ed. dj. EX. B13. $50.00

WRIGHT, Eric. *Body Surrounded by Water.* 1987. Collins Crime Club. 1st ed. dj. VG. P1. $15.00

WRIGHT, Eric. *Man Who Changed His Name.* 1986. Scribner. 1st ed. dj. EX. P1. $13.95

WRIGHT, Eric. *Night the Gods Smiled.* 1983. Scribner. 1st ed. dj. EX. P1. $15.00

WRIGHT, Eric. *Question of Murder.* 1988. Scribner. 1st ed. dj. EX. P1. $15.95

WRIGHT, Eugene. *Great Horn Spoon.* nd. Garden City. 320 p. VG. B10. $3.75

WRIGHT, F.L. *Autobiography.* 1932. London/NY/Toronto. 1st ed. VG. G1. $95.00

WRIGHT, F.L. *Autobiography.* 1943. NY. Revised/Expanded ed. 1st print. EX. $100.00

WRIGHT, F.L. *Genius & Mobocracy.* 1949. NY. 1st ed. VG. B3. $60.00

WRIGHT, F.L. *Natural House.* 1954. NY. Ils. dj. VG. T1. $30.00

WRIGHT, F.L. *Testament.* 1957. NY. 1st ed. folio. dj. EX. G1. $110.00

WRIGHT, F.L. *Work of Frank L Wright.* 1965. Bramhall House. sm folio. VG. R5. $55.00

WRIGHT, F.L. *60 Years of Living Architecture.* 1953. Guggenheim Mus. 1st ed. pictorial wrp. VG. T1. $30.00

WRIGHT, G.F. *Ice Age in N Am.* 1890. NY. Ils. VG. T1. $40.00

WRIGHT, G.F. *Man & the Glacial Period.* 1899. Appleton. Ils. 385 p. VG. F2. $15.00

WRIGHT, G.T. *7 Am Stylists From Poe to Mailer: An Intro.* 1973. MN U. sgn. dj. H3. $75.00

WRIGHT, Grahame. *Jog Rummage.* 1974. Random House. 1st ed. dj. EX. P1. $10.00

WRIGHT, H.B. *Devil's Highway.* 1932. NY. VG. B3. $95.00

WRIGHT, H.B. *Exit.* 1930. NY. 1st ed. dj. VG. B3. $27.50

WRIGHT, H.B. *Eyes of the World.* 1914. Book Supply. 1st ed. VG. $10.00

WRIGHT, H.B. *Mine With the Iron Door.* 1923. Appleton. 1st ed. VG. $10.00

WRIGHT, H.B. *Re-Creation of Brian Kent.* nd. Book Supply. VG. R3. $25.00

WRIGHT, H.B. *When a Man's a Man.* nd. (1916) Book Supply. 348 p. VG. B10. $4.00

WRIGHT, H.B. *Winning of Barbara Worth.* 1911. Burt. 511 p. VG. B10. $3.00

WRIGHT, H.S. *Old-Time Recipes for Home-Made Wines.* c 1909. Boston. 12mo. 156 p. VG. G4. $18.00

WRIGHT, J.L. *My Father Who Is on Earth.* 1946. NY. 1st ed. dj. VG. B3. $50.00

WRIGHT, Jack. *On the 40-Yard Line.* 1932. World. dj. EX. $7.00

WRIGHT, James. *Gr Wall.* 1957. New Haven. 1st ed. inscr. dj. EX. C4. $300.00

WRIGHT, James. *Shall We Gather at the River.* 1968. NC Wesleyan U. 1st ed. dj. EX. B13. $65.00

WRIGHT, James. *St Judas.* 1959. Middletown. Wesleyan. 1st ed. sgn. dj. EX. K2. $300.00

WRIGHT, June. *Devil's Caress.* 1952. Hutchinson. 1st ed. VG. P1. $20.00

WRIGHT, Kenneth. *Mysterious Planet.* 1953. Winston. 1st ed. dj. VG. R3. $15.00

WRIGHT, L. *Clean & Decent: Unruffled Hist of Bathroom & Water Closet.* 1960. NY. dj. VG. $20.00

WRIGHT, M.O. *My NY.* 1926. NY. 1st ed. sgn. EX. G1. $22.00

WRIGHT, Marcus. *Wright's Official Hist of Spanish-Am War.* 1900. WA. Ils. 617 p. fair. T5. $95.00

WRIGHT, Norman. *Mexican Kaleidoscope.* 1948. London. Ils. 175 p. F2. $12.50

WRIGHT, O.L. *Our House.* 1959. NY. 308 p. dj. VG. T5. $35.00

WRIGHT, Peter. *Spy Catcher.* 1987. Viking. 9th print. dj. VG. P1. $15.00

WRIGHT, R.V. *Locomotive Cyclopedia of Am Practice.* 1925. NY. 7th ed. G. T5. $95.00

WRIGHT, Richard. *Blk Boy: Record of Childhood & Youth.* nd. Harper. Book Club ed. dj. EX. B10. $4.00

WRIGHT, Richard. *Clr Curtain.* 1956. London. Dobson. 1st ed. dj. VG. B13. $85.00

WRIGHT, Richard. *Letters to Joe C Brn.* 1968. Kent State. 1st ed. wrp. EX. $25.00

WRIGHT, Ronald. *Cut Stones & Crossroads.* 1986. Penguin. 1st ed. 239 p. wrp. F2. $10.00

WRIGHT, S.F. *Deluge.* 1927. London. 1st ed. VG. R3. $22.50

WRIGHT, S.F. *Deluge.* 1928. Cosmopolitan. 1st ed. VG. P1. $25.00

WRIGHT, S.F. *Elfwin, a Romance of Hist.* 1933. Harrap. G. P1. $20.00

WRIGHT, S.F. *Island of Capt Sparrow.* nd. Grosset Dunlap. dj. VG. P1. $30.00

WRIGHT, S.F. *Island of Capt Sparrow.* 1928. Cosmopolitan. 1st ed. dj. EX. R3. $50.00

WRIGHT, S.F. *Prelude in Prague.* 1935. London. 1st ed. G. R3. $25.00

WRIGHT, S.F. *Throne of Saturn.* 1949. Arkham House. 1st ed. dj. VG. P1. $30.00

WRIGHT, S.F. *World Below.* 1949. Shasta. Ltd ed. sgn. dj. EX. R3. $60.00

WRIGHT, S.F. *World Below.* 1949. Shasta. 1st ed. dj. EX. R3. $30.00

WRIGHT, S.F. *World Below.* 1949. Shasta. 1st ed. dj. VG. P1. $25.00

WRIGHT, Stephen. *Meditations in Gr.* 1983. Scribner. ARC. wrp. EX. C4. $30.00

WRIGHT, T.M. *Strange Seed.* 1978. Everest House. 1st ed. dj. EX. F5. $50.00

WRIGHT, T.M. *Woman Next Door.* 1981. Playboy Pr. 1st ed. wrp. EX. F5. $8.00

WRIGHT, Thomas. *Hist of King Arthur.* 1866. London. Smith. 1st ed? very scarce. C1. $49.50

WRIGHT, Thomas. *Life of Charles Dickens.* 1936. Scribner. Ils. 8vo. H3. $175.00

WRIGHT, Thomas. *Works of James Gillray the Caricaturist...* c 1873. Chatto Windus. rebacked. VG. $180.00

WRIGHT, W.H. *Blk Bear.* 1910. NY. Ils Kerfoot/author. 1st ed. 127 p. T5. $22.50

WRIGHT & CORBETT. *Pioneer Life in W PA.* 1940. Pittsburgh. Ils 1st ed. 251 p. VG. T5. $17.50

WRIGHT & FAYLE. *Hist of Lloyd's From Founding of Lloyd's Coffee House...* 1928. London. 1st ed. 475 p. T5. $95.00

WRIGHT & GREEN. *Native Son.* 1941. Harper. 1st Play ed. dj. H3. $175.00

WRIGHTSON, Patricia. *Down to Earth.* 1965. Harcourt Brace World. 1st ed. Lib bdg. xl. P1. $5.00

WRIGHTSON, Patricia. *Down to Earth.* 1965. Hutchinson. dj. xl. P1. $7.50

WU & MURPHY. *SF From China.* 1989. Praeger. 1st ed. dj. RS. P1. $18.95

WURST, Werner. *Exakta: Kleinbild-Fotografie.* 1956. Verlag. 1st ed? 415 p. VG. B10. $5.00

WURTZ, Gideon. *Foolish Dictionary.* 1904. Grosset. VG. B10. $3.50

WYETH, Betsy. *Stray.* 1979. NY. Ils Jamie Wyeth. sgns. dj. EX. $55.00

WYETH, Betsy. *Wyeth at Kuerners.* 1976. Boston. 1st ed. dj. VG. B3. $65.00

WYETH, Betsy. *Wyeths.* 1971. NY. 1st ed. dj. VG. B3. $47.50

WYETH, N.C. *Robinson Crusoe.* 1920. Cosmopolitan. 1st ed. 13 pls. VG. B3. $95.00

WYETH, N.C. *Wht Co.* 1922. Cosmopolitan. 1st ed. 14 pls. VG. B3. $65.00

WYLD, Lionel. *Erie Canal: 150 Years.* 1967. Rome, NY. 1st ed. 54 p. wrp. VG. B10. $5.00

WYLIE, Philip. *Corpses at Indian Stones.* 1943. Farrar Rinehart. 1st ed. G. P1. $20.00

WYLIE, Philip. *Corpses at Indian Stones.* 1943. Farrar Rinehart. 1st ed. xl. $7.50

WYLIE, Philip. *Corpses at Indian Stones.* 1943. NY. 1st ed. dj. VG. B3. $35.00

WYLIE, Philip. *Denizens of the Deep.* 1953. NY. 1st ed. dj. VG. B3. $25.00

WYLIE, Philip. *End of the Dream.* 1972. Doubleday. 1st ed. dj. EX. R3. $35.00

WYLIE, Philip. *Essay on Morals.* 1951. NY. sgn. dj. VG. B3. $25.00

WYLIE, Philip. *Generation of Vipers.* 1955. NY. 1st ed. dj. VG. $10.00

WYLIE, Philip. *Opus 21.* 1949. Rinehart. 1st ed. 375 p. G. B10. $5.00

WYLIE, Philip. *Tomorrow!* 1954. Rinehart. 1st ed. VG. P1. $20.00

WYLIE & BALMER. *When Worlds Collide.* 1939. Triangle. 2nd ed. dj. VG. P1. $15.00

WYND, Oswald. *Death, the Red Flower.* 1965. Cassell. 1st ed. dj. xl. P1. $6.00

WYND, Oswald. *Ginger Tree.* nd. Book Club. dj. EX. P1. $4.50

WYND, Oswald. *Ginger Tree.* 1977. Collins. 1st ed. dj. xl. P1. $5.00

WYND, Oswald. *Hawser Pirates.* 1970. Cassell. 1st ed. dj. xl. P1. $6.00

WYNDHAM, John. *Chocky.* nd. Book Club. 1st ed. dj. VG. P1. $4.50

WYNDHAM, John. *Day of the Triffids.* nd. Book Club. dj. VG. $4.50

WYNDHAM, John. *Jizzle.* 1954. London. Dennis Dobson. 1st ed. dj. VG. K2. $85.00

WYNDHAM, John. *Midwich Cuckoos.* 1969. Walker. dj. xl. P1. $7.50

WYNDHAM, John. *Seeds of Time.* 1956. London. 1st ed. dj. EX. $80.00

WYNNE, Anthony. *Gr Knife.* 1939. Caxton House. VG. P1. $12.50

WYNNE, N.B. *Agatha Christie Chronology.* 1976. Ace 10445. PB Orig. wrp. EX. T9. $20.00

YAGGY & HAINES. *Mus of Antiquity.* 1885. Alexandria, VA. 8vo. 944 p. VG. $18.00

YAPLE, G.R. *Perry at Erie.* 1913. Erie, PA. Ils. 39 p. wrp. G. T5. $25.00

YARBRO, C.Q. *Blood Games.* nd. Book Club. dj. VG. P1. $5.00

YARBRO, C.Q. *Blood Games.* 1979. St Martin. dj. EX. $25.00

YARBRO, C.Q. *False Dawn.* nd. Book Club. dj. EX. P1. $4.50

YARBRO, C.Q. *False Dawn.* 1978. Doubleday. 1st ed. dj. EX. P1. $17.50

YARBRO, C.Q. *Flame in Byzantium.* 1987. Tor Books. 1st ed. dj. EX. P1. $17.95

YARBRO, C.Q. *Floating Illusions.* 1986. Harper. 1st ed. dj. EX. F5. $18.00

YARBRO, C.Q. *Hotel Transylvania.* nd. Book Club. dj. EX. P1. $7.50

YARBRO, C.Q. *Hyacinths.* 1983. Doubleday. 1st ed. dj. VG. P1. $15.00

YARBRO, C.Q. *Locadio's Apprentice.* 1984. Harper Row. 1st ed. dj. EX. P1. $15.00

YARBRO, C.Q. *Palace.* nd. Book Club. dj. VG. P1. $4.00

YARBRO, C.Q. *Path of the Eclipse.* nd. Book Club. dj. VG. P1. $5.00

YARBRO, C.Q. *Signs & Portents.* 1984. Dream Pr. 1st ed. 1/250. sgn. M. R3. $50.00

YARBRO, C.Q. *4 Horses for Tishtry.* 1985. Harper Row. 1st ed. dj. EX. P1. $15.00

YARDLEY, J.H.R. *Before the Mayflower.* 1931. NY. Ils. 408 p. dj. VG. T5. $12.50

YARDLEY. *Am Blk Chamber.* 1931. London. 1st UK ed. VG. B3. $27.50

YARROW, C.H. *Quaker Experiences in Internat Conciliation.* 1978. New Haven. 1st ed. 8vo. 308 p. dj. V1. $14.00

YATES, Brock. *Dead in the Water.* 1975. Farrar Straus Giroux. 1st ed. dj. EX. F5. $13.00

YATES, Dornford. *Blind Corner.* 1927. Hodder Stoughton. 3rd ed. VG. P1. $20.00

YATES, Dornford. *Jonan & Co.* 1976. Ward Lock. dj. EX. P1. $12.00

YATES, Elizabeth. *Up the Golden Stair.* 1966. Dutton. 1st ed. 64 p. VG. B10. $5.00

YATES, G.W. *Body That Wasn't Uncle.* 1941. Triangle. 2nd ed. VG. P1. $10.00

YATES, R.F. *ABC of Television; or, Seeing by Radio.* 1929. NY. Henley. 1st ed. octavo. 210 p. VG. H3. $175.00

YATES, Richard. *William Styron's Lie Down in Darkness.* 1985. Ploughshares Books. Special Sgn ed. 1/50. sgns. M. H3. $150.00

YATES, Richard. *William Styron's Lie Down in Darkness.* 1985. Watertown, MA. ARC. presentation. wrp. EX. T9. $45.00

YEATS, Dornford. *Blind Corner.* 1927. Hodder Stoughton. 3rd ed. VG. P1. $20.00

YEATS, Dornford. *Jonan & Co.* 1976. Ward Lock. dj. VG. P1. $12.00

YEATS, Dornford. *She Fell Among Thieves.* 1949. Ward Lock. 13th print. dj. VG. P1. $15.00

YEATS, J.B. *Collected Plays.* 1971. Bobbs Merrill. 1st Am Collected ed. dj. EX. H3. $45.00

YEATS, J.B. *Plays for an Irish Theatre...* 1911. Shakespeare Head. 1st ed. 1st issue. H3. $200.00

YEATS, J.B. *2 Plays for Dancers.* 1919. Cuala Pr. 1st ed. 1/400. 38 p. VG. H3. $200.00

YEATS, J.B. *4 Plays for Dancers.* 1921. Macmillan. 1st ed. VG. H3. $150.00

YEATS, W.B. *Broadsides: Collection of Old & New Songs 1935.* 1935. Cuala Pr. Ils Jack Yeats/others. Ltd ed. sgns. H3. $750.00

YEATS, W.B. *Collected Works.* 1908. Shakespeare Head. 8 vols. octavo. G. H3. $350.00

YEATS, W.B. *Later Poems.* 1924. Macmillan. Ltd ed. 1/250. sgn. H3. $300.00

YEATS, W.B. *Plays & Controversies.* 1924. Macmillan. Ltd 1st ed. 1/250. sgn. H3. $250.00

YEATS, W.B. *Reveries Over Childhood & Youth/Trembling of the Veil.* 1927. Macmillan. New Revised ed. 477 p. dj. VG. B10. $35.00

YEATS, W.B. *Trembling of the Veil.* 1922. London. 1/1000. sgn. dj. VG. H3. $400.00

YEATS & JOHNSON. *Poetry & Ireland.* 1908. Cuala Pr. quarto. w/sgn poem. H3. $650.00

YELTSIN, Boris. *Against the Grain: An Autobiography.* 1990. 1st ed. EX. B3. $7.50

YEP, Laurence. *Child of the Owl.* 1977. Harper Row. dj. VG. P1. $15.00

YEP, Laurence. *Sea Demons.* 1977. Harper Row. 1st ed. dj. VG. P1. $12.50

YEREX, Cuthbert. *Christopher Brand: Looking Forward.* 1934. Wetzel. 1st ed. dj. EX. R3. $25.00

YODER, R.M. *Saturday Evening Post Carnival of Humor.* 1958. Prentice Hall. 2nd ed. dj. VG. P1. $20.00

YOLEN, Jane. *Dragon's Blood.* nd. NY. 1st ed. dj. M. C1. $12.00

YOLEN, Jane. *Heart's Blood.* 1984. NY. 1st ed. dj. M. C1. $11.50

YOLEN, Jane. *Magic 3 of Solatia.* 1974. Crowell. 1st ed. dj. EX. P1. $20.00

YOLEN, Jane. *Merlin's Book.* 1986. Ils Tom Canty. 1st ed. 1/200. sgns. dj. EX. C1. $44.50

YOLEN, Jane. *Shape Shifters.* 1978. Seabury. 1st ed. dj. EX. F5. $12.00

YOLEN, Jane. *Spaceships & Spells.* 1987. Harper Row. 1st ed. dj. EX. P1. $12.95

YOLEN, Jane. *Tales of Wonder.* 1983. 1st ed. dj. C1. $12.50

YOLEN, Jane. *Tales of Wonder.* 1983. Schocken. 1st ed. dj. P1. $14.95

YOLEN, Will. *Heroes of Our Times.* nd. (1968) Stackpole. 1st ed. 245 p. dj. EX. B10. $4.50

YORICK. *Sentimental Journey Through France & Italy.* 1927. London. Peter Davies. Ils Willoughby. Ltd ed. 8vo. 198 p. EX. R4. $40.00

YORK, Andrew. *Captivator.* 1974. Crime Club. 1st ed. dj. VG. P1. $10.00

YORK, Andrew. *Eliminator.* nd. Lippincott. 2nd ed. dj. EX. P1. $10.00

YORK, Andrew. *Fascinator.* 1975. Crime Club. 1st ed. dj. xl. P1. $5.00

YORK, Andrew. *Predator.* 1968. Lippincott. 1st ed. dj. EX. P1. $15.00

YORK, Andrew. *Talent for Disaster.* 1978. Crime Club. 1st ed. dj. VG. P1. $12.00

YORK, James. *Making Up.* 1905. NY. Witmark. 179 p. VG. J3. $12.00

YORK, Robert. *Swords of December.* 1978. Scribner. 1st ed. dj. EX. F5. $13.00

YORK, Scott. *Scott York Lecture.* 1975. Busby Magic. 52 p. NM. J3. $6.00

YORKE, Margaret. *Come-On.* 1978. Harper Row. 1st ed. dj. VG. P1. $15.00

YORKE, Margaret. *Speak for the Dead.* nd. Book Club. dj. VG. P1. $4.50

YOUNG, A.S. *Negro 1sts in Sports.* 1969. Chicago. Johnson Pub. 2nd print. dj. VG. B13. $30.00

YOUNG, Al. *As Me Now.* 1980. McGraw Hill. 1st ed. dj. EX. K2. $40.00

YOUNG, Al. *Song Turning Back Into Itself.* 1971. Holt Rinehart Winston. UP. wrp/proof dj. EX. scarce. B13. $100.00

YOUNG, Collier. *Todd Dossier.* 1969. Delacorte. 1st ed. dj. VG. P1. $60.00

YOUNG, Collier. *Todd Dossier.* 1969. Macmillan. 1st ed. dj. xl. P1. $20.00

YOUNG, E.R. *My Dogs in the Northland.* 1902. NY/Chicago/Toronto. 1st ed. G. $15.00

YOUNG, F.B. *Century of Boys' Stories.* nd. Hutchinson. VG. P1. $30.00

YOUNG, F.B. *My Brother Jonathan.* 1928. Heinemann. inscr. dj. H3. $100.00

YOUNG, F.B. *Portrait of Clare.* 1927. Heinemann. inscr. dj. H3. $100.00

YOUNG, G.O. *AK Yukon Trophies Won & Lost.* 1947. Huntington. 1st ed. dj. VG. B3. $150.00

YOUNG, Gordon. *Devil's Passport.* 1942. Triangle. dj. VG. P1. $20.00

YOUNG, J.H. *Toadstool Millionaires.* 1961. Princeton. 1st ed. 282 p. dj. VG. B3. $25.00

YOUNG, J.S. *Weather Tomorrow.* 1982. Random House. 1st ed. dj. EX. H3. $60.00

YOUNG, J.W. *Projective Geometry.* 1930. Open Court Pub. 1st ed. bl bdg. EX. $15.00

YOUNG, Marguerite. *Angel in the Forest: Fairy Tale of 2 Utopias.* 1945. NY. 1st ed. 313 p. dj. VG. T5. $17.50

YOUNG, P.B. *Undine.* 1964. Longman Canada. 1st ed. dj. xl. P1. $5.00

YOUNG, Perry. *Mistick Krewe.* 1931. Carnival Pr. 1st ed. octavo. 268 p. H3. $150.00

YOUNG, Perry. *Mistick Krewe.* 1931. New Orleans. 30 clr pls. VG. C2. $75.00

YOUNG, Stark. *So Red the Rose.* 1934. NY. 1st ed. dj. VG. $25.00

YOUNG & GOLDMAN. *Puma: Mysterious Am Cat.* 1946. WA. 1st ed. VG. B3. $40.00

YOUNG & GOLDMAN. *Wolves of N Am.* 1944. WA. 1st ed. dj. VG. B3. $67.50

YOUNG & JACKSON. *Clever Coyote.* 1951. WA. 1st ed. dj. VG. B3. $75.00

YOUNG & STIRLING. *Capt Swing: Romantic Play of 1830.* 1919. London. Collins. 1st ed. wrp. slipcase. H3. $40.00

YOUNGBLOOD & MOORE. *Devil To Pay.* 1961. Coward McCann. 1st ed. 320 p. dj. F2. $10.00

YOUNT, John. *Hardcastle.* 1980. Marek. 1st ed. sgn. M. $25.00

YOUNT, John. *Hardcastle.* 1980. NY. ARC. wrp. VG. T9. $65.00

YOURCENAR, Marguerite. *Abyss.* 1976. Farrar Straus. 1st Am ed. inscr. dj. EX. K2. $85.00

YUILL, P.B. *Hazell Plays Solomon.* 1975. Walker. 1st ed. dj. VG. P1. $12.50

YURICK, Sol. *Island Death.* 1975. Harper Row. 1st ed. dj. EX. F5. $13.00

YUTANG, Lin. *Hist of the Pr & Public Opinion in China.* 1936. Shanghai. inscr. dj. H3. $200.00

Z

ZAFFO, G.J. *Big Book of Real Fire Engines.* 1950. Grosset Dunlap. sm folio. 24 p. VG. $22.00

ZAGAT, A.L. *7 Out of Time.* 1949. Fantasy. 1st ed. dj. VG. P1. $30.00

ZAHARIAS, Babe. *This Life I've Led.* 1955. NY. 1st ed. dj. VG. B3. $20.00

ZAHARIAS, Babe. *This Life I've Led.* 1955. NY. 1st ed. presentation. dj. VG. B3. $45.00

ZAIDENBERG, Arthur. *Studies of Figure Drawing.* 1950. Garden City. sm folio. EX. $25.00

ZAKI, H.M. *Phoenix Renewed.* 1988. Starmont. 1st ed. wrp. M. R3. $9.95

ZANE, J.M. *Grandeur That Was Rome.* 1927. Chicago. Ltd ed. 1/300. boxed. B3. $25.00

ZANTO, Lewis. *Treasury of Magic From Out of the Past.* 1969. Waverly, OH. Zanto. 1st ed. sgn. 36 p. NM. J3. $4.00

ZANUCK, Darryl. *Tunis Expedition.* 1943. 2nd print. VG. C1. $7.50

ZARA, Louis. *Blessed Is the Man.* 1935. Bobbs Merrill. presentation. dj. H3. $50.00

ZARA, Louis. *Give Us This Day.* 1936. Bobbs Merrill. inscr. gilt blk bdg. dj. H3. $50.00

ZAREK, Otto. *Quakers.* 1945. London. Religious Book Club. 12mo. 216 p. dj. VG. V1. $12.00

ZARIN, Cynthia. *Swordfish Tooth: Poems.* 1989. Knopf. UP. wrp. EX. C4. $25.00

ZEBROWSKI, George. *Macrolife.* 1979. Harper Row. Ltd ed. 1/250. sgn. M. R3. $30.00

ZEBROWSKI, George. *Macrolife.* 1979. Harper Row. 1st ed. dj. EX. P1. $15.00

ZEBROWSKI, George. *Sunspacer.* 1978. Harper Row. 1st ed. dj. EX. P1. $15.00

ZEIGFRIED, Karl. *No Way Back.* 1968. Arcadia. dj. xl. P1. $5.00

ZELAZNY, Roger. *Blood of Amber.* 1986. Arbor House. 1st ed. dj. EX. P1. $14.95

ZELAZNY, Roger. *Changeling.* nd. Book Club. dj. EX. P1. $4.50

ZELAZNY, Roger. *Chronicles of Amber.* nd. Book Club. dj. VG. P1. $10.00

ZELAZNY, Roger. *Courts of Chaos.* 1978. Doubleday. 1st ed. dj. EX. P1. $35.00

ZELAZNY, Roger. *Courts of Chaos.* 1980. Faber. 1st ed. dj. VG. P1. $30.00

ZELAZNY, Roger. *Creatures of Light & Darkness.* 1969. Doubleday. 1st ed. dj. xl. P1. $10.00

ZELAZNY, Roger. *Damnation Alley.* 1969. Putnam. 1st ed. dj. EX. R3. $50.00

ZELAZNY, Roger. *Doorways in the Sand.* nd. Book Club. dj. VG. P1. $4.50

ZELAZNY, Roger. *Doorways in the Sand.* 1976. Harper. 1st ed. dj. EX. R3. $25.00

ZELAZNY, Roger. *Doorways in the Sand.* 1977. WH Allen. 1st ed. dj. EX. P1. $20.00

ZELAZNY, Roger. *Eye of Cat.* 1982. Timescape. 1st ed. dj. VG. P1. $20.00

ZELAZNY, Roger. *Hand of Oberon.* 1976. Doubleday. 1st ed. dj. EX. P1. $40.00

ZELAZNY, Roger. *Hand of Oberon.* 1978. Faber. 1st ed. dj. VG. P1. $45.00

ZELAZNY, Roger. *Ils Roger Zelazny.* 1978. Baronet. 1st ed. sgn. no dj issued. EX. P1. $60.00

ZELAZNY, Roger. *Jack of Shadows.* nd. Book Club. dj. VG. P1. $6.00

ZELAZNY, Roger. *Lord of Light.* nd. Book Club. dj. VG. P1. $7.50

ZELAZNY, Roger. *Madwand.* nd. Book Club. dj. EX. P1. $4.50

ZELAZNY, Roger. *Madwand.* 1981. Phantasia. 1st ed. 1/750. sgn. M. R3. $40.00

ZELAZNY, Roger. *Road Marks.* 1979. Del Rey. 1st ed. dj. EX. P1. $25.00

ZELAZNY, Roger. *Sign of Chaos.* 1987. Arbor House. 1st ed. dj. EX. P1. $15.95

ZELAZNY, Roger. *To Die in Italbar.* nd. Book Club. dj. VG. P1. $5.00

ZELAZNY, Roger. *Unicorn Variations.* nd. Book Club. dj. EX. P1. $5.00

ZELAZNY, Roger. *9 Princes in Amber.* 1970. Doubleday. 1st ed. dj. xl. VG. R3. $125.00

ZELMAN, Anita. *Right Moves.* 1988. St Martin. 1st ed. dj. EX. F5. $12.00

ZEMPEL & VERKLER. *1st Eds: Guide to Identifications.* 1985. Spoon River. dj. EX. $20.00

ZETFORD, Tully; see Bulmer, Kenneth.

ZEVI & KAUFFMAN. *Casa Sulla Cascata di FL Wright.* 1965. Milan. L'Architeturra. 2nd ed. Eng/Italian text. 4to. 80 p. dj. EX. R4. $75.00

ZIEMANN, H.H. *Accident.* 1979. St Martin. 1st ed. dj. EX. P1. $15.00

ZIEROLD, Norman. *3 Sisters in Blk.* 1968. Little Brn. 1st ed. 240 p. dj. VG. B10. $4.25

ZILG. *Dupont: Behind the Nylon Curtain.* 1974. NY. 1st ed. dj. VG. B3. $22.50

ZIMMER, J.T. *Catalog of Edward E Ayer Ornithological Lib.* 1926. Chicago. Field Mus Nat Hist. 2 vols. wrp. VG. T3. $65.00

ZIMMERMAN, Arthur. *Francisco de Toledo, 5th Viceroy of Peru 1569-1581.* 1938. Caxton. 1st ed. 307 p. dj. F2. $25.00

ZIMMERMAN, Dick. *Creative Magic.* 1973. Los Angeles. 1st ed. 11 p. SftCvr. NM. J3. $3.00

ZIMMERMANN. *Solitude Considered With Respect to Its Influence...* 1796. Albany. sm 8vo. 280 p. VG. G4. $39.00

ZINDEL, Paul. *When a Darkness Falls.* 1984. Bantam. dj. VG. P1. $12.50

ZOCHERT, Donald. *Man of Glass.* 1981. Holt Rinehart Winston. 1st ed. dj. VG. P1. $12.50

ZOLOTOW, Maurice. *Great Balsamo.* 1946. Random House. 1st print. 431 p. fair. J3. $4.00

ZUCKER, A.E. *Chinese Theater.* 1925. Little Brn. 1/750. 8vo. 234 p. G. V1. $125.00

ZUCKERLANDL. *Atlas & Epitome of Operative Surgery.* 1902. Phil. Saunders. Revised 2nd ed. 40 pls. 410 p. VG. $65.00

ZUCKMAYER, Carl. *Carnival Confession.* 1961. Methuen. 1st ed. dj. VG. P1. $20.00

ZUMBRO, Ralph. *Tank Sergeant.* 1986. Presidio Pr. Ils 1st ed. 182 p. dj. VG. T5. $12.50

ZVER, D.E. *Book 1 of the Dark Side Chronicles of Sabastian N Krypt.* 1990. Sorceries Ltd. 1st ed. M. J3. $15.00

ZWEIG, Stephan. *Conqueror of the Seas: Story of Magellan.* 1938. Literary Guild. 335 p. F2. $10.00

ZWINGER & TEALE. *Conscious Stillness: 2 Naturalists on Thoreaus Rivers.* 1982. Harper. 1st ed. 243 p. dj. EX. B10. $10.00

ZYKE, Cizia. *Oro.* 1985. St Martin. 1st Am ed. 281 p. dj. F2. $10.00

BOOKBUYERS

In this section of the book we have listed buyers of books and related material. When you correspond with these dealers, be sure to enclose a self-addressed stamped envelope if you want a reply. Do not send lists of books for appraisal. If you wish to sell your books, quote the price you want or send a list and ask if there are any on the list they might be interested in and the price they would be willing to pay. If you want the list back, be sure to send a S.A.S.E. large enough for the listing to be returned. When you list your books, do so by author, full title, publisher and place, date, edition, and condition, noting any defects on cover or contents.

Advance Review Copies
Paperbacks.
The American Dust Company
47 Park Court
Staten Island, NY 10301

Alcholics Anonymous
1939-1954.
Paul Melzer Fine Books
12 E Vine St.
Redlands, CA 92373
714-792-7299

The Book Baron
1236 S Magnolia Ave.
Anaheim, CA 92804

Americana
Art Source International
1237 Pearl St.
Boulder, CO 80302
303-444-4080

Bowie & Weatherford, Inc.
314 First Ave. S
Seattle, WA 98104
206-624-4100

The Bookseller Inc.
521 W Exchange St.
Akron, OH 44302
216-762-3101

Gene Vinik Books
2213 E Copper St.
Tucson, AZ 85719

Jim Hodgson Books
908 S Manlius St.
Fayetteville, NY 13066

Terry Harper, Bookseller
P.O. Box 37
Bristol, VT 05443-0037

Fritz T. Brown Books
5 Claremont Pl.
Cranford, NJ 07016
908-276-4753

The Book Inn
6401-D University
Lubbock, TX 79413
806-793-0342

18th & 19th C.
Gordon Totty
Scarce Paper Americana
347 Shady Lake Pkwy.
Baton Rouge, LA 701810
504-766-8625

Renaissance to reconstruction.
Sandlin's Books & Bindery
Jeff Sandlin, Bookbinder
70 W Lincolnway
Valparaiso, IN 46383-5522

Southern.
The Captain's Bookshelf, Inc.
P.O. Box 2258
Asheville, NC 28802-2258
704-253-6631

Antiquarian
Robert Mueller Rare Books
8124 W 26th St.
N Riverside, IL 60546

Printed before 1800.
Gordon Totty
Scarce Paper Americana
347 Shady Lake Pkwy
Baton Rouge, LA 70810
504-766-8625

Fine & hard-to-find books.
Arnold's of Michigan
218 S Water St.
Marine City, MI 48039
313-765-1350

The Book Baron
1236 S Magnolia Ave.
Anaheim, CA 92804

Bowie & Weatherford, Inc.
314 First Ave. S
Seattle, WA 98104
206-624-4100

Terry Harper, Bookseller
P.O. Box 37
Bristol, VT 05443-0037

Appraisals
Lee & Mike Temares
50 Heights Rd.
Plandome, NY 11030

Archaelogy
Flo Silver Books
8442 Oakwood Ct. N
Indianapolis, IN 46260

Architecture
Cover to Cover
P.O. Box 687
Chapel Hill, NC 27514

Gene Vinik Books
2213 E Copper St.
Tucson, AZ 85719

Also related materials.
Robert Schweitzer
3661 Waldenwood Dr.
Ann Arbor, MI 48105
313-668-0298

Art
AL-PAC
HC 1, Box 7120
Yucca Valley, CA 92284-9489

Cary Loren
Book Beat
26010 Greenfield Rd.
Oak Park, MI 48237

The Captain's Bookshelf, Inc.
P.O. Box 2258
Asheville, NC 28802-2258
704-253-6631

Lee & Mike Temares
50 Heights Rd.
Plandome, NY 11030

Significant Books
3053 Madison Rd.
Cincinnati, OH 45209

Gene Vinik Books
2213 E Copper St.
Tucson, AZ 85719

Heritage Book Shop, Inc.
8540 Melrose Ave.
Los Angeles, CA 90069

Fine & applied.
L. Clarice Davis
P.O. Box 56054
Sherman Oaks, CA 91413-1054
818-878-1322

Art Deco
Moderne Books
111 N 3rd St.
Phil., PA 19106

Arthurian
Camelot Books, Charles E. Wyatt
P.O. Box 2883
Vista, CA 92083
619-940-9472

Atlases
Art Source International
1237 Pearl St.
Boulder, CO 80302

Before 1870.
Gordon Totty
Scarce Paper Americana
347 Shady Lake Pkwy.
Baton Rouge, LA 70810
504-766-8625

Autographs
Paul Melzer Fine Books
12E Vine St.
Redlands, CA 92373
714-792-7299

Heritage Book Shop, Inc.
8540 Melrose Ave.
Los Angeles, CA 90069
213-659-3674

Michael Gerlicher
1375 Rest Point Rd.
Orono, MN 55364

Automobilia
Hank Loescher
52 Melrose Ave.
Bridgeport, CT 06605

Aviation
Cover to Cover
P.O. Box 687
Chapel Hill, NC 27514

Hank Loescher
52 Melrose Ave.
Bridgeport, CT 06605

The Bookseller Inc.
521 W Exchange St.
Akron, OH 44302
216-762-3101

Baseball
Brasser's
8701 Seminole Blvd.
Seminole, FL 34642

Big Little Books
Jay's House of Collectibles
75 Pkwy. Dr.
Syosset, NY 11791

Biographies
Gene Vinik Books
2213 E Copper St.
Tucson, AZ 85719

Black Americana
Mason's Rare & Used Books
115 S Main St.
Chambersburg, PA 17701

Black Hills
Allen J. Petersen, Books
809-20 St. S
Fargo, ND 58103

Book Search Service
Avonlea Books
P.O. Box 74, Main Station
White Plains, NY 10602
914-946-5923

Fritz T. Brown Books
5 Claremont Pl.
Cranford, NJ 07016
908-276-4753

Passaic Book Center
594 Main Ave.
Passaic, NJ 07055

Books About Books
Bowie & Weatherford, Inc.
314 First Ave. S
Seattle, WA 98104
206-624-4100

Books With Maps
Art Source International
1237 Pearl St.
Boulder, CO 80302

Bottles
Homebiz Books & More
2919 Mistwood Forest Dr.
Chester, VA 23831-7043

Brazil
The Midnight Bookman
1908 Seagull Dr.
Clearwater, FL 34624

British History
Sandlin's Books & Bindery
Jeff Sandlin, Bookbinder
70 W Lincolnway
Valparaiso, IN 46383-5522

California
Paul Melzer Fine Books
12 E Vine St.
Redlands, CA 92373
714-792-7299

Carnivals & Ephemera
Betty Schmid
485 Sleepy Hollow Rd.
Pittsburgh, PA 15228

Cartoon Art
Jay's House of Collectibles
75 Pkwy. Dr.
Syosset, NY 11791

Catalogs

Architecture related.
Robert Schweitzer
3661 Waldenwood Dr.
Ann Arbor, MI 48105
313-668-0298

Cave Books

D. Snyder
3079 Main St.
Neffs, PA 18065

Celtic

Camelot Books; Charles E. Wyatt
P.O. 2883
Vista, CA 92083
619-940-9472

Central America

Flo Silver Books
8442 Oakwood Ct. N
Indianapolis, IN 46260

Marc Chagall

Paul Melzer Fine Books
12E Vine St.
Redlands, CA 92373
714-792-7299

Children's Illustrated

Noreen Abbot Books
2666 44th Ave.
San Francisco, CA 94116
415-664-9464

Children's Series

Bob Dittmeier
Science Fiction Dept.
25 William St.
Farmingdale, NY 11735

Lee & Mike Temares
50 Heights Rd.
Plandome, NY 11030

China

J.G. Wetterling
P.O. Box 965
Los Molinos, CA 96055

Agatha Christie

Dale Weber Books
5740 Livernois
Rochester, MI 48306

Sir W.S. Churchill

Dale Weber Books
5740 Livernois
Rochester, MI 48306

Cinema & Films

Murphy's Books
3113 Bunker Hill Rd.
Marietta, GA 30062-5421

Circus & Ephemera

Betty Schmid
485 Sleepy Hollow Rd.
Pittsburgh, PA 15228

Civil War

Brasser's
8701 Seminole Blvd.
Seminole, FL 34642

Karl M. Armens
740 Juniper Dr.
Iowa City, IA 52245

Jim Hodgson Books
908 S Manlius St.
Fayetteville, NY 13066

K.C. Owings
P.O. Box 19
N Abington, MA 02351

Elder's Book Store
2115 Elliston Pl.
Nashville, TN 37203

Also ephemera before 1900.
Gordon Totty
Scarce Paper Americana
347 Shady Lake Pkwy.
Baton Rouge, LA 70810
504-766-8625

Mason's Rare & Used Books
115 S Main St.
Chambersburg, PA 17701

Color Plate Books

Art Source International
1237 Pearl St.
Boulder, CO 80302

Bowie & Weatherford, Inc.
314 First Ave. S
Seattle, WA 98104
206-624-4100

Comics

Passaic Book Center
594 Main Ave.
Passaic, NJ 07055

Decorative Arts

Gene Vinik Books
2213 E Copper St.
Tucson, AZ 85719

Moderne Books
111 N 3rd St.
Phil., PA 19106

Detective

First editions.
Karl M. Armens
740 Juniper Dr.
Iowa City, IA 52245

Disney

Jay's House of Collectibles
75 Pkwy. Dr.
Syosset, NY 11791

Entertainment

Murphy's Books
3113 Bunker Hill Rd.
Marietta, GA 30062-5421

Exhibition Catalogs

L. Clarice Davis
P.O. Box 56054
Sherman Oaks, CA 91413-1054
818-787-1322

Exploration

Terry Harper, Bookseller
P.O. Box 37
Bristol, VT 05443-0037

Flo Silver Books
8442 Oakwood Ct. N
Indianapolis, IN 46260

Heritage Book Shop, Inc.
8540 Melrose Ave.
Los Angeles, CA 90069
213-659-3675

Paul Melzer Fine Books
12 E Vine St.
Redlands, CA 92373
714-792-7299

Western.
Art Source International
1237 Pearl St.
Boulder, CO 80302
303-444-4080

Fantasy

The Book Baron
1236 S Magnolia Ave.
Anaheim, CA 92804

Camelot Books; Charles E. Wyatt
P.O. Box 2883
Vista, CA 92083
619-940-9472

Farming & Farm Toys

Henry Lindeman
4769 Bavarian Dr.
Jackson, MI 49201

First editions.
Karl M. Armens
740 Juniper Dr.
Iowa City, IA 52245

Fiction

19th & 20th C American.
Mason's Rare & Used Books
115 S Main St.
Chambersburg, PA 17701

Fine Bindings

Terry Harper, Bookseller
P.O. Box 37
Bristol, VT 05443-0037

Paul Melzer Fine Books
12E Vine St.
Redlands, CA 92373
714-792-7299

Firearms

Melvin Marcher, Bookseller
6204 N Vermont
Oklahoma City, OK 73112

First Editions

Between the Covers
132 Kings Hwy. East
Haddonfield, NJ 08033

Modern or signed.
AL-PAC
HC 1, Box 7120
Yucca Valley, CA 92284-9489

The Book Baron
1236 S Magnolia Ave.
Anaheim, CA 92804

Heritage Book Shop, Inc.
8540 Melrose Ave.
Los Angeles, CA 90069
213-659-3674

Karl M. Armens
740 Juniper Dr.
Iowa City, IA 52245

Robert Mueller Rare Books
8124 W 26th St.
N Riverside, IL 60546

Yesterday's Books
25222 Greenfield
Oak Park, MI 48237

Modern.
Ken Lopez, Bookseller
51 Huntington Rd.
Hadley, MA 01035

Harrison Fisher
Parnassus Books
218 N 9th St.
Boise, ID 83702

Fishing
Jim Hodgson Books
908 S Manlius St.
Fayetteville, NY 13066

Melvin Marcher, Bookseller
6204 N Vermont
Oklahoma City, OK 73112

Florida
Brasser's
8701 Seminole Blvd.
Seminole, FL 34642

Football
Brasser's
8701 Seminole Blvd.
Seminole, FL 34642

Freemasonry
Mason's Rare & Used Books
115 S Main St.
Chambersburg, PA 17701

Gambling & Gaming
Gambler's Book Shop
630 S Eleventh St.
Las Vegas, NV 89101
800-634-6243

Games
Card or board.
Bill Sachen
927 Grand Ave.
Waukegan, IL 60085

Gardening
The Captain's Bookshelf, Inc.
P.O. Box 2258
Asheville, NC 28802-2258
704-253-6631

Genealogy & Local History
Elder's Book Store
2115 Elliston Pl.
Nashville, TN 37203

Fritz T. Brown Books
5 Claremont Pl.
Cranford, NJ 07016
908-276-4753

General Out-of-Print
The Abstract
4850 W Mooresville Rd.
Indianapolis, IN 46241

Bicentennial Book Shop
820 S Westnedge Ave.
Kalamazoo, MI 49008
616-345-5987

Buck Creek Books, Ltd.
838 Main St.
Lafayette, IN 47901

Passaic Book Center
594 Main Ave.
Passaic, NJ 07055

Significant Books
3053 Madison Rd.
Cincinnati, OH 45209

The Book Baron
1236 S Magnolia Ave.
Anaheim, CA 92804

The Bookseller Inc.
521 W Exchange St.
Akron, OH 44302
216-762-3101

Tuttle Antiquarian Books, Inc.
P.O. Box 541
26 S Main St.
Rutland, VT 05701

Grave Matters
P.O. Box 32192-08
Cincinnati, OH 45232

Geology
Art Source International
1237 Pearl St.
Boulder, CO 80302
303-444-4080

Golf
Brasser's
8701 Seminole Blvd.
Seminole, FL 34642

David Goodis
The American Dust Company
47 Park Court
Staten Island, NY 10301

Heritage Press
Lee & Mike Temares
50 Heights Rd.
Plandome, NY 11030

Hippie
Black Ace Books
1658 Griffith Park Blvd.
Los Angeles, CA 90026
213-661-5052

History
Local & regional.
Significant Books
3053 Madison Rd.
Cincinnati, OH 45209

Camelot Books, Charles E. Wyatt
P.O. Box 2883
Vista, CA 92083
619-940-9472

British.
Sandlin's Books & Bindery
Jeff Sandlin, Bookbinder
70 W Lincolnway
Valparaiso, IN 46383-5522

Horticulture
The Abstract
4850 W Mooresville Rd.
Indianapolis, IN 46241

Horror
The Book Baron
1236 S Magnolia Ave.
Anaheim, CA 92804

Pandora's Books Ltd.
P.O. Box BB-54
Neche, ND 58265

Yesterday's Books
25222 Greenfield
Oak Park, MI 48237

House Plan
Robert Schweitzer
3661 Waldenwood Dr.
Ann Arbor, MI 48105
313-668-0298

L. Ron Hubbard
AL-PAC
HC 1, Box 7120
Yucca Valley, CA 92284-9489

Humanities
Reprint editions.
Dover Publications
Dept. A 214
E Second St.
Mineola, NY 11501

Hunting
Allen J. Petersen, Books
809-20 St. S
Fargo, ND 58103

Melvin Marcher, Bookseller
6204 N Vermont
Oklahoma City, OK 73112

Jim Hodgson Books
908 S Manlius St.
Fayetteville, NY 13066

Idaho
Parnassus Books
218 N 9th St.
Boise, ID 83702

Illustrated
Bowie & Weatherford, Inc.
314 First Ave. S
Seattle, WA 98104

Noreen Abbot Books
2666 44th Ave.
San Francisco, CA 94116
415-664-9464

Juvenile.
Cover to Cover
P.O. Box 687
Chapel Hill, NC 27514

Indian Wars
K.C. Owings
P.O. Box 19
N Abington, MA 02351

Indians
Plains, Black Hills, etc.
Allen J. Petersen, Books
809-20 St. S
Fargo, ND 58103

Flo Silver Books
8442 Oakwood Ct. N
Indianapolis, IN 46260

Iowa
Karl M. Armens
740 Juniper Dr.
Iowa City, IA 52245

James Joyce
Paul Melzer Fine Books
12 E Vine St.
Redlands, CA 92373
714-792-7299

John Deere
Henry Lindeman
4769 Bavarian Dr.
Jackson, MI 49201

Juvenile Series
Lee & Mike Temares
50 Heights Rd.
Plandome, NY 11030

Stephen King
Dale Weber Books
Amalienstrasse #81
D8000 Munich 40
Germany
#011 49 89 280 2060

Latin Americana
Flo Silver Books
8442 Oakwood Ct. N
Indianapolis, IN 46260

Limited Editions Club
Lee & Mike Temares
50 Heights Rd.
Plandome, NY 11030

Literature
Mason's Rare & Used Books
115 S Main St.
Chambersburg, PA 17701

The Captain's Bookshelf, Inc.
P.O. Box 2258
Asheville, NC 22802-2258
704-253-6631

African-American.
Between the Covers
132 Kings Hwy. East
Haddonfield, NJ 08033

First editions.
Karl M. Armens
740 Juniper Dr.
Iowa City, IA 52245

Classical.
Sandlin's Books & Bindery
Jeff Sandlin, Bookbinder
70 W Lincolnway
Valparaiso, IN 46383-5522

Paperbound.
Black Ace Books
1658 Griffith Park Blvd.
Los Angeles, CA 90026
213-661-5052

Southern.
Elder's Book Store
2115 Elliston Pl.
Nashville, TN 37203

Modern.
Yesterday's Books
25222 Greenfield
Oak Park, MI 48237

Ken Lopez, Bookseller
51 Huntington Rd.
Hadley, MA 01035

Magazines
Passaic Book Center
594 Main Ave.
Passaic, NJ 07055

Robert A. Madle
4406 Bestor Dr.
Rockville, MD 20853

Mystery only.
Grave Matters
P.O. Box 32192-08
Cincinnati, OH 45232

Relating to decorative arts.
Moderne Books
111 N 3rd St.
Phil., PA 19106

Manuscripts
Heritage Book Shop, Inc.
8540 Melrose Ave.
Los Angeles, CA 90069
213-659-3674

Maps
Bowie & Weatherford, Inc.
314 First Ave. S
Seattle, WA 98104
206-624-4100

Art Source International
1237 Pearl St.
Boulder, CO 80302
303-444-4080

The Bookseller Inc.
521 W Exchange St.
Akron, OH 44302
216-762-3101

Pre-1900 Florida.
Brasser's
8701 Seminole Blvd.
Seminole, FL 34642

Mathematics
Significant Books
3053 Madison Rd.
Cincinnati, OH 45209

Medieval
Camelot Books; Charles E. Wyatt
P.O. Box 2883
Vista, CA 92083
619-940-9472

Metaphysics
AL-PAC
HC 1, Box 7120
Yucca Valley, CA 92284-9489

Mexico
Flo Silver Books
8442 Oakwood Ct. N
Indianapolis, IN 46260

Hank Loescher
52 Melrose Ave.
Bridgeport, CT 06605

The Bookseller Inc.
521 W Exchange St.
Akron, OH 44302
216-762-3101

Significant Books
3053 Madison Rd.
Cincinnati, OH 45209

Brasser's
8701 Seminole Blvd.
Seminole, FL 34642

Before 1900.
Gordon Totty
Scarce Paper Americana
347 Shady Lake Pkwy.
Baton Rouge, LA 70810
504-766-8625

Miscellaneous
Bridgman Books
906 Roosevelt Ave.
Rome, NY 13440

Movies
Murphy's Books
3113 Bunker Hill Rd.
Marietta, GA 30062-5421

Mystery
Bob Dittmeier
Science Fiction Dept.
25 William St.
Farmingdale, NY 11735

Karl M. Armens
740 Juniper Dr.
Iowa City, IA 52245

Pandora's Books Ltd.
P.O. Box BB-54
Neche, ND 48265

Yesterday's Books
25222 Greenfield
Oak Park, MI 48237

Natural History
Melvin Marcher, Bookseller
6204 N Vermont
Oklahoma City, OK 73112

The Abstract
4850 W Mooresville Rd.
Indianapolis, IN 46241

Non-Fiction
Pre-1950.
Brasser's
8701 Seminole Blvd.
Seminole, FL 34642

North Dakota
Allen J. Petersen, Books
809-20 St. S
Fargo, ND 58103

Novels
Lane Books
Arundel
Peaks Island, ME 04108

Occult
AL-PAC
HC 1, Box 7120
Yucca Valley, CA 92284-9489

Ohio
The Bookseller Inc.
521 W Exchange St.
Akron, OH 44302
216-762-3101

aperbacks

he American Dust Company
7 Park Court
taten Island, NY 10301

ob Scherl
.O. Box 7124
an Nuys, CA 91409
18-780-2072

arby Curtis
29 Broadway
ackson, OH 45640

or Collectors Only
028B Ford Pkwy.
ept. 136
t. Paul, MN 55116

Michael Gerlicher
375 Rest Point Rd.
rono, MN 55364

andora's Books Ltd.
.O. Box BB-54
eche, ND 58265

ime.
d LeBlanc
7 School St.
all River, MA 02720

intage.
uck Creek Books, Ltd.
38 Main St.
afayette, IN 47901

intage, beat, hippie, & counterculture.
ack Ace Books
558 Griffith Park Blvd.
os Angeles, CA 90026
13-661-5052

intage.
rave Matters
O. Box 32192-08
incinnati, OH 45232

erforming Arts

owie & Weatherford, Inc.
14 First Ave. S
eattle, WA 98104
06-624-4100

hotography

gnificant Books
053 Madison Rd.
incinnati, OH 45209

ary Loren
ook Beat
5010 Greenfield Rd.
ak Park, MI 48237

he Captain's Bookshelf, Inc.
O. Box 2258
sheville, NC 28802-2258
04-253-6631

laying Cards

ll Sachen
27 Grand Ave.
aukegan, IL 60085

dgar Allan Poe

ale Weber Books
740 Livernois
ochester, MI 48306

Pre-Columbian Art

Flo Silver Books
8442 Oakwood Ct. N
Indianapolis, IN 46260

Press Books

Heritage Book Shop, Inc.
8540 Melrose Ave.
Los Angeles, CA 90069
213-659-3674

Prints

Art Source International
1237 Pearl St.
Boulder, CO 80302
303-444-4080

Private Presses

American.
Richard Blacher
209 Plymouth Colony, Alps Rd.
Branford, CT 06405

Pulps

Science fiction & fantasy before 1945.
Robert A. Madle
4406 Bestor Dr.
Rockville, MD 20853

Quaker

Vintage Books
117 Concord St.
Framingham, MA 01701

Railroading

Mason's Rare & Used Books
115 S Main St.
Chambersburg, PA 17701

Rare & Unusual Books

Art Source International
1237 Pearl St.
Boulder, CO 80302
303-444-4080

Heritage Book Shop, Inc.
8540 Melrose Ave.
Los Angeles, CA 90069
213-659-3674

Paul Melzer Fine Books
12 E Vine St.
Redlands, CA 92373
714-792-7299

Terry Harper, Bookseller
P.O. Box 37
Bristol, VT 05443-0037

Reprint editions.
Dover Publications
Dept. A 214
E Second St.
Mineola, NY 11501

Revolutionary War

K.C. Owings
P.O. Box 19
N Abington, MA 02351

Roycroft Press

Richard Blacher
209 Plymouth Colony, Alps Rd.
Branford, CT 06405

Dale Weber Books
Amalienstrasse #81
D8000 Munich 40
Germany
#011 49 89 280 2060

Tim Ward
3232 #8 Denver Ave.
Merced, CA 95348

Scholarly Books

Reprint editions.
Dover Publications
Dept. A 214
E Second St.
Mineola, NY 11501

Sciences

Cover to Cover
P.O. Box 687
Chapel Hill, NC 27514

Reprint editions.
Dover Publications
Dept. A 214
E Second St.
Mineola, NY 11501

Significant Books
3053 Madison Rd.
Cincinnati, OH 45209

Science Fiction

AL-PAC
HC 1, Box 7120
Yucca Valley, CA 92284-9489

Bob Dittmeier
Science Fiction Dept.
25 William St.
Farmingdale, NY 11735

Karl M. Armens
740 Juniper Dr.
Iowa City, IA 52245

Hank Loescher
52 Melrose Ave.
Bridgeport, CT 06605

Pandora's Books Ltd.
P.O. Box BB–54
Neche, ND 58265

Robert A. Madle
4406 Bestor Dr.
Rockville, MD 20853

Yesterday's Books
25222 Greenfield
Oak Park, MI 48237

Set Editions

Bowie & Weatherford, Inc.
314 First Ave. S
Seattle, WA 98104
206-624-4100

Ships

Hank Loescher
52 Melrose Ct.
Bridgeport, CT 06605

Show Business

Bob Dittmeier
Science Fiction Dept.
25 William St.
Farmingdale, NY 11735

South America

Flo Silver Books
8442 Oakwood Ct. N
Indianapolis, IN 46260

Speciality Publishers
Arkham House, Gnome Press, Fantasy Press, etc.
Robert A. Madle
4406 Bestor Dr.
Rockville, MD 20853

Statue of Liberty
Mike Brooks
7335 Skyline
Oakland, CA 94611

Technology
Cover to Cover
P.O. Box 687
Chapel Hill, NC 27514

Significant Books
3053 Madison Rd.
Cincinnati, OH 45209

Tennessee History
Elder's Book Store
2115 Elliston Pl.
Nashville, TN 37203

Tennis
Brasser's
8701 Seminole Blvd.
Seminole, FL 34642

Jim Thompson
The American Dust Company
47 Park Court
Staten Island, NY 10301

Trades & Crafts
19th C.
Cover to Cover
P.O. Box 687
Chapel Hill, NC 27514

Travel
Terry Harper, Bookseller
P.O. Box 37
Bristol, VT 05443-0037

Jim Hodgson Books
908 S Manlius St.
Fayetteville, NY 13066

Flo Silver Books
8442 Oakwood Ct. N
Indianapolis, IN 46260

Heritage Book Shop, Inc.
8540 Melrose Ave.
Los Angeles, CA 90069
213-659-3675

With discoveries before 1900.
Gordon Totty
Scarce Paper Americana
347 Shady Lake Pkwy.
Baton Rouge, LA 70810
504-766-8625

UFO
AL-PAC
HC 1, Box 7120
Yucca Valley, CA 92284-9489

Vargas
Parnassus Books
218 N 9th St.
Boise, ID 83702

Voyages
Jim Hodgson Books
908 S Manlius St.
Fayetteville, NY 13066

Terry Harper, Bookseller
P.O. Box 37
Bristol, VT 05443-0037

Heritage Book Shop, Inc.
8540 Melrose Ave.
Los Angeles, CA 90069
213-659-3675

Western Americana
Bowie & Weatherford, Inc.
314 First Ave. S
Seattle, WA 98104
206-624-4100

K.C. Owings
P.O. Box 19
N Abington, MA 02351

J.G. Wetterling
P.O. Box 965
Los Molinos, CA 96055

Terry Harper, Bookseller
P.O. Box 37
Bristol, VT 05443-0037

Karl M. Armens
740 Juniper Dr.
Iowa City, IA 52245

Charles Willeford
The American Dust Company
47 Park Court
Staten Island, NY 10301

World War II
Cover to Cover
P.O. Box 687
Chapel Hill, NC 27514

Zeppelins
Also any ephemera & artifacts.
Ford U. Ross
11020 SW 15th Manor
Village of Harmony Lakes
Davie, FL 33324

BOOKSELLERS

This section of the book lists names and addresses of used book dealers who have contributed the retail listings contained in this edition of *Huxford's Old Book Value Guide.* The code (A1, S7, etc.) located before the price in some of our listings refers to the dealer offering that particular book for sale. Given below are the dealer names and their codes.

A1
Adobe Books
11325 Chicot
Dallas, TX 75230

A2
Allen J. Peterson, Books
809-20 St. S
Fargo, ND 58103

A3
Antique Books
3651 Whitney
Hamden, CT 06518

A4
Arnold's of Michigan
218 S Water St.
Marine City, MI 48039
313-765-1350

A5
Art Source International
1237 Pearl St.
Boulder, CO 80302
303-444-4080

A6
Artis Books
P.O. Box 822
Alpena, MI 49707-0822
517-354-3401

A7
Avonlea Books
P.O. Box 74, Main Station
White Plains, NY 10602
914-946-5923

A8
AL-PAC
HC 1, Box 7120
Yucca Valley, CA 92284-9489

B1
Betty Schmid
485 Sleepy Hollow Rd.
Pittsburgh, PA 15228

B2
Bev Chaney Jr. Books
73 Croton Ave.
Ossining, NY 10562

B3
Bicentennial Book Shop
820 S Westnedge Ave.
Kalamazoo, MI 49008
616-345-5987

B4
Black Ace Books
1658 Griffith Park Blvd.
Los Angeles, CA 90026
312-661-5052

B5
Bob Adelson
13610 N Scottsdale Rd., #10
Scottsdale, AZ 85254

B6
Bob Dittmeier
Science Fiction Dept.
25 William St.
Farmingdale, NY 11735

B7
Book Treasures
P.O. Box 121
E Norwich, NY 11732

B8
Bowie & Weatherford, Inc.
314 First Ave. S
Seattle, WA 98104
206-624-4100

B9
Brasser's
8701 Seminole Blvd.
Seminole, WA 98104

B10
Bridgman Books
906 Roosevelt Ave.
Rome, NY 13440

B11
British Stamp Exchange
12 Fairlawn Ave.
N Weymouth, MA 02191

B12
Buck Creek Books, Ltd.
838 Main St.
Lafayette, IN 47901

B13
Between the Covers
132 Kings Hwy. East
Haddonfield, NJ 08033

B14
Bob Scherl
P.O. Box 7124
Van Nuys, CA 91409
818-780-2072

B15
Bill Sachen
927 Grand Ave.
Waukegan, IL 60085

B16
Burke's Book Store
1719 Poplar Ave.
Memphis, TN 38104

C1
Camelot Books, Charles E. Wyatt
P.O. Box 2883
Vista, CA 92083
619-940-9472

C2
Cover to Cover
P.O. Box 687
Chapel Hill, NC 27514

C3
Chimney Sweep Books
419 Cedar St.
Santa Cruz, CA 95060-4304

C4
The Captain's Bookshelf, Inc.
P.O. Box 2258
Asheville, NC 28802-2258
704-253-6631

C5
Cary Loren
Book Beat
26010 Greenfield Rd.
Oak Park, MI 48237

D1
D. Snyder
3079 Main St.
Neffs, PA 18065

D2
Dale Weber Books
Amalienstrasse #81
D8000 Munich 40
Germany
#011 49 89 280 2060

D3O
Darby Curtis
229 Broadway
Jackson, OH 45640

D4
L. Clarice Davis
P.O. Box 56054
Sherman Oaks, CA 91413-1054
818-787-1322

D5
Don Smith
3930 Rankin St.
Louisville, KY 40214

D6
Dover Publications
Dept. A 214
E Second St.
Mineola, NY 11501

E1
Ed LeBlanc
87 School St.
Fall River, MA 02720

E2
Elder's Book Store
2115 Elliston Pl.
Nashville, TN 37203

F1
Fanta Co. Enterprises, Inc.
21 Central Ave.
Albany, NY 12210

F2
Flo Silver Books
8442 Oakwood Ct. N
Indianapolis, IN 46260

F3
Fritz T. Brown Books
5 Claremont Pl.
Cranford, NJ 07016
908-276-4753

F4
Ford U. Ross
11020 SW 15th Manor
Village of Harmony Lakes
Davie, FL 33324

F5
For Collectors Only
2028B Ford Pkwy.
Dept. 136
St. Paul, MN 55116

G1
Gene Vinik Books
2213 E Copper St.
Tucson, AZ 85719

G2
Grave Matters
P.O. Box 32192-OB
Cincinnati, OH 45232

G3
G.M. Books
45 Halsey St.
Newark, NJ 07102

G4
Gordon Totty
Scarce Paper Americana
347 Shady Lake Pkwy.
Baton Rouge, LA 70810
504-766-8625

G5
Gambler's Book Club
630 S 11th St.
Las Vegas, NV 89101
800-634-6243

H1
Hank Loescher
52 Melrose Ave.
Bridgeport, CT 06605

H2
Henry Lindeman
4769 Bavarian Dr.
Jackson, MI 49201

H3
Heritage Book Shop, Inc.
8540 Melrose Ave.
Los Angeles, CA 90069
213-659-3674

H4
Homebiz Books & More
2919 Mistood Forest Dr.
Chester, VA 23831-7043

H5
Hidden Treasures
P.O. Box 643
31580 Hwy. 97 N
Tonasket, WA 98855
509-486-4496

J1
Jay's House of Collectibles
75 Pkwy. Dr.
Syosset, NY 11791

J2
Jim Hodgson Books
908 S Manlius St.
Fayetteville, NY 13066

J3
John A. Greget Magic Lists
1124 Cymry Dr.
Berwyn, PA 19312

J4
J.G. Wetterling
P.O. Box 965
Los Molinos, CA 96055

K1
Karl. M. Armens
740 Juniper Dr.
Iowa City, IA 52245

K2
Ken Lopez, Bookseller
51 Huntington Rd.
Hadley, MA 01035

K3
Key Books
P.O. Box 58097
St. Petersburg, FL 33715-8097

K4
K.C. Owings
P.O. Box 19
N Abington, MA 02351
617-857-1655

L1
Lane Books
Arundel
Peaks Island, ME 04108

L2
Lee & Mike Temares
50 Heights Rd.
Plandome, NY 11030

L3
Lucius Farish
Rte. 1, Box 220
Plumerville, AR 72127

M1
Mason's Rare & Used Books
115 S Main St.
Chambersburg, PA 17701 717-261-0541

M2
Melvin Marcher, Bookseller
6204 N Vermont
Oklahoma City, OK 73112

M3
Michael Gerlicher
1375 Rest Point Rd.
Orono, MN 55364

M4
Mike Brooks
7335 Skyline
Oakland, CA 94611

M5
Moderne Books
111 N 3rd St.
Philadelphia, PA 19106

M6
Movie Memories Poster Shop
502 Waverly
Palo Alto, CA 94301

M7
Murphy's Books
3113 Bunker Hill Rd.
Marietta, GA 30062-5421

N1
Noreen Abbot Books
2666 44th Ave.
San Francisco, CA 94116
415-664-9464

P1
Pandora's Books Ltd.
P.O. Box BB-54
Neche, ND 58265

P2
Parnassus Books
218 N 9th St.
Boise, ID 83702

P3
Passaic Book Center
594 Main Ave.
Passaic, NJ 07055

P4
Paul Melzer Fine & Rare Books
12 E. Vine St.
Redlands, CA 92373
714-792-7299

R1
Raintree Books
432 N Eustis St.
Eustis, FL 32726

R2
Richard Blacher
209 Plymouth Colony, Alps Rd.
Branford, CT 06405

R3
Robert A. Madle
4406 Bestor Dr.
Rockville, MD 20853

R4
Robert Mueller Rare Books
8124 W 26th St.
N Riverside, IL 60546

R5
Ron's Reading Room
235 Wilbar Dr.
Stratford, CT 06497

R6
Robert Schweitzer
3661 Waldenwood Dr.
Ann Arbor, MI 48105
313-668-0298

R7
R.G. Wilborn
Health Research
P.O. Box 70
Mokelumne Hill, CA 94245

S1
Sandlin's Books & Bindery
Jeff Sandlin, Bookbinder
70 W Lincolnway
Valparaiso, IN 46383-5522

S2
Significant Books
3053 Madison Rd.
Cincinnati, OH 45209

T1
Terry Harper, Bookseller
P.O. Box 37
Bristol, VT 05443-0037

T2
The Abstract
4850 W Mooresville Rd.
Indianapolis, IN 46241

T3
The Book Baron
1236 S Magnolia Ave.
Anaheim, CA 92804
714-527-7022

T4
The Midnight Bookman
1908 Seagull Dr.
Clearwater, FL 34624

T5
The Bookseller, Inc.
521 W Exchange St.
Akron, OH 44302
216-762-3101

T6
Tuttle Antiquarian Books, Inc.
P.O. Box 541, 26 S Main St.
Rutland, VT 05701

T7
Tim Ward
3232 #8 Denver Ave.
Merced, CA 95348

T8
The Book Inn
6401-D University
Lubbock, TX 79413
806-793-0342

T9
The American Dust Company
47 Park Court
Staten Island, NY 10301

T10
The Old Map Gallery
Paul F. Mahoney
1746 Blake St.
Denver, CO 80202
303-296-7725

V1
Vintage Books
117 Concord St.
Framingham, MA 01701
508-875-7517

V2
Volume I Books
407 Augusta St.
Greenville, SC 29601

Y1
Yesterday's Books
25222 Greenfield
Oak Park, MI 48237